MAIN
CURRENTS
OF
MARXISM

MAIN CURRENTS OF MARXISM

THE FOUNDERS ❦ THE GOLDEN AGE ❦ THE BREAKDOWN

LESZEK KOŁAKOWSKI

Translated from the Polish by P. S. Falla

W · W · Norton & Company

New York   London

First published in Polish as *Glowne Nurty Marksizmu* (Paris; Instytut Literacki, 1976) and in English as *Main Currents of Marxism* (London: OUP, 1978)

Manufacturing by RR Donnelley, Bloomsburg Division
Book design by Margaret M. Wagner
Production manager: Julia Druskin

Library of Congress Cataloging-in-Publication Data

Kolakowski, Leszek.
   [Glówne nurty marksizmu. English]
   Main currents of Marxism : the founders, the golden age, the breakdown / Leszek Kolakowski ; translated from the Polish by P.S. Falla.
      p. cm.
   Originally published: Oxford : Clarendon Press, 1978.
   Includes bibliographical references and index.
   ISBN 0-393-06054-3 (hardcover)
   1. Socialism—Europe—History. 2. Communism—Europe—History. 3. Marx, Karl, 1818–1883.
4. Engels, Friedrich, 1820–1895. I. Falla, P. S. (Paul Stephen), 1913– II. Title.
   HX36.K61813 2005
   335.4'09—dc22
   2005020823

W. W. Norton & Company, Inc., 500 Fifth Avenue, New York, N.Y. 10110
www.wwnorton.com

W. W. Norton & Company Ltd., Castle House, 75/76 Wells Street, London W1T 3QT

1 2 3 4 5 6 7 8 9 0

New Preface

ABOUT THREE DECADES have elapsed since these volumes, now combined in this new edition, were written and it is not out of place to ask whether the events that have occurred in the meantime have made my interpretation obsolete, irrelevant or plain wrong. To be sure, I was clever enough to avoid making predictions that could now be proved false. The question remains valid, however, what, if anything, can be still interesting in the intellectual or political history my volumes tried to depict.

Marxism was a philosophical or semi-philosophical doctrine and a political ideology which was used by the communist state as the main source of legitimacy and the obligatory faith. This ideology was indispensable, regardless of whether people believed in it. In the last period of communist rule it hardly existed as a living faith; the distance between it and reality was so great, and hopes for the joyful future of the communist paradise were fading so rapidly, that both the ruling class (i.e., the party apparatus) and the ruled were aware of its emptiness. But it remained officially binding, precisely because it was the main instrument of the legitimacy of the system of power. If the rulers really wanted to communicate with their subjects, they did not use the grotesque doctrine of "Marxism-Leninism"; they appealed, rather, to nationalist sentiments or, in the case of the Soviet Union, to imperial glory. Eventually the ideology fell apart, together with the empire; its collapse was one of the reasons that the communist system of power died out in Europe.

It may seem that after the demise of this multi-national machine, intellectually inept but efficient as an instrument of repression and exploitation, Marxism as a subject of study is buried for good, and that there is no point in digging it out from oblivion. But this is not a good argument. Our interest in the ideas of the past does not depend on their intellectual value, nor on their persuasive power in the present. We study various mythologies of long-dead religions, and the fact that there are no longer any believers does not make this study any less interesting. As a part of the history of religions, and of the history of culture, such study gives us insight into the spiritual activity of mankind, into our soul and its relations with other forms of human life. Inquiry into the history of ideas, whether religious, philosophical or political, is a search for our self-identity, for the meaning of our mental and physical efforts. The history of utopias is no less fascinating than the history of metallurgy or of chemical engineering.

And as far as the history of Marxism is concerned, there are additional and more pertinent reasons that make it worthy of study. Philosophical doctrines that for a long time enjoyed considerable popularity (and what was called Marxist philosophical economics was not really economics in today's meaning of the word but a philosophical dream) never die out entirely. They change their vocabulary but they survive in the underground of culture; and though they are often poorly visible, they are still able to attract people or to terrify them. Marxism belongs to the intellectual tradition and the political history of the nineteenth and twentieth centuries; as such it is obviously interesting, together with its endlessly repeated, often grotesque, pretensions to being a scientific theory. However, this philosophy entailed some practical conse- quences which would bring indescribable misery and suffering to mankind: private property and the market were to be abolished and replaced by uni- versal and all-embracing planning—an utterly impossible project. It was noticed towards the end of the nineteenth century, mainly by anarchists, that so conceived, the Marxist doctrine was a good blueprint for converting human society into a giant concentration camp; to be sure, this was not Marx's inten- tion, but it was an inevitable effect of the glorious and final benevolent utopia he devised.

Theoretical dogmatic Marxism drags on its poor existence in the corridors of some academic institutions; while its carrying capacity is very poor, it is not unimaginable that it will gain in strength, supported by certain intellectually mis- erable but loud movements which have in fact lost contact with Marxism as a theoretical body, but look for issues that can, however vaguely, be presented as issues of capitalism or anticapitalism (these concepts are never defined, but they are employed in such a way that they seem to derive from Marxist tradition).

The communist ideology seems to be in a state of rigor mortis, and the regimes that still use it are so repulsive that its resurrection may seem to be impossible. But let us not rush into such a prophecy (or anti-prophecy). The social conditions that nourished and made use of this ideology can still revive; perhaps—who knows?—the virus is dormant, waiting for the next opportunity. Dreams about the perfect society belong to the enduring stock of our civilization.

．　．　．

THESE three volumes were written in Polish in the years 1968–1976, when their publication in Poland could only be dreamed of. They were published by the Institut Littéraire in Paris in 1976–78 and then copied by underground publishers in Poland. The next Polish edition was published in London in 1988 by the publishing house Aneks. It was not until 2000 that the book was published legally in Poland (by the publishing house Zysk), when censorship and the communist regime had disappeared. The English version, translated by P.S Falla, was published by the Oxford University Press in 1978. Later on, German, Dutch, Italian, Serb and Spanish translations appeared. I am told that a Chinese version exists, but I have never seen it. In French translation only two volumes were published; why the third volume has never appeared, the publishers (Fayard) failed to explain, but I can guess the reason: the third volume would provoke such an outrage among French Leftists that the publishers were afraid to risk it.

Leszek Kołakowski
Oxford
July 2004

Contents

BOOK TWO

THE GOLDEN AGE
351

BOOK THREE

THE BREAKDOWN
785

Preface to the 1981 Edition

THE PRESENT WORK is intended to serve as a handbook. In saying this I am not putting forward the absurd claim to have succeeded in presenting the history of Marxism in a non-controversial manner, eliminating my own opinions, preferences, and principles of interpretation. All I mean is that I have endeavoured to present that history not in the form of a loose essay but rather so as to include the principal facts that are likely to be of use to anyone seeking an introduction to the subject, whether or not he agrees with my assessment of them. I have also done my best not to merge comment with exposition, but to present my own views in separate, clearly defined sections.

Naturally an author's opinions and preferences are bound to be reflected in his presentation of the material, his selection of themes, and the relative importance he attaches to different ideas, events, writings, and individuals. But it would be impossible to compile a historical manual of any kind—whether of political history, the history of ideas, or the history of art—if we were to suppose that every presentation of the facts is equally distorted by the author's personal views and is in fact a more or less arbitrary construction, so that there is no such thing as a historical account but only a series of historical assessments.

This book is an attempt at a history of Marxism, i.e. the history of a doctrine. It is not a history of socialist ideas, nor of the parties or political movements that have adopted one or another version of the doctrine as their own ideology. I need not emphasize that this distinction is a difficult one to observe, especially in the case of Marxism where there is manifestly a close link between theory and ideology on the one hand and political contests on the other. However, a writer on any subject is bound to extract from the 'living whole' separate portions which, as he is well aware, are not wholly self-contained or independent. If this were not permitted we should have to confine ourselves to writing histories of the world, since all things are interconnected in one way or another.

Another feature that gives the work the character of a handbook is that I have indicated, though as briefly as possible, the basic facts showing the connection between the development of the doctrine and its function as a political ideology. The whole is a narrative strewn with my glosses.

There is scarcely any question relating to the interpretation of Marxism that is not a matter of dispute. I have tried to record the principal controversies, but it would altogether exceed the scope of this book to enter into a detailed analysis of the views of all historians and critics whose works I have studied, but whose opinions or interpretations I do not share. The book does not pretend to propose a particularly original interpretation of Marx. And it is easy to see that my reading of Marx was influenced more by Lukács than by other commentators, though I am far from sharing his attitude to the doctrine.

It will be observed that the book is not subdivided according to a single principle. It proved impossible to adhere to a purely chronological arrangement, as I found it necessary to present certain individuals or tendencies as part of a self-contained whole. The division into volumes is essentially chronological, but here too I had to permit myself some inconsistency in order, as far as possible, to treat different trends in Marxism as separate themes.

The first volume was originally drafted in 1968, during the leisure time at my disposal after dismissal from my professorship at Warsaw University. Within a year or two it became clear that the draft required a good deal of supplementing, amendment, and alteration. The second and third volumes were written in 1970–6, during my Fellowship at All Souls College, Oxford, and I am almost certain that it could not have been written but for the privileges I enjoyed as a Fellow.

The book does not contain an exhaustive bibliography, but only indications for the reader who wishes to refer to the sources and principal commentaries. In the works I have mentioned it will be easy for anyone to find references to literature which today, unfortunately, is altogether too extensive for a single reader to master.

The second volume has been read in typescript by two of my Warsaw friends, Dr. Andrzej Walicki and Dr. Ryszard Herczyński. The former is a historian of ideas, the latter a mathematician; both have made many valuable critical remarks and suggestions. The whole work has been read, prior to translation, only by myself and my wife, Dr. Tamara Kołakowska, who is a psychiatrist by profession; like all my other writings, it owes much to her good sense and critical comments.

Leszek Kołakowski
Oxford

BOOK ONE

THE
FOUNDERS

Bibliographical Note

Sources of quotations used in the text:

St. Anselm, *Proslogium* etc., trans. S. N. Deane, Kegan Paul, London, 1903.

Engels, F., *Herr E. Dühring's Revolution in Science*, Martin Lawrence, London, 1935.
  Dialectics of Nature, Progress Publishers, Moscow, 1954.

Hegel, G. W. F., *Phenomenology of Mind*, trans. Baillie, Allen & Unwin, London, 1910.
  Philosophy of Right, trans. T. M. Knox, Oxford, 1942.
  Science of Logic, trans. A. V. Miller, Allen & Unwin, London, 1969.
  Lectures on the Philosophy of History, trans, J. Sibree, Dover, New York, 1956.

McLellan, D., *Karl Marx: his Life and Thought*, Macmillan, London, 1973.
  (ed.), *Karl Marx: Early Texts*, Blackwell, Oxford, 1971.

Marx, K., *Selected Works*, 2 vols., Lawrence & Wishart, London, 1942.
  Capital, trans. in 3 vols., Lawrence & Wishart and Progress Publishers, Moscow, 1970.
  Grundrisse, trans. M. Nicolaus, Penguin, London, 1973.
  Surveys from Exile, ed. Fernbach, Penguin, London, 1973.
  and F. Engels, *Selected Works*, Lawrence & Wishart, London, 1968.

Plotinus, *Enneads*, trans. S. McKenna, Faber, London, 1962.

Introduction

K<small>ARL</small> M<small>ARX</small> was a German philosopher. This does not sound a particularly enlightening statement, yet it is not so commonplace as it may at first appear. Jules Michelet, it will be recalled, used to begin his lectures on British history with the words: 'Messieurs, l'Angleterre est une île.' It makes a good deal of difference whether we simply know that Britain is an island, or whether we interpret its history in the light of that fact, which thus takes on a significance of its own. Similarly, the statement that Marx was a German philosopher may imply a certain interpretation of his thought and of its philosophical or historical importance, as a system unfolded in terms of economic analysis and political doctrine. A presentation of this kind is neither self-evident nor uncontroversial. Moreover, although it is clear to us that Marx was a German philosopher, half a century ago things were somewhat different. In the days of the Second International the majority of Marxists considered him rather as the author of a certain economic and social theory which, according to some, was compatible with various types of metaphysical or epistemological outlook; while others took the view that it had been furnished with a philosophical basis by Engels, so that Marxism in the proper sense was a body of theory compounded of two or three parts elaborated by Marx and Engels respectively.

We are all familiar with the political background to the present-day interest in Marxism, regarded as the ideological tradition on which Communism is based. Those who consider themselves Marxists, and also their opponents, are concerned with the question whether modern Communism, in its ideology and institutions, is the legitimate heir of Marxian doctrine. The three commonest answers to this question may be expressed in simplified terms as follows: (1) Yes, modern Communism is the perfect embodiment of Marxism, which proves that the latter is a doctrine leading to enslavement, tyranny, and crime; (2) Yes, modern Communism is the perfect embodiment of Marxism, which therefore signifies a hope of liberation and happiness for mankind; (3) No, Communism as we know it is a profound deformation of Marx's gospel and a betrayal of the fundamentals of Marxian socialism. The first answer corresponds to traditional anti-Communist orthodoxy, the second to traditional Communist orthodoxy, and the third to various forms of critical, revisionistic, or 'open' Marxism. The argument of the present work, however, is that the question is wrongly formulated and that attempts to answer it are not worth while. More precisely, it is impossible to answer the questions 'How can the various problems of the modern world be solved in accordance with Marxism?', or 'What would Marx say if he could see what his followers have done?' Both these are sterile questions and there is no rational way of seeking an answer to them. Marxism does not provide any specific method of solving questions that Marx did not put to himself or that did not exist in his time. If his life had been prolonged for ninety years he would have had to alter his views in ways that we have no means of conjecturing.

Those who hold that Communism is a 'betrayal' or 'distortion' of Marxism are seeking, as it were, to absolve Marx of responsibility for the actions of those who call themselves his spiritual posterity. In the same way, heretics and schismatics of the sixteenth and seventeenth centuries accused the Roman Church of betraying its mission and sought to vindicate St. Paul from the association with Roman corruption. In the same way, too, admirers of Nietzsche sought to clear his name from responsibility for the ideology and practice of Nazism. The ideological motivation of such attempts is clear enough, but their informative value is next to nothing. There is abundant evidence that all social movements are to be explained by a variety of circumstances and that the ideological sources to which they appeal, and to which they seek to remain faithful, are only one of the factors determining the form they assume and their patterns of thought and action. We may therefore be certain in advance that no political or religious movement is a perfect expression of that movement's 'essence' as laid down in its sacred writings; on the other hand, these writings are not merely passive, but exercise an influence of their own on the course of the movement. What normally happens is that the social forces which make themselves the representatives of a given ideology are stronger than that ideology, but are to some extent dependent on its own tradition.

The problem facing the historian of ideas, therefore, does not consist in comparing the 'essence' of a particular idea with its practical 'existence' in terms of social movements. The question is rather how, and as a result of what circumstances, the original idea came to serve as a rallying-point for so many different and mutually hostile forces; or what were the ambiguities and conflicting tendencies in the idea itself which led to its developing as it did? It is a well-known fact, to which the history of civilization records no exception, that all important ideas are subject to division and differentiation as their influence continues to spread. So there is no point in asking who is a 'true' Marxist in the modern world, as such questions can only arise within an ideological perspective which assumes that the canonical writings are the authentic source of truth, and that whoever interprets them rightly must therefore be possessed of the truth. There is no reason, in fact, why we should not acknowledge that different movements and ideologies, however antagonistic to one another, are equally entitled to invoke the name of Marx—except for some extreme cases with which this work is not concerned. In the same way, it is sterile to inquire 'Who was a true Aristotelian—Averroës, Thomas Aquinas, or Pomponazzi?', or 'Who was the truest Christian—Calvin, Erasmus, Bellarmine, or Loyola?' The latter question may have a meaning for Christian believers, but it has no relevance to the history of ideas. The historian may, however, be concerned to inquire what it was in primitive Christianity that made it possible for men so unlike as Calvin, Erasmus, Bellarmine, and Loyola to appeal to the same source. In other words, the historian treats ideas seriously and does not regard them as completely subservient to events and possessing no life of their own (for in that case there would be no point in studying them), but he does not believe that they can endure from one generation to another without some change of meaning.

The relationship between the Marxism of Marx and that of the Marxists is a legitimate field of inquiry, but it does not enable us to decide who are the 'truest' Marxists.

If, as historians of ideas, we place ourselves outside ideology, this does not mean placing ourselves outside the culture within which we live. On the contrary, the history of ideas, and especially those which have been and continue to be the most influential, is to some extent an exercise in cultural self-criticism. I propose in this work to study Marxism from a point of view similar to that which Thomas Mann adopted in *Doktor Faustus vis-à-vis* Nazism and its relation to German culture. Thomas Mann was entitled to say that Nazism had nothing to do with German culture or was a gross denial and travesty of it. In fact, however, he did not say this: instead, he inquired how such phenomena as the Hitler movement and Nazi ideology could have come about in Germany, and what were the elements in German culture that made this possible. Every German, he maintained, would recognize with horror, in the bestialities of Nazism, the distortion of features which could be discerned even in the noblest representatives (this is the important point) of the national culture. Mann was not content to pass over the question of the birth of Nazism in the usual manner, or to contend that it had no legitimate claim to any part of the German inheritance. Instead, he frankly criticized that culture of which he was himself a part and a creative element. It is indeed not enough to say that Nazi ideology was a 'caricature' of Nietzsche, since the essence of a caricature is that it helps us to recognize the original. The Nazis told their supermen to read *The Will to Power*, and it is no good saying that this was a mere chance and that they might equally well have chosen the *Critique of Practical Reason*. It is not a question of establishing the 'guilt' of Nietzsche, who as an individual was not responsible for the use made of his writings; nevertheless, the fact that they were so used is bound to cause alarm and cannot be dismissed as irrelevant to the understanding of what was in his mind. St. Paul was not personally responsible for the Inquisition and for the Roman Church at the end of the fifteenth century, but the inquirer, whether Christian or not, cannot be content to observe that Christianity was depraved or distorted by the conduct of unworthy popes and bishops; he must rather seek to discover what it was in the Pauline epistles that gave rise, in the fullness of time, to unworthy and criminal actions. Our attitude to the problem of Marx and Marxism should be the same, and in this sense the present study is not only a historical account but an attempt to analyse the strange fate of an idea which began in Promethean humanism and culminated in the monstrous tyranny of Stalin.

. . .

THE chronology of Marxism is complicated for the chief reason that many of what are now considered Marx's most important writings were not printed until the twenties and thirties of the present century or even later. This applies, for example, to the full text of *The German Ideology*; the full text of the doctoral thesis on the *Difference between the Democritean and Epicurean Philosophy of Nature*; *Contribution to the Critique of the Hegelian Philosophy of Law*; the *Economic and Philosophic Manuscripts* of 1844; *Foundations of the Critique of Political Economy (Grundrisse)*; and also Engels's *Dialectic of Nature*. These works could not affect the epoch in which they were written, but today they are regarded as important not only from the biographical point of view but also as integral components of a doctrine which cannot be understood without them. It is still disputed whether, and how far, what are considered to be Marx's mature ideas, as reflected especially in *Capital*, are a natural development of his philosophy as a young man, or whether, as some critics hold, they represent a radical intellectual change: did Marx, in other words, abandon in the fifties and sixties a mode of thought and inquiry bounded by the horizon of Hegelian and Young Hegelian philosophy? Some believe that the social philosophy of *Capital* is, as it were, prefigured by the earlier writings and is a development or particularization of them, while others maintain that the analysis of capitalist society denotes a breakaway from the utopian and normative rhetoric of the early period; and the two conflicting views are correlated with opposing interpretations of the whole body of Marx's thought.

It is a premiss of this work that, logically as well as chronologically, the starting-point of Marxism is to be found in philosophic anthropology. At the same time, it is virtually impossible to isolate the philosophic content from the main body of Marx's thought. Marx was not an academic writer but a humanist in the Renaissance sense of the term: his mind was concerned with the totality of human affairs, and his vision of social liberation embraced, as an interdependent whole, all the major problems with which humanity is faced. It has become customary to divide Marxism into three fields of speculation—basic philosophic anthropology, socialist doctrine, and economic analysis—and to point to three corresponding sources in German dialectics, French socialist thought, and British political economy. Many are of the opinion, however, that this clear-cut division is contrary to Marx's own purpose, which was to provide a global interpretation of human behaviour and history and to reconstruct an integral theory of mankind in which particular questions are only significant in relation to the whole. As to the manner in which the elements of Marxism are interrelated, and the nature of its internal coherence, this is not something which can be defined in a single sentence. It would seem, however, that Marx endeavoured to discern those aspects of the historical process which confer a common significance on epistemological and economic questions and social ideals; or, to put it another way, he sought to create instruments of thought or categories of knowledge that were sufficiently general to make all human phenomena intelligible. If, however, we attempt to reconstruct these categories and display Marx's thought in accordance with them, we run the risk of neglecting his evolution as a thinker and of treating the whole of his work as a single homogeneous block. It seems better, therefore, to pursue the development of his thought in its main lines and only afterwards to consider which of its elements were present from the outset, albeit implicitly, and which may be regarded as transient and accidental.

The present conspectus of the history of Marxism will be focused on the question which appears at all times to have occupied a central place in Marx's independent thinking: viz. how is it possible to avoid the dilemma of utopianism versus historical fatalism? In other words, how can one articulate and defend a viewpoint which is neither the arbitrary proclamation of imagined ideals, nor resigned acceptance of the proposition that human affairs are subject to an anonymous historical process in which all participate but which no one is able to control? The surprising diversity of views expressed by Marxists in regard to Marx's so-called historical determinism is a factor which makes it possible to present and schematize with precision the trends of twentieth-century Marxism. It is also clear that one's answer to the question concerning the place of human consciousness and will in the historical process goes far towards determining the sense one ascribes to socialist ideals, and is directly linked with the theory of revolutions and crises.

The starting-point of Marx's thinking, however, was provided by the philosophic questions comprised in the Hegelian inheritance, and the break-up of that inheritance is the natural background to any attempt at expounding his ideas.

I

The Origins of Dialectic

ALL LIVING TRENDS of modern philosophy have their own prehistory, which can be traced back almost to the beginnings of recorded philosophical thought. They have, in consequence, a history which is older than their names and clearly distinguishable forms: it is meaningful to speak of positivism before Comte, or existential philosophy before Jaspers. At first sight it may appear that Marxism is in a different position, since it derives its name from that of its founder: 'Marxism before Marx' would seem to be as much of a paradox as 'Cartesianism before Descartes' or 'Christianity before Christ'. Yet even intellectual trends that originate with a given person have a prehistory of their own, embodied in a range of questions that have come to the fore, or a series of isolated answers that are knitted into a single whole by some outstanding mind and are thus transformed into a new cultural phenomenon. 'Christianity before Christ' may, of course, be a mere play on words, using 'Christianity' in a sense different from that which it normally bears; there is general agreement, after all, that the history of early Christianity cannot be understood without the knowledge that scholars have been at pains to acquire concerning the spiritual life of Judaea immediately before the advent of Christ. Something analogous may be predicated of Marxism. The phrase 'Marxism before Marx' has no meaning, but Marx's thought would be emptied of its content if it were not considered in the setting of European cultural history as a whole, as an answer to certain fundamental questions that philosophers have posed for centuries in one form or another. It is only in relation to these questions, to their evolution and the different ways in which they have been formulated, that Marx's philosophy can be understood in its historical uniqueness and the permanency of its values.

In the last quarter of a century many historians of Marxism have done valuable work in studying the questions that classical German philosophy presented to Marx and to which he offered new answers. But that philosophy itself, from Kant to Hegel, was an attempt to devise new conceptual forms for basic, immemorial questions. It makes no sense except in terms of such questions, though certainly it is not exhausted by them—if such a simplification were possible the history of philosophy would cease to exist, as every philosophical development would be deprived of its unique relation to its own time. In general the history of philosophy is subject to two principles that limit each other. On the one hand, the questions of basic interest to each philosopher must be regarded as aspects of the same curiosity of the human mind in the face of the unaltering conditions with which life confronts it; on the other hand, it behoves us to bring to light the historical uniqueness of every intellectual trend or observable fact and relate it as closely as possible to the epoch that gave birth to the philosopher in question and that he himself helped to form. It is difficult to observe both these rules at once, since, although we know they are bound to limit each other, we do not know precisely in what manner and are therefore thrown back on fallible intuition. The two principles are thus far from being so reliable or unequivocal as the method of setting up a scientific experiment or identifying documents, but they are none the less useful as guidelines and as a means of avoiding two extreme forms of historical nihilism. One is based on the systematic reduction of every philosophical effort to a set of eternally repeated questions, thus ignoring the panorama of the cultural evolution of mankind and, in general, disparaging that evolution. The second form of nihilism consists in that we are satisfied with grasping the specific quality of every phenomenon or cultural epoch, on the premiss, expressed or implied, that the only factor of importance is that which constitutes the uniqueness of a particular historical complex, every detail of which—although it may be indisputably a repetition of former ideas— acquires a new meaning in its relationship to that complex and is no longer significant in any other way. This hermeneutic assumption clearly leads to a historical nihilism of its own, since by insisting on the exclusive relationship of every detail to a synchronic whole (whether the whole be an individual mind or an entire cultural epoch) it rules out all continuity of interpretation, obliging us to treat the mind or the epoch as one of a series of closed, monadic entities. It lays down in advance that there is no possibility of communication among such entities and no language capable of describing them collectively: every concept takes on a different meaning according to the complex to which it is applied, and the construction of superior or non-historical categories is ruled out as contrary to the basic principle of investigation.

In seeking to avoid both these nihilistic extremes, it is the purpose of this inquiry to understand Marx's basic thoughts as answers to questions that have long exercised the minds of philosophers, but at the same time to comprehend them in their uniqueness both as emanations of Marx's genius and as phenomena of a particular age. It is easier to formulate such a directive than to apply it successfully; to do so to perfection, one would have to write a complete history of philosophy, or indeed of human civilization. As a modest substitute for that impossible task, we propose to give a brief account of the questions in regard to which Marxism can be described as constituting a new step in the development of European philosophy.

1. *The contingency of human existence*

IF THE aspiration of philosophy was and is to comprehend intellectually the whole of Being its initial stimulus came from awareness of human imperfection. Both this awareness and the resolve to overcome man's imperfection by means of understanding the Whole were inherited by philosophy from the realm of myth.

Philosophical interest centred on the limitations and misery of the human condition—not in its obvious, tangible, and remediable forms, but the fundamental impoverishment which cannot be cured by technical devices and which, when once apprehended, was felt to be the cause of man's more obvious, empirical deficiencies, the latter being mere secondary phenomena. The fundamental, innate deficiency was given various names: medieval Christian philosophy spoke of the 'contingency' of human existence, as of all other created beings. The term 'contingency' was derived from the Aristotelian tradition (the *De interpretatione* refers to contingent judgements as those which predicate of an object something which may or may not apply to it without altering its nature) and denoted the state of a finite being that might or might not exist but was not necessary, i.e. its essence did not involve existence. Every created thing has a beginning in time: there was a time when it did not exist, and consequently it does not exist of necessity. For the Scholastics, following Aristotle, the distinction between essence and existence served to distinguish created beings from the Creator who existed necessarily (God's essence and existence were one and the same), and was the most evident proof of the transitoriness of creation; but it was not regarded as a misfortune or a manifestation of decay. The fact that man was a contingent or accidental being was a cause for humility and worship of the Creator; it was an inevitable, ineradicable aspect of his being, but it did not denote a fall from a higher state. Man's bodily and temporal existence was not the result of any degradation, but were the natural characteristics of the human species within the hierarchy of created beings.

In the Platonic tradition, on the other hand, the term 'contingent' was seldom or never used, and the fact that man as a finite, temporal being was different from the essence of humanity signified that 'man was other than himself', i.e. his empirical, temporal, factual existence was not identical with the ideal, perfect, extra-temporal Being of humanity as such. But to be 'other than oneself' is to suffer from an unbearable disjunction, to live in awareness of one's own decline and in perpetual longing for the perfect identification from which we are debarred by our existence in time and in a physical body subject to corruption. The world in which we live as finite individuals, conscious of our own transience, is a place of exile.

2. *The soteriology of Plotinus*

PLATO and the Platonists formulated in philosophical language the question, originating in religious tradition and pervading the whole history of European civilization: is there a remedy for the contingent state of man? Is his life incurably accidental, as Lucretius thought and as the existentialists maintain today, or has man, despite his duality, preserved some discoverable link with non-accidental and non-contingent Being, so that he may entertain a hope of self-identification? Or, in other terms, is he summoned or destined to return to a state of completeness and non-contingency?

For the Platonists, especially Plotinus, and also for St. Augustine, the deficiency of human existence is most evident in its temporal character—not only in the fact that man has a beginning in time, but also in his being subject to the time-process at all. Plotinus follows up a line of thought originated by Parmenides, and although his intellectual construction culminates in a stage higher than Being as Parmenides conceived it (which Plotinus treats as secondary to the One or the Absolute), his basic philosophical outlook is nevertheless the same as his predecessor's. Plotinus does not argue, like the Aristotelians, *ex contingente ad necessarium;* that is, he does not try to show that the reality of the One can be conclusively deduced from observation of finite beings, as a logical presupposition of their existence. The reality of the One is inexpressible yet self-evident, since 'to be' in its most basic sense signifies to be immutably and absolutely, to be undifferentiated and outside time. That which truly *is* cannot be subject to time, to the distinction of past and future. Finite and conditional beings, on the other hand, are constantly moving from a past that has ceased to be into a future that does not yet exist; they are obliged to see themselves in terms of memory or anticipation; their self-knowledge is not direct, but mediated by the distinction of what was and what will be. They are not self-identical or 'all of a piece': they live in a present that vanishes even as it comes to be, and can then only be revealed through memory. The One is truly self-identical and for that reason cannot be properly understood in opposition to the transitory world, but only in and through itself. ('We cannot think of the First as moving towards any other; He holds his own manner of being before any other was; even Being we withhold, and therefore all relation to beings': *Enneads*, VI. 8. 8. 'Certainly that which has never passed outside its own orbit, unbendingly what it is, its own unchangeably, is that which may most strictly be said to possess its own being' (ibid. 9).) Composite beings, on the other hand, are not self-identical, inasmuch as it is one thing to say that they exist and another to say that they are such and such. That which is what it is is not amenable to language: even 'the One', even 'Being' are clumsy attempts to express the inexpressible; those who have experienced this

Being know what they are speaking of, but can never communicate their experience. The *Enneads* revolve with infinite persistence around this fundamental intuition which perpetually eludes the grasp of speech. It cannot truly be said of finite creatures that they 'are', since they fade away at each moment of their duration and cannot perceive themselves as identities, but are obliged to go forwards or backwards beyond themselves to achieve self-understanding. But the term 'existence' is inappropriate to the Absolute also, since in ordinary language it is applied to that which can be grasped by means of concepts, whereas the One is not a conceptual entity. Our reason approaches the One by way of negation, and with our insufficient minds we apprehend it as that which is radically other than the world of limitations—not merely the sensual one, but even the world of eternal rational ideas. But this negative approach is only an unfortunate necessity, and in reality things are the other way about: it is the world of transitory objects which is negative, characterized by limitation and by participation in non-being. The One is not 'something', for to be something is merely not to be some other thing: it is to be definable by qualities that the object possesses and that are opposed to those it does not possess. To be something is to be limited, in other words to be in some measure nothing.

The hypostases of reality are so many stages of degradation. Being or intellect, as a secondary hypostasis, represents the One degraded by multiplicity, since it involves taking cognizance of oneself and hence a kind of duality between that which apprehends and that which is apprehended. (We cannot speak of knowledge in the One, since the act of cognition distinguishes a subject and an object: *Enn.* v. 3. 12–13 and v. 6. 2–4.) The soul, which is the third hypostasis, consists of mind degraded by contact with the physical world, that is to say with evil or non-existence. Matter, and the bodies which are its qualitative manifestation, are the last stage of degradation, representing radical passivity and non-self-sufficiency: incomplete, divested of harmony, little more than shadows, their Being signifies virtually no more than non-being (*Enn.* I. 8. 3–5). The attenuation of existence is measured by the descent from unity to multiplicity, from immobility to motion and from eternity to time. Movement is a degradation of quiescence, activity is enfeebled contemplation (*Enn.* III. 8. 4), time is a corruption of eternity. The human mind can only conceive eternity as non-time, but in fact time is non-eternity, the negation or dilution of Being. To be in time signifies not to be all at once. Strictly speaking, according to the intricate exposition of *Enn.* III. 7, it is not souls which are in time but time which is in them, for they have created time by concerning themselves with objects of sense. Plotinus's definition of eternity, foreshadowing the celebrated language of the *Consolations* of Boethius, is that it is 'the Life—instantaneously entire, complete . . . which belongs to the Authentic Existent by its very existence' (*Enn.* III. 7. 3). It knows no distinction between what was and what is not yet, and is therefore identical with true Being: for 'to be in reality' signifies 'never not to be' and 'never to be different', i.e. to be self-identical and unchangeable (III. 7. 6).

But the soul imprisoned in transience, impelled without ceasing from the nothingness of what was to the nothingness of what is to be, is not after all condemned to endless exile. The sixth *Ennead* is not only a description of the infinite distance between supreme reality and the life of our minds and senses, speech and concepts: it also points the way by which we may return from exile to union with the Absolute. This return, however, is not an exaltation of man above his natural state (the conception of the supernatural cannot in general be read into Plotinus's thought), but is a reversion of the soul to its own self. 'It is not in the soul's nature to touch utter nothingness; the lowest descent is into evil and, so far, into non-being; but into utter nothing, never. When the soul begins again to mount, it comes not to something alien but to its very self; thus detached, it is in nothing but in itself' (*Enn.* VI. 9. 11). Even at its lowest descent, the soul is not cut off from its source and is always free to return. 'We have not been cut away; we are not separate, though the body-nature had closed about us to press us to itself; we breathe and hold our ground because the Supreme does not give and pass but gives of its bounty for ever, so long as it remains what it is' (VI. 9. 9). The road to unity does not mean a quest for something outside the seeker: it involves, on the contrary, casting off all ties with external reality, first with the physical world and then with that of ideas, so that the soul may commune with that which constitutes its inmost being. Plotinus's work is not a metaphysical system, since language cannot express the most important truths; it is not a theory but a work of spiritual counsel, a guide for the use of those who wish to set about liberating themselves from temporal being.

Plotinus, Iamblichus, and other Platonists exerted influence both directly and to the extent that their ideas were accepted by early Christian thinkers. The conception which they thus disseminated, and which has never disappeared from our culture, was a philosophical articulation of the mythopoeic longing for a lost paradise and faith in One who Is—who presents himself to man not only as a creator or a self-sufficient being but also as the supreme good, as the fulfilment of man's fine purpose and as a voice summoning him to itself. The Platonists familiarized philosophy with categories intended to express the difference between empirical, factual, and finite existence and man's true Being, self-identical and free from the shackles of time: they pointed to a 'native home' beyond everyday reality, a place where man might be what he truly was. They explained the process of decline and reascent, the difference between man's contingent and his authentic Being, and sought to show how he might overcome this duality by an effort of self-deification. They refused to accept contingency as the human lot, and believed that the way lay open to the Absolute.

At the same time Plotinus pointed out the link between the duality of man's nature and the limitation which obliges us to regard the known world as essentially different from ourselves, so that our thoughts and perceptions move in an alien universe. If we can overcome the soul's alienation from itself (an alienation forced upon it by time, since we can only know ourselves as we are no longer, or as we have yet to be), then we shall also have overcome the alienation between the soul and everything it knows, loves, or desires. Plato wrote in one of his *Letters* that 'he who is not linked by a tie of kinship with the object will not acquire insight through ease of apprehension or a good memory; for basically he does not accept the object, as its nature is foreign to him' (*Letter* 7, 344a). In true knowledge, by contrast, the subject is not merely an absorber of information about realities that are completely external to him: he enters into an intimate contact with the object, and this cognition is his mode of becoming better than he was before. For Plato and the Platonists, therefore, the soul's urge to liberate itself from contingency involves overcoming the alienation between the soul and its object. Whatever makes the world alien and essentially different from me is, by the same token, a cause of my own limitation, insufficiency, and imperfection. To rediscover oneself is to make the world one's own again, to come to terms with reality. My own unity signifies my unity with the world, and my ascent to knowledge is identical with the aspiration of the universe to a lost unity. As the human mind is the guiding light of creation, logic, that is to say the movement of my thoughts about reality, is the process by which reality seeks its own reintegration. This may sound like a piece of Hegelian exposition, but it is quite in accordance with Plotinus's thinking: 'Dialectic does not consist of bare theories and rules: it deals with verities; Existences are, as it were, Matter to it, or at least it proceeds methodically towards Existences, and possesses itself, at the one step, of the notions and of the realities' (*Enn.* 1. 3. 5). Since the cosmic odyssey is the history of the soul, and the soul's activity is logical thought, ideas and reality tend to converge in their evolution and there is no longer any distinction between dialectics and metaphysics. Thought, in the true sense, is and must be self-directed. 'If the intellectual act is directed upon something outside, then it is deficient and the intellection faulty' (*Enn.* v. 3. 13).

To resume: the only single reality, for Plotinus, is that which is absolute, non-contingent, and identical with its own existence. The contingency of man's Being lies in the fact that his true essence is outside himself and differs from his empirical life, as is most evident in the latter's subjection to time. A return to non-contingency signifies a return to unity with the Absolute, in a way which cannot be more closely defined and is indeed inexpressible. The return involves liberation from time, so that memory ceases to exist (*Enn.* IV 4. 1). The process by which the soul frees itself from time is likewise an evolution of the whole of reality from a conditional to an absolute state. The effect of the process is to obliterate the distinction between knower and known; the subject and object are once more unified, and the world ceases to be a foreign realm into which the soul makes its entrance from outside.

3. Plotinus and Christian Platonism. The search for the reason of creation

THE Christian version of Platonism, i.e. the philosophy of St. Augustine, differs fundamentally from that of Plotinus in that it is based on the Incarnation and Redemption and the idea of a personal God who calls the world into being by his own free choice. But for Augustine, too, the contingency of man is most evident in his temporal being. Book XI of the *Confessions,* which is doubtless influenced by Plotinus, reflects the overwhelming experience of becoming aware of one's existence between the unreal past and the unreal future. Time must be subjective, an attribute of the soul experiencing its own Being, since that which was and that which will be have no existence except what is apprehended by human thought. It is only in relation to the soul, therefore, that we can speak intelligently of a distinction between past and future reality. But this distinction itself betrays the contingency of a being who is aware that his own life is a perpetual evanescence, represented at any given time by a point which has no extension and is isolated between two stretches of nothingness. Augustine, like Plotinus, depicts the insufficiency of man, but the idea of Providence alters the picture. Since the one basic dichotomy is that between the personal God and the created world, and since that world is encompassed by God's providence; since, moreover, the earth is a place of exile to which we are relegated on account of sin and not by an ineluctable process of emanation, while our liberation from sin is the work of the incarnate Redeemer, it is not surprising that Augustine's writings are a cry for help rather than, like Plotinus's, a summons to effort. Augustine's thought, profoundly influenced by the controversy with Manichaeism, lays paramount weight on the omnipotence of God watching over his creation, whereas for Plotinus reality is, first and foremost, 'a road leading both upwards and downwards'. Plotinus's Absolute is, in the sense we have indicated, 'human nature': man discovers it within him as his true self and recognizes that Eternity is his native home, whereas Augustinian man identifies himself as a helpless, miserable being incapable of self-liberation. As we have seen, a division between the natural and the supernatural would be meaningless in Plotinus's system, whereas in Augustine's it is the basic framework of metaphysics. God is not the essence of man, but a Ruler and a source of help. Temporal existence is the visible token of man's insignificance, through which he becomes aware of his need for protection and support.

In short, the return to a lost paradise means different things to the two philosophers, and they give different accounts of how it is to be achieved. For Plotinus it signifies identification with the Absolute, and can be attained by the unaided effort of any man who can free himself from the bonds of corporeal and intellectual being; in principle, the Absolute is 'within us'. For Augustine the return is only possible with the help of grace, and the exertion of the individual will plays a secondary part or no part at all. Moreover, it does not do away with the difference between the Creator and creation, nor is there any question of recovering a lost identity between them; on the contrary, the first step towards returning is the soul's awareness of the gulf which separates fallen man from God.

Both systems, however, the emanational and that of Christianity, leave unanswered the question which they regard as beyond the power of human mind to solve, although they make some attempt to do so: namely, how did the degradation of Being take place? The way this question is formulated varies according to the conception of the Absolute: in the first case it is 'Why did the One give rise to the manifold?', in the second 'Why did God create the world?' The One in Plotinus's thinking, like the Creator in Augustine's, is characterized by absolute self-sufficiency, and it would be blasphemous to suppose that they needed other beings or lacked anything that could be supplied by the created world. Nor can the question 'Why?' be asked in the sense of discovering an external cause that could influence the will of God or the emanational activity of the Absolute. A being which is completely self-sufficient, lacking and needing nothing, unable to be more perfect than it is, cannot display to the human mind any 'reason' prompting the act of creation. The very notion of an Absolute Creator contains within itself a kind of contradiction: if absolute, why does he or it create human kind? If created reality includes evil—even though we regard this evil as mere negation, defect, or insufficiency—how can we explain its presence in a world brought into being by an Absolute which is itself supreme Power and supreme Goodness?

Plotinus and Augustine give essentially the same answer to this question, by which they are both equally baffled. According to Plotinus, everything depends on the Good and aspires to it, as all things need it while it needs nothing (*Enn.* 1. 8. 2). Since there exists not only the Good but that which radiates from it, the limit of that radiation must of necessity be Evil, that is to say pure deficiency, which is matter. ('As necessarily as there is something after the First, so necessarily there is a Last; this Last is Matter, the thing which has no residue of good in it': *Enn.* 1. 8. 7). The road leading downwards from the One to lower and lower hypostases has a kind of inevitability about it, entailing successive degrees of deficiency or evil. But as to why the Supreme Good had to go outside itself in order to produce a reality that it does not need and, in so doing, to introduce the disturbance of evil into the closed autarky of the Absolute—of this Plotinus has nothing to say except for a laconic remark about 'superfluity' or 'superabundance' (*hyperpleres*). ('Seeking nothing, possessing nothing, lacking nothing, the One is perfect and, in our metaphor, has overflowed, and its superfluity has produced the new: this product has turned again to its begetter and been filled and has become its contemplator and so an intellectual principle [*nous*]': *Enn.* v. 2. 1).

This enigmatic notion of a 'superfluity' of existence or of goodness has continued to serve Christian philosophy as a solution to the awkward problem, although its inadequacy is obvious enough—we may ask, for instance, 'superfluity' in relation to what? Augustine himself does not seem to be bothered by the problem or to see that there is anything to answer, and he expresses astonishment at what he calls Origen's errors on the subject. God, he declares, does not experience any lack; the creation is the effect of his goodness; he did not create the world from necessity or from any need of his own, but because he is good and because it is fitting for the Supreme Good to create good things. (*Conf.* XIII. 2. 2; *Civitas Dei*, XI. 21–3).

This motif recurs, almost without change, throughout the course of Christian philosophy in so far as it is free from suspicion of unorthodoxy. As St. Thomas Aquinas puts it, '. . . excessus autem divinae bonitatis supra creaturam per hoc maxime exprimitur quod creaturae non semper fuerunt' (*Summa contra Gentiles*, II. 35). This indeed is all that can be said, given the premiss of God's perfect self-sufficiency, but the flimsiness of the explanation could not go altogether unperceived. What exactly can be the *excessus bonitatis* which creates a universe that nobody needs? Kindness, or bounty, is a relative quality, at any rate to the human mind; it is impossible for us to comprehend the goodness of a self-sufficient God without any creature to which it can be extended, and we are thus led to conclude that the goodness of God without the universe is a virtual and not an actual goodness—but this conflicts with the principle that there is no potentiality in God. We might suppose that the act of creation was necessary to God in order that his goodness might manifest itself, so that in creation God attains to a higher perfection than before; but this in turn conflicts with the principle that God's perfection is absolute and cannot be increased. Theology, of course, has answers to these objections, pointing out that it is meaningless to speak of God 'before' the act of creation, because time itself is part of the created universe and God is not subject to temporality; as Augustine says, he does not precede his creation. In any case, the theologians continue, our minds are not capable of fathoming the depths of God's nature, but can only understand him in relation to the work of his hands—as Creator, as almighty, kind, and merciful; while, on the other hand, it is certain that no relative attributes can pertain to God, that he exists in and by himself and that the universe cannot modify his Being. These answers, however, amount merely to an admission that no answer can be given. For if we are only able to know the divine nature in relation to ourselves, and if we know that this relativity is not a reality in God himself, then it follows that the question we are seeking to answer concerning the essence of God in himself and its relation to his essence 'after' the creation is not a question that can properly be asked, and that we must fall back on the sacred formulas without attempting to probe their meaning.

But there is yet another difficulty in explaining creation by the 'excess of divine goodness', namely the existence of evil. True, the whole of Christian theology since the controversies with Gnosticism and Manichaeism agrees in holding that evil is not a reality in itself but is pure negativity, deficiency, the absence of good. Evil is the lack of what ought to be, and the notion of evil thus introduces a normative idea to which reality itself is inadequate. The inequality of created things is not an evil, but a matter of order and degree. Evil in the strictest sense, i.e. moral evil, proceeds solely from beings endowed with reason and is caused by the sin of disobedience. Such beings are able to exert their own will against that of the Creator, and thus evil is not God's work. The various passages of Holy Writ, debated over the centuries, which suggest plainly and disquietingly that God is the author of evil as well as of good (e.g. Isa. 45: 7; Eccles. 7: 14 (in the Vulgate); Ecclus. 33: 12; Amos 3: 6) can of course be reconciled with orthodoxy by skilful exegesis (God permits evil but does not perform it), but this does not explain the creation of a world which itself produces evil. Christian theodicy wavers between two basic solutions. The first argues that evil is an indispensable component of the cosmos as a whole; this amounts to suggesting that in fact there is no such thing as evil, or that it only appears to exist from a partial point of view and vanishes when the universe is contemplated in its entirety—a standpoint characteristic of doctrines that verge upon pantheism. The second solution argues that although evil is mere negation, *privatio* or *carentia*, its source is the corruption of the will that disobeys the divine commands. (Both forms of theodicy, as Bréhier has shown, are present, unreconciled, in the philosophy of Plotinus.) The second version, which denies the responsibility of God for evil, suggests by the same token that man is endowed with a spontaneous creative initiative, albeit restricted to evil, so that the freedom whereby he disobeys God is complete and equal to the freedom of God himself, though naturally man does not share God's goodness and omnipotence. The effect is to regard man as a source of completely independent initiative, an Absolute on a par with the Deity. This ultimate conclusion is first explicitly brought out in the Cartesian theory of freedom.

The first version, according to which good presupposes evil, is hard to accept in so far as it implies that there is no such thing as evil pure and simple. It can only be sustained on the basis of a dynamic view of the universe, i.e. on the premiss that evil is an essential condition of the final efflorescence and complete realization of good. The answer to the problem of evil, and also to that of contingency, thus leads to dialectic of negation, i.e. to the idea that evil and contingency must exist if all the possibilities of being are to be realized. This dialectic provides an answer to the questions why the world was created, why evil exists, and why human beings are imperfect, but it does so in a way that places it outside the bounds of orthodox Christianity. It involves believing that God needed the world, that he only achieves fulfilment in creation and that his perfection depends on giving life to imperfect reality. This again is contrary to what Scripture tells us of God's self-sufficiency (Acts 17: 25). It means introducing the divine principle into history and subjecting it to the process of self-multiplication through creation.

4. Eriugena and Christian theogony

THIS idea probably found expression for the first time, though incompletely, in the work of Eriugena. It has since been essential to all Northern mysticism of the pantheistic kind, and we can trace it in different variations almost from one generation to another, from the Carolingian renaissance to Hegel. Speaking in the most general terms, it is the idea of the potential Absolute (a semi-Absolute, if this expression can be permitted) which attains to full actuality by evolving out of itself a non-absolute reality characterized by transience, contingency, and evil; such non-absolute realities are a necessary phase of the Absolute's growth towards self-realization, and this function of theirs justifies the course of world history. In and through them, and above all in and through mankind, the Deity attains to itself: having created a finite spirit it liberates that spirit from its finitude and receives it back into itself, and by so doing it enriches its own Being. The human soul is the instrument whereby God achieves maturity and thereby infinitude; at the same time, by this process the soul itself becomes infinite, ceases to be alien to the world, and liberates itself from contingency and from the opposition between subject and object. Deity and humanity are thus alike fulfilled in the cosmic drama; the problem of the Absolute and that of creation are resolved at a single stroke. The prospect of the final consummation of the unity of Being gives a meaning to human existence from the point of view of the evolution of God, and also from the point of view of man himself as he attains to the realization of his own humanity or divinity.

This, of course, is a simplified schema, expressed in terms that cannot be found in the actual writings of Eriugena, Eckhart, Nicholas of Cusa, Böhme, or Silesius—to mention the principal philosophers and mystics who come into question here. Nevertheless, despite the differences of exposition, their works can be seen as formulations of the same basic intuition which constitutes the historical background of the Hegelian dialectic and therefore of Marxian historiosophy. Naturally we cannot describe the history of that dialectic, in all its variations, in an account confined to the antecedents of Marx's thought, but some aspects of its history should be briefly noted here.

Eriugena's principal work, *De divisione naturae*, by its initial distinction of four natures in effect introduces the concept of a historical God, a God who comes into existence in and through the world. God as Creator (*natura naturans non naturata*), and God as the location of the ultimate unity of creation (*natura non naturata non naturans*), is not presented under a twofold guise for didactic reasons or because the infirmity of our understanding requires it thus: the juxtaposition of the two names signifies the actual evolution of God, who is not the same at the end of all things as he was at the beginning.

Eriugena makes frequent appeals to tradition: to the Cappadocian Fathers, St. Augustine and St. Ambrose, sometimes Origen, but most often the Pseudo-Dionysus and Maximus the Confessor. The most important borrowing from the Pseudo-Dionysus is the whole idea of negative theology as expressed in *De nominibus Dei* (the royal road to knowledge of God consisting in knowing what he is not). But from all these sources Eriugena constructs an original theogony of a neo-Platonist kind, which he attempts, despite immense difficulty and incessant contradictions, to reconcile with the truths of faith.

De divisione naturae is in fact a prototype of Hegel's *Phenomenology of Mind*, which it precedes by almost a thousand years—a dramatic history of the return of the Spirit to itself through the created world; a history of the Absolute recognizing itself in its works and drawing them into unity with itself, to the point at which all difference, all alienation, and all contingency is removed, yet the wealth of creation is not simply annihilated but incorporated in a higher form of existence, a higher form which entails a previous decline.

Eriugena accepts the premiss, common to all Platonists and all Christian theologians, that God is not prior to the world in time, since time itself is part of creation: God exists in a *nunc stans* where there is no distinction of past and future (*De divisione naturae*, III. 6, 8). God is unchangeable and the act of creation does not make any alteration in him, nor is it accidental in relation to his Being (v. 24). However, though Eriugena pays lip-service to God's unchangeability, it is called into question as soon as we come to consider the reason for creation: for at this stage it appears that

God, in a marvellous and inexpressible way, is created in creation in so far as he manifests himself and becomes visible instead of invisible, comprehensible instead of incomprehensible, revealed instead of hidden, known instead of unknown; when instead of being without form or shape he becomes beautiful and attractive; from super-essential he becomes essential, from supernatural natural, from uncompounded compound, from non-contingent contingent and accidental, from infinite finite, from limitless limited, from timeless temporal, from spaceless located in space, from the creator of all things to that which is created in all things. (III.17)

Eriugena makes clear that he is not speaking merely of the Incarnate Word but of the whole manifestation of Deity in the created universe. This indeed is intelligible on the premiss that God alone truly *is*, that he is 'the being of all things' (1. 2), the form of all things (1. 56), so that everything that exists is God as far as its Being is concerned. On the other hand, the statement that 'God is' is itself misleading in so far as it suggests that he is some one thing and not another (III. 19). If, however, the Being is divinity itself, it will be true to say that

the divine nature both creates and is created. For it is created by itself in the primordial causes and thereby creates itself, that is to say it begins to manifest itself in its own theophanies, desiring to pass beyond the most secret boundaries of its nature, in which it is as yet unknown to itself and recognizes itself in nothing, inasmuch as it is unlimited, supernatural and supereternal and is above all things that can and cannot be understood. (iii. 23)

We can thus comprehend the reasons for creation as it relates to God himself: God enters into nature in order to manifest himself, to become 'all in all', and thereafter, having called everything back into himself, to return into his own Being.

But not all created things participate in this process directly and on an equal footing. The whole visible world has been called into existence for man's sake, in order that he may rule over it; consequently, human nature is present in the whole of created nature, all creation is comprised in human nature and is destined to achieve its freedom through man (IV. 4). Man, as a microcosm of creation, contains in himself all the attributes of the visible and invisible world (V. 20). Mankind is, as it were, the leader of the cosmos, which follows it into the depths and back into union with the divine source of all Being.

It is clear that Eriugena sees the creative act of God as a satisfaction of the creator's own need, and that he regards the circuit whereby creation returns to the creator as a process which restores God's nature to him in a form other than its original one. In one passage he actually puts the question: why was everything created from nothingness in order to return to its first beginning? Having stated that the answer to this question is beyond human understanding, he at once proceeds to offer an answer: everything was created in order that the fullness and immensity of God's goodness should be manifested and adored in his works. If the divine goodness had remained inactive and at rest there would have been no occasion to glorify it, but, as it overflows into the wealth of the visible and invisible world and makes itself known to the rational creation, the whole of creation sings its praises. Moreover, the Good which exists in and by itself had to create another Good that only participates in the original bounty, otherwise God would not be lord and creator, judge and fountain of all benefits (V. 33).

Thus the Absolute had to exceed its own boundaries and create a contingent, finite, and transient world in which it could contemplate itself as in a mirror, so that, having reabsorbed this exteriorization of itself, it might become other than it originally was, richer by the totality of its relationship with the world: instead of a closed self-sufficient system it becomes an Absolute known and loved by its own creation. We have here a complete schema of 'enriching alienation', serving to explain the whole history of being; the vision of a Deity who develops by a process of decline and reascent.

The term 'decline' must, however, be used with reservation. For the Deity to enter into the world of creation is in itself, of course, a descent into a lower form of existence; but are we to understand that evil, or non-being, is also part of the universal cycle? Does it too perform a necessary part in the process of emanation and return? Eriugena nowhere says expressly that it does. The fall of man cannot, of course, be ascribed to his nature, which is good; nor can it be the effect of free will, which is also good (V. 36), even though it belongs to man's animal nature (IV. 4). It is the result of evil desires, which are harmless in animals but contrary to man's true nature (V. 7). Eriugena does not explain specifically how the fall was possible, but concentrates on man's return to his lost perfection. 'Paradise' signifies no more or less than human nature as it was created by God and destined to immortal life; death and all the consequences of our exile are the effect of sin, but the exile itself is a manifestation of the mercy of God, whose desire is not to condemn but to renew and sanctify mankind and enable us to eat of the tree of life (V. 2). Eriugena repeats time and again that when fallen man returns to God he will recover his original greatness and dignity, and he explains that this return consists of five stages: corporal death, resurrection, the transformation of the body into spirit, the return of the spirit and of man's whole nature to its 'primordial causes', and finally the return of these 'causes' (principles, ideas), and all else with them, to God (V. 7). The 'causes' or essential forms have nothing about them that is contingent, changeable, or composite; every species comes into being by participation in its form, which is one and one only and is fully present in every individual of the species; every human being contains in himself one and the same form of humanity (III. 27). It might seem, therefore, that the unity of mankind with God signifies a loss of individuality, the whole species being identified with its universal, which belongs to the divine essence. This 'monopsychism' is suggested by various remarks on the unity and simplicity of the 'first principles', which are not creatures and are not bounded in space and time (V. 15, 16), and by the statement that a thing which begins to be what it was not ceases to be what is was—including presumably human individuals as differentiated by the contingent attributes of each (V. 19). We are also told expressly (V. 23, 27) that in heaven there will be no contingent differences. However, different human beings will enjoy different stations in heaven according to the degrees of their love of God, even though they will all be saved and evil will cease to exist. Evidently the nature of our unification with the Deity is not clear to Eriugena, and he is unable to say whether or to what extent human individuality will survive in that final unity. It is certain, however, that whatever has been created by God cannot cease to be, though it may change its character. The lower will be absorbed by the higher, but will not be destroyed; the corporal will become spiritual, not losing its nature but ennobling it, and in the same way the soul will be united with God (v. 8). There will thus be a complete resorption of each lower level of Being by the next higher or more perfect, but nothing that has been created will be lost: this is the pattern of Hegel's *Aufhebung* or 'sublation'.

The whole process of return, in which man takes the lead, is in no way enforced by God upon nature: on the contrary, it is engrafted upon humanity, as the philosopher shows by a fanciful piece of medieval etymology, equating *anthropia* with *anotropia* or ascent (V. 31). Resurrection is a natural phenomenon (Eriugena disclaims his previous opinion that it was the effect of grace alone: V. 23), and so is our return to the house of God, in which there is room for all. The supernatural gift of grace will consist merely in the fact that the elect, sanctified in Christ, will be received into the very heart of paradise and will undergo deification.

But in the same way as God, when the cosmic epic is concluded, will find himself in a different state than before, enriched by his own creatures' knowledge of him, so also man, though he returns to his 'first beginnings', will not be purely and simply in his original state: for he will be in a condition in which a second fall is impossible and his unity with God is eternal and indissoluble (*theosis* being, however, reserved for the elect). It also appears that the work of the Incarnate Word does not consist, for Eriugena, simply in restoring men to the bliss of paradise by erasing the consequence of sin. Christ's incarnation has effects over and above redemption: Christ has set all men free, but while some will merely be restored to their primal state, others will be deified, thus raising humanity to the dignity of Godhead (V. 25).

It thus appears that the degradation of Being was not in vain. In the final result, the duality of man (who, as a composite being, cannot be a true image of God, who is uncompounded: V. 35) is a condition of his return to God and thereby to his own self. Humanity recovers its lost nature and even surpasses it by being deified. The drama ends with the attainment of godlike existence, self-identification, the abolition of the division between forms of Being, and hence the coincidence, once again, of the soul with its object. In accordance with the spirit of his dialectic, Eriugena finally declares that evil is only apparent when we view things in part; when we consider the whole there is no such thing as evil, since it plays its part in the divine plan and enables the good to shine with brighter radiance (V. 35). In this theodicy everything finds its justification and, in the eschatological perspective, the history of the cosmos is ultimately the history of God's growth in the human spirit and man's ripening into divinity—in short, a history of the salvation of Being by negation. If creation is the negation of divinity by reason of its finitude, differentiation, and lack of unity, divinity as the point of return—*natura non naturans non naturata*—may be called the 'negation of a negation'. Eriugena himself does not use this expression, which probably appears for the first time in Eckhart.

There are many hesitations and contradictions in Eriugena's work: we read, for instance, that evil has no cause, and also that it is caused by the corruption of will; that no one is condemned, and that some will suffer eternal sadness; that all will be one in God, and that there will be a system of ranks in heaven; that eternal ideas are part of creation, and that they are infinite, and so forth. Nevertheless, he was the first Latin philosopher to propound a system of categories, based on the Greek patristic tradition, which made it possible to link the history of mankind with that of a self-creating God, thus justifying the miseries of life by the hope of deification and offering man the prospect of final reconciliation with himself through reconciliation with Absolute Being.

No such majestic theogony as the *De divisione naturae* was composed in the Christian world between Eriugena's time and that of Teilhard de Chardin. None the less, its main themes can be traced again and again—not always in the same arrangement—throughout Christian philosophy, theology, and theosophy in so far as these are influenced directly or indirectly by the ideas of Plotinus, Iamblichus, and Proclus, or, in later centuries, by Arabic and Jewish thought which was inspired by those ideas. Among the themes in question are these:

Only the Absolute is perfectly identical with itself; man suffers from disjunction and, as a temporal being, cannot achieve self-identification.

Man's essence lies outside him or, which is the same thing, is present in him as an Absolute that is unrealized and aspires to realization.

It is possible for man to escape from the contingency of existence by union with the Absolute.

This escape, to which man is called, signifies a return to his own Being; and it is also the way in which the Absolute attains fulfilment, which was not possible without the defective world of creation.

Thus the process whereby conditional existence evolves from the Absolute is, for the Absolute, a loss of itself in order to achieve self-enrichment; and degradation is a condition of the furtherance of the highest mode of Being.

Hence the history of the world is also the history of unconditional Being, which attains to its final perfection as a result of being reflected in the mirror of the finite spirit.

In this final phase the difference between finite and infinite disappears, as the Absolute reassimilates its own works and they are incorporated in the divine Being.

Consequently the difference between subject and object also disappears, as does the estrangement between the soul that knows and loves and the rest of Being; the soul puts on infinitude, and ceases to be 'something' in opposition to something else which it is not.

All these thoughts recur persistently in Christian philosophy, despite various criticisms and condemnations, and were taken up in due course by the dissidents of the Reformation.

'Thou alone, O Lord,' says St. Anselm, 'art what thou art; and thou art he who thou art. For that which is one thing in the whole and another in the parts, and in which there is any mutable element, is not altogether what it is. And that which begins from non-existence, and can be conceived not to exist, and unless it subsists through something else, returns to non-existence; and which has a past existence that is no longer, or a future existence that is not yet,—this does not properly and absolutely exist.' (*Proslogium*, XXII.)

However, although this opposition between God and man is strictly orthodox, it at once raises the question: Can man be saved unless he is delivered from contingency, yet is not contingency a necessary correlative of his particular mode of existence? In other words, can man achieve self-identification without losing that which makes him a separate entity and becoming passively transformed into the divine Being?

5. Eckhart and the dialectic of deification

THIS consequence was accepted by Northern mysticism, which freed itself in this respect from a certain ambiguity of Eriugena's Platonism. To Eckhart the maxim of 'co-operation with one's own God' signifies the same as self-annihilation—a mystic kenosis that is not a mere moral precept but an ontological transformation. 'He who desires to possess everything must renounce everything'; to possess everything means to possess God, and to renounce everything involves renouncing oneself. God himself desires only to belong to me, but to belong wholly. When the soul achieves the fullness of inner poverty or denudation it makes God wholly its own, and he belongs to it in exactly the same way as to himself. There is then nothing in the soul that is not God. But the soul also achieves release from itself as a creature, that is to say from nothingness: for all creation (according to the well-known formula from Eckhart's sermon on James 1: 17, quoted in the bull of John XXII) is pure nothingness, not in the sense of being insignificant but in the literal sense of non-being. Thus the self-annihilation of the mystic is, paradoxically, the destruction of nothingness or, if we may so express it, the overcoming of the resistance that the void opposes to Being. When the soul is completely emptied of its particular nature, God gives himself to it in the fullness of his Being and belongs to it as to himself. But by this self-destruction the soul attains to that which it truly is: for there is within it a latent spark of divinity, obscured by the link with created things and by attachment to its individual, limited form. There is present in the soul that which is not created, namely the Son of God; and therefore any man can, like Christ himself, be united with the Father. Thus for a man to be one with himself is the same as to be one with God. In this way man's will is identified with God's and shares in his omnipotence. For the soul which has thus found itself, or found God in itself, there ceases to be any problem of the relationship between its will and that of the Absolute—both are fundamentally the same, and the question of obedience or disobedience does not arise. Eckhart distinguishes the particular, contingent self-will that tries to maintain a partial, isolated, subjective existence from the real will which is identical with that of universal Being, the only Being that truly deserves to be so called (although, unlike Aquinas, Eckhart regards Being as secondary in relation to the mind of God).

Eckhart's thought is dominated by the intense, unremitting conviction that Being and God are one and the same. The multitude of individual existence is nothing in so far as each of them is limited and partial; in so far as each one is possessed of Being, it is identical with God. Hence the question as to the reason of creation does not figure, properly speaking, in his sermons and writings. At the same time, he makes a distinction between the Godhead or indescribable Absolute—the One of Plotinus—and the personal Absolute which is God. This God—corresponding to Plotinus's second hypostasis, Being or Mind—realizes himself as God in creation; or, more precisely, it is only in the human soul that God, as its hidden nature, becomes what he is. In this sense we can speak of the meaning of creation from the standpoint of God himself. But the final aim of human endeavour is not to discover God in oneself but to destroy him, i.e. to destroy the last barrier that separates the soul from Godhead and prevents it returning into the inexpressible unity of the Absolute. This return takes place in the form of cognition and is consummated in a state in which all difference between the knower and known is obliterated.

In this way Eckhart's pantheistic mysticism embodies some of the basic ideas we have been considering. The contingency of human existence is only apparent ('Man is essentially a heavenly being'—sermon on Hebrews 11: 37), but this appearance must be overcome by the soul exercising its faculty of knowledge, and only in this way can the soul discover itself. In so doing it loses itself as a partial being and enters into possession of itself as an entirety, as divinity, as the Absolute. The particularization of Being pertains to the history of God realizing his own Being, which he can only do in and through the soul, but it does not pertain to the history of the Godhead or first hypostasis, which is not subject to any process of becoming.

6. Nicholas of Cusa. The contradictions of Absolute Being

NORTH EUROPEAN spiritual writing in the fourteenth century preserves much of the Eckhart tradition, but in terms of practical devotion rather than specu-lation. We cannot deal here with the social and ecclesiastical conditions which encouraged this type of mystic piety in the late Middle Ages. A substantial attempt at a new, speculative neo-Platonic theogony is found in the fifteenth century in the work of Nicholas Cusanus, who speaks, more clearly perhaps than his predecessors, of God's need for creation. God desired to manifest his glory, and for this he needed rational beings to know and worship him. 'Nihil enim movit creatorem ut hoc universum conderet pulcherrimum opus nisi laus et gloria sua, quam ostendere voluit; finis igitur creatoris ipse est, qui et principium. Et quia omnis rex incognitus est sine laude et gloria, cognosci voluit omnium creator, ut gloriam suam ostendere posset. Immo qui voluit cognosci, creavit intellectualem naturam cognitionis capacem' (Letters written in 1463 to a monk at Monte Oliveto; published by W. Rubczyński in *Przegląd Filozoficzny*, V. 2).

This, however, suggests too strongly the idea of a God who needs something other than himself, which is contrary to the principle of divine self-sufficiency. In his chief work, *De docta ignorantia*, when discussing the question of God's relationship to created beings, Cusanus avows himself defeated by the mystery of contradictions in the divine essence. The absolute unity of God is all that there can be, i.e. it is complete actuality, and is therefore not multipliable. ('Haec unitas, cum maxima sit, non est multiplicabilis, quoniam est omne id quod esse potest'—*Doct. ign. 1.* 6). On the other hand, God (as *rerum entitas, forma essendi, actus omnium, quidditas absoluta mundi*, etc.) descends into the manifold, differentiated world and creates the whole of its existential reality. Creation in itself is nothing; in so far as it exists, it is God; one cannot speak of it as a combination of Being and non-being. As the *esse Dei* it is eternal; as something temporal, it is not of God (II. 2). It is, as it were, a finite infinitude or a created God: 'Ac si dixisset creator "Fiat," et quia Deus fieri non potuit, qui est ipsa aeternitas, hoc factum est, quod fieri potuit Deo similius . . . Commu-

nicat enim piissimus Deus esse omnibus eo modo quo percipi potest' (ibid.).
God is the *complicatio* (wrapping-up, involution) of all things, as unity is that
of number, rest of motion, presentness of time, identity of diversity, equality of
inequality, simplicity of divisibility. In God, however, unity and identity are not
opposed to the multiplicity of the world that is 'involved' in him. The converse
relationship is *explicatio* or unfolding: thus the world is the *explicatio* of God,
multiplicity is that of unity, motion of rest, etc. But, Cusanus explains, the character of this mutual relationship is beyond our comprehension; for, as understanding and Being are in God one and the same, then in understanding
multiplicity he should himself be multiplied, which is impossible. ('. . . videtur
quasi Deus, qui est unitas, sit in rebus multiplicatus, postquam intelligere eius
est esse; et tamen intelligis non esse possible illam unitatem, quae est infinita
et maxima, multiplicari'–II. 3). It would seem that God cannot 'unfold' himself
in multiplicity without violating his absolute unity or his complete actuality, or
the exclusiveness of his Being; yet one of these attributes, and hence all of
them, must be forfeited if we accept that the development from unity to multiplicity, or, more simply, the process of creation, involves turning potential into
actual Being. Yet the actual fact is that amid the multiplicity of things all that
has Being consists of God alone. Thus we know only that everything is in God,
since he is the *complicatio* of all things, and God is in everything, since creation
is the *explicatio* of God; but we cannot fathom how this is so. The universe considered as an intermediary between God and the manifold or *unitas contracta*–
the undifferentiated Being that is no particular thing but is, in everything, that
thing itself ('universum, licet non sit nec sol nec luna, est tamen in sole sol et
in luna luna'–ibid.)–does not resolve the contradiction, since the Being of all
things is God and nothing else.

The difficulty felt by Cusanus is that of all monism. He seeks in vain for a
formula that will make it possible to regard the development from unity into
multiplicity as a real development, but not as a change from potential to actual
Being, which would imply the ascription of potentiality to God himself.
Cusanus's thought is in a state of tension between two extremes, neither of which
can be reconciled with even the loosest form of orthodoxy. On the one hand is
the eternal temptation to regard the whole manifold universe as an illusion and
a mere semblance of being, while the only reality is the unity of the Absolute.
Alternatively, the world must be regarded as God in a state of evolution, from
which it follows that God is not fully actual, nor is he the Absolute, but that he
merely becomes so at the end of the history of creation and by virtue of that
history. Pantheists often waver between these opposing views, which represent
the dilemma of all monistic thought. The first alternative leads to the contemplative morality of self-annihilation; the second to religious Prometheanism,
animated by the hope of achieving deification by one's own efforts.

There is no doubt that Cusanus was more attracted by the idea (though he does not express it outright) of God realizing himself in his creation than by that of the created world as an illusion. Like all 'emanationists' he regards the human spirit as the medium through which the Deity achieves actuality, which means that the Absolute is at the same time the true fulfilment of humanity. The soul returns into the actualized Absolute by means of knowledge, specifically knowledge of the whole and its relation to the parts: a paradoxical form of knowledge, discarding the principle of contradiction in favour of the *coincidentia oppositorum* which finds its prototype in the mathematics of infinitely large or limiting quantities. With the aid of knowledge the soul discovers itself as divinity and adopts the infinite object of its knowledge as its own self.

Cusanus found an ineradicable contradiction in the divine nature, but it was, to use Hegelian language, an immobile contradiction, i.e. the result of a speculation leading to an antinomy. Reflection on the divine nature leads to the conclusion that it must contain within itself qualities that are incompatible in finite beings: for, as God is pure actuality and at the same time embraces the whole of reality, there can be nothing in that reality that is not actualized, in some unfathomable way, in the divine unity. Cusanus's thought thus led him to the antinomy that results from simply developing the notion of the Absolute. The contradiction appeared under a logical, not a dynamic form: it was not a collision of real forces whose antagonism gives rise to something new. Nor was it an explanation of God's creation, but rather a recognition of the absurdity in which the finite mind becomes involved when it seeks to probe the infinite.

7. Böhme and the duality of Being

CONTRADICTION, or rather antagonism, conceived as an ontological category makes its first appearance in the works of Böhme, which resemble a dense, swirling cloud of vapours, yet which open a new chapter in the history of dialectic. The picture of the world as a scene of cosmic conflict between hostile forces was of course a traditional one, and recurred from time to time in different versions of Manichaean theology. But it is one thing to regard the whole of reality as a battlefield between rivals, and another to ascribe the conflict to a rift within a single Absolute.

Böhme's visionary writings are a continuation of the Platonism which was active among the pantheistic dissidents of the Reformation and which, as in the cases of Franck and Weigel, repeated in different language many ideas found in Eckhart and the *Theologia germanica*. Within this school of thought Böhme was something of an innovator. Following the tradition of the alchemists, he regarded the visible world as a collection of sensory and legible signs revealing invisible realities; but this revelation was in his view a necessary means whereby the Deity exteriorized and displayed itself. The 'eternal self-seeker and self-discoverer' duplicates himself, as it were, and emerges from a state of undifferentiated immobility to become truly God. Thus we find in Böhme's notion of divinity the same ambiguity as in Eckhart's works, an echo of the two first hypostases of Plotinus. God as revealed is the God who transmutes himself into creation, but he can only do so in such a way that what is actually unity in him appears in the guise of opposing forces of light and darkness. 'In the light, this power is the fire of divine love; in the darkness it is the fire of God's wrath, and yet there is only one fire. It divides itself into two principles, so that one should become manifest in the other. For the fire of wrath is a manifestation of great love: we perceive light in darkness, otherwise it could not be seen' (*Mysterium magnum*,VIII. 27). By emerging from his solitude and overstepping his own boundaries in search of himself, God inevitably creates a divided world in which qualities can only be recognized thanks to their opposites. Böhme has chiefly in mind the internal antagonism aroused in the human soul by conflicting desires. The essential drama of creation is played out within the individual torn by opposing forces. The soul's true home is in God, who has sown in it the seed of grace, but at the same time it longs to assert its own will. Thus there is no return to God without an internal conflict in which, by means of self-denial, the desire for harmony finally conquers the urge towards self-affirmation.

Böhme's theosophy is, as it were, the obscure self-knowledge of a central antinomy inherent in the idea of an unconditional being creating a finite world: the latter is both a manifestation and a denial of its creator, and cannot be one without the other. In so far as the absolute spirit chooses to become manifest, it is bound to contradict itself. The world of finite beings, inspired by the unity of its source, cannot altogether resist the force that bids it return to its origin; but, as it has come into existence, it also cannot escape the urge to assert itself in its own finitude. In Böhme's theosophy this conflict is for the first time clearly presented as the antagonism of two cosmic energies arising from a cleavage in the primal impulse of creation.

8. *Angelus Silesius and Fénelon: salvation through annihilation*

THE dialectic of God's self-limitation and the idea of the non-self-identity of man's Being recur throughout the seventeenth and eighteenth centuries, chiefly in Northern mysticism; they can be traced without difficulty in Benedictus de Canfield and in Angelus Silesius. However, while the former emphasizes the 'nothingness' of all created beings and the exclusive reality of God, Silesius in *Der cherubinische Wandersmann*, written no doubt before his conversion to Catholicism, is not content with this and returns to Eckhart's theme of the divinity as man's true essence and final home. The call of eternity is constantly present within each of us; in answering it we become 'essential' instead of 'contingent', putting off the particularity of individual existence and becoming absorbed in absolute being. The contrast between 'essential' and 'contingent' is clearly expressed: 'Mensch, werde wesentlich! denn wenn die Welt vergeht—So fällt der Zufall weg, das Wesen, das besteht' (*Cher. Wand.* II. 30). But whereas in some of Silesius's epigrams the contingency of individual Being appears simply as an evil whose presence is incomprehensible and which must be cured by voluntary renouncing all attachment to one's 'selfhood' (*Selbstheit, Seinheit*), in others we find Eriugena's notion of a cycle wherein creation restores to God his own Being in an altered form. Only in me can God find his 'double', equal to him for all eternity (I. 278); I alone am the image in which he can contemplate himself (I. 105); only in me does God become something (I. 200). It may be said that God descends into the world of chance and wretchedness in order that man in his turn may achieve divinity (III. 20). We thus have the same model of the Absolute exteriorizing itself into finitude so as ultimately to put an end to that finitude and return to unity with itself, but a unity enriched by all the effects of the polarization of the spirit, and hence, we may suppose, a reflective unity of self-contemplation. Contingency, evil, finitude—which all mean the same thing—are not a gratuitous, inexplicable decline on the part of the Deity, nor are they the work of any rival or adversary of his. They belong to the last phase of the circular dialectical movement, involving first a negation of divinity and then a counter-negation by the finite soul which wills its own annihilation. Once again, therefore, the return of God to himself is also a return of the human spirit to itself, to that eternity which is its true nature and resting place but which is eclipsed by temporal existence. Self-annihilation terminates the unbearable disruption which is inseparable from the process whereby God becomes himself, but which is destined to be finally remedied.

However, we need not prolong examples unduly. The theme of the contingency of man is found in all pantheistic literature and mystical writing, whether by orthodox Catholics, Protestants, or adherents of no denomination. 'I am not, O my God, that which is,' wrote Fénelon,

Alas! I am almost that which is not. I see myself as an incomprehensible middle point between nothingness and existence; I am one that was and one that will be, I am he who no longer is what he was and is not yet what he will be; and in that betweenness what am I?—a thing, I know not what, which cannot be contained in itself, which has no stability and flows away like water; a thing, I know not what, which I cannot grasp and which slips through my fingers, which is no longer there when I try to grasp it or catch a glimpse of it; a thing, I know not what, which ceases to exist even as it comes to be, so that there is never a moment at which I find myself in a state of stability or am present to myself in such a way that I can say simply 'I am' (Traité de l'existence et des attributs de Dieu, Œuvres, 1820, 1. 253–4)

The non-sectarian Dutch mystic Jakob Bril (*Alle de Werken* . . . , 1715, p. 534) declares that 'All things in nature are what they are except for man, who, considered in himself, is not the thing that he is; for he imagines himself to be something when he is not. All things are what they are, not in themselves but in their creator; man imagines himself to be something in himself, but this is only a false idea of his.' The conception of man as a divided being whose true existence is in God is a common one and is always associated with the hope of return. The view that contingent existence is a negative stage of the evolution of the Absolute clearly entails additional premisses, which can only be found in the writings of those who consciously step outside the confessional orthodoxy of the great Churches or who are branded as apostates.

9. The Enlightenment. The realization of man in the schema of naturalism

IT might seem that both these schemata could only be products of religious thought, that they involve an interpretation of the physical world as a theophany, and an explanation of man in terms of his relationship—be it positive, negative, or, more usually, twofold—to absolute spirit. But this is not so, for the theory of man's return to himself is also found as a constituent element of the naturalistic philosophy of the Enlightenment. It appears in fact that the theory in question, together with the paradigmatic image of a lost paradise, is an unchanging feature of man's speculation about himself, assuming different forms in different cultures but equally capable of finding expression within a religious or a radically anti-religious framework.

In the literature of the Enlightenment we find the notion of man's lost identity and the summons to recover it, both in utopian writings and in multifarious descriptions of the state of nature. The scepticism and empiricism inculcated by Locke and Bayle provided a negative basis for the notion of an ideal harmony which man has the power and the duty to restore on the natural plane. The acceptance of human finitude proved compatible with the conviction that it was possible to discover what man truly was, or what were the exigencies of his Being. Even though man's existence must be regarded as accidental in the sense that it is not the work of some spirit anterior to nature, nevertheless Nature herself provides information concerning the perfection of humanity, showing us what man would be if he were fully obedient to his proper calling; so that any particular civilization can be evaluated against the standard observable in nature. Instead of comparing earth to heaven, existing cultures were compared with the natural state of humanity. Whereas the mystics contrasted the general condition of humanity, irrespective of particular cultures, with the true fulfilment of humanity in the Absolute, the naturalists judged every form of civilization, and especially their own, in the light of authentic humanity as prescribed by Nature's imperatives. It is immaterial from this point of view whether they believed that the imperatives were actually fulfilled in some time or place, as in theories of the noble savage, or whether they regarded them as constituting a pattern to be obeyed—not, however, a pattern devised by mere speculation, but one discovered in the laws of nature. The attitude of detachment from one's own culture and criticism of it as 'unnatural' had, it is true, already appeared in the late Renaissance (for example Montaigne) and was transmitted to the Enlightenment by the more or less continuous tradition of Libertinism. It was not till the eighteenth century, however, that it took on such a massive, consistent, and radical form as to constitute a whole new intellectual system. The device of portraying one's own civilization through the eyes of others (Goldsmith's Chinese, Montesquieu's Persians, Swift's Houyhnhnms, and Voltaire's traveller from Sirius) was associated with the belief that there was a true standard for all humanity and that the civilization in question was contrary to nature. An exception should, however, be made for Swift's bitter satire: by placing his ideal state among horses and not men, he showed clearly enough that it was 'utopian' in the full sense of the term's derivation and of its popular use.

The claims of 'natural man' *vis-à-vis* the prevailing civilization involved various assertions of rights and qualitative comparisons. But man's natural equality, his right to happiness and freedom and to the use of reason, were currently accepted themes and were sufficient to constitute an apparatus of criticism. Nevertheless, it turned out before long that the conceptual framework of the Enlightenment ideals was inadequate and that its components did not jibe with one another. The key concepts of 'nature' and 'reason' proved, on closer analysis, not to combine in a consistent whole: for how was the cult of reason as the gift of nature to be harmonized with the cult of nature as itself reasonable? If, as the materialists held, human reason was a prolongation of animal nature and there was no essential difference between tricks performed by monkeys and the reasoning of mathematicians (de la Mettrie), and if all moral judgements are reducible to reactions of pleasure and pain, then human beings with their abstract reasoning and moral laws are indeed the work of nature but are no more than blind pieces of natural mechanism. If, on the other hand, Nature, as many contend, is a rational, purposeful, protective entity, then she is merely another name for God. Hence either reason is not reason or nature is not nature; we must either regard thought as irrational or credit Nature with Godlike attributes. How can it be accepted that human impulses are no less natural than the moral laws that regulate and control them? We are back to the eternal dilemmas with which atheists have taunted worshippers of the gods since Epicurus's time: since the world is full of evil, God must be either evil or powerless or incompetent or all three; and the same can be said of 'good and omnipotent' Nature. If, on the other hand, nature is indifferent to man and his fate, there is no reason to believe that evil can be vanquished: it may be that the only natural law is that of the jungle and that human societies are no better off than plant or animal species. At this point the *idées-forces* of the Enlightenment begin to diverge, and we encounter the pessimistic attitudes of Mandeville, Swift, and the later Voltaire. The notion of a benevolent natural harmony which, once discovered, will remove all conflict and misfortune, begins to falter.

10. Rousseau and Hume. Destruction of the belief in natural harmony

ROUSSEAU, Hume, and Kant are all exponents of this loss of confidence. Rousseau believes in the archetype of man living in self-identity, but he does not believe it possible to erase the effects of civilization and return to natural happiness. Natural man felt no sense of alienation, as his relationship to life was not mediated by reflection; he lived straightforwardly without having to think about life; he accepted, but in an unconscious manner, his own situation and his own limitations. Thus his fellowship with others developed spontaneously and needed no special institutions to preserve it. Civilization introduced man's detachment from himself and ruined the original harmony of society. It made selfishness universal, destroyed solidarity, and degraded personal life to a system of conventions and artificial needs. In this society the self-identity of the individual is unattainable; all he can do is to attempt to escape its pressures and contemplate the world independently of received opinion. Co-operation and solidarity with others does not deprive the individual of a true personal life, whereas the negative bond of selfish interest and ambition destroys both community and true personality. Man's proper duty is both to be himself and to live in willing solidarity with others. Since we cannot undo civilization, we must attempt a compromise: let each man discover the natural state within himself and educate others in the same spirit. There is no historical law to assure us that our efforts will lead to the restoration of true community and that society will be reborn in individuals, but it is not quite impossible that this will be so.

Rousseau does not embark on any historical theodicy or attempt to integrate the evil in the world with the hope of a harmonious order blossoming out of the horrors of the past. The rupture of the original harmony is in his eyes evil pure and simple, without justification and without purpose. There is no dialectic of 'spiral progress' to foster an uncertain hope of improvement.

Rousseau thus has his own model of authentic humanity, but he does not acknowledge any reasons justifying a breach with that model. The fall of man is not, in his view, a self-correcting phase in the advance towards perfection. In this respect he is closer to ordinary Christianity than to theogonists after the manner of Plato: evil is evil, it is the fault of man and has no hidden significance for the history of the cosmos. There is, on the other hand, a summons addressed to man, which is prior to history and not dictated by it; the ultimate reality of that summons is an open question.

Hume's doctrine, in its turn, represents the cleavage between two other basic elements of eighteenth-century thinking: the categories of experience and those of the natural order. When the premises of empiricism were carried to their logical conclusion, it became clear that the notion of a natural order was untenable. If there can be no knowledge except what is conveyed by the senses, and if our sense-data provide no evidence for any causal connection or law of necessity, then it is clear that our minds are incapable of apprehending reality as anything but a collection of separate phenomena. Nor can we, in that case, perceive any natural order which it would be legitimate to regard as an immanent feature of the universe rather than simply a 'law' of the scientific type, i.e. the subjective fixing in the mind, for reasons of practical convenience, of certain recurrent sequences of events. Nor, again, is there any reason to suppose that we are bound by moral laws possessing a validity independent of our own sensations of pain and pleasure. In short, both the 'physical order' and the 'moral order' are imaginations above and beyond what is or can be conveyed to us by experience. In the same way, it is useless to suppose that there is any human standard, obligation, or purpose independent of the actual course of human history.

Hume does not assert the contingency of either man or the universe: on the contrary, when rebutting the cosmological proofs of the existence of God, he states that we cannot know from experience that the universe is contingent. But this means only that it is not contingent in the schoolmen's sense, i.e. that it has no qualities to indicate that it must be dependent on a necessary creator. To the Scholastics the 'contingency' of the world serves as a demonstration of necessity. Considered in itself the world has nothing necessary about it, but the necessity must be there, since the world exists; its contingency is only apparent, as we see when we relate it to the existence of God. Considered, as it should be, in relation to God, the world is not contingent, since nothing can exist by accident. Thus when Hume tells us that there is nothing in experience to show that the world is contingent, he is really saying that the world *is* contingent, i.e. there is nothing that obliges us to relate it to any necessary or absolute reality. In other words, the expression 'contingent' is only meaningful in opposition to the expression 'necessary'. Hume's position is that the world is what it is, and the antithesis between contingency and necessity has no basis in experience. The universe, for Hume, is contingent in exactly the same sense as it is for Sartre: it is not founded on any 'reason' and does not authorize us to seek for any.

Hume's criticism finally shook the foundations of the eighteenth-century system which had appeared to reconcile empiricism with belief in natural harmony, moral utilitarianism with the belief that man was destined for happiness, reason as a gift of nature with reason as a sovereign power. If the attempt was to be made to restore the legitimacy of belief in the unity and necessity of Being and in an authentic human standard as distinct from empirical and historical humanity, it would have to take account of the devastating implications of Hume's analysis. This was the problem facing Kant, by whom the attempt was actually made.

11. Kant. The duality of man's being, and its remedy

KANT opted for the sovereignty of human reason as against belief in a natural order of which reason is a part or a manifestation. In his philosophy he rejected the hope that reason could discover the natural law, a pre-existing harmony, or a rational God, or could interpret itself within that harmony. This did not mean, as Hume would argue, that all our knowledge is reduced to the contingency of separate perceptions. Not all our judgements are empirical or merely analytic: synthetic *a priori* judgements, i.e. non-empirical ones which tell us something about reality, form the backbone of our knowledge and assure it of regularity and general validity. But—and this is one of the main conclusions of the *Critique of Pure Reason*—synthetic *a priori* judgements relate only to objects of possible experience. This means that they cannot provide a basis for a rational metaphysic, since a metaphysic would have to consist of synthetic *a priori* judgements if it were possible at all. All we can hope for is an immanent metaphysic in the shape of a code of natural laws that are not abstracted from experience but can be ascertained *a priori*. All thought is ultimately related to perception, and the *a priori* constructions that our mind necessarily forms are meaningful only in so far as they can be applied to the empirical world. Thus the order of nature, as far as its constituent determinants are concerned, is not found in nature but is imposed on it by the order of the mind itself. To this order belongs the arrangement of objects in time and space, as the basis of pure apprehension, and also the system of categories, i.e. non-mathematical concepts which give a unity to the empirical world but are not derived from it.

Experience is thus only possible through the unifying force of the intellect. The order of nature bears witness to the mind's sovereignty over it, but the sovereignty is not complete. Every piece of knowledge, apart from analytical judgements which convey no fresh information, has a content derived from two sources. Perception and judgement are radically different activities. In sensual perception objects are simply given to us and we passively undergo their effect, whereas in intellectual activity we exercise the mind upon them. Both these aspects of human presence in the world, the active and the passive, are necessarily involved in every act of cognition. There is no valid thought that is not related to perception, and no perception without the unifying activity of the intellect. The first of these propositions means that there is no legitimate hope of theoretical knowledge extending beyond the empirical world to absolute realities, and also that the variety of experience cannot be wholly subordinated to the power of the intellect. The second proposition brings out the legislative superiority of the mind over nature considered as a system.

The ineradicable duality of human knowledge is not directly perceptible, but once it has been discovered it reveals the basic duality of all human experience, whereby we assimilate the world, at one and the same time, as legislators and as passive subjects. Within the limits of the legitimate use of our intellect, we cannot do away with the inexplicable contingency of the data of experience. That contingency is something given; we are obliged to recognize it and abandon any hope of finally mastering it. Consequently we cannot bestow a final unity on ourselves or on the world. My own ego as I perceive it in introspection is subject to the condition of time and is therefore not identical with my ego in itself, which is inaccessible to theoretical knowledge. Behind the ego of introspection, it is true, we can discern a transcendental unity of apperception, the condition of the uniting activity of the subject, a self-awareness that is capable of accompanying all perceptions; but of this we only know that it exists, and not how it is constituted. In general, the whole of our organized experience presupposes a realm of unknowable reality which affects the senses but which we perceive not in its real shape but in a form ordered by our *a priori* categories. The presence of the world-in-itself is not deduced from empirical data but is simply known; my awareness of my own existence is at the same time a direct awareness of objects. But we can know nothing of independent reality except the mere fact that it exists; nor can we do away with the contingency of the knowable world or the duality to which the human intellect is subject.

The human spirit, however, is not content with the knowledge of its own limitations or with a jejune metaphysic confined to awareness of the *a priori* conditions of experience. Our minds are so constituted that they strive unremittingly after the unity of absolute knowledge; they seek to understand the world not only as it is but as it must be, and to overcome the distinction, entailed by the postulates of empirical thought, between what is possible, what is real and what is necessary. For this distinction cannot be expelled from the mind: the possible is everything that is compatible with the formal conditions of experience, the real is that which is actually given in its material conditions, the necessary is that part of reality which proceeds from the general conditions of experience. The realities of the world thus include contingency, which we could only eliminate if we had access to unconditional being, to the absolute unity of the subject and object of knowledge. We strive incessantly to attain this, although our striving is in vain; the delusions of metaphysics, even when revealed as such, live on in the human mind. They find expression in the construction of concepts which not only are not abstracted from experience (for *a priori* concepts are legitimate and essential to knowledge) but are not even applicable to it. These concepts or ideas of pure reason—such as God, freedom, and immortality—are a perpetual temptation to the human spirit, although they cannot be significantly used within the bounds of theoretical reason. In terms of pure reason they have a certain meaning, but a regulative and not a constitutive one. That is to say, we cannot know any reality that corresponds to these concepts, but can only use them as unattainable limits or pointers indicating the direction of our cognitive activity.

The legitimate use of these ideas, therefore, lies in their constant summons to the mind to exceed its previous efforts; their illegitimate use lies in the supposition that any effort, however great, will enable us to achieve absolute knowledge. For every judgement in a syllogistic chain, the mind seeks to discover a major premiss; the law of the syllogism requires that we seek a premiss for every premiss, a condition for every condition, until we arrive at that which is unconditional. This maxim is a proper one for the purpose of governing the operations of the mind, but it should not be confused with the erroneous supposition that there is in fact a first, unconditioned link in the chain of premisses. For it is one thing to know that every member of an intellectual sequence has a preceding condition, and quite another to maintain that we can comprehend the sequence in its entirety including a first, unconditioned member. (We may elucidate Kant's thought here by pointing out that while it is true to say that, for any particular number, there is a number greater than it, it is not true to say that there exists a number greater than any other number whatsoever.) The failure to distinguish the syllogistic maxim from the fundamental, but false premiss of pure reason is the source of three typical errors corresponding to the three types of syllogism. In the sphere of the categorical syllogism, this premiss states that in seeking successive conditions for predicative judgements we can finally come upon a subject that is not a predicate. In the sphere of the hypothetical syllogism, it tells us that we can come to an assertion that presupposes nothing; and in the sphere of the disjunctive syllogism, that we can discover such an aggregate of the members of the division of a concept as requires nothing further to complete the division. In this way we delude ourselves that we can establish in the domain of knowledge three kinds of absolute unity: in psychology that of the thinking subject, in cosmology that of the sequence of the causes of phenomena, and in theology that of the subjects of thought in general. But within the boundaries of finite experience there is no object corresponding to any of these three ideas. We cannot apprehend theoretically either the substantial unity of the human soul, or the unity of the universe, or that of God.

There can scarcely be any example in history of a philosopher going to so much trouble as Kant to invalidate arguments in favour of propositions to the truth of which he was so deeply attached. Belief in the existence of God, the freedom and immortality of the soul were not, to him, indifferent matters in respect of which he was only concerned to declare his neutrality. On the contrary, he regarded them as of vital importance, but he believed that the mind deludes itself when it is tempted to imagine that it has laid hold of the Absolute. The Absolute is a beacon to the endless progress of knowledge, but cannot itself become a possession of the mind.

To attain to the Absolute by cognition is the same as to become absolute. But the division of man into a passive and an active part, and the corresponding division of the world into what is perceived and what is thought, what is contingent and what is intellectually necessary—this division can only be resolved at the point of infinity; and the same is true of the opposition in our moral life between free will and law, happiness and duty. For our life as beings endowed with will is divided in the same way between two orders in which we participate unavoidably: the phenomenal, natural world subject to causality, and the world of things in themselves, freedom and total independence of the mind. That which is called duty, and expresses itself in the form of an imperative, is not only quite independent of our inclinations but, by its very character as an imperative, must be contrary to them.

> For a command that something must be done willingly involves a contradiction, since if we knew of ourselves that we are obliged to do something and also knew that we would do it willingly, the command would be superfluous; while if we performed the action unwillingly and only out of respect for the law, then the command which makes that respect the motive of the maxim would operate in a manner contrary to the disposition commanded. (*Critique of Practical Reason*, 1. 3)

But the conformity of will to law must be possible; it is a condition of supreme goodness, which itself must be possible, bringing about a harmonious synthesis of happiness and virtue, which in the empirical world tend, as we all know, to limit each other. The reason perceives the moral law directly, i.e.

independently of knowledge of the subjective conditions that make it possible to fulfil the law. This is to say, man knows what he should do before he knows that he possesses freedom of action; from the fact that he *ought*, he learns for the first time that he *can*, i.e. that he is free. But the freedom thus apprehended is an object of practical reason, which has a wider field of action than speculative reason. Everyone will agree that it is in his power to obey the moral imperative, even if he is not certain that he will in fact do so; 'he believes that he can perform an action because he knows that it is his duty, and he recognizes in himself a freedom which would remain unknown to him if it were not for the moral law'. (*Crit. Prac. Reason,* 1. 1, 6). The practical reason has its own *a priori* principles which cannot be derived from theoretical knowledge, and their validity makes it necessary to accept certain fundamental truths which are inaccessible to the intellect, whose power to form concepts is limited by their empirical applicability. Since the will, subject to the moral law, has the supreme good as its necessary object, the supreme good must be possible. And, as this good demands absolute perfection, which is only possible as the result of infinite progress, the validity of the moral law necessarily presupposes the infinite duration of the human individual, i.e. personal immortality. Similarly, the postulate of the supreme good requires for its validity that man's happiness should coincide with his duty, but no natural conditions afford evidence that this will certainly be so. Hence the supreme good as a necessary object of the will presupposes the existence of a free, rational cause of nature that is not part of nature, i.e. the existence of God. Thus, thanks to our awareness of the moral law, the ideas of speculative reason acquire an objective reality that theory could never have secured for them. Our immortality, our participation in the world of *intelligibilia*, unconditional freedom, and the Creator's supremacy over nature—all these are shown to be realities whose existence is demanded by the moral law.

To sum up, the division of man between two opposite orders—that of nature and that of freedom, that of desire and that of duty; a passive existence full of contingent things, an active existence in which the contingency of the object disappears—this division is curable, but on the condition of an infinite progress. The prospect before us is that of an unlimited striving towards self-deification, not in the mystic sense of achieving identity with a transcendent God, but in the sense of attaining absolute perfection, which destroys the power of contingency over freedom. The achievement of a God-like condition in which the reason and will are completely dominant over the world is the horizon towards which the infinite progress of each human individual is directed.

Kant's philosophy does not include the history of a lost paradise and the fall of man. It offers a prospect of the realization of essential humanity, not by obedience to nature but by emancipation from it. Kant opens a new chapter in the

history of philosophy's attempt to overcome the contingency of human existence, setting up freedom as man's realization and establishing the independence of the autonomous reason and will as the ultimate goal of man's unending
pilgrimage towards himself, a self that will then be divine.

12. *Fichte and the self-conquest of the spirit*

JOHANN GOTTLIEB FICHTE sought to remove the limitations of the Kantian
doctrine of man's summons to freedom and expounded the view that it is
within man's power, and is his duty, to achieve a radical awareness of his own
unbounded domination over the conditions of Being, the absolute primacy of
his own existence, and his complete independence of any pre-existing order. As
Fichte said in his address 'On the Dignity of Man' (1794), 'Philosophy teaches
us to discover everything in the ego'; 'only through the ego can order and harmony be instilled into the inert, formless mass'; man, 'by virtue of his existence,
is utterly independent of everything outside him and exists absolutely in and
through himself; . . . he is eternal, existing by himself and by his own strength'.
However, this awareness by man of his own status as the unconditional author
of Being is not something provided ready-made but is a moral precept, a call
to incessant self-transcendence and to an ever-repeated effort which regards
each form of Being in turn not as a finality but as a fresh obligation.

This philosophical emancipation of spirit from nature, and the conception
of the world as a perpetual moral task, were subsequently decried by Marx and
others as symptomatic of the weakness of German political radicalism and of a
civilization which, lacking the courage for a practical revolutionary effort,
transposed action into the realm of thought and envisaged practice in moralistic terms. However, by virtue of its basic position, German philosophy did not
regard the world as a source of optimistic anticipation or as the work of a
benevolent nature which prescribed values and provided for their vindication,
but as a problem and a challenge. Reason was no longer a copy of nature and
did not find in it a pre-established harmony. Philosophy was able to discern in
man, as a subject of cognition, a part or aspect of the whole man and of his
practical being; and in this way cognition came to be interpreted as a form of
practical behaviour.

Fichte's opposition to the philosophy of the Enlightenment was based on a
Kantian motif. If man is constrained by the pressure of existing nature, to which
he himself corporally belongs, then there can be no morality beyond a utilitarian calculation of pleasures and pains, that is to say no morality at all. If the
world is to be an object of obligation, man must be free from the determinism
of nature. Consequently, metaphysical and epistemological options imply a
moral question. We are constantly tempted by what Fichte calls 'dogmatism',

i.e. the viewpoint that explains consciousness by means of objects, since this frees us from responsibility and tells us to rely on the supposed laws of causality to be found in nature; anyone who cannot free himself from dependence on objects is, by inclination, a dogmatist. Idealism, on the other hand, treats consciousness as the point of departure and appeals to it for an understanding of the world of things; the idealist is a man who has achieved awareness of his own freedom, accepts his responsibility for the world, and is prepared to grapple with reality. Those who identify self-awareness with man's objective existence among things, i.e. the materialists, are not so much in error as weak and incapable of assuming the role of initiators of Being. Idealism is not only morally superior but is also a natural starting-point for the philosopher, as it avoids unanswerable questions. It does not have to inquire for whom the original fact of experience arises, for from this point of view subject and object coincide; the primary state of Being, self-consciousness, is being-for-itself and requires no explanation.

But this being-for-itself of self-consciousness is not given to our reflective faculty as a thing or a substance: it appears only as an activity. Fichte rejects the observational point of view that substance must precede action, while action presupposes an active substance. On the contrary, action is primary and in relation to it substantial being is only a secondary product or concrement. Consciousness is itself action, the movement of a creative initiative not prescribed from outside; it is *causa sui*. The world of objects has no independent existence; Kant's 'thing in itself' is a relic of dogmatism. In the awareness of his own unlimited freedom man recognizes himself as absolutely responsible for Being, and he recognizes Being as something which, taken as a whole, makes sense because of man. Freedom is also the condition of a true human community, based on voluntary solidarity and not on the negative bond of interest, which is the only bond if we accept the view that man's Being is defined by the needs marked out for him by nature. Fichte's ideal, like Rousseau's, is a society in which the ties between human beings are based on free co-operation and not regulated by a contract imposed from without.

If, however, consciousness is the absolute starting-point, it cannot be the awareness of perceptions, as in Berkeleyan idealism, but must be the awareness of acts of will. Its first and essential postulate is the obligation of thought towards itself, and this requires the ego to create its own counterpart, in which it recognizes itself as its own self-limitation. Consciousness, the ego, brings into existence the non-ego in order to establish itself in creative self-awareness. The mind is not content with its directly given self-identity but demands a reflective self-identity, turned in upon itself and perceived by itself; to achieve this, however, it must first divide into two and objectify itself by creating the world, which then appears to it as something external and enables it to know itself.

This dialectic of self-cancelling exteriorization is a direct anticipation of the Hegelian schema, but it is also rooted in the whole history of neo-Platonic theogony and in all doctrines that present God as coming into existence through his own creative activity. In Fichte's version the attributes of the divine Being are transferred to the human mind, which in its boundless autonomy is the standard to which all other reality is related. As far as the ego is concerned, the opposition between activity and passivity is no longer applicable. In the first version of his *Wissenschaftslehre* (*Theory of Science*; 1794; II. 4. E III) Fichte writes: 'Since the essence of the ego consists exclusively in the fact that it posits itself, self-positing and existence are for it one and the same . . . The ego can only avoid positing something in itself by positing it in the non-ego . . . The activity and passivity of the ego are one and the same.'

The ego is not identical with the empirical, psychological, individual subject: it is a transcendental ego, i.e. humanity considered as a subject, but it cannot be called a collective subject inasmuch as there is no autonomous being (like, for example, the 'universal mind' of the Averrhoists) independent of the individual consciousness. In other words, humanity is present as the nature of every individual man, the consciousness which each must discover in himself. It is thanks to this that human community is possible; the task of every individual is to know himself as Humanity.

The ego must in this way establish the world of things, which is a product of the ego's freedom but which, once established, is a restriction upon it and requires to be lifted. Hence the creation of the world is not a single event but an unceasing effort whereby the objectified products of the mind are reabsorbed into it. In overcoming the resistance of its objectifications—a resistance which is necessary for its own development—the mind thus attains to the state of absolute self-knowledge, through an unending process of setting itself fresh limits to be successfully transcended. The ultimate end of this process is expressed by absolute consciousness, but this end cannot in fact be reached: as in Kant's philosophy, it is a horizon marking the goal of an infinite progress. The positive conquest of freedom in human affairs thus requires a perpetual antagonism of the mind *vis-à-vis* each established form of civilization. The mind is the eternal critic of its own exteriorizations, and the tension between the inertia of established forms and the mind's elemental creative activity cannot cease to be, since it is a condition of the mind's existence or even, we may say, a synonym for it.

The Fichtean philosophy sought in this way to interpret man as a practical being, and introduced into epistemology the supremacy of the practical, i.e. the moral, point of view. Human cognition is determined as to its content by the practical perspective; man's relation to the world is not receptive but creative; the world is given as an object of obligation, not a ready-made source of perceptions. As, however, the true purpose of the ego is to perfect itself, man's true obligations lie in the sphere of education and self-education.

The ego being understood as freedom perpetually overcoming its own limitations, human history can be interpreted as the history of the mind's struggle for freedom. For Fichte, as later for Hegel, history becomes meaningful if it is conceived as progress towards the awareness of freedom. From unreflecting spontaneity via the power of tradition, the domination of individual particularism, and the final discovery of reason as an external governor, history moves towards a state in which individual freedom will coincide completely with universal reason and the sources of human conflict will dry up. History thus considered is a kind of theodicy, or rather anthropodicy: we can either interpret the evil we find in it as a factor of progress in relation to the dynamism of the whole, or we can argue that it is completely irrational and devoid of existential consistency, that in short it is nothing and does not belong to history.

The Fichtean picture of man as freedom, man discovering his proper calling in a perpetual contest with the inertia of his own alienations, provided the basis for a critique of all tradition and appeared to favour aspirations towards freedom in cultural and political life. It turned out, however, that the same philosophy could be made to yield conclusions quite opposite to its apparent intentions; and indeed Fichte himself did so at a later stage of his career. During the Napoleonic Wars his criticism of the utilitarianism of the Enlightenment and his apologia for non-utilitarian bonds between human beings were combined with a cult of the Nation as the embodiment *par excellence* of a non-utilitarian and non-rational community. In this respect Fichte anticipated Romantic thought. The idea that particular nations are the exponents of the main values of each epoch in the march of history led him into German messianism, and the idea of humanity as the essence of man led him to advocate compulsory state education as a means of aiding the discovery by the individual of his own true path in life. The totalitarian Utopia sketched in Fichte's *Der geschlossene Handelsstaat* (*The Closed Commercial State*; 1800) can be basically justified by his philosophy of freedom. The connection may be traced hypothetically as follows. What is required of man is to discover in himself his own absolutely free and creative humanity. This is not an arbitrary ideal but a real, ineluctable call to self-knowledge, progress towards which is identical with human existence itself. Since individuals and peoples do not develop equally towards their destined aim, but differ widely in the degree of self-knowledge they attain, it is quite natural that the education of the less by the more advanced should hasten the development of the former towards full humanity. If it is the task of the state to educate its nationals in the community spirit and in humanity, it is not strange that the rulers, who know the meaning of humanity better than the ruled, should use compulsion to bring out the humanity that lies dormant in every individual. This compulsion will be no more than the social expression of the compulsion that resides in every individual as his own essence, of which he is as yet unaware; it will in fact, therefore, not be compulsion at all, but the realization of humanity. As man is endowed with humanity by nature, compulsion to join in the community is not a violation of the individual's freedom but a release from the prison of his own ignorance and passivity. In this way Fichte's philosophy of humanity as freedom makes it possible to proclaim the police state as the incarnation of liberty.

Fichte was the true author of the immanent dialectic, i.e. the dialectic which does not extend beyond human subjectivity but makes that subjectivity its absolute point of departure (although in the last stage of his work Fichte returned to the idea of an extra-human Absolute, in whose freedom the human mind participates). Subject and object were, in his view, the result of a duality which sought to find a synthesis in infinite progress; however, as the subject was a human one, the synthesis could not realize itself in the contemplation of an extra-human Absolute, but only in the irreplaceable activity of human individuals. Since Fichte regarded humanity as unconditional existence, he could—and indeed, strictly speaking, had to—regard it as practical existence, defined basically by an active attitude towards its own world, which possessed a conditional existence in relation to creative subjectivity. In this way he laid the foundation of the interpretation of human history as the self-creation of a species, the meaningful, unidirectional ascent of freedom to self-knowledge. History is of course the medium through which non-historical consciousness, directly identical with itself, moves towards a reflective self-identity. History, therefore, is not an end in itself; it does not embrace all humanity without exception, but is a bridge between two non-historical realities, viz. consciousness as it was at the beginning and as the final goal of human evolution. The transcendental human subject, rooted in itself as freedom, by its practical exertion divides itself into the world of subject and object, and, through history, returns in an infinite progress to self-conscious freedom—such is the essential content of Fichtean metaphysics.

The possibility of interpreting this doctrine as an apologia for the totalitarian state depends primarily on two of its presuppositions. In the first place, Fichte holds that the purpose of each human individual and that of humanity as a whole are completely identical, that the realization of each and every one of us is exhausted in the realization of the universal humanity which resides in the individual as his own nature although he is not fully aware of it. Further, human beings are more or less advanced according to the degree to which they have realized their own essential humanity. Although, in Fichte's mind, education was to be primarily maieutic and to bring out the human dignity inherent in each individual, nevertheless, given the latitude with which the more enlightened were permitted to specify the kind of humanity to be aimed at, it was easy to interpret his programme as a system whereby everyone was to be coerced into realizing his own freedom. In other words, as freedom is in no way linked with differentiation and as the realization of the individual is no more or less than the realization of undifferentiated humanity, the achievement of freedom does not depend at all on the free self-expression of the individual as an irreducible entity. The transcendental ego is not a product of empirical human experience, but is sovereign *vis-à-vis* human life and can make demands on it by virtue of its own freedom; it can also, like God, hasten the progress of its own freedom by coercing the empirical human being.

13. Hegel. The progress of consciousness towards the Absolute

DESPITE the opposition between Kant's and Fichte's attempts to autonomize human existence, they both maintained an essentially dualistic point of view. In Kant this was a dualism between the contingency of the world of sense and the necessary forms of the intellect, and between duty and nature in man; in Fichte it was the dualism of duty and reality, which is a permanent condition of the development of the mind and is prolonged endlessly in an infinite movement of progress. However, neither Kant nor Fichte overcame the dilemma: either the mind comes to grips with the contingency of existence, and in cognizing it is, so to speak, infected with contingency, or it does away with contingency and thereby does away with the manifoldness of existence.

Hegel's majestic system was intended, among other things, to interpret the nature of Being in such a way as to deprive contingency of its effect while at the same time preserving the richness and variety of the universe. Contrary to Schelling's idealism, Hegel did not wish to reduce Being to the undifferentiated identity of the Absolute, in which the variety and multiplicity of finite reality must be lost or dismissed as an illusion; and again, in opposition to Kant, he refused to regard the thinking subject as abandoned helplessly to the experience of that variety and multiplicity, presented to him endlessly as a datum without reason or meaning. His purpose was to interpret the universe as entirely meaningful without sacrificing its differentiation. This required, as he wrote, 'a self-origination of the wealth of detail, and a self-determining distinction of shapes and forms' (*Phenomenology of Mind*, Preface).

But a Mind free from contingency is the same as an infinite Mind. For in so far as the object is something alien to the subject it is a limitation of it, a negation; a limited consciousness is finite, and the object, as foreign, is, so to speak, its enemy. Only when the Mind perceives itself in the object, thus removing the latter's alienness and objectivity, does it free itself from restrictions and achieve infinity; in this way the variety of Being ceases to be accidental. But, in order for that variety to maintain its richness, the process of removing the alienness and objectivity of the world must not be based on annihilating the created universe or proclaiming it as an illusion that is bound finally to merge into the unity of the all-absorbing Absolute; it must persist even as it passes away, that is to say the negation of it by the Mind must be an assimilating negation. The term *Aufheben* or 'sublation' denotes this particular kind of preserving negation, which safeguards both the independence of the Mind and the manifoldness of Being. But these are to be safeguarded not merely by putting forward an arbitrary definition of the Mind that meets these conditions, but by means of a historical description comprising the whole development of Being and capable of giving an integral sense to the history of the world and especially of human civilization. This historical system must present the development of Mind, through the travail of history, towards absoluteness. Such is the purpose of Hegel's *Phenomenology*, the most important of those of his works which together contain the germ of Marxism. It presents the successive phases of the necessary development of consciousness, which evolves from pure consciousness to absolute knowledge by way of self-awareness, Reason, Spirit (or Mind), and religion, and in that knowledge fulfils the purpose of the world, which is identical with knowledge of the world.

Apart from its immensely complicated and abstract language, which sets the reader's mind off on conflicting tracks and involves him in monstrous ambiguities, the *Phenomenology* has the further defect that it is not clear in which parts of the work the successive phases of the evolution of Mind are intended to correspond to actual phases of cultural development, and in which they are schemata constructed independently of that development. In some passages Hegel corroborates his account of particular phases by referring to specific events in the history of philosophy, religion, or politics, as when he speaks of Stoicism or scepticism, Greek religion, the Renaissance, the Enlightenment, etc. This might suggest that he is tracing the successive stages of the incarnate Mind in the history of civilization. On the other hand, we find that the phenomenological time-scheme does not correspond with actual history. For example, religion is presented as a phase of development subsequent to the evolution of self-knowledge, Reason, and Spirit—an evolution that comprises many elements of modern times, whereas religion dates back to antiquity. A 'phenomenology', however, is, properly speaking, not a timeless classification but a presentation of the sequence in which phenomena make their appearance and come to maturity. There are many such ambiguities in Hegel's *Phenomenology*, and they affect the question of the proper place of this work in Hegel's system as a whole. None the less we may draw attention to some essential tendencies in the sphere with which our own study is concerned.

Hegel regards it as evident that the spiritual is the starting-point of the whole evolution of Being: in this he is following a tradition that goes back to the beginnings of European philosophy in Parmenides, Plato, and the Platonists. The first principle must be something that depends for its Being on nothing else, that is self-supporting and related only to itself, the manner of this relationship being left for further investigation. It cannot therefore be composed of parts that limit one another or are mutually indifferent; being-in-itself and being self-related is a mode of Being that pertains to the spirit. That which is absolute is by definition free of all restriction or limitation, i.e. it is infinite, and only the Mind can be infinite in this sense. But Hegel goes further: the Mind is not only the first principle but is the only reality. This means that every manifestation of Being, every form of reality is intelligible only as a phase of the development of Mind, as its instrument or as a manifestation of the manner in which it combats its own imperfection.

For the Mind, though self-existent, is not self-sufficient. Hegel avoids the difficulty of the Platonists and Christians who had to account for the finite world while premising the self-sufficiency of the Absolute. He does so on the basis that the Absolute is self-sufficient in the sense that its self-existence does not require support from anything, but in the sense that it expresses the fullness of its own possibilities. It must also come to exist *for* itself, i.e. as the plenitude of knowledge of itself as Mind. In other words, it must become an object so that it can then do away with its own objectivity and assimilate it completely, when it will be a sublated object, self-directed and existentially identical with self-knowledge. Now—and this is the most distinctive feature of Hegelian thought—our reason, reflecting on the way in which the Absolute comes into being, must regard its own activity as a constituent of that process; for otherwise the evolution of Mind and of our own thinking concerning that evolution would be two separate and disparate realities—our thought would be accidental in relation to the evolution of Mind, or vice versa. This accounts in part for the error of the Kantian criticism, which involves first examining the nature of our cognitive powers and then using them to consider the nature of Being, after Reason has determined the limits of its own validity. This is an impracticable endeavour based on a false assumption. It is impracticable because our finite Reason cannot draw the bounds of its own validity without some prior means of doing so, nor can it exist before it exists. The false assumption is to suppose that man and the Absolute are 'on opposite sides' in the process of cognition, which is represented as a link between them. Reason, thinking of the Absolute, must be able to give a meaning to its own thought by relating itself to the Absolute; otherwise it condemns itself to a contingent role, by the illusory attempt to embrace an Absolute which does not comprise the activity of our intellect concerning it. In thinking about the world we must be aware that our thought is itself part of the evolution of the world, a continuation of the very thing to which it relates. Hegel is not writing *about* the Mind: he is writing the Mind's autobiography.

Thinking in this way, we see that the way to grasp the sense of any process of evolution is to relate the part to the whole. Truth can only be expressed in its entirety; meaning can be understood only in relation to the complete process, 'truth is the whole' (*das Wahre ist das Ganze*). This phrase has a double sense. In the first place, apart from any Hegelian interpretation it means that the knowledge of any part of the universe is significant only in so far as that part relates to the total history of Being. Secondly, the specifically Hegelian meaning is that the truth of every individual being is contained in the concept of that being, and that in realizing itself a being displays the fullness of its nature, which was previously concealed; it conforms progressively to the concept of itself and is finally identical with knowledge of itself. This last point, too, has a different meaning according to whether it is applied to a component of the universe or to the whole. We can say of any particular being that in developing itself it actualizes what was at first only a possibility (but a specific possibility, not a choice of different ones) and in this way attains to its own truth. In this sense, the truth of a seed is the tree that grows out of it, and the truth of an egg is a chicken. By achieving what was only a possibility, an object becomes its own truth. But Hegel goes further: in the development of Being, considered as a single process, truth, or the attainment of conformity with the concept, is not a mere casual conformity, i.e. the coincidence of two realities that the Mind might compare from outside as it compares a picture with its original or the plan of a house with the house itself. Where the whole process of the evolution of Mind is concerned, this conformity consists of the identity of a being with the concept of itself, i.e. the final situation in which the Being of Mind is the same thing as knowledge of that being: the Mind, having cast off its own objectivized form, returns into itself as the concept of itself, but a concept which is not merely abstract but is also awareness of that concept.

The progress of the Mind is thus circular: it ends as it began, which signifies that it is its own truth or has become conscious of what it was in itself. This final state is what is called absolute knowledge.

But this substance in which spirit consists is the development of itself explicitly to what it is inherently and implicitly; and only by this process of reflecting itself into itself is it then essentially and in truth spirit. It is inherently the movement which constitutes the process of knowledge—the transforming of that implicit inherent nature into explicitness and objectivity, of Substance into Subject, of the object of consciousness into the object of self-consciousness, i.e. into an object that is at the same time superseded and transcended—in other words, into the notion [*Begriff*]. This transforming process is a cycle that returns into itself, a cycle that presupposes its beginning, and reaches its beginning only at the end. (*Phen. of Mind*, DD. viii. 2)

If, however, the operation in which Mind creates the true content of history and finally returns into itself is not an empty one, that is to say if Mind does not simply revert to its original state as though nothing had happened, this is because the final outcome forms an integral whole with the process that has led to it, so that the Mind preserves at the end of the journey all the wealth it has accumulated on the way. The operation is one of continual 'mediation', i.e. the self-differentiation of the Mind, which produces from itself ever new forms which it then reassimilates by de-objectivizing them. At each successive stage the Mind thus proceeds by a continual self-negation; the negation is itself negated, but its values persist although they are absorbed into a higher phase.

> But the life of mind is not one that shuns death, and keeps clear of destruction; it endures its death and in death maintains its being. It only wins to its truth when it finds itself in utter desolation [*Zerrissenheit*] . . . Mind is this power only by looking the negative in the face, and dwelling with it. This dwelling beside it is the magic power that converts the negative into being. (*Phen. of Mind*, Preface)

The first form of the existence of Mind is awareness that is still not self-awareness. It goes through a phase of sensual certainty, in which consciousness is distinguished from the object, so that for consciousness there is such a thing as being-in-itself. What was an object has become knowledge of an object, so that Being has become being-in-itself-for-consciousness. At the same time consciousness changes in character and gradually frees itself from the illusion that it is burdened by something alien. Then, when consciousness grasps things in their specific character and understands their unity, it becomes a perceiving consciousness, or simply perception. In perception consciousness attains to a new phase, that of apprehending generality in the individual phenomenon. Every actual perception contains a general element: in order to grasp that a present phenomenon is present, we must apprehend the 'now' as something distinct from the perception itself, thus deriving an abstract element from the concrete datum. In the same way, when we apprehend the individuality of things we can do so only by means of an abstract conception of individuality, and we are on the level of generalized knowledge when we become aware of individuality as such. The actual 'thing out there' is inexpressible: language belongs to the realm of generality, and so therefore does every perception as soon as we express it. Perception, by imparting generality to the world of sense, surpasses the concreteness of the given object yet at the same time preserves it. Again, the object is distinguished by its particular qualities from other objects, and this opposition gives it its independence; yet at the same time it deprives it of independence, for the independence that consists in being different from other things is not absolute independence but a negative dependence on something else. The object dissolves into a set of relationships to other objects, so that it is a being-in-itself only in so far as it is a being-for-something-else, and vice versa. The comprehension of this form of generality in the world of sense signifies the entry of consciousness into the domain of intellect. Intellect is capable not only of apprehending the general in the concrete but also of apprehending generality as such, in the full content of its conceptual existence. It comprehends the supersensual world by its opposition to the sensual. In this opposition both worlds are made relative to each other in consciousness: each can only be understood as the negation of the other, each thus contains in itself its own opposite and thereby becomes infinite—for infinity is the lifting of the barriers imposed on Being by anything alien to it; a world becomes infinite by containing within itself what was previously its limitation. Then, when the conception of infinity becomes an object of consciousness, the latter becomes self-awareness or self-reflection.

Self-knowledge is aware that the object's being-in-itself is its manner of existing for another; it endeavours to possess itself of the object and cancel its objectivity. Self-knowledge tends by its nature towards that infinity which it has conceptually made its own. On the other hand, self-knowledge exists in and for itself only by virtue of the fact that it is recognized as such by another self-knowledge. Every self-knowledge is a medium through which every other is linked with itself. In other words, the self-knowledge of a human individual exists only in the process of communication and mutual understanding among human beings; it is a delusion to imagine a self-knowledge that treats itself as an absolute point of departure. But the presence of another self-knowledge as a condition of the first is also a limitation of the latter and a hindrance to its attainment of infinitude. Hence there is a natural tension and antagonism among self-knowledges in one another's presence. It is a fight to the death, in which each self-knowledge voluntarily exposes itself to destruction, and which results in one of them losing its independence and being subdued by the other. There arises a master-and-slave relationship, and this mutual dependence is the beginning of the process of the development of the spirit by human labour. The master has enslaved the independent object, using the slave as an instrument. The slave subjects things to treatment which has first been planned deliberately, i.e. in the Mind; but he performs the role imposed by the master and commander, and it is the latter alone who truly assimilates the object to himself by using it. But in this process, which seems to realize the object as a spiritual extension of the master, there occurs the reverse of what one would expect from the master-slave relationship. Labour signifies abstention from enjoyment, the repression of desire; in the slave's case it is a perpetual abstention for fear of the master, but in that fear the slave's self-knowledge achieves being-in-itself, and the repression gives form to objects; the slave regards the Being of things as an exteriorization of his own consciousness, and in this way being-in-itself is restored to consciousness as its own property. In labour, which is as it were the spiritualization of things, the slave's self-knowledge discovers its own meaning, although it appeared only to be actualizing the meaning of another. In servile work man perfects himself in humanity by the active spiritual assimilation of the object and by aptitude for ascesis. This phase, however, is not one of freedom or of the unity of subject and object: self-knowledge as an independent object is distinct from the independent object as self-knowledge.

The next form of self-knowledge is the thinking consciousness which apprehends itself as infinite and is therefore free. When I think, I am within myself and am free; the object becomes my being-for-myself. This form of free self-knowledge is that of Stoic philosophy, which refuses to recognize slavery and holds that spiritual freedom is independent of external conditions. The essence of this freedom is thought in general; thought withdraws into itself, relinquishes the attempt to assimilate the object, and declares itself indifferent to the question of natural existence. This moral negation of things is carried to an extreme by scepticism, which denies them intellectually as well, declares the non-existence of everything 'other', and annihilates the multiplicity of the universe. The sceptical consciousness would destroy both the object and its own relation to it. It suffers from a contradiction, however, since it purports to achieve self-identity by denying the fact of differences in the world, yet in that very act it becomes aware of its own contingency, which is the opposite of self-identity. When this contradiction is perceived we have an unhappy consciousness, torn between awareness of itself as an autonomous being and as a contingent one. This divided state is exemplified by Judaism and early Christianity. Consciousness is confronted by the otherworldly Being of God, in which it beholds itself indeed, but in opposition to God's immutability; it humbly acknowledges its own individual contingency in the presence of divinity, but does not know its own individuality in its truth and universality. Powerless individuality perceives renunciations on God's part even in the results of its own activity, but in the consequent acts of thanksgiving it rediscovers its own reality and attains to the next stage of spiritual evolution, that of Reason.

Reason is the affirmation of the individual consciousness as a consciousness that is antonomous and sure of itself; it expresses this certainty in idealistic doctrines which aim at regarding the whole of reality as something comprehended by the individual consciousness. However, this rationalistic idealism is unable to find room within its boundaries for all the variety of experience, and declares this variety to be of no concern to it. In so doing it falls into a contradiction, for, while seeking to affirm the independence of Reason, it acknowledges, if only by its indifference, the existence of something that, as in Kant's doctrine, is outside the unity of apperception. In addition, it is obliged to take cognizance of another's ego as different from its own and thus as a limitation of its Being. Reason, however, is confident of discovering itself in the world and removing the 'otherness' of natural being; it sets about doing this, firstly in scientific observation (Reason as observer), with the purpose of turning the evidence of the senses into concepts, and then seeks to establish laws that will eliminate sensual being, so as to recognize as real only that which purely and simply fulfils the conditions of the law. However, unassimilated reality cannot be invalidated in this fashion. Reason is constantly faced with a contradiction between its demands and the world as it is encountered. Consciousness is thus again subjected to an inner conflict, due to the chronic opposition between that which is given and the purposes devised by reason. The issue is between individuality and universality, between law and the individual, between virtue and the actual course of history.

This last point is of especial importance, as it raises the whole general question of the relation between moral imperatives and existing reality. In the contest between virtue and history, the former is bound to succumb.

> Virtue will thus be overpowered by the world's process, because the abstract unreal essence is in fact virtue's own purpose . . . Virtue wanted to consist in the fact of bringing about the realization of goodness through sacrificing individuality; but the aspect of reality is itself nothing else than the aspect of individuality. The good was meant to be what is implicit and inherent, and opposed to what *is*; but the implicit and inherent, taken in its real truth, is simply *being* itself. The implicitly inherent element is primarily the abstraction of essence as against actual reality: but the abstraction is just what is not true, but a distinction merely for consciousness; this means, however, it [the implicitly inherent element] is itself what is called actual, for the actual is what essentially is for another—or it is being. But the consciousness of virtue rests on this distinction of implicitness and explicit being, a distinction without any true validity . . . The way of the world is, then, victorious over what, in opposition to it, constitutes virtue; it is victorious over that whose nature is an unreal abstraction. (*Phen. of Mind*, C. v. B, c, 3)

This is an expression, in more complicated terms, of the classic aphorism in the Preface to the *Philosophy of Right*: 'What is rational is actual, and what is actual is rational.' Hegel regards it as a delusion of Reason to set up a basic opposition between the actual course of history and the 'essential' demands of the world—an opposition in the form of a conflict between the normative ideal derived from Reason itself and the realities of the spirit as it evolves into Being. This criticism of Hegel's is levelled both against Fichte and against the Romantics: the error of postulating an eternal conflict between the rational imperative and the existing world lies in the fact that Reason is not yet able to comprehend reality as the gestation of Reason, so that reality constantly appears to it as something contingent and to be overcome. It is over this question that the

most important conflicts of interpretation have arisen among Hegel's successors. Did Hegel mean to declare that it is in accordance with Reason to assent
ex animo to reality as we encounter it in all its detail, the world at any given
moment being simply a necessary stage in the evolution of Mind, so that his
doctrine is a logodicy devoted to proving that 'whatever is, is right'? Or, on the
contrary, is it the duty of Reason to investigate what parts of existing reality are
truly in accordance with the principles of its evolution, and thus reserve to
itself the right to judge any particular situation? It is difficult to resolve the
ambiguity of Hegelianism on this fundamental point. Hegel does not in fact
seek to apply moral judgements to past history, but rather to understand it, with
all its horrors, as the travail of Mind struggling to be free. On the other hand,
he restricts philosophy to awareness of the past historical process and denies it
the right to peer into the future, while claiming that his own philosophy represents the final emancipation of Mind from the trammels of objectivity. We
may thus say that as regards the past his philosophy is a reasoned justification
of history in relation to its final goal, while as regards the future he, as it were,
chooses to suspend judgement.

This point of view is confirmed when it comes to transferring the accord
between developing essence and actual existence to the case of a human individual. The individual knows himself only through his own action: his nature
is revealed in his attitude to the world and the way he expresses that attitude
in practice. What he does *is* himself: activity is merely the bringing of possibility into existence, the awakening of latent potential. But if so, we cannot find
rules in the Hegelian system that enable us, in a practical situation, to distinguish what is 'essential', either in the individual's case or in the context of history, from what is a distortion and corruption of that essence. It appears natural
to suppose, indeed, that factual reality is generally the fulfilment of the developing possibilities of Mind, which exists just in so far as it manifests itself ('The
essence must reveal itself', as Hegel says in his *Logic*), and which is not presented with a choice between different roads of development, but brings to
fruition the single possibility that it contains within itself.

To proceed: when Reason has attained the certainty that it is itself its own
world and that the world is it, and when it thus knows that it is objective reality and that this reality is at the same time its being-for-itself, Reason then
becomes Mind in the narrower sense of the term, i.e. as limited to the developmental phase of consciousness. Reason in the form of Mind recognizes itself
in the world, i.e. it sees the world as rational and frees it of contingency, but at
the same time it does not regard the world as a delusion but as a reality in
which it actualizes itself. It is not the kind of Reason which separates itself
from the world and places itself above or beside it, which is not prepared
either to entrust its own contingency to the world of Being or, on the other

hand, to obtain for itself an illusory autonomy by declaring the world to be a mere appearance. It stands in opposition to Kant's solution as to those of the Romanticists and idealists. The spirit actualizes itself in the world of ethics, culture, and the moral conscience. 'But only spirit which is object to itself in the shape of Absolute Spirit is as much aware of being a free and independent reality as it remains therein conscious of itself' (*Phen. of Mind*, CC. VII, Introduction). The Mind conscious of itself as Mind is the mind that functions in religion, that is to say in the action of the Absolute Being in the guise of Mind's self-knowledge. The first actuality of Mind is natural religion; the elimination of that naturalness leads to the religion of art, and when the one-sidedness of both these stages is done away with there appears a revealed synthetic religion in which the 'I' of the spirit is directly present and reality is identified with it. Religion, however, is not the final fulfilment of the activity of Mind, for in it the Mind's self-knowledge is not an object of its consciousness, its own consciousness has not yet been overcome. The final form of Mind is absolute knowledge, i.e. the pure being-for-itself of self-knowledge. Being, truth, and certainty of truth have all become one; the full content of Mind, accumulated in the course of history, takes on the form of the ego. Objectivity has been eliminated as such, and Mind discourses with itself, imbued with the fullness of variety created through history and at the same time freed from all 'otherness' by which it was limited and from all the differences that arose at particular stages between Being, concept, and conceptual consciousness.

Despite all the ambiguities of the *Phenomenology of Mind*, the uncertainty as to the relationship between the developmental necessities of consciousness and the actual history of civilization, and the immense difficulty of following the transitions between the successive phases of Mind's self-denial and the reassimilation of its own exteriorizations—despite all this, Hegel's metaphysical epic affords sufficient clues as to its general intentions. Hegel insists that our acts of cognition include not only the object of knowledge but also the fact that it is known; in the cognitive act whereby the Mind assimilates things, it must understand its present relation to them. He thus aims at an observational standpoint from which reality and the thought of reality are alike explicable, a standpoint that comprehends both Being and the understanding of Being. Only from such a standpoint, if it can be achieved, will the world and the intellect lose their contingency; alternatively, one or other of them must be inexplicable or arbitrarily written off as mere appearance. At the same time we perceive that even the phrase 'observational stand-point' is incorrect; if the intellect were able to contemplate its own relation to the world, this contemplation would be a new kind of relationship, not comprised by self-understanding, and there would be no end to the process of ascending to higher and higher vantage-points, while consciousness would always remain in some inexplicable place outside the world and outside itself. Therefore the final elimination of the estrangement between Mind and object must at the same time be the effective elimination of the object's own objectivity, and not a mere theoretical understanding of the object as of an alienated consciousness; the object and knowledge of it must coincide in unity.

If the elimination of the opposition between subject and object were merely a regulative ideal for the purposes of thought, and not a state of affairs that can actually be attained in the course of a finite development, then the operation of Mind would be in vain. Progress might go on for ever, but it would be no real progress, as the goal would still be infinitely far away. From this point of view Hegel, especially in his *Logic*, denounces the idea of 'spurious infinity' which he finds in the doctrines of Kant and Fichte. In their view of progress the antagonism between the order of nature and that of freedom, between duty and Being, is eternalized, so that finitude becomes something absolute and unvanquishable.

> The understanding persists in this sadness of finitude by making non-being the determination of things and at the same time making it imperishable and absolute. Their transitoriness could only pass away or perish in their other, in the affirmative; their finitude would then be parted from them; but it is their unalterable quality, that is, their quality which does not pass over into its other, that is, into its affirmative; it is thus eternal . . . But certainly no philosophy or opinion, or understanding, will let itself be tied to the standpoint that the finite is absolute; the finite is only finite, not imperishable; this is directly implied in its determination and expression. (*Science of Logic*, Bk. 1, 2, B, c, a)

If we regard infinity as merely the negation of finitude, then the very concept of the former is dependent on finitude considered as the basic reality; infinity is merely the extremity of finitude, from which it cannot free itself, and is therefore a finite or 'spurious' infinity. As against this, an affirmative, true infinity is the negation of finitude conceived as a negation: it is thus the negation of a negation, a real victory over finitude, an issuing of finitude beyond itself. Only when finitude by reasons of its contradictions shows itself to be infinite, and when the finite by becoming truly itself puts on infinity—only then will infinity assume a positive sense. Hence 'progress to infinity', or the idea of unlimited self-perfection, the eternal approximation of reality to an ideal, is an internal contradiction but an inert one, repeating itself over and over again without change and leading nowhere. It is the tedium of monotonous non-fulfilment; whereas authentic infinity, 'as the consummated return into self, the relation of itself to itself, is being—but not indeterminate, abstract being, for it is posited as negating the negation; . . . the image of true infinity, bent back into itself, becomes the circle, the line which has reached itself, which is closed and wholly present, without beginning and end' (ibid., Ch. 2, C, c).

As we have seen, Hegel regards the notion of infinite progress as encumbered by an internal, non-dialectic contradiction. If the idea of an ascending development is to make any sense in general, it must be a development with an effective terminus in view. The elimination of the contingency of Mind and the conquest of freedom must be actually possible; to say that they can be reached at infinity is the same as to say that they cannot be reached at all. If the history of Being is intelligible, if any sense can be given to the dialectic in which Mind wrestles with its own objectifications, this can only be in relation to a *real* Absolute—not an Absolute which is merely a signpost to a place that the Mind knows it will never reach, that is to say a place that does not exist.

To sum up, the Hegelian dialectic is not a method that can be separated from the subject-matter to which it is applied and transferred to any other sphere. It is an account of the historical process whereby consciousness overcomes its own contingency and finitude by constant self-differentiation.

14. Hegel. Freedom as the goal of history

THIS overcoming of contingency is the same as freedom of the spirit. From this point of view the evolution of Mind is dealt with especially in Hegel's *Lectures on the Philosophy of History*. Published after his death, the *Lectures*, along with the *Philosophy of Right*, are the most popular and most often read of his works. Unlike the *Phenomenology of Mind*, they are written in fairly clear and uncomplicated language, and have thus had a major effect in forming the stereotype of Hegel's doctrine. His philosophy of history is an account of the spirit's search for freedom through the variety of past events.

According to Hegel the meaning of history can be discovered, but it is a meaning that is not indicated by history: rather it uses history as an instrument. Freedom is proper to the Mind, as gravity is to matter; but Mind must first realize its own nature by elevating its freedom to the dignity of freedom-for-itself, self-knowing freedom. This freedom is equivalent to being-within-itself, i.e. the state of being unlimited by any alien objectivity. In the course of human history the Mind becomes that which it was in itself; it does not, however, throw away the riches it has accumulated on the journey, like a ladder that is no longer needed after the ascent, but preserves them all. 'The life of the ever-present Spirit is a circle of progressive embodiments [*ein Kreislauf von Stufen*], which looked at in one aspect still exist beside each other, and only as looked at from another point of view appear as past. The grades [*Momente*] which Spirit seems to have left behind it, it still possesses in the depths of its present' (*Lectures on the Philosophy of History*, Introduction).

Nature does not contain in itself the element of freedom, and consequently there is no progress in it, only changes and endless repetition of the same thing.

Nature is an indispensable condition for the operation of the human spirit, and as such has its place in the divine economy. But the actual progress of Mind takes place in human history and particularly in the evolution of civilization, in which the human spirit attains to an increasing self-knowledge of freedom. History becomes intelligible as a whole if we regard it as the development of the consciousness of freedom, a development which in its main lines is necessarily determined. In the ancient Orient only one man, the despotic ruler, enjoyed freedom, and all that world knew of freedom was expressed in the tyrant's whim. Ancient Greece and Rome had an elementary notion of freedom in general and knew that some of their citizens were free, but they did not ascend to the concept that man as such is free. This concept was recognized only in Christian-Germanic civilization, and is an essential, inalienable conquest of the human spirit.

World history is also the history of Reason: i.e. its course follows a rational design which the philosopher's eye is capable of perceiving. At first sight, it is true, history appears to be a chaos of surging passions and confused struggles, in which the collision of individual or group interests produces irrational, accidental results; the mass of human suffering and misfortune serves no useful purpose and is engulfed by the indifference of time. But in fact the situation is quite otherwise. Individual passions, which are the mainspring of human activity, play their part, independently of anyone's intention, in the progress of evolution and are instruments of the wisdom of history, which cunningly uses for its own purpose actions motivated by private designs. History is thus not intelligible if we present it in a psychological light by examining the motives of particular agents; its meaning consists in the process that is not contained in any of these motives, but uses them to fulfil the purpose for which Mind exists. The subjective motives of human acts are not accidental, inasmuch as they relate to an overriding purpose that precedes both history and the individual subject. Hegel says, it is true, that 'reason is immanent in historical existence and fulfils itself in and through it' (*Lectures*, Introduction), but this does not mean that the rules of the operation of universal Reason were created for the first time by empirical history. Reason is immanent in history in the same way as the Christian God, incarnate in human form; his purpose is fulfilled only through history, which is, as it were, the body of the Deity, but it is not by history that the purpose is determined.

It is by no means the purpose of the operation of the spirit in history to satisfy human desires. 'The history of the world is not a scene [*Boden*] of happiness. Periods of happiness are blank pages in it, for they are periods of harmony—periods when the antithesis is in abeyance' (ibid.). Humanity undergoes struggles and antagonism, suffering and oppression in order to fulfil its own calling, which is also that of the universal spirit. For 'man is an object of existence in himself only in virtue of the Divine that is in him—that which was designated at the outset as Reason and which, in view of its activity and power of self-determination, was called Freedom' (ibid.).

Once we understand this we can evaluate for ourselves the utopias or ideals which men, following their own whims, have opposed to the poverty of reality. Reason justifies history when discerned in it, and condemns to vanity and ineffectiveness all arbitrary models of a perfect society. Even if these are in accordance with the just demands and rights of the individual, 'the claim of the world-spirit rises above all particular claims'. And this right of the spirit actualizes itself with inexorable necessity, according to the self-determination to which the spirit is subject.

All forms and aspects of civilization—law and the state, art, religion, philosophy—have their defined place in the progress of Mind towards freedom. Thanks to them, the rational consciousness of the individual is not condemned, like that of the Stoics, to the kind of freedom that consists of withdrawing helplessly into oneself and accepting the inevitability of external, alien, accidental, and uncontrollable events. Hegelian freedom is the understanding of necessity, but it is quite different from what the Stoics meant by this. The human spirit desires to reconcile itself with reality, but not through humble resignation which eternalizes the opposition between a closed-off, autarkic self-awareness and the indifferent course of events. The subjective human will has a means of reconciling itself to the world by understanding it and realizing itself in it, rather than turning away from it in a spurious dignity which is merely a cloak for despair. This means consists of civilization and especially the state. The state is the 'ethic whole' in which the individual can realize his own freedom as a part of the community, at the price of giving up the whims of self-will and the making of arbitrary demands on the world as his fancy may dictate. The state is not merely an institution invented for the settling of conflicts or the organization of collective enterprises in accordance with a social contract. As the locus of the reconciliation of the subjective will with universal Reason it is the realization of freedom, an end in itself, 'the divine idea as it exists on earth' and the reality which alone gives value to the individual life. 'Every value and every reality that man possesses, he owes to the state alone' (ibid.). As the highest form of objectivization of Mind, the state represents the general will, and the freedom of the individual is a reality when it is based on obedience to the law, for then the will is obeying itself. In this subordination the opposition between freedom and necessity ceases to exist, since the necessity prescribed by the Reason of history comes about not through compulsion but through free will. Hegel did not assert that the private sphere must be completely absorbed into the collective will embodied in the organs of the state: he believed, on the contrary, that the state is a mediator between the spheres of private and collective life and that its institutions are the embodiment of that mediation, for the private interest of the state's servants is identical with the collective interest. In the case of other members of society, the restrictions imposed on their personal wishes and impulses, far from being a limitation of freedom, are a condition of it. The state, it is true, has no other reality than its citizens, but this does not mean that the will of the state can be determined by the collectivity of their private, individual opinions. The general will is not the will of the majority but the will of historical Reason.

Hegel's historiosophy was criticized from the beginning, as it still is today, on two main grounds. In the first place, there was the complaint that it denied the independent value of personal human life, allowing to the individual only the role of complying with the demands of universal Reason, and, in the name of those demands, authorizing the state to coerce individuals as much as it liked for the sake of a higher freedom. Secondly, critics pointed out that the doctrine justified every actual reality as praiseworthy by the very fact of its existence, which proved it to have been planned by the divine Mind. The first of these objections relates chiefly to the introduction to *Lectures on the Philosophy of History*, the second to the introduction to the *Philosophy of Law*.

The objection which represents Hegel as an apologist of the totalitarian state is weakened to a certain extent by the fact that he regarded the development of society not only as the development of absolute spirit through historical events, but also as the gradual reconciliation of the subjective will with the general will. This means that no state acting by means of violence could fulfil the supreme commands of Reason. It is true that in the earlier stages law appears, from the individual's point of view, as an external system of restriction and constraint, but the whole tendency of the development of the spirit is to overcome this opposition and so interiorize the general will. The course of history does not begin with a Golden Age; the mythology of a happy state of nature or a lost paradise is completely alien to Hegel's thought. On the contrary, the state of nature is one of barbarity and lawlessness, and it is by the gradual perfecting of politico-legal institutions that this gives place to rational thought and the subduing of private impulses. But, in Hegel's view, Reason tolerates only the compulsion of reasoning itself. That is to say, the systematic coercion of individuals is the mark of an immature society, and progress leads to a situation in which the subjective will and the general will coincide spontaneously as a result of acts of understanding of the world by those who form the collectivity of the state. It is impossible for Reason to rule in a situation where it has to assert its demands by violence so as to triumph finally in opposition to the consciences of individuals; its triumph can only be assured by the intellectual maturity and reformed consciousness of the state's citizens.

If it is true, however, that Hegel was by no means a champion of the tyrannic power which forces its subjects to obey the dictates of historical Reason, the practical application of his doctrine means that in any case where the state apparatus and the individual are in conflict, it is the former which must prevail. For as long as the individual consciousness is not fully transformed and is still subject to egoistical impulses, so that there is not yet a complete and voluntary accord between the subjective will and universal Reason, the question must arise: who is to decide, in a particular situation of conflict, what the universal will requires? Since there is no other institution but the state which could assume this role, and since the state by definition is the incarnation of Reason, in cases of conflict it must play the role of the medieval Church, i.e. the sole authorized interpreter of the divine message. Hence, although Hegel's ideal was certainly the complete interiorization of historical Reason in the soul of every individual, and the perfection of the state as an institution was to manifest itself by the disappearance of the need for compulsion, nevertheless in actual cases of conflict where there is no practical question of appealing to the 'majority will' or the voice of the people, the state apparatus, independent of the changing opinions of citizens, must be the final court from which there is no appeal. Hegel supposes, of course, that it is an apparatus functioning according to law and not by the whim of a tyrant or a civil servant; but in cases where the law is ambiguous or it is a question of changing the laws, the state apparatus for the time being has the last word. In this sense, despite Hegel's emphasis on legal and constitutional forms of communal life, the state apparatus is privileged in his eyes and is entitled to assert itself not only against any individual but against all together, since the force of Reason resides in it and not in the will of the majority. Historians have pointed out, it is true, that Hegel's apologia for the Prussian monarchy as the ideal state is qualified inasmuch as he describes institutions that Prussia at that time did not possess. Nevertheless, and although he recognized legality as the essential feature of the state, in which all men were to be equal before the law (though not in making the laws), Reason as embodied in particular individuals or even a majority of them was bound to be nonsuited when it came into conflict with the authorities. Thus, while Hegel demanded that reality should be answerable to the tribunal of Reason, there was no possibility of finding Reason in this sense elsewhere than in the state apparatus.

Hegel does not answer clearly the question whether, and to what extent, the value of the human individual is preserved in the triumphal progress of Mind through history. On the one hand, Mind in the course of becoming itself loses none of the wealth of its exteriorization, and the instruments it uses for its purposes are not simply cast aside, but endure as part of its infinite richness. It might seem therefore that individual life is permanently valuable in itself. But, on the other hand, the value of the individual consists only in the 'element of divinity' within him, and it thus actualizes itself *as a value of the Absolute;* moreover, it seems to disappear completely in the final consummation of the destinies of being. Mind, in completing its progress, attains to infinitude, i.e. the removal of all limitations by anything that is not itself; it appears therefore that in Hegel's view the final destiny of every separate individual is to be absorbed in universal Being, since otherwise the Absolute would be limited by the self-knowledge of individuals and would not accomplish its own purpose. At this central point Hegel appears once again to follow the tradition of neo-Platonic pantheism: the abolition of the contingency of man and the fulfilment of man in his essence, his self-reconciliation, must signify his total absorption into universal Being. It is not clear how individuality as such could be preserved in all its richness when all difference between subject and object disappears; in other words, how is it possible for an infinite being, which has attained to full self-knowledge and reabsorbed all its own objectifications, to be other than *one* being? We must finally conclude that in the Hegelian system humanity becomes what it is, or achieves unity with itself, only by ceasing to be humanity.

We can, of course, consider Hegel's philosophy of history in the light of its partial conclusions, concentrating on the rationalistic determinism of the historical process, its indifference to individual human desires, and its development through successive negations, while abstracting our minds from the final result. But to ignore the eschatological perspective is to deprive the doctrine of its specifically Hegelian character: neither Hegel's dialectic nor its application to history make sense without the eschatology, the vision of the final salvation of Being in a return into itself.

The question of the rationality of the world as such, in all its details, also requires some differentiation. Hegel in fact believes that only the actual historical process is creative of values—that is to say, it is vain and foolish to imagine ideals independently of the actual state of history, or to postulate a radical opposition between the world as it ought to be and as it is. In this respect his anti-utopianism is emphatic and unambiguous. Those who defend him against the charge of conservative bias point out with truth that he believes in a tribunal of Reason to distinguish between what is truly real and what appears real but is no longer 'essential', maintaining a purely empirical existence and destined soon to be swept away. 'Reality', to Hegel, does not mean any fact that happens to present itself: for instance, he excludes from his definition of the civilizing process various forms of behaviour, such as personal caprices, which are not rooted in the will of history. What appears to be an overwhelmingly evident and inescapably real feature of the present situation may be, from Hegel's point of view, no more than the empty shell of a bygone reality, while something that is barely emerging from a dormant or virtual state, and is hardly accessible to empirical inquiry, may actually contain more reality. In the same way an egg which is about to hatch into a chicken looks as though it would remain an egg for ever, but in fact it is on the point of giving birth to a new form which, though invisible, is already mature and is the one important thing about it. In this sense Hegel taught that we must look for what is 'truly' real as opposed to the superficial reality that is passing away. This distinction is, in his view, a matter of scientific reflection and does not call for any value-judgements opposed to the actuality of the facts. Such evaluation, abstracted from historical necessity, was in Hegel's opinion a symptom of the sterile recalcitrance of Fichte and the Romantics. This does not mean that his prescription was to find out what was necessary and at once infer that it was desirable, but rather that he rejected the dichotomy of facts and values. It is not necessary first to discover what is real and then to evaluate it. Acts of comprehension of the world are undivided: in the very act in which we perceive something as a portion of evolving Reason, we accept that something. The positivistic distinction between judgements of fact and of value does not arise in Hegel's system any more than in dogmatic religion: once we know what the will of God is, we do not have to express our approval of it by a separate intellectual act. The perception of the world which relates every detail to the will of the Absolute does not involve any such dichotomy either: it consists of acts of comprehension merged with practical acts of affirmation. The submission of the intellect to the authority of the Absolute is an indivisible whole composed of simultaneous understanding and trust in its wisdom.

While, however, it would be wrong to think of Hegel as approving any and every part of existing reality simply because it is there, the question immediately arises: by what criteria are we to judge whether a particular feature is 'real' or not? Who is to decide, and on what basis, whether a particular state of affairs is a sham from which the energy has gone out, or is still full of vitality? Certainly purely empirical criteria will not suffice. How then are we, in practice, to appeal to universal Reason to tell us, for example, whether an institution or form of state has outlived its usefulness or is still rational? The Hegelian system does not provide an answer to this question. As Mind endeavours to interiorize its freedom in individual intellects, it might seem that a form against which empirical individuals are in rebellion must for that reason be irrational, and we should therefore condemn political systems that are unquestionably opposed by the generality of people. But, on the other hand, we are told that the *consensus omnium* is not a valid criterion and that all men, or nearly all, may be in opposition to right Reason, since 'the affairs of the state are matters of knowledge and education and not of its people' (*Lectures*, Introduction). We are thus led back to a conservative apologia for existing institutions as such, from which there is no appeal to any other empirical reality for the purpose of interpreting the decrees of Reason.

Although Hegel's thought on this fundamental point is beset by ambiguity, it is clear that fewer difficulties and glosses are required if we choose to interpret it in a conservative sense: for this provides an indication of the principles on which things are to be condemned, whereas if we seek to adopt the 'critical principle' we are left uncertain which criteria to apply.

The question can be seemingly avoided by reference to the famous passage in the preface to the *Philosophy of Right* where Hegel says that philosophy always comes too late and can only interpret a completed process: 'By philosophy's grey in grey, [a shape of life] cannot be rejuvenated but only understood'. From this point of view our thoughts about the world are of no significance for the purpose of practical evaluation, since we cannot judge the future but can only try to understand the past. There is no point in debating whether we should accept the present as simple reality or judge its empirical qualities by the transcendental demands of Reason, since we are concerned as philosophers only with what is irrevocably past and not with the present world or its prospects. But for practical purposes this attitude itself amounts to a conservative acceptance of the *status quo*, since it prohibits us from speculating as to what might be better. The final message of Hegelianism, therefore, is not the opposition between Reason and an unreasonable world, but contemplation of the world as *a priori* reasonable. We do not know what parts of the existing world are or are not true instruments of Mind: we cannot be sure, for example, that it has ceased to use criminals for its purposes. The individual has no rules of morality which he can oppose to the supremacy of the historical process. In Hegel's system, rebellion against the existing world *may* be justified in a particular case, but we have no means of telling whether it is or not until its destiny is accomplished. If it proves successful, this shows that it was historically right; if crushed, it will evidently have been only a sterile reaction of 'what ought to have been' (*Sollen*). The vanquished are always wrong.

. . .

UP TO this stage of our exposition we have been concerned with doctrines which presuppose that man is not the same in his empirical being as he is in reality or in essence, and that the basic imperative is that the two should once more become identical. This leads to two alternatives: either the essence of man is not only outside empirical human life but outside humanity altogether, so that man's 'return to himself' is not a return to himself but a realization of the Absolute, in which the particular character of humanity disappears without trace; or else, as in Kant and Fichte, the realization of man's essence is an infinite process. In both cases the progress of humanity towards fulfilment was either dictated by the Absolute, as preceding humanity, or by humanity as preceding actual human nature: human existence was not rooted in itself as a natural form of Being. A new philosophical possibility and a new eschatology came into view with the conception of humanity self-present as an Absolute in its own finitude, and the rejection of all solutions that involve man realizing himself by the actualization, or at the command, of an antecedent absolute Being. This new philosophical prospect is that displayed in the work of Marx.

II

The Hegelian Left

1. The disintegration of Hegelianism

LIKE ALL other such philosophies, Hegel's attempt at a universal synthesis of Being soon led to discordant results. Immediately after his death in 1831 it became clear that both the general theory of consciousness and its application to the meaning of history and to problems of law and politics were capable of different and contradictory interpretations. In particular, it was not at all clear how far Hegel's political conservatism was the natural consequence of his philosophy of history, or whether it could be distinguished from it as a private and personal opinion. To Hegel's radically minded interpreters it seemed evident that a philosophy which proclaimed the principle of universal negativism, treating each successive phase of history as the basis of its own destruction, a philosophy which presented the critical and self-annihilating process as the eternal law of spiritual development, could not consistently tolerate the endorsement of a particular historical situation, or recognize any kind of state, religion, or philosophy as irrefutable and final.

Hegel's doctrine, apart from the explicit political views it contained, embodied two essential themes which seemed hard to reconcile and likely to prove contradictory in some at least of their consequences. On the one hand, Hegelianism was inexorably anti-utopian: it expressly condemned the viewpoint which, in the face of a particular historical reality, puts forward exigences based on arbitrary normative ideals, moralistic presumptions, and notions of how the world ought to be. Hegel's dialectic was a method of understanding past history but did not pretend to gaze into the future; in fact it condemned any such extrapolation and did not aspire to shape the course of human affairs. From this point of view it might seem that Hegelianism amounted to recognizing history and the *status quo* as realities no less unshakeable than the rules of logic, so that any protest against the present world in the name of an imaginary one must be rejected as the caprice, understandable certainly but sterile, of an immature consciousness. On the other hand, the Hegelian apologia for Reason could equally be taken as postulating a reasonable world, as demanding that reality should be made rational and empirical history coincide with the requirements of the spirit struggling to be free. On the first interpretation the Hegelian system tended towards contemplative acceptance of the historical process as something natural and inevitable, any revolt against which was condemned to futility. On the opposite interpretation it encouraged a spirit of mistrust and criticism, requiring the confrontation of any existing world with the imperatives of Reason, and contained within itself standards which entitled mankind to judge and criticize reality and to demand that it be reformed.

For a few years after Hegel's death his system functioned as, in effect, the official doctrine of the Prussian state; apologists for that state drew on its wealth of theory, and the authorities began to fill university chairs with Hegelians. This situation rapidly altered in the middle thirties when it became clear that the most active of Hegel's disciples had ideas that were unpalatable to the Prusso-Christian monarchy, and that the intricacies of his thought involved elements of radicalism as regards, in particular, the critique of established religion. The celebrated and often-interpreted aphorism 'what is actual is rational' could be taken as sanctifying any factual situation simply because it existed, or contrariwise as meaning that an empirical fact only deserved to be called 'actual' if it conformed to the demands of historical Reason: on this view, elements contrary to Reason were not truly actual, although they might empirically be more obvious than the rational ones. This interpretation was the one that finally prevailed, chiefly owing to the works of the Hegelian Left; but it does not answer the question, by what signs are we to distinguish actual and rational features of the universe from illusory, irrational ones? Are these criteria to be established independently of the facts of history, according to the arbitrary dictates of pre-historical Reason, or are they to be inferred from history? And, in the latter case, how do we define the role of historical knowledge in the opinion-forming or normative operation of the spirit? In other words, how far and in what sense can rules be derived from a knowledge of history so as to enable us to judge the rationality of the world as it now is? If rules cannot be so derived, they are as emptily formal as the Kantian imperative.

The Young Hegelian movement, as it is called, singled out as the dominant theme of Hegel's philosophy the principle of permanent negation as the ineluctable law of spiritual development. This led by degrees to an attitude of radical criticism in politics, certain forms of which supplied the philosophical basis of communism. Engels observes in one of his early writings that the Hegelian Left was the natural approach to communism, and that Hegelian communists such as Hess, Ruge, and Herwegh were a proof that the Germans must adopt communism if they were to remain faithful to their philosophical tradition from Kant to Hegel. This remark, it is true, belongs to a time when Engels was himself connected with the Young Hegelians, and is contrary to opinions he expressed after those ties were broken; nevertheless, it is typical of the hopes that were cherished in the early stages for a radicalization of the master's system.

Young Hegelianism was the philosophical expression of the republican, bourgeois-democratic opposition which criticized the feudal order of the Prussian state and turned its eyes hopefully towards France. Prussia's western provinces, the Rhineland and Westphalia, had been under French rule for the best part of two decades and had benefited from the Napoleonic reforms— abolition of feudal estates and privileges, equality before the law. After their annexation to Prussia in 1815 they were a natural centre of lively conflict with the monarchical system. In the domain of literature the opposition was led in the early thirties by the group known as Junges Deutschland (Heine, Gutzkow, Börne), and later by the Hegelian radicals who, at that time, were mostly concentrated in Berlin. They included a club of young philosophers and theologians (Köppen, Rutenberg, Bruno Bauer) who reinterpreted Christianity in a Hegelian spirit, and with whom Marx came into contact at the time when he was beginning to formulate his own ideas.

2. David Strauss and the critique of religion

ONE of the chief literary manifestations of the Hegelian Left was David Strauss's *Life of Jesus* (*Das Leben Jesu*, 1835), which attempted to apply Hegelianism to a philosophical reconstruction of the origins of Christianity. For the generation brought up on Kant, Fichte, and Hegel the fact that the universe is ruled by Spirit was so obvious as scarcely to need proof, but it had to be explained exactly how that rule was exercised. The Young Hegelians, especially in their later phase (1840–3), were to 'Fichteanize' Hegel, if we may so put it, by reintroducing the aspect of obligation (*Sollen*) in their approach to history. That is to say, they regarded Hegelian Reason as having above all a normative sense: all social realities should be subjected to the irrefragable criteria of rationality. Christianity was the first victim of this attack. Strauss used Hegelian premises to overthrow the Hegelian belief in the absolute character of the Christian religion; he thus applied the Hegelian method against its inventor in a particular question of exceptional importance. His argument was that no one religion, the Christian or any other, could claim to be the bearer of absolute truth. Christianity, like other faiths, was only a transitional phase, though a necessary one, in the evolution of the spirit. The Gospels were not a system of philosophical symbols, but a collection of Jewish myths. In his mythical interpretation of the Gospels, Strauss went so far as to question the existence of a historical Jesus. At the same time he was convinced of the complete immanent presence of God in history, and rejected whatever remained in Hegelianism of the notion of a personal God. In particular, the myth of a single incarnation of the Absolute in a historical person was absurd: infinite Reason could not express itself fully in any finite human being.

Strauss's critique and the polemics it aroused led to the crystallization of the Hegelian Left and made it conscious of its separate identity. This was expressed first and foremost in the conviction that Hegel's dialectical method could not, without contradicting itself, permit of belief in the finality of history or of any one civilization. (The rejection of the Christian belief in an incarnate God was an essential instance of this view, though only a particular one.) Accordingly, the dialectic of negation could not stop at the interpretation of past history but must address itself to the future, being not merely a clue to understanding the world but an instrument of active criticism; it must project itself into unfulfilled historical possibilities, and be transformed from thought into action.

3. Cieszkowski and the philosophy of action

IN the transformation of Hegel's dialectic of negation into a 'philosophy of action', or rather a call to abolish the difference between action and philosophy, an essential role was played by a Polish writer, Count August Cieszkowski, especially in his early work *Prolegomena zur Historiosophie* (1838). Cieszkowski (1814–94) studied in Berlin from 1832 onwards and became interested in Hegelianism through Karl Ludwig Michelet, whose lectures he attended and whose life-long friend he became.

The *Prolegomena* were intended as a revision of the Hegelian philosophy of history, breaking with its contemplative and backward-looking tendencies. Philosophy was to become an act of will instead of merely reflection and interpretation, and was to turn itself towards the future instead of the past. According to Cieszkowski, Hegel's rationalism had forbidden philosophy to consider what would be, and commanded it to content itself with what had been. But Hegel's universal synthesis was itself only a particular historical phase of intellectual development, which it was now necessary to surmount. Cieszkowski divided human history into three phases after the fashion of medieval millenarians such as Joachim of Fiore, to whom he refers in his later works. The period of antiquity had been dominated by feeling: the spirit then lived in a state of pre-reflective, elemental immediacy and unity with nature, and expressed itself pre-eminently in art. The spirit was 'in itself' (*an sich*) and had not yet experienced the division of mind and body. The second era, lasting to the present time, was that of Christianity—a period of reflection in which the spirit turns toward itself, moving from natural, sensual immediacy to abstraction and universality. In spite of all changes and reversals, since the advent of Christ humanity has essentially remained at the level of the spirit 'for itself (*für sich*). The supreme and final work of the spirit in this phase is Hegel's own philosophy, the absolutization of thought and universality at the expense of individual existence, will, and matter. Throughout the Christian centuries humanity has been in a state of intolerable duality, in which God and the temporal world, spirit and matter, action and thought have been opposed to each other as antagonistic values. But that era has now come to an end. It is time for a final synthesis surmounting both Christianity and Hegelianism—but surmounting them in a Hegelian sense, preserving all the wealth of past ages. This will put an end to the dualism of matter and spirit, cognition and will. Philosophy, properly speaking, came to an end with Hegel: that is to say, in future the spirit will not express itself in philosophical speculation, but what was hitherto manifested as philosophy will coincide with the creative activity of man. It is not so much a question of the 'philosophy of action', i.e. philosophy glorifying action, as of the real merging of philosophical activity in the synthesizing practice of life. The spirit, developing its potentialities out of itself (*aus sich*), will assimilate to itself both nature, which was despised in the Christian era, and thought, which that era one-sidedly worshipped. The new era of the final synthesis will also mean a rehabilitation of the body: it will reconcile subjectivity with nature, God with the world, freedom with necessity, elemental desires with external precepts. Heaven and earth will join in eternal friendship, and the spirit, fully aware of itself and completely free, will no longer distinguish its active life in the world from its thought concerning it.

If the Christian centuries plunged humanity into a painful state of disruption, this does not mean that that suffering could have been avoided. History unfolds itself according to the innate necessity of the spirit, and original sin— *felix culpa*—had to precede the great resurrection that is to come. In the light of the final synthesis all past events will be seen as tending to salvation, and all the conflicting manifestations of the spirit will appear as contributions to the future rebirth.

Cieszkowski's main part in the evolution of Hegelianism consisted in the idea of identifying philosophy with action, and thus superseding the former as it had hitherto been understood. It is debatable how far, if at all, he should be considered as belonging to the Hegelian Left. Inasmuch as the identification of philosophy with action appeared subsequently in the work of Hess and became, through him, a cornerstone of Marxism, it seems natural to regard Cieszkowski as a Left Hegelian, and some writers, such as A. Cornu, have done so. Others, such as J. Garewicz, have objected on the ground that in his later works (*Gott und Palingenesie*, 1842, and especially *Ojcze nasz* (*Our Father*), vol. i, 1848) Cieszkowski formulates his triad in terms of sacred history (the periods of God the Father, of the Son, and of the Holy Ghost) and thus comes down in favour of a personal God (who, however, achieves perfection in human history) and of personal immortality, or rather reincarnation. In Germany the

Hegelian Left and Right were distinguished above all by their respective attitudes to religion and Christianity, and from this point of view Cieszkowski
could clearly not be ranked with the Left. Nor did the latter regard him as one
of their own, even though the unity of philosophy and action soon became
a radical war-cry. Michelet, on the other hand, defended Cieszkowski, while
taking the view that his ideas did not go beyond orthodox Hegelianism.
Cieszkowski himself, when attacking Feuerbach, treated the latter's naturalism
and atheism as natural consequences of Hegelianism, and by so doing placed
himself, according to German criteria, to the 'right' of Hegel. As for Hess, while
following Cieszkowski on the crucial issue, he did not accept his historiosophy
altogether. He held, in particular, that syntheses of thought and action have
taken place ever since the beginning of history and that the new era is not simply a matter of the future, but was inaugurated by the German Reformation.

Some scholars, such as A. Walicki, observe that while in Germany the Left
and Right were distinguished by their attitude towards religion, this was not
the case in France, whence Cieszkowski derived much of his inspiration. The religious interpretation of socialism and the conception of a new epoch as the fulfilment of the true content of Christianity were, in fact, current coin in the French
socialism of the 1830s and 1840s. Cieszkowski was much influenced by Fourier
and the Saint-Simonists, and incorporated into his soteriology an elaborate
system of social reforms.

The question of Cieszkowski's place on the map of post-Hegelian disputa-
tion is not especially significant to the history of Marxism; nor, from this point
of view, does much importance attach to his later philosophical fortunes and
his contribution to Polish culture. It is true that his division of history into
three phases and his belief in a future, final synthesis of spirit and matter were
not new, but were quite common in French philosophical literature. Nevertheless, he played an essential part in the prehistory of Marxism by expressing in
Hegelian language and in the context of the Hegelian debates the idea of the
future identification (not merely reconciliation) of intellectual activity and
social practice. It was out of this seed that Marx's eschatology grew. Marx's
most frequently quoted saying—'The philosophers have only interpreted the
world in various ways; the point, however, is to change it'—is no more than a
repetition of Cieszkowski's idea.

4. Bruno Bauer and the negativity of self-consciousness

THE idea of the spirit which, as simply spirit, is always opposed to the existing
world, always creative, critical, and in a state of disquiet, served the Left
Hegelians as an instrument of political and religious criticism. The Hegelians
hoped and expected that the irresistible force of their ideas would eventually

do away with anachronistic institutions and bring the state into conformity with the demands of Reason. On the political side their criticism was of a general and abstract kind, largely inspired by the ideals of the Enlightenment. But the hopes of an early transformation, to be brought about by philosophical criticism alone, were soon disappointed. The authorities gradually withdrew their support for Hegelianism as the Young Hegelian movement came to show its destructive attitude towards the system, and its philosophers were subjected to increasing harassment.

Bruno Bauer (1809–82), who began as an orthodox Protestant theologian, forsook the orthodox line in 1838 (*Die Religion des Alten Testaments*) and was soon writing pamphlets of a more anti-Christian character than anything else in Germany at the time, including the works of Feuerbach. He moved from Berlin to Bonn, where he was a *Privatdozent* at the university and where his attacks on Christianity grew even sharper. Bauer interpreted history in general, in the Hegelian style, as an expression of the developing self-consciousness of Mind. At the same time the whole of empirical reality presented itself to him on Fichtean lines as a collection of negatives, a kind of necessary resistance for the spirit to overcome in the course of its infinite progress. The meaning of everything that empirically *is* consists in the fact that it can and must be overcome, that it constitutes a centre of resistance against which the critical activity of the spirit is directed. The principle of this activity is a never-resting negation, a perpetual criticism of what exists simply because it does exist. History is determined by the permanent antagonism between what is and what ought to be, the latter being expressed by the spirit in its quest for self-consciousness. This principle, which is eminently Fichtean and non-Hegelian, formed the nucleus of Bauer's critique of religion. The Gospel narrative, in his view, contained no historical truth whatever but was merely the expression of a transient stage of self-consciousness, a fanciful projection of the latter's own vicissitudes into historical events. Christianity was of service to the development of spirit in that it awakened a consciousness of values that belongs to every human individual; but at the same time it created a new form of servitude by requiring individuals to accept subjection to God.

The growth of state power in imperial Rome obliged men to recognize their impotence *vis-à-vis* the outside world. Self-consciousness withdrew into itself and declared that world to be contemptible, as the only way of escaping its pressure. (It should be noted that in Bauer's view the idea of Christianity was itself a product of Roman culture; he minimized the part played in its origins by the Jewish tradition, ascribing a much more important role to popular Stoic philosophy.) In Christianity, religious alienation reaches an extreme form: man divests himself of his own essence and entrusts it to mythical forces to which he regards himself henceforth as subservient. The main task of the present phase of history is to restore to man his alienated essence, by liberating the spirit from the bonds of Christian mythology and freeing the state from religion. A practical consequence of Bauer's historiosophy was the call for the laicization of public life. He was never an adherent of communism, however; on the contrary, he held that if it were possible to create a system based on communist principles, it would tend to subject all human activity and thought to itself, so that freedom of thought and human individuality would be destroyed and the creative activity of mind replaced by a code of official dogma.

In 1841, during his lectureship at Bonn, Bauer published anonymously a satirical pamphlet entitled *Die Posaune des jüngsten Gerichts über Hegel den Atheisten und Antichristen. Ein Ultimatum (The Trump of the Last Judgement upon Hegel, the Atheist and Anti-Christian. An Ultimatum)*. Marx had a share in this work, but it is not known how much of it is his: probably not a large amount, as the work is full of biblical quotations and references to theological literature which are evidently due to Bauer's erudition. The book was ostensibly a critique of Hegel from the standpoint of orthodox Protestant theology, denouncing the atheistic implications of his doctrine. With pretended indignation the author showed that Hegel's pantheism was bound to develop in the direction of radical atheism and that its true purport had been revealed by the Young Hegelians, the only faithful expounders of his philosophy. Hegel was an enemy of the Church, of Christianity, and of religion altogether. Even his pantheism was a mere show: religion played no part in his system except as the relationship of self-consciousness to itself, and anything that differed from self-consciousness must be interpreted as an element (*Moment*) in it. Hegel's criticism of the 'sentimental religion' of Jacobi or Schleiermacher was misleading: he accused it of subjectivism, as though he himself were a champion of the reality of God's existence, but this was quite untrue. By representing the finite spirit as a manifestation of universal spirit, Hegel made the latter a projection of historical self-consciousness, while infinity appeared as merely the self-negation of finitude—i.e. God, in the last analysis, is merely a creation of the human ego, which with diabolic pride lays claim to almighty power. Hegel's 'world spirit', too, acquires reality only thanks to the operation of human historical self-consciousness. Human history is thus self-sufficient and has no significance beyond its own self-development. So, according to Hegel, God is dead and the only reality is self-consciousness. All this, Bauer continues, fits perfectly with the other ingredients of Hegel's system: his glorification of Reason and philosophy, his violent critique of all that exists simply because it exists, his worship of the French Revolution, his love of the Greeks and French, his hatred and contempt for the Germans (as a nation of cowards, incapable of doing without religion even in their most radical and rationalistic moods), even his dislike of Latin. Religion, the Church, and belief in God are presented as obstacles that the spirit must overcome in order to achieve absolute mastery; humanity must realize in the end that when it thinks it is contemplating God it is only looking at its own face in a mirror, and behind that mirror there is nothing.

Although Bauer's work purported to be the lament of a believing Christian at the wickedness of a blasphemer, its basic argument was perfectly sincere: Hegel was interpreted as an *alter ego* of Bruno Bauer, a mocker and an atheist, a worshipper of nothing but Self-Knowledge. Hegel's Absolute Idea was merely the self-consciousness that the spirit strives to attain through successive manifestations of itself. The *Weltgeist* is actualized only in the human spirit; each stage of its operation ends in the assumption of a form that begins to encumber it, and requires to be surmounted, as soon as it comes to fulfilment. Every form of the life of the spirit soon becomes anachronistic and irrational, by its very existence challenging the spirit to a fresh effort of criticism and opposition. Philosophy is the criticism which knows how things ought to be, and on the strength of that knowledge it is philosophy's business to condemn and destroy the world as it finds it, attacking especially the established forms of religious mythology. These were Bauer's own views, and it is not surprising that, holding the destruction of Christianity to be the most urgent task of mankind, he was looked at askance in the faculty of Protestant theology and was eventually deprived of his lectureship.

As can be seen, Bauer's philosophy treats the operation of the intellect as a purely negative one. Whereas Hegel's philosophy of history sought to maintain a positive link between the Idea and empirical reality, Bauer and other Hegelians of his school reintroduced a radical dualism between the critical mind and the existing universe. In this interpretation, the spirit is no more than the agent of an eternal dissolution to which every feature of the empirical world is bound to be subjected. The spirit has no positive support in reality itself: its only such support consists in the imperatives of reason which are at all times in advance of reality. The Idea is a tribunal judging the world in accordance with its own suprahistorical laws: every empirical reality is an object of condemnation in the eyes of the spirit. The spirit is defined by its destructive function, and the world is essentially the inertia that opposes criticism; thus the spirit and the world are defined negatively by their relation to each other. History cannot of itself unfold the principles whereby each of its stages is to be judged, but, in order to be changed, it must be judged on the basis of suprahistorical demands. The grounds of historical change lie outside history. The spirit must break through the shell imposed on it by the empirical world, but it cannot derive from that world the strength it needs for its destructive task.

Bauer's critique of religious alienation was strongly reflected in Marx's early thought, including the famous comparison of religion to opium. At the same time the philosophy of self-knowledge was one of the main points in opposition to which Marx came to adopt his own distinctive philosophy.

5. Arnold Ruge. The radicalization of the Hegelian Left

OTHER Left Hegelian writers reinterpreted the master's philosophy on similar lines. Arnold Ruge, as the editor of a journal, did most to consolidate Young Hegelianism as a political movement. Along with others he went through the evolution which gradually radicalized the anti-religious critique and transferred its impact to the sphere of politics. In 1838–41 he edited the Young Hegelian philosophical journal, *Hallische Jahrbücher*, which at first shared Hegel's delusion that Prussia was the embodiment of historical Reason. The Young Hegelians originally believed that historical self-consciousness was the prerogative of the Prussian system, and that the development of freedom which historical Reason demanded could take place there gradually by means of peaceful reforms. The ideal towards which Prussia should evolve was, in the journalists' opinion, a Protestant constitutional monarchy; its Protestantism, however, should not signify the domination of any organized Church, but the conformity of all public institutions to the demands of Reason, and the voluntary subjection of religion to scientific principles. The Young Hegelians' philosophy was reflected in anti-feudal postulates: the abolition of privileged estates, public office open to all, freedom of speech and property—in short, a bourgeois egalitarian state. They envisaged a rational state in accordance with the ideas of the Enlightenment, as expressed in the career of their hero Frederick the Great; this did not appear to them as a mere speculative Utopia, but as part of the natural course of history in which Prussia for the time being enjoyed a special mission. From this point of view they attacked Catholicism as a religion of bygone times, exalting dogma above reason; they also attacked orthodox Protestantism and pietistic sentimentalism, as well as Romantic philosophy, which set reason below emotion and subjected the spirit to a cult of unreasoning Nature. The change in the Young Hegelians' political orientation brought with it a modification of the belief in historical Reason. The Prussian government showed no enthusiasm for their vision of itself as the embodiment of Reason which was to sweep away feudal inequality and political slavery. The Young Hegelians' appeals were met with repressive measures especially after 1840, when the new king, Frederick William IV, on whom the radicals had pinned their hopes, proved to be a staunch defender of the old, class-ridden order and the Prussian hereditary monarchy, and curtailed political freedom and religious tolerance more drastically than ever. Arnold Ruge and other contributors to the *Hallische Jahrbücher* (later the *Deutsche Jahrbücher*, edited by Ruge from 1841 to 1843) ceased to believe that Prussia was evolving of its own accord towards the kingdom of Reason, and they saw what a gulf lay between their ideals and the stagnant social situation. It was then that they adopted the theory of an inevitable disharmony between the demands of Reason and the empirical world. Reason was no longer an instrument of reconciliation with reality, the latter being rational by definition; it was a source of obligation, a standard with which to confront the world. Practical action and conscious criticism were categories expressing the opposition between the world as it should be and as it was. Ruge proclaimed that Hegel had betrayed his own idealism when he absolutized particular forms of social and spiritual life (the Prussian state, Protestant Christianity) as the ultimate fulfilment of the demands of reason; he had abandoned the principle of eternal criticism and turned his system into an apologia for a merely contemplative, conformist attitude towards the universe.

The radicalization of Young Hegelianism took three main forms. In philosophy it appeared as a breach with Hegel's doctrine of the self-fulfilment of history, and an acceptance of the opposition between the facts of history and normative Reason. In the religious sphere the Young Hegelians rejected the Christian tradition even in diluted, pantheistic forms and adopted a position of out-and-out atheism, first formulated by Bauer and Feuerbach. In politics they abandoned reformist hopes and accepted the prospect of revolution as the only way to regenerate humanity and Germany in particular. However, if we leave aside Hess and the uninfluential Edgar Bauer, this radicalism did not have any socialist content: the expectation of revolution was confined to political change and was unconnected with any hope of a transformation in the system of property and production. Unlike Hegel, who saw an inevitable division between the state with its political institutions and 'civil society' as the totality of private and particular interests, the Young Hegelians in their radical phase believed that in the perfect society of the future the division and even the difference between these two aspects would disappear. Hegel himself did not think it possible to do away with all tension between the general interest and the conflicting private interests of individuals, but only that this tension could be lessened by the mediation of the official machine identifying its own interest with that of the state. In Hegel's view the state as a mode of collective being did not have to justify itself by the interest of the individuals who composed it; on the contrary, their highest and absolute good consisted in membership of the state. It followed that the state's function of overruling the discordant interests of civil society could be justified by the value of the state in and for itself. Hegel's political doctrine expressed the ideology of the Prussian bureaucracy, and in his view the general good, i.e. the good of the state, was independent of private interests and did not derive from them; on the contrary, the individual's interest and his essential value lay in being a citizen of the state. The Young

Hegelians, however, completely rejected this view. In proclaiming their own republican ideal and demanding the general participation of the people in political life, with universal suffrage on a basis of equality, freedom of the Press and public criticism, and a freely elected government which truly represented the whole community—in advocating all this, they believed that when it came to pass there would be no difference between the general good and private interests. When political institutions were a free emanation of the people, they could not appear to individuals as alien forces; a state in which education aroused the universal consciousness of every individual citizen and made him aware of the dictates of Reason would signify the unity of private and public interests. In this way the Young Hegelians revived the republican idealism of the eighteenth century, believing that education and political liberties would solve all social problems without any need to alter the system of property on which material production and economic exchanges were based.

The Young Hegelians played an important part in awakening Germany intellectually and spreading democratic ideas. In spite of the attention they aroused, however, they did not succeed in making their philosophy the nucleus of a political movement in which the country's significant social forces were involved. The break-up of the Hegelian Left, which began after the *Deutsche Jahrbücher* were suppressed in 1843, took the form of ideas which postulated a general opposition between abstract thought and politics. The beginning of this dissolution of the movement coincided in time with the early thinking of Marx, who grew up amid the Hegelian Left but, even when he still accepted its philosophical categories and its identification of the problems to be solved, showed clearly that he took an essentially different view of history.

III

Marx's Thought in Its Earliest Phase

1. Early years and studies

WHEN MARX came into contact with the Hegelian Left, it was already aware of itself as an independent movement. At the university he was able to witness the conflict between Hegelian rationalism and the conservative doctrine of what was called the Historical School of Law (Historische Rechtsschule). His upbringing and his own critical temperament were conducive to the early development of a radical outlook.

Karl Marx was born at Trier on 5 May 1818, the child of Jewish parents with a long rabbinical tradition on both sides. His grandfathers were rabbis; his father, a well-to-do lawyer, changed his first name from Herschel to Heinrich and adopted Protestantism, which in Prussia was a necessary condition of professional and cultural emancipation. The young Marx was brought up in a liberal democratic spirit. In the autumn of 1835, after leaving the Trier Gymnasium, he enrolled as a law student at Bonn University. The influence of Romantic philosophy, popularized at the university by August von Schlegel, can be seen in Marx's early poetic efforts. However, he received his first real intellectual stimulus at Berlin University, to which he moved in the following year. Although still a law student, he was more absorbed by lectures on philosophy and history. The former subject was taught by, among others, Eduard Gans, who was regarded as belonging to the liberal centre of the Hegelian movement. Hegelianism, in his view, was the interpretation of history as a progressive rationalization of the world in accordance with the ineluctable laws of the spirit; the chief purpose of philosophical thought was to observe this evolution, in which empirical reality was seen gradually to conform to universal reason. Gans was also one of the few Hegelians of his time to profess socialist views, which he had absorbed in Saint-Simon's version. Thus Marx was introduced from the outset to a form of Hegelianism that by no means required obedient acceptance of the *status quo*, but demanded that it be judged by the dictates of Reason.

A directly opposite viewpoint was represented at Berlin University by Friedrich Karl von Savigny (1779–1861), the main theoretician of the Historische Rechtsschule and the author of works on the history of Roman law; he also wrote the pamphlet *Vom Beruf unserer Zeit für Gesetzgebung und*

Rechtswissenschaft (*On the Mission of Our Times for Legislation and Jurispru-
dence*, 1814). Savigny's philosophy expressed the view that obligation should be
derived from actual being, and in particular that all law should be based on
positive enactments, customs, and rules sanctified by tradition. His conservatism was sharply opposed to the Enlightenment doctrine that laws and institutions must be justified by abstract norms before the tribunal of sovereign
Reason, regardless of which laws and institutions are actually valid by force of
historical tradition. Political radicalism was expressed in the cult of reason and
the systematic refusal to acknowledge the authority of history, and the republican ideals exhibited the vision of a world as it ought to be. For Savigny, on the
other hand, the factual, positive institutions and customs that were 'given' by
history and rooted in it were authoritative for that very reason. The source of
law, from this point of view, could not be an arbitrary legislative act based on
the assumed needs of a rational social order; the rightful source of all legislation was customary law and history. This conservative doctrine provided a justification and sanctification of the existing political order simply because it did
exist in a positive form, while any attempt to improve it in the name of a better, imagined order was condemned *a priori*. All the feudal elements of backward Germany deserved to be revered, their very antiquity proving them to be
legitimate. Savigny combined this irrational cult of 'positiveness' with a belief
in the 'organic', suprarational nature of a social community and particularly a
national one. Human societies were not instruments of rational co-operation
but were welded together by a non-rational bond that is its own justification
irrespective of any utilitarian purpose.

The legislating subject is the nation, which spontaneously evolves and modifies its laws. The nation is an indivisible whole, and the laws, like its customs
and language, are only one expression of its collective individuality. There cannot be, as the utopians would have it, a single 'rational' form of legislation for
all peoples, regardless of their different traditions. Lawgiving is not an arbitrary
matter: the legislator finds a particular legal system in being, and can only formulate changes in legal awareness that have occurred as a result of the community's organic growth. In sharp opposition to utilitarian and rationalistic
theories, and in close alliance with Romantic philosophy, Savigny was the true
promulgator of the notion that 'whatever is, is right'—the doctrine, in fact, that
was ascribed to Hegel by some of his disciples and opponents as a possible
interpretation of his dictum that what is actual is also rational. In point of fact
Savigny did not derive his inspiration from Hegel, who criticized his conservative views. Hegel, although he refused to oppose the arbitrary dictates of Reason to the real process of history, was not willing to accept the existing order as
rational and worthy of respect simply because it existed.

The Young Hegelian radicals, who claimed to judge empirical reality by the abstract requirements of reason, and Savigny, who demanded that reality should be accepted as given, represent opposite solutions of the problem on which Marx's early thought was focused. Hegel, with his ambiguities and incomplete utterances, stood between the two extremes, and Marx's position on this key question was closer to Hegel than to the Young Hegelians. The conservative outlook of the Historical School of Law was quite foreign to Marx, and in the summer of 1842 he satirized it directly in an article in the *Rheinische Zeitung* on Gustav Hugo's philosophy of history. ('Everything that exists is an authority in [Hugo's] eyes, and every authority is an argument . . . In short, an eruption on the skin is no less valuable [*positiv*] than the skin itself'.) But equally Marx never adopted in an extreme form the Young Hegelian, or rather Fichtean, opposition between what ought to be and what historically is, between the dictates of Reason and the actual social order, though this point of view was certainly more congenial to him than the other. At a very early stage he endeavoured to interpret the revolutionary principle of the permanent negativity of the spirit in such a way as not to imply the latter's absolute sovereignty. He did not accept the Absolute in the form of a rational standard imposing itself on the world from outside and taking no account of historical fact; he sought to preserve Hegel's anti-utopian standpoint and to safeguard the respect for the undeniable factual characteristics of the world as we know it.

2. Hellenistic philosophy as understood by the Hegelians

MARX's efforts to find a position for himself between the rationalist utopia and the conservative cult of 'positiveness' can be traced in his early studies of post-Aristotelian Greek philosophy. There was a sound reason for his interest in this subject. The Young Hegelians were much interested in Hellenistic philosophy, as they perceived an analogy between the period after Alexander the Great, marked by the twilight of pan-Hellenistic ideas and the decay of the great Aristotelian synthesis, and their own time, which had witnessed the failure of the Napoleonic union of Europe and the collapse of Hegel's attempt at a universal philosophy. The Young Hegelians, as it were, rehabilitated the post-Aristotelian schools—the Epicureans, Sceptics, and later Stoics—and brought to light their values which Hegel had neglected. Hegel, in fact, had accused all these schools (which he mostly considered in their Roman forms) of eclecticism and irrelevance, declaring that their purpose was merely to teach the soul indifference in the face of a cruel and hopeless social reality. They provided an imaginary reconciliation with the world by means of thought which turned in upon itself and lost contact with the object, and a will whose only purpose was to have no purpose. The Hellenistic philosophies were a purely negative defence against the despair aroused by the dissolution of political and social ties in imperial Rome.

In Hegel's view, a mode of being in which the intellect withdrew into sterile self-contemplation was condemned to an abstract individuality, whereas concrete individuality was bound to refresh itself by constant contact with universality and with the outside world.

In Bruno Bauer's opinion, on the other hand, these 'philosophies of self-consciousness' were far from being mere negative expressions of impotence. If they made it possible for the individual, engulfed by the collapse of his former world, to achieve a certain spiritual emancipation by returning into himself, and if they could in some degree protect his consciousness against the onslaughts of the world, then, by providing a basis for spiritual autonomy, they opened up a new and necessary phase in the development of spirit; they endowed the individual mind with autonomy, enabled it to assert itself against the world, universalized and liberated it, and made it conscious of its own freedom in and by the critical faculty which it opposed to the corruption of reality. In short, Hegel and the Young Hegelians gave a similar interpretation to the Hellenistic philosophies, but took a different view of their historical and philosophical importance. According to Hegel the absolutization of individual self-consciousness merely showed the impotence of the philosophical spirit, whereas to Bauer it represented the victory of the critical intellect over the pressure of the external world.

3. Marx's studies of Epicurus. Freedom and self-consciousness

AT AN early stage in his Berlin studies Marx underwent a conversion to Hegelianism and frequented a club of young graduates who interpreted the master's doctrine in a radical spirit. For his doctoral thesis he orginally intended to analyse all three schools of Hellenistic thought. However, the subject grew unmanageable and he finally restricted himself to a single aspect of Epicureanism, viz. a comparison between the natural philosophy of Epicurus and the atomism of Democritus. He worked on his dissertation from the beginning of 1839, and in April 1841 was awarded a doctor's degree by Jena University. He intended to print the dissertation, but was soon absorbed by other occupations. The work remained in a manuscript state, with several gaps; it was published in part by Mehring in 1902, and appeared in 1927, with introductory notes, in the *Marx-Engels Gesamtausgabe*.

The work was entitled *On the Differences between the Natural Philosophy of Democritus and of Epicurus*; it is written in a romantic style and in accordance with the categories of Hegelian logic. It is clear that as regards the relationship between the spirit and the world, Marx was a long way from articulating the viewpoint that he was to express three or four years later. Nevertheless, if we compare the dissertation with his subsequent writings we can trace the beginnings of a departure both from the Young Hegelian faith in the supremacy of the critical spirit and from Hegelian conservatism. Using Marx's writings of 1843-5 as a key to the dissertation, we can see it as an attempt to declare his connection with a particular philosophical tradition: that which requires that the spirit should not remain submissive to existing facts, nor yet believe in the absolute authority of normative criteria which it discovers freely in itself without regard to those facts, but should make of its own freedom a means wherewith to influence the world. Marx criticizes Epicurus but is a great deal more severe upon the latter's critics, especially Cicero and Plutarch who, he thinks, quite misunderstood the Epicurean philosophy. In some passages he appears carried away by the rhetorical sweep of Lucretius, his revolt against religion and his Promethean faith in human dignity rooted in freedom.

In opposition to the tradition which, following Plutarch and Cicero, regarded Epicurus' atomism as a corruption of Democritean physics by the arbitrary and fantastic theory of deviations in the movement of atoms (*parenclisis, clinamen*), Marx argues that the apparent similarity of the two philosophers conceals a deep and fundamental difference. Epicurus' theory of accidental deviation is not a mere caprice but an essential premiss of a system of thought centred upon the idea of the freedom of self-consciousness. On the basis of laboriously collected material (editions of the scattered writings of Greek philosophers, such as those of Diels and Usener, did not exist at the time) Marx sought to prove that the philosophical intentions of Democritus and Epicurus were quite different from each other. Democritus opposes the world of atoms, which is inaccessible to the senses, to perception, which is inevitably illusory. He turns to empirical observation, although aware that it does not contain the truth; truth, to him, is empty, however, because the senses cannot grasp it. He prefers to rest content with an illusory knowledge of nature, which he treats as an end in itself. Epicurus' view is different: he regards the world as an 'objective phenomenon' and accepts the evidence of perception uncritically (exposing himself to undeserved mockery by the champions of 'common sense'). His concern, however, is not to know the world but to achieve the ataraxia of self-knowledge through the consciousness of individual freedom. *Parenclisis* is the actualization of freedom, which is essential to the atom. The actualization is fraught with a contradiction, since in Epicurus' view the atom entails the negation of all qualities; but its actual existence is necessarily subject to all qualitative determinations, such as size, shape, and weight. The atom—as the principle of being, not as a physical unit—is, to Epicurus, a projection of the absolute freedom of self-knowledge, but at the same time he is concerned to point out the unreality and fragility of nature conceived as a world of atoms. His theory of meteors was intended to show, according to Marx, that, contrary to traditional belief, the heavenly bodies were not eternal, unchangeable, and immortal; if they were, they would overwhelm self-knowledge by their majesty and permanence and would deprive it of freedom. Their movements can be explained by many causes, and any non-mythical explanation is as good as any other. Epicurus thus robs nature of its unity and makes it feeble and transient, because the serenity of self-consciousness would otherwise be disturbed. The down-grading of nature (in which Epicurus is not interested from the viewpoint of physical science) signifies the removal of a source of disquiet; it gives the mind a sense of its own supremacy and of total freedom from the world. The atom, which is a metaphysical principle, is degraded in the most perfect form of its existence, namely the heavens. The most important source of terror is removed by the destruction of the myths which oppose the frailty of self-consciousness to the immortality of superterrestrial nature. The enemy, to Epicurus, is any form of definite being that is relative to, or determined by, something other than itself. The atom is being-for-itself, and its very nature therefore entails the necessity of deviating from a straight course. Its law is the absence of law, i.e. chance and spontaneity. *Parenclisis* is not a sensual quality (as Lucretius says, it does not occur in any particular place or time), but is the soul of the atom, the resistance that is inseparable from it and therefore from ourselves.

Marx sees Epicurus as a destroyer of the Greek myths and as a philosopher bringing to light the break-up of a tribal community. His system destroyed the visible heaven of the ancients as a keystone of political and religious life. Marx allies himself, so to speak, with Epicurean atheism, which he regards at this stage as a challenge by the intellectual élite to the cohorts of common sense. 'As long as a single drop of blood pulses in her world-conquering and totally free heart, philosophy will continually shout at her opponents the cry of Epicurus: "Impiety does not consist in destroying the gods of the crowd but rather in ascribing to the gods the ideas of the crowd."'

The dissertation, moreover, introduces the theme of religious alienation in its analogy with the alienation of economic life. Referring in an incidental (and critical) passage to Kant's refutation of the ontological argument for the existence of God, Marx writes:

> The ontological proof merely amounts to this: 'What I really imagine is for me a real imagination' that reacts upon me, and in this sense all gods, heathen as well as Christian, had a real existence. Did not Moloch reign in antiquity? Was not the Delphic Apollo a real power in the life of the Greeks? Kant's *Critique* does not make any sense here. If someone imagines that he has one hundred pounds, and if for him this is no arbitrary fancy but he really believes in it, then the one hundred imagined pounds have the same worth for him as one hundred real ones. He will, for example, contract debts on the strength of his imaginings, they will have an effect, just as the whole of humanity has contracted debts on the strength of its gods . . . Real

pounds have the same existence as imagined gods. Surely there is no place where a real pound can exist apart from the general, or rather collective, imagination of men. Take paper money into a land where the use of such money is not known, and everyone will laugh at your subjective imagination. Go with your gods into another land where other gods hold sway, and it will be proved to you that you are suffering from fanciful dreams. Rightly so . . . What a particular land is for particular foreign gods, the land of reason is for God in general, an area in which his existence ceases.

As this passage shows, the image *à la* Feuerbach of a man who is ruled by his own imaginations and is not aware that he is their creator, so that their domination over him is real and not merely supposed, is linked in Marx's mind at this period with the necessary role of 'imagination' involved in the power of money. This is a kind of early, obscure prefiguration of Marx's later theory of 'commodity fetishism'.

While, however, Marx paid tribute to Epicurus and Lucretius for liberating the ancient world from the terrors of alien deities and an alien Nature, and restoring the mind's awareness of its own freedom, he regarded Epicurean freedom as a flight from the world, an attempt by the mind to withdraw to a place of refuge. In Epicurus' philosophy the ideal of the sage and the hope of happiness are rooted in a desire to sever links with the world. They are an expression of the mind of an unhappy era when

their gods are dead and the new goddess has as yet only the obscure form of fate, of pure light or of pure darkness . . . The root of the unhappiness, however, is that the soul of the period, the spiritual monad, being sated with itself, shapes itself ideally on all sides in isolation and cannot recognize any reality that has come to fruition without it. Thus, the happy aspect of this unhappy time lies in the subjective manner, the modality in which philosophy as subjective consciousness conceives its relation to reality. Thus, for example, the Stoic and Epicurean philosophies were the happiness of their time; thus the moth, when the universal sun has sunk, seeks the lamplight of a private person.

Marx regards the monadic freedom of Epicurus as escapism: he objects not to the belief in the freedom of the spirit, but to the idea that this freedom can be attained by turning one's back on the world, that it is a matter of independence and not of creativity. 'The man who would not prefer to build a world by his own strength, to create the world and not simply remain in his own skin—such a man is accursed by the spirit, and with the curse goes an interdict, but in the reverse sense: he is cast out from the sanctuary of the spirit, deprived of the delight of intercourse with it and condemned to sing lullabies about his own private happiness, and to dream of himself at night.'

Marx's first work is almost wholly within the limits of Young Hegelian thought. The sweeping attack on religion, and the conviction of the creative role of the spirit in history, do not go beyond the Young Hegelian horizon, nor does the critique of Epicureanism as a philosophy in which the mind seeks to shake off the yoke of nature and envelop itself in a purely subjective autonomy. For the Young Hegelians, too, the supremacy of the spirit was not related to a desire for isolation, but was the precondition of a critical attack on the irrationality of the empirical world. However, we can perceive in Marx's dissertation the germ of what later emerged as the 'philosophy of praxis' in contrast to the critical philosophy of the Young Hegelians. The crucial difference between the latter and Marx's philosophy in its full development may be described as follows. In critical philosophy the free spirit enters the world as a permanent negation of it, a normative act of judgement upon factual life, a statement of what reality ought to be, irrespective of what it actually is. Thus understood, critical philosophy is unalterably supreme over the world. It does not seek to be separate from it, but to affect it and break up its stability; but at the same time it preserves the autonomy of a judge, and the standards by which it measures reality are not derived from that reality but from itself. The philosophy of praxis, on the other hand, declares that in so far as philosophy is purely critical it is self-destructive, but that its critical task is consummated when it ceases to be mere thinking about the world and becomes part of human life. Its function is thus to remove the distinction between history and the intellectual or moral critique of history, between the praxis of the social subject and his awareness of that praxis. As long as theory is the sovereign judge of practice there is a rift between the individual mind and its surroundings, between thought and the world of men. To remove this division is to do away with philosophy and with 'false consciousness'; for as long as consciousness signifies the understanding of an irrational world from outside, it cannot be the self-understanding of that world or the self-awareness of its natural development. If the identification of self-awareness with the historical process is to be a real prospect, that self-awareness must emerge from the immanent pressure of history itself and not from extra-historical principles of rationality. We must therefore find in history itself conditions that can make it rational— i.e. conditions thanks to which its empirical development can coincide with the consciousness of its participants and do away with false consciousness, with that consciousness which contemplates the world but is not as yet the world's self-consciousness.

Some passages of Marx's doctoral thesis contain an embryonic expression of the 'philosophy of praxis' in this sense. He observes, for instance, that when philosophy *as will* turns itself against empirical reality, then it is an enemy of itself *as a system*: in its active form, it is opposed to its own ossified self. This contradiction is resolved by a process in which the world 'philosophizes itself' while philosophy turns into world history. In this conflict philosophical self-consciousness takes a double form: on the one hand positive philosophy, which seeks to cure philosophy of its deficiencies and turns in upon itself, and on the other hand a liberal attitude, which addresses itself critically to the world and, while affirming itself as an instrument of criticism, tends unconsciously to eliminate itself as a philosophy. It is only this latter method which is capable of bringing about real progress. An antique sage who sought to oppose his own free judgement to 'substantial' reality was bound to suffer defeat because he could not escape from that 'substantiality' and, in condemning it, was all the time unconsciously condemning himself. Epicurus tried to free mankind from dependence on nature by, in effect, transforming the immediate aspect of consciousness, its being-for-itself, into a form of nature. But in fact we can only become independent of nature by making it the property of reason, and this in turn requires us to recognize the rationality of nature in itself.

When we consider these remarks in the dissertation we perceive the rudiments of a new outlook: the prospect of philosophy being incorporated into history and thus abolished, and the conviction that mind must look to the 'rationality' of the world as a support for its own emancipation, that is to say its absorption by the reality upon which it is directed. We can see in this outline the future ideal in which there ceases to be a difference between life and thinking about life, so that man is set free by the reconciliation of self-consciousness with the empirical world. We see also the germ of what was to become the theory of false consciousness. Marx was aware that philosophers have, in addition to the overt structure of their ideas, a substructure which is unknown to them; their thought as they themselves present it is different from the crystallization of systems in which the mole-like activity of true philosophical knowledge, finds expression. To discover this unconscious, underlying structure is the proper task of the historian of philosophy, and is the task that Marx set himself in regard to Epicurus.

However, this early work contains no reference, even in general terms, to the social causes that lead philosophers to deceive themselves, or the social conditions that may eliminate false consciousness and restore the unity of experience and self-knowledge. Marx is still thinking in terms of an abstract opposition between the spirit and the world, self-consciousness and nature, man and God. His philosophy did not crystallize further until he had made closer contact with political realities and engaged in the political journalism of his day.

IV

Hess and Feuerbach

In the year 1841, in which Marx completed his dissertation on Epicurus, there were published at Leipzig two important books by different authors which were to influence his early activity and enable him gradually to free himself from the current schemas of Young Hegelian thought. Moses Hess, author of *The European Triarchy*, made the first attempt to integrate the Hegelian philosophical inheritance with communist ideals; Ludwig Feuerbach, author of *The Essence of Christianity*, rescued the Hegelian Left from its bondage to the philosophy of self-consciousness and not only led the critique of religious belief to its ultimate conclusion, but extended it to all forms of philosophical idealism and unequivocally espoused the point of view which treats all spiritual life as a product of nature.

1. Hess. The philosophy of action

Moses Hess (1812–75), the self-educated son of a Rhineland merchant, was brought up in strict Jewish orthodoxy. In youth he was attracted by the writings of Spinoza and Rousseau; the former taught him to believe in the unity of the world and the identity of reason and will, while from the latter he imbibed a conviction of the natural equality of man. He came into contact with socialist ideas in France, but was soon drawn into the Young Hegelian movement, and from all these sources composed his own, communist philosophy. His writings, including those of the period when he was active in the German socialist movement and was under Marx's influence, are always stamped with a visionary quality. The gaps in his education, and his enthusiastic temperament, prevented him from giving his thoughts a coherent and methodical shape; but many of his ideas helped considerably to form Marx's conception of scientific socialism.

In his first book, *The Sacred History of Mankind* (1837), Hess predicted a new era of man's covenant with God, when, by the operation of unfailing historical laws embodied in the conscious acts of men, there was to be a final reconciliation of the human race, a free and equal society based on mutual love and the community of goods. He suggested for the first time that the social revolution would come about as the result of an inevitable deepening of the contrast between growing wealth on the one hand and misery on the other. In *The European Triarchy* (1841) he based his communism on a Hegelian schema, while endeavouring to strip Hegelianism of its contemplative, backward-looking tendencies and transform it into a philosophy of action. Like other Young Hegelians (including, as we shall see, the young Marx) he desired to see an alliance between the German speculative genius and French political sense, so that German philosophy could take on a substantial form instead of remaining in the field of theoretical meditation. The 'philosophy of action' as Hess conceived it was a development of Cieszkowski's ideas. The history of humanity was divided into three stages. In antiquity, spirit and nature were allied to each other, but unconsciously; the spirit operated in history without any intermediary. Christianity introduced a division whereby the spirit withdrew into itself. In our own day the unity of spirit and nature is being restored; it will, however, no longer be elemental and unreflecting, but conscious and creative. The inaugurator of the modern era is Spinoza, whose Absolute realized, though still only in theory, the unity of being-in-itself and being-for-itself, the identity of subject and object. In Hegelianism this understanding of the identity between subject and object reached its height, but only as an act of understanding: Hegel confined himself to interpreting past history and had not the strength to make philosophy an instrument for the conscious moulding of the future. The transition from the philosophy of the past to that of the future, from interpretation to action, is the work of the Hegelian Left. The essence of the last stage is that what is planned by the spirit to take place in history should be the result of free action. In this stage, human freedom and historical necessity coincide in a single act: that which *must* take place by virtue of historical law, *can* only take place through absolutely free activity. Sacred history, or the work of the spirit in human history, then becomes the same thing as history *tout court*. The surmounting of Hegelianism consists primarily in this, that philosophy henceforth lays claim to the future—aware of historical necessity, but also of the fact that only through freedom can this necessity embody itself in actual history. In this way past history will likewise be sanctified through its relationship to the future, which will be the accomplishment of mankind's historical mission. Hegel ruled out this relationship by decreeing that the dialectic could not apply to the future, and consequently he was unable to sanctify the past even though he desired to do so. The freedom of the spirit, initiated by the German Reformation and brought to theoretical perfection by German philosophy, must ally itself with the freedom of action inaugurated by the French Revolution. When it does, Europe will undergo a swift regeneration, the fulfilment of Christianity and the authentic religion of love. The religion of the new world will not need churches or priests, dogmas or a transcendent

Deity, belief in immortality or education through fear. God will not help men from outside, punishing or instructing, but will manifest himself in them in the spontaneity of love and courage. The separation of Church and State will have no purpose, since, unlike the medieval situation in which their unity was only contingent, they will henceforth be identified with each other in a fundamental social unity: secular and religious life will be the same, and particular creeds will be revealed as anachronisms. In a society united voluntarily from within, without coercion, there will no longer be any antagonism between public order and freedom, which will support instead of limiting each other. A prior necessity is that the principle of love should triumph in human life, and Hess regards the transformation of minds as a pre-condition of communism. 'Moral and social slavery proceeds only from spiritual slavery; and, contrariwise, legal and moral emancipation is bound to result from spritual liberation.' The society of the future will not need to protect itself by any repressive laws or institutions, as it will be based on a voluntary harmony and on the identity of the individual and collective interest as a result of the development of self-awareness.

2. Hess. Revolution and freedom

In later articles and books Hess gave a clearer description of the communist society he envisaged, and attempted a deeper analysis of the economic causes of contemporary ills; he also expressed his atheistic outlook more emphatically. He remained convinced that the perfect society was simply the realization of the essence of humanity, i.e. that it would consist of bringing empirical existence into harmony with the normative pattern contained in the conception of man; this, he believed, would remove all possibility of social conflict, as the essence of humanity is equally binding upon all. He sought to show that the principle of social unity combines absolute freedom of the individual with the perfect equality aimed at by Fourier, and that the ideal of authentic freedom excludes private property as contradictory to the universal essence of humanity. For this reason he believed that communism, as a scheme for the abolition of property, was justified by faith in the community of man as a species. This community, when realized in practice, would do away with the need for religion and politics (i.e. political institutions) at a stroke, since both are instruments and manifestations of the servitude endured by men and women who are set at variance by conflicting egoisms. When man is conscious of himself as essential man there ceases to be a distinction between thought and action, which are absorbed in the undifferentiated process of living; in Hess's (quite arbitrary) interpretation of Spinoza, the identity of reason and will is the philosophical basis of this identity between action and thought. The free spirit will recognize itself in all objects of its own thought and action and will thus make the whole world its own; the alienness between nature and man, or one man and another, will cease to exist; man will truly be 'at home' in the universe. In the world as it has been till now, 'generalities' have dissipated real human contact into religious and political abstractions; communism will remove the contradiction between the individual and the community, by enabling the individual to regard the general patrimony as the work of his own hands. There will no longer be alienation, i.e. the domination of human products over men and women who do not realize that this is what they are dominated by. Negative freedom, which is no more than a margin secured by struggling against coercion, will be replaced by the voluntary self-limitation that constitutes true freedom; for 'freedom consists in overstepping external boundaries by means of self-limitation, the self-awareness of active spirit, the replacement of natural determination by self-determination . . . In humanity every self-determination of the spirit is merely a degree of development that oversteps itself.' But freedom is indivisible: social servitude and spiritual servitude, i.e. religion, go hand in hand; misery and oppression lead to the illusory panacea of religious 'opium'. Consequently servitude cannot be abolished in only one of its forms, such as religion: the evil must be exterminated at the roots, and it is primarily a social evil. Criticizing Feuerbach, who regarded the illusions of religion as the root of social servitude, Hess argued that money was a no less primary form of alienation than God. The influence of Proudhon can be seen here. The alienated essence of man, dominating its own creator, is not only and not primarily God, but money—the blood and sinew of the working man, turned into an abstract form and acting as a standard of human value. Proletarians and capitalists are alike obliged to sell their own vital activity and to feed, like cannibals, on the product of their own blood and sweat in the abstract shape of a medium of exchange. The money-alienation is the most complete inversion of the natural order of life. Instead of the individual being a means, as nature requires, and the species being an end in itself, the individual subordinates the species to himself and makes of his generic essence an unreal abstraction, which takes the form of God in religion and money in social life.

Hess's work bears the mark of hasty and ill-digested reading and of transient influences which affected his thought but were not brought into a synthetic harmony. It is not clear how we are to reconcile the Young Hegelian belief in the species-essence of man, realizing itself in time in every individual and, as Rousseau hoped, removing the possibility of a conflict between the individual and society, with Hegel's own principle of the primacy of the species over the individual. Nor is it clear whether, in Hess's view, spiritual liberation is in the last resort a prior condition of social liberation, or the other way about. His ideal of communism as a perfect harmony ensured by the abolition of private property and the right of inheritance appears clear enough; but his Utopia does not extend beyond themes that were current in France in his day, if not in Prussia. Socialism as a social movement was, in his view, mainly the result of poverty, although the opposition between rich and poor already ceases to dominate his picture of society, yielding to the opposition between capitalist and proletarian.

Hess was the first writer to express certain ideas which proved especially important in the history of Marxism, even though in his works they appear only in a generalized and aphoristic form. Above all, he expressed the conviction that the social revolution would be the result of polarized wealth and poverty, with a gradual disappearance of the middle classes. He suggested the analogy between religious and economic alienation, which was the germ of later Marxist analyses of commodity fetishism. He attempted to resolve the philosophical opposition between necessity and freedom, especially in the philosophy of action which proclaims that in the new phase of history what is necessary will come about through free creative activity, and which identifies self-consciousness with the historical process. This thought was expressed in the context of the philosophical self-consciousness of humanity as such, but it recurred with Marx in the form of a conviction of the identity of class-consciousness with the historical process in the privileged case of the proletariat. The prospect of philosophy being absorbed in its own realization is also found in Marx and is already present in Hess's work: 'When German philosophy becomes practical it will cease to be philosophy.' The importance of Hess is that he made the first attempt to synthesize Young Hegelian philosophy with communist doctrine and, in the name of social revolution, took issue with Young Hegelian expectations of a purely political change. Hess's work is linked with the German movement of 'true socialism' (Karl Grün, Hermann Pütmann, Hermann Kriege), which was more than once branded by Marx (for example in *The German Ideology* and *The Communist Manifesto*) as a reactionary Utopia: the movement regarded actual economic conditions as mere manifestations of spiritual servitude, and looked for the arrival of socialism as men became aware of their own species-essence. Hess, who met Marx in the autumn of 1841 and became his friend and collaborator for some years, later adopted to some extent the class orientation of Marxian socialism. They thus influenced each other, but Hess did not keep up with the theoretical development of socialism over which Marx presided, and did not adopt either the materialistic interpretation of history in the Marxist sense, or the Marxist theory of proletarian revolution.

3. Feuerbach and religious alienation

LUDWIG FEUERBACH (1804–72) was already a well-known writer in 1841. He had studied at Berlin under Hegel and Schleiermacher, but abandoned Hegelian idealism and Christianity at an early stage. In *Thoughts on Death and Immortality* (1830) he criticized theories of eternal life, and in *A History of Modern Philosophy from Bacon to Spinoza* (1833) and studies of Bayle and Leibniz he manifested his sympathy with the freethinking tradition. He opposed independent reason to all forms of dogmatism, called for the philosophical rehabilitation of nature, and criticized Hegelianism on the ground that, as it began with the spirit, it was bound to confine itself to the spirit and to define nature as a secondary manifestation (*Anderssein*) of the latter. But he first became celebrated with *The Essence of Christianity* (1841), a naturalistic critique of religion expressed in Hegelian language. Feuerbach did not care for the term 'materialism' because of its unfavourable moral associations, but on the basic issue he adopted a materialistic standpoint. He argued that 'the secret of theology is anthropology', i.e. that everything men have said about God is an expression in 'mystified' terms of their knowledge about themselves. If the real truth of religion is uttered it will prove to be atheism, or simply the positive affirmation of humanity. In general everything that man can apprehend in thought is the objectification of his own essence. 'Man becomes self-conscious in the object: consciousness of the object is man's self-knowledge . . . the object is the manifest essence of man, his true, objective self. And this applies not only to spiritual objects but also to those of sense. Even the objects that are furthest from man, in so far as they are objects to him, are a manifestation of his essence.' This of course does not mean that things owe their being to human consciousness, but only that the definitions whereby we apprehend them are definitions of ourselves projected on to the object, so that things are always perceived in human terms and are a projection and image of our self-consciousness. On the other hand, 'man is nothing without an object': it is only in objectivity that he recognizes himself. This idea of the mutual dependence of subject and object (the subject constituting itself in self-knowledge through the object, the object constituting itself in the projection of self-knowledge) is not further analysed by Feuerbach; in general he expresses it in the formula that man belongs to the essence of nature (despite vulgar materialism) and nature to the essence of man.

But Feuerbach was interested above all in the particular kind of objectification that occurs in religious alienation. When men relate to the object in an essential and necessary manner, when they affirm in it the fullness and perfection of their species-essence, that object is God. God is thus the imaginative projection of man's species-essence, the totality of his powers and attributes raised to the level of infinity. Every species-essence is 'infinite', i.e. as an essence it is full of perfection and is a model or standard for individual beings. Man's knowledge of God is an attempt to perceive himself in the mirror of exteriority; man exteriorizes his own essence before he recognizes it in himself, and the opposition between God and man is a 'mystified' version of the opposition between the species and the individual. God cannot in principle have any other predicates than those which men have abstracted from themselves; he is real in so far as these predicates are real. Religion, however, inverts the relationship between subject and predicates, giving human predicates—in the shape of Deity—the primacy over what is real, human, and concrete. Religion is a self-dichotomy of man, his reason, and feelings, the transference of his intellectual and affective qualities on to an imaginary divine being which asserts its own independence and begins to tyrannize over its creator. Religious alienation, the 'dream of the spirit', is not only an error but an impoverishment of man, since it takes away all his best qualities and faculties and bestows them on the Deity. The more religion enriches the essence of God, the more it devitalizes man; the nature of religion is most clearly symbolized in the ritual of blood-sacrifice. Humanity must be humiliated, degraded and stripped of its dignity in order that the Deity may be revealed in majesty. 'Man asserts in God what he denies in himself.' Moreover, religion paralyses men's ability to live together in concord, for it diverts the energy of love on to the divinity and rejects the real fellowship of man into an imaginary heaven. It destroys the feeling of solidarity and mutual love, encourages egoism, depreciates all the values of earthly life, and makes social equality and harmony impossible. To overthrow religion is to realize the true values of religion, which are those of humanity. When people come to themselves and realize that the personifications of religion are the fruit of their own childish imagination, they will be able to form genuinely humanistic societies, in the light of Spinoza's principle *homo homini Deus*. The cult of fictitious other-worldly beings will give place to the cult of life and love. 'If the essence of man is the supreme essence for man, then the first and supreme law of action must be man's love for man.'

The Essence of Christianity was an attempt to apply the Hegelian category of alienation to the formulation of a purely naturalistic and anthropocentric viewpoint. Unlike Hegel, Feuerbach regarded alienation as an altogether negative phenomenon. In Hegel's view, Being realizes its essence by first excluding and then reabsorbing it in a process of self-enrichment; what it potentially contains must be made external before it can be actualized. The Absolute Idea attains to self-consciousness through its own alienated manifestations; it is not pure act, like the God of the Scholastics, but comes to fulfilment only through history and the successive phases of alienation. To Feuerbach, on the other hand, alienation is purely evil and erroneous and possesses no positive value. Religious mystification divides man from his species and opposes the individual to himself; it wastes human energy in the cult of unreal beings and distracts it from the one true value, that of man in and for himself.

4. Feuerbach's second phase. Sources of the religious fallacy

FEUERBACH's later writings display an ever-widening rift with Hegelianism and a more and more explicit materialism of the eighteenth-century kind. In the preface to the second edition of *The Essence of Christianity* (1843) he rejects the theory that subject and object condition each other, declaring that our apprehension of things is primarily sensual and passive, and only second-arily active and conceptual. In *Lectures on the Essence of Religion* (1848–9, published in 1851) he repeats this view and also emphasizes that religious imaginations result from man's feeling of dependence on nature, whereas he had previously treated them as an objectification of the 'essence of humanity'. Originally he envisaged that the overthrow of religion would put an end to human egoism; now he asserted that egoism is a natural and inevitable human trait, present in even the most altruistic of actions, i.e. he reverted to the Enlightenment stereotype of 'natural egoism'. In his earlier work he had described the process of God-creating projection but had not explained its causes. He now tried to fill the gap, but did not go further than stating that the source of religious imagination is generally ignorance and man's inability to interpret aright his own situation in nature. Realizing his dependence on nature, which is eternal and inescapable, man fails to comprehend this dependence in rational categories; instead he devises anthropomorphic fan-cies to express his fear of Nature's incalculable caprices and the positive feel-ings of gratitude and hope that she arouses in him. Religion is an ersatz satisfaction of human needs that cannot be met in any other way: men seek to compel nature to obey them by using magic or appealing to divine goodness, i.e. they try to achieve by imagination what they cannot have in reality. As knowledge increases, religion, which is an infantile state of mind, gradually yields to a rational world-view, and men are able, by the arts of civilization and technology, to control forces that were previously untameable. At the same time Feuerbach draws attention to the sources of religious imagination that lie in the very nature of the cognitive processes, especially that of abstraction. Since we can only think or express ourselves in terms of abstracts, we are apt to credit them with an independent existence *vis-à-vis* individual, which are in fact the only reality. In the same way God and other religious figments, per-sonifying human ideas, feelings, and abilities, are an illegitimate autonomiza-tion of the legitimate instruments of cognition. 'The idea or generic concept of God in the metaphysical sense is based on the same necessity and the same foundations as is the concept of things or of fruit... The gods of polytheists are nothing but names and collective or generic concepts imagined as actual beings'; but 'in order to understand the meaning of general concepts it is not necessary to deify them and turn them into independent beings that differ from individual essences. We can condemn wickedness without at once personifying it as the devil.'

In *Lectures on the Essence of Religion* there is no longer any trace of Feuerbach's Hegelian upbringing. Religion is explained in simple Enlightenment terms as the result of fear and ignorance, and Feuerbach also takes over the Enlightenment theory of perception as merely sensual and empirical. The *Lectures* were a novelty in German philosophy, dominated as it was by the categories of Kant and Hegel, but to the rest of Europe they were merely a repetition of well-known theories. The essential feature was that Feuerbach consistently saw religion as the root of all social evil. He believed that when religious mystification was done away with there would be an end of the sources of social inequality, exploitation, egoism, and slavery. Religion was the source and epitome of all the evil in history; and he expected that public enlightenment, sweeping away religious prejudice, would at the same time eradicate social servitude. This was one of the main points, though not the only one, on which Marx soon took up a sharply critical attitude towards Feuerbach's philosophy.

By the end of the 1840s Feuerbach had completely rejected Hegelianism, regarding it, like all other forms of idealism, as nothing but a continuation of religious fiction. All the creations of classic German philosophy, such as Hegel's Idea, Fichte's Ego, or Schelling's Absolute, appeared to him simply as substitutes for the Deity, reduced to a more abstract form by philosophical imagination. Interpreting humanity in purely zoological categories, he saw the social community as a form of natural co-operation within the species, distorted or depraved by religious prejudice, while in moral speculation he did not advance beyond the eudaemonistic schema of the Enlightenment. The sweep of his rhetoric, with its humanistic and freethinking ideas, won him many adherents. *The Essence of Christianity* had immense influence in Germany and played a large part in transforming the Young Hegelian camp by radicalizing its anti-religious orientation. To Marx in particular, Feuerbach's philosophy was not only a point of repulsion but also one of the main stimuli that enabled him to reject Hegelian categories in his own thinking. He also owed much to Feuerbach as regards knowledge of the history of philosophy, especially in the sixteenth and seventeenth centuries. He adopted the critique of Hegelianism as a philosophy that 'put the predicate where the subject should be' and gave human creations priority over man himself, and made use of it in his analysis of Hegel's philosophy of law.

It might be thought that after Marx's criticisms the philosophy of Feuerbach was completely outdated, especially in view of his rather dull and repetitive style. Yet it continues to excite interest among seekers after a universal humanistic formula, and even among theologians. The radical anthropocentrism which is its chief feature may be summed up as follows. Firstly, man is the only value; all others are instrumental and subordinate. Secondly, man is always a live, finite, concrete entity. Thirdly, there are permanent features of human nature which make it possible for men to live in a harmonious community based on mutual love and respect for life. Fourthly, the abolition of religion in the dogmatic and mystical forms in which it has hitherto been known will open the way to a new, authentic religion of humanity, enabling men to attain what has been their true object in all religions, namely the satisfaction of their need for happiness, solidarity, equality, and freedom.

V

Marx's Early Political and
Philosophical Writings

AFTER COMPLETING his studies Marx returned to Trier in the spring of 1841 and afterwards moved to Bonn, where he began to write for Young Hegelian journals. His first article, on the Prussian government's new decree concerning Press censorship, was written for the *Deutsche Jahrbücher*, the issue of which was confiscated as a result; it appeared in 1843 in a collective work published in Switzerland. However, Marx was able to publish a series of articles on this subject in the *Rheinische Zeitung*, a liberal bourgeois journal founded at Cologne at the beginning of 1842 and dominated by Young Hegelian writers: among its contributors were Adolf Rutenberg, Friedrich Engels, Moses Hess, Bruno Bauer, Karl Köppen, and Max Stirner. Marx himself edited the paper from October 1842 to March 1843. During this time, apart from articles on the freedom of the Press, he wrote analyses of the debates in the Landtag (provincial assembly), in which for the first time he devoted his attention to economic questions and the standard of living of the deprived classes. Adopting a radical democratic standpoint, he denounced the pseudo-liberalism of the Prussian government and stood up for the oppressed peasantry.

1. The state and intellectual freedom

FROM the point of view of the development of Marx's theories, his early journalistic writings are important for two main reasons. In his sharp attacks on the censorship law he spoke out unequivocally for the freedom of the Press, against the levelling effect of government restriction ('You don't expect a rose to smell like a violet; why then should the human spirit, the richest thing we have, exist only in a single form?'), and also expressed views concerning the whole nature of the state and the essence of freedom. Pointing out that the vagueness and ambiguity of the press law placed arbitrary power in the hands of officials, Marx went on to argue that censorship was contrary not only to the purposes of the Press, but to the nature of the state as such.

The freedom of the Press has quite a different basis from censorship, for it is the form of an idea, namely freedom, and is an actual good; censorship is a form of servitude, the weapon of a world view based on appearances against one based on the nature of things. Censorship is something purely negative ... Freedom lies so deeply in human nature that even the opponents of freedom help to bring it about by combating its reality ... The essence of a free press is the rational essence of freedom in its fullest character. A censored press is a thing without a backbone, a vampire of slavery, a civilized monstrosity, a scented freak of nature. Is there any further need to prove that freedom is in accordance with the essence of the Press, and that censorship is contrary to it?

Thus, Marx continues, 'Censorship, like slavery, can never be rightful, even though it existed a thousand times in the form of laws', and a Press law is a true law only when it protects the freedom of the Press. Censorship is contrary to the very nature of law and of the state, for a free Press is an indispensable condition of a state fulfilling its own nature: it is embodied civilization, the individual's link with the state, a mirror of the people. A censored Press depraves public life and means that the government hears only its own voice. Freedom does not require arguments to justify it, for it is part and parcel of man's spiritual life. 'In a free system every separate world revolves round the central sun of freedom as, and only as, it revolves upon itself ... For is it not a denial of one person's freedom to demand that he should be free after the manner of another?' The written word is not a means to an end, but an end in itself, and must not be confined by laws that have in view any interest other than spiritual development.

In this argument, as will be seen, Marx distinguishes the 'real' law and state, those which correspond to their own proper nature, from laws and institutions which are maintained by police methods but are only binding in an external sense. This distinction belongs to the Hegelian tradition: a state and a law which are not the realization of freedom are contrary to the very concept or essence of state and law and are thus not truly such, even though upheld by force. Marx, however, unlike Hegel, denies that freedom of speech and writing can be limited by the overriding interest of the 'true' state, since he claims that this freedom is an essential part of the concept of a state. Thus, while he uses the normative concept of the state as a model with which existing states are to be compared so as to determine whether they are 'real' or merely empirical, in applying this method he parts company with Hegel by asserting that the freedom of diversity is an essential human value which carries with it its own justification.

Another main theme appears at this time in Marx's comments on the Landtag debate on the law concerning the theft of timber (this was a revocation of the custom allowing peasants to gather brushwood in the forests without pay-

ment). Defending the peasantry and the customary law, Marx adopted a philanthropic viewpoint but also argued that the Landtag was degrading the laws
and the authority of the state to the role of an instrument of the private interests of landowners, and was thus contravening the very idea of the state. In this
way he opposes the state, representing the whole community, to institutions
which turn it into the agent of one sectional group or another. At this stage,
however, it is not clear that he has any answer to the question as to how state
institutions can be brought into conformity with the general interest, or how, if
at all, the state is capable of solving social questions, especially poverty and the
inequality of incomes.

2. Criticism of Hegel. The state, society, individuality

MARX's concern with politics led him to make a deeper study of Hegel's philosophy of law. His lengthy *Critique of Hegel's Philosophy of Right*, written in
1843 (and first published in 1927), remained unfinished, but some of its main
ideas can be found in two articles entitled *On the Jewish Question* and *Introduction to a Critique of Hegel's Philosophy of Right*. These were written towards
the end of 1843 and appeared in the *Deutsch-Französische Jahrbücher*, which
Marx was then editing in collaboration with Arnold Ruge and Hess. He had
moved to Paris in the autumn of that year, accompanied by his newly wedded
wife Jenny, the daughter of Baron Ludwig von Westphalen, a City Councillor of
Trier, and was in contact with local socialist organizations of French and German workers. Before this he probably knew something of communist propaganda in France from Lorenz von Stein's *Socialism and Communism in
Present-Day France* (1842). Stein, a conservative Hegelian, had been investigating socialist movements on the instructions of the Prussian government,
which was interested in subversive activity among German workers in Paris. He
was anti-socialist and regarded the class hierarchy as a precondition of organized society, but his book, which contained a large amount of information, was
widely known in radical circles in Germany.

In his long critique of Hegel, Marx attacked especially the idea that the state
was, in its origin and value, quite independent of the empirical individuals who
composed it. Hegel had argued that the functions of the state were connected
with the individual in an accidental manner, whereas in fact there was between
them an essential link, a *vinculum substantiale*. Hegel conceived the functions
of the state in an abstract form and in themselves, treating empirical individuals as an antithesis to them. But in fact

> the essence of a human person is not that person's beard or blood or abstract phys-
> ical nature, but his or her social character, and the state's functions are nothing more

or less than the forms of existence and operation of man's social characteristics. It is reasonable, therefore, to consider individuals as representatives of the functions and authority of the state, from the point of view of their social and not their private character.

In the second place Marx, following Feuerbach, criticizes the 'inversion of the relationship of predicate and subject' in Hegel's philosophy, where human individuals, who are real subjects, are turned into predicates of a universal substance. In reality everything that is general is merely an attribute of individual being, and the true subject is always finite. To Hegel, the individual man is a subjective and secondary form of the existence of the state, whereas 'democracy starts from man and makes the state into objectified man. Just as religion does not make man, but man makes religion, so the constitution does not make the people, but the people makes the constitution.' Marx thus endeavours to reduce all political institutions, as a matter of theory, to their actual human origins. At the same time he seeks to subordinate the real state to human needs, and to strip it of the appearance of independent value apart from its function as an instrument to serve the needs of empirical individuals. The aim of democracy as Marx understands it is to make the state once more an instrument of man, i.e. to dealienate political institutions. Only a state which is a form of the existence of its people, and not a foreign body over against them, is a true state, one which conforms to the essence of statehood. An undemocratic state is not a state. Hegel perpetuates the gulf between man and state by regarding society not as the realization of personality but as a goal approached by the state; the empirical human being is thus the supreme reality of the state, but not its creator. 'In Hegel it is not subjects who objectify themselves in the common cause, but the common cause itself becomes a subject. It is not subjects who need the common cause as their own true cause, but the common cause is in need of subjects as a condition of its own formal existence. It is the business of the common cause to exist as a subject also.' The purport of this criticism is clear: if human individuals are only 'moments' or stages in the development of universal substance, which through them attains the supreme form of being, then they are mere instruments of that universal substance and not independent values. The Hegelian philosophy thus sanctions the delusion that the state as such is the embodiment of the general interest, which is only the case if the general interest is completely alienated from the interests and needs of actual individuals. This question is closely connected with that of the state bureaucracy. Hegel believed that the spirit of the state and its superiority to the particular interests of its citizens were embodied in the consciousness of officialdom; for officials identified their particular interest with that of the state as a whole and thus, as an organ of the state, effected a synthesis between the common good and that of particular sections or corporations. To Marx this was an illusion, a reflection within Hegelianism of the ideology of the Prussian bureaucracy which persuaded itself that it was the supreme embodiment of the general good. The fact was, on the contrary, that

> wherever the bureaucracy is a principle of its own, where the general interest of the state becomes a separate, independent and actual interest, there the bureaucracy will be opposed to the corporations in the same way as every consequence is opposed to its own premises . . . The purpose of a true state is not that each citizen should devote himself to the general cause as though to a particular one, but that the general cause should be truly general, i.e. the cause of every citizen.

Hegel distinguished two separate spheres of contemporary life, viz. civil society and the political state. In this division, which Marx accepted, civil society was the totality of divergent particular interests, individual and collective—empirical daily life with all its conflicts and disputes, the forum in which every individual carried on his day-to-day existence. At the same time, as a citizen he was a participant in the organization of the state. Hegel believed that the conflicts within civil society were held in check and rationally synthesized in the supreme will of the state, independent of particular interests. On this point Marx strongly opposes the Hegelian illusion. The division into two spheres is real, but a synthesis between them is not possible. The state in its present form is not a mediator between particular interests, but a tool of particular interests of a special kind. Man as a citizen is completely different from man as a private person, but only the private person who belongs to civil society possesses real, concrete existence; as a citizen he is part of an abstract creation whose apparent reality is based on a mystification. This mystification did not exist in the Middle Ages, for in those days the division into estates was also an immediate political division: the articulation of the civil community coincided with the political division. Modern societies, which have altered or abolished the political significance of the division into estates, have brought about a dualism which affects every human existence and creates within every human being a contradiction between his private capacity and his capacity as a citizen. Marx does not set out, however, merely to describe this contradiction but to explain its origin.

3. The idea of social emancipation

IN his essay *On the Jewish Question* Marx repeats this theme more clearly, in the form of a description and a plan of action. Commenting on Bauer's critique of the subject, he expresses his own idea of human as distinct from political emancipation. Bauer, in Marx's opinion, turned social questions into theological ones; he called for religious emancipation as the chief precondition of political emancipation and was content with a programme for liberating the state from religion, i.e. disestablishing the latter. But, Marx objected, religious restrictions were not a cause of secular ones, but a manifestation of them. By freeing the state from religious limitations we do not free mankind from them: the state may free itself from religion while leaving the majority of its citizens in religious bondage. In the same way the state may cancel the political effect of private property, i.e. abolish the property qualification for voting, etc., and may declare that differences of birth and station have no political significance, but this does not mean that private property and differences of birth and station will cease to have any consequences. In short, a purely political and therefore partial emancipation is valuable and important, but it does not amount to human emancipation, for there is still a division between the civil community and the state. In the former, people live a life which is real but selfish, isolated and full of conflicting interests; the state provides them with a sphere of life which is collective, but illusory. The purpose of human emancipation is to bring it about that the collective, generic character of human life is real life, so that society itself takes on a collective character and coincides with the life of the state. Bauer does not penetrate to the real source of antagonism between individual and collective life; he combats only the religious expression of that conflict. The freedom he proclaims is that of a monad, the right to live in isolation; as in the Declaration of the Rights of Man, it is based on mutual self-limitation (my freedom is bounded by the freedom of someone else). Given the separation of the two spheres, the state does not help to abolish the egoistic character of private life but merely provides it with a legal framework. Political revolution does not liberate people from religion or the rule of property, it merely gives them the right to hold property and to profess their own religion. Political emancipation thus confirms the dichotomy of man. 'The actual individual man must take the abstract citizen back into himself and, as an individual man in his empirical life, in his individual work and individual relationships, becomes a species-being; man must recognize his own forces as social forces, organize them and thus no longer separate social forces from himself in the form of political forces. Only when this has been achieved will human emancipation be completed.'

In this way Marx came upon the idea which, in the political context, enabled him to go beyond the purely political, republican, anti-feudal programme of the Young Hegelians and to proclaim the objective of a social transformation which would remove the conflict between private and political life. From the philosophical point of view this was based on the idea of an integrated human being overcoming his own division between private interest and the community. Marx's conception of humanity goes far beyond Feuerbach, since the mystification of religion appears to him merely as a manifestation, not a root, of social servitude. He does not, like Feuerbach, regard man from a naturalistic point of view; he does not imagine a return to innate rules of co-operation which would, of their own accord, prevail in human society once the religious alienation was overcome. On the contrary, he regards the emancipation of man as a specifically human emancipation made possible by the identification of private with public life, the political with the social sphere. The conscious absorption of society by the individual, the free recognition by each individual of himself as a bearer of the community is, in Marx's view, the way in which man rediscovers and returns into himself.

However, as these postulates are expressed in the *Critique of Hegel's Philosophy of Right* and the essay *On the Jewish Question,* they remain utopian (in the sense in which Marx later used this word) inasmuch as they simply oppose the actual state of man's dichotomy to an imaginary unity, described in very abstract terms. The question of how and by means of what forces that unity is to be attained remains open.

4. The discovery of the proletariat

THE *Introduction to a Critique of Hegel's Philosophy of Right* is regarded as a crucial text in Marx's intellectual development, as it is here that he expresses for the first time the idea of a specific historical mission of the proletariat, and the interpretation of revolution not as a violation of history but as a fulfilment of its innate tendency.

The latter idea appears in a letter from Marx to Ruge written in September 1843.

> Let us develop new principles for the world out of its own principles. Let us not say to it 'Cease your nonsensical struggles, we will give you something real to fight for.' Let us simply show the world what it is really fighting for, and this is something the world must come to know, whether it wishes to or not. The reform of consciousness consists only in the world becoming aware of its own consciousness, awakening it from vague dreams of itself and showing it what its true activity is . . . Then it will be seen that the world has long been dreaming of things that it only needs to become aware of in order to possess them in reality.

It may be seen that the tremendous role that Marx ascribes to the awakening of consciousness does not signify—as it did with most of the Young Hegelians, with Feuerbach, and the majority of socialist writers of the thirties and forties—that people could be offered an arbitrary ideal of social perfection, so sublime and irresistible that they would at once seek to put it into practice. In Marx's view, a reformed consciousness was a basic condition of social transformation because it was, or could be, the revealing and explication of what had been merely implicit; because it gave recognizable form to what had all along been the aims of the struggle for liberation, and thus converted an unconscious historical tendency into a conscious one, an objective trend into an act of will. This is the basis of what Marx later called scientific socialism, as opposed to the utopian variety which confined itself to propounding an arbitrarily constructed ideal. In calling for a revolution as a result of men coming to understand the meaning of their own behaviour, Marx turned his back on the utopianism of contemporary socialists and on Fichte's opposition, which the Young Hegelians had taken over, between obligation and reality.

In the *Introduction* Marx pursued this theme and at the same time emphatically opposed Feuerbach's critique of religion. He accepts that man is the creator of religion, but adds that

> Man is the world of man, the state, society. This state, this society, produce religion's inverted attitude to the world, because they are an inverted world themselves. Religion is . . . the imaginary realization of human being, because human being possesses no true reality. Thus the struggle against religion is indirectly the struggle against that world whose spiritual aroma is religion. . . . Religion is the opium of the people. The real happiness of the people requires the abolition of religion, which is their illusory happiness. In demanding that they give up illusions about their condition, we demand that they give up a condition that requires illusion. . . . Once the holy form of human self-alienation has been unmasked, the first task of philosophy, in the service of history, is to unmask self-alienation in its unholy forms. The criticism of heaven is thus transformed into criticism of earth, the criticism of religion into the criticism of law, and the criticism of theology into the criticism of politics.

Having thus exposed the delusions of the anti-religious criticism which claims to possess in itself the power to abolish human servitude, Marx repeats his critique of conditions in Germany, where the only revolutions have been philosophical ones—a state of political anachronism, with all the drawbacks and none of the advantages of the new order. The liberation of Germany can only be brought about by ruthless awareness of its true position. 'We must make the actual oppression even more oppressive by making people conscious of it, and the insult even more insulting by publicizing it. . . . We must force these petrified relationships to dance by playing their own tune to them. To give people courage, we must teach them to be alarmed by themselves.' A German revolution would mean the realization of German philosophy by its own abolition. But philosophy can only be realized in the sphere of material action.

> The weapon of criticism is no substitute for criticism by weapons: material force must be opposed by material force. But theory, too, will become material force as

soon as it takes hold of the masses. This it can do when its proofs are *ad hominem*, that is to say when it becomes radical. To be radical is to grasp the matter by the root; and for man, the root is man himself.

The social revolution can only be carried out by a class whose particular interest coincides with that of all society, and whose claims represent universal needs. That class is the proletariat,

> which has a universal character by reason of the universality of its sufferings, and which does not lay claim to any specific rights because the injustice to which it is subjected is not particular but general. . . . It cannot liberate itself without breaking free from all the other classes of society and thereby liberating them also . . . It stands for the total ruin of man, and can recover itself only by his total redemption.

Thus the liberation of the proletariat signifies its abolition as a separate class and the destruction of class distinctions in general by the abolition of private property. Marx believes that Germany is the destined birthplace of the proletarian revolution because it is a concentration of all the contradictions of the modern world together with those of feudalism. To abolish a particular form of oppression in Germany will mean the abolition of all oppression and the general emancipation of mankind. 'The head of this emancipation is philosophy, its heart is the proletariat. Philosophy cannot realize itself without transcending the proletariat, the proletariat cannot transcend itself without realizing philosophy.'

It is noteworthy that the idea of the proletariat's special mission as a class which cannot liberate itself without thereby liberating society as a whole makes its first appearance in Marx's thought as a philosophical deduction rather than a product of observation. When Marx wrote his *Introduction* he had seen very little of the actual workers' movement; yet the principle he formulated at this time remained the foundation of his social philosophy. He also formulated at this early stage the idea of socialism, not as the replacement of one type of political life by another but as the abolition of politics altogether. In articles published in the Paris journal *Vorwärts* in the summer of 1844 he declared that there could not be a social revolution with a political soul, but there could be a political revolution with a social soul. Revolution as such was a political act, and there could be no socialism until the old order was overthrown; but 'When the organization of socialism begins and when its true purpose and soul are brought to the forefront, then socialism will cast off its political integument.'

It should be observed that from start to finish Marx's socialist programme did not, as his opponents have often claimed, involve the extinction of individuality or a general levelling for the sake of the 'universal good'. This conception of socialism was indeed characteristic of many primitive communist doctrines; it can be found in the utopias of the Renaissance and the Enlightenment, influenced as they are by traditions of monastic communism, and in socialist works of the 1840s. To Marx, on the other hand, socialism represented the full emancipation of the individual by the destruction of the web of mystification which turned community life into a world of estrangement presided over by an alienated bureaucracy. Marx's ideal was that every man should be fully aware of his own character as a social being, but should also, for this very reason, be capable of developing his personal aptitudes in all their fullness and variety. There was no question of the individual being reduced to a universal species-being; what Marx desired to see was a community in which the sources of antagonism among individuals were done away with. This antagonism sprang, in his view, from the mutual isolation that is bound to arise when political life is divorced from civil society, while the institution of private property means that people can only assert their own individuality in opposition to others.

From the outset, then, Marx's criticism of existing society makes sense only in the context of his vision of a new world in which the social significance of each individual's life is directly evident to him, but individuality is not thereby diluted into colourless uniformity. This presupposes that there can be a perfect identity between collective and individual interests, and that private, 'egoistic' motives can be eliminated in favour of a sense of absolute community with the 'whole'. Marx held that a society from which all sources of conflict, aggression, and evil have been thus extirpated was not only thinkable, but was historically imminent.

VI

The Paris Manuscripts. The Theory of
Alienated Labour. The Young Engels

In Paris in 1844 Marx was engaged in composing a critique of political economy in which he attempted to provide a general philosophical analysis of basic
concepts: capital, rent, labour, property, money, commodities, needs, and
wages. This work, which was never finished, was published for the first time in
1932 and is known as the *Economic and Philosophical Manuscripts of 1844*.
Although merely an outline, it has come to be regarded as one of the most
important sources for the evolution of Marx's thought. In it he attempted to
expound socialism as a general world-view and not merely a programme of
social reform, and to relate economic categories to a philosophical interpretation of man's position in nature, which is also taken as the starting-point for
the investigation of metaphysical and epistemological problems. In addition to
German philosophers and socialist writers, Marx addressed himself in this
work to the writings of the fathers of political economy, whom he had begun
to study: Quesnay, Adam Smith, Ricardo, Say, and James Mill.

It would, of course, be quite wrong to imagine that the Paris Manuscripts
contain the entire gist of *Capital*; yet they are in effect the first draft of the book
that Marx went on writing all his life, and of which *Capital* is the final version.
There are, moreover, sound reasons for maintaining that the final version is a
development of its predecessor and not a departure from it. The Manuscripts,
it is true, do not mention the theory of value and surplus value, which is
regarded as the corner-stone of 'mature' Marxism. But the specifically Marxist
theory of value, with the distinction between abstract and concrete labour and
the recognition of the labour force as a commodity, is nothing but the definitive version of the theory of alienated labour.

1. Critique of Hegel. Labour as the foundation of humanity

Marx's negative point of reference is contained in Hegel's *Phenomenology*, in
particular the theory of alienation and of labour as an alienating process. The
greatness of Hegel's dialectic of negation consisted, in Marx's view, in the idea

that humanity creates itself by a process of alienation alternating with the transcendence of that alienation. Man, according to Hegel, manifests his generic essence by relating to his own powers in an objectified state and then, as it were, assimilating them from the outside. Labour, as the realization of the essence of man, thus has a wholly positive significance, being the process by which humanity develops through externalization of itself. Hegel, however, identifies human essence with self-consciousness, and labour with spiritual activity. Alienation in its original form is the alienation of self-consciousness, and all objectivity is alienated self-consciousness; so that the transcendence of alienation, in which man reassimilates his own essence, is the transcendence of the object and its reabsorption into the spiritual nature of man. Man's integration with nature takes place on the spiritual level, which makes it, in Marx's view, an abstraction and an illusion.

Marx, following Feuerbach, bases his own view of humanity on labour, understood as physical commerce with nature. Labour is the condition of all spiritual human activity, and in it man creates himself as well as nature, the object of his creativity. The objects of human need, those in which he manifests and realizes his own essence, are independent of him; that is to say, man is also a passive being. But he is a being-for-himself, not merely a natural being, so that things do not exist for him simply as they are, irrespective of their being human objects. 'Human objects are not natural objects, therefore, in the form in which they are immediately given; and human sense, as it is immediately given in its objective form, is not human sensibility and human objectivity.' Consequently, the transcendence of the object as alienated cannot be, as Hegel maintained, the transcendence of objectivity itself. In order to show how man can reabsorb nature and the object into himself, it is necessary first to explain how the phenomenon of alienation actually arises, through the mechanism of alienated labour.

2. The social and practical character of knowledge

SINCE, in Marx's view, the basic characteristic of humanity is labour, i.e. contact with nature in which man is both active and passive, it follows that the traditional problems of epistemology must be looked at from a fresh standpoint. Marx denied the legitimacy of the questions posed by Descartes and Kant: it is wrong, he argued, to inquire how the transition from the act of self-consciousness to the object is possible, since the assumption of pure self-awareness as a starting-point rests on the fiction of a subject capable of apprehending itself altogether independently of its being in nature and society. On the other hand, it is equally wrong to regard nature as the reality already known and to consider man and human subjectivity as its product, as though it were possible to contemplate nature in itself regardless of man's practical relation to it. The true starting-point is man's active contact with nature, and it is only by abstraction that we divide this into self-conscious humanity on the one hand and nature on the other. Man's relationship to the world is not originally contemplation or passive perception, in which things transmit their likeness to the subject or transform their inherent being into fragments of the subject's perceptual field. Perception is, from the beginning, the result of the combined operation of nature and the practical orientation of human beings, who are subjects in a social sense and who regard things as their proper objects, as designed to serve some purpose.

> Man assimilates his many-sided essence in a many-sided way, and thus as a whole man. His whole human attitude to the world—sight, hearing, smell, taste and touch, thought, contemplation and sensation, desire, action and love—in short, all the organs of his personality, and those that in their form are directly social organs, constitute in their objective relationship, or their relation to the object, an assimilation of that object, an assimilation of human reality; their relation to the object is a manifestation of human reality . . . The eye became a human eye, and its object became a social and human object, created by man and destined for him. Thus the senses, in practice, became directly theoreticians. They relate themselves to things with regard to the thing itself, but the thing itself is an objective, human relationship to itself and also to man, and vice versa . . . An object is not the same to the eye as it is to the ear, and the object of the eye is different from that of the ear. The peculiarity of every essence is its own peculiar essence, and hence also its peculiar way of objectifying it, its own objectively real, live being . . . To the unmusical ear the finest music means nothing—it is not an object for it. To be an object for me, a thing must be a confirmation of one of the forces of my being; it can exist for me only as a force of my being exists for itself, as a subjective faculty, since the significance of the object for me can extend no further than my own senses extend. The senses of a social man, then, are different from the senses of an unsocial one.

Marx, it may be seen, takes up the basic question posed by Kant and Hegel, viz. how can the human mind be 'at home' in the world? Is it possible, and if so how, to bridge the gulf between the rational consciousness and the world which is simply 'given' in a direct, irrational form? If the question is put in such general terms as this, we may say that Marx inherited it from classical German philosophy; but the specific questions he asks are different, especially from those of Kant. In the latter's doctrine, the alienness of nature *vis-à-vis* the free and rational subject is insuperable: the duality of the subject-matter of cognition, i.e. the fundamental difference between what is given and *a priori* forms, cannot be overcome in real terms, the manifoldness of the data of experience cannot be rationalized. The subject, which is self-determining and therefore free, encounters nature, which is constrained by necessity, as something other than itself, an irrationality which it has to tolerate. In the same way ideals and moral imperatives cannot be derived from the world of irrational data, so that the real and the ideal are bound to be in conflict. The unity of the world comprising subject and object, sense and thought, the freedom of man and the necessity of nature—such unity is a limiting postulate which reason can never actually bring about, but towards which it must strive without ceasing. Thus reality is an unceasing limitation for the subject, its mental faculties, and its moral ideals. In Hegel's view the Kantian dualism was an abdication of rationalism, and the postulate of unity as the unattainable limit of endless striving represented an anti-dialectic view of the world. If the gulf between the two worlds to which man belongs remains equally wide in every single cognitive or moral act, then the striving to overcome it is a sterile infinitude in which man's inability to heal his internal rift is endlessly reproduced. Hegel therefore seeks to represent the process whereby the subject gradually assimilates reality as a progressive discovery of its latent rationality, i.e. its spiritual essence. Reason is impotent if it cannot discover rationality in the very facticity of Being, if it wraps itself up in its own perfection and is at the same time encumbered with an irrational world. But when it discovers emergent rationality in that world, when it perceives reality as a product of self-consciousness and of the self-limiting activity of the Absolute, then it is able to recover the world for subjectivity; and this is the task of philosophy.

It was perhaps Feuerbach who first made Marx aware of the arbitrary and speculative character of the solution proposed by Hegelian idealism to the dualism of Kant. Hegel presupposes that actual existence is alienated self-consciousness, merely in order to recover the world for the thinking subject. But self-consciousness cannot, by alienating itself, create more than an abstract semblance of reality; and if, in human life, products of this self-alienation come to acquire power over men, it is our task to put them back in their proper place and recognize abstractions for what they are. Man is himself part of nature, and if he recognizes himself in nature it is not in the sense of discovering in it the work of a self-consciousness that is absolutely prior to nature, but only in the sense that, in the process of the self-creation of man by labour, nature is an object *for* man, perceived in a human fashion, cognitively organized in accordance with human needs, and 'given' only in the context of the practical behaviour of the species. 'Nature itself, considered in the abstract, fixed in separation from man, is nothing as far as he is concerned.' If the active dialogue between the human species and nature is our starting-point, and if nature and self-consciousness as we know them are given only in that dialogue and not in a pure inherent sense, then it is reasonable for nature as we perceive it to be called humanized nature, and for mind to be called the self-knowledge of nature. Man, a part and product of nature, makes nature a part of himself; it is at once the subject-matter of his activity and a prolongation of his body. From this point of view there is no sense in putting the question as to a creator of the world, since it presupposes the unreal situation of the non-existence of nature and man, a situation which cannot be posited even as a fictive starting-point.

> By enquiring as to the creation of nature and man, you abstract from both man and nature. You assume their non-existence and yet wish to have it proved that they exist. Let me tell you, then, that if you give up your abstraction you will likewise abandon your question . . . Since, for socialist man, the whole of so-called universal history is nothing but the formation of man by human labour, the shaping of nature for man's sake, man thus possesses a clear, irrefutable proof that he is born of his own self, a proof of the process whereby he has come to be. Since the essentiality of man and nature has become something practical, sensual and evident; since man has become for man practically, sensually and evidently the being of nature, and nature has become for man the being of man, the question of a foreign being over and above both man and nature . . . has become a practical impossibility. Atheism, as a denial of that non-essentiality, is also meaningless, for atheism consists in denying the existence of God and establishing man's being on that denial. But socialism as such no longer needs such assistance; it takes as its starting-point the theoretical and practical sensual awareness of man and nature as an essence. It is the positive self-consciousness of man which no longer stands in need of the abolition of religion, just as real life is the positive reality of man which no longer stands in need of the abolition of private property—that is to say, communism.

Thus, in Marx's view, epistemological questions in their traditional form were no less illegitimate than metaphysical ones. A man cannot consider the world as though he were outside it, or isolate a purely cognitive act from the totality of human behaviour, since the cognizing subject is an aspect of the integral subject which is an active participant in nature. The human coefficient is present in nature as the latter exists for man; and, on the other hand, man cannot eliminate from his intercourse with the world the factor of his own passivity. Marx's thought on this point is equally opposed to the Hegelian theory of self-consciousness constituting the object as an exteriorization of itself, and to the versions of materialism which he encountered, in which cognition was, at its source, a passive reception of the object, transforming it into a subjective content. Marx describes his own view as consistent naturalism or humanism, which, he says, 'differs equally from idealism and materialism, being the truth which unites them both'. It is an anthropocentric viewpoint, seeing in humanized nature a counterpart of practical human intentions; as human practice has a social character, its cognitive effect—the image of nature—is the work of social

man. Human consciousness is merely the expression in thought of a social relationship to nature, and must be considered as a product of the collective effort
of the species. Accordingly, deformations of consciousness are not to be
explained as due to the aberrations or imperfections of consciousness itself:
their sources are to be looked for in more original processes, and particularly
in the alienation of labour.

3. The alienation of labour. Dehumanized man

MARX considers the alienation of labour on the basis of capitalistic conditions
in their developed form, in which land-ownership is subject to all the laws of a
market economy. Private property is, in his view, a consequence and not a cause
of the alienation of labour; however, the Paris Manuscripts as they have survived do not examine the origins of this alienation. In the developed conditions
of capitalist appropriation the alienation of labour is expressed by the fact that
the worker's own labour, as well as its products, have become alien to him.
Labour has become a commodity like any other, which means that the worker
himself has become a commodity and is obliged to sell himself at the market
price determined by the minimum cost of maintenance; wages thus tend
inevitably to fall to the lowest level that will keep the workmen alive and able
to rear children. The situation which thus arises in the productive process is
analogous to that which Feuerbach described in connection with the invention
of gods by the human mind. The more wealth the worker produces, the poorer
he gets; the more the world of things increases in value, the more human beings
depreciate. The object of labour is opposed to the labour process as something
alien, objectified, and independent of its producer. The more the worker assimilates nature to himself, the more he deprives himself of the means of life. But
it is not only the product of labour that is alienated from the subject: labour
itself is so alienated, for instead of being an act of self-affirmation it becomes
a destructive process and a source of unhappiness. The worker does not toil to
satisfy his own need to work, but to keep himself alive. He does not feel truly
himself in the labour process, i.e. in that form of activity which is specifically
human, but only in the animal functions of eating, sleeping, and begetting children. Since, unlike animals, 'man produces even when he is free from physical
need, and indeed it is only then that he produces in the true sense', the alienation of labour dehumanizes the worker by making it impossible for him to produce in a specifically human manner. Work presents itself to him as an alien
occupation, and he forfeits his essence as a human being, which is reduced to
purely biological activities. Labour, which is the life of the species, becomes
only a means to individual animalized life, and the social essence of man

becomes a mere instrument of individual existence. Alienated labour deprives man of his species-life; other human beings become alien to him, communal existence is impossible, and life is merely a system of conflicting egoisms. Private property, which arises from alienated labour, becomes in its turn a source of alienation, which it fosters unceasingly.

The reification (as it would be called later) of the worker—the fact that his personal qualities of muscle and brain, his abilities and aspirations, are turned into a 'thing', an object to be bought and sold on the market—does not mean that the possessor of that 'thing' is himself able to enjoy a free and human existence. On the contrary, the process has its effect on the capitalist, too, depriving him of personality in a different way. As the worker is reduced to an animal condition, the capitalist is reduced to an abstract money-power: he becomes a personification of this power, and his human qualities are transformed into aspects of it.

> My power is as great as the power of money. The attributes and essential strength of money are those of myself, its owner. It is not my own personality which decides what I am and what I can afford. I may be ugly, but I can buy the prettiest woman alive; consequently I am not ugly, since money destroys the repellent power of ugliness. I may be lame, but with money I can have a coach and six, therefore I am not lame. I may be bad, dishonest, ruthless and narrow-minded, but money ensures respect for itself and its possessor. Money is the supreme good, and a man who has it must be good also.

The effect of the alienation of labour is to paralyse man's species-life and the community of human beings, and therefore it paralyses personal life also. In a developed capitalist society the entire social servitude and all forms of alienation are comprised in the worker's relationship to production; the emancipation of workers is therefore not simply their emancipation as a class with particular interests, but is also the emancipation of society and humanity as a whole.

However, the emancipation of the worker is not simply a question of abolishing private property. Communism, which consists in the negation of private property, exists in different forms. Marx discusses, for instance, the primitive totalitarian egalitarianism of early communist utopias. This is a form of communism which seeks to abolish everything that cannot be made the private property of all, and therefore everything that may distinguish individuals; it seeks to abolish talent and individuality, which is tantamount to abolishing civilization. Communism in this form is not an assimilation of the alienated world but, on the contrary, an extreme form of alienation that consists in imposing the present condition of workers upon everybody. If communism is to represent the *positive* abolition of private property and of self-alienation it must mean the adoption by man of his own species-essence, the recovery of himself as a social being. Such communism resolves the conflict between man and man, between essence and existence, the individual and the species, freedom and necessity. In what, however, does the 'positive' abolition of private property consist? Marx suggests an analogy with the abolition of religion: just as atheism ceases to be significant when the affirmation of man is no longer dependent on the negation of God, in the same way socialism in the full sense is the direct affirmation of humanity independent of the negation of private property: it is a state in which the problem of property has been solved and forgotten. Socialism can only be the result of a long and violent historical process, but its consummation is the complete liberation of man with all his attributes and possibilities. Under the socialist mode of appropriation man's activity will not be opposed to him as something alien, but will be, in all its forms and products, the direct affirmation of humanity. There will be 'wealthy man and wealthy human need'; 'a rich man is at the same time a man needing the manifestations of human life in all their fullness'. Whereas in conditions of alienated labour the increase of demand multiplies the effect of alienation—the producer strives artificially to arouse demand and to make people dependent on more and more products, which in such circumstances only increase the volume of servitude—in socialist conditions the wealth of requirements is indeed the wealth of mankind.

While the Paris Manuscripts thus attempt to establish socialism as the realization of the essence of humanity, they do not present it as an ideal pure and simple but as a postulate of the natural course of history. Marx does not regard private property, the division of labour, or human alienation as 'mistakes' that could be rectified at any time if men came to a correct understanding of their own situation; he regards them as indispensable conditions of future liberation. The vision of socialism outlined in the Manuscripts involves the full and perfect reconciliation of man with himself and nature, the complete identification of human essence and existence, the harmonization of man's ultimate destiny and his empirical being. It may be supposed that a socialist society in this sense would be a state of complete satisfaction, an ultimate society with no incentive or need for further development. While Marx does not express his vision in these terms, he does not rule out such an interpretation either, and it is encouraged by his view of socialism as the removal of all sources of human conflict and a state in which the essence of humanity is empirically realized. Communism, he says, 'is the solution to the riddle of history and is aware of that fact'; the question then arises whether it is not also the termination of history.

4. Critique of Feuerbach

THE philosophy of the Manuscripts is confirmed and completed by Marx's *Theses on Feuerbach*, written in the spring of 1845. Published by Engels in 1888, after Marx's death, they were regarded as an epitome of the new world-view and are among the most frequently quoted of their author's works. They contain the most trenchant formulation of Marx's objections to Feuerbachian materialism, especially his opposition of a purely contemplative theory of knowledge to a practical one and the different meaning he ascribed to religious alienation. The reproach that Marx levelled against Feuerbach and all previous materialists was that they envisaged objects merely in a contemplative way and not as 'sensuous, practical, human activity, not subjectively', with the result that it was left to idealism to develop the active side—'but only abstractly, since of course idealism does not know real, actual, sensuous activity as such'. This objection repeats the thought expounded in more detail in the Manuscripts: perception is itself a component of man's practical relationship to the world, so that its object is not simply 'given' by indifferent nature but is a humanized object conditioned by human needs and efforts. The same practical standpoint appears in Marx's refusal to enter into a speculative dispute on the conformity of thought with its object. 'In practice man must prove the truth, that is, the reality and power, the this-sidedness [*Diesseitigkeit*] of his thinking. The dispute over the reality or non-reality of thinking which is isolated from practice is a purely scholastic question.' As might be expected, and as *The German Ideology* later confirms, the cognitive function of practice does not merely signify that the success of an activity confirms the accuracy of our knowledge, nor that practical life expresses the range and purpose of human interests; it means also that veracity is itself the 'reality and power' of thought, i.e. that those ideas are true in which man confirms himself as a 'species-being'. On this ground Marx dismisses as 'scholastic' the Cartesian question as to the conformity between a pure act of thought and reality. The epistemological question is not a real question, because the pure act of perception or thought which it premises is a mere speculative fiction. Since the mind, having achieved self-understanding, apprehends itself as a coefficient of practical behaviour, it follows that the questions that may legitimately be put to it as to the meaning of its acts are also questions as to its effectiveness from the point of view of human society.

Marx also repeats in the *Theses* his criticism of Feuerbach's theory of religion, viz. that it reduces the world of religion to its secular basis but does not explain the duality in terms of the internal disharmony of man's situation in the world, and is therefore unable to offer an effective cure: the mind can only be freed from mystification if the negativities of social life from which it arises are removed by practical action.

Further, Marx criticizes Feuerbach's conception of the essence of man as 'an abstraction inherent in a particular individual', whereas it is in fact 'the totality of social relationships'. The effect of Feuerbach's conception is that he takes as his point of departure the individual in his species-characteristics, and reduces the tie between human beings to a natural tie. The same thought appears in the tenth *Thesis*, having previously been expressed in Marx's essay *On the Jewish Question:* 'The standpoint of the old materialism is "civil" society; the standpoint of the new is human society, or socialized humanity.' This corresponds to Marx's previous contention that civil society must coincide with political society, so that both of them cease to exist in the old form: no longer will the first be a mass of conflicting egoisms, the second an abstract, unreal community; man, himself a true community, will absorb his own species-nature and realize his personality as a social one.

In the important third *Thesis* Marx expounds his opposition to the doctrines of utopian socialism based on eighteenth-century materialism. It is not sufficient to say that human beings are the product of conditions and upbringing, since conditions and upbringing are also the work of human beings. To assert only the former proposition amounts to 'dividing society into two parts, of which one is superior to society (in Robert Owen, for example). The coincidence of the changing circumstances and of human activity can be conceived and rationally understood only as revolutionary praxis.' This statement means that society cannot be changed by reformers who understand its needs, but only by the basic mass whose particular interest is identical with that of society as a whole. In the revolutionary praxis of the proletariat the 'educator' and 'educated' are the same: the development of mind is at the same time the historical process by which the world is transformed, and there is no longer any question of priority between the mind and external conditions or vice versa. In this situation of revolutionary praxis the working class is the agent of a historical initiative and is not merely resisting or reacting to the pressure of the possessing classes.

The same 'practical' viewpoint is dominant in Marx's conception of the cognitive functions of the mind and its role in the historical process; 'practical' is always regarded as implying 'social', and 'social life is practical by its very essence'. So is the task of philosophy as defined in the eleventh *Thesis*, in what are perhaps Marx's most-quoted words: 'The philosophers have only interpreted the world in various ways; the point, however, is to change it.' It would be a caricature of Marx's thought to read this as meaning that it was not important to observe or analyse society and that only direct revolutionary action mattered. The whole context shows that it is a formula expressing in a nutshell the viewpoint of 'practical philosophy' as opposed to the 'contemplative' attitude of Hegel or Feuerbach—the viewpoint which Hess, and through him Cieszkowski, suggested to Marx and which became the philosophical nucleus of Marxism. To understand the world does not mean considering it from outside, judging it morally or explaining it scientifically; it means society understanding itself, an act in which the subject changes the object by the very fact of understanding it. This can only come about when the subject and object coincide, when the difference between educator and educated disappears, and when thought itself becomes a revolutionary act, the self-recognition of human existence.

5. Engels's early writings

THE year 1844 saw the beginning of Marx's friendship and collaboration with Friedrich Engels, whom he had already met briefly in Cologne. Engels had been through a similar spiritual evolution to Marx, though their early education was different. Born on 28 November 1820, Engels was the son of a manufacturer at Barmen (Wuppertal, near Düsseldorf). He grew up in a stifling atmosphere of narrow-minded pietism, but soon escaped from its influence, leaving school before his final year to work in his father's factory; in 1838 he was sent to Bremen to gain business experience. As a result of practical contact with trade and industry he soon became interested in social questions. In the course of private study he imbibed liberal-democratic ideas and was attracted to Young Hegelian radicalism. His first Press articles were written in 1839 for the *Telegraph für Deutschland,* published by Gutzkow at Hamburg, and the Stuttgart *Morgenblatt.* He attacked German bigotry and the hypocrisy of petty-bourgeois pietism, but also described industrial conditions and the oppression and poverty of the workers. He was attracted by the sentimental pantheism of Schleiermacher and did not at first wholly abandon Christianity, but became an atheist under the influence of Strauss's *Life of Jesus.* During his military service at Berlin in 1841 he joined the philosophical radicals and wrote three pamphlets criticizing Schelling from a Young Hegelian point of view. Later, when he regarded himself as a communist, he declared that communism was the natural fruit of German philosophical culture. Towards the end of 1842 he went to his father's works in Manchester for further commercial training, and spent much time observing the conditions of the British working class and studying political economy and socialism. The number of the *Deutsch-Französische Jahrbücher* to which Marx contributed his articles on Hegel's *Philosophy of Right* and *The Jewish Question* also contained an essay by Engels entitled *Outline of a Critique of Political Economy.* This argued that the contradictions of capitalist economy could not be resolved on the basis of that economy; that periodical crises of overproduction were the inevitable consequence of free competition; that competition led to monopoly, but monopoly in turn created new forms of competition, etc. Private property led necessarily to antagonism between classes and between individuals in each class, and to an incurable conflict between private and public interests; it was also bound up with anarchy in production and the resultant crises. Economists who defended private property could not understand this chain of causes and were driven to invent groundless theories, such as that of Malthus which blamed social evil on the fact that population grew faster than production. The abolition of private property was the only way to save humanity from crises, want, and exploitation. Planned production would do away with social inequality and the absurd situation in which poverty was caused by an excess of goods. 'We shall liquidate the contradiction', wrote Engels, 'simply by removing it. When the interests that are now in conflict are merged into one, there will be no contradiction between the excess of population at one end of the scale and the excess of wealth at the other; we shall no longer experience the amazing fact, more extraordinary than all the miracles of all religions put together, that wealth and an excess of prosperity cause peoples to die of hunger; we shall no longer hear the foolish assertion that the earth cannot maintain the human race.'

Engels remained rather less than two years at Manchester, and published his observations at Leipzig in *The Situation of the Working Class in England* (1845). In this book, which was revelation for its time, he painted a broad picture of the result of the industrial revolution in Britain and described graphically the cruel poverty of the urban proletariat and the starvation brutality, and hopelessness of working-class life. He did not write as a moralizer or philanthropist, but inferred from the conditions of the working-class that the latter was bound to bring about a socialist revolution by its own efforts within a few years. His prediction of socialism was thus based not on general ideas about human nature or the need to bring human existence into conformity with the essence of humanity, but on actual acquaintance with working-class conditions and trends of development. He was convinced that the middle classes would disappear, that capital in Britain would concentrate more and more and that there would soon be an inevitable and blood-thirsty war between the needy and the rich. Engels set his prediction within the framework of a clear-cut division of classes, the proletariat being not only the most oppressed and afflicted but also destined to put an end to all oppression. At the same time, while describing with a wealth of detail the villainy of the English bourgeoisie, Engels did not treat their behaviour as being due simply to moral depravity, but as an inevitable effect of the situation of a class of men obliged by cut-throat competition to exploit their fellows to the maximum degree.

VII

The Holy Family

Marx's meeting with Engels in Paris in August 1844 was the beginning of forty years' collaboration in political and literary activity. While Marx's powers of abstract thought were superior to those of his friend, Engels surpassed him in relating theory to empirical data, whether social or scientific. Their first joint work, entitled *The Holy Family, or a Critique of Critical Criticism: against Bruno Bauer and Co.*, was published at Frankfurt-on-Main in February 1845; only a small part of it was the work of Engels, who had returned to Barmen after a short stay in Paris.

The Holy Family is a radical and, one may say, ruthless challenge to Young Hegelianism. It is a virulent, sarcastic, and unscrupulous attack on Marx's former allies, especially Bruno and Edgar Bauer. The work is diffuse and full of trivial mockery, puns on his adversaries' names, etc. It sets out to display the naïvety and intellectual nullity of the Hegelian 'holy family' and the speculative character of its criticism; unlike *The German Ideology*, it contains little in the way of independent analysis. Nevertheless it is an important document, bearing witness to Marx's final break with Young Hegelian radicalism: for its proclamation of communism as the working-class movement *par excellence* is presented not as a supplement to the critique of Young Hegelianism, but as something opposed to it. It even declares in the Introduction that 'True humanism has no more dangerous enemy in Germany than spiritualism or speculative idealism, in which the actual individual human being is replaced by "self-consciousness" or "spirit."' In some important ways *The Holy Family* confirms, but with greater emphasis, Marx's theoretical standpoint as formulated in previous works, while in others it introduces new elements.

1. Communism as a historical trend. The class-consciousness of the proletariat

Marx expresses more plainly than hitherto the idea of the historical inevitability of the movement towards communism. Private property, by endeavouring to prolong itself indefinitely creates its own antagonist, the proletariat. In the self-alienation which is strengthened by private property the possessing class enjoys the satisfaction procured by the outward show of humanity, while the working class is humiliated and impotent. Private property tends to destroy itself irrespective of the knowledge or will of the possessing class, since the proletariat which it creates is a dehumanization that is conscious of itself. The victorious proletariat does not simply turn the tables and substitute itself for the possessors, but puts an end to the situation by eliminating itself and its own opposition. It represents the maximum of dehumanization, but also awareness of that dehumanization and the inevitability of revolt. The misery of the proletariat obliges it to free itself, but it cannot do so without at the same time freeing the whole of society from inhuman conditions.

Marx's emphasis on the self-awareness of the proletariat in the process of emancipation is important in connection with the objection, sometimes put forward at a later date, that he appeared to believe that the revolution would come about as the result of an impersonal historical force, irrespective of the free activity of man. From his point of view there is no dilemma as between historical necessity and conscious action, since the class-consciousness of the proletariat is not only a condition of the revolution but is itself the historical process in which the revolution comes to maturity. For this reason the authors of *The Holy Family* join issue with any personification of history as an independent force. Bauer, Engels says, transforms history into a metaphysical being which manifests itself in individual men and women; but in actual fact 'history does nothing, has no "enormous wealth", wages no battles. It is not "history" but live human beings who own possessions, perform actions and fight battles. There is no independent entity called "history", using mankind to attain its ends: history is simply the purposeful activity of human beings.' These observations are the point of departure for the later controversy on Marx's alleged historical determinism. They leave room for differences of interpretation, as do subsequent statements of his: in particular, that men make their own history but do not make it irrespective of the conditions they are in. Are we to understand that man's ability to affect the historical process is limited, that existing conditions are not wholly obedient to human action but can to some extent be governed by the organized will of the community; or is it rather the case that the conditions in which a man acts are themselves the determinants of his consciousness and his action? These are key questions for the understanding of historical materialism, and we shall have occasion to revert to them in due course.

2. Progress and the masses

AN essential topic of Marx's criticism of Bauer is the latter's opposition between the masses and progress, between the masses and the critical spirit. In Bauer's view the masses as such are an embodiment of conservatism, reaction, dogmatism, and mental inertia. Any ideas they assimilate, including revolutionary ones, are turned into conservatism; any doctrine absorbed by the masses becomes a religion. A creative idea is no sooner adopted by the masses than it loses its creativity. Ideas that need their support are foredoomed to distortion, degeneration, and defeat; all great historical enterprises that have come to grief have done so because the masses took possession of them. This analysis, in Marx's view, is an absurd attempt to condemn the course of history. Successful ideas, he contends, must be the expression of some mass interest ('The "idea" has always been a fiasco when divorced from "interest"'); but whenever 'interest' takes the form of an idea it goes beyond its real content and must present itself delusively as a general interest and not a particular one. By opposing progress to the conservatism of the masses, Bauer's criticism is condemned to remain a thing of the mind instead of an instrument of social transformation. In any Case, Marx contends, the undifferentiated category of progress is itself without content. Socialist ideas originated in the historical observation that what is called progress has always come about in opposition to the majority of society and led to more and more inhuman conditions. This suggested that civilization was radically diseased; it pointed to a fundamental criticism of society, coinciding with a mass movement of social protest. We must not, then, be content with phrases about progress, since no absolute progress can be identified in history.

Marx here introduces for the first time a thought that recurs more than once in his later work. Instead of an incurable antagonism between the masses and the critical spirit—a parody, in his opinion, of the traditional opposition between 'spirit' and inert 'matter', the former being represented by the individual and the latter by the masses—he puts forward the idea of a fundamental antinomy that has pervaded history hitherto, whereby actual progress, especially in the technical field, has been effected at the expense of the great mass of toiling humanity. While Bauer's historiosophy is obliged by its nature to confine itself to purely theoretical ideas of liberation, socialist criticism is aimed at the material conditions which have produced a contradiction between the advance of civilization and the needs of the immediate creators of wealth. Ideas by themselves, Marx argues, can never burst the bonds of the old world; human beings, and the use of force, are necessary before ideas can be realized.

3. The world of needs

IN *The Holy Family* Marx returns to the problem of the opposition between the true human community and the imaginary community of the state. Bauer holds that human beings are egoistic atoms which have to be welded into an organism by the state. To Marx this is a speculative fiction. An atom is self-sufficient and has no needs; a human individual may imagine himself to be an atom in this sense, but in fact he never can be, for the world of men is a world of needs and, despite all mystification, it is they which constitute the real links between members of the community. The social bond is not created by the state but by the fact that, although people may imagine themselves to be atoms, they are actually egoistic human beings. The state is a secondary product of the needs which constitute the social bond; this latter is not a product of the state. Only if the world of needs gives rise to a conflict, if needs are satisfied by means of a struggle between egoisms, and if the social bond assumes the aspect of social discord—only then does the question arise as to the possibility of a real human community. Bauer, however, is content to maintain the Hegelian opposition between the state as a community and civil society as a tangle of egoisms, and regards this opposition as an eternal principle of life.

4. The tradition of materialism

IN *The Holy Family* Marx also expresses for the first time his awareness of the link between socialist ideas and the tradition of philosophical materialism. He distinguishes two trends in the history of French materialism: the first, which goes back to Descartes, is naturalistic in inspiration and evolves in the direction of modern natural science. The second, that of Lockean empiricism, represents the direct tradition of socialism, whose ideological premises derive from the anti-metaphysical critique of the eighteenth-century materialists and their attacks on the dogmatism of the previous century. Locke's sensationalism implied the doctrine of human equality: every man who comes into the world is a *tabula rasa*, and mental or spiritual differences are acquired and not innate. Since all men are by nature egoists and morality can only be rationalized egoism, the problem is to devise a form of social organization that will reconcile the selfish interests of each with the needs of all. As human beings are entirely the product of their education and conditions of life, they can only be changed by changing the social institutions that fashion them. Fourier's doctrine is the fruit of the French materialism of the Enlightenment, while Owen's socialist ideas are rooted in Bentham and, through him, in Helvétius. The principles of empiricism and utilitarianism, which lay down that human beings are neither good nor bad by nature but only by upbringing, that interest is the mainspring of morality, and so forth, naturally lead us to inquire what social conditions are necessary to make the community of mankind a reality.

In this way Marx invokes the materialist tradition against Bauer, who, following Hegel, makes self-consciousness into a substantive entity (whereas it is in fact only an attribute of man and not a separate form of Being) and imagines that he has thus ensured the spirit's independence of nature. By the same token Bauer reduces human life to intellectual activity and turns all history into the history of thought, whereas it is, first and foremost, the history of material production.

The Holy Family thus contains, though as yet only in laconic and general formulas, the seminal ideas of the materialist interpretation of history: that of the mystification that befalls human interests when they are expressed in ideological form, and that of the genetic dependence of the history of ideas on the history of production. We find here the application to a new historiosophy of the classic schema of Hegel's dialectic, the negation of a negation. As private property develops it necessarily creates its own antagonist; this negative force is itself dehumanized, and as its dehumanization progresses it becomes the precondition of a synthesis that will abolish the existing opposition together with both its terms—private property and the proletariat—and will thus make it possible for man to become himself again.

■　■　■

THE basis of the materialist interpretation of history was expounded in the next joint work by Marx and Engels, *The German Ideology*. Marx remained in Paris until the beginning of 1845, taking an active part in the meetings of socialist organizations and especially the League of the Just, while in Germany Engels spread the word of communism in speeches and writings and endeavoured to weld scattered socialist groups into a single organization. In February 1845 Marx was deported from Paris at the instance of the Prussian government and took up his abode in Brussels, where Engels joined him in the spring. In summer they visited England, where they made contact with the Chartists and took steps to establish a centre of co-operation of the revolutionary movements of different countries. Returning to Brussels, they continued to work for the unification of revolutionary associations and to carry on polemics with German philosophers.

VIII

The German Ideology

Marx and Engels finished *The German Ideology* in 1846, but were not able to publish it. Parts of the manuscript were lost; the remainder was published in an incomplete form by Bernstein in 1903, and in its entirety in the *MEGA* edition in 1932. The work was primarily an attack on Feuerbach, Max Stirner, and so-called 'true socialism'; Bruno Bauer is only referred to incidentally. From the philosophical point of view the most important sections are those criticizing Feuerbach's 'species-man' and Stirner's 'existential' conception of man. These also contain the most positive expression of the authors' own views; Feuerbach is in fact criticized indirectly, by the exposition of their own standpoint. To Feuerbach's anthropology they oppose the idea of humanity as a historical category; to Stirner's absolute of the individual self-consciousness, the idea of man actualizing his social nature in his own unique and individual character. The central ideas of *The German Ideology*, or at any rate those which gave rise to the liveliest discussion in the later development of Marxism, are those concerning the relationship between human thought and living conditions; these contain the basis of the materialist interpretation of history, which was developed later in fuller detail.

1. The concept of ideology

The term 'ideology' dates from the end of the eighteenth century, when it was introduced by Destutt de Tracy to denote the study of the origin and laws of operation of 'ideas' in Condillac's sense, i.e. psychic facts of all kinds, and their relation to language. The name 'idéologues' was given to the scholars and public men (Destutt, Cabanis, Volney, Daunou) who carried on the tradition of the *Encyclopédistes*; Napoleon applied the expression to them in the pejorative sense of 'political dreamers'. The Hegelians occasionally used 'ideology' to denote the subjective aspect of the cognitive process.

In the work of Marx and Engels 'ideology' is used in a peculiar sense which was later generalized: they do not define it expressly, but it is clear that they give it the meaning later expounded by Engels in *Ludwig Feuerbach* (1888) and in a letter to Mehring dated 14 July 1893. 'Ideology' in this sense is a false consciousness or an obfuscated mental process in which men do not understand the forces that actually guide their thinking, but imagine it to be wholly governed by logic and intellectual influences. When thus deluded, the thinker is unaware that all thought, and particularly his own, is subject in its course and outcome to extra-intellectual social conditions, which it expresses in a form distorted by the interests and preferences of some collectivity or other. Ideology is the sum total of ideas (views, convictions, *partis pris*) relating, first and foremost, to social life—opinions on philosophy, religion, economics, history, law, utopias of all kinds, political and economic programmes—which appear to exist in their own right in the minds of those who hold them. These ideas are in fact governed by laws of their own; they are characterized by the subject's unawareness of their origin in social conditions and of the part they play in maintaining or altering those conditions. The fact that human thought is determined by the conflicts of material life is not consciously reflected in ideological constructions, or they would not truly deserve the name of ideology. The ideologist is the intellectual exponent of a certain situation of social conflict; he is unaware of this fact and of the genetic and functional relationship between the situation and his ideas. All philosophers are ideologists in this sense; so are religious thinkers and reformers, jurists, the creators of political programmes, etc. It was not until much later, in Stalin's time, that Marxists came to use 'ideology' to denote all forms of social consciousness, including those that were supposed to present a scientific account of the world, free from mystification and distortion. In this sense it was possible to speak of 'scientific' of 'Marxist' ideology, which Marx and Engels, given their use of the term, could never have done.

The original Marxist concept was the basis of the twentieth-century theory of ideology and, more generally, the sociology of knowledge (Mannheim), i.e. the study of ideas irrespective of whether they are true or false—for ideological mystification is not the same as error in the cognitive sense; to define a product of the mind as ideology does not involve any judgement as to its truth or falsehood. Instead, this science considers ideas as manifestations of certain group interests, practical instruments whereby social classes and other sections of the community uphold their own interests and values. The study of ideology investigates social conflicts and structures from the standpoint of their intellectual expression; it considers ideas, theories, beliefs, programmes, and doctrines in the light of their dependence on the social situations that give rise to them, thought being a disguised version of reality. As Mannheim observed, this idea goes back beyond Marx; the hypocrisy of moral ideals, religious beliefs, and philosophical doctrines was pointed out by Machiavelli, and between Marx and Mannheim we can find similar ideas in Nietzsche and Sorel. In the modern analysis of ideas it is generally accepted that the ideological content must be distinguished from the cognitive value, that the functional-genetic conditioning of thought is one thing and its scientific legitimacy another. Marx was the pioneer of this distinction; he was concerned, however, not only with pointing out the dependence between thought and interests but also with identifying the particular type of interest that exerts the strongest influence on the construction of ideologies, namely that connected with the division of society into classes.

Marx begins by dealing with the central delusion of German ideologists who believe that while humanity is governed by false ideas and imaginations and men are enslaved to the creations of their own minds ('gods' in Feuerbach's sense), it is within the power of philosophy to expose and destroy these wrong ideas and revolutionize the society based upon them. The basic position of Marx and Engels is, on the contrary, that the authority of delusions over human minds is not a result of mental distortion that can be cured by working upon the consciousness, but is rooted in social conditions and is only the intellectual expression of social servitude.

2. Social being and consciousness

In this way, taking up a theme already sketched in their Previous writings, Marx and Engels set out to overthrow the view of the Young Hegelians and Feuerbach that mental aberrations and distortions were the cause of social servitude and human misfortune, and not the other way about. They attempted to analyse the origin of ideas, not in Condillac's sense but by investigating the social conditioning of consciousness. The Hegelians, in their delusions, had not confined themselves to believing in the omnipotence of thought in social history. Holding as they did that the relations between human beings are the result of wrong ideas about the world and themselves—whereas in fact the contrary is the case—the Hegelians from Strauss to Stirner had reduced all human ideas on politics, law, morals, or metaphysics to the denominator of theology, making all social consciousness a religious consciousness, and seeing in the critique of religion a panacea for every human ailment.

The contention of Marx and Engels was that the distinguishing mark of humanity, that which primarily characterizes men as opposed to beasts, is not that they think but that they make tools. This is what first made man a separate species; then, in the course of history, men were distinguished by their way of reproducing their own life, and hence by their way of thinking. Human beings are what their behaviour shows them to be: they are, first and foremost, the totality of the actions whereby they reproduce their own material existence. ('As individuals express their lives, so they are. What they are, therefore, coincides with their production, both with what they produce and how they produce it. The nature of individuals thus depends on the material conditions of their production'.) The level of production determined by the productive forces, i.e. by the quality of tools and technical skill, itself determines the social structure. This latter consists primarily in the division of labour, and the historical development of humanity is divided into phases by the different forms that the division of labour assumes. Each of these forms in turn creates a new form of property. The tribal ownership of primitive times, the ancient world with communal and state property, feudalism with its estates, crafts and landed property, and finally capitalism—all these are forms of society owing their origin to the type of productive capacity available to the human race at each period. We cannot consider rationally any conscious human life except as a component of the whole of life as defined in the first place by the method of satisfying elementary needs, the widening of the range of needs, the method of reproducing the species in family life, and also the system of co-operation which is itself to be reckoned as a productive force. Consciousness is nothing but human existence made conscious; but the self-delusion of consciousness which imagines that it only defines itself in its own work is in fact conditioned by the division of labour. It is only when the level of production makes it possible to separate physical and intellectual labour that consciousness can imagine itself to be other than awareness of practical life and can devise pure, abstract forms of mental activity such as philosophy, theology, and ethics. In addition, the ruling thoughts of a particular era gradually become separate from the ruling individuals, i.e. intellectual labour becomes a distinct occupation and the profession of the ideologist is born. This encourages the idea that it is thought which governs history and that it is possible to deduce human relationships, as Hegel did, from the concept of humanity itself.

> The imaginary creations of the human brain are the inevitable sublimations of the material process of existence, which can be observed empirically and which depends on material causes. Morality, religion, metaphysics and all other forms of ideology and the related forms of consciousness thus lose the independence they appeared to have. They have no history or development of their own; it is only people, developing their material production and mutual material relations, who as a result come to think different thoughts and create different intellectual systems. It is not consciousness that determines life, but life that determines consciousness . . . and all consciousness is that of live individuals.

These first, somewhat crude formulations of the materialist interpretation of history foreshadow subsequent debates on the sense in which Marx regarded thought as dependent on social conditions. If such aspects of social life as religion, morality, and law have no history of their own, it would seem that for Marx human ideas are no more than a natural secretion of social life embodying no active principle, a mere by-product of the true history which consists in the material productive processes and the property relationships that correspond to them; or, as critics of Marxism later put it, that the life of the mind is an epiphenomenon of the conditions of production. There has been a controversy in this sphere between economic materialism and the version of Marxism which ascribes an active and independent historical function to 'subjective' factors, i.e. the workings of the intellect and freely directed political activity.

Clearly Marx cannot be saddled with the view that all history is the effect of 'historical laws', that it makes no difference what people think of their lives, and that the creations of thought are merely foam on the surface of history and not truly part of it. Marx speaks of the active function of ideas as an indispensable means of maintaining and transforming social life, and he includes human skill and technology among 'productive forces'. He does not, it is true, regard humanity as constituted by self-consciousness: the latter is 'given' as a product of life, not in a pure form but as articulated in language—i.e. as communicative self-knowledge, its form determined by the means of collective communication. In this sense consciousness is always a social product. But, Marx says, 'Circumstances create people in the same degree as people create circumstances.' Both social servitude and the movement towards its abolition have as their condition certain subjective factors. Material subjugation requires spiritual subjugation; the ideas of the dominant class are dominant ideas; the class which commands material force also commands the means of intellectual coercion, as it produces and propagates the ideas that express its own supremacy.

Marx, then, cannot be regarded as maintaining that history is an anonymous process in which conscious intentions and thoughts are a mere by-product or casual accretion. Yet there is room for controversy over his theory even if we accept that thoughts, feelings, intentions, and the human will are a necessary condition of the historical process. For this view is compatible with strict determination on the basis that although 'subjective' factors are necessary causal links, they are themselves entirely due to non-subjective factors; thoughts and feelings, on this assumption, have an auxiliary role in history but not an originating one. In short, even if we do not interpret Marx's position as one of economic determination, there is still room for argument as to the role of free action in the historical process. This controversy has in fact made its appearance in various forms of Marxism in the present century, and cannot by any means be regarded as settled.

3. The division of labour, and its abolition

IN Marx's view the division of labour is, genetically speaking, the primary source of social conflict. It brings about inevitable disharmony between three aspects of life: productive forces, human relations, and consciousness. It leads to inequality, private property, and the opposition between individual interests and the general interest arising from the mutual dependence of human beings. As long as the division of labour runs riot and is outside human control, its social effects will be an alien force dominating individuals like an independent, superhuman power.

Marx, it will be seen, generalizes the concept of alienation, extending its operation to the whole historical process. Not only the imaginations of religion, as Feuerbach maintained, but the whole of history is alienated from mankind, since human beings cannot control its course; their actions result in a mysterious, impersonal process which tyrannizes over those who have brought it about. To remove this alienation man must be given power once more to shape the effects of his own actions—to turn history into something human, something controlled by man.

As the division of labour is the primary source of social inequality and private property, the chief purpose of communism must be to abolish the division of labour. Communism requires conditions in which men are not restricted to a particular type of work, but can take part successively in all types and thus achieve all-round development. The reification of human products, by which they come to dominate the individual, is one of the chief factors in the historical process; it also means that the 'general interest' assumes independent existence in the form of the state, which is at present necessary to enable the bourgeoisie to hold on to its own property. Political struggles within the state are an expression of the class conflict; every class aspiring to power must present its own interest as that of the whole community, and the purpose of its ideology is to confirm this mystification.

Marx later compared the situation of humanity faced with the alienation of history to that of the sorcerer's apprentice in Goethe's poem, who called up magic powers which he could no longer control and which turned into a threat to himself. But to abolish alienation, two conditions are required. Firstly, the state of servitude must become intolerable, the masses must be deprived of possessions and totally opposed to the existing order. Secondly, technical development must have reached an advanced stage: communism in a premature state would only be generalized poverty. Moreover, this development must be worldwide: communism can only come about when the world is a single market and all countries are economically interdependent. It must be brought about by simultaneous revolution in the most advanced and dominant countries; a proletariat capable of effecting the revolution must be a class that exists on a world scale. (This last point, which is basic to Marx's theory of revolution, was hotly debated at the beginning of the Stalin era, when the possibility of building 'socialism in one country' was mooted.)

But the social conditions that make communism possible also mean that there will be an irresistible movement towards it. 'Communism is not merely a state to be brought about or an ideal to which reality should conform; what we call communism is an actual movement which is sweeping away the present state of things.' This view of Marx's, which he afterwards repeated in various forms, has given rise to another essential controversy. Should the communist movement await the spontaneous development of mass opposition and then impose a form on it, or should it organize that opposition from outside and not wait for the masses to become aware of their predicament? Should current political activity be geared to the achievement of a certain final state, or, as the reformists would have it, should the working-class movement be content with such piecemeal gains as can be extracted from particular situations? These problems were developed in later polemics. At the time of *The German Ideology* Marx and Engels were chiefly concerned to argue that communism is not an arbitrarily constructed ideal of a better world, but a natural part of the historic process. Until such time as the social preconditions of an upheaval are fully realized it is of no consequence how, and how often, the idea of that upheaval is proclaimed. But the communist revolution is fundamentally different from all that have gone before. Previous revolutions have altered the division of labour and the distribution of social activity; but the communist revolution will abolish the division of labour and the class division, and will abolish classes and nations as divisions of the human race. Communism will for the first time bring about a universal transformation of the terms of production and exchange; it will treat all previous forms of social development as the work of man, and will subject them to the authority of united individuals.

4. Individuality and freedom

THE restoration of man's full humanity, removing the tension between individual aspirations and the collective interest, does not imply a denial on Marx's part of the life and freedom of the individual. It has been a common misinterpretation by both Marxists and anti-Marxists to suppose that he regarded human beings merely as specimens of social classes, and that the 'restoration of their species-essence' meant the annihilation of individuality or its reduction to a common social nature. On this view, individuality has no place in Marxist doctrine except as an obstacle in the way of society attaining to homogeneous unity. No such doctrine, however, can be derived from *The German Ideology*, in which Marx distinguishes, as a fact of history, between the individual and the contingent nature of life. The opposition between the individual and the system of human relations is a continuation of the opposition between productive forces and productive relationships. As long as this contradiction does not exist, the conditions in which the individual operates do not appear to him as an external reality but as part of his individuality. Up to the present time the social relationships in which individuals of this or that class were involved were such that people stood to them not as individuals but as specimens of a class. At the same time, as the products of their activity escaped their control, the conditions of life were subordinated to a reified, extra-human power and the individual became a victim of absolute contingency, to which was given the name of freedom. Personal ties were transformed into material ones; people confronted one another as representatives of the impersonal forces that ruled the world—goods, money, or civil authority—while the individual's 'freedom' meant a lack of control over the conditions of his own life, a state of impotence *vis-à-vis* the external world. To reverse this reification and restore man's power over things is likewise to restore his individual life, the possibility of all-round development of his personal aptitudes and talents. In such a community people will for the first time be truly individuals and not merely specimens of their class.

While it is certain, therefore, that Marx does not follow the Cartesian tradition of conceiving man in terms of self-consciousness (which he regards as secondary both to physical and to social existence), it is also certain that he seeks to preserve the principle of individuality—not, however, as something antagonistic to the general interest, but as completely coincident with it. This should not be mistaken for a new version of the theory of 'enlightened self-interest', which holds that a properly organized system of laws can obviate the conflict between the individual, conceived as essentially selfish, and the collectivity, by so arranging matters that anti-social acts turn against their perpetrators, so that the true self-interest is to behave in a socially constructive manner. Marx for his part rejects the notion of 'innate egoism', and in this respect is closer to Fichte than to the Enlightenment. He believes that the abolition of dependence on alienated forces will restore to man his social nature, i.e. the individual will accept the community as his own interiorized nature. But this community, consciously present in each of its members, is not intended to be a merging of personality in an anonymous, homogeneous whole. There is no question of uniformity being either imposed or voluntarily accepted; this idea, in Marx's view, belongs to primitive utopian communism—not a state in which private property has been abolished, but one in which it has not yet developed. True communism, on the other hand, will enable everyone to deploy his abilities to the maximum: it will do away with the obstacles created by the power of things over human beings, the contingency of personal life, and the alienation of labour which reduces individuals to a dead level of mediocrity. At the same time, it was Marx's view that under communism men's individual possibilities would display themselves only in socially constructive ways, so that conflicts among individuals would lose all *raison d'être*.

5. Stirner and the philosophy of egocentrism

QUESTIONS of personality and personal freedom are treated in *The German Ideology* in the form of a polemic with Max Stirner (1806–56; real name Johann Kaspar Schmidt). Stirner was one of the Berlin Young Hegelians, but his work *Der Einzige und sein Eigentum* (*The Ego and His Own*, 1844) belongs to the period of the dissolution of Left Hegelian views and reinterprets the cult of humanity in terms of extreme egocentrism. Prior to this, in 1841–2, Stirner wrote articles, reviews, and letters to various journals, especially the *Rheinische Zeitung* and the *Leipziger Allgemeine Zeitung*. He failed to obtain a post in the state educational system, and for some time taught in a private boarding-school for girls. Later he made a rich marriage and embarked on commercial specu- lation, which led to bankruptcy and imprisonment for debt. By what may seem a malicious irony of fate, the apostle of the absolute sovereignty of the Ego died of a gnat-bite. Subsequently to his main work he wrote some short articles and polemics and a compilation entitled *The History of Reaction* (1852). *The Ego* was celebrated for a short time in Germany and then forgotten till the 1890s, when it was the subject of extensive commentary and became a classic of anar- chist literature. Some branches at least of the anarchist movement adopted Stirner as their chief ideologist, and today he is often thought of as an existen- tialist *avant la lettre:* his basic principle that personal self-consciousness can- not be reduced to anything other than itself may indeed be regarded as the keynote of existentialism in its earliest version. This is a matter of coincidence rather than historical continuity; there is, however, a link between Stirner and modern existentialism through Nietzsche, who had read Stirner's work though he nowhere expressly refers to it.

Stirner's book is a proclamation of absolute egoism, a philosophical affir- mation of the Ego considered not as a distinct individual, body or soul, but as pure self-consciousness, an ego in which existence and the awareness of exis- tence are identical. '*Der Einzige*'—'the unique one'—is deliberately opposed to '*der Einzelne*', the 'individual' of liberal philosophy. Stirner's apologia for the uniqueness of personality is an extreme reaction to Hegel's reduction of indi- viduals to the role of instruments of the universal Idea; but it also stands in opposition to Feuerbach's cult of humanity as a species, to Christianity which subordinates mankind to values imposed by God, to liberalism with its demo- cratic faith in the common nature of man, to socialism, and to some extent even to Marx, whom Stirner once quotes as the author of *Introduction to a Critique of Hegel's Philosophy of Right*.

Stirner maintains that the whole effort of philosophy has been, in one way or another, to subject the authentic human individual to some form of impersonal general Being. Hegel deprived human individuals of reality by treating them as manifestations of universal spirit. Feuerbach liberated man from religious alienation only to replace the tyranny of God by that of the species, man in his universal aspect. As Feuerbach opposed species-man to God, so Stirner sets up against Man the irreducible Ego, uniquely and solely present to itself in each particular case. All religions, philosophies, and political doctrines require me to fix my attention on outside things—God, man, society, the state, humanity, truth—and never simply on myself; yet my self is all that matters to me, and it requires no justification, precisely because it is mine. Hence Stirner adopted as his motto the line from Goethe 'Ich hab' mein Sach auf Nichts gestellt' ('I have put my trust in Nothing'). The Ego is not describable in words that are used to describe other things; it is absolutely irreducible, the self-sufficient plenitude of subjectivity, a perfect self-contained universe. In affirming my Ego I am simply myself; it is for me the only reality and the only value. My Ego is sovereign, it recognizes no authority or constraint such as humanity, truth, the state, or any other impersonal abstraction. All general values are foreign to myself and do not concern me. From this point of view the differences between moral or philosophical doctrines are insignificant. Christianity condemned self-love, egoism, and self-indulgence; so does liberalism, although on a different principle, and the result is the same. The idea of equality is no less destructive of the sovereign Ego than is the despotism of God. By reducing individuals to the level at which they share equally in the impersonal nature of humanity, I am circumscribing human personality and destroying it by turning it into a mere instance of a species. Socialism does the same when it seeks to reduce the unique Ego to the anonymity of social Being, subordinating its own values to those of the community. From the fundamental standpoint of the emancipation of the Ego, it is much the same whether I am enslaved to impersonal Hegelian Reason or to Humanity, to a divine being or to the mass of my fellow creatures. All these purport to reduce subjective human existence to some kind of universal essence, and to resolve the conflict between the thinking subject and society by destroying the former. The true way to put an end to human alienation is to abolish whatever subjects the Ego to universal, impersonal values. Stirner's philosophy is thus an affirmation of total egoism and egocentrism, in which the whole universe is only taken into account as a means to the realization of the individual's private values.

Is any community life possible on this basis? Yes, says Stirner, but the relations between individuals must be personal, i.e. not mediated by society or by institutions, and free from reified forms. The proper business of education, accordingly, is not to train people to render services to society. The kind of education which seeks to make 'good citizens', as in liberal doctrine, is an enslavement of the Ego, a triumph of generality over true existence. From this point of view liberalism is a continuation of Christianity, and communism of liberalism. The human individual is alienated, according to Stirner, whenever he is subjected to anything outside himself, including 'goodness' or 'truth' considered as values binding on everyone. There is no general good and no moral law that can be imposed on me as a duty; even the rules of logic are a tyranny over my unique existence. Language itself is a threat, being a reification of life. It is hard to see, indeed, how Stirner's programme of total egoism can be realized in practice. The whole of civilization, in his view, is a system of manifold pressure on the Ego, and a man's self-affirmation involves rejecting the *mores* and the scientific and cultural achievements of the community, which are all instruments of servitude as far as he is concerned. Apparently, therefore, a return from alienation to authenticity would mean the denial of civilization and a return to animality and the unbridled sway of individual passions. Since specifically human behaviour is the outcome of a collective civilization, the wholesale rejection of the norms of that civilization must mean a regression to a pre-human state. Stirner does not spell out this conclusion, but merely speaks of the Ego's need to rebel against enslavement. This it does, not by endeavouring to alter external conditions in any way, but by the emancipation of its personal self-consciousness independently of the outside world. My act of rebellion is a self-affirmation in which I oppose my Ego to every form of generality; it neither expects nor requires any external success. (Raskolnikov, in Dostoevsky's *Crime and Punishment*, may be taken as an embodiment of the Ego as conceived by Stirner.) The theory thus implies that in the last resort the source of each man's servitude lies within him: he is fettered by his own false imagination and deference to universals, and can accordingly liberate himself by a purely spiritual act.

In Stirner's system the Ego is always unique. This means not only that it possesses qualities peculiar to itself and to be found nowhere else, but that it is actually inexpressible in words. Its specific, irreducible subjectivity cannot be defined or conceptually understood, since language consists of signs denoting what is common to two or more objects. Subjectivity is beyond the reach of human utterance. The life of the Ego consists of recognizing oneself and one's thoughts simply as one's own and not as impersonal general truths. Man becomes exclusively himself, self-rooted and self-justified—not an individual in a community, but an Ego living its own life. The Ego's values are in complete opposition to such 'universal' notions as law or the public good. My freedom is an enemy to the general freedom; my Ego apprehends itself as a negation of the rest of the universe. The Ego's desires or whims are its own law; it is not bound by any state ordinances or 'rights of man'. It seeks no justification from society and acknowledges no obligation towards it; it has a right to everything it can lay hands on. If a criminal can get away with his crime, he is in the right as far as he is concerned; if he is punished, he has no call to blame anyone; what happens is proper in either case. 'Crime' is a politico–legal notion expressing the viewpoint of the generality, but the real crime is to violate the Ego. For the egoist in Stirner's sense, community life is worth while in so far as it increases his own strength. A community of egoists is conceivable, but it is not a stable polity founded on institutions, merely a constant process of uniting and disuniting. The Ego refuses to be measured by the yardstick of humanity: it asserts its own uniqueness and recognizes nothing outside itself, not even thought; my own thoughts are myself and acknowledge no master, no standard to which they must conform. In a community, or assembly, of egoists there are no ties between any man and his fellows, and hence no conflicts, since a conflict is itself a kind of tie.

Stirner's work represents a final breach between Young Hegelianism and the doctrine of Hegel himself; the criticism of Hegel is pushed to absurd lengths by the condemnation of human society and culture in the name of the monadic sovereignty of the subject. In his violent attack on Hegel Stirner invokes a theme that we also find in Marx, the protest against reducing individual human beings to instruments of the Absolute; but they apply this protest in quite different ways. Marx too denies that there is such a thing as 'humanity' over and above individuals, but he regards individuality as the product of civilization. To Stirner, on the other hand, individuality is the same thing as the experience of subjectivity; to exist is no more or less than to be aware that one exists. To this extent he is rightly to be regarded as a forerunner of existentialism. At the same time his philosophy is an attack on the value of all ties among human beings and the whole historical process of collective development. As recent studies by Helms have shown, Stirner's doctrine inspired not only anarchists but various German groups who were the immediate precursors of fascism. At first sight, Nazi totalitarianism may seem the opposite of Stirner's radical individualism. But fascism was above all an attempt to dissolve the social ties created by history and replace them by artificial bonds among individuals who were expected to render implicit obedience to the state on grounds of absolute egoism. Fascist education combined the tenets of asocial egoism and unquestioning conformism, the latter being the means by which the individual secured his own niche in the system. Stirner's philosophy has nothing to say against conformism, it only objects to the Ego being subordinated to any higher principle: the egoist is free to adjust to the world if it appears that he will better himself by doing so. His 'rebellion' may take the form of utter servility if it will further his interest; what he must not do is to be bound by 'general' values or myths of humanity. The totalitarian ideal of a barrack-like society from which all real, historical ties have been eliminated is perfectly consistent with Stirner's principles: the egoist, by his very nature, must be prepared to fight under any flag that suits his convenience.

6. Critique of Stirner. The individual and the community

In *The German Ideology* Marx and Engels criticize Stirner unmercifully, contrasting the sterility and hopelessness of the egoist's inward 'rebellion' with the act of revolution in which the individual participates with the community and liberates himself by so doing. This argument is in some respects an anticipation of the quarrel in our own day between Marxists and existentialists. Apart from its bitter sarcasm, the polemic of Marx and Engels contains some passages of key importance to the understanding of Marxism. Marx does not attack Stirner from the Hegelian point of view, or combat his doctrine of the sovereign Ego by subordinating the individual to any form of universal reason, society, or the state. Instead, he advances the outline of a theory in which true individuality (and not merely a fictitious, self-contained, and self-sufficient subject) is enabled to find a place in the community without sacrificing the uniqueness of its own essence.

Marx denounces as unreal the notion of a human being whose whole life is only a kaleidoscope of self-consciousness and who can be indifferent or insensitive to the physical and social changes which in fact condition mental ones. Stirner's 'Ego' is beyond understanding, and his acts are barren by definition. In Marx's opinion, Stirner expresses no more than the impotent, sentimental discontent of the *Philister* who rebels against the sanctities of his time, but keeps his thoughts to himself and does not attempt to turn them into reality. Stirner imagines that he can destroy the state by an intellectual act, when he is really only displaying his inability to criticize it in a material fashion. The difference between revolution and a revolt *à la* Stirner is not that one is a political act and the other an egoistic one, but that the latter is a mere state of mind and not an act of any sort. Stirner imagines that he can divest himself of human ties and that the state will collapse of its own accord when its members secede from it; he sets out to overcome the world by an attack in the realm of ideas. He seeks to liberate himself from all communal institutions as the embodiment of a 'general will' whereas the 'general will' is in fact the expression of the social compulsion which requires the governing class to invest its rule with an ideological aura of universality, although its position does not depend on its own preference in any way. Stirner's programme of liberation through egoism comes simply to this, that the egoist would like to do away with the world in so far as it hinders him, but has no objection to using it to further his career.

It is a pious illusion, Marx argues, to expect individuals to live together with-out the aid of the community and its institutions. It is not in the power of the individual to decide whether his relations with others are to be personal or institutional; the division of labour means that personal relations are bound to transform themselves into class relations, and the superiority of one individual over another is expressed in the social relationship of privilege. Whatever indi-viduals may intend, the nature and level of needs and productive forces deter-mine the social character of their mutual relations.

> Individuals have always and in all circumstances stood on their own feet, but they were not 'unique' [*einzig*] in the sense of not needing one another: their needs (sex, trade, the division of labour) are such as to make them mutually dependent, and so they have been obliged to enter into relationships. This they did not as pure egos but as individuals at a particular stage of development of their productive forces and needs, which were in turn determined by their mutual intercourse. In this way their personal, individual behaviour towards one another has created their existing relationships and renews them day by day. . . The history of an individual cannot be detached from that of his predecessors or contemporaries, but is deter-mined by them.

For Marx, then, the intentions of individuals are of little account in deter-mining the effect and social significance of their behaviour in a situation in which it is not individuals that regulate social ties, but the ties they have cre-ated become an independent, alien force regulating the lives of individuals. In the present age individuality is overwhelmed by material forms or by 'contin-gency'; this constraint has reached an extreme form and has thereby imposed on humanity the necessity of bringing about a revolution which will destroy the element of contingency and give individuals the power once again to control their mutual relations. That is what communism means: restoring the control of individuals over the material, reified forms in which their mutual ties are expressed. In the last analysis, the task facing humanity consists of abolishing the division of labour; and this presupposes the attainment of a stage of tech-nological development at which the system of private property and division of labour presents itself as a hindrance, so that technology itself requires their abolition. 'Private property can only be abolished on condition of an all-round development of individuals, since the existing forms of exchange and produc-tive forces are universal and only individuals developing in a universal manner can assimilate them, that is to say transform them into free vital activity.' In a communist society the universal development of individuals is no empty phrase, but it does not mean that the individual is to seek self-affirmation inde-pendently of others (which is in any case impossible), in monadic isolation and in the assertion of his rights against the community. On the contrary, 'This development is conditioned by the existing link between them—a link constituted partly by economic premises, partly by the necessary solidarity of the free development of all, and finally by the universal nature of the activity of individuals on the basis of the productive forces existing at a given time.'

For this reason the idea of individual liberation based on Stirner's category of the unique Ego is an idle fantasy. If 'uniqueness' is merely the consciousness of uniqueness, this can of course be realized in any conditions, as an act of pure thought, without any change of external reality. If it merely signifies the obvious fact that everyone is different from everyone else in some respect or other, then it cannot be a programme, since, for what it is worth, it is already the case. As Leibniz observed, there are no two identical things; even the passports of no two men are alike, and in this way even officialdom or the police ensure the identity and uniqueness of every human being. But we are not concerned with such commonplace matters. For the notion of 'uniqueness' to be any use it should denote originality, a particular skill or ability; but these can only display themselves as social values, within the community. 'Uniqueness in the sense of originality implies that the individual's activity in a particular sphere is unlike that of other individuals of the same kind. La Persiani is an "incomparable" singer precisely because, as a singer, we compare her with others.'

In the light of this analysis we can easily perceive the error of those totalitarian interpretations of Marx, less frequent now than formerly, which represent his ideal of communism as a society in which the individual is identified with the species by the extinction of all creative initiative and all qualities that might distinguish him from his fellows. On the other hand, Marx does not believe that individuals can determine or assert their true personality by a mere act of self-knowledge. Self-affirmation of this kind can take place in any conditions, it calls for no change in the world of social ties, and therefore it cannot eradicate human servitude or the process by which human beings eternally forge and re-forge the bonds of their own alienation. In Marx's view, the affirmation of one's own individuality involves the restoration of man's 'social character' or 'species-nature' as distinct from, and opposed to, the state of 'contingency', i.e. enslavement to alienated forces. Under communism, the disappearance of the antagonism between personal aspirations and the species is not a matter of identification, whether forced or voluntary, between the two, and thus of generalized mediocrity and uniformity. What it means is that conditions will be such that individuals can develop their aptitudes fully, not in conflict with one another but in a socially valuable way, instead of superiority turning itself, as now, into privilege or the subjugation of others. 'Depersonalization', if we may introduce this modern term, derives from the subjection of individuals to the work of their own hands and brains; it cannot be cured by a mere reform of ideas, but by reasserting control over inanimate forces which have gained the upper hand over their creators.

However, to say that Marx did not intend the totalitarian version of his theory is not to say that that version is a mistake and nothing more. We shall have to consider in due course whether Marx's vision of social unity did not contain elements contrary to his own intention, and whether he is not to some extent responsible for the totalitarian form of Marxism. Can that unity in fact be imagined in any other way than that of a totalitarian state, however little Marx himself supposed this to be the case?

7. *Alienation and the division of labour*

IN *The German Ideology* and subsequent writings Marx uses the term 'alienation' less frequently, and some critics infer from this that he no longer thought of society in the same categories as before. This, however, appears to be a mistake. According to the Paris Manuscripts the process that engenders all other forms of servitude is that of alienated labour, to which private property is secondary; Marx does not inquire, however, what gives rise to alienated labour itself. In *The German Ideology* the root of all evil is the division of labour, private property being once again a secondary phenomenon. It should not be supposed, however, that the 'division of labour' is only a more precise formulation of the rather vague term 'alienation'. Marx's view is that the division of labour consequent on the improvement of tools is the first source of the alienating process and, through it, of private property. This happens because the division of labour leads necessarily to commerce, i.e. the transformation of objects produced by man into vehicles of abstract exchange-value. When things become commodities, the basic premiss of alienation already exists. Inequality, private property, alienated political institutions for the protection of privilege—all these are a continuation of the same process. The phenomenon of 'alienated labour' continues to operate and to be created in production. A particular form of alienation ensues when physical and mental work are separated from each other. This leads to the self-delusion of ideologists who believe that their thoughts are not dictated by social needs but derive their power from immanent sources; the very existence of ideologists as a group increases support for the notion that ideas have an inherent validity of their own.

A note appended to Part I of *The German Ideology* provides evidence that Marx did not abandon the category of alienation and did regard the division of labour as its primary source. It runs:

Individuals have always regarded themselves as the point of departure, their relations are part of the real process of their lives. How can it be, then, that their relationships become independent of them, that the forces of their own lives gain control over them? The answer, in a word, is—the division of labour, the degree of which depends on the extent to which productive forces have developed.

Although the word 'alienation' occurs less often, the theory is present in Marx's social philosophy until the end of his life; 'commodity fetishism' in *Capital* is nothing but a particularization of it. When Marx writes that commodities produced for the market take on an independent form, that social relations in the commercial process appear to the participants as relations among things over which they have no control (exchange value being falsely represented as inherent in the object and not as an embodiment of labour), and that the supreme type of this fetishism is money as a standard of value and means of exchange—in all this Marx is reproducing the theory of self-alienation that he had formulated in 1844. That social relationships and the whole of history are the work of human beings, which escapes from their control and takes on a more and more autonomous aspect—this, to the very end, was a fundamental determinant of Marx's ideas on the degradation of mankind under capitalism and the social function of the proletarian revolution.

8. The liberation of man and the class struggle

THERE is another point which some critics have taken as signifying a change of attitude in *The German Ideology*, viz. that whereas in the Manuscripts and earlier writings Marx spoke of the emancipation of mankind in general, this idea is now replaced by that of the class struggle between the proletariat and the bourgeoisie. But here too there is no real alteration. Marx continued throughout his life to regard communism as the liberation of the whole of mankind; the proletariat was to be the conscious instrument of that liberation, as being the class which had suffered the extreme degree of dehumanization. It is generally recognized as essentially Marx's view that communism meant the abolition of the class system, not merely the substitution of one ruling class for another; and this view is in complete accordance with his early idea of liberation. Dehumanization cannot affect one class alone; it applies to all classes, though in different degrees, and although the possessing class turns it into a source of pride. It is true, indeed, that the aspect of universal liberation is less prominent in Marx's later works than that of the revolution inspired by the class interest of the proletariat. This is already the case in *The German Ideology*, and is easily explained by the polemical context and particularly the critique of 'true socialism'. According to this doctrine the socialist Utopia, which involved the general liberation of mankind, could and ought to be attained by a universal moral appeal to all social classes without distinction. In other words, 'true socialism' meant socialism without the class struggle and without a revolution inspired by class interests. Marx was convinced, however, that the particular interest of the proletariat and its struggle against the possessing classes was the motive force of the socialist revolution, and that while the revolution would bring about the final disappearance of classes and social antagonism, there must be a transitional period during which the proletariat would continue to oppose its exploiters. As Marx became more closely acquainted with political realities he took more interest in organizing the revolution than in portraying the ideal society, let alone planning the details of communism in action after the manner of Fourier and others; he was more interested, therefore, in the class struggle than in social eschatology. Nevertheless, the whole theory of the class struggle made no sense without that eschatology, and Marx adhered throughout his life to the basic premises of communism as he had formulated them in 1844. He believed that in the class struggle it was no good appealing to general human interests, but only to those of the oppressed. Later, and especially in the *Critique of the Gotha Programme*, he expressly distinguished the first, negative, post-revolutionary phase from the universal community of the future. But the prospect of that community was continuously in his mind, as we may see, for example, from the third volume of *Capital*, and it is not inconsistent either with the class struggle or with the belief that the proletariat, by defending its own class-interest, will be the liberator of the whole human race.

9. The epistemological meaning of the theory of false consciousness

'FALSE CONSCIOUSNESS' is not regarded by Marx as 'error' in the cognitive sense, just as the emancipation of consciousness is not a matter of rediscovering 'truth' in the ordinary sense. In *The German Ideology* as in the Paris Manuscripts, Marx refuses to concern himself with epistemological questions. For him there is no problem of the world being 'reflected' in the mind, except in the sense of his repeated statement that consciousness signifies people's awareness of the nature of their lives. Questions of the correspondence between thought and reality-in-itself are meaningless, as is the opposition of subject and object considered as two independent entities, one absorbing images produced by the other. As Marx says in the *Theses on Feuerbach*, the question of the reality of the world as distinct from practical human interests is a 'purely scholastic' one and is the result of ideological mystification. ('The whole problem of the transition from thought to reality, and thus from language to life, exists only as a philosophical illusion: it is justified only to the philosophic mind, puzzling over the origin and nature of its supposed detachment from real life.') Since extra-human nature is nothing to man, who knows nature only as the objectification of his own activity (which does not mean, of course, that he has physically created it), and since cognition signifies imparting a human sense to things, the difference between false and liberated consciousness is not that between error and truth but is a functional difference related to the purpose served by thought in the collective life of mankind. 'Wrong' thinking is that which confirms the state of human servitude and is unaware of its own proper function; emancipated thought is the affirmation of humanity, enabling man to develop his native abilities. Consciousness is the mental aspect of human life, a social process (for consciousness is realized only in speech) whereby men communicate with one another and assimilate nature in a humanized form. It can either intensify the slavery of man, imprisoned and dominated by material objects, or help towards his liberation. Consciousness determines things, but does not make them objective. As Marx puts it in his critique of Hegel, 'From the point of view of self-knowledge, what is unacceptable in alienation is not that the object is definite, but that it is objective.' Or as he says in one of his early articles: 'The character of things is a product of reason. Every object, in order to be something, must distinguish itself and remain distinguished. By imposing a definite form on every object of discourse and, as it were, giving Permanent shape to flowing reality, reason creates the manifoldness of the world, which would not be universal without many one-sidednesses.'

For Marx, then, there is no question of knowledge having an epistemological value distinct from its value as an organ of human self-affirmation. The restoration of a sound consciousness is one aspect, and not merely a result, of the de-alienation of labour. Marx's epistemology is part of his social utopia. Communism does away with false consciousness, not by substituting a correct image of the world for an incorrect one, but by dispelling the illusion that thought is or can be anything other than the expression of a state of life. It is not a matter of providing new answers to questions of metaphysics and epistemology, but of denying their validity—whether the question be that of God's creation of the world, or that of 'being-in-itself' and the relation to it of subjective data. When we understand the genesis and function of human thought, purely epistemological questions fall to the ground. Thought is always an articulation of its own time in history, but whether it is 'good' or 'bad' does not depend merely on whether it is helpful to the governing class (those who govern materially and therefore intellectually) at that time—for if this were so, we should have to regard bourgeois thought as 'good' at the present day. Thought can and must be judged from an absolute standpoint—not, however, as related to a reality separate from man, but as related to the emancipated consciousness, affirming in an absolute manner the 'species-essence' of man. Consciousness may thus be false even when it correctly expresses the historical situation in which it arises; and we can only speak of false consciousness, or ideology, with reference to the absolute state of emancipation. Having in mind Marx's conception of reason as a practical organ of collective existence, and of the object as something defined though not objectivized by reason, we may describe his epistemology as one of generic subjectivism.

IX

Recapitulation

WE MAY ATTEMPT at this stage to recapitulate Marx's thought in the form it had assumed by 1846. From 1843 onwards he developed his ideas with extreme consistency, and all his later work may be regarded as a continuation and elaboration of the body of thought which was already constituted by the time of *The German Ideology*.

1. Marx's point of departure is the eschatological question derived from Hegel: how is man to be reconciled with himself and with the world? According to Hegel this comes about when Mind, having passed through the travail of history, finally comes to understand the world as an exteriorization of itself; it assimilates and ratifies the world as its own truth, divests it of its objective character, and actualizes everything in it that was originally only potential. Marx, following Feuerbach, places in the centre of his picture the 'earthly reality' of Man, as opposed to the Hegelian Spirit developing through empirical individuals or using them as its instrument. 'For man, the root is man himself'—the basic reality, self-derived and self-justified.

2. Marx, like Hegel, looks forward to man's final reconciliation with the world, himself, and others. Again following Feuerbach against Hegel, he does not see this in terms of the recognition of being as a product of self-knowledge, but in the recognition of sources of alienation in man's terrestrial lot and in the overcoming of this state of affairs. Rejecting the Young Hegelian 'critical principle', he refuses to accept the eternal conflict between negative self-knowledge and the resistance of an unresponsive world, but envisages a de-alienated state in which man will affirm himself in a world of his own creation. On the other hand, he disagrees with Feuerbach's view that alienation results from the mythopoeic consciousness which makes God the concentration of human values; instead, he regards this consciousness as itself the product of the alienation of labour.

3. Alienated labour is a consequence of the division of labour which in its turn is due to technological progress, and is therefore an inevitable feature of history. Marx agrees with Hegel against Feuerbach in seeing alienation not merely as something destructive and inhuman but as a condition of the future all-round development of mankind. But he dissents from Hegel in regarding

history up to the present time not as the progressive conquest of freedom but as a process of degradation that has reached its nadir in the maturity of capitalist society. However, it is necessary for man's future liberation that he should undergo the extremes of affliction and dehumanization, since we are not concerned with regaining a lost paradise, but with the re-conquest of humanity.

4. Alienation means the subjugation of man by his own works, which have assumed the guise of independent things. The commodity character of products and their expression in money form (cf. Hess) has the effect that the social process of exchange is regulated by factors operating independently of human will, after the fashion of natural laws. Alienation gives rise to private property and to political institutions. The state creates a fictitious community to replace the lack of real community in civil society, where human relations inevitably take the form of a conflict of egoisms. The enslavement of the collectivity to its own products entails the mutual isolation of individuals.

5. Alienation is thus not to be cured by thinking about it, but by removing its causes. Man is a practical being, and his thoughts are the conscious aspect of his practical life, although this fact is obscured by false consciousness. Thought is governed by practical needs, and the image of the world in a human mind is regulated not by the intrinsic quality of objects but by the practical task in hand. Once we realize this we perceive the nullity of questions which have only arisen because philosophers did not understand the conditions that gave rise to them, namely the separation of intellectual from practical activity. We deny the validity of metaphysical and epistemological problems engendered by the false hope of attaining to some absolute reality beyond the practical horizon of human beings.

6. The transcendence of alienation is another name for communism—a total transformation of human existence, the recovery by man of his species-essence. Communism puts an end to the division of life into public and private spheres, and to the difference between civil society and the state; it does away with the need for political institutions, political authority and governments, private property and its source in the division of labour. It destroys the class system and exploitation; it heals the split in man's nature and the crippled, one-sided development of the individual. Contrary to Hegel's view, the distinction between the state and civil society is not eternal. Contrary to the views of the liberal Enlightenment, social harmony is to be sought not by a legislative reform that will reconcile the egoism of each individual with the collective interest, but by removing the causes of antagonism. The individual will absorb society into himself: thanks to de-alienation, he will recognize humanity as his own internalized nature. Voluntary solidarity, not compulsion or the legal regulation of interests, will ensure the smooth harmony of human relations. The species (cf. Fichte) can then realize itself in the individual. Communism

destroys the power of objectified relations over human beings, gives him control again over his own works, restores the social operation of his mind and senses, and bridges the gulf between humanity and nature. It is the fulfilment of the human calling, the reconciliation of essence and existence in human life. It also stands for the consciousness of the practical, humane and social character that belongs to all intellectual activity, and repudiates the false independence of existing forms of social thought: philosophy, law, religion. Communism turns philosophy into reality, and by so doing abolishes it.

7. Communism does not deprive man of individuality or reduce personal aspirations and abilities to a dead level of mediocrity. On the contrary, the powers of the individual can only flourish when he regards them as social forces, valuable and effective within a human community and not in isolation. Communism alone makes possible the proper use of human abilities: thanks to the variety of technical progress it ensures that specifically human activity is freed from the constraint of physical need and the pressure of hunger and is thus truly creative. It is the realization of freedom, not only from exploitation and political power but from immediate bodily needs. It is the solution to the problem of history and is also the end of history as we have known it, in which individual and collective life are subject to contingency. Henceforth man can determine his own development in freedom, instead of being enslaved by material forces which he has created but can no longer control. Man, under communism, is not a prey to chance but is the captain of his fate, the conscious moulder of his own destiny.

8. Contrary to what the utopian socialists claim, communism is not an ideal in opposition to the real world, a theory which might have been invented and put into practice at any time in history. It is itself a trend in contemporary history, which is evolving the premises of communism and moving unconsciously towards it. This is because the present age stands for the maximum of dehumanization: on the one hand it degrades the worker by turning him into a commodity, on the other it reduces the capitalist to the status of an entry in a ledger. The proletariat, being the epitome of dehumanization and the pure negation of civil society, is destined to bring about an upheaval that will put an end to all social classes, including itself. The interest of the proletariat, and that of no other class, coincides with the needs of humanity as a whole. The proletariat, therefore, is not a mere agglomeration of suffering, degradation, and misery, but also the historical instrument by which man is to recover his heritage. The alienation of labour has operated through the ages to create the working class, the agent of its destruction.

9. But the proletariat is more than the instrument of an impersonal historical process: it fulfils its destiny by being conscious of that destiny and of its own exceptional situation. The consciousness of the proletariat is not mere passive

awareness of the part assigned to it by history, but a free consciousness and a fount of revolutionary initiative. Here the opposition of freedom and necessity disappears, for what is in fact the inevitability of history takes the form of a free initiative in the proletariat consciousness. By understanding its own position the proletariat not only understands the world but *ipso facto* sets about changing it. This consciousness is not a mere Hegelian acknowledgement and assimilation of past history; it is turned towards the future, in an active impulse of transformation. At the same time it is not, as Fichte and the Young Hegelians would have it, a mere negation of the existing order, but an urge to create a movement that is already potentially there—an innate trend of history, but one that can only be set in motion by the free initiative of human beings. In this way the situation of the proletariat combines historical necessity and freedom.

10. While communism is the final transformation of all spheres of life and human consciousness, the motive force of the revolution that brings it about must be the class-interest of the exploited and destitute proletariat. The revolution has a negative task to perform, and this devolves on the proletariat as long as it is necessary to carry on the struggle with the possessing classes. Communism is not established merely by abolishing private property; it requires a long period of social convulsion, which is bound to result in the consummation demanded by history and by the improvement of instruments of production. Communism has as its precondition advanced technical development and a world market, and will itself result in more intensive technical development; this, however, will not turn against its creators as in the past, but will help them to full self-realization as human beings.

▪   ▪   ▪

THESE are the fundamental principles of Marx's theory, from which he never departed. The whole of his work, down to the last page of *Capital*, was a confirmation and elaboration of these ideas. Engels, from a more empirical point of view, gave expression to the same vision of a classless communist society, to be brought about by the initiative of the working class activating the natural trend of history. On the other hand, Engels adopted a different standpoint as regards the cognitive and ontological link between man and nature. In his later works the idea of the 'philosophy of praxis' as we have discussed it gives place to a theory which subjects humanity to the general laws of nature and makes human history a particularization of those laws, thus departing from the conception of man as 'the root' (in Marx's phrase) and of the 'humanization' of nature. In so doing Engels created a new version of Marxist philosophy, differing as much from its original as did post-Darwinian European culture from the age that preceded it.

X

Socialist Ideas in the First Half of the Nineteenth Century as Compared with Marxian Socialism

1. The rise of the socialist idea

FROM 1847 onwards Marx occasionally reverted to philosophic speculations of the kind that dominate his early writings. The instances of this are important, as they confirm the essential continuity of his thought and enable us to relate his political and economic ideas to the trends of his earliest thinking. However, his mature writings are directly focused on an increasingly precise analysis, of which *Capital* provides the most finished version, of the functioning of the capitalist economy, together with polemics against various socialist doctrines and programmes which, in his opinion, misinterpreted the historical and economic facts and impeded the development of the workers' revolutionary movement. Having joined issue with German 'true socialism' he proceeded to challenge Proudhon, utopian socialism, Bakunin, and Lassalle. All these quarrels and controversies were of great importance to the history of the workers' movement, but not all of them involved new departures in the realm of theory.

At the time when Marx came into the field as a theoretician of the proletarian revolution, socialist ideas already had a long life behind them. If we sought to provide a general definition of socialism in historical as opposed to normative terms, i.e. to identify the common features of the ideas that went under that name in the first half of the nineteenth century, we should find the result extremely jejune and imprecise. The mainspring of the socialist ideas that arose under the combined influence of the Industrial and the French Revolution was the conviction that the uncontrolled concentration of wealth and unbridled competition were bound to lead to increasing misery and crises, and that the system must be replaced by one in which the organization of production and exchange would do away with poverty and oppression and bring about a redistribution of the world's goods on a basis of equality. This might imply the complete equalization of wealth, or the principle of 'to each according to his labour', or, eventually, 'to each according to his needs'. Beyond the general conception of equality, socialist programmes and ideas differed in every respect. Not all of them even proposed to abolish private ownership of the means of production. Some advocates of socialism regarded it as essentially the cause of the working class, while others saw it as a universal human ideal which all classes should help to bring about. Some proclaimed the necessity of a political revolution, others relied on the force of propaganda or example. Some thought that all forms of state organization would soon be done away with, others that they were indispensable. Some regarded freedom as the supreme good, others were prepared to limit it drastically in the name of equality or efficient production. Some appealed to the international interest of the oppressed classes, while others did not look beyond the national horizon. Some, finally, were content to imagine a perfect society, while others studied the course of historical evolution in order to identify the natural laws which would ensure the advent of socialism.

The invention of the term 'socialism' was claimed by Pierre Leroux, a follower of Saint-Simon, who used it in the journal *Le Globe* in 1832; it was also used in Britain in the 1830s by the disciples of Robert Owen. As the name and the concept became widely known, theorists and adherents of the new doctrine naturally turned their attention to its antecedents in Plato's Republic, the communist ideas of medieval sectarians and the Renaissance utopianists, especially Thomas More and Campanella. In these writers and their imitators in the seventeenth and eighteenth centuries it was possible to discern a continuity of ideas despite their very different philosophies. Plato's hierarchic society was a long way from the egalitarian tenets of most modern socialists, and the ascetic ideals of medieval doctrinaires were specifically religious in character. But More's Utopia owed its origin to reflection on the first symptoms of capitalist accumulation, and the advocates of socialism found much to sympathize with in its ideals: the abolition of private property, the universal obligation to work, the equalization of rights and wealth, the organization of production by the state, and the eradication of poverty and exploitation. From the sixteenth to the eighteenth century socialist ideas were generally inspired not merely by reflection on the sufferings of the downtrodden classes, but by a philosophical or religious belief that antagonisms and conflicts of interest, inequality and oppression were contrary to God's plan or Nature's, which intended men to live in a state of peace and harmony. Some exponents of these ideas went so far as to maintain that the perfect society required all its members to be completely uniform in all respects—not only their rights and duties, but their way of life and thought, food and clothing, and even (according to Dom Deschamps and others) their physical appearance. In some cases the ideal of static perfection excluded any notion of creativity or progress.

Campanella was an exception: his *Civitas Solis*, unlike More's *Utopia*, left plenty of room for scientific and technical discovery.

2. Babouvism

THE first active manifestation of socialism after the Revolution of 1789 was the conspiracy of Gracchus Babeuf. Filippo Buonarroti, who took part in the conspiracy, published an account of it in 1828, thanks to which its ideas became for the first time generally known. Babeuf and the Babouvists took their philosophy in the main from Rousseau and the utopianists of the Enlightenment, and regarded themselves as the successors of Robespierre. Their basic premiss was the idea of equality: as Buonarroti wrote, 'the perpetual cause of the enslavement of peoples is nothing but inequality, and as long as it exists the assertion of national rights will be illusory as far as the masses are concerned, sunk as they are beneath the level of human dignity' (*Conspiration pour l'égalité dite Babeuf*, i. 100). As all men have by nature the same right to all earthly goods, the source of inequality is private property and this must be done away with. In the future society wealth will be distributed equally to all, irrespective of the work they do; there will be no right of inheritance, no large cities; all will be compelled to do physical work and to live in the same manner. In addition to laying down the principles of the new society, the Babouvists planned the way to it by organizing, under the Directory, a conspiracy to overthrow the existing order. Since the masses were not yet liberated from the spiritual influence of the exploiters they could not at once exercise power, which would be wielded for them by the conspirators. Later, when education became universal, the populace would govern itself through elected bodies. Babeuf's conspiracy was detected in 1796, and he was tried and guillotined. His ideas were to some extent carried on by Louis Blanqui. The Babouvist programme was not expressed in specific class-categories, but merely distinguished rich and poor, or peoples and tyrants; its egalitarian rhetoric, however, was one of the first attempts at an economic criticism of private property as the foundation of society.

The Babouvist movement is also important because it reflected for the first time a conscious conflict between the revolutionary ideal of freedom and that of equality. Freedom meant not only the right of assembly and the abolition of legal differences between estates of the realm, but also the right of every man to carry on economic activity without hindrance and to defend his property; freedom, therefore, meant inequality, exploitation, and misery. Babeuf's conspiracy was in its immediate origin a reaction of the Jacobin Left to the *coup* of Thermidor, but ideologically it went far beyond the Jacobin tradition. The Babouvists took over the Jacobin conception of society in terms of political power acquired by force, and bequeathed this to the French socialist movement. (British socialism, originating as it did not from a political revolution but from the process of industrialization, was dominated from the outset by a reformist tendency.) The *Manifeste des égaux* drawn up in 1796 by Sylvain Maréchal described the French Revolution as the prelude to another, much greater and final revolution. The leaders would not allow this document to be published, as they drew the line at two of its statements. The first was 'Let all the arts perish, if need be, so that we may have true equality'; the second called for the abolition of all differences not only between rich and poor, masters and servants, but also between rulers and the ruled. The former statement reveals a tendency that was often to recur in communist movements. Equality is the supreme value, and in particular equality in the enjoyment of material goods. Taken to an extreme, this means that it matters less whether people have much or little so long as they all have the same. If there is a choice between improving the lot of the poor but allowing inequality to subsist, or leaving the poor as they are and depressing everyone to their level, it is the second alternative that must be chosen. The various communist and socialist groups did not actually envisage the matter in these terms, since they were all certain that the equalization of wealth would produce, if not abundance, at any rate a sufficiency for all. Most of them also naïvely assumed that the deprivation of the workers was due to the conspicuous consumption of the rich, and that if all the goods enjoyed by the privileged classes were distributed among the people, the result would be general prosperity. In the first stage of socialist ideas, however, moral indignation at poverty and inequality was not distinguished from economic analysis of capitalist production, but rather took the place of such analysis. As with the utopianists of the Enlightenment, Morelly or Mably, the principle of the community of goods was deduced from a normative theory according to which human beings, simply as such, have an identical right to whatever the earth provides. Whether this view was defended by quotations from the New Testament (as in many socialist writings) or by the materialist tradition of the Enlightenment, the conclusion was the same: inequality of consumption is contrary to human nature, and so is rent, interest, and any unearned income.

As to abolishing the difference between the rulers and the ruled, this, as an immediate revolutionary aim, belongs rather to the tradition of anarchism. The Babouvists rejected it, as they envisaged a period of dictatorship in the general interest for as long as might be necessary to destroy or disarm the enemies of equality.

Altogether, the Babouvist movement marks the point at which liberal democracy and communism began to part company, as it came to be seen that equality was not a completion of liberty but a limitation of it. This does not mean, however, that the dilemma was at once obvious to all. For some time, liberal democracy and socialism were present in mixed and intermediate forms;

only 1848 drew a clear line between them. Similarly, the terms 'communist' and 'socialist' were for a long time not clearly distinguished. By the 1830s, however, the former name was in general used by those radical reformers and utopians who demanded the abolition of private property (at first chiefly the ownership of land, then also factories) and absolute equality of consumption, and who did not rely on the goodwill of governments or possessors, but on the use of force by the exploited.

After 1830, in both France and England—the parent countries of socialism—socialist ideas and the embryonic workers' movement appeared in combination in various ways. Even before this, however, ideas of a radical reform of society on socialist though not communist (i.e. not Babouvist) lines were ventilated in both countries in the form of theoretical reflections on the development of industry. This type of socialism, in which the chief names are Saint-Simon, Fourier, and Robert Owen, had an important influence on Marx's thought, both positively and negatively. It was not itself a protest by the deprived classes, but sprang from the observation and analysis of social misery, exploitation, and unemployment.

3. Saint-Simonism

CLAUDE HENRI, comte de Saint-Simon (1760–1825), was the real founder of modern theoretical socialism, conceived not merely as an ideal but as the outcome of a historical process. He was a descendant of the famous Duke, fought in the American War of Independence and, after the Revolution, engaged in trade operations which led to bankruptcy. He had a lifelong interest in philosophical subjects and in the possibility of reforming society by reforming the method of studying it. He also formulated the idea, taken up afterwards by Auguste Comte, of reducing every branch of knowledge to a positive state, having first liberated it from its theological and metaphysical phases. In his early works, including *Lettres d'un habitant de Genève* (1803) and *Introduction aux travaux scientifiques du XIXe siècle* (1807), he called for a form of political science that would be as positive and reliable as the physical sciences. Another Newton was needed to impose unity on the body of knowledge accumulated since his day; scholars would in time lead the nations on their path towards happiness. In 1814–18, aided by the future historian Augustin Thierry, he drew up plans of political reform on a European scale (*De la réorganisation de la société européenne*, 1814); these included parliamentary government on British lines and a supranational European assembly to ensure peace, cooperation, and unity on the medieval lines, but inspired by liberalism instead of theocracy. As time went on he took an increasing interest in broad problems of economic organization. He reached the conclusion (*L'Industrie*, 1817) that the proper function of the state was to look after productivity and that it should apply methods of industrial management to all social questions. Developing this subject with the assistance of Auguste Comte, who was his secretary from 1818 to 1822, he finally abandoned economic liberalism and formulated the principle of a future 'organic' social community, which gained many adherents and was the basis of his fame.

Saint-Simon believed that the future of humanity was to be discerned in the light of past historical changes and trends. The conclusion he came to, although he did not work it out systematically, was similar to that of historical materialism, viz. that all political change has been due to the evolution of the instruments of production, and today's technology calls for corresponding political change. Poverty and crises are caused by free competition and the resulting anarchy of production and exchange. This anarchy, however, subjects those who contribute to production—manufacturers, merchants, industrial and agricultural workers—to the authority of incompetent drones and idlers. The most important dividing line, in Saint-Simon's opinion, was between producers and those who merely consumed the fruits of others' labour. The future society, to which industrial concentration was leading, would be one in which industry was managed by the producers of wealth; production would be planned and measured by social needs, and private property, while still permitted, would change its character, as its use would be subordinated to the general good and not left to the owner's whim; inheritance would be abolished, so that property would be enjoyed only by those who had earned it by their abilities and application. Competition would give way to emulation; private interest would become an instrument of self-improvement, devoted to serving the community instead of opposing it. The social hierarchy would be preserved but would no longer be hereditary; the highest positions would be held by bankers allocating investment resources and wise men supervising the general development of society. The new industrial order would put an end to the poverty and humiliation of the most afflicted class of society, the proletariat; however, Saint-Simon did not look to the oppressed workers to carry out his plans, but believed that society would be transformed for their benefit by manufacturers, bankers, scholars, and artists, once they had been convinced by the new doctrine. Political power would undergo a complete change: it would not be a matter of governing people but of administering things, i.e. ensuring that human beings made the best possible use of Nature's gifts. To bring about this change, nothing more was needed than peaceful reforms such as the acquisition of parliamentary power by industrialists; from time to time Saint-Simon also appeared to the governing class to support his plan. In his last major work (*Le Nouveau Christianisme*, 1825) he declared that political science must be based on still more fundamental principles, namely religious ones. Far from spelling the ruin of Christian civilization, the industrial society would fulfil its essential meaning and especially the precept to 'love one another'. Self-interest was not enough as a basis for social organization; sentiment and religion were necessary, and religious life was a permanent feature of human existence and could never become obsolete.

The religious strain in Saint-Simon's programme was emphasized by his immediate followers, who systematized his thought and contributed elements of their own. In the *Exposition de la doctrine de Saint-Simon* by Enfantin and Bazard, of which the first volume appeared in 1830, we see clearly the process by which his social philosophy transformed itself into a dogma and his adherents into a sect; we also find there a detailed exposition of ideas which in some cases were no more than outlined by Saint-Simon himself.

The Saint-Simonist school regards history as a continual progress in which, however, two phases alternate: the organic and the critical. 'Organic' periods are those in which certain principles of thought are generally accepted, there is a clear-cut social hierarchy and an unbroken unity of faith. 'Critical' periods are necessary transitional phases of disharmony and disunity, in which the sense of community is lost and the bonds of society are relaxed. Europe has been in this state since the Reformation but is now moving into a new organic period, which will be permanent and not succeeded by one of anarchy. It will be a kind of return to medieval theocracy, but without its contempt for the body and for temporal needs. Instead, the new Christianity will be imbued with the spirit of science and technical progress and will regard productive work as essentially valuable. Belief in God and a future life will be maintained, as will the priesthood, but the whole system of religion will be harmonized with man's concern for his earthly welfare.

This prospect, according to the Saint-Simonians, is not an arbitrary one but can be deduced from the whole of history, in which we may trace the gradual development of co-operative principles. The growth of industry and its increasing centralization call for a fundamental change in the organization of production. Idlers are sharing less and less in the fruits of labour, as we see from the falling rates of interest in industrial countries. But the seeds of future development must be encouraged to sprout. At present competition and anarchy are widening the gap between classes, since manufacturers reduce wages in order to cut prices. Thanks to the hereditary principle the means of production are controlled by incompetent persons and the irrational privilege of birth has replaced that of estates of the realm. In the new society, instead of man exploiting man the earth will be made to fructify by co-operating producers, and their output will not be consumed by idlers. This will be achieved by doing away with the right of inheritance, especially as regards the means of production, abolishing interest on capital, and organizing productivity on a state-centralized basis. The state will allocate investment credits and all the means of production to manufacturers in accordance with their abilities and with social needs. The right to use the means of production will depend on ability, and the exercise of that right under state supervision will be the sole form of property. Men will not be governed by selfish interests alone but by sentiment and enthusiasm, willingness to work for others, morality and religion. Incomes will not be equal, since the principle is 'To each according to his labour', but this inequality will not be due to exploitation and will therefore not be injurious to the community or tend to revive classes and class antagonisms. The illusory freedom which means nothing to the starving, and the equality before the law which is nullified by the privilege of wealth, will be superseded by the universal brotherhood of working man. Industrialists, artists, and men of learning will work harmoniously to improve the human race and satisfy its material, moral, and intellectual needs, while preserving the invaluable link with Divinity that alone enables man to be happy and to love and help his neighbour.

Like other moral and philosophical doctrines, Saint-Simonism showed itself capable of evolving in opposite directions. Its authoritarian elements—the emphasis on social hierarchy, and a theocratic strain—contributed, partly through Comte, to a conservative school of thought which stressed everything connecting Saint-Simon with de Maistre and other traditionalist critics of the post-Revolutionary order. But, on the other hand, Louis Blanc was a disciple of Saint-Simon and so, through him, was Lassalle. Socialist ideas, wherein the state was expected to play an important part in resolving class antagonisms, were largely an intellectual legacy of Saint-Simon. As far as Marxian socialism is concerned, the most important features of his doctrine may be listed as follows: the firm belief in the regularity of history and its inexorable march towards socialism; the ruinous consequences of anarchic competition and the necessity of state economic planning; the replacement of political government by economic administration; science as the instrument of social progress; and the internationalist approach to politico-economic problems. What is contrary to Marxism, on the other hand, is the idea that the state as it now exists can be used to bring about a socialist transformation; likewise Saint-Simon's appeal for co-operation between classes, and the religious overtones of his 'industrial order'. The formula 'From each according to his ability, to each according to his needs' was taken over by Marxist socialism from Louis Blanc, who modified Saint-Simon's doctrine on this point.

Like early Marxism, Saint-Simon's doctrine requires to be judged within the framework of the Romantic movement or rather as an attempt to overcome Romanticism from within. His critique of post-Revolutionary society reflected not only sympathy with the downtrodden masses, but also alarm at the dissolution of the bonds which had held the old society together. The Romantics,

Saint-Simon, and the young Marx condemned industrial civilization not only for its social injustice but because it replaced almost every link between human beings by the negative principle of private interest. The new world was one in which everything was for sale and was worth just what it would fetch in the market, while selfish motives took the place of human solidarity and fellow-feeling. The Romantics for the most part blamed this state of affairs on technical progress, and idealized the rural or chivalrous communities of pre-industrial times. The Saint-Simonists agreed with the Romantics in disliking the new industrial order, or rather disorder, but they saw the answer not in calling back the past but in a rational organization of production. They also believed, like Marx, that technical progress would cure its own destructive effects and restore to humanity—by which they meant mainly Europe—an organic unity based on scientific development instead of, as in former times, on the stagnation of a primitive agricultural community.

The later fortunes and extravagances of the Saint-Simonists—a priestly hierarchy, sexual mysticism, the Near Eastern quest for a female Messiah—are irrelevant to the history of socialism. However, some manufacturers were attracted to the doctrine by the cult of industrial organization, technical efficiency, and the entrepreneurial spirit. In France, unlike Britain, the dawn of industrialization was associated with a semi-Romantic ideology in which engineers and businessmen figured as the knights-errant and explorers of the new world of applied science. The 'Père Enfantin' ended his career as the manager of a railway line, and another of Saint-Simon's disciples, Ferdinand de Lesseps, built the Suez Canal.

Of all pre-Marxist doctrines Saint-Simonism had the strongest effect in diffusing socialist ideas among the educated classes. Two or three generations grew up on the novels of George Sand, who was among the converted. It was chiefly due to the Saint-Simonists that a belief in socialism spread to the intellectuals of the great European countries, including German Romantics, British utilitarians, and Russian and Polish radicals.

4. Owen

UNLIKE most of the socialist thinkers of his day, Robert Owen (1771–1858) had been an industrialist and in direct contact with working-class life for many years before he put pen to paper. As compared with the French socialists, moreover, he lived in a country which suffered much more grievously from the ill-effects of industrialization and mechanization.

The son of a poor craftsman, Owen began to earn his living at an early age. By dint of great energy and ingenuity he set up a workshop of his own in Manchester. He later became the manager of a large cotton mill, married a manufacturer's daughter, and became manager and co-owner of a large textile factory at New Lanark in Scotland. There, from 1800 onwards, he carried on social and educational experiments designed to rescue workers and their families from poverty, degradation, and debauchery. His career as a manufacturer and philanthropist continued for many years. He reduced working hours to ten and a half, employed no children under 10 years of age, introduced free primary education and relatively hygienic working conditions, and eliminated drunkenness and theft by persuasion instead of punishment. To the general surprise he showed that on this basis he could achieve better results in production and trade than employers in whose factories adult and child workers were decimated by cruel and inhuman conditions, while disease, starvation, drunkenness, crime, and slave-driving methods degraded the labouring class to the level of animals.

Owen described his experiments and their philosophical basis in *A New View of Society, or Essays on the Principle of the Formation of the Human Character* (1813–14). In this work he sought to convince manufacturers and the aristocracy of the need for a reform of the industrial and monetary system, wages and education, in the interest not only of workers but of capitalists and the whole of society. In numerous subsequent pamphlets, periodicals, articles, memorandums and appeals to Parliament he continued to advocate his reformist ideas, exposing the horrors of industrialization and urging the adoption of social and educational measures which would remedy abuses without hindering technical progress. Above all he sought to relieve the cruelty of the system which obliged children of 6 to work fourteen or sixteen hours a day in spinning mills. With great difficulty he succeeded in obtaining the passage of the Factory Act of 1819, the first law in England to limit child working hours in the textile industry. In speeches and writings from 1817 onwards he attacked the Established Church for keeping the masses in a state of poverty and superstition; the most erroneous and harmful of its doctrines, in his opinion, was that of the individual's responsibility for his character and actions. In later years Owen turned from philanthropy to organizing trade unions and co-operatives and planning a new type of society based on voluntary mutual aid without exploitation or antagonism. Pilloried for his attacks on private property and religion, he went to America in 1824 and attempted unsuccessfully to set up communist settlements there. He returned to England in 1829 and spent the rest of his life promoting the trade union and cooperative movement, being thus the first outstanding organizer of the British proletariat in its economic struggle. He advocated a 'labour currency' to enable the price of products to be fixed at their real value, i.e. the average labour-time required for their manufacture, and organized a 'labour exchange' for the direct marketing of goods. Although the British trade unions and co-operatives subsequently changed the basis of their activity, they had in Owen not only a champion and theoretician but also their first large-scale organizer.

The aims for which Owen fought were the practical ones of eliminating poverty, unemployment, crime, and exploitation. In this he was inspired by a few simple principles, the recognition of which would, in his opinion, suffice to cure all the ills of humanity. Above all, he took over from the eighteenth-century utilitarians the view that man does not form his own character, feelings, opinions, or beliefs but is irresistibly influenced by environment, family, and education. It is a fatal error to hold, as all religions do, that a man's will has any effect on his opinions or that the individual is responsible for his character and habits; experience shows that people are conditioned by upbringing and circumstances, and criminals, no less than judges, are the product of their environment. Man has an innate desire for happiness, he has intellectual powers and animal instincts, and everyone comes into the world with different abilities and inclinations. But knowledge and convictions are wholly the work of education, and man's prosperity and adversity depend on the knowledge he receives. The only source of the evil and unhappiness that have beset mankind through the ages is ignorance, particularly ignorance of human nature, and knowledge is the cure for all human ills. From all this it follows that a man cannot achieve happiness by acting against his neighbour, but only by means of actions directed to the happiness of all.

The idea that man can be moulded at will, and that there can be a social harmony which does not do away with private interests but reconciles them through education, is part of the stock-in-trade of the Enlightenment; but Owen derived from it practical conclusions which were intended to revolutionize the social system. The essential need, in his view, was to transform the educational milieu. Children, if properly taught, would imbibe lifelong instincts of co-operation and charity towards their fellows; but for this they must be given training at an early age and not driven to work in factories where they were physically degraded and kept in ignorance.

> Children are, without exception, passive and wonderfully contrived compounds; which, by an accurate previous and subsequent attention, founded on a correct knowledge of the subject, may be formed collectively to have any human character. And although these compounds, like all the other works of nature, possess endless varieties, yet they partake of that plastic quality which, by perseverance under judicious management, may be ultimately moulded into the very image of rational wishes and desires. (*New View of Society*, Second Essay)

The reform of education must be accompanied by a reform of labour conditions. It is in the manufacturers' own interest to improve the lot of the workers, since they provide a mass demand for the goods they themselves produce. Poverty and low wages lead to crises of overproduction, in which goods remain on the market and employers are ruined. Owen at first hoped that by convincing capitalists of this he could enlist their support for his reforms. He finally decided, however, that the workers would have to rely on their own efforts for any improvement in their lot, although he never ceased to believe that reform was in the interest of the whole of society and could be brought about without revolution, by gradual change and peaceful propaganda.

In his later years Owen put his trust in communist settlements engaged in agriculture and industry, the nuclei of a future harmonious society. Here, thanks to good organization and loyal co-operation, people would produce more willingly, in greater quantity, and at a cheaper rate than elsewhere. Education would inculcate love of the community from the child's earliest years, and would eliminate religious intolerance and sectarian strife. The desire to help one's neighbour would be a sufficient incentive to work, without the stimulus of competition or public honours. Value would be measured by labour; the currency in circulation would correspond to the amount produced, and the economy would thus be immune to crises, overproduction, depression, or inflation. There would be no crime, drunkenness, or debauchery, no punishments, prisons, or executions. It was not true, as Malthus contended, that food supplies could not keep up with natural increase and that part of the population was therefore condemned to undernourishment and starvation. People could produce far more than they consumed; there was no known limit to the fertility of the soil, and production was increasing at an ever-faster rate.

Owen believed that if these simple truths were not universally accepted, it was only because people's minds were not ready for them: thanks to ignorance, mankind had for centuries been in a kind of conspiracy to work its own undoing. Now that the moment of clarity had come, the whole of life could be reformed easily and quickly. In time the reform would spread all over the world, since it applied to the whole human species. National prejudices and enmities, belief in the inequality of man and the class system—all this was the fruit of superstition, and would disappear when superstition was eradicated.

Owen's belief that human nature was unchangeable did not conflict with his theory that character can be moulded, since he maintained that the permanent factor in humanity was its liability to change and also the desire for happiness. He often uses the term 'human nature' in a normative rather than a descriptive sense, signifying man's duty to live in harmony and concord despite individual differences.

Although it originated in practical experience, Owen's doctrine, like that of

the French socialists, centred round the conviction that socialism was a unique
and heaven-sent discovery, so manifestly right that it was bound to be
accepted by all classes as soon as proclaimed. Since Owen is never tired of
repeating that innate determinism puts men at the mercy of inherited beliefs
and prejudices, it is not clear how some of them, like Owen himself, are able
suddenly to break free and to show others the way to social reform. These
defiers of omnipotent tradition are, it would seem, endowed by the spontaneity of genius with the power to inaugurate a new era. Owen himself did not discuss this problem; he was only interested in philosophy in so far as it related
directly to his plans for society, and even then contented himself with general
formulas drawn from the Enlightenment tradition. He does not discuss the
function of class-consciousness, and is inclined, like most of the system-
builders of socialism, to ascribe to himself the role of a demiurge in the historical process. This is the chief point of difference between Owenite socialism
and Marxism, and is the source of such other important differences as that
concerning the respective role of economic and political reforms. Marx shared
the view of Owen and others that in a socialist society the power of the state
over men would in the end be superseded by the administration of things, i.e.
of the productive process, but he held that this could only come about after a
political upheaval. Owen, on the other hand, thought that a radical economic
reform in a socialist spirit could be effected by appealing to universal human
interests and with the aid of the existing state power. The British trade union
movement is still marked by this outlook, which directly subordinates the
political struggle to economic interests. The social democratic theories which
treated workers' political parties as organs of the trade unions are a continuation of the same doctrine. In a more developed form the question was to
become a source of polemics at the time of the Second International.

Owen's doctrine initiated a new phase of the British workers' movement, in
which it ceased to be merely an outburst of despair and became a systematic
force which in the end brought about immense social changes. Moreover, his
attack on capitalism and his plans for a new society contained enduring features, although some of his ideas—for example, that of a labour currency, developed by his followers John Gray and John Francis Bray—were soon discarded
as they proved to be based on entirely false economic diagnoses.

Meanwhile, at the end of the 1830s a political workers' movement made its
appearance in England in the form of Chartism, which remained in the public
view for the next ten years. Engels wrote for its newspaper the *Northern Star*,
founded in 1838 by Feargus O'Connor. The main Chartist demand was for
equal and universal male suffrage; this they did not achieve, but their agitation
led to the passage of further legislation against exploitation in industry.

5. Fourier

CHARLES FOURIER (1772–1837), who enjoys the deserved reputation of a visionary and crank of the first order, described the future socialist paradise in more grandiose detail than any of the utopians who preceded him throughout history. Nevertheless, he was the first to make certain observations that proved of importance in the evolution of socialist ideas. He was an eyewitness and to some extent a victim of the economic crises, destitution, and speculation of the Revolutionary and Napoleonic era; these experiences formed the background to his system, which he regarded as the most important event in the history of the human race.

Born at Besançon, the son of a rich merchant, Fourier was destined against his will for a business career. He became a commercial agent at Lyons in 1791, and in this capacity travelled extensively in France, Germany, and Holland. Eventually he founded a firm of his own, but was ruined by the events of the Revolution and thereafter held its ideas in abhorrence. Conscripted into the army, he was discharged in 1796, and became once more an agent at Lyons and subsequently a broker. After some years he moved to Paris, then returned to Lyons as a bank cashier, and finally settled in Paris, first as a trade official and then as a modest *rentier*. The last four decades of his life were spent in elaborating and publicizing his ideal of a perfect society: nearly all his spare time was devoted to writing, and only a small fraction of it to reading. He sought incessantly for a patron who would invest a few million francs in the first 'phalanstery' or cell of the new society; it it were once set up, he was convinced that the example would prove irresistible in four years at the longest. Though embittered by failure he continued his efforts and managed to recruit a small band of disciples, the chief of whom was Victor Considérant (1808–93). Fourier began writing in 1800, and in 1808 expounded his system in the anonymous *Théorie des quatre mouvements et des destinées générales*. In 1822 he published his *Traité de l'association domestique et agricole,* and in 1829 *Le Nouveau Monde industriel et sociétaire*. He left a number of manuscripts, some of which were published by his followers, while others have only recently seen the light of day.

Fourier's extraordinary cast of mind is well illustrated by the account he gives of the manner in which he hit upon the basic principle of his system. Travelling from Rouen to Paris in 1798, he noticed a wide difference in the price of apples from one place to another, although the climate was the same. This brought home to him the harmful and destructive effect of middlemen, and thus inspired the whole conception of the new society. Fourier goes on to observe that in the history of the world there have been two pernicious apples,

those of Adam and Paris (the apple of discord), and two beneficial ones, Newton's and his own; the latter is more salutary than all previous human inventions put together. The world might, he adds, have been organized on his
system at almost any time in the past, for instance in the age of Pericles, and
this would have saved much suffering and unhappiness. Fourier was not the
only theoretician of his time to see himself in the role of a saviour, but he was
more open about it than most.

Fourier's doctrine was inspired by the phenomena of crisis, speculation,
exploitation, and the misery of the workers. All this, he thought, was not an
inevitable consequence of human nature but was due to a wrongful system of
labour and exchange. Human needs and passions were ineradicable, but they
only led to unhappiness because society was badly organized; the problem was
to order matters in such a way that they conduced to the general good instead
of to antagonism. Modern civilization was contrary to the natural order as
established by God; we must rediscover Nature's demands and organize public
life accordingly. The society of the future would be composed of settlements
called phalansteries', in which all passions would be satisfied and would serve
constructive ends. Altogether twelve passions were common to human beings,
though in varying proportion: four related to sentiment (friendship, love, ambition, and family feeling), one to each of the five senses, and the remaining three
were 'distributive': the desire for change, love of intrigue, and the tendency to
unite in competing groups. By means of elaborate calculation Fourier showed
that the combinations of these passions produced 810 types of character, and
the basic unit of his society, which he called the 'phalanx', should consist, for
maximum variety, of twice this number of individuals plus a reserve, making a
total of 2,000. Production was to be organized in such a way that everyone had
an occupation congenial to his character. Work would not be a form of drudg-
ery but a stimulus and a source of pleasure. No one would be obliged to stick
at the same job; everyone would have at least forty different aptitudes, and
could change employment several times a day if he felt like it. Unpleasant jobs
like killing animals or cleaning sewers and drains could be performed by children, who like playing in the dirt. The phalanstery was to be an agricultural and
industrial unit. Life would be communal, but privacy would not be sacrificed;
the dwellings would be hotels rather than barracks; everyone would be completely free to follow his own bent. Women would enjoy full equality with men;
family life would be abolished, and children brought up communally at public
expense; burdensome domestic cares would cease, and all restrictions on sexual life would be removed. This was a basic feature of the new society: people
could live monogamously if they wanted to, but love was to be absolutely free
and brothels would be among the most respected institutions of the new order.

Private property, inheritance, and economic inequality would not be done away with, but would lose their antagonistic character. The phalanx would provide minimum subsistence for all, even if they did not wish to work (but everyone would wish to, for all work would be pleasurable). Production would be by cooperatives whose share in the general wealth would be determined by the usefulness of their output, the enjoyment of creating it etc. Each individual would work in several groups and be paid differently in each according to his ability. There would be inequality but no envy, only zeal and healthy competition. All were entitled to share in the capital of the co-operative, but this could not give rise to exploitation. The education of all children free of charge would ensure that they engaged in useful work at an early age. The organs of political authority would become superfluous; public affairs would be decided on democratic principles and government would be reduced to economic administration; however, for the sake of variety and emulation, the new order would maintain a system of titles, dignities, and representative functions. Fourier calculated with precision how many phalanxes, combined in units of increasing size, would be necessary to comprise the world state of 'omnarchy' (*sic*, i.e. rule of all). Since the evils of the present system had affected the animal and vegetable kingdoms as well, the new order would see a transformation of these and the assertion of man's dominion over them. The seas would turn into orangeade, deserts would blossom and glaciers melt, spring would be eternal, and wild beasts would die out or become friends of man, 'anti-lions' and 'anti-whales' to do his bidding. There would be a single language for all mankind; all would live life to the full, developing their personality in all directions, in a happy and harmonious community embracing every kind of sentiment and avocation.

The extravagance of Fourier's description and the naïvety with which he attributed his own tastes to other (sexual promiscuity, gluttony, love of flowers and cats, etc.) caused him to be regarded as a hopeless crank, with the result that some of his acuter observations were overlooked. His whole theory was enveloped in a speculative cosmology and theology which sought to explain human affairs by universal laws. The pursuit of knowledge was to him a form of worship, and the laws of nature were divine decrees. Newton's law of gravity applied to souls as well; all human passions were instances of 'attraction', all were natural, therefore divine and deserving of satisfaction. The universe was a kind of phalanstery composed of heavenly bodies in a hierarchical order: the planets copulated, the stars had souls, and so on. Fourier adopted Schelling's view that the world was a unity, and he believed that the human soul and the universe were constructed according to an identical schema.

Despite these absurdities, Fourier's critique of 'civilization' (a term he always uses in a pejorative sense) and his ideas of a future harmonious state contain many elements that became part of the socialist tradition. His view that exploitation and poverty are due to a discrepancy between social conditions and the developed instruments of production appears in a more precise form in Marx's writings. Fourier pointed out the parasitic nature of trade in conditions of economic anarchy, and also the harm done by tiny land-holdings. He showed that technical progress increased the poverty of the proletariat (the remedy being not to halt progress but to alter the property system), and that wages gravitated to a minimum subsistence level. His ideal was a unified economic system which would prevent human energies being wasted in intermediary occupations and would eliminate the chaos of unplanned production leading to a glut of merchandise and pauperizing the workers. Fourier criticized the republican doctrines that extolled political freedom, which, he pointed out, was of little use without social freedom, i.e. liberty to develop one's own inclinations. He argued that hired labour is a form of slavery, that humanity aspires to freedom based on conformity between the individual's desires and the work he does, and that the aim is a voluntary society of harmonious co-operation. All these ideas are close to those of Marx. As to Fourier's conception of an all-round man liberated from occupational one-sidedness, capable of performing a variety of tasks, and living in a system which enables him to do so, this too can be found many times in Marx, from the Paris Manuscripts to *Capital*. Again, Fourier was one of the first to advocate the emancipation of women: he believed that human progress depended on the liberation of the sex, and, like the Marxists, he condemned the element of prostitution in bourgeois marriage. His Utopia was the antithesis of the monastic imaginations of the Renaissance and Enlightenment; he held that asceticism was contrary to nature and that the liberation of man signified, not least, the liberation of his passions. In this respect he appears to have more in common with Rabelais than with the classical utopianists. He is close to Marxian socialism, again, in the important place assigned in his ideal world to aesthetic experience and artistic creation.

Fantastic though some of his answers were, Fourier posed a real and important problem: as men are endowed with different desires and with aggressive and selfish impulses, how are these natural rivalries to be turned into constructive channels instead of leading to social antagonism? Unlike most utopianists, Fourier saw the remedy in terms of a new social order and not of transforming human nature. He believed that the conflict of interests was a universal law and that it was no use trying to prevent it, but that society must be so organized that conflict invariably led to harmony. He thought it useless to contemplate a general levelling and the equalization of man, and from this point of view he disagreed with both Saint-Simon and Owen; the idea of complete equality and community of goods seemed to him chimerical. He was convinced, however, that partial reforms of civilization were no good. Society must be transformed root and branch, or nothing would be changed; yet he believed that this transformation could be brought about by the mere force of example.

Fourier's disciples were not interested in the religious and cosmological trappings of his system, but they upheld the view that political struggles could not lead to any change and that it was only social reform that counted. They tried in various ways to modify Fourier's ideas in the direction of realism. Workers' consumer co-operatives were an outcome of his system, as were attempts to establish producer co-operatives in which the workers were shareholders.

Victor Considérant published Fourierist journals (*Le Phalanstère*, 1832–4, and *La Phalange*, 1836–49) and tried to start model colonies in Texas (many utopians sought to put their theories into practice in the New World, including Owen, Cabet, and Weitling). Another disciple of Fourier's was Flora Tristan (1803–44), an early feminist known for the amorous adventures described in her autobiography.

6. Proudhon

PIERRE JOSEPH PROUDHON (1809–65) is noteworthy among the early socialists for the many directions in which his influence extended, a fact largely due to the incoherence of his writings and the contradictions they contain. His lifelong passion for social justice was not equalled by his education (he was largely self-taught) or powers of historical analysis. Born at Besançon, the son of a brewery workman, he was sent to school by benefactors and became a printer. Subsequently he received a scholarship and migrated to Paris. In 1840 he published the pamphlet *Qu'est-ce que la propriété?*, which aroused fury and admiration in equal measure. Henceforth, to his pride, he was identified with the slogan 'Property is theft', though these exact words had in fact been used by Brissot before the Revolution. He was tried and acquitted, and soon published two further pamphlets on the same subject (*Lettre à M. Blanqui sur la propriété*, 1841; *Avertissement aux propriétaires*, 1842), for which he was again tried and acquitted. Until 1847 he earned his living as the agent of a transport firm, and in these years published two important books: *De la création de l'ordre dans l'humanité, ou Principes d'organisation politique* (1843) and the lengthy *Système des contradictions économiques, ou Philosophie de la misère* (1846). The latter work provoked a crushing reply from Marx entitled *Misère de la philosophie* (1847). Marx had met Proudhon and, in the course of long conversations, imparted to him, or so he claimed, the ideas of Hegelian philosophy. Proudhon did not know German, but he may also have heard about Hegel from the lectures and books of Heinrich Ahrens, who was then teaching in Paris.

After the Revolution of 1848 Proudhon went into politics in the hope of persuading the republican government to enact his programme of social reform. In June he was elected to the constituent assembly, where he became the chief representative of the Left; however, he was shortly sentenced to three years' imprisonment for articles criticizing Louis Napoleon. He continued to work in prison, and in 1851 published *L'Idée générale de la révolution au XIXe siècle*. After the *coup d'état* in December of that year he hoped for a while that he might use the Prince-President to carry out his socialist plans. Undeterred by failure, poverty, and obloquy he continued to agitate and published numerous writings. In 1858 he was again sentenced to three years' imprisonment for his large work *De la justice dans la révolution et dans l'église*, but escaped by fleeing to Belgium. Four years later he was expelled from Belgium and returned to France, where he again attempted unsuccessfully to found a party and a literary organ. He died at Passy.

Proudhon, as he admitted, never reread his own works and did not seem aware of their contradictions. His plan belongs to the category of socialist utopias in so far as it is purely normative and invokes ideals of justice and equality, but he sought to found it on an analysis of contemporary economic life and to assess the possibility of change in practical terms. It was he who coined the expression 'scientific socialism'.

Proudhon believed in a 'natural' social harmony and in the inalienable rights of man, which were violated by the existing economic system: the right to freedom, equality, and the sovereignty of the individual. These were part of man's destiny as prescribed by the will of God (though elsewhere Proudhon represents himself as God's enemy). The system of competition, inequality, and exploitation is incompatible with human rights, and economists who confine themselves to describing it are ratifying a state of chaos. However, the contradictions of the system cannot be simply removed by an act of synthesis. Proudhon, in his limited acquaintance with Hegel's dialectic, was especially attracted by the well-known schema of thesis, anti-thesis, and synthesis; this in fact plays quite a secondary role in Hegel's philosophy, but has always appealed to the imagination of those who know little of it. In Proudhon's opinion, the Hegelian 'synthesis' by which the terms of a contradiction are assimilated is thought of in such a way as logically to precede those terms. The belief that all contradictions are resolved by the synthesizing movement of progress is the foundation of Hegel's cult of the state and of the absolutism which subordinates the value and dignity of the human personality to the state apparatus. To this logic Proudhon opposes his own negative dialectic based on the view that antagonistic terms are not dissolved in synthesis, but balance each other without ceasing to be distinct; such balance, moreover, is not an inevitable law of progress but only a possibility of which people may or may not succeed in taking advantage. Men and women are not instruments of progress, working itself out independently of their will; if progress occurs, it is the result of human effort.

Despite Marx's scornful criticism, it is not the case that Proudhon regarded actual social conditions and economic forces as the embodiment of abstract philosophical categories antecedent to social reality. On the contrary, he is at pains to state that the intellectual organization of social reality in abstract categories is secondary to that reality. The first determinant of human existence is productive work, while intellectual activity is the outcome of such work. If spiritual life has become alienated from its true origins, and if ideas are not aware that their source lies not in themselves but in the world of labour, this is a symptom of an illness in society that must be cured.

However, 'labour' in Proudhon is a normative as well as a descriptive category. His criticism of property is based on the moral indignation aroused by unearned income. 'Property is theft' may sound like a call to do away with all private property, but Proudhon was far from actually being a communist. When he sets out to prove in his pamphlet that 'property is a physical and mathematical impossibility', what he really has in mind is that the system which permits the enjoyment of unearned income is immoral and leads to social contradictions. To draw dividends, interest, rent, etc. on the mere ground that one possesses capital is as though one were creating something out of nothing. It is irrelevant whether the property-owner performs productive work or not; if he does, he is entitled to a proper reward, but anything he enjoys over and above this, merely as an owner of wealth, represents a theft from other workers. Property in a monopolistic form, i.e. the privilege of unearned income, is a source of inequality and wrong and destroys personal life; it owes its origin to violence, of which it is the crystallization. The antithesis of a system based on property, however, is not communism but the abolition of incomes not justified by labour, i.e. a society in which goods are exchanged among producers at a rate determined by the amount of labour that has gone into them.

In this respect Proudhon claims to modify the theories of Ricardo and Adam Smith. Ricardo held that labour was the only measure of value, and the market value of any product was a crystallization of the man-hours required to manufacture it; the proceeds were then shared out between capitalists (in the form of return on capital), landowners (as rent), and workers (as wages). This led British socialist reformers of the 1820s and 1830s to point out that the immediate producer of goods was at the same time the only creator of value, and that he was entitled to the whole of the value he created; it was equally unjust that goods were manifestly not exchanged according to their value and that some people enjoyed what they had not created. Proudhon for his part did not entirely accept this naïve interpretation of Ricardo, but he accepted its ultimate consequence. His view was that none of the three factors of production—tools, land, and labour—created value by itself, but only all three together. Tools and land had no productive force without labour, but the mere expenditure of energy was unproductive too unless it were used to change the face of nature by means of tools. The sea, the fisherman, and his net are all needed before we can have fish to eat. Present-day economy, however, was based on the false premiss that capital (tools and machinery) or land are in themselves productive forces, so that the owners of land, capital, or buildings are entitled to charge for their use. In a just economy this could not be, nor could it happen that goods were bought and sold in accordance with the fluctuations of supply and demand instead of at their true value. As to what that value is, Proudhon is not altogether clear. On the one hand he says it depends on utility, on the other that it derives from all three factors of production, or again from labour alone. But the guiding principle of his economic Utopia is clear, even if its theoretical foundation is shaky. What it requires is that each person should receive, from the products of others' labour, the exact equivalent of what he himself produces, and this equivalence must be measured in hours of work. Unearned income must be abolished, and a system of exchange created on the basis of the number of work-hours embodied in a given product, so that each producer receives an income sufficient to buy what he himself produces.

Thus property in the sense of monopoly is done away with, but not in the sense of the producer's right to use the means of production as he wishes—a right which is the condition of personal freedom and individual sovereignty. The concentration of wealth in the hands of a few, and the resulting pauperization of the working masses, can only be remedied by the abolition of monopoly income. The Malthusians are mistaken in regarding overpopulation as the cause of poverty, for overpopulation is relative to the quantity of resources shared among the non-property-owning classes. It cannot be cured so long as goods are not exchanged on a basis of equivalence and the working man's wage will only buy part of what he produces. In such conditions, no matter how many people emigrate from a country it will still be overpopulated in the sense that the masses will be in a state of impoverishment.

It thus appears that Proudhon (like Fourier, though his moral and philosophical reasons are quite different) does not really wish to abolish property but to generalize it. Communism, he believed (having chiefly Cabet and Blanc in mind), would never be compatible with the dignity of the individual and the values of family life; its outcome would be universal poverty and the suffocating mediocrity of a regimented existence. The advocates of communism were power-thirsty fanatics who aimed to set up an omnipotent state on the basis of public property. Far from abolishing the harmful effects of property, the communists would carry it to an absurd extreme: the individual, in their system, would have no property, but the whole lawlessness of its use would be conferred upon the state, which would own the country's wealth and the bodies of its citizens as well. The lives, talents, and aspirations of human beings would, at a stroke, become state property, and the monopoly principle, the source of all social evil, would be intensified to the utmost. Communism, in short, had nothing to offer but the extremity of police despotism.

In order to ensure 'equivalent exchange' and eliminate competition, the first necessity was to reorganize the credit system and do away with interest, which was an especial cause of injustice. Proudhon proposed to create a people's exchange bank which would make interest-free loans to small producers and thus turn the whole of society into property-owners, assuring them of freedom, equality, and a fair share in the fruits of their own activity. The bank would issue bonds or coupons which would serve as a means of exchange between producers on the principle 'To each according to his labour'. From some of Proudhon's writings it might be inferred that his ideal was a petty-bourgeois community of small individual producers, as the only way to ensure social justice. However, it appears elsewhere that he did not contemplate a return from mechanized industry to craftsmanship. He was concerned rather with what he called 'industrial democracy', i.e. that the workers should retain control over the means of production. Productive units must be the collective property of all those employed in them, and the whole of society would consist of a federation of producers, both industrial and agricultural. This, among other things, would resolve the contradiction inherent in machinery, which on the one hand was a triumph of the human spirit over matter, but on the other hand spelt unemployment, low wages, overproduction, and the ruin of the working class. The plan would also resolve the contradiction in the division of labour, which was an instrument of progress yet which degraded human beings into mere parts of themselves.

The new 'mutualistic' society would thus reconcile, for the first time in history, property with equality and freedom with co-operation. Proudhon made light of purely political problems, regarding the social issue as the only important one. In his early writings he takes an anarchistic view of the state as an instrument of the possessing classes, to be replaced by a system of free agreements among economic co-operatives. Later he came to acknowledge the need for state power, not as the weapon of a class but as the organizer of production for the common good. His ideal, however, continued to be decentralized production and a state consisting of a loose federation of communities.

For the translation of his dreams into reality Proudhon relied neither on political nor on economic action by the proletariat. He was opposed to revolutions and even strikes, on the ground that violent action against the 'haves' would lead to disorder and despotism and would only exacerbate class hostility. He believed that, as his ideals were rooted in human nature and their realization would be no more than the fulfilment of human destiny, he could reasonably direct his appeal to all classes without distinction. In several places he invites the bourgeosie to take the lead in bringing about the desired reform, and he also relied from time to time on the state as an auxiliary factor. He continued for many years to believe in co-operation among different classes. However, in his posthumous work *De la capacité politique des classes ouvrières* (1865) he reverted to the idea of the uniqueness of the proletariat and called for a combination of the economic and the political struggle (and, as before, a boycott of state institutions). On the other hand, his theories show no trace of internationalism: his plans for reform are geared to French conditions, he had no quarrel with French national values, and in one work (*La Guerre et la paix*, 1861) he even glorified war as a strengthener of moral fibre and developer of the highest virtues.

Proudhon's work as a whole presents a chaotic and incoherent aspect, and its inconsistencies were fully reflected in its subsequent influence. Marx, who greeted his first publication as a political event comparable with Sieyès's *Qu'est-ce que le Tiers Etat?*, was mercilessly sarcastic at the expense of *La Philosophie de la misère*, reproaching Proudhon with ignorance of economics, the fanciful use of misunderstood Hegelian schemas, a moralistic conception of socialism, and a reactionary petty-bourgeois Utopia. Proudhon regarded this attack as a farrago of coarse slander, misrepresentation and plagiarism, but he did not join issue with Marx in public. There was clearly a wide difference between them as regards the interpretation of economic life, their ideas of the future of socialism, and their choice of political tactics.

While Marx's criticism was unjust and dishonest in some respects, he was intellectually far superior to Proudhon, who had all the faults of the clever autodidact: self-assurance, unawareness of the limitations of his knowledge, incomplete or desultory reading, lack of skill in selecting and organizing material, and the hasty condemnation of authors whom, for the most part, he did not properly understand. Nevertheless, his influence was of considerable duration. It was clearly felt in the French syndicalist movement of the 1860s, which rejected political action and hoped to liberate the workers by organizing co-operatives and credit on a mutual basis. Most of the French members of the First International, notably Tolain and Fribourg, were Proudhonists and upheld the principle of 'mutuality' in preference to strikes, let alone political revolution. Proudhon also exerted a strong influence over Bakunin, particularly from the anarcho-syndical point of view, and many of his followers were active in the Paris Commune; he was also looked up to by later anarchists such as Kropotkin. In the years before the First World War his teaching was acknowledged by the Action Française monarchists under Charles Maurras, who perceived in it the spirit of the first counter-revolutionary ideologists, de Maistre and Antoine de Rivarol: the defence of individual and family property, French patriotism and the praise of war, domestic virtues and a patriarchal system (together with the natural inferiority of women), the decentralization of power, hostility to the unification of Germany and Italy (Proudhon was also opposed to the cause of Polish independence), and finally racism and anti-Semitism. Georges Sorel, the advocate of revolutionary syndicalism, invoked the authority of Proudhon, who opposed strikes on principle.

After the Paris Commune there was no 'Proudhonism' properly so called in the workers' movement itself, but particular ideas and proposals featured in French socialism for a considerable time. Anti-centralist and anti-etatistic tendencies are part of Proudhon's heritage; the objection to communism as a system of extreme political and economic centralization is a theme that he implanted in the French workers' movement and that has retained its actuality from his time onwards. He originated the idea of 'industrial democracy' and also what is called *ouvriérisme*—the tendency to disparage purely political and parliamentary action, to mistrust intellectuals in the workers' movement, and to look with suspicion on all ideologies that do not serve the immediate material interests of the proletariat.

7. *Weitling*

THE works of Wilhelm Weitling (1808–71) stand out amid the communist utopias of the 1840s not because he was in any sense a forerunner of Marx, but because he was himself a member of the working class and therefore a better exponent of its attitude at the time than were theorists belonging to the privileged classes. His form of communism was less close to Babouvism than to the German anabaptists of the early sixteenth century.

After an impoverished childhood, Weitling left his native Magdeburg at an early age and earned his living as an itinerant tailor. His travels took him to Vienna, Paris, and Switzerland. Paris was at that time the home of thousands of working-class German *émigrés*, and Weitling made contact with two clandestine communist organizations, the League of Outlaws (Bund der Geächteten) and its offshoot the League of the Just (Bund der Gerechten). In 1838 he published in Paris a pamphlet in German on *Humanity as it is and as it ought to be* (*Die Menschheit wie sie ist und wie sie sein sollte*). Fearing prosecution he fled to Switzerland, where he published *Guarantees of Harmony and Freedom* (*Garantien der Harmonie und Freiheit*; 1842) and *The Gospel of a Poor Sinner* (*Das Evangelium eines armen Sunders; 1843*); the latter earned him some months' imprisonment at Zurich. He later went to London and collaborated for a time with Karl Schapper, the leading spirit in German *émigré* worker organizations there. By this time his writings were known throughout Europe, but their religious and prophetic strain was equally uncongenial to the more down-to-earth workers' leaders and to sophisticated theorists. In the spring of 1846, on his return to the Continent, Weitling encountered Marx, who was at Brussels organizing a liaison centre for European communist groups. The meeting was a disaster, as Marx attacked the self-taught worker with the arrogance of an intellectual, accusing him of ignorance and naïvety; Weitling, for his part, thought that having shared the sufferings of the proletariat he was able to understand its position and prospects better than a doctrinaire scholar. After a short visit to America Weitling returned in time to take part in the 1848 Revolution in Berlin, after which he emigrated to America for good.

Weitling's works are a typical example of primitive evangelical communism, in the form of sermons on justice and the need to rebel against tyranny. They make ample use of everything in the Gospels that can be turned against the rich and the oppressor, and present a picture of Christ as a communist urging the destruction of the system of exploitation and injustice. The world is governed by the selfishness of the rich, while the workers who create their wealth live in poverty and insecurity. It is not machines that are to blame: in a just society technical progress would be a blessing, but as things are it makes the poor worse off than before. The real cause of social misery is the unequal distribution of goods and obligations and the craving for luxury. When wealth is held in common and all are obliged to work, all evil will disappear in a twinkling; working hours will be greatly shortened, and work will be a delight instead of a curse. There will be no money or accumulation of wealth; class differences will vanish, all benefits of body and soul will be available to everyone. This is the true message of Christianity. Not surprisingly, the Gospel teaching has been distorted and falsified by kings and priests who have used it to defend their own privileges; but the time has come to unmask their imposture and to build a new world of freedom, equality, and Christian love. We must not expect governments and capitalists, however, to recognize this ideal and bring it about of their own accord; the workers can rely only on themselves and their own strength. From the medieval preachers of the millennium, Weitling takes over the division of history into three ages: the ancient times of primitive communism, the present era of private property, and the communism of the future. He describes in some detail the earthly paradise in which there will be no hatred or envy, no crime or evil desires. Men will be brothers again, and the national languages that divide them will die out within three generations. As all will have equal obligations, wealth and luxury will be accessible to all. Anyone, for instance, who wishes to wear different clothes from those provided by the community will be able to afford them by working overtime, especially as the compulsory working day will soon be no longer than three hours.

In this way Weitling naïvely reflected the current notions and day-dreams of the poor. Marx, inevitably, was irritated by his lay-preacher's tone. Yet Weitling imparted to the German working class something of the ethos of medieval chiliasm, and, while he could contribute nothing to the scientific analysis of capitalism, undoubtedly helped to awaken the rudimentary class-consciousness of the proletariat in his country.

8. Cabet

IF Weitling embodies the traditions of sectarian revolutionism of the pre-capitalist era, Étienne Cabet (1788–1856) provided the early industrial age with a specimen of a classic literary genre in his utopian description of a communist island.

Cabet, who was trained as a lawyer, took part in the Revolution of 1830, and his political and literary activity belongs almost entirely to the period of the July Monarchy. In 1839–40 he published a four-volume *Histoire populaire de la Révolution française*. In 1840 his best-known work, *Voyage en Icarie*, appeared under a pseudonym in England, where he had emigrated for fear of prosecution and where he was influenced by Owen's ideas. On returning to France he resumed publication of the journal *Le Populaire*, advocating non-revolutionary communism as the teaching of Christ. He emigrated to America at the beginning of 1849 and established communist settlements in Texas and later in Illinois; one of these lasted for several decades. He died at Saint Louis.

Cabet's 'Icaria' is an egalitarian community with some totalitarian features, like many utopias of the Renaissance and Enlightenment. Since inequality is the cause of all social evils and can only be remedied by holding goods in common, and since the equality of rights and duties is commanded by 'true' human nature and by the Christian faith, it follows that in the ideal society there is no private property and no monetary system. All social production is the work of a single organism of which individuals are parts. All are equally obliged to work according to their powers and to share in the general revenue according to their needs. The community must do its best to see that everyone eats the same food, wears the same clothes, and lives in the same kind of dwelling; obligatory living standards are laid down by the authorities, and all towns look alike. The people as a whole is the sovereign power in its territory, and elects for a limited period administrators to look after production. There are no parties or political clubs (there would be nothing for them to do), and the written word is strictly supervised to prevent any danger to morale. All this is brought about without violence and without a revolution. Cabet expressly dissents from Babeuf and believes that revolutions, conspiracies, and *coups* have brought mankind more unhappiness than gain. Since the perfect society is based on the dictates of natural law and all men are equally partakers in it, it would be a fatal mistake to inaugurate it with force, oppression, and hatred. Rich men and oppressors are the victims of a faulty social system, and their prejudices must be cured by education and not repression. The better world is not to be brought about by violence and conspiracy, but by gradual reform and through a transitional system which will merge into the ideal society of the future.

Among Cabet's other works are *L'Ouvrier, ses misères actuelles, leur cause et leur remède* (1845); *Comment je suis communiste* (1845); and *Le Vrai Christianisme suivant Jésus-Christ* (1846). Together with 'Icaria', they have all the attributes of utopianism in the pejorative sense generally given to this term in Marxist literature. However, as a widely read writer in a popular style, he did much to spread communist ideals: he had no influence whatever on Marx, but helped to acquaint French readers with the basic values of communism.

9. Blanqui

IN the history of socialism Blanqui is of importance not so much as a theoretician but because he transmitted the heritage of Babouvism to the generation of 1848 and its successors, thus providing a link between the Jacobin Left and the nineteenth-century radicals and introducing the idea of revolutionary conspiracy into the workers' movement. He was also the originator of the idea (though not the phrase) of a 'dictatorship of the proletariat', to be exercised in its name by an organized minority.

The son of a Girondin, Louis-Auguste Blanqui (1805–81) studied law and medicine in Paris. He became acquainted with the various socialist doctrines that were going about, and took an active part in the July Revolution. In the thirties he organized clandestine societies of a radical-democratic nature, inclining more and more to socialism. He was put on trial in January 1832 and made a celebrated speech of accusation rather than defence, proclaiming the just war of the proletariat against the rich and the oppressor. He was imprisoned for a year, after which he resumed conspiratorial activity and led an unsuccessful revolt against the monarchy in May 1839. Sentence of death was passed, but commuted to life imprisonment. Liberated by the 1848 Revolution, he became one of the chief leaders of the Paris working class, but was soon behind bars again. He was released in 1859 for a brief period, but spent most of the sixties in gaol. Under Thiers's regime he was released, and again arrested in March 1871; he was elected *in absentia* to the leadership of the Paris Commune, in whose ranks his followers were the most active and resolute faction. He remained in prison till 1879, and thereafter continued to agitate for the remaining two years of his life.

Those of Blanqui's writings that appeared during his lifetime were of a more propagandist than theoretical character, except for the philosophical work *L'Eternité par les astres* (1872). This was based on the mechanistic materialism of the Enlightenment and put forward the Stoic notion of the unceasing repetition of worlds—the state of the universe is entirely determined by the

arrangement of its material particles, and, as the number of such arrangements is finite, each one must repeat itself an infinite number of times in the
course of history. In 1885 the two-volume *Critique sociale* appeared posthumously. Blanqui's critique of capitalism does not go beyond the usual rhetoric
of his day and is fairly simplistic on the economic side. He shared the view that
inequality and exploitation occur because goods are not exchanged at their
'true' value as determined by labour-content; as to the future communist society, he has no more than generalities to offer. His chief role in the history of
socialist movements is that he inculcated the importance of revolutionary
organization and helped to improve the technique of conspiracy. The term
Blanquism' in socialist parlance came to mean much the same as 'revolutionary voluntarism'—that is to say, the belief that the success of a communist
movement does not depend on 'objective' economic circumstances, that a
properly organized conspiratorial group may seize power if the political situation is favourable, and that it may then proceed to exercise a dictatorship on
behalf of the working masses and establish a communist system regardless of
other social conditions. 'Blanquism' in this sense was a pejorative label affixed
by reformists to revolutionaries, notably in Russia after the split in the social
democratic party in 1903, when the Mensheviks accused Lenin of following a
non-Marxist, conspiratorial strategy of revolution.

10. Blanc

BLANQUI and Blanc were the nineteenth-century protagonists of two sharply
opposed tendencies in the socialist movement, both of which are contrary to
Marxism. Blanqui believed in the all-conquering force of the revolutionary will
embodied in an armed conspiracy, while Blanc trusted that gradual reform by
the state would abolish inequality, exploitation, crises and unemployment. The
former doctrine is derived from Babouvism; the latter from Saint-Simon, with
some attenuation as regards democracy and the take-over of all means of production by the state. Blanqui's ideas were adopted by Tkachev and afterwards
by Lenin; those of Blanc by Lassalle and the modern social democrats. The former was a conspirator, the latter a reformer and scholar. Lenin was accused of
'Blanquism' by Plekhanov and Martov, and retorted on many occasions
between the February and the October Revolution by comparing the attitude
of his Menshevik opponents to that of Blanc in 1848, with his indecision,
proneness to compromise, and lack of revolutionary will-power.

Louis Blanc (1811–82) studied in Paris under the Restoration and in 1839
founded the *Revue du progrès*, in which he published in instalments *L'Organisation du travail*, one of the most popular socialist texts of the 1840s. Besides
major works on the revolutions of 1789 and 1848, the Empire, and the July

Monarchy, he published *Le Socialisme. Droit au travail* (1848) and many articles on political and social questions. He was a member of the Provisional Government in 1848 and put forward an extensive programme of reforms and public works to overcome unemployment and poverty. After the savage repression of the June insurrection the right wing accused him of responsibility for the outbreak (although he had hoped to prevent riots by reforms); he fled the country and spent the next two decades in England, returning in 1870 after the collapse of the Second Empire. His attempts to reconcile the Commune and Versailles brought on him the obloquy of both sides. He was a deputy of the moderate republican Left from 1876 until his death, and in 1879 inspired the law granting amnesty to the Communards.

His classic work, *L'Organisation du travail*, argued that revolution was inevitable, but by this he meant radical social reform and not violent political change. Unlike the utopianists with their detailed plans for a perfect social order, Blanc set out to be a practical reformer and to indicate what steps might be taken on the basis of the existing state of affairs. He did not want to provoke a violent upheaval, but to prevent one; however, an explosion was bound to occur soon if the starving, desperate masses could not find jobs, and the most urgent need was to cure unemployment. The system based on unimpeded competition among entrepreneurs led infallibly to crises, poverty, ignorance and crime, the barbarous exploitation of children, and the decay of family life. Unless Malthus's doctrine was to be applied by simply killing off workers' children in excess of a certain number, the state must use all its power to carry out social reform, of which political reform was a necessary prerequisite. History had shown that violent revolutions whose leaders started with no definite plan but imagined that they could work one out after seizing power resulted merely in pointless slaughter: it sufficed to compare 1789 with 1793 and the following years. The proposals of Owen, Saint-Simon, and Fourier contained many useful ideas but were lacking in practical sense, and the changes they advocated could not be put into effect in a short time. What could be done was for the state to assume control over production immediately, and to put an end by degrees to unbridled competition. A grand design for industry, based on public property, should be set on foot with the aid of a national loan; workers whose earnings depended on productivity and the success of the concern they worked for would display far more energy than when driven by private capitalists. The competition between socialized and private enterprises would soon be resolved in favour of the former, which would produce better articles more cheaply. No more competition, no more crises, no more so-called overpopulation; technical progress, instead of harming the workers' interests, would lessen the weight of toil and shorten the working day. Free compulsory education would bring benefits to all. Wage rates would have to be differentiated for some time to come, as faulty education had so conditioned people that they had to be tempted to work harder. The administrative hierarchy would be elective, and the units of production would enjoy autonomy. The right to work would be universally recognized as the basic principle of social organization.

Blanc may justly be considered one of the chief precursors of the welfare state. He believed that it was possible, without violence or mass expropriation, to carry out peaceful economic reforms within a system of political and industrial democracy which would eliminate poverty and harmful competition and would gradually lead to social equality and to the socialization of means of production. Of all the writers discussed in this chapter he was certainly the least 'utopian' in the usual sense, and indeed the only one whose ideas proved to some extent workable—apart from the idea of political dictatorship, which became a reality but not for the purposes that its authors intended.

11. Marxism and 'utopian socialism'

As MAY be seen from this rapid survey, the socialist writers of the first half of the nineteenth century can be classified in various ways. We may oppose reformists to conspirators, novelists to theoreticians, democrats to advocates of revolutionary despotism, and working-class leaders to philanthropists. On the other hand, the division into those whose philosophy is based on eighteenth-century materialism and those, such as Weitling, Cabet, and Lamennais, who invoke Christian values, is not essential. In both cases their Utopia is founded on the premiss that all human beings possess the same dignity by virtue of their humanity, and that, whatever the innate differences among individuals, they are identical as far as their rights and duties are concerned. This conception of human nature is both descriptive and normative. We may deduce from it what a man needs, and is entitled to receive, in order to be truly a man, but we know in advance that the answer will be the same for every individual. The idea of human nature presupposes equality, whatever its other implications may turn out to be.

The conception of human nature is at the same time a description of man's proper calling. Throughout utopian literature it is assumed that men are intended to live in a state of equality and mutual love, and that exploitation, oppression, and conflict of all kinds are contrary to nature's ordinance. The question of course arises: how can it be, in that case, that men have lived for centuries in a manner at variance with their true destiny? This is the hardest question to answer from the utopian point of view. Even if we suppose that somebody at some time happened to devise the system of private property, which would otherwise not have been instituted, how are we to explain the fact that his crazy and inhuman notion was unanimously adopted? If we lay the blame on 'evil desires', how is it that such desires came to dominate society? If it is man's nature to live in amity and equality with his fellows, why is it that we seldom or never find him doing so? How can a majority of mankind 'truly' want something which, as a matter of experience, they do not want? On the utopian view, the whole of human history is a monstrous calamity, and incomprehensible to boot. For traditional Christianity there is no problem, on account of the doctrine of original sin and the corruption of humanity at its source. But the Utopians of this period, even when they called themselves Christians, did not believe in original sin; they were thus deprived of this explanation, and had no other to offer. They wanted the good, but evil was to them inconceivable and inexplicable. They fell back, without exception, on a confused idea of human nature as something already 'given' and not a mere arbitrary norm (for in that case there would be no reason to expect people to conform to it)—a kind of reality or 'essence', dormant in every individual.

Thinking in this way, the utopians were naturally attracted to the idea of communist despotism. If we know that human nature is fulfilled by the communist system, it is of no importance, in establishing this system, what proportion of humanity wants to accept it. Jean-Jacques Pillot, at the end of his pamphlet *Ni châteaux ni chaumières* (1840), puts the question 'What if people do not want this?', and replies 'What if the inmates of Bicêtre [lunatic asylum] refuse to have baths?' If people are out of their minds, they must be cured by force. The utopians did not put the further question, which calls to mind Poe's story of Professor Tarr and Dr. Fether—how do we decide which are the lunatics and which are the keepers? Is a man really entitled to claim that everyone is out of step except himself? To say that mankind should decide its own destiny may mean that history is to be left in the hands of lunatics, but if we disagree with our fellow men we must prove that we ourselves are sane. As long as it was possible to appeal to the divine will as an irrefragable authority, the matter was simple enough. The utopians do so appeal when it suits them; but, as we know, Scripture has been used for centuries to justify inequality and the hierarchical order of society.

The same objection could be put to all the utopians, not only the advocates of communist despotism, and it was in fact put to Owen by Marx: who is to educate the educators? In the answer to this question lies the principal difference between Marx's Utopia and those of all his predecessors, between the heir of Hegelian phenomenology and the heirs of French materialism.

.   .   .

IT is not difficult to select from the works of the utopian socialists a series of propositions that seem to anticipate the most important ideas of Marx, though they are not set out in the same order or expounded in the same way. They comprise three main topics: historiosophical premises, the analysis of capitalist society, and the depiction of the future socialist order.

Under the first two headings we may list the following points:

No essential change is possible in the system of the distribution of wealth without a complete change in the system of production and property relations.

Throughout history, constitutional changes have been conditioned by technological ones.

Socialism is the outcome of inevitable historical laws.

The organization of capitalist society is in contradiction with the state of development of productive forces.

Wages, under capitalism, tend naturally to remain at the minimum level consistent with survival.

Competition and the anarchic system of production lead inevitably to exploitation, overproduction crises, poverty, and unemployment.

Technical progress leads to social disaster, not for inherent reasons but because of the property system.

The working class can only free itself by its own efforts.

Political freedom is of little value if the mass of society is enslaved by economic pressure.

As regards the socialist future—whether this goes by the name of Harmony, mutualism, or the industrial system—we may enumerate the following ideals:

The abolition of private ownership of the means of production.

A planned economy on a national or world scale, subordinated to social needs and eliminating competition, anarchy, and crises.

The right to work, as a basic human entitlement.

The abolition of class divisions and social antagonisms.

The whole-hearted, voluntary co-operation of associated producers.

Free education of children at the public expense, including technical training.

The abolition of the division of labour and the degrading consequences of specialization; instead, the all-round development of the individual, and free opportunity for the use of human skills in every direction.

Abolition of the difference between town and country, while permitting industry to concentrate as at present.

Political power to be replaced by economic administration; no more exploitation of man by man, or rule of one man over another.

Gradual effacement of national differences.

Complete equality of rights and opportunities as between men and women.

The arts and sciences to flourish in complete freedom.

Socialism as a boon to humanity as a whole; the exploitation of the proletariat as the chief factor tending to bring about socialism.

Impressive as these analogies are, there is a basic difference between Marx and all other socialist thinkers of the first half of the nineteenth century. Moreover, this difference affects the meaning of many ideas which, in themselves, show a striking similarity and no doubt testify to the utopians' influence on Marx's thought. It is often said that he and they were not at variance as regards the end to be attained but only as regards the means, i.e. revolution versus peaceful persuasion; but this is a superficial and misleading view. It is, in fact, incorrect, since Marx never adopts the ethical, normative point of view which first establishes an aim and then seeks the best means of achieving it. On the other hand, it is not the case that he regarded socialism as the inevitable result of historical determination and was not interested in whether it was desirable or not. It is an essential feature of Marx's thought that he avoided both the normative and the purely deterministic approach, and it is in this that he shows himself to be a Hegelian and not a member of the utopian school. The utopians, admittedly, did not always regard socialism as a 'free' ideal; we may find references to historical necessity in Owen, Fourier, and the Saint-Simonists; but they do not probe the question to any depth or indicate how their deterministic fancies are to be reconciled with the conception of socialism as an ideal or as a moral imperative. On the one hand they insist that socialism (or whatever name they give it) is bound, in the nature of things, to conquer the world, on the other they regard its discovery as a happy effect of intellectual genius; and they oscillate between these points of view without seeming to perceive their inconsistency. Again, the utopians are convinced that political changes cannot by themselves bring about the new economic order and the redistribution of wealth; they believe that economic reforms must be achieved by economic action, and in consequence they undervalue politics and reject the prospect of a revolution. The starting-point of their reflections is poverty, especially that of the proletariat, which they are bent on relieving.

Marx's starting-point, however, is not poverty but dehumanization—the fact that individuals are alienated from their own labour and its material, spiritual, and social consequences in the form of goods, ideas, and political institutions, and not only from these but from their fellow beings and, ultimately, from themselves. The germ of socialism in capitalist society consists in the working class's awareness of dehumanization, not of poverty. This comes about when dehumanization has reached its uttermost limit, and in that sense the proletariat's class-consciousness is an effect of historical development. But it is also a revolutionary consciousness, the awareness of the working class that its liberation must come from its own efforts. The proletariat cannot do away with the system of wage-labour and competition by peaceful persuasion, because the consciousness of the bourgeoisie, which is likewise determined by its part in the productive process, prevents it from abandoning its role voluntarily. Dehumanization, although in a different form, is also an attribute of the possessing class, but the privileges that class enjoys prevent it from being clearly aware of its own dehumanized condition, in which it rejoices instead of chafing at it. Socialism is the effect of history in the sense that history gives birth to the revolutionary consciousness of the proletariat, but it is the effect of freedom inasmuch as the act of revolution is free, so that, in the revolutionary workers' movement, historical necessity expresses itself in free action. Revolution, a political act, is the indispensable condition of socialism, for the institutions that purport to represent the community in fact embody the particular interest of the possessing classes and cannot be the instrument by which that interest is overthrown. Civil society, or the collectivity of actual individuals with their private interests, is destined to 'absorb' the ostensible community and turn it into a real one. Free human action cannot bring about a radical change of conditions if it is only a question of ideals and an attempt to reform society from outside; it is constructive only when it proceeds from that society's awareness of itself as a dehumanized society, and this awareness can only arise in the working class, which experiences the acme of dehumanization. It is a demystified consciousness, presenting itself from the outset as awareness of actual reality, and by the same token a revolutionary consciousness, that is to say a practical attempt to change the world by violently destroying the political institutions that protect the existing order. In that consciousness, but not otherwise, historical inevitability and freedom of action are the same: as we read in the *Theses on Feuerbach*, 'The coincidence of the changing of circumstances and of human activity can be conceived and rationally understood only as revolutionary praxis.'

The suggestion that Marx differs from the utopians in soteriology but not in eschatology, i.e. that he more or less shares their ideal of the future while not agreeing that it can be achieved by peaceful means, is thus seen to be erroneous. As a disciple of Hegel he knew that truth is not only a result but also a way. The picture of a harmonious community, a society without conflict in which all human needs are satisfied, and so forth—all this can be found in Marx in similar formulas to those of the utopians. But socialism means more to Marx than a welfare society, the abolition of competition and want, the removal of conditions that make man an enemy to man: it is also, and above all, the abolition of the estrangement between man and the world, the assimilation of the world by the human subject. In the class-consciousness of the proletariat society attains to a state in which there is no longer any opposition between subject and object, educator and pupil, for the act of revolution is one in which society transforms itself by being conscious of its own situation. There is no longer a difference between ideologists above the community, and the community itself; consciousness knows itself to be part of the conditions that have produced it, and it also knows that men's fetters are forged, and can only be broken, by themselves. Socialism is not a mere matter of consumer satisfaction, but the liberation of human forces—the forces of each and every individual, aware that his own energy is likewise social energy. The fact that productive forces determine productive relationships and, through them, political institutions does not mean, in Marx's view, that socialism can be brought about by direct action in the economic field: for political institutions are not simply the outcome of the system of production but are its means of self-defence, and they must be swept away before it can be altered. Socialism, therefore, can only result from a political revolution with a 'social soul'. As we have seen, it is neither an arbitrary goal nor the mere result of history working in the manner of a natural law, but is the outcome of the conscious struggle of dehumanized man to recover his humanity and to make the world a human place again. The proletariat, as the spearhead of that struggle, is not a mere tool of history but a conscious agent; nevertheless, it was necessary for the historical process to dehumanize it completely before the struggle was possible.

12. Marx's critique of Proudhon

MARX's critique of Proudhon in *La Misère de la philosophie* may be summed up under three heads.

In the first place, Proudhon fails to perceive the inevitable consequences of competition and, in his anxiety to eliminate its 'evil aspects', adopts a moralistic point of view at the expense of economic analysis. The same substitution of moral indignation for economic thought appears in the slogan 'Property is theft'—which, moreover, is not accurate in itself, for theft by definition presupposes property. It is a utopian fantasy to hope to establish the true value of commodities in accordance with a labour standard, while maintaining the system of individual production and exchange and therefore of competition. Proudhon constantly confuses labour-time as a standard of value with the value of labour itself. Since labour is itself a commodity (Marx at this stage still held the view that wage-labour is a sale of labour, and not of labour-power as in the final formulation of his theory of surplus value), it is not clear how it, more than any other commodity, can be a standard of value. The true standard of value is labour-time—not the time it actually takes to make a particular article, but the shortest time in which it could be made in present conditions of technology and the organization of production. Competition fixes the price of goods on the basis of socially necessary labour-time, and thus necessarily involves inequality among competing producers. As long as competition exists, there can be no equivalent exchange because, as Marx later argued in more detail, the movement of capital evens out the rate of profit while fixing prices at a level above or below the actual value (it is impossible to maintain prices corresponding to value and at the same time ensure equal profit rates in different branches of production). In competitive conditions, moreover, the system of exchange serves the needs of production and not consumption, and industry does not await demand but creates it. To attempt to maintain private property and competition while abolishing their 'evil aspects' is a moralist's chimera.

Secondly, Marx accuses Proudhon of a reactionary and hopeless endeavour to revive medieval production methods based on individual craftsmanship. The ideal of individual exchange on a value basis is as utopian in the industrial age as is the ideal of abolishing the division of labour in conditions of small-scale production. Marx himself regards the division of labour in its present form as a source of physical and mental degradation, and envisages that it will somehow be abolished; but on Proudhon's view this can only happen if the worker carries out the entire process of producing a given article, i.e. if he reverts to being a craftsman. Industry dominated by competition entails ever-increasing division of labour for the sake of increased output, and one can only imagine its abolition if competition is done away with and production regulated by actual human needs. Proudhon's doctrine is a petty-bourgeois fantasy—a dream of preserving the bourgeoisie while eliminating the proletariat, in other words turning everybody into a bourgeois.

Thirdly, Proudhon attempts to apply Hegelian schemata in a fantastic and arbitrary manner. Having taken over from Hegelian idealism the notion that economic categories are independent historical factors, spiritual forces to which actual phenomena are secondary, he imagines that social reality can be transformed by the intellectual manipulation of categories. But the latter are no more than abstractions, the reflection in human minds of social conditions at a given moment in history; the only reality of social life are human beings, who form links determined by history and then convert them into mental 'categories'. Above all, it is quite wrong and contrary to the Hegelian dialectic to suppose that one can set out to abolish the 'evil aspect' of a particular category while preserving its positive values. The contradictions that belong to each historical era are not ordinary blemishes that can be removed by simply taking thought; they are indispensable conditions of social development and of society's evolution towards maturity.

Suppose that the economists of the feudal era, captivated by all that was good in feudalism—the virtues of chivalry, the harmony of rights and obligations, the patriarchal life of the cities, the flourishing of cottage industry in the villages, the
development of production in guilds, corporations and fraternities—suppose they
had decided to preserve all this and simply remove the blemishes of serfdom, privilege and anarchy, what would have been the result? They would have rooted out all
the elements of conflict and stifled the bourgeoisie at its very origin. They would
have set themselves the absurd task of eliminating history.

Marx here follows the Hegelian interpretation of progress as the result of internal conflict, a process incompatible with the simple elimination of defects.
'Since the dawn of civilization,' Marx writes, 'production has been based on the
antagonism of groups, estates and classes, and finally the antagonism between
accumulated labour and direct labour. Where there is no antagonism there is
no progress. This has been the rule of civilization until our own time. Up to this
very day, class antagonism has been the cause of the development of productive forces.' It was absurd for Proudhon to seek to turn everyone into a capitalist and thereby cure the defects of capitalism—inequality, exploitation, and the
anarchy of production—since this amounted to 'removing' social antagonisms
while retaining their basic cause, or abolishing the proletariat while preserving
the bourgeoisie.

All three of Marx's chief criticisms are aspects of a single idea: the historical process has a dynamic of its own, which is governed by the level of technology ('The hand-mill gives you society with the feudal lord; the steam-mill,
society with the industrial capitalist') and which works itself out by means of
the class struggle. It follows that a social upheaval cannot be brought about by
moralizing, that outworn structures cannot be revived, and that social conflicts
cannot be resolved by eliminating one of the contenders. The struggle must be
allowed to reach its final form, in which both antagonists will give place to a
higher type of organization: the proletariat, in the revolution, will liquidate
itself as a class and by so doing will destroy all class differences.

13. The Communist Manifesto

IN 1847–8 events took place which decisively affected the communist movement and its propaganda on Marxist lines. A group of German communists in
Brussels, with whom Marx collaborated, were in contact with similar bodies in
other countries, including the Bund der Gerechten, which at the end of 1846
had transferred its headquarters from Paris to London. One of its leaders,
Joseph Moll, invited Marx and Engels to join the League and draft a programme: the League at this time was operating on the basis of an eclectic mix-

ture of socialist ideas and lacked a coherent theoretical basis. In June 1847 Engels attended the League's congress in London. On the advice of Marx and Engels its name was changed to The Communist League, and its motto 'All men are brothers' was replaced by the class-conscious slogan 'Proletarians of all countries, unite!' Marx and Engels organized branches in Brussels and Paris respectively, and Engels drew up a programme in question-and-answer form entitled 'Principles of Communism': this dealt with capitalist exploitation and the inevitability of crises and described the future society based on community of goods, political democracy, equal wages, and planned industrial production. The document also spoke of the necessity of a simultaneous political revolution in all civilized countries. At the end of November and beginning of December Marx and Engels both attended the League's second congress in London and were entrusted with the task of composing what became a fundamental text of scientific socialism—the *Manifesto of the Communist Party*. This masterpiece of propagandist literature was first published in February 1848, and in subsequent editions was entitled *The Communist Manifesto*.

The *Manifesto* deals in turn with relations between the bourgeoisie and the proletariat, between the communists and the proletariat, and between communism and existing socialist doctrines. The first section contains the classic sentence: 'The history of all hitherto existing society is the history of class struggles.' After the antagonisms in the ancient world between freeman and slave, patrician and plebeian, after the lords and serfs of the feudal era, the basic structure of the present age consisted in the opposition between the bourgeoisie and the proletariat. Modern society had simplified the class situation: the division into two basic classes was more and more evident and was becoming more and more widespread. The discovery of America and the rise of industry had created a world market and, after long struggles, had given the bourgeoisie a commanding role in political life. The bourgeoisie had accomplished a revolutionary task without precedent by destroying the patriarchal, so-called 'natural' ties between human beings and reducing their mutual relations to the level of unabashed self-interest. It had turned the working man's 'vocation' into wage labour and had impressed a cosmopolitan stamp on trade, industry, and the whole of civilization, breaking down national barriers and involving the world in a breathless rush of technical and cultural progress. 'The bourgeoisie . . . has been the first to show what man's activity can bring about.' But, unlike the dominant classes of earlier times, the bourgeoisie is neither able to preserve the means of production unchanged nor desirous of doing so. It can only exist if technology, and therefore social relations, are being constantly revolutionized. More and more it subordinates agricultural production to itself, concentrates the means of production in general, and organizes, to serve its own interest, national states with uniform legislative systems. But just as the victory of the bourgeoisie was due to the incompatibility of the social and legal institutions of feudal society with the productive forces that evolved in that society, so its downfall will be due to the contradiction between its own technology and the property relationships of capitalism. This contradiction manifests itself in periodic crises of overproduction which are overcome by the destruction of productive forces and the conquest of new markets, but these methods in turn lead to more and graver crises. 'Not only has the bourgeoisie forged the weapons that bring death to itself; it has also called into existence the men who are to wield those weapons—the modern working class, the proletariat.' The workers are obliged to sell themselves to the bourgeoisie at a price equal to the cost of reproducing their labour, i.e. the minimum that will keep them alive; they have become an appendage to the machine. Exploited by manufacturers, tenement owners, tradesmen, and usurers, they rise in revolt, firstly against the new machines which throw them out of jobs and increase their insecurity, then against exploitation by their own employers, and finally against the capitalist system itself. At this stage their struggle becomes a political one, embracing ever-wider areas and uniting the proletariat on a national and then a worldwide basis. The proletariat is the only class that is truly revolutionary. The particular interests of the middle classes—peasants, craftsmen, small traders—are conservative; they would, if they could, arrest the inevitable process whereby capital is centralized and concentrated and they themselves are forced down into the proletariat. They are in a state of gradual disappearance and can only be a revolutionary force in so far as they are proletarianized. The bourgeoisie, as industry develops, creates worse and worse conditions for the workers and thus drives them into solidary, united action. In this way it creates, unconsciously but inevitably, its own grave-digger. The bourgeoisie has proved that it cannot maintain itself as the ruling class and is doomed to destruction. The workers, for their part, can only gain control of productive forces by demolishing the whole system by which wealth has hitherto been acquired. 'The proletarians . . . have nothing of their own to secure and fortify; their mission is to destroy all previous securities for, and insurances of, individual property.'

Communists have no interests apart from those of the proletariat, and they are distinguished from other proletarian parties by the fact that they stand for the proletariat's interest as a whole, irrespective of national differences. They are in advance of the proletarian masses owing to their theoretical understanding of the world in which the struggle is going on. Their aim is to lead the proletariat in the conquest of political power, to destroy the bourgeois property system which enables the capitalist to appropriate others' labour, and to abolish the bourgeoisie and the proletariat as social classes. In addition, the *Manifesto* replies as follows to the accusations most often levelled against communism:

1. 'The abolition of private property will lead to general idleness and the col-

lapse of production.' But private property does not exist today for the masses, yet society exists and maintains itself.

2. 'Communism is a denial of individuality.' Yes—of such individuals as are enabled by the system to use their own property as an instrument for the enslavement of others.

3. 'Communism destroys the family.' It destroys the bourgeois family, based on property-ownership on the one hand and on prostitution and hypocrisy on the other. Big business has destroyed the family life of the proletariat.

4. 'Communism is against nationality.' But the working man has no fatherland, so how can he be deprived of one? In any case the world market is effacing national differences, and the victory of the proletariat will intensify this process. When the exploitation of man by man is abolished we shall also see an end of exploitation, oppression, and enmity among nations. National oppression is the outcome of social oppression.

5. 'Communism seeks to destroy the eternal truths and sublime ideas of religion, ethics, and philosophy.' But all the ideas bequeathed by history are absolute only in so far as exploitation and oppression have persisted despite all changes in political systems. The spiritual output of mankind is as changeable as the conditions of human existence; ideas are permanent in so far as particular social relations have hitherto been permanent. Communism overthrows 'eternal' ideas by destroying the class system which, by existing from time immemorial, gave them the appearance of eternity.

The socialist propaganda of the time is criticized in the *Manifesto* according to its class origin. In the first place there is feudal socialism, which opposes capitalism from the standpoint of the aristocracy ruined by the bourgeois property system (the French legitimists, 'Young England'): invoking the patriarchal bliss of olden times, it attacks the bourgeois for subverting the ancient order and, above all, for creating the revolutionary proletariat. The same may be said of Christian socialism, 'holy water with which the priest consecrates the heart-burnings of the aristocrat'. Petty-bourgeois socialism (Sismondi) reflects the small producers' fear that industry will drive them out of existence. It argues that increased mechanization, the concentration of capital, and the division of labour infallibly lead to crises, poverty, gross inequality, war, and moral disintegration; this is true, but the proposed remedy of a return to the pre-capitalist system of production and exchange, with guilds and a patriarchal peasant economy, is reactionary and useless. As for the 'true socialism' of Grün and other German writers, it is a sentimental tissue of speculation and generalities about mankind regardless of class divisions and the particular interests of the workers. Socialists of this school attract the approval of the feudal classes who still govern Germany by attacking the liberal bourgeoisie which, in that country, is the true vehicle of progress.

Such are the brands of reactionary socialism. Then there is the bourgeois socialism of Proudhon and others, which seeks to preserve existing conditions by eliminating everything that tends to revolutionize society—'to keep the bourgeoisie and get rid of the proletariat'. It relies on philanthropic slogans and administrative reforms, making no effort whatever to abolish the bourgeois property system.

Lastly, utopian socialism or communism as preached by Saint-Simon, Owen, and Fourier, while aware of the class struggle and the oppression of the proletariat, fails to perceive the latter's key historical role and makes it a mere passive object of reformist plans. These theorists reject the prospect of revolution and fix their sights on the community as a whole or on the privileged classes. They have played a useful part in criticizing bourgeois society and advocating reforms, but, having attempted to rise above the actual class struggle, their successors in later generations turn into reactionary sects whose aim is to extinguish class antagonisms and prevent independent political action by the proletariat.

Communists in different countries support various political movements, but only those which aim at a radical transformation of existing conditions. Germany is especially important to them, as the imminent bourgeois revolution in that country will take place against the background of more advanced social conditions, in Europe and even in Germany herself, than did the bourgeois revolutions in France and England: so much so that the German bourgeois revolution 'can only be the direct prelude to a revolution of the proletariat'.

Marx and Engels saw little cause to revise subsequent editions of the *Manifesto* as far as its theoretical bases were concerned. Apart from their oversanguine expectations of revolution in Europe and their failure to foresee developments which could not have been predicted at the time (the *Manifesto* does not mention either Russia or America as potentially revolutionary countries), their later prefaces or amendments only involve one important point of theory: the experience of the Paris Commune convinced them that the revolutionary proletariat cannot capture the state machine and use it for its own purposes, but must start by destroying it.

As regards the controversy with socialists of the earlier part of the century, Engels reverted to this in 1878 in the *Anti-Dühring*, which repeats the *Manifesto*'s main criticisms of utopian socialism. This doctrine, he says, is the product of a situation in which the working class has not yet matured to the point of taking a historical initiative of its own, and appears merely as an oppressed and suffering group and not as the vehicle of social revolution. Utopian socialism is precluded, by the very conditions of its origin, from envisaging socialism as a historical necessity of the present time rather than an ingenious theory, an intellectual windfall which might have occurred at any period. Whenever Marx and Engels, the creators of scientific socialism, revert to the subject of their utopian predecessors they repeat the three basic charges of philanthropism towards the working class, rejection of the prospect of revolution, and the conception of socialism as an accidental theory. To these errors they oppose their own view of socialist theory as the self-awareness of the actual revolutionary initiative of the working class, a free activity which is nevertheless historically necessary. Engels pays tribute to the utopians, however, for the sharpness and boldness of their attack on the contemporary world and the inventiveness of their predictions of the future; he does not look down on them from the height of a superior revelation, since he is aware of the historical conditions that restricted their field of vision.

With the appearance of *The Communist Manifesto*, we may say that Marx's theory of society and his precepts for action had attained completion in the form of a well-defined and permanent outline. His later works did not modify what he had written in any essential respect, but enriched it with specific analyses and transformed what were sometimes no more than aphorisms, slogans, or heads of argument into a massive theoretical structure. We may, therefore, after a short review of relevant historical events, abandon our chronological exposition for one based on subject-matter. Special attention is due, however, to Engels's theory of the dialectic of nature and his interpretation of philosophical materialism, since these may be regarded as a substantive change in Marxism as it existed in the years before 1848. Naturally, the principles that were established then and elaborated later were at no time so expressed as to preclude mutually inconsistent interpretations. As the socialist movement and socialist theory progressed, it often happened that Marx's views on this or that subject—historical determinism, the theory of classes, of the state, or of revolution—were understood differently by different people. This is the natural fate of all social theories without exception—at all events those that have been a real force in politics and social development, and from this point of view no modern theory can rival Marxism. However, the most important controversies as to the exact interpretation of Marx's theory took place after his own lifetime.

XI

The Writings and Struggles of
Marx and Engels after 1847

1. Developments in the 1850s

THE PUBLICATION of *The Communist Manifesto* coincided with the political convulsions of 1848. After the February Revolution in Paris the Belgian government adopted repressive measures against the *émigré* revolutionaries; Marx was expelled from Brussels and returned to Paris, where he worked for the German revolutionary cause on behalf of the Communist League. After the Vienna and Berlin revolutions in March many German *émigrés* made their way from France to Germany; Marx and Engels established themselves in Cologne, where communist propaganda was most active, and from June onwards published a newspaper, the *Neue Rheinische Zeitung*, with a programme based on a flysheet previously composed by them, entitled *Demands of the Communist Party in Germany*. These aims were not communistic as such, but radical-democratic and republican: they included the confiscation of large estates, free universal education, a progressive income tax, and the nationalization of railways. The paper, of which Marx was chief editor, condemned the pliant and irresolute attitude of the bourgeoisie and advocated a united Germany under a republican constitution with direct and universal suffrage; it championed the oppressed national minorities, especially the Poles, and called for war with Russia as the mainstay of reaction in Europe. The programme of alliance between the proletariat and the republican bourgeoisie for the sake of a democratic revolution was looked at askance by many German communists, who feared that if the working class did not maintain itself as a separate political entity it would be merely the instrument of a revolution in the bourgeois interest.

The victory of reaction in Europe and the collapse of the Frankfurt parliament put an end to Marx's revolutionary activity in Germany. The *Neue Rheinische Zeitung* closed down in May 1849; Marx was expelled from Prussia and made his way, not without difficulty, back to Paris, where he expected a fresh revolutionary outbreak at any moment. The French government, however, put obstacles in the way of his remaining, and in August, with no money and no means of livelihood, he embarked on a new life of exile in London. He was to spend the rest of his days there, wrestling with poverty, illness, and domestic troubles. Engels settled in Manchester in 1850 and remained there for twenty years, drawing an income from the cotton mill of which his father was co-owner. For many years he supported Marx financially, sacrificing his own literary work in order that his friend might be able to devote himself to academic writing.

Soon after their arrival in London Marx, Engels, and a few friends set about resuscitating the Communist League, which had been dissolved during the revolution. The manifesto they wrote for this purpose advocated a different programme from that of the *Neue Rheinische Zeitung*: it urged that the proletariat should organize itself independently of the republican bourgeoisie and, while supporting all democratic claims, should aim at a state of 'permanent revolution' which would enable it eventually to seize political power. Marx and Engels believed that the growing economic crisis was bound to touch off revolution in Europe, and especially in France, at an early date. When this hope proved vain, the League was condemned to an early demise; it was in fact wound up in 1852. The *Neue Rheinische Zeitung*, with the sub-title *Politisch-ökonomische Revue*, appeared in London for a few months only, in 1849. During the next two decades the European socialist movement subsisted in the margin of political life, but thanks to Marx's efforts it acquired a new theoretical basis which enabled it to spring vigorously into life when conditions changed. During the 1850s Marx reverted to economic studies and did not himself take part in any political organization, though he maintained some links with the Chartist leaders.

The first important work of Marx's to be published during his London period was *The Eighteenth Brumaire of Louis Bonaparte*, an essay on the *coup d'état* of December 1851: it constituted the first number of a New York journal, the *Revolution*, which had been started by Marx's friend Joseph Weydemeyer. The essay formed a sequel to *Class Struggles in France, 1848–50*, which had appeared in London in the *Neue Rheinische Zeitung*; in his new work Marx analysed the class situation which had enabled such a 'mediocrity' as Louis Napoleon to seize power. It is rich in general observations and contains some of Marx's most frequently quoted aphorisms.

The trial of a group of communists in Cologne in 1852, in which evidence was produced purporting to incriminate Marx, provoked him to expose the fabrications of the Prussian police; the most important document, *Revelations concerning the Communist Trial in Cologne*, appeared anonymously at Basle in 1853. From 1851 to 1862 Marx contributed articles on current affairs to the *New York Daily Tribune*, some of which were by Engels though they appeared over Marx's signature. This did not suffice to provide a livelihood, but it helped to mitigate the family's direst poverty. For years on end they were short of money for rent, paper, and footwear; Marx was notoriously incapable of keeping accounts, and Jenny was a regular customer of the London pawnbrokers. Marx at one stage tried for a job as a railway official, but was rejected on account of his execrable handwriting.

Marx's chief occupation during these years, however, was the elaboration of his critique of political economy which had begun with the Paris Manuscripts of 1844. Again and again he believed that he had come to the end of the work, but his restless thoroughness impelled him constantly to seek fresh data and new sources with which to improve the draft. The economic crisis of 1857 prompted him to compose a revised version, but this was never completed and was not published in his lifetime. The Introduction to this work was published in 1903 by Kautsky in *Die Neue Zeit* (Stuttgart), and is Marx's fullest and most important study of the problems of method in the social sciences. The whole work, entitled *Grundrisse der Kritik der politischen Ökonomie* (*Outline of a Critique of Political Economy*), was first published in Moscow in 1939–41, an unpropitious time for academic study. It was republished in East Berlin in 1953, but was not subjected to thorough examination and discussion till the 1960s. It is of interest as showing the continuity of Marx's thought from the Paris Manuscripts to *Capital*; it contains, for instance, a new version of the theory of alienated labour which throws light on the significance of this category in Marx's later work.

In general the text of the *Grundrisse* shows that Marx had not abandoned his anthropological ideas of the 1840s but was attempting to translate them into economic terms. We also know from a letter of his that the method of the work was influenced by a rereading of Hegel's *Logic*, a copy of which had happened to come his way. The Introduction contained a general plan of the work he intended to write, and as this plan is only partially fulfilled in *Capital* there has been discussion as to whether, or how far, he subsequently changed his mind. However, the recent studies of McLellan and others have shown clearly that there is no reason to think he made any essential change. The three volumes of *Capital*, which deal with the theory of value, money, surplus value, and capital accumulation (Volume I), circulation and reproduction (Volume II), and profits, rent, and credit (Volume III), constitute a portion of the structure as originally planned, while the *Grundrisse* is the first sketch, and the only one, covering the whole ground, i.e. it provides the most comprehensive exposition of Marx's economic doctrine that we possess. It contains the first statement of some important ideas that appear in *Capital*—for example, the theory of the average rate of profit and the distinction between constant and variable capital—and also some themes that are not to be found in the later work. Among these—apart from the earliest portion, criticizing Carey and Bastiat— are the observations on foreign trade and the world market and the philosophical passages scattered through the work, in the style of the 1844

Manuscripts. The publication of the *Grundrisse* has not altered the general picture of Marxist doctrine in any important respect, but it has upheld the view of those who believed in the continuity of Marx's philosophical inspiration, and not of those who postulated a radical breach between the anthropological theories of his youth and the economic tenets of his maturer years.

Another economic work of Marx's did see the light of day at this time, viz. *Zur Kritik der politischen Ökonomie (Contribution to a Critique of Political Economy)*, published with Lassalle's help at Berlin in 1859. Here Marx expressed for the first time his theory of value, different from Ricardo's, though he did not develop it to a conclusion. The Preface to this work is one of Marx's most-quoted texts, as it contains the most concise and general formulation of what was later called historical materialism.

In 1859–60 much of Marx's energy was devoted to a polemic with Karl Vogt, a German politician and naturalist who was then teaching at the University of Berne. The immediate cause of the quarrel was that Marx accused Vogt–without much evidence, but, as later events showed, correctly–of intriguing in support of Napoleon III at the time of the Franco-Austrian War. Apart from this, Vogt was the advocate of a crude and vulgar form of materialism ('Thought is a secretion of the brain just as bile is of the liver'). Marx's work *Herr Vogt*, published in 1860, denounced him for intrigue, slander, and double-dealing; it is now, however, of no more than biographical interest.

2. Lassalle

APART from Proudhon, Marx's chief rival as a theoretician in the 1860s was Lassalle, who for many years outclassed him as far as ideological influence in Germany was concerned.

Ferdinand Lassalle (1825–64) was the son of a Jewish trader from Breslau. He studied philosophy and philology in Berlin and Breslau in 1843–6 and intended to embrace an academic career. He became a Hegelian (though not a Young Hegelian), read socialist literature, and decided at an early age that he was destined to be an eminent philosopher and to transform social conditions in Germany. However, his energies were for a long time absorbed by personal affairs. He fell in love with Countess Sophie von Hatzfeld, who was nearly twice his age, and for ten years chivalrously defended her financial interests against her estranged husband in innumerable German courts. In this connection he was arrested early in 1848 for complicity in the theft of certain documents. He was released six months later, but reimprisoned for some months in November for incendiary speeches in support of the revolution. From 1849 to 1857 he lived at Dusseldorf. During this time he corresponded with Marx (they had first met in 1848) and also wrote a large work on Heraclitus (*Die Philosophie*

Herakleitos des Dunklen von Ephesos, 1857); Marx in a letter to Engels, dismissed this as a diluted version of the relevant part of Hegel's *History of Philosophy*. In 1859 Lassalle published a historical drama, *Franz von Sickingen*, on the subject of a sixteenth-century knight who headed a league to spread the Reformation in Germany; his tragic fate was apparently intended to symbolize the defeat of the 1848 Revolution. The work is full of patriotic sentiment and faith in the German mission. In 1860 Lassalle wrote articles on Fichte and Lessing, and in 1861 he published his most important work, *The System of Acquired Rights*—a philosophical, historical, and political treatise which was well received by the academic world. After reviewing the history of the Roman and Germanic laws of inheritance Lassalle discussed the question which had also been raised by Savigny: in what circumstances can acquired rights lose their validity? This had a clear bearing on current politics, as the defenders of privilege invoked the classic rule that a law cannot act retrospectively: from this they deduced that new laws could not extinguish rights acquired under earlier ones. Lassalle's counter-argument was on the following lines. Acquired rights are those created by the deliberate activity of an individual; but the law tacitly presupposes that they are valid only for so long as such rights are allowed in general by the legal system in force, and the legal system derives its legitimacy from the consciousness of the nation as a whole. If a certain type of right or privilege is forbidden by later laws, the individual cannot appeal to the formula *lex retro non agit* and claim, for instance, that he has a right to keep slaves or serfs or to be immune from taxation, simply because 'it has always been so'. In this way Lassalle defended the legality of social changes that involved the abolition of privilege.

Lassalle's activity as a politician and ideologist of the workers' movement began, properly speaking, in 1862 and lasted (owing to his early death) for little more than two years. He was now living in Berlin and took an active part in the Prussian constitutional controversy, attacking the liberals of the Progressive party (Deutsche Fortschrittspartei). In the spring of 1862 he published an address to the workers, later known as the *Arbeiterprogramm*, which became the classic exposition of his views; also a speech on the constitution and a lecture on Fichte.

The Progressive party had a strong following in the Prussian working class; one of its leaders, Schulze-Delitzsch, was a promoter of friendly societies, insurance funds, and consumer co-operatives as methods of improving the lot of the proletariat within the framework of co-operation between capital and labour. However, some groups were not content with the patronage of the liberal bourgeoisie, and one of these, in Leipzig, appealed to Lassalle to state his position in regard to the workers' movement. Lassalle responded in January 1863 with an Open Letter which became a kind of charter of the first German working-class socialist party, the Allgemeiner Deutscher Arbeiterverein, founded in May of that year.

At the same time, as became known afterwards, Lassalle entered into contact with Bismarck in the evident hope of contracting an alliance with the conservatives against the bourgeoisie. In a speech in the Reichstag in 1878, Bismarck said he had had several talks with Lassalle at the latter's request, but these had not been negotiations, for the simple reason that Lassalle represented no political force and had nothing to offer; he described Lassalle, however, as a man of intellect and a true patriot.

The Arbeiterverein had no special success during Lassalle's lifetime, but it grew to a membership of about a thousand and was the first independent political expression of the German working class. In August 1864 Lassalle was killed in Geneva in a duel over a girl of seventeen whom he wished to marry; her aristocratic family refused to receive him, she herself changed her mind and returned to a previous fiancé, and Lassalle wrote an insulting letter which resulted in a challenge and his death.

Marx and Lassalle met in Berlin in 1861 and in London in the following year. They were never on cordial terms; Marx distrusted Lassalle and criticized him repeatedly in letters to Engels and others, while his political disagreement was expressed most notably in 1875, years after Lassalle's death, in the *Critique of the Gotha Programme*. There were also personal grounds of dislike and irritation. Lassalle was a man of outstanding powers, but he was also an ostentatious parvenu and something of a play-actor. In 1860 he wrote, to a woman with whom he was in love at the time, a 'confession' which is an extraordinary specimen of naïve self-praise. He represents himself as a genius adored by the people, the leader of a revolutionary party (which then existed only in his imagination), a new Robespierre, the terror of his enemies; a man of thirty-five with the experience of a sage of ninety, and the possessor of an income of 4,000 talers a year.

However, Marx's conflicts with Lassalle were not mainly due to personal antipathy. They differed on almost every point of substance: economic doctrine, political tactics, their attitude to the state in general and the Prussian state in particular. In general it may be said that the points on which their views coincided had nothing specifically Marxist about them. Some of their dissensions were as follows.

Firstly, the economic diagnosis of the situation of the proletariat. Lassalle stated in his Open Letter of 1863 that the liberals were mistaken in thinking they could liberate the working class by means of insurance funds, co-operatives, and so on; this, of course, was in accordance with Marx's view. However, Lassalle went on to prove his point by the 'iron law of economics' that, when wages are determined by the supply of labour and the demand for it, they are bound to gravitate to the 'physiological minimum' necessary to keep the workers and their children alive. If wages rise for any reason, the working classes will have more children and the increased supply of labour will push down wages; if wages fall below the minimum the workers will have fewer children, the demand for labour will exceed supply and wages will go up. The vicious circle is inevitable as long as supply and demand govern the wage level.

Lassalle took this doctrine over more or less literally from Malthus and Ricardo. Marx never professed it in this form, and although he sometimes took the view (especially in his earlier works) that wages must tend towards the physiological minimum, he did not accept Lassalle's supporting argument, which gave sole weight to the demographic factor in determining labour supply and demand. It was clear, indeed, that supply and demand could not be measured absolutely but only in relation to the whole economic picture, including such matters as boom and slump, the state of world markets, technical progress, the proletarianization of the peasantry and the petty bourgeoisie, and finally the effect of working-class pressure on wages. According to circumstances these factors might collectively push wages up or down, but in any case it was a gross over-simplification to reduce the whole problem to that of the birth-rate of an existing proletariat. Moreover, Lassalle contradicted himself in the same document when he said that minimum needs increase as general progress increases, so that one cannot speak of an improvement in the workers' lot by comparing their present position with the past: workers may be earning more in absolute terms, yet be worse off in relation to their total needs. It follows that the minimum is not merely a physiological but also a social and cultural one. Thus understood, the theory of 'relative pauperization' is close to Marx's views as he expressed them in the fifties and sixties.

Secondly, Lassalle differs radically from Marx in inferring from the 'iron law of economics' that the right way to emancipate the workers is to develop producer co-operatives, in which they will be paid wages equal to the value of the goods they produce. As the proletarians cannot set these up by their own efforts, the state must help them with credit institutions. For this to happen the workers must be able to exert pressure on the state, which they can only do if there is universal, direct, and equal suffrage.

This programme was contrary to Marx's theory in at least three important respects. In his view the domination of the economy by producers' associations was simply a repetition of Proudhon's Utopia: units of this kind, even if they belonged to the workers, could only exist in a state of competition like that which now prevailed. The laws of the market would continue to operate; there would still be crises, bankruptcies, and the concentration of capital. In any case, wages could never be fully equal to the value of the goods produced, since part of that value must be devoted to public needs, necessary unproductive work, reserves, etc. Finally, the programme whereby the state was to be the agent of working-class emancipation under capitalist conditions was contrary to Marx's idea of the state as a defensive weapon of the privileged classes.

Lassalle criticized the liberal theory of the state from a Hegelian point of view: as he wrote in the *Arbeiterprogramm*, the state's only function according to the bourgeoisie was to protect the freedom and property of individuals, so that if there were no criminals it would have nothing to do. In reality, however, the state was the highest form of human organization, in which all human values were actualized, and its function was to lead the human race to freedom; it was a unity of individuals in a single moral entity, and the instrument whereby man is to fulfil his destiny. In writing this, Lassalle had in mind the Prussian state; unlike Marx, he was a German patriot and saw the events of his time, including wars, from a national viewpoint rather than a proletarian international one. He believed German unity to be an issue of supreme importance, and thought Bismarck's policies would bring more gain than loss; moreover, the true antagonist of the proletariat was the bourgeoisie, so an alliance with the conservatives might well be desirable. This was directly contrary to Marx's general line that when the claims of the liberal bourgeoisie conflict with the interests of conservative, feudal, or monarchist elements, the proper course for the proletariat is to ally itself with the former.

The philosophical basis of Lassalle's nationalism is seen most clearly in his lectures on Fichte, where he says that the latter's ideas embody the spiritual greatness of the German people. The endeavour of all German philosophy is to overcome the duality of subject and object, to reconcile the spirit with the world and to achieve the mastery of 'spiritual inwardness' (*die Innerlichkeit des Geistes*) over reality. Fichte had proclaimed the mission of the German people to march in the forefront of human progress and to vindicate the divine plan of creation by attaining national independence. Germany was not only a necessary aspect (*Moment*) of world history but was destined to be sole champion of the idea of liberty on which the future of mankind depends. Precisely because it had had no proper history for centuries, being a 'pure metaphysical inwardness' and not a state, it had become the birthplace of the philosophical idea which set out to reconcile thought and being.

The metaphysical nation, the German nation, has had bestowed on it, throughout its development and in the perfect accordance of its internal and external history, the supreme metaphysical destiny and the uttermost honour in world history—namely, that of creating a national territory out of the spiritual concept of a nation, and evolving its own being out of pure thought. To a metaphysical nation belongs a metaphysical task, an achievement no less than that of the divine creation. Pure spirit not only informs the reality presented to it but creates a territory, the very seat of its own existence. There has been nothing like this since the beginning of history. ('Die Philo-sophic Fichtes', in F. Lassalle, *Reden und Schriften*, ed. Hans Feigl, 1920, p. 362)

The Fichtean–Romantic conception of state and nation took precedence, in Lassalle's thinking, over his semi-Marxist vision of the proletariat as the liber-ator of the world. He appears to have felt his Jewish origin as a stigma, though he made no attempt to hide it—he used to say that he had always hated two kinds of people, Jews and literary men, and that unfortunately he himself was both—and he lost no opportunity of proclaiming his patriotic feelings. In his glorification of the state, the organic unity of the nation, and the spiritual lead-ership of Germany he was, like Fichte before him, a pioneer of national social-ism. His inflated, prophetic style exasperated Marx no less than their theoretical disagreements. Yet his practical success is beyond dispute: his insistence on an independent proletarian movement laid the foundations of organized socialism in Germany. Among later orthodox Marxists opinions on him were divided. Mehring emphasized Marx's personal dislike of Lassalle and minimized the political and theoretical differences between the two, whereas Kautsky held that their ideas of socialism were completely different. At all events it was clear that Lasalle's theoretical horizon, unlike Marx's, was limited to Germany; so was his political influence, but in that country it was powerful and lasting. Even in later years, when German social democracy had finally abandoned Lassalle's programme, his spirit was still discernible in the party, both in the strain of nationalism which persisted beneath the surface and in the belief that the existing machinery of the state could be made to serve the interest of the proletariat.

3. The First International. Bakunin

FROM the mid-sixties onwards Marx was less involved in combating Lassalles's views than in polemics against other schools of thought within the Interna-tional, especially those of Proudhon and Bakunin.

The International Working Men's Association, to give it its full title, was estab-lished at a public meeting in London in September 1864. A year earlier the first organizational links had been formed between British and French trade union-ists on the occasion of demonstrations in support of the Polish insurrection against Russia. The meeting in 1864 was attended by German, Polish, and Ital-ian *émigrés* as well as the British and French, and it was decided to create an international body to co-ordinate the working class struggle in different coun-tries. A General Council of thirty-four members was elected, with George Odger, a London trade unionist, as its president. Marx was elected to the Council and was made corresponding secretary for Germany; he also played a leading part in drafting the Rules and Inaugural Address. The latter described briefly the fortunes of the European proletariat since 1848. It pointed out that the working class was increasingly impoverished and property more concentrated, that there had nevertheless been successes in reducing working hours and in the co-operative movement, but that the emancipation of the proletariat depended on its conquering political power. This could only be achieved by the international action of the workers, who were a class with common interests independent of country or nationality. They were not fighting to replace existing privileges by others, but to put an end to class domination. However, the approved texts contained no express revolutionary demands.

During the next few years the International endeavoured with moderate success to organize sections in various European countries: outside Britain, these were formed in various towns in France, Belgium, and Switzerland, generally on the basis of existing organizations. Lassalle's party remained outside the International, largely owing to disagreement over its attitude to Bismarck and to German bourgeois democracy. The British unions, some of which joined the International, pursued a separate policy of their own. The French were mostly Proudhonists, and expressed their differences from Marx at the congresses at Geneva (September 1866) and Lausanne (September 1867). Among other things they objected to the Polish question being discussed at meetings or mentioned in manifestos; Marx, on the other hand, believed that Polish independence was inseparable from the cause of the European workers and that the most urgent task was to break the reactionary power of the Tsardom. The Proudhonists, like their master, were mistrustful of political action in general and held to the belief in 'mutualism', which in Marx's eyes was purely utopian.

The Rules of the International were loose enough to permit the membership of a large variety of groups. Besides the British unions and the Proudhonists it included, for some years, French radicals and the partisans of Mazzini. The federation was a loose one, and the General Council had no executive powers over its members. Throughout its existence Marx devoted the greater part of his time to its affairs, with three chief objectives that were especially evident in the later years. He wanted the International to become a centralized body that could impose a uniform policy on its sections; he strove to make the whole movement accept the ideological bases he had himself worked out; and he hoped to turn the International into a weapon against Russia. Despite his prestige he failed in all three of these aims, and his policies led to a breach within the International which was a major cause, if not the main cause, of its collapse. Marx himself attended only one congress of the International, the final one, held at The Hague in 1872.

The economic crisis of 1867 and the wave of strikes in many European countries were propitious to the International: new sections were created in Spain, Italy, Holland, and Austria, while in Germany a new social democratic party was formed, alongside the Lassallists, by Liebknecht and Bebel; this did not formally join the International, but was closer to Marx on the main issues. The influence of the Proudhonists grew weaker; at the Brussels Congress in September 1868 the International called for the collective ownership of arable land, forests, roads, canals, and mines, and declared itself in favour of the strike weapon.

The year 1869 marked the zenith of the International's activity and influence, but also witnessed the beginning of the fatal split between the outstanding figures of the nineteenth-century revolutionary movement, Marx and Bakunin. These two leaders held diametrically opposite views on strategy and on the subject of the working class, revolution, the state, and socialism.

■   ■   ■

MIKHAIL ALEXANDROVICH BAKUNIN (1814–76) had a long and adventurous political past behind him when he joined the International in 1869. Born in the province of Tver, of aristocratic family, he began his education at a military school but left it after a short time. He spent some years in Moscow, where he frequented intellectuals who discussed the future of Russia and the world in the light of Hegel's philosophy of history. For a time he was a Hegelian conservative, believing in the rationality of actual history and holding that the individual has no right to assert his accidental subjectivity against the decrees of universal reason. Soon, however, he passed to the opposite extreme, which was certainly more suited to his temperament. He went to Berlin in 1840, met the Young Hegelians and was infected by their ideas. In further travels to Switzerland, Belgium, and France he met the chief socialist writers of the time: Cabet, Weitling, Proudhon, and finally Marx and Engels. He also met many Poles of the post-1830 emigration, and from then onwards devoted much attention in his writings to the cause of Polish independence. In the 1840s he agitated for a Slav federation, an idea which he later rejected as ineffective or reactionary. He never abandoned his hatred of Germany, however, which was as violent as Marx's hatred of Russia.

The two men clashed for the first time during the 1848 Revolution, when an article in the *Neue Rheinische Zeitung* accused Bakunin of being a Tsarist agent—a libel which the newspaper was compelled to withdraw. Bakunin took an active part in the revolutionary struggle in Prague and Dresden; he was twice condemned to death and finally expelled to Russia, where he spent the next twelve years in prison and exile. From one of his prisons he addressed an extraordinary Confession to Tsar Nicholas I, (first published after the October

Revolution), expressing repentance for his subversive activity but warning that the fearful conditions in Russia might lead to revolution. In 1862 he escaped from Siberia to Japan and made his way via America to London. His career as a theoretical and practical anarchist dates from 1864, when he founded a clandestine group known as Fraternité Internationale—a loose organization of his friends and adherents, chiefly in Spain, Italy, and Switzerland. In September 1868 he established an overt anarchist association, the Alliance Internationale de la Démocratic Socialiste, which applied to join the International. The latter's Council refused to accept the Alliance as such, but in 1869 it agreed that individual sections might join, including the Geneva one to which Bakunin belonged and which was the only properly organized group. From then on Marx and Bakunin were engaged in a conflict in which it is hard to distinguish political from personal animosities. Marx did his best to persuade everybody that Bakunin was only using the International for his private ends, and in March 1870 he circulated a confidential letter to this effect. He also saw the hand of Bakunin (whom he never met after 1864) on every occasion when his own policies were opposed in the International. Bakunin, for his part, not only combated Marx's political programme but, as he often wrote, regarded Marx as a disloyal, revengeful man, obsessed with power and determined to impose his own despotic authority on the whole revolutionary movement. Marx, he said, had all the merits and defects of the Jewish character; he was highly intelligent and deeply read, but an inveterate doctrinaire and fantastically vain, an intriguer and morbidly envious of all who, like Lassalle, had cut a more important figure than himself in public life.

Politics apart, the history of Marx's relations with Bakunin does not show the former in a favourable light. His charge that Bakunin was using the International for personal advantage was groundless, and his efforts to have Bakunin expelled were finally successful (in 1872) thanks in the main to the Nechayev letter, for which Marx must have known that Bakunin bore no responsibility. Bakunin, of course, worked for the victory of his own ideas in the International, just as Marx did. At the Basle Congress in 1869 the Bakuninists secured the adoption (contrary to Marx's standpoint) of a proposal declaring that the abolition of the right of inheritance was a basic feature of the social revolution. From 1870 there was increasing dissension within sections of the International, and in Switzerland, Italy, and Spain Bakunin's adherents predominated over those of Marx. Bakunin's last years were mainly devoted to writing. In 1870 he published *L'Empire knouto-germanique et la révolution sociale*, and in 1873, in Russian, his only work of any size, *Statehood and Anarchy* (translated as *Etatisme et anarchie*). This was intended as the introduction to a larger work (which he never wrote), and contains all the important ideas of his anarchist period. It is an unsystematic collection of remarks on the most varied subjects: European and world politics, Russia, Germany, Poland, France, China, the 1848 Revolution, the Paris Commune, attacks on communism, and various philosophical observations.

Bakunin had not the gifts of a theoretician or a founder of systems. He was full of inexhaustible revolutionary energy, bent on destructive aims and inspired by anarchistic Messianism. He could not endure situations which required long-term political calculations, tactical manoeuvres, and temporary alliances. He expressed, as he was well aware, all the spirit of revolt which grew among the most deprived elements of the working class, the lumpenproletariat and the peasantry. According to him, 'state communism', i.e. Marx's variety, was supported by the better-off, relatively secure workers who had acquired bourgeois habits, while he himself appealed to the ragged paupers who were still uncorrupted and had nothing to lose. He referred repeatedly to the rebellions of Pugachev and Stenka Razin in Russia—elemental, instinctive uprisings of the desperate peasantry led by 'bandits' (his own expression). Marx's adherents, he declared, despised the people; had not Lassalle written that the suppression of the peasant revolt in sixteenth-century Germany had been a major contribution to historical progress? Marx and Lassalle, who were divided by nothing but Marx's personal jealousy, were the upholders of a new state despotism which was bound to develop out of their 'scientific socialism'.

Bakunin's whole doctrine centred in the word 'freedom', while the term 'state' epitomized all the evil which must be banished from the world. He accepted to some extent the theory of historical materialism, in the sense that human history depends on 'economic facts' and that men's ideas are a reflection of the material conditions in which they live. He also espoused philosophical materialism (under this name), based on atheism and the rejection of any notion of 'another world'. But he believed that the Marxists absolutized the principle, in itself correct, of historical materialism into a kind of fatalism which left no room for the individual will, for rebellion, or for moral factors in history.

Maintaining the primacy of 'life' over 'ideas', Bakunin rejected the doctrine of 'scientific socialism' which assumed that it was possible to organize social life on the basis of schemata devised by intellectuals and imposed on the people. Political or moral propaganda could only convince the masses in so far as it accorded with what was in their minds and hearts but had not yet found expression. It was no use hoping to enlighten the Russian people by means of academic theories; they would only accept what they already knew after a fashion but had not been able to articulate. In general, science was no more than a function of life and could not claim supremacy over its other manifestations. It was necessary and should be respected, but it could not grasp phenomena in their fullness: it reduced them to abstractions and ignored individuality and human freedom. Life was creative; science was uncreative and was no more than a facet of reality. The social sciences in particular, which were still in their infancy, could not claim to foretell the future or impose ideals on mankind. History is a process of spontaneous creation, not the working-out of scientific schemes; it develops like life itself, instinctively and in an unrationalized manner.

Bakunin's idea of the revolt of life against science, though hedged with reservations concerning the value of knowledge, was to serve as the basis for versions of anarchism which regarded all academic thought as a crafty invention of the intelligentsia to maintain their privileges under the cloak of mental superiority. Bakunin did not go so far as this, but he inveighed against universities as the abodes of élitism and seminaries of a privileged caste; he also warned that Marxist socialism would lead to a tyranny of intellectuals that would be worse than any yet known to man.

'Life', in Bakunin's sense, is an endless, indefatigable endeavour towards freedom for every individual, every community, and the whole human race. Freedom in turn presupposes equality, not merely before the law but in reality, that is to say economic equality. Freedom and equality are opposed by the system of privileges and private property safeguarded by state power. The state is a historically necessary form of communal life, but it is not eternal and is not merely a superstructure imposed on 'economic facts'; on the contrary, it is an essential factor in maintaining privilege, exploitation, and all forms of slavery. The state by its very nature signifies the enslavement of the masses by a despotic, privileged minority, whether priestly, feudal, bourgeois, or 'scientific'. 'Any state, even the most republican and the most democratic, even the pseudo-popular state imagined by Marx, is essentially nothing but the government of the masses by an educated and therefore privileged minority, which is supposed to understand the people's needs better than they do themselves' (*Statehood and Anarchy*, pp. 34–5). The task of the revolution, accordingly, is not to transform the state but to abolish it. The state is not to be confused with society: the former is an artificial means of oppression, the latter a natural extension of the instinctive ties that bind human beings together. To abolish the state does not mean abolishing all forms of co-operation and organization; it means that every social organization must be built up entirely from below, without authoritarian institutions. Bakunin does not accept Stirner's doctrine that in the society of the future everyone will pursue his own private interest; on the contrary, human beings have a natural, instinctive solidarity which makes them capable of self-sacrifice and concern for others. The state not only does not foster this solidarity but opposes it: at most, it organizes the solidarity of the privileged classes in so far as they have a common interest in maintaining exploitation. When the machinery of the state is destroyed, society will be organized in small autonomous communes which will allow their members absolute freedom. Any larger units will be formed on a completely voluntary basis, and every commune will be able to withdraw from the federation whenever it wishes. No administrative functions will be permanently assigned to any individuals; all social hierarchies will be abolished, and the functions of government will be completely merged in the community. There will be no law or codes, no judges, no family as a legal unit; no citizens, only human beings. Children will not be the property of their parents or of society, but of their own selves as they are destined to be: society will take care of them and remove them from their parents if they are in danger of being depraved or hampered in their development. There will be absolute freedom to maintain any views, even false ones, including religious beliefs; freedom, too, to form associations to propagate one's views or for any other purpose. Crime, if any there still is, will be regarded as a symptom of disease and treated accordingly.

Since it is clear that all privilege is connected with the right to bequeath one's property and that the state serves to perpetuate this unjust arrangement, the first step towards destroying the present system must be to abolish the right of inheritance. This is the road towards equality, which is unthinkable without freedom; and freedom is indivisible.

In the light of these principles the state communism of the German doctrinaires—Marx, Engels, Lassalle, and Liebknecht—is revealed as the threat of a new tyranny of self-styled 'scientists' in a new form of state organization. 'If there is a state, there is bound to be domination and therefore slavery. A state without slavery, open or disguised, is unthinkable—that is why we are enemies of the state.' (*Statehood and Anarchy*. p. 280.) In one way or another, the minority will govern the majority.

> But, the Marxists say, this minority will consist of the workers. Yes, no doubt—of former workers, who, as soon as they become governors or representatives of the people, cease to be workers and start looking down on the working masses from the heights of state authority, so that they represent not the people but themselves and their own claim to rule over others. Anyone who can doubt this knows nothing of human nature . . . The terms 'scientific socialist' and 'scientific socialism', which we meet incessantly in the works and speeches of the Lassallists and Marxists, are sufficient to prove that the so-called people's state will be nothing but a despotism over the masses, exercised by a new and quite small aristocracy of real or bogus 'scientists'. The people, being unlearned, will be completely exempted from the task of governing and will be forced into the herd of those who are governed. A fine sort of emancipation! . . . They [the Marxists] claim that only a dictatorship, their own of course, can bring the people freedom; we reply that a dictatorship can have no other aim than to perpetuate itself, and that it can engender and foster nothing but slavery in the people subjected to it. Freedom can be created only by

freedom, that is by a rising of the whole people and by the free organization of the working masses from below. (*Statehood and Anarchy*, pp. 280–1.)

In short, the object of the revolutionary movement cannot be to gain control of the existing state or to create a new one, for in that case the outcome would defeat the idea. For the same reason, the movement cannot pin its faith on a political struggle within the framework of existing state and parliamentary institutions. Liberation can only be attained by a single apocalyptic upheaval sweeping away the whole apparatus of the state, law, and private property. From this point of view the coming social revolution differs fundamentally from all its predecessors and especially the French Revolution, which turned into a despotism inspired by the sick mind of Rousseau. Bakunin speaks of Rousseau and Robespierre in tones of abhorrence; nor has he much good to say of any socialist thinker except for Proudhon, who knew the value of freedom.

Must there not, however, be a state organization and means of compulsion or restriction so as to limit conflicts and keep human egoism within bounds? No, Bakunin replies: it is precisely because the state exists that even the best individuals, emerging from the mass of humanity, become tyrants and executioners. In a society based on freedom even the most selfish and ill-disposed will be cured of their vices; for a society without a state and without privileges is not only better but is the only mode of life compatible with human nature, spontaneous, creative, and unrestricted. Anarchy is more than an ideal, it is the realization of man as he was meant to be. This does not signify, however, that it is guaranteed by the laws of history or part of a destined plan: it is essentially the work of human purpose, but there is every reason to think that purpose will prevail. Bakunin believed strongly in the natural revolutionary instinct of the working masses, and he considered the problem chiefly as it affected Russia. Revolution required as a prior condition extreme poverty and desperation, plus the ideal of a new society: this ideal could not be imposed on the people from outside, but must already be dormant within them. What the people needed was not teachers to invent ideals, but revolutionaries to arouse them from their slumbers. The Russian people, i.e. the peasantry, had a deeply rooted sense of anarchy: they felt that the land belonged to everyone and that the village commune, the *mir*, should be completely autonomous, and they were naturally hostile to the state. This feeling, however, was overlaid by the patriarchal tradition, by their faith in the Tsar, and by the fact that the *mir* absorbed human personality and hampered its development, while the opium of religion kept the peasants in spiritual bondage. Consequently, the village communes were inert and isolated from one another; but there might arise from among the people rebels who would stir it up and awaken its natural revolutionary tendencies. Moreover, the same natural ideals were dormant among the poor of other countries, as was most clearly seen in Italy, where the anarchist revolution became more imminent every day. The great exception was Germany, where there were always plenty of theoreticians chattering about revolution but not enough people working for it. The Germans were natural state-worshippers, delighting to obey as much as to command, and it was not surprising that they could rise no higher than the state socialism of Marx and Lassalle, or that Bismarck's Germany was now the bastion of world reaction. The Tsardom, whatever Marx might say, did not compare with Germany in this respect: it was certainly always trying to meddle in European affairs, but with very little success.

Bakunin's statements about Russia do not form a consistent whole. On the one hand, he says that the Slavs are incapable of forming states and that all their political systems have been created by foreigners. But, on the other hand, he maintains that Russia is not only a military state (as opposed to a commercial one like Britain) but has evolved a system in which the interests of all classes, and the whole of industrial and agricultural activity, are subordinated to the central power, so that the nation's wealth is no more than a means to aggrandize the state. On this point Bakunin repeats an observation that had often been made in the nineteenth century: the primacy of the Russian state *vis-à-vis* the civil community was so absolute that even the distinction of classes was secondary to it. But it is hard to see how this can be reconciled with the view that the Slavs have no state-forming abilities.

From this brief review of Bakunin's ideas it will be clear that he differed widely from Marx as regards both theory and tactics. Apart from their dispute over the leadership of the International, each accusing the other of dictatorial aims, and apart from the question whether Russia (as Marx insisted) or Prussia (as Bakunin maintained) was the headquarters of world reaction, they disagreed on several points of key importance to the socialist movement.

In the first place, Marx regarded the call for the immediate abolition of inheritance as putting the cart before the horse, since the right to bequeath property was only a particular aspect of the property system itself. Secondly, Marx held that the state is not the independent source of all social evil but merely the instrument by which existing privileges are maintained. On this point the disagreement was not essential, for Marx, like Bakunin, considered that existing political institutions would have to be destroyed, while Bakunin agreed that the state had arisen historically as an instrument of private property, though he also held that in the course of time it had become an independent force and a necessary bulwark of the class system. The dispute therefore came down to whether the socialist revolution could do away with all forms of statehood at the outset. Marx believed that the state of the future would not be concerned with 'governing people' but with 'administering things', i.e. organizing production. To Bakunin, this amounted to extreme etatism: there could be no centralized economic administration without political centralization and therefore slavery. Thirdly, Marx's strategic plan included political activity within existing systems, parliamentary and other, and permitted temporary alliances with the democratic bourgeoisie when its interests happened to coincide with those of the proletariat; whereas for Bakunin the only kind of political activity that revolutionaries should undertake was to destroy all forms of statehood. Fourthly, Bakunin's idea of completely free economic activity carried on by small autonomous communes appeared to Marx no better than a Proudhonist Utopia, and open to the same objections: on the one hand the natural tendency is for production to be centralized, and, on the other, an economy composed of independent units would be bound to reproduce the system of competition and capital accumulation.

Marx's ideas on all these questions altered and matured over a long period. It was not until after the Paris Commune that he came round to the view, which was to be central in Lenin's version of Marxism, that the existing state machine must be destroyed. Bakunin's Swiss follower Guillaume welcomed this as signifying Marx's conversion to anarchism; but he was mistaken, as Marx remained convinced of the necessity of a central economic administration, though he believed the future state would have no political functions. It is true, however, that Marx did not explain clearly on what basis social life would be organized when the state had been abolished and the whole economy centralized. Bakunin himself had only the crudest ideas of political economy, believing simply that once people were free of the state their natural solidarity and bent for co-operation would come into play and conflicts of interest would be impossible. He envisaged democracy on the lines of the Swiss cantons and villages in which the whole adult population assembled from time to time to decide matters of common concern; but his writings give no indication of how this could be applied on the scale of a province, a country, or the whole world, assuming that representative democracy was done away with.

In these disputes Marx's strength lay in the field of economic criticism and in his conviction that a system of independent productive units would mean reviving all the harmful aspects of a commodity economy. Bakunin, on the other hand, had a strong point in his criticism of the overt or implied etatism in Marx's programme. He raised the very real question to which Marx gives no answer: how can a centralized economic power be imagined without political coercion? And, if the future society is still divided into rulers and ruled, how can it fail to recreate the system of power privilege, which has a natural tendency to perpetuate itself? These objections were to recur frequently in criticisms of Marx by anarchists and syndicalists. It is clear enough that Marx did not himself imagine socialism as a despotic system in which the political apparatus would maintain its privileges on the basis of a monopoly of the means of production; but he did not answer Bakunin on this point, and the latter deserves credit for being the first, as it were, to infer Leninism from Marxism.

Bakunin believed naïvely that men, left to themselves, would behave as they ought and would live in harmony, since evil did not come from human beings but from the state and private property; he did not explain how man, being good by nature, had come to create such an evil system. Marx for his part thought the question of natural goodness irrelevant and naïve. He was concerned with the Promethean expansion of the human race in its growing mastery over nature, and he thought personal development had no meaning except in relation to the development of the species. He was far from being an advocate of despotism, but he failed to answer the charge that it was implicit in his system.

The First International was destroyed by internal conflicts on the one hand and, on the other, by the Franco-German War and the Paris Commune. The Commune was not the child of the International, still less of the Marxists. Most of its leaders were Blanquists, while those members of the International who joined it were mainly Proudhonists. Marx saw from the beginning that it was doomed to failure, but after the defeat and massacre of the Communards he composed a pamphlet entitled *Class Struggles in France* in which, besides paying tribute to their heroism, he analysed the significance of their spontaneous movement from the viewpoint of the future of communism. The Paris Commune, being in a sense the first proletarian regime in history, had, by a natural process as it were, exemplified some of the basic principles of the future socialist society: the replacement of the standing army by an armed citizenry, the transformation of the police into a popular organ, the electivity of all magistrates and officials, a maximum wage, free education, the disestablishment and expropriation of the Church. Nevertheless, Marx did not regard the Commune as specifically either socialist or proletarian; Engels in 1891 referred to it as a dictatorship of the proletariat, but Marx never did so. (Its name, of course, is simply French for the Paris municipality, and has no ideological significance.) In February 1881, in a letter to F. Domela Nieuwenhuis, Marx said expressly that the majority of the Commune was not socialist and that its only right and possible course had been to compromise with Versailles in the interest of the French people as a whole.

The defeat of the Commune gave encouragement to reaction throughout Europe and accentuated the dissensions which broke up the First International. Workers' organizations in France and Germany were subjected to harassment, and the International lost the effective support of the British trade unions, who had joined it for tactical rather than ideological reasons and were chiefly concerned to establish a legal position for themselves within the existing order. At its London Conference in September 1871 the International

endorsed Marx's call for combined political and economic action by the working class and for independent workers' parties in all countries; the congress at
The Hague in September 1872 showed that Marx's followers were a majority in
the General Council. But the International was by now fatally weakened by dissensions and persecution, and was incapable of directing workers' organizations in conditions that differed widely from one country to another. On a
proposal by Engels the General Council transferred itself to New York, where
the organization lingered on for a few years before it was formally dissolved in
1876. A rival International formed by Bakunin's followers fell to pieces a year
later; however, throughout the 1870s anarchism was stronger than Marxism,
not only in Spain and Italy but also in France.

Apart from the conflict of influences in the International it may be said that
from the 1860s Marxism was the most important of the rival socialist ideologies, in the sense that doctrines and programmes throughout the world defined
their position by reference to it. Marxism presented the most consistent and
elaborate body of doctrine, and this was due in part to the publication at
Leipzig in 1867 of the first volume of Marx's *Capital*. This volume reverted,
inter alia, to the problems discussed in the *Critique of Political Economy*
(1859), and revealed the sources of exploitation by analysing the basic phenomena of the capitalist economy: commodities, exchange- and use-value, surplus value, capital, wages, and accumulation. The fundamental thesis of
Capital is that exploitation derives from the sale of labour-power by hired
workers. Labour is a commodity of a special kind in that the value of its product is much greater than the cost of reproducing it, i.e. of the worker's subsistence; and the exploitation that this involves can only be done away with by
abolishing wage-labour.

Marx intended to finish the second and third volumes of his work in a short
time. The second was to analyse the circulation of capital and the market,
while the third was to deal with the sharing of profit among different groups
of exploiters, the origin of the average rate of profit, the tendency of the rate of
profit to fall, and the transformation of surplus profit into ground rent. Parts
of these volumes were written before the first was published, but although
Marx continued working on them till 1878 they were not completed at the time
of his death. The manuscripts, arranged and edited by Engels, were published
in 1885 and 1894, while *Theories of Surplus Value* was published by Kautsky
as the fourth volume of *Capital* in 1905–10.

After the break-up of the International, and as the hope of an early European revolution once more receded, Marx concentrated on theoretical work to
the extent permitted by frequent illness, visits to health resorts, money troubles, and domestic misfortune. He read extensively, but in his last years was
almost incapable of writing; however, he continued to follow closely the devel-

opment of European socialism. In 1875 the two German workers' parties, the Lassallists and the Eisenach group, united to form the Socialist Workers' party. Their programme elicited a devastating attack by Marx in the form of a letter to the Eisenach leaders: this *Critique of the Gotha Programme*, first published by Engels in 1891, repeated Marx's objections to Lassallian socialism and contained more trenchant formulations than are found elsewhere in his works on such matters as the state, internationalism, and the nature of a proletarian authority. The document had little effect on the final version of the programme, but it became one of the principal texts invoked by the revolutionary wing of the Second International against reformism and revisionism: its use of the phrase 'dictatorship of the proletariat' made it especially valuable to Lenin and his followers. In 1880 Marx helped Jules Guesde to draft the programme of the French workers' party; in 1881–2 he wrote some letters on the prospects of revolution in Russia, which were afterwards much debated and disputed over by Russian Marxists.

Marx died in London on 14 March 1883. Some of his papers were published posthumously by Engels; after the latter's death in 1895 a vast amount of material remained in the hands of Bernstein and Bebel, who did not do much to make it available. Mehring republished some articles of the 1840s which were difficult of access, and also published the manuscript of Marx's doctoral dissertation, though without the preliminary notes. Bernstein published portions of *The German Ideology*. The first edition of Marx's correspondence, by Mehring and Bernstein, was inaccurate and incomplete. Kautsky, as already mentioned, published *Theories of Surplus Value* and (in 1903) the Introduction to the *Grundrisse*. A great deal of work was done in collecting scattered manuscripts and letters, and publishing them in scholarly form, by David Ryazanov, who created the Marx–Engels Institute in Moscow and was its director until 1930. He also founded the great critical edition of the works of Marx and Engels (*M.E.G.A.*), which, although never completed, made available several texts that were previously unknown, including the whole of *The German Ideology*, the Paris Manuscripts of 1844, and Engels's *Dialectic of Nature*.

■   ■   ■

ENGELS survived Marx by twelve years. During the long period of their friendship and collaboration he was content to remain in Marx's shadow, regarding the latter as the founder of scientific socialism and modestly underrating his own contribution. None the less, subsequent generations of Marxists made more use, in expounding and advocating their doctrine, of Engels's writings than of Marx's, always excepting the first volume of *Capital*. Engels was a man of great breadth of knowledge and intellectual capacity. Besides history, politics, and philosophy, which occupied the bulk of his time, he wrote numerous articles on military problems and the technical aspects of current operations of war, and also followed developments in natural science from the viewpoint of his own philosophical reflections. As a writer he is much more digestible than Marx; he endeavoured more than once to set out the main ideas of scientific socialism in a generally accessible form, and his works were widely read by socialists everywhere.

His first important work after 1848 was *Der deutsche Bauernkrieg* (*The German Peasant's War*, 1850), on the subject of the sixteenth-century rising under Thomas Münzer. Based on the history by Wilhelm Zimmermann published in the 1840s, this work attempted to interpret the most important popular rising in German history in terms of the class struggle and to suggest analogies between it and the revolutionary situation of 1848-9. Engels's views on the events of those years, in which he himself took part, were summed up in a series of articles published in 1851-2 over Marx's signature in the *New York Daily Tribune*, entitled *Revolution and Counter-Revolution in Germany*; these were first published in book form (still attributed to Marx) in 1896.

Among Engels's best-known works is *Herrn Eugen Dührings Umwälzung der Wissenschaft*, known as the *Anti-Dühring* (1878). Dühring (1833-1921), who was blind, was dismissed from his lectureship at the University of Berlin for his violent attacks on academic philosophy. His writings were popular among the German social democrats, and for a time he was regarded as one of the party's chief theorists. Engels, who considered Dühring a dangerous influence, attacked his views in a sharply polemical work in which he gave a clear exposition of dialectical materialism as the basis of Marxian economics, and of scientific socialism as opposed to the utopian tradition. The *Anti-Dühring* became a kind of Marxist handbook after Dühring himself had been quite forgotten (though Nazi propagandists were to revive his memory on account of his anti-Semitic views).

After Marx's death Engels, who had moved to London in 1870, devoted much of his energy to editing the remaining portions of *Capital*, but also wrote philosophical works of his own. In 1886 he published in *Die Neue Zeit* an article on 'Ludwig Feuerbach and the End [*Ausgang*] of Classic German Philosophy', in which he related scientific socialism to the German intellectual tradition; this, too, is one of the most popular expositions of Marxism. It was republished in book form in 1888 together with Marx's *Theses on Feuerbach*, which had not previously appeared.

Another classic work by Engels is *The Origin of the Family, Private Property and the State* (1884). This made considerable use of the work of Lewis H. Morgan, who for the first time had systematically analysed primitive society on the basis of direct observation of North American Indians, and in *Ancient Society* (1877) outlined a theory of the stages of human development from savagery to civilization. Using these and other works, Engels endeavoured to present the origins of the basic institutions of civilized life.

In the early seventies Engels conceived the plan of a critique of vulgar materialism which would apply the dialectical method to scientific observation. He wrote some chapters and notes for this work between 1875 and 1882, but did not succeed in completing it. All this material, finished and unfinished, was first published in 1925 in Moscow under the title *Dialectic of Nature*.

The works mentioned here constitute that part of Engels's literary output— a small proportion of the whole—which has become widely read on account of its systematic character and the permanence of its themes. Along with *Capital*, these works are the basic source from which three or four generations of readers have imbibed their knowledge of scientific socialism and its philosophic background.

Engels died in London on 5 August 1895. Unlike Marx, he is not buried there; he was cremated by his own wish, and his ashes, in an urn, were cast into the sea off Beachy Head.

XII

Capitalism as a Dehumanized World.
The Nature of Exploitation

1. The controversy as to the relation of Capital *to*
Marx's early writings

MARX'S EXPOSITION of the functioning and prospects of the capitalist economy cannot be studied in isolation from his anthropological ideas and his philosophy of history. His theory is a general one embracing the whole of human activity in its various interdependent spheres. The behaviour of human beings in all ages—whether active or passive, whether intellectual, aesthetic, or engaged in labour—must be understood integrally or not at all. *Capital* is the culmination of a series of works in which Marx applied his basic theory of dehumanization to the phenomena of economic production and exchange. His successive 'critiques'—the Paris Manuscripts of 1844, *The Poverty of Philosophy* (1847), *Wage Labour and Capital* (1849), the *Grundrisse* (1857-8), the *Critique of Political Economy* (1859), and finally *Capital* itself (1867)—are more and more elaborate versions of the same thought, which may be expressed as follows. We live in an age in which the dehumanization of man, that is to say the alienation between him and his own works, is growing to a climax which must end in a revolutionary upheaval; this will originate from the particular interest of the class which has suffered the most from dehumanization, but its effect will be to restore humanity to all mankind.

There is no doubt that Marx's terminology and the mode of his exposition underwent changes between 1844 and 1867, and there has been much discussion as to how far these correspond to changes in his ideas. In particular, it has been suggested that the theory of a 'return to species-essence', which is prominent in the texts of 1843-4, and which implies a normative, anthropological view, was abandoned by the later Marx in favour of a structural description.

Some commentators, such as Landshut and Meyer, Popitz and Fromm, consider that the early writings express a richer, more universal philosophical theory and that the later ones, by comparison, are intellectually more restricted. Many others, such as Sydney Hook, Daniel Bell, and Lewis Feuer, maintain that there was a break in the development of Marx's ideas and that *Capital* differs from the Paris Manuscripts not only in scope but also in substance; this view is denied by such critics as Calvez, Tucker, McLellan, Fetscher, and Avineri. A distinct but closely related question is whether, despite the frequent sharpness of Marx's attacks on Hegel, his ideas were in fact derived from Hegelian sources, and whether in this respect too there was a breach in his intellectual development. Croce, Löwith, and Hook maintain that he parted company with Hegelianism after 1844, while Lukács, Fetscher, Tucker, and Avineri hold that he was inspired by it more or less consciously to the very end. These views are equally compatible with a sympathetic or unsympathetic approach to any particular 'phase' of Marx's thinking, or to the whole of it. Other critics again, such as Jordan, believe that Marx's relationship to Hegel went through different stages: that a short period of fascination was followed by radical criticism and the almost complete abandonment of Hegelianism, but that he subsequently reverted to a middle view.

The literature of this controversy already amounts to a considerable library, and we cannot study the arguments in detail here. It may, however, be briefly stated why the present author agrees with those who hold that there is no discontinuity in Marx's thought, and that it was from first to last inspired by basically Hegelian philosophy.

It must be made clear that the question is not whether Marx did or did not change during his forty years as a writer, since he obviously did change in many respects. Nor is it whether the whole substance of *Capital* can be found in the Paris Manuscripts by anyone who chooses to look hard enough—for Marxism without the theory of value and surplus value is clearly not the same as Marxism with this theory elaborated. The question is whether the aspects of his early thinking which Marx subsequently abandoned are important enough to justify the idea of an intellectual break, and whether the theory of value and its consequences are a basic innovation, either contrary to Marx's philosophy of the early forties or in no way anticipated therein. To this question we would reply as follows.

The fundamental novelty of *Capital* consists in two points which entail a wholly different view of capitalist society from that of the classical economists with their labour theory of value. The first of these is the argument that what the worker sells is not his labour but labour-power, and that labour has two aspects, the abstract and the concrete. But this view is itself the final version of Marx's theory of dehumanization, first sketched in 1843–4. Exploitation consists in the worker selling his labour-power and thus divesting himself of his own essence: the labour process and its results become alien and hostile, a deprivation of humanity instead of a fulfilment. In the second place, having discovered the dual nature of labour as expressed in the opposition between exchange-value and use-value, Marx is able to define capitalism as a system in which the sole object of production is to increase exchange-value without limit; the whole of human activity is subordinated to a non-human purpose, the creation of something that man as such cannot assimilate, for only use-value can be assimilated. The whole community is thus enslaved to its own products, abstractions which present themselves to it as an external, alien power. The deformation of consciousness and the alienation of the political superstructure are consequences of the basic alienation of labour—which, however, is not a 'mistake' on history's part but a necessary precondition of the future society of free beings in control of the vital process of their own lives.

In this way *Capital* may be regarded as a logical continuation of Marx's earliest views; and this continuity is attested by his reference, in the Afterword to the second edition of Volume I (1873), to his criticisms of Hegel 'almost thirty years ago', i.e. no doubt to the Manuscripts themselves.

Admittedly, such expressions as 'man's recovery of his own species-essence' and 'the reconciliation of essence and existence' do not appear in Marx's writings after 1844. This, as we have seen, is best explained by his controversy with the German 'true socialists', who regarded not only socialism itself but the movement towards it as all humanity's concern, putting their faith in action by all social classes and not only the proletariat with its special interests. Marx, however, once he had come to the conclusion that socialism would be achieved not by humanitarian sentiment but by the paroxysm of the class struggle and if necessary by revolutionary force, from then on avoided any expressions which might suggest the idea of class solidarity or imply that the world could be transformed by ideals and emotions which transcended class enmity. Nevertheless, his original intention remained the same. He still believed that socialism was the concern of humanity as a whole and would do away with classes and privilege; and, though he was naturally most moved by the oppression of the working class, he analysed the process of dehumanization and reification from the point of view of the capitalist as well.

The idea of man's recovery of his own self is in fact comprised in that of alienation, which Marx continued to employ: for alienation is nothing but a process in which man deprives himself of what he truly is, of his own humanity. To speak in these terms implies, of course, that we know what man 'truly' is as opposed to what he empirically is: what the content of human nature is, conceived of not as a set of features which may be empirically ascertained but as a set of requirements that must be fulfilled in order to make human beings genuinely human. Without some such standard, vague though it may be, 'alienation' has no meaning. Accordingly, whenever Marx uses this term he presupposes, expressly or otherwise, a non-historical or prehistorical norm of humanity. This, however, is not a collection of permanent, unchanging qualities belonging to some arbitrary ideal, but a conception of the conditions of

development enabling men to display their creative powers to the full, untrammelled by material needs. The fulfilment of humanity is not, in Marx's view, a
matter of attaining some final, imagined perfection, but of freeing man for ever
from conditions that hamper his growth and make him the slave of his own
works. The idea of freedom from alienation, and thus of alienation itself,
requires a preliminary value-judgement and an idea of what 'humanity' means.

The term 'alienation' still occurs frequently in the *Grundrisse* (1857-8) but
is less common in Marx's writing thereafter, and is seldom used in *Capital*.
This, however, is a change of language and not of substance; for the process
whereby man's labour and its products become alien to him is described in
Capital in terms which clearly show that Marx has in mind the same phenomenon as that described in the Manuscripts.

It is important to note, in Marx's early criticism of Hegel, that he did not at
any time identify alienation with externalization, i.e. the labour process
whereby human strength and skill are converted into new products. It would
clearly be absurd to speak of abolishing alienation in this sense, since in all
imaginable circumstances men will have to expend energy to produce the
things they need. Hegel, as we have seen, did identify alienation with externalization, and he could therefore only conceive man's final reconciliation
with the world by way of abolishing the objectivity of the object. To Marx, however, the fact that people 'objectivize' their powers does not mean that they
become the poorer by whatever they produce; on the contrary, labour in itself
is an affirmation and not a denial of humanity, being the chief form of the
unending process of man's self-creation. It is only in a society ruled by private
property and the division of labour that productive activity is a source of misery and dehumanization, and labour destroys the workman instead of enriching him. When alienated labour is done away with, people will continue to
externalize and 'objectivize' their powers, but they will be able to assimilate
the work of their hands as an expression of their collective ability.

Again, there appears to be no contradiction between the young Marx's
praise of the self-affirmation that a productive worker enjoys or may enjoy, and
the argument in the third volume of *Capital* that future progress would consist
in the gradual reduction of necessary work, i.e. that involved in satisfying elementary physical needs. The time thus saved was not to be spent in idleness
but in free creative activity, the earnest, absorbing toil which, for Marx, was typ-
ified by that of the artist. Man would continue to assert his humanity in the
form of labour, but would spend less and less time producing food, clothing,
and furniture and more and more on the products of art and science.

There is also good ground for saying that Marx continued to hold the view
he expressed in 1844 that man is acquainted with nature not as it is in itself but
through the medium of a socially created system of needs. In one of his last

works, a commentary (written in 1880) on Adolph Wagner's handbook of political economy, he argues that man regards the external world as a means of satisfying his needs and not a mere object of contemplation, and that the features he perceives in it and embodies in language, in other words all his conceptual categories, are related to his practical requirements. It is clear from this that Marx never accepted the view that the world in itself is simply reflected in human minds and that the images found there are then transformed into abstract concepts.

It can be argued, on the other hand, that the Romantic idea of man once more achieving unity with nature does not appear in Marx's writings after 1844, and it may seem from the *Grundrisse* that he shifted to a utilitarian or similar viewpoint. In one of his many descriptions (such as we find both in *The Communist Manifesto* and in *Capital*) of the tremendous part played by capitalism in advancing civilization, he says that capital for the first time made it possible for men to 'assimilate' nature in a universal way, i.e. to treat it as an object of use and not of idolatry. But here too it is difficult to speak of a real change of view. Marx himself did not share the idolatrous view of nature that he commended capitalism for destroying, or regard the world in its primal, untamed state as deserving of human worship. He believed that man perceives and organizes the world in accordance with his needs, and that as humanity progresses so nature becomes more humanized, more obedient, and less incalculable. The expression of his view may have changed, but not the view itself.

As we have already said, the publication of the *Grundrisse* went a long way to refute those who held that there was a major discontinuity in the evolution of Marx's ideas. It was clear, in particular, that his theory of value and of money combined harmoniously with the concept of alienation. No doubt two separate traditions are here synthesized: those of Hegel and of the classic British economists, whom Marx began to study while still in Paris. It was in fact one of his greatest achievements to express the theory of alienation, derived from Bauer, Feuerbach, and Hess, in conceptual categories which he took over, though with substantial modification, from Ricardo.

2. *The classical economic tradition and the theory of value*

THE theory of value, which is the core of *Capital*, has a history which may be traced back to Aristotle's time. It was of interest for both theoretical and practical reasons. The theoretical question is: since goods are exchanged for one another at a particular rate, they must have some property that makes them quantitatively comparable, despite all their differences of quality; what, then, is this common feature which reduces the multiplicity of things to a single measure? The practical question, which was much debated in the Middle Ages, is that of a 'just price'. Although expressed in normative terms—how should the just price of a given article be determined?—this is really the same question as how to define the conditions of 'equivalent exchange', in which the purchaser pays the price to which the seller is 'really' entitled. This was directly related to another question frequently posed by medieval theologians, moralists, and political writers: was it lawful to lend money at interest, and, if so, on what ground? Clearly, the question of a 'just price' and of interest could only be answered by determining what constituted the 'real' value of a commodity, and how it was to be measured.

The idea that the value of an article is to be measured by the amount of labour that went into its production was advanced by various thinkers before the eighteenth century. Marx, who had made a thorough study of the history of the problem, took as the starting-point of his own theory two classic works which he regarded as the bases of economic science: Adam Smith's *Inquiry into the Nature and Causes of the Wealth of Nations* (1776) and Ricardo's *Principles of Political Economy and Taxation* (1817).

Smith's main work is devoted *inter alia* to the question of how national wealth increases and how it can be measured objectively, regardless of price fluctuations. He assumed that increasing wealth was desirable, and sought to prove that state intervention in production and trade could only impede its growth. He distinguished between productive and non-productive labour, including in the former not only agricultural labour (as did the physiocrats) but all occupations which involved the processing of material objects for useful purposes—i.e. excluding services, administration, political and intellectual activities, etc.—and which produced 'surpluses' that could be used for further production. The question of how to measure the value of a product depended, in Smith's view, on how the national product was calculated. He distinguished the use-value of an object, i.e. its power to satisfy a human need, from its exchange-value, which was the proper subject-matter of economics; for it was clear that some objects, such as air, were of great use but were not objects of exchange, while others, though of very small use, fetched enormous prices.

However, Smith argued, exchange-value is not the same as the actual price of a commodity; on the contrary, it is necessary to find out in what conditions prices correspond to 'real' value, and what causes them to vary from it. The real or 'natural' value of an article is measured by the quantity of work that has gone into producing it; such, at least, was the case in primitive societies, where goods were exchanged on the basis of labour-time, for example the time spent in hunting game. But in modern societies other factors come into play besides labour, namely capital and land; so that the value or 'natural price' of a product includes remuneration for the worker, a return on the capital used, and an element for rent. The distribution of profits between capitalists, landowners, and workers is thus in accordance with nature. The increase of wealth is in the general interest of all classes engaged in production: Smith did not believe that wages were bound to gravitate to the bare subsistence level, as Malthus and, at least for a time, Marx were subsequently to contend. It is also in the interest of all for market prices to be as close as possible to 'natural' ones, and the market itself ensures automatically that they will tend to this level despite fluctuations; artificial regulation of the market by administrative action is more likely to disturb the process than to assist it. The market also provides a common measure for unequal forms of human labour, which must be rewarded not simply on a time basis but according to the complexity of the task and the skill put into it.

Smith did not indicate any way in which 'natural' prices and national revenue could be calculated independently of market prices. Nevertheless, his work was the first attempt to arrive at a complete system of categories applicable to the analysis of economic activity, on the premiss that that activity obeys laws of its own, independent of human volition, and is regulated by the 'invisible hand' of the market. *The Wealth of Nations* is one of the most important documents in the history of liberalism, though Smith came to modify in some respects his belief in the automatically favourable effects of competition and the market; he did not, moreover, draw a clear line as yet between economic and moral aspects.

Ricardo put somewhat different questions from those of Smith, but for a time at least used the same instruments of analysis. He was less interested in calculating the national income than in discovering the basis of its distribution among different classes. He believed that in theory the value of commodities could be expressed in terms of labour units (machines too being treated as the sum of labour involved in making them), but he recognized that such a calculation was impracticable in respect of large-scale economic processes. He also perceived a contradiction between the dependence of prices on labour and the tendency for rates of profit to even out as regards different branches of production; for it is clear that the amount of capital per labour unit varies in different sectors of industry, so that there cannot be a uniform rate of profit if prices are proportionate to labour input. In the last resort, the labour theory of value was not so important to Ricardo as it subsequently was to Marx.

Ricardo saw, much more clearly than Smith, the conflict of interest between capitalists and wage-earners. He recognized that technical progress might lead to a fall in employment and so reduce the workers' total income. He was also inclined to share Malthus's view that wages tend to fall to the bare subsistence level, as otherwise the workers will breed more children, the supply of labour will increase, and wages will drop once more.

Marx regarded the works of the classic British economists as a model of unprejudiced analysis, endeavouring without sentiment to discover the actual mechanisms of social life. He understood, indeed, that their doctrine was grounded in economic liberalism and the belief that it was 'natural' for owners of land and capital to be rewarded for their share in production. But what interested him in Smith and Ricardo was their description of the interrelation between the various elements in the production process: investment, population growth, wages, food costs, foreign trade, etc. The classic economists believed, like Hegel, that one could not understand much of human society by observing people's intentions in their individual relationships; the laws that governed its working were not intended by anyone, but it was they and not men's thoughts which determined human behaviour.

Marx, however, used the theory of value in a different way from any of the economists who preceded him. Instead of applying it to the question of how the national product is to be estimated or how it is distributed, he used the theory chiefly to investigate the nature of exploitation in a society based on private property.

Thus, apart from the two points already mentioned (the two-fold character of labour, and the contention that what the wage-earner sells is not labour but labour-power), the theory of value was transformed by Marx in two other essential respects. In the first place, unlike Ricardo, he held that labour is not only the measure of value but its only source. Secondly, he maintained that the phenomenon of exchange-value is not a natural and inseparable part of society or civilization, but is a historical and transitory form of the organization of production and exchange. Such are the four main respects in which Marx altered the traditional theory of value.

Marx spent many years amending, correcting, and completing his economic doctrine. As Ernst Mandel has shown, his first notes of 1844–5 indicate that he then regarded Ricardo's theory of value as erroneous because it failed to explain the maladjustment of supply and demand, and hence economic crises, and also as morally suspect because it implied that the natural value of human labour was defined by the subsistence level.

Marx arrived at his own formulation of the theory of value by various stages; we shall not, however, pursue them here, but will describe the theory as it appears in its final form in *Capital*.

3. *The double form of value and the double character of labour*

AT the outset of *Capital* Marx observes that every useful object may be looked at from a qualitative or a quantitative point of view: we may either consider the properties that make it useful as bread, cloth, furniture, etc., or simply the amount of work, of whatever kind, that has gone into it. In this way human products have a double value, or rather two incommensurate kinds of value: use-value, the characteristics that enable them to satisfy human needs, and the value which derives from the amount of labour-time that has gone to make them. When articles are compared with each other in the process of exchange, their value takes the form of exchange-value. Particular useful objects are thus endowed with abstract exchange-value, the crystallization of labour-time irrespective of the difference between one form of labour and another. It is only labour as such that constitutes exchange-value. Objects that are useful but are not man-made (natural resources, water-power, virgin soil, and forests) have no value, even though they have a price—a point which Marx explains later in the context of surplus value.

As exchange-values, things are comparable quantitatively in terms of the amount of labour-time embodied in them; they can thus form the object of an exchange in which they are reduced to the homogeneous aspect of labour-time. However, this does not mean the time actually employed in making them: it could not be the case that one loaf of bread was worth twice as much as another because the baker was less skilful or had less good equipment and therefore took twice as long to make it. What we are concerned with is not actual labour but socially necessary labour-time, defined as the average amount of time necessary to produce a given article at a particular historical stage of human ability and technical progress. This necessary labour-time is the quantitative standard of the relative values of things, permitting them to be bought and sold at a determinate rate. Goods embodying the same amount of work in this sense have the same value, however different their uses and physical qualities.

It is clear that the possession of use-value is a necessary, though not a sufficient, condition of the possession of exchange-value: no product can be exchanged, and thus become a commodity, unless it satisfies some need and is good for something. To put it another way: a thing does not become an exchange-value without assuming the character of a commodity, and it does not become a commodity without entering into the process of exchange. People have been making useful things since the dawn of history, but until there is a system of exchange based on homogeneous labour-time there are no commodities and no exchange-value. Exchange-value is not an intrinsic quality of objects, but derives from their involvement in the social process of circulation and exchange. Products are converted into values by being exchanged for one another.

The general form of value results from the joint action of the whole world of commodities, and from that alone. A commodity can acquire a general expression of its value only by all other commodities, simultaneously with it, expressing their values in the same equivalent; and every new commodity must follow suit. It thus becomes evident that, since the existence of commodities as values is purely social, this social existence can be expressed only by the totality of their social relations, and consequently that the form of their value must be a socially recognized form. (*Capital*, I, Ch. I, 3C,1)

The commodity form of objects is thus the effect of a particular kind of social nexus, viz. the situation in which people engaged in an exchange confront each other as private owners,

> whose will resides in those objects and who behave in such a way that each does not appropriate the other's commodity and part with his own except by means of an act done by mutual consent . . . All commodities are non-use-values for their owners, and use-values for their non-owners. Consequently, they must all change hands. But this change of hands is what constitutes their exchange, and the latter puts them in relation with each other as values, and realizes them as values. Hence commodities must be realized as values before they can be realized as use-values. (*Capital*, I, Ch. II)

The quality of things that we call value, which is unknown to nature and conferred on them by the conditions of human society, is the basis, in Marx's theory, of the twofold character of human labour. On the one hand, labour is a concrete activity of a specific kind, issuing in a specific product; on the other hand, it is labour in general, the simple expenditure of human labour-power. This abstract, homogeneous labour is the true creator of exchange-value, while differentiated labour creates use-value. In considering the production of commodities, i.e. production for exchange, we abstract our attention from the difference between a baker's work and that of a spinner or a woodcutter, treating them as identical from the point of view of the exertion of labour-power for a time that can be exactly measured. In this way the most complex forms of labour are reduced to labour *tout court*, or labour-time. It is thus that disparate products can be compared and exchanged, and that a change in productivity affects the total amount of use-value created, but not that of exchange-value. When technology improves, the same amount of effort produces more goods, but the value of each article falls correspondingly, so that the total sum of values remains the same. At whatever stage of technical development, society produces the same quantity of values in the same amount of working time.

Since all products of labour manifest their value only in exchange, i.e. in comparison with one another, it follows that any of them is equally suitable as a standard with which to measure the others. The appearance of a universal standard of value in the form of money was possible owing to the prior existence in things of the abstract quality created in the process of exchange. The fact that in the course of time precious metals acquired a privileged position as standards of value was due to the physical properties of uniformity, divisibility, resistance to corrosion, etc., which made them more suitable than other things previously used as money, for example cattle. In itself gold is no different from any other commodity as an exchange-value, and its value derives not from any magic properties but from its being the product of abstract human labour; it had first to be a commodity like any other, before it was promoted to the role of a universal standard. Yet in money—considered as a standard of value, a means of payment, exchange, and accumulation—exchange-value somehow becomes autonomous and its origin in labour is lost to view. The fact that the products of labour can be appropriated in the form of money creates the illusion that money or gold is an intrinsic, original source of wealth. Quoting, in *Capital*, the tirade against gold by Shakespeare's Timon which he had used in the 1844 Manuscripts, Marx observes: 'Just as every qualitative difference between commodities is extinguished in money, so money, like the radical leveller that it is, does away with all distinctions. But money itself is a commodity, an external object, capable of becoming the private property of any individual. Thus social power becomes the private power of private persons.' (Ibid., Ch. III, 3a.)

When considering exchange-value in itself we make the fictitious assumption that goods are exchanged according to their value. The creation of money, however, introduces the factor of price, i.e. the amount of currency for which other articles are exchanged. When value is converted into price, goods express their quantitative relationship to one another in the form of a quantitative relationship to money. It thus becomes possible for value and price to diverge, i.e. for goods to be exchanged at a rate higher or lower than their value expressed in money terms.

> The price-form, however, is not only compatible with the possibility of a quantitative incongruity between magnitude of value and price, i.e. between the former and its expression in money, but it may also conceal a qualitative inconsistency, so much so that, although money is nothing but the value-form of commodities, price ceases altogether to express value. Objects that in themselves are no commodities, such as conscience, honour etc., may be offered for sale by their holders and thus acquire, through their price, the form of commodities. Hence an object may have a price without having value . . . On the other hand, the imaginary price-form may sometimes conceal either a direct or an indirect real value-relation; for instance, the price of uncultivated land, which is without value because no human labour has been incorporated in it. (*Capital*, I, Ch. III, 1)

The money-form thus makes possible, and actually brings about, an incongruity between value and the price which is supposed to express it. As Marx states in Volume III of *Capital*, the sum total of the prices of the whole social product must be equal to the sum of its values; but, in a commodity economy, this equation not only permits but actually presupposes inequality in particular cases, i.e. prices that tend to equal values but constantly fluctuate above or below them. The contrast between values and prices expresses the basic contradiction of capitalist production and exchange. This inequality, however, is not the explanation of profit: selling an article above its value is not the true origin of profit, only the origin of one form of it. The phenomenon of profit must be explained on the assumption that all commodities are sold at their true value. This sounds paradoxical, but, as Marx observes in *Wages, Price and Profit*, 'it is also a paradox that the earth moves round the sun and that water consists of two highly inflammable gases. Scientific truth is always paradoxical if judged by everyday experience, which catches only the delusive appearances of things'.

4. Commodity fetishism. Labour-power as a commodity

BEFORE investigating the source of profit, however, we may note the effect of the money form on human thought-processes. Neither the exchange of commodities nor the existence of money is a sufficient condition of capitalist production, which requires in addition the free sale of labour-power and a production system aimed essentially at increasing exchange-value. But the commodity and money-form assumed by objects is the root of the particular illusion which Marx calls commodity fetishism, and which accounts for a large part of the false consciousness of human beings in regard to their own social existence.

The essence of commodity fetishism is that, in measuring the output of energy by labour-time, we introduce into the products of labour the measure which originally relates to the life-process itself. Thus the mutual relations of human beings as exchangers of goods take on the form of relations between objects, as though the latter had mysterious qualities which of themselves made them valuable, or as though value were a natural, physical property of things.

> The relation of the producers to the sum total of their own labour is presented to them as a social relation, existing not between themselves but between the products of their labour. This is the reason why the products of labour become commodities, social things whose qualities are at once perceptible and imperceptible by the senses . . . The existence of things *qua* commodities, and the value-relation between the products of labour which stamps them as commodities, have absolutely no connection with their physical properties and with the material relations arising therefrom. Here it is a particular social relation between men that assumes, in their eyes, the imaginary form of a relation between things. To find an analogy we must have recourse to the mist-enveloped regions of the religious world, where the productions

of the human brain appear as independent beings endowed with life, and entering into relation both with one another and with the human race. (*Capital*, I, Ch. I, 4)

This process whereby social relations masquerade as things or relations between things is the cause of human failure to understand the society in which we live. In exchanging goods for money men involuntarily accept the position that their own qualities, abilities, and efforts do not belong to them but somehow inhere in the objects they have created. In this way they are the victims of the deformation of consciousness called alienation, and more particularly of reification, which confers objective reality on social relationships. Marx no longer uses the term 'alienation', but the description of the phenomenon is the same as in his earlier works, and so is the analogy with religion which he owes to Feuerbach.

Commodity fetishism, then, is the inability of human beings to see their own products for what they are, and their unwitting consent to be enslaved by human power instead of wielding it. Fetishism contains in embryo all other forms of alienation—the autonomy of political institutions which turn into instruments of oppression, the autonomy of creations of the human brain in the shape of religious fantasies: in short, the whole sum of man's enslavement to his own works. All social progress—scientific development and the organization of labour, improved administration and the multiplication of useful products—turn against man and are transformed into quasi-natural forces. Every genuine advance only serves to increase man's subjugation, as though to confirm Hegel's doctrine of the contradictions of progress.

However, the deluded consciousness which mistakes social relations for things finds particular expression in a phenomenon typical of the capitalist mode of production, namely the reification of labour-power—a situation in which human persons, real subjects, appear in the context of labour as commodities bought and sold on the market according to the rules dictated by the law of value.

As we have seen, the socialists had argued from Ricardo's labour theory of value that exploitation consisted in labour being sold at too low a price, and that the cause of social injustice was this non-equivalent exchange between the wage-earner and the capitalist. What must be done, therefore, was to reorganize production and exchange on a basis of equivalence, so that labour was sold at its true value.

However useful this reasoning might be for the purpose of agitation among the workers, Marx regarded it as quite erroneous. Exploitation, in his view, did not consist in the worker selling his labour below its value. To explain the phenomena of profit and exploitation it was necessary to start from the principle of equivalent exchange in the circulation of commodities as well as in the sale of the particular commodity known as labour-power. For—and this is the corner-stone of Marx's analysis of capitalism in its mature form—wage-labour is based on the sale of labour-power, not the sale of labour. Labour creates values, but does not itself possess value. To elucidate this, Marx propounds the question of the origin of capitalist profit. How is it that the owner of the means of production can get more exchange value out of them than he puts into the whole production process? How is it that a man with money can, simply because it is his, multiply it by lending at interest? How is it that a landowner is entitled to rent without any expenditure of labour on his part? It might appear to the simple-minded that capital is an autonomous source of value with a mysterious power of self-multiplication: a view which supports the theory of three independent sources of value, namely land, capital, and labour. Theories of this kind are used to justify the capitalist system and to suggest that capitalists, landowners, and workers have a common class interest as co-producers. They are, however, based on a confusion of thought, as in Condillac's theory that value is increased by the exchange process itself. It is true that the excess of a commodity's value over the cost of producing it is only realized in circulation, in the act of exchange, and this has given rise to the delusion that it originates in the act of exchange. But value, being exclusively the effect of the work of production, cannot be increased by merely commercial operations. Some socialists have argued that a merchant who buys cheap and sells dear is, in effect, a swindler, and that all his profit would at once disappear in conditions of equivalent exchange. But the fact is that profit can exist even when the exchange is strictly equivalent: it does not arise from circulation, though it only manifests itself when goods are exchanged. A man with money can multiply it thanks to the fact that there is on the market a particular commodity whose use-value is a source of value, and which creates exchange-value as its use-value is realized, i.e. in the process of consumption. This commodity is labour-power or capacity for labour, 'the aggregate of those mental and physical capabilities existing in a human being, which he exercises whenever he produces a use-value of any description' (*Capital*, I, Ch. IV, 3; English edn., Ch. VI). Wage-labour is the sale of labour-power for a fixed time. For this exchange to take place there must be a class of wage-earners who are free in a double sense: legally free to dispose of their labour-power and sell it to whomever they like, and also free from ownership of the means of production, i.e. possessing nothing but their labour-power and consequently obliged to sell it. This situation, in which the free wage-earner sells his labour-power to the owner of the instruments of production, is the characteristic feature of capitalism. It is a system which had a beginning in history and will have an end, but meanwhile it has revolutionized the whole historical process.

The value of labour-power is determined in the same way as that of any other commodity, by the amount of labour-time necessary to reproduce it. The reproduction of labour-power consists in maintaining the labourer in a condition in which he is able to work and to rear a fresh generation of non-property-owning producers. In other words, the value of labour-power is the value of the products necessary to keep the labourer and his children alive and able-bodied. Consequently, the sale of labour-power is an equivalent exchange when the wage-earner receives, in return, an amount equal to the cost of his subsistence. This amount is not determined solely by the physiological mini-mum but also by needs that vary historically; yet the physiological minimum constitutes the lower limit of wages. Thus the utopian socialists are wrong to argue that exploitation arises because the worker sells his labour for less than its value. As long as his wage enables him to remain alive and fit, he has not sold his labour for less than its value; the exchange is an equivalent one.

But this does not mean there is no such thing as exploitation. On the contrary, it is much more prevalent than the utopians thought, but it is due, not to a non-equivalent exchange between the seller and buyer of labour-power, but to the fact that at a certain technological level the application of labour-power can create exchange-values far greater than the values of the products neces-sary to maintain it. Or, to put if differently, the working day may be much longer than would be necessary to produce the commodities that keep the workman in an active state. The use-value of labour-power consists in the fact that it cre-ates an exchange-value greater than its own. As in any purchase, the seller of labour-power parts with its use-value, which he makes over to the capitalist, in return for its exchange-value. The owner of the means of production pays the value of a day's work and acquires the right to use the worker's labour-power for anything up to twenty-four hours. The excess of the value so created over the cost of the worker's maintenance is 'surplus value', and this is acquired by the capitalist even in conditions of equivalent exchange. If half the worker's day corresponds to the value of the products necessary to reproduce his labour-power, the other half is unrequited labour—i.e. the consumption of labour-power (for the labour *is* the consumption) which creates the surplus value acquired by the owner of the means of production. This explains how exploita-tion can be consistent with equivalent exchange, and also why there is bound to be a class struggle against exploitation—a struggle which cannot be won sim-ply by raising wages, but only by abolishing the whole system of wage-labour.

> The capitalist maintains his rights as a purchaser when he tries to make the working day as long as possible, and to make, whenever possible, two working days out of one. On the other hand, the peculiar nature of the commodity sold implies a limit to its consumption by the purchaser, and the labourer maintains his right as seller when he wishes to reduce the working day to one of definite normal duration. There is here,

therefore, an antinomy: right against right, both equally bearing the seal of the law of exchanges. Between equal rights, force decides. Hence it is that in the history of capitalist production the determination of what is a working day presents itself as the result of a struggle between collective capital, i.e. the class of capitalists, and collective labour, i.e. the working class. (*Capital*, I, Ch. VIII, 1; English edn., Ch. X, 1)

The system of wage-labour, in which the capitalist buys labour-power for the time during which it is exercised, obscures the division of the working day into the work necessary to reproduce labour-power and the extra, unpaid labour that creates surplus value. To outward appearance the employer pays for the whole of the worker's labour, but in fact he does not; the situation is the reverse of that which obtains under slavery, the slave appears to be working entirely for his master when in fact part of his working day is devoted to producing the values necessary for his own maintenance. In regular conditions of serfdom, on the other hand, the serf's labour for his lord and the work he does for his own benefit are clearly divided in time, and it is clear which part of his labour is unremunerated. The unrequited labour-time of the wage-earner is concealed in the homogeneous process of production, and it is necessary to analyse the situation to discover the source of surplus value. The capitalist expends a certain sum on the worker's wages, and the values created over and above that sum accrue to him as profit, which, however, only becomes actual in the circulation of commodities. The sum total of these surplus values is called 'absolute surplus value'; the ratio between it and the total amount of capital expended by the employer on wages is called 'relative surplus value'.

5. *The alienation of labour and of its product*

THE one and only source of value, then, is productive labour, the shaping of material objects that satisfy human needs. All secondary forms of capital—that of merchants, bankers, and landowners—are used in the acquisition of surplus value, but play no part in its production. 'Industrial capital is the only mode of the existence of capital in which the latter's function consists not only in the appropriation of surplus value or surplus product, but likewise its creation' (*Capital*, II, Ch. 1, 4). Industrial capital includes the organization of transport. 'The actual transport industry and expressage can be, and in fact are, industrial branches entirely distinct from commerce; and purchasable and saleable commodities may be stored in docks or in other public premises, the cost of storage being charged to the merchant by third persons in so far as he has to advance it . . . The express company owner, the railway director and the shipowner are not "merchants"' (Ibid. III, Ch. XVII). Transport and storage, then, are part of production; but no commercial activity in the strict sense, i.e.

no act of exchange, can endow commodities with additional value. Only the
workman processing or transporting commodities, or of course the peasant
labourer, creates new exchange-values and increases the sum total of value at
the community's disposal.

We have thus discovered the social nexus on which the whole edifice of capitalist production is based, namely the commodity character of labour-power.
The fact that labour-power is a commodity means that man functions as a
thing, that his personal qualities and abilities are bought and sold like any
other commodity; his brains and muscle, his physical energy and creative powers are reduced to a state in which only their exchange value counts for anything. This reification, the turning of a personality into a thing, is the measure
of human degradation under capitalism. In this part of *Capital* Marx returns to
the ideas he formulated as far back as 1843, when he saw in the working class
the epitome of dehumanization and also the embodied hope of a restored
humanity. In Chapter I of *Wage Labour and Capital* (1849) he wrote: 'The exercise of labour power, labour, is the worker's own life-activity, the manifestation
of his own life. And this life-activity he sells to another person in order to
secure the necessary means of subsistence. Thus his life-activity is for him only
a means to enable him to exist. He works in order to live.' So in *Capital*:

> The means of production are at once changed into means for the absorption of the
> labour of others. It is no longer the labourer that employs the means of production,
> but the means of production that employ the labourer. Instead of being consumed
> by him as material elements of his productive activity, they consume him as the fer-
> ment necessary to their own life-process, and the life-process of capital consists only
> in its movement as value constantly expanding, constantly multiplying itself.' (*Capi-
> tal*, I, Ch. IX; English edn., Ch. XI)

In Volumes I and III of *Capital* Marx returns again and again to the theme
of the alienation of labour—the vital productive process is nothing to the
worker except as a means of maintaining himself—and the alienation of the
fruits of labour: the objectification of the worker's energy, creating surplus
value for others, is to him only the means of perpetuating his own poverty and
dehumanization.

> The relationships of capital . . . place the labourer in a condition of utter indiffer-
> ence, isolation and alienation vis à vis the means of incorporating his labour . . .
> The labourer looks at the social nature of his labour, at its combination with the
> labour of others for a common purpose, as he would at an alien power; the condi-
> tion of effecting this combination is alien property, the squandering of which would
> be totally indifferent to him if he were not compelled to economize with it. (*Capi-
> tal*, III, Ch. V, 1)

Capitalist production is in itself indifferent to the particular use-value and distinctive features of any commodity it produces. In every sphere of production it is only concerned with producing surplus value, and appropriating a certain quantity of unpaid labour incorporated in the product of labour. And it is likewise in the nature of the wage-labour subordinated to capital that it is indifferent to the specific character of its labour and must submit to being transformed in accordance with the requirements of capital and to being transferred from one sphere of production to another. (ibid., Ch. X)

Capitalism separates the product of labour from labour itself, the objective conditions of the productive process from human subjectivity. The worker creates values but has no way of realizing them for himself or enriching his life by appropriating them as use-values.

Since . . . his own labour has been alienated from himself by the sale of his labour power, has been appropriated by the capitalist and incorporated with capital, it must, in the [production] process, be realized in a product that does not belong to him. As the process of production is also the process by which the capitalist consumes labour power, the labourer's product is incessantly converted, not only into commodities, but into capital, into value that sucks up the value-creating power, into means of subsistence that buy the person of the labourer, into means of production that command the producers. The labourer therefore constantly produces material, objective wealth, but in the form of capital, of an alien power that dominates and exploits him; and the capitalist as constantly produces labour power, but in the form of a subjective source of wealth, separated from the objects in and by which it can alone be realized—an abstract source, existing only in the labourer's person; in short, the capitalist produces the labourer, but as a wage-labourer. This incessant reproduction, this perpetuation of the labourer, is the *sine qua non* of capitalist production. (*Capital*, I, Ch. XXI; English edn., Ch. XXIII)

Consequently, the worker's vital functions are realized outside the production process, and it is only when not at work that he belongs to himself; as a worker, he belongs to the capitalist and functions only as a living reproducer of capital. This corresponds precisely to the picture drawn by Marx in the Paris Manuscripts. Even the worker's individual consumption, though motivated by his private needs, is, from the point of view of the economic process, a part of the activity of reproducing his labour-power, like greasing a wheel or supplying a steam-engine with coal. 'The labourer exists to satisfy the needs of self-expansion of existing values, instead of, on the contrary, material wealth existing to satisfy the needs of the labourer's development. As, in religion, man is governed by the emanation of his own brain, so in capitalist production he is governed by the work of his own hand.' (*Capital*, I, Ch. XXIII, 1; English edn., Ch. XXV, 1.) Since surplus value merely goes to swell the mass of existing capital, labour confers no kind of ownership. The right of property turns into its opposite: for the capitalist it becomes the right to appropriate values created by others, while for the worker it means that his own product does not belong to him. Consequently, the exchange relationship is completely illusory.

In the worker's situation we observe in its most blatant form the enslavement of man by his own works and by technical progress.

> Machinery, considered alone, shortens the hours of labour, but in the service of capital it lengthens them; in itself it lightens labour, but when employed by capital it heightens the intensity of labour; in itself it is a victory of man over the forces of nature, but in the hands of capital it makes man the slave of those forces; in itself it increases the producers' wealth, but in the hands of capital it makes them paupers. (*Capital*, I, Ch. XIII, 6; English edn., Ch. XV, 6)

The effect of disjoining human labour from property, and creating a situation in which the worker's personal life is external to his work, is that the social process of production cannot take the form of a community. Co-operation itself is alienated *vis-à-vis* the co-operating producers: it presents itself to them as a form of compulsion, not alleviating their mutual isolation but intensifying it. 'The behaviour of men in the social process of production is purely atomic, and hence their relations to one another in production assume a material character independent of their control and conscious individual action. The chief manifestation of this is that products in general take the form of commodities.' (*Capital*, I, Ch. II.) Here Marx again repeats an idea from the Manuscripts. The alienation of labour is the source of the commodity form of production, not the other way about; by the same token it is the source of capital, i.e. of the value which increases itself by surplus value thanks to the purchase of labour-power.

6. The alienation of the process of socialization

THE social character of labour under capitalist conditions is thus apparent only; it is a technological process, not a human one, and does nothing to overcome the isolation of producers.

> The connection between [the workers'] various labours appears to them, ideally, in the shape of a preconceived plan of the capitalist, and practically in the shape of the authority of the same capitalist, the powerful will of one who subjects their activity to his own aims . . . Being independent of one another, the labourers are isolated persons who enter into relations with the capitalist, but not with one another. This co-operation begins only with the labour process, but by that time they have ceased to belong to themselves. Once involved in that process, they are incorporated with

capital. As co-operating members of a working organism, they are merely a special mode of the existence of capital. Hence the productive power developed by the labourer when working in co-operation is the productive power of capital. (*Capital*, I, Ch. XI; English edn., Ch. XIII)

Thus the characteristic and essential function of capitalism which consists in the exchange of variable capital (i.e. capital used to pay employees) for the labour-power of human beings is the true cause of producers being turned into things and prevented from forming a human community; for their community takes the form only of enforced co-operation between elements of their personal existence which have already been sold in the shape of labour-power, and are no longer their property. 'It is a result of the division of labour in manufactures that the labourer is confronted with the intellectual potencies [*Potenzen*] of the material process of production as the property of another and as a power to which he is subjugated.' (*Capital*, I, Ch. XII, 5; English edn., Ch. XIV, 5.) Whatever contributes to increasing man's power over the forces of nature likewise contributes, under the special conditions of wage labour, to destroying the producer himself; this applies both to technical progress and to the increased division of labour.

The division of labour in manufacture . . . not only increases the social productive power of labour for the benefit of the capitalist instead of the labourer, but it does this by crippling individual labourers. It creates new conditions for the lordship of capital over labour. While, therefore, on the one hand it presents itself historically as a factor of progress and a necessary phase in the economic development of society, on the other hand it is a refined and civilized method of exploitation' (*Capital*, I, Ch. XII, 5; English edn., Ch. XIV, 5)

The mechanical automaton . . . is the subject, and the workmen are merely conscious organs, co-ordinated with the unconscious organs of the machine and, together with them, subordinated to the central moving power. . . . The lightening of the labour, even, becomes a kind of torture, since the machine does not free the labourer from work, but deprives the work of all interest . . . It is not the workman that employs the instruments of labour, but the instruments of labour that employ the workman . . . By means of its conversion into an automaton, the instrument of labour confronts the labourer during the labour process itself in the guise of capital, of dead labour that enslaves the power of living labour and pumps it dry.' (Ibid., Ch. XIII, 4; English edn., Ch. XV, 4)

The division of labour becomes a fragmentation of man himself, shackled for life to part-activities whose function of creating use-value is of no concern to him, since the subjective purpose of his work is not to produce useful articles but to satisfy his own elementary needs. Indeed, the capitalist system prefers a stupid, mechanized worker who has no human skills beyond ability to perform the task imposed upon him.

But it is not only the worker who is turned into an instrument for the increase of capital; the same thing happens to the personality of the capitalist. Marx says in his Preface that he is concerned with human beings only as personifications of economic categories, embodiments of particular class-relations and class-interests. This is of course simply a methodological principle, excluding psychology from economic analysis and examining, not the motives of actions, but the laws which govern them and which, like those of natural science, do not depend on anyone's intentions. But this approach is only possible because the factual situation is such that the motives of individual capitalists are only manifestations of the tendency of capital to multiply itself, so that the capitalist as such is literally nothing but an embodiment of capital with no subjective or human qualities. 'As capitalist, he is only capital personified. His soul is the soul of capital. But capital has one single life impulse, the tendency to create value and surplus value and to make its constant factor, the means of production, absorb the greatest possible amount of surplus labour. Capital is dead labour, which, vampire-like, only lives by sucking living labour, and lives the more, the more labour it sucks.' (*Capital*, I, Ch. VIII, 1; English edn., Ch. X, 1.) 'Free competition brings out the inherent laws of capitalist production, in the shape of external coercive laws having power over every individual capitalist.' (Ibid. 5.) In the production process the worker and the capitalist are living representatives of variable capital and constant capital respectively, and this causes them to behave in a predetermined fashion. For the same reason, the utopian reformers are mistaken in thinking that the capitalist system can be changed by appealing to the goodwill or human feelings of the exploiters. The capitalist's personal character and intentions play no part in the economic process; he is subject to a force which inexorably shapes his ends, at all events where action on a socially significant scale is concerned. In capitalist production neither the worker nor the capitalist is a human being: their personal qualities have been taken away from them. Thus, when the class-consciousness of the proletariat evolves from awareness of poverty to a revolutionary consciousness and a sense of its historical mission to destroy capitalism, by the same token the worker becomes a human individual once again, throwing off the domination of exchange-value which turned him into a mere object. As for the capitalists, they cannot as a class take up arms against their own dehumanization, since they rejoice in it and in the wealth and power it brings. Thus, although both sides are equally dehumanized, only the wage-earner is spurred by this state of affairs to protestation and social combat.

It can thus be seen that, in Marx's view, not poverty but the loss of human subjectivity is the essential feature of capitalist production. Poverty indeed has been known throughout history, but awareness of poverty and even the revolt against it are not sufficient to restore man's subjectivity and membership of a human community. The socialist movement is not born of poverty, but of the class antagonism which arouses a revolutionary consciousness in the proletariat. The opposition between capitalism and socialism is essentially and originally the opposition between a world in which human beings are degraded into things and a world in which they recover their subjectivity.

7. The pauperization of the working class

THE law which governs the sale of labour-power does not appear in itself to entail that the workers will remain poor or grow poorer. If they sell their labour-power at its true value—and there is nothing in capitalism to prevent this—it might seem that their standard of living can be maintained or even improved, inasmuch as that value is partly determined by non-physiological needs that vary from one period of history to another. But in fact the workers grow more and more impoverished, owing to the accumulation of capital. Moreover, their impoverishment is not only relative, involving a decreasing proportionate share of socially created values, but is also absolute: the working class either receives a diminishing sum total of values, or at all events is increasingly down-graded in the social scale.

All methods for raising the social productiveness of labour are brought about at the cost of the individual labourer; all means for the development of production transform themselves into means of domination over, and exploitation of, the producers; they mutilate the labourer into a fragment of a man, degrade him to the level of an appendage of a machine, destroy any remnant of attraction in his work and turn it into a hated toil; they estrange from him the intellectual potentialities of the labour process in the same degree as science is incorporated in it as an independent power [*Potenz*]; they distort the conditions under which he works, and subject him during the labour process to a despotism the more hateful for its meanness; they transform his lifetime into working-time, and drag his wife and child beneath the wheels of the Juggernaut of capital. But all methods for the production of surplus value are at the same time methods of accumulation; and every extension of accumulation becomes again a means for the development of those methods. It follows therefore that in proportion as capital accumulates, the lot of the labourer, be his payment high or low, must grow worse. The law that always equilibrates the relative surplus population, or industrial reserve army, to the extent and energy of accumulation, this law finally rivets the labourer to capital more firmly than the wedges of Vulcan did Prometheus to the rock. It establishes an accumulation of misery, corresponding with accumulation of capital. Accumulation of wealth at one pole is therefore at the same time accumulation of misery, agony of toil slavery, ignorance, brutality and moral degradation at the opposite pole, i.e. on the side of the class that produces its own product in the form of capital. (*Capital*, I, Ch. XXIII, 4; English edn., Ch. XXV, 4)

Marx put the point with equal clarity in *Wages, Price and Profit*: 'The general tendency of capitalist production is not to raise but to sink the average standard of wages, or to push the value of labour more or less to its minimum limit.' Hence, while the workers' economic struggle against pauperization may modify the downward trend of wages, and while it is necessary and important in itself, it cannot affect the basic development of capitalism or achieve the liberation of the proletariat.

The doctrine of the impoverishment of the proletariat is one of those that have excited most controversy among twentieth-century Marxists. The different references to the subject in Marx's works are by no means unequivocal. In his earlier writings, such as *Wage Labour and Capital* and the *Manifesto*, he appears to have believed in absolute impoverishment, or at least that wages in a capitalist economy were constantly governed by the principle of the physiological minimum. In the *Grundrisse*, however, he observes that the value of labour-power is partly determined by cultural factors, including the increase of needs to which capitalism itself gives rise: the satisfaction of previously unknown needs becomes part of the minimum living standard. In *Wages, Price and Profit* he also emphasizes that the conception of the minimum standard varies according to the traditions of different countries; and in the same work he introduces the idea of a relative fall in wages, i.e. a fall in workers' incomes compared with those of capitalists. The passage just quoted from *Capital* ('the lot of the labourer, be his payment high or low') is often used to argue that Marx finally abandoned the theory of absolute pauperization. But a distinction must be made between the level of wages and other factors governing the standard of living. The sense of the quoted passage is that whether wages are 'high' or 'low', the worker's position is bound to deteriorate both relatively and absolutely; not necessarily in terms of food and clothing, but by spiritual degradation and increasing subjection to economic tyranny.

The conclusion thus is that (1) Marx abandoned the theory that wages are bound to fall to, or remain at, the bare subsistence level; (2) he continued to believe in absolute impoverishment as far as the worker's spiritual and social degradation were concerned; and (3) he maintained the doctrine of relative impoverishment. This doctrine, however, as we may see from Marx's writings and from later discussions among his followers, can be defined in at least three ways. It may mean, firstly, that total wages constitute a diminishing proportion of the national product; or, secondly, that the average worker's income decreases constantly in proportion to the average capitalist's income; or, thirdly, that the worker earns an ever-decreasing amount relative to his own growing needs. Clearly these situations are not interdependent, and any one of them could exist without the other two. It also appears clear that the first might result from various causes, for example a relative fall in the working-class population, in which case it would be misleading to speak of impoverishment. In the third situation impoverishment is defined by subjective criteria which cannot be measured: if, for any reason, consumer aspirations are rapidly rising, any or all classes of the population may feel 'impoverished' except for a handful of the very rich, who need not be members of the bourgeoisie in the strict sense.

It is clear, however, that Marx was determined to find in capitalism a relentless tendency to degrade the worker, and that he resisted facts which indicated that the worker was getting better off. Bertram Wolfe has pointed out that in the first edition of *Capital* various statistics are brought down to 1865 or 1866, but those for the movement of wages stop at 1850; in the second edition (1873) the statistics are brought up to date, again with the exception of those on wages, which had failed to bear out the impoverishment theory. This is a rare but important case of disingenuousness in Marx's treatment of factual data.

In the twentieth century, discussion could not blink the obvious fact that there was no such thing as absolute pauperization in the capitalist economy. The question thus arose whether this also meant that Marx was at fault in his whole theory of accumulation and of the functioning of capitalism. Those who wished to defend his doctrine, and who believed that the theory of absolute pauperization flowed inevitably from it, were at pains to show that despite appearances such pauperization did exist. However, this point of view is seldom met with among Marxists today. Others argue that although the working class, by exerting pressure on the capitalists, has obliged them to lower the rate of profit, this does not mean there has been any change in the nature of capitalist production or the dehumanization that it inevitably brings. As Marx pointed out, wages and working hours are limited in two directions. On the one hand, the worker's elementary physical needs must be met if he is to go on living and if capitalist production is to subsist; on the other, the maximum wage level is determined by the success of the proletariat's struggle at any given time and the amount of pressure it is able to exert on the bourgeoisie. Hence, although Marx's forecast of absolute pauperization has proved wrong, this is not because of any flaw in the doctrine of accumulation and the tendency of capital to increase without limit, but only because Marx underrated the power of the working class to exert pressure within the capitalist framework.

In general, however, it must be borne in mind that material pauperization was not a necessary premiss either of Marx's analysis of the dehumanization caused by wage-labour, or of his prediction of the inescapable ruin of capitalism. That prediction was based on his belief that the internal contradictions of capitalism would destroy the system by bringing about an intensified class struggle, irrespective of whether material poverty increased or not.

8. The nature and historical mission of capitalism

As we saw, the essential characteristic of capitalism in Marx's eyes was its unlimited urge to multiply exchange-value, the insatiable appetite for self-increase by the exploitation of surplus labour. Capital is indifferent to the specific nature of the goods it produces or sells; it is interested in their use-value only in so far as it may serve to increase their exchange-value. Again and again Marx refers in his chief work to the 'wolfish hungering after surplus value' that is the hallmark of capitalism. Societies in which commercial exchange was practised for the purpose of acquiring use-value could not be characterized by this limitless hunger for growth. People who produce commodities to trade against things they want for themselves are, in effect, producing in order to create use-values. But

> the circulation of money as capital is, on the contrary, an end in itself, for the expansion of value takes place only within this constantly renewed movement. The circulation of capital has therefore no limits. As the conscious representative of this movement, the possessor of money becomes a capitalist . . . The expansion [*Verwertung*] of value which is the objective basis of circulation, becomes his subjective aim; and it is only in so far as the appropriation of ever more and more wealth in the abstract becomes the sole motive of his operations that he functions as a capitalist, that is as capital personified and endowed with consciousness and a will. Use-value must therefore never be looked upon as the real aim of the capitalist; neither must the profit on any single transaction. The restless never-ending process of profit-making alone is what he aims at. (*Capital*, I, Ch. IV, 1; English edn., Ch. IV)

It is understandable, therefore, that the capitalist system required as a precondition the generalization of the monetary form of value, which sets no limit to the possibility of accumulation. The capitalist, however, 'fanatically bent on making value expand itself, ruthlessly forces the human race to produce for production's sake; he thus forces the development of the productive powers of society, and creates those material conditions that alone can form the real basis of a higher form of society based on the full and free development of every individual'. (*Capital*, I, Ch. XXII, 4; English edn., Ch. XXIV, 3.) It is not even the case that the capitalist behaves in this way for the sake of his own consumption; on the contrary, as a rule he regards enjoyment as the destruction of value and a form of waste, this kind of ascetic morality being especially common in the first phase of capitalism.

But the same insatiable hunger for exchange-value which degrades and impoverishes the working class is the cause of the amazing technological advance of capitalism.

> Production for value and surplus value implies . . . the constantly operating tendency to reduce the labour time necessary for the production of a commodity. i.e. its value, below the social average prevailing at the time. The pressure to reduce cost-price to the minimum becomes the strongest lever for raising the social productiveness of labour, which, however, is seen only as a continual increase in the productiveness of capital. (*Capital*, III, Ch. LI)

It is for this reason that former societies could exist for centuries in a state of technological stagnation, reproducing their way of life from one generation to another, whereas capitalism, as the *Communist Manifesto* pointed out, cannot exist without constantly revolutionizing the means of production. Technological progress is vital to it because the expansionist tendencies of capital obliges the entrepreneur to seek higher and higher profits by reducing the labour-time necessary to produce a commodity to a lower level than that which is socially necessary; he then markets his commodity at the current price and in so doing makes a profit higher than the average, i.e. that obtainable in average technological conditions.

> When surplus value has to be produced by the conversion of necessary labour into surplus labour, it by no means suffices for capital to take over the labour process in the form in which it has been historically handed down, and then simply to prolong the duration of that process. The technical and social conditions of the process, and consequently the very mode of production, must be revolutionized before the productiveness of labour can be increased. Only thus is it possible to decrease the value of labour power and reduce the portion of the working day necessary for the reproduction of that value. (*Capital*, I, Ch. X; English edn., Ch. XII)

'Modern industry never looks upon and treats the existing form of a production process as final. Its technical basis is therefore revolutionary, while all earlier modes of production were essentially conservative.' (Ibid., Ch. XIII, 9; English edn., Ch. XV, 9.) For this reason 'the capitalist mode of production presents itself historically as a necessary condition of the transformation of the labour process into a social process.' (Ibid., Ch. XI; English edn., Ch. XIII.)

Capitalism, in short, is the necessary historical condition of progress in technology and the organization of labour. The 'wolfish hunger' for surplus value lies at the root of modern industry and modern co-operative methods, although that progress has been attained at the cost of unspeakable suffering, exploitation, poverty, and dehumanization. Fearful as are Marx's descriptions of the victimization of adults and children by the capitalist system, he regards that system not as a historical mistake which could have been avoided if someone, long ago, had devised a better form of social organization, but as a necessary condition of the re-establishment of a true community of mankind. Hence, though he believed the economic struggle of the proletariat to be indispensable, he did not regard it as an end in itself but, above all, as a means of hastening the revolutionary process. The accumulation of capital, by aggravating the workers' poverty, was also bringing closer the day of their liberation. For the hope of destroying capitalism did not lie only in spontaneous action by the working class. The internal contradictions of the system were bringing about a situation in which it could no longer subsist, and this was due to the self-increasing process which was its most vital principle.

9. *The distribution of surplus value*

IN the first volume of *Capital* Marx analyses capitalist production in isolation from the process of circulation and the distribution of profit. He distinguishes between the rate of profit and the rate of surplus value, the former being the ratio of the surplus value obtained in production to the whole of the capital expended—i.e. constant capital (the value of the raw materials, equipment, etc.) plus variable capital (that spent on wages). The defenders of capitalism generally address themselves to the rate of profit, since the capitalist is interested in the ratio between his total investment and the resulting increase of value; exploitation of the worker is a means of maximizing value, not an end in itself. But, according to Marx, the degree of exploitation is not to be measured by the rate of profit but by the rate of surplus value, i.e. the ratio of surplus value to variable capital only: for it is this which shows how much of the value produced by the worker accrues to him and how much he forfeits to the capitalist by the sale of his labour-power. If, for example, the value he creates in a working day is double the price of his labour-power, i.e. the amount of variable capital expended, then the rate of surplus value, or the degree of exploitation, is one hundred per cent. Variable capital alone creates surplus value; the condition of its doing so, however, is the existence of constant capital, 'dead labour' in the form of equipment and the materials of production. There is no linear relationship between the rate of profit and the rate of surplus value; one may rise while the other falls, or vice versa.

The realization of surplus value depends, in reality, on circulation as well as production: the capitalist must sell his product in order to enjoy the excess of value over the production cost. But this complicates the issue in many ways, for commodities do not automatically find a purchaser and there is no guarantee that production, which is not planned on a social scale, will coincide with social demand. As Marx shows in the second volume of *Capital*, the circulation of commodities affects the rate of profit: it takes place over a period of time, during which larger or smaller portions of capital are inactive. Thus the surplus value created by the capital used in production is diminished to the extent of this inactivity, expressed, for example, in raw material stocks or unsold goods. The more rapid the capitalist's turnover, the greater the surplus value and the rate of profit. The market is a race to turn goods into money, in conditions where demand and supply are never exactly matched and consequently prices are never the same as values.

Indeed, capitalist production could not exist if commodities were sold at their true value. The rate of profit varies in different branches of production: different amounts of capital are necessary to hire the same number of workers and thus produce a given quantity of surplus value. Depending on variations in the 'organic composition' of capital (the ratio of the variable to the constant element), and on the different time that it takes for capital to circulate in different spheres of production, there would be vast differences in the rate of profit, i.e. the ratio of the increase of surplus value to the whole of the capital invested. Capital of course flows to where the rate of profit is highest. If there is too much capital in a particular branch of production compared with the market's absorptive power, the product will remain unsold; circulation will be impeded or slowed down, thus reducing the rate of profit and diverting capital to other branches where its value-producing power will be greater. This constant movement of capital creates the 'average rate of profit' applying to all branches of industry despite differences in the organic composition of capital. Competition evens out the rate of profit, but in so doing causes the price of commodities to diverge considerably from their value.

But the entrepreneur does not enjoy the whole of the profit accruing from production. Part of it is taken by the merchant, who does not help to produce surplus value but enables the producer to realize his profit. In this way the average rate of profit is affected by commercial capital. Again, the lending of money at interest does not mean that capital increases by some innate power. Interest is a share in the surplus value created by industrial capital, and reflects the fact that the circulation period affects the rate of profit. By borrowing money the capitalist is able to put into production an additional amount of value; he shares the resulting profit with his creditor, and thus the average rate of profit determines the rate of interest.

A further share in the distribution of profit (the absolute value of which equals the absolute quantity of surplus value produced) is assigned to the landowner. Marx regards agriculture, for the purpose of his argument, as a purely capitalist form of production, a kind of industry in which the entrepreneur invests means of production and employs a work force in the same way as the factory owner. The farmer divides his profit with the owner of the land, who receives part of the surplus value in the form of rent: it makes no difference here whether the land is arable or used for building etc. Thus rent also constitutes a share of the surplus value created by wage-labourers, and land is no more an independent source of increased value than is capital. The landowner is privileged inasmuch as the supply of land is limited and he can therefore demand a share in the profits of industrial capital. Rent is thus a by-product of the capitalist economy; and this also explains the fact that land can have a price, though it has no value. The price of land is anticipated rent, arising from the landowner's power to demand a share in the profits of capital though he has played no part in creating them; just as the price of a slave in antiquity was an anticipation of the surplus value to be got out of his labour.

XIII

The Contradictions of Capital
and Their Abolition. The Unity of
Analysis and Action

1. The falling rate of profit and the inevitable collapse of capitalism

IN ITS STRIVING after unlimited growth (Marx's argument continues), capitalism involves itself in an inextricable contradiction. As technology progresses and the amount of constant capital increases, less and less work is necessary to produce the same volume of goods; the ratio of variable to constant capital decreases, and so does the average rate of profit. This law of the diminishing rate of profit is a universal feature of capitalist production. On the one hand, capital increases only thanks to the growth of surplus value, and its chief concern is to maximize this value in proportion to the resources used; on the other hand, it is obliged by competition and improved technology to create conditions which constantly lower the rate of profit. It strives to prevent this effect by increasing exploitation, lengthening the workers' day and paying them less than their labour-power is worth. Another factor which helps to maintain profits is that increased productivity, while it tends on the one hand to lower profits, also creates a 'reserve army of labour'—a state of relative overpopulation which forces workmen to compete with one another and so depresses the wage level. The profit rate is also assisted by foreign trade in so far as it helps to lower the price of some ingredients of constant capital or reduce the cost of subsistence. Nevertheless, in spite of all these factors the profit rate tends increasingly to decline. The effect of this is to aggravate exploitation and encourage the concentration of capital, as small capitalists find it harder to make ends meet and are swallowed up by big ones. The fall in the profit rate also leads to over-production, excess capital, relative overpopulation, and economic crises. The employers' alarm in this situation springs from the feeling

'that capitalist production encounters, in the development of its productive forces, a barrier which has nothing to do with the production of wealth as such. This peculiar barrier testifies to the limitations and the merely historical, transitory character of the capitalist mode of production; it shows that it is not an absolute method of producing wealth, but rather, at a certain stage, prevents it increasing any further' (*Capital*, III, Ch. XV, 1).

The law of the falling rate of profit is, according to Marx, one of the internal contradictions of capitalism which are bound to lead to its downfall; but he never argued, as has been alleged, that the fall in the rate of profit would in itself make capitalism an economic impossibility. A falling profit rate is quite compatible with an increasing total volume of profit, and it is hard to see how it could be the direct cause of the system breaking down. The principal factor working against a fall in the profit rate is a decline in the value of the components of constant capital, owing to the same technical progress which reduces the relative importance of wages in production costs—this being a basic aspect of Marx's analysis. In view of the difficulty of quantifying the factors working in either direction, there is no firm ground for asserting that those tending to produce a fall in the rate are stronger; and the alleged 'law' appears to be no more than an expression of Marx's hope that capitalism would be destroyed by its own inconsistencies. Only empirical observation, and not deduction from the nature of the profit rate, can tell us whether it does tend permanently to decline; and such observation is not found to confirm Marx's theory.

Marx often repeats (for example, in *Capital*, I, Ch. XXI (English edn., Ch. XXIII); III, Ch. LI) that the capitalist production process reproduces the social conditions that estrange the worker from his own labour and its product, and perpetuates itself by depriving producers of a share in the values they create. This does not mean, however, that the process can go on *ad infinitum*. The fall in the rate of profit and increasing accumulation create artificial overpopulation; at the same time the fall in the rate slows down accumulation and provides an incentive to reactivate it by every possible means, with the result that capital repeats the very processes that it desires to prevent. The upshot is a paradoxical situation in which there is both an excess of capital available for production and an excess of working-class population. Consumption cannot keep pace with the increase of production that springs from the insatiable greed for surplus value, since this greed itself prevents a corresponding increase in the purchasing power of the masses. The sum total of wealth produced is by no means too great for real needs, but it is chronically more than the market can absorb. The falling rate of profit is a constant obstacle to the development of the productive force of labour. As capital accumulates, so it is more and more concentrated as a result of small producers being driven out of business. Capital overcomes its contradictions by means of periodic crises of overproduction which ruin the mass of small owners and wreak havoc among the working class, after which the balance of the market is restored for a time.

These crises, due to the anarchic character of production and the fact that its sole purpose is to increase exchange-value, are an essential feature of the capitalist economy.

It is not the case, as spokesmen of the working class have often maintained, that crises could be averted by raising wages and enabling the market to absorb more goods, and that therefore it is in the employers' interest to pay higher wages; this is refuted, as Marx argues in the second volume of *Capital*, by the fact that crises regularly occur after a period of relative prosperity and rising wages, which would prevent them if the argument were correct. The fact is that the greed for expansion is such that the market cannot possibly go on absorbing the products of capitalism—especially as the bulk of these, in value terms, consists of means of production, which do not become easier to sell because of a rise in wages. Economic crises involve the squandering of the community's wealth on a vast scale, demonstrating that capitalism cannot cope with its own contradictions. They are the expression of a conflict between the technological level and social conditions of technical progress, between the forces of production and the system within which they work. The capitalist, controlling the means of production and concerned only to increase surplus value to the utmost, is no longer, as he was in the first stage of accumulation, an organizer who plays a necessary part in efficient production; as often as not, he now leaves it to others to run his enterprise for him. Property and management are increasingly disjoined. As production becomes more and more social in character, the private appropriation of the fruits of labour is seen to be more and more anachronistic.

> Thus grows the power of capital—the alienation, personified by the capitalist, of the conditions of social production from the real producers. Capital comes increasingly to the fore as a social power whose agent is the capitalist and which no longer stands in any possible relation to what the labour of a single individual can create. It is an alienated, independent force which stands opposed to society as an object and as the means whereby the capitalist wields his power. The contradiction between the general social force into which capital develops, on the one hand, and the power of individual capitalists over the social conditions of production, on the other, becomes ever more irreconcilable; yet it contains the germ of a resolution of the situation, in the shape of a transformation of the conditions of production into general, common, social conditions. (*Capital*, III, Ch. XV, 4)

Capital seeks frantically for new markets and endeavours to expand into non-capitalist areas, but the more its productive capacity increases, the more obvious is its conflict with the narrow limits of consumption. Marx holds that capitalism is doomed from the purely economic point of view, independently of the class struggle, since the contradiction, inherent in its production system, between use-value and exchange-value is bound to cause ever-recurring crises. As Engels put it,

> We have had many of these revulsions, happily overcome hitherto by the opening of new markets (China in 1842), or the better exploiting of old ones, by reducing the cost of production (as by free trade in corn). But there is a limit to this, too. There are no new markets to be opened now; and there is only one means left to reduce wages, namely, radical financial reform and reduction of the taxes by *repudiation of the national debt*. And if the free-trading mill-lords have not the courage to go the length of that, or if this temporary expedient be once exploded, too, why they will die of repletion. It is evident that, with no chance of further extending markets, under a system which is obliged to extend production every day, there is an end to mill-lord ascendancy. And *what next?* 'Universal ruin and chaos,' say the free-traders. *Social revolution and proletarian ascendancy, say we.* (*Democratic Review*, London, Mar. 1850)

The issue here raised was to be much debated by Rosa Luxemburg and her critics: was capitalism bound to collapse as soon as it could no longer expand into non-capitalist markets? If so, there was a well-defined limit beyond which capitalism could not endure, whether or not one held (as Marx, Engels, and Rosa Luxemburg did) that it would not simply destroy itself like an erupting volcano but would have to be overthrown by the revolutionary working class. While Engels appears to answer the question in the affirmative, it does not seem to be a necessary deduction from Marx's views that capitalism can no longer exist when there are no further non-capitalist markets left to conquer. All that follows is that capitalism must be destroyed by its own inconsistencies, especially the conflict between private ownership and the development of instruments of production and technical co-operation; that it is becoming a brake on technological progress, which it did so much to foster in the past, and that this fact must be its downfall.

The proletarian revolution, Marx believed, would spring from the same antagonism, *mutatis mutandis*, as had the bourgeois revolutions. At a certain stage bourgeois technology had become irreconcilable with the social condi-tions of feudalism—the restrictive guild system, local and hereditary privileges, and checks on the free employment of labour. In the same way, as technology progressed, the bourgeoisie itself had created a situation which was bound to ruin it as a class, doing away with capitalist ownership and, finally, all class differences.

> Along with the constantly diminishing number of the magnates of capital, who usurp and monopolize all the advantages of this process of transformation, grows the mass of misery, oppression, slavery, degradation, exploitation; but with this too grows the

revolt of the working class, a class ever increasing in numbers and disciplined, united, organized by the very mechanism of capitalist production itself. The monopoly of capital becomes a fetter upon the mode of production, which has sprung up and flourished along with it and under it. Centralization of the means of production and socialization of labour at last reach a point where they become incompatible with their capitalist integument. This integument is burst asunder. The knell of capitalist private property sounds. The expropriators are expropriated. (*Capital*, I, Ch. XXIV, 7; English edn, Ch. XXXII)

2. *The economic and political struggle of the proletariat*

It is clear from this that economic analysis alone brought Marx to the conclusion that capitalism was beyond reform, and that despite all political and economic struggles the working class would remain in bondage as long as the capitalist production system continued. As Marx and Engels wrote in 1850 in an appeal from the Central Committee to the Communist League: 'For us the issue cannot be the alteration of private property but only its abolition, not the smoothing over of class antagonisms but the abolition of classes, not the improvement of existing society but the foundation of a new one.' In articles on 'The Housing Question' published in the Leipzig *Volksstaat* in 1872–3, Engels wrote: 'As long as the capitalist system of production exists, it will be absurd to attempt to solve the housing question or any social question affecting the workers. The solution is to destroy the capitalist system of production.' It might seem that as no social question could be solved under capitalist conditions and as the blind onrush of the system was leading it to its doom, Marx and Engels were in effect, as their reformist critics held, adopting a position of 'the worse, the better', i.e. welcoming exploitation and poverty because they brought the revolution closer. This touches on a crucial problem of Marxist theory, the relationship between the 'objective', quasi-natural laws of economics on the one hand and free human initiative on the other. If capitalism is to transform itself into socialism by a spontaneous explosion independent of human will, there is no need to do anything but wait until its contradictions reach their height and the system chokes itself by its own expansion. In actual fact, however, capitalism can only be abolished when the class-consciousness of the proletariat is sufficiently developed. Perhaps Marx's clearest statement of this view is in an article on Russian policy towards Turkey, published in the *New York Daily Tribune* on 14 July 1853:

> There exists a class of philanthropists, and even of socialists, who consider strikes as very mischievous to the interests of the 'working-man [*sic*] himself', and whose great aim consists in finding out a method of securing permanent average wages. Besides the fact of the industrial cyclus, with its various phases, putting every such

average wages [*sic*] out of the question I am, on the very contrary, convinced that the alternative rise and fall of wages, and the continual conflicts between masters and men arising therefrom, are, in the present organization of industry, the indispensable means of holding up the spirit of the labouring classes, of combining them into one great association against the encroachments of the ruling class, and of preventing them from becoming apathetic, thoughtless, more or less well-fed instruments of production. In a state of society founded upon the antagonism of classes, if we want to prevent Slavery in fact as well as in name, we must accept war. In order to rightly appreciate the value of strikes and combinations, we must not allow ourselves to be blinded by the apparent insignificance of their economical results, but hold, above all things, in view their moral and political consequences. Without the great alternative phases of dullness, prosperity, over-excitement, crisis and distress, which modern industry traverses in periodically recurring cycles, with the up and down of wages resulting from them, as with the constant warfare between masters and men closely corresponding with those variations in wages and profits, the working-classes of Great Britain, and of all Europe, would be a heart-broken, a weak-minded, a worn-out unresisting mass, whose self-emancipation would prove as impossible as that of the slaves of Ancient Greece and Rome.

Marx's position is thus clear: the disarray of capitalist production affords the opportunity for the working class to organize itself in a movement of protest and become conscious of its own revolutionary future. The laws of capitalism that operate against the workers may be weakened in their effects, but cannot be neutralized as long as the system lasts. Hence the economic struggle cannot be expected to yield triumphant results. Its main purpose is to foster the political consciousness of the proletariat; for, as Marx writes in *Wages, Price and Profit*, 'In its merely economic action, capital is the stronger side.' The economic struggle is above all a preparation for the decisive political struggle, not an end in itself. At the same time, the political movement is not an end in itself either, but a means of economic liberation, as was emphasized in the Rules of the First International (1871): 'The economic emancipation of the working class is the great end to which every political movement ought to be subordinate as a means.' Thus, while Marx held that 'though temporary defeat may await the working classes, great social and economical laws are in operation which must eventually insure their triumph' ('The English Middle Class', *New York Daily Tribune*, 1 Aug. 1854), he did not draw the conclusion that the workers could sit back and await final success as a gift from History. On the contrary, political consciousness prepared by the economic struggle was an indispensable condition of success. 'Economic laws' in themselves were sufficient to ensure the possibility of victory, but political initiative had its place as an autonomous factor in the historical process. We find here, in a more specific form, a theme present in Marx's writings since the earliest period. In the class-consciousness of the proletariat, historical necessity coincides with freedom of action; the opposition between human will and the 'objective' course of events ceases to exist, the dilemma of utopianism and fatalism is resolved. The working class, and it alone, enjoys the privilege that its hopes and dreams are not condemned to beat against the wall of inexorable destiny; its will and initiative are themselves part of the necessary course of history. This means in practical terms that the economic struggle is a means to political action (the main point on which the reformists dissented from Marxism), while political action is a means to economic emancipation after the revolution; for, under socialism, there will in any case be no separate sphere of political life.

It is absurd, therefore, to say that from the Marxist point of view the working class should welcome crises, unemployment, and falling wages as steps leading to the destruction of capitalism. On the contrary, it must combat the effects of crises, while realizing that it is impossible for capitalism, by reforming itself, to obviate the enslavement of the proletariat. The workers' task is not to invite economic disasters but to use them, when they occur, for revolutionary purposes. In the same way the expropriation of small owners, including peasant ones, is an inevitable law of capitalist accumulation ('The smallholder, like any other survival of an outdated production system, is doomed to extinction and to become the proletariat of the future'—Engels, 'The peasant problem in France and Germany', *Die New Zeit*, Nov. 1894); but it does not follow that socialists should do their best to ruin the peasantry, only that they should take advantage of the inevitable process to increase their own political strength. In short, in the political struggle and in the economic struggle which is an instrument of it, the proletariat must defend its own interests from a strictly class point of view; but by doing so it becomes the champion of humanity as a whole, since the revolution that it brings about leads to the socialization and thus the liberation of mankind. In exactly the same way, the bourgeois revolutions inspired by the interest of a single class furthered the cause of all humanity. As Marx wrote in 'The Bourgeoisie and the Counter-revolution' (*Neue Rheinische Zeitung*, 11 Dec. 1848), 'The revolutions of 1648 and 1789 were not English and French revolutions, but European ones. The were not just the victory of a particular social class over the old political order, but the proclamation of a political order for a new European society.' The service they rendered to humanity did not consist, however, in liberating society by allowing capital to develop freely; what has happened is that the immense progress of technology and political organization has prepared the way for a socialist revolution, which can only take place in the conditions created by capitalism.

Capitalism creates the preconditions of the new society not only by revolutionizing technology and evolving new forms of co-operation: as we read in Volume III of *Capital,* joint-stock companies in which property and management are separate, and likewise co-operative factories, are to be regarded as 'transitional forms' or instances of the abandonment of the capitalist mode of production within the system itself, in this sense socialism is not simply the negation of capitalism but also a continuation of it and of the socializing process based in the technological development of the present age.

3. The nature of socialism, and its two phases

CAPITALISM, then, creates the necessary preconditions of socialism. Its historical mission was to bring about a tremendous development of technology due to the unbridled urge to increase exchange value to the maximum. By constantly transferring masses of workers from one occupation to another, capitalism calls for a certain versatility in the working class and thus creates conditions for an upheaval in which the division of labour will be abolished: cf. *Capital,* I, Ch. XIII (XV in English edn.), 9. But, as Engels wrote, 'it is only at a certain stage, and in modern conditions a very advanced one, of the development of social conditions that production can be increased to a point at which the abolition of class differences can constitute a real progress and can be achieved permanently without causing a standstill or a regression in the community's method of production' ('Social Conditions in Russia', *Volksstaat,* 1875). Socialism reaps the harvest of capitalism, and without the latter it could only be an empty dream. The new society will arise out of the catastrophe towards which capitalism is swiftly yet unconsciously tending.

'The working class has conqured nature; now it must conquer man' (Marx in the *People's Paper,* 18 Mar. 1854). This is a concise expression of the Marxian idea of socialism. To 'conquer man', as Marx indicated on many occasions, is to create conditions in which men are in full control of their own labour process and its physical and spiritual product, so that the results of their actions cannot in any circumstances turn against themselves. Man ruling over himself and no longer subjected to material forces of his own creation—man identified with the social process, overcoming the opposition between blind necessity and his own free behaviour—such will be the effect of the socialist revolution. Socialism, as we saw, does not consist essentially in abolishing material poverty or the luxurious consumption of the bourgeoisie, but in abolishing human alienation by doing away with the division of labour. If the bourgeois standard of living were equated with that of the workers, this in itself would not bring about any significant change. It is not a question simply of redistributing the same income produced in the same old way. Nor, as Marx emphasized against the Lassalleanists, is it a matter of the worker receiving for his own benefit the whole of the value that he creates, for that is an impossibility. There are many occupations that create no value, yet are socially necessary and must be preserved in the socialist system. So, as we read in the *Critique of the Gotha Programme*, there can be no question of demanding 'the undiminished proceeds of labour'. Considerable sums must always be deducted from the social product for the renewal of consumed values, the expansion of production, insurance against emergency, administrative costs, collective consumption (schools and hospitals), and the care of those unfit to work. The basic difference between the capitalist and socialist modes of production is that in the latter the system of wage labour, i.e. the sale of labour-power, is abolished and the whole of material production is devoted to use-value. In other words, the scale and character of production in all its branches will be governed purely by social needs and not by the desire to accumulate the maximum exchange-value; and this, of course, requires the social planning of production.

> By abolishing the capitalist form of production, the length of the working day could be reduced to the necessary labour time. But, even in that case, the latter would extend its limits. On the one hand, because the notion of 'means of subsistence' would considerably expand and the labourer would lay claim to an altogether different standard of life. On the other hand, because a part of what is now surplus labour would then count as necessary labour, viz. the labour of forming a fund for reserve and accumulation. (*Capital*, I, Ch. XV [English edn., Ch. XVII], IV)

The distinction between necessary and surplus labour would in fact lose its meaning in socialist conditions: not all labour would be directly remunerated in the form of wages, but all of it would accrue to society in the collective satisfaction of various needs.

But the liberation of humanity does not consist solely in the satisfaction of material needs, however much their scope may be extended, but rather in achieving a full and many-sided life for all. This is why Marx was so concerned to abolish the division of labour, which crippled human beings physically and spiritually and condemned individuals to a stultifying one-sidedness. The prime task of socialism is to liberate all the powers latent in every human being, and develop his personal abilities to the utmost in the social context. This being so, in what sense are we to understand the claim that socialism is the 'final' state of man? As Engels wrote in *Ludwig Feuerbach*, I: 'Just as knowledge is unable to reach a perfected termination in a perfect, ideal condition of humanity, so is history unable to do so.' Socialism is not 'final' in the sense of a stagnant society providing for the satisfaction of a fixed total of needs and therefore containing no incentive to development. But it is 'final', according to Marx, in that it would ensure that society was in full control of the conditions of its own existence, so that there was no occasion for any further transformation; there would no longer be any difference between rulers and ruled, and no

limitation on human creativity. Socialism does not mean that human development and creativity cease to exist, but that there are no longer any social
restrictions upon them. However, the development of creative forces does not
mean simply, or even chiefly, the increase of material wealth. The well-known
passage in Volume III of *Capital* is very significant here:

> The realm of freedom actually begins only where labour which is determined by
> necessity and mundane considerations ceases; thus in the very nature of things it
> lies beyond the sphere of actual material production. Just as the savage must wres-
> tle with Nature to satisfy his wants, to maintain and reproduce life, so must civilized
> man, and he must do so in all forms of society and under all possible modes of pro-
> duction. With his development this realm of physical necessity expands as a result
> of his wants; but, at the same time, the forces of production which satisfy these wants
> also increase. Freedom in this field can only consist in socialized man, the associ-
> ated producers, rationally regulating their interchange [*Stoffwechsel*] with Nature,
> bringing it under their common control, instead of being ruled by it as by a blind
> force; and achieving this with the least expenditure of energy and under conditions
> most favourable to, and worthy of, their human nature. But it nevertheless still
> remains a realm of necessity. Beyond it begins that development of human energy
> which is an end in itself, the true realm of freedom, which, however, can blossom
> forth only with this realm of necessity as its basis. The shortening of the working day
> is its basic prerequisite. (*Capital*, III, Ch. XLVIII, III)

We thus have a schema of the values that Marx associated with the socialist
transformation. Socialism as a mode of organization consists in removing the
obstacles which prevent human beings from developing their creative abilities
to the full. This free expansion in all spheres is the true purpose of humanity.
The production of physical requirements belongs to the 'realm of necessity',
and the time spent therein is the measure of man's dependence on nature. This
of course cannot be completely overcome, but its effect can be minimized and,
more important, it is possible to eliminate the forms of compulsion connected
specifically with social existence, i.e. so to order things that social life will be a
fulfilment of individuality and not a curb on it. This identification of personal
and collective existence will not be a matter of compulsion—for then it would
be contrary to its own premises—but will spring from the consciousness of
each and every individual, who will regard his own life as value-creating in
respect of others. There will no longer be a gap between social and private life—
not because the individual is absorbed into a single, grey, uniform collectivity,
but because social life will no longer create forms that are alienated from the
individual: it will cease to arouse antagonisms and will present itself to every
man as his own personal creation. Social relations will become transparent to
all instead of wrapped in the mystification of religious forms.

The religious reflex of the real world can only then finally vanish, when the practical relations of workaday life offer to man none but perfectly intelligible and rational relations with his fellow-man and Nature. The life-process of society, i.e. the process of material production, does not strip off its mystical veil until it takes the form of production by freely associated men, and is consciously regulated by them in accordance with a settled plan. This, however, demands for society a certain material groundwork, or set of conditions of existence, which in their turn are the spontaneous product of a long and painful process of development. (*Capital*, I, Ch. I, 4)

The socialist movement thus leads to a revolution without precedent in history—the greatest transformation of all and, in the sense explained above, the final one. Socialism is *novissimus*, the end of history as it has hitherto been known and the beginning of the adventure of mankind. It makes a radical break with the past and has no need of any existing tradition to justify it or bring it to self-awareness. 'The social revolution of the nineteenth century can only create its poetry from the future, not from the past. It cannot begin its own work until it has sloughed off all superstitious regard for the past. Earlier revolutions have needed world-historical reminiscences to deaden their awareness of their own content. In order to arrive at its own content the revolution of the nineteenth century must let the dead bury their dead.' (*The Eighteenth Brumaire of Louis Bonaparte*, I.)

From 1848 onwards Marx went through alternate phases of expecting an early European revolution and reconciling himself to a longer wait. Every new period of disturbances, war, or economic depression increased his hopes. Shortly after 1848 he gave up the optimistic conviction that the death-knell of capitalism had already sounded; instead, he told the advocates of 'direct action' that the workers had fifteen, twenty, or fifty years of hard struggle to face before they would be ready for power. Again and again he was encouraged by political or economic crises to hope that in one place or another, in Germany, Spain, Poland, or Russia, a revolutionary spark might touch off a fire that would sweep across Europe. In accordance with his theory he expected most from the more developed countries, but he also hoped at times that even backward Russia might witness the breaking of the storm that would herald the worldwide transformation. Among his followers many sterile disputes arose as to the conditions which, according to the doctrine, were most likely to presage a world revolution of the proletariat. Marx himself did not formally indicate what these were, and his scattered remarks on the subject over many years do not form a consistent whole. It is evident that there was a conflict in his mind between revolutionary impatience and the theory that capitalism must first attain its 'economic maturity'—which, he apparently thought, had not taken place in any European country except Britain—and one or other of these viewpoints prevailed according to the turn of events. He never indicated, however, by what signs economic maturity was to be recognized. In 1871–2, moreover, he took the view that in advanced countries such as Britain, the U.S.A., and Holland the transition to socialism might be achieved by peaceful propaganda, without violence or rebellion.

All in all, Marx came in time to believe that there could be no immediate transition to a socialist system as he imagined it. In the *Critique of the Gotha Programme* he observed that there would have to be an intermediate period between the revolution and the final realization of socialist hopes. In the first stage, human rights would be proportionate to labour. 'This equal right is an unequal right for unequal labour. It recognizes no class differences, because everyone is only a worker like everyone else; but it tacitly recognizes unequal individual endowment and thus productive capacity as natural privileges. It is therefore a right of inequality in its content, like every right.' The transitional period would bear the mark of the society out of which it had grown. Economically it would be based on the principle 'To each according to his labour'; politically it would be a dictatorship of the proletariat, a system in which a particular class exercised authority and used force for the purpose of abolishing class distinctions. Only in the higher phase of communist society, when men would no longer be enslaved by the division of labour and when the difference between physical and intellectual work would be done away with—when the development of productive forces ensured a sufficiency for all, and labour was the most vital requirement of a man's being—only then could the slogan become a reality, 'From each according to his ability, to each according to his needs.'

Although Marx did not leave any detailed description of the organization of the future society, its basic principle is clear: socialism stands for complete humanization, restoring man's control over his own powers and his own creative energy. All its specific features can be derived from this principle: the gearing of production to use-value, the abolition of the division of labour in so far as it impedes the acquisition of a diversity of skills (but not, of course, in the sense of reverting from industry to craftsmanship), the dismantling of the state apparatus as distinct from the administration of production, the abolition of all social sources of inequality (equality, as Engels wrote, means doing away with class differences but not with individual ones) and of all social conditions that in any way restrict human creativity. It is significant that, according to Marx, the abolition of capitalism 'does not re-establish private property for the producer, but gives him individual property based on the acquisitions of the capitalist era: i.e. on co-operation among free workers and their possession in common of the earth's resources and the means of production, themselves produced by labour'. (*Capital*, I, Ch. XXIV, 7; English edn., Ch. XXXII.) 'Individual property' stands in contrast to capitalist property: the latter is non-individual in the sense that its transformation and growth are not controlled by particular human beings and that it develops its own laws in the anonymous force of capital, subjugating even the capitalist himself. Socialism, by contrast, is the return to a situation in which only individual human subjects truly exist and are not governed by any impersonal social force; property is individual, and society is no more than the assemblage of the individuals who own it. The notion that Marx regarded socialism as a system for depressing individuals into a Comtean universal being deprived of all subjectivity is one of the absurdest aberrations to which the study of his work has given rise. What can be said with truth is that in Marx's view personality is not a mere matter of self-experience on the lines of the *cogito ergo sum*, since there is no such thing as pure self-knowledge apart from consciousness of the social life in which the individual has his being. The contrary supposition could only arise in conditions in which intellectual work has been so completely severed from productive work that the links between them were forgotten. Every individual was a social being; man realized himself in the community, but this did not mean that the latter derived its creative forces from any other source than that of personal, subjective existence.

4. *The dialectic of* Capital: *the whole and the part, the concrete and the abstract*

THESE views do not in any way conflict with Marx's over-all analysis of capitalism. Throughout history material forces have dominated human beings, and in considering capitalist society each separate element must be related to the whole and each phenomenon treated as a phase in a developing process. In *Capital* Marx more than once recalls this global aspect of his method of inquiry. No economic act, however trivial, such as the buying and selling that occurs millions of times a day, is intelligible except in the context of the entire capitalist system.

> Every individual capital forms but an autonomous fraction, endowed with individual life, as it were, of the aggregate social capital, just as every individual capitalist is but an individual element of the capitalist class. The movement of the social capital consists of the totality of the movements of its fractional parts, the turnovers of individual fragments of capital. Just as the metamorphosis of the individual commodity is a link in the series of metamorphoses of the commodity-world—the circulation of commodities—so the metamorphosis of the individual capital, its turnover, is a link in the circulation of social capital. (*Capital*, II, Ch. XVIII, I)

Accordingly, the existence of an average rate of profit means that each capitalist makes a profit proportionate to his share of the aggregate social capital and not to the organic composition of capital in his particular branch of production. The whole functioning of the capitalist economy is geared to creating the maximum exchange-value in conditions of the interdependence of every link in the process of production and the circulation of capital; the economy has become a single process and can only be understood as such.

But the dialectical rule that a phenomenon can only be understood in relation to the whole does not mean that the starting-point of analysis must be an empirical 'whole' untouched by theory, a mere confused jumble of perceptions. On the contrary, such a 'whole' is incapable of being an object of cognition. It is the function of analysis to reproduce the concrete on the basis of abstractions, viz. of the simplest social categories, which take shape in the first instance as isolated phenomena and are only afterwards enriched by the perception of their mutual relations. The argument is summarized in a passage in the Introduction to the *Grundrisse:*

> It would seem to be correct to begin with the real and concrete, the real precondition, and thus, in economics, to begin with e.g. the population, which is the foundation and subject of the entire social act of production. However, on closer examination this proves false. The population is an abstraction if I leave out, for example, the classes of which it is composed. These are in turn an empty phrase if I am not familiar with the elements on which they are based, e.g. wage labour, capital etc . . . Thus, if I were to begin with the population, this would give a chaotic picture of the whole; I would then, by means of further definition, move analytically towards ever more simple concepts, from the imagined concrete towards ever thinner abstractions until I had arrived at the simplest formulations . . . The economists of the seventeenth century always begin with the living whole, with population, nation, state, several states etc.; but they generally conclude by discovering through analysis a small number of determinant, abstract, general relations such as division of labour, value, money etc. Once these individual factors were more or less firmly established and abstracted, there began the economic systems, which ascended from simple relations, such as labour, division of labour and exchange value, to the level of the state, exchange between nations and the world market. This is obviously the scientifically correct method. The concrete is concrete because it is the concentration of many determinations, hence unity of the diverse. It appears in the process of thinking, therefore, as a process of concentration, as a result and not a point of departure even though it is the point of departure in reality and hence also the point of departure for observation and conception. . . . Abstract determinations lead towards a reproduction of the concrete by way of thought. In this way Hegel fell into the illusion of conceiving the real as the product of thought concentrating itself, probing its own depths, and unfolding itself out of itself; whereas the method of rising from the abstract to the concrete is only the way in which thought appropriates the concrete, reproduces it as the concrete in the mind. But it is by no means in this way that the concrete itself comes into being.

Thus in Marx's view the order of exposition of social phenomena is the reverse of the order of factual observation. The former begins with the simplest and most abstract qualitites of social life, for example value, and from these it reconstructs concrete phenomena in the form in which they are assimilated by the mind and subjected to theory. The 'whole' thus reproduced is not the chaotic mass of direct perception but a conceptually linked system. To achieve this result we make use, as in any other science, of the method of ideal situations which assume for the sake of argument certain simple relationships undisturbed by any outside factor, so that their complexity may afterwards be analysed.

In this way Marx attempts to transfer to political economy the basic method of modern science which originated in Galileo's perception that mechanics cannot be an account of actual experience (as was believed by the empiricists of the sixteenth and seventeenth centuries, including Gassendi), but must presuppose ideal situations that never occur in actual experimental conditions: namely situations involving limiting values, like the investigation of the course of a projectile discharged in a vacuum so that there is no air resistance, or the movement of a pendulum on the supposition that there is no friction at the point of suspension, etc. This method is universally acknowledged although the conditions it assumes are imaginary ones: there is no such thing in nature as a vacuum, a perfectly elastic body, an organism affected by only a single stimulus at a time, and so on, but these must be assumed in order to measure the deviations from the norm that take place in empirical circumstances. In the same way Marx begins by considering the creation of value in a notional society consisting purely of a bourgeoisie and a proletariat, and examines the process of the creation of surplus value abstracting from circulation and the variations it causes; then he considers circulation in isolation from supply and demand, and so forth.

> In reality, supply and demand never coincide; . . . but political economy assumes that they do, so that we may study phenomena in their fundamental relations, in the form corresponding to their conception, that is independently of the appearances caused by the movement of supply and demand. The other reason for proceeding thus is to find out and to some extent record [*fixieren*] the actual tendencies of these movements. Since the deviations are of an opposite nature, and since they continually succeed one another, they balance out through their mutual contradiction. (*Capital*, III, Ch. X)

There is, however, an essential difference between the use of this method in physics and in political economy. In the case of Galileo's pendulum the limiting conditions were such that deviations could be observed in experimental conditions. But nothing of the sort is possible with complex social phenomena, where there are no instruments to measure the deviation of reality from the ideal model. Hence Marx's exposition in *Capital* has given rise to the question: is he describing a real society or a purely theoretical one (apart, of course, from the historical passages which clearly relate to particular, non-recurring situations)? From some of his remarks it might be inferred that he was not analysing capitalism as it actually was, but only a schema with no real existence. In that case the analysis would be, so to speak, in the air, since we do not know how to compare the model with historical reality or in what way the two are related. But it cannot actually have been Marx's intention to describe an 'ideal' capitalist society (in the sense of a theoretical one, not of course in the normative sense) irrespective of whether it explained the workings of the real one or, above all, how it was likely to develop. What theoretical or practical use could there be, for instance, in saying that in the capitalist 'model' the profit rate must fall or the classes become polarized, if, owing to interference of one sort or another, this does not happen in a real capitalist economy? The model is only of value if it enables us to say: 'Capitalism under such and such conditions would undergo such and such changes, but as the conditions are affected in certain ways, the changes will take place somewhat differently, as follows . . .' But this is precisely what we cannot say; for, if capitalism in real life undergoes different changes, in some respects at least, from theoretical capitalism, then, even if we can explain the differences *ex post facto*, the analysis of the model has been no good to us. At all events, it is very doubtful whether Marx regarded the diminishing profit rate or the polarization of classes as merely tendencies of 'ideal' capitalism which, according to circumstances, might or might not occur in practice. He certainly believed that the rate of profit was bound to fall in real-life capitalism and that the middle classes were historically bound to die out. Attempts to interpret *Capital* as relating only to 'ideal' capitalism sometimes serve as a means of resisting the empirical evidence that refutes Marx's predictions which are thus represented merely as statements of what would happen in a non-existent ideal form of capitalism. But such interpretations protect Marxism against the destructive results of experience only by depriving it of its value as an instrument of real-life social analysis.

The laws of physics serve to explain observational data by postulating unreal limiting values. The ideal conditions expounded by Marx, on the other hand, are intended to display the 'essence' of reality underlying 'appearances': this may be seen from the passage quoted above and from other statements, including his remark that there would be no need for science if the essence of things always coincided with appearances. But, it may well be asked, what is the status of an 'essence' that may be contradicted by phenomena, and how do we make sure that we have discovered it when, *ex hypothesi*, we cannot do so by empirical observation? The fact that, for example, the existence of atoms and genes was accepted before it was confirmed by direct observation is not a sufficient answer. Atoms and genes bore a clear logical relation to empirical data and served to explain factual observations; they were not the result of mere abstract deduction. In the case of discoveries that purport to explain the 'essence' of things it is important to inquire whether their status is like that of atoms in the time of Ernst Mach (who questioned their existence) or genes in the time of T. H. Morgan, or, on the contrary, like that of 'phlogiston' in the seventeenth and eighteenth centuries—a mere verbal pseudo-explanation which there can be no question of confirming empirically.

It is certain, however, that Marx's holistic approach to social phenomena, relating all categories to a single system, permeates every stage of his analysis. He emphasizes again and again that the qualities he is concerned with have no 'natural being' discernible by perception, but only a 'social being', and that value in particular is not a physical attribute but a social relation which takes on the form of a quality of things. 'In the analysis of economic forms, neither microscopes nor chemical reagents are of use. The force of abstraction must replace both. But in bourgeois society the commodity-form of the product of labour—or the value-form of the commodity—is the economic cell-form' (*Capital*, I, Preface to the first German edn.). 'The value of commodities is the very opposite of the crude materiality of their substance: not an atom of matter enters into its composition. Turn and examine a single commodity by itself as we will, yet in so far as it constitutes an object of value it is impossible to grasp it. If, however, we bear in mind that the value of commodities has a purely social reality, and that they acquire this reality only in so far as they are expressions or embodiments of one identical social substance, viz. human labour, it follows as a matter of course that value can only manifest itself in the social relation of commodity to commodity.' (Ibid., Ch. I, 3.) Value is not something that inheres in a commodity independently of its circulation; it is not accessible to perception, being the crystallization of abstract labour-time—a fact that appears in the relation between commodities on the market, compared as objects of exchange. 'In a sort of way, it is with man as with commodities. Since he comes into the world neither with a looking-glass in his hand nor as a Fichtean philosopher to whom "I am I" is sufficient, man first sees himself reflected in other men. Peter only recognizes himself as a man by first relating himself to Paul as being of like kind.' (Ibid., Ch. I, 3A, 2a.) When a coat expresses the value of a quantity of cloth it does not denote an innate property of the two things but their value, which is purely social in character. (Ibid., 2b.) 'The form of wood, for instance, is altered when we make a table out of it; yet, for all that, the table continues to be that common, everyday thing, wood. But, so soon as it takes the form of a commodity, it is changed into something material yet transcendent [*ein sinnliches übersinnliches Ding*].' (Ibid., Ch. I, 4.)

These arguments contain, it will be seen, an anti-naturalistic premiss according to which social life creates new qualities that are irreducible to those of nature and inaccessible to direct perception, yet are real and determine historical processes. They are not, strictly speaking, new attributes of natural objects, or they are such only in conditions of commodity fetishism; they are inter-human relations which create laws of their own. Such relations cannot be explained *à la* Feuerbach as continuations or specific forms of those existing in pre-human nature. They form complexes which obey their own laws, and they confer on the human beings concerned qualities which cannot be discovered in the non-human world. In this sense the human individual cannot be understood, either by himself or by theoretical analysis, as a mere natural being, or in any way except as a participant in the social process. Thus it is the case, as Marx wrote in 1843, that 'For man, the root is man himself.' Objects, moreover, when involved in human relationships, become different from what they are 'in themselves'. 'A negro is a negro; he only becomes a slave in certain relationships. A cotton-spinning jenny is a machine for spinning cotton; it becomes capital only in certain relationships. Torn from these relationships it is no more capital than gold in itself is money, or sugar the price of sugar.' (*Wage-Labour and Capital*, III.)

We can thus understand more precisely Marx's idea of a return to humanity as a result of socialist revolution. Under socialism, when all useful labour is subordinated to use-value, a cotton-spinning machine is indeed a machine for spinning cotton, an instrument used by human beings to provide themselves with clothing. It is also the crystallization of a certain amount of human labour-time, but it does not constitute exchange-value, at least in the more advanced phase of socialist society, because products in general will not be exchanged by value but distributed in accordance with real need. Hence what happens to the machine, as to any other product, does not depend on its relation to other objects in terms of value. Things which in a commodity economy are humanized in appearance, i.e. assume qualities that are in fact human relations, lose this appearance under socialism and are humanized in reality: they are acquired by people as objects of use and become true individual property. Man continues to be a 'political animal', or a city-dwelling one (Marx refers expressly to Aristotle's phrase); he realizes his creative possibilities as social values, but under socialism abstractions cease to dominate human beings. In this sense socialism is a return to the concrete. The process of inversion whereby objectified labour increasingly extends its power over living labour, so that human activity is not merely a matter of objectification but primarily of alienation, is, as Marx explains in the *Grundrisse*, a process inherent in society itself and not only in the imagination of workers and capitalists. This inversion is indeed a historical necessity without which productive forces could not have developed as they have done, but it is by no means an absolute necessity of all production.

> With the suspension of the immediate character of living labour, as merely individual, or as general merely internally or merely externally, with the positing of the activities of individuals as immediately general or social activity, the objective moments [*Momente*] of production are stripped of this form of alienation; they are thereby posited as property, as the organic social body within which the individuals reproduce themselves as individuals, but as social individuals. (*Grundrisse*, III, 3)

5. The dialectic of Capital: consciousness and the historical process

THE dialectic method of *Capital*, however, does not consist merely in regarding every part of capitalist reality as a component of a whole that functions according to its own laws. It is a no less important feature, and indeed the principal one in Marx's view, that every existing form is considered as a stage in a continuing process, i.e. phenomena are observed in terms of historical evolution. Marx never gave a separate exposition of his dialectic—like Hegel's, it cannot be described in isolation from its subject—but from time to time he indicates its general character in the course of a specific argument. One of the most frequently quoted passages is in the Afterword to the second German edition of *Capital*, where he says: 'My dialectic method is not only different from the Hegelian but is its direct opposite. To Hegel the thought-process, which he actually transforms into an independent subject under the name of the Idea, is the demiurge of the real world, and the real world is only the external, phenomenal form of the Idea. With me, on the contrary, the ideal is nothing else than the material world reflected in the human mind and translated into forms of thought.' In the same Afterword he quotes with approval an account of his method given by a Russian reviewer of *Capital* in 1872, who observed that 'Marx treats the social movement as a process of natural history governed by laws independent of human will, consciousness and intentions', and that in his system each historical period has its own laws, which give way in due course to those of the next. However, Marx says, his dialectic 'in its comprehension and affirmative recognition of the existing state of things, at the same time comprehends the negation of that state and its inevitable breaking up; it regards every historically developed social form as in fluid movement, and therefore takes into account its transient nature no less than its momentary existence; it lets nothing impose upon it, and is in its essence critical and revolutionary.'

However, the doctrine of the transitoriness of social phenomena is not in itself a sufficient basis for analysis. The whole of history must in addition be interpreted in relation to its highest forms; in particular, former systems can only be understood in terms of their outcome in bourgeois society.

> Bourgeois society is the most developed and the most complex historic organization of production. The categories which express its relations, the comprehension of its structure, thereby also afford insight into the structure and the relations of production of all the vanished social formations out of whose ruins and elements it built itself up . . . Human anatomy is the key to the anatomy of the ape. The intimations of higher development among the subordinate animal species can be understood only when the higher development is already known. In the same way the bourgeois economy supplies the key to the ancient, etc.; but not after the manner of those economists who blur all historical differences and see bourgeois relations in all forms of society. One can understand tribute, tithe etc. if one is acquainted with ground rent; but one must not identify them. (*Grundrisse*, Introduction)

Not only are bygone social forms intelligible only in relation to present ones, but present-day society can only be understood in the light of the future, i.e. the form that will take its place after its inevitable collapse. In this important respect Marx's thought differs from Hegel's, which was essentially confined to interpreting the past. The idea of extending the dialectic into the future and interpreting the present in terms of its own dissolution was adopted by Marx from the Young Hegelians.

From time to time Marx, in *Capital*, invokes Hegelian formulas. For example, having argued that in given social conditions an accumulation of value can only be described as 'capital' if it is large enough to employ wage-labour, he cites this as an instance of the Hegelian transformation of a quantitative change into a qualitative one: value, beyond a certain quantitative level, acquires the power to command living labour and to create surplus value. Again, having described capitalist property as the negation of individual private property based on labour, he refers to socialism as the 'negation of a negation'—i.e. the return to individual property, based, however, on joint ownership of the means of production instead of on private ownership.

To Marx as to Hegel, however, the dialectic is not a collection of rules independent of one another and of the subject-matter to which they are applied. If it were simply a method applicable to any subject and capable of being expounded in isolation, there would be no reason for Marx to say that his own dialectic was contrary to Hegel's because of the latter's idealism; for its laws could be formulated in the same way whether history was interpreted in an idealist or a materialist fashion. But, in Marx's view, the relationship of consciousness to the historical process is part of the very content of the dialectic. Whereas for Hegel the dialectic was a history of the diffraction of ideas in the course of which the mind comes to understand being as its own creation, for Marx it is a history of the material conditions of life in which mental and institutional forms are vested with an apparent autonomy before returning, as they are bound to do, into union with their substructure. The dialectic as a means of understanding the world is secondary to the actual dialectic of the world itself, inasmuch as the theory of the dialectical movement of social reality is aware of its own dependence on the historical process that gave it birth. Marx repeats several times that a theory reflecting working-class interests can only spring from observation of the changing situation of the workers. The theory is in fact the self-conscious superstructure of that situation; it knows itself to be merely a reflection of the real historical process, a product of social praxis and not an independent contemplation of it. The Marxian dialectic ends in the 'unity of subject and object', but in a different sense from Hegel's. It restores to man his true function as a conscious historical subject, by abolishing the situation in which the results of his free, conscious initiative are turned against himself. The subject will be in full command of the process whereby he objectifies himself in production and creative work; this objectification will not degenerate into alienation; real human individuals will possess the work of their own hands and will no longer be subjected to an independent objectified power. The course of history will be completely governed by the conscious human will; the latter will know itself for what it is, namely consciousness of the life-process. The historical process and the free development of consciousness will be one and the same.

Marx's dialectic is a description of the historical evolution leading to this unity of consciousness and social Being. As with Hegel, it is the description of a movement in which contradictions arise and are overcome, giving place to fresh contradictions. The advance through contradictions is essential to the dialectical interpretation of the world. But these are not logical contradictions or a different term for social conflict: the latter has been with us throughout history, but no one built a dialectical system of interpretation on it. Class antagonism in conscious political forms is an effect of the contradictions underlying an unconscious, 'objective' process. In Hegel's theory, concepts as they developed revealed internal contradictions, the resolution of which gave rise to higher forms of consciousness. In Marx's view, contradictions 'occur' in the historical process independently of whether they are translated into consciousness or conceptual forms; they consist in the fact that a phenomenon gives rise to situations contrary to its own nature and basic tendency. The most important feature of the dialectic of the internal contradictions of capitalism is Marx's analysis of the falling profit rate and of economic crises, in which he shows that the urge to maximize the rate of profit defeats its own object by increasing the amount of constant capital and so causing the profit rate to fall steadily. The same urge to increase surplus value in absolute terms leads to crises and the collapse of capital, despite the 'inborn tendency' of capital itself (a different matter from the intentions of capitalists, which are secondary here). Thus capital, which originally displayed a single, undifferentiated tendency, gives rise to phenomena which work in the opposite direction to itself, and the contradiction finally reaches a point, in spite of all efforts, at which capital can no longer exist. This is analogous to the Hegelian disjunction of concepts, but it is a pattern that history develops of its own accord, independently of anyone's consciousness. Consciousness, indeed, has figured in the process up to now only as a complex of delusion and mystification. The return to the unity of subject and object does not mean, as with Hegel, depriving the world of its objective character and of objectivity altogether; man will still objectivize his powers by means of labour and will still be confronted by independent Nature. What it does mean is depriving social phenomena of their thing-like character, their independence of real, individual human subjects. The dialectic that explains this process is the consciousness of the working class raised to the level of intellectual understanding.

Having come this far, we can define the Marxian dialectic in its entirety as follows. The dialectic is the consciousness of the working class, which, aware of its own condition and its opposition to bourgeois society, perceives the entire functioning of that society, and the whole of past history, as a recurrent process of the emergence and resolution of contradictions. The dialectical consciousness, by a process of abstraction, strips social phenomena of their contingent character and apprehends their basic structure; it relates every component of the historical process to the whole, and in this way understands itself likewise. In its final stage it reflects the intensified contradictions which—including itself *qua* dialectical consciousness—will be swept away in a revolutionary explosion; this event will terminate the prehistory of the human race and restore the unity of society as subject and object of history, or, to put it another way, the unity of the consciousness of history with history itself.

It may be seen from this formulation that the dialectic is not a method, like those of mathematics, that can be applied to any subject-matter in any conditions. It exists as a method only in so far as it is conscious of its functional relation to the class-situation that it reflects, and in so far as it not only understands history but at the same time anticipates it by the revolutionary abolition of existing contradictions. The dialectic cannot exist outside the practical struggle for a future society whose ideal image it contains within itself.

It can be seen why Marx need not, and indeed cannot in terms of his own method, provide socialism with an ethical basis, i.e. present it simply as a collection of desirable values. This is not because he thought of socialism merely as a 'historical necessity' and was not interested in whether it was good or bad, nor because he took the absurd view that it was people's duty to follow the course of history wherever it led. The reason why ethical justification is irrelevant is that in Marx's theory the understanding of bourgeois society comes into being as a practical ʻ act, or rather it is the reflection in consciousness of revolutionary action and cannot appear independently of it. It is foreign to Marx's conception to divide his theory into separate elements of fact, obligation, and method—to determine first what the world is like, then what it should be like to satisfy certain norms, and finally by what means it can be transformed. The capitalist world presents itself to the proletariat in the latter's act of understanding which springs from the practical act of destroying it. The workers' movement came into being before the theory which reflects its real though at first unconscious tendencies: when the theory takes shape, it does so as the self-knowledge of the movement. Those who adopt the theory do not thereby come into possession of a set of values in the form of an external imperative; they become aware of the aim they were in fact pursuing, though they had no clear theoretical understanding of it. There is no room here for the process of fixing an aim and then considering how to attain it, as with a technical problem where the objective is arbitrarily given and the rational solution is devised afterwards, or again as in the moralizing socialism of the utopians. In Marx's theory, awareness of the aim takes the form of an act in which the participants in the historical process acquire theoretical insight into the means they have already begun to employ. Since men do in fact strive to liberate themselves from oppression and exploitation, and afterwards become aware of their action as part of the 'objective' movement of history, they have no need of a separate imperative telling them that they should strive for liberation in general or that freedom from oppression is a good thing. It is only in action that man becomes aware of himself—although he may be deceived, and indeed notoriously has been, as to the true content of that self-knowledge. The movement to free mankind from slavery recognizes itself at once for what it is and identifies its own position as a fighting movement; it could not put to itself the question 'What is the fight for?' without first ceasing to fight, and if it did that it would cease to exist. The dichotomy between fact and value, observation and appreciation has no place here. It belongs to those whose ideals and dreams go far beyond reality and are not anchored in history—the Epicureans who see a great gulf fixed between themselves and the real world. But, in the case of the working class, the understanding of the historical world and its practical transformation are a single undifferentiated act: there is not and cannot be a separate perception of what is and what ought to be. Understanding history and participating in it are one and the same, and require no separate justification. The dialectic is a rule of observation, but it is also the self-knowledge of the historical process; it cannot escape this role by setting itself up as an instrument for the mere observation of history, still less of the natural world in general.

6. Comments on Marx's theory of value and exploitation

MARX's theory of value has been much criticized from several points of view, especially that of its unsuitability for empirical analysis. This objection was voiced by Conrad Schmidt and after him by Bohm-Bawerk (to whom we shall return), Sombart, Struve, Bernstein, and Pareto, and in recent years by Joan Robinson and Raymond Aron. Some lines of argument recur frequently in the various criticisms. We cannot go into all the details here, but will mention the main points.

To begin with, it has been observed that value in Marx's sense is unmeasurable, i.e. it is impossible to state the value of any commodity in units of necessary labour-time. This is so for two independent reasons. The first is that the value of any product, on Marx's theory, includes the value of the tools and materials used to make it, those used to make the tools and materials in question, and so on *ad infinitum*. It is true that, according to Marx, instruments do not create fresh value but only transfer to the product part of the value crystallized in them; but, if we have to calculate the value of the product in units of labour-time, we should have to reduce the value of the tools to such units also, which is clearly impossible. The second reason is that different kinds of work cannot be reduced to a common measure. Human labour involves varying degrees of skill, and on Marx's showing we should have to add to the quantity of labour expended in making the product the amount of labour which went into the worker's training; but this too is impossible. The usual Marxist defence that the labour market automatically reduces complex and simple labour to a common measure is of no avail here, since it means that value cannot be calculated independently of price, which is exactly the point of the objection. In any case the price of labour-power (assuming, with Marx, that it is labour-power and not labour which is exchanged in a commodity economy) depends, like other values, on numerous factors and especially the laws of supply and demand; so there is no reason to suppose that wage differences between skilled and unskilled labour correspond to the amount of labour-time required to produce a skilled workman.

If value cannot be calculated independently of price, there is no way of verifying the statement that the actual prices of commodities fluctuate around their real value. Marx of course knew that prices are determined in practice by various factors, including labour productivity, supply and demand, and the average rate of profit. If he disregarded these in the first volume of *Capital*, it was for methodological reasons and not because he thought value and price were the same thing; thus he cannot be reproached with inconsistency as between Volume I and Volume III, which deals *inter alia* with the average rate of profit. But the point is that it is impossible to measure quantitatively the respective effect of the various factors on market prices. If Adam Smith thought that primitive men exchanged products in accordance with the time it had taken to make them, or if Engels strove to maintain that this still happened in the late Middle Ages, the Marxian theory of value is still in no better case. If we accept these historical statements we can only assert that while they are true for primitive economies, in a developed commodity economy labour-time is one of the factors determining price, but not the only one. Yet Marx, while aware of the other factors, maintained that real value is determined only by socially necessary labour-time. In other words, he was not answering the question 'What determines prices?' but the question 'What is value?' We have, in that case, to investigate the meaning of the latter question and whether it is possible to give a reasoned answer to it.

A second difficulty that is often raised is how we can imagine a proof of the assertion that the 'real' value of a commodity (what the Middle Ages called a 'just price', and the classical economists a 'natural price') is determined by labour-time. What does Marx mean, in fact, when he speaks of the 'law of value'? A natural law is generally a statement that certain phenomena occur in certain circumstances; but it is not clear that Marx's definition of value can be expressed as a law. The most general statement that might deserve this name, though it cannot have a quantitative character, would be that variations in the productivity of labour generally affect prices. But this is not the same as Marx's theory, which holds not that labour-time affects prices but that it is the only constituent of value. This is not a law, but an arbitrary definition which cannot be proved and is of no use for the empirical description of economic phenomena. As there is no transition from value to price, so there is no transition from the theory of value to the description of any actual economic process.

Many Marxists, such as Lukács, have maintained, for example, that the ruin of small firms by large ones is a confirmation of the law of value or even proves that Marx's 'abstract labour' is a genuine economic phenomenon. This, however, is a misuse of words. If small firms fail to compete with large ones because of lower productivity, this can be explained by the notion of production costs without bringing in the law of value. If labour-consuming techniques are replaced, in many cases at least, by others that are less so, this can be explained by the analysis of prices, which, unlike values, are an empirical phenomenon. To state that the 'law of value' operates in such cases does not make the process easier to understand—especially when we do not know what is meant by the 'law of value' if it is something different from a definition of value, which is certainly not a law.

For this reason economists of an empirical turn consider Marx's theory of value to be useless, as it cannot be applied to the empirical description of phenomena. Their point is not that Marx gave the wrong answer to the question 'What is real value?', but that this question has no meaning in economic science if it refers to anything but the factors governing prices. On this ground Marx's theory has been criticized as 'metaphysical' in the pejorative sense given to this term by the positivists: i.e. it claims to reveal the 'essence' hidden beneath the surface phenomena, but provides no way of empirically confirming or refuting what it says. The objection that Marx was, in this sense, hunting after the 'substance' of value has been denied by Marxists who point out that he defined it as a social relation having no existence except in the exchange of commodities. But this is not a good answer to the objectors, even if they use the word 'substance' improperly. Marx, it is true, expressly rejects the idea that exchange-value is immanently present in a commodity, independently of the social process of exchange to which it is subjected. But if we distinguish value from exchange-value we can say that any commodity 'represents' or is the embodiment or vehicle (or any similar metaphor) of the total sum of labour that has been put into it, while exchange-value is the manifestation of value as between goods on the market. Exchange-value thus depends on there being a commodity economy (and in this sense, according to Marx, it is a transient historical phenomenon) and also on the existence of value itself, which is 'crystallized labour time'. The existence of value does not depend on the system of production and exchange; men have always expended labour on making various objects, and value, in consequence, is an immanent quality of things, manifested in certain social conditions as exchange-value. But if Marx's 'law' is meant to signify anything more than two logically independent empirical statements—that most useful objects are the fruit of labour, and that labour-time is one element in price; if it is supposed to mean that there is a 'real', unmeasurable value independent of price, then this is no better than a 'latent property' of the type condemned by science since the seventeenth century. Yet there can be no doubt that Marx did mean more than the above two statements, and intended to throw light on the true nature of value and exchange-value. The assertion that true value is crystallized labour-time is on a par with the statement that opium puts people to sleep because it is soporific. We are told of a hidden quality that manifests itself empirically (opium puts people to sleep, goods are exchanged); but the information does not explain the empirical phenomena or enable us to predict them better than we can without it.

There is another formula that might seem to give content to the law of value, viz. Marx's statement that the sum of prices equals the sum of values. This too, however, is not supported by any argument, and its meaning is not clear. If objects are sold which possess no value—for example, land, the price of which is anticipated rent—this must mean that the equality of prices and values is not actual at any particular moment, but only over a period of time that is not and cannot be determined. In this sense the statement has no definable meaning, and in any case it is not clear how it could be verified, since value cannot be quantitatively expressed.

As an interpretation of economic phenomena Marx's theory of value does not meet the normal requirements of a scientific hypothesis, especially that of falsifiability. It may, however, be defended on a different basis, as a piece of philosophic anthropology (or, as Jaurès put it, social metaphysics)—a continuation of the theory of alienation and an attempt to express a feature of social life which is important to the philosophy of history: namely that when human skill and effort are transformed into commodities they become abstract vehicles of currency and are subject to the impersonal laws of the market over which producers have no control. The theory of value, then, is not an explanation of how the capitalist economy works, but a critique of the dehumanization of the object, and therefore of the subject, in a system wherein 'everything is for sale'. On this view the theory is part of the Romantic attack on a society enslaved by the money-power.

It should be observed that those analyses of Marx's which can be checked empirically with some degree of rigour, such as the falling rate of profit or the schemata of reproduction in Volume II of *Capital*, do not (whatever Marx himself believed) depend logically on the theory of value, which can be ignored in appraising them.

As already mentioned, Marx's theory of value includes the statement, peculiar to himself, that labour is not only the measure of value but its only source. Logically the two parts of this proposition are separable: labour might be the measure but not the only source, or vice versa.

The statement that human labour is the only source of value, and the connected distinction between productive and non-productive labour, are not supported by argument either. It is not clear why, when a farmer uses a horse to plough his land, he himself creates new values but the horse does no more than transfer part of its own value to the product. The motive for this arbitrary assertion appears to lie in the conclusion, so important to Marx, that capital does not create value. Marx knew, and indeed emphasized in the *Grundrisse*, that capital as an organizing force greatly increases the productivity of labour; yet he maintained, following Ricardo, that it contributes only to use-value and not to exchange-value. But if so, capital is in fact a source of real wealth, i.e. the increase of usable objects—although the sum total of the values of that wealth will be the same whatever its quantity, if they represent the same number of labour hours (reduced to 'simple labour'). Thus the increase of social wealth has nothing to do with the increase of values. We can imagine a society in which all production was perfectly automatized, so that the society produced no values in Marx's sense, though it produced great quantities of wealth or use-value. There is no logical, physical, or economic reason why such a society should not be based on capitalist ownership, even though it employed no 'living labour' or productive labourers at all.

Thus Marx's ridicule of the idea that money has a magic power of self-multiplication because it can be lent at interest is over-facile. The proposition that capital does not increase values follows logically from Marx's definition of value, and must be assented to if we accept that definition; but there are no sufficient logical or empirical grounds for accepting it. The fact that capital increases use-values by organizing labour is not contrary to Marx's premises. But, for that very reason, the growth and distribution of social wealth are unrelated to the theory that labour is the only source of value; for the increase of exchange-values, as distinct from the question of prices and the multiplication of commodities, is in itself of no interest to society. What is of interest is the quantity of goods produced, the manner of their sale and distribution and the question of exploitation. But the theory that the workman is the only creator of value throws no light on these matters; it merely serves to arouse indignation at the fact that the 'only real producer' gets so small a share of the result of his work, while the capitalist, who contributes nothing to value, rakes in profits on the strength of being a property-owner. Apart from this moral interpretation it is not clear how the theory is supposed to throw light on the mechanism of the capitalist economy; and, it should be repeated, Marx did not agree with the Ricardian socialists who deduced from the theory of value that the workman was entitled to the equivalent of what his labour produced.

The distinction between productive and unproductive labour appears in Marx in two forms. In one sense, as we read in the *Grundrisse*, productive labour is labour that helps to create capital; and in this sense the distinction applies only to capitalist production. In another sense productive labour is labour which creates values of any kind, irrespective of social conditions. The distinction has been much debated by Marxists, as the dividing line between the two kinds of labour is very hard to draw. In general we gather from Marx that productive labour is physical labour applied to material objects; but from occasional remarks it appears that he was prepared to count as producers those who did not directly work on the material themselves but enabled others to do so—for example, engineers or designers in factories. In this case, however, the distinction is highly obscure and has given rise in the socialist countries to practical as well as theoretical dilemmas. It could be disputed, for instance, whether a doctor's work was 'productive' or not: from the economic point of view it means restoring or reproducing labour-power and is thus productive, but the same can be said of begetting children, which throws a doubtful light on the argument. Again, a teacher's work may help to produce important industrial skills, so presumably it too creates values. The practical aspect of the question is that in societies that try with greater or less (usually less) success to apply criteria derived from Marx's theories, labour regarded as productive is more highly respected and better paid; so, as long as teachers and medical staff were officially non-productive, the wretched level of their salaries could be theoretically justified. Another consequence of the theory was that the whole services sector was reckoned to be non-productive and was therefore totally neglected in planning.

At the present time, the distinction is more and more anachronistic and its purpose is not very clear. The proportion of those whose work consists in the direct physical processing of material objects grows less as technology improves, and the increase in total wealth depends less and less on the number of such workers.

It is also not clear on what Marx bases his view that what the worker sells is not labour but labour-power. Even if we agree with him that labour, while it is the source of value, has no value of its own, it does not follow that it cannot be sold: according to Marx many objects and activities are sold though they have no value as he defines it. What he probably meant to emphasize was that when the capitalist buys labour-power according to the laws of capitalist economy he is the owner of the labourer's person for the stipulated time and is entitled to make him work up to and beyond his physical capacity and endurance. But the capitalist's right to exploit the labourer and prolong the working day is not a built-in feature of capitalism as such, but only belongs to an early phase of it. How far it exists in practice depends on legislation and the amount of pressure the working class is able to exert; in the capitalist world at present there is no country where the employer can be said to have such a right. Even if he believes himself entitled to all he can squeeze out of the labourer, legal or other reasons prevent the claim being made good, and it is not clear how Marx's assertion helps towards an understanding of present-day capitalism. Nor is his theory necessary to explain the workers' struggle for shorter hours and fairer wages.

The distinctions and concepts most clearly linked with Marx's theory of value are an ideological expression of his belief that capitalism cannot be reformed and that it tends inexorably to depress wages to the minimum value of labour-power and to work labourers to the physical maximum. (Any rise in wages is due to the increase of needs, to which no limit is set, so that whatever the wage-level it can be maintained that the worker is selling his labour-power at its market value.) However, at the present time when resistance to exploitation has not only been successful but has radically transformed social life, the theory of value and its corollaries merely obscure the picture, as Marxists feel obliged to maintain the validity of laws that bear no relation to the facts. This does not mean, of course, that the capitalist is not out to make the highest profit he can; but this is a common-sense principle which has nothing to do with any particular theory of value.

As for exploitation, it can be defined consistently with Marx's intentions without any logical need to invoke his theory. He explains it as a matter of unpaid labour, i.e. the surplus value appropriated by the capitalist after deducting the cost of materials, wages, and the replacement of constant capital. Yet Marx himself ridiculed the utopians and Lassalle for holding that the worker should receive in the form of wages the whole equivalent of the values produced by him, as this would be impossible in any society. The abolition of exploitation meant, in his view, not that workers should receive the equivalent of what they produced, but that the surplus value they do not receive in wages should accrue to society in the form of fresh investments, emergency reserves, payment for necessary 'unproductive' services, administration, etc., plus provision for those unable to work. But under capitalism surplus values over and above what is consumed by the bourgeoisie do revert to society in all these forms. The moral aspect of exploitation comes to the fore when there is a blatant contrast between bourgeois luxury and the poverty of the workers. But Marx did not contend, like the leaders of earlier people's movements, that it would help to solve social problems if the goods consumed by the bourgeoisie were divided among the whole population. Bourgeois consumption in the face of workers' poverty is a moral issue, not an economic one; the distribution, once and for all, of rich men's wealth among the poor would not solve anything or bring about any real change. Such a measure only made sense as regards landed property, which could be divided among the peasantry and has been so divided in several countries. If the homes, furniture, clothing, and valuables of the bourgeoisie were distributed among the poor it would only be an isolated act of revenge, not a solution of social problems—yet this is the only sharing that would result from the socialization of property. For this reason Marx avoided encouraging the facile but false idea that to abolish exploitation meant simply to strip the rich of their movable possessions: this was contrary to his own theory and only served to foster the envious and predatory mentality of peasant movements and the lumpenproletariat.

Exploitation, in fact, does not signify either that the worker receives less than the equivalent of his product, or that incomes in general are unequal—since there is no known way of making them perfectly equal in an advanced industrial society—or even that the bourgeoisie pay for their luxuries out of unearned income. Exploitation consists in the fact that society has no control over the use made of surplus product, and that its distribution is in the hands of those who have an exclusive power of decision as to the use of means of production. It is thus a question of degree, and one can speak of limiting exploitation not merely by increasing wages but by giving society more control over investment and the division of the national income. Bourgeois luxury is not itself exploitation but is a consequence of it: those who control the means of production, and therefore the distribution of surplus product, naturally seize a large share of the cake.

Although this account of exploitation appears to be in accordance with Marx's own views it is hard to reconcile with orthodox Marxism, since it implies that the nationalization of means of production does not necessarily prevent exploitation and, in certain circumstances that have actually occurred, may increase it to a considerable degree. For, if exploitation can be limited in so far as society controls the distribution of surplus product, it must be greater to the extent that the machinery for such control is weakened. If, instead of private ownership, the power to control the means of production and distribution is confined to a small ruling group uncontrolled by any measure of representative democracy, there will be not less exploitation but a great deal more. The important thing is not the material privileges that the rulers keep for themselves, just as it is not important what clothes the bourgeoisie wear or how much caviar they eat; what matters is that the mass of society is excluded from decisions as to the use of means of production and the distribution of income. Exploitation, in short, depends on whether there is or is not effective machinery to enable the workers to share in decisions concerning the product of their labour, and hence it is a question of political freedom and representative institutions. From this point of view socialist communities at the present day are examples not of the abolition of exploitation but of exploitation in an extreme degree, since by cancelling the legal right of ownership they have destroyed the machinery which gave society control over the product of its own labour. In capitalist communities, by contrast—at all events the more advanced ones—this machinery makes it possible to limit exploitation by progressive taxation, partial control of investment and prices, welfare institutions, increasing the social consumption fund, etc., even while private ownership of the means of production continues and exploitation has not been abolished.

XIV

The Motive Forces of the Historical Process

1. Productive forces, relations of production, superstructure

In his description in *Capital* Marx referred to the causal connection between the advance of technology and the unlimited expansionism of capital. At the same time he argued that this tendency could only arise and become universal in certain technological conditions, and not at any period of history without distinction. The functioning and the expansionist tendency of capitalism was a special case of the more general system of relations that had governed social life in all its forms, past and present. Marx's description of that system goes by the name of historical materialism or the materialist interpretation of history. It was first clearly set out in *The German Ideology*, but the best-known general formulation is in his Preface to *A Contribution to the Critique of Political Economy* (1859); the doctrine is also stated in different versions in the popular writings of Engels. Here is Marx's classic exposition:

In the social production which men carry on they enter into definite relations that are indispensable and independent of their will; these relations of production correspond to a particular stage of development of their material forces of production. The sum total of these relations of production constitutes the economic structure of society—the real foundation, on which rises a legal and political superstructure and to which correspond particular forms of social consciousness. The mode of production in material life determines the social, political and intellectual life processes in general. It is not the consciousness of men that determines their being, but, on the contrary, their social being that determines their consciousness. At a certain stage of their development the material forces of production in society come into conflict with the existing relations of production, or—what is but a legal expression for the same thing—with the property relations within which they have been at work before. From forms of development of the forces of production, these relations turn into their fetters. Then begins an epoch of social revolution. With the change of the economic foundation the entire immense superstructure is more or less rapidly transformed. In considering such transformations a distinction should always be made between the material transformation of the economic conditions of production, which can be determined with the precision of natural science, and the legal, political, religious, aesthetic or philosophic—in short, ideological forms in which men become conscious of this conflict and fight it out. Just as our opinion of an individual is not based on what he thinks of himself, so we cannot judge of such a period of transformation by its own consciousness; on the contrary, this consciousness must be explained rather from the contradictions of material life, from the existing conflict between the social forces of production and the relations of production. No social order ever disappears before all the productive forces for which there is room in it have been developed; and new higher relations of production never appear before the material conditions of their existence have matured in the womb of the old society itself. Therefore mankind always sets itself only such tasks as it can solve; since, looking at the matter more closely, we shall always find that the task arises only when the material conditions necessary for its solution already exist or are at least in the process of formation. In broad outlines we can designate the Asiatic, the ancient, the feudal and the modern bourgeois modes of production as so many epochs in the progress of the economic formation of society. The bourgeois relations of production are the last antagonistic form of the social process of production—not in the sense of individual antagonism, but of one arising from the social conditions of life of the individuals; at the same time the productive forces developing in the womb of bourgeois society create the material conditions for the solution of that antagonism. The present formation constitutes, therefore, the closing chapter of the prehistoric stage of human society.

In the history of human thought there are few texts that have aroused such controversy, disagreement and conflicts of interpretation as this one. We cannot retrace the whole intricate debate here, but will note some of the main points.

In *Socialism, Utopian and Scientific* (Introduction to English edn., 1892) Engels defines historical materialism as 'that view of the course of history which seeks the ultimate cause and the great moving power of all important historic events in the economic development of society, in the changes in the modes of production and exchange, in the consequent division of society into distinct classes, and in the struggle of these classes against one another'.

Historical materialism is thus an answer to the question: what circumstances have had the greatest effect in changing human civilization?—this word being understood in a broad sense covering all social forms of communication, from categories of thought to the social organization of labour and political institutions.

The starting-point of human history from the materialist point of view is the struggle with nature, the sum total of the means employed by man to compel nature to serve his needs, which grow as they are satisfied. Man is distinguished from other animals by the fact that he makes tools: the brute creation may use tools in a primitive way, but only such as they find in nature itself. Once equipment is perfected to the extent that an individual can produce more goods than he consumes himself, there is a possibility of conflict as to the sharing of the excess product and of a situation in which some people appropriate the fruits of others' labour—that is to say, a class society. The various forms that this appropriation may take determine the forms of political life and of consciousness, i.e. the way in which people apprehend their own social existence.

We thus have the following schema. The ultimate motive force of historical change is technology, productive forces, the whole of the equipment available to society plus acquired technical ability plus the technical division of labour. The level of productive forces determines the basic structure of the relations of production, i.e. the foundation of social life. (Marx does not regard technology itself as part of the 'base', since he speaks of a conflict between productive forces and the relations of production.) The relations of production comprise, above all, property relations: i.e. the legally guaranteed power to dispose of raw materials and the instruments of production and, in due course, of the products of labour. They also include the social division of labour, wherein people are differentiated not by the kind of production they are engaged in, or the particular phase of a production process, but by whether they take part in material production at all or perform other functions such as management, political administration or intellectual work. The separation of physical from intellectual work was one of the greatest revolutions in history. It was able to occur because of the social inequality which permitted some men to appropriate the work of others without taking part in the process of production. The volume of leisure thus created made possible intellectual work, and thus the whole spiritual culture of mankind—the arts, philosophy, and science—is rooted in social inequality. Another component of the 'base', or the relations of production is the way in which products are distributed and exchanged between producers.

The relations of production further determine the whole range of phenomena to which Marx gives the name of superstructure. This includes all political institutions, especially the state, all organized religion, political associations, laws and customs, and finally human consciousness expressed in ideas about the world, religious beliefs, forms of artistic creation, and the doctrines of law, politics, philosophy, and morality. The principal tenet of historical materialism is that a particular technological level calls for particular relations of production and causes them to come about historically in the course of time. They in turn bring about a particular kind of superstructure, consisting of different aspects which are antagonistic to each other: for the relations of production based on appropriation of the fruits of others' labour divide society into classes with opposing interests, and the class struggle expresses itself in the super-structure as a conflict between political forces and opinions. The superstructure is the sum total of the weapons employed by the classes fighting one another for a maximum share in the product of surplus labour.

2. Social being and consciousness

THE objections most frequently raised against historical materialism in the nineteenth century were: (1) it denies the significance of conscious human action in history, which is absurd; (2) it declares that men act only from motives of material interest, which is also contrary to all evidence; (3) it reduces history to the 'economic factor' and treats all other factors such as religion, thought, feeling, etc. either as unimportant or as determined by economics to the exclusion of human freedom.

Some formulations of the doctrine by Marx and Engels might indeed seem open to these objections. The critics were answered partly by Engels and partly by later Marxists, but not in such a way as to remove all ambiguity. However, the objections lose much of their force if we recall what questions historical materialism does and does not set out to answer.

In the first place, it is not and does not claim to be a key to the interpretation of any particular historical event. All it does is to define the relations between some, but by no means all, features of social life. In a review of Marx's *Critique* in 1859 Engels wrote: 'History often proceeds by jumps and zig-zags, and, if it were followed in this way, not only would much material of minor importance have to be included but there would be much interruption of the chain of thought . . . The logical method of treatment was therefore the only appropriate one. This, however, is essentially no different from the historical method, only divested of its historical form and disturbing fortuities.' In other words, Marx's account of the dependence of the superstructure on the relations of production applies to great historical eras and fundamental changes in society. It is not claimed that the level of technology determines every detail of the social division of labour, and thus in turn every detail of political and intellectual life. Marx and Engels thought in broad historical categories and in terms of the basic factors governing the change from one system to another. They believed that the class structure of a given society was bound sooner or later to manifest itself in basic institutional forms, but the course of events which brought this about would depend on a multitude of chance circumstances. As Marx wrote in a letter to Kugelmann (17 April 1871), 'World history. . . would be of a very mystical nature if "accidents" played no part in it. These accidents fall naturally into the general course of development and are compensated by other accidents. But acceleration and delay are very dependent upon such "accidents", including the "accident" of the character of those who at first stand at the head of the movement.' Engels too, in some well-known letters, warned against exaggerated formulations of so-called historical determinism. 'While the material mode of existence is the *primum agens*, this does not preclude the ideological spheres from reacting upon it in their turn, though with a secondary effect.' (Letter to Conrad Schmidt, 5 Aug. 1890.)

> The determing element in history is, in the last resort, the production and reproduction of real life. More than this neither Marx nor I have ever asserted. If therefore somebody twists this into the statement that the economic element is the only determining one, he transforms it into a meaningless, abstract and absurd phrase. The economic situation is the basis, but the various elements of the superstructure—political forms of the class struggle and its consequences, constitutions established by the victorious class after a successful battle, etc.; forms of law, and even the reflexes of all these actual struggles in the brains of the combatants: political, legal philosophical theories, religious ideas and their further development into systems of dogma—all these exercise their influence upon the course of the historical struggles and in many cases preponderate in determining their form. There is an interaction of all these elements in which, amid all the endless host of accidents . . . the economic movement finally asserts itself as necessary. (Letter to Joseph Bloch, 21 Sept. 1890)

In the same way, great individuals who appear to shape the course of history actually come upon the scene because society needs them. Alexander, Cromwell, and Napoleon are instruments of the historical process; they may affect it by their accidental personal traits, but they are unconscious agents of a great impersonal force which they did not create. The effectiveness of their action is determined by the situation in which it takes place.

If, then, we can speak of historical determinism, it is only in the context of major institutional features. The technological level of the tenth century being what it was, there could not have been at that time a Declaration of the Rights of Man or a *Code Napoléon*. As we know, there can in fact be widely differing political systems in societies where the technological level is much the same. Nevertheless, if we consider the essential features of these societies and not the accidental details of personal character, tradition, and circumstance, it will appear from the point of view of historical materialism that in all decisive respects they resemble one another or show a tendency to do so.

As to the reflex action of the superstructure on the mode of production, here, too we must remember the qualification 'in the last resort'. The state may, for instance, act in such a way as either to help or to hinder the social changes required by the level of productive forces. The effectiveness of its action will vary according to 'accidental' circumstances, but in the fullness of time the economic factor will prevail. If we consider history in panoramic form it appears as a tumult of chaotic events, amid which the analyst is able to perceive certain dominant trends, including the basic interrelations of which Marx spoke. It will be seen, for instance, that legal forms approximate steadily to the situation in which they best serve the interests of the ruling classes, and that these interests are constituted according to the mode of production, exchange, and ownership which obtains in the society in question; it will also be seen that philosophies and religious beliefs and observances vary according to social needs and changes in political institutions.

As to the part played by conscious intentions in the historical process, the view of Marx and Engels appears to be as follows. All human acts are governed by specific intentions—personal feelings or private interests, religious ideals or concern for the public welfare. But the result of all these multifarious acts does not reflect the intentions of any one person; it is subject to a kind of statistical regularity, which can be traced in the evolution of large social units but does not tell us what happens to their components as individuals. Historical materialism does not state that personal motives are necessarily perverse or selfish, or that they are all of a kind; it is not concerned with such motives at all, and does not attempt to predict individual behaviour. It is only concerned with mass phenomena which are not consciously willed by anyone but which obey social laws that are as regular and impersonal as the laws of physical nature. Human beings and their relations are, nevertheless, the sole reality of the historical process, which ultimately consists of the conscious behaviour of individuals. The sum total of their acts forms a pattern of diachronic historical laws, describing the transition from one social system to the next, and also functional laws showing the interrelation of such features as technology, forms of property, class barriers, state institutions, and ideology. 'Men make their own history, but they do not make it just as they please; they do not make it under circumstances chosen by themselves, but under circumstances directly found, given and transmitted from the past.' (*The Eighteenth Brumaire of Louis Bonaparte*, I.)

Strictly speaking, it is wrong to represent materialism as distinguishing various 'factors' in history and then 'reducing' them to a single one or claiming that all the others depend on it. The misleadingness of this approach was pointed out by Plekhanov among others. So-called historical 'factors' are not substantive entities but abstractions. The historical process is one and all important events are made up of the most varied influences and phenomena: mental attitudes, traditions, interests and ideals. According to historical materialism, on the stage of world history men's opinions, customs and institutions are predominantly affected by the prevailing system of production, exchange, and distribution. This, of course, is an extremely general statement and scarcely does more than signify its opposition to the type of theory which regards institutions and social organization as ultimately the product of opinions or the Spirit of History working towards its goal. Nor does the statement indicate in what way men's 'social being determines their consciousness': many interpretations of this saying are possible, even apart from the rejected notion that men are consciously motivated by nothing but material interest. In particular it is not clear whether the 'determination' is teleological or merely causative. If we say that forms of consciousness such as religious and philosophical doctrines 'reflect' or 'express' the interests of the community or class in which they arise, this may either mean that they serve the interests of that community, i.e. it derives advantage from believing them, or simply that they are what they are because of the community's situation. Marx and Engels explained, for instance, that the ideals of political freedom served the interests of the bourgeoisie because they included the idea of free trade and freedom to buy and sell wage-labour. In this sense it can be said that the idea of freedom was a device to support bourgeois expansionism. But when Engels says that the Calvinistic theory of predestination was a religious expression of the fact that commercial success or bankruptcy does not depend on the businessman's intentions but on economic forces, then, whether we agree with his statement or not, we must regard it as asserting a merely causal connection: for the idea of absolute dependence on an external power (viz. the market in the 'mystified' shape of Providence) does not seem to further the businessman's interest, but rather to set the seal on his impotence. As a rule, however, when the founders of historical materialism interpret the phenomena of the superstructure, they do so in order to show that the ideas, trends, or institutions are not only caused by the interests of the class in question but actually serve those interests, i.e. they are functionally adapted to that class's needs. The analogy, moreover, is with a physical organism rather than with a human purpose. The ideas conduce to the advantage of those who hold them even though, or rather because, the fact that they do so is not perceived or is misunderstood. Part of their function is in fact one of mystification, transforming interests into ideals and concrete facts into abstractions, so that those who make use of them do not understand what they are doing and why.

At this point, of course, the interpretative possibilities of historical materialism begin to show certain limitations. In explaining, for example, the history of religion it accounts not so much for the genesis of a particular idea as for the fact of its becoming widespread. It cannot tell us why a certain conception of Deity and salvation occurred to a Jew living on the confines of the Roman Empire in the time of Augustus and Tiberius, but it purports to explain the social process whereby Christianity spread throughout the Empire and finally prevailed over it. The theory cannot interpret every dogmatic dispute that has arisen among the innumerable Christian sects, but it explains the main tendencies of those sects in terms of the social classes to which their adherents belonged. It cannot account for the appearance and nature of a particular artistic talent, but it can interpret the principal trends in the history of art in the light of the 'world-view' that each represents and the origins of that view in class ideology. The limitations on the use of the theory are important, for it would be a delusion to suppose that the division of society into classes could ever provide an explanation of all its differentiations without exception. Even political struggles and controversies are full of details which cannot be explained by the class conflict, although the method of historical materialism can be applied to fundamental disputes or periods when society is more than usually polarized in class terms.

What, then, in the last resort is the determining influence of the base on the superstructure, and what is the 'relative independence' possessed by the various forms of superstructure according to Engels and most theoretical Marxists? The influence in question relates only to certain features of the superstructure, but they are important ones. For instance, the possessing class in any political system will do its best to order the law of inheritance so as to keep estates intact, and it will be able to do this unhindered if it enjoys full political power. However, even when this class's material interest and the law are thus openly linked, its freedom of action may be limited by accidental circumstances such as the traditional laws and customs of the society in question, or religious beliefs which arose in other times but have not lost their effect. Within the superstructure of class societies there are always antagonistic forces at work, so that political and legal institutions are generally the fruit of a compromise among discordant interests. These, moreover, are as a rule distorted by tradition acting as an independent force, which will be all the stronger in so far as the different elements of the superstructure are not embodied in institutions. The force of tradition will be strongest in purely ideological matters, for example philosophical or aesthetic opinions: here the influence of the base on the superstructure will be relatively weaker than, for example, in the case of legal institutions. It must not therefore be inferred from historical materialism that the relations of production unequivocally determine the whole of the superstructure: they only do so in broad lines, excluding some possibilities and encouraging certain tendencies at the expense of others. Some elements of a given superstructure may persist apparently unchanged through various economic formations, though their significance may be different in different circumstances: this is true of religious beliefs and philosophical doctrines. In addition, elements of the superstructure become autonomous because human needs take on an independent form and instrumental values become ends in themselves. As Marx observed, the sum of needs is not constant but grows with the advance of production. 'The need which consumption feels for the object is created by the perception of it. An object of art, in the same way as every other product, creates a public which is sensitive to art and enjoys beauty. Production thus not only creates an object for the subject, but also a subject for the object.' (*Grundrisse*, Introduction.) 'At the dawn of civilization the productiveness acquired by labour is small, but so too are wants, which develop with and by the means of satisfying them.' (*Capital*, I, Ch. XIV; English edn., Ch. XVI.) It is in no way contrary to Marx's ideas or to historical materialism to hold that aesthetic needs, for instance, have come to require satisfaction for their own sake, as opposed to being merely 'apparent' or subordinate to some other, more fundamental needs. However, if some instrumental values have in this way become independent ones alongside elementary physical needs, the biological conditions of existence, it is quite natural that the process of creating them should largely cease to be dependent on relations which are ultimately based on those elementary needs.

The functional character of various elements of the superstructure is not inconsistent, in Marx's view, with the permanence of the creations of human culture. To explain the immortality of Greek art he suggests that humanity, like the individual, returns with pleasure to the imaginations of its childhood, which it knows to be past for ever but for which it still feels affection. From this it would follow that according to Marx cultural activity is not merely accessory to socio-economic development, but contains values independent of its role in subserving a particular order of society.

Nor should it be supposed that 'Social being determines consciousness' is an eternal law of history. The *Critique of Political Economy* describes the dependence of social consciousness on the relations of production as a fact that has always existed in the past, but it does not follow that it must be so for ever. Socialism, as Marx saw it, was vastly to enlarge the sphere of creative activity outside the production process, freeing consciousness from mystification and social life from reified forces. In such conditions, consciousness, i.e. the conscious will and initiative of human beings, would be in control of social processes, so that it would determine social being rather than the other way about. The maxim, in fact, appears to relate to ideological consciousness, i.e. that which is unaware of its own instrumental character. On the other hand, *The German Ideology* assures us that consciousness can never be anything other than conscious life, i.e. the manner in which men experience situations that arise independently of consciousness. It may be, however, that these two views can be reconciled. The rule that social being determines consciousness can be regarded as a particular case of the more general rule that consciousness is identical with conscious life—a particular case applying to the whole of past history, in which the products of human activity have turned into independent forces dominating the historical process. When this domination ceases and social development obeys conscious human decisions, it will no longer be the case that 'social being determines consciousness'; but it will still be the case that consciousness is an expression of 'life', for this principle is one of epistemology and not of the philosophy of history. Consciousness of life is a function of 'pre-conscious' life, not of course in the sense of Schopenhauer or Freud but in the sense that thought and feeling and their expression in science, art, and philosophy are instruments related positively or negatively to man's self-realization in empirical history. In other words, the situation in which social being determines consciousness is one in which consciousness is 'mystified', unaware of its true purpose, acting contrary to man's interest and intensifying his servitude. When consciousness is liberated it becomes a means of strength instead of enslavement, aware of its own participation in the realization of man and of the fact that it is a component of the whole human being. It controls the relations of production instead of being controlled by them. It is still the expression and instrument of life aspiring towards fullness, but it furthers that aspiration instead of impoverishing life, and is a source of creative energy instead of a brake on it. In short, the liberated consciousness is de-mystified and aware of its contribution to the expansion of human opportunities. Consciousness at all times is an instrument of life, but throughout history up to now (prehistory) it has been determined by relations of production that are independent of the human will. This interpretation, at all events, is consistent with Marx's writings, though he does not anywhere expressly adopt it.

3. Historical progress and its contradictions

THE whole of progress up to the present time (so the theory continues) has been beset by an internal contradiction: it has increased man's total power over nature while depriving the majority of the fruits of that power, and enslaving all mankind to objectified material forces. Contrary to Hegel's view, history is not the gradual conquest of social freedom but rather its gradual extinction. 'At the same pace that mankind masters nature, man seems to become enslaved to other men or to his own infamy. Even the pure light of science seems unable to shine except against the dark background of ignorance.' (Speech delivered by Marx at the anniversary of the Chartist organ, the *People's Paper*, on 14 Apr. 1856.) Engels wrote in a similar strain in his *Origin of the Family* (Ch. II): 'Monogamy was a great historical advance, but at the same time it inaugurated, along with slavery and private wealth, that epoch, lasting until today, in which the well-being and development of the one group are attained by the misery and repression of the other.' Again: 'Since the exploitation of one class by another is the basis of civilization, its whole development moves in a continuous contradiction. Every advance in production is at the same time a retrogression in the condition of the oppressed class, that is, of the great majority.' (Ibid., Ch. IX.) 'Indeed, it is only by dint of the most extravagant waste of individual development that the development of the human race is at all safeguarded and maintained in the epoch of history immediately preceding the conscious reorganization of society.' (*Capital*, III, Ch. V, II.)

This negative, anti-human side of progress is an inseparable consequence of alienated labour. But for this very reason, even in the cruellest aspects of civilization we can perceive history working towards the final liberation of man. From this point of view, perhaps the most characteristic of Marx's observations are contained in his articles on British rule in India. After describing its devastating effect on the peaceful, stagnant Indian communities he goes on to say:

> Sickening as it must be to human feeling to witness those myriads of industrious patriarchal and inoffensive social organizations disorganized and dissolved into their units, thrown into a sea of woes, and their individual members losing at the same time their ancient form of civilization and their hereditary means of subsistence, we must not forget that these idyllic village communities, inoffensive though they may appear, had always been the solid foundation of Oriental despotism; that they restrained the human mind within the smallest possible compass, making it the unresisting tool of superstition, enslaving it beneath traditional rules, depriving it of all grandeur and historical energies . . . We must not forget that these little communities were contaminated by distinctions of caste and by slavery, that they subjugated man to external circumstances instead of elevating man to be the sovereign of circumstances, that they transformed a self-developing social state into never-changing natural destiny and thus brought about a brutalizing worship of nature, exhibiting its degradation in the fact that man, the sovereign of nature, fell down on his knees in adoration of Hanuman, the monkey, and Sabbala, the cow . . .
>
> The question is, can mankind fulfil its destiny without a fundamental revolution in the social state of Asia? If not, whatever may have been the crimes of England she was the unconscious tool of history in bringing about that revolution. Then, whatever bitterness the spectacle of the crumbling of an ancient world may have for our personal feelings, we have the right, in point of history, to exclaim with Goethe: '*Sollte diese Qual uns quälen,/Da sie unsre Lust vermehrt?*' ['Should we be grieved by this pain that increases our pleasure?'] (*New York Daily Tribune*, 25 June 1853)

This argument is an important clue to the understanding of the Marxian interpretation of history. We find in it the Hegelian doctrine of the historical mission fulfilled unconsciously, despite their crimes and passions, by particular nations or classes. There is also the idea of the historical mission of humanity, the vocation of mankind as a whole. We see, further, that Marx constantly regarded the historical process from the point of view of the future liberation of mankind, which was the sole touchstone of current events: in particular he attached no importance to the economic conquests of the working class under capitalism except in relation to this ultimate purpose. Finally it should be noted that Marx's historical appraisal of human actions in terms of the part they play in bringing about liberation had nothing to do with a moral judgement: the crimes of the British imperialists were not palliated by the fact that they brought the day of revolution nearer. This is also the viewpoint of the whole of *Capital*, in which moral indignation at the cruelty and villainy of exploitation is found side by side with the conviction that this state of affairs was helping on the revolution. Increasing exploitation was bringing about the downfall of capitalism, but it did not follow that the workers who resisted it were acting 'against history'. However, their action was progressive not because it improved their lot and this improvement was good in itself, but because it helped to develop the workers' class-consciousness, which was a precondition of revolution.

Marx and Engels believed in the rights of a higher civilization over a lower one. The French colonization of Algeria and the U.S. victory over Mexico seemed to them progressive events, and in general they supported the great 'historical' nations against backward peoples or those which for any reason had no chance of independent historical development. (Thus Engels expected Austria-Hungary to swallow up the small Balkan countries; Poland, as a historical nation, should, he thought, be restored and include in its dominion the less developed peoples to the east—Lithuanians, White Russians, and Ukrainians.) The future liberation on which their historical optimism was based was not merely a matter of abolishing poverty and satisfying elementary human needs, but of fulfilling man's destiny and ensuring his dignity and greatness by giving him the maximum control over nature and his own life. We see how, despite Marx's abandonment of the old formulas about restoring man's nature, his faith in humanity and its fulfilment in the course of history lived on and determined his attitude to current events. Capitalism, through all its negative features and manifold inhumanity, had prepared the technological basis enabling man to escape from the compulsion of material needs and develop his intellectual and artistic faculties as ends in themselves.

> The surplus labour of the mass has ceased to be the condition for the development of general wealth, just as the non-labour of the few has ceased to be the condition for the development of the general powers of the human brain. With that, production based on exchange value breaks down, and the direct, material production process is stripped of the form of penury and antithesis. [It is] the free development of individualities, and hence not the reduction of necessary labour time so as to posit surplus labour, but rather the general reduction of the necessary labour of society to a minimum, which then corresponds to the artistic, scientific etc. development of the

individuals in the time set free, and with the means created, for all of them. (*Grundrisse*, III, 2, Notebook VII)

Thus the martyrdom of history would not be in vain, and future generations would enjoy the fruits of their predecessors' sufferings.

It should be emphasized that to Marx the concept of 'modes of production' is a basic instrument for the division of history into periods and also for the comprehension of it as a single whole. There is one point, however, which has given trouble to commentators, namely the 'Asiatic mode of production', to which Marx refers in the *Grundrisse* and in certain articles and letters of 1853. The essence of the Asiatic system, found historically in China, India, and some Muslim countries, is that private ownership of land was almost unknown, as geographical and climatic conditions called for an irrigation system that could only be provided by a centralized adminstration. Hence the special autonomous role of the despotic state apparatus, on which the economy largely depended; commerce developed to a very small extent, towns did not exist as centres of trade and industry, and there was scarcely any native bourgeoisie. The traditional village communities lived on through the ages in social and technical stagnation. The gradual dissolution of these communities and of the state despotism was due to European capitalism rather than internal causes.

In Stalin's time orthodox Marxism altogether excluded the 'Asiatic mode of production' from its schema of history, for the following reasons: Firstly, if a large part of humanity had lived for centuries with an economy of a type all its own, there could be no question of a uniform pattern of development for all mankind. The progression from slave-owning through feudalism to capitalism would apply only to one part of the world and not the rest, so that there could be no universally valid Marxist theory of history. Secondly, according to Marx the peculiarities of the Asiatic system were due to geographical factors; but how could the primacy of technology over natural conditions be maintained, if the latter could bring about a different form of social development in a large part of the globe? Thirdly, the Asiatic system was said by Marx to have involved the countries concerned in stagnation from which they were only rescued by the incursion of peoples whose economic development had been on different lines; apparently, then, 'progress' is not a necessary feature of human history but may or may not happen, according to circumstances. Thus the 'Asiatic mode of production' appeared contrary to three of the fundamental principles that orthodox Marxists generally attributed to historical materialism: the primary role of productive forces, the inevitability of progress, and the uniformity of human evolution in society. It might seem that the doctrine applied only to Western Europe and that capitalism itself was an accident—a system that had happened to arise in a particular, not very large part of the world and had subsequently proved strong and expansive enough to impose itself on the whole planet. Marx did not himself draw this influence, although, significantly, he observed at a later stage that the analysis in *Capital* applied only to Western Europe. But the conclusion follows naturally enough from what he says about the Asiatic system. It may appear no more than a detail in his philosophy of history, but if it is accepted it calls for the revision of a number of stereotypes, especially those connected with historical determinism and the idea of progress.

4. The monistic interpretation of social relationships

HISTORICAL materialism, as we have seen, provides a theoretical account of the main determinants and can be used to predict general lines of development, but not specific occurrences. Like any other philosophy of history, it is not a quantitative theory and cannot inform us of the relative strength of the factors at work in a particular social process. It purports to enable us, however, to discern the fundamental structure of any society by analysing its relations of production and the class divisions based directly thereon. As to the meaning of 'relations of production', this does not appear unequivocally from the writings of Marx and Engels. The latter, in *The Origin of the Family*, refers to 'the immediate production and reproduction of life' as including not only the making of tools and means of subsistence, but also the biological reproduction of the species—a doctrine frequently criticized by later Marxists; and in his letter to Starkenburg of 25 January 1894 Engels includes among 'economic conditions' the entire technique of production and transport and also geography. This is not merely a verbal question of the precise definition of such terms as 'relations of production' or 'economic conditions': the point is whether a single type of circumstance determines the whole superstructure, or several independent types. For instance, is the social aspect of the increase of the species, i.e. family institutions and the demographic situation, completely dependent on the mode of production and distribution, or does it present biological or other features with an independent effect on other social phenomena in the realm of the superstructure? Similarly, how far can geography be regarded as an independent factor in social processes? Marx observes in *Capital* (Vol. I, Ch. XIV; English edn., Ch. XVI) that capitalism arose in the temperate zone because the luxuriance of the tropics did not spur mankind to the efforts which gave rise to technology. It thus appears that, to Marx, some natural circumstances are at least a necessary condition of a particular social development. But in that case the level of technology, which in its primitive form has been achieved by all branches of the human race, cannot be a sufficient condition of changes in the relations of production. What has been said of geography applies equally to demographic phenomena. The message of historical materialism would seem to be that a given technology is a sufficient cause of particular relations of production provided certain other conditions of geography or demography are present. In the same way, such relations of production are a sufficient cause of essential features of the political superstructure if certain other conditions are fulfilled, for example as regards the consciousness and traditions of a people or its present situation. Hence the interpretative value of historical materialism appears only in particular analyses in which various concurrent factors can be discerned, and not in the general premisses which only dictate the direction of investigation.

Finally, historical materialism as a set of guidelines drawing attention to a particular type of interrelation must be distinguished from historical materialism as a theory which traces the basic course of human events from the first community to the classless society. This survey of world history is based on the premiss that if developments are considered on a large enough scale they can be explained by changes and improvements in the production of means wherewith to satisfy material needs, and that above a certain technological level these developments take the form of a struggle between classes with conflicting interests.

5. *The concept of class*

IN his letter of 5 March 1852 to Joseph Weydemeyer, Marx declares that it was not he who discovered the existence of classes or the class struggle: what he did was to prove that the existence of classes is bound up with particular phases in the development of production, that the class struggle leads to the dictatorship of the proletariat, and that this dictatorship constitutes the transition to a classless society.

Neither Marx nor Engels ever clearly defined the concept of class, and the last chapter of Volume III of *Capital*, which was to treat of this question, breaks off after three or four paragraphs. In it Marx poses the question 'What makes wage-labourers, capitalists and landlords constitute the three great social classes?' It would seem at first sight, he goes on, that they are characterized by the identity of sources of revenue within each class—wages, profit, and ground-rent respectively. But, he goes on, from this point of view doctors, officials, and many others would constitute separate classes defined in each case by their source of revenue: so this criterion is in any case insufficient.

Kautsky, who took up the argument where Marx left off and tried to reconstruct his thoughts, arrived at the following conclusion (*The Materialist Interpretation of History*, IV, i, 1–6). The concept of class has a polarized character, i.e. a class exists only in opposition to another class. (It would therefore be absurd to speak of a one-class society: a society can only be classless or com-

posed of at least two hostile classes.) A collectivity does not become a class simply because its members' revenue comes from the same source; it must also be
in a state of conflict with another class or classes over the distribution of revenue. But this is not sufficient either. Since workers, capitalists, and landowners in fact all derive their revenue from the same source, namely the value
produced by the workers' labour, and since the way this value is distributed
depends on who owns the means of production, it is this ownership that constitutes the ultimate criterion. Thus we have on the one hand the possessing
classes who own the means of production and therefore the surplus value created by the workers' labour, and on the other hand the class of the exploited,
who own nothing but their own labour-power and are obliged to sell it. On this
criterion we can also distinguish intermediate classes of those who, like small
peasants or craftsmen, possess some means of production but do not employ
wage-labour; they do not enjoy the results of others' unpaid labour, but create
values by employing themselves or their families. These classes have a divided
consciousness: the ownership of means of production inclines them towards
solidarity with the capitalists, but they are likened to the workers by the fact
that they live from their own efforts and not from the surplus value produced
by others. Capitalism tends constantly to deprive these middle classes of their
small possessions and depress them to the status of the working class, allowing
only a small minority to enter the ranks of the exploiters.

Marx approached the question of classes from the standpoint of conditions
in Britain, while Kautsky had in view Germany and the rest of central Europe.
The criterion as to ownership of the means of production and the employment
of wage-labour enables us to distinguish between the exploiters, the
exploited, and those in between, but it does not distinguish capitalists from
landowners, both of whom, by their ownership of the means of production
including land, appropriate unpaid hours of surplus labour. In point of fact
the class opposition between these two is different from that between them
and the workers: for both the possessing classes are interested in maximizing
exploitation and surplus value. Hence at times of crisis they present a common front against the proletariat, although the latter may temporarily ally
itself with one of them against the other, for example with the bourgeoisie to
secure political freedom in situations where feudal institutions retain their
power. The ultimate source of the capitalist's and the landowner's revenue is
the same—the surplus value created by the workers; and, according to Marx,
this is also the case with financiers, merchants, and lenders of money at interest. The exploiting classes differ, however, in their way of appropriating profit.
Only industrial capital does so by exchanging objectified labour for living
labour, while the landowner or the usurer subsists on rent while taking no
part in the process of exchange.

It would seem to be in accordance with Marx's intentions, therefore, to distinguish between primary and secondary criteria in the class division of society. The primary criterion is the power to control the means of production and therefore to enjoy the values created by others' surplus labour. This criterion places on one side all the exploiting classes, i.e. those which profit by surplus labour, including industrial and commercial capitalists and landowners. On the other side are the sellers of labour-power, i.e. wage-earners, and small peasants, craftsmen, etc. using their own means of production. The first category is divided by a secondary criterion into the direct acquirers of labour-power (industrial capitalists) and those who appropriate surplus value indirectly by the possession of land or capital. Within the second category, wage-earners are divided from the rest by the fact that they do not own any means of production.

The primary criterion in its general form is also applicable to pre-capitalistic class formations, such as serfdom and feudalism; while the secondary criteria are peculiar to the capitalist mode of production.

The definition of class is by no means a purely verbal or methodological question. The need for a definition arises from observation of the facts of the class struggle; it is a question of ascertaining the criteria which in practical terms distinguish the groups whose antagonisms define the basic historical processes.

Another essential feature of a class is that it shows spontaneous solidarity in its opposition to other classes, though this does not prevent its members from being rivals to one another. In Volume III of *Capital* Marx describes the economic basis of capitalist class solidarity: as the rate of profit evens itself out in all spheres of production, and every capitalist shares in profit according to the amount of his capital,

> in each particular sphere of production the individual capitalist, and capitalists as a whole, are involved in the exploitation of the total working class by the totality of capital and in the degree of that exploitation, not only out of general class sympathy, but also for direct economic reasons ... A capitalist who did not in his line of production employ any variable capital or, therefore, any labour (in reality an exaggerated assumption) would nevertheless be as much interested in the exploitation of the working class by capital, and would derive his profit quite as much from unpaid surplus labour, as a capitalist who (another exaggeration) employed only variable capital and thus invested his entire capital in wages. (*Capital*, III, Ch. X)

The clash of interests between particular capitalists is naturally repressed in situations dominated by antagonism between the exploiters and the exploited as a whole. None the less their individual interests are bound to conflict, and so do those of the workers, for example when there is grave unemployment. But, while the rivalry between capitalists does not in itself harm the interests of capital as a whole, competition between workers does harm the interests of the working class. Hence the latter's class-consciousness is much more important to the realization of its class-interest than that of the exploiters is to theirs.

Finally, an essential feature of Marx's concept of class is that he rejects the utopian-socialist classification according to scale of income or relative share in the whole social product. The utopian division according to wealth is quite alien to Marx's thought. A person's share in the national revenue does not determine his place in the class system but is determined by it. A small craftsman may in some circumstances earn less than a skilled worker, but this does not affect the class they belong to. Luxury consumption is not a determinant of class either, as witness the 'heroic asceticism' of the bourgeoisie in its early period. In the second place, class is not determined by Saint-Simon's distinction between idlers and workers. The capitalist may perform essential functions of management or may hire others to do so for him; which he does may be of importance to the efficiency of his firm, but does not affect his class position. The performance of managerial functions is neither a necessary nor a sufficient condition of belonging to the capitalist class.

An essential condition of the existence of a class is, however, that there should be at least the germ of class-consciousness, an elementary sense of common interest and shared opposition to other classes. A class may indeed exist 'in itself' without being a class 'for itself', i.e. aware of its role in the social process of production and distribution. But before one can speak of class there must be a real community of interest, manifesting itself in practice. If its members are isolated from one another, a class has no more than a potential existence. As Marx wrote in *The Eighteenth Brumaire*, sect. VII:

> The small peasants form a vast mass, the members of which live in similar conditions but without entering into manifold relations with one another. Their mode of production isolates them from one another instead of bringing them into mutual intercourse . . . In this way the great mass of the French nation is formed by simple addition of homologous magnitudes, much as potatoes in a sack form a sackful of potatoes. In so far as millions of families live under economic conditions that divide their mode of life, interests and culture from those of the other classes, and put them in hostile contrast to the latter, they form a class. In so far as there is merely a loose interconnection among these small peasants, and the identity of their interests begets no unity, no national union and no political organization, they do not form a class. They are consequently incapable of enforcing their class interest in their own name, whether through a parliament or through a Convention. They cannot represent themselves, they must be represented. Their representative must at the same time appear as their master, as an authority over them, as an unlimited governmental power.

On the other hand, the existence of a political class struggle is not, in Marx's view, a necessary condition of the reality of class division. 'In ancient Rome the class struggle took place only within a privileged minority, between the free rich and the free poor, while the great productive mass of the population, the slaves, formed a purely passive pedestal for these combatants' (ibid., Preface to second edn.). None the less, Marx regarded the slaves as a class.

Marx regarded the class division as the essential, but not the only, division in every society in which classes exist. Within each class there are groups whose interests may conflict, for example industrial capital and finance. Among those who draw their revenue from ground-rent there are separate divisions of land-owners, mine-owners, and property-owners. The working class is divided by branches of industry and by different degrees of skill and rates of pay. The pro-fessions and trades are divided from one another. The intelligentsia, as Marx conceived it, is not itself a class but is divided according to the class whose interest it serves. In short, the divisions of society are infinitely complex. None the less, Marx contended that throughout the history of antagonistic societies—i.e. all except primitive classless communities—class divisions were the chief factor determining social change. The whole sphere of the superstructure—political life, wars and conflicts, constitutional and legal systems, and intellec-tual and artistic production of every kind—was dominated by the class division and its consequences. Here too, of course, it is only possible to operate with qualitative characteristics, for we cannot measure the relative importance of different forms of social stratification in determining particular aspects of the superstructure.

It would seem to follow that the mere removal of the class division by abol-ishing private ownership of the means of production would not abolish all sources of social antagonism, but only the most important ones due to differ-ent degrees of control over surplus value. Marx believed, however, that the domination of the class system was such that its removal would do away with all other sources of antagonism and bring about a unity of social life in which the freedom of one man would not be limited by that of another.

6. The origin of class

As to the origin of class distinctions, a necessary though not a sufficient con-dition was the achievement of a state of technology in which it was possible to appropriate the fruits of surplus labour. Engels considers this question in *The Origin of the Family* and the *Anti-Dühring*. Dühring had suggested that classes owed their origin to the use of force, and had offered the example of two indi-viduals unequally endowed by nature. Engels opposed this theory, which he thought erroneous and unfounded. Neither property nor exploitation, he said, were the result of violence. Property was based on production exceeding the producer's needs, and exploitation presupposed the inequality of property. As for classes, they had arisen in various ways. In the first place, commodity production led to the inequality of possessions, which were bequeathed from one generation to another and thus made it possible for a hereditary aristocracy to spring up, not by violent means but as a result of custom. Secondly, primitive communities had to entrust their defence to individuals appointed for the purpose, and the offices thus created were the germ of political power. What were at first socially necessary institutions of defence and administration became in time hereditary estates, independent of society and, as it were, above it. Thirdly, the natural division of labour took on a class form when technical progress and economic development made it possible to use slave labour obtained by conquest. Slavery made possible for the first time a real division between industry and agriculture, and hence the whole political system and culture of the ancient world; it was thus a condition of the huge progress of civilization up to the present day. But in all the forms in which class divisions arose, their ultimate origin lay in the division of labour. This was the condition of the whole evolution of mankind, and was therefore the cause of private property, inequality, exploitation, and oppression.

7. *The functions of the state and its abolition*

THE division of classes led in time to the creation of a state apparatus. Tracing the development of primitive society on the lines of Morgan's explorations, Engels suggests that the state arose as a result of the breakdown of the democratic organization of the tribe. Several factors were at work in this process: to begin with, the transformation of offices into hereditary estates as already described, and the need to defend fortunes acquired through various contingencies. The state, as an instrument of coercion in defence of class interests, presupposes at least the elements of a class division. The apparatus of authority and the use of force to control slaves are economic in origin. Conquest is one way in which a state may come into being, but in its typical form it arises from class antagonisms within a single community. The state sanctifies acquired wealth and privilege, defending them against the communist tradition of earlier societies and creating conditions in which private fortunes and inequality increase. 'Because the state arose from the need to hold class antagonisms in check, but because it arose, at the same time, amid the conflict of these classes, it is, as a rule, the state of the most powerful, economically dominant class, which, through the medium of the state, becomes also politically dominant, and thus acquires new means of holding down and exploiting the oppressed class' (*Origin of the Family*, IX). In relation to the bourgeois state, this function of defending the privileges of the possessing class is highly conspicuous and vital to its political structure. As Marx and Engels wrote in 1850 in a review of a book by E. de Girardin, 'The bourgeois state is nothing but the mutual insurance of the bourgeoisie against its own individual members and the class of the exploited—an insurance that must become ever more costly and, in appearance, independent of bourgeois society, which finds it increasingly hard to keep the exploited in a state of subservience' (*Neue Rheinische Zeitung, Politisch-ökonomische Revue*, 4, 1850). Hence, although the original, socially necessary functions which, by becoming autonomous, gave rise to political power have still to be performed, it is not these which determine the character of the state. For these functions themselves contain no element of political power, and their autonomization would not have led to the creation of a state apparatus if it were not for the need to defend the privileged classes.

It can also happen in bourgeois society, as Marx observes in connection with Louis Napoleon's *coup d'état*, that the bureaucratic machine asserts its independence of the class it serves. But such situations can also be explained by class interests. The bourgeoisie may give up parliamentary power and entrust the direct exercise of political authority to an autonomized bureaucracy, if this is necessary to maintain its own economic position as a class.

If we define the meaning of the state in this way, two conclusions follow which are of great importance for Marx's doctrine: viz. the disappearance of the state in a classless society, and the necessity of destroying the existing state machine by a revolution.

The first conclusion is evident. Once class division has been abolished, there is no need for the institutions whose function is to maintain it and oppress the exploited classes.

> The first act in which the state really comes forward as the representative of society as a whole—the taking possession of the means of production in the name of society— is at the same time its last independent act as a state. The interference of the state power in social relations becomes superfluous in one sphere after another, and then ceases of itself. The government of persons is replaced by the administration of things and the direction of the processes of production. The state is not 'abolished', it withers away. (*Socialism, Utopian and Scientific*, III)

The state is not eternal, but a transient feature of civilization which will disappear with class divisions—as Engels puts it, 'into the museum of antiquities, by the side of the spinning-wheel and the bronze axe' (*Origin of the Family*, IX).

As we see, the abolition of the state does not mean abolishing the administrative functions necessary for the management of production; but these functions will not be an exercise of political power. Putting the matter in this way implies a situation in which all social conflicts have disappeared; and this confirms the interpretation according to which Marx and Engels held that the abolition of class divisions would at the same time abolish all other sources of conflict.

In the second place, the political superstructure as an apparatus of coercion cannot be reformed in such a way as to start serving the interests of the exploited class; it must be destroyed by revolutionary violence. This conclusion, as we have seen, forced itself on Marx at the time of the Paris Commune. The abolition of the bourgeois state is a step towards the abolition of the state in general, but, during the period when the victorious working class is still fighting the exploiters, it must possess its own means of coercion, which for the first time in history will be an instrument of the majority. This is the dictatorship of the proletariat, in which the latter will use force without concealment for the purpose of doing away with class altogether. The transition to a socialist society, even though it is prepared by the development of the capitalist economy, cannot be effected by the economic process alone but only in the realm of the superstructure. The positive prerequisite of socialism in a capitalist economy is a high degree of technology and of co-operation in the productive process; its negative causes are the internal contradictions of capitalism and the class-consciousness of the proletariat. The transition itself is a political and not an economic act; however, according to Marx's aphorism, 'Force is the midwife of every old society pregnant with a new one. It is itself an economic power [*Potenz*]' (*Capital*, I, Ch. XXIV, 6; English edn., Ch. XXXI).

In 1895, a few months before his death, Engels wrote an Introduction to the second edition of Marx's *The Class Struggles in France, 1848–50*, which has been invoked by reformists as a proof that Engels replaced the idea of revolutionary force by that of achieving power for the proletariat by parliamentary means. In this text he states that since the repeal of the Anti-Socialist Law in Germany and in view of the success of social democracy at the polls, 'rebellion in the old style, the street fight with barricades, which up to 1848 gave everywhere the final decision, is to a considerable extent obsolete'. Insurgents were worse off in street-fighting than previously, and in any case a rebellion by a small vanguard could not bring about the transformation of society. This required the conscious, rational participation of the masses, and it was therefore a mistake to sacrifice the most enlightened part of the proletariat in street-fighting: what must be done was to continue the advance by legal means in parliament and in the field of propaganda, accumulating strength for the decisive conflict. 'We, the "revolutionaries", the "rebels", are thriving far better on legal methods than on illegal methods and revolt.'

Engels certainly laid great emphasis on peaceful means of strengthening the workers' movement; and he did not exclude the possibility, in Germany at all events, that power might be achieved by non-violent means. But the change of

viewpoint brought about by the electoral success of the German social democrats is not so great as it at first seems. In the first place, Engels confines his
hopes to Germany, as Marx had once confined them to Britain, the U.S.A., and
Holland. Secondly, he did not think it a foregone conclusion that power would
be achieved by parliamentary means: this depended entirely on the attitude of
the bourgeoisie, and a violent revolution was still a possibility. Thirdly, while
he expected a 'decisive conflict' in the form of a seizure of power by the working class, he believed that this might be a bloodless act owing to the latter's
strength, its highly developed consciousness, and its ability to enlist the support of the lower middle classes. He did not reject the idea of a revolution as
necessary in principle and inevitable in practice, but he believed that it might
be a non-violent one. He did not say expressly that he thought the working class
might achieve power simply by obtaining a majority at the polls, and it is hard
to be certain whether he envisaged this; but he undoubtedly attached more
importance than previously to peaceful instruments of the class struggle. If he
did expect that power would be taken over by electoral means, this would signify a radical change in his position; but even in this case we cannot attribute to
him the idea of co-operation between classes or the extinction of class conflict.

Whatever the means by which the proletariat was to achieve victory, Marx
and Engels always saw the state power as an instrument only: unlike Hegel or
Lassalle, they did not regard the state as a value in itself or identify it with society, but saw it as a historical, transient form of social organization. Man's social
existence was by no means the same as his political existence; on the contrary,
the state as such was the political expression of a situation in which man's powers, embodied in his works, were opposed to him—i.e. social alienation in the
highest degree. If the proletariat should need a temporary means of coercion,
this would consist in the domination actually exercised by the great bulk of
society. But the whole purpose of such domination would be to terminate its
own existence and put an end to politics as a separate sphere of life. Marx's theory of the state is thus a repetition and development of what he wrote in philosophical language in 1843 in *The Jewish Question*. Real human individuals,
who are the only true 'subjects', will absorb into themselves the species-essence
which has hitherto existed in the alienated sphere of political life. The social
character of men's individual energies will not express itself as an alienated
political creation; men and women will perform their mission in society in a
direct manner and not in a realm specially created for the purpose—in short,
private and community life will be integrated at the level of each and every
human being. Man's species-essence will resolve itself completely into the lives
of individuals, and there will be no more distinction between private and public life. The abolition of class divisions is a necessary and sufficient condition
of this return to concreteness.

8. Commentary on historical materialism

IN the foregoing account of the main principles of historical materialism we have been at pains to interpret the doctrine as sympathetically as possible. We have not, for instance, taken in a literal sense certain compressed or aphoristic statements by Marx and Engels which appear to assert dogmatically and without proof that every detail of history is the outcome of the class system, determined in its turn by the technological development of society. When Marx says in *La Misère de la philosophie* that the handmill 'produces' feudal society and the steam-mill capitalism, we are clearly not meant to take this literally. What the handmill and steam-mill produce is flour, and both kinds of mill may coexist in a society which, in its turn, may have predominantly feudal or capitalist features. When Engels said in his funeral oration that Marx's great merit was to have discovered that 'mankind must first of all eat, drink, have shelter and clothing before it can pursue politics, science, art, religion etc.', it is hard to use such expression as a proof of historical materialism or to see why it should be an immortal discovery to repeat the maxim *primum edere, deinde philosophari*. But it would be petty to attack the doctrine on the strength of such formulas in isolation. On the other hand, doubts and objections arise at a more fundamental level. The great majority of Marxist theoreticians have followed Engels in speaking of the 'reciprocal influence' of the base and superstructure, the 'relative independence' of the latter, and the fact that it is determined by economic factors 'in the last resort'. As we have seen, the exact meaning of 'economic factors', 'base', and 'superstructure' is by no means unequivocal, and the statement itself is in any case open to serious controversy. It would seem that to say there is an interaction between the relations of production and the 'superstructure' is to utter a truism which all would accept and which has nothing particularly Marxist about it. Historic events—wars, revolutions, religious changes, the rise and fall of states and empires, artistic trends and scientific discoveries—can be rationally explained by many circumstances, not excluding technology and class conflicts: this is a matter of common sense and would not be denied by a religious believer, a materialist, or any philosopher of history unless he were a fanatical champion of some 'unique factor' or other. That books and plays cannot be understood without knowledge of the historical circumstances and social conflicts of the time was known, long before Marx, to many French and other historians, some of whom were conservative in politics. We must ask then, what exactly is historical materialism? If it means that every detail of the superstructure can be explained as in some way dictated by the demands of the 'base', it is an absurdity with nothing to recommend it to credence; while if, as Engels's remarks suggest, it does not involve absolute determinism in this sense, it is no more than a fact of common knowledge. If interpreted rigidly, it conflicts with the elementary demands of rationality; if loosely, it is a mere truism.

The traditional way out of this unhappy dilemma is, of course, the qualification 'in the last resort'; but Engels never explained precisely what he meant by this. If it only means that the relations of production determine the superstructure indirectly, through other factors, then we may still object that the theory is one of absolute determinism: it makes no difference whether one wheel acts directly on another or whether it does so by means of a conveyor belt. Most probably, however, Engels meant that the determination was not absolute: not all features of a civilization were dictated by the class structure, and not all relations of production by the technological level, but only the chief ones in each case. But then, how do we decide which features are more important and which less? We may choose to regard as important those relationships of which historical materialism tells us, but then we are involved in a tautology or a vicious circle: the base determines those parts of the superstructure that are determined by the base. We can of course say, for instance, that what is important in Verlaine's poetry is not the versification, which is 'contingent' or traditional, but the poet's melancholy, which can be accounted for in terms of the class situation (a stock example of literary history as expounded by the materialist school). But historical materialism cannot tell us why one is important and not the other, except on the ground that it is able to account for the latter—and this is clearly a vicious circle.

Again, if the relations of production determine only some features of the superstructure and not all, the doctrine cannot explain any particular historical phenomenon—for any historical fact is an accumulation of many circumstances—but only certain broad lines of the historical process. This, it appears, was in fact the main intention: not to explain a particular war, revolution, or movement of any kind, but only the fact that one major socio-economic system gave place to another. Everything else—the 'zigzags' and reversals of history, the fact that a process occurred when it did and not a few centuries sooner or later, the particular struggles and efforts that accompanied it—all this would be relegated to the status of contingency, with which the theory need not concern itself. In that case historical materialism could not claim to be an instrument of prognostication. It could state, for instance, in the most general way that capitalism must be replaced by socialism; but when and how this would be, in how many decades or centuries and after what wars and revolutions—as to these 'contingent' aspects it could offer no prediction whatever.

But even if the scope of historical materialism is thus limited, we have not done with the objections to it. The course of history is one and unrepeatable: it does not, therefore, permit the formulation of a rule that, for example, a slave-owning society must everywhere and at all times be superseded by a society based on feudal landownership. If, on the other hand, we say that history consists of many independent processes, since different parts of the world have lived for centuries in more or less complete isolation from one another, this tends rather to refute historical materialism than to confirm it: for Asiatic or Amerindian societies before the European invasions did not in fact evolve in the same manner as our own, and it would be a gratuitous fancy to assert that they would have done so if they had been left alone for long enough.

All the more detailed historical and political analyses by both Marx and Engels show that they were not themselves prisoners of their 'reductionist' formulas but took into account all kinds of factors—demography, geography, national characteristics, and so on. When, for instance, Engels in a letter of 2 December 1893 attributes the absence of a U.S. socialist movement to ethnic considerations, he shows clearly that he did not regard the bourgeois–proletariat conflict as the determinant of all social processes, though he expected it finally to take much the same political form in America as in Europe. If this expectation was not fulfilled, as it has not been for the past eighty years, the fact can of course be ascribed to 'secondary factors', and Marxists can preserve indefinitely their faith in the validity of the doctrine despite accidental interferences. Any failure of their predictions can be explained away by saying that the theory is not a schematic one, that a multiplicity of factors have to be considered, etc. But, if it is easy to dismiss inconvenient facts in this way, it is not because of the theory's profundity but because of its vagueness—a quality which it shares with all universal theories of history that have ever been put forward.

This same vagueness enables the theory to make various unprovable historical assumptions. When Engels says that great men like Alexander, Cromwell, and Napoleon appear when the social situation requires them, this is the merest speculation: for by what signs could such a 'requirement' be recognized, other than by the fact that these men actually did appear? Clearly, a deduction of this kind, based on universal determinism, cannot help us to understand any single phenomenon.

There also exists an even less rigorous interpretation of historical materialism. Marxists have often asserted that, according to the doctrine, relations of production do not bring about the superstructure but 'define' it in the negative sense of limiting the options at society's disposal, without prejudicing its choice between them. If Marx and Engels meant no more than this, the doctrine is again in danger of becoming a truism. All would agree that the legal, political, artistic, and religious forms that we know from history cannot be imagined irrespective of social conditions: to take an example already quoted, the Declaration of the Rights of Man could not have happened among the Aztecs or in the technical and social environment of tenth-century Europe. Yet the fact that some aspects of the superstructure preserve their continuity in spite of profound social changes is relevant to the validity of even this diluted version of historical materialism. Christianity, like Islam, has persisted through many social and economic systems. It has of course changed in many ways, in the interpretation of Scripture, in its organization and liturgy and the development of dogma; it has gone through crises, schisms, and internal conflict. Yet, if the term 'Christianity' can still be used with meaning, it is because it has not changed in every respect and has preserved its essential content despite the vicissitudes of history. Every Marxist, of course, admits that tradition possesses an autonomous force of its own, and there are plenty of passages in Marx to confirm this. But if the objection can be brushed aside in this manner, it merely shows that the doctrine is so imprecise that no historical investigation and no imaginable facts can refute it. Given the variety of factors of all kinds, the 'relative independence of the superstructure', 'reciprocal influence', the role of tradition, secondary causes, and so forth, any fact whatever can be fitted into the schema. As Popper observes, the schema is in this sense irrefutable and constantly self-confirming, but at the same time it has no scientific value as a means of explaining anything in the actual course of history.

Furthermore, it seems highly improbable that any fact or series of facts in the realm of ideology could be explained or understood without reference to other circumstances which are of an ideological or biological nature, or otherwise not covered by Engels's 'in the last resort'. To take a simple example: in the fifteenth century there arose in Catholic Christianity a demand for communion under both kinds, and this was taken up by an important heretical movement (the Utraquists). It is contended, with some truth, that the demand expressed a desire to efface the difference between the clergy and laity, and can thus be regarded as a manifestation of egalitarianism. But the question then arises: 'Why do men desire equality?' To reply 'Because they are unequal' would be a tautological pseudo-explanation. We must therefore take for granted that, at some periods of history, men have regarded equality as a value worth fighting for. If the fight is carried on by men who are starving or otherwise deprived of essentials, we can say that it is explicable on purely biological grounds. But, if it is more than a question of satisfying physical needs, we cannot explain that men fight for equality 'because of economic conditions' without positing the existence of an egalitarian ideology, for otherwise they would have no reason to desire it. Or, to take an even simpler example, already quoted: the possessing classes in any community try to influence legislation so as to minimize death duties, and it is regarded as 'obvious' that they will do this. But in fact their action is due not only to particular relations of production and the existence of private property, but also to concern for their own posterity. This concern, being universal, is considered obvious, but it does not appear in itself to be an economic fact; it can be interpreted biologically or ideologically, but not related to any particular economic system or to the collectivity of systems based on the profit motive.

Both Marxists and their critics have often pointed out that the concept of technical progress as the 'source' of changes in the relations of production is doubtful and misleading. The steam-engine was not created by the stage-coach but by the intellectual labour of its inventors. The improvement of productive forces is obviously the result of mental labour, and to ascribe to it the primacy over the relations of production and, through them, over mental labour is consequently absurd if the words are taken literally. Orthodox Marxists of course reply that technical progress and the intellectual labour that produces it result from the 'requirements' of society, and that the creative mind which devises more perfect instruments is itself an instrument of social situations. But if this were so it would still not mean that the 'primacy' belonged to technical progress; one could speak of a multiplicity of links between intellectual labour and social environment, but this does not entail any specifically Marxist theory of interdependence between the different aspects of social life. In any case, even the idea of society 'requiring' improved technology is of limited application. It is true that modern technical progress is broadly dictated by clear social requirements; but Marx himself points out that there was no incentive to technical progress in pre-capitalist economic forms, because they did not subordinate production to the increase of exchange-value. On what basis, then, do we assume that technical progress 'must' occur and that capitalism was bound to make its appearance? Why could not feudal society have gone on for ever in a condition of technical stagnation? Marxists generally reply: 'Well, capitalism did make its appearance'; but this does not answer the question. If, by saying that it had to appear, they mean simply that it did, this is a misuse of language. If they mean something more, in the shape of 'historical necessity', then the appearance of capitalism does not prove that it was necessary unless, of course, we hold that everything happens because it must—an unproven metaphysical doctrine that anyone is free to hold, but which does not help to explain history in any way whatever.

Considered as a theory explaining all historical change by technical progress and all civilization by the class struggle, Marxism is unsustainable. As a theory of the interdependence of technology, property relationships, and civilization, it is trivial. It would not be trivial if this interdependence could be expressed in quantitative terms, so that the effect of the various forces acting upon social life could be measured. Not only have we no means of doing this, however, but it is impossible to imagine how these forces could be reduced to a single scale. In interpreting past events or predicting the future, we are obliged to fall back on the vague intuitions of common sense.

All this does not mean, however, that Marx's principles of historical investigation are empty or meaningless. On the contrary, he has profoundly affected our understanding of history, and it is hard to deny that without him our researches would be less complete and accurate than they are. It makes an essential difference, for example, whether the history of Christianity is presented as an intellectual struggle about dogmas and interpretations of doctrine, or whether these are regarded as a manifestation of the life of Christian communities subject to all manner of historical contingency and to the social conflicts of successive ages. We may say that although Marx often expressed his ideas in radical and unacceptable formulas, he made a tremendous contribution by altering the whole fashion of historical thought. It is one thing, however, to point out that we cannot understand the history of ideas if we do not consider them as manifestations of the lives of the communities in which they arose, and quite another to say that all the ideas known to history are instruments of class struggle in the Marxian sense. The former statement is universally acknowledged to be true and we therefore think of it as obvious—but it has become so largely as a result of Marx's thought, including his hasty generalizations and extrapolations.

Marx is of course partly to blame, if we may so put it, for the over-simplified and vulgarized notions that can be defended by many quotations from his works. If we believe literally that 'the history of all societies that have existed up to now is the history of class struggles', we can indeed interpret Marxism as contending that every feature of the history of all civilizations in every sphere is an aspect of the class struggle. Whenever Marx himself went into detail, he certainly did not push his hypothesis to such an absurd extreme. He did, however, coin some formulas that gave colour to this simplistic interpretation. It was possible to deduce from these formulas that men were deluded whenever they imagined that they were actuated by anything but the material interests of the class with which they identified, consciously or otherwise; that men never 'really' fought for power or freedom for their own sakes, or for their country as such, but that all these values, aspirations, and ideals were disguises for class-interests. It could likewise be inferred that political bodies did not evolve any interests independent of the classes they 'represented' (despite Marx's observations on bureaucracy), and that if the state appeared to play an autonomous part in social conflicts, it was only (as Marx argued in the case of Louis Bonaparte) the result of a momentary balance of forces in an acute class struggle.

Some contemporary historians and some sociologists, like T. B. Bottomore, suggest that Marxism should be treated not as an all-embracing theory of history but as a method of investigation. Marx himself would not have agreed with this limitation—he regarded his theory as a complete account of world history, past and present—but it is an attempt to rationalize Marxism and strip it of its prophetic and universalist claims. However, the word 'method' also requires qualification. Historical materialism, conceived loosely enough to be free from the objections we have mentioned, is not a method in the proper sense, i.e. a set of rules that will lead to the same result if applied by anyone to the same material on different occasions. In this sense there is no general method of historical research except, of course, the method of identifying sources. Historical materialism in the sense just defined is too vague and general to be called a method; but it is a valuable heuristic principle, enjoining the student of conflicts and movements of all kinds—political, social, intellectual, religious, and artistic—to relate his observations to material interests, including those derived from the class struggle. A rule of this kind does not mean that everything is 'ultimately' a matter of class-interest; it does not deny the independent role of tradition, ideas, or the struggle for power, the importance of geographical conditions or the biological framework of human existence. It avoids sterile debate on the question of 'determination in the last resort', but it takes seriously Marx's principle that men's spiritual and intellectual life is not self-contained and wholly independent but is also an expression of material interests. If this seems obvious, we repeat, the reason is that Marxism has made it so.

Needless to say, the account we have given considerably limits the validity of Marxism as an instrument for interpreting the past. We now turn to consider it as a means of predicting the future, and here its limitations are perhaps even more serious.

No student can fail to recognize that in Marx's view history as he knew and analysed it derived its meaning not from itself alone but from the future that lay before mankind. We can understand the past only in the light of the new world of human unity to which our society is tending—this is the Young Hegelian point of view, which Marx never abandoned. Marxism, then, cannot be accepted without the vision of the communist future: deprived of that, it is no longer Marxism.

But we should consider on what the prophecy is based. Rosa Luxemburg was the first Marxist to point out that Marx never specified the economic conditions that make the downfall of capitalism inevitable. Even if we accept his view that capitalism will never be able to prevent crises of overproduction, his analysis of such crises and their devastating consequences does not prove that such an uncontrolled system of adjusting production to demand cannot continue indefinitely. Most Marxists have rejected Rosa Luxemburg's theory that capitalism depends for its existence on non-capitalist markets which are ruined by it. But neither poverty, nor uncontrolled production, nor a falling profit rate give ground for believing that capitalism 'must' collapse, still less that the result of its collapse must be a socialist society as described by Marx.

For Marx, it is true, the collapse of capitalism and the communist millennium were 'necessary' in a different sense from that in which capitalism had, as he believed, evolved from feudalism. No one, at the time, had set himself the aim of 'establishing capitalism'. There had been merchants, all of whom wanted to sell dear and to buy cheap. Navigators and discoverers had sailed the seas for adventure or treasures or to enlarge their country's dominions. Later there had been manufacturers out for profit. Every one of these men had been bent on his own interest, but none of them was concerned for 'capitalism', which was the gradual, impersonal outcome of millions of individual efforts and aspirations—an 'objective' process, in which human consciousness was not involved except in a 'mystified' form. But the necessity of socialism, as Marx saw it, was of a different kind. Socialism could only be brought about by men who knew what they were doing; the fulfilment of 'historical necessity' depended on the proletariat being aware of its role in the productive process and its historical mission. In this one privileged case, necessity would take the form of conscious action: the subject and object of historical change were one, and the understanding of society was itself the revolutionary movement of that society.

Although the revolutionary consciousness of the proletariat was identical with the latter's revolutionary movement, it would of necessity arise from the development of capitalist society. The proletariat's historical mission could not be fulfilled unless it were a fully conscious one, in a different way from that of the conquistadors of capitalism; but this consciousness was an inevitable result of the historical process.

Marx was convinced that the proletariat was destined by history to establish a new classless order; but this conviction was not based on any argument. It was not a question of perceiving that the proletariat would go on fighting for its interests against the employers. Awareness of a conflict of interests was not, in Marx's view, the same thing as revolutionary consciousness, which required the conviction that there was a fundamental worldwide opposition between two classes and that this could and must be resolved by a worldwide proletarian revolution. The proletariat was a 'universal' class, not only as the bourgeoisie had been when its aspirations coincided with the needs of 'progress' (whatever this word meant), but also because it restored the universality of the human species; it was appointed to realize the destiny of mankind and terminate 'prehistory' by removing the source of social antagonisms. It was also a universal class in the sense that it would free humanity from ideological mystification, making social relationships transparent to all; it would put an end to the duality that had dominated human affairs from the beginning of time, between the impotent moral consciousness and the uncontrolled, unfathomable course of 'objective' history.

Marx's conviction that the proletariat would evolve a revolutionary consciousness in this sense was not a scientific opinion but an ungrounded prophecy. Having arrived at his theory of the proletariat's historic mission on the basis of philosophical deduction, he later sought empirical evidence for it.

The first empirical premiss was his belief that the classes were bound to become increasingly polarized. This at least was capable of verification; it actually proved to be untrue, but even if it had not, it is hard to see how it proved that a worldwide socialist revolution was inevitable. Nor does this conclusion follow from the fact that the working class is the agent of production and is dehumanized to the maximum extent, for in both these respects it is no different from the slaves of antiquity. If it were true that the social degradation of the working class was bound to increase, the prospects for a world socialist revolution, as Marx's critics often pointed out, would not become any the brighter: for how could a class that was kept in a state of ignorance and debility, humiliated, illiterate, and condemned to exhausting labour, find the strength to bring about a universal revolution and restore the lost humanity of mankind? Least of all, as Marx himself maintained, could the proletariat hope for victory because it had justice on its side—at least if past history was to be any guide to the future.

In point of fact Marx did not believe that the proletarian revolution would be the result of poverty, nor did he ever entertain the idea that an improvement in the workers' condition would affect their 'natural' revolutionary tendency. Later orthodox Marxists did not accept this idea either, though several of them expressed contempt for the 'working-class aristocracy' who, thanks to higher wages and security, came under the ideological influence of the bourgeoisie—which, according to theory, they ought not to have done.

Even if Marx's two premisses that were capable of being tested in practice—that society would approximate more and more to a two-class model, and that the lot of the proletariat could not really improve—had been vindicated by the facts, this would still not have shown that the working class must, by virtue of its position, evolve a revolutionary consciousness; but it would have given ground for thinking that there would be a state of ferment among the proletariat which might lead to the overthrow of the existing property system. Failing the presence of the two factors in question, Marx's prophecy had no firm foundation, which is not to say that it had no social effects. However, the success of political movements that have invoked Marx's doctrine, whether or not they have deformed it in the process, does not prove that the doctrine is true: in the same way, the victory of Christianity in the ancient world, foretold by its own prophets, did not prove the doctrine of the Trinity but, at most, showed that the Christian faith was able to articulate the aspirations of important sections of society. There is no need to demonstrate that Marxism had a powerful effect on the workers' movement, but this does not mean that it is scientifically true. We have no empirical confirmation of Marx's predictions, as there has never been a proletarian revolution of the kind described, brought about by the conditions his theory required—'contradiction' between productive forces and the relations of production, inability of capitalism to develop technology, etc.

Even assuming, however, that for economic reasons capitalism cannot last indefinitely, it would still not follow that it must be replaced by Marxian socialism. There might instead be a general breakdown of civilization (and the alternative 'socialism or barbarism' suggests that Marx did not always believe in the historic necessity of socialism), or a technologically stagnant form of capitalism, or some other form of society that did not depend on constant technical progress but was not socialist either. Marx's argument that capitalism must collapse because it had lost or would soon lose the capacity for technological improvement involves at least two assumptions: first, that technical progress is bound to continue, and secondly, that the working class is its agent. Both these assumptions are improbable. The first is merely the extrapolation of a historical fact (not a law) that for long periods men have continued to improve the instruments of production; but there is no certainty that they will do this for ever, and there have been times of stagnation and regress. As for the second assumption, in capitalist society the working class is not the exponent of any superior form of technology. The supposition would therefore have to be that socialism will owe its success to a higher degree of labour productivity than is possible under capitalism. This is hardly borne out by the socialist record, nor can it be deduced from anything in capitalism. Altogether, it is difficult to imagine the mechanism of a revolution based on these premisses.

The idea that half a million years of man's life on earth and five thousand years of written history will suddenly culminate in a 'happy ending' is an expression of hope. Those who cherish this hope are not in a better intellectual position than others. Marx's faith in the 'end of prehistory' is not a scientist's theory but the exhortation of a prophet. The social effect of his belief is another question, which we shall examine in due course.

XV

The Dialectic of Nature

1. The scientistic approach

In the 1860s European intellectual life entered a new phase, as Lothar Meyer, Helmholtz, and Schwann were succeeded by Darwin, Virchow, Herbert Spencer, and T. H. Huxley. The natural sciences appeared to have reached a point at which the unitary conception of the universe was an incontestable fact. The principle of the conservation of energy and the laws governing its transformation were, it appeared, close to providing a complete explanation of the multiplicity of natural phenomena. Studies of the cellular structure of organisms gave promise of the discovery of a single system of laws applying to all basic organic phenomena. The theory of evolution afforded a general historical schema of the development of living creatures, including man with his specifically human attributes. Fechner's studies opened the way to the quantitative measurement of mental phenomena, which had previously been most rebellious to investigation. The day seemed close at hand when the unity of nature, hidden beneath the chaotic wealth of its diversity, would be laid bare to human view. The worship of science was universal; metaphysical speculation seemed condemned to wither away. The methods of the physicists were held to be applicable to all branches of knowledge, including the social sciences.

Engels, who followed the progress of natural science with enthusiasm, shared the hope that a new *mathesis universalis* was about to dawn. A student of Hegel in his youth, he never ceased to admire and respect the great master of dialectics, but he believed that the rational content and value of the latter's speculations would come to light through the development of experimental science, every new stage of which pointed to the dialectical understanding of nature. However, the philosophic interpretation of the new discoveries called for a theoretical examination of the breakdown of former methods, especially the mechanistic viewpoint which had dominated scientific investigation since the seventeenth century but was now an anachronism. From his earliest writings onwards, Engels strove to maintain the strictest possible relation between theoretical concepts and empirical data. This is especially clear in all his works expounding and popularizing the ideas of Marx, who was more concerned with theoretical consistency than with relating his doctrine to the facts of experience.

It is not surprising that Engels was infected by the scientistic enthusiasm of his day, and sought to create an image of the world in which the same basic methods would apply to physical and social science, the latter being a natural prolongation of the former. In his search for unity of method and content, and for concepts linking human history, in Darwinian fashion, with natural history, Engels was close to the positivists of his day. However, he did not propose to find this unity by reducing the whole of knowledge to mechanistic schemata (after the manner of many physicists, such as Gustav Kirchoff), but by discovering dialectical laws appropriate equally to all fields of inquiry. This can be seen in his three most important works written between 1875 and 1886: the *Anti-Dühring, Ludwig Feuerbach*, and *Dialectics of Nature*. The last of these, an unfinished collection of short essays and notes, was begun with a view to controversy with Ludwig Büchner, whose mechanistic materialism was seen by Engels as furnishing the opportunity to formulate a new dialectical materialism; subsequently, however, he went beyond his polemical intention. All three works, unlike those of Marx, deal with questions traditionally regarded as belonging to philosophy, and provide the outline of a doctrinal stereotype which, under the name of dialectical materialism, came to be officially regarded as the 'Marxist ontology and theory of knowledge'. From Plekhanov's time onwards, Marxism was more and more generally defined as a doctrine composed of Engels's philosophical ideas, the economic theory of *Capital*, and the principle of scientific socialism. It has been a matter of dispute for some decades whether these form a consistent whole, and in particular whether Engels's dialectic of nature is in harmony with the philosophical basis of Marx's work.

2. Materialism and idealism. The twilight of philosophy

ACCORDING to Engels—who inherited this view from Leibniz, Fichte, and Feuerbach—the opposition between materialism and idealism is the central question on which philosophy has always turned. In the last analysis it was, in his opinion, a debate concerning the creation of the world. The idealists were those who maintained that spirit (whether a divine creator, or the Hegelian Idea) existed prior to nature, whereas the materialists held the opposite. Berkeleyan subjectivism, according to which being consists in being perceived, falls, of course, on the idealistic side of the division.

Although the history of philosophy is filled with the debate between these two views, they do not occur in identical terms at all periods. There have been times, for example the Christian Middle Ages, when civilization knew nothing of materialism in the strict sense. Yet even in the basic controversies of that time we can detect something akin to materialism in the nominalist view concerning universals, which reveals a certain interest in physical nature and in concreteness. There have also been many doctrines in the history of philosophy which tried to find a compromise or middle way between the two main views, irreconcilable as they are. It is difficult, therefore, to distinguish two main currents expressing the adverse opinions in all their purity and, between them, comprising the whole history of thought. Nevertheless, we always find two conflicting tendencies of which one is closer to the materialist viewpoint or contains more of the elements which usually accompany materialism in its pure form. The fact that idealist or spiritualist tendencies are more frequently met with in philosophy is due, Engels tells us, to the division between physical and intellectual labour, the resulting autonomy of mental pursuits, and the existence of a class of professional ideologists who, in the nature of things, tend to ascribe the primacy to mind rather than matter.

How is the materialistic view to be more closely defined? Since Engels maintains that the essential opposition in philosophy is between nature and spirit, it would seem that both the opposing views express a kind of dualism: so that although the materialists regard mind as genetically secondary to nature, they must also regard it as something separate and different. But Engels does not in fact take this view. He holds that the opposition between nature and spirit is not that of two different substances in a particular genetic relation: consciousness is not a thing in itself, but an attribute of material objects (human bodies) organized in a certain way, or a process which takes place in them. His standpoint is thus a monistic one, rejecting the belief in any form of being that cannot be called material.

But, to know what materialism is, we must first define matter. In some passages Engels appears to take a purely scientistic or phenomenalistic view and to dispense altogether with the category of substance. He says, for instance: 'The materialistic outlook on nature means nothing more than the simple conception of nature just as it is, without alien addition' (*Dialectics of Nature*, 'From the History of Science'); and again: 'Matter as such is a pure creation of thought and an abstraction. We leave out of account the qualitative differences of things when we lump them together as corporeally existing things under the concept 'Matter' . Hence matter as such, as distinct from definite existing pieces of matter, is not anything that exists in the world of sense' (Ibid., 'Forms of Motion of Matter'). From this it would follow that materialism as understood by Engels is not an ontology in the usual sense but an anti-philosophical scientism which sees no need to ask questions about 'substance' and is content with the bare facts of natural science, purged of all speculative additions. From this point of view all philosophy is idealism, an imaginative embellishment of scientific knowledge; and, sure enough, Engels prophesies the decline and extinction of philosophy. 'If we deduce the world schematism not from our minds, but only through our minds from the real world, deducing the basic principles of being from what is, what we need for this purpose is not philosophy but positive knowledge of the world and what goes on in it; and the result of this deduction is not philosophy either, but positive science' (*Anti-Dühring*, I, 3). 'With Hegel philosophy comes to an end: on the one hand because his system sums up its whole development most admirably, and on the other because, even though unconsciously, he showed us the way out of the labyrinth of systems to real positive knowledge of the world' (*Ludwig Feuerbach*, I). 'Modern materialism . . . is not a philosophy but a simple conception of the world [*Weltanschauung*] which has to establish its validity and be applied not in a "science of sciences" standing apart, but within the actual sciences. Philosophy is thus "sublated" [*aufgehoben*], that is "both abolished and preserved"— abolished as regards its form, and preserved as regards its real content' (*Anti-Dühring*, I, XIII). 'As soon as each separate science is required to understand clearly its position in the totality of things and of our knowledge of things, there is no longer any need for a special science dealing with this totality. Of all former philosophy, all that now independently survives is the science of thought and its laws, i.e. formal logic and dialectics. Everything else is merged in the positive science of nature and history' (Ibid., Introduction).

Engels thus regards philosophy as either a purely speculative description of the world or an attempt to perceive general connections between phenomena over and above those established by natural science. Philosophy in this sense is to disappear, leaving behind it nothing but a method of ratiocination which has this much in common with 'former philosophy' that it was traditionally considered part of it, though not the most essential part. Engels does not express himself quite unequivocally, but basically his views are in line with the positivism that was widespread in his day: philosophy is a superfluous adjunct to the individual sciences, and there will soon be nothing left of it but the rules of thought, or logic in a broad sense. But there is a different side to this. While, in the passage quoted, Engels speaks of 'dialectics' as meaning simply the laws of thought, he elsewhere uses the term to denote a comprehensive and legitimate system of knowledge of the most general laws of nature, of which our thought processes are a particular exemplification. In this sense, he is a good deal less anti-philosophical than at first appeared. Philosophy, it would seem, is the science of the most general laws of nature; its conclusions derive logically from data furnished by the 'positive' sciences, though they may not have been formulated by any one of those sciences.

Engels's writings alternately support the more ruthless and the more tolerant view of philosophy; but even the latter was in tune with contemporary positivism, which did not wish to abandon philosophy altogether but only to reduce it to what could be deduced from the natural sciences. Either way,

materialism is not an ontology but a method prohibiting the addition of speculation to positive knowledge. None the less, Engels uses the term 'matter' to
denote either the totality of physical beings or what is left of things when they
are stripped of qualitative differentiation. 'The real unity of the world consists
in its materiality' (*Anti-Dühring*, I, 4): that is to say, all that *is* is the physical
world perceptible by the senses; there is no invisible Nature or behind-the-
scenes world different in kind from that observed by the scientist. Engels does
not discuss whether materialism in the purely methodical or phenomenalistic
sense is identical with the view that the world is a material unity, or whether
this view is the same as that of the primacy of matter over mind. He oscillates
between scientistic phenomenalism unburdened by metaphysical categories,
and a substantialist materialism which holds that there is one true original
form of Being whose different manifestations constitute the events of the
empirical world. Matter, which is this original Being, is permanently and essentially characterized by 'motion', including change of all kinds; for otherwise the
source of change would have to be looked for outside matter, in something like
the 'first impulse' (*primum mobile*) of the deists. Motion is the form of matter,
uncreated and indestructible as itself.

3. *Space and time*

IN addition to change, matter possesses the inseparable attributes of space and
time. The theories which, in Engels's day, set out to explain space and time
jointly, i.e. apart from the psychological aspect of time, may be reduced, very
broadly, to three types: (1) Space and time are autonomous and independent of
physical bodies. Space is the container of bodies, but there could be empty
space with the same properties as physical space; time is the container of
events, but there could be time in which nothing happens. This is Newton's
doctrine. (2) Space and time are subjective, *a priori* forms (Kant): they originate in cognition, but are not derived from experience; they are transcendental conditions of experience, prior to any possible factual knowledge. (3) Space
and time are subjective and empirical (Berkeley, Hume); they are ways of
ordering experience *ex post*, i.e. combining empirical data so that the mind
may operate on them more efficiently. Engels does not share any of these views:
he holds that space and time are 'basic forms of being' and are therefore objective (contrary to Hume and Kant), but (contrary to Newton) they are inseparable properties of material bodies and events. Strictly speaking, this implies that
there is no such thing as time in itself but only relations of succession (before
and after), 'time' being a secondary abstraction from these; similarly, there is
no space as such but only relations of distance, direction, and extent. Engels
does not say this explicitly, but it appears to be his thought. 'The two forms of

the existence of matter are naturally nothing without matter, empty concepts, abstractions which exist only in our minds' (*Dialectics of Nature*, 'Dialectical Logic and the Theory of Knowledge'). The temporal and spatial infinity of the universe are natural consequences of the doctrine that matter is uncreated and indestructible.

4. The variability of nature

THERE exists, therefore, nothing except material bodies in a state of constant change and differentiation. Engels writes, it is true, that 'the world is not to be comprehended as a complex of ready-made things, but as a complex of processes in which things, though apparently no less stable than the concepts which are our images of them, incessantly change, come into being and pass away' (*Ludwig Feuerbach*, IV). But we must not take this literally, on the lines of some modern theories where events are primary and things are momentary condensations of events: for Engels elsewhere defines matter as 'the totality of material things, from which this concept [matter] is abstracted' (*Dialectics of Nature*, 'Dialectical Knowledge and the Theory of Knowledge'). His purpose in describing nature as a complex of processes and not of things is rather to emphasize the eternal changefulness and instability of the material world.

The principle of constant change is a keynote of dialectical thinking. In Engels's view it was Hegel's greatest achievement to point out that every form of Being turns into another, and that only the universe as a whole is exempt from the law of birth, change, and passing-away. Early modern scientists such as Copernicus, Kepler, Descartes, Newton, and Linnaeus were dominated by faith in the immutability of basic natural processes and classifications, whether in the heavens or in the structure of the earth and of organic beings. This view was revolutionized by their successors, starting with Kant's astronomical theory developed by Laplace, Lyell's discoveries in geology, J. R. Mayer and Joule in physics, Dalton in chemistry, Lamarck and Darwin in biology—all of whom demonstrated the perpetual variability of nature and the impossibility of hard-and-fast classification. Every observable fragment of reality proved to be only a phase in its unceasing development; all categories were approximate; more and more intermediate and transitional forms came into view. Man himself was seen to be the product of natural variations, and all his many sided faculties were the continuation of forces to which Nature herself had given birth. It was labour that distinguished man from the rest of the animal creation and was the source of all his proper pride: manual effort was the cause of mental development. The observation of constant change assures us that man, like the earth and the whole solar system, is sentenced to destruction; but the law according to which matter evolves ever higher forms of existence assures us that these forms in which we participate—conscious reflection and social organization—will reappear somewhere in the universe, and will in due course again cease to be.

5. Multiple forms of change

BUT the dialectic of nature is not only a matter of constant change. The main difference between the mechanistic and the dialectical viewpoints is that the latter distinguishes change in multiple forms. The mechanicism of the seventeenth and eighteenth centuries, transmitted to the nineteenth by the German materialists Vogt, Büchner, and Moleschott, maintained that everything that happens in the world is nothing other than mechanical motion, i.e. the displacement of material particles, and that all qualitative differentiations in nature are subjective or merely apparent. They concluded from this that all branches of knowledge should pattern themselves on mechanics: the processes observed by them would prove to be particular cases of mechanical motion, obedient to the laws governing the movement of bodies in space. Engels was far from accepting this position, even as an ultimate ideal. He believed that the qualitative differentiation of forms of change was a real phenomenon, and that the higher or more complex forms could not be reduced to the lower. The higher, in fact, is defined as that which presupposes the lower but is not presupposed by it. Chemical phenomena, for this reason, are higher than mechanical ones, and those of the organic world are higher still; in the same way, there is an ascent from biology to mental phenomena and social processes. There is thus a multiplicity of forms of change or motion, and a corresponding natural hierarchy of sciences. The forms differ in quality: each of them presupposes all the lower ones, but these do not exhaust it.

However, this all-pervading hierarchy and irreducibility of higher forms is not explained by Engels in a manner free from ambiguity. When he distinguishes the various forms of motion (mechanical processes, molecular movement, chemical, biological, mental, and social phenomena, on the ascending scale indicated by Comte), he does not state clearly in what their irreducibility consists. Is it because the laws of the higher forms cannot be logically deduced from those of the lower (for example, the laws of social history from those of chemistry) or are not logically equivalent to them? Or is it an ontological irreducibility, in that there is something in the 'higher' processes which is not mechanical motion and cannot be causally explained by it? The first interpretation is weaker, for it does not exclude the hypothesis that the higher processes are no more than mechanical ones which occur statistically in a particular way; on the ontological level mechanical motion would then be the only form of change, but science would content itself for observational purposes with statistical laws concerning its manifestation in particular conditions. The second interpretation excludes this hypothesis, but it is not at once clear how the ontological irreducibility comes about, given the starting-point of a homogeneous material substratum of all processes without exception.

Whatever be the answer to this question, it is clear that Engels does not regard nature as uniform in all its changes, or reduce its multiplicity to a single pattern: the manifoldness is real, not merely subjective or due to the temporary insufficiency of our knowledge. Genetically, all higher forms are derivations of the lower (and the history of science to some extent reflects this order), and they are in some sense inherent in them; in other words, matter tends by its very nature to evolve higher forms of Being in the manner observable on earth. Engels does not explain, however, in what way the higher forms are potentially contained in the elementary attributes of matter.

6. Causality and chance

THE view that the manifoldness of nature is real makes it possible to conceive the problem of causality in a different way from that of mechanistic materialism. The latter in its classical form reduced determinism to the principle that every event is conditioned in every detail by the totality of circumstances at the moment when it happens. If we call something an accident, we can only mean that we do not know its cause; the category of contingency is a subjective one. A perfect intellect, as Laplace suggested, could give a complete and accurate description of the universe at any time, past or future, if it knew the exact mechanical coefficients (position and momentum) of every particle at the present moment or any other. There can be no question of undetermined phenomena or, in particular, free will except as a purely subjective and erroneous sense of freedom. This form of determinism, represented in modern philosophy by Descartes (as regards the material world), Spinoza, and Hobbes, had many adherents among nineteenth-century mechanists.

Engels, however, took a different view. He believed in universal causality in the sense that he rejected the possibility of uncaused phenomena and also the existence of design in nature, conceived as the realization of a conscious intention: this would have been contrary to materialism, as it involved the primacy of mind over matter. But he regarded the general formula of universal determinism as completely sterile from the scientific point of view. If we say that there are five peas and not six in a certain pod, or that a particular dog's tail is five inches long and no more or less, or that a particular flower was fertilized by a particular bee at a certain moment, and so forth, and that all these facts were determined by the state of the particles in the original nebula from which the solar system developed, we are making a statement that is useless to science, and are not so much overcoming the contingency of nature as universalizing it.

Explanations like these leave us exactly where we were; they do not enable us to predict anything or improve our knowledge in any way. The business of science is to formulate laws operating in particular spheres so that we can understand phenomena, foresee them, and affect them. Small differentiations are the effect of an infinite number of reactions and may be thought of as accidental; but science is concerned not with them but with the general laws that can be discerned amid the mass of deviations. 'In nature, where chance also seems to reign, there has long ago been demonstrated in each particular field the inherent necessity and regularity that asserts itself through this chance. What is true of nature holds good also for society' (*Origin of the Family*, IX). Engels did not formulate precisely his idea of chance, but his thought seems to be that it is neither an event of whose causes we are ignorant (as the mechanists hold) nor an event with no causes (the indeterminist view). If a phenomenon is contingent, it is so objectively but relatively. Phenomena that form part of a series of events subject to a certain regularity are inevitably disturbed by events belonging to a different type of regularity, i.e. a different form of motion. These disturbances are called accidents, not in themselves but from the point of view of the process to which the former events belong. A cosmic catastrophe which destroyed all life on earth would be accidental in relation to the laws of organic evolution, which do not, so to speak, provide for such an event; but it would not itself be unconditioned. An isolated fact such as the presence of five peas in a pod is the result of many detailed circumstances which we need not and cannot investigate, including the state of the wind, the dampness of the soil, etc. All these combine to produce a particular fact which is therefore not determined by purely botanical laws, for example that a certain seed grows into a pea and not a pine-tree. A general statement that every detail of every process is governed by strict necessity is a mere metaphysical phrase without explanatory value. Science is concerned with laws which operate, of course, in slightly different situations each time, the variations being the effect of chance, but which are nevertheless dependable in spite of deviations and disturbances; it is the laws that matter, not their precise functioning in every separate case.

This being Engels's view of regularity and causality, he approaches the question of freedom in a different manner from the usual one. Freedom does not mean the absence of causation, nor is it a permanent human attribute; it is not a question of suspending the laws of nature, or of enjoying a margin of free play around their edges. With one important modification Engels follows the conception of freedom that arose among the Stoics and reached Hegel through Spinoza: freedom is the understanding of necessity.

> Freedom does not consist in the dream of independence of natural laws, but in the knowledge of those laws and in the possibility thus afforded of making them work

systematically towards definite ends . . . Freedom of the will means nothing but the capacity to make decisions with real knowledge. The freer a man's judgement is in relation to a particular question, so much the greater is the necessity with which the content of his judgement is determined. (*Anti-Dühring*, I, XI)

It appears from this that freedom as the understanding of necessity has a different meaning for Engels than for the Stoics, Spinoza, and Hegel. The free man is not he who understands that what happens must happen, and reconciles himself to it. A man is free to the extent that he understands the laws of the world he is living in and can therefore bring about the changes he desires. Freedom is the degree of power that an individual or a community are able to exercise over the conditions of their own life. It is therefore a state of affairs, not a permanent attribute of man. It presupposes an understanding of the environment and its laws; but it does not consist merely of such understanding, for in addition it requires the individual to affect his environment, or at all events it is only visible when he does so. A man or a community are not free or unfree in themselves, but relatively to their situation and their power over it. There can, of course, never be such a thing as absolute freedom, i.e. unlimited power over all aspects of every situation; but human freedom may increase indefinitely as the laws of nature and social phenomena are better known. In this sense socialism is a 'leap from the realm of necessity into the realm of freedom', wherein society takes control over the conditions of its being and the productive system, which have hitherto run riot and operated against the majority.

Engels thus puts the question of free will in a different way from his predecessors. He does not ask whether a conscious act of choice is always determined by circumstances independent of consciousness, but rather in what conditions human choices are most effective in relation to the end proposed, whether practical or cognitive. Freedom is the degree of effectiveness of conscious acts—not the degree of independence with regard to the laws which govern all phenomena, whether men are conscious of their operation or not; for, according to Engels, such independence does not exist.

7. The dialectic in nature and in thought

DIALECTICS, as understood by Engels, are the study of all forms of motion or activity in nature, in human history, and in thought. Thus there is an objective dialectic which governs nature, and a subjective dialectic which is the reflection of the same laws in the human mind. The term 'dialectic' is used in a double sense, either for the processes of nature and history or for the scientific study of those processes. If we are able to think dialectically, it is because our minds obey the same laws as nature does: 'the dialectic of the mind is only the reflection of the forms of motion of the real world, both of nature and of history' (*Dialectics of Nature*, 'Natural Science and Philosophy'). As this implies, Engels accepted the psychological view of logic in accordance with the naturalist doctrines of his time: i.e. he regarded its laws as facts, empirical regularities of the functioning of the nervous system. Only man, however, is able to think dialectically. Animals can perform operations involving 'reason' in the Hegelian sense, i.e. the elementary abstractions of induction, deduction, analysis, synthesis, and experiment—cracking nuts is the beginning of analysis, and performing animals demonstrate the power to synthesize; but dialectical thinking involves the ability to examine concepts, and this is peculiar to man.

Dialectics—in the sense of thought which perceives phenomena in their development, their internal contradictions, the interpenetration of opposites, and qualitative differentiation—came into being gradually during the ages. We find it in embryo in Greek and Oriental thought, and even in popular sayings like 'extremes meet'; but only German philosophy, and above all Hegel, gave it the form of a complete conceptual system. This, however, had to be reinterpreted in a materialist sense before it could be useful to science. Concepts had to be stripped of their self-generating power and recognized as the reflection of natural phenomena; the method which consisted in dividing ideas into contraries and synthesizing these in a higher unity was thus seen as an image of the laws governing the real world.

The laws of the dialectic may be reduced to three: the transition from quantity to quality and vice versa; the interpenetration of opposites; and the negation of the negation. These are the laws formulated by Hegel and apprehended as governing nature, history, and the human mind.

8. Quantity and quality

THE law that quantity becomes quality, or, more precisely, that qualitative differences arise from the accumulation of quantitative ones, may be explained as follows. Quantitative differences are those which can be exhaustively characterized by the distance between points on a single scale—temperature, pressure, size, number of elements, etc. Differences that cannot be expressed merely in figures are qualitative. Now it is found throughout the natural world that the increasing or diminishing of the quantitative aspect of a thing leads at a certain point (usually clearly defined) to a qualitative change. The dialectic states, moreover, that qualitative changes are brought about *only* by quantitative increases or decreases. Changes of this kind occur in all fields of reality. A difference in the number of atoms of a given element in a molecule of a chemical compound produces a substance with quite different properties (for example, the series of hydrocarbons, alcohols, acids, etc.). Current of a certain strength causes a filament to become incandescent; bodies change their consistency according to temperature, and melt or freeze at a definite point. Light and sound waves are perceptible to human receptors within certain limits of frequency, and here again the threshold of perception represents a qualitative difference due to a quantitative change. The slowing-up of intracellular motion, and the consequent loss of heat, at a certain point causes a cell to die, which is a qualitative change. A sum of money has to be of a certain size in order to become capital, i.e. to produce surplus value; the co-operation of men at work is not merely a combination, but a multiplication of the strength of each. (Not all these examples come from Engels, but they are in accordance with his thought.) In general, qualitative changes resulting from a quantitative increase or decrease may be seen in all cases where we distinguish between an agglomeration and an integrated whole. Nature and society afford innumerable examples of situations in which the whole is not merely the sum of its parts, but the latter acquire new properties by being part of an integrated system, while the system creates new regularities that cannot be deduced from the laws governing its elements. This concept of the whole became, after Engels's day, an important subject of methodology and an essential category in such forms as *Gestalt* psychology, holism in biology, etc.; it can also be found in Greek thought, for instance Aristotle draws attention to the difference between an integral whole and a combination of elements. But the law of the transformation of quantity into quality sets out to generalize these simple observations into a universal principle. The fact that the structure of organisms depends partly on their size is also a particular case of the law: an animal with the structure of an ant could not be as large as a hippopotamus, and conversely. Even in mathematics, Engels argues, there are qualitative differences, for example roots and powers, the incommensurability of infinitely large or small magnitudes with finite ones, and so on.

The opposition of qualitative and quantitative differences throws a clear light on the contrast between Engels's materialism and that of the mechanists. The latter—for example, Descartes, Hobbes, Locke, and most of the French eighteenth-century materialists—endeavoured to show that qualitative differentiation is not inherent in the world itself but is a feature of our perception, and that the authentic or 'primary' attributes of things are 'geometrical' ones of size, shape and motion; everything else is an illusion caused by our subjective reaction to mechanical stimuli. Engels, on the other hand, reproduces to some extent, of course in a more exact form, the ideas of Francis Bacon, who believed that qualitative differences could not be reduced to quantitative co-ordinates. The law of the transformation of quantity into quality states merely, it would seem, that there are non-additive features in nature and society, or perhaps that there are no purely additive qualities, i.e. none that can be intensified indefinitely without causing new properties or the disappearance of existing ones.

9. Contradictions in the world

THE second of Engels's dialectical laws is that of development through contradiction and the interpenetration of opposites. His remarks on this subject are in a more condensed form than the rest of his argument. He observes that 'the two poles of an antithesis, like positive and negative, are just as inseparable from each other as they are opposed, and despite all their opposition they mutually penetrate each other' (*Anti-Dühring*, Introduction). The phenomenon of polarity occurs in magnetism, electricity, mechanics, chemistry, the development of organisms (heredity and adaptation), and social life. It is not a question, however, of merely noting this fact but of arguing that nature contains in itself contradictions, the opposition and interpenetration of which is the source of all development. In Engels's opinion the existence of contradictions in nature is a refutation of formal logic, one of whose primary laws of thought, as they were called, was the principle of non-contradiction. As he writes, 'Motion itself is a contradiction: even simple mechanical change of place can only come about through a body at one and the same moment of time being both in one place and in another place, being in one and the same place and also not in it' (*Anti-Dühring*, I, XII). This is still more evident in more complex phenomena. 'Life consists precisely in this, that a living thing is at each moment itself and yet something else. Life itself, therefore, is a contradiction that is objectively present in things and processes, and is constantly asserting and resolving itself' (ibid.). Even the science of mathematics is full of contradictions. 'It is for example a contradiction that a root of A should be a power of A, and yet A to the power of one-half is the square root of A. It is a contradiction that a negative quantity should be the square of anything, for every negative multiplied by itself gives a positive . . . . And yet the square root of minus 1 is in many cases a necessary result of correct mathematical operations' (ibid.). In the same way, societies develop through the unceasing emergence of contradictions.

Engels was criticized for his view that contradictions are so present in nature that they cannot be described without violating logic, i.e. that logical contradictions are a feature of the universe. The great majority of contemporary Marxists hold that the principle of 'development through contradiction' does not involve rejecting the logical rule of non-contradiction; and they observe that, following Hegel, Engels spoke of motion being a contradiction he was repeating the paradox of Zeno of Elea, the only difference being that Zeno declared motion to be impossible because contradictory, while Engels declared contradiction to be in the nature of things. Many Marxists now hold that it is possible to speak of contradiction in the sense of conflict or contrary tendencies in nature and society, and of these being the cause of development and the evolution of higher forms, without necessarily rejecting formal logic. There is nothing illogical in the fact that contrary tendencies exist in practice; we are not asked to believe that two propositions contradicting each other are true, but only that nature is a system of tensions and conflict.

10. The negation of the negation

ENGELS's law of the 'negation of the negation' is intended to give a more exact account of the stages of development through contradiction, and *mutatis mutandis* it agrees with Hegel's formulation. The law states that every system has a natural tendency to produce out of itself another system which is its contrary; this 'negation' is negated in its turn so as to produce a system that is in some important respects a repetition of the first, but on a higher level. There is thus an evolution in the form of a spiral: the opposition of the thesis and antithesis is resolved, and they are merged in a synthesis which preserves them in a more perfect form. A seed, for instance, develops into a plant, which is the negation of it; this plant produces not one seed but many, after which it dies; the seeds collectively are the negation of the negation. With insects we have the similar cycle of egg, larva, imago, and eggs in large number. Numbers are negated by the minus sign, which in turn is negated by squaring; it makes no difference that we can arrive at the same number by squaring the positive, 'for the negated negation is so securely entrenched in A^2 that the latter always has two square roots, A and minus A' (*Anti-Dühring*, I, XIII). History develops according to the same rule, from common ownership among primitive peoples to private property in class societies and public ownership under socialism. The negation of the negation consists in restoring the social character of property, not by returning to a primitive society but by creating a higher and more developed system of ownership. In the same way, the primitive materialism of ancient philosophy was negated by idealistic doctrines so as to return in the more perfect form of dialectical materialism. Negation in the dialectical sense is not simply the destruction of the old order, but its destruction in such a way as to preserve the value of what is destroyed and raise it to a higher level. This, however, does not apply to the phenomenon of physical death. Life contains the germ of destruction, but the death of an individual does not lead to his renewal in a higher form.

11. *Critique of agnosticism*

THE basic problem of philosophy has also, as Engels said, its 'other side': the question whether the world is knowable, whether the human mind is capable of forming a true image of relations in independent nature. On this point the new materialism is firmly opposed to all agnostic doctrines such as, in particular, those of Hume and Kant. It rejects the idea that there is any absolute limit to knowledge, or that phenomena are radically different from unknowable 'things in themselves'. According to Engels, the agnostic viewpoint is easy to refute. Science is constantly transform-ing 'things in themselves' into 'things for us', as when it discovers new chemical substances that existed in nature but were not previously known. The difference is between reality known and unknown, not between the knowable and unknowable. If we are able to apply our hypotheses in practice and use them to foretell events, this confirms that the area under observation has been truly mastered by human knowledge. Practice, experiment, and industry are the best argument against agnostics. It has indeed happened that agnosticism played a useful part in the history of philosophy, as when French scientists of the Enlightenment sought to free their own studies from religious constraint by declaring that metaphysical problems were insoluble and that science was neutral *vis-a-vis* religion. But even this attitude smacked of evading real problems by pretending that they could never be solved.

12. *Experience and theory*

THE prior condition of knowledge is experience. Engels, like J. S. Mill before him, adopts an empirical standpoint even in mathematics, at least as regards the origin of its fundamental notions:

> The concepts of number and form have not been derived from any source other than the world of reality . . . Pure mathematics deals with the space forms and quantity relations of the real world—that is, with material which is very real indeed . . . But, as in every department of thought, at a certain stage of development the laws abstracted from the real world become divorced from that world and set over against it as something independent, as laws coming from outside, to which the world has to conform. (*Anti-Dühring*, I, III)

However, Engels's empiricism is a long way from that of most phenomenalists and positivists of his time. He does not hold that knowledge proceeds unidirectionally from raw fact to theory, nor does he regard theoretical generalizations as 'passive' constructions, i.e. as arising from accumulation and induction and exercising no reflex effect on the observation of new facts. Here as elsewhere, there is an interaction between facts and theories. Engels did not expatiate on the problems involved, but the main lines of his thought are clear. He is opposed to what he calls 'bare empiricism', i.e. uncritical belief in facts as, so to speak, interpreting themselves. In 'Natural Science in the Spirit World' (*Dialectics of Nature*) he points out that strict empiricism cannot provide an answer to the beliefs of spiritualists, who appeal to experiment and observation. Theory is essential to the interpretation of facts, and contempt for it is fatal to science. (For this reason Engels called Newton an 'inductive ass'.)

Facts do not interpret themselves, and to perceive their connections we need theoretical instruments which derive, it is true, from observation, but in time become independent elements of knowledge. In the progress of science there is a kind of mutual corroboration between experience and theory, though the former is always genetically prior to the latter. It appears that Engels does not regard the laws of science as merely the logical sum or economical formulation of individual statements of fact but as embodying something further, namely the necessity of the connection which they describe—a necessity which is not inherent in any one fact, nor in all together. There is in nature a 'form of universality'.

> All real, exhaustive knowledge consists solely in raising the individual thing in thought from individuality into particularity and from this into universality, in seeking and establishing the infinite in the finite, the eternal in the transitory. The form of universality, however, is the form of self-completeness, hence of infinity; it is the comprehension of the many finites in the infinite. We know that chlorine and hydrogen, within certain limits of temperature and pressure and under the influence of light, combine, with an explosion, to form hydrochloric acid gas; and as soon as we know this, we know that it takes place wherever and whenever these conditions are present, no matter whether the phenomenon occurs once or is repeated a million times, or on however many heavenly bodies. The form of universality in nature is law. (*Dialectics of Nature*, 'Dialectical Logic and the Theory of Knowledge')

The necessity of a law concerning a particular causal connection is not, as Hume would argue, a mere habituation of the mind; it is inherent in the natural connection itself, and we recognize this by the fact that we not only observe the regular sequence of particular events but are able, as a result, to produce the events ourselves.

Engels's remarks on the empirical background of theoretical constructions are rather summary, but their general trend is clear enough. He is a radical empiricist as regards the genesis of knowledge (no valid knowledge is derivable elsewhere than from experience) and a moderate empiricist as far as method is concerned. The social process of knowledge leads to the forging of theoretical instruments, thanks to which we do not submit passively to facts but interpret and combine them. (The second law of thermodynamics, for instance, appeared to Engels an absurdity, as it posited an over-all diminution of energy in the universe.) Science is not merely the concise recording of facts, but the comprehension of something universal and necessary in the world of nature.

13. *The relativity of knowledge*

AT the same time, Engels holds, it is impossible either for the whole of our knowledge or for elements of it such as natural laws to attain absolute validity. While accepting the traditional view that truth signifies agreement with reality, Engels follows Hegel in expounding the idea of truth as a process and as something essentially relative.

But in what does this relativity consist? Engels does not hold that the accuracy of a judgement is a matter of time or personality in the sense that it is true or false according to who pronounces it or in what circumstances. His belief in relativity is formulated in different ways. In the first place, knowledge is relative in the obvious sense that it is always incomplete, that man in his finitude cannot discover all the secrets of the universe. A second, more important aspect of relativity is one which applies especially to scientific laws. The way in which science usually advances is that theoretical explanations of observed facts are replaced in course of time by others which do not contradict the former ones but narrow the sphere of their validity. Thus Boyle's and Mariotte's law on the relation between the pressure, volume, and temperature of gases was corrected by Regnault's discovery that it does not apply outside certain limits of temperature and pressure. But we can never be certain that we have discovered once and for all the limits of applicability of a particular law, or that it may not have to be reformulated more precisely in the future. In this sense all scientific laws are relative, or are true only in a relative sense.

Thirdly, we can speak of the relativity of knowledge in the sense that the same collections of facts admit of different theoretical explanations, the scope of these explanations becoming narrower as science progresses, though it never disappears altogether. Fourthly, although there is a difference between a law of nature and a hypothesis (unless we deny the reality of causal connection, in which case every law is hypothetical), yet the basis of scientific generalizations can never be complete, since they comprise an infinity of possible individual facts. Hence any items of knowledge that lay claim to absolute validity must either be commonplaces like 'All men are mortal', or particular facts like 'Napoleon died on 5 May 1821'. Truly absolute knowledge, either in the sense of mentally reproducing the whole universe or of formulating a law of unalterable and final validity, is an unattainable goal to which we can only approximate indefinitely. In so doing, however, we come to possess an increasingly full and accurate picture of reality as a whole.

14. Practice as the criterion of truth

IN Engels's view, the truest confirmation of the accuracy of our knowledge is the effectiveness of our actions. If, on the strength of certain information, we set about changing the world in some particular, and if we succeed in doing so, that is the best vindication of our knowledge. Practice, in this sense, is the criterion of truth, and we thus have a reason for eschewing any mental speculation which does not lend itself to practical confirmation. In some passages Engels interprets the notion of 'practice' so broadly as to include the verification of hypotheses in cases where there is no question of our acting upon the external world, for example in astronomical observation. But the importance of practice in cognitive activity is even wider than this. It is not only the best criterion but itself a source of knowledge, inasmuch as real, socially felt needs direct human beings to particular fields of inquiry and determine the range of the questions they seek to answer. In this way, practice supplies the true purpose and social motivation of the quest for knowledge. Thought, in this sense, is practically oriented, which does not mean that it is not 'objective'—i.e. capable of reflecting, subject to its historical and other limitations, the real, factual attributes and relationships of nature itself, independent of the human mind. On the other hand, Engels writes in 'Dialectical Logic and the Theory of Knowledge': 'Natural science, like philosophy, has hitherto entirely neglected the influence of men's activity on their thought; both know only nature on the one hand and thought on the other. But it is precisely the alteration of nature by men, not solely nature as such, which is the most essential and immediate basis of human thought, and it is in so far as man has learnt to change nature that his intelligence has increased.'

From this interesting remark we might suppose that Engels was inclined to regard the content of human knowledge as the result of interaction between man and nature, and not simply a reflection of nature in which practical action plays the part of a touchstone and a determinant of interests. That would mean, however, that the object of our knowledge is not reality itself but man's relations with nature. This is hard to reconcile with the belief that human thought is a more and more perfect reflection of the world as it exists independently of man's cognitive and practical activity. The passage, however, is not so unambiguously expressed as to justify far-reaching inferences, and Engels nowhere developed the idea, nor is it clear exactly what he meant by such terms as 'basis of human thought'. Nevertheless, we find here a hint of a concept significantly different from his opinion that thought is a copy of the real world.

15. The sources of religion

BY this dialectical transformation of materialism Engels stands opposed to the whole of idealistic philosophy and to all his materialist predecessors, who did not advance beyond a mechanistic interpretation of the world. This applies to some extent even to Feuerbach: while crediting the latter with a large part in overcoming German idealism, Engels criticizes him for simply rejecting the Hegelian dialectic instead of discovering its rational content. In addition Feuerbach, like all previous materialists, was 'a materialist from below and an idealist from above': that is to say, he was unable to explain human history except in terms of ideology, in particular the figments of religion, which he regarded as the mainspring of historical change. Modern materialism is consistent in this respect too, that it accounts for historical events by regarding social consciousness as the product of material conditions of life. It would even seem, though Engels does not expressly say so, that he regarded historical materialism as the logical consequence of philosophic materialism. As for religion, which Feuerbach made the efficient cause of great historical changes, Engels, in accordance with positivist evolutionism, saw it as the fruit of human misconception and ignorance.

> From the very early times when men, still completely ignorant of the structure of their own bodies, under the stimulus of dream apparitions came to believe that their thinking and sensation were not activities of their bodies, but of a distinct soul which inhabits the body and leaves it at death—from this time men have been driven to reflect about the relation between this soul and the outside world. If upon death it took leave of the body and lived on, there was no occasion to invent yet another distinct death for it. Thus arose the idea of its immortality . . . Not religious desire for consolation, but the quandary, arising from universal ignorance, of what to do with this soul, once its existence had been accepted, after the death of the body, led to the empty notion of personal immortality. In exactly the same way the first gods arose through the personification of natural forces and, as religion developed, assumed more and more an extra-mundane form. (*Ludwig Feuerbach and the End of Classical German Philosophy*, II)

Engels, after the fashion of the Enlightenment thinkers, saw religion as the fruit of ignorance or want of understanding. He thus abandoned the Marxian view of religion as a secondary alienation due to the alienation of labour, in favour of an intellectualist explanation. In this respect he also shared the ideas of nineteenth-century evolutionism as to the origin and nature of religion.

XVI

Recapitulation and Philosophical Commentary

1. Marx's philosophy and that of Engels

ENGELS'S VIEWPOINT may be described in summary terms as both naturalistic and anti-mechanistic. He presents the universe as evolving dynamically towards higher forms, manifold in differentiation and enriching itself by inner conflict. His version of the dialectic is an anti-philosophical, anti-metaphysical one (though with some inconsistency on this point), which accepts the multiplicity of the universe as irreducible to a single pattern. It is allied to scientism and positivism by its confidence in natural science and mistrust of philosophy as anything but a set of intellectual rules; also by its general empiricist and determinist trend and by a (less definite) inclination to phenomenalism. On the other hand, it diverges from typical positivism by its critique of radical empiricism and its theory of the multiple forms of motion. (Yet even on this point Comte, for whom Marx and Engels expressed such profound contempt, anticipated Engels's views: he refused to reduce all phenomena to mechanistic models, and his classification of sciences was taken over by Engels with little modification.)

It should be added that Engels's evolutionism is apparently related to the separate parts of the universe and not to the universe as a whole. As we read at the end of the Introduction to *Dialectics of Nature*, the universe is infinite and eternal, reproducing the same forms in a never-ending cycle of birth and destruction. Particular fragments of the universe, particular astral systems, by force of internal necessity evolve higher forms of organic life and consciousness; but the universe as a whole does not evolve in this way. We may suppose that, as dwellers on the earth, we are now living in a part of the cosmos which is in a state of upward evolution; but from the point of view of nature as a whole this is a mere passing efflorescence, bound to repeat itself without ceasing in some nook or cranny of the universe.

Engels's observations were of course made in the light of contemporary science and mathematics, and many of them are now out of date. But the general lines of his thought—naturalism, cognition as a reflection of reality, knowledge as relative, the dialectic of nature—were upheld by later Marxists and regarded especially by the Russians (Plekhanov, Lenin) as the Marxist philosophy *par excellence*. At the same time, the dialectic of nature was criticized by some Marxists. The first to attack Engels's philosophy as radically different from Marx's was probably Stanislaw Brzozowski, while Max Adler also spoke of important divergences between the two founding fathers. Subsequently Lukács attacked the dialectic of nature, arguing that the idea that nature itself behaved dialectically was incompatible with Marx's view that the dialectic was an inter-action between subject and object, leading ultimately to their unification. According to Marx, nature was not something ready-made and assimilated by man in the process of cognition; it was the counterpart of a practical effort, and was 'given' only in the context of that effort. The evident fact that man trans-forms nature does not itself invalidate the contemplative theory of knowledge, if praxis is merely the exploitation of natural forces or a criterion for verifying hypotheses. The dialectic, which according to Marx is the unity of theory and practice, cannot be formulated so as to relate to nature in itself as it presup-poses the activity of consciousness.

The issue here raised as to whether the founders of scientific socialism saw eye to eye in their epistemological views may, it appears to me, be analysed as follows.

Engels's dialectic was formulated under the influence of Darwin's discover-ies and in the intellectual atmosphere of Darwinism. The main trend of opin-ion, shared by Engels, was to interpret life, knowledge, and social phenomena from the point of view of naturalism, which treats human history as a prolon-gation and a special case of natural history, and assumes that the general laws of nature apply, in specific forms, to the destiny of mankind. Engels, of course, does not question that human history has special features, nor does he assert that the laws of the animal kingdom suffice to explain human society or can be applied to it without modification; indeed, he expressly rejects such a proce-dure, holding that evolving nature creates new qualities and that human soci-ety is an instance of this differentiation. None the less, writing in *Ludwig Feuerbach* of the difference between the history of the organic world in general and that of mankind, he observes that men, unlike animals, act according to conscious intentions, but that their intentions and acts as a whole conform to the 'objective' regularities of history, which are independent of whether men realize them or not. This last thought is in harmony with many of Marx's state-ments, but the passage itself is not in accordance with Marx if it means that the conscious character of individual acts, which does not affect the laws govern-ing history as a whole, is the only feature that distinguishes the history of mankind. For it does not appear that the philosophical bases of Marx's Marxism are compatible with belief in general laws of nature having, as particular applications, the history of mankind and also the rules of thought, identified with psychological or physiological regularities of the brain. Whereas Engels, broadly speaking, believed that man could be explained in terms of natural history and the laws of evolution to which he was subject, and which he was capable of knowing in themselves, Marx's view was that nature as we know it is an extension of man, an organ of practical activity. Man, of course, did not create nature and it is not a subjective imagination; but the object of our knowledge is not nature in itself but our contact with it. In other words, when Marx spoke of knowledge having a practical character he did not simply mean that interest is determined by practical needs and hypotheses are confirmed by practical action. Human praxis is the true object of our knowledge, which can never free itself from the practical, situational manner in which it is acquired. We cannot contemplate the subject in itself, free from historical involvement; the *cogito* is an impossibility. But equally the object cannot be purged of the fact that it presents itself to man in the practical context, as a purely human object. Practical contact with nature is the horizon that our knowledge cannot overstep, and in this sense there is no ready-made nature that we can contemplate and then act upon. Nature, as far as we are concerned, is known only in terms of our acts and needs; knowledge cannot be divested of the fact that it is human, social, and historical knowledge. Or again: there is no transcendental viewpoint from which the subject can apprehend natural forms as they are, in order then to duplicate them in his own mind. The materialist interpretation of consciousness according to Marx is that knowledge and everything else in the mind—feelings, desires, imaginations, and ideals—are the product of social life and history. Man, therefore, cannot adopt a cosmic or divine viewpoint, throwing aside his own humanity and comprehending reality as it exists in itself and not as an object of human praxis.

There is thus a clear difference between the latent transcendentalism of Engels's dialectic of nature and the dominant anthropocentrism of Marx's view. The difference is also seen in the significance they respectively attach to Hegel and the Hegelian dialectic. Engels, who extolled Hegel's part in elaborating the conceptual framework of the dialectic, and who regarded the German workers' movement as the sole legitimate heir of classic German philosophy, saw it as the great merit of Hegelianism to have emphasized the transience of all forms of social existence. He criticized Hegel, on the other hand, for the non-dialectical conception of nature as repeating its cycle of evolution without a break, and especially, following the radical Young Hegelians of the 1840s, for the 'contradiction between system and method'. By this they meant that the dialectic speaks of ceaseless development and negation, so that no form of Being or society can be final, and the Absolute is always out of reach; yet Hegel represents certain forms of religion, philosophy, and the state as final and unimprovable, and thus sins against his own method.

But the supposed conflict between method and system cannot be resolved by recognizing the transience of all forms and the impossibility of final ones. Hegel's thought is not comprehensible without its fulfilment in the Absolute, and negativity as the Young Hegelians understood it is no longer Hegelian. The whole burden of Hegel's criticism of Kant and Fichte, especially of the 'bad infinity' or the notion of unending growth, was that any phase of development can only be understood in relation to a final state, without which so-called 'progress' is merely eternal repetition. Only an Absolute which is actually attainable, not somewhere dimly visible on the horizon, can provide the reference system that gives meaning to any stage of spiritual evolution. The notion that it is possible to salvage from the Hegelian dialectic the idea of eternal progress while jettisoning the conservative idea of an ultimate goal is analogous to a philosophy which, confronted with the contradiction between God's omnipotence and man's free will, should abolish God and claim that it had preserved the genuine essence of Christianity, namely atheism. The contradiction, or tension, is itself the essence of Christianity, and to remove one of its terms is not to accommodate Christianity to critical thought but simply to destroy it. In the same way, the notion of infinite progress without that of the final unification of Being is not a critical absorption of Hegelianism but a denial of it, and the first term of the 'contradiction' is not even specifically Hegelian: it comes from Kant and Fichte, and if it is to be the kernel of dialectical thought, such a dialectic has no need of the Hegelian tradition.

Marx's assimilation of Hegel, however, is not based on keeping the method while rejecting the system, but on 'standing Hegel on his feet instead of his head', which is a different thing. Marx in his own fashion took over from Kant and Hegel the idea of history culminating in the complete unity of man, the identification of existence with essence and the abolition of contingency in human life. Man, according to Marx, is not doomed to contingency, as Stirner maintained (and as do modern existentialists, at least of the atheistic kind); on the contrary, what has hitherto been contingent, though miscalled freedom, derives from the power of objectified forces over man. To remove these forces and subject man's existence to his own freedom, abolishing the difference between empirical Being and species-essence, is to destroy the contingency of existence. Man is no longer at the mercy of alienated forces of his own creation; the individual is not a victim of anonymous society, nor the owner of its objectified labour in the form of capital; in short, man's Absolute Being is fully realized in actual being. The latter, in consequence, ceases to be accidental; its individuality expresses the universal essence of humanity, and its freedom is historical necessity. Man's fundamental disunity can thus be overcome, but not in the way Hegel suggested. Hegel, having reduced man and his works to self-consciousness and the externalization thereof, and regarding humanity as a stage in the evolution of spirit, could not, on the basis of his own method, reconstruct man as an integral being. Man's contingency cannot be healed by an Absolute outside himself, and accordingly Hegel does not cure the contingency of individual life, or else he does so only in the context of that life: in effect, he condemns empirical human individuality to a state of contingency throughout its existence, as may be seen in the permanent dichotomy between the state and civil society in Hegel's philosophy of law. To do away with contingency it is necessary, firstly, to take man as a complete physical being, working and contending with nature, and secondly, to comprehend that man's only reality consists in his being an individual—any other form of existence is the effect of the alienation of labour, an aberration of fortune which, however, is historically inevitable and is the condition of his liberation. Only when Hegelianism has thus been transformed in the sense of materialism (consciousness as a component of the complete man and an effect of practical activity) and individualism (the individual as the only subject, all other modes of existence being predicates of the actual man)—only then is it possible to look forward to man's true unification as predicted in the Paris Manuscripts and in *Capital*. Hegel has been 'stood on his feet'—the individual is the subject and universal Being is the predicate, instead of the other way round, and the starting-point of historical development is not the externalization of consciousness but that of natural human forces in the form of labour.

Marx, therefore, does not take over Hegel's method without his system, but transforms both together. In the new schema we still have the prospect of a kind of ultimate goal, namely what Marx calls the end of the past and the beginning of true history. It is a consummation in the sense that it puts an end once and for all to the historic duality between the individual and reified social Being, between self-objectification in labour and the alienation of its products. The healing of disunity and return to full integration are no less essential to Marx's doctrine than to Hegel's, although the disunity and therefore the return are conceived in different terms. The finality of the socialist transformation, as we have seen, does not imply the cessation of development but the extinction of all conflict between man's empirical life and his nature—the removal of all obstacles that alienated labour and the contingency of life opposed to the true, creative objectification of man's natural powers.

In a similar way to that in which Marx differs from Hegel, his idea that 'philosophy will be abolished by being realized' is different from the scientistic belief that philosophy will be superseded by the positive sciences. In Marx's view the abolition of philosophy is a natural element in the reintegration of man, as it consists in depriving thought processes of their autonomy *vis-à-vis* life as a whole. Thought becomes a direct affirmation of life, aware that it is itself conscious life and nothing else; the division between physical and intellectual work is done away with; thought can no longer withdraw to an 'independent' realm of its own; philosophy, which is the mind's aspiration towards the integrality of man, will disappear when that aspiration is realized. This is quite different from the view that philosophy will no longer have the right to a separate existence, and that anything worth while in it will be taken over by the various positive sciences.

The difference between these two interpretations of the human condition is clear, as is the sharpness of the division, in Marx's view, between the present world and that which is to come. On his own philosophical premises he could never have made any concession to reformist strategy; the new society had to make a complete break with the old, and a revolutionary upheaval was the only valid form of social criticism. By contrast, on the assumption that progress continues throughout history but never reaches an absolute goal, it is easier to understand the view that reform within the framework of capitalism may be of value in itself.

To sum up the difference in the attitudes of Marx and Engels we may say that they exhibit a contrast, firstly, between naturalistic evolutionism and anthropocentrism; secondly, between the technical interpretation of knowledge and the epistemology of praxis; thirdly, between the idea of the 'twilight of philosophy' and that of its merging into life as a whole; and, fourthly, between infinite progression and revolutionary eschatology. Many critics have taken the view that Marx never uses the term 'materialism' in the same sense as Engels, as he always means by it the dependence of consciousness on social conditions and not the metaphysical primacy of matter over mind. Some, such as Z. Jordan, even argue that Marx had a much better title than Engels to be called a positivist, as he rejected any kind of 'substantialist' metaphysics. To some extent this is a question of terminology: Marx was certainly not a positivist in the historical sense of the word, as he did not share the phenomenalist theory of knowledge or the prohibition against looking for an 'essence' behind phenomena, and indeed often expressed himself to the contrary. It is true, however, that, unlike Engels, he did not concern himself with metaphysical questions about the primal substance and the origin of the world. In his early writings he expressly rejected metaphysical questioning, and it is of course one thing to do this and another to answer the question negatively. Certainly Marx is a 'materialist' in the broad sense of one who does not believe in spirit existing prior to matter, or who rejects the question of such existence as meaningless. As a rule, however, the term is used to denote a 'substantialist' belief in 'matter' as the substratum of all that can meaningfully be said to exist; or, more precisely, the belief that all objects have the properties that scientific and everyday experience ascribe to physical bodies. It is hard to call Marx a materialist in this sense, and Engels himself, as we saw, varies between scientistic phenomenalism (which is not a metaphysical doctrine but an intellectual rule) and true materialism, which goes beyond the reach of scientific rigour and, according to how it is formulated, is either obscure or unprovable.

A point of view represented especially by Catholic critics of Marxism, and recently defended also by L. Coletti, is that materialism is incompatible with Engels's dialectic of nature because the latter predicates the existence in nature of qualities, such as creativity, that belong only to spiritual beings. This criticism, however, is open to objection. The idea that nature can evolve forms that are qualitatively new (in the sense we have considered), and that some parts of nature obey laws that cannot be deduced from the universal laws of physics, does not involve any logical contradiction with materialism in the above sense. At all events, the theory of a multiplicity of irreducible qualities does not in itself conflict with materialism. There is, however, another way in which materialism may be found incompatible with the dialectic. Engels clearly expresses the view that logical contradiction is a property of certain natural phenomena. Now the statement that a certain logical relationship occurs in nature may be reconciled with the philosophy of Hegel, Leibniz, or Spinoza (in the latter's case, with the proposition that *cogitatio* is an attribute of the whole universe), but none of these is compatible with Engels's form of materialism. If we interpret 'contradiction' and 'negation' in the non-logical sense of conflict or destruction, this point falls to the ground. It would seem, however, that Engels's casual identification of logical relationships with physical ones is due to his inadequate training in philosophy rather than to a deliberate theory. With all his wide knowledge and agility of mind, Engels was an amateur in philosophy. His critique of Kant's 'agnosticism' is astonishingly naïve: he shows complete misunderstanding by arguing that according to Kant new chemical substances could never be discovered because, if they were, a 'thing in itself' would become an object of Knowledge. It is also not clear how Engels could reconcile his psychologistic interpretation of logic (which is expressed in summary form and does not go beyond the commonplace views of his time) with his belief that human knowledge is a reflection of nature as it 'really' and independently exists. For, if the laws of thought are not obligatory rules independent of experience and of the existence of things, but are merely the way in which the human brain works and are thus particular cases of some general law of nature, the question whether knowledge is 'true' in the traditional sense has no meaning: cognitive activity would be a form of biological reaction and nothing more, and could be evaluated only from the point of view of its usefulness.

Despite Engels's inconsistencies and reckless generalizations, can the 'dialectic of nature' in some sense preserve its validity? Those Marxist critics who dispute the possibility have pointed out that in Marx's usage 'dialectic' refers to an interplay between the mind and its social environment: this cannot be transferred to nature, or constitute a set of universal laws whereof the laws of social life are only a manifestation. If it were so, the development of society and above all its revolutionary transformation would be the effect of 'natural laws', which is the opposite of Marx's view. However, if this criticism be accepted, it does not follow that orthodox Marxism forbids consideration of the irreducibility of various natural processes to a single model; all that is shown is that the term 'dialectic' does not apply to such consideration in the way that it does to social phenomena. With this reservation there seems to be no reason why Engels's speculations should be condemned out of hand, though it is a further question how far and in what sense they are true in detail. His ideas of logical contradictions in nature, or the dialectic in arithmetic, are certainly naïve; but the question of the multiplicity of qualities is not, nor does it seem improper to speak of an accumulation of quantitative changes leading to qualitative ones (in the sense suggested above, i.e. that most or even all the parameters by which natural phenomena are described are not indefinitely additive).

Certainly Engels's 'dialectic of nature' is full of obsolete examples and unfounded speculation in the realm of philosophic cosmology. He maintains that the emergence, in the history of the earth, of higher forms from lower represents an immanent necessity and that nature 'must', by virtue of some unknown law, produce the same forms in similar conditions. Although Engels himself at other times condemned this kind of arbitrary speculation, at all events in general terms, it belongs to a traditional philosophy of nature that was fairly widespread in the nineteenth century. This is not to say, however, that Engels's philosophy made any contribution to the development of science. As historians of science point out, there have in the past been moments of crisis when philosophical ideas played an important part in this way, for example the influence of Platonism on Galilean physics or of empiriocriticism on the theory of relativity. But no such heuristic role can be ascribed to Marx's or Engels's philosophy of nature; and its effect in the Soviet Union has been to stifle sciences, not bring them to birth. It may even be said that Engels is not wholly innocent in this respect: on the one hand, he emphasized that philosophic generalizations are valueless if they are not based on scientific experience, but on the other, in his critique of empiricism, he ascribed to philosophy a supervisory role *vis-à-vis* 'plain experience'. He failed to explain clearly how these principles could be reconciled or on what basis philosophy was entitled to criticize experience. The idea that it is so entitled could easily furnish a pretext for the subjection of science to ideology, which has in fact happened—of course, in political circumstances that have nothing to do with this part of Engels's doctrine.

Questions connected with the dialectic of nature constitute a much-publicized part of what is now codified as 'dialectical materialism'. How far they are scientifically and philosophically fruitful at the present time is a topic to be considered later.

2. Three motifs in Marxism

As with all great thinkers we can perceive in Marx's own doctrine, considered as a whole, a degree of tension between heterogeneous strains of thought, and also between the sources which he wrought into a synthesis. From this point of view we may distinguish three principal motifs.

(1) The Romantic motif. In the main lines of his criticism of capitalist society, Marx is an heir to the Romantic movement. The Romantics attacked industrial society from a conservative point of view, deploring the loss of 'organic' ties and loyalties and the fact that human beings confronted one another not as individuals but as representatives of impersonal forces and institutions or the money power. On the one hand, personality was lost in anonymity and men tended to treat one another as embodiments of their social function or the wealth they possessed. On the other hand, genuine collective life disappeared as well: there were no true communities of the traditional kind, moral entities united not only by interest but by spontaneous solidarity and direct contact between individuals. The opposition between such organic communities and 'society' as a mechanical aggregate held in balance by nothing but the negative bond of interest is a theme that runs through pre-Romantic and Romantic philosophy, from Rousseau and Fichte to Comte. The dream of a return to perfect harmony and to a state in which no middle term intervened between the individual and the community, or the individual and himself, was an attack, expressed or implied, on liberalism and its theoretical basis in the social contract. Liberal philosophy assumes that men's conduct is necessarily governed by selfish motives and that their conflicting interests can only be reconciled by a rational system of laws which safeguards the security of all by limiting the freedom of each. This implies that men are one another's natural enemies, each one's freedom being the limit of everyone else's. Unlimited freedom would be self-destructive, for if no one agreed to respect the rights of others, all would be exposed to aggression and none would be safe; the social contract, in Hobbes's sense, prevents this by organizing the community on the basis of men respecting one another's freedom. Society is thus an artificial creation, a system of legislation to restrain natural egoism and provide security for all at the price of a partial relinquishment of freedom. In the Romantics' view this was

indeed a true picture of industrial society, but it did not answer to the require-ments of human nature. Man's natural destiny was to live in a community based not on the negative bond of interest but on the independent, spontaneous need to communicate with others. Coercion and control would not be necessary in a society in which each individual freely identified with the whole.

Marx adopted the destructive part of the Romantics' view of contemporary society: witness his theory of alienation and of the power of money, and his belief in a future unity in which the individual would treat his own forces directly as social forces. The aspects of society that he attacked were the same as those whose devastating consequences had been noted by the Romantics: men were dominated by their own energies and skills in the form of the anony-mous laws of the market, the abstract tyranny of money, and the ruthless process of capitalist accumulation. To Marx, as to the Romantics, the freedom contained in the Declaration of the Rights of Man, which allowed the individ-ual to do what he liked so long as he did no harm to others, was the hallmark of a society dominated by the negative bond of self-interest.

Not only this, but the main features of the communist Utopia are also bor-rowed from the Romantics. Marx's basic principle is that all mediation between the individual and mankind will cease to exist. This applies to all constructions, rational or irrational, that interpose themselves between the individual and his fellows, such as nationality, the state, and law. The individual will voluntarily identify himself with the community, coercion will become unnecessary, the sources of conflict will disappear. The removal of mediating forms does not mean the destruction of individuality—on the contrary. As in the Romantic view, the restoration of organic links will at the same time restore the authenticity of per-sonal life. As things are now, the individual wrenched from the community and enslaved to anonymous institutions is robbed of his personal life and obliged to treat himself as a mere object. The worker sees his whole effort as a means of biological survival, while the creative part of his work becomes alien to him; his personal qualities and abilities take on the form of a commodity bought and sold on the market like any other. The capitalist loses his own personality in a different but equally pernicious way: as the personification of money he is not master of his behavior but must do as the market tells him, irrespective of whether his intentions are good or bad. On both sides of the gulf personality is extinguished as individuals turn into servants of alienated forces. The abolition of capitalism does not mean exalting the community at the expense of the indi-vidual, but restoring both at once. Instead of freedom being conceived in the liberal fashion as the private sphere of non-interference with others, it becomes the voluntary unity of the individual with his fellow men.

But the agreement between Marxism and Romanticism is only partial. Romanticism in its classic form is a dream of attaining social unity by reviving some idealized feature of the past: the spiritual harmony of the Middle Ages, a rural Arcadia or the happy life of the savage, ignorant of laws and industry and contentedly identifying with the tribe. This kind of nostalgia is, of course, the reverse of Marx's viewpoint. Although he shows traces of the Romantic belief in the felicity of the savage, these are not numerous or important and there is no suggestion in his work that mankind could or should revert to a primitive life-style. Unity will be recovered not by destroying modern technology or invoking primitivism and rural idiocy, but by further technical progress and by obliging society to put forward its utmost efforts to perfect its control over natural forces. It is not by retreating into the past but by strengthening man's power over nature that we can salvage what was of value in primitive society: the process is a kind of spiral, involving the maximum negativity of the present system. The destructive effects of the machine cannot be cured by abolishing machines, but only by perfecting them. Technology itself, by its negative aspects as it were, makes it possible to revive what it destroyed.

Because future unity will be obtained not by jettisoning the achievements of social development but by continuing it, that unity will reside in the human species as a whole and not in traditional forms like the nation or the village. The national community, which so many Romantics regard as the paradigm of organic life, is already being dissolved by the progress of capitalism, which sweeps away everything that does not serve its own expansion. The workers have no fatherland, and neither has capital: on both sides of the great conflict of the age, patriotism has lost its relevance. Nationalism may be exploited for political or other short-term ends or to justify protectionist policies, but its strength is collapsing under the remorseless pressure of cosmopolitan capital and the internationalist consciousness of the proletariat. From this point of view also capital, the destroyer of tradition, is clearing the way for the new society.

(2) If Marx parted company with the Romantics in this important feature of his Utopia, it was because of what may be called the Faustian–Promethean motif—a strong influence and, in some ways at least, a rival to Romanticism. It is hard to refer this motif to any particular school of thought: it appears in a wide variety of philosophies, including some strands of neo-Platonism (man as the head of created Being) and in texts of Lucretius and Goethe that were well known to Marx. We find it in Giordano Bruno and other Renaissance writers whom Marx regarded as models of fulfilled humanity, universal giants who had overcome the penury of the division of labour and had not only assimilated the entire culture of their day but had raised it to a higher level by their own efforts. This strain in Marx's thinking appears clearly from the answers he gave to his daughters' 'questionnaire'—favourite poets, Shakespeare, Aeschylus, Goethe; favourite heroes, Spartacus, Kepler; idea of happiness, fighting; most hated quality, servility. The Promethean idea which recurs constantly in Marx's work

is that of faith in man's unlimited powers as self-creator, contempt for tradition and worship of the past, history as man's self-realization through labour, and the belief that the man of tomorrow will derive his 'poetry' from the future.

Marx's Prometheanism is of course of a special kind, and above all it relates to the species and not the individual. Marx believed, as he made clear in his defence of Ricardo against the sentimental critique of Sismondi, that the idea of 'production for production's sake' meant developing the riches of human nature as an end in itself, and that the progress of the species must not be held up by considerations of individual happiness. Even if the development of the species took place at the expense of a majority of individuals, it was in the end synonymous with the development of every individual; the progress of the whole always involves detriment to some, and the callousness ascribed to Ricardo was a proof of his scientific honesty.

Marx was certain that the proletariat as the collective Prometheus would, in the universal revolution, sweep away the age-long contradiction between the interest of the individual and that of the species. In this way, too, capitalism was the harbinger of socialism. By smashing the power of tradition, brutally rousing nations from their slumbers, revolutionizing production, and liberating fresh human forces, capitalism had made a civilization in which man for the first time was able to show what he could do, although as yet his prowess took non-human and anti-human forms. It was pitifully sentimental to upbraid capitalism in the hope of stopping or diverting its victorious advance. The conquest of nature must go forward; in the next stage, men would achieve mastery over the social conditions of progress.

A typical feature of Marx's Prometheanism is his lack of interest in the natural (as opposed to economic) conditions of human existence, the absence of corporal human existence in his vision of the world. Man is wholly defined in purely social terms; the physical limitations of his being are scarcely noticed. Marxism takes little or no account of the fact that people are born and die, that they are men or women, young or old, healthy or sick; that they are genetically unequal, and that all these circumstances affect social development irrespective of the class division, and set bounds to human plans for perfecting the world. Marx did not believe in the essential finitude and limitation of man, or the obstacles to his creativity. Evil and suffering, in his eyes, had no meaning except as instruments of liberation; they were purely social facts, not an essential part of the human condition.

In the 1844 Manuscripts, it is true, Marx refers to sexual relations, i.e. presumably a biological tie, as the paradigm of the truly human links which are apparently to be dominant in communist society. But the parallel is at once explained in a contrary sense from what we expect. It is not that the biological tie is a model for the social one, but that it has taken on a social character: man discovers in sexual relations to what extent his nature has been 'humanized', i.e. socialized—in what way his biology has become human, and his biological needs have become social needs. Contrary to social Darwinism and to liberal philosophy, Marx not only does not derive the social tie from biological needs, but represents the latter, and the biological conditions of human existence, as elements of the social tie. 'Socialized nature' is not a metaphor. Everything in man's being is social: all his natural qualities, functions, and behaviour have become virtually divorced from their animal origins.

For this reason Marx can scarcely admit that man is limited either by his body or by geographical conditions. As his argument with Malthus showed, he refused to believe in the possibility of absolute overpopulation, as determined by the earth's area and its natural resources. Overpopulation was a purely social fact relating to the conditions of capitalist production, as technical progress and exploitation caused relative overpopulation in the shape of a reserve army of workers. Demography was not an independent force but an element in the social structure, to be evaluated accordingly.

Marx's ignoring of the body and physical death, sex and aggression, geography and human fertility—all of which he turns into purely social realities—is one of the most characteristic yet most neglected features of his Utopia. Among other things, it means that the popular analogy between Marx's soteriology and that of Christianity (the proletariat as redeemer, total salvation, the chosen people, the Church, etc.) is erroneous in one crucial respect. Salvation, for Marx, is man's salvation of himself; not the work of God or Nature, but that of a collective Prometheus who, in principle, is capable of achieving absolute command over the world he lives in. In this sense man's freedom is his creativity, the march of a conqueror overcoming both nature and himself.

(3) But Prometheanism too has its limits, at all events in the interpretation of the past: it is rivalled by the third motif, that of the rationalist, determinist Enlightenment. Marx often speaks of the laws of social life, operating in the same way as the laws of nature. By this he does not mean that they are a continuation of the laws of physics or biology, but that they impose themselves on human individuals with the same inexorable necessity as an avalanche or a typhoon. It is for objective scientific thought to study these laws as a naturalist does, without preconceived dogma, sentiment, or value-judgements, as Marx considered himself to have done in *Capital*. The normative concepts of alienation and dehumanization thus present themselves as the neutralized, non-evaluating concepts of exchange-value, surplus value, abstract labour, and the sale of labour-power. In the questionnaire we have already quoted, Marx's rationalism and philosophical scepticism appear in his favourite maxim, *De omnibus dubitandum*.

In this scientistic approach we recognize the third conception of freedom, as formulated by Engels: freedom is the understanding of necessity, the extent to which men are able to turn the laws of nature to their own use, the level of material and social technique.

Here too, however, there is a reservation to be made. Belief in the 'laws' governing society is grounded in the interpretation of history up to the present, the 'prehistory' of mankind. Up to now men have been governed by forces they have created but do not control—currency, the market, religious myths. The gulf between the tyranny of economic laws and the mind which impotently observes them is closed by the appearance of the proletariat, conscious of its mission. From then on necessity is not imposed from without, and does not consist in the technical utilization of existing laws by enlightened social engineers. The very difference between necessity and freedom ceases to exist, and so presumably do 'social laws' as hitherto understood, i.e. as something like the law of gravitation. The latter, however, while it can be known and put to use, cannot be abolished, and operates whether we know about it or not. The term 'law' in this sense cannot apply to a social process that occurs only on condition of being understood, and this is precisely the case with revolutionary praxis. There is a crucial distinction here: the laws that have governed society up to now were independent of human knowledge; the fact that they are now known does not mean that they cease to operate. But the revolutionary movement of the proletariat is not the exemplification of a law in this sense, for although it is caused by history it is also the awareness of history.

While, then, the Romantic side of Marxism applies equally to the past and to the future (criticizing the dehumanization of man by capitalism, and looking forward to a state of unity), and while Prometheanism looks primarily to the future (for, although man has at all times been his own creator, he was not and could not have been aware of this fact), the deterministic aspect of Marxism relates to the past which still weighs upon mankind, though it is destined soon to be thrown off altogether.

The whole of Marx's thought can be interpreted in terms of these three motifs and their interrelation. They do not coincide, however, with the conventional 'sources' of Marxism. The Romantic strain derives variously from Saint-Simon, Hess, and Hegel; the Promethean from Goethe, Hegel, and the Young Hegelian philosophy of praxis and self-knowledge (man as creator of himself); the determinist and rationalist from Ricardo, Comte (whom Marx derided), and again from Hegel. All three motifs are influenced by Hegelian thought, but in all of them it is transformed from Hegel's intention.

The three motifs are present uninterruptedly in Marx's work, but their respective strength varies at different times. There can be no doubt that Marx laid more weight on the purely scientific, objective, deterministic aspect of his observations in the sixties than in the forties. The other two strains did not lose their force, however, but continued to affect the direction of his work, the concepts he used, the questions he put and the answers he gave to them—even though, as often happens in such cases, he was not fully aware of their constant influence.

Marx was convinced that he had synthesized all the intellectual values available to him in a single picture. In the light of his own conception of his work, such questions as whether he was a determinist or a voluntarist, or whether he believed in historical laws or the power of human initiative, have no meaning. Ever since, as a student at Berlin, he came to the conclusion that with Hegel's help he had overcome the Kantian dualism between what is and what ought to be, he was in an intellectual position which enabled him to reject such questions.

3. Marxism as a source of Leninism

ALL these considerations, however, belong to the domain of social philosophy, and it was difficult to derive a precise political strategy from them at a time when there was already a strong movement in being which professed Marxism as its ideology. The philosophy required interpretation and specification, and this brought to light tensions and contradictions within Marxism which had not been noticeable on the plane of general soteriology and eschatology. The debate between necessity and freedom could be resolved in theory, but at a certain point it had to be decided whether the revolutionary movement must wait for capitalism to mature economically or whether it should seize power as soon as the political situation permitted. General principles were of little use in resolving this question. Marxism promised that society would become one and that all barriers between the individual and society would be removed; the next step was to draw practical conclusions and translate the promise into the language of a political programme. It was also necessary to define more clearly the idea of civilization as conditioned by class and at the same time universal. What exactly was meant by the state 'withering away', and how was this to be brought about in practice? Those who relied on the gradual and automatic development of capitalism into communism, and those who stressed the creative historical role of revolutionary initiative, could both find support in Marxist writings. The former accused the latter of seeking to violate the laws of history as laid down by Marx; the latter retorted that the former expected the impersonal process of history to make their revolution for them, which might mean waiting till the end of the world. Marx was quoted on either side of the argument, but, taken together, the quotations did not prove much, and, as usually happens, they were used to buttress positions adopted for other reasons.

Still more troublesome was the practical interpretation of all Marx's prophecies concerning the nature of communism. It was possible to argue as follows: according to Marx, all social antagonisms were based on class conflicts. When private ownership of the means of production was abolished, there would be no more classes and no social conflict except that due to the lingering resistance of the possessing classes. Marx envisaged that there would be no 'mediacy' in socialist society: this meant, in practical terms, the abolition of the liberal bourgeois separation of powers and the unification of the legislature, executive, and judiciary. Marx also envisaged the disappearance of the 'national principle': so any tendency to cultivate national separateness and national culture must be a survival of capitalism. Marx had declared that the state and civil society would become identical. Since the existing civil society was a bourgeois one, the simplest way to interpret this was by the complete absorption of civil society into the new state, which was by definition a working-class state ruled by the party that professed Marxism, the proletarian ideology. Marx had said that the negative freedom of the liberal bourgeois tradition would have no place in socialist society, as it only expressed the antagonistic character of society. The building of the new world could thus begin by substituting for negative freedom a higher form of freedom based on the unity of the individual and society. As, by definition, the proletariat's aspirations were embodied in the proletarian state, those who failed in any way to conform to the new unity deserved destruction as survivals of bourgeois society. What else, after all, was the meaning of the principle that human progress is always at the expense of the individual, and that this cannot be otherwise until absolute communism is achieved?

By arguing on these lines, the whole Marxist–Romantic theory of unity, classes, and the class struggle could be used (which does not mean that this was historically inevitable) to justify the establishment of an extreme despotism which professedly embodied the maximum possible freedom. For if, as Engels taught, the freest society is that which has most control over the conditions of its life, it is not a gross distortion of the theory to infer that society will be free in proportion as it is governed more despotically and subjected to more numerous regulations. Since, according to Marx, socialism deposes objective economic laws and enables men to control the conditions of their lives, it is easy to infer that a socialist society can do anything it likes—i.e. that the people's will, or the will of the revolutionary party, can ignore economic laws and, by its own creative initiative, manipulate the elements of economic life in any way it pleases. Marx's dream of unity could thus take the form of a despotic party oligarchy, while his Prometheanism would appear in the attempt to organize economic life by police methods, as Lenin's party did at the outset of its rule. Economic voluntarism, which was only abandoned when the new society was on the brink of ruin, was an application, and not too much a caricature, of Marxian Prometheanism—Chinese communism went through a very similar period, inspired by the same ideology and no less catastrophic in its results. Under socialism economic failure can only be seen as due to the ill-will of the governed, which in turn must be an effect of resistance by the possessing classes. The rulers had no need to seek the reasons for failure in doctrinal errors: as true Marxists they could blame them on the bourgeoisie and intensify repressive measures against the latter, as in fact they did. In short, the Leninist–Stalinist version of socialism was a possible interpretation, though certainly not the only possible one, of Marx's doctrine. If freedom equals social unity, then the more unity there is, the more freedom; as the 'objective' conditions of unity have been achieved, namely the confiscation of bourgeois property, all manifestations of discontent are relics of the bourgeois past and should be treated accordingly. The Promethean principle of creative initiative divided the field with historical determinism: initiative was vested in the political machine, while the backward masses were expected to accept their lot as a historical necessity which, once understood, was identical with freedom. There is nothing easier than to find passages in Marx which support the view that the superstructure is an instrument of the base and that both must be described in class categories. If there are new relations of production reflecting the interests of the proletariat, the superstructure—politics, laws, literature, art, and science—must conform to the demands of these relations as interpreted by the conscious vanguard of the proletariat. Thus the abolition of law as a mediating institution between individuals and the state, and the principle of servility in every manifestation of culture, could be regarded as a perfect embodiment of Marxist theory.

It is easy to reply to objections such as these that Marx (except perhaps for a short time after the revolutions of 1848) not only did not question the principles of representative democracy but regarded them as a necessary part of popular rule, and that although on two occasions he used the term 'dictatorship of the proletariat' (without saying what he meant by it), he had in mind the class content of the power system and not, as Lenin did, the liquidation of democratic institutions. It follows that the despotic socialism of history is not socialism as Marx intended it; the question, however, is how far it represents the logical outcome of his doctrine. To this it may be answered that the doctrine is not wholly innocent, though it would be absurd to say that the despotic forms of socialism were a direct outcome of the ideology itself. Despotic socialism arose from many historical circumstances, the Marxist tradition among them. The Leninist–Stalinist version of Marxism was no more than a version, i.e. one attempt to put into practice the ideas that Marx expressed in a philosophical form without any clear principles of political interpretation. The view that freedom is measured in the last resort by the degree of unity of society, and that class interests are the only source of social conflict, is one component of the theory. If we consider that there can be a technique of establishing social unity, then despotism is a natural solution of the problem inasmuch as it is the only known technique for the purpose. Perfect unity takes the form of abolishing all institutions of social mediation, including representative democracy and the rule of law as an independent instrument for settling conflicts. The concept of negative freedom presupposes a society of conflict. If this is the same as a class society, and if a class society means a society based on private property, then there is nothing reprehensible in the idea that the act of violence which abolishes private property at the same time does away with the need for negative freedom, or freedom *tout court*.

And thus Prometheus awakens from his dream of power, as ignominiously as Gregor Samsa in Kafka's *Metamorphosis*.

Selective Bibliography

The relevant works by Marxist authors whose writings are discussed in Volumes II and III are listed in the bibliographies of those volumes. When an edition of collected works of an author is available, individual works are not mentioned.

I General Works. General Anthologies and Bibliographies

Bibliographie marxiste internationale, Paris: Centre d'études et de recherches marxistes, 1964–.

Cole, G. D. H., *A History of Socialist Thought*, 5 vols., London, 1953–60.

Drachkovitch, M. M., (ed.), *Marxism in the Modern World*, London, 1965.

Drahn, E., *Marx-Bibliographie*, Charlottenburg, 1920.

Fetscher, I., *Der Marxismus. Seine Geschichte in Dokumenten*, Munich, 1967 (an anthology with a copious bibliography).

Karl Marx und der Marxismus, Munich, 1967 (Eng. trans. 1971).

Howe, I., *Essential Works of Socialism*, 2nd edn., New Haven and London, 1976.

Jordan, Z. A., *The Evolution of Dialectical Materialism*, London and New York, 1967.

Lachs, J., *Marxist Philosophy, a Bibliographical Guide*, Chapel Hill, 1967.

Lichtheim, G., *Marxism. A Historical and Critical Study*, London, 1961.

Masaryk, T. G., *Die philosophischen und soziologischen Grundlagen des Marxismus*, Vienna, 1899.

Papaioannou, K., *Marx et les marxistes*, Paris, 1970 (an anthology).

Plamenatz, J., *German Marxism and Russian Communism*, London, 1954.

Vranicki, P., *Geschichte des Marxismus*, 2 vols., Frankfurt, 1972–4.

Wolfe, B., *Marxism: 100 years in the life of a doctrine*, New York, 1965.

II Works by Marx and Engels

Marx–Engels, *Historisch-kritische Gesamtausgabe (M.E.G.A.)*, Frankfurt, 1927–35 (incomplete).

Werke, 39 vols., Berlin, 1956 ff. (incomplete).

Collected Works, Moscow, New York, and London, 1975 ff. (planned to comprise 50 vols.).

Anthologies in English:

Marx–Engels, *Selected Writings in Sociology and Social Philosophy*, ed. T. Bottomore and M. Rubel, London, 1956.

Basic Writings on Politics and Philosophy, ed. L. Feuer, New York, 1959.

Marx, Karl, *Early Writings*, ed. T. Bottomore, London, 1963.

The Essential Writings, ed. D. Caute, London and New York, 1967.

The Early Texts, ed. D. McLellan, Oxford, 1971.

Economy, Class and Social Revolution, ed. Z. A. Jordan, London, 1971.

III General Works on Marx and Engels; Biographies

Berlin, I., *Karl Marx*, 3rd edn., Oxford, 1973.

Blumenberg, W., *Karl Marx*, London, 1971.

Calvez, J.-Y., *La Pensée de Karl Marx*, Paris, 1956.

Cornu, A., *Karl Marx et Friedrich Engels*, 3 vols., Paris, 1955–62.

Künzli, A., *Karl Marx, eine Psychographie*, Vienna, Frankfurt, and Zurich, 1966.

McLellan, D., *The Thought of Karl Marx. An Introduction*, London, 1971.

    Karl Marx. His Life and Thought, London, 1973.

Mayer, G., *Friedrich Engels. Eine Biographie*, 2 vols., The Hague, 1934.

Mehring. Fr., *Karl Marx. Geschichte seines Lebens*, Leipzig, 1918 (Eng. trans. 1936).

Meyer, A. G., *Marxism: The Unity of Theory and Practice*, Ann Arbor, 1963.

Nikolaevsky, B. I. and Maenchen-Helfer, O., *Karl Marx, Man and Fighter*, London, 1936.

Payne, R., *Marx: A Biography*, London, 1968.

Raddatz, F. J., *Karl Marx, Eine politische Biographie*, Hamburg, 1975.

Rubel, M., *Bibliographie des œuvres de Karl Marx*, Paris, 1956.

    Karl Marx. Essai de biographie intellectuelle, Paris, 1957.

IV The Hegelian Left, Feuerbach, The Young Marx,
The Marx–Hegel Relationship

Avron, H., *Feuerbach ou la transformation du sacré*, Paris, 1957.

Bauer, B., *Kritik der evangelischen Geschichte des Johannes*, Bremen, 1840.

    Kritik der evangelischen Geschichte der Synoptiker, Leipzig, 1841.

    Das entdeckte Christenthum, Zurich, 1843.

Berlin, I., *The Life and Opinions of Moses Hess*, Cambridge, 1959.

Cieszkowski, A. Graf von, *Prolegomena zur Historiosophie*, Berlin, 1838, 2nd edn. 1908.

    Gott und Palingenesie, 1842.

Dupré, L., *The Philosophical Foundation of Marxism*, New York, 1966.

Feuerbach, L., *Sämtliche Werke*, 10 vols., ed. W. Bolin und F. Jodl, Leipzig, 1903–11; 2nd edn.
    1959.

Friedrich, M., *Philosophie und Ökonomie beim jungen Marx*, Berlin, 1960.

Garewicz, J., *August Cieszkowski w oczach Niemców . . . (August Cieszkowski in the eyes of the
    Germans)*, in *Polskie Spory o Hegla (Polish Controversies about Hegel)*, Warsaw, 1966.

Grégoire, Fr., *Aux sources de la pensée de Marx: Hegel, Feuerbach*, Louvain, 1947.

Hess, Moses, *Philosophische und sozialistische Schriften, 1837–1850*, ed. A. Cornu und W. Monke,
    Berlin, 1961.

Hillmann, G., *Marx und Hegel*, Frankfurt, 1966.

Hook, S., *From Hegel to Marx*, Ann Arbor, 1962 (1st edn. 1936).

Hyppolite, J., *Études sur Marx et Hegel*, Paris, 1955 (Eng. trans. 1969).

Istituto G. Feltrinelli, *Annali*, vii, 1964–5 (contains a bibliography).

Jodl, F., *Ludwig Feuerbach*, Stuttgart, 1921.

Kühne, W., *August Graf von Cieszkowski*, 1938.

Löwith, K., *Die Hegelsche Linke*, Stuttgart, 1962.

    Von Hegel zu Nietzsche, Stuttgart, 1959.

McLellan, D., *Marx before Marxism*, London, 1970.

Maguire, J., *Marx's Paris Writings: An Analysis*, Dublin, 1972.

Panasiuk, R., *Filozofia i Państwo. Studium myśli polityczno-społecznej lewicy heglowskiej i
    młodego Marksa 1838–1841 (Philosophy and State. A Study of the Social and Political
    Thought of the Hegelian Left and the Young Marx 1838–1841)*, Warsaw, 1967 (with a good
    bibliography).

Popitz, H., *Der entfremdete Mensch*, Basle, 1953.

Rosen, Z., *Bruno Bauer and Karl Marx. The Influence of Bruno Bauer on Marx's Thought*, The Hague, 1977.

Silberner, E., *Moses Hess. An annotated Bibliography*, New York, 1951.

Strauss, D. F., *Das Leben Jesu*, 2 vols., Tübingen, 1835–6.

Streitschriften zur Verteidigung meiner Schrift über das Leben Jesu, Tübingen, 1838.

Die christliche Glaubenslehre, 2 vols., 1840–1.

Thier, E., *Das Menschenbild des jungen Marx*, Göttingen, 1957.

Tschiżewskij, D., *Hegel bei den Slaven*, Reichenberg, 1934.

Tucker, R. C., *Philosophy and Myth in Karl Marx*, Cambridge, 1961.

Walicki, A., 'Cieszkowski–filozoficzna systematyzacja mesjanizmu' ('Cieszkowski–a Philosophical Systematization of Messianism'), in *Filozofia Polska (Polish Philosophy)*, Warsaw, 1967.

'Two Polish Messianists: Adam Mickiewicz and August Cieszkowski', in *Oxford Slavonic Papers*, vol. ii, Oxford, 1969.

Złocisti, T., *Moses Hess, der Vorkämpfer des Sozialismus und Zionismus*, Berlin, 1921.

Żółtowski, A., *August Graf von Cieszkowski's Philosophie der Tat*, Posen, 1904.

V Pre-Marxian Socialism

Abendroth, Wolfgang, *Sozialgeschichte der europäischen Arbeiterbewegung*, 1965.

Advielle, V., *Histoire de Gracchus Babeuf et du babouvisme*, Paris, 1884.

Angrand, P., *Étienne Cabet et la République de 1848*, Paris, 1948.

Babeuf, G., *Textes choisis*, Préf. et Comment. par G. et I. Willard, Paris, 1950.

Beer, M., *A History of British Socialism*, London, 1953.

Bernstein, S., *The Beginning of Marxian Socialism in France*, New York, 1965.

Blanc, L., *Organisation du travail*, Paris, 1839.

Le Socialisme. Droit au travail, Paris, 1848.

Blanqui, A., *Critique sociale*, 2 vols., Paris, 1885.

Bouglé, C., *La Sociologie de Proudhon*, Paris, 1911.

Bravo, G. M., *Wilhelm Weitling e il communismo tedesco prima del quarantotto (Wilhelm Weitling and German Communism before '48)*, Turin, 1963.

Les Socialistes avant Marx, 3 vols., Paris, 1970 (an anthology, with a copious bibliography).

Charléty, S., *Histoire du saint-simonisme*, Paris, 1931.

Cole, G. D. H., *The Life of Robert Owen*, London, 1930.

Cole, M. I., *Robert Owen of New Lanark*, London, 1953.

Del Bo, G., *Charles Fourier e la scuola societaria. Saggio bibliografico (Charles Fourier and the 'societaria' School. A Bibliographical Essay)*, Milan, 1957.

Dommanget, M., *Les Idées politiques et sociales d'Auguste Blanqui*, Paris, 1957.

Victor Considérant. Sa Vie, son œuvre, Paris, 1929.

Fourier, Ch., *Œuvres complètes*, Paris, 1841–5.

Fournières, E., *Les Théories socialistes au XIXe siècle de Babeuf à Proudhon*, Paris, 1904.

Garewicz, J., *Między marzeniem a wiedzą. Początki myśli socjalistycznej w Niemczech (Between Dream and Knowledge. Beginnings of Socialist Thought in Germany)*, Warsaw, 1975.

Gray, A., *The Socialist Tradition*, London, 1963.

Gurvitch, G., *Proudhon, sociologue*, Paris, 1955.

Les Fondateurs français de la sociologie contemporaine: Saint-Simon et P. J. Proudhon, Paris, 1955.

Proudhon et Marx: une confrontation, Paris, 1964.

Halévy, E., *Histoire du socialisme européen*, Paris, 1948.

Harris, D., *Socialist Origins in the United States. American Forerunners of Marx 1817–1832*, 1966.

Harrison, J. F. C, *Robert Owen and the Owenites in Britain and America*, London, 1969.

Harvey, R. H., *Robert Owen, Social Idealist*, Berkeley, 1949.

Jackson, J. H., *Marx, Proudhon and European Socialism*, New York, 1962.

Labrousse, C. E., *Le Movement ouvrier el les théories sociales en France de 1815 à 1848*, Paris, 1861.

Landauer, C., *European Socialism*, Berkeley, 1959.

Leroy, M., *Le Socialisme des producteurs. Henri de Saint-Simon*, Paris, 1924.

    Histoire des idées sociales en France, 2nd edn., Paris, 1962.

Lichtheim, G., *The Origins of Socialism*, London, 1969.

Loubère, L. A., *Louis Blanc. His Life and his Contribution to the Rise of French Jacobin-Socialism*, Evanston, 1961.

Manuel, F. E., *The New World of Henri Saint-Simon*, Cambridge, Mass., 1956.

    The Prophets of Paris, Cambridge, Mass., 1962.

Mazauric, C., *Babeuf et la conspiration pour l'égalité*, Paris, 1962.

Morton, A. L., *The Life and Ideas of Robert Owen*, London, 1962.

Owen, R., *A New View of Society, and Other Writings*, Intro. by G. D. H. Cole, London, 1927.

    The Book of the New Moral Worlds, London, 1836–1844.

    The Future of the Human Race, London, 1853.

Pollard, S. and Salt, J., (eds.), *Robert Owen. Prophet of the Poor*, London, 1971.

Proudhon, P. J., *Œuvres complètes*, Paris, 1923, ff. (incomplete).

Renard, E., *Bibliographie relative à Louis Blanc*, Toulouse, 1922.

    Louis Blanc, sa vie, son œuvre, Paris, 1928.

Spitzer, A. B., *The Revolutionary Theories of L. A. Blanqui*, New York, 1957.

Saint-Simon, H., *Œuvres de Saint-Simon et d'Enfantin*, 47 vols., Paris, 1865–78.

    Selected Writings, trans. F. M. H. Markham, Oxford, 1952.

Talmon, J. L., *The Origins of Totalitarian Democracy*, London, 1952.

Vidalenc, J., *Louis Blanc*, Paris, 1948.

Walch, J., *Bibliographie du saint-simonisme*, Paris, 1967.

Weitling, W., *Das Evangelium eines armen Sünders. Die Menschheit wie sie ist und wie sie sein sollte*, ed. W. Schäfer, Reinbek bei Hamburg, 1971.

Wittke, C., *The Utopian Communist. A Biography of W. Weitling, Nineteenth Century Reformer*, Louisiana State U.P., 1950.

VI The First International, Bakunin, Lassalle

Archives Bakounine, Textes établis et annotés par Arthur Lehning, The Hague, 1961 ff.

Bakunin, M., *Œuvres*, 6 vols., Paris, 1895–1913.

    Gesammelte Werke, 3 vols., Berlin, 1921–4.

    Sobranie sochineniy i pisem (Collected Works and Letters), ed. Y. Steklov, 4 vols., Moscow, 1934–5.

Braunthal, J., *History of the International*, vol. i, 1864–1914, London, 1966.

Carr, E. H., *Michael Bakunin*, London, 1937.

Collins, M. and Abramsky, C., *Karl Marx and the British Labour Movement*, London, 1965.

Footman, D., *Ferdinand Lassalle*, New York, 1969.

Freymond, J. (ed.), *La Première Internationale*, 2 vols., Geneva, 1962.

Guillaume, J., *Karl Marx, pangermaniste, et l' Association Internationale des Travailleurs de 1864 à 1870*, Paris, 1915.

Lassalle, Ferdinand, *Gesammelte Reden und Schriften*, 12 vols., hg. und eingeleitet von E. Bernstein, Berlin, 1919–20.

    Reden und Schriften . . . im Auswahl, hg. von H. Feigl, Vienna, 1920.

Lehning, A., *From Buonarroti to Bakunin, Studies in International Socialism*, London, 1970.

Molnar, M., *Le Déclin de la Première Internationale*, Geneva, 1963.
Oncken, H., *Lassalle. Zwischen Marx und Bismarck*, Stuttgart, 1966 (1st edn. 1904).
Pyziur, E., *The Doctrine of Anarchism of M. A. Bakunin*, Milwaukee, 1955.
Ramm, T. (ed.), *Der Frühsozialismus*, Stuttgart, 1955.
Temkin, H., *Bakunin i antynomie wolności (Bakunin and the Antinomies of Freedom)*, Warsaw, 1964.

VII Various Aspects of Marx's and Engels's Doctrines

Avineri, S., *The Social and Political Thought of Karl Marx*. Cambridge, 1968.
Amsterdamski, S., *Engels*, Warsaw, 1965.
Becker, W., *Kritik der Marxschen Wertlehre*, Hamburg, 1972.
Bober, M. M., *Karl Marx's Interpretation of History*, Cambridge, Mass., 1950.
Bottomore, T., *The Sociological Theory of Marxism*, London, 1972.
Croce, B., *Historical Materialism and the Economics of Karl Marx*, London, 1922.
Dahrendorf, R., *Marx in Perspektive. Die Idee des Gerechten im Denken von Karl Marx*, Hanover, 1952.
Eilstein, H. (ed.), *Jedność materialna świata (The Material Unity of the World)*, Warsaw, 1961.
Feuer, L. S., *Marx and the Intellectuals*, New York, 1969.
Fleischer, H., *Marxismus und Geschichte*, Frankfurt, 1969 (Eng. trans. 1973).
Gamble, A. and Walton, P., *From Alienation to Surplus Value*, London, 1972.
Heller, A., *The Theory of Need in Marx*, London, 1976.
Hommes, J., *Der technische Eros: das Wesen der materialistischen Geschichtsauffassung*, Freiburg, 1955.
Horowitz, D. (ed), *Marx and Modern Economics*, London, 1968.
Jaroslawski, J., *Theorie der sozialistischen Revolution von Marx bis Lenin*, Hamburg, 1973.
Kamenka, E., *The Ethical Foundation of Marxism*, London, 1963.
Kedrov, B. M., *Engels i dialektika yestestvoznania (Engels and the Dialectics of Natural Science)*, Moscow, 1970.
Klages, H., *Technischer Humanismus*, Stuttgart, 1964.
Krajewski, W., *Engels o ruchu materii i jego prawidłowości (Engels on the Movement of Matter and its Laws)*, Warsaw, 1973.
Lifshitz, M., *Karl Marx und die Aesthetik*, Dresden, 1967.
Lobkowicz, N., *Theory and Practice. The History of a Marxist Concept*, Notre Dame, 1967.
Mandel, E., *The Formation of the Economic Thought of Karl Marx*, London, 1971.
Morawski, S., *Il Marxismo e l'estetica (Marxism and Aesthetics)*, Rome, 1973.
Ollman, B., *Alienation: Marx's Critique of Man in Capitalist Society*, Cambridge, 1971.
Plamenatz, J., *Karl Marx's Philosophy of Man*, Oxford, 1975.
Post, W., *Kritik der Religion bei Karl Marx*, Munich, 1969.
Prawer, S. S., *Karl Marx and World Literature*, Oxford, 1976.
Reiprich, K., *Die philosophisch-naturwissenschaftlichen Arbeiten von Karl Marx und Friedrich Engels*, Berlin, 1969.
Robinson, J., *An Essay in Marxian Economics*, 2nd edn., London, 1967.
Rosdolsky, R., *Zur Entstehungsgeschichte des Marxschen 'Kapitals'*, Frankfurt, 1968.
Schmidt, A., *Der Begriff der Natur in der Lehre von Karl Marx*, Frankfurt, 1962 (Eng. trans. 1971).
Schwann, G., *Die Gesellschaftskritik von Karl Marx*, Stuttgart, 1974.
Tucker, R., *The Marxian Revolutionary Idea*, London, 1970.
Witt-Hansen, J., *Historical Materialism: the Method, the Theories*, New York, 1960.

BOOK TWO

THE
GOLDEN AGE

Bibliographical Note

Sources of quotations used in the text:

Lenin, V. I., *Collected Works*, 45 vols., Lawrence & Wishart, London, 1960–70.
McLellan, D., *Karl Marx: Early Texts*, Blackwell, Oxford, 1971.
Marx, K., *Capital*, Lawrence & Wishart, London, 1974.
Sorel, G., *Reflections on Violence*, trans. T. E. Hulme and J. Roth, The Free Press, Glencoe, Ill., 1950.
Trotsky, L., *The Defence of Terrorism*, Labour Publishing Co. and Allen & Unwin, London, 1921.

I

Marxism and the Second International

THE PERIOD of the Second International (1889–1914) may be called without exaggeration the golden age of Marxism. Marxist doctrine had been clearly enough defined to constitute a recognizable school of thought, but it was not so rigidly codified or subjected to dogmatic orthodoxy as to rule out discussion or the advocacy of rival solutions to theoretical and tactical problems.

Certainly the Marxist movement cannot, at this time or at any other, be identified simply with the ideology of the socialist parties that belonged to the International. The many sources of European socialism had by no means dried up, though they seemed of little importance compared with the apparently self-consistent, universally applicable theories of Marx. Only in Germany was it possible, despite the strong tradition of Lassalleanism, to frame and maintain for a considerable time a uniform ideology based on Marxist premises, or what were generally regarded as such. The French party led by Guesde could lay claim to orthodoxy inasmuch as its programme had been drawn up under Marx's own auspices and with his assistance; but the French socialist movement was in a state of disruption for some time, and the Marxist tradition was more lively in some sections than in others. In Austria, Russia, Poland, Italy, Spain, and Belgium, and wherever else there was a working-class socialist movement, its ideology was permeated by Marxism to a greater or lesser degree. The influence of Marxism was least strong in Britain, the country in which its basic doctrine had been formulated: British socialism owed far more of its character to the ideas of Owen, Bentham, and J. S. Mill. In Europe generally, to be a socialist was not necessarily to be a Marxist, but, except in Britain, socialist theory was in general the work of men who called themselves Marxists, though each understood the term in his own way. There was no clear distinction between theorists and practical socialists: in addition to the many theoreticians, party leaders such as Bebel, Guesde, Victor Adler, and Turati, who were not intellectuals and had no ambition to develop socialist theory on their own account, were nevertheless educated men and quite capable of joining in theoretical discussions. The general intellectual calibre of party leaders never again reached such a high level, either among social democrats or communists. Marxism seemed to be at the height of its intellectual impetus. It was not the religion of an isolated sect, but the ideology of a powerful political movement; on the other hand, it had no means of silencing its opponents, and the facts of political life obliged it to defend its position in the realm of theory.

In consequence, Marxism appeared in the intellectual arena as a serious doctrine which even its adversaries respected. It had redoubtable defenders such as Kautsky, Rosa Luxemburg, Plekhanov, Bernstein, Lenin, Jaurès, Max Adler, Bauer, Hilferding, Labriola, Pannekoek, Vandervelde, and Cunow, but also such eminent critics as Croce, Sombart, Masaryk, Simmel, Stammler, Gentile, Böhm-Bawerk, and Peter Struve. Its influence extended beyond the immediate circle of the faithful, to historians, economists, and sociologists who did not profess Marxism as a whole but adopted particular Marxist ideas and categories.

The main characteristics of Marxist doctrine were of course connected with its social situation and political function. There were many factors which contributed to its development as an ideology of the workers' movement, but at the same time, as that development was affected by current political pressures, its scope was in some respects limited. The quarter-century of the Second International saw the publication of many important theoretical works on the general problems of historical materialism, the Marxist interpretation of particular ages and historical events, and the economics of imperialism. A Marxist school of aesthetics and art criticism came into being (Plekhanov, Lafargue, Mehring, Klara Zetkin, and Henriette Roland Holst), and works were published on the theory of religion and ethnology (Cunow, Krzywicki, and Kelles-Krauz). There was, however, no such efflorescence in the more strictly philosophical fields of epistemology and anthropology. Those who considered themselves Marxists may be divided into two groups according to their attitude towards the philosophical premises of Marxism. One group took the view that Marxism was a theory of social development and especially of capitalist society and its inevitable collapse, and that this theory could without inconsistency be supplemented and enriched by philosophical doctrines derived from other sources, in particular Kantianism and positivism. They thus attempted to link historical materialism with Kantian ethics (as in ethical socialism) or empiriocritical epistemology (for example, the Russian Machists and Friedrich Adler). The orthodox majority, however, maintained that Marxist doctrine itself contained the answers to all or most of the problems of philosophy, and that Engels's works, in particular the *Anti-Dühring* and *Ludwig Feuerbach*, were the natural completion of Marx's economic and sociological theories. Those who thus regarded Marxism as a single, uniform theoretical whole—for instance, Kautsky, Plekhanov, and Lenin—did not add much to Engels's popular philosophy and were generally content to echo his summary conclusions or apply them to the criticism of new idealistic trends. After Engels's death the German socialists published many of Marx's works that were not previously known—

such as *The Theory of Surplus Value*, part of *The German Ideology*, correspondence with Engels and others, and the doctoral dissertation—but other texts of great philosophical value remained unpublished, for instance the Paris Manuscripts of 1844, the *Critique of Hegel's Philosophy of Right*, and the *Grundrisse*. Attempts were made, by Sorel and Brzozowski among others, to distinguish the materialism of Engels from Marxian anthropology, but these were not in the main stream of Marxism and played no decisive role. On the whole, therefore, Marxism as a general philosophical theory remained a dead letter or took the form of eclecticism, despite the vast body of literature interpreting the premisses of historical materialism. The *Theses on Feuerbach* were known and quoted, but rather as pieces of rhetoric than as statements to be seriously analysed. Categories such as alienation, reification, and praxis, which are today so frequently met with, received scarcely any mention in Marxist literature.

The Second International was not a uniform, centralized organization with an elaborate body of doctrine acknowledged by all its members, but rather a loose federation of parties and trade unions, working separately though united by their belief in socialism. Nevertheless, the International seemed to be the first true embodiment of Marx's dream, which was also Lassalle's, of a marriage between socialist theory and the workers' movement, between the class struggle and the scientific analysis of social processes—two phenomena of independent origin, condemned to impotence unless they could achieve this state of symbiosis or identity. Although non-Marxist traditions of socialism had not lost their strength (Lassalleanism in Germany, Proudhonism and Blanquism in France, anarchism in Italy and Spain, utilitarianism in Britain), it was Marxism that stood out as the dominant form of the workers' movement and the true ideology of the proletariat. Unlike the First International, which was an ideological centre rather than an organization of the workers' movement, the Second was an assemblage of parties representing the masses.

What, however, did it mean to be a Marxist in the twenty-five years preceding the First World War? In relation to the stereotypes of the period, the notion of Marxism may be most simply defined by enumerating some classic ideas that distinguished Marxists from the adherents of all forms of utopian socialism and anarchism, and *a fortiori* from liberal and Christian doctrines. A Marxist was one who accepted the following propositions:

· · ·

THE tendencies of capitalist society, in particular the concentration of capital, have activated the natural tendency of the historical process towards socialism, which is either the unavoidable or the most probable consequence of the processes of accumulation.

Socialism involves public ownership of the means of production and thereby the abolition of exploitation and unearned income, of privilege and inequality deriving from the unequal distribution of wealth. There must be no discrimination of race, nationality, sex, or religion, and no standing armies. There must be equal opportunities for education, democratic freedom for all—freedom of speech and assembly, popular representation at all levels—and a comprehensive system of social welfare.

Socialism is in the interest of all mankind and will make possible the universal development of culture and welfare, but the standard-bearer in the fight for socialism is the working class as the immediate producer of all basic values and as the class most strongly and directly interested in abolishing wage-labour.

The advance towards socialism calls for an economic and political struggle on the part of the proletariat, which must fight for the short-term improvement of its lot within the capitalist system and must make use of all political forms, expecially parliamentary ones; in order to fight for socialism, the proletariat must organize itself into independent political parties.

Capitalism cannot be radically altered by the accumulation of reforms, and its catastrophic consequences of depression, poverty, and unemployment are unavoidable. Nevertheless, the proletariat must fight for reforms in the shape of labour legislation, democratic institutions, and higher wages, since these make conditions more tolerable and also provide training in class solidarity and in the technique of battles to come.

Capitalism will finally be swept away by revolution, when economic conditions under capitalism and the class-consciousness of the proletariat are ripe for this. The revolution, however, is not a *coup d'état* to be carried out by a handful of conspirators, but must be the work of an overwhelming majority of the labouring population.

The interests of the proletariat are identical on the world scale, and the socialist revolution will come as an international event, at all events in the advanced industrial societies.

In human history, technical progress is the deciding factor in bringing about changes in the class structure, and these changes determine the basic features of political institutions and the reigning ideology.

Socialism is not only a political programme but a world-view based on the premiss that reality is susceptible of scientific analysis. Only rational observation can reveal the nature of the world and the meaning of history. Religious and spiritualist doctrines are the expression of a 'mystified' consciousness and are bound to disappear when exploitation and class antagonisms are abolished. The world is subject to natural laws and not to any kind of Providence; man is the work of nature and is to be studied accordingly, although the rules that govern his being cannot be simply reduced to those of the pre-human universe.

■   ■   ■

THE main lines of Marxist doctrine as thus formulated were, however, open to important differences of interpretation, and in certain conditions these led to the formation, within Marxism, of political movements and theoretical positions that were radically hostile to one another. Within the framework of the general definition it was possible to hold quite different views as to, for example, the degree of validity of historical materialism or the relationship between the 'base' and the 'superstructure'. Socialism might be regarded either as a 'natural inevitability' or as a possibility within the historical tendency of the capitalist economy. The struggle for reform might be treated as valuable in itself or merely as training for the revolution to come. It was possible to advocate the political exclusivism of socialist parties or to admit, with greater or less freedom, the legitimacy of alliances of various kinds with non-socialist movements. The revolution could be envisaged either as a civil war or as the result of non-violent pressure by the majority. It was possible to hold either that the socialist world-view was an all-embracing, self-contained system providing the answer to every important philosophical question, or that philosophical criticism might draw freely on pre-Marxist or non-Marxist thought in respect of questions that Marxism itself did not decide one way or the other. All these differences were of great importance in defining the objectives and policy of socialist parties. The latter were not mere discussion groups but had to take many practical decisions. They were constantly confronted by situations which Marx's doctrine had, so to speak, not foreseen; this obliged them to draw particular conclusions from the master's principles, and they did not always agree as to the mode of doing so.

From the doctrinal point of view the most important stages of theoretical development in the Second International may be reduced to three: the struggle against anarchism and revisionism in the first and second phases respectively, and the conflict between orthodoxy and the left wing after the Russian Revolution of 1905. From the point of view of the fate of Marxism and the socialist movement the decisive conflict was of course that waged against revisionism in all its ramifications. (In these introductory remarks we take no account of Russia, which requires separate and more detailed treatment.)

The most important factors of the European situation affecting the development of socialist thought during the period of the Second International may be summarized briefly as the retreat from liberalism in ideology and economic practice; the democratization of political institutions, especially the introduction of equal and universal suffrage in many European states; the economic expansion of Western Europe; and the growth of imperialist tendencies.

The decline of liberalism was expressed above all in the abandonment of two principles that had been fundamental to liberal social philosophy. The first of these laid down that the main function of state institutions was to protect the safety, freedom, and property of the individual: questions of production and exchange lay outside their competence and should be left to private initiative, which gave the best assurance of prosperity. The second, more specific principle was that the relationship between the employer and the wage-earner was a particular kind of free contract between free individuals and must be left subject to the laws of such contracts: it was an infringement of freedom for the law to interfere in labour agreements or for trade unions to exert collective pressure on employers to improve conditions. These two principles, expressing what may be called the 'pure' doctrine of capitalism and free competition, were scarcely defended by anyone in the closing years of the nineteenth century. This was partly the result of socialist propaganda and partly because changes in the world economy had made the ideal of unrestricted free trade unworkable. Socialist ideas had effectively destroyed the fiction that the employer and the wage-earner met on equal terms, and most liberal theorists had also abandoned this position. It was consequently recognized as the right and duty of legislative bodies to regulate the system of wage contracts and restrict certain forms of exploitation, and it was equally conceded that workers were entitled to form associations for the collective defence of their interests against employers.

The recognition of the principle of state intervention between workers and employers, and the possibility of exerting pressure through freely elected legislative bodies, faced the socialist parties of Western Europe with a situation to which Marxist strategy provided no clear-cut answer. If socialists became members of bourgeois parliaments and helped to pass laws in the working-class interest, were they not participating in the reform of capitalism? The anarchists charged them with doing so and admitting, by implication, that capitalism was remediable, whereas Marx had stated the contrary. To this the orthodox replied that capitalism could not be reformed in the sense that it would cease to be capitalism and evolve of its own accord into a socialist order, but it was nevertheless essential to fight for the improvement of workers' conditions under capitalism so as to develop their class-consciousness. Workers who were left to the mercy of capitalists, deprived of education and stupefied by toil, would never be capable of playing their part in the socialist revolution.

The dilemma was especially acute as regards temporary alliances with non-socialist parliamentary groups. If the socialists refused, on principle, any association with parties of the centre, they lost all hope of obtaining concessions in the interest of the working class and were in practice favouring the conservatives and the right wing. But if they agreed to such associations it meant co-operating with the bourgeoisie to improve the capitalist system, and thereby blunting the edge of class antagonism. In countries such as Russia, where the parliamentary system either did not exist or was ineffectual from the socialist point of view, this problem scarcely arose: parliament might be a sounding-board for propaganda, but could not be looked to for effective social reform. But where such reforms proved to be practicable, it was hard to draw a line between the struggle to improve conditions and 'reformism' in the pejorative sense. The anarchists held that any form of political action, especially in parliament, demoralized the workers by suggesting that capitalism was changing for the better; the distinction drawn between one bourgeois party and another obscured, in the eyes of the proletariat, the basic cleavage between hostile classes. To this the orthodox retorted that it was not a matter of indifference to the future of socialism whether the workers lived in an empire, a tyranny, or a republic. It was not contrary to the principles of the class struggle to defend republicanism and bourgeois democracy against reaction, clericalism, and military cliques: a bourgeois republic could not itself carry out the socialist programme, but it provided better conditions for the proletariat to carry on the fight.

The history of the socialist movement is that of a continuing debate between these two points of view. Either side could find statements by Marx supporting its attitude. If it were held that the proletariat does not belong to bourgeois society and cannot amend that society, but only destroy it—that the natural laws of capitalist production operate against the workers, and that this state of things can no more be altered than physical bodies can be made to fall up instead of down—then any struggle for reform, any temporary parliamentary alliance, any distinction between one bourgeois party and another is a betrayal of the proletariat and an abandonment of the revolution. But, on the other hand, did not Marx expressly reject Lassalle's view that all the non-proletarian classes form a single reactionary mass? Did he not approve of the proletariat fighting not for total revolution but for democratic rights or factory laws, and did he not condemn the absurd principle 'The worse, the better'?

The anarchists, and particularly the anarcho-syndicalists, set their faces against parliamentary tactics and any idea of reforming capitalism or coming to terms with the bourgeoisie. The older generation of orthodox socialists, such as Guesde, and the young German Left accepted the need for political action but were against temporary alliances, and they regarded the struggle for reforms as valuable not in itself but only in relation to the ultimate aim. The orthodox of the centre persuasion accepted political alliances provided the working-class party remained fully independent, and they recognized the fight for short-term objectives as valid in itself. The right wing (Jaurès, Turati) were not only prepared to come to terms with anyone in the immediate interest of the proletariat, but regarded reforms within capitalist society as having a socialist significance, i.e. as implanting elements of socialism in the midst of bourgeois reality. There was a clear divide between the syndicalists and the rest of the movement, as there was between the socialism of Jaurès and the orthodox position. Between intermediate schools of thought the barriers were more fluid and made themselves felt occasionally, in particular controversies.

Throughout its existence the Second International was dominated by German social democracy. The German socialist movement was the most numerous and uniform and the best equipped doctrinally. Lassalle's party founded in 1863 enjoyed considerable support among the workers even after the death of its leader, but it did not produce any outstanding theoreticians or men of action. It held dogmatically to the views of its founder, who thought the social question could be solved by establishing producer co-operatives with the help of the state and gradually eliminating the system of hired labour. For this purpose Lassalle believed that the working class would first have to gain a parliamentary majority, and the prospect of this was so remote that the party's programme seemed devoid of practical content. A new party, the Sozialdemokratische Arbeiterpartei, was formed in 1869 at Eisenach under the aegis of August Bebel and Wilhelm Liebknecht. Bebel (1840–1913) was a turner by occupation and spent some years in his youth as a travelling journeyman, but at an early age became active in workers' associations at Leipzig. There in 1864 he met Liebknecht (1826–1900), who acted as a mentor to his younger friend and introduced him to Marxist theory. Liebknecht had lived abroad for a dozen years after the 1848 Revolution: he met Marx and Engels in England and adopted their social theories. Bebel and Liebknecht were subsequently elected to the Reichstag and opposed the war with France and the annexation of Alsace and Lorraine. Bebel was not a theoretician, but his chief work apart from memoirs, *Die Frau und der Sozialismus* (1883; translated as *Woman under Socialism*), was popular with two or three generations of socialists: its importance was that it led the socialist movement as a whole to embrace the cause of women's emancipation and equal rights. Bebel enjoyed moral authority in the German and European socialist movement and displayed tactical skill in the intricate disputes that arose within the party. He was concerned above all to preserve unity, and it was mainly thanks to his influence that the later conflict with revisionism did not disrupt the party organization.

In 1875 the Lassalle and Eisenach parties united at Gotha to form the Socialist Workers' party. The Gotha Programme, severely criticized by Marx, was a compromise between Lassalle's strategy and Marxism, in which the former's basic principles were maintained; in practice, however, the influence of Marxism was increasingly strong. Neither Bebel nor Liebknecht was a doctrinaire by nature: they accepted the fundamental principles of Marxian socialism, but were not interested in the absolute correctness of theoretical formulas without direct application to the practical struggle. They believed that socialism would eventually conquer by revolutionary means, but this was more a general hope than a political directive. Between them they organized the German socialist movement into a powerful force which set an example to the rest of Europe.

In 1878 Bismarck used the pretext of an attack on the Emperor's life to enact an emergency law prohibiting socialist meetings and publications and dissolving local party organizations. Many leaders were forced to emigrate, but the party did not give in and, as was seen in due course, managed to maintain and extend its influence. At this time Kautsky founded at Stuttgart the monthly *Die Neue Zeit*, ostensibly a private venture, which became a focus for the whole European Marxist Movement. Bernstein at Zurich edited the *Sozialdemokrat*, a less theoretical publication which became one of the chief organs of party life during the period of repression. The Anti-Socialist Law was repealed in 1890, and in that year the party obtained a million and a half votes at the polls and 35 seats in the Reichstag. In the following year the Congress at Erfurt adopted a new programme drafted by Kautsky and Bernstein: this was purged of Lassalleanism and faithfully reflected Marxist doctrine in the current version approved by Engels. It asserted that capital was bound to become more concentrated, squeezing out small businesses and accentuating the class struggle. It spoke of the exploitation of the proletariat, economic crises, and the growing incompatibility between private ownership of the means of production and the efficient use of existing technology. The programme set out the need to fight for reforms in preparation for the revolution which would bring about the socialization of property and the subordination of all production to social needs. It also declared the unity of proletarian interests on a world scale. A second section dealt with practical objectives: universal and equal suffrage, a direct, secret ballot, proportional representation; replacement of the standing army by a people's militia; freedom of speech and assembly; equal rights for women; secular, free, and compulsory education; religion to be treated as a private matter; free legal aid, election of judges and magistrates; abolition of the death penalty; free medical care; progressive taxation; an eight-hour working day; no child labour under fourteen years of age; supervision of working conditions.

It soon became evident that the relationship between the practical and the theoretical part of the programme was far from clear. The dispute between the orthodox and the revisionists may be reduced to the question which part of the Erfurt Programme truly expressed the party's mind and policy.

The second pillar of the International was France. French socialism had a richer and more varied tradition than that of Germany, but was in consequence more subject to ideological disputes, and Marxist doctrine did not enjoy a monopoly position. The Parti Ouvrier Français led by Guesde was fundamentally closer to German social democracy. Jules Guesde (1845–1922; real name Jules Bazile) grew up under the Second Empire, which he hated from his early years, and soon became a republican and atheist. From 1867 he worked as a journalist for various republican publications, and in 1870 he helped to found *Les Droits de l'homme*, a democratic but not socialist journal. Sentenced to five years' imprisonment for supporting the Commune, he escaped to Switzerland, where he encountered Bakuninist groups and spread anarchistic ideas among French *émigrés*. He was still an anarchist while at Rome and Milan in 1872–6, but after returning to France became a Marxist and the chief organizer of the party founded on Marxist doctrine. In 1877–8 two workers' congresses were held in France, both dominated by reformist tendencies. The third, held at Marseilles in October 1879, adopted the main premisses of Marxian socialism and decided upon the creation of a workers' party. In May 1880 Guesde went to London to discuss the party programme with Marx, Engels, and Lafargue. This document, to which Marx himself wrote the theoretical introduction, was less elaborate than the subsequent Erfurt Programme, but embodied similar practical objectives. It was adopted with small amendments at a congress at Le Havre in November 1880, but it soon became clear that the party was by no means unanimous as to its interpretation. Some argued that the party should adjust its programme to real possibilities and only set itself tasks that could be carried out in the foreseeable future: these members were called 'possibilists' by their orthodox revolutionary opponents, and retorted by calling the latter 'impossibilists'. The former group was not interested in direct action towards the 'ultimate goal', but preferred to concentrate on local and municipal issues as the proper field of party activity. A split took place in 1881–2: the adherents of the Parti Ouvrier Français under Guesde took the line of awaiting a global revolution which would sweep away capitalism, while the possibilists in the Parti Socialiste Français set their sights on immediate objectives. The former emphasized the purely proletarian character of the movement and were basically opposed to alliances with non-socialist radicals, while the latter aimed to increase their influence among the petty bourgeoisie and were ready for local and tactical alliances of all kinds. There soon came into being a new group of possibilists led by Jean Allemane, which was essentially revolutionary but in the manner of Proudhon rather than Marx: unlike the followers of Guesde, this group disbelieved in the effectiveness of political action, but it was also opposed to the pure reformism of the possibilists. Meanwhile Blanqui had formed a group of his own, which was led after his death in 1881 by Édouard Vaillant. The Blanquist group eventually joined the Guesdists, but Vaillant continued to insist on the division between himself and the Marxists. Besides these four groups there were, at a later stage, independent socialists such as Jaurès and Millerand.

At the beginning of the twentieth century French socialism was divided into three main streams: the Parti Socialiste Français, with Jaurès as its chief ideol-

ogist, the Parti Socialiste de France (Guesdists and Blanquists), and the syndicalists. Of the first two groups, the Guesdists were concerned with prolaterian
purity and were opposed to tactical understandings with non-socialist parties,
or to intervention in disputes within the bourgeois camp. They disbelieved in
the value of reformist action and firmly rejected the idea that any reforms
within the existing system could be of significance for socialism. Jaurès and his
followers, on the other hand, while they saw the transition to socialism in terms
of revolution, believed that some socialist institutions could be established and
maintained in bourgeois society, as socialism was not the negation of republicanism but a development of its principles. They were also prepared to contract
alliances with non-socialist forces in the interests of any cause currently
defended by the socialists. The syndicalists, the least important of the three
groups, were opposed in principle to all political activity and especially to parliamentary action. Their periodical, the *Mouvement socialiste*, was edited from
1899 to 1914 by Hubert Lagardelle, and the chief ideologist of the movement,
although he stood outside it, was Georges Sorel. The Guesde and Jaurès groups
united in 1905, but this did not put an end to ideological differences within
French socialism.

Marxism, however, did not produce any important theoreticians in France
during the period of the Second International. Guesde was not a scholar, and
Lafargue, no doubt the chief French Marxist in the 'classic' sense of the term,
was more of a popularizer than an independent thinker. Jaurès and Sorel, who
were genuinely original writers, could only be called Marxists in a very loose
sense, but both influenced French intellectual life by their different interpretations of Marxism as well as in other ways.

British socialism, as already mentioned, was hardly affected by Marxian doctrine. Strictly speaking, there is nothing in the ideological basis of Fabianism
that can be called specifically Marxist. *Fabian Essays in Socialism* (1899), which
struck the keynote of British socialism for generations to come, comprised a
programme of reform which was either contrary to Marxist theory or rooted in
principles drawn from the general arsenal of nineteenth-century socialism. The
Fabians were not interested in social philosophy unless it was directly related
to feasible reforms. Their main ideals were equality and rational economic planning, and they believed that these could be achieved by democratic pressure
within the framework of existing political institutions and their gradual improvement. They accepted that the concentration of capital created the natural economic pre-conditions of socialism, but they believed that social reform and the
gradual limitation of unearned income would make it possible to give this
process a socialist sense without the revolutionary destruction of the existing
state. It would seem that in the course of time the idea of rational, scientific
social organization and economic efficiency came to loom larger in Fabian ide-

ology, at the expense of democratic values. Despite the great importance of the British movement in the history of socialism, it made no significant contribution at this time to the evolution of Marxist doctrine, except of course for the British role in the formation of European revisionism.

The Belgian socialist movement was more Marxist than the British, but less doctrinally consistent than the German. The Parti Ouvrier Belge, formed in 1885, had as its chief theoretician Émile Vandervelde (1866–1938), chairman of the International from 1900 to 1914. He considered himself a Marxist, but felt free to diverge on points of theory that he regarded as doctrinaire: Plekhanov, for one, denied that he was a Marxist at all. But he was not a leader of the type, common in the Second International, that was interested in doctrine only for its direct relation to political and reformist action. On the contrary, he strove after an 'integral' world-view and regretted that socialism, unlike Catholicism, had not evolved one. In *L'Idéalisme dans le marxisme* (1905) he gave an extremely loose interpretation of historical materialism, retaining only the general idea of the 'reciprocal influence' of all historical circumstances—technical, economic, political, and spiritual: a position which almost everyone at that time accepted, but which left no room for Marxian monism. He also argued, following Croce, that the term 'historical materialism' was misleading. No type of historical change was absolutely 'prior' to any other, and in different circumstances different kinds of change might give the initial impetus. Demographic processes or changes of geographical environment might of themselves affect social developments. Nor was it true that spiritual phenomena were simply the consequence of changes of economic structure: they could not exist outside that structure, just as a plant had to have soil in which to grow, but it was absurd to say that the soil was the cause of the plant. Technical development was itself conditioned by man's intellectual activity, which was a spiritual phenomenon. Moral factors, too, played an independent part in historical change: Marx and Engels, in attacking capitalism, had been moved by moral considerations. Historical materialism was a useful device for seeking out the hidden causes of social ideas and institutions, but it was wrong to regard it as providing the sole cause of the entire historical process. Arguing in this way Vandervelde rejected the determinist aspect of the doctrine, while accepting that the general tendency of capitalist economy led towards the socialization of industry. This did not mean that he accepted the theory of 'increasing misery', or of socialism as requiring the transfer of all production to public ownership, or, above all, the inevitability of revolution. On the contrary, all the signs were that socialism would come about gradually, in different ways and not necessarily in the same form everywhere. Socialization was not the same as nationalization: one of its most essential elements was the gradual elimination of political authority centralized in the state. The development of socialism was more likely to be aided by local groupings and forms of self-government which permitted genuine social control over the productive process. Vandervelde was not an outstanding theorist, and his views on theoretical questions are generally cursory and commonsensible. In politics he stood perhaps closest to Jaurès, but he had not the latter's analytical mind or rhetorical gifts.

The Austrian socialist movement was, next to the German, the most active from the theoretical point of view. The social democratic party, formed in 1888, was led for many years by Viktor Adler (1852–1918), a doctor by profession. He was not an original theorist, and on important questions generally took up a position near the centre of German orthodoxy. The great achievement of the Austrian party was the enactment of universal suffrage in 1907, an event helped to a large extent by the Russian Revolution. In the multinational Habsburg monarchy the social democrats had to cope incessantly with conflicts between nationalities, both in the state and in the party, and their ideologists naturally spent much time analysing the national problem from a Marxist point of view. The best-known writings on this subject are by Otto Bauer and Karl Renner. Both were leaders of so-called Austro-Marxism, a movement generally regarded as including also Max Adler, Rudolf Hilferding, Gustav Eckstein, and Adler's son Friedrich. The Austro-Marxists produced important theoretical works which, for the most part, were looked on askance by the orthodox, as they refused to treat Marxism as an all-embracing system and had no hesitation in combining it with other sources: in particular (though they were not alone in this) they sought to incorporate Kantian moral and epistemological categories into the Marxist philosophy of history. Most of them belonged to the generation born in the 1870s, as did Lenin, Trotsky, Rosa Luxemburg, and many other leaders of Russian socialism. Scarcely any of this generation were orthodox Marxists of the stamp of Kautsky, Plekhanov, Lafargue, and Labriola; the polarization which took place as a consequence was to be the ideological cause of the division of socialism into two hostile camps.

In Italy the workers' movement, after some false starts, achieved separate existence in opposition to anarchism in 1882, but it was not until 1893, after two changes of name, that it adopted a socialist programme in the Marxian sense. Its chief leader was Filippo Turati (1857–1932), who was not a theoretician but stood for a decidedly reformist policy, or 'gradualist' as it was then called. The only important Marxist theoreticians at this period of Italian socialism were Antonio Labriola and Enrico Ferri. The former represented the main stream of Marxist orthodoxy, while the latter was even more of a 'Darwinist' than Kautsky.

Poland, too, was an important centre of the Marxist movement. It may in fact be said that it was here that socialism for the first time split up in accordance, more or less, with the principles that subsequently divided social democracy from communism. The Social Democratic Party of the Kingdom of Poland (i.e. Russian Poland) and Lithuania, known from its Polish initials as SDKPiL, was the first independent party of communist type inasmuch as it emphasized the purely proletarian character of the socialist movement, refused to have anything to do with Polish (or any other) nationalism, and professed absolute fidelity to Marxian doctrine. On the other hand, it lacked the features which were to distinguish Lenin's form of social democracy, viz. the idea of the party as vanguard and the use of peasant demands as a weapon in the revolutionary struggle. The party's co-founder and chief theoretician was Rosa Luxemburg, but although of Polish birth she belongs essentially to the German socialist movement. Another theoretician of the SDKPiL was Julian Marchlewski, who studied the history of the physiocrats and also the theory of art. However, the main stream of Polish socialism was represented by the Polish Socialist party (PPS), which as a whole can hardly be considered Marxist; its chief Marxist theoretician was Kazimierz Kelles-Krauz. Ludwik Krzywicki, an unorthodox Marxist and the most eminent sociologist of his generation in Poland, was also close to the PPS. Another writer who belongs in part to Polish Marxist literature is Edward Abramowski, a philosopher and psychologist and a theoretician of the anarcho-cooperative movement. Finally a special place in the history of Marxism belongs to Stanisław Brzozowski, who made a highly original and unorthodox attempt to interpret Marx in terms of voluntarism and collective subjectivism.

The Dutch socialist movement began as a struggle on two fronts, being opposed on the one hand to Catholic trade unions based on the doctrines of Leo XIII's *Rerum Novarum* and, on the other, to a strong anarchist tendency whose chief exponent was Domela Nieuwenhuis. As in Poland, a strong leftist group arose within Dutch social democracy and eventually formed an independent party, the nucleus of the future Communist party. Its chief ideologist, Anton Pannekoek (1873–1960), was an implacable opponent of the 'parliamentary delusion' and the pitfalls of reformism, insisting that socialism required the violent overthrow of the bourgeois state machine and could not be built piecemeal in capitalist conditions. Pannekoek sided with Lenin at the Zimmerwald Conference in 1915, and later belonged to the left-wing, anti-parliamentary section of the Dutch Communist movement.

Although larger or smaller groups of Marxists were active in almost every European country, it is more or less true to say that the Marxist movement was a phenomenon of Central and Eastern Europe. The Second International can be called Marxist only in a very approximate sense, nor was it ever centrally organized and directed like the Comintern. The criteria for membership of the International were not clear-cut, as in some countries there was no clear division between political parties and trade union movements. Nevertheless, its inaugural congress at Paris in July 1889 was attended by the whole élite of European Marxism including Engels, although he had expressed in letters his misgivings at setting up an international organization. Strictly speaking, the conflict between the Guesdists and possibilists meant that the founding congress broke in two from the beginning, a fact which led to general confusion. Yet it was only the Marxist congress that really mattered to the subsequent history of socialism. Among the twenty countries represented were Germany (Bebel, Liebknecht, and others), France (Guesde, Vaillant), Russia (Plekhanov, Lavrov), Austria (Viktor Adler), Britain (William Morris), Belgium, Poland (Mendelson, Daszyński), and the Netherlands. Resolutions were passed concerning the eight-hour day, the replacement of standing armies by a general militia, the First of May holiday, the fight for social legislation and universal suffrage as a means to the seizure of power. From 1889 to 1900 the International had no real existence except in the form of successive congresses; at the fifth of these a permanent organ was set up, the International Socialist Bureau, but this was only a clearing-house for information, not a directive body. The list of congresses between 1889 and 1914 is: Brussels 1891, Zurich 1893, London 1896, Paris 1900, Amsterdam 1904, Stuttgart 1907, Copenhagen 1910, and Basle 1912.

The crucial issue during the first phase of the International, up to the London Congress, was the controversy with the anarchists. The latter had done much to break up the First International but, partly because of their own ideology, did not set up a lasting independent organization. Accordingly, the anarchist wing of the First International soon ceased to exist. In the early 1880s an anarchist association (the Alliance Internationale Ouvrière) came into existence, numbering among its members Kropotkin, Malatesta, and Élisée Reclus, but it had no precisely agreed doctrine or means of co-ordinated action. The anarchist movement was largely defined in negative terms, there being about as many sub-groups as there were individual writers or political activists. Their main common ground was the belief that human beings left to their own inclinations were capable of forming harmonious communities, but that the root of all evil lay in impersonal institutions and particularly the state. It might seem that the opposition of actual individuals to faceless institutions was in accordance with Marx's social philosophy, but the two cases are not the same. Marx believed that socialism would restore man's individual life in all its fullness and would do away with autonomized political organisms, thus replacing sham forms of community by the direct association of individuals. But he also held that the return to an 'organic' community could not consist in the mere liquidation of existing institutional forms, but required the reorganization of civil society on the basis of the technique and organization of labour created in the capitalist world. The state as an instrument of coercion would become superfluous, but not the centralized administration of material resources and production. In Marx's view the overthrow of the state and political authority did not imply the destruction of social and industrial organization; but he believed that the socialization of property would prevent the organization of society from degenerating into an apparatus of violence and a source of inequality. If the state were destroyed and the processes of production were at the same time handed over to the uncoordinated initiative of groups or individuals, the result would be bound to be a return to capitalism in all its forms.

This view of Marx's implies the existence of certain natural laws governing a commercial economy independently of the will of individuals. The anarchists, on the other hand, generally believed that the aptitude of human beings for friendly co-operation would prevent all injustice once the institutions of tyranny were swept away. Kropotkin, in his *Ethics* and in *Mutual Aid, a Factor of Evolution*, argued in opposition to the Darwinists that within a given species the law of life is not force and rivalry, but aid and co-operation: from this he drew the comforting conclusion that the natural inclinations of individuals would ensure the harmony of society. Only a few anarchists professed absolute egoism *à la* Stirner: the majority thought there was no basic conflict between individual interests, and that disputes would come to an end when men perceived their own nature and threw off the religious and political mystification and corruption that tyranny imposed upon them. Hence the anarchists often attacked Marxist socialism as a new form of tyranny designed to replace that of the bourgeoisie. The Marxists claimed that their objective was a social organization in which all forms of democracy would not only be preserved but would come into their own for the first time, as legal democracy was reinforced by democratic production; the state, however, as a means of organizing production, exchange, and communication could not be abolished without destroying society. To this the anarchists retorted that a 'democratic state' or a 'state based on freedom' was a contradiction in terms, since any form of state was bound to give rise to privilege, inequality, and violence. In the same way the anarchists were opposed to agitation for reforms such as the eight-hour day, since small concessions of this sort only served to strengthen and perpetuate the organization of oppression. Political action, too, in the sense of socialist parties engaging in current rivalries, elections, parliamentary contests, etc., was a fraud at the expense of the downtrodden classes. To seek the verdict of the ballot was to endorse the legality of existing political institutions. Thus the anarchists were equally opposed to the political struggle and to the economic struggle for immediate ends. They rested their hopes either on a transformation of the moral consciousness of the oppressed which would cause the breakdown of coercive institutions, or on a violent revolution engineered by a terrorist conspiracy. Their ideal was complete equality and the abolition of all organizational forms beyond the range of immediate democracy, i.e. the complete decentralization of public life. In addition the anarchists, and especially the syndicalists, were mistrustful of middle-class intellectuals in the revolutionary movement, as they suspected them of seeking to dominate the workers. Some anarchist groups professed violent hatred of intellectuals as such, of the whole body of scientific knowledge and art: it was the duty of the working class, they believed, to sever all continuity with culture as it had hitherto existed. This tendency was represented only by a few writers and groups, but it is in accordance with the spirit of a movement which sought to begin human history anew, to go back to the sixth day of creation and restore mankind to a state of paradisal purity.

The anarchists were influential in France, owing in part to Proudhonist tradition. They were stronger still in Spain and Italy, and had active groups in Holland and Belgium; they were least firmly rooted in Germany. At the Zurich and London congresses they were finally excluded from the International, since a rule was adopted confining membership to parties which accepted that political activity was indispensable.

In 1896–1900, between the London and Paris congresses, events took place which brought to light or exacerbated profound differences within the socialist movement: the Dreyfus case, the controversy over Millerand joining the Waldeck-Rousseau government of 1899–1902, and the debate over revisionism in Germany. The agitation over Dreyfus and 'ministerialism' might appear purely tactical, but in fact these issues involved fundamental questions of the class interpretation of the French socialist movement. Those who, headed by Jaurès, demanded that the party commit itself without reserve to the defence of Dreyfus argued that socialism, as the cause of all mankind and of the moral values created throughout history, must take up arms against injustice wherever it appeared, even if the victim was a member of the governing class. Guesde and his followers objected that if the party sprang to the defence of a particular member of the military caste it would blur the distinction between the proletarian party and bourgeois radicalism and, by weakening class-consciousness, would play into the hands of the bourgeoisie. The dispute, although it was not so formulated, can be seen as reflecting two different interpretations of Marxism. Marx himself, especially after his polemic with German 'true socialism', held that although socialism is the affair of all humanity and not just of a single class, the advance towards socialism is the concern of the working class and must therefore be inspired by its class-interests and not by humane moral values in general. This could be interpreted to mean that socialists should not get involved in conflicts that did not affect proletarian interests, especially those between different sections of the bourgeoisie who, by definition, could not be upholders of socialist values. It was possible, following Guesde, to defend the political exclusivism of the working class and treat the possessing classes as essentially a single, uniform, hostile camp. (Some socialists also pointed out that the party would suffer needlessly at the polls if it came out too strongly for Dreyfus, but Guesde rejected this consideration as unworthy.) But strategic and theoretical arguments could also be advanced, from a Marxist point of view, in the opposite direction. Marx did not accept the over-simple and ruinous principle that it was all one to the proletariat what kind of system prevailed until the day of revolution: on the contrary, he and Engels repeatedly distinguished between reaction and democracy, royalists and republicans, clericals and radicals in the political groupings of the propertied classes. As they were well aware, for the working class to look on passively while the bourgeois quarrelled among themselves not only brought the revolution no closer but condemned the workers to impotence. (A basically similar dispute, though more clearly articulated, was that between Russian Marxists on the role and participation of the working class in a bourgeois revolution.)

Jaurès, however, based himself on other grounds which were more doubtful from the Marxist point of view: viz. that the party must take an active part in all conflicts involving universal moral values because by defending those values it was building socialist reality in the midst of bourgeois society. While the *ouvriérisme* professed by Guesde and his followers was no doubt a false and over-simplified interpretation of Marxism, Jaurès was guilty of unorthodoxy when he represented the party's moral commitment as itself a realization of socialism. In Marx's view the socialist revolution was to be a violent breach of continuity with bourgeois institutions, and could certainly not be realized in whole or in part within bourgeois society. To an orthodox Marxist, then, it would seem that support for Dreyfus might be justified on strategic or tactical grounds but not on moral ones. On the other hand, it was hard to find a text in Marx stating that the revolution meant a breach of moral as well as institutional continuity. If Marx had taken this view, it would have implied that socialists enjoyed complete moral freedom *vis-à-vis* bourgeois society. But had not Engels on this very ground condemned Bakunin for treating all moral precepts as strategic weapons, holding, for instance, that the sanctity of contracts was a bourgeois prejudice? Here again, it was difficult to judge the question unequivocally by appealing to the fathers of scientific socialism.

The problem of Dreyfus was, however, less acute than it might have been inasmuch as none of the socialists found it necessary to pose the question 'For or against?' Moreover, not even Guesde proposed that the party should ignore the *Affaire* completely. The opponents of Dreyfus stood for black reaction, militarism, chauvinism, and anti-Semitism, and there were no two opinions about them in the socialist camp. The Millerand issue was a more delicate one, raising the question whether, and on what conditions, a socialist was justified in joining a bourgeois cabinet—in the present case, a cabinet which included among its members General Galliffet, the bloodthirsty suppressor of the Paris Commune. Those who defended Millerand's action argued that the presence of one socialist in the government could not alter its class character but might help to curb the more reactionary elements and promote reforms within the existing system, a policy which enjoyed the party's basic approval. The opponents of this view replied that the participation of a socialist confused the proletariat by giving the impression that the party was throwing in its lot with those in authority; moreover, it would mean that the party bore some responsibility for the actions of a bourgeois government.

The Millerand question was debated at the Paris Congress of the International in 1900, where Vandervelde, like Jaurès, argued that agreements between socialists and other parties were justifiable in defence of democratic freedoms (the issue of the Italian emergency laws) or the rights of the individual, or for electoral purposes. The Congress adopted a compromise resolution by Kautsky to the effect that socialists might join a non-socialist government in exceptional circumstances provided they remained under party direction and that their action was not treated as a partial transfer of power.

The dispute over revisionism was the most important event in the ideological history of the Second International and calls for a separate discussion. The International was less concerned with the theoretical sources of antagonism between the revisionists and the orthodox than with the question of reformism and the significance of reforms, which from the theoretical point of view reflected more fundamental divergences. The German social democrats passed a resolution against revisionism at their congress in Dresden, and at the Amsterdam Congress Guesde proposed that the International adopt the same resolution. On this occasion Jaurès made his famous speech declaring that the doctrinal rigidity of the German socialists was only a mask for their practical ineffectiveness (the French socialist movement was in fact much smaller, but also much more militant, than the German). The anti-revisionist resolution was adopted by a majority, but the revisionist movement continued to grow. The German party did not expel its revisionists: neither Bebel nor Kautsky wanted a split, and the strength of revisionism lay not in Bernstein's theoretical arguments but in the practical situation of the German working class. Those party activists who supported Bernstein were not interested in his critique of the dialectic, or even in the theory of value or the concentration of capital, but rather expressed that state of mind of the workers' leaders who saw a gulf between the austere revolutionary formulas of the party's programme and its actual policy, and who could no longer ascribe a practical meaning to traditional Marxist dogmas. In theory, of course, neither the increased importance of parliamentary institutions (which was much greater in Britain, France, or Belgium than in

Germany) nor the achievement of labour legislation and other social reforms should have affected the revolutionary outlook of the proletariat. According to the doctrine, everything the working class was able to secure under capitalism, in the way of social reforms or democratic freedoms, should have helped to awaken the revolutionary consciousness, and no orthodox Marxist could admit that this was not so. But the crisis over revisionism emphasized the problem of the social significance of reforms and gave an impetus to the study of the theoretical premises of Marxism in this area. It soon became clear that the dispute affected, directly or indirectly, many of the basic categories of Marxism. The idea of revolution, classes, and the class struggle, the continuity and discontinuity of culture, the state, historical inevitability, historical materialism, and the meaning of socialism itself—all these were called in question. Once the debate on revisionism was engaged, orthodox Marxism was no longer the same as before. Some of its adherents held by the old positions, but new forms of orthodoxy gradually supplanted the 'classic' Marxism of Kautsky, Bebel, and Labriola.

The last years of the Second International were overshadowed by the approach of war. The threat of a European conflict and the problem of socialist policy were discussed many times, especially at the Stuttgart Congress in 1907. The question was closely bound up with that of nationalities and self-determination. Some general principles were accepted by all socialists. All but a group of the German social democrats were opposed 'in principle' to militarism and colonialism, and all opposed national oppression. But this did not suffice to determine a common attitude towards war or particular international conflicts. The International had condemned militarism in general terms at Brussels in 1891, and at London in 1896 it adopted a resolution for the replacement of standing armies by peoples' militias. But as the respective socialist parties were organized on national lines and were obliged in the event of war to take up a position in view of the policy of their own governments, such resolutions had no tangible consequences for any of them. As regards the discussions of war and peace, the following general points may be singled out.

Guesde, faithful as ever to his dogmatic Marxism, was unenthusiastic about any special anti-war campaign: wars were inevitable under capitalism, and the way to stop them was to abolish it. This was in effect a repetition on the international plane of Guesde's position in regard to the Dreyfus case. Socialists should not interfere in disputes among the possessing classes; imperialist war is an instance of such a dispute, and is not the proletariat's concern. This was also the view of some German social democrats, but it meant abandoning all hope of exerting a socialist influence on events. If war broke out, a large part of the proletariat was bound to be mobilized and take part in the general slaughter, and if the socialists stood aside in the name of doctrinal purity they would in practice be endorsing the actions of governments. Several leaders accordingly urged that the International should adopt a definite policy of preventing war. Jaurès and Vaillant were for active resistance, including rebellion if necessary; but they also held that if a country was attacked it had a right to defend itself and it was the duty of socialists to take part in the defence. At Stuttgart in 1907 Gustave Hervé proposed a resolution calling for a general strike and mutiny in the event of war; but the Germans opposed this, chiefly for fear that their party might be outlawed. Even the call to strike and rebel was within the bounds of a 'reformist' policy; the left wing, represented by Lenin, Rosa Luxemburg and Karl Liebknecht, put forward more radical proposals. In their view the business of socialists, should a war break out, was not to attempt to stop it, whether by means of strikes or invoking international law, but to use it to overthrow the capitalist system. The resolution adopted at Stuttgart spoke in general terms of acting to stop a war or using it to hasten the downfall of capitalism, but these were purely ideological statements and comprised no specific plan. The idea of taking advantage of the imperialist conflict could be interpreted, as it afterwards was by Lenin, in the sense of turning it into a civil war, but the great majority of socialist leaders were not thinking on these lines. At the Basle Congress in 1912, although the First Balkan War had broken out, the mood was one of concord and optimism. A further anti-war resolution was passed, the slogan 'war on war' was vociferated, and the delegates dispersed in the conviction that the socialist movement was strong enough to prevent the carnage plotted by imperialist governments.

The International was also divided, though along different lines, on the question of national self-determination. National oppression was of course condemned by all, but neither this nor Marxist theory provided a solution to the complicated ethnic problems of Central and Eastern Europe. In general it was accepted that while national oppression and chauvinism were contrary to socialist ideas, the former was only a 'function' of social oppression and would vanish along with it; the nation-state was likewise associated with the development of capitalism, and there was no reason for Marxists to regard it as a guiding principle. The Austrian Marxists put forward the idea of cultural autonomy within a multinational state: there was no need for the state to be organized on a national basis, but every ethnic community was entitled to maintain its cultural traditions and language without interference. Rosa Luxemburg violently attacked the principle of self-determination on the ground that socialism would do away with national quarrels in due course: while the fight for socialism was going on, to raise the national question as a separate problem would distract the proletariat from its proper objective and assist the bourgeois policy of national unity. Lenin and the left wing of the Russian social democrats upheld the right of every nation to form a state of its own. Rosa Luxemburg's dogmatism on this issue was similar to the rigid attitude of Guesde towards other disputes: as all important historical processes were determined by the class struggle there was no such thing as a separate national problem, and in any case it was not a proper object of attention for the working-class movement. As for Lenin, he did not advocate the idea of the nation-state for its own sake, but regarded national tension and oppression as a powerful source of strength that could be exploited in the interest of the social struggle.

The collapse of the International in the face of the 1914 war was the more unexpected and depressing as the socialists had built such high hopes on the strength of their movement. The left wing did not expect it either: Lenin at first refused to believe that the German social democrats had obeyed the fatherland's call to arms. In every country of Europe the great majority had instinctively adopted a patriotic attitude. Even among the Bolshevik *émigrés* in the West, a large number did so without hesitation. Plekhanov, the father of Russian Marxism, had no doubt that Russia must be defended against invasion, and almost all the Mensheviks thought likewise. At the beginning of August the large social democratic party in the Reichstag voted for war credits: a minority which had been outvoted at a previous party meeting conformed to the majority line. At the next Reichstag vote in December, Karl Liebknecht alone broke the ranks of party solidarity. During the next two years the number of active dissidents rose to the point at which there was a split: the opponents of war were expelled and, in April 1917, formed the Independent German Socialist party (USPD), which drew its members from all parts of the German Socialist party (SPD). The war brought about new political divisions: the USPD included orthodox centrists like Kautsky and Hugo Haase (chairman of the SPD since Bebel's death in 1913), revisionists like Bernstein, and the left wing, which had formed itself into the Spartacus League at the beginning of 1916 and now joined the USPD in a body. In France the anti-patriotic opposition was if anything even weaker than in Germany. Jaurès, who might have hesitated, was murdered on the eve of the war. Guesde and Sembat joined the war government, as did Vandervelde in Belgium. Hervé, the most radical of French anti-war agitators, changed almost overnight into an ardent patriot. The International was in ruins.

In the summer of 1914 the socialist movement suffered the greatest defeat in its history, when it became clear that the international solidarity of the proletariat—its ideological foundation—was an empty phrase and could not stand the test of events. Both on the side of the Entente and on that of the Central Powers attempts were made to justify the upsurge of patriotism on Marxist grounds. Marx had often denounced Russia as a bulwark of barbarism and reaction, and a war against her could well be represented as defending European democracy against Tsarist despotism. On the other hand, Prussian militarism and feudal survivals in the German lands had traditionally been the object of socialist attack from Marx onwards, and it was easy to present France's struggle as that of republicanism against reactionary monarchy.

Lenin and the later Zimmerwald Left attributed the collapse of the International to treachery and opportunism on the part of the social democratic leaders. None of the Marxists posed the question whether the débâcle of the socialist movement in the face of national conflicts was of any significance for Marxist doctrine itself.

The summer of 1914 saw the beginning of a process whose consequences are still with us and whose final outcome cannot be foreseen. Two fundamentally different interpretations of socialism, which for years had made themselves felt in a variety of questions, had suddenly collided with such force as to destroy the International. Marxists at the time did not clearly examine or decide the question whether, and in what sense, socialism is a continuation of human history and in what sense it represents a breach with all that has gone before; or, to put it another way, how far and in what sense the proletariat is part of bourgeois society. Different answers to these questions were implicit in the philosophical conflicts within the socialist movement, and Marx's doctrine was by no means unambiguous on the point. In some important respects it supported the view of revolutionaries who refused to have any dealings with existing society or to attempt to reform it, but who counted on a great historical apocalypse that would sweep away oppression, exploitation, and injustice and begin history anew on the ruins of capitalism. On the other hand, Marx did not envisage socialism as something built in the void, and he believed in the continuity of civilization, both technical and cultural. He thus provided support to those who regarded socialism as the gradual increase of justice, equality, freedom, and community of ownership within the present system. The workers' movement, organized into parties adhering more or less strictly to Marxist ideology, had obtained real successes in the fight for labour legislation and civil rights: this seemed to show that existing society was reformable, whatever the doctrine might say, and thus to knock the bottom out of revolutionary programmes. The idea of socialism as a radical break was more natural in countries such as Russia, the Balkans, and Latin America, where there was little or no prospect of improving conditions by gradual pressure for reform. In Western Europe it was hard to argue that the proletariat was a pariah class with no place in society or the national community and no expectation of better conditions under the present system. Marxism had in fact helped on its own dissolution as an ideological force by contributing to a workers' movement that had achieved successes under capitalism and so refuted the view that the latter was incapable of reform.

This is of course a simplified schema, and does not take account of the intricate changes that took place in the socialist movement after the collapse of the

Second International. It gives an idea, however, of the subsequent polarization leading to a state of affairs that still exists: on the one hand, reformist social-ism bearing only a tenuous relation to Marxism, and, on the other hand, the monopolization of Marxism by Leninism and its derivatives. The latter, despite the traditional doctrine, displays its main strength in parts of the world that are backward from the technological, democratic, and cultural points of view—countries that are only on the threshold of industrialism and where the main pressure comes from non-proletarian claims, especially those of the peasants and subject nationalities. This polarization appears to have shown that the clas-sic version of Marxism which held the field up to the First World War is unten-able as a practical ideological force. From this point of view the present situation is, in spite of all changes, essentially the outcome of the drama that took place in the summer of 1914.

II
German Orthodoxy: Karl Kautsky

THE FIGURE of Karl Kautsky dominates the theoretical development of Marxism for the whole period of the Second International. While certainly not an outstanding philosopher, he was the chief architect and, so to speak, the embodiment of Marxist orthodoxy. He defended it against all extraneous influences popularized it skilfully and intelligently, and applied it successfully to the interpretation of past history and to new phenomena connected with the evolution of capitalist imperialism. He played the main part in creating a stereotype of Marxism which, especially in Central and Eastern Europe, held the field for decades and has only begun to give ground to other stereotypes in the last ten or fifteen years. Generations of Marxists were brought up on his books, which became classics of Marxist literature and—doubtless a unique case—remained so even after Lenin had denounced their author as a renegade for attacking the October Revolution. Kautsky was not orthodox in the sense of feeling obliged to defend every particular thought expressed by Marx or Engels, or of treating quotations from their works as arguments in themselves; indeed, no theoreticians of his generation were orthodox in this sense. In some matters, not of the first importance but not wholly trivial either, he criticized Engels's views, for example by maintaining that the state most frequently comes into existence as the result of external violence. But he was pedantically orthodox in the sense that Marxism as a theory and a method of historical investigation was the only system that he regarded as valid for the analysis of social phenomena, and he opposed all attempts to enrich or supplement Marxist theory by elements from any other source, except Darwinism. Thus, while not a strict dogmatist in respect of all Marx's or Engels's ideas, he was a rigorous defender of doctrinal purity. It was thanks to his interpretative work that the stereotype known as scientific socialism—the evolutionist, determinist, and scientistic form of Marxism—became universally accepted in its main lines.

1. Life and writings

KARL KAUTSKY (1854–1938) was born in Prague of a Czech father and a German mother. As a youth in Vienna he became acquainted with socialist ideas by reading the novels of George Sand and the historical works of Louis Blanc. He entered the University in 1874, and joined the social democratic party in the following year. He studied history, economics, and philosophy and was attracted by Darwinism as an explanation of the general principles governing human affairs. His first book, *Der Einfluss der Volksvermehrung auf den Fortschritt der Gesellschaft* (*The Influence of Human Increase on Social Progress*, 1880), was a critique of the Malthusian view that poverty is the result of overpopulation.

While still a student Kautsky wrote for the socialist Press in Vienna and Germany and met Liebknecht and Bebel. In 1880 he moved to Zurich, where he became a friend of Bernstein and worked for the German-language periodicals *Sozialdemokrat* and *Jahrbuch der Sozialwissenschaft und Sozialpolitik*. In 1881 he spent some months in London, where he met Marx and Engels. In the following year he returned to Vienna, and at the beginning of 1883 founded the monthly (later weekly) *Die Neue Zeit*, which he edited until 1917 and which was, throughout this period, the chief Marxist journal in Europe and therefore in the world. No other periodical did so much to popularize Marxism as the ideological form of the workers' movement in Germany and the rest of Europe. Many articles by socialist theoreticians that appeared in *Die Neue Zeit* later became part of the Marxist canon. The journal was first published at Stuttgart, but was subsequently transferred to London owing to the anti-socialist laws. After the laws were repealed Kautsky returned to Stuttgart at the end of 1890, and moved to Berlin seven years later.

The Erfurt Programme adopted at the German social democratic congress in October 1891—the first party programme based strictly on Marxist premisses—was the work of Kautsky and Bernstein, the former being responsible for the theoretical section. Kautsky attended every congress of the German party and of the International, defending his conception of orthodoxy against the anarchists, Bernstein, the revisionists, and the left wing. In matters of political strategy he was the chief exponent of what was then usually called the centre point of view, opposing the reformist idea that socialism could be introduced into capitalist society by way of gradual reforms and co-operation between the proletariat, the peasantry, and the petty bourgeoisie; at the same time he opposed the revolutionary theory that the party's proper task was to prepare for a single violent upheaval at a moment dictated by political circumstances. In the same way, when the war came and the International fell apart Kautsky took up a middle position between the nationalism of the German party as a whole and the revolutionary defeatism of the left wing. His sharp criticism of the October Revolution in Russia caused him to be branded as a traitor by Lenin and his followers. In the 1920s he returned to politics and took a prominent part in drafting the programme adopted by the German social democratic party at Heidelberg in 1925. He lived in Vienna until shortly before the Anschluss, and died at Amsterdam.

Kautsky's writings cover all the important problems that confronted Marxism and the socialist movement in his time. Amid his huge output of books and articles those on history and economics achieved the most permanent reputation. In 1887 he published *Karl Marx's ökonomische Lehren* (*The Economic Doctrines of Karl Marx*)—in effect a summary of Volume I of *Capital*, which served for some decades as a handbook of Marxist economic theory for beginners. Four historical works, applying the Marxist method of class analysis to the study of ideology and political conflict, are perhaps the most important part of his theoretical activity: these are *Thomas More und seine Utopie* (*Thomas More and his Utopia*, 1888; English translation 1927); *Die Klassengegensätze von 1789* (*The Class Antagonisms of 1789*, 1889); *Die Vorläufer des neueren Sozialismus* (*The Forerunners of Modern Socialism*, two volumes, 1895); and *Der Ursprung des Christentums* (*The Foundations of Christianity*, 1908). The first of these works analysed the state of England under Henry VIII and the life and best-known work of Thomas More in terms of the class conflicts of the age of primitive accumulation. The third work is a historical review of socialist ideas from Plato's *Republic* to the French Revolution, with particular attention to revolutionary anabaptism; while the fourth is concerned with the historical significance of early Christian ideas.

Kautsky's most important work of general theory published before 1914 is *Ethik und materialistische Geschichtsauffassung* (*Ethics and the Materialist Interpretation of History*, 1906), which contains a history of ethical doctrines and an exposition of Darwinist and Marxist views on the biological and social significance of moral ideas and behaviour. Works dealing directly with political theory and the strategy of social democracy are his extensive commentary on the Erfurt Programme (*Das Erfurter Programme in seinem grundsätzlichen Teil erläutert*, 1892); and polemics against Bernstein and the Left on the reformist-revolutionary dilemma (*Bernstein und das sozialdemokratische Programm*, 1899; *Die soziale Revolution*, 1907, translated 1909; *Der politische Massenstreik*, 1914; *Der Weg zur Macht*, 1909). His criticism of the Russian Revolution can be found in *Die Diktatur des Proletariats* (1918, translated 1918, 1964); *Terrorismus und Kommunismus* (1919); and *Von der Demokratie zur Staatssklaverei* (1921). In 1927 he summed up his theoretical ideas in *Die materialistische Geschichtsauffassung* (*The Materialist Interpretation of History*). This vast work had far less influence than his earlier treatises, on account of its size and because its popularity suffered from the ban pronounced on Kautsky by the highest authority in the Communist world. Moreover, the social democrats, having broken with the Communists, were less interested in the philosophical foundation of socialist ideas and their own links with the Marxist tradition.

Marxist doctrine had been almost monopolized by the Leninist and Stalinist brand of socialism, in which there was no longer room for Kautsky's later ideas. In consequence, the most impressive exposition of historical materialism ever written had virtually no audience and no effect on those it was meant for.

2. Nature and society

KAUTSKY'S views changed remarkably little in the course of his career. In his youth he had embraced Darwinism and a naturalistic view of the world; he soon discovered historical materialism, and wove the two elements into an integral whole which satisfied him for the rest of his life. Having written his commentary on the Erfurt Programme in 1892 he could still reaffirm its validity not only in 1904 but also in the preface to the seventeenth edition in 1922, after the European war, the Russian Revolution, and the disintegration of international socialism. His last, monumental work contains scarcely anything by way of modification or correction of the views he expressed in the preceding fifty years. This early rigidification and satisfaction with his own conclusions made him insensitive to new political and philosophical ideas. However, he preserved the spirit of inquiry and intellectual honesty, which enabled him to remain clear-sighted in polemics: he eschewed demagogy and the replacement of logic by insult, and marshalled his vast knowledge of history into convincing arguments. His writing is marked by pedantry and a hankering after systematization: when he sets out to explain the Marxist view of ethics he begins by attempting (with very poor success) to give a compressed history of ethical doctrines and the whole history of manners and customs. Denouncing the terrorism of the Russian Revolution, he traces the history of France's Revolution of 1789 and the Paris Commune. He always goes back to first beginnings, is imbued with didactic purpose, and attaches great importance, as did Lenin, to the correct formulation of the theoretical basis of the socialist movement.

A striking feature of Kautsky's work is the complete lack of understanding of philosophical problems. His remarks on purely philosophical subjects do not go beyond what may be read in the summary essays of Engels: from his comments on Kant it is clear that he had no idea of the true meaning of the latter's philosophy. The key problems of metaphysics and epistemology, including the epistemological basis of ethics, are unknown to him. The strongest aspects of his intellect are seen in his analysis of past events and social conflicts in the light of Marxist theory.

The peculiar nature of Kautsky's thought is best seen by comparing him with a writer like Jaurès. To Jaurès, socialism, and Marxism as the modern theoretical expression of socialism, was above all a moral notion, a value-concept, the highest expression of man's eternal longing for freedom and justice. To

Kautsky, Marxism was primarily the scientific, deterministic, integral apprehension of social phenomena. Kautsky was fascinated by Marxism as a coherent theoretical system by which the whole of history could be comprehended
and its events reduced to a single schema: he was a typical child of the scientistic era in which he grew up, inspired by Darwin and Herbert Spencer and
the advance of physics and chemistry. He believed in the unlimited capacity of
science to synthesize knowledge into a more and more extensive yet concentrated system of facts and explanations. The scientistic and positivistic version
of Marxism developed in Engels's later writings was adopted by Kautsky without modification; his world-view was dominated by scientific rigour devoid of
sentiment and value-judgements, a belief in the unity of scientific method, the
strictly causal and 'objective' interpretation of social phenomena, the world of
men considered as an extension of organic nature. Thinking in this way, he naturally regarded the Hegelian origins of Marxism as a historical accident of
small importance; like Engels, he saw no more in Hegel's contribution to the
Marxist tradition than a few banal reflections on the interdependence of all
phenomena, the development and variability of the universe, etc.

Thus the foundation of the scientific world-view was, in Kautsky's eyes, strict
determinism and a belief in unchanging universal laws. Even more strongly than
Engels he emphasized the 'natural necessity' (*Naturnotwendigkeit*) of all social
processes. He was not a 'social Darwinist' in the sense of denying the specific
character of human society or reducing social conflicts and class struggles to a
mere Darwinian fight for survival. But his reservations concerning the reduction of human society to the level of animal communities are of far less importance than the analogy that he sees between them. All specifically human
characteristics, i.e. those that appear throughout history, are shared by mankind
with other animals: this is a frequent motif in Kautsky's works, from the *Ethics*
to *The Materialist Interpretation of History*. Kautsky adopted without reserve
Darwin's view of evolution as a process resulting from chance mutations that
permit the survival of the individual best adapted to its environment. Nature
has no purpose in the sense either of a conscious force governing evolution or
of a definite over-all tendency. Organisms that undergo favourable mutations
transmit their power of adaptation to their descendants, and this process
accounts for the whole course of evolution. All typically human functions can
be found in the animal world: intelligence, sociability, social instincts, and moral
feelings. Intelligence is a weapon in the struggle for existence, and the cognitive faculty has no other purpose than to ensure the preservation of the species.
Animals show a knowledge of natural laws and the relations of cause and effect,
and human knowledge is a development and systematization of this.

Kautsky does not ask himself how it is that a purely biological ability to associate events and to express this association in terms of 'natural laws', articulated

in the form of language, can claim the status of a discovery of the truth about the universe, or how the idea of knowledge as truth can be derived from its role as an instrument of adaptation. Two basic instincts, those of self-preservation and the preservation of the species, are a sufficient explanation of the whole range of animal and human behaviour, both moral and cognitive. The instinct for co-operation within the species is what, in the human race, we call the moral law or the voice of conscience. Among human beings as among animals, it is often in conflict with the instinct of self-preservation. It is therefore not the case that man is 'naturally' egoistic or altruistic, since both tendencies, though they may conflict in particular cases, coexist in him as in all the higher animals. The division of labour and the use of tools are observable among beasts in embryonic forms, as is production in the sense of transforming the environment to suit one's purposes. In short, human beings are in no way different from animals as cognitive, moral agents and producers. There is nothing in specifically human nature that cannot be found also in the non-human universe. The specific powers achieved by man, or rather specific developments of animal powers, can be explained by adaptation and the interaction of the organism with its environment. These powers—namely language and the invention of tools—have fostered each other's development, making possible the accumulation of thought, experience, and ability; but they are no more than the prolongation of animal faculties. The whole progress of civilization can be explained by the working of the same laws of adaptation. When primitive man emerged from the jungle into open country he had to make clothing, build houses, discover fire and the art of cultivation. Language was a strengthener of social ties and co-operation within the tribe, but it led to differences of speech and social groups and hence to the peculiarly human institution of wars within a single species.

The division of labour, a continuation of the process begun in animal communities, made it possible to produce in excess of essential needs: this led men to fight for control of such surpluses, and also to the formation of class divisions based on the possession of means of production. Technical developments determined the changing forms of such divisions, but these were also determined in part by other factors, especially the natural environment. Class divisions take one form where centralized irrigation works are required, for example in the Nile delta, another where the chief problem is to ward off the attacks of neighbouring tribes; they will be different among mountaineers and in coastal settlements. In all cases, however, the principle of adaptation to the environment determines specific forms of human behaviour, governed by the unvarying instincts of self-preservation and co-operation.

The delusion that there are eternal and absolute values that humanity finds ready-made or, at any rate, preserved throughout history arises from the fact that for thousands of years social progress was extremely slow, so that particular commands and prohibitions remained unchanged until they came to be regarded as valid for all time and in all circumstances. In reality the only immutable factors of this sort are general biological instincts, whereas specifically human moral norms and values are all dependent on modes of production. It is true that in the struggle carried on by the oppressed classes throughout history certain uniform circumstances can be discerned, and hence a similarity in the values created by those classes. But this similarity is more apparent than real. In primitive Christianity, equality meant an equal distribution of goods, while freedom meant idleness; in the French Revolution, equality meant an equal right to property and freedom meant the free use of one's possessions. Under socialism, however, equality means an equal right to use the products of social labour, while freedom is the reduction of necessary labour, i.e. the gradual shortening of the working day.

It can happen, indeed, that opinions or values outlive the conditions from which and in which they arise, and in which case they act as a clog on social progress. As a rule, however, human behaviour in society is not determined by ideals but by the material exigencies of life. A moral ideal 'is not an aim, but a weapon in the social struggle'. In general no ideals can be ascertained by scientific observation, which is by definition morally neutral and concerned only with necessary connections in nature and human history. Scientific socialism demonstrates the inevitability of a classless society as a result of economic laws, but it cannot erect this into a moral purpose. This fact, however, does not detract from the greatness and sublimity of the vision of a socialist world for which the working class is fighting, impelled by irresistible economic necessity.

Kautsky appears to have failed to understand the epistemological problem of moral values or the fact that, when a historical process has been presented as inevitable, the question of its value remains open. Hence his criticism of Kant and of ethical socialism is beside the point. As Cohen, Vorländer, and Bauer pointed out, from the fact that something is necessary it does not follow that it is desirable or valuable. We need a special cognitive faculty to tell us that socialism is not only historically necessary but also a good thing; Marx having demonstrated the former proposition, Kantian ethics might show us a way to believe the latter. Kautsky replied, however, that values are outside the province of science. He agreed with the neo-Kantians that Marxism proved the historical necessity of socialism, and this, in his view, was all that required to be shown. The working class was bound to develop a consciousness that would regard socialism as an ideal, but this attitude of mind was itself no more than the consequence of a social process. The question why a person should regard as desirable what he believes to be inevitable is ignored by Kautsky, who gives no reason for not answering it. He maintained that Kant's categorical impera-

tive rested on a delusion, in the first place, because it purported to be independent of experience, whereas it presupposed the existence of other people,
which could only be known empirically to the philosopher. (In actual fact the
categorical imperative is independent of experience in the sense that it cannot
be logically derived from empirical data, but not in the sense that it can be
effectively formulated without any empirical knowledge.) Secondly, Kautsky
declares, the categorical imperative is unworkable in a society torn by antagonisms and conflicting loyalties. In fact, however, it is presented by Kant as a formal norm constituting the necessary condition of any concrete rule, and not an
empirical assertion excluding moral conflicts or presupposing the existence of
a harmonious society; nor does it purport to be a sufficient basis for the construction of a moral code. The extent of Kautsky's failure to understand Kant
is shown by a remark in his *Ethics* to the effect that the Kantian precept of
treating every individual as an end and not as a means is realized among animals, with the proviso that the community protects only those individuals
whose survival is advantageous to the species. Kautsky does not notice that this
proviso is contrary to the whole principle of the intrinsic value of the individual, who is treated, in this case, not as an end in himself but as a means to the
preservation of the species.

3. Consciousness and the development of society

THE principle of strict determinism, and the belief that human history is a continuation of natural history and can be explained by the same laws, led Kautsky to a purely naturalistic interpretation of human consciousness. Kautsky
does not regard consciousness as an 'epiphenomenon' (as critics of Marxism
frequently assert), i.e. as a phenomenon that is not part of 'objective' history
but appertains only to the perception, true or false, of historical events. On the
contrary, he regards it as an essential link in the chain of necessary processes;
but, he says, there is no such thing as a human consciousness differing from
that of animals. Human consciousness consists of intelligence, knowledge, and
moral sensibility, all of which evolved at the pre-human stage as organs of
adaptation. It is therefore wrong to say that conscious processes are an inessential 'extra' without which human history would be exactly the same as it is now.
But this is also true of pre-human history, which in the case of higher animals
involves conscious processes enabling them to survive in a hostile environment. From this point of view, he declares, the human species, despite its faculties of language and tool-making, is no different from other intelligent
beings. In particular—and here Kautsky seems to be mistaken in imagining that
he is faithful to Marx's ideas—the necessity of the downfall of capitalism and
the transition to socialism is no different from the necessity whereby techno-

logical progress has in the past brought socio-economic systems into existence. Of course Marx's idea that socialism will be consciously brought about by the organized working class, when it has acquired knowledge of social processes, remains in force. But neither Kautsky nor his neo-Kantian adversaries realized the true sense of Marx's attempt to transcend the opposition between necessity and freedom, between description and prescription. Neither the Kantians nor the determinists assimilated the Marxian eschatology involving the identification of the subject and the object of history—the idea of man's return to his 'species-nature', and the theory of alienation which is inseparable from it.

Marx, as we have seen, did not regard socialism merely as a new system that would do away with inequality, exploitation, and social antagonism. In his view it was the recovery by man of his lost humanity, the reconciliation of his species-essence with his empirical existence, the restoration to man's being of his 'alienated' nature. History up to the present time involved the participation of human beings and their conscious intentions, but was subjected to its own laws, which were valid whether or not they were consciously apprehended (as in fact they could not be, at all events not completely). But in the consciousness of the working class we have not merely to do with the increased knowledge of social processes, which, like any other knowledge, can be used to transform society in the same way as it transforms technology. The consciousness of the working class actually *is* the process of the revolutionary transformation of society: it is not a reservoir of information, first acquired and then put into practical use, but is the self-knowledge of the new society, in which the historical process coincides with awareness of that process. Socialism is necessary in the sense that capitalism, like all previous systems, is fated to lose control over the technological conditions it has itself created; but the necessity of socialism realizes itself as the free, conscious activity of the working class. Since the consciousness of the proletariat is the self-awareness of humanity recovering its lost nature (a nature that really exists, not a normative ideal), this consciousness cannot be divided into a descriptive or informational aspect and a normative or imperative one. The act by which men become aware of their own being, or return to their own essence, is a self-affirmation of humanity and, as such, cannot be reduced to awareness of the natural inevitability of the historical process, or to a normative ideal, or to a combination of these two. Marx's specifically Hegelian belief in 'essence' as something more real than empirical reality, and not simply an imagined ideal, was ignored in the argument between the determinists and the Kantists. The latter's position was that Marx had shown that socialism was an objective necessity, and they held that awareness of this fact must be supplemented by the socialist norm of value. Kautsky contended that Marx had shown socialism to be an objective necessity, and that one factor in this necessary process was the proletariat's awareness and approval of that necessity: this awareness and approval were inevitable, and nothing more was required. Marx's real view, however, was that the consciousness of the proletariat, being the consciousness of humanity returning to its own essence, was identical with that return as an objective process: in the revolutionary activity of the proletariat, the opposition between necessity and freedom ceased to exist.

To put it another way: Kautsky, following Engels, took a naturalistic and positivistic view of consciousness as knowledge which, being itself the result of the necessary development of society, was part of that development inasmuch as it provided the indispensable basis for effective social technology. Knowledge of society, and the practical application of that knowledge, were distinguished from each other in the same way as in any technology. Hence the specific meaning of the term 'scientific socialism': socialism was a theory that could only be the result of scientific observation and not of the spontaneous evolution of the proletariat. Socialist theory was bound to be the creation of scholars, not of the working class, and must be introduced from outside into the workers' movement as a weapon in the struggle for liberation. This theory, later adopted by Lenin, of socialist consciousness implanted in the spontaneous working-class movement from outside is a direct consequence of the naturalistic interpretation of consciousness and the Darwinist interpretation of social processes in general. It also became a political instrument by supplying a theoretical basis for the new idea of a proletarian party directed by intellectuals versed in theory—a party expressing the authentic, scientific consciousness of the proletariat, which the working class was unable to evolve for itself. Kautsky drew different consequences from the theory of 'scientific socialism' than did Lenin; but in his case, too, the view that the proletarian class-consciousness can only take shape outside the proletariat, in the minds of the intelligentsia, was a reflection and theoretical justification of a socialist party transforming itself into a party of professional politicians and manipulators.

4. Revolution and socialism

BELIEF in historical necessity, and in particular the 'objective' necessity of socialist society, was to Kautsky the corner-stone of Marxism and the essential difference between scientific and utopian socialism. (In fact, however, the opinion that socialism is objectively inevitable is not exclusively Marxist: it can be found in the works of some utopians, for example the Saint-Simonists.) Kautsky was especially careful to remain faithful to Marx's doctrine on this point, and he never ceased to emphasize that political fantasy is no substitute for economic necessity: socialism can only proceed from the economic maturity of capitalism and the resulting polarization of classes. Kautsky's political attitude was essentially determined by this principle of 'maturity', which indeed was accepted by all theoreticians of the Second International except the Leninist wing: it appeared to follow as a matter of course from the anti-utopian and anti-Blanquist elements in Marx's teaching.

Both in his criticism of utopian socialism and of revisionism Kautsky empha-sized the difference between the class division of society and its division according to criteria of consumption, i.e. participation in the national income; in this he was fully in accord with Marx. The proletariat's struggle is not the result of poverty but of class antagonism, and the condition of socialist victory is not the absolute impoverishment of the working class but the sharpening of class antagonism, which is not the same thing. At various points in his histor-ical analyses Kautsky shows that the class struggle may become more acute in cases where the exploited workers' lot is improving, so that its intensity is not a function of poverty. On this ground he rejects all revisionist arguments show-ing that the workers were relatively better off and predicting that class antago-nism would therefore diminish. The theory of the absolute pauperization of the working class was thus, in Kautsky's view, not an essential part of Marxist doc-trine, such that the latter would have to be abandoned if the theory proved to be untrue. What was essential, however, was the view that class polarization would increase and that the middle class would be squeezed out by the con-centration of capital. Kautsky was uncompromising on this point, and strove to refute Bernstein's contention that in spite of the concentration process the middle class, and especially the small owners, were not becoming less numer-ous. In his polemics with the revisionists and in his exposition of the theoreti-cal portion of the Erfurt Programme Kautsky argued that the development of bourgeois society was bound to eliminate small enterprises; when told that sta-tistics did not confirm this, he replied that the new owners were not petty bour-geois but men thrown out of work by the concentration of capital, who strove to keep afloat by establishing small workshops and co-operatives. He admitted that in agriculture the disappearance of small holdings was not proceeding so fast as had been predicted, but here too he thought it was bound to come about in time.

Kautsky held that the collapse of capitalism would not be a result of the fall in the profit rate, which was compatible with a rise in the absolute level of prof-its. Capitalism would break down because private ownership of the means of production did not permit the efficient use and development of the techniques that humanity had evolved. Capitalism could not avoid anarchy, recurrent crises of overproduction, and mass unemployment; moreover, it was bound to develop the consciousness of the working class, which was organizing itself not only to obtain short-term improvements but to seize political power and estab-lish public ownership of the means of production for the good of society.

On the two basic questions of the relation between the political and the

economic struggle, and that between fighting for reforms and awaiting the revolution, Kautsky's position was that of orthodox Marxism. As to the first question, he opposed the Marxist viewpoint to the equally false extremes of
Proudhonism on the one hand and Blanquism on the other. The Proudhonists were not interested in the political struggle, for they held that the conquest
of political power by the proletariat would not do away with exploitation: as
long as there was capitalism the proletariat would gain nothing by democracy,
as political democracy would not bring economic liberation. The workers must
therefore have nothing to do with political and parliamentary issues, but concentrate on freeing themselves by organizing production independently of capitalism. The Blanquists, on the other hand, were interested only in the conquest
of political power, irrespective of economic conditions. Marx, as Kautsky
explains, avoided both these one-sided views and adopted the only position
consonant with the scientific method, viz. that the proletariat's assumption
of political power is the necessary condition and means of economic liberation, but this power can only be used to overthrow capitalism when the latter is ripe for destruction. If the moment is premature from the economic point
of view the seizure of power cannot lead to the overthrow of capitalism, for
objective economic laws cannot be overruled by decrees or violence. An example of this is the Jacobin dictatorship, which Kautsky regarded as a dictatorship of the proletariat. The Terror was supposed to smash profiteering and keep
up the revolutionary enthusiasm of the masses, but it only brought fear and disillusionment. When the Thermidor reaction came, the Jacobins had no support
and the revolution returned to the base established for it by economic conditions, i.e. the rule of the bourgeoisie. The Paris Commune was bound to collapse for the same reason.

Kautsky, however, was unable, or did not try, to explain precisely how the
ripeness of capitalism for political revolution was to be recognized. He maintained against the reformists that socialism could not simply develop as a natural continuation of capitalism, by partial reforms and concessions on the part
of the possessing classes. A revolution, in the sense of a conscious seizure of
political power by the organized proletariat, was an essential and inevitable precondition of socialism. But social democrats must not tie their hands by any
precise definition of the character and duration of the revolutionary process. In
particular it need not signify a once-and-for-all act of violence, an armed rebellion or a bloody civil war. On the contrary, the more the proletariat was capable of organized action, aware of historical processes and trained in the working
of democratic institutions, the more likely it was that the revolution would take
a non-violent form. The precise situation, however, was hard to predict. As for
the social democratic party, since it could not itself create the economic conditions that made revolution possible, it was, in Kautsky's words, a revolution-

ary party but not a party that was making or preparing a revolution. For a revolution could not simply be made at will or from purely political ingredients.
The social democrats rightly rejected the absurd doctrine of 'The worse, the
better': the struggle for social and political reforms under capitalism was in the
highest interest of the proletariat and of its eventual victory, developing its class-
consciousness and enabling it to gain experience of economic administration
and political life. Reforms were not a substitute for revolution, but they were a
necessary preparation for it. It was contrary to Marxist strategy either to set a
course towards catastrophe or to rely on co-operation between classes in the
hope that capitalism would turn into socialism by gradual evolution.

Kautsky was certainly faithful to Marx when he insisted that the revolution
could not be enacted by decree, and that the mere transfer of political power
would not bring about the economic liberation of the proletariat unless capitalism were economically and technically ripe for the change. But he seems to
have overlooked the fact that the strategy, tactics, and organization of the
worker's movement would have to be quite different according to whether it set
about preparing for a political upheaval or chose to await the conditions, whatever they were exactly, for the economic collapse of capitalism. Kautsky's
refusal to prejudge the character and duration of the revolution was quite reasonable on the premiss that the proletariat must wait for the ripening of conditions under capitalism. But a party that calls itself revolutionary cannot act
rationally if, on whatever grounds, it refuses to prejudge the meaning of the
term 'revolution'. If it signifies a peaceful process, perhaps lasting for decades,
in which the proletariat gradually gains control of political institutions, the
party's educational and organizational tasks must be quite different than if the
revolution is to be a once-and-for-all act of violence. The party, therefore, cannot in practice refrain from choosing on the mere ground that historical events
are unpredictable. It may leave both alternatives open in its programme, but in
political life it is bound to opt for one or the other. For this reason Kautsky's
centrist position, based on his scientific attitude and reluctance to take decisions without rational foundation, amounted in practice to acceptance of the
reformist standpoint. The theory of a revolution prepared by capitalism itself
and not by the proletariat was a reflection, in Kautsky's doctrine, of the practical situation of the party, which adhered to revolutionary phraseology in its
programme but took no action suggesting that it meant what it said. Bernstein
was quite right when he observed that German social democracy was in actual
fact a reformist organization and that the revolutionary elements in its programme were at variance with its actions and even with the practical objectives
set forth in the programme itself. The eventual defeat of centrism—as a matter
of practice, not of phraseology—and the party's dissolution into a revolutionary
and a reformist wing were due to the fact that centrism, under the appearance

of scientific open-mindedness, was a philosophy of indecision and was incapable of taking up a clear position on questions that had to be decided—and that were decided, if not in the party programme, at all events in political life. This fault was not obvious while the party was peacefully building up its strength, and so Kautsky's orthodox Marxism prevailed over the reformist programme at congresses although the party continued in practice to take a reformist line. The inconsistency came fully into view at the moment of crisis, which swept away the foundation of Kautsky's policy.

The idea that the revolution must await the ripening of economic conditions appeared to Kautsky a perfectly natural consequence of the Marxist theory of historical processes. It was not his view that in the relationship between the 'base' and the 'superstructure' the former alone played an active role and the latter was a mere adjunct. On the contrary, he emphasized, following Engels, that the division between the two was not identical with that between 'material' and 'spiritual' factors in the historical process. The base, which he regards as including means of production and tools, develops in accordance with the advance of knowledge and comprises all human productive faculties including 'spiritual' resources. The superstructure, on the other hand, i.e. legal and political relationships and socially formed opinions, has a great deal of influence on economic conditions. There is thus a continuing process of reciprocal influence, and the 'primacy' of the base *vis-à-vis* the superstructure applies only 'in the last resort'—a phrase which Kautsky, like Engels before him, does not explain precisely. He only adds that technological progress and the accompanying changes in property relations do not account for every detailed change in the superstructure, though they do account for the appearance of new ideas, social movements and institutions. Having thus limited the interpretation of the 'primacy' of the base, Kautsky still does not explain how the new is to be distinguished from the old, or how we can be sure that ideas or institutions that may come into being long after the relevant changes in technology or property relations are in fact a consequence of these.

In interpreting single events in the history of the revolutionary movement Kautsky suggests many convincing explanations, but in the case of more extended processes his suggestions often appear arbitrary. He argues, for instance, that the Kantian principle of treating every human being as an end and not a means is the expression of a bourgeois protest against personal dependence in a feudal society. But the opposite ethical principle voiced by the utilitarians of the Enlightenment is equally characteristic of the rising bourgeoisie, asserting its epicureanism against the asceticism of Christian morality. On the other hand, epicureanism is also typical of the declining aristocracy, while Kant's principle is rooted in Christianity; and again, the liberal doctrine of the survival of the fittest is of bourgeois origin. It is easy to see that if the sense of intellectual phenomena can be manipulated thus freely it is possible to defend any interpretation of them in class or economic terms, which in itself shows up the weakness of the theory. If, as Kautsky argues, Christian ethics reflected the misery of the oppressed classes in ancient Rome and also the situation of the decadent aristocracy of those times, and if it could then be an instrument of the rulers of feudal society, and later an inspiration of protest against that society; or if the bourgeois mentality could equally well be expressed by Kant's personalism, Bentham's utilitarianism, and Calvin's asceticism—then the theory is certainly capable of accounting for all historical phenomena and is covered against falsification, but only because it is arbitrary and lacking in precise criteria for the correlation of spiritual phenomena with their material origins.

In Kautsky's evolutionist doctrine there is of course no room for eschatology or any belief in the general 'meaning' of history. Like Marx, he regards socialism as the cause of all mankind and not merely of a class, but he also follows Marx in insisting on the class character of the movement that is to bring socialism about. The working class may conclude temporary alliances with the bourgeoisie or lower-middle class to secure political or social reforms, but it would be lost if it did not at the same time preserve its independence and separate character. (Kautsky was especially mistrustful of any alliance with the peasantry, which he regarded, above all in Germany, as a pre-eminently conservative class.) Socialism is in the interest of all, but the fight for socialism is in the interest of the working class alone. This idea (not formulated by Kautsky in so many words, but expressing his teaching and that of Marx) is self-consistent on the assumption that only the proletariat is so privileged by history that its immediate and ultimate aims are in harmony with each other, whereas the short-term objectives of the peasantry and the lower-middle class, not to mention the bourgeoisie, are contrary to the interest of all humanity embodied in the idea of a socialist society. The contradiction does not lie in the doctrine, but in the interests of the possessing classes.

Socialism signifies emancipation for the whole human race: this is true, first and foremost, because public ownership of the means of production and control of the production process in accordance with social needs will shorten the working day and give people more time to develop their personal aptitudes and aspirations. Socialism does not mean the abolition of the state, as the anarchists would have it, or a return to small self-contained communities, which would revive all the consequences of anarchic production and competition. The state, transformed into an organ of the social administration of things as opposed to people, must be centralized and capable of looking after the whole range of material production; artistic and intellectual production, on the other hand, will develop in perfect freedom. Kautsky, like most Marxists of his time, saw no conflict between the central regulation of trade and industry and the independence of culture. Democracy, freedom of the spoken and written word, the right of assembly, and cultural freedom were generally regarded by Marxists as automatic features of socialist organization. Kautsky often expressed his view on this subject, and always in the same sense. Although, as a matter of history, democratic freedoms have been secured by the bourgeoisie fighting feudal oppression, they belong to the permanent achievement of progress, and socialism without democracy would be a parody of its own first principles. For this reason socialism must never be imposed by a revolutionary minority, for it would then contradict itself. It must be the undisputed work of a majority, which should respect the right of the minority to express and advocate different opinions.

5. Critique of Leninism

KAUTSKY'S basic conviction that socialism could not prevail until economic conditions were right for it, and his belief that socialism entailed democracy, combined to make him firmly opposed to the October Revolution and the Leninist conception of the dictatorship of the proletariat.

Like most of Lenin's socialist critics Kautsky held that Lenin was wrong in claiming Marx's support for the idea of the dictatorship of the proletariat as a particular form of government, opposed to democratic forms: to Marx and Engels, he maintained, it signified not the form of government but its social content. This was shown by the fact that Marx and Engels used the term 'dictatorship of the proletariat' to describe the Paris Commune, which was based on democratic principles, a multiparty system, free elections, and the free expression of opinion. In resolving to build socialism in a backward country by means of terror and oppression the Bolsheviks were in opposition to the views of Marx and Engels—who, for instance, had sharply criticized the Bakuninists for attempting to start a Communist rising in Spain in 1873—and also to those of Russian Marxists like Plekhanov and Akselrod, who hold that a revolution in Russia could only be of a bourgeois character, even if the proletariat played a decisive role in it. The destitution of the Russian people and the chiliastic hopes that went with it, the brutalization caused by war, and the general backwardness of the proletariat meant that socialism, if introduced there, was bound to turn into its opposite. Instead of organizing the proletariat for practicable aims and raising it to a higher level the Bolsheviks had incited it to take revenge on individual capitalists, destroyed all elements of democracy, and allowed the immaturity of the movement to bear fruit in universal savagery and banditry. They were trying ineffectually, like the Jacobins before them, to cure economic difficulties by mass terror and forced labour, which they falsely called the dictatorship of the proletariat. Thus, as Kautsky wrote in 1919, there was growing up amid despotic conditions a new class of bureaucratic exploiters, no better than the Tsarist chinovniks; and the workers' future struggle against tyranny would be even more desperate than under traditional capitalism, when they could exploit divergences of interest between capital and the state bureaucracy, whereas in Bolshevik Russia these two had coalesced into one. This kind of regimented socialism could only maintain itself by denying its own principles, which it was most likely to do, given the Bolsheviks' notorious opportunism and the ease with which they changed their tune from one day to the next. The most probable result would be a kind of Thermidor reaction which the Russian workers would welcome as a liberation, like the French in 1794. The original sin of Bolshevism lay in the suppression of democracy, abolition of elections, and denial of the freedom of speech and assembly, and in the belief that socialism could be based on a minority despotism imposed by force, which by its own logic was bound to intensify the rule of terror. If the Leninists were able to keep their 'Tartar socialism' going long enough, it would infallibly result in the bureaucratization and militarization of society and finally in the autocratic rule of a single individual.

6. Inconsistencies in Kautsky's philosophy

NEXT to Engels, Kautsky was certainly the chief exponent of the naturalist, evolutionist, determinist, Darwinist version of Marxism. At first glance his philosophy appears to form a consistent whole and to be reducible to a few main principles covering the whole history of nature and of mankind. All development is the result of interaction between organisms and their environment; those that are best adapted survive and transmit their characteristics to the next generation; the competition among species creates universal instincts of aggression and intra-species solidarity; the human race has achieved a special place in nature owing to its ability to make tools and to the power of articulate speech; the development of tools led to the origin of private property and classes fighting each other for the appropriation of surpluses; this in turn leads to the concentration of capital and class polarization; private ownership prevents further technical progress and intensifies the antagonism between the exploiting minority and the exploited majority; and this process is bound to end in the establishment of public ownership and of a new society which will preserve the technical and social achievements of capitalism, especially the democratic way of life, but will de-antagonize the process of socialization, restore the solidarity of the human race, do away with basic social conflicts, and enable individuals to develop without restraint.

On closer inspection, however, the theory proves to be full of gaps and inconsistencies, some of which are peculiar to the evolutionist brand of Marxism as opposed to that contained in Marx's early writings, while others are common to the naturalist and anthropocentric versions.

In Kautsky's view the whole development of the organic world, and human history as a subdivision of natural history, are to be explained by the interaction of organisms with their environment. Kautsky regards this theory of interaction as the true, rational content of the dialectic, and for this reason he criticizes the idea of the dialectic as the theory of the dichotomy of Being, due to its latent inner contradictions: self-negation as an explanation of development is, in his view, a survival of Hegelian idealism. Changes in nature and history are not brought about by a self-generated movement of contradiction but by the interaction of distinct elements of the universe. There is no such thing in reality as the paradigm of human nature returning into itself after an age-long state of fission and restoring the unity between the object and subject of history. We are the spectators of a necessary process of changes which have no 'meaning' in themselves and cannot reveal any to scientific investigation, for science has nothing to do with values and is only concerned with necessity or the 'laws' of nature.

This naturalistic determinism, which is not fully worked out from the philosophical point of view, gives rise to important inconsistencies, or arbitrary assumptions, affecting the whole of Kautsky's thought. To begin with, it is not clear whether 'historical necessity' comprises every detail of history or only its general direction. If the former, then, leaving aside the arbitrariness of this form of determinism, it must be the case that each particular event or process is inevitable and predetermined in exactly the same sense. It follows that there is no point, for example, in Kautsky criticizing the Russian Revolution, for this was a no less necessary event than the transformation of a commodity economy into capitalism. Human volition may indeed be a necessary link, but its nature and effect are as much determined as everything else, and it is no different in function from any other factor of historical change. It is meaningless to criticize a revolutionary movement for taking no account of whether the situation is ripe, since its ripeness is demonstrated by the movement's very success. If, on the other hand, historical necessity is only a matter of general tendencies, while the particular form of events is subject to unconditioned human volition, then the criticism is meaningless for another reason. Since we cannot say precisely what constitutes 'ripeness' for the change-over to socialism, and since conscious human activity may bring the favourable moment closer, no one can say for certain at what time the moment has in fact arrived. Hence Kautsky's criticism of Blanquism and Leninism is not justified, as it purports to be, by his theory of historical determinism.

Furthermore, as scientific consciousness arises independently of the social movement that leads to socialism and must be introduced into that movement from without, there is no reason not to draw the same conclusion from this state of affairs as Lenin did. The truly proletarian, i.e. the scientific, consciousness can develop independently of the actual proletariat, and the political organism which possesses that consciousness is entitled to regard itself as embodying the 'will of history' whatever the actual working class thinks of the matter. Lenin's theory of the party as a vanguard was based on the doctrine formulated by Kautsky and cannot be accused of inconsistency. In Marx's own thought the problem does not arise, as he identifies the scientific doctrine that arises in the minds of scholars with the movement which makes that doctrine its own. In Marx's view the scientific consciousness is an articulation of the elemental consciousness: it is not simply awareness of a process that is going on outside it, but is itself that process; in the consciousness of the proletariat the object and subject of history coincide, and the proletariat, by becoming aware of itself and thus of the whole historical process, *ipso facto* transforms the historical situation. In the proletarian consciousness knowledge of the (social) universe and political activity are not two separate things, like the knowledge of natural laws and the application of that knowledge to technological purposes; they are one and the same.

For the same reason, as already stated, there is no problem for Marx of the dichotomy between facts and values, or knowledge and duty. As, in this particular case, the act of cognizance of the world is the same as the act of changing it or of taking a practical part in the cognitive process, there is no room for the dichotomy to manifest itself, for there is no question of a perception followed by a separate act of evaluation. But since Kautsky, like his neo-Kantian opponents, regards knowledge as independent of its application and free from any value-judgement, he does not really come to grips with his critics' objections but fends them off with general statements, without perceiving the real nature of the problem. If men are convinced by scientific knowledge that socialism is a historical necessity, they must then ask themselves why they should help to bring it about: the mere fact that it is necessary does not answer this question. For Marx there is no problem, as humanity personified in the proletariat becomes aware of the necessity of the revolution in, and only in, the very act of bringing it about—theoretical awareness of the revolutionary movement *is* that movement. But Kautsky's deterministic philosophy makes it necessary to cope with the difficulty that the Kantians formulated but Kautsky himself failed to perceive. He also failed to notice that approbatory terms such as 'humanism', 'liberation', the 'greatness' or 'sublimity' of the socialist ideal—all of which he often employed—were inadmissible on his own premises.

Kautsky was profoundly attached to democratic values; he hated violence and war, and, while recognizing that future forms of the class struggle could not be foreseen, he hoped that mankind would advance into the realm of socialist freedom as a result of peaceful pressure, without violence or bloodshed. He tried to provide a theoretical backing for his hopes, but here too his doctrine is not free from essential weakness. The case for democracy, in his view, was based on the incurable limitation of human knowledge. No group or party could claim a monopoly of truth; all knowledge was partial and subject to change, and it would impede progress if any party were to reserve the exclusive right to express its views and to suppress criticism and discussion. These are sound arguments from the common-sense point of view, but they are combated by Kautsky's own theory of the social basis of knowledge. He maintained that there is no such thing as classless knowledge, at any rate in social questions, but that a true understanding of social processes can only be had by adopting the proletarian viewpoint. This raises epistemological problems that Kautsky never faced: if all knowledge of society is class-conditioned, how can knowledge acquired from the proletarian viewpoint in particular lay claim to universal validity? If it cannot, however, then all the scientific pretensions of Marxism are baseless; at best it can only rate as the formulation of a particular interest, albeit the interest of humanity in general, but it cannot, in addition, claim superiority over all other theories as the possessor of 'objective truth'. If, however, the proletarian viewpoint also entails a purely cognitive superiority, i.e. if it alone makes it possible to apply universal criteria of knowledge and if all other attitudes are not only class-conditioned but inevitably lead to the distortion of reality, then the demand for democracy, pluralism, free speech, etc. is groundless; for the party of the proletariat has, by definition, a monopoly of truth as against every other political organism, and all the privileges it claims and the despotism it imposes are fully justified in the interest of truth itself. But on this point too Kautsky failed to notice his own inconsistency.

Again, it is not clear why despotism and violence should be condemned from the point of view of Kautsky's historiosophy, although undoubtedly he himself was opposed to them. If mankind, unlike the rest of nature, has evolved various forms of intra-species aggression as a result of the very factors to which its pre-eminence is due, if man is endowed by nature with an aggressive instinct as well as an instinct of solidarity with his fellows, and if he has given free rein to the former instinct throughout his history, why should this state of things suddenly come to an end? Why should we believe in a law of history tending to lessen the use of coercion in intra-human relations? Even if we accept that capitalist forms of appropriation and the sharing of the surplus product must give way to public ownership, it does not follow that the same struggle will not be continued by other means in a socialized state, since the instincts that caused it will still be there. Kautsky's faith in the gradual elimination of violence and the increase of human solidarity is no more than faith, and cannot be vindicated by his theoretical principles.

Kautsky's position is also ambiguous as to the relation between reform and revolution. At first sight he appears in general to follow Marx in holding that there is no contradiction between the prospect of revolution and the policy of fighting for reforms; social progress, the shorter working day, greater prosperity for the workers, and democratic rights enabling them to defend their interests collectively, are all ways of developing class-consciousness and training the workers to take over the state in due course. But the consistency of this position is only apparent. The real question is whether reforms are *only* of value in relation to the coming revolution, or whether they are also valuable in themselves since they improve the lot of the proletariat. Kautsky took the latter view, holding that the intrinsic value of reforms was quite consistent with their value as an instrument of the revolutionary struggle. The course of practical politics, however, was to show that this supposed consistency was an illusion. A party which treated the struggle for reform seriously and which was successful in its efforts naturally became a reform party, its revolutionary slogans surviving only as embellishment. Kautsky was able to show that there were cases in history when the class struggle had intensified although the lot of the exploited workers was at the same time improving. But he was wrong in thinking that the improvements obtained by the working class through economic pressure were, as a general principle, without effect on the sharpness of class conflict and the state of revolutionary ardour. No doubt revolutionary situations are always the result of an unexpected coincidence of many circumstances, and better conditions for the workers do not rule out such situations *a priori*. But the practical difficulty is that a party which works for reforms instead of for revolution, which achieves reforms and therefore treats them as a serious objective, will find that its revolutionary theory becomes atrophied, and when the moment for revolution arrives the party will be incapable of seizing its opportunity. The objectives of reform and revolution can be reconciled in general doctrinal formulas, but not in social and psychological reality. Hence a socialist movement that achieves success in the economic struggle and in reformist endeavours tends inevitably to turn into a reform movement. As Bernstein saw but Kautsky did not, the achievements of German social democracy meant that it virtually ceased to be a revolutionary party.

The keynote of Kautsky's philosophy and that of the Marxists who thought like him is the 'naturalization' of human consciousness, i.e. its complete subordination to natural determinism, so that it plays the part of a mere factor of organic evolution. The main features of Kautsky's political theory and historiosophy are determined by this Darwinian version of Marxism: belief in the gradual and continuous evolution of capitalism to the point at which it destroys itself; confidence in historic inevitability, perceived from outside by the theoretical consciousness; dichotomy between theoretical awareness and the social process to which it is directed; the notion of a proletarian consciousness imported from without, and the rejection of the eschatological spirit of socialism. Kautsky's policy may be summed up as: 'Let us improve capitalism for the time being; socialism is guaranteed by the law of history in any case. It does not matter that we cannot prove separately the moral superiority of socialism: it simply so happens that what is necessary is also what appears desirable to me and to other persons of good sense.' Having introduced into Marxism the Enlightenment belief in continuous progress and the Darwinian view of consciousness as a biological organ, Kautsky was insensitive to the dramatic reversals of progress and failed to realize that consciousness itself is the cause of breaches of historical continuity that can easily be explained with the aid of hindsight, but which no one is ever able to foresee.

7. *A note on Mehring*

FRANZ MEHRING (1846–1919) was, after Kautsky, the principal pillar of orthodox German Marxism. He became a social democrat in middle age, in the early 1890s, having made a considerable name as a publicist and writer for the liberal Press. From then on he devoted his vast historical knowledge and literary skill (in which he stood foremost among the orthodox writers) to the cause of socialism. His works include the voluminous classic *Geschichte der deutschen Sozialdemokratie* (*History of German Social Democracy*, 1897–8); a no less classic, though somewhat hagiographic, life of Marx (*Karl Marx, Geschichte seines Lebens*, 1918; translated 1936); *Deutsche Geschichte vom Ausgange des Mittelalters* (*History of Germany from the End of the Middle Ages*, 1910–11); and *Die Lessing-Legende* (1893), perhaps the finest work of Marxist historiography of the period. He also left many studies of literary history and criticism, and helped to create the Marxist theory of literature (articles on Schiller, Heine, Tolstoy, and Ibsen). From time to time he dealt with the general principles of historical materialism, for example in the appendix to *Lessing*, in different parts of his book on German social democracy, in the life of Marx, and in critical articles against the neo-Kantists. On these occasions he showed a leaning towards very simplified or 'reductionist' formulations—a fact to which we owe Engels's famous letter of 1893, in which the patriarch of scientific socialism corrected 'one-sided' interpretations of historical materialism and the rather crude formula which he himself and Marx had employed on occasion for purposes of controversy. Mehring's historico-literary analyses also contain some remarkable simplifications, as when he says that the *Oresteia* merely reflects the victory of the patriarchal principle over the matriarchal, or that the whole of classical German literature—Klopstock and Lessing, Goethe and Schiller—represents 'nothing but' the fight of the bourgeoisie for emancipation. If this is so, it is hard to see how

Aeschylus can be read with pleasure and understanding by people who have not the faintest interest in the conflict between the patriarchate and the matriarchate in ancient Greece, or why Goethe and Schiller are still part of German culture although the political struggles of the last century have been forgotten. But it would be unfair to judge Mehring purely on the strength of such utterances. As a theoretician of historical materialism he did not, it is true, contribute anything to the evolution of Marxism, but he was of great importance as a historian and literary critic who, when it came to particular analyses, shook off the stiffness of doctrinal generalizations. The *Lessing-Legende* is not only a work about Lessing, but a review of the conventional views of German historians on the Enlightenment and an attack on the idolators of Frederick the Great and those who called Lessing the 'scribe of the Prussian monarchy'. Mehring tries to show that Lessing embodied in the most perfect and radical form all the virtues and progressive aspirations of the German bourgeoisie in its most militant and therefore creative period. His work has also an ideological purpose: it ends by declaring that Lessing's legacy 'belongs to the proletariat', as the bourgeoisie has jettisoned all his enlightened ideals.

Mehring joined issue with Marx on one point, namely his opinion of Lassalle. He recognized that Marx stood far above Lassalle as a scholar, writer, and revolutionary, and that Lassalle had his faults both as a historian and as a man of action, but he regarded Marx's judgement of him as offensive and largely due to personal prejudice. In Mehring's opinion, Lassalle had done a permanent service to German socialism both by his work as a theoretician and by creating a workers' party.

In his works on literature Mehring generally endeavoured to show that the greatness of a writer was measured by his success in presenting the aspirations and ideals of the class which he historically represented. But he did not identify artistic value with the class standpoint or with the social function that served to explain it. He held that no artistic values or tastes were permanent irrespective of history, but that all were relative to social situations. What he called 'emergent classes', i.e. those that were just beginning to fight for their social rights, tended in his opinion to show similar tastes in literature and art, in the shape of a desire for truth and realism. But naturalism, which had once been a weapon of the progressive bourgeoisie, had at times degenerated into the slavish imitation of casual reality and had deprived literature of the greatness that comes from a historical perspective. Naturalism had shown, sometimes very convincingly, the horrors of capitalism, but given its class origin it could not offer any way of escape from the bourgeois predicament. It had therefore given place to neo-Romanticism, which was an escape from the unfeeling world into capricious subjectivism and a capitulation before social problems. Along with historical perspective, the bourgeoisie had lost its spiritual creativity and no longer produced great works of the mind. Contemporary art and literature were alien to the proletariat, which turned to the great classics for the sound of warfare, the passion and fighting spirit by which it was itself animated. The art which would express specifically proletarian ideals and aspirations was still in an embryo state. Mehring did not believe, however, that sympathy for the workers' cause sufficed to produce literature of high quality: he did not identify artistic value with a correct political tendency, but more than once deprecated any such 'reduction'. Good intentions were not a substitute for artistic ability. Thus, although Mehring emphasized the value of art that expresses the proletarian point of view (Freiligrath's poems, Hauptmann's *Die Weber*), he was mistrustful of proletarian literature produced for direct political or propaganda ends and detached from the classical literary tradition.

It is not clear, however, how there can be a 'scientific aesthetic' such as Mehring desiderates, since he declares on the one hand that art cannot be evaluated by its social genesis and intentions, and, on the other, that there can be no purely aesthetic, non-historical criteria. Mehring was a well-read and percipient critic and quite aware of the difference between great and mediocre art. He defined the greatness of a work of art by the success with which it reflected the conflicts of its time, but he also questioned the possibility of other criteria than those based on the genesis of the work. On this basic point it is hard to clear him of inconsistency. For if all works of literature are born of class conflict, their genesis cannot permit us to distinguish good works from bad. The fact that a work expresses the tendencies of the 'progressive' class is also not enough. There is still a need for criteria independent of the genetic explanation; but according to Mehring there cannot be any such criteria, for in that case we should have to acknowledge that there were non-historical standards of beauty, which would mean falling into Kantianism or worse.

Here again, however, Mehring should not be too severely blamed for inadequacies that he shared with all contemporary Marxist writers on this subject. The value of his work does not consist in theoretical generalizations but in particular analyses in which he explained, skilfully and convincingly, the social background of creative literature. The genetic approach remains legitimate even when it is not clear exactly how it relates to artistic evaluation.

Kautsky, Mehring, and Heinrich Cunow were the most eminent theoreticians of orthodox Marxism as it was understood in their day. During and after the war, however, their political paths diverged. Kautsky maintained his 'centrist' position, Mehring declared for Spartacus, and Cunow for the right wing of the party. There was no direct correlation between theoretical orthodoxy on the one hand and politics on the other.

III

Rosa Luxemburg and the
Revolutionary Left

Rosa Luxemburg occupies an ambiguous place in the tradition of socialist thought. She was the principal theoretician of the small revolutionary group which combated both revisionists and orthodox centrists, but she differed from the Leninist wing on certain important points. The group in question, the left wing of German social democracy, had no real prolongation in the later history of the socialist movement, in the time of polarization after 1918. Rosa Luxemburg's uncompromising revolutionism, and her violent criticism of the treachery of most of the socialist leaders in 1914, separated her completely from reformist social democracy. At the same time her sharp attacks on Lenin's programme and tactics meant that, in spite of dying a martyr's death, she was never quite admitted to the Communist pantheon. Verbal tribute was paid to her as a revolutionary and critic of revisionism, but from a practical point of view she was disregarded.

None of her writings is expressly philosophical: she was a theoretician of socialist strategy and tactics and of political economy. One may, however, regard 'Luxemburgism' as a particular variant of Marxism which, though not possessing an articulate philosophical basis, occupies a place of its own in the history of socialist doctrine, including its theoretical foundations.

1. Biographical information

Rosa Luxemburg, a Polish Jewess, was born at Zamość in 1870. Although she spent very little of her adult life in Poland she maintained close links with the Polish revolutionary movement, as a pillar of the Social Democratic Party of the Kingdom of Poland and Lithuania and, indirectly, as one of the founders of the Polish Communist party. Her links with socialism began in her early youth. After leaving high school in Warsaw in 1887 she joined a clandestine socialist youth group and, to escape arrest, fled to Switzerland in 1889. She studied at Zurich University and lived there till 1898, when she moved to Berlin and became one of the most active theorists and leaders of German social democracy. In Zurich she met the Polish socialists Warski, Marchlewski, and Tyszka-Jogiches, and wrote for the Paris paper *Sprawa Robotnicza* (*The Workers' Cause*), which became the organ of SDKPiL when the latter was founded in 1894. From 1893 onwards she took part in all the congresses of the Second International except the final one at Basle, and afterwards in all those of the German social democratic party. From the outset she devoted much time to combating the Polish Socialist party and its programme for the independence of Poland. In 1897 she wrote a doctoral thesis at Zurich on Polish industrial development (published as *Die industrielle Entwicklung Polens*, 1898): this formed the historical background to her future tactics, which were unalterably opposed to any attempt at reconstituting an independent Polish state. Her argument was that the development of capitalism in Russian Poland was mainly the result of the conqueror's policy, which had linked the fate of the Polish bourgeoisie with the Tsarist empire and its economic expansion to the east; plans for an independent Poland, as she maintained in subsequent writings, were contrary to the 'objective economic trend' which had irrevocably drawn Polish capitalism into the Russian orbit. Rosa Luxemburg's opposition to the movement for Polish independence supplied the main ideological theme of SDKPiL in contrast to that of the PPS.

From the time she settled in Berlin Rosa Luxemburg's career was linked with the German socialist movement, but she remained active in the leadership of SDKPiL, carried on political propaganda in Prussian Poland, which she visited several times, and wrote for Polish socialist papers; *Przegląd Socjaldemokratyczny* (*Social Democratic Review*), published legally at Cracow, and the illegal Warsaw journal *Czerwony Sztandar* (*Red Flag*). From 1895 she wrote for *Die Neue Zeit*, the *Leipziger Volkszeitung*, and other German socialist organs. From 1898, when the world of German social democracy was dominated by the controversy over Bernstein's views, Rosa Luxemburg's writings and speeches were largely devoted to combating revisionism as advocated by Bernstein and other reformists. Her most important theoretical work of this period was the pamphlet *Sozialreform oder Revolution?* (*Social Reform or Revolution?*) published in 1900 (second edition 1908), containing the fullest expression of her disbelief in the possibility of reforming capitalism and her conviction that any struggle for economic reform must be of purely political significance.

Up to 1906 revisionism was attacked by all orthodox German socialists, but the first Russian revolution caused, or rather brought to light, a divergence of view resulting in the formation of a left-wing group with Rosa Luxemburg as its chief theorist; other members were Karl Liebknecht, Clara Zetkin, and Franz Mehring. It was not until 1910, however, that the differences between the radicals and the centre took on an acute form and led to a new balance of political forces within the party, with the centre group (Bebel and Kautsky) in general closer to the Right than to the revolutionaries.

The events in Russia prompted Rosa Luxemburg to work out a new idea of revolution in the light of the spontaneous uprising of the workers of the Tsarist empire. At the end of 1905 she went illegally to Warsaw to take part in the revolutionary movement. Arrested after two months, she was released on bail in July 1906 and returned to Berlin via Finland. In a pamphlet *Massenstreik, Partei und Gewerkschaften* (1906) she attempted to draw conclusions from the events of the past year. Apart from this, both before and after the 1905 Revolution she expressed her views on matters related to the state of socialism in Russia. In articles published in *Die Neue Zeit* in 1903–4 she criticized the 'opportunism' of Lenin's ultra-centralist policy and his distrust of the workers' movement. At the same time she defended the Bolsheviks against the charge of Blanquism that was brought by Plekhanov and the Mensheviks. Like Lenin she opposed the doctrine that, in view of the bourgeois character of the coming Russian revolution, the socialists should not attack the liberals but should allow them to gain power without hindrance; this issue was debated, for example, at the London Conference of the Russian Social-Democratic Workers' Party (RSDWP) in May 1907. Rosa Luxemburg believed that the defeat of the Russian revolution was only temporary, that the revolutionary process would continue and that Russia was a pattern for the German working class as well— which Bebel and Kautsky both denied. The centrists and the radicals, however, were agreed in their attitude towards militarism and the threat of war, until it actually materialized. At the Stuttgart Congress of the Second International in 1907 Rosa Luxemburg caused the anti-war resolution to be amended in the sense that if war did break out despite the efforts of the working class, it should be transformed into an anti-capitalist revolution.

In 1912 she wrote her principal theoretical work *Die Akkumulation des Kapitals* (published in 1913; English translation, *The Accumulation of Capital*, 1951), which analysed the process of reproduction and demonstrated the economic inevitability of the collapse of capitalism. In 1913, with Marchlewski and Mehring, she founded the *Sozialdemokratische Korrespondenz*, a revolutionary organ of the German Left. She was sentenced to a year's imprisonment in 1914 for anti-war speeches, but was not actually imprisoned until later. The outbreak of war, the action of the social democrats in voting for war credits, and the dissolution of the International had placed the internationalist Left in the position of a helpless minority; but Rosa Luxemburg continued the struggle, convinced that the revolutionary potential of the world proletariat would eventually turn the war into a social upheaval. Sentenced to another year's imprisonment in February 1915, she wrote in her cell a pamphlet analysing the causes of the war and condemning the social democratic leaders for destroying the socialist movement by accepting the *Burgfriede* ('civic truce') and supporting the imperialist war. She went on to define the basis on which the workers' movement should be revived: wars, imperialism and militarism could not be abolished as long as capitalism lasted, but could only be overcome by a socialist revolution; the most urgent task was to free the proletariat from the state of spiritual dependence on the bourgeoisie in which it had been placed by its time-serving leaders. This work, published under the title *Die Krise der Sozialdemokratie* but generally known as the 'Junius pamphlet', was the ideological foundation of the Spartacus League, which was formed early in 1916 and was the nucleus of the future German Communist party (KPD). In 1917 the League, while remaining a separate body, joined the left wing of the social democrats who had formed the USPD: after the war the USPD dissolved, its members joining either the KPD or the reconstituted SPD.

Rosa Luxemburg was released from prison in February 1916 but was arrested again less than four months later for taking part in anti-war demonstrations; she remained in gaol until the last days of the war (8 November 1918). While there she wrote a reply (the *Antikritik*) to criticisms of her *Accumulation of Capital*, and an unfinished analysis of the October Revolution in Russia. The latter work was first published in 1922, after Rosa Luxemburg's death, by her friend Paul Levi, a former member of the Spartacus League and a leader of the KPD, who, however, was afterwards expelled from the latter and returned to the SPD. The pamphlet, entitled *Die russische Revolution*, hailed the events in Russia as a sign that world revolution was close at hand, but attacked the Bolsheviks for their policy towards the peasants and the national question, and above all for their despotic rule and suppression of democratic freedoms. It was chiefly on account of this work that Rosa Luxemburg became a *bête noire* of the Stalinists (who never quoted it, however). In general the pamphlet was little known before the Second World War, and was only translated into other languages after 1945 (English version 1959).

Rosa Luxemburg was set free by the German revolution, but did not enjoy her liberty for long. She imagined that the revolution would at once develop into a socialist phase, but the attempted rising by the Spartacus League, which was weak in itself and had scarcely any roots in the working class, was a fiasco. During the rising the League transformed itself into the KPD, while the Workers' and Soldiers' Councils formed the basis of the social democratic government of Germany. On the night of 15–16 January 1919 the two chief Communist leaders, Rosa Luxemburg and Karl Liebknecht, were murdered by *Freikorps* troops, and two months later Leo Tyszka-Jogiches met a similar death at the hands of the police. The lectures on economics which Rosa Luxemburg had delivered at the party school and written up while in prison were published posthumously in 1925 (*Einführung in die Nationalökonomie*).

2. The theory of accumulation and the inevitable collapse of capitalism

ALTHOUGH Rosa Luxemburg's chief theoretical work was not published until 1913, its main ideas can be found in many earlier texts, including *Social Reform or Revolution?*, and most of her theoretical and political opinions derive logically from her views on accumulation, which we shall therefore begin by examining.

The theory expounded in *The Accumulation of Capital* is commonly referred to as that of the 'automatic collapse of capitalism'. This term, however, was coined by Rosa Luxemburg's opponents, chiefly Leninists and Stalinists: it does not occur in her own work, and it is misleading in so far as it suggests that capitalism will collapse by virtue of its own contradictions and irrespective of the political struggle of the proletariat. Far from taking this view, Rosa Luxemburg believed that the revolution would overthrow capitalism long before the latter's economic possibilities were exhausted. She held, however, that the capitalist system could only work as long as it had at its disposal a non-capitalist market, whether internal or external, and, as it was in the nature of the system to destroy its non-capitalistic environment, it was inevitably preparing its own economic ruin. There could be no such thing as 'pure capitalism' on a world scale: if the capitalist economy developed to that extent it would cease to exist.

Marx had maintained that capitalism was bound to destroy itself by its own contradictions, especially those connected with the concentration of capital and the impoverishment of the working class, but he never defined the exact conditions under which capitalism would become an economic impossibility. Rosa Luxemburg set out to do this, partly by supplementing Marx's views and partly by modifying them.

The starting-point of her theory of accumulation consists in the schemata of reproduction set out in Volume II of *Capital*. This is the most arduous and the least-read portion of Marx's work, but from Rosa Luxemburg's point of view it was fundamental to the crucial question of scientific socialism, viz. 'Why is capitalism doomed to destruction on economic grounds?'—or, to put it the other way round, 'Can the process of compound reproduction (*erweiterte Reproduktion*) as it exists in capitalism develop, theoretically, to infinity?' Rosa Luxemburg's argument is as follows.

According to Marx the value of any commodity consists of three components, expressed in the formula $C + V + S$. C (constant capital) stands for the value of the means of production, i.e. tools and raw materials, that have gone into making the product; V (variable capital) represents wages, and S (surplus value) is the increase of value due to the unremunerated portion of wage-labour. In contrast to previous systems in which reproduction was governed by social needs, capitalism is concerned only with the maximum increase of surplus value, and therefore tends constantly to increase production irrespective of need. Accumulation, or the conversion of surplus value into fresh, active capital, belongs to the nature of capitalist production. It is a condition of compound reproduction, however, that the goods produced should be converted into money: for this purpose further quantities of goods must be marketed, a process over which the individual capitalist has little influence. Let us assume that the annual production is expressed in the proportion:

$$40C + 10V + 10S = 60$$

In this formula the amount of constant capital is four times that of variable capital, and the rate of surplus value, or rate of exploitation, is 100 per cent. The value of the commodities produced is 60 units. If the capitalist now devotes 5S, or half the surplus value, to increasing production, i.e. adds it to his constant capital, then, the organic composition of capital remaining the same, the next phase of production will be expressed by the formula

$$44C + 11V + 11S = 66$$

This process can go on as long as the capitalist can get hold of sufficient means of production and labour force and secure an outlet for his goods. Hence, if in conditions of simple reproduction money plays only the part of an intermediary in the exchange of commodities, under capitalism it is an element in the circulation of capital: for accumulation to be possible, surplus value must assume a monetary form. In addition capitalism tends naturally to drive wages down to subsistence level, so that S tends to increase in relation to V.

If, following Marx, we divide the whole of social production into two 'departments'—I production of means of production, and II production of consumption goods—then we see that the two are interdependent, i.e. they must remain in a specific proportion so that the process of production may continue harmoniously. Department I produces means of production for both departments I and II, while department II produces consumption goods for the workers and capitalists of both departments. The necessary proportion is illustrated by the following pattern:

Department I: $4,000C + 1,000V + 1,000S = 6,000$
Department II: $2,000C + 500V + 500S = 3,000$

For simple reproduction the value of the products in department I, i.e. 6,000, must equal the value of the constant capital of both departments (4,000 + 2,000), while the value of the products of department II, i.e. 3,000, must equal the combined income of workers and capitalists in both departments, i.e. 1,000 + 1,000 + 500 + 500. This is so in the above example, but it is not so in capitalist reality, which is based on 'compound reproduction', i.e. the capitalization of a part of S in both departments. If we have

$$\text{Department I: } 4,000C + 1,000V + 1,000S = 6,000$$
$$\text{Department II: } 1,500C + 750V + 750S = 3,000$$

it will be seen that the value of the production of means of production (6,000) exceeds by 500 the value of the means of production used in the given productive cycle (i.e. 4,000 + 1,500), while the value of consumption goods (3,000) is 500 less than the total incomes of capitalists and workers in both departments (1,000 + 1,000 + 750 + 750). The application of this unconsumed portion of S to the new productive cycle, the proportion between the two departments remaining the same, causes a corresponding increase in all elements of the value of the totality of commodities. For this, however, the commodities must first be transformed into money. Accumulation depends on an increasing demand for the goods produced, and the question is, how does this demand arise? Industry cannot go on creating its own market *ad infinitum*; what is produced must in the end be consumed. An increase of population does not solve the problem of demand, for the numerical increase of the capitalist class is included in the absolute magnitude of the consumable portion of surplus value, while working-class consumption is limited by the wage-level; nonproducing sections of the population, such as landowners, civil servants, soldiers, professional men, and artists, are maintained either from surplus value or from wages. Nor does foreign trade provide the solution, for the analysis of compound reproduction applies to world capitalism, for which all countries are an internal market. In other words, for the surplus value of both departments of production to realize itself in money-form, there must be a market external to both departments and capable of absorbing goods at a rate increasing with the rate of accumulation.

Marx, according to Rosa Luxemburg, did not come to grips with this problem. He believed that capitalists collectively provide a market by buying one another's means of production; but they cannot increase surplus value indefinitely except by increasing the rate of consumption, and the workers cannot help towards this end, since all they have is their wages, which figure in the equation already. Marx, it is true, never stated that accumulation can go on to an unlimited extent: his schemata are only designed to illustrate the proportion between accumulation in the two departments and their dependence on each other. But, as he never answered the basic question, For whom does compound reproduction occur?, the schemata may be falsely interpreted as indicating that production is capable of absorbing the whole increase of surplus value: the industry of department I expands to increase production in department II, and the latter is increased so as to maintain the growing army of workers in both departments. Thus the Russian Marxists—Struve, Bulgakov, and Tugan-Baranovsky—use the Marxian schemata to infer that capitalist accumulation can go on increasing indefinitely. But to admit this is to give up the whole idea of scientific socialism. For if there is no limit to accumulation within capitalist forms of production, it follows that capitalism is economically invincible, that it is an inexhaustible source of economic and technical progress; socialism is not a historical necessity, and there is no economic reason for the collapse of capitalism. (The idea that capitalism would collapse because of the falling rate of profit seemed to Rosa Luxemburg absurd. It was impossible to imagine the scenario of this breakdown, the more so as the tendency for the profit rate to fall was quite compatible with an absolute increase in total profits; it was hard to suppose that capitalists would one day cease production because the profit rate was too low, even though they were making larger profits than before.)

Thus, in Rosa Luxemburg's opinion, Marx overlooked the question which is vital to the existence of scientific socialism, viz. that of the precise economic reason why capitalism is bound to destroy itself. He wrote, indeed, that the increase of productive power conflicts increasingly with the limited possibilities of consumption, but his schemata of compound reproduction do not reveal the contradiction between the creation of surplus value and its realization. The schemata presuppose that capitalists and workers are the only consumers, i.e. they assume for theoretical purposes a fictional society of 'pure' capitalism, consisting of capitalists and workers only. Such a fiction is admissible in the analysis of individual capital but not, Rosa Luxemburg argues, in regard to capital as a whole: for it conceals the fundamental point that compound reproduction takes place in a world in which there is still a non-capitalist market, and the social classes or countries that live outside the capitalist system are necessary to the latter as consumers of its surplus production in both departments I and II. The surplus value must realize itself outside the sphere of capitalist production, in pre-capitalist spheres such as backward countries, the rural economy, and handicrafts: mature capitalism depends on the existence of non-capitalist classes and countries. But capitalist expansion tends inexorably to eliminate pre-capitalist economic forms by drawing peasants and craftsmen into its own orbit. Capitalism thus unconsciously prepares its own downfall by destroying the forms on which it depends. When capitalism succeeds in assimilating the whole of production, accumulation will become impossible and capitalism will be economically unfeasible. 'Pure capitalism' is incapable of surviving. At the present time there are many non-capitalist areas of the world, and the struggle to possess these as sources of raw materials and cheap labour, and above all as outlets for European goods, takes the form of imperialism. The field for expansion still exists, but it is contracting rapidly. By the fight for mar-

kets capitalism is steadily destroying all remnants of the pre-capitalist environment which is the condition of its own being.

It is noteworthy that although Rosa Luxemburg's intention was to establish once and for all the economic inevitability of the collapse of capitalism,
none of the Marxist theoreticians who believed in the historical necessity of
socialism endorsed her argument, and the most important of them opposed
it—Hilferding, Kautsky, Gustav Eckstein, Otto Bauer, A. Pannekoek, Tugan-
Baranovsky, and Lenin. Tugan-Baranovsky held that the anti-human character of capitalism, and the fact that it makes increased production an end in
itself instead of a means of satisfying social needs, meant that accumulation
could go on indefinitely, as industry was able to provide itself with outlets by
continuing to increase production, absorbing more and more of the means of
production, employing more and more workers, and so forth. No one denied,
of course, that capitalism was beset by marketing difficulties that resulted in
crises of overproduction, cut-throat competition, the struggle for markets, and
imperialist wars, and that militarism, beside the immediate purpose of conquering markets, itself afforded a sphere of capital accumulation. But Marxists
generally took the view that although capitalism would eventually be
destroyed by its own manifold contradictions, it was not possible to predict the
exact economic circumstances in which this would happen; and they were
inclined to attach more importance to the concentration of capital, the pauperization of the working class, and the extinction of the middle class than to
any insufficiency of demand, which capitalism seemed able to remedy in various ways despite its undoubted difficulties and crises. Rosa Luxemburg's
Leninist critics were suspicious of the theory of accumulation precisely
because it seemed to imply that capitalism would break down automatically. If
capitalism was bound to destroy itself by its own expansion, irrespective of the
political role of the proletariat, this would encourage a policy of passive expectation and would tend to relax the party's zeal instead of spurring it to revolutionary activity. Rosa Luxemburg herself never drew this conclusion from her
theory. The critics also objected that she underrated the possibility of compound reproduction thanks to the armaments industry and military expansion,
and this has been confirmed by the later development of capitalism.

In general it appears that the theory of accumulation involves assumptions
concerning capitalism that were either unreal or have been disproved by subsequent events.

Rosa Luxemburg frequently makes the point that she is concerned with
capitalism as an all-embracing system, a single worldwide market, and for this
reason she ignores any modifications that might be due to external markets.
Capitalism in a single country may be able to survive by expanding into the
non-capitalist world, but if capitalism is worldwide there are no markets to

expand into. But for 'pure capitalism' to exist in this sense, it is not sufficient for capitalist production to embrace every country in the world. It is necessary in addition for the rate of profit to be the same throughout the world: for, on Rosa Luxemburg's theory, the developed countries may expand into areas which, although capitalist, are backward and where the rate of profit is therefore higher. In other words, her schema presupposes a world in which there is no difference in economic development between the Congo and the U.S.A. One may imagine a world as uniform as this, but it scarcely affords a solid basis for economic predictions. Not only is the prospect remote and unreal, but it ignores the fact that the gap between developed and backward nations is getting larger rather than smaller. This being so, to assert that capitalism will break down when this prospect becomes a reality is no less arbitrary than, for example, to suppose that capitalism can content itself with simple reproduction and could therefore survive if there were insufficient outlets to permit of compound reproduction. Rosa Luxemburg derides those who believe that the fall in the profit rate will lead to the collapse of capitalism, on the ground that one cannot see the capitalists committing suicide because their profit rates are less high than they used to be. But she fails to observe that her own theory is open to the same taunt: if capitalists one day find they cannot market an increased volume of goods, will they hang themselves sooner than be content with simple reproduction? The answer to this in Marxian terms is of course that it is in the nature of capitalism to seek after compound reproduction; but if 'nature' is not a purely metaphysical entity, we may ask whether capitalism is really unable to change its spots as an alternative to complete destruction. Such a hypothesis is no less extraordinary than Rosa Luxemburg's imaginary world in which all countries are at the same level of industry, technology, and civilization.

From today's standpoint we can see how far her theory of accumulation was based on a false estimate of the future development of capitalism. This estimate, however, unlike her specific theory of the collapse of capitalism, was shared by most of her Marxist contemporaries. The theory of accumulation assumed a growing class polarization approximating to the condition in which society consisted exclusively of capitalists and workers. As we know, things happened differently; not only were small businesses not squeezed out, but, above all, in the more developed countries the proportion of workers in the population has tended to decrease, while there has been a huge increase of what Marx called non-productive workers, i.e. those engaged in trade, administration, education, services, etc. Rosa Luxemburg disposes of these non-productive elements by saying that they are remunerated either from the uncapitalized portion of surplus value or out of wages, but that there is always a portion of surplus value that is turned into capital and so increases production in the next cycle. But it is not clear why the increased consumption of the non-productive workers should have no effect on the realization of surplus value, even if we accept Marx's increasingly doubtful distinction between productive and non-productive labour and suppose that the latter is 'in the last resort' paid out of surplus value created by the working class.

Another false assumption of the theory of accumulation is that wages under capitalism would always be close to subsistence level: the argument being that although the laws of exploitation might be weakened from time to time they would 'in the last resort' always prevail over working-class resistance, so that a genuine increase in workers' consumption was unlikely to occur.

Further, Rosa Luxemburg did not believe that a state controlled by the bourgeoisie could regulate the process of accumulation to any important extent. But the evolution of capitalism has shown that she was mistaken. Even if, following Marx, we regard the state as a whole as the political embodiment of global capital, experience has shown that this state can play the part of an organizer, using economic and legal means to affect the distribution of investment resources, and that it can, under political pressure for instance, enlarge the internal market. That is to say, it can act as a socialist state in so far as it controls the process of production in accordance with social needs, instead of leaving everything to the 'wolfish greed for surplus value' as the sole motive force of capitalist production.

For the above reasons Rosa Luxemburg's theory of accumulation cannot, in its literal form, be accepted as an explanation or forecast of the economic development of capitalism. It does not follow, however, that her work was of no effect. As Michael Kalecki observes in the collective work (in Polish) *The economic theories of Marx's 'Capital'* (1967), the rival theories of reproduction put forward by Rosa Luxemburg and Tugan-Baranovsky were both erroneous but both helped to illustrate certain features of economic growth under capitalism. Tugan-Baranovsky held that there are no absolute barriers to capitalism in the form of limited outlets, and that its output can be marketed at any level of consumption as long as the ratio of consumption to investment is maintained. There is nothing absurd, in capitalist terms, in production being undertaken simply in order to increase production: on the contrary, production regardless of need is the strength of the system. But, Kalecki observes, Tugan-Baranovsky overlooked the fact that a system which entirely ignored the level of consumption would be very unstable, since any drop in investment would mean a decrease in the use made of the existing apparatus of production, hence a further drop in investment, and so on in a vicious spiral. On the other hand, Rosa Luxemburg's theory that compound reproduction depends wholly on non-capitalist markets has been refuted by our experience of the state's power to create, in the form of arms production, a huge market that may have a decisive effect on economic growth. In addition she was wrong in supposing that the whole volume of goods exported to non-capitalist markets contributes to the realization of productive surpluses, whereas what actually counts is the excess of exports—both goods and capital, but especially the latter—over imports; for imported goods also absorb purchasing power. However, in a limited sense the two theories supplement each other: one shows up the absurdity of a system whose viability depends on producing for profit instead of need, while the other demonstrates the importance of foreign markets for capitalist growth. At the same time, neither theory provides a sufficient explanation of the process of compound reproduction.

To Rosa Luxemburg, however, the theory of accumulation was of fundamental importance not only as the sole possible scientific vindication of Marx's prophecy of the downfall of capitalism, but also as an ideological weapon: for it meant that capitalists could do nothing to avert the destruction of their class and that no human power could prevent the final victory of socialism, which, as she and all Marxists believed, would replace capitalism.

This belief was, it would seem, based on a more general conviction by which her thought was permeated—an unshakeable, doctrinaire fidelity to the concept of iron historical laws that no human agency could bend or break. The belief in historical laws is, of course, a classic theme of Marxism, and all Marxists at the time professed it, but some held it more uncompromisingly than others. Most of them attenuated the literal sense of the doctrine, for instance by invoking Engels's formula of the 'relative independence of the superstructure', or, like Lenin, emphasizing the role of 'subjective' factors—i.e. organized willpower—in hastening social change; or again, pointing out in a common-sense fashion the many social conflicts that do not fall into the general category of 'contradictions of capitalism' yet undeniably do affect history. Rosa Luxemburg, however, was determined to find a single key to all historical problems and believed that Marx's analysis of the dynamics of capitalism provided this key, at any rate when supplemented by an exact account of the conditions of reproduction. Her adamant refusal to believe in any individual or even collective human actions that were not pre-determined by the 'laws of history' was manifested in all important questions in which she took a different stand from her fellow Marxists. Just as no capitalist efforts could hinder the blind anarchic forces of accumulation that were bringing the whole system to ruin, so too it was impossible for any organized movement to bring about a revolution by artificial means. Men and women were instruments of the historical process, and their task was to understand it and their own part in it. No purely ideological phenomena could of themselves affect the course of history; in particular, national ideologies were powerless to deflect history from its progress towards the great transformation of all time, the worldwide socialist revolution.

Owing to this doctrinaire belief Rosa Luxemburg was frequently blind to the empirical reality of social events and showed an extraordinary lack of political understanding in regard to national questions and to the revolution itself. Her writings show a theoretical consistency of the kind which can only come from extreme dogmatic rigidity and insensitivity to facts.

3. Reform and revolution

IF Rosa Luxemburg had believed in the 'automatic breakdown' of capitalism in the sense imputed by her critics, it would have been in glaring contradiction to the position she took up in the debate on 'reform versus revolution'. But, although she held with Marx that capitalism was condemned to self-destruction in that it would sooner or later become a brake on technical progress and economic growth, it did not follow that capitalism would collapse without the need for revolutionary action. It was rather the case that imperialism must develop to a point at which it would awaken the revolutionary consciousness of the proletariat, without which capitalism could not be overthrown. Its overthrow was a historical necessity, but so was the revolutionary movement that must bring it about. This view was shared by Rosa Luxemburg and other orthodox Marxists of her time.

The question of the significance and prospects of 'reformist' action—i.e. the workers' economic struggle for better conditions, and the campaign for democratic measures within bourgeois society—was, in Rosa's Luxemburg's opinion, vital to the whole socialist movement. Her position was essentially the same as Marx's: the value of reforms was not that they brought an alleviation of conditions but that the struggle itself afforded the proletariat the necessary practice for the decisive battle. Those who regarded reforms as an end in themselves were denying the prospect of socialism and turning their backs on the ultimate goal.

Many orthodox Marxists took the view that the revolution would come when economic conditions were ripe and that meanwhile their task was to fight for democracy in public life and better conditions for the working class. The reformists, while not expressly abandoning the hope of revolution, were vague about the time and circumstances in which it would occur. The essence of Rosa Luxemburg's position (like that of all the left wing of the International, including Lenin) was that she combated both these views, although her opposition to the orthodox viewpoint took shape at a later date. In the controversy with Bernstein and those party leaders and trade unionists who supported him in practice though without evolving any special theoretical views—for example, Georg von Vollmar, Wolfgang Heine and Max Schippel—Rosa Luxemburg in effect directed her attack not only against 'revisionist' reformism but also against the orthodox variety. Her main point was that reforms were meaning-less if they were not a means to the conquest of power; they must not be treated, even partially, as an end in themselves, and those who did so, whatever their professions, were abandoning the revolutionary cause. Any struggle for reform that was not subordinated to the coming revolution was a hindrance rather than a help to socialism, whatever its immediate outcome might be. As Rosa Luxemburg declared at the party congress at Stuttgart in 1898, the unions' fight for better terms for the sale of labour-power, pressure for social reform and democratic methods were forms of activity within the capitalist system and therefore had no specifically socialist meaning except as part of the struggle for the ultimate conquest of political power. To Bernstein's dictum that 'The goal is nothing, the movement everything' she replied with the opposite formula: 'The movement as an end in itself, unrelated to the ultimate goal, is nothing to me; the ultimate goal is everything.' Concentration on short-term effects led reformists like Schippel to support militarism, as the growth of armies and war production would reduce unemployment and prevent crises by increasing pur-chasing power. This, Rosa Luxemburg said, was absurd economically, as crises were not due to an absolute imbalance between consumption and production, but to the inherent tendency of production to exceed the possibilities of the market, and military costs would be borne in one way or another by the work-ing class. But the theory was also politically dangerous, as it suggested that the workers could or should give up their principal aims for the sake of temporary gains that would finally be to their detriment ('Miliz und Militarismus', *Leipziger Volkszeitung*, February 1899).

Rosa Luxemburg's most general treatment of this question is in her pam-phlet *Social Reform or Revolution?* There is no opposition, she declares, between the struggle for reform and the struggle for political power: the former is a means, the latter an end in itself. Social democracy is distinguished from bourgeois reformism by its awareness of the ultimate goal. To treat reforms as an end in themselves means accepting the indefinite continuance of capitalism, enabling it to escape destruction at the cost of a few modifications. For example, Konrad Schmidt held that the workers' political and economic struggle would lead in time to public control over production and would limit the role of capitalists. But in fact the workers' influence on capitalist production could only have a reactionary effect: it would hold up technical progress, or align workers and capitalists against consumers. 'In general,' Rosa Luxemburg wrote in 1900, 'the trade union movement is not moving into a period of victorious development but into one of increasing difficulties. When the development of industry reaches its zenith and worldwide capitalism begins to go downhill, the unions' task will be doubly difficult. In the first place the objective state of the labour market will be worse, as demand will increase more slowly and supply more rapidly than now. Secondly, capital will be even more unscrupulous in seizing that part of the product which is the workers' due, so as to recoup its losses on the world market.' The state cannot intervene in any other interest than that of capital, since it is an organ of the capitalist class and can only pursue general policies in so far as they accord with the interests of that class. This applies equally to democratic political institutions, which the bourgeoisie will maintain as long as, and to the extent that, it suits them to do so. Hence no amount of reform can overthrow capitalism or achieve revolutionary objectives by degrees. The proletariat's economic and political struggle can only help to bring about the subjective conditions of revolution; it does not, as Bernstein argues, lead objectively towards socialism or restrict exploitation. What the struggle achieves is not the transformation of society but the transformation of the consciousness of the proletariat. To treat short-term successes as ends in themselves is contrary to the class viewpoint and can only breed illusions; 'in the capitalist world, social reform is and always will be a nut without a kernel'. In despite of Bernstein, Marx's predictions concerning the development of capitalism are being fulfilled to the letter. The fact that there are no crises of overproduction at the moment does not invalidate his views or signify that capitalism is changing or is capable of adaptation. The crises that Marx knew at first hand were not the same as those he predicted: the former were crises of the growth and expansion of capitalism, not its exhaustion—the real crises of overproduction have yet to come. The system of share capital is not, as Bernstein maintains, a sign that small capitalists are on the increase: it is a form of the concentration of capital and therefore intensifies contradictions instead of curing them. The proletariat cannot avert or invalidate the laws of capitalist economy: its defensive struggle for the right to sell labour-power on normal terms is a Sisyphean task, though necessary to prevent wages falling still more. But, whatever the workers' efforts, their share in the wealth of society must diminish 'with the inevitability of a natural process, as the productivity of labour increases'.

Thus revolution and reform are different in nature, not merely in degree: reform does not amount to a gradual revolution, or revolution to a telescoped reform. To think otherwise is to believe that capitalism need only be amended, and that its overthrow is unnecessary.

Rosa Luxemburg's refusal to admit that reforms had any value in themselves, and her mistrust of any conspicuous success in the proletariat's economic struggle, inclined her to make pessimistic forecasts and to disparage the results obtained. Her revisionist adversaries, such as Bernstein and David, regarded Britain as a model country as far as the workers' struggle was concerned; she, on the other hand, saw in it a pernicious example of how the proletariat could be corrupted by temporary gains. In an article in the *Leipziger Volkszeitung* in May 1899 she declared that the British trade unions had achieved successes by abandoning the class viewpoint and bargaining within the framework of the capitalist economy. The British proletariat had adopted bourgeois ideas and sacrificed class objectives for immediate gain. But we are now at the end of this period, and the class struggle—in the true, not the reformist sense—is about to begin again.

All this is fully in accord with Marx's theory, but not with the celebrated text from Engels on which the reformists relied. At the first congress of the German Communist party on 30 December 1918 Rosa Luxemburg made no attempt to interpret Engels in a sense favourable to her own views, but criticized him for taking a reformist line in the Introduction to Marx's *The Class Struggles in France*, under pressure, as she claimed, from Bebel and the social democrats in the Reichstag. The text in question had done harm to the socialist movement by providing a permanent excuse to those who based their hopes on purely parliamentary action and in practice ignored the prospect of revolution.

Rosa Luxemburg did not speculate deeply as to the basis of Marx's view that the working class, by virtue of its position, must evolve a revolutionary consciousness. Marx formed this opinion in 1843 on purely philosophical grounds, and never abandoned it. Its only basis at that time, however, was the conviction that because the working class is subject to the maximum of dehumanization it cannot liberate itself as a separate class but only as a movement restoring the humanity of mankind as a whole. This is scarcely a cogent argument. Because a particular class is oppressed, exploited, and dehumanized it does not follow *a priori* that that class must aspire to world revolution, still less that its aspiration will succeed. In any case, the modern working class is no more dehumanized than the slaves of antiquity. In his later writings Marx used what appeared to be more pragmatic arguments. The capitalist system would soon lose control over technological progress, and the working class stood for a society that would remove obstacles to such progress and subordinate production to human needs instead of to the multiplication of value for its own sake. But this argument involves premises which are far from obvious. It assumes that indefinite technical progress is in the nature of things, or rather that the desire for technical improvement is an inseparable part of human nature—for technical progress is a human activity: as Lévi-Strauss puts it, one axe does not produce another. But Marx did not make this assumption; on the contrary, he believed that the urge for technical improvement was peculiar to capitalism and had not existed in other economic systems. Thus, if he was right in holding that capitalism was bound to lose the power to improve technology, the consequence would be that capitalism would cease to exist in its present form, i.e. as characterized by technical progress; but it would not follow that its role would be inherited by the working class, still less that the working class would inherit the ability to control technical progress and that this ability would ensure its political triumph. It could equally well be supposed that capitalism would go on existing in a stagnant form or be replaced by another society that might not necessarily depend on the continual improvement of productive forces and need not be socialist in Marx's sense.

This, it is true, was not the whole of Marx's argument. He also thought that the historical prelude to the proletarian revolution would be the increasing polarization of classes, the disappearance of the intermediate class, the increasing size of the 'reserve army' and of the proletariat, and the development of the latter's class-consciousness. But even on Marx's premises these events are not sufficient to justify belief in the inevitability of a proletarian revolution. Poverty does not in itself produce a trend towards revolution, nor does the preponderance of the exploited class, nor, least of all, the fact that justice is on its side. On the other hand, according to Marx the growth of revolutionary consciousness depends on social conditions 'objectively' tending towards revolution: it is not a spontaneous mental phenomenon, but must be the reflection of an actual historical trend. In order to know whether to expect an upsurge of revolutionary consciousness, we must first find out whether a socialist upheaval is on the way in accordance with the historical process. But it has not been shown that this condition is fulfilled, since the proletarian revolution as predicted by Marx has not yet occurred anywhere and there is no reason to expect it soon, or indeed at all.

Neither Marx nor Rosa Luxemburg makes it clear which statement logically comes first: that capitalism cannot be reformed, or that the working class is bound to destroy it by revolution. Since the two propositions are not the same, either they must be proved independently or one must follow from the other. In her polemics with the reformists, Rosa Luxemburg appears to make most use of the former proposition. Her theory of accumulation supplies proof (which, according to her, Marx failed to give) that for purely economic reasons capitalism cannot go on indefinitely. But even if we accept that theory for the sake of argument, it is not clear how it follows that there must be a proletarian revolution. Assuming that capitalism must collapse because private ownership of the means of production leads to overproduction and crises, it is still not proved that the system of ownership must be transformed in that particular way. The conclusion is more likely, though still not certain, on the further assumptions that society is coming closer to a state in which it consists of nothing but the bourgeoisie and the proletariat, that the latter's situation cannot be really improved, and that the bourgeoisie is bound to resist any attempt to break its monopoly of the means of production. But of these three additional assumptions, only the last is credible.

Since, however, Rosa Luxemburg believed unalterably that the working class was revolutionary by nature, her account of social reality was often based more on theory than on observation. She was convinced that revolutionary consciousness was on the increase, and when the facts belied this she was more inclined to blame the leaders' opportunism than objective circumstances. Believing that the workers were 'essentially' revolutionary, she placed more hope in an elemental outbreak than in organized party action.

4. The consciousness of the proletariat and forms of political organization

THE question of spontaneity versus party organization was the crux of Rosa Luxemburg's most violent disagreement with the Bolsheviks; but she saw similar dangers in every branch of social democracy. Lenin, Kautsky, Jaurès, and Turati were all guilty in her eyes of underrating the spontaneity of the masses and tending to discourage it by the doctrine of 'leadership'. Here again, she was almost the only one of her opinion in the social democratic movement.

By spontaneity, however, she did not mean a blind impulse devoid of ideological self-awareness. Not only had Marx predicted the proletarian revolution, but his prediction must itself become part of the proletarian consciousness in order for the revolution to come about. 'It is fundamental to the historic upheaval as formulated in Marx's theory that this theory should become the form of the working-class consciousness and, as such, a historical factor in its own right' (article on Marx in *Vorwärts*, 14 March 1903). Since the revolutionary consciousness that is to be, or is now taking shape, has already been formulated in terms of theory, the working class has every opportunity to become aware of its own destiny, and there is no need of leaders to educate the masses or look after their consciousness for them. Lenin's ultracentralism was a piece of opportunism, typical of the intelligentsia—so Rosa Luxemburg declared in 'Problems of the organization of Russian social democracy' (*Die Neue Zeit*, No. 42-3, 1903-4). According to Lenin, the Central Committee could arrogate to itself full power *vis-à-vis* party organizations, turning the whole party into a mere passive instrument.

> The centralization of social democracy, based on these two principles—firstly the blind subjection of all party organs and their activity, down to the minutest detail, to a central authority which thinks, acts and decides for everyone, and secondly the strict separation of the organized core of the party from the surrounding revolutionary *milieu*, as Lenin would have it—seems to us no more or less than a mechanical transference of the Blanquist principles of the organization of conspiratorial groups to the social democratic movement of the working masses. Lenin has defined his own point of view more trenchantly, perhaps, than any of his opponents could have done when he speaks of his 'revolutionary democrat' as a 'Jacobin linked with

an organization of the proletariat conscious of its class interests'. But social democracy is not 'linked' with the organization of the working class, it is itself the working-class movement.

Lenin failed to distinguish the mindless discipline of the barrack-room from conscious class-action, and his centralism was imbued with the 'sterile attitude of a night-watchman'. Revolutionary tactics could not be invented by leaders, they must develop spontaneously: history came first, leaders' consciousness second. The effect of the Bolshevik policy was to paralyse the free development of the proletariat, deprive it of responsibility, and make it an instrument of the bourgeois intelligentsia. The agency of revolution must be the collective mind of the workers and not the consciousness of self-styled leaders. The errors of the true workers' movement were more fruitful than the infallibility of a Central Committee.

The Russian Revolution of 1905 convinced Rosa Luxemburg that mass strikes were the most effective form of revolutionary action. In her view, that revolution afforded a pattern for other European countries: an elemental outbreak without a leader, a plan, or a co-ordinated programme, and not initiated by any political party. In 1914 Kautsky, in *Der politische Massenstreik*, decried Rosa Luxemburg's views as an aberration: how could she suppose that a few months of accidental, disorganized strikes, without a unifying idea or plan, could teach the workers more than thirty years of systematic work by parties and trade unions? But this was precisely what Rosa Luxemburg believed; and she held that the revolutionary potential of the working masses was indestructible, though it might be temporarily stifled by arrogant leaders. This did not mean that the party was superfluous, however. The concept of an advance guard of the proletariat was a sound one; but it should be a group of active members, not a sovereign body. The party's task was not merely to await the revolution but to hasten the course of history; this, however, was not a matter of conspiracies and *coups d'état*, but of cultivating the revolutionary consciousness of the masses, who would in the end decide the fate of socialism without help from their leaders.

Although Rosa Luxemburg criticized Lenin for his barrack-room ideas and manipulation of the socialist movement, she did not join issue directly with Kautsky's doctrine which Lenin adopted as the basis of his theory of the party, viz. that revolutionary consciousness should be instilled into the workers' movement from without. Lukács, in his article 'Rosa Luxemburg as a Marxist' in *Geschichte und Klassenbewusstsein* (*History and Class-Consciousness*, 1923), maintained that she herself accepted this doctrine, as she held that the party was the vehicle of the proletariat's class-consciousness and that its task was to turn theory into practice by imbuing a spontaneous movement with the truth already implicit therein. Rosa Luxemburg would probably have agreed with this formulation, but she would not have gone on to say that the intelligentsia was the prime source of the consciousness of the proletariat, or that the party in its role of standard-bearer could be replaced by a group of leaders. To her the party was the self-organizing proletariat, not the proletariat organized by professional functionaries of the revolution. In her comments and criticisms she maintained the position that Marxism was not merely a theory of the historical process but an articulation of the consciousness, latent though it might be as yet, of an actual workers' movement. When that consciousness took shape, i.e. when the spontaneous movement achieved theoretical self-knowledge, the distinction between theory and practice would cease to exist: the theory would become a material force, not in the sense of being a weapon in the struggle, but as an organic part of it. There is in this sense a kind of pre-established harmony between Marx's doctrine and the revolutionary movement that was to make it its own. Marx did not 'invent' the philosophy of history: he expressed the content of the proletariat's self-awareness, which was still dormant, and was, one may say, the instrument by which that content was first manifested.

This account of the matter is consistent with Marx's view of his own theory and with Rosa Luxemburg's dominant idea, but she did not herself use this or similar language. It is clear that the above interpretation does not remove the difference between Leninism and Rosa Luxemburg's philosophy of the party, but is compatible with either of them. If the party's function is to inspire a spontaneous movement with the truth that is immanent in that movement, we are still free either to accept Lenin's view of the party as a manipulator or to agree with Rosa Luxemburg that the workers' movement is always a spontaneous process and that all the party has to do is to explain to the workers their true objectives as laid down by history.

Rosa Luxemburg's belief that the workers' movement should not be manipulated or forced into a tactical mould by party leaders was the basis of her criticism of the Bolsheviks after their first year of rule in Russia. This fell under three main heads: their policy towards the peasants and towards the nationalities, and the question of democracy in the state and party.

Rosa Luxemberg criticized Bolshevik tyranny in the same way as Kautsky, but not for the same reasons. Kautsky defended democracy on general grounds that were not specifically Marxist but might also be recognized by liberals, whereas Rosa Luxemburg was actuated by her Marxist faith in the unique value of the spontaneous political activity of the masses. She brushed aside the arguments of Kautsky and the Mensheviks about Russia's economic backwardness and the desirability of a coalition with the liberal bourgeoisie. This, she said, would be a desertion of the revolutionary cause. The Bolsheviks had been right to start the revolution when they did and to bank on its spreading to the rest of the world. Here Rosa Luxemburg was in agreement with Trotsky and Lenin: the party should seize power when it was politically feasible to do so, regardless of doctrinaire objections about economic maturity—always on the assumption, which was generally accepted, that a socialist revolution in Russia could only succeed if it touched off a revolution throughout Europe. She also rejected the social democratic principle that the party must first gain a majority and only then think about taking power. This was 'parliamentary cretinism': the proper course was to use revolutionary tactics to gain a majority, not the other way round.

This did not mean, however, that the party, having seized power despite the majority of the population, should maintain itself by terror and reject all normal forms of political freedom and representation. The turning-point of the Russian Revolution was the dispersal of the Constituent Assembly. Lenin and Trotsky had done away with general elections altogether, basing their power on the Soviets. Trotsky declared that the Assembly summoned before October was reactionary and that universal suffrage was needless as it did not truly reflect the state of feeling of the masses. But, Rosa Luxemburg replied, the masses could influence their representatives after the elections and make them change course, and the more democratic the system, the more effective such pressure could be. Democratic institutions were not perfect, but to abolish them was much worse, as it paralysed the political life of the masses. The restriction of the suffrage to those who worked for their living was absurd in the general state of chaos, with industry in ruins and unemployment on a huge scale. The curbs on the Press and on the right of assembly turned the rule of the masses into a fiction. 'Freedom only for supporters of the government, only for members of a single party, however numerous—this is not freedom. Freedom must always be for those who think differently' (*The Russian Revolution*). Socialism was a live historical movement and could not be replaced by administrative decrees. If public affairs were not properly discussed they would become the province of a narrow circle of officials and corruption would be inevitable. Socialism called for a spiritual transformation of the masses, and terrorism was no way to bring this about: there must be unlimited democracy, a free public opinion, freedom of elections and the Press, the right to hold meetings and form associations. Otherwise the only active part of society would be the bureaucracy: a small group of leaders would give orders, and the workers' task would be to applaud them. The dictatorship of the proletariat would be replaced by the dictatorship of a clique.

For Lenin and Trotsky, Rosa Luxemburg wrote, democracy was the opposite of dictatorship, as it was for Kautsky. Because of this opposition Kautsky thought the proletariat should give up the power it had seized in an unripe situation; because of it, Lenin and Trotsky decided that power should be wielded by means of coercion. But the proletariat is supposed to exercise the dictator-ship of a class, not of a party or a clique, and it should do so openly, in demo-cratic conditions. 'If we have revealed the bitter kernel of inequality and slavery beneath the husk of formal equality and freedom, it is not in order to throw the husk away, but to persuade the working class not to be satisfied with it but to press on to the conquest of political power and fill it with a new social content . . . Dictatorship is not a matter of abolishing democracy but of applying it cor-rectly' (ibid.). True, the Bolsheviks had come to power in circumstances in which full democracy was impossible. But they were now making a virtue of necessity by seeking to impose their own tactics on the whole workers' move-ment, turning the distortion of an exceptional situation into a universal rule. They were to be commended for seizing power in Russia, but the socialist cause was a matter for the whole world and not for a single country.

Rosa Luxemburg's criticism of the Bolshevik dictatorship was consistent with her earlier critique of Leninism. In 1906 she wrote that 'the very idea of social-ism excludes minority rule' ('Blanquism and social democracy', *Czerwony Sztan-dar*, 27 June). She also said at that time that when the Tsardom was overthrown the Russian proletariat, after seizing power, would hand it over to a government elected by a majority of the population, and, as the proletariat was a minority in Russia, this government could not be predominantly social-democratic. It is not clear how she imagined the Bolsheviks could keep themselves in power in 1918 while allowing free elections, since the proletariat was only a minority and it could not by any means be supposed that the whole of it would vote for them. Martov and Kautsky did not have to meet this difficulty in their criticism of the Bolshevik dictatorship, since they took the view that authority must derive from general representative institutions, so that there could only be a government of the proletariat if the latter constituted the bulk of society. Rosa Luxemburg, on the other hand, seemed to believe that the Bolsheviks could have held on to power by democratic means under a system of popular representation. This strange notion could only be based on her mythical, unshakeable belief in the innate revolutionary character of the masses, which, left to themselves, were bound to evolve socialist forms of public life. Lenin and Trotsky were a good deal more circumspect and realistic than this.

5. The national question

THE question of nationality was a permanent, unsolved theoretical difficulty of Marxism and a practical difficulty of socialist movements. It was not easy to rec-oncile the principle that class divisions were fundamental to social analysis and prediction and to problems of practical policy, with the historical fact that peo-ple were and always had been divided on a national basis. Ethnic units were divided by quite other criteria than those of class, and a nation was historically a unit transcending class; how then could a purely class viewpoint be combined with the traditional recognition of the right of nations to independence? The brotherhood of peoples against their exploiters had been a popular slogan in the mid-nineteenth century and no doubt expressed the natural attitude of the democratic revolutionaries of the Age of Emancipation, but on inspection it clearly failed to solve the inveterate problems of national frontiers and minorities and colonial exploitation. When countries were ruthlessly exploiting their colonies it was hard to show in despite of all practical experience that the interests of the subject peoples were 'in the nature of things' identical with those of the metropolitan population.

Marx and Engels left nothing that could be called a theory of the nationality question. Their attitude to the problem was a mixture of Hegelian reminiscences, the slogans of 1848, and their personal likes and dislikes, which they expressed forcibly at times, especially in letters. Their views are marked by a strong European orientation and by contempt for small 'unhistorical' peoples, which are doomed to destruction as nations and are meanwhile supporters of darkest reaction and puppets of great-power intrigue. Marx was systematically hostile to Russia, believing that the desire for world domination was the mainstay of her policy; he suspected the British government of conniving at Russian expansionism, and regarded Britain's part in the Crimean War as due to proletarian pressure. He was little interested in ancient civilizations other than that of Greece, dismissing them as infantile periods of spiritual weakness and barbarism: both India and China were written off in this way. He once wrote in a letter that the Orient had given us nothing but religion and the plague. He had no doubt that socialism was the mission of the advanced and dominant countries. By creating a world market the bourgeoisie was setting the stage for revolution, and when it took place in the developed countries the rest would follow. Engels welcomed the United States' conquest of territory from Mexico and the French colonization of Algeria: the Bedouin were a race of bandits anyhow. Marx emphasized Britain's revolutionary role in India, roused by colonization from its millennial slumbers. In a letter of 9 August 1882 he rebuked Bernstein for taking a sentimental view of Egyptian nationalism. Engels made no secret of his contempt for the Balkan peoples: the Bulgarians were a race of swineherds who would do best to keep quiet under Turkish rule pending the European revolution. All these small nations were allies of the Tsar and enemies of the developed West. The 'historic' peoples—Germans, Poles, Hungarians—should rule over the other Slavs (except Russia); Poland should be restored to her pre-1772 frontiers, including Lithuania, White Russia, and a large part of the Ukraine. The Hungarians were entitled to rule over the Slovaks and Croats, the Austrians over the Czechs and Moravians. All these small subject peoples had played no part in European history and would never be independent. France should rule over Belgium, Alsace, and Lorraine; Germany over Schleswig. In general the higher civilization should prevail over the lower, progress over barbarism and stagnation. Both Marx and Engels were especially interested in the Polish question. Engels thought the Poles had done more for the revolution than Germany, Italy, and Hungary put together. Both men regarded the partition of Poland as the corner-stone of European reaction: the freeing of Poland from Russian rule would be the first step towards overthrowing the Tsardom and destroying reaction throughout the world.

Engels's distinction between historical and non-historical peoples is a reflection of the mood of 1848 rather than a deliberate historical theory, and the same may be said of his sympathy for Poland and his belief that it would play a key part in the revolution. Marx, however, towards the end of his life became seriously interested in the prospect of a revolution in Russia; he also thought the Irish question might hasten the revolution in England. However, national questions in general played no part in his theory of revolutionary strategy.

The socialists of the Second International, especially those from the multinational empires of Russia and Austria-Hungary, could not fall back on general formulas and summary classifications of nations into 'progressive' and 'reactionary', especially as they canvassed for support from the proletariat of the subject nationalities. It was thus natural for the Russians, Poles, and Austrians in particular to endeavour to find a socialist solution to the national question. Lenin, Otto Bauer, Karl Renner, Stalin, and Rosa Luxemburg all in their different ways sought to integrate the national problem into the corpus of Marxist doctrine.

The theme is one which naturally recurs incessantly in Rosa Luxemburg's correspondence. The SDKPiL proclaimed itself first and foremost, in opposition to the PPS, to be against the policy of Polish independence. Not that Rosa Luxemburg was indifferent to the oppression of one nation by another, but she regarded it as a consequence and a function of the rule of capital. After the socialist revolution the problem would solve itself, as socialism by definition would do away with all forms of oppression. In the meantime it was no use fighting for national independence, and it would be harmful to the revolutionary cause as it would divide the movement into sections, destroy the international solidarity of the proletariat, and divert its attention to nation-building, which was supposed to be the concern of the whole nation and not only of the oppressed classes. In general, concern over the national question as a separate problem was the result of bourgeois infiltration and tended to undermine the class viewpoint which was the *raison d'être* of social democracy. Marx's attitude towards Poland was understandable as a matter of policy in his time, but it was outdated or erroneous and in conflict with Marxist theory, which forbade the

labelling of Poland and Russia, regardless of class divisions, as respectively progressive and reactionary. The attempts of Limanowski, continued by the PPS,
to link the cause of socialism with that of an independent Poland were reactionary in the highest degree. The PPS sought to involve the international
workers' movement in the cause of a reconstructed Polish state by foisting on
it the traditions of the Polish nobility's struggle for independence. As early as
1896 Rosa Luxemburg protested against the introduction of a 'Polish' resolution at the London Congress of the Second International, arguing that it was
not true that Russia's strength depended on the subjugation of Poland and that
the Tsardom would collapse if she were freed. The strength of the Tsardom
depended on conditions inside Russia, and the development of capitalism
would lead to its downfall in due course.

The idea of restoring Poland was not only reactionary inasmuch as it tended
to destroy the class solidarity of the proletariat in the Tsarist empire, but it was
utopian and hopeless as well. In all her writings Rosa Luxemburg never ceased
to emphasize that Polish capitalism was an integral part of Russian capitalism;
two-thirds of Polish exports went to the east; the irreversible process of economic integration could not be arrested by childish patriotic dreams. No social
class in Poland was interested in independence: neither the bourgeoisie, whose
livelihood depended on Russian markets, nor the gentry, fighting desperately
to preserve as much as they could of their way of life, nor the proletariat, whose
concern was the class struggle, nor the majority of the petty bourgeoisie, nor
the peasants. At the most, some small groups of the intelligentsia who lacked
social advancement, or of the reactionary petty bourgeoisie threatened by the
rise of capitalism, dreamt impotently of an independent Poland. In general,
national problems had no significance of their own; national movements were
always in the interest of particular classes. Since there was no class that could
represent the national cause on the basis of strong, irrefutable economic principles, that was the end of the matter: an independent Poland was an impossibility. What was true of Russian Poland applied equally to the provinces ruled
by Prussia and Austria. Polish capitalists attempted to turn the workers'
thoughts to ideas of independence so as to cloud their minds and persuade
them that the enemy was not capitalism but the Germans and the Hakata (an
organization for eroding Polish rights in the Poznań province).

Holding these views, Rosa Luxemburg combated from the outset the principle of national self-determination that figured in the programme of the Russian social democrats; she inclined instead to the Austro-Marxist idea of
cultural autonomy as a solution to the national question after the revolution.
Her opinions were set out in an article 'The nationality question and autonomy' in *Przegląd Socjal-demokratyczny* (No. 6, August 1908), and in her pamphlet on the Russian revolution. In the former she states that the right of

self-determination is a slogan of bourgeois nationalism, implying that every nation has an equal right to decide its own destiny. In fact, national movements are progressive or reactionary according to historical circumstances. This was recognized by Marx and Engels when they emphasized the reactionary character of national aspirations on the part of the southern Slavs and Czechs, the Swiss revolt against the Habsburgs in the fourteenth century, or the separatism of Scots, Bretons, and Basques; many of these movements supported reactionary monarchies against republicans. The natural tendency of history was for small nations to be absorbed by larger ones; cultural and linguistic unity was bound to be the ultimate goal, and it was reactionary and utopian to seek to reverse this process. 'Can one speak seriously of "self-determination" for the Montenegrins, Bulgars, Romanians, Serbs and Greeks, or even to any real extent of the Swiss?' In any case a nation was not an integrated social whole, but a congeries of hostile classes opposing one another in everything.

Rosa Luxemburg held that the recognition of the right of nationalities to self-determination was one of the Bolsheviks' gravest mistakes. This so-called right was 'no more than an idle petty-bourgeois phrase and humbug': the Bolsheviks had hoped by it to secure the support of the non-Russian peoples of the empire, but the result was that the Poles, Finns, Lithuanians, Ukrainians, and the peoples of the Caucasus used their freedom to combat the revolution, though formerly they had been active in its cause. Instead of defending the integrity of the Russian state, now the bulwark of the revolution, and 'crushing separatism with an iron hand', the Bolsheviks had allowed the bourgeoisie of the non-Russian peoples to decide their own fate and had even stirred up national feeling among peoples like the Ukrainians, who had never been a nation.

The acerbity with which Rosa Luxemburg fought the idea of national independence, especially for the Poles, brought her and the Leninists into sharp opposition, but it must be emphasized that this was a question of strategy and not of different views as to the intrinsic value of nations and national culture. Lenin's attitude on this point was the same as Rosa Luxemburg's. He conceded the right to self-determination, but he regarded it as the duty of socialists to fight against the separatism of their own nation; in any case self-determination was far less important than the interest of the revolution, i.e. of keeping the Bolsheviks in power. The proletariat of a nation should speak for it as regards separation versus integration, and the mouthpiece of the proletariat was its party, which expressed the most progressive tendencies of any national group. Lenin's disapproval of the brutality of the Soviet occupation of Georgia in 1921 had no practical effect, and the party's programme afforded ample justification of the violent measures by which most of the Russian patrimony was regained. However, Rosa Luxemburg's quarrel with the PPS was a fundamental one.

With hindsight it may appear incredible that she could be so blind to social realities, but this was not the only instance of its kind: she was a doctrinaire intellectual through and through. Her accounts of social phenomena are deductions from a Marxist schema, with the minimum of correction in the light of experience. Since capitalist society was in the nature of things divided into hostile classes, and as the interest of each class was identical throughout the world, at least as far as the class war was concerned, it was a theoretical impossibility for any nation 'as a whole' to aspire to independence, for aspirations on the national plane simply could not exist. Rosa Luxemburg was not shaken in this opinion by the outburst of nationalism in 1914 and the resulting collapse of the International: she merely blamed the social democratic leaders for betraying international ideals. Like many doctrinaire Marxists, she ceased to think in terms of social analysis when experience failed to bear out her theoretical presuppositions; instead, she looked for 'guilty men' and blamed the discrepancy on subjective factors. Since nations did not exist as integrated communities, there could be no such thing as a true national movement. If there appeared to be, it was a case of 'bourgeois fraud' or 'revisionist treachery', and the Marxist schema remained unscathed. The working class was essentially revolutionary, and any appearance to the contrary must be due to corrupt leaders instilling reformist ideas in the workers: the disparity between the essence of things and superficial experience could be ignored or attributed to individual bad faith, or explained as a 'dialectical contradiction'. Reasoning in this way, Rosa Luxemburg was able to preserve her views unaltered even though her predictions were almost always falsified by events.

Lenin for his part criticized Rosa Luxemburg on the ground that by onesidedly combating Polish nationalism she was favouring the more dangerous nationalism of Great Russia. Others who criticized her were the PPS theorists, Feliks Perl and Kazimierz Kelles-Krauz. The latter wrote in 1905 that the 'economic conditions' that were supposedly an obstacle to Polish independence were no more than a matter of trade between provinces, and that Rosa Luxemburg was in effect advocating that the proletariat should adapt its activity to the temporary requirements of the bourgeoisie. National states were in the natural interest of capitalism, but independence was also necessary to the working class, as it was a necessary condition of democracy.

The Polish Communists, on the other hand, wholeheartedly accepted Rosa Luxemburg's doctrine on the subject of national independence. The later criticism of 'Luxemburgism', which was of a general and summary character, accused her of 'underestimating' the bourgeoisie's interest in the internal market and that of other classes in the national cause. But this criticism never went so far as to call in question the principle that the class struggle is 'in the last resort' the only decisive historical conflict; national questions are either transient, unimportant issues or a disguise for 'real', i.e. class, interests, or else they represent a potential source of revolutionary energy that must be used for tactical reasons but can hardly be taken seriously 'in a historical perspective'. In short, Marxism in its Communist version never came to terms with national realities.

. . .

ROSA LUXEMBURG is an outstanding example of a type of mind that is often met with in the history of Marxism and appears to be specially attracted by the Marxist outlook. It is characterized by slavish submission to authority, together with a belief that in that submission the values of scientific thought can be preserved. No doctrine was so well suited as Marxism to satisfy both these attitudes, or to provide a mystification combining extreme dogmatism with the cult of 'scientific' thinking, in which the disciple could find mental and spiritual peace. Marxism thus played the part of a religion for the intelligentsia, which did not prevent some of them, like Rosa Luxemburg herself, from trying to improve the deposit of faith by reverting to first principles, thus strengthening their own belief that they were independent of dogma.

Rosa Luxemburg's main theme was the theory of accumulation, linked closely with her belief that capitalism must bring about increasing class polarization. (All orthodox Marxists shared this belief, and in Kautsky's view Marxism would have collapsed without it.) She endeavoured to give Marxism a final consistent shape by defining the circumstances in which capitalism becomes an economic impossibility. Marxism was to her the universal key to the meaning of history, enabling the mind to reject as insignificant trifles any adventitious factors that might disturb its course. In this way historical materialism could be looked on not as an extreme impoverishment of reality but as a process of scientific abstraction, preserving the essence of things and eliminating what was merely accidental. No one seemed to notice, however, that this meant treating the whole of actual history as a series of unimportant contingencies, leaving science to contemplate only the general framework of the transition from one economic system to another. All the rest—wars, national and racial conflicts, constitutional and legal forms, religions, artistic and intellectual life—was relegated to the scrap-heap of 'accidents', of no concern to the theoretician brooding over the majestic phases of 'great' history. In this way the barrenness of simplistic schemata was endowed with a false sublimity.

The fate of Rosa Luxemburg's writings illustrates the tragedy of the attempt to preserve the integrality of Marxism while rejecting the only means of doing so, viz. an institutional body with authority to distinguish finally between truth and error. Rosa Luxemburg sought to be the champion of orthodoxy, but instead of regarding the party as the infallible fount of orthodoxy she preferred to believe in the revolutionary mission of the masses as the spontaneous source of truth. Lenin was not guilty of this inconsistency, and his form of Marxism was effective in practice because its doctrine was made the exclusive property of an organization of professional revolutionaries. In the case of Rosa Luxemburg, strange results followed from believing absolutely in the predetermination of history and also in the 'essentially' revolutionary character of the masses. In her pamphlet on the Russian revolution she urged Lenin to introduce unfettered democracy and at the same time to crush all nationalist movements with an iron hand, not suspecting for a moment that there might be any inconsistency in these two demands.

On the basis of her theory of accumulation Rosa Luxemburg foresaw increasing market difficulties and pressure of capital on wages, the radicalization of the working masses, and the class polarization of society. This is why she attached no practical importance to national and peasant movements, whose effect must diminish as capitalism expanded, and she neglected the role of colonial territories as theatres of revolution. In short, she believed in a proletarian revolution in the classic Marxian sense, whereas Lenin realized that no 'pure' proletarian revolution would ever occur and that as capitalism approached the 'ideal' of two-class society the socialist revolution became less probable, not more. Thus Rosa Luxemburg opposed Lenin on three points, each of which was a necessary precondition of the Bolsheviks' success in 1917: their policy towards the peasants and the nationalities, and their military conception of the party.

In an article written in 1922 and published posthumously in 1924 Lenin drew a picture of Rosa Luxemburg which was accepted as definitive by the Communist movement: she was an 'eagle of the Revolution', but she had been wrong in her opinions concerning accumulation, the national problem, the Mensheviks and Bolsheviks, and the October Revolution itself. (Her ideas on 'spontaneity' and the role of the party do not figure in this list of her mistakes.) The German Communists, after their failure to bring about a rising in 1920 and 1923, blamed their miscalculation on the ideology of 'Luxemburgism': prominent in this were Ruth Fischer and Maslow, the former of whom compared Rosa Luxemburg to a syphilis germ. The whole tradition of the Spartacus League was written off as a series of theoretical and tactical errors. In 1926, when factional and personal conflicts in the Soviet party leadership brought the so-called 'rightists' to power in the German Communist party, Rosa Luxemburg was rehabilitated for a brief period, while Ruth Fischer and Maslow lost their influence; but soon the old stereotypes were revived and intensified. In an article in 1931 Stalin closed the discussion by stating that Rosa Luxemburg was responsible for the theory of 'permanent revolution', later adopted by Trotsky in opposition to the doctrine of 'socialism in one country'.

In consequence, all that was distinctive in Rosa Luxemburg's political and theoretical views became a dead letter, and she was remembered only in verbal tributes by Polish and German Communists commemorating her martyrdom for the revolution. Her critique of revolutionary despotism was not noticed until long after the Second World War, when such criticism had become current coin, and was treated as a historical curiosity rather than an incentive to change. In the 1960s, however, some interest in her ideas was shown by the so-called 'New Left' in its search for an alternative model of Marxist orthodoxy which, while rejecting Lenin's theory of the party, would set its face against revisionism and continue to rely on the inexhaustible revolutionary potential of the proletariat.

IV

Bernstein and Revisionism

1. The concept of revisionism

THE TERM 'revisionism' has never been precisely defined, but has been used in a wider or narrower sense according to circumstances. In present-day Communism it is no more than an arbitrary label affixed to any group or individual who in any way criticizes the policy, programme, or doctrine of a particular party; but at the turn of the century 'revisionism' existed as a specific phenomenon, though with fluid boundaries, in Central and East European socialism. The term denoted those writers and political figures who, while starting from Marxist premises, came by degrees to call in question various elements of the doctrine, especially Marx's predictions as to the development of capitalism and the inevitability of socialist revolution. 'Revisionists' were not people who abandoned Marxism completely or had never been Marxists, but those who sought to modify the traditional doctrine or who held that some of its essential features were no longer applicable in the present state of society. Jaurès, for instance, was seldom called a revisionist, because he never set up to be an orthodox Marxist in the German sense. Later the term was also applied to those who attempted to supplement Marxism on Kantian lines. In general, however, revisionism is typically found within the parties that insisted on their fidelity to Marx's theory, i.e. especially those of Germany, Austria, and Russia.

Strictly speaking, revisionism was regarded as a theoretical position, but its articulation by Bernstein in the later 1890s was preceded by political tendencies which led to the same direction. The first sign of the revisionist crisis in the German party appeared in a discussion of the agrarian question in the early 1890s. At the Frankfurt Congress in 1894 the Bavarian social-democratic leader Georg von Vollmar (1850-1922) urged that the party should defend the interests of peasants as well as workers. This appeared to be a purely tactical question, but it involved an essential point of theory. The orthodox, following Marx and Engels, held that agriculture under capitalism must develop on broadly the same lines as industry, i.e. that fewer and fewer owners would hold more and more of the land, and that small peasant proprietors would be squeezed out of existence. Hence Kautsky and those who thought like him were against taking up the cause of the small farmers, who were doomed to extinction as a class and were therefore 'reactionary' in the eyes of history. This meant, however, that the socialists could never enlist peasant support, a fact which greatly weakened them in electoral terms, especially as most of the Prussian peasants allied themselves with the reactionary Junkers against the bourgeoisie. But the issue was not only a tactical one: it was also a question of whether the expected concentration of agriculture was really taking place. Eduard David (1863–1930), a socialist expert on agricultural questions, argued that it was not, and that the family farm was the ideal form of rural production. Kautsky disputed both these points, but agreed many years later that David was right in holding that there was no 'necessary' process of concentration in landownership.

It soon appeared, however, that the correctness of Marx's predictions could be doubted with regard to industry as well as agriculture. The traditional doctrine was that capitalism involved the increasing polarization of classes and concentration of capital, the ruin of small concerns, and the proletarianization of the masses, and that this was an irreversible process: all reforms within the framework of capitalism were superficial and impermanent, and the main task of socialists was to organize their forces for the coming revolutionary conflict. But the growth of mass socialist parties, parliamentary successes, and social reforms prompted a large section of the leadership to see their task in terms of immediate advantages to the working class, and to lose sight of the prospect of a final decisive battle. This 'reformist' attitude was widespread in practical socialism before Bernstein gave it a theoretical basis. Note was taken of the record of British socialism, which had no revolutionary doctrine but had scored undoubted successes over the years. Thus the revisionist doctrine, when it came, fell on fertile ground among party and trade union leaders. Their practical revisionism had various motives and took various directions. Parliamentarians were interested in forming alliances with non-socialist forces for electoral or reformist purposes, and all such alliances were suspect from the orthodox point of view. Local party and union representatives were less interested in electoral tactics, but they were also generally indifferent to the 'ultimate goal' of socialism and the whole theoretical side of the party programme. Among the leaders their way of thinking was represented by Ignaz Auer (1846–1907). Others again, such as Schippel and Heine, questioned the party's anti-militarist and anti-colonial programme on grounds of nationalism and in the belief that a strong army and the acquisition of colonies and markets were in the interest of the German proletariat. In general, the practical basis of this loosely formulated revisionism was that socialists should build the new society 'by degrees', concentrating on day-to-day improvements and not merely waiting for a revolution. Bernstein's theories could never have had such an earth-shaking effect if they had not been a crystallization of ideas which were already in the air.

2. Biographical information

EDUARD BERNSTEIN (1850–1932) was born in Berlin, the son of an engine-driver; both his parents were non-practising Jews. After leaving the Gymnasium at an early age he worked in a bank from 1869 to 1878. He joined the Eisenach party in 1872 and took part in the Gotha Congress of 1875. For a time he adhered to Dühring's philosophy, but was put off by the latter's dogmatic intolerance and anti-Semitism. Engels's *Anti-Dühring* (1878) converted him to Marxism, and he became a zealous exponent of orthodoxy as then understood. After the anti-socialist laws were promulgated he went to Lugano and then to Zurich as secretary to Karl Höchberg, a rich German who sympathized with the social democrats and helped them financially, though not himself a Marxist. In Zurich Bernstein wrote for the *Sozialdemokrat*, and became its editor from 1880 to 1890. He also met Kautsky, who came from Vienna with Höchberg's help, and the Russian socialist *émigrés*. The *Sozialdemokrat* was an orthodox revolutionary journal and played an important part in maintaining the party's continuity in conditions of illegality or semi-legality. In 1880 Bernstein accompanied Bebel to London, where he met Marx and Engels. He visited Engels again in 1884 and they maintained a lively correspondence, which Bernstein did not publish until 1925. In 1887 he published in Zurich a work on the Chartists (*Die Chartisten-Bewegung in England*). In the middle of 1888 he was deported from Switzerland and went to London; he was one of Engels's closest friends for the next few years, and was an executor of his will.

Bernstein remained in England till the beginning of 1901. His stay there fundamentally altered his views on Marxism and the philosophy of socialism: he was much influenced by the Fabians, with whom he remained in close contact. His experience of conditions in England convinced him that the idea of a once-and-for-all break-up of capitalism was a doctrinaire illusion, and that socialists should place their hopes in gradual social reforms and socialization as the result of democratic pressure. These conclusions soon took the form of an entire system in which many of the philosophical and political premises of Marxism were modified. Bernstein's critique had much in common with the *Kathedersozialismus* of Brentano, Schulze-Gävernitz, and Sombart, who attempted to combine socialism with liberalism and looked to social legislation as a means of reform instead of a single 'qualitative' jump from capitalism to socialism. Bernstein expounded his views in a series of articles entitled 'Problems of Socialism' which appeared in *Die Neue Zeit* from the end of 1896, and later in a book *Die Voraussetzungen des Sozialismus und die Aufgaben der Sozialdemokratie* (*The Premisses of Socialism and the Tasks of Social Democracy*, 1899), which became the fundamental revisionist text and the object of innumerable polemics. Bernstein replied to the first attacks in a letter to the party congress at Stuttgart, which he could not attend as he was still wanted for trial in Germany. His views were denounced at the congress by Kautsky, Clara Zetkin, and Rosa Luxemburg, and soon the whole of the European social dem-ocratic movement was involved in a debate which led finally to the crystalliza-tion of two opposing tendencies. In spite of the succession of anti-revisionist resolutions and condemnations, and although Bernstein was opposed by most of the party theorists, his influence was already clearly increasing within the party and the trade unions.

Bernstein returned to Germany in 1901, and was elected to the Reichstag in 1902 as member for Breslau. He ceased to contribute to *Die Neue Zeit* but wrote frequently for *Sozialistische Monatshefte*, which Julius Bloch edited from 1897 and which became the chief theoretical organ of reformism. He was not expelled from the party (only a small group of radicals pressed, unsuccessfully, for the expulsion of the revisionists), and as time went on his adherents secured more and more influential posts in the party administration.

From then on Bernstein divided his activity between parliamentary work (he was a deputy to the Reichstag from 1902 to 1918 and again from 1920 to 1928) and writing and publishing. In London he had published works by Las-salle, and a complete edition in twelve volumes subsequently appeared in Berlin. He endorsed the programme for a mass political strike (*Dér politische Massenstreik und die politische Lage der Sozialdemokratie in Deutschland,* 1905), wrote a three-volume history of the Berlin workers' movement (*Geschichte der Berliner Arbeiterbewegung,* 1907–10), collaborated with Bebel in publishing the correspondence of Marx and Engels in four volumes, and founded and edited the periodical *Dokumente des Sozialismus* (1902–5). He criticized Marxism more and more outspokenly, and in the last few years before 1914 was closer to the liberal reformers than to the Marxists. During the war he belonged to the anti-war minority of the party and joined the USPD along with Kautsky and Haase. He rejoined the SPD after the war and took part in draft-ing its first programme. He was the real founder of the social democratic ideol-ogy as that term was generally understood between the wars, in opposition to Communism. He died in Berlin.

3. *The laws of history and the dialectic*

IN Bernstein's opinion, it was the misfortune of Marxist theory that it derived from Hegelianism. Marx, he thought, had never quite shaken off the Hegelian tendency to make deductions about social conditions from abstract, *a priori* dialectical schemata, with insufficient regard to actual facts. This had led him to believe in historical determinism and in a single factor governing the course of history, in relation to which human beings were merely instruments or organs. But Engels had considerably attenuated the original formulas of historical materialism by his doctrine of 'ultimate causes', which implied that there were also mediate causes affecting history: the more numerous and varied these were, the less absolute must be the preponderance of the 'ultimate causes'. This was confirmed by experience: the multiplicity of forces affecting society limited the sphere of necessity and enabled human beings to exercise increasing influence on social processes. This being recognized, Marxism could no longer be regarded as a purely materialist doctrine, still less as teaching that history was absolutely governed by the 'economic factor'; though Marx deserved immense credit for having shown the importance of changes in technology and production methods for the understanding of history.

Hegel was also responsible for the Blanquist element in Marxism, the belief in total revolution and the creative role of political violence. *The Communist Manifesto* made no mention of Babeuf among the socialist authors whose views it criticized. The Address of the Central Committee to the Communist League made in March 1850 was Blanquist in spirit: it appeared to assume that the will to revolution and the organization of terrorism were sufficient to provide the driving force of a socialist upheaval. In general, Marx had tried to find a compromise between two socialist traditions. The first was constructive and evolutionary: it had been developed in utopian literature and in nineteenth-century socialist sects and workers' associations, and aimed at emancipating society by means of a new economic system. The second principle was destructive, conspiratorial and terrorist, and its aim was to transform society by the political expropriation of the governing classes. Marxism was rather a compromise than a synthesis of the two principles, and Marx's thought oscillated between them, presenting different features at different times.

Bernstein's view that Hegel was to blame for the Blanquist elements in Marxism was, it may be noted, the opposite of Plekhanov's opinion. The latter held that Hegel's tradition, with its anti-utopian trend and its emphasis on the natural 'logic' of history, was the most effective weapon against political adventurism, Blanquist conspiratorial tactics, and the expectation of a lightning leap to socialism, before the relations of production under capitalism had matured to the point where an organic change was possible.

Another blemish in Marx's philosophy, according to Bernstein, was his theory of value, suggesting as it did that value as defined by labour-time was a real phenomenon governing the terms of exchange and not merely a convenient expository device. Value in Marx's sense was unmeasurable and was at best an abstract conceptual instrument, not an economic reality. Engels had held that in the Middle Ages goods were still exchanged according to their value, but Parvus had shown that even then there were various factors limiting the effect of value on prices. The law of value was truly in force only in primitive societies. The rightness or wrongness of Marx's theory in this respect was not essential to the analysis of surplus value, but here too the doctrine was misleading: by identifying the rate of surplus value with the rate of exploitation, he gave the impression that the former was the index of social injustice. This was incorrect, for the workers' standard of life was not directly geared to the rate of surplus value—they might be in a state of destitution when the rate was low, or comparatively well off although it was high; moreover, socialism could not be justified by the fact that wages did not equal the full value of the product, since they could not do so anyway.

In his later articles Bernstein took issue even more emphatically with the theory of value expressed in *Capital*. The point that Marx's definition of value was an expository device and not a real social phenomenon had made previously by Schmidt and Sombart, and in his main treatise Bernstein followed their argument. Later he went further and declared that value in Marx's sense did not exist; price was the sole economic reality, and commodities had value because they had a price. Marx had underestimated the use-value of commodities, and his concept of value was useless because it was not quantitative: one of the reasons for this was that one can measure labour-time but not the intensity of labour.

Bernstein's critique of the philosophical basis of Marxism and its derivation from Hegelianism is summary in the extreme. He does not in fact seem to have known any more of Hegel's work than he could gather from the absurd simplifications of Engels. In this he was not alone among his contemporaries: the Marxists knew next to nothing of Hegel, and the latter's contribution to Marx's world-view was reduced to a few platitudes or ignored. (Labriola and Plekhanov were among the few who mentioned the dependence of Marx on Hegel, but Plekhanov's view of Hegel was also simplified out of all recognition.) The general trend of Bernstein's critique of Marx is clear, however. It is an attack on all speculative systems which purport to explain history by a single abstract principle, and on the 'philosophic' mentality which, instead of studying empirical economic tendencies, subordinates all to the expectation of a single tremendous qualitative change which is to transform and save the world.

Bernstein did not endeavour to show that he was faithful to Marx's views: he openly criticized what he regarded as the 'negative' element of Marxism, the belief in speculative historical schemata and in the advent of socialism as a complete break with the previous history of mankind.

4. The revolution and the 'ultimate goal'

THE critique of Hegelian blemishes in Marx's thought would not in itself have been a grave threat to party ideology, but the brunt of Bernstein's attack lay elsewhere. He argued that Marxist predictions as to the concentration of capital were erroneous, as was the theory of class polarization and a single revolutionary change sweeping away the existing order; that the task of social democracy was gradually to socialize political institutions and property, and that the party had already accepted this in practice, though it had not the courage to jettison the time-honoured revolutionary theory. Such was the true substance of the revisionist doctrine, which was clearly inconsistent with the letter and spirit of Marxism and with the theoretical section of the party programme.

Marx's statements concerning the falling rate of profit, overproduction, crises, concentration and the periodical destruction of capital were undoubtedly based on fact, Bernstein observed, but he ignored or underrated the contrary tendencies that were to be found in capitalism. The concentration of enterprises was not the same as the concentration of wealth: the former was taking place, but not the latter. Owing to the joint-stock system, the growth of large industrial concerns did not mean the corresponding growth of large fortunes. On the contrary, the number of property-owners was increasing in both relative and absolute terms. Thus, if the prospects of socialism depended on the concentration of wealth, social democracy would be fighting against an objective economic process. In reality, however, the chances of socialism did not depend on the validity of the theory of concentration. As Bernstein emphasized to the Stuttgart Congress, in stating that the number of owners was increasing he did not mean to justify the present system. What was decisive for socialism was not the concentration of wealth but the productivity of labour. If the increase in the number of owners acted as a brake on productive forces, it was not conducive to socialism; but the increase must be recognized as a fact, whatever its social significance.

In the same way, the predictions of class polarization were erroneous. On the contrary, social stratification was increasingly complex as technology and the organization of society produced a more numerous middle class. It was therefore hopeless and utopian to expect socialism as a result of capital squeezing out the intermediate class. As the class of technicians and functionaries was increasing rapidly, so the ratio of the proletariat to the total population tended to fall. Nor was rural property tending to concentrate in fewer hands.

The prospects of socialism did not depend on a major crisis bringing about the collapse of capitalism. Such crises were less and less probable, as capitalism grew more capable of adapting itself to market difficulties. The belief of many socialists that crises were due to under-consumption by the masses was incorrect and was contrary to the views of Marx and Engels. Sismondi had put forward this idea, and Rodbertus after him; but Marx himself had pointed out that crises usually occur at a time when wages are going up. Volume III of *Capital*, however, described crises as the result of a conflict between the purchasing power of the masses and the urge of capitalism to improve and increase the forces of production. But the development of world trade had vastly increased the power of capital to react to local crises by mobilizing credit at short notice. Foreign markets were growing intensively rather than extensively, and there was no reason to foresee an absolute end to this increase. Rosa Luxemburg held that Marx's theory related to future crises of decline, whereas hitherto crises had been those of growth; but if this were so it would follow that Marx's theory of crises had a different meaning than he himself ascribed to it, and also that it was a mere speculative deduction unproved by evidence. As it was, the elaborate system of credit, cartels, and protective duties that helped to maintain exploitation was also an effective guard against crises and nullified the hope of an economic cataclysm.

According to Marx there were two main conditions of socialism: a high degree of socialization of the productive process under capitalism, and the political power of the proletariat. The first of these conditions, Bernstein argued, was far from being fulfilled. As to the second, it should be made clear whether the party expected to gain power through democratic electoral institutions or by revolutionary force. The basic trends of social development were not favourable to hopes of revolution. Contrary to prediction, social functions were becoming more differentiated, both generally and amid the working class. The theory that the workers' condition under capitalism was hopeless and could not undergo any real improvement had also been refuted. Marx had not been quite consistent here: he recognized the existence of tendencies that might limit exploitation and improve the wage-earner's lot, but as often as not he ignored them because they were inconsistent with his *a priori* theories. At the present time there was certainly no ground to expect class antagonisms to become more acute owing to increasing exploitation and poverty. But again, the prospects of socialism did not depend on this expectation: they depended on the increasing social productivity of labour as a result of general progress, and on the moral and intellectual maturity of the working class. Socialism was a gradual process of increasing socialization with the aid of democratic institutions and the strength of the organized proletariat. Democracy was not merely a weapon in the political struggle but an end in itself, the form in which socialism was to become a reality. It was not an automatic solution to all social problems, but a powerful and necessary instrument of progress. Since the social democratic movement had taken its stand on parliamentary ground, phrases about the 'dictatorship of the proletariat' were meaningless. Nor could there be any question of the working class building socialism by using force against the rest of society; on the contrary, the socialists should try to interest the petty bourgeoisie and peasants in their programme. The right course was to take advantage of the growing influence of social democracy on state institutions in order to reform the organization of the economy, remove obstacles to co-operative production, secure the right of trade organizations to control production, and establish safeguards against monopoly and guarantees of employment. If these things were achieved it would not matter that production was partly socialized and partly not. Private enterprises would socialize themselves by degrees, but a single wholesale conversion to public ownership would involve waste and terror on a large scale. This did not mean, Bernstein insisted, that the revolution was 'forbidden': revolutions were spontaneous, elemental processes and no one could stop them. But a policy of reform made no difference in this respect. The important thing was to recognize that the party was in fact working towards the socialist transformation of society through democratic and economic reforms, and it should have the courage to show itself in its true colours. Bebel, for instance, denied the charge that the party intended to use political violence; Kautsky had drawn up a reformist agrarian programme, and in the Reichstag the party had called for the establishment of arbitral courts. It was not the case, anyway, that threats of force and strikes were the most effective mode of action: the British workers had gained the vote not in the revolutionary days of Chartism but by allying themselves with the radical section of the bourgeoisie.

Bernstein summed up his attitude in a formula which became famous as the target of orthodox attack: 'What is generally called the ultimate goal of socialism is nothing to me; the movement is everything.' In his letter to the Stuttgart Congress he explained this as follows: the party at the present time should not rely on a great cataclysm but on the general extension of the workers' political rights and their participation in economic and administrative bodies; the conquest of power and the socialization of property are not ends, but means. In his principal work, however, he explains himself somewhat differently. Marx, he says, wrote that the working class has no ready made Utopia to be introduced by a decree; it has no arbitrarily fashioned ideals; it knows that its emancipation will require long struggles and many historical processes, altering circumstances as well as people; we must bring into action the elements of the new society that have already developed under capitalism. To hold fast to traditional Utopias is injurious to social progress, as it distracts attention from the practicable reforms for which we should be fighting.

As can be seen, the formula 'the goal is nothing, the movement everything' is not clear in itself, and it distorts the idea of Marx's on which it is based. In *Class Struggles in France*, in *The German Ideology*, and in other writings Marx emphasized that scientific socialism did not set out to allure people with arbitrary models of a perfect society; its purpose was to ascertain existing economic and social tendencies in order to stimulate or activate the real forces by which society was changed. It was necessary to study 'natural' historical tendencies in embryo or, as he put it in 1843, to 'force these petrified relationships to dance by playing their own tune to them'. This attitude of Marx's was certainly opposed to all sentimental and moralizing Utopias, but not to the hope of a single violent revolution. It did not mean that socialists should limit their horizon to urgent or immediately attainable ends, but only that their aims, including the 'ultimate goal' and the hope of a political revolution, should be based on observation of real historical tendencies and not arbitrary imaginings of a perfect world. In particular Marx made clear the way in which capitalism, as he believed, was creating the 'premisses' for a new order, viz. the collectivization of productive processes, class polarization, and the revolutionary training of the proletariat by the very conditions of its existence. These premisses made socialism possible and even necessary, but no changes in capitalism had any socialist significance prior to the political victory of the proletariat.

Bernstein was thus not justified in invoking Marx's authority for his views, though there was some colour for them in the writings of Engels. The essential question was not whether to accept or reject revolutionary violence, but whether processes of socialization within the capitalist economy were 'already' part of the building of socialism. If socialism could be realized 'little by little' under capitalism, there was no reason why the transformation should not turn out, one day, to be complete. Thus there would no longer be an impassable gulf between the two systems. The movement towards socialism was not the prelude to a great expropriation but simply meant more collectivization, more democracy, equality, and welfare—a gradual trend with no predetermined limit and, by the same token, no 'ultimate goal'. When Bernstein said that the goal was nothing and the movement everything, he was not expressing a banal demand that the party should only set itself practicable tasks. He meant, first and foremost, that the 'ultimate goal' as understood in Marxist tradition—the economic liberation of the proletariat by its conquest of political power—had no definite content. The socialist movement was capable of fighting successfully for many changes which would mean the realization of more and more socialist values; if it were to live merely on the expectation of a once-and-for-all cataclysm, it would not be serving the interests of the proletariat.

Moreover, according to Bernstein, the SPD was already a reformist party in many of its political attitudes. The revolutionary formulas in its programme were inconsistent with its actual policy and could only act as a brake on the latter. It was not a question of the party changing its policy, but rather of understanding the policy it was in fact pursuing, and adapting traditional ideas to current realities.

Furthermore, Bernstein rejected the formula in *The Communist Manifesto* to the effect that the workers had no fatherland. This might have been true in the 1840s, when the proletariat had no political rights and took no part in public life, but it was an anachronism when the workers had asserted their rights as citizens and could affect their country's destiny. The present-day worker had a fatherland and had good reasons to defend it. In the same way, colonialism should not be condemned by socialists out of hand, without regard to circumstances and to the form in which it was exercised. Marx had written that human societies are not the owners but the usufructuaries of the land they inhabit, and are in duty bound to hand it on to posterity in an improved and not a wasted condition. Thus, Bernstein argued, the right to a particular territory did not depend on conquest but on the ability to make good economic use of it. Civilized peoples who could cultivate the land to advantage had a better right to it than savages, so long as they did not rule with brutality or to the detriment of the natives.

5. *The significance of revisionism*

BERNSTEIN'S writings provoked an unprecedented flood of attack from orthodox Marxists of all shades. Scarcely any important socialist writer failed to join in: Kautsky, Rosa Luxemburg, Plekhanov, Bebel, Labriola, Jaurès, Adler, Mehring, Parvus, Clara Zetkin—all felt it their obligation to give tongue, which in itself showed that Bernstein's views were not a casual aberration but the expression of a tendency genuinely rooted in the socialist movement.

The philosophical critique of Marx's views played a very small part in these polemics; Bernstein's own remarks in this field were trite and lacking in understanding. The aspect of his writings that aroused indignation was that which disputed the theory of the concentration of capital and argued that the existing order might be gradually reformed by an alliance between the proletariat and the peasants and petty bourgeoisie. Plekhanov objected that the abandonment of the Marxist premiss that the workers had no hope of improving their lot under capitalism meant that socialism was no longer a revolutionary doctrine but a programme of legislative reform. If Bernstein was right, said Kautsky, socialism had no *raison d'être*. Labriola argued that Bernstein had thrown in his lot with the liberal bourgeoisie, and Rosa Luxemburg pointed out that socialism would be unnecessary if the capitalist economy had powers of adaptation enabling it to avoid crises of overproduction. Criticisms of this kind were purely ideological and expressed no more than a well-grounded fear that if Bernstein was right, classic revolutionary Marxism would cease to exist. But most of the critics also maintained that Bernstein was arguing from false premisses. Kautsky, Bebel, and Rosa Luxemburg held to the traditional theory of concentration, and in so doing showed that this term could be interpreted in different ways. Bernstein had not disputed that capital mergers and combinations were taking place in such a way as to increase the number of big industrial enterprises and their share in production. But he denied that there was a tendency for capital to accumulate in the hands of fewer and fewer owners, while small capitalists were squeezed out. Rosa Luxemburg objected that the shareholding system meant the concentration and not the deconcentration of capital; this was true, but did not refute Bernstein's argument. Apart from this, however, all the orthodox critics perceived that if the polarization of classes and the disappearance of the middle class were called in question, the whole of Marxist doctrine would collapse. The universal practice of issuing small shares was, they said, only the method used by capital to attract small savings, and had nothing to do with the class division of society. Even Jaurès questioned Bernstein's view that class divisions were becoming more fluid: in spite of all differentiations, he claimed, the basic division between haves and have-nots remained in force. Jaurès feared, moreover, that if Bernstein's views were adopted the socialist movement would lose its class character and dissolve into vague radicalism. On this account Jaurès broadly supported Kautsky, although his own views were closer to Bernstein's as regards the socialist significance of reforms and the right and duty of social democrats to ally themselves with non-socialists in the pursuit of short-term objectives.

Rosa Luxemburg formulated the crux of the dispute most clearly. If it is supposed that capitalism can be reformed either by gradually removing the consequences of anarchical production or by improving the workers' standard of life, then there is no point in working for a revolution. But such reform is impossible, for anarchy and crises are in the nature of capitalism, and the worker is exploited by virtue of the fact that he sells his labour-power. This state of things cannot be eliminated or improved without expropriating the capitalists, which can only be done by a revolutionary seizure of power. There is a qualitative difference between revolution and reforms of any kind.

The critics' views did not prevent revisionist ideas from becoming wide-spread among German social democrats, the majority of whom had in practice been reformists before Bernstein published his theories. True, there were many party and union leaders who were uninterested in theory or the revision of party doctrine: the latter was neither a help nor a hindrance in the everyday process of struggle, bargaining, and reform, and could be left as it stood for purposes of rhetoric. None the less, once the new formula was uttered they accepted it without resistance. The revolutionary idea was much more the property of the party intellectuals than of the working masses. In the first years of the dispute the future left wing did not clearly take shape within the party, and up to the war period it was represented only by a few theorists and publicists who had no organizational role or practical influence and did not form a permanent group among themselves. To the orthodox Marxists who provided the party with its organization and doctrine, like Bebel and Kautsky respectively, Bernstein's views were of course a challenge to the revolutionary faith which they professed with full sincerity: the party was in their eyes a true embodiment of its programme, both on the practical and on the theoretical side. If, however, they were able to obtain majority support for anti-revisionist formulas, it was not because the party was imbued with revolutionary spirit but because most of its members regarded the traditional slogans as harmless and of little practical consequence.

Lenin took the view, which is still treated as a dogma by the Communist movement, that revisionism came into being as an ideology reflecting the interests of the aristocracy of the working class, whom the bourgeoisie permitted to enjoy the 'left-overs' of their feast of prosperity. This would suggest that only a small privileged part of the German working class lent a willing ear to reformist doctrine, while the great majority were fervent revolutionaries. But in fact, what was later called by its opponents 'practical' revisionism was chiefly found among the trade unions, the most immediately class-based organization of the proletariat; moreover, the unions at that time did not yet possess the elaborate bureaucracy which was later made the scapegoat for opportunism and revisionism. In any case, if Lenin's explanation were true it would be highly unfortunate for Marxist doctrine. Since the 'aristocracy of the working class' are wage-earners like their fellow workers, and differ from them only in earning more, it would appear that a higher standard of living turns workers from revolutionaries into reformists; but, according to traditional Marxism, poverty is not the source of the class struggle and the revolutionary consciousness, and a short-term improvement in the workers' lot has no significant effect on their innate revolutionism.

When Bernstein was writing, the German working class had behind it a long period of increasing real wages and the successful struggle for welfare measures and a shorter working day. It also had a powerful political organization, whose influence was steadily increasing. The Reichstag, it is true, did not carry much weight, and Prussia had not introduced universal suffrage, but elections, political mobilization, and the comparison of forces encouraged hopes of a successful struggle for republicanism and even of seizing power. The actual experience of the German working class by no means supported the theory that its position was essentially hopeless and could not be reformed under capitalism. In Russia, too, a revisionist tendency made its appearance when the social democrats were no longer a handful of intellectuals and a genuine workers' movement had begun to take shape. The history of revisionism does not suggest that the working class is naturally revolutionary because it is forced to sell its labour-power and is incurably alienated in consequence. Thus it was not only in the doctrinal field that revisionism called into question the traditional belief in the revolutionary mission of the proletariat: the belief was challenged, perhaps more effectively still, by the success of revisionism as a social phenomenon, which robbed socialism of the glamorous prospect of a 'final battle' for universal liberation. Instead of a new Fourteenth of July bringing human 'prehistory' to an apocalyptic close and ushering in the new era, the reformists offered a programme of laborious, gradual, and unspectacular improvement.

Thus was created the ideological foundation of a new social democracy, the further development of which had very little to do with the history of Marxist doctrine. Although this form of socialism derives genetically from Marxism, in part at least, its origin soon became unimportant. The new doctrine was a compromise between liberalism and Marxian socialism, or a socialist variant of liberalism. It was applied to situations other than those envisaged by classical Marxism, and appealed to different psychological motivations. The increasing dominance of revisionism in German social democracy spelt the end of Marxism as socialists had understood it before the First World War. The centre of gravity was soon to be transferred eastward, where revolutionary doctrine was embodied in new dynamic forms.

V

Jean Jaurès: Marxism as a Soteriology

1. Jaurès as a conciliator

AS A THEORETICIAN, Jaurès counts for little among orthodox Marxists. He is
of course generally recognized as one of the key figures of French socialism,
but his views are regarded as a 'synthesis' (by his admirers) or a 'conflation' or
'patchwork' (by the more orthodox) of a variety of sources, especially French
ones, among which Marxism occupied no more than a position of equality. Certainly he never treated Marxism as a self-sufficient and all-embracing system
from which the interpretation of all social phenomena could be deduced, still
less as a metaphysical key to the universe, explaining its every feature and providing moral and practical guidance as to how it should be changed. On the
contrary, Jaurès made conscious efforts to combine the most varied philosophical and political traditions into a single vision of the world, believing as
he did in the essential unity of intellectual and moral trends that presented
themselves in apparent diversity at different stages of history. He was by nature
a universal conciliator, and was aware of this fact. His political and philosophical opponents accused him of glossing over social and doctrinal differences,
obscuring contrasts, being all things to all men, blunting the edge of the class
struggle by a naïvely moralizing attitude, and so on. From the orthodox point
of view, a writer and politician who invoked the authority of Proudhon and
Blanqui, Michelet and Saint-Simon, Kant and Fichte, Lassalle and Comte,
Rousseau and Kropotkin, instead of treating them all as enemies or naïve
'predecessors', was obviously not to be ranked as a Marxist, which in orthodox
eyes is an all-or-nothing position. But if we do not approach the matter from a
dogmatic standpoint, our judgement as to whether Jaurès was a Marxist will
depend on which of Marx's thoughts, and which interpretation of them, we
regard as containing the essence of his doctrine; and on this point there is no
agreed conclusion, even among those who claim to have remained faithful to
the spirit and letter of Marxism.

Unlike the most typical Marxists of his own day, Jaurès never believed that
the idea of socialism could be fully objectivized as a scientific theory similar to
that of evolution, or actually as an extension of the latter. Nor was Marxism, in
his view, a theory of social development and nothing more: it was an impas-

sioned moral appeal, a new and more perfect expression of man's eternal thirst for justice, unity, and brotherly love. Jaurès's ambition was not to intensify but to assuage conflicts, antagonisms, and enmity of every kind: the fundamental ideas of Marxism, he believed, did not signify a breach of historical continuity but appealed to the deepest moral instincts of mankind. Since men basically shared the same feelings, desires, and habits of thought, and since socialism to Jaurès was above all a moral concept, he naturally addressed his appeals and explanations to all social classes, the bourgeoisie included. This was not because he imagined that all social problems could be solved by philanthropy or the goodwill of the privileged classes, or that socialism could be achieved by a moral transformation alone instead of by pressure and fighting, but because he believed that all human beings possessed common values that were not those of any specific class. If they took those values seriously and drew practical conclusions from them, they would be bound to see that socialism offered the only chance of their fulfilment. Socialists, therefore, should take advantage of any support they might find outside the working class, among people whose moral instincts prompted them to support the socialist cause.

Socialism, to Jaurès, was essentially a question of morals and human values, an ideal to which mankind had more or less consciously aspired throughout the ages. Consequently he was repelled by an interpretation of it in terms of a break with man's spiritual and cultural heritage. Spiritual values, he believed, were continuous and grew stronger as history progressed. In the coming synthesis all human values and achievements would turn out to be part of the same culture, even though they were rooted historically in conflict and hatred. Trends that appeared contrary or irrelevant to one another would one day blend into a harmonious unity. Nothing, therefore, that the human spirit had ever created should be despised or overlooked. This vision of an ultimate synthesis is the most characteristic feature of Jaurès's thought. In his more enthusiastic moments he may be called the Pangloss of socialism, believing in the final unity of science and religion, idealism and materialism, national and class values, the individual and society, spirit and matter, man and nature. Even before the final synthesis it was possible to combine revolution and evolution, the political struggle and moral education—to work on man's feelings as well as his intellect, and to appeal to proletarian interests as well as to universal human values.

Moreover, the unity of human progress was not only a matter of the final synthesis but could be seen already in the gradual prevalence of the idea which was to find its fulfilment in socialism. Progress up to the present time consisted not only in technological change but in the embodiment of basic values in increasingly perfect forms, though their ultimate perfection of course lay in the future. Jaurès shared with Marx the belief that human affairs would one day be harmonized in a socialist world, and that past history and present conflicts were meaningful only in relation to this prospect. But he differed from Marx in his view of the continuity and cumulative character of the whole of past history, as opposed to the Hegelian belief that progress is realized by its 'bad aspect'. Jaurès believed in the steady upward progress of humanity, supported by an increasing accumulation of spiritual and social values, and not in a descent into the abyss, to be followed by a sudden, apocalyptic renascence.

2. Biographical outline

JAURÈS's political career belongs wholly to the period of the Second International, and his death occurred at the moment of its dissolution. Born in 1859 at Castres in the South of France, he attended the *lycée* there and subsequently the École Normale in Paris. In 1881 he was third on the list of *agrégés;* the candidate with the highest marks had a career of no special distinction, while the runner-up was Henri Bergson. In the same year Jaurès became a teacher of philosophy in the *lycée* at Albi, and two years later he was made a lecturer at Toulouse University. In 1885 he was elected to the Chamber as a republican deputy, in opposition to the monarchist and clerical parties. Partly as a result of his political activities he became attracted to socialist ideas, which he regarded from the start as the legitimate development of the ideals of the Revolution. In 1889 he lost his seat to a conservative candidate and returned to Toulouse, where he spent the next two years working on his doctoral theses. The first of these, entitled *De la réalité du monde sensible* (published 1891, second edition 1902) was a philosophical discourse in the strict sense and expressed his basic metaphysical views, which are important for the understanding of his public life. The second thesis was in Latin: *De primis socialismi germanici lineamentis apud Lutherum, Kant, Fichte et Hegel* (1891; a French translation, *Les Origines du socialisme allemand*, was published in 1892 in the *Revue socialiste*). This is more directly related to Jaurès's socialist views, giving his interpretation of the philosophical sources that inspired the social theories of Marx and Lassalle. At this period he also wrote socialist articles, chiefly in the *Dépêche de Toulouse*. When re-elected to the Chamber in 1893 he was a socialist not only in the sense of upholding the principles of a socialist order, but in believing that the future of those principles depended on action by the working class. During the next five years he became an acknowledged leader of the socialist group in parliament, and until 1914 his life was an integral part of French history. In the main issues of the time—the Dreyfus case and the Millerand affair, questions of war and peace, Morocco and the French colonial empire, the role and significance of the International—Jaurès's attitude was always important and sometimes decisive. Generally his views can be traced to philosophical principles which he appears to have had constantly in mind. If he was whole-heartedly involved in the Dreyfus case, without regard to considerations of tactics, it was because he held, unlike Guesde, that the socialist movement should be the mouthpiece of any cause in which human rights were at stake, no matter who the victim was or to what class or group he belonged: for socialism was responsible for all human values, not only 'after the revolution' but here and now. When, after much hesitation and to the indignation of the whole socialist left wing, he supported Millerand's action in joining Waldeck-Rousseau's government, it was because of his view that advantage should be taken of every means of influencing existing forms of public life: if co-operation with class enemies seemed likely to pay off in a particular case, it should not be rejected on grounds of strategic exclusivism. His socialist opponents retorted that he was abandoning the class viewpoint and was prepared to accept the shadiest allies for the sake of some immediate gain; he was, they claimed, a reformist and an opportunist. Jaurès was not a reformist, however, in the sense of abandoning the 'ultimate goal' or limiting his sights to the short-term, partial interests of the working class. On the contrary, he insisted at every turn on the basic principles and objectives of socialism. However, unlike the revolutionary syndicalists and the extreme Left of the International, but in agreement with most of the centre group, he regarded reforms not merely as a preparation for the final conflict but as an improvement of the workers' lot here and now. He did not consider that the proletariat embodied the whole virtue of society, since human values could not be the monopoly of a single class, even though that class might enjoy the historical privilege of bringing them to a state of complete fulfilment. A policy of conciliation, compromise, and piecemeal agreements did not, as he saw it, signify opportunism or lack of principle but was an expression of faith in the power of the socialist ideal. The opponents of socialism were bound to recognize that in many matters it had right on its side, and in this way it could enlist support outside its natural home in the working class.

Both Jaurès and Guesde lost their seats in the election of 1898, when the Dreyfus agitation was at its height. Re-elected in 1902, Jaurés spoke frequently in parliament and at meetings and wrote innumerable pamphlets and articles on current politics and problems of socialism. He no longer had time to produce large single works, and most of the volumes he published at this period were collections of short pieces. They include Les Preuves (1898, on the Dreyfus case); Études socialistes (1901, second edition 1902: mainly theoretical); Action socialiste (1897); and L'Organisation socialiste de France. L'Armée nouvelle (no date). In addition he edited, and partly wrote, a Histoire socialiste de la Révolution française, published in instalments from 1879 to 1900; Jaurès's contributions were republished separately by A. Mathiez in 1922-4. Many articles scattered through various periodicals—Revue socialiste, Mouvement social-

iste, Humanité, Petite République, Matin, Revue de Paris—have not yet been collected and republished. An edition of Jaurès's works by M. Bonnafous appeared in nine volumes from 1931 onwards, but was not completed.

Jaurès's last years were overshadowed by the approach of war, which aroused anxiety throughout the European socialist movement. He was shot dead by a nationalist fanatic in a Paris cafe on 31 July 1914, the last day of the nineteenth century. He was certainly one of the liveliest and most versatile minds in the socialist movement, interested in all aspects of public life and culture. Although frequently attacked both by socialists and by others, according to most accounts he aroused friendly feelings in all those whom he met personally.

3. The metaphysics of universal unity

UNLIKE most socialist leaders except Lassalle, Jaurès was also a philosopher in the professional sense of the word. His thesis *De la realité du monde sensible* shows no trace of Marxist influence but is inspired by neo-Kantian ideas and particularly by Jules Lachelier. This does not mean that it is irrelevant to his activity as a writer and politician: on the contrary, it serves as a metaphysical background to the latter, but at the same time it illustrates the unorthodoxy of his view of Marxism. It was not Marxist studies that led him to socialism, but moral motivations that he shared long before he had heard of Marxism. Marxism to him was not a philosophy or a metaphysic, but the theoretical expression of the socialist movement; and he was never a Marxist in the sense of expecting the doctrine to provide a key to all human problems. His philosophical *magnum opus*, couched in the diffuse rhetorical style of the École Normale, is an attempt to reconcile almost every conflicting metaphysical standpoint and to show that all of them are basically right, but each is incomplete in the light of his universal theory of Being. It expresses a kind of evolutionary pantheism which, however, does not sacrifice individual Being to the Absolute but defends the rights of subjectivity amid the general trend of the universe towards final unity. When Jaurès tackles the classic problem of the 'primacy' between sense and intellect in the act of perception, he adopts a kind of popular Kantianism: as sensual qualities present themselves in permanent associations the mind is constrained to regard objects as substances, and the idea of substance is present in every mind, including the minds of those philosophers who declare there is no such thing. Certainly the mind would not have evolved the idea of the substantial unity of objects if this were not suggested to it by sensual perception, but the latter could not of itself give rise to the idea of substance, which is due to the operation of the intellect. In this sense 'the real' and 'the intelligible' are one and the same.

However, Jaurès goes beyond this purely epistemological standpoint and develops a positive metaphysic over and above the Kantian critique. The mind does not create the organization of the universe, but neither does it simply reflect that organization as a result of perception. The perception of the order that pervades all Being is possible only because the mind is itself a part of that order, a product and a co-author of it. The different forms and levels of universal organization combine in a single purposeful whole: the astral system, chemical compounds, the organic world, and the world of mankind are all part of a rational evolution towards divine harmony and unity. At the highest level of Being, thought and reality are the same; the mind coalesces with the universe. This ultimate unity is a condition of the meaning of every particle of reality, and it also determines that meaning. There is no such thing as 'chance', which term only signifies the mind's perplexity in the face of events that spring from multiple causes. But to explain the meaning of existence it is not sufficient to reject the idea of chance, nor even (and here Jaurès parts company with Lachelier) to accept the view that all change is for a purpose. There must also be a category of 'progress' to which all events contribute after their fashion, and this is not contained in the idea of purpose as such. Progress implies a distinction between potentiality and actuality. The reality of each particular event is then determined not merely by its cause or even its purpose in relation to other events, but also by the part it plays in the progressive realization of the Absolute, the rational movement towards final harmony. Reality *is* the Absolute as it lives and develops. Human reason perceives the meaning of evolution and thus helps to cause it; so does the act of understanding in which sense is revealed. Thus, strictly speaking, there is no 'primacy' of truth or reason as opposed to Being, for in the last resort they are one and the same: Being affirms itself by taking on intellectual form.

Examining in turn the various elementary forms of the mental and physical world, Jaurès tries to show the meaningfulness of all that we experience with the mind and senses, but always from an eschatological point of view. For instance, he puts the question why there are three dimensions, and replies that this is so that the postulate of freedom can be realized in the physical world. If there were only one dimension, change could only take the form of movement forwards or backwards, and from the teleological point of view this would mean a simple increase or decrease of the distance to the ultimate goal, i.e. slavish virtue or absolute wickedness. Freedom, however, requires the possibility of a departure from the straight path in the direction 'most opposed' to it, i.e. at right angles to the original line. Moreover, freedom also requires that there be an infinite number of lines at right angles to the original one, i.e. that there be three dimensions. 'These three are both necessary and sufficient, expressing in the order of spatial extension the infinite freedom of infinite activity' (*De la réalité du monde sensible*, p. 32).

The starting-point of Jaurès's metaphysical system is self-identical Being (not, he emphasizes, the idea of Being), i.e. Being as understood by Parmenides and Hegel. All forms of partial existence are related to Being in a manner that is not specifically defined, but in which there is no place for a distinction between real and apparent existence: everything that seems to be an appearance or illusion exists in its own way, more particularly human subjectivity. Even dreams are not mere illusion: they are perceived, and therefore have a reality of their own. Consciousness does not reduce Being to an illusion, nor is it itself an illusion or a mere fleeting manifestation of Being. On the contrary, it can—as Descartes observed—arrive at the fact of Being by merely contemplating itself, and in so doing it shows that its own existence is not merely a fact but a necessity. Impressions are no less real, though they are real in a different way, than the physical movements that are their 'objective' counterpart. The evolution of Being comprises everything, gives it a meaning and in some sense justifies it. It tends towards perfect unity, but not so as to destroy the wealth of diversity in which Being is manifested. That unity is God, of whom it may be said that he is above the world but also, in a sense, that he *is* the world: he is the self in every self, the truth in every truth, the consciousness in every consciousness. The human mind needs God and finds him in spite of the sophists, just as it needs justice and finds it in spite of the sceptics. Faith is not a sign of weakness or ignorance; on the contrary, those who have no faith or do not feel the need for it are mediocrities.

Jaurès's thesis does not appear to have been influenced by Hegel, though in some respects it shows Hegelian tendencies: in particular the idea that the act by which Being is apprehended must be regarded as itself a *Moment* or aspect of the development of Being. In other words, thought does not turn Being into an illusion, nor is it merely a passive reflection of it, but, by understanding the evolution of Being, it acts as a necessary co-author and sharer in that evolution. Jaurès, when he wrote his principal thesis, does not seem to have known the *Phenomenology of Mind;* in his second dissertation he mentions Hegel's philosophy, but only in regard to the state. The general idea of the fundamental unity of all Being seems to have taken shape in his mind under the influence of Spinoza and the French neo-Kantians. But his evolutionary conception of the Absolute, which so strikingly recalls the pantheism of the Christian neo-Platonists, was probably worked out independently rather than borrowed from tradition. Today it also brings to mind the cosmology and cosmogony of Teilhard de Chardin. The importance of Jaurès's metaphysical pantheism does not lie in the field of Marxist theory, on which it had no influence whatever, but in the fact that it led him to embrace socialism and that he never departed from it in later years. On many occasions, in more or less popular writings, he returned to the ideas expressed in his doctoral thesis. In an article in the

Dépêche de Toulouse of 15 October 1890, at the time of the thesis itself, he summed up his social and religious hopes in a vision of the triumph of socialism and of universal concord, joy, and human dignity. In that day

> men will understand the profound meaning of life, whose secret aim is the harmony of all minds and forces and of every individual freedom. They will understand history better and will love it more, for it will be their own history, as they will be the heirs of the whole human race. And they will understand the universe better too: for as they behold the triumph of mind and spirit in humanity, they will soon realize that the universe out of which humanity is born cannot be fundamentally brutal and blind, that there is soul and spirit everywhere, that the universe itself is nothing but an obscure, infinite yearning and progress towards harmony, beauty, freedom and goodness.

In a speech in the Chamber in favour of secular education, on 11 February 1895, Jaurès declared that he understood the new generation which sought to reconcile naturalism and idealism with the aid of Spinoza and Hegel, for he himself could not accept the doctrine that the explanation of the universe lay in matter, 'cette suprême inconnue'. Nor could he regard the great religions as the result of mere calculation or deceit: although exploited for class purposes they had their roots in human nature and were, so to speak, an appeal to the future which might be heard some day. In *Socialisme et liberté* (*Socialism and Freedom*, 1898) he returned to the same ideas. The future order would be a supreme affirmation of the rights of the individual, and would differ from Christianity in that it would not conceive of God as a transcendental ruler over mankind. But human minds would not be content with mere negation. Many socialists were tending towards idealistic monism, regarding the world as an integrated progress of man and nature towards final harmony. Socialism would unite men with one another, and all men with the universe.

> The advent of socialism will be like a great religious revelation. Will it not be a miraculous event when men and women who have grown up in the brutal obscurity of our planet attain justice and wisdom; when man by natural evolution rises above nature, that is to say above violence and conflict; when warring forces and instincts blend into a harmony of wills? And how can we forbear to ask ourselves whether there is not, at the root of all this, a secret of unity and kindliness that gives meaning to the world? . . . A revolution of justice and goodness, carried out by that part of nature which we now call mankind, will be, as it were, a challenge and a signal to nature itself. Why should not the whole creation strive to free itself from inertia and confusion, since in the form of humanity it will already have achieved consciousness, enlightenment and peace? Thus, from the height of its triumph, humanity will proclaim words of hope to reach the very depths of nature, and will give ear to the

voice of universal longing and expectation that will answer its cry. (*Œuvres*, ed. Bonnafous (9 vols., 1931–9), vi, 96–8.)

Similar thoughts are expressed in a lecture *L'Art et le socialisme* (1900) and in other writings. In Jaurès's view socialism is part of the universal trend towards harmony which gives a meaning to all the struggles and sufferings of which history is full. This, as he himself acknowledged, is a religious viewpoint, though pantheistic rather than Christian. It is as though Jaurès in his intellectual development unconsciously retraced the long road from neo-Platonic pantheism to Marxian soteriology: not only the step from Hegel to Marx, which was all Marx himself regarded as important, but the preceding stages as well. Marx in his early writings speaks, it is true, of a restoration of unity between man and nature, but in a different sense. Nature, to him, has no significance prior to that of mankind. It is not man who in his spiritual development reveals the spirituality of nature, its latent aspirations or unconscious goodness and wisdom; rather, by exercising his own wisdom man confers a human significance on nature. If the spirit is the work of nature, it does not therefore constitute a manifestation of nature as spirit. In the same way socialism is not the product of feeling, least of all an unconscious feeling by which the development of the universe is inspired and permeated. Marx could never have said that the revolution would take place 'in the name of justice and goodness', for these were not part of history and had no share in determining its meaning. Jaurès's belief in a purposeful harmony of the universe is of course foreign to Marxism, although it was the cause of Jaurès becoming a Marxist. Holding this belief, he considered that in the last resort there was no conflict between scientific knowledge of the world and the religious faith of pantheism. His attitude to religion was not that of Saint-Simon's followers, who in effect accepted the basic doctrine of Christianity. But Jaurès believed, it would seem, that historical soteriology was of no value except as part of a universal soteriology of Being. Like most pantheists he believed in universal salvation and the ultimate reconcilability of all things, i.e. the non-reality of evil.

4. The directing forces of history

As in general metaphysics, so in the philosophy of history Jaurès sought to reconcile two apparently opposite concepts: those of historical idealism and Marxism. In the preface to the *Socialist History of the Revolution* he argued that while history has economic 'foundations', economic forces act on human beings who impart to history the variety of their passions and ideas, living not only on a social but on a cosmic plane. Certainly the evolution of ideas depends in some measure on that of economic forms, but that dependence does not explain everything. Marx himself had believed that humanity in future times would be able to determine the course of its own development: this was not yet so, but even today superior souls were able to rise to freedom, and the dignity of the spirit played an increasingly important part in history. Arguing thus, Jaurès declared that his interpretation of history was 'materialist with Marx and mystical with Michelet'. As the historian of France and especially of the Revolution, Michelet was an important figure to Jaurès in that he emphasized the role of collective inspiration in bringing about great events.

In his critical writings Jaurès often takes a similar line to many of his Marxist contemporaries. For instance, he opposes the interpretation of historical materialism according to which every detail of history can be fully explained by the development of technology causing changes in the system of ownership, production, and exchange, and hence in class-relationships and the whole ideological superstructure. In a lecture of February 1900 on 'Bernstein and the evolution of socialist method' he states that particular branches of human spiritual activity have their own logic and are in some degree independent of economic processes. In *Socialism and Freedom* he writes: 'Just as a weaver, although bound by the shape of his loom, is able to weave fabrics of varying design and colour, so history, with the same equipment of economic forces, can fashion human destiny in various ways. The economic form conditions all human activities, but that is not to say they can be deduced from it.' In many other passages he makes clear, however, that he is concerned with more than Engels's 'relative independence of the superstructure'. He also holds that human history must be understood as a process of the steadily increasing prevalence of ideal values and their influence on events. There is no place for this idea in Marx's historiosophy, even as diluted by Engels. In the preface to a book by Benoît Malon, Jaurès observes that in spite of all conflicts human beings have an instinct of mutual sympathy that expresses itself in religion and philosophy and, most fully of all, in the working-class movement. In a lecture of December 1894 on the idealistic and materialistic views of history he says that historical development arises from the conflict between man and the use that is made of him, and that this development will come to an end when man is used according to what he is. 'Humanity thus realizes itself in economic forms that conflict less and less with its own idea. And in human history there is not only necessary evolution, but also an ideal sense and a purposeful direction.' Through all the moral changes due to the pressure of economic forces, humanity preserves an unchanging impulse and an undying hope of rediscovering itself. There is no conflict between materialism and historical idealism: history is affected by mechanical laws, but it also reflects a moral urge and an ideal law. Recalling Marx's critique of Bentham, Jaurès observes that Marxism itself would be meaningless if it were a mere description of indifferent historical 'necessities', and not also an affirmation of the human values enshrined in socialism. It would be contrary to common sense to suppose that the socialist idea could assert itself automatically, without the aid of human faith and enthusiasm. Capitalism, it is true, prepares the way for socialist forms of life and draws the lines of the future state, but we cannot confer the stamp of natural necessity on historical evolution. Socialism would not exist without the forces set in motion by capitalism in the form of technology, labour organization, and property; but it would also not exist if it were not for the conscious will of humanity, athirst for freedom and justice and inspired by the energy to transform the opportunities offered by capitalism into reality.

In discussing the problem of 'socialism as historical necessity' and 'socialism as a value' Jaurès does not resort to the typical categories of 'ethical socialism', i.e. he does not put the question 'Assuming that we know socialism to be the inevitable result of historical laws, how does it follow that we must approve its values?' Unlike the neo-Kantians he rejects the dualism of 'what is' and 'what ought to be', claiming to have overcome this by his pantheistic theory of development. Since the universe develops in accordance with ideal laws determined 'in the last resort' by a future harmony, and since goodness, beauty, and love are not immanent in human history but are part of the creative surge of nature itself, while humanity brings to its fullness the divine potentiality of Being, it follows that the apprehension by man of his future destiny is not a purely intellectual act, to be complemented by a subsequent act of moral approbation. The end to which mankind has aspired more or less consciously throughout history, and to which it still aspires, is not an arbitrary creation of the mind: it is the articulation of the aspirations of universal Being. Men are part of nature not only as organisms but as creatures endowed with mind, feeling, and desires; once they are aware of their own unity with the cosmos, their self-understanding is at the same time an acceptance of nature and of its necessities, which must be benevolent in their effect. There is no contradiction between the indifferent course of nature, subject to mechanical laws, and the rules of morality which must derive from sources other than theoretical knowledge; hence there is no longer any duality or separation between that which is and that which ought to be.

Marx too rejected the Kantian dualism, but not for the same reasons as Jaurès. Marx believed that in the last phase of 'pre-history', in which the proletarian movement paved the way for a general revolution, the duality of necessity and freedom would disappear, as what was historically necessary would be carried out by free revolutionary activity. He believed that in this way he had overcome the Kantian dualism, but he did not thereby do away with the problem whether what was historically necessary was also good. The question why this should be so cannot in fact be answered, or even asked, within the framework of Marx's views, because the fact (if such it is) that what is necessary is also good in this case is a contingent one: the historical necessity of socialism is not based on the proposition that it is good for mankind, nor can its value be deduced from its quasi-natural inevitability. The two aspects are logically and historically distinct, and each is accidental with respect to the other. There is no 'law' which lays down that man must achieve liberation or unity with himself and nature; historical necessity does not assure us *a priori* that man is not bound to endure slavery, poverty, and unhappiness for ever. The fact that men desire to free themselves from these things does not prove that they will succeed, for history does not depend on human wishes. Hence, although the changes scheduled to take place in the last phase are due to revolutionary will and not to anonymous 'laws', the efficacy of that will derives from objective circumstances and not from the fact that it stands for justice and freedom. In this sense it can be said that the ultimate beneficence of historical necessity is a matter of chance: it happens to be the case that the laws of history favour the accomplishment of what human beings regard, or will regard, as satisfying their desires, and that this same end will, independently of their wishes, in fact constitute the fulfilment of human nature. Jaurès is concerned to avoid this element of contingency, because his vision of universal harmony leaves no room for a necessity which is devoid of purpose or neutral as between good and evil: in his view, intelligence and the invincible force of goodness are constantly shaping the course of the entire universe. There is no stage of evolution at which the universe is a blind force that men can only exploit or curb for their own ends. In short, Jaurès believes that universal Being desires the same ends as humanity does, and that this is so not by chance but because of man's place in the order of being and the fact that his desires and aspirations are the articulation of what the universe as a whole desires and aspires to.

5. Socialism and the republic

IT IS easy to see how closely Jaurès's political reactions are linked with his philosophy. Believing as he did in the over-all unity of history and the march of progress in all spheres of human life, he also held that the liberated society of the future would not be a radical negation of existing forms but a continuation and development of values that were already burgeoning. Thus he constantly reiterated, in one form or another, the view that socialism was the full realization of principles that were already discernible in history and especially in the 1789 Revolution. The Declaration of the Rights of Man and the Constitution of 1793 contained in essence all the ideas of socialism, which only had to be developed to their proper conclusion: in particular, freedom, equality, and justice must be extended from the political field to that of ownership and the sys-

tem of production, and this was the proper meaning of socialism. The individual freedom guaranteed by the Revolution did not apply to economic affairs,
and privileges of ownership remained although political privilege had been
swept away. In justice, every human being had an equal right to the enjoyment
of all the resources accumulated by humanity since the beginning of time. As
Marx had contended, under socialism accumulated labour should serve to
enrich workers' lives, whereas under private ownership living labour only went
to increase the accumulation of labour in the form of capital. The aim of socialism was to subordinate the achievements of the past to life in the present. As
Jaurès wrote in an article on 'Socialism and Life' (7 September 1901), 'Life does
not cancel the past, but makes use of it. The revolution is a conquest, not a new
rupture.' But the logic of the Declaration of the Rights of Man was a dead letter until the proletariat came on the political scene, and thus the plans of Saint-
Simon and Fourier had come to nothing. Since 1848 it was clear that the
socialist order could not be created merely by dreams of justice but only by the
organized working class putting an end to the contradiction between the political sovereignty of the people and its economic enslavement. The 'political
republic' must be turned into a 'social republic' by the extension of democracy
to the whole of economic life.

The frequency with which Jaurès insisted that socialism was a continuation
and not a negation of the republican idea was partly due to his anxiety to
refute the anti-socialist argument that 'collectivism' was a denial of individual
freedom, but partly also to the fact that, in France at least, socialists themselves were by no means unanimous on the point. The idea of socialism as the
'direct opposite' of the existing order suggested that socialists wanted to
destroy the bourgeois republic with its democratic institutions, or to replace
the rule of bankers and capitalists by that of bureaucrats in charge of nationalized industry—a fear expressed in many quarters at this time, not least by the
anarchists. Hence Jaurès insisted that individual human values were the sole
criterion of the values of social institutions. 'Socialists relate the value of every
institution to the human individual. It is he who, by asserting his will to freedom and development, confers strength and vitality on institutions and ideas.
The individual is the measure of all things: the fatherland, the family, property, humanity, God himself. This is the logic of revolutionary thought. This is
what socialism means' (Socialism and Freedom). The collectivization of property would be a travesty of socialism if it meant that the political authorities
were put in charge of the economy as well. 'If the politicians and administrators who already control the nation's diplomacy and armed forces were also
given authority over the whole labour force, and if they could appoint managers at all levels in the same way as they now appoint army officers, this
would confer on a handful of men such power as Asian despots never dreamt

of—for they controlled only the surface of public life and not the economy of their countries' (*Socialist Organization*). Socialists did not propose to strengthen the state as an instrument of coercion but, on the contrary, to place state institutions and production once more under the control of associated individuals. The abolition of classes meant the abolition of those private interests that fought for control of the administrative machine, and hence an end to its corruption and oppressive function. Everyone would be, in the same sense, a worker for the public good: there would be no separate caste or group of administrators tyrannizing over the public. Freedom to work and enjoy the fruits of one's labour, freedom of speech and the printed word, freedom of assembly, of the arts and sciences—all this could be guaranteed incomparably better by socialism than by a system where these freedoms were curtailed by the privileges of private ownership. There was no reason to fear that people would be reluctant to do unpleasant or laborious work: rates of pay could take account of the nature of the job, and anyhow there might be people who felt a vocation to be dustmen. Nor should it be feared that producers would be deprived of initiative or that workers would lack incentive to increase and improve production, for it was easy to devise rewards for productivity and invention. In any case production would not be wholly centralized: there would be increased scope for corporations covering different branches of production, and for municipal and regional bodies. Representative institutions, both on a national scale and on the basis of smaller geographical or industrial units, would ensure that the people as a whole were able to supervise the entire economy. Freedom would not be curtailed but greatly extended when the basic social functions of production and distribution were placed under public control. The state would remain in charge of public services which required to be administered from the centre, but it would be a state of a different kind. Instead of private owners, as now, using the state's social functions for their own ends, the state would act for the benefit of society as a whole and would, as socialists had always maintained, cease to exercise political authority over individuals. It was not the purpose of socialism to impose on the public any particular idea of happiness, but to create conditions in which everyone could pursue his own happiness as he saw fit.

Socialism preserved and maintained all the values that mankind had created over the centuries, and had no intention of sacrificing anything that would increase man's dignity, freedom, and energy or further the quest for harmony. In particular, contrary to what was often asserted, it did not seek to diminish the idea of nationality, to deprive people of a fatherland or of patriotic feelings. The famous remark on this subject in *The Communist Manifesto* was no more than a *boutade*. Now that the proletariat enjoyed universal suffrage and education and had become a political power, it was absurd and insulting to suggest that it

did not form part of the existing state and nation or that it must 'remain nothing until it became everything'–so Jaurès declared in Chapter X of *L'Armée
nouvelle*. It was indeed counter-revolutionary to assert that the proletariat did
not belong to the *patrie*, for it meant denying the value of the day-to-day struggle and of partial gains, without which there could be no final liberation. Since
the Revolution the national and the democratic idea had been inseparable. The
unity of a nation was not a matter of landownership, as some pretended, but the
natural, almost physical longing of human beings to live in a community larger
than the family; the whole of mankind was too large a unit to satisfy that need.
Socialism was not out to destroy patriotism but to enlarge it. Abstract internationalism, ignoring national differences, was a chimera: mankind could only
achieve unity by the federation of free nations. It was natural, therefore, that
socialists defended the right of every nation to independence. The international
character of the workers' movement in no way conflicted with patriotism or the
desire to defend one's country against threats and aggression. The nation was
not the primary object of socialism, which was concerned above all with individual freedom, but it was nevertheless an essential form of life without which
socialism would wither away. It was impossible to imagine social liberation in
conditions of national enslavement, or a socialist movement that did not operate on the national plane before it became international. Chauvinism, wars,
aggression, and hatred were not part of the national idea but were a contradiction of it. Socialism presupposed France and the French Republic, as it presupposed every other human value.

As socialism thus laid claim to everything of value that the human race had
ever produced, it may be said that in Jaurès's mind all such values were, consciously or otherwise, a contribution to socialism. He did not perhaps assert
this in so many words, but he seems concerned to persuade everyone that they
are 'really' socialists at heart and that if they attack socialism it is because they
have not thought out their own ideas properly. Republicans, anarchists, Christians, intellectuals, patriots–all would be socialists if they reflected sufficiently
on the best way of preserving the values that they hold most dear. In the past
as well as in the present, Jaurès is constantly discovering more or less conscious
socialist tendencies, hampered by ignorance or inconsistency. In the French
Revolution he finds them among Babouvists, Girondists, and Jacobins. In his
thesis on the origins of German socialism he detects the germ of socialist ideas
at every point in the history of German idealism, beginning with Luther. The
idea of Christian equality paved the way for that of civic equality; fighting
against the tyranny of Rome, Luther taught his countrymen to fight tyranny of
every kind. The Lutheran notion of freedom as circumscribed by the divine law
is part of the critique of false freedom in the economic sphere. Kant and Fichte,
too, contributed to socialism by reconciling the freedom of the individual with

the authority of the state and its right to control economic affairs. Even Kant's idea that property is a precondition of citizenship was consistent with socialism in the sense that wage-labourers who own nothing are not full citizens. Fichte's *geschlossener Handelsstaat* embodied a kind of moral socialism, for it involved the social regulation of production in the common interest of its citizens. Hegelian philosophy was another source of socialism, especially when it distinguished abstract freedom, which was no more than individual caprice, from freedom governed by reason and universal law. Perfect freedom was not, as the liberals claimed, freedom short of injuring others: its true definition implied that freedom of the individual, instead of separating people, involved universal aspirations. Hegel came close to socialism when he defended the organic unity of a society in which individual values are preserved and subjected to the law of reason. Finally, Lassalle and Marx resolved the contradiction between the moral and historical interpretations of socialism, reconciling Fichte and Hegel and—especially in Lassalle's case—discovering eternal justice in the dialectical movement of the world.

Socialism could not become a live movement until there was an active, self-conscious working class to uphold its values. But, as Marx had shown, socialism was in the interest of all mankind and not only of the workers. It was even in the interest of today's exploiters—sick men refusing to be cured, who were victims of the system despite their privileges. When communism arrived the children of today's bourgeoisie would not only see in it the negation of what their fathers had done: they would also realize that the bourgeois themselves, by their bold and energetic improvement of technology, had unconsciously prepared for the liberation that would bring their endeavours into harmony with those of the revolutionary proletariat.

Since every human being was an *anima naturaliter socialista*, it was right and necessary for socialists to appeal to human values of all kinds and not only those peculiar to the present situation of the proletariat. The revolution could not, without self-contradiction, be the work of a minority or the result of a *coup d'état*, even if this were technically possible. The changes involved by socialism would be far more profound than those of the bourgeois revolution, and they could not be brought about without the unequivocal support of a large majority of the population. General elections revealed the true strength of different groups in society and made a successful *coup* less and less likely. But in any case socialism required the whole-hearted co-operation of society, for it was not enough to overthrow the old order and then allow economic life to be governed by the free play of individual forces: the new organizational forms must be planned in advance and must embrace the whole system of production and distribution. Thus the revolution must be preceded by moral changes that would arouse the socialist consciousness and inspire enthusiasm for the values of the new order.

The socialists therefore must seek support among other classes, especially the farmers and petty bourgeoisie. Jaurès recalled that in Liebknecht's view the working class should be taken to include all those who lived wholly or mainly by the work of their hands, i.e. the peasantry and the petty bourgeoisie as well as the industrial proletariat. Moreover, Liebknecht maintained, the socialist party should be more interested in whether its members professed socialist ideas than in whether they were wage-earners. If the movement were based exclusively on the industrial proletariat it could not become a majority or achieve its aims. It must be a movement of the whole people other than the nobility, clergy, and upper bourgeoisie, who together formed only a small percentage of society. Jaurès thought on similar lines: socialism, by its universality, would attract almost the whole people, and the socialist revolution, unlike the bourgeois one, could therefore be accomplished without violence, bloodshed, or civil war. Co-operation with the bourgeoisie and bourgeois parties on particular issues was possible and desirable not only on tactical grounds but because the spirit of co-operation was the guiding principle of socialism. 'We want a revolution,' said Jaurès in a lecture on Bernstein's views,

> but we do not want everlasting hatred. If, for the sake of some great cause—trade unions, co-operatives, art or justice, even bourgeois justice—we can get the bourgeoisie to march with us, how strong we shall feel when we can say to them: 'What a joy it is that those who were divided by hatred and mistrust can join forces even in a temporary fashion, for a single day—and how much more sublime and lasting will be our joy at the final encounter of all mankind!' ... What I wish, what we wish is that the socialist party should be the geometrical locus of all great causes and all great ideas. This does not mean that we are abandoning the fight for social revolution: on the contrary, we are arming ourselves in strength, dignity and pride so that the hour of revolution may strike all the sooner. (*Bernstein et l'évolution de la méthode socialiste*, 10 February 1900; *Œuvres*, vi. 139–40.)

This was the theoretical basis of Jaurès's activity in regard to the Dreyfus case, and also his attitude to the controversy over 'ministerialism'. Many French socialists of the *ouvriériste* persuasion took the view that the *Affaire* was a quarrel among bourgeois, with a member of the military caste as its protagonist, and was therefore no concern of the socialist movement. Guesde did not share this view and took a similar line to Jaurès at the outset, but he afterwards came to think that the party should not commit itself to the defence of a single individual in the opposing camp, as its proper task was to stand up for the whole oppressed working class: the bourgeois intrigues of which Dreyfus was a victim were not a good reason for abandoning the class struggle. The opposing arguments of Guesde and Jaurès were subsequently published in the pamphlet *Deux méthodes* (1900). Guesde's position was summed up in the contention that 'the proletariat should be guided solely by its own class egoism, since its interests are identical with the ultimate, universal interests of the whole human race'; 'there has been and can be no change in society until capitalist ownership is abolished'; 'we do not believe in negotiations: the class struggle excludes agreements between classes'; 'the revolution is only possible if you remain yourselves, a class against a class—a class that has never known, and is determined to avoid, the divisions that exist in the world of capital'.

Jaurès, on the contrary, held that the universal character of the proletariat's struggle was not something that only came into play after the revolution, but that it must manifest itself here and now, in all matters, in order that the revolution might come about. The proletariat, as an oppressed class, was already the mouthpiece of universal justice and the ally of all who had justice on their side, even if they were not its allies on other issues. It must therefore join forces in the present case with those sections of the bourgeoisie who stood for progress against reaction. It must defend the secular state against clericalism, even though this was the cause of the bourgeois radicals as well as its own; it must defend the republic against monarchists, and the cause of justice even when the victim was a member of the opposing camp.

A similar issue was raised in a more doubtful form by the Millerand affair. The latter's opponents maintained that his action in joining a bourgeois government was a deception of the working class, as it suggested that the proletariat already shared in political power; moreover, the socialist movement would be compromised if one of its leaders shared responsibility for the acts of a bourgeois regime which he could not prevent and which were bound to be in the interest of the exploiting classes. Jaurès replied that Millerand's act in joining the government would certainly not induce the latter to change its course basically, but it nevertheless bore witness to the strength of the socialist movement, and the latter's struggle against militarism and the reaction was aided by temporary alliances with the more progressive elements of the bourgeoisie.

The controversy brought to light two fundamentally different approaches to the idea of the political independence of the proletariat, and it also revealed the ambiguity of this idea in the context of the parliamentary activity of the socialist movement. There was a strong tradition, for which it was easy to find support in Marx's writings, in favour of treating the proletariat as a foreign enclave in bourgeois society—a class for which there could be no 'partial' liberation but which was destined to overthrow the entire political establishment and could therefore not ally itself with any of the other, hostile classes. But this exclusivism could not be consistently maintained in a situation in which socialist parties took part in parliamentary life and secured improvements in the condition of the working class by legislative means. Every improvement of this kind was to some extent an 'improvement of capitalism', and if Guesde consistently believed in his own principle that such improvements should be left to the capitalists, he ought not to involve the socialist party in parliamentary life or the struggle for immediate economic and legislative gains. The revolutionary syndicalists were more consistent in this respect, but by the same token they had no hope of influencing conditions in France. In any case, once the principle of attempting to 'reform capitalism' had been accepted it was impossible to draw an exact dividing line between tactical co-operation with other parties and an 'opportunist' policy of grafting socialism on to the existing order.

Jaurès was far from holding that the political independence of the proletariat was of no consequence. Arguing in general support of Kautsky against Bernstein, he accused the latter of submerging the proletariat among the other classes on the ground that both the working class and the bourgeoisie were far from being homogeneous. This was fallacious, Jaurès claimed, as there was a clear distinction between the haves and the have-nots. These two basic classes were radically opposed, but socialists need not be afraid of temporary alliances provided they kept in mind that their ultimate objective was not to improve the present system but to transform it. Socialism was unthinkable except as an achievement of the working class, and the hopes of such men as Fourier, Louis Blanc, and Owen could only be idle dreams. But—and this perhaps is the kernel of the dispute between Jaurès and the 'exclusivists'—the working class was building elements of socialism within the capitalist system. Jaurès seems to have had no doubt that the final transformation of society could only come about by revolution, but he did not understand this as entailing an act of violence or civil war. By 'revolution' he meant simply the radical transformation of the property-owning system in a socialist sense. The proposition that socialism can only come about by revolution thus becomes a tautology; Jaurès failed to notice this, and dismissed the question as to what form the revolution would take as a barren speculation relating to the unforeseeable future. But on this argument the revolution might take the form of a gradual evolutionary change from capitalism to socialism, although Jaurès seems to have denied this possibility. In his view socialism was taking shape within capitalism in many ways, thanks in particular to the workers' growing historical sense and power of self-organization, but also to democratic reforms in the working-class interest: universal education, labour laws, improved living standards, the secularization of public life, and the effect of unions and co-operatives in curbing exploitation. The 'ultimate goal' of socialism was distinct from these reforms, but the latter were more than a mere process of training for the decisive battle: they constituted the objective foundations of a socialist society, and it was not clear therefore why they should not in course of time lead, in a continuous and gradual progress, to the achievement of the goal.

6. Jaurès's Marxism

JAURÈS did not consider himself a revisionist, although he often emphasized his debt to French socialist sources independent of Marxism. He defended against Bernstein the idea of the political independence of the proletariat, and he upheld the Marxian dialectic as a theory of natural evolution whereby one social formation engenders another as the result of its internal contradictions. A belief in this natural movement of history was necessary to an oppressed class, giving it faith in the success of its efforts. Jaurès accepted the Marxian theory of exploitation as the appropriation of the unremunerated part of the working man's labour, and the Marxian theory of value as a piece of 'social metaphysics' though not as a theory of prices. The idea that socialism is the cause of all humanity and not of the working class alone, but that it is the latter's mission to bring socialism about, is of course one of the traditional pillars of Marxist doctrine. It is also consistent with this idea to hold—though perhaps no one did so as emphatically as Jaurès—that the value of socialism resides ultimately in its effect on the spiritual development of every human individual.

What essentially divides Jaurès from Marxism is his belief in continuous and universal progress. Apart from the pantheist metaphysic which treats historical progress as part of a universal soteriology of Being, the progress in which Jaurès puts his trust applies to all periods of history and every aspect of civilization. The future salvation and absolute unity of the world are not, as he foresees them, the result of a violent historical break but of a gradual improvement in every sphere, especially that of political and legal institutions. Marx, it is true, did not limit progress to technological change, but expected that the victorious proletariat would take over from bourgeois society its scientific and, in part at least, its artistic achievements. He also believed that past history was a preparation for socialism, especially in the technique and organization of labour. But he did not believe in a gradual and irreversible build-up of socialism through the ages, with social and legal ideas and institutions steadily approximating to the perfection that would supervene after a final upheaval. This, however, is precisely what Jaurès seems to have believed in, justifying in this way his policy of contracting alliances on all hands, his appeals to all social classes, and his role of a universal conciliator. Jaurès did not accept the Marxian vision of progress using evil as a necessary instrument, and the Hegelian tragedy of history was quite alien to him. His philosophy of history, as we have seen, combined in a coherent whole the notion of socialism as the salvation of the world with that of socialism as the result of an immanent historical trend, whereas in

Marx's theory these two were contingent with regard to each other. But Jaurès's consistency is achieved at the cost of a prophetic optimism which enables him to believe that the future world of universal unity will absorb the whole of past history, and that it will one day be seen that no human labour has been in vain, no effort of the spirit has spent itself against the indifference of nature. His socialism and his metaphysic of salvation sprang from his love of the world and of his fellow men. If this last statement is an appraisal it relates to Jaurès as a human being, but not to the analytical coolness of his mind.

VI

Paul Lafargue: a Hedonist Marxism

LAFARGUE is certainly one of the principal *scriptores minores* of the Marxist canon. By the orthodox of the present day he is treated with the respect due to a minor authority. As the co-founder, with Guesde, of the French socialist party, as a polemicist against anarchists, Christians, and Jaurès, as a propagandist of Marxism and finally as Marx's friend and son-in-law, he fully merits a place in the second rank of the Marxist pantheon. True, his Marxism was highly simplified and it is hard to find anything in his writings that could be called a 'development' of the doctrine. But of all French Marxist writers he was closest to German orthodoxy, and in his day this was the touchstone of doctrinal purity.

Paul Lafargue (1842–1911) was a planter's son from Cuba: his father was partly negro, and he had Indian blood on his mother's side. When he was a boy the family came to France, where he was educated. He studied medicine at Paris, but was expelled from the University for socialist activities, after which he went to London and took his degree in 1868; in the same year he married Marx's daughter Laura. Returning to France at the end of 1868, he took up journalism and practised as a doctor. He was a member of the Commune and, after its defeat, fled to Spain, where he was active in the small socialist party led by Pablo Iglesias. At the end of 1872 he returned to London, where he stayed for ten years. He made his living as a photographer, wrote articles and pamphlets and helped Marx and Guesde to draw up the French party programme. After the amnesty for the Communards he returned to France in the spring of 1882, worked as a civil servant, and was an active propagandist of Marxism: he wrote extensively, gave lectures in the provinces, and assisted Guesde as party leader. In 1891 he was elected to the Chamber. He and Laura committed suicide, not from despair but in order to escape the onset of senile decay.

As a writer and theorist Lafargue was a gifted and versatile dilettante, one of many examples in the history of Marxism. His articles and pamphlets popularized a certain style which, like that of Plekhanov, contributed to diluting the intellectual values of Marxism. He wrote on almost every branch of social science: philosophy, history, ethnology, linguistics, religion, economics, and literary criticism. He was not an expert on any of these subjects, but knew something about all of them at second hand. Like most Marxists he believed that as Marx had provided a universal key it could be used by anyone to unlock the secrets of all sciences, however little particular knowledge he might possess. He also believed that he was contributing to the triumph of Marxism by discovering elements in non-Marxist works that seemed to confirm the truth of historical materialism by relating political and literary phenomena or social customs to this or that mode of economic production. He did not realize that it is easy to point to such relationships in large number but that they do not prove Marx's general theory, any more than a theory of genetics can be established by accumulating instances of the likeness between parents and their children.

In short, it cannot be said that Lafargue enlarged or improved upon Marxist doctrine in any way. None the less he is of some importance in the history of Marxism, both because he did more than anyone else to make it known in France and because his writings, simplified as they are, brought into prominence an aspect of Marxism that is less evident in writers of a more serious stamp. He was one of the first to criticize literature in a Marxist spirit, and his amusingly malicious pamphlet on Victor Hugo is still quite readable.

There is as yet no complete edition of Lafargue's writings. His most important works are Le Déterminisme économique: la méthode historique de Karl Marx (1907), a popular pamphlet Le Droit à la paresse (1883; translated as The Right to be Lazy, 1907), Le Programme du parti ouvrier (written jointly with Guesde, 1883), and a discussion with Jaurès on historical materialism (1895).

Lafargue's philosophical works do not go beyond popular sensationalism and the materialism of the Enlightenment. He lays great stress on the derivation of all abstract ideas from sensual perception, using the arguments of Locke, Diderot, and Condillac. He maintained that the Platonist idea that abstracts can be intuited independently of perception was not only false but socially reactionary, as it regarded man as something more than a physical being and thus opened the way to religious mystification. This was why the bourgeoisie, having fought Christianity under the banner of materialism and sensationalism, had dropped its old iconoclasm as soon as it achieved power, turning to an alliance with the Church and reinstating the Platonic-Christian belief in supersensual cognition. Such had been the evolution of Maine de Biran and Cabanis; while the whole Romantic movement, from Chateaubriand onwards, was nothing but an attempt to reconcile the bourgeoisie with Catholicism. The bourgeoisie needed the fiction of eternal truths and supersensual knowledge in order to consecrate and perpetuate the social order that served its ends. Meanwhile the materialism of the Enlightenment was taken over by the proletariat, as a weapon against the ascetic morality preached by the Church in order to maintain class divisions and exploitation. Lafargue's materialism is expressed in crude formulas similar to those of de La Mettrie, Cabanis, or Moleschott, i.e. to what Marxist tradition stigmatizes as 'vulgar materialism'.

He says, for instance, that 'the brain is an organ for thinking as the stomach is for digesting' (*Recherches sur l'origine et l'évolution des idées de justice, du bien . . .*), or that 'the brain transforms impressions into ideas as a dynamo transforms motion into electricity' (discussion with Jaurès). The epistemological problem of the independent function of abstraction is not touched on in his writings. The only valid objection, in his opinion, to the views of the eighteenth-century sensationalists is that the brain, thanks to the inheritance of acquired experience, has a 'disposition' to assimilate abstract ideas and is therefore not a mere *tabula rasa*. An argument he frequently advances in favour of sensationalism is that etymology shows that terms denoting abstract ideas such as justice, goodness, and the other virtues, as well as the idea of number and all other universals, are all derived from the names of empirical objects or qualities apprehended by the senses.

In his philosophical argumentation Lafargue is closer to Feuerbach than to Marx—a late Feuerbach, freed from any 'encumbrance' of Hegelianism. Idealistic philosophy and the history of religion are nothing to him but a system of delusions and an instrument of class division. Unlike Marx, he sees no cognitive value in the history of idealism; as for the age-long controversy between sense and spirit, beginning with the opposition between Zeno the Stoic and Plato, it is simply the history of truth versus error. Religion is the projection of human passions, *mores*, and social conditions into a world of supernatural beings. The idea that a soul inhabits the body arises from primitive attempts to explain the nature of dreams: the existence of dream-figures led men to imagine supernatural beings and deities and to conjecture that the soul was immortal. The belief in an incorporeal soul was characteristic of matriarchal society and disappeared as the patriarchal system prevailed, but revived as the latter declined, thus preparing the way for Christianity. Elsewhere, in his commentary on the party programme, Larfargue explains religion as being due to fear of the unbridled forces of nature: it is the reaction of primitive man, still half an animal, to his own helplessness in the face of elemental powers. As men succeed in extending their power over nature, so religion declines; it will disappear completely when the socialist revolution enables man fully to control the conditions of his own existence.

In his treatment of 'economic determinism' Lafargue again simplifies Marxism out of all recognition. He understands by historical materialism, firstly, that there is in social development no pre-existing purpose or intention: everything, including human behaviour, is the effect of natural, ineluctable causality. Free will is a delusion: men's acts are wholly determined by their natural circumstances or those they have created for themselves. In the man-made environment changes occur most frequently in the mode of production (which Lafargue appears to identify with productive forces, or rather the whole productive apparatus). These changes inevitably bring about corresponding changes in social institutions and ideologies; if the latter are not completely identical in different societies at the same level of technology, it is because of differences in the natural environment. In general, however, Lafargue agrees with Vico, who observed that all human societies go through the same phases of development. Matriarchate, patriarchate, slave-owning, feudalism, capitalism—all human communities pass through these stages on the way to communism, and the last is as necessary as its predecessors.

The starting-point of social development is primitive communist equality, in which the ideas of justice and property are unknown, as are moral restrictions of all kinds. Along with other stereotypes of the Enlightenment Lafargue to some extent revived the myth of the noble and contented savage, which was unusual among Marxists of his day, though traces of it can be found in Engels. In almost all respects, he maintained—in physical development, happiness, and purity of soul—primitive men were on a far higher level than those of today. 'It has been proved that men and women in communities felt neither jealousy nor parental affection: they lived polygamously, the woman having as many husbands as she pleased and the man as many wives as he could; travellers tell us that all these people lived in a state of greater contentment and fellowship than do the members of sad, selfish monogamous families.' So Lafargue declares in the discussion with Jaurès, while in *The Right to be Lazy* he writes: 'Consider the noble savage whom the missionaries of trade and the traders in religion have not yet depraved by Christianity, syphilis and the dogma of labour, and then look at our wretched servants of the machine . . . The physical beauty and the noble bearing of members of primitive tribes, as yet uncorrupted by what Pöppig calls the "poisonous breath of civilization", arouses the admiration and amazement of European observers.' Similarly, Le Play remarks that 'The tendency of the Bashkir people to indolence, the habit of reflection and the inactivity of nomadic life . . . have endowed them with a subtlety of mind and judgement and a distinction of manner such as is seldom met with on the same social level in more developed civilizations.'

Lafargue, like most of his predecessors, held up the idyllic picture of primitive man in order to criticize industrial civilization rather than actually to start a 'back to nature' movement. Nevertheless, not a few of the Arcadian clichés are present in his depiction of the future Communist paradise. The perfect society is not to be an embodiment of the idea of justice, but one in which that idea has no meaning, since it is bound up with private property and the regulation of property relationships. In primitive communism social life was subject to the instinct of revenge, which is rooted in biology. This lawless instinct was then transformed into a socially regulated system of retribution; but, as this was insufficient to settle all private accounts, the institution of private property was created so that individual claims and rights could be satisfied without recourse to blows. This is how the idea of justice first arose. Its original purpose was to sanction existing social equality, but under the system of private property it began to sanctify privilege and thus became anti-human.

As will be seen, Lafargue in effect reproduces Hobbes's theory of the social contract in the belief that he is offering a Marxist view of the rise of civilization; but, unlike Hobbes, he believes that the socialization of property to which capitalism is leading will restore mankind to a blessed state of innocence free from laws, claims, and obligations. This is perhaps especially clear in his controversy with Jaurès. The latter argued that in the interpretation of history materialism and idealism can and must be reconciled: for, on the one hand, human ideals can only be realized by economic changes, while, on the other, men need ideals in order to recognize historical necessity as beneficial. Rational ideas are known to us only as embodied in the world; equally, whatever happens in the world is the embodiment of a rational idea. The life of the mind reflects economic phenomena, but at the same time economic change is in part due to moral forces present in the mind: the desire for unity, beauty, and justice act as *idées-forces* throughout the course of history. In short, we must acknowledge both the theory that evolution is causally determined and the idea that gives it meaning and sees in it the embodiment of values. Whether as a means of understanding historical change or as a theory describing it, idealism is not a rival to Marxian materialism but a complement to it.

Lafargue's reply brings out clearly the irreconcilable conflict between two fundamentally different ways of thinking (or even mentalities), the naturalistic and the moralistic. There is, he declares, no inherent purpose in historical evolution and no aspiration towards ideals as an efficient cause, for evolution is not a specifically human phenomenon. The human species came into existence not by any conscious intention but because men developed hands. All abstract ideas, and in particular moral values and the idea of justice, derive from sensual perceptions interpreted in accordance with dominant economic conditions. 'The ideas of justice, based on the notions of "mine" and "thine", that cloud the minds of civilized human beings will vanish like a dream when private property gives way to common property.' (*Recherches sur l'origine . . .*) The true, living ideal is not justice but peace and happiness, in a society in which everything belongs to all men. This is a modern version of the paradisal conditions of primitive communism, but only now will these aspirations become a reflection and counterpart of the actual course of economic change.

Lafargue's picture of the new order is most clearly drawn in *The Right to be Lazy*. Men will be happy under communism because they will not have to work. In the past they have been taken in by bourgeois and clerical propaganda telling them that work is meritorious in itself; but in fact work is a curse, and so is the love of work. 'All individual and collective woes are due to man's passion for work . . . For the proletariat to realize its own strength it must shake off the prejudices of Christian, economic and free-thinking morality. It must rediscover its natural instincts and proclaim that the right to idleness is a thousand times more sacred and noble than the rights of man devised by the metaphysical lawyers of the bourgeois revolution. It must firmly refuse to work more than three hours a day, and spend the rest of the twenty-four in repose and revelry.' Modern technology makes it possible to reduce labour to a minimum while satisfying all human needs; under communism there will be no need for international trade, as 'Europeans will consume their goods at home instead of exporting them to the ends of the earth, and therefore sailors, dockers and transport workers will be able to lead a life of leisure . . . The working class, like the bourgeoisie before it, will have to curb its taste for asceticism and develop its aptitude for consumption. Instead of the workers getting, at best, a small bit of tough meat every day, they will eat large juicy steaks. Instead of inferior wine mixed with water they will drink bumpers of fine claret and burgundy; water will be the drink of animals.'

In this way Lafargue, unlike Marx, envisages communism from the angle of consumption only. Marx, it is true, regarded the progressive shortening of the working day as a basic feature of the coming society, but he was thinking of men having to do less necessary work and enjoying more time for free creative activity. Communism in his eyes was not primarily an opportunity for carefree consumption but for self-fulfilment in action. For Lafargue it was more like the Abbaye de Thélème, as he suggests in his introduction to the French party programme: 'Rabelais was a far-sighted man. He foresaw the communist society of the future, in which we shall produce more than we need and all will be able to consume as much as they like.' Communism was a matter of liberating man's natural instincts from the inhibitions of a civilization based on private property. It was a true return to nature, to a life of natural inclination free from the trammels of morality.

We may see from this how naïve and trivial was Lafargue's interpretation of historical materialism, the Marxian theory of knowledge, and socialism itself. His writings, however, present one possible version of the simplified naturalism which quite commonly passed for Marxism in his day. Assuming that man's being is determined by inclinations due to his biological makeup, and that human history had tended to distort these rather than gratify them, it was reasonable enough to believe that social liberation would take the form of a liberation of natural instincts: this was likewise the principle of Fourier's socialism. The unique and specific character of human existence which played so large a part in Marx's theory was ignored in schemes like these: it was indeed hard to maintain on the basis that man was a product of evolutionary laws governing the whole of nature. This assumption, however, was not peculiar to Lafargue but was current coin among post-Darwinian Marxists. In his naïve optimism and his consumption-oriented doctrine of communism, Lafargue expressed in simplified terms a possible variant of naturalist philosophy. His ideas were a popularized blend of eighteenth-century sensationalism and the myth of the noble savage, of post-Darwinian evolutionism and Marxism—the latter serving rather to buttress eighteenth-century ideals than to correct them. It is in this that the originality of his Marxism consists, if indeed he is to be regarded as a Marxist at all.

VII

Georges Sorel: a Jansenist Marxism

1. The place of Sorel

How far do Sorel's writings belong to the history of Marxism? He was not a member of any political movement that claimed spiritual descent from Marx, and, although he took part in all the great polemics of his day, he did so from the outside as it were, so that the guardians of orthodox Marxism were not much concerned to refute his views. He kept aloof from political and party quarrels, and wrote no treatises on historical materialism. He did not consider himself an orthodox Marxist, and criticized both the master and his disciples as he thought fit to do so. He remains vaguely associated with Italian Fascism, as Mussolini and other ideologists for a time acknowledged him as a prophet of the movement. From the viewpoint of Marxism he may be considered an accidental oddity: at the outset of his literary career he had nothing in common with it, and his name hardly figures in the later development of the doctrine.

At the time of his main writings, however, Sorel not only considered himself a Marxist but believed that he could extract the core of Marx's philosophy—the class war and the independence of the proletariat—and oppose Marx himself to the whole body of contemporary orthodoxy, whether reformist or revolutionary. His unfulfilled ambition was to be the Luther of the Marxist movement, which he saw as corrupted by the struggle for power and privilege, as Rome had appeared to the German reformer in the guise of the Whore of Babylon. He dreamt of a Marxism that would be morally and doctrinally pure; his own version, though it drew on a great variety of sources, was not a patchwork but an extremely coherent whole. He undoubtedly influenced the first ideologists of Italian Communism, such as Antonio Gramsci, and also Angelo Tosca and Palmiro Togliatti.

However, Sorel differed from his Marxist contemporaries not merely by interpreting Marx in his own way, nor even by sometimes criticizing him, since this happened even to such fanatics of orthodoxy as Rosa Luxemburg. The main point of difference was that all the orthodox regarded Marxism as scientifically true in the same sense as, for instance, evolution or the quantum theory, whereas for Sorel it was true in a pragmatic sense, as the ideological expression of a movement to liberate and rejuvenate the human race. That it was true meant that it was the one irreplaceable instrument that history had put into the hands of the proletariat, though there was no guarantee that the proletariat would make successful use of it. Marxism was the truth of its own age in the same sense as early Christianity had been—the hope of a fresh dawn for mankind, not a 'scientific' account of history, a means of accurate prognosis, or a reliable source of information about the universe. At the present stage of history it was the instrument best calculated to put into effect the supreme values of humanity; but these values, in their substance and origin, owed nothing to Marxism. Hence Sorel was free to change his mind about Marxism without changing his mind about values. He could be a Marxist or a nationalist and still remain faithful to the ideal in respect of which Marxism was only an instrument forged by history at a particular moment. From this point of view, even when most fervently devoted to Marxian philosophy he was not a Marxist in the same sense as Kautsky or Labriola—not because he construed the doctrine differently, but because he took a different view of its historical significance and was not afraid to interpret Marx in the light of quite other authorities such as Proudhon or Tocqueville, Bergson or Nietzsche. He was one of the few who tried to adapt Marxism to the philosophical style of the neo-romantic era, i.e. to interpret it in a pragmatic and activist sense, with emphasis on psychological factors and respect for the independent role of tradition, in a spirit radically opposed to positivism and rationalism.

Sorel's thoughts on social problems are dominated by the idea of greatness, dignity, heroism, and authenticity, and he treats the revolution, the proletariat, and the class war as historical instances of these supreme values. Radicalism and intransigence are in his eyes valuable for their own sakes, irrespective of object. He seems to approve everything in history that proceeds from strong authentic impulses, disinterested fervour, lofty aspirations, and generous hopes. He respects the ardour of religious faith but despises religion when it appears in the form of scholasticism or politics or is tainted by calculation or a spirit of rationalism and appeasement. He is an enthusiast for the workers' movement as a revolt in the name of a great revivifying myth, but he scorns parliamentary manoeuvres and the feebleness of half-hearted reformism. He rejects the tradition of anti-clericalism as a bridge between socialists and petty-bourgeoisie radicals, but also as a hangover of eighteenth-century rationalism with its optimistic faith in steady, inevitable progress. He opposes nationalism as a device for depriving the proletariat of its absolute separateness; but when estranged from the syndicalists, he turns towards nationalist radicalism with the same hope that made him a Marxist, namely that of recreating the world in its pristine image. In all struggles he is more interested in the heroism of the contendants than in who wins or who is in the right. The conquering spirit of the proletariat excites him more than the vision of socialism. When he joins the proletarian movement it is not for the sake of improving the lot of the oppressed, but because the surge of historic events promises a rebirth of greatness. He stands for the complete spiritual separation of the proletariat from the bourgeoisie and all its works.

Different as Sorel's intellectual sources are, they form a coherent pattern in his work. His Jansenist upbringing no doubt gave him a dislike of any optimistic faith in the natural goodness of mankind, an easy triumph of good over evil, or the attainment of great ends at small cost. From the same source came his contempt for Jesuitical tactics of conciliation, his general intransigence, the all-or-nothing rejection of compromise, and the belief in a sharp distinction between the elect and the rest of the world. In opposition to the doctrine of automatic progress he was attached to the tradition of radical Christianity, i.e. the Christianity of the martyrs.

His technical education and work as an engineer instilled into him a cult of expertise and efficiency, a dislike of dilettantism and empty rhetoric, a conviction that it was production and not exchange that mattered, and an admiration for capitalism in its early, ruthless, expansionist forms, before it was contaminated by philanthropy and the spirit of compromise.

From Marx he learnt to believe that the revolution that would restore society was to be carried out by the proletariat—a clearly differentiated class of direct producers, obliged to sell their labour-power and embodying the hope of a total revolution that would liberate mankind. The basic tenets of Sorel's Marxism are class war, contempt for utopianism, a literal belief in the abolition of the state, and the expectation of a total revolution carried out by the proletariat alone, in isolation from the rest of society.

Giambattista Vico contributed the notion of *ricorso*, the cyclical return of mankind to its own forgotten sources. The proletarian revolution was to be a 'reversion' of this kind, a rediscovery of the primal values rooted in tribal morality.

Another influence was Proudhon, from whom Sorel learnt to regard socialism as primarily a moral question, that of breeding a new type of man (the producer ethic), and to consider the proletariat as a kind of race apart, called on to divide the world between itself and all the rest. The importance Sorel attaches to family and sexual morality in social life is due to Proudhon, as is the habit of characterizing socialism in terms of justice and dignity rather than welfare.

Bergson was the chief philosophical exponent of the style of thought that dominates the work of Sorel: the opposition between 'global' intuitive perception and analytical thought, which in Sorel takes the particular form of opposing 'myth' to 'Utopia'. Bergson also provided Sorel with the conceptual means of contrasting scientific determinism, combined with a belief in the predictability of social processes, with the idea of unforeseeable spontaneity. In addition Sorel derived from Bergson a conviction of the inexpressibility of the concrete, which enabled him to protect his idea of the 'myth' against rational argument.

The influence of Nietzsche is clearly felt in Sorel's cult of greatness, his hatred of mediocrity, and of party huckstering in political life.

The great exponents of liberal conservatism—Tocqueville, Taine, Renan—exercised a strong influence on Sorel in his early period, and to some extent in his Marxist phase as well. From them he learnt to approach politics soberly, to perceive the corruption of democratic institutions and the interests that underlay humanistic rhetoric. From these authors too he imbibed an understanding of early Christianity, the Revolution, and the *ancien régime*.

From these various sources of inspiration Sorel created an ideological whole which shattered traditional agglomerations of values and combined ideas in a different way from any of his predecessors. It was as a Marxist that he stood up for values traditionally associated with the Right: the dignity of marriage and of the family, tribal solidarity, honour and tradition, customary law and the sanctity of religious experience. As a writer he paid little attention to coherence and structure and was more of an apostle than a controversialist. His thoughts appeared to develop without a plan, gropingly as it were, but always in accordance with certain ruling tendencies and values. His works make laborious reading, not because they are obscure but because they lack literary unity. Sometimes he begins by stating a problem and then plunges into digressions, long quotations, aggressive polemics, and violent challenges, in the course of which he seems to forget the point at issue. As a writer he stood far above the orthodox Marxists, but he had insufficient command over his talent. His polemical ardour and lack of logical discipline make it especially hard to summarize his thought, but some recurrent themes can be clearly identified. Brzozowski, himself a writer of a similar kind, thought this spontaneity and lack of preconceived system a great merit in Sorel. The latter's style is reminiscent of Bergson's 'creative evolution', developing in obedience to a governing tendency but without a predetermined goal.

The easiest way to present, or re-present, Sorel's thought in a systematic fashion is to list in parallel columns the ideas and values which he opposed or criticized and those which he advocated. This produces a result on the following lines:

utopianism	Marxist historical realism
epistemological rationalism	Bergsonian intuition and thinking in terms of 'wholes'
sociological rationalism	respect for tradition
determinism	spontaneity
happiness	dignity and greatness

political socialism	syndicalism
dilettantism	professionalism
cult of the French Revolution	cult of early Christianity
reform	revolution
belief in progress	voluntarism, individual responsibility
inter-class alliances	separateness of the proletariat
politics and power	production and the organization of production
optimism	pessimism
intellectuals and politicians	the proletariat
political parties	working-class syndicates
political revolution	general strike
Utopia	myth
democracy	freedom
consumer morality	producer morality
scholastic religion	the religion of mystics and martyrs
decadence	*ricorso*, a return to the sources
social sciences	the activist myth
the state	an association of producers

This set of antitheses may seem strange to anyone acquainted with the stereotypes and conceptual associations of classical Marxism, but Sorel's positive values, taken together, define his polemical attitude with great clarity. He was opposed to contemporary socialist politicians, the leaders of the International, who in his eyes were a mere band of self-seekers out to enjoy the flesh-pots of office once they had wrested them from the bourgeoisie. Jaurès, in particular, he pilloried in almost all his writings as a symbol of petty-bourgeois socialism seeking to win over the bourgeoisie in order to appease the proletariat, to destroy the idea of the class struggle, and to introduce a new system of privilege on the basis of a spurious unity.

2. Biographical outline

GEORGES SOREL was born of bourgeois parents at Cherbourg in 1847. He studied at the École polytechnique and became an engineer in the Département des ponts et chaussées, where he worked until 1892. His first writings were published shortly before he retired: *Le Procès de Socrate* (1889), *Contribution à l'étude profane de la Bible* (1889), *La Ruine du monde antique* (1888). In about 1893 he became interested in Marx and afterwards in an anti-political syndicalist movement based in part on Proudhonist and anarchist traditions, its chief organizer being Fernand Pelloutier. In 1898 Sorel published *L'Avenir socialiste des syndicats*, later reissued as part of *Matériaux d'une théorie du prolétariat* (third edition 1919): this was the first attempt at a theoretical analysis of the experience of the syndicalist movement developing independently of the socialist parties and even in opposition to them. In the 1890s Sorel wrote for *L'Ère nouvelle* and *Devenir social*, where in 1895–6 he published studies of Durkheim and Vico. Active in the defence of Dreyfus, he was disillusioned to find that the socialist *Dreyfusards* exploited the *Affaire* for purely party ends. Bernstein's work to some extent led him to criticize orthodox Marxism, but his own objections soon developed along quite different lines. (Although basically opposed to reformism he continued to admire and respect Bernstein, and agreed whole-heartedly with his contention that the policy of the German socialists had nothing to do with their revolutionary programme.) As time went on he became increasingly severe in his criticism of the socialist party, parliamentary democracy, and what he called 'political socialism' as opposed to syndicalism. His chief Marxist writings are: *Réflexions sur la violence* (*Reflections on Violence*, 1908 and later, enlarged editions), *Les Illusions du progrès* (1908), *Matériaux d'une théorie du prolétariat* (1908: essays dating from 1898 onwards), and *La Décomposition du marxisme* (1908). The first two of these originally appeared in serial form in *Le Mouvement socialiste*, edited by Hubert Lagardelle. The fourth edition of *Réflexions sur la violence* (1919) contains an appendix with an enthusiastic defence of Lenin and the Bolshevik revolution. (Lenin himself took no interest in Sorel, whom he mentions only once and in a disparaging tone.)

In the course of time Sorel lost faith in French syndicalism, but he hoped for a while that a similar movement might win the day in Italy. He had close contacts with that country, having contributed to Italian socialist periodicals from 1898 onwards: he wrote articles on Vico and Lombroso, and his own books, translated into Italian, were praised by Croce and Pareto and attacked by Labriola. In 1910, however, deciding that syndicalism was irretrievably corrupted by reformist trends, he switched to support of radical nationalist movements in France and Italy and for a time co-operated with the Action Française; he also influenced the national-syndicalist groups in Italy which helped to provide the basis of Fascism. He welcomed the first beginnings of the latter movement in 1912 and reiterated his sympathy in 1919, seeing in Fascism the promise of a social rebirth inspired by nationalist mythology. For the same reason he hailed the Bolshevik revolution as a retreat from Westernism to the true spirit of Muscovy. The Fascists, after they came to power, paid lip-service to Sorel as their spiritual patron, but the real trend of their movement was to assert the brutal authority of dictatorial government, which Sorel abominated. On the other hand the first Italian Communist periodical, *Ordine Nuovo*, edited by Gramsci at Turin from 1919 onwards, regarded Sorel as an ideologist of the proletariat.

Sorel died in 1922 at Boulogne-sur-Seine, where he had lived for some years. Since the end of the 1920s his ideas have had no effective influence on any branch of the socialist movement or on the Communist International.

3. Rationalism versus history. Utopia and myth. Criticism of the Enlightenment

THE 'rationalism' to which Sorel was opposed was not a particular philosophical statement but an intellectual attitude which drew its strength from Cartesianism, flourished in the eighteenth-century *salons*, and, in his opinion, had a pernicious effect on the contemporary interpretation of Marxism. Rationalism, thus understood, consists of creating simplified, abstract patterns of thought and making them do duty for the real, complex world. Examples of such patterns are theories of human nature which regard man as an assemblage of permanent, general characteristics and types of behaviour, regardless of the historical circumstances which in practice affect human actions. By reducing society to the speculative universal of 'man', rationalists are able to conjecture at will as to the nature of the perfect community and to construct utopian models of the future, free from conflict, contingency, and rival aspirations. Engels was not exempt from this way of thinking, for he too 'reduces the world to a single human being'. Rationalists also believe that all actions are governed by rational motives, and they thus blind themselves to the real-life complexity of psychological differences, the importance of tradition and custom, and the role played in social development by biological (particularly sexual) and many other factors. They regard the French Revolution, for instance, as the triumph of an idea over historical reality, oblivious of the many actual forces, especially those rooted in the plebeian levels of society, which combined to overthrow the old regime. Rationalism is a simplified, schematic mode of thought based on a legalistic form of reasoning which reduces human beings to the status of juridical units. The history of communist Utopias is full of rationalist preconceptions, and that is why they have never seriously competed with existing forms of government. As Pascal pointed out, rationalism is not, as the Cartesians would have us believe, a synonym of scientific thinking. Cartesianism was successful and popular because it turned science into a drawing-room topic. Like the Scholastics, Descartes set up between man and reality ingeniously devised intellectual machines which prevented man from using his mind to any purpose. He provided the uninstructed laity with a simple formula for discoursing on scientific subjects in the belief that the 'natural light' enables everyone, however amateur, to pass judgement on everything. The Enlightenment writers adopted the same style: for Condorcet as for Fontenelle the object was not to instruct men how to be farmers or manufacturers, but merely *salon* philosophers. The dominant ideology of the eighteenth century was that of men in the service of the monarchy, with the philosopher playing the role of court jester: '*causeurs*, satyrists, panegyrists, clowns in the pay of a degenerate aristocracy'—to quote Sorel's summing-up. To justify the moral depravity of the *salons* Diderot taught that the only instincts in nature were those of self-preservation and generation, and in Sorel's day Darwinism was interpreted in the same sense. The *Encyclopédie* contributed nothing to the development of science, but was a mere farrago of dilettantism for the purposes of polite conversation. The communist fantasies of Enlightenment authors were no threat to anyone. It was dangerous to criticize inhuman conditions in the mines, but the monarchy and its hangers-on had no objection to abstract praise of communism, republican virtues, and the natural law, or to those who disparaged tradition in the name of some paradisal Utopia.

Utopian literature from Plato onwards was, Sorel argued, a typical and sterile product of rationalist delusion. 'Since the Renaissance, Utopias have become a literary genre which, by simplifying economic, political and psychological questions to the extreme, has had a deplorable effect on the intellectual formation of revolutionaries' (*Matériaux* . . . third edn., p. 26). Utopias are sterile because they postulate an abstract human individual uninfluenced by history, religion, inherited custom, or any national, biological, or psychological traits, and they create an imaginary state made up of such beings; they are also harmful, since their authors appeal to the prudence, enlightenment, or philanthropy of the privileged classes and weaken the proletariat's understanding of the class struggle. Marxism is closer to the Manchester school of bourgeois economics than to the utopian writers, for it is a realistic look at society torn by the class struggle, which can neither be avoided nor mitigated. Marx's occasional lapses into utopian naïvety, as in the *Critique of the Gotha Programme*, are contrary to the true spirit of Marxism, which does not appeal to a universal sense of justice or attempt to compress society into a logical schema, but takes account of the forces that have actually affected history in all their complexity. Thanks to Marxism, socialism has parted company with utopian ideas. It no longer seeks to be a 'scientific' blueprint for a future society, or to compete with the bourgeoisie in theorizing on the organization of production: its purpose is to provide the ideology of a radical class war.

Instead of constructing abstract plans for a perfect society, our task is to discover how social institutions have come into being spontaneously in the course of history, and to interpret them in the light of all the psychological and economic circumstances. This was done by Savigny when, in opposition to the rationalist doctrine of a social contract, he expounded the notion of law arising in the form of local custom, gradually accumulating and adapting itself to new conditions in the course of history. The utopians were ready with draft constitutions for the whole of mankind because they took little heed of actual history; Marxism offered an analysis of history as it really was, not as it appeared in a rationalist schema.

In *Reflections on Violence* Sorel devotes special attention to those aspects of social life that offer most resistance to rationalization and form, as it were, a core of mystery, yet have more effect on social development than all the rest. In the field of morality the clear, rational element comprises relationships of reciprocity analogous to commercial exchanges, while sexual life, by contrast, remains opaque and difficult to reduce to simple formulas. In legislation the most easily rationalized measures are those relating to debts and contracts; the most refractory are those concerning the family, which affects the whole of social life. In economics, trade is a lucid area but production, which is the final determinant, is obscurely embedded in local and historical traditions. The rationalists come to grief whenever they try to reduce to simple legal formulas aspects of life which belong to the 'dark areas' of experience and whose qualitative differences are the result of historical contingency. True history is more like a work of art than a pellucid logical construction.

The contrast between the rationalistic and the historical mentality is very similar to that between optimism and pessimism, in the special sense in which Sorel uses these terms. Among the optimists he includes Socrates, the Jesuits, the *philosophes*, the ideologists of the French Revolution, the utopians, believers in progress, socialist politicians, and Jaurès; among pessimists the early Christians, Protestants, Jansenists, and Marxists. Optimists believe that the evil in the world is due to inadequate legislation, a lack of enlightenment and of human feeling. They are convinced that legal reform will soon bring about the earthly paradise, but in practice their delusions and ignorance of social reality lead them to adopt policies of terror like those of the Revolution. Pessimists, on the other hand, do not believe in any all-embracing theory or infallible method of introducing order into the universe: they are conscious that human projects operate within narrow limits set by the weight of tradition, human weakness, and the imperfection of our knowledge. Aware of the interrelation of all aspects of life, they regard social conditions as forming an indivisible whole that cannot be reformed piecemeal, but must either be left alone or destroyed in a catastrophic explosion. In ancient Greece pessimism was the philosophy of warlike mountain tribes—poor, proud, uncompromising, and wedded to tradition—while optimism was that of prosperous city traders. The early Christians were pessimists; believing that no human effort could reform the world, they withdrew into themselves and impassively awaited the Second Coming. Protestantism began as an attempt to revive Christian pessimism, but later it fell under the spell of Renaissance humanism and adopted the latter's values. The pessimism of true Marxism lies in the fact that it does not believe in any automatic law of progress, in the possibility of gradual reform, or in the attainability of general happiness by a simple process of imposing on society some arbitrary construction of the mind. Marxism is an apocalyptic challenge to the proletarian consciousness, not in the name of some utopian programme but in that of an apocalyptic 'myth'.

A myth, in Sorel's sense, is not a kind of Utopia but the very opposite: not the description of a perfect future society, but the call to a decisive battle. Its value is not cognitive in the ordinary sense; it is not a scientific prediction, but a force inspiring and organizing the militant consciousness of a self-contained group. The myth of the proletariat is the general strike. Only by means of a myth can a fighting group maintain its solidarity, heroism, and the spirit of self-sacrifice. It is a state of mind that expects and prepares for the violent destruction of the existing order at a single blow, but has no ready-made paradise to set up against it. Unlike utopias, a myth is primarily negative, regarding the present world as a coherent whole that can only be destroyed root and branch: it represents a spirit of total opposition and cannot be criticized as though it were a plan of reform or a blueprint for the future. It must be wholly accepted or wholly rejected, and its devotees are impervious to any doubt that may be cast on its effectiveness. Utopians and social scientists imagine that they can foresee and plan the future, but the myth is an act of creation, not of prediction. The myth of a general strike embodies the whole idea of socialism and the self-consciousness of the proletariat, which radically severs its connection with the present society and seeks no help or allies of any kind.

> These results could not be produced in any very certain manner by the use of ordinary language; use must be made of a body of images which, by intuition alone, and before any considered analyses are made, is capable of evoking as an undivided whole the mass of sentiments which correspond to the different manifestations of the war undertaken by socialism against modern society. The syndicalists solve this problem perfectly, by concentrating the whole of socialism in the drama of the general strike; there is thus no longer any place for the reconciliation of contraries in professorial gibberish [*la conciliation des contraires dans le galimatias par les savants officiels*]. (*Reflections on Violence*, Ch. IV)

The myth is not a matter of thinking about the future or planning it: it lives in the present, which it also helps to form. 'The myth must be judged as a means of acting on the present; any attempt to discuss how far it can be materially applied to the course of history is devoid of sense. It is the myth in its entirety which is alone important: its parts are only of interest in so far as they bring out the main idea.' (Ibid.)

As will be seen, while Sorel criticizes the rationalism of Descartes or the Enlightenment he does not expressly oppose to it an irrationalist point of view: he regards rationalist delusions as simply a mark of historical dilettantism, the mentality which prefers elegant speculation to complex reality. But when he contrasts social planning with the mythopoeic act he is no longer opposing historical reason to *a priori* abstractions, but upholding the claims of sentiment against analytical reasoning in general. The myth is an indivisible, inexpressible whole that can only be grasped in a single act of intuitive perception as described by Bergson. Acceptance of the myth is not an intellectual act, but an expression of readiness for destructive action. The myth is proof against argument, discussion, or compromise. It is anti-intellectual in a more radical sense than we find in Bergson, who did not condemn analytical reason as a source of decadence but merely defined the limits of its usefulness as an instrument for technical manipulation in describing physical or social reality. In Bergson's view rational and analytical thought on social problems was far from valueless, though it could not take account of historical breaches of continuity due to spontaneous creativity. For Sorel, however, belief in the myth was to be a complete substitute for sociological knowledge, and all practical acts must be subordinate to the expectation of an undefined, indescribable apocalypse. By thus setting up a mythology immune to rational criticism Sorel gave advance endorsement to political movements founded on 'instinct': from this point of view the Fascists were right to claim him for their own, whereas his connection with Marxism must be regarded as accidental.

4. 'Ricorsi.' The separation of classes and the discontinuity of culture

ALTHOUGH Sorel's myth is a negation of the present in the name of a future catastrophe, it also has some roots in the past, though not in the manner of religious myths. It purports to be a revival of what formerly was, a rejuvenation of the world by stripping it of the accumulated layers of civilization. This is what Vico called a *ricorso*, when a people reverts to its primitive state and all its works are creative, instinctive, and poetic, as in early Christianity or the decline of the Middle Ages. Revolutionary syndicalism is to bring about a universal rebirth of this kind, based on the proletariat as a self-contained enclave within an alien society.

Sorel laid especial emphasis on the separateness of the proletariat, but in a different sense from that of orthodox Marxism. When the leaders of the Second International spoke of the independence of the proletariat they had in mind the political distinctness, the independence of the workers' parties, the movement developing according to its own interests and pursuing its own goals. Neither Kautsky, Rosa Luxemburg, nor even Lenin and Trotsky ruled out tactical alliances with non-proletarian parties in particular circumstances, nor did they advocate a break with existing civilization: on the contrary, it was taken for granted that this included human values that socialism was capable of assimilating and to which it was indeed the sole rightful heir. To Sorel, on the other hand, the point at issue was not the political separateness of the workers' party, since he was opposed to parties as such and regarded them as a badge of bourgeois society. The party expressed, naturally and inevitably, the subjection of the proletariat to professional politicians. Not only could it not assist in liberating the proletariat but it was bound to frustrate its liberation, at best replacing the former tyranny by that of party officials, parliamentary orators, and journalists' clubs. The proletariat's hope lay not in parties, or in trade unions striving to improve conditions for the time being, but in revolutionary syndicates—expressly non-political, indifferent to parliamentary tactics, refusing to play the bourgeois game, devoting all their efforts to forming the consciousness and solidarity of the working class against the day when society would be totally transformed.

The syndicalist movement (or anarcho-syndicalist, as it is usually called) developed in France in the 1890s, in Italy and Spain a little later; in Germany it did not prevail to any extent. In keeping with the Proudhonist tradition it rejected any kind of political activity or participation in bourgeois institutions, and subordinated the economic struggle of the proletariat to the coming revolution, which would not replace existing political institutions by new ones of the same kind, but by loosely federated producers' associations governed exclusively by workers. Marx stigmatized this as a petty-bourgeois Utopia, arguing that workers' self-government could not in itself put an end to competition and anarchy in production, and that if Proudhon's ideal were realized it would bring back all the horrors of capitalist accumulation. To Sorel, however, syndicalism offered the only hope of a genuine victory of the proletariat. He did not join the movement, believing that middle-class intellectuals could only do harm as members of workers' organizations, but he provided it with an ideology from outside.

The business of the syndicalist movement, then, was to imbue the workers with a sense of alienation from bourgeois society, to break with bourgeois morality and modes of thought, to have nothing to do with party and parliamentary intrigue, and to defend proletarian purity against ideologists and rhetoricians. The proletariat would never free itself if it tried to ape the bourgeoisie: its first rule must be to 'preserve its exclusively working-class character by keeping out intellectuals, whose leadership would bring about the re-establishment of hierarchies and create divisions among the workers' (*Matériaux*, p. 132). It is not only a question of organizational purity, however, but still more of spiritual purity. 'My friends and I are never tired of urging the workers to avoid being drawn into the rut of bourgeois science and philosophy. There will be a great change in the world when the proletariat discovers, as did the bourgeoisie after the Revolution, that it is capable of thinking in a manner appropriate to its own mode of life' (*Illusions*, p. 135). The new proletarian culture will be founded on labour, and 'will afford no cause to regret the disappearance of bourgeois culture. The war that the proletariat is called on to wage against its masters is, we know, calculated to arouse in it a sense of sublimity that today's bourgeoisie completely lacks . . . We must make every effort to ensure that the rising class is not poisoned by bourgeois ideas, and for that reason we cannot do enough to free the people from the shackles of eighteenth-century literature' (ibid., pp. 285–6). The new philosophy is 'one of arms and not of heads' (*Décomposition du marxisme*, p. 60), its purpose being to convince the working class that its whole future lies in the class struggle. It is a philosophy that comes into being spontaneously: the revolutionary syndicalist movement is created by men who know little of Marxism, but it expresses the truest need of the class of producers. Without it the proletariat would be exposed to the same fate as the ancient Germans who, after conquering Rome, felt ashamed of their barbarism and succumbed to the decadent culture of the rhetoricians, or the men of the Reformation who let themselves be corrupted by the values of humanism. The proletariat, engaged in the class war, must firmly understand that all other classes without exception are opposed to its liberation. The society of the future will inherit capitalist technology, but there will be no place in it for the spiritual culture of capitalism. Any ideological or political battle, however justified in other ways, will do the workers more harm than good if it involves their co-operating with bourgeois radicals—for instance, in combating the Church and clericalism, not to speak of defending patriotic causes—since it will weaken the sense of class separateness and foster the dangerous illusion that the proletariat can effectively join forces with liberals to bring about social change. The revolution will be 'an absolute separation between two historical eras' (*Reflections*, Ch. IV), and the proletariat, which is to carry it out, must have no moral scruples *vis-à-vis* other classes. 'People who have devoted their lives to a cause which they identify with the regeneration of the world could not hesitate to make use of any weapon which might serve to develop to a greater degree the spirit of the class war' (ibid., Ch. VI).

5. Moral revolution and historical necessity

THIS does not mean, however, that the proletariat is, or can be, indifferent to morality. On the contrary, the basic purpose of the revolution and of the preparatory period is to effect a moral transformation of the working class that will restore its dignity, pride, independence, and sense of mission and exclusivity. Although his best-known work is largely an apologia for violence, Sorel regards violence as being morally right only in so far as it plays a part in the moral education of its users. It is a military and not a police type of violence that he has in mind, devoid of cruelty and certainly not motivated by envy of

the wealthier classes, which would be immoral and degrading to the proletariat. Far from seeking to replace the present form of government by one
equally authoritarian, the object of proletarian violence is to do away with government altogether. Morally commendable violence is evinced, he argues, in
spontaneous acts of popular justice by Norwegian mountain-dwellers, in lynch-
law or the Corsican vendetta. It is the advocates of *political* revolution, such as
the socialists who wish to supplant the privileged minority of today, who are
liable, as the Revolution showed, to adopt inquisitorial methods of cruelty and
terror as a cure for political or economic difficulties. In this absurd and hopeless course the Jacobins were encouraged by Rousseau's doctrine of the social
contract, since they regarded themselves as the embodiment of the 'general
will' and therefore entitled to do whatever they chose. Being morally unpre-
pared to rule, the best thing they could think of was to imitate the *ancien
régime*. The same kind of despotism would result if power were placed in the
hands of Jaurès and others like him, who use humanistic rhetoric to imbue the
proletariat with a bourgeois desire to see its party in power, instead of preparing it to smash the machinery of public authority.

For these reasons syndicalism is against democracy, which encourages the proletariat to take part in bourgeois institutions, especially parliament, and is a source
of demoralization, corruption, and the undermining of class solidarity.

The general strike, which is the proper aim of the proletarian struggle, is
thus to be distinguished from political revolution. In this conception of Sorel's
the conventional opposition between an economic and a political strike does
not apply. The general strike is not an economic one in the sense of an attempt
to improve the situation of the working class in capitalist conditions, but it is
also the contrary of a political revolution. The purpose of the latter is to attain
power, and it is subject to all the laws of a fight for power, including tactical
alliances, but it does not premise the division of society into only two camps.
Besides the syndicates it presupposes other organizations, committees, or parties with programmes and ready-made forms for the future: it must be planned,
and can therefore be criticized in detail. Moreover, a political revolution is not
based on the Marxian doctrine of class division but on an anti-Marxist opposition between rich and poor; it appeals to base instincts of envy and vindictiveness, instead of the sublime heroism of popular champions. A general strike
means the destruction of the existing order without any idea of setting up a new
authority: its purpose is to restore control of production to free men who have
no need of masters. It is a single, indivisible action, not to be broken down into
stages or conceived as a strategic plan. The definition of socialism in terms of
a general strike 'means that politicians' revolutions have had their day; the proletariat refuses to have new hierarchies set up over it. Our formula has nothing
to say concerning the rights of man, absolute justice, political constitutions and

parliaments: it rejects not only bourgeois capitalistic government, but any hierarchy that at all resembles that of the bourgeoisie' (*Matériaux*, pp. 59–60). Syndicalism cares nothing for doctrines or 'scientific' preparation: 'it proceeds as circumstances dictate, regardless of dogma, not fearing to commit its forces in ways that prudent men deplore. A sight calculated to discourage those noble minds who believe in the supremacy of science in modern times, who expect the revolution to be brought about by a mighty effort of thought, who imagine that the world has been ruled by pure reason since it was freed from clerical obscurantism.' But 'all experience has shown that revolution does not possess the secret of the future: it acts in the same way as capitalism, rushing to occupy every outlet that presents itself' (ibid., p. 64).

Revolutionary syndicalism is thus equally opposed to utopianism and to the Blanquist doctrine that a group of conspirators claiming a mandate from the proletariat may take advantage of circumstances to seize power and then transform society by means of force and repression. Blanquism or Jacobinism stands for a revolution of the poor against the rich, not a Marxian revolution carried out by producers alone. The latter is by no means aimed at a party dictatorship: Bernstein is right when he says that the assumption of power by the social democrats would not make the people sovereign, but merely dependent on professional politicians and newspaper owners. Until such time as the workers have a strong economic organization and attain a high standard of moral independence, the dictatorship of the proletariat can only mean the dictatorship of party orators and men of letters.

Again, the syndicalist revolution cannot be simply the result of the economic decadence of capitalism. Revolutions that take place when the old regime is in a state of impotence and collapse do not lead to improvement, but petrify the state of decay. The syndicalist revolution requires capitalism to be expansive—to suffocate by its own energy, not to die of inanition. It is not, therefore, in the workers' interest to weaken capitalism by forcing legislative concessions and reforms: it is best for them that capitalists should be overcome by a ruthless, predatory spirit of expansion, like the American conquistadors of capitalism. This is the way to foster the sense of absolute class division, the solidarity of the oppressed, inflexible heroism, the grandeur and dignity of a historical mission—everything that socialist politicians sacrifice when they cheat the exploiters into making petty concessions and in so doing demoralize the working class.

Nor should we be deluded by 'so-called scientific socialism' into thinking that victory is assured by historical necessity. As Bergson showed, history proceeds by unforeseeable acts of creation. The illusions of determinism are due to the exaggerated hopes aroused by the progress of natural science in the nineteenth century: the utopians naïvely imagined that the future course of society could be plotted like the movements of heavenly bodies. But, as Berg-son's theory of personality and evolution makes clear, the future is constantly taking a fresh start as the result of freely creative action. The revolutionary movement is directed towards the future, but it foresees it only in terms of its own spontaneous action, guided by a single, indivisible, unanalysable idea—the sublime myth of a total transformation of the world in a final, apocalyptic bat-tle. Such was the inspiration of early Christianity, which refused to compromise with the world or to regard itself as part of society, withdrawing instead into the myth of the Parousia. But the Church's later history shows how, defying the predictions of the wise, it periodically renewed itself in bursts of vigorous expansion, as initiated by the great reformers and founders of new monastic orders. The syndicalist movement is likewise a spontaneous process of renewal which may regenerate the working class, corrupted by politicians and legisla-tion, and in due time bring salvation to all mankind.

The purpose of the new revolution is not to bring prosperity and abundance, or to make life easy. Sorel makes fun of Destrée and Vandervelde, who imag-ine the future socialist state as a Land of Cockaigne or a place where the inhab-itants may do as they please, as in the Abbaye de Thélème. The mainspring of the revolutionary movement is not poverty but class antagonism, and the work-ers' cause is not that of the poor who want to take away the property of the rich, but that of direct producers who wish to be the organizers of production. The principal values of socialism are those of morality and not of well-being, and it may be noticed that the poorest members of the proletariat are the least, not the most, revolutionary-minded. A just society must, as Proudhon put it, acknowledge the 'law of poverty'; a frugal life is an honest and happy one. Proudhon saw the future society as a loose federation of agricultural and indus-trial associations, with public life based on communal and provincial units, freedom of the Press and of assembly, and no standing armies. Sorel despised all planning for the future and vouchsafed no details of the 'perfect society', but as an exponent of Proudhon he no doubt imagined it on similar lines. In *L'Avenir socialiste des syndicats* he says that society will be 'organized accord-ing to the plan of production', and that the object of socialism is to 'apply the workshop system to public life' (*Matériaux*, p. 70), so that all social issues will present themselves in terms of production units.

From the moral and organizational points of view Sorel's ideal seems to have been one of isolated mountain clans or Swiss communes practising direct democracy, more or less self-sufficient in production, and not involved in com-mercial exchanges on such a scale as to affect their customs and traditions. The morality of the proletariat was a morality of producers as opposed to mer-chants; modern democracy was still modelled on the stock exchange, whereas the democracy of the future would be analogous to co-operative manufacture.

These comparisons are not devoid of foundation. The history of democratic ideas and institutions is certainly related to the history of trade, and the whole Mediterranean culture arose and developed in terms of ports and commercial towns. Trading encourages habits of compromise, negotiation and bargaining as well as deceit and hypocrisy, rhetoric and demagogy, prudence and competition, love of wealth and comfort, rationalism and disregard for tradition, shrewd calculation and prediction, and the ideal of success. The subordination of production to exchange-value, which according to Marx is the essence of capitalism, is a natural culmination of these trends. The society in which 'everything is for sale', and in which family, tribal, and local links, irreducible to exchange relationships, count for nothing, was attacked by all the Romantics including Marx in his young days. Sorel, like Nietzsche, was a sworn enemy of this type of society and to that extent an heir of the Romantics, but the upshot of his criticism was very different from Marx's. He was attracted by the picture of untamed warrior clans fighting for survival rather than wealth or comfort, valiant but not cruel, proud in spite of their poverty, devoted to their tribal customs and their freedom, ready to fight to the death against foreign rule. The main purpose of socialism, in Sorel's mind, was to revive this type of morality as opposed to that of commercial society. 'Socialism is a moral issue in that it provides a new way of judging all human acts, or, in Nietzsche's famous phrase, a revaluation of all values' (*Matériaux*, p. 170, quoting from his own preface to the French translation of a work by Saverio Merlino). The new morality takes shape in the working class under capitalist conditions, and is in fact a prior condition of revolution and of economic change: here Sorel agrees with Vandervelde, who says that a victory of the workers without a radical moral transformation would plunge the world into a state of suffering, cruelty, and injustice as bad as the present, if not worse. The chief points at which the new morality comes into play are the family, war, and production, and in all these spheres it means an increase of dignity, solidarity, heroism, generosity, and personal responsibility. Sorel attaches especial importance to sexual restraint and family virtues, the weakening of which he regards as a natural reinforcement of bourgeois society. 'The world will become a juster place only in so far as it becomes more chaste—I believe there is nothing more certain than this' (ibid., p. 199). The ideal to which he looks up is that of the Homeric heroes as seen by Nietzsche.

6. Marxism, anarchism, Fascism

As we have already observed, the interrelation of values and ideas in Sorel's work is quite different from that of the orthodox Marxists or any critic of Marxism. In this respect he stands unique. His attacks on reformism are sometimes very like those of the orthodox social-democratic Left, but his criticism of

Marxist orthodoxy has much in common with that of the anarchists. He attacks anarchism from a Marxist standpoint, yet on some points he criticizes Marx from the angle of Bakunin or Proudhon. The usual classifications of socialist thought at this period do not apply to him.

Like Marx, Sorel regarded socialism not merely as a better form of social organization but as a complete transformation of every aspect of life, morality, thought, and philosophy: not a mere set of reforms, but a reinterpretation of human existence. The socialists of his time did not, in his opinion, take a serious interest in human nature and the final aim of life. They adopted the shallow metaphysics of the eighteenth-century free-thinkers and failed to realize the importance of evil in Marx's historiosophy; their rationalistic optimism prevented them from matching the Church in understanding men, but it was necessary for socialism to offer all the values that the Church did if it was to prevail. Sorel, following Gustave Le Bon, did not hesitate to ascribe to socialism a religious and charismatic character: in this he differs from Marx's views, at all events in *Capital*.

Marxism, to Sorel, was above all the poetry of the Great Apocalypse which he identified with social revolution. He combated reformism not because it was ineffectual—on the contrary, he knew it to be effective—but because it was prosaic and unheroic. He believed in the class basis of socialism and the unique role of the producers as agents of the revolution. The proletariat, as a militant sect, must guard above all things its independence of existing society. Sorel dreamt of a free society, i.e. an association of producers with no bosses over them, its basic values deriving from the fact that it was devoted to material production; Marx, on the other hand, thought the great achievement of socialism would be the conquest of leisure, enabling people to devote themselves to creative work as the labour hours necessary for material production were progressively shortened. Marx put his faith in technology, which he thought would liberate mankind from the cares of material existence; Sorel, on the contrary, regarded productive activity as the source of all human dignity, and the desire to be free from such cares was, to him, no better than bourgeois hedonism. Marx was a rationalist inasmuch as he believed in scientific socialism, i.e. that a rational analysis of the capitalist economy would show that it was bound to be replaced by a collective system; he also believed in the continuity of civilization. Sorel regarded the idea of the historical necessity of socialism as a survival of the Hegelian *Weltgeist*; he accepted Bergson's theory of spontaneity and advocated a complete break in cultural continuity, yet at the same time he wished to preserve the traditions of the family and tribal solidarity. His arbitrary treatment of Marxist doctrine may be seen in the definition, which he ascribes to Marx, of a class as 'a collectivity of families united by traditions, interests and political views, and possessing a degree of solidarity such that they may be regarded as forming a single personality, a being endowed with reason and acting accordingly' (*Matériaux*, p. 184).

Sorel did not profess to be an anarchist: the anarchists of his day were not well defined from a class point of view, but tended to enlist support among the lumpenproletariat and the *déclassé* intelligentsia. A movement led by lawyers, journalists, and students clearly had nothing to do with revolutionary syndicalism as Sorel understood it, and he was also repelled by the anarchist groups of Bakuninist persuasion who combined conspiratorial methods with authoritarian principles. At the same time, he shared with the anarchists their basic premiss of the need to do away with all state institutions and their refusal to take part in parliamentary life or to support 'political socialism'. From Bakunin's time onward it was a constant feature of anarchist propaganda, emphasized, for example, by Machajski, that 'political' or 'party' socialism was only the prelude to a new tyranny, and that the 'dictatorship of the proletariat' as a form of state organization meant subjecting the workers to the despotism of professional politicians. Sorel also agreed with those anarchists who insisted on a 'moral revolution' as an integral part of the social revolution. 'Social democracy is cruelly punished today for having fought so hard against the anarchists, who tried to bring about a revolution of minds and hearts' (*Matériaux*, p. 380, commenting on a letter from Proudhon to Michelet). The nationalization of means of production was valueless in itself as far as liberating the workers was concerned, for it merely increased the power of politicians over producers.

It may appear strange that a writer who so fiercely attacked the idea of patriotism, state institutions, and party organization should have been recognized as an ideologist of the budding Fascist movement and should have supplied arguments to the functionaries and apologists of a brutal nationalist tyranny— the more so as, unlike Nietzsche, Sorel accepted the basic doctrines of Marxism. Yet his link with Fascism is a real one, though clearly it was impossible to judge the first intimations of Italian Fascism in 1912 with the eyes of those who witnessed the Second World War. Everything in Sorel's work that related to the revolution and the free post-revolutionary society belongs, it is true, to the realm of 'myth', which in principle admits of no discussion or explanation. Fascism drew its strength from the sense of desperation and desire for absolute change, the disillusionment with democracy and disbelief in the possibility of reform, the obscure need for some radical break with the existing scheme of things. Sorel's appeals were well adapted to the spiritual conditions out of which Fascism was bred. He did not set up to be the planner of a new order, but the herald of catastrophe. He called for a break in the continuity of civilization in the name of a better culture, a return to the popular sources of legislation and morality; in so doing he unconsciously showed that an attack on the whole of an existing culture is in effect an invitation to barbarism unless it is based on already existing values and a clear knowledge of what the new order is supposed to comprise. Sorel aims many shrewd blows at the naïvety of the rationalists; but if an attack on rationalism is not clearly distinguished from an attack on reason, if it appeals to a *philosophie des bras* which is not so very different from a philosophy of the mailed fist, then it becomes a rebellion against the mind and a plea for violence pure and simple. Sorel's advocacy of violence related, in his mind, to the warlike variety as opposed to that of a *gendarmerie*; but the distinction is a fine one, based on literary stereotypes and the idealization of Grecian or Viking heroes. A morality that regards violence in itself as a source of heroism and greatness is very near to being an instrument of despotism. The same is true of Sorel's criticism of parliamentary democracy: there was much truth in it, but the same could be said of Hitler's writings on the subject. The criticism of pervading corruption, abuses, cant, petty squabbling, and the competition for jobs masquerading as a conflict of ideas—all these have been denounced by anarchists, communists, and Fascists in very similar terms. But a criticism of democracy that wraps itself in 'myth' and advances no tangible alternative, merely the absence or the negation of democracy, can be nothing but an apologia for tyranny, at any rate when it descends from the realm of literature into practical politics.

As a professed Marxist who supplied inspiration to Fascism, Sorel is important in that the destiny of his idea reveals the convergence of extreme forms of leftist and rightist radicalism. If leftist radical phraseology confines itself to attacking bourgeois democracy without offering a better democracy in its place, if it merely opposes rationalism without setting up new cultural values, if it advocates violence unhampered by moral restrictions, then its programme is merely that of a new despotism and is essentially the same as that of the radical Right. If, as in Sorel's doctrine, the ultimate catastrophe is represented as an object in itself, or even as the supreme object, irrespective of the consequences it may produce, then the proletariat's role is, first and foremost, that of the expected agent of cataclysmic change. Since it failed to play this part, Sorel could without inconsistency turn to nationalism as a more promising embodiment of the cause, which in his eyes was still 'total revolution' and not the nation as such. Thus his passionate defence of Lenin and the Bolsheviks was highly ambiguous. He admired the Russian Revolution as a dramatic apocalypse, a death-blow to intellectuals, a triumph of willpower over alleged economic necessity, and an assertion of native Muscovite traditions over Western ones. 'The sanguinary object-lesson in Russia will prove to all workers that there is a contradiction between democracy and the mission of the proletariat. The idea of a government of producers will not perish; the cry "Death to intellectuals", for which the Bolsheviks are so much abused, may in the end be taken up by workers the world over. Only a blind man could fail to see that the

Russian revolution is the dawn of a new era' (*Matériaux*, postscript to Preface of 1919 edn.). In the 1919 appendix to *Reflections on Violence* we read:

> When the time comes to evaluate present-day events with historical impartiality, it will be recognized that Bolshevism owed a great part of its power to the fact that the masses regarded it as a protest against an oligarchy whose greatest concern had been not to appear Russian; at the end of the year 1917, the former spokesman of the Black Hundred said that the Bolsheviks had 'proven that they were more Russian than the rebels Kaledin, Roussky etc., who betrayed the Tsar and the country' (*Journal de Genève*, 20 December 1917) . . . One may speak as a historian of the process of revolutionary repression in Russia only by keeping in mind the Moscovite character of Bolshevism . . . the national traditions provided the Red Guards with innumerable precedents, which they believed they had the right to imitate in order to defend the Revolution . . . If we are grateful to the Roman soldiers for having replaced abortive, strayed or impotent civilizations by a civilization whose pupils we are still in law, literature and monuments, how grateful will not the future have to be to the Russian soldiers of socialism!

Sorel knew little of Leninist doctrine: he admired Lenin as a prophet of the Apocalypse, and Mussolini for the same reason. He was ready to support anything that seemed heroic and promised to destroy the hated system of democracy, party strife, compromise, negotiation, and calculation. He was not interested in the petty question of human welfare, but in discovering the circumstances most propitious to an outburst of energy. The penetrating critic of rationalism ended as a worshipper of the great Moloch into whose jaws the blind, fanatic, jubilant mob advanced, in a warlike frenzy, to its own destruction.

VIII

Antonio Labriola: an Attempt at
an Open Orthodoxy

1. Labriola's style

ANTONIO LABRIOLA played a similar role in Italy to that of Plekhanov in Russia and of Lafargue in France: he was the first in his country to expound Marxism as a system, and had an important influence on the form in which it was accepted there. When Labriola became a Marxist he already had behind him a long career as an academic philosopher. Although chiefly influenced in his formative years by Hegel and Herbart, he was strongly attached to the Italian tradition and imparted its peculiar features to his version of Marxism. It was also of importance that he was never a party activist, but only a publicist and theoretician.

Owing to the fragmentation of Italy before 1870 and its relative economic backwardness, the workers' movement took shape much later there than in the rest of Western Europe. Socialist ideas and slogans figured for some time as part of general radical ideologies which also expressed what Marxists were wont to regard as typical aspirations of the 'progressive' bourgeoisie. Confronted by the powerful opposition of the Church and clericalism, socialists and bourgeois radicals found themselves 'on the same side of the barricade' for much longer than in other countries, and were more conscious of the values they had in common. The division of Italy into a conservative-Catholic and a progressive camp remained fundamental even after the socialist movement became an organized political force on its own account. By virtue, therefore, of historical circumstances and of his own life-story, Labriola remained strongly attached to the radical Italian tradition in politics and philosophy, with its cult of such figures as Garibaldi and Giordano Bruno.

Labriola's philosophical style is also typically Italian in both its attractive and its less acceptable features. In the homeland of Thomas Aquinas, more perhaps than in any other country, secular philosophy from the sixteenth century onwards broke radically with scholastic modes of thought and logical skills. Outside the powerful but sterile domain of late scholasticism there was a distaste for schemes and systems and a preference for 'global' thinking as opposed to

analysis: a predilection for discursive essays, and a strong emphasis on the didactic and rhetorical aspects of philosophical writing. All these tendencies can be
found in Labriola's works. The boundaries between epistemology, psychology,
ethics, and pedagogy are fluid, and he is clearly not concerned to make philosophy a separate, self-contained preserve of professional thinkers. The distrust of specialization within the domain of humanism, which even today makes
itself felt in Italian culture and the Italian university system, was enhanced in
the nineteenth century by the Hegelian tendency to think in global terms and
relate every specific problem to some large, panoramic vision of history. This
tendency allied itself in Italy with Renaissance-style universalism and the attitude of the *eroici furiosi* for whom the basic problems of existence were at stake
in every particular question.

The literary style and global thinking of Italian philosophers, their dislike of
rigid classification, specialization, and hierarchies of ideas, may help to explain
the success in Italy of the historicist, anti-positivist version of Marxism which
was championed by Labriola and upheld in the next generation by Gramsci.
The attraction of this form of Marxism, as opposed to the scientistic and positivistic approach, was not so much that it raised the study of social problems to
the dignity of natural science, but that it enabled all aspects of material and
spiritual culture to be interpreted as expressions or manifestations of a single
universal process or a particular historical epoch. This propensity to relate
social phenomena to great historical 'totalities' was not specifically Marxist, but
in combination with other principles it could be presented as a natural part of
historical materialism. At the same time it fitted in with the relativist tendencies that seem to be a distinctive mark of Italian philosophy.

Such generalizations, of course, are highly simplified. Positivism and scientism duly made their appearance in Italy, and with Enrico Ferri we encounter
a positivist, Darwinist, scientistic version of Marxism. In Italy, although
nowhere else, there was a period during which positivism and Hegelianism
were united rather than divided as regards their effect on society: both represented lay, radical, rationalist thought as against clerical reaction, and were on
the same side of the cultural divide which ran through the nation. None the
less, from the present-day viewpoint at least it would seem that the most fertile
sources of Italian intellectual life derive from the tradition of historicism rather
than scientism.

It was particularly hard for Italians, whether Marxist or not, to believe in a
theory of uninterrupted historical progress, since the whole history of their
country in modern times went to prove the contrary. After the three centuries
of regression and stagnation which followed the Counter-Reformation, the
whole radical intelligentsia was imbued with a sense of the country's economic
and cultural backwardness. The hopes aroused by the Risorgimento were not

such as to encourage the conviction that progress was an inevitable consequence of 'historical laws', and Italian philosophers, including Marxists, tended to be more sensitive to the variety, dramatic complexity, and unexpectedness of the historical process. From this viewpoint also, Labriola instilled into Italian Marxism a sceptical attitude towards comprehensive explanations of universal history.

2. *Biographical note*

ANTONIO LABRIOLA (1843–1904) was born at Cassino, the son of a teacher. He was brought up on the ideals of 'Young Italy' (the secret society founded by Mazzini) and dreamt from his youth of the independence and unification of his country. He entered the University of Naples in 1861 and was influenced by Hegelianism, the chief exponents of which in Italy were Bertrando Spaventa and Augusto Vera. In an essay afterwards published by Croce, Labriola criticized Zeller and the neo-Kantians and argued that Kant's doctrine was finally superseded by Hegelianism. After graduating he became a schoolteacher at Naples, where he lived until 1874. His first philosophical work during this period was an analysis of the theory of affections in Spinoza (1865). In 1869 he wrote a more elaborate work on Socratic philosophy, which won a prize in a competition organized by the Naples Academy of Moral and Political Sciences. He continued his studies and became erudite in philosophy, history, and ethnography; he was also interested in Herbart's associationist psychology, which he adopted to a large extent, and in the works of Vico, which influenced him all his life. In the early 1870s he took up political journalism in a liberal and anticlerical vein. In 1873 he published *Moral Liberty* and *Morality and Religion*, which show a departure from the Hegelian viewpoint though they are in no way specifically Marxist. In the following year he was appointed to a professorial chair in Rome, where he spent the rest of his life teaching, writing, and joining in all the important controversies of the day.

His conversion to Marxism was not sudden but gradual. In 1889 he wrote in a lecture *On Socialism* that he had criticized liberalism from 1873 onwards and had embraced a 'new intellectual faith' in 1879, based especially on his studies of the preceding three years. His essay *On the Idea of Freedom* (1887) shows no clearly Marxist tendency, but his writings of the 1890s reflect the viewpoint of a definite 'school'. *On Socialism* is an explicit political declaration in which he criticizes bourgeois democracy and defends internationalist socialism, the cause of the world proletariat. His best-known Marxist work is *Essays on the Materialist Conception of History*, containing a general account of historical materialism and a discussion of *The Communist Manifesto*: this was published in 1896, and to the second edition in 1902 he added a polemical article against Masaryk's book on the foundations of Marxism. The work was soon translated into French and became a classic of European Marxist literature. Labriola intended to write a fourth section based on his lectures of 1900–1 and giving a general account of the nineteenth century. He did not live to complete this, but the parts he had written were published by his great pupil Benedetto Croce in 1906 in a collection of Labriola's unpublished or little-known works entitled *Various Writings on Philosophy and Politics*, while the remaining notes were published in 1925 by Luigi dal Pane, who subsequently wrote a monograph on Labriola. The latter's Marxist philosophy is also set out in a collection of letters to Sorel, published in 1897 under the title *Talking of Socialism and Philosophy*. It is noteworthy that of the many articles Labriola published in the last fifteen years of his life, some clearly stress his Marxist position (critique of Bernstein and of Millerand, article on the difference between socialism and radicalism), while others could equally well have been written by a radical rationalist (lecture on the freedom of science, speech commemorating Giordano Bruno). In this respect too Labriola differs from the orthodox German Marxists, who proclaimed their allegiance in everything they wrote.

3. *Early writings*

LABRIOLA's essay on Spinoza's theory of affections is of no special importance, being merely a summary for school purposes of the relevant part of the *Ethics*. It is worth noting that he emphasizes the moral background of Spinoza's metaphysics and the latter's general naturalistic viewpoint, while adding that the significance of Spinoza's doctrine lies in the fact that he denies the metaphysical basis of value-judgements and derives the noblest human impulses from egoism as the sole creative force; he is also concerned to validate the category of freedom within the limits of a deterministic view of the universe.

The essay on Socrates, a much more important work, is an erudite and in part polemical dissertation on the theme, borrowed from Hegel and Zeller, that the key to Socrates' thought is to be found in Xenophon and not in Plato, and that we must resist the temptation to ascribe Plato's metaphysics to the elder philosopher. Labriola regards Socrates as a pedagogue first and foremost, and interprets his personality in terms of the internal contradictions of Athenian culture. He is not concerned with finding out Socrates' implicit metaphysical views, but with describing those that were consciously articulated in his mind. In Labriola's opinion, Socrates' activity is to be understood as an attempt to resolve the conflict between traditional conservatism and the scepticism and relativism produced by the variety and richness of Athenian culture. The humanism and relativism of the sophists was a symptom of the break-up of traditional communities, while Socrates' endeavour was to discover absolute norms of morality independent of human beings. He was not fully aware how far his own investigations transcended traditional values, but in fact he was looking for a new interpretation of the world that would afford support against the sophists. Socrates' belief in the chronic inadequacy of human knowledge was necessary in order to justify his search for absolute cognitive and moral norms independent of the arbitrary decisions of individuals. This search was evinced particularly in his revaluation of the concept of deity, which made him—following Aeschylus, Pindar, and Sophocles—the herald of a new religious consciousness, turning by degrees from the traditions of the old mythology towards monotheism. But the functions of the Socratic deity were exclusively moral: it was to be the repository of absolute values, proof against relativism and subjectivism. In the same way Socrates' logical investigations and his endeavours to elucidate concepts were not born of disinterested curiosity but were inspired by the same pedagogical purpose: hence his contempt for natural science. He had himself no metaphysical intentions and was purely pragmatic; nevertheless, he provided a basis for Plato's theory of ideas and metaphysic of the Good.

Labriola's views on Socrates illustrate his indebtedness to Hegel for the belief, which became part of his Marxist faith, that philosophical ideas are the expression of changing historical needs, arising from the internal contradictions of a particular phase of civilization. The influence of Hegel is also visible, besides that of Kant and Herbart, in Labriola's treatise on moral freedom. This is an obscure work as regards both argument and conclusions, which indeed is generally the case with philosophical treatments of this subject. However, it is clear that Labriola regards the question concerning free will (*liberum arbitrium*) as wrongly framed, and that in Hegelian fashion he seeks to replace the question of freedom in the sense of indifference by that of freedom conceived as the conformity between choice and conscience. He tries in this way to distinguish between determinism and fatalism, but does not get beyond vague general formulas. He regards as self-evident Kant's rule which makes moral judgements entirely independent of utilitarian factors and of the evaluation of the results of human actions. The imperative of obligation is implied in moral freedom, which realizes itself in acts of conscious obedience to that imperative. However, as the human will is the result of many social and psychological factors, it is assailed by conflicting spiritual aspirations, and its freedom does not consist in a potential ability to determine itself as it pleases, but in an actual choice conforming to an absolute norm. Unlike animals, whose actions are determined merely by the strength of habit or of this or that desire, man is free in the sense that he possesses a moral consciousness enabling him to resist natural impulses. The fact, and not the mere abstract possibility, of such self-determination entitles us to call him free. Labriola expressly protests against the 'naturalization' of the human conscience and the idea that it consists of a mere collection of instincts that are 'ultimately' attributable to animal needs. Like Herbart, however, he rejects the idea of the soul as a metaphysical entity or of separate spiritual powers, but is content to analyse the motivations that constitute an expression or a denial of freedom according as they do or do not conform to the individual's awareness of the moral imperative. There is, strictly speaking, no contradiction between the principle of causality and moral freedom, provided we regard human acts, in Leibnizian fashion, as self-determined (as opposed to external, mechanical, or 'natural' determination), or, following Schopenhauer, as causality 'seen from the inside'. It is easy to see in this way that freedom can and must be the purpose of an education that inculcates a moral consciousness and assimilates it to habit. To treat freedom as an innate quality of the soul is not only misleading but pernicious in practice, as it dispenses with the obligation to educate men to freedom: such education is the supreme purpose of the state, which in its ideal form is, above all, a pedagogical institution.

The essay on *Morality and Religion* shows clearly the influence of Kant and to a lesser extent that of Hegel. Its main points are three. First, 'practical judgements' are not derivable from theoretical ones and cannot be based either on psychological premises (the content of an empirical moral consciousness) or on utilitarian grounds, but must be *a priori*; morality is founded on those practical judgements which run most contrary to instinctive desires. The multiplicity of moral opinions is an empirical fact and does not invalidate the contention that there is only one morality *par excellence*. Second, moral values belong exclusively to the good will, regarded as autonomous in all respects including its relation to the hypothetical will of God: moral imperatives based on the will of God are not truly moral, since they imply the submission of one will to another. Third, morality is wholly independent of religious faith. Religion is a universal and inseparable part of the spiritual life, and rationalists who criticize a particular historical form of it are missing the point when they attack religion in general. The purpose of religion is 'to compensate with a different form of idealism the discordance between our ethical demands and the natural world in which we live'. It can and does reinforce moral values and the moral consciousness, but it contributes nothing to the content of ethical norms, which must be derived from sources independent of any revelation or mythology. Religious faith has its own field of activity, and can coexist freely with other forms of spiritual life provided the division of functions is respected; the educational system should not be opposed to religious feelings, but should on the contrary encourage them. But the natural sense of goodness, independent of religious and metaphysical opinions, is a sufficient basis for morality. This sense is not the product of knowledge either, since value-judgements are radically different from cognitive acts, and moral norms are not to be derived from scientific observation. The moral consciousness involves ideals that are in a sense contrary to the natural course of things; their validity does not depend on empirical factors, though they vary in specific content according to social and psychological circumstances.

In retrospect it can be said that Labriola's attraction to Marxism and socialism was a natural outcome of his intellectual background and that, both in philosophy and in politics, it represented a strengthening and specialization of already existing tendencies. Philosophically he was most influenced from this point of view by two very different teachers, Hegel and Herbart. From the former he learnt to think in terms of great historical concepts and to interpret cultural values as manifestations of the eras to which they belonged: to adopt a relativistic viewpoint and to regard ideas as historical instruments rather than the subjective embodiment of ideal patterns. Hegel also taught Labriola to accept the category of progress while regarding the historical process as a tragic spectacle. Herbart, by contrast, inspired him with a distrust of metaphysics and speculative philosophy, and with a belief in empirical psychology as necessary to the interpretation of civilization. From the political point of view Labriola's socialism stemmed from his radical anticlerical outlook and identification with the people's cause. Even in his Marxist days, however, his anticlericalism was combined with an understanding and a certain sympathy for religious sentiment, though not for the Church as an institution or a political instrument.

4. Philosophy of history

APART from his role as a propagandist, can Labriola be regarded as an independent theoretician or the author of a specific variant of Marxism? It might be said by an ill-disposed reader of his works that their chief difference from contemporary orthodoxy lay in the vague and elusive manner in which he expressed his views. But if we read with closer attention and more goodwill we may come to the conclusion that the generality of his style is not due merely to a preference for rhetoric over precision of thought, but to a distrust of cut-and-dried formulas and a conviction that Marxism is not a 'final', self-sufficient rationalization and schematization of history, but rather a collection of pointers to the understanding of human affairs; these must be imprecise if they are not to degenerate into a dogmatic contempt for the variety of forces at work in history, and thus to reduce complicated social processes to a handful of bloodless 'universal' categories. The individuality of Labriola's Marxism does not consist so much in any combination of theses to be found in his work, as in the elasticity and openness of general formulas which enable Marxism to be enriched by ideas from other sources. It is easier, perhaps, to characterize his philosophy by those elements of hard-core orthodoxy that are absent from it. Contrary to Togliatti's claim, Labriola did not seek to make Marxism an integrated, self-contained system, but wished to preserve a certain degree of imprecision so as to prevent the doctrine from ossifying into self-satisfaction and an imagined mastery over universal knowledge. He took seriously the description of scientific socialism as a 'critical' theory—not in the sense that it attacked other doctrines, for the most obscurantist sect may do this, and the more obscurantist it is, the more violent the attack—but in the sense that it regarded no truths as everlasting, recognized that all established principles were provisional, and was ready to drop or modify its own ideas if experience should so dictate.

It is characteristic of Labriola that he approached Marxism from a historical and not a sociological point of view. In his eyes it was not a matter of discovering general, permanent relationships between artificially distinguished aspects of social life, but of describing a single, unique, actual historical process, having regard to the whole variety of forces at work in it. As he wrote in his lectures of 1902–3,

> History is always concerned with the heterogeneous—with nations conquering other nations, classes oppressing other classes, priests ruling the laity and layfolk getting the better of priests. All these are sociological facts, but they do not fit into sociological schemata: they can only be understood empirically, and this is the whole difficulty of historical investigation. The abstractions of sociology give us no clue as to why, in the general process of the development of the bourgeois classes, it was only in France that the events occurred which we call the Great Revolution.

Labriola was thus very far from believing that the notion of 'class' enables us to interpret the whole of past history and to foretell the future. He accepted the Marxist position that individuals do not choose their social links at will, and he opposed the rationalist delusion that social phenomena can be reconstructed on the basis of deliberate behaviour of individuals. The social bond is not the result of anyone's intention. 'Society is given *a priori*, since we know nothing of man as a *ferus primaevus*. The original datum is society as a whole: classes and individuals appear as elements in that whole and as determined by it.' (*Da un secolo all'altro*, VI.) But it is one thing to recognize the objectivity of the social bond and another to claim that it can be reduced to a mere relationship of classes. Schemes of history which represent it as a uniform, continuous, self-contained process are criticized by Labriola on four main grounds: the independence of the national principle, the irreducibility of religious sentiment, the discontinuity of progress, and the unpredictability of the future.

Nationality signifies to Labriola not only a social reality *sui generis* but also a value *sui generis*, irreducible to other ties and values. As he wrote to Sorel (14 May 1897),

Languages are not accidental variants of some universal Volapük but, on the contrary, are much more than purely external methods of denoting and communicating thoughts and feelings. They determine the conditions and limits of our internal life, which for this and many other reasons expresses itself in national forms and not in merely accidental ones. If there are 'internationalists' who are unaware of this they can only be called amorphous and woolly-minded—like those who derive their knowledge not from old apocalyptic sources but from Bakunin, the master of appearances, who even wanted equalization of the sexes.

In his lectures of 1903 Labriola used Hegel's division of nations into those historically passive and historically active, but did not seek to justify this in specifically Marxist terms. The category of nationhood is not, with him, merely a feature of tactical reasoning (though of course he defended self-determination, especially for Italy and Poland), but stands for an independent historical reality; in this he differs from the majority of Marxists.

As to religion, while he was less explicit during his Marxist period than in *Morality and Religion*, it is clear that he regarded religious sentiments (as distinct from theological systems and church institutions) as something other than the self-delusion of primitive minds, or a deception practised upon mankind, or the result of a transitory class situation. In a lecture on popular education (1888) he advocated non-religious schools but emphasized that he did not want to introduce anti-religious elements. 'It is an historical misfortune that we have in our country the Pope, a spiritual leader claiming territorial power; but let us not add to this the misfortune that would result from turning tens of thousands of teachers into anti-Popes.' The problem in any case was not a purely political one. Essentially there was no opposition between religion and other forms of culture. 'Culture is no enemy to any sincere, healthy manifestation of the spirit, and it is certainly no barrier to deep religious feelings. These have nothing to do with theological systems imposed by the orthodox, or with priestly rule: indeed, I will go further and say that all forms of priesthood which elevate it into a caste and a system of privilege are a denial of those feelings.' Similarly, in the lecture *On Socialism* he declares that socialists are the truest disciples of Jesus and the only Christians of the present age. These are not mere rhetorical flourishes, as may be seen from Labriola's notes for the lectures that were to form the last part of his *magnum opus* on historical materialism. Here we read:

Is religion a permanent fact or simply an invention, an aberration and a deceit? Certainly it is a need. Were the nineteenth-century rationalists therefore mistaken? Yes. It is not true, then, that the last century was an age of science? This is only partially the case. Is it then impossible to suppress religion? The fact that it is sometimes suppressed proves a certain thesis but does not define its limits. Is it the case, then, that man can never become master of the natural and historical world by virtue of his own intellect, moral autonomy and aesthetic sensibility? Yes and no.

These remarks are not clear enough to serve as the basis of an explicit theory of religion. They indicate, however, that Labriola never accepted the conventional Marxist view that religion is a historically explicable self-delusion and an instrument of mystification for class purposes, and is destined to die out as class antagonisms fade away and minds become more enlightened. Labriola distinguished clericalism and theological rationalizations of faith from the religious sense itself, and seemed to regard the latter as a permanent form of spiritual culture. This in itself suffices to create doubts as to whether he should be reckoned as a member of the Marxist camp by the criteria of his time. True, in a letter to Sorel of 2 July 1897 he says that the men of the future 'will probably give up any transcendent explanation of the practical problems of daily life, since *primus in orbe deos fecit timor*'. But this does not conflict with the remarks quoted above, since he did not regard the religious sense as offering 'explanations' of any kind: it was not for religion, he thought, to compete with science or to usurp its role in any way.

As regards the idea of progress, Labriola considers it necessary to the understanding of history but emphasizes that its role is a normative one. He repeatedly rejects the prejudice that history is a tale of continuous progress, in particular if this means that it is free from regression or that all civilizations have to go through the same stages of development. In *Problems of the Philosophy of History* (1887) he observes that faith in progress was a superstition that took the place of theology and was encouraged by Hegel's monistic philosophy of history: this, however, became a Procrustean bed for the historical sciences concerned with forms of social life such as law, language, and art. There was in fact no unity of history or constant trend for the better.

> The original centres of civilization are many in number and cannot be reduced by any sleight of hand: that is, the sources of civilized life cannot be brought to an identity of form or of origin. Civilizations, linked by particular relationships, develop in accordance with their own traditions and by the interchange of values: we must therefore recognize that primary factors have a modifying effect on secondary influences ... The consideration of so many separate and independent series of events, so many factors that resist simplification, so many unintended coincidences ... makes it seem highly improbable, in fact no better than a delusion, to suppose that there is at the root of everything a real unity, a permanent subject of experience, constituting the essential meaning of every kind of impulse and activity from the earliest times to the present.

In short, there is no over-all 'meaning' of history, no rationalization of its actual course. 'The observation of human affairs obliges us to recognize that there is both progress and regression: many nations have been destroyed, many enterprises have failed and much human effort has been expended in vain.' The idea of progress enables us to say that some things have improved—for example, slavery has been abolished, men are equal before the law—but it is not a universal law of history, and indeed there are no such laws.

> People have sought to extend to the whole human race the schema, worked out in France, of the transition from a serf economy to an economy of subjects and then of wage-earners; but anyone using this sacred formula will understand nothing, for instance, about fourteenth-century England. And what about the brave Norwegians, who were never serfs or subjects? How is it that in Germany beyond the Elbe, serfdom arose and developed *after* the Reformation, or that the European bourgeoisie instituted slavery afresh in America? (*Da un secolo all'altro*, IV)

Labriola in his Marxist phase believed more strongly than ever that the category of progress is not inherent in events but is a way of interpreting them—it provides us with an evaluating perspective, but does not emerge from the facts themselves.

This is particularly important when we are considering the future as well as the past. Labriola believed that there was good ground for expecting the advent of socialism, but he also believed that the future was undecided. A remark in his last work is directed not only against Hegel but against the commonest interpretations of Marxism: 'The wisest and most telling objection to all systems of the philosophy of history is that put forward by Wundt, namely that we do not know where history ends. That is, if I understand him rightly, we never see history as a completed whole' (ibid. I). And, further on: 'Socialism is an active reality so long as it is the manifestation and war-cry of an actual struggle; but when it starts to regard prophesies of the future as a measure and criterion of the present, it becomes no more than a Utopia' (ibid. III).

Since Labriola disputes the continuity, unity, and regularity of the historical process, it clearly may be asked in what sense he accepts the Marxist philosophy of history. He professes to be a historical materialist, but he gives an elastic sense to this concept and to the relationship between the base and the superstructure. According to him, the essence of historical materialism is contained in two statements. First, men have created political and legal institutions 'in proportion to the prevailing economic structure'. Second, religious and moral ideas 'always correspond to particular social conditions'; this statement he describes as 'more hypothetical', and he draws from it the unexpected inference that 'the history of religion and ethics is psychology in the broad sense of the term' (lectures of 1902). In his principal work he states that history 'is based' on technical development, that ideas 'do not fall from heaven', that moral ideas 'in the last resort' correspond to economic conditions, and so on. Such loose formulations as these were to be found in Marxist literature, but by the end of the century they were no longer specifically Marxist except for Engels's reference to determination 'in the last resort', the meaning of which has never been elucidated. Labriola's work on historical materialism is largely a critique of what he considered vulgar interpretations of Marxism as a theory of the 'preponderance' or 'dominance' of the 'economic factor' in history. The historical process, he argues, develops 'organically', and the so-called 'factors' therein are conventional abstractions and not social realities. They are necessary to the historian as conceptual instruments and to delimit the sphere of his investigation, but they should not be hypostatized into separate historical forces as a prelude to assigning one of them causal priority over all the rest. Historical events cannot be 'translated' into economic terms, although 'in the last resort' they may be explained by economic structures and these structures may, in the long run, give rise to 'corresponding' political and legal institutions.

In general, it must be acknowledged that Labriola did not help to dispel the obscurity of the general tenets of historical materialism, though he tried to give them as undogmatic a sense as possible. Like Engels, he believed in the interrelation of all fields of human activity, and the independent force of the crystallized tradition of institutions and ideologies. It is not clear, however, what boundaries he assigns to determination by 'economic structures' and how far historical materialism, thus understood, differs from the contention, which was already a commonplace by the late nineteenth century, that both institutions and ideas are affected by the relations of production.

Another characteristic feature of Labriola's ideas—thought here again he expresses himself in generalities—is his opposition to the naturalist interpretation of history. In his view, to say that human history is a continuation of natural history is so abstract as to be meaningless. History is concerned with the artificial environment which men have created and which reacts upon them. Social ties, it is true, are formed independently of human intentions, but human beings develop both actively and passively, determining historical conditions and being determined by them.

Observations in this sense ('Man is both the subject and object of history', etc.) are too indefinite, however, to serve as the basis of an investigatory method. The Marxists who use them generally refer to them as a 'dialectic', as though this term denoted no more than common-sense, all-purpose formulas such as 'not only . . . but also', 'both . . . and', 'on the one hand . . . on the other', and so forth. Historical materialism in such watered-down terms may provide a contrast to the type of history, such as St. Augustine's, which relates everything to designs of Providence; but it does not constitute a specific method over and beyond what every historian is prepared to recognize.

As to the meaning of socialism, Labriola does not seem to go beyond the views commonly formulated by socialists in his day. It denotes the collective ownership of means of production, the right to work, the abolition of competition, the principle 'to each according to his deserts'. It does not mean abandoning any of the achievements of modern times as regards political emancipation and the rights of the individual. Socialists do not set out to abolish freedom and equality before the law, but to enrich them by destroying the bondage and inequality that result from privilege and private ownership. The general tendency of socialism is to decentralize power and economic institutions, not to centralize them. The state will disappear with the class struggle; socialism will remove contingency from human life. While endorsing all this, Labriola avoids committing himself to the 'historical necessity' of socialism. He writes that capitalism 'prepares the way' for a socialist society, that socialist ideas are not a moral condemnation of capitalist exploitation but the recognition of a historical tendency, and that socialism 'is not a subjective critique of things, but the discovery of a self-criticism inherent in them'. All this, however, does not add up to a belief in the inevitability of a socialist future. Labriola also did not hold that socialism could only come about by a violent revolution, but hoped that the new social forms could be grafted by degrees on to the 'common stock of liberal institutions' (lectures of 1902), a view close to Bernstein's 'evolutionism'. True, he opposed revisionism in a letter to Hubert Lagardelle published in *Le Mouvement socialiste*, but the grounds of his objection are not clear, except that he accuses Bernstein of writing about everything at once and of being the spokesman of those who abandon socialism in disappointment because changes do not come soon enough. In the same way Labriola's polemics against writers such as Masaryk, Croce, and Sorel, who claimed that Marxism was breaking down, are very general in character and are rather a proclamation of loyalty to the Marxist camp than an objective contribution to its defence.

One of the reasons which, on his own showing, inclined Labriola towards Marxism was his dislike of metaphysical speculations and the *esprit de système*; he also emphasized the role of positivism in providing the basis for a philosophy that 'does not anticipate reality, but is contained in it' (letter to Sorel, 24 May 1897). The theme that philosophy is the self-revelation of reality rather than the intellectual pursuit of a hidden essence recurs frequently in Labriola's writings, where it is linked to the special position of Marxism as a philosophy of praxis. Labriola uses this term in a different sense from most of the orthodox, who were content with Engels's remarks on the practical role of human activity as a means of checking the validity of knowledge and identifying the scientific problems that required solution. 'The process of praxis comprehends nature or the historical evolution of man, but in speaking of praxis from the integral point of view we imply the overcoming of the opposition between theory and practice as it is vulgarly conceived' (Labriola to Sorel, 10 May 1897). Historical materialism 'takes as its point of departure praxis, i.e. the development of effectuality, and, as it is a theory of labouring mankind, it treats science itself as labour' (ibid., 28 May 1897). These remarks too are somewhat disconnected and reflect a tendency of mind rather than a clear-cut theory. It may, however, be said in very general terms that Labriola conceives of human intellectual activity, whether philosophy or science, as an aspect of practical life and not as the quest for a 'truth' waiting to be discovered: his historicism thus apparently admits of no cognitive values other than pragmatic ones, from the point of view of society and history as opposed to the individual. In other words, he appears to think that human thought is part of a historical process, and not a description of the world that can lay claim to 'objective' accuracy independent of time and circumstances. Historicism of this type dispenses with the notion of transcendental truth and ascribes a functional character to all human knowledge. If this was Labriola's view, he was in agreement with the young Marx and not with Engels's positivism. For, if praxis signifies the whole of man's part in history, the value of intellectual production as an aspect of that whole is to be measured by the mind's ability to 'express' changing historical situations, and not by the correspondence between some 'objective' universe and the description of it. This line of reasoning was later followed by Gramsci, probably under Labriola's influence.

Labriola's critique of agnosticism is on similar lines. He does not adopt the naïve attitude of Engels, who argued that when we learn something we did not know before, the 'thing in itself' becomes a 'thing for us'; but he considered agnosticism to be not so much false as meaningless. His view was that the category of the Unknowable is one that our minds simply cannot frame, so that any agnostic formula involves a concept to which no meaning can be attached. 'We can only think about what is given in experience, taking that term in its widest sense': thus he wrote to Sorel on 24 May 1897, and in the next letter he expressed his view more fully. 'Everything that is knowable can be known and will be known "at infinity", and anything that is not knowable does not concern us in the realm of knowledge . . . It is mere fantasy to suppose that our minds can apprehend, as existing *in actu*, an absolute difference between what is knowable and unknowable in itself.' Hence the absurdity of Herbert Spencer, who spoke of the Unknowable as the limit of the knowable, and in so doing implied that something could be known about it. This criticism is in harmony with Labriola's functional and historical view of knowledge and his treatment of cognition not as unlocking the secrets of Being 'in itself 'but as an articulation of the practical behaviour of human societies. From this point of view there can certainly be no such category as that of the Unknowable. Labriola, however, did not attempt, as he should on his own premises, to discover the social and historical significance of agnosticism: he merely stigmatized it as 'cowardly resignation', while not accepting the crude explanation that it was a symptom of the decline of bourgeois civilization.

Despite his dislike of metaphysics and his radical 'humanization' and historicization of knowledge, Labriola did not advance any theory of the 'demise of philosophy'. In his view the conformity of philosophy with science was an ideal result that could hardly be expected in the foreseeable future; meanwhile philosophical reflection had its own purpose, namely to anticipate problems not yet taken up by science or, as Herbart observed, to build general concepts that imparted unity to the results of experience.

■ ■ ■

In spite of the imprecision of his writings, Labriola played an important part in the history of Marxism. His was probably the first attempt to reconstruct Marxism as a philosophy of historical praxis, treating this as a concept in terms of which all aspects of human life should be interpreted, including intellectual activity and its product. He was thus opposed to the scientistic ideology that dominated Marxism in his day. The doctrine outlined in his works was revived in the twentieth century by Gramsci and Lukács among others, inspired by the publication of Marx's early writings. This version gave new life to the idea of humanism as an epistemological standpoint, treating human history as the boundary of attainable knowledge and re-stressing the relativistic aspect of Marxist doctrine.

IX

Ludwik Krzywicki: Marxism as an Instrument of Sociology

MARXIST THEORETICIANS may be divided into two broad intellectual categories. The first consists of those whose interest centres on Marxism itself, and who study the problems of philosophy, history, economics, or sociology for the purpose of demonstrating the correctness of Marxism. They are, as it were, professional Marxists, concerned to vindicate the doctrine in every branch of human thought. They may interpret it in different ways, but each of them is determined to prove that his interpretation is closest to the spirit of Marxism conceived as a pre-existing whole. They are imbued with 'orthodoxy' in the sense that, whatever they are engaged in, they never forget that the purpose of all their endeavours is to defend and exalt the doctrine of which they are custodians. They generally regard Marxism as self-sufficient and embracing every need, and they seldom refer to any other philosophy except to criticize it (apart, of course, from the pre-Marxist writers who have been canonized as 'sources'). At the time we are concerned with, the outstanding representatives of this type were Plekhanov, Lafargue, Lenin, and Rosa Luxemburg.

The second category comprises sociologists, philosophers, or historians who make use of Marxist conclusions as an aid to solving the problems of their respective disciplines. Marxism is to them a means, not an end: they are not interested in proving it right, but in understanding social phenomena. They are not regarded as orthodox by writers of the former class, who treat them with suspicion or disdain, realizing that they cannot be counted on to support the cause at any given moment. They do not assume that Marxism implicitly contains the answers to all important questions and that one has only to look properly in order to find them; they are indifferent to doctrinal purity and are prepared to use the work of Marxists and non-Marxists alike.

Ludwig Krzywicki was one of the outstanding members of this second category. His numerous works are almost entirely in Polish, except for a few Russian translations and minor contributions in other languages, and he therefore had no direct influence on the main stream of European Marxism. In Poland, however, he had a strong intellectual and moral influence on two or three generations of the intelligentsia, and played the chief part in familiarizing social and human scientists with Marxist concepts.

Krzywicki belonged to the last generation in which it was possible for a highly gifted and industrious person to master almost the whole of contemporary knowledge on social problems. Accordingly, he covered an extremely wide field as an investigator, teacher, and publicist. The subjects of his works include Slav archaeology, demography and statistics, fairy-tales and folklore, primitive societies, modern literature, the details of political and economic life in many countries of the world, questions of the family, religion, and education, the psychology of artists, parapsychology, agriculture, and foreign exchange problems. His chief interest, however, was social anthropology, the beliefs and customs of primitive peoples and the psychology of communities. He paid much attention to phenomena of social pathology, in which he hoped to discern causes and effects that were less evident in normal conditions: cases of mass delusion, moral infection, collective hallucination, panic, massacre, ecstasy, religious and political crazes, the psychology of martyrs, sadists, and cannibals. His literary style, apart from some youthful articles, is descriptive and not aggressive, but is permeated by an ideological approach: a sense of solidarity with the downtrodden, revulsion against capitalist society in which everything was for sale, disgust with urban civilization, and the dream of a society bound together by goodwill after the fashion of primitive communism. He did not engage in party activities, however, and only belonged for a brief period to the political socialist movement.

1. Biographical note

Ludwik Krzywicki (1859–1941) was born at Płock in Russian Poland: like most of the Polish intelligentsia of his generation, he belonged to a family of impoverished gentry (*szlachta*). He grew up under the shadow of repression following the 1863 insurrection: police terror, enforced Russification of the educational system, and a general atmosphere of impotent discontent. The landowning classes were falling into economic and cultural decline; industry, however, was on the up grade. Politically and culturally, Russian Poland did not begin to revive until the late 1870s. Meanwhile, as a result of the growth of industry and the defeat of hopes for early political liberation, there came into being the slogan of 'organic work'; Poland's national life was to be rebuilt by means of education, industrial activity, technical skills and rationalist attitudes in place of romanticism, rebellion, and conspiracy. The philosophical basis of this outlook was Western evolutionary positivism as expounded by Spencer, Darwin, and Taine. Krzywicki, as a young publicist, made it the first object of his attack, while at the same period young student groups began to seek new ideologies inspired by either nationalism or socialism.

In 1878 Krzywicki entered the University of Warsaw, where he studied mathematics. While still at school he had come into contact with socialist ideas, chiefly in a Saint-Simonist form; at the University he read *Capital* and was convinced by its arguments. Together with Stanisław Krusiński (1857–86) and Bronisław Białobłocki (1861–88), both of whom studied in Russia, he founded the first Marxist group in Poland and introduced its ideas to the reading public; either he nor his fellow students, however, were orthodox Marxists in the strict sense. Białobłocki published essays on aesthetics and the theory of literature under the general influence of Chernyshevsky, while Krusiński's background was mainly positivist and scientistic. Both died too young to exert any real influence on Marxist thought. They and Krzywicki were in loose touch with the first Polish socialist party, known as the Proletariat. This was an underground body, founded in 1881 by Ludwik Waryński and others; it was broken up by the authorities and its leaders were hanged in 1885, the first of a long line of martyrs for Marxist socialism. (Socialist ideas had been current in Polish intellectual life for the past half-century, especially among the *émigrés* who fled from Poland after the insurrection of 1830.)

Krzywicki began his career as a publicist in 1883 with articles criticizing Herbert Spencer and his Polish followers. In the same year he was expelled from the University for taking part in a political demonstration. He emigrated to Leipzig, where he prepared for publication a Polish translation of Volume I of *Capital* by the Krzywicki-Krusiński group; this appeared in parts between 1884 and 1890. After studying anthropology, sociology, and political economy at Leipzig Krzywicki went to Switzerland (where he met German and Russian socialist *émigrés*, including Kautsky and Bernstein) and, at the beginning of 1885, to Paris. During this period he published in Polish *émigré* journals several articles in a revolutionary Marxist vein. In 1885 he returned to Poland, but to avoid arrest stayed for the first year in Galicia (under Austrian rule). He moved to Płock towards the end of 1886 and settled in Warsaw in the middle of 1888, writing extensively and taking part in numerous educational activities, legal and underground. Clandestine socialist organizations were just beginning to re-form in Poland: Krzywicki was closely connected with the Union of Polish Workers, founded in 1889, which concentrated on the economic struggle. When the workers' movement crystallized into two mutually hostile camps, the PPS and the SDKPiL, Krzywicki became a member of neither, though he contributed to PPS journals from time to time. Between 1890 and 1910 his political writing became distinctly milder in tone as his mind moved in the direction of evolutionary socialism. At this time he also wrote his most important theoretical works on historical materialism, published in 1923 as *Sociological Studies,* and several books on ethnography and anthropology: *Peoples. An Outline of Ethnic Anthropology* (1893); *A course of Systematic Anthropology. Physical*

Races (1897); *Psychic Races* (1902); *The Wisdom of Primitive Peoples* (1907); 'The Sociology of Herbert Spencer' (in *Przegląd filozoficzny*, 1904). His articles on literary subjects and on urban civilization were collected in a volume *In the Abyss* (1909).

Except for visits to Berlin and the U.S.A. in 1892–3 Krzywicki remained in Warsaw until the First World War, becoming an acknowledged authority on scientific and social questions. After the war he taught at Warsaw University and elsewhere and was Director of the Institute of Social Economy, which studied conditions in Poland for the purpose of working out economic guidelines and which, in 1922, produced under Krzywicki's editorship the first serious studies of economic and social life in Soviet Russia. During the post-war years he completely abandoned the idea of revolution and, like many European socialists, regarded the Soviet regime as an attempt to violate economic laws. He remained a socialist to the end, however, while believing that socialist ideals could be realized gradually by the rationalization and democratization of the capitalist economy. He also continued to believe in the validity of the principal Marxist criteria for the study of social conditions. He died in Warsaw during the German occupation.

2. Critique of the biological theory of society

KRZYWICKI's writings in the 1880s did much to spread the knowledge of Marxism in Poland, but they did not contribute a great deal to theory and for the most part followed the standard version of historical materialism. They are largely polemical in tone. In his critique of Spencer and social Darwinism Krzywicki argued that the evolutionists, constructing models of society after the pattern of a living organism, were in effect propagating the ideology of class solidarity, endeavouring to put an end to the class struggle, and closing their eyes to the dissolution of traditional bonds in a society rent by contradictions and competition. He also joined issue with the social-Darwinist ideas invoked by ideologists of the Manchester school. Competition and the social conflict could not be treated as a particular case of the biological struggle for survival of the fittest: they were caused not by biological circumstances, but by the anarchy of production, which was a phase of social development and not an eternal law of nature. Nor was it true that the fittest survived in present conditions: what ensured survival was, as a rule, not ability but privilege. Krzywicki attacked the biological view of society on other occasions also, for example in reply to Gobineau's racialist philosophy of history and anthropological concept of the nation, and Lombroso's theory of criminality. The so-called 'spirit of a race' was not, Krzywicki held, a biological category but the legacy of historical conditions. Racialism could not account for changes in social institutions, or the fact that they differed in societies that were racially akin, or were similar in societies of different race; but all these things could be explained if social institutions and ideologies were seen as dependent on changes in the method of production and exchange. As for nations, Krzywicki agreed with Kautsky that they were not anthropological entities, but cultural and therefore historical ones. The national idea in Europe was mainly the creation of the commercial class, for whom a centralized nation-state provided an advantageous legal framework: true, ethnic unity had preceded the growth of national markets, but the latter had stimulated it into awareness of itself.

In the same way, Krzywicki held, the fashionable theories of Lombroso were vitiated by being based on a class approach instead of a scientific one: the Italian physician held that crime was due to heredity or innate anthropological traits, whereas it was in fact due to social conditions, poverty, and ignorance.

The anarchist ideology too was based on erroneous biological theories. It was a mistake to hold that anarchism differed from socialism as to means but agreed with it as to the purpose of the struggle. The anarchists believed in a permanent conflict between the individual and society, and saw history as a process in which human beings were constantly subjugated by institutions. They therefore refused to take part in a struggle that involved using political and parliamentary institutions, preferring to employ all their efforts to paralyse the existing state machine in the hope that men's benevolent instincts would then suffice to do away with social bondage and privileges. Proclaiming the slogan 'The worse, the better', they regarded all means as legitimate, including wholesale pillage, and welcomed to their ranks the lumpenproletariat and other *déclassé* elements. The socialists, by contrast, regarded social development not in terms of pathology but as a necessary evolution, and they expected the liberation of the individual to be brought about not by kindly instincts or eternal moral precepts, but by human beings exercising collective authority over the powers of nature. Anarchism, in their view, was a sterile revolt by pre-capitalist forms of production, ruined by the progressive concentration of capital.

3. Prospects of socialism

KRZYWICKI's attack was directed, finally, against all solidaristic doctrines and movements—whether attempts at a Christian pseudo-socialism, combating capitalism in the name of feudal institutions and seeking a solution of social problems in a system of tutelage over the workers, or democratic ideologies which glossed over the class system by the undifferentiated concept of the 'people'. What such democrats called the 'people' consisted of several strata whose interests by no means always coincided: workers, rich peasants, small tradesmen, craftsmen, etc. Only in backward Poland was it possible for such a vague form of democracy to survive: in the more developed countries the various strata had separated and were at odds with one another. Only capitalists and the working class really stood for progress in the sphere of production, while the other classes, especially the peasantry, represented bygone forms that were doomed to destruction by the development of modern industry.

In all these arguments Krzywicki's viewpoint is that of classical Marxism. He stands for the independence of the proletariat as the only class that can liberate society on the basis of technical progress and not of hopeless attempts to revive a pre-capitalist system. He confidently expects the middle classes to disappear as the concentration of capital increases. He accepts the basic principles of historical materialism and especially the view that historical development takes place when spontaneous technical progress comes into conflict with the politico-legal system and calls forth ideas which lead to the alteration of that system. In all societies, from the most barbarous onwards, the distribution of goods, and hence the class division, depends on the mode of production. Economic conditions 'account for' the genesis of ideologies or 'are the basis' of political institutions; moral and political ideas arise in response to social needs as the necessary forms in which men envisage their own interests and are capable of uniting to defend them. Ideas are not only a powerful agent of social development but a necessary condition of institutional change; however, they are secondary in the sense that they come into being as an articulation of previously unconscious interests, and can only become instruments of social cohesion if the necessary material conditions of such cohesion are already present, namely the community of certain interests and the divergence of others. Ideas that are not thus rooted in social needs are condemned to impotence, and this applies to all utopias and dreams of a perfect society. But ideas that organize and bring into the light of consciousness men's existing conditions and needs are necessary for the destruction of any social order that has become a brake on technical progress and thus an enemy of the class which stands for such progress.

The socialist revolution does not figure largely in Krzywicki's early works, even those published out of reach of the Tsarist censorship. It is clear, however, that on this point too he shared the view of orthodox European Marxists, namely that at a certain stage of development the contradiction between technical progress and the system of private property would lead to the revolutionary overthrow of capitalism. The crisis could not be brought about artificially but must be the result of the spontaneous maturing of capitalism; the business of socialists was to organize the class-consciousness of the proletariat and take control of the revolutionary process at the right moment. However, even in his early period Krzywicki does not appear to have believed in the inevitability of progress or of socialism itself. In an article entitled 'An Outline of Social Evolution', which appeared in *Głos* in 1887, he wrote that new productive forces did not always succeed in breaking up old societies, as witness India, where the caste system had proved stronger than other factors and condemned the country to centuries of stagnation. In his preface to the Polish translation of Kautsky's book on the *Economic Doctrines of Karl Marx* he stated that the new order that would result from the evolution of capitalism and the polarization of classes might be the work of either the proletariat or the bourgeoisie. In the former case there would be collective ownership of the means of production; in the latter, private ownership and wage-labour would remain but be subordinated to the state organization. In later articles he repeated this view more than once. His ideal was a socialist society with industrial democracy as its chief feature; he thought it possible, however, that capitalism would succeed in curing the anarchy of production and competition by transforming the whole of production into a state monopoly. This would mean a kind of state capitalism more or less similar to that envisaged by Rodbertus or Brentano: the workers would enjoy social security and economic planning would be introduced, but the basic features of socialism would be missing, namely the abolition of wage-labour and the control of production by the entire working class.

In his discussion of early society Krzywicki shows special sympathy towards primitive communism, which he considered to be the most democratic system known to history. Lafargue, who shared this view, was not an ethnologist by profession; but Krzywicki's scientific interest was no doubt reinforced by the vision of a community of equals, united in mutual respect and eschewing slave labour. His investigations were based on the theories of Lewis H. Morgan, whose classic work Krzywicki translated into Polish. The study of primitive societies, which he continued throughout his life, led him in course of time to conclusions that were hard to reconcile with historical materialism, or at any rate limited its scope.

4. Mind and production. Tradition and change

KRZYWICKI regarded himself as an adherent of the materialist interpretation of history. However, when we look at his best-known expositions of the theory we are struck by the extent of the reservations with which he accepts the rules of Marxist historiosophy.

In the first place, he regarded historical materialism as completely independent of any specific philosophical viewpoint, materialistic or other. To emphasize this point he referred to historical 'materialism' with the second word in quotation marks, indicating that he regarded it as conventional and misleading. He seldom dealt with epistemological or metaphysical problems, but from certain articles ('The Economy Principle in Philosophy', 1886; 'Qui pro Quo' in *Widnokręgi* (*Horizons*), 1914), it is clear that, like many in his time, he took a phenomenalist view, close to that of the empiriocritics and certain Kantists. He states that we apprehend the world in our own human fashion, making distinctions and categories that are instruments of prediction but not objective realities: we create 'objects' out of impressions, distinguish 'force' from 'matter' and impose 'laws' on nature after the manner of human legislation. There are in fact no natural laws independent of human perception, but within the limits of that perception we can express the relations between phenomena in cause-and-effect terms that admit of prediction: all this is to be understood as independent of metaphysical assumptions, particularly 'materialistic' ones. The whole evolution of the world is originally a construction of the mind, and the reason we project it on to reality is that in present-day society men are the servants and not the masters of the machines they have created.

The 'secondary' nature of mental phenomena thus has nothing to do with any metaphysical opposition between spirit and matter, but is a sociological fact signifying that material needs exist before they are consciously articulated.

The question arises, however, within what limits we are justified in accepting the dependence of mental phenomena on 'material' conditions of life. Krzywicki does not refer here to the Marxist opposition between base and superstructure, but he illustrates by various examples, some classic and others less so, the way in which technical changes give rise to new needs that cannot be satisfied within the existing legal order. The new problems arise spontaneously but can only be solved by conscious activity, with the aid of an ideology that plays an indispensable part in organizing social forces hemmed in by the political system of the day. Throughout history there have been arbitrary Utopias or ideals unrelated to any real economic tendencies: these are mere 'chips and shavings' of the historical process. The seminal ideas of history do not operate by any immanent power of their own but because they express the as yet unconscious aspirations of new sections of society for whom the old conditions have become a strait-jacket. In this way Krzywicki accounts on classical lines for such principles as personal freedom and equality before the law, the condemnation of theft, the right to lend at interest, and the cult of knowledge—all resulting from the development of trade and the increased importance of the bourgeoisie in Western Europe. He cites the case of Thomas Münzer, who dreamt of an egalitarian evangelistic community but, when it came to practical reforms, could propose no more than changes that were feasible because they reflected the interests of the merchant class.

This does not mean, however, that ideological phenomena can do no more than 'express' existing needs and organize forces that are already present in society. Historical materialism explains the genesis of ideas, or rather of those ideas that have had an effect on history. But the idea, once come to maturity, has a life of its own and may call forth new social forces in countries where material conditions have not developed to the point of generating them independently. As a striking example of social evolution being thus hastened by ideas imported from outside, Krzywicki quotes the adoption of Roman civil law by European countries in the late Middle Ages. This system of law belonged to a society in which commerce was well established, and it was therefore suited to late medieval society, where the commercial economy was rapidly gaining ground. But the adoption of Roman law itself did a great deal to accelerate the 'material' process that was then beginning. 'But for the monuments of Roman law the development of Europe might have taken place some centuries later and followed a different course' ('Movements of Ideas', 1897, in *Sociological Studies*, p. 47). Thus a legal doctrine or any other ideology, while 'secondary' at the time of its origin, might subsequently, in other circumstances, become a 'primary', creative force—not a mere barometer of change, but a cause of it. In the same way, the socialist ideology in Russia was not the result of the ripening of social conditions there; it was imported from the West and itself contributed to the ripening process, though this fact in turn caused it to assume a different and more 'subjectivist' form.

Another important factor which debars us from assuming a simple correspondence between material and spiritual forms of social life is the independent force of tradition. Institutions, customs, and beliefs that begin as rational attempts to solve the problems of social life generally remain in being and petrify after the circumstances that justified them have changed. Survivals of this kind accumulate through the ages, each generation adding something to the pile, and the total result, which Krzywicki calls the 'historical substratum', is a powerful curb on all human activity. Men are bound by outdated forms long after they could, materially speaking, be jettisoned. The metal axe continues for a long time to be made in the less efficient shape of the stone hatchet; stone buildings and tombs are made to imitate wooden ones; as Morgan pointed out, the names of family relationships in primitive languages reflect a pattern that has ceased to exist in the society in question. New social forces rebel against the weight of tradition, opposing the law of nature to that of history and norms of rationality to inherited standards, but the past continues to impede all our actions and hold up social progress. The final result of any historical process is not what it would be if 'objective conditions' were the sole determinant: it is affected in a marked degree by traditions, made up of customs, beliefs, institutions, local variations of temperament or what is called the 'spirit of a race', which in turn results from the long-term effects of environment on human nature. In consequence, the actual development of society is varied in the extreme and it is hard to discern a uniform schema of evolution. Krzywicki's studies of primitive societies led him to conclude that there was no universal law and that, for example, serfdom was not a necessary stage in all cases. In his later years he reached the unexpected conclusion that conscious human intentions have a greater effect on social processes in primitive societies than in civilized ones, because the former are less encumbered by accumulated material institutions and social ties are therefore less rigid. This observation is in accordance with Krzywicki's frequent criticism of industrial society, in which human personality is almost completely subdued to 'reified' ties and impersonal forms of co-operation, and creativity is stifled by the money-power. This degeneration was especially visible in the big cities, where individuality was drowned in a sea of mediocrity. Like Engels and many other nineteenth-century socialists, Krzywicki thought that one of the chief effects of the new order would be to deurbanize mankind and allow city-dwellers to get 'back to nature'. He did not define socialism in metaphysical terms, but he hoped that human labour and creativity would cease to depend on commercial conditions and that human relations would again be spontaneous and direct. His criticism of contemporary literature was based on the same opposition between personal and anonymous social ties: modernism in art seemed to him a typical product of big-city culture, a rebellion against the omnipotence of exchange-value and the degradation of human beings to the status of machines. It was a fruitless revolt, however, for its only answer to utilitarian culture was to take refuge from the world in a subjective attitude of *soi-disant* independence.

There may be discerned in Krzywicki's writings a tension between two recurrent themes. On the one hand, he makes much use of the category of 'progress', i.e. the extension of man's mastery over natural forces; but, on the other, he emphasizes that as this mastery increases human relations become more and more degraded and impersonal, the mind comes to depend on things, and there is less and less room for individual creativity. No doubt he hoped, like Marx, that the socialization of production would make it possible to reconcile man's dominion over nature with the claims of his personal life, and effect a synthesis of the two. But he did not develop this subject, and his attraction towards primitive peoples and rural life (though elsewhere he insists on its poverty) seems to betray regret for the lost innocence of the 'natural' life.

Another factor which to some extent limits the historical primacy of productive forces is that 'natural selection' in the psychological field continues to operate after the conditions which made it appropriate have ceased to exist. Historical circumstances throw up, for instance, such specific psychological types as the Girondists and the Jacobins, and the results of this selection may in their turn have a significant effect on history. Biological selection, too, may be important in this way. One instance is cannibalism, which Krzywicki, following Krafft-Ebing, considers to be, as a rule, a pathological form of sexual libido rather than the effect of superstition or shortage of food; whatever its causes, it appears that natural selection produces whole pathological peoples imbued with a cannibalistic urge.

Comparing Krzywicki's statements on the importance of various forces in the historical process, we find that the role of productive forces and relations of production in determining change is hedged in with so many restrictions that it is hard to accommodate his views to the canons of Marxism in his day. No particular process or event can in practice be explained simply by the development of productive forces or the conflict between them and political conditions, since there is always a whole series of other factors at work: demography, geography, psychology, tradition (this above all), and ideas from outside the given society. For the same reason there can be no historical schema to fit all societies, and no such thing as historical necessity. What then is left of the idea that the historical process depends on technical change? Krzywicki does not invoke any such vague formula as Engels's reference to determination 'in the last resort'. His view is probably best expressed as follows. All actual social processes are the result of a large variety of causes including technical progress; the special feature of the latter is that, in 'historical' societies at all events, changes take place sooner in this field than in others, so that technical change is the most rapid agent of change in general. There is as yet no mention of 'primacy', but this can be affirmed in the sense that some, though by no means all, important features of political and legal institutions are brought about by human needs arising from progress in the field of production. As to the 'secondary' character of the ideological product, this is not to be taken as meaning that *all* social, religious, or philosophical ideas have come into existence in order to meet material needs (since many utopias, for instance, serve no such purpose), or that the social importance of an idea is necessarily proportionate to the strength of such needs (for ideas themselves may stimulate social processes in the 'material' order. All that is meant by calling ideas or doctrines 'secondary' seems to be that those which show the greatest effectiveness in harnessing human passions, desires and energies owe their strength to preexisting 'material' ties in which human beings are involved irrespective of their will or intention. This, of course, is a very much diluted version of historical materialism. No doubt it enabled Krzywicki to criticize biological theories of history, or those of Tarde or especially Le Bon, who attributed the basic social processes to the human instinct of mimicry. But what remains of Marxism in Krzywicki's theory is little more than what thinkers of every shade were soon taking for granted. Since every process that takes place is the result of various causes and since there is no quantitative measure of the relative importance of those singled out by Marxism, the contention that they are the 'main' or 'most decisive' factor is meaningless. Since 'accidental' facts (i.e. those not due to a 'material' cause) like the adoption of Roman law can affect human destiny for centuries, the importance of 'material' determinants can only be predicated in the most general terms. The technical level of a society and the pattern of material interests can only have a vague bearing on its history: the course and outcome of social conflict and even the ultimate effect of 'objective conditions' are not predetermined by historical laws but belong to the realm of contingency. Historical materialism in this form is not a theory of history or a self-sufficient method of investigation: it is a very general reminder that we should as far as possible look beyond political institutions and ideologies to discern factors and interests arising out of production methods, while not expecting that the latter will provide a complete explanation of the former or enable us to predict their evolution. It is also a reminder that historical processes do not depend on the arbitrary decisions of individuals, that not every plan for reforming the world has any hope of success, that not all ideas take root, and that the social effectiveness of an idea does not depend on its authorship, value, or accuracy. But these propositions too, thanks to the arguments of Marx and his followers, were soon to become generally accepted and were no longer even regarded as specifically Marxist.

Krzywicki's role in the dissemination of Marxist theory is thus an ambiguous one. He did much to introduce Marxist ideas and methods into Polish intellectual life, but the flexibility and eclecticism of his approach was one of the reasons why Polish Marxism failed to take on orthodox forms and tended to dissolve into a general rationalist or historicist trend. In this sense Krzywicki—like Labriola in Italy, though for slightly different reasons—was perhaps, from the Marxist point of view, not so much a battering-ram as a Trojan horse.

X

Kazimierz Kelles-Krauz:
a Polish Brand of Orthodoxy

KAZIMIERZ KELLES-KRAUZ was the chief theoretician and ideologist of the main stream of the Polish socialist movement, i.e. the PPS. Among the Polish Marxists who played an important part in formulating and disseminating the doctrine he also stood closest to the German orthodoxy of his day, though he deviated from it on some major points. Throughout his short adult life he was a party propagandist and advocate of Marxism in a form acceptable to those left-wing socialists who also strongly supported the cause of Polish independence.

Kazimierz Kelles-Krauz (1872–1905) was born at Szczebrzeszyn in the south-eastern part of Russian Poland. While attending the *gimnazjum* at Radom he joined one of the many socialist groups that were being formed among young people in the eighties. Expelled from school and refused entry to Warsaw University, he went to study in Paris in 1892 and there worked for the Association of Polish Socialists Abroad. He published theoretical and political articles in French, German, and *émigré* Polish periodicals defending Marxism against critics of various kinds, including nationalists in the PPS, revisionists, and Rosa Luxemburg. He died of tuberculosis in Vienna. The most important of his many writings are: 'The Law of Revolutionary Retrospection as a Consequence of Economic Materialism' (in *Ateneum*, 1897); *The Class Character of Our Programme* (1894); 'The So-Called Crisis of Marxism' (in *Przegląd filozoficzny*, 1900); and the posthumous works *Economic Materialism* (1908, with a preface by Ludwik Krzywicki) and *Some Basic Principles of the Development of Art* (1905).

Like many Marxist theoreticians of his time Kelles-Krauz took the view that Marxism does not claim to decide philosophical or epistemological questions in the traditional sense but merely asserts its own phenomenalist standpoint, so that historical materialism has only the name in common with materialism considered as a 'substantialist' theory in contrast to a spiritualist one. He agreed with Labriola that Marxism was concerned with the relations between social consciousness and the external world, both regarded as phenomena, and not between 'mind' and 'matter'. The cognitive process was of interest to Marxism only as a social and historical phenomenon, not as a means of getting at 'things in themselves'. Accordingly, Marxism must accept that any given state of knowledge was meaningful only in relation to the whole of a given civilization, and that its truth consisted in its historical function; this meant, however, that the principle of relativism applied to Marxism itself. With reference to the slogan of a 'return to Kant', Kelles-Krauz wrote:

> We should in any case understand this idea somewhat differently: what we would wish to do is to translate the critical standpoint into social terms. We would recall that any society or group, and, what concerns us most, the class to which an individual belongs, imprints a certain stamp on his consciousness, imposing on it *a priori* a certain conception of society and the world, from which he can no more free himself than he can see things otherwise than through his own retina. It follows that the proletariat too must have its own class-conditioned apperception and that its philosophy, like that of all previous classes, is essentially relative and transient: it will cease to be true, or to appear true, when—but not before—the new social apperception of the future classless society takes the place of that resulting from the class struggle. The philosophy of that future society, while deriving from Marxism, must in the nature of things be different and in some ways at least contrary to Marxism as we know it today, but what exactly it will be we cannot tell. (*Economic Materialism*, p. 34)

Kelles-Krauz did not believe, therefore, in any privileged historical situation in which the class viewpoint of the proletariat coincides with a universally scientific or 'objective' viewpoint: in his recognition of the *a priori* principle in history and social affairs he is perhaps closer to Simmel than to Marxism. Within the limits of this relativism he supported the Marxist interpretation of history, while complementing it with observations of his own.

Historical materialism was, in his view, essentially a monistic theory, i.e. it asserted that a single form of human activity, namely the production of the necessities of life and of tools, was sufficient to account for the origin of all other aspects of life: the division of labour, the class structure, the distribution of goods, and all features of the superstructure. Following Cunow and Tugan-Baranovsky, he criticized Engels for holding that, besides material production, the propagation of the species and the forms of family life were a fundamental aspect of human activity that helped to determine social processes. In arguing thus Engels had abandoned the monistic standpoint which was the greatest achievement of Marxism. His mistake had been to confuse the natural process of human reproduction with the socially conditioned forms of the family: the former, being purely physiological, was unchanging and therefore could not explain social evolution, while the latter were dependent on economic conditions. In the same way Kautsky had departed from the monistic standpoint when he maintained that economic conditions could only account for the genesis of the common features of an epoch, but not for particular circumstances or the behaviour of individuals.

It would seem that Kelles-Krauz advocated a highly rigorous interpretation of Marxist 'monism', but in fact he is not consistent on this crucial point. He says that human life is governed by three main factors—the biological characteristics of the species, the natural environment, and social conditions—but that historical changes are the result of technical changes. 'Ethics, law, politics, religion, art, science, philosophy—all these are utilitarian in their origin and essence, and therefore they cannot conflict with the mode of production but must be adapted to it' (*Economic Materialism*, p. 10). But we find in history a tendency for needs to become autonomous. Certain forms of activity, especially intellectual and artistic life, which were originally the instruments of more basic needs, acquire a life of their own: the superstructure reacts on the base and becomes partially independent of it. It is none the less true that forms of social life, deprived of their economic basis, are bound to die out in time, but they generally survive the economic conditions that have brought them about.

All these considerations are consistent with the Marxist stereotypes of the period. Kelles-Krauz, like other Marxists, did not ask how far it made sense to speak of a 'monistic' interpretation of history while at the same time accepting the common-sense view that changes in art, science, philosophy, or religion depend on other factors besides changes in the relations of production—especially the logic of their own internal development and the operation of 'autonomized' needs in respect of each. His thought probably was that all forms of social life can be explained genetically in terms of the relations of production, but he did not see that it is misleading to use the term 'monism' in such a restricted sense.

Comparing the philosophy of Comte to Marxism, Kelles-Krauz says that the two agree in explaining human individuals as the result of many social influences, but also in ascribing a spiritual nature to all social phenomena: from the Marxist point of view, therefore, it is all the same whether we refer the superstructure to the base or 'express' new economic phenomena by new phenomena in the domain of the superstructure. If this is so, it is hard to see in what sense the 'primacy' of relations of production *vis-à-vis* the superstructure can be maintained.

One of the phenomena that are hard to explain on the basis of Marxist schemata is Marxism itself. How is it that the proletarian ideology could come into being and influence large numbers of workers at a time when there was no basis for it in the relations of production? Unlike the capitalist economy, which had a strong basis within the politico-legal framework of feudalism, socialism does not arise spontaneously under capitalism, but is only a dream of the future.

Kelles-Krauz explains this paradox by what he calls, rather pretentiously, the law of 'revolutionary retrospection', whereby 'the ideals that any reform movement seeks to substitute for existing social norms are always similar to the norms of a more or less distant past'. It is of course true enough, though it was known before Kelles-Krauz and hardly deserves to be called a 'law', that new ideologies generally seek support in tradition and present themselves as the revival of modes of thought that have existed at some former time. Such reversions, or *ricorsi* in Vico's language, can be observed throughout the ideological history of the European bourgeoisie, one example being the adoption of a Roman disguise—first republican, then imperial—by revolutionary France. As to the proletariat, the object of its 'retrospect' is primitive communism. Thus, according to Kelles-Krauz, human development proceeds in a spiral fashion by the constant revival of old forms which bear an affinity to new ideas. This explains, among other things, the fact that reactionary ideologies closely resemble those which look towards the future, since both, though for different reasons, criticize the *status quo* in the light of values derived from the past. In France, for instance, the defenders of the medieval guild system join with the syndicalists to attack the liberals. In the same way, ideas that were to form the basis of Marxism—anti-individualism, belief in the regularity of social life, the historical sense as opposed to naïve rationalist utopias—could all be found in the writings of conservatives like Vico, or the French counter-revolutionaries such as de Maistre, Bonald, and Ballanche. Socialism is a reversion to pre-classical antiquity, and this is why the development of Marxism has been so strongly influenced by the investigators of primitive societies—Morgan, Taylor, and Bachofen.

Kelles-Krauz believed that his 'law' could be explained in Marxist terms, but he does not seem to have realized that it limited the application of historical materialism by recalling the importance of autonomous tradition in social development. While upholding the view that Marxism was a 'monistic' philosophy, in his replies to critics he emphasized, like other Marxist writers of his day, that it was a mistake to interpret historical materialism as denying that the superstructure had any effect on the evolution of the base. Like his fellow Marxists he ignored the question how the relative independence of the spiritual life, and of the institutions of the superstructure, could be reconciled with a belief in the 'ultimate cause' of human history, and what limits it imposed on the general formulas of historical materialism.

The same ambiguity may be seen in Kelles-Krauz's arguments on the social significance of art, a subject to which he devoted much attention. On the one hand, art may be explained genetically by utilitarian considerations, whether related to biology (the rudiments of artistic activity can be seen in animals) or to production (rhythm as an aid to work). The development of art is related to conditions of production, for it adapts itself to political or religious aims which in turn depend on class-interests: thus, for instance, the Doric and Ionic styles respectively express the simplicity of patriarchal conditions and the aspirations of a rising class of craftsmen. On the other hand, art itself has played an important part in social change since the very beginning, first as a means of socialization and later as a form for the organization of political and religious needs. In the end it becomes autonomous to such a degree, and aesthetic needs assert themselves so strongly, that the dependence of art on the mode of production, though it never quite ceases, is much reduced. Elsewhere Kelles-Krauz inclines to the opinion that independent aesthetic needs exist from the earliest stage of social life, and even among animals. These various opinions do not form a coherent whole. On this and other subjects Kelles-Krauz was one of the many who, in a praiseworthy attempt to overcome the schematic one-sidedness and 'reductionism' of primitive versions of Marxism, ended by unconsciously reducing historical materialism to the trivial statement that the various aspects of social life to some extent depend, and to some extent do not depend, on methods of production and the conflict of class-interests.

He regarded himself, however, as a Marxist in the full sense of the term, defending the doctrine against such eminent critics as Croce, Sombart, Masaryk, and Kareyev. He opposed the German revisionists but thought the resolutions of the Dresden Congress, condemning revisionism, were ambiguous. The Congress rejected any concession or adaptation to the existing order of society, but, Kelles-Krauz argued, any reformist activity could be described as 'adapting' to capitalism. The Italian socialist party had adopted a better and clearer standpoint at its congress at Imola: the party was reformist because revolutionary, and revolutionary because reformist. In other words, Kelles-Krauz agreed with most socialist theoreticians of the time that the purpose of reforms was to prepare the way for revolution: he did not enter into the complex problems raised by the attempt to combine a revolutionary and a reformist point of view. He combated the revisionism of Eduard David on the agricultural question, sharing the orthodox view that a collectivized economy was better for the land as well as for industry. He also fought against Rosa Luxemburg and the SDKPiL for their opposition to Polish independence, holding that national and social liberation constituted a single aim for the Polish socialist movement. The latter, however, must preserve its class character and not allow the bourgeoisie to exploit it for the purpose of achieving political independence only. Independence was a condition of the social liberation of the proletariat; free Poland was for the proletariat, not the other way about. Rosa Luxemburg was wrong in contending that as Poland was economically integrated with the Russian empire, the revival of an independent Poland would be contrary to objective economic trends. Capitalism developed best in national states, and the bourgeoisie therefore had an interest in Polish independence, while the proletariat would be in a much better position to fight if it were not subjected to national as well as social oppression. Socialists, however, must prevent the proletariat from being used merely for the overthrow of the Tsardom, in such a way that its class identity was obscured.

Kelles-Krauz did not live long enough to write any important books, but, in addition to his role as a popularizer of Marxism, a polemist, and an ideologist of Polish left-wing socialism, he helped to inspire what may be called the conservative side of Marxism. His 'law of revolutionary retrospection' is not a law and is merely commonplace in its general formulation, as is his notion of socialism as a 'spiral regression' to primitive society. But his more detailed observations on tradition as an autonomous force in history, and on the antirationalist historicism of the great conservatives as an important source of Marxism, helped to establish a somewhat different view of Marxism than that of Kautskyan orthodoxy. Kelles-Krauz's version sought to take into account not only history as the realization of 'laws' but also history as contingency: that is, he generally kept in view the fact that the present and future of human societies depend not only on the laws of evolution and on what had to happen according to the doctrine, but also on what simply happened. As to his phenomenalist outlook and interpretation of Marxism as a social theory that did not attempt to solve epistemological or metaphysical problems, Kelles-Krauz was not alone in holding these views: they were shared by many Marxists of his time, especially in the Austrian school. But in this respect too he helped to present a different picture than that offered by Plekhanov, Kautsky, or Lafargue. It is worth noting that during the period of the Second International the idea of Marxism as a form of philosophical materialism scarcely existed in Poland.

XI

Stanisław Brzozowski: Marxism as Historical Subjectivism

꧁

THE WORK of Stanisław Brzozowski is scarcely known outside his own country, yet the intellectual history of twentieth-century Poland cannot be understood without reference to the bizarre and disparate effects of his dynamic writings and personality. A philosopher, critic, and novelist who died of consumption before he was thirty-three and whose activity covered a span of barely ten years, he remains a controversial and painful subject as regards both the value of his work, concerning which opinions are fiercely divided, and the more mysterious elements of his life-story, which are still a puzzle to historians. A provocative writer who was regarded for a time as a prophet of the youthful intelligentsia in revolt against both positivism and Romanticism, he found himself at odds with all the political forces of his day—conservatives, socialists, and national democrats. His style is violent and appears to be constantly at boiling-point: whatever the object of his attention, he seems to be capable only of fervent admiration or unqualified contempt. Some critics thought the explosiveness of his manner was a mask for dilettantism, a want of originality or the power to discipline his mind and digest his thoughts—the more so as he changed his opinions with dizzying swiftness, evidently as the result of hasty writing, wide but superficial reading, and self-identification with the latest philosopher or writer who came within his ken. More attentive readers, however, detected a certain logic in all these changes, and an imprint of personality which gave an individual stamp to all his borrowings from the intellectual store of West European, German, Russian, and Polish thinkers. In passing on the ideas of others he paraphrased them and tinged them with his own style to such an extent that they sometimes appeared unrecognizable: this was the case with Kant and Spencer, Hegel and Marx, Avenarius and Nietzsche, Proudhon and Sorel, Bergson and Newman, Dostoevsky, Loisy, and many others. The ambiguity and variability of Brzozowski's influence extended beyond the grave.

Young people of the Left were brought up on his novels and other writings (*The Flames*, a story of the heroic conspirators of the Narodnaya Volya, was required reading for each generation of revolutionaries), yet before and during the Second World War he was successfully claimed as a prophet by the radical nationalist camp. In this respect Brzozowski resembled Sorel, who in fact influenced him greatly.

Was he a Marxist, and if so, to what extent? He wrote of himself that he had never been orthodox and that when he joined the Marxists it was in the capacity of a dissident. He believed, however, that the 'philosophy of labour' which he professed in 1906–9 was a development of Marx's ideas, and he contrasted Marxism as it had figured in his life with the evolutionism of the orthodox and, above all, the whole tradition stemming from Engels. He was one of the first to contrast Marx and Engels as minds of a completely opposite stamp. Marxism, it may be said, was only one phase in his highly complicated intellectual history, but it was the phase of his maximum intellectual independence and influence on Polish culture. Marxism cannot be treated as the main line of his biography but only as a section of it, unintelligible without some reference to the remainder. His most important work from the standpoint of the history of Marxism is *Ideas*.

It is almost impossible to summarize Brzozowski's views without distortion. He believed that philosophy was not merely a process of reflecting on life but an enhancement of it, and that the meaning of philosophy was determined by its social effectiveness. Hence to describe the content of his writings irrespective of their personal and social genesis and function is to turn them into something they were meant not to be, namely an abstract doctrine. On the other hand, a philosopher who believes that philosophizing is an entirely immanent part of history has no right to complain that his ideas are 'distorted' by critics: for if meaning is always created and not extracted from something ready-made, there can be no question of 'distortion' when he proclaims his vision of the world or when others comment upon it.

Brzozowski's thought may be defined negatively in relation to certain intellectual positions which he opposed. In the first group of these are positivism, evolutionism, naturalism, and the theory of progress, all of which purport to interpret human life and make it intelligible as a function or extension of a natural process. Secondly, he opposed the Romantic tradition which contrasts the independent 'interior' of man with nature, alien to him and governed by its own laws. Brzozowski was, it is true, the most active exponent in Poland of modernist or 'neo-Romantic' thought, but he would have nothing to do with that aspect of it which he regarded as a continuation of the 'bad side' of Romanticism, i.e. the view that art should be completely free and unfettered by any consciousness of its social functions. He was equally opposed to the positivist, utilitarian approach and to the doctrine of 'art for art's sake'. He wished to preserve a place for artistic creation which was not determined by the laws of 'progress' and did not owe its significance to other than human powers, yet at the same time did not represent a breach of historical continuity or claim to be exempt from social responsibility.

1. Biographical note

STANISŁAW BRZOZOWSKI (1878–1911), the son of minor gentry, was born in the village of Maziarnia in south-eastern Poland. After a high school education he entered the Science Faculty of Warsaw University in 1896, but was expelled a year later for helping to organize a patriotic demonstration of students. Arrested in autumn 1898 for underground educational activities, he was released a few weeks later but kept under police supervision. Next year he contracted tuberculosis, and from then till 1905 he lived partly in Warsaw and partly at the nearby resort of Otwock. From 1901 he was extremely active as a writer of books and articles on subjects of popular philosophy, novels, plays, literary criticism, and drama reviews. In the first few years he published pamphlets on the philosophy of Taine, essays on Amiel, Śniadecki, Kremer, Avenarius, and Żeromski, and polemics against Sienkiewicz and Miriam-Przesmycki. At the beginning of 1905 he went to Zakopane in the Tatras and spent a year in Galicia, giving lectures at Zakopane and Cracow. At this time he wrote a pamphlet (published in 1924) on the philosophy of Polish Romanticism, essays on Norwid and Dostoevsky, and a course of logic. At the beginning of 1906 he went for a cure to Nervi near Genoa, then to Lausanne, Germany, and Lwów (Lemberg); during that year he published several articles and a book, *The Modern Polish Novel.* He returned to Nervi at the beginning of 1907 and then spent six months at Florence. While in Italy he wrote a study of Nietzsche and an essay on historical materialism; he met Gorky and Lunacharsky and published two books, *Culture and Life* and *Modern Polish Literary Criticism.* He also took up the intensive study of Marxism and read the works of Sorel.

The following year was that of the 'Brzozowski affair', which beclouded the philosopher's last years and shook the Polish intelligentsia to its foundations. In April 1908 a former Okhrana agent named Mikhail Bakay gave to Vladimir Burtsev, a Russian *émigré* in Paris and the editor of a socialist journal, a list of informers for the Okhrana which included Brzozowski's name. The heinous charge was repeated in *Czerwony Sztandar*, the organ of the SDKPiL, and both the socialist and the National Democratic (right-wing) Press unleashed a campaign against the 'spy'. Brzozowski at once denied the charge and demanded that it be investigated by a 'citizens' court' representing all the socialist parties. After much preparation the court was constituted: it met at Cracow in February and again in March 1909, but Brzozowski was struck down by illness before the next session. The only witness against him was Bakay, who gave confused evidence. The court passed no sentence; controversy raged meanwhile, with many eminent writers defending Brzozowski against the charge of treason. After his death the matter was re-opened many times with inconclusive results. Feliks Kon, a Polish communist and a member of the Cracow court, investigated the Okhrana archives after the October Revolution and found no evidence that Brzozowski had been a traitor. The general opinion today is that either there was a confusion of identity (both his Christian name and surname are very common in Poland) or the charge was a 'plant' by the Russian police. In any case, it had a catastrophic effect on Brzozowski's personal fortunes and those of his writings. (During the affair it came to light that Yevno Azev, the leader of a terrorist organization of the Russian Social Revolutionaries, was an Okhrana agent; his name had also been on Bakay's list, but the ins and outs of this matter are not clear either.)

Despite persecution, poverty, and illness Brzozowski did not cease to work. In 1908 he published *The Flames*, in 1909 *The Legend of Young Poland*, perhaps his best-known work of philosophical criticism, and in 1910 the volume of essays *Ideas*, a summing-up of his philosophical reflections. He died in Florence. Many of his writings appeared posthumously, including memoirs written in the last months of his life, an unfinished novel, and an essay on Newman prefaced to a Polish translation of the *Grammar of Assent*.

2. Philosophical development

LIKE most of his contemporaries, Brzozowski was infected for a time by the positivist outlook of Darwin and Spencer. Soon, however, he not only abandoned evolutionism, determinism, and 'scientific' optimism, but made them the chief target of his attack. For his own part he adopted an individualist philosophy of 'action' which dispensed with objective criteria of cognitive, aesthetic, and moral values, relating them exclusively to the self-assertion of the individual in his uniqueness, and sought to preserve the idea of creativity as a challenge to all forms of naturalist determinism. He articulated this philosophy with the aid of the same sources as most of his contemporaries drew upon—Fichte, Nietzsche, Avenarius—and also of traditional Polish Romanticism, in which the cult of 'action' afforded an ideological compensation for the country's enslavement.

At this time Brzozowski's chief masters were Avenarius and Nietzsche. The former was one of those who had drawn unexpected, and in Brzozowski's view tragic, conclusions from evolutionist positivism. The Darwinists interpreted the whole of civilization and all intellectual activity as a weapon in the struggle of the human race for survival. This view facilitated, if it did not necessitate, a pragmatic attitude towards knowledge: since cognition, and its results preserved and codified in the form of science, were 'nothing but' the response of the species to its natural environment, the notion of truth, like that of goodness or beauty, ceased to have any transcendental meaning; things were valuable in the cognitive, aesthetic, or moral sense in so far as they helped to prolong and strengthen the life of the species. In the same way no scientific opinions, including the theory of evolution itself, could be regarded as 'true' in the every-day sense: they were merely organs of 'life', which in itself is neither good nor bad, true nor false, but simply exists through time. Yet this argument was based on a biological theory which claimed to be 'true' in the transcendental sense of everyday usage. The whole structure of 'scientific philosophy' turned out to be a vicious circle.

Empiriocritical philosophy did not overcome these difficulties, and Brzo-zowski, who for a time attached great weight to this philosophy, took the view that any theory of knowledge was bound to involve a vicious circle, as the gen-eral rules of its evaluation could not be formulated without prior assumptions. He accepted the empiriocritical negation of the concept of truth, while believ-ing that it entailed the once-and-for-all abandonment of any claim to discover 'objective' values in the rationalist sense of the term. In Avenarius's view the predicate 'true', like 'good' or 'beautiful', did not denote a quality found in expe-rience but merely a certain interpretation given by men to their perceptions and thoughts: truth was a 'character', not an 'element'. The epistemological question as to the nature of truth, regarded as an attribute of human judge-ments irrespective of the biological function of those judgements or the cir-cumstances in which they were formed, was not a question that could be meaningfully put. There were no valid questions outside the sphere of empiri-cal description, and no such thing as 'reason' considered and designed to form a picture of the world as it is 'in itself'. The task of philosophy was not to inves-tigate the attributes of Being, but to generalize the data of experience while taking care not to endow its abstractions with any but a purely instrumental sig-nificance. It was for man to systematize experience in scientific form, not as the passive recipient of pre-existing reality but as its active organizer.

Brzozowski held at this time that we are obliged to accept these conclusions and abandon any claim to discover the 'truth'. What we regard as valuable is not so because it gives us a true picture of the world but because it is useful to us in the fight with nature, and the question why it is useful is the fruit of an addic-tion to metaphysics and has no real meaning. The world as we know it is our own creation, cut to our measure. We cannot intelligibly put questions about any other world or invent, as Spencer did, a category of the Unknowable, for the existence of such a category implies, absurdly, that we have knowledge of what we cannot know.

However, Brzozowski's biological relativism at this time was conceived in terms of the individual and not the species, and was thus ultimately closer to

Nietzsche than to Avenarius. All that is true, good, or beautiful is referred not to the interests of the community but to the irreducible subjectivity of each human being. It is each one's business to create the world for himself, and he is entitled to apply the term 'good' or 'true' to whatever he regards as favourable to his own development. In science, art, and morality there are no universal criteria, only that of the individual who designs his own world in an act of unfettered creation.

In this phase Brzozowski's thought did not go beyond the stereotypes of neo-romanticism, except for the dramatic rhetoric in which he clothed them. In 1906–7, however, without apparently quite realizing the extent of the change, he moved away from the solipsistic theory of value and the Nietzschean slogan of creativity, towards an anthropocentric viewpoint which he called the 'philosophy of labour', and in which he was most influenced by Marx, Sorel, and Bergson.

Although he never expressly unfolded the reasons for this change, they may be tentatively reconstructed by comparing his early views on the Romantic philosophy with his later criticism of it. It would seem that he perceived the contradiction between his own critique of modernist art, which proclaimed its independence of society and thereby rejected social responsibility, and, on the other hand, a philosophy which postulated the freedom of the individual to create a world for himself as his own will or caprice dictated. If creativeness is defined by the lack of any connection with existing culture or responsibility for it, and if the mind proclaims itself as creative in so far as it breaks off continuity with the universe, then we are back to the Romantic vision that opposed the 'internal' and spiritual, to which alone it attached importance, to the indifferent world of objectivized nature and civilization, the realm of natural or sociological determinism. A philosophy based on this assumption is not a creation forming part of the world, but a flight from its imperatives. If, as Nietzsche contended, the existing world has no meaning for us, then the freedom of the creative subject is mere contingency, an irresponsible refusal to inquire what social conditions make creativity possible, how far and in what circumstances we can be masters of our fate.

The ontology of culture which Brzozowski adumbrated at this stage was opposed both to evolutionist positivism and to Romanticism: these appeared diametrically opposed to each other but, in his opinion, shared a common base. Both believed that external reality does not have a meaning of its own but is subject to its own laws, irrespective of mankind: to the positivists it was something to be manipulated for technical purposes, to the Romantics it was an insensible world of necessity possessing no interest for us. But in either case the idea of man as a creative being could not be saved: in the former because creativity was only an adaptation to the demands of the natural environment and was determined by the general laws of 'progress' in the same way as changes in that environment, in the latter because creativity was not supposed to apply itself to the external world but to reject it in favour of the illusory autarky of a human monad. The 'philosophy of labour' transcended both the evolutionist faith in progress and the Romantic cult of the self-sufficient ego: it regarded the world as existing only by virtue of the significance conferred on it by collective human effort, and it sought in this way to preserve the dignity of man as the initiator of the world, as unconditionally responsible for himself and for external reality—as a collective Absolute, to whom no ready-made laws afford a promise of triumph over destiny. This is a kind of Marxist version of Kantianism: nature as we know it and can meaningfully speak of it proves to be the creation of man, but its human coefficient derives from labour and not from transcendental conditions of experience.

The philosophy of labour was not the end of Brzozowski's spiritual evolution. The last years of his life were largely filled with religious speculations and a growing interest in Catholicism as presented by Newman and the modernists. To be sure, Brzozowski had never been a 'progressive freethinker' or a militant atheist in the old-fashioned positivist or Marxist style. He never set out to 'fight religious superstition', as he took seriously all forms of the spiritual life and saw in Catholicism an important and fruitful source of cultural values. In a certain undefined sense he regarded himself as a religious man: shortly before his death he wrote in a letter that he had never lost faith in the immortality of the soul. But for a long time Catholicism was to him only a historical creation, a concentration of values and a seed-bed of philosophical, artistic, and literary production: he interpreted it in an immanent fashion, within the limits of self-contained human history. He did not believe at any time that cultural values could be wholly detached from their historical roots, the form and manner in which they had come to be, or that everything of value in Christianity could be simply taken over, without its Christian integument, into secular civilization. But in his last years his thoughts took a different turn; he was attracted by Christianity not only as an important cultural factor and a transmitter of values, but also as a means of intercourse with the supernatural. One can hardly speak of an outright conversion, nor can the nature of the change be exactly determined from the notes and letters dating from the last months of Brzozowski's life. It would seem, however, that there was no breach of continuity with his previous ideas but that he was still preoccupied, as he had been all his life, with the question: How can man give an absolute meaning to that which he himself creates? He appears to have decided that this absolute meaning, on which depends also man's faith in his own absolute dignity, can only come from the belief that our endeavours are capable of reaching the divine, timeless foundations of all being. Any realistic metaphysic of Christianity, or attempt at rationalizing faith, was alien to his mind. If he died as a Catholic it was the continuation of his philosophical pilgrimage, not a break with what had gone before.

3. The philosophy of labour

LOOKING more closely at the variant of Marxism outlined by Brzozowski, we see first of all that it is based on opposition to the then dominant evolutionist version popularized by Engels and Kautsky. In Brzozowski's view all the Marxist writings of his day, except those of Labriola and Sorel, were a successful attempt to distract attention from the essential problems that Marx had raised. 'There was not a single concept, vision or method which, in the transfer from Marx's mind to Engel's, did not become completely different, and indeed diametrically opposite as far as the philosophical nature of concepts is concerned' (*Ideas*, p. 264). Engels shared with the positivists a belief in the natural evolution of the world, of which human history was one aspect: history could be explained by the laws of nature, and there was an objective law of progress, independent of human will, which ensured that man would sooner or later attain a blessed state on earth. This positivist optimism, said Brzozowski, was not only a gratuitous invention but was degrading to man, as it signified that he was not the real master of his fate but was being steered by the 'law of progress' towards an earthly paradise which had a sort of quasi-existence already: it robbed man of the sense that he was the active subject of his own destiny, and of the will to be so. Engels's theory thus maintained the essential alienness of man *vis-à-vis* the world, just as all the conservative metaphysics of the positivists had done. 'To Marx the victory of the working class was necessary because he had convinced himself that he knew how to create and construct that victory, that he was laying its foundations and taking part in the work of achievement. To Engels the whole of this construction, including Marx's will animating it from the inside, was a matter of knowledge, a cognitive complex that maintained itself in his mind because it satisfied his demands, covered all the facts known to him and had an answer to every objection. The workers' victory was a necessity because it took shape in his mind as a logical inference from what he knew ... We are back at the same stage as though Marx had never existed' (ibid., pp. 348–9). 'To Engels it sufficed to feel that he represented, logically and intellectually, a form of life that was worthy of victory and power. He saw the world as a theatre of errors out of which there would finally emerge, necessarily and by the nature of things, that error which dominated his own mind' (p. 384). 'Basically he regards human beings as insignificant creatures, whose function is to be happy and free and not cause any logical perturbation in Engels's mind ... He loved the working class because it furnished him with a necessary argument; apart from this he had no spiritual attachment except to Marx' (p. 389).

Marx by contrast, according to Brzozowski, had no doctrine that made it possible to predict historical events on the basis of ascertained 'natural' laws, valid alike for human affairs and for inanimate nature. This does not mean, however—and the point is worth stressing—that Brzozowski opposed the 'determinism' of Engels to the 'voluntarism' of Marx. He ascribed to Marx, not a voluntarist doctrine as the negation of determinism, but a philosophy that conceived itself as historical praxis. That is to say, Marxism was not a theory about praxis but was a form of social activity comprehending both history and itself as a historical factor, or, to put it otherwise, contemplating the historical process from the inside. In this way Brzozowski's interpretation is more radical than the collective subjectivism of the Russian empiriocritical Marxists: he not only regards the world as a meaning created by the collective effort of human beings, but relativizes his own meaning in the same manner. Brzozowski was perhaps the first who, anticipating Lukács and Gramsci, rejected the dispute among Marxists between determinists and followers of Kant. Both sides in this dispute regarded Marxism as a sociological attempt to ascertain social laws; but to Brzozowski the sense of Marxism consisted not in what it described or predicted, but in what it brought about.

Brzozowski had not much ground for taking this view, except the *Theses on Feuerbach*: he relied more on intuition than on Marx's writings. He believed firmly, however, that he had rediscovered the basic philosophical impulse which Marx himself had, as it were, forgotten when he came to concentrate on the problem of attaining power.

The first target of attack by the philosophy of praxis as thus understood was the idea of a 'ready-made world' subject to laws of its own which mankind was capable of ascertaining in so far as it could exploit them for its own use. Such a world was an intellectualist delusion, a means of evading responsibility for the fate of humanity. What we know as nature, he argues, is not being-in-itself but is, at each particular stage of our knowledge, the degree of the power we exercise over Being. He expresses this idea in different variants in several places. 'From the point of view of the critique of knowledge, nature in the scientific sense of the term is the power achieved by human technical ability over the outside world' (*Ideas*, p. 7). 'Nature, as an idea, is experience envisaged in categories created by our real power over the surrounding universe . . . Nature, as an idea, is experience envisaged as the work of man, the world as a possible object of technical activity' (p. 119). 'Man does not acquaint himself with a ready-made world, but first unconsciously creates various forms of activity and later becomes aware of them' (p. 154). 'The reality encountered by human thought is nothing but human activity and human life. What lies beyond

humanity is something against which only human labour can assert itself . . .
Man has no resources other than himself and that which he deliberately creates. Science is the awareness, the plan and method of our activity and there
are no boundaries to it, as human life and labour endure and develop' (p. 164).

In other words, man's contact with reality is primarily active contact, i.e.
labour: all the rest, including the perception and understanding of the world,
is secondary. We know the world, from the beginning and at every successive
stage, as that upon which our labour is directed, as a focus of resistance and
effort. This practical dialogue with our environment is the absolute, intrans-
gressible reality. There is no way of passing beyond it to discover the 'real' face
of Being, nor can the external world, unaffected by us, come within the range
of our conscious perception and create a subjective image there; nor is there
any pure self-knowledge in which we arrive at an unclouded, substantive ego
that is perfectly transparent to itself. The world, Brzozowski maintains, is 'coex-
tensive with labour'. In the same way we cannot, in our intellectual activity, separate perception from evaluation: for there is no perception or theoretical
reflection that does not have a human, partial, evaluative slant, working within
the horizon which is bounded from the outset by man's practical need to control the world. Labour is an 'Absolute' for human beings in the sense that no
theoretical reflection can go beyond the realities created by labour and organized according to its requirements. In the most general sense Kant is right:
objects conform to our concepts, because the very presence of an object presupposes a human faculty of organizing experience. But this faculty does not
consist in a set of *a priori* forms, nor is it due to any transcendental rationality:
it is simply the practical ability to transform the environment in accordance
with our needs.

Humanity, therefore, cannot itself be explained. We cannot interpret man by
referring his origin, existence, and perceptions to pre-human conditions (such
as a body without consciousness, or the history of species), since these conditions can only be known to us within the practical perspective brought about
by the totality of human efforts to maintain life and enhance its quality. We
know things as the counterpart of our practical activity, and our own selves in
the same state of interlocking tension. Neither the self nor the object is at any
time 'given' in the form of a separate 'image': both are inescapably relativized
vis-à-vis each other, and this interrelation is the final, unanalysable basis of all
our knowledge of the history of men and nature and the laws of the universe.

This, in Brzozowski's view, is not simply another attempt to solve epistemological questions, but involves a radically new conception of our relation to the
world. To believe that we find a 'ready-made world' obeying its own laws and
waiting for us to observe or exploit it is to accept, as it were, the consolidated

results of human activity ('dead labour', in Marxian terms) as an inescapable necessity, and thereby to accept that human labour must be enslaved for ever. To believe that man is, in a radical sense, the creator of the universe is to accept responsibility for the future, rejecting the domination of the results of past labour over the world that our own efforts are bringing to birth. The whole of the past—the necessities of cause and effect as we know them, the world organized into objects by a particular system of connections—is nothing but 'dead labour', a deposit created by past human activity. 'What we know as reality is no more than the result of past history. When we say, then, that reality imposes certain bounds on our historical activity, we should say that past history or reality as it is, or the ideas occasioned by that reality, set absolute limits to our thinking . . . For any philosophy of history, or metaphysics of being, or theory of knowledge that purports to abstract from history, is only possible on the basis of labour that has not recognized itself as the sole human activity that has consequences in the realm of being' (*Ideas*, p. 131).

It is easy to see that if we take the view that there is nothing which is not immanent in human history the dispute between materialism and idealism falls to the ground, since both are based on a false assumption. 'Both these opinions regard the content of the mind as constituting the essence of the universe. Idealism tells us how the world is created by what is in our minds, while materialism accepts the result and tries to forget the "process". Bergson, quite rightly, points out that evolutionism *à la* Spencer is essentially the same thing as evolutionism *à la* Fichte' (ibid., pp. 202–3). 'History is the creator of what we call our minds and nature: it is the ground on which we stand and which prevents us from falling into the abyss; we are from it, and only through it have we any contact with what is not human' (p. 207).

All the attributes that ignorant conservatism, with its eyes fixed on the past, would have us regard as features of a ready-made world are, from the point of view of the philosophy of labour, secretions of human effort, and this radically alters their significance. This applies in particular to the notion of time, which is neither a 'natural' frame within which events occur, nor a relationship between them independent of ourselves. We create the category of time in order to make ourselves aware of the possibility of controlling our own destiny, by opposing the human effort crystallized in past history to the energy which is free to project itself as it chooses: the past is what we have already done, the future is the open realm of our hopes and intentions. To the conservative way of thinking which dominates the evolutionist version of Marxism, time is not a reality: the future, in some mysterious way, already exists and is determined; human happiness and contentment are already inscribed on some future part of the unwinding scroll of progress. But this optimistic philosophy is a self-delusion and a flight from reality in the eyes of those who have learnt from Bergson that the future does not exist in any form and that only duration is real, i.e. nothing is real that has not appeared in actual duration. It is absurd, Brzozowski says, to attribute to Marx a belief in time as something that only actualizes eternal 'laws' and thus entrusts human fate to higher powers of which men are the compliant instruments. 'Teach me to feel myself the tree, And not the withered leaf'—the quotation from Meredith prefaced to Brzozowski's *Ideas* is central to his understanding of Marxism. To him it was above all a way in which men could comprehend the dependence of all forms of culture, including science and nature itself, on labour conceived as an original datum, not analysable into independent elements; and at the same time it signified the acceptance by men of responsibility for their own collective lot.

The understanding of culture must therefore be both genetic and functional. There are no transcendental or pre-existing rules determining the value of what men produce in the way of knowledge, religious myths, works of art, or systems of philosophy. Forms of civilization cannot be discussed without a knowledge of their origin. The question of truth, again, is not that of a connection, independent of ourselves, between the content of certain ideas and a self-existing object: truth is whatever strengthens society and aids it in the fight for survival. This, of course, is close to the pragmatist approach; but Brzozowski differs from James, whose philosophy he knew, in that he does not derive the meaning and truth of the products of culture and knowledge from particular situations or individual needs, but always relates them to the community. Only the whole labouring people can impart the dignity of 'truth' to anything they produce, in so far as it proves able to survive in their world and serves to further its development. In the same way Brzozowski, in accordance with his argument, refuses to accept the category of 'use' or 'life-value' in relation to pre-cultural, biological needs or instincts: for as humanity cannot be defined, or its origin explained, in terms of pre-human factors, so it cannot be treated as a complex of instincts or animal needs to which consciousness is superadded at a later stage. Needs and the demands of 'life' are historical, human categories, and the pragmatic significance of civilization relates to man as the creator of himself, not as a creature who grafts cultural institutions on to his animal existence. However, Brzozowski shares with pragmatism the fundamental conviction that the same value-criterion applies to scientific knowledge as to art, morals, social systems, religious sentiments and institutions: viz. their utility to humanity as the master of its own destiny.

This view does away with the traditional dichotomies of rationalism, positivism, and free thought as between religion and science, fact and value, art and knowledge, cognition and creation. If 'life' is the sole touchstone of value, no

branch of culture can claim supremacy over another or set up universal criteria, but all deserve equally to be judged as instruments of the human struggle
to survive and create a more abundant life; they are good if they enhance
energy, and bad if they dissipate it in backward-looking delusions.

Since humanity is its own final basis and there is nothing beyond it to which
we can appeal, it is no good looking for any guarantee in the shape of historical necessity or a pre-established order. 'The present state of humanity is the
profoundest metaphysical work of man; it is reality *par excellence*. Our towns,
factories, wars, arts and sciences are not a dream behind which something more
profound waits to liberate us: they are absolute reality, irreducible to anything
else' (*Ideas*, p. 215). 'There is no such thing as relations "to the world", "to
nature", "to logic"; there are only intra-historical, intra-social relations between
different efforts, tensions and directions of the will. What we call the world is a
certain property of the human will: we take it for the world because we do not
so much create it as find it' (p. 443). But what we find is brittle and uncertain:
we can and do preserve ourselves daily by fresh efforts: nothing is truly ours,
no satisfaction is permanent, no gain is everlasting. The meaning and value
accumulated by centuries of human effort has to be maintained by an effort
constantly renewed. The human condition is not a steady progress towards final
satisfaction, happiness, or the enjoyment of benefits acquired once and for all:
it is an unceasing struggle, the result of which is not and never will be certain.
All we can hope to do in that struggle is to preserve our own dignity. We have
no 'calling' other than what we actually decide our 'calling' to be.

If there is no criterion of truth and value outside 'life' itself, rationalism
stands revealed as a conservative illusion. For, in Brzozowski's view, rationalism is the belief that actual forms of culture can be evaluated by criteria independent of the cultural process and can be explained by factors that are not the
work of man. But such criteria and explanations do not in fact exist. There is
no such thing as pure thought or pure aesthetic sensibility which can then be
applied to real life. 'Social existence is not the application of thought and perception, but is itself the reality which creates the faculty and the content of perception. Each and every mental phenomenon is only a phase in the history of a
particular social group, and the life of the group is its essential content' (*Ideas*,
p. 419). Once again, the meaning and cognitive value of any product of culture
can only be judged by its origin and functions and not by extra-historical criteria. Moreover, if the organic crystallization of a culture can be expressed in
rational form, this signifies that it has already lost its creative force and
belongs to the lifeless accumulation of the past. Live cultural tendencies can
never be confined in perfectly rational and convincing forms. Rationalism is
the attitude of those who wish to entrench themselves in ready-made positions

and persuade others that these positions cannot be questioned. But thought and artistic creation, in their formative stages, are characterized by lack of self-confidence and by the imperfect logic of its forms.

4. Socialism, the proletariat, and the nation

THE philosophy of labour is, in Brzozowski's view, a kind of metaphysic of socialism and a motivation, or rationalization, of his adherence to it. He was not an active party worker at any time, partly because he disapproved of social-ist particularism and current versions of Marxism, but also because he believed, especially in his last years, that all political forms that derived organ-ically from the life of a nation were in some way necessary to it, and none of them could claim a monopoly of the truth. He declared himself to be a social-ist in the sense of holding that the workers would conquer if they could show that the mass of free labour could outweigh that which was possible with enslaved labour. This highly vague form of socialism was expressly neutral with regard to current ideas of the nature of the future order. He believed that as the whole of civilization must be interpreted as the self-organization of the work-ing community, and as it was only from the point of view of labour that men could understand the meaning of their own efforts, it was from the class of direct producers that humanity must learn to understand itself and be imbued with the necessary hope and confidence to govern its own destiny. In this gen-eral sense Brzozowski believed in the special mission of the proletariat, and his Prometheanism on its behalf was expressed in formulas close to the syndical-ism of Sorel. 'The class separatism of the proletariat is the only way to bring about a moral atmosphere among mankind, to rediscover the meaning of the word "humanity". The proletariat's increasing class consciousness is the one great, metaphysically genuine spiritual reality of our time. This is the point at which man's tragic dilemma is decided. We do not demand justice—no one knows what it is—nor do we promise or look for happiness: mankind never will be happy. Suffering has its absolute values which we do not want to lose. But we believe that man must exist because he has loved and valued his existence—because he creates himself as that reality whose existence he desires, as his own absolute meaning and as the purpose of the world' (Ideas, p. 222).

Socialism is thus expressed not in terms of welfare, security, and content-ment, but of human dignity. The struggle for dignity is a struggle for 'free labour', defined as the opposite of labour 'controlled from above', or as a state in which the labourer, while at work, is not subject to any higher authority. Like Sorel, Brzozowski did not go beyond this general formulation, which is, of course, in accordance with Marxist tradition as far as it goes. He was not inter-ested in the question of the seizure of political power by the proletariat, or of economic organization. What was needed was for the 'mind and will of the working class' to rise to a level at which the workers were in full control of the vital processes of society based on the productivity of labour. Political and economic changes that did not lead to the spiritual transformation of the workers, or increase their readiness and ability to take control of the productive process, were of no account. From this point of view Brzozowski, like Sorel and the anarcho-syndicalists, distinguished the socialism of the intelligentsia from that of the proletariat. The intelligentsia was merely a consuming class that produced nothing; but, as its activity took place in the mental sphere, it was naturally inclined to believe that forms of life are produced by consciousness and not the other way round. What the intelligentsia called socialism was only an attempt to secure for itself a dominant place in society, using the workers as an instrument to maintain its privileges. The hegemony of intellectuals in the socialist movement was a result of the spiritual immaturity of the proletariat. Brzozowski dreamt of a mass struggle of the proletariat, not led by the intellectuals but fully capable of fighting for itself.

No historical law guaranteed the success of socialism. If 'free labour' showed itself to be more productive, socialism would be possible; if not, not. The productivity of labour was to be the final criterion of social progress, but not—and this is a particular feature of Brzozowski's thought—because increased productivity would make possible an increase of consumption. The advance of technology and increased productivity meant the growth of man's power over his environment: this was to Brzozowski an end in itself, not simply the means to a more comfortable life. His whole conception of socialism was heroic and adventurous: man's conquest of nature needed no material gain to justify it; production was not a means to consumption, but to the maintenance of man's position as the independent lord of creation. The proletariat, in his eyes, was a collective warrior with the traits of a Nietzschean hero, the idealized embodiment of humanity as a metaphysical entity. Human ideals and values made sense and were historically momentous in so far as they helped man to wrestle with refractory nature, but that wrestling itself was in the last resort justified on spiritual grounds, as a self-assertion of the will.

To critics brought up on Marxist orthodoxy, this Prometheanism with its metaphysical and prophetic tone appeared highly suspect. Faced with the popularity of Brzozowski's writings amongst left-wing youth, Polish communist intellectuals attached importance to destroying his influence and, in effect, wrote him off as an ideologist of the Right. Andrzej Stawar, for instance, declared that the undifferentiated cult of labour belonged to the ideology of class solidarity. This was an exaggeration in that Brzozowski strongly emphasized the separate cultural identity of the proletariat and its special role in social development. It was true, however, that unlike the Marxists he defined the proletariat by the fact that it performed physical labour, and not by its place in the scheme of production or, especially, the sale of its labour as a commodity. In general, Brzozowski did not pay attention to the class division of society and the social conditions of production. In the last resort we cannot say exactly what he meant by the proletariat, 'free labour', or socialism. He used these terms as metaphysical categories to aid in the description of man as the conqueror of nature: labour, and the struggle itself, were their own reward. 'By means of labour the ideal becomes a fact. Labour is the divine element in which nature—for labour is a fact of nature—becomes the body of an ideal. Labour is the fruit of the will, the basis of its domination over the world' (letter to Salomea Perlmutter, March 1906). In this sense the reproach that Brzozowski levelled against the socialist parties—that they treated the proletariat as a means to the conquest of power by intellectuals who were professional politicians—can, *mutatis mutandis*, be directed against himself: to him the proletariat was the instrument of a Promethean ideal derived from metaphysical reflection and not from observation of the actual tendency of the workers' movement. He was not concerned with what the workers actually wanted, but with what they must become in order that the conquistador's vision of human destiny might be fulfilled.

Another point of contention with Polish Marxists was Brzozowski's attitude to the national question. As time went on the ideas of 'nation' and 'fatherland' became more prominent in his writing, as did the role of traditional culture. Moreover, he used biological metaphors which, vague as they were, became increasingly suspect when radical-nationalist movements of a more or less Fascist type began to use similar metaphors in defence of national values. On such grounds Paweł Hoffman, another orthodox communist, denounced Brzozowski as a forerunner of Fascism.

Brzozowski gave no thought to the tensions that might arise from an attempt to reconcile the national and the class points of view in social philosophy. It seemed clear to him that his loyalty to the workers' cause in no way conflicted with his belief in Poland as a source of national and cultural values; on this subject he wrote:

> People have been at pains to show that the workers' movement can be, and is, a national movement. I do not know that their efforts were necessary. Poland is the field of action of the motive forces in Polish life and the resources which sustain it. To argue that the workers' movement can be independent of the nation's life and destiny is to say that it does not matter what range of forces and means of action it has at its disposal. As long as the Polish community is deprived of its rights, so long will our working class be an amorphous body of degraded paupers—not occupying the fourth rank in the social order, but the fifth, sixth or even lower. What is the issue

here? To renounce one's national existence is to give up hope of influencing human reality: it means destroying one's own soul, for the soul lives and acts only through the nation. The so-called question of nationality does not arise, for it is the same as to ask whether we wish to lose our human dignity. There are no opinions, interests or values that can dispense us from loyalty to this supreme value. A man without a country is a soul without substance—he is lukewarm, dangerous and harmful. For the human soul is the result of a long collective struggle, a long process of creation, and all its significance is due to the length of time that has gone into making it. The older our soul is, the more creative it will be. That is why the workers must consciously arouse themselves to love their country and remember its history. (*Ideas*, p. 225)

If this argument had simply meant that the liberation of the working class could not take place in conditions of national oppression, it would have been commonplace enough and would have been endorsed by Polish socialists in general. But it is clear that Brzozowski meant more than this, and in his discussion of Sorel and Bergson he developed his thought more fully. His point was that there could be no approach to culture except through national tradition, and 'culture' here included all forms of knowledge. Our relationship to the world is such that we perceive everything not only in terms of human history but also of national history, and we delude ourselves if we think we can step outside this. Summarizing Sorel's views, with which he evidently agrees, Brzozowski writes:

The idea of knowledge as the contemplation of some reality above or beyond human life is a fiction: in no circumstances can thought be independent of the community in which it comes to birth, or express anything but a certain sum of human activity . . . Metaphysics came into being as a surrogate for patriotism, as its destruction; today the mother-country comes into its own again . . . We cannot communicate with anyone except through the nation: there is no road to life except through that body-spirit by which we are sustained and exalted. Knowledge is international only inasmuch as it affects the conditions of life of every nation; it cannot be attained by any shallow mind, or by anyone who has not been involved in the stern and tragic aspects of the life of his own people . . . Poland, our language and our soul are not accidental figures of inanimate, uncaring nature: they are a great reality in their own right, a fundamental aspect of being, and will remain so as long as there are Poles on this earth. There are things that are even older and more profound than nations, but man as such can only know himself through the nation, for there are no non-national, international organs of spiritual life. (*Ideas*, pp. 248–51)

This passage clearly goes far beyond what would have been accepted by even the least orthodox of Marxists, suggesting as it does that even science, not to speak of other forms of culture, depends on the national tradition as a necessary medium. To Brzozowski these thoughts were simply an expression of his belief in the value of the nation as a continuous, irreducible reality in which all its members participated. It is hard to deny, however, that his views gave a handle to nationalist radicalism with all its dangerous consequences. The attempts of extreme Rightists to claim him for their own cannot be dismissed as simply mistaken, and it is not easy to acquit him of all blame for this. On the other hand, none of the Marxists was able, either in theory or in practical politics, to resolve the conflict between the internationalism of the workers' movement and the intrinsic value of the national community, except by arbitrarily denying the latter as Rosa Luxemburg did. Nor did any of them apparently suspect that history might have thrown up social forms which were not necessarily reducible to a single pattern.

5. Brzozowski's Marxism

THERE is no need to demonstrate that Brzozowski's ideas of the proletariat and of socialism were very different from Marx's. Moreover, he was certainly wide of the mark in interpreting Marx's intention as follows: 'Nobody can understand Marx's thought who does not feel that he identifies himself with certain constructions of his own such as "productive forces", the "concentration of capitalism", etc. These cognitive concepts are really myths that Marx uses in the first place to represent to himself the trend and content of his own will; he then endeavours to impose this will on others, to build it up and sustain it in them' (*Ideas*, pp. 347–8).

However, irrespective of the later reception of Brzozowski's ideas and the many arbitrary features in his interpretation of Marxism, it can be said that he was the first to attempt to divert Marxist thought from the channel in which it had been flowing without arousing any misgiving, and to impel it in the direction that was afterwards followed in different ways by Gramsci and Lukács. Both the evolutionists and the Kantians accepted as axiomatic that Marxism was an account of the social reality of capitalism and its future, as 'objective' as any other scientific theory. Almost all were likewise agreed that Marxism was based on a kind of common-sense realistic metaphysic and that it interpreted human existence and perception in the way generally assumed in evolutionist theories. Brzozowski, arguing from a shaky factual basis, challenged both these axioms and proposed an interpretation of his own which is remarkably close to the philosophic outlook of Marx's early writings that have since come to light. He contended that Marxism could not in principle treat the social process as 'natural' reality independent of the act of perceiving it. The understanding of the world was itself a factor in changing it, and therefore the determinist explanation of social phenomena, as usually understood, could not be maintained. From the Marxist point of view the social universe and the knowledge of that universe were one and the same, and therefore the course of history could not be 'predicted' like the weather.

In addition, Brzozowski argued, Marxism was incompatible with the idea of a world that preceded and produced human reality and was then able to imprint its own image, together with that of human existence, upon human minds. Man perceived the world from a human angle and could not impartially observe himself as a part of it, for this would mean casting off his human skin and his whole dependence on history. There was no knowledge independent of the human situation in which it was acquired, and we could not even so much as form a concept of the world 'in itself'. The subjection of our perceptions to historical and social conditions was irrevocable, and we must reconcile ourselves to this as to an absolute reality.

However, Brzozowski's religious 'conversion' threw doubt on the possibility of consistently maintaining this strictly anthropocentric viewpoint. It was not, as we have mentioned, a conversion in the usual sense, or a commonplace effect of mental stress in a man close to death. In a letter of 2 May 1910 to Witold Klinger he wrote that he felt no need for revelation, as Catholicism satisfied him intellectually. However, in another letter to Klinger on 19 April 1911, a few days before his death, he wrote: 'My Catholicism includes many important aspects of my Marxism, not to speak of Darwinism, Nietzscheanism and all the other "isms".' Brzozowski did not leave a detailed account of the last phase of his philosophical evolution, but if we regard his conversion as a part of this and not merely a psychological phenomenon, we may perhaps explain the background to it as follows.

The leitmotiv of Brzozowski's thought was the desire to safeguard the absolute value of humanity and endow it with absolute meaning. He expressed this desire first in the Fichtean–Nietzschean category of creativeness and 'action', which appeared to provide a basis for asserting the absolute independence of the creative individual spirit. He abandoned this viewpoint after coming to the conclusion that creativeness was self-contradictory if it did not spring from a sense of obligation towards existing tradition and the centres of social energy that have arisen in the course of history. To defend the subjective, lyrical autarky of the personal 'interior' as an absolute value meant abandoning the world to the indifferent laws of nature: creativity would no longer signify making one's mark on the world, but running away from it. The answer to this was the Marxist vision of man as a collective creator, asserting his own absolute significance in and through his struggle with the external world, and treating the whole of reality as a factor in his own situation. The meaning of the universe was referred wholly to human existence, which took on the role of Atlas and would not, indeed could not, know or perceive anything unrelated to its own self-regarding determination to endure as a species.

It turned out, however, that even this point of view did not suffice to vindicate the absolute meaning of human existence, simply because it was a meaning arbitrarily asserted by a being who could regard himself as absolute only in his manner of envisaging the world and not in Being itself. Since man is condemned to fight for mastery over nature and affirms his dignity in conflict with the non-human world, so that his existence is neither necessary nor independent, his ascription to himself of an absolute position in the scale of values may appear to be no more than a caprice, and may be cancelled by irrational forces if ever they should prove stronger. Faith in the absolute meaning of human existence can only be preserved if it is based on the non-contingent existence of God. Radical anthropocentrism is impossible and self-contradictory because it implies that human existence is at the same time both contingent and absolute.

This hypothetical reconstruction may indicate the road which led Brzozowski from activistic narcissism, via the collective solipsism of Marxist doctrine, to the Church as a historical organism through which humanity is in touch with unconditional Being and is able, in the only possible way, to maintain its own unconditional significance.

XII

Austro-Marxists, Kantians in the
Marxist Movement, Ethical Socialism

1. The concept of Austro-Marxism

THE TERM 'AUSTRO-MARXISM' was coined in 1914 by the American socialist
Louis Boudin and has become generally accepted; it was also used by members of the school itself. The Austro-Marxists are distinguished by certain common tendencies and particular interests; they were not, however, a 'school' in
the scholastic or rabbinic sense of a group of scholars acknowledging or professing a set of tenets by which they can be identified.

The chief theoreticians of Austrian social democracy—Max Adler, Otto
Bauer, Rudolf Hilferding, Karl Renner, Friedrich Adler—all considered themselves Marxists in the full sense of the term, but they did not regard Marxism
as a closed, self-contained system. In the preface to the first volume of *Marx-
Studien* (1904) the editors, Max Adler and Hilferding, declared that they were
faithful to the spirit of Marx's work but were not necessarily concerned with
fidelity to the letter. This does not, of course, mean much in itself, as such statements were common even among the most dogmatic and pious Marxists
('Marxism is not dogma', 'We must creatively develop the Marxian heritage', and
so on). The degree of flexibility of the various schools of thought must be measured not by professions of this kind but by how far they were put into practice,
and in this respect the Austrians differed essentially from typical orthodox
believers. Not only did they emphasize the links between Marxism and earlier
thinkers—especially Kant—whom Marx had not authorized as 'sources', but
they also saw no harm in using ideas, concepts, and questions that had come
to the fore since Marx's time in non-Marxist philosophy and sociology, especially among the neo-Kantians. This, in their view, was not a betrayal of the
doctrine but a corroboration and enrichment of it. They were anxious to show
that Marxism and socialist ideas were an integral part of the European cultural
tradition, and preferred to emphasize not the novelty of Marxism but its affini-
ties and points of contact with various trends of European philosophy and
social thought.

Another characteristic of the Austro-Marxists was their interest in re-examining the broad theoretical and epistemological foundations of Marxism, which Kantian criticism in particular had shown to be full of gaps and loose ends. While accepting the basic principles, including the theory of value, the class struggle, and historical materialism, they did not agree that Marxism logically presupposed a materialist philosophy or that its validity depended on the philosophical arguments of Engels, to which they objected as 'uncritical' in the Kantian sense. Their general attitude was a transcendentalist one, opposed to positivism and empiricism. They held that Marxism was a scientific theory in the fullest sense, but that this did not mean it had to conform to the criteria of knowledge advanced by the empiricists: these were arbitrary and could not provide science with an 'absolute' foundation, simply because they ignored the Kantian questions.

All Marxist theoreticians were obliged to answer, expressly or otherwise, the question whether Marxism was a scientific theory or an ideology of the proletariat. The orthodox replied without embarrassment that it was both, and that the class and the scientific viewpoints converged perfectly; but on reflection this simple answer gave rise to doubts. If Marxism was a scientific theory, then in order to recognize its truth it was sufficient to apply the generally accepted rules of scientific thought, without having first to adopt any political or class standpoint: Marxism, like the theory of evolution, would be accessible to one and all. It was generally added, as a rider to this, that although Marxism was scientifically true it was bound to be resisted by the possessing classes, as it prophesied their downfall. Nevertheless, its truth did not depend logically on any political attitude but on the correct application of rules of intellectual procedure. While it also served the interests of the proletariat, this fact added nothing to its intellectual content and could not logically strengthen the case for accepting it. If, on the other hand, Marxism was the 'ideology of the proletariat', then its acceptance was not merely a theoretical position but a political commitment, and one was impossible without the other. Those who took this view—Lenin in particular—continued to emphasize the scientific nature of Marxism, but they treated it as an instrument of political warfare and refused to admit even in theory that its development had an immanent logic that was independent of politics and might in some circumstances conflict with political expediency. In spreading the doctrine, those of Lenin's school appealed purely to class-interests and not to intellectual principles independent of class. The Austrian Marxists took a precisely opposite view, appealing to all rational minds and not only those who were interested in the theory by reason of their class position. In the field of ethics, similarly, they stressed the intellectual and moral universality of Marxism. To be a Marxian socialist it was sufficient to think aright and to respect humane values that were not those of any particular class but would be embodied most perfectly in socialism. Their attitude on this point resembled that of Jaurès, though they were much more rigid doctrinally. They regarded Marxism as the continuation of the 'natural' development of social knowledge, and socialism as the 'natural' interpretation of traditional human values in terms of present-day society.

Here again, it was accepted doctrine that Marxism was valid for all mankind, but this principle was differently interpreted in practice. Since socialists also agreed that the working class was the unreplaceable champion of human values, it was possible to treat the 'universality' of Marxism as an inessential flourish and bend all one's forces towards annihilating the political adversary. Contrariwise, it was possible to take the view of the Austrians and others who, while accepting the principle of the class struggle, believed that everyone who took seriously the ideals of liberty, equality, and fraternity must, to be consistent with himself, adopt a socialist attitude whatever his own class-interests.

To the Austrians universality was a major principle and not a mere piece of rhetoric. Consequently, when they wrote about the society of the future they had less to say about authority and institutional changes than about the free self-government of workers. They regarded the collectivization of property as an instrument of socialist change but not as the whole of socialism, which also involved socialization of the productive process itself and thus the control of all economic life by the society of producers. They believed that the Kantian rule of treating the individual always as an end and not a means was fully in accord with the principles of socialism, and that socialism would be a parody of itself if it did not have as its sole aim the free development of human persons in association.

At the same time the Austrians were opposed to Bernstein's revisionism and belonged in politics to the radical wing of European Marxism, or rather constituted a radical variant of their own, which included the idea of a democratic dictatorship of the proletariat and rejected that of the gradual building of socialist institutions within capitalist society. During and after the First World War the main theoreticians of Austro-Marxism went different ways in politics. Hilferding and Renner became social democrats in the present-day sense, while Max Adler and Bauer (and also Friedrich Adler) maintained their position on the radical socialist Left, identifying with neither social democracy nor with Leninist communism, but unsuccessfully attempting to mediate between them.

In addition to the monthly *Der Kampf* (from 1907) the Austrian Marxists published the volumes of *Marx-Studien*, already mentioned, which contained some of the most important theoretical works of Marxist literature: Adler's *Kausalität und Teleologie im Streite um die Wissenschaft* (1904) and *Die Staats-*

auffassung des Marxismus (1922), Bauer's *Die Nationalitätenfrage und die Sozialdemokratie* (1907), Hilferding's controversy with Böhm-Bawerk on Marx's theory of value (1904), and Hilferding's *Finanzkapital* (1910).

2. The revival of Kantianism

AUSTRO-MARXISM should not be identified with Marxist neo-Kantism. Those of the Austrians who concerned themselves with epistemology and ethics—i.e. especially Max Adler, but also Bauer to some extent—may, it is true, be regarded as belonging to the Kantian-Marxist movement, but Austro-Marxism as such has other distinguishing marks besides a leaning towards Kant, and many Kantian Marxists cannot be regarded as members of the Austrian school.

The curious phenomenon of Marxist neo-Kantianism, or Marxism with Kantian overtones, is to be viewed not only within the history of Marxism but as an important part of the general revival of Kant's influence which began in the 1860s and led in the next few decades to an almost complete monopoly of Kantianism in German universities. Among the first leaders of this movement were Friedrich Albert Lange and Otto Liebmann. Before long, however, Kantianism divided into various trends and schools which differed both in their interests and in the interpretation of Kant's philosophy.

Kantianism was not merely a philosophical trend but, above all, a bid to rehabilitate philosophy as such against the scientistic outlook of the positivists. Positivism and German materialism were not so much philosophies as attempts at philosophical suicide. They asserted that the methods used by natural science were the only means of attaining reliable knowledge, and that therefore philosophy either had no *raison d'être* or could only consist of reflection on the results of science. Kantianism, on the other hand, offered an intellectual method within which philosophy was not only legitimate but indispensable, but was at the same time limited in its aspirations: it did not pretend to be a metaphysic and was not exposed to the reproach levelled against Hegel, Schelling, and their successors that their ideas were vague, futile *Schwärmerei*, an exercise of fancy untrammelled by logic. The Kantians taught that philosophy should concentrate on the critique of knowledge; natural science did not interpret itself, and there was nothing in it which guaranteed the validity of its results and methods; particular sciences were concerned with knowing the world, but they did not study the fact of cognition, which required special investigation to prove its validity.

Kantianism thus shared with scientism a general opposition to metaphysics, but did not hold with its nihilistic approach to philosophy as a whole. In the second place, it was particularly concerned with the theory of ethic values. The purely empiricist outlook seemed to lead naturally to a radical moral relativism: as science observes and generalizes 'facts' it knows the world of values only as a collection of social or psychological phenomena and has no means of forming value-judgements, any set of which is equally right or wrong so far as science is concerned. Here too Kantianism seemed to offer a protection against relativism: it promised to show that the realm of facts was indeed quite distinct from that of values (so far the Kantians agreed with the positivists), but that human reason is able to define at least the formal conditions that our ethical judgements must satisfy, so that we are not at the mercy of the arbitrary workings of human caprice.

The Kantians, then, were opposed to all-embracing ontological constructions but held, in opposition to scientism, that the critique of knowledge must logically precede all particular knowledge if the latter is to claim universal validity.

3. Ethical socialism

KANTIANISM in its original version was psychological rather than transcendental. That is to say, the *a priori* conditions of knowledge that Kant investigated passed simply for universal attributes of the human mind, which is so constructed that we cannot perceive objects without imposing on them the forms of time and space, causality, substantial unity, etc. This, however, does not do away with relativism but only shifts it to a higher level: for it means that science's picture of the world is universally valid in the sense that it conforms to the requirements of the species-structure of man, but not that it would be equally valid for any possible rational being.

Consequently, the next generation of Kantists, especially the Marburg school (Hermann Cohen and Paul Natorp), passed from the psychological interpretation to a transcendental one, arguing that Kant's *a priori* forms were not psychologically or zoologically contingent and not peculiar to the human species or any other, but were inherent in reason as such and were necessary conditions of any act of cognition. Moreover, reason could not function on the basis of empirical 'facts' as ready-made data. Philosophical criticism was based on science not, as the positivists claimed, in order to 'generalize' its results but in the sense that it investigated the epistemological conditions that made science possible. The Marburg school looked mainly to mathematics and theoretical physics to confirm its generally rationalist outlook. Everything in our knowledge that has universal validity derives from the pure activity of reason and not from contingent, empirical material. Pure reason is the foundation of natural science, and every intelligible idea of reality relates to reality as known. This does not mean that reality is relative *vis-à-vis* individuals or the human species, but that it is relative *vis-à-vis* pure, impersonal thought. Kant's 'thing in itself' is only a regulative concept, a kind of fiction serving to organize knowledge, or else it can be dropped altogether without philosophy suffering any loss.

However, the interest that the Marburg school aroused among certain German and Austrian Marxists was due less to its radical apriorism than to its attempt to found socialist ethics on Kant's theory of practical reason. Cohen and Natorp did not consider themselves Marxists, but they were socialists and believed that socialism could only be grounded in ethical idealism.

Cohen held that Kant had provided socialism with a moral foundation by showing, in the first place, that ethics could not be based on anthropology, for man's natural drives could not give rise to the idea of humanity and of the unique value of the individual. Humanity was not an anthropological but a moral concept: i.e. we cannot admit on the basis of purely natural inclinations that we are parts of a collectivity in which every individual has equal rights. Secondly, Kantian ethics were independent of religious dogma and faith in God: belief in the authority of divine commandments was the basis of a legal system, not a specifically moral one. Only man was a moral lawgiver, but his law could claim universal validity provided it was based on the equality of human beings as objects of moral behaviour. The Kantian ethic that commanded us to treat every human being as an end and not a means was the very essence of socialism, for it meant that the worker must not be treated as a commodity, and this was the basis of the doctrine of socialist liberation. The socialist idea of human brotherhood, in which all men were equal and were free—freedom being defined within legal order—was a logical deduction from Kantian doctrine.

Cohen was one of the originators of the idea of 'ethical socialism', which was adopted by most of those who sought to graft the Kantian tradition on to the Marxian theory of social development. Ethical socialism may be reduced to two main tenets. The first, and the more general, is that even if the Marxian philosophy of history is true and socialism is therefore inevitable, it does not follow that socialism must be accepted as a good. The inevitability of an event or a process does not mean that it is necessarily desirable or that we must support it. In order to accept socialism in addition to foreseeing it, we must have some value-judgements based on grounds other than historical materialism or any other theory of history. The Kantian ethic can provide such a ground, as it shows that the socialist order in which society has no aims other than the human person is a real value. The second principle of ethical socialism, though this was not stated by all its adherents, was that ethical precepts have universal validity, i.e. they apply to all individuals without exception, both as subjects and as objects of moral behaviour. From this it follows that socialism as an ethical postulate is unrelated to social class, and that every human being as such, regardless of class interests, can only preserve his humanity by recognizing the moral value of the socialist ideal. This of course did not mean, as the orthodox claimed, that ethical socialism denied the existence of the class struggle, or that its adherents believed that moral propaganda would suffice to bring about socialist changes. It meant, however, that they could and should advocate the ideals of socialism by appealing to universal human values and not only to working-class interests.

4. Kantianism in Marxism

As ALREADY stated, there were many neo-Kantists who considered themselves (unlike Cohen) to be Marxists as well as socialists, and who in one way or another reconciled historical materialism and scientific socialism with Kantian ethics or epistemology.

This curious symbiosis of Kantian and Marxian ideas may be accounted for by various circumstances. Marxism was less isolated from the rest of the world than it afterwards became, and it was natural that philosophical trends which gained in popularity outside socialist circles should affect Marxist thinking also. In the same way, half a century later, when Communist orthodoxy became diluted after the death of Stalin, attempts were made to infuse new life into the withering tree by drawing on external sources such as existentialism, phenomenology, structuralism, and even Christianity. However, the immanent logic of the doctrine might have led to the same result even without external influence. The principle that socialism is a universal value and not merely a class one led naturally to speculation as to how the two aspects could be combined. The particular interest of the working class was, on the face of it, easy to determine, but it was not obvious what the universal human interest was, and the canonical texts did not throw much light on this question. It seemed clear, however, that as Marxism admitted such a category as this universal interest it must also presuppose the idea of man in general, undifferentiated by class, since otherwise it made no sense to say that socialism would satisfy the aspirations of humanity. The workers, who were the historical standard-bearers of the universal cause, were supposed to fight exclusively for their own interests, which would coincide with those of humanity in some undetermined millennial future. But if the universal interest was to be an intelligible category it must exist here and now in the shape of a tangible reality and specific claims: humanity must, at the present moment, be a visible attribute of every human individual, and there must be moral precepts applying to everyone and not only to comrades in arms. This inference was a hard one for those fundamentalists of Marxism who, in the name of revolutionary purity and intransigence, demanded the complete separation of the socialist movement from 'bourgeois' culture.

The neo-Kantians, seeking formulas to express the universalist aspect of

Marxism, seized upon and developed what had been something of a dead letter or an empty piece of rhetoric in the Marxist canon. But in so doing they came up against the question of the relationship between the universal and the class aspects of socialism, and were accused by the orthodox in general of advocating class solidarity, glossing over mortal antagonisms, and giving a handle to reformist tendencies. As a rule these attacks were couched in vague generalities, but there was some truth in the charge, unspecific as it was, that neo-Kantianism played into the hands of the reformist wing of social democracy. The neo-Kantians, however, at all events in the Austrian school, did not reject the idea of revolution: on more than one occasion they argued that Kant's own views were not opposed to revolution either logically or in a historical sense, and they adduced as evidence his attitude to the Revolution in France. In this they were right: it cannot be deduced from Kant's philosophy that it is illegitimate to overthrow an existing regime by force. But the Kantians, in conformity with their transcendentalist premises, defined socialism in terms of morality rather than institutions, and their theory thus suggested strongly that the moral changes which the workers were capable of bringing about 'here and now' under capitalism would amount to the actual building of socialism. This was anathema to the orthodox, who believed that all the working class could do under capitalism was to prepare the way for revolution: socialism could not be built piecemeal, it was indivisible and consisted in taking over political power and expropriating the capitalists. The effect of defining socialism in moral terms was to blur the sharpness of the transaction from one era to another. To this extent neo-Kantianism, like Bernstein's revisionism, reflected an optimistic faith in 'socialism by degrees', though many or even most of the neo-Kantian Marxists did not express this in so many words.

The neo-Kantian movement was probably also rooted in German national pride. The socialist idea turned out to be the most genuine product of the German Enlightenment, and not only Kant but Lessing, Fichte, Herder, Goethe, and Schiller were often cited among its ancestors.

An outstanding and typical philosopher of the movement was Karl Vorländer (1860–1928), who wrote several works comparing and synthesizing the views of Kant and Marx (for example, *Kant und der Sozialismus*, 1900; *Kant und Marx*, 1911; *Kant, Fichte, Hegel und der Sozialismus*, 1920; *Marx, Engels und Lassalle als Philosophen*, 1921). His arguments may be summed up under three main heads.

In the first place Vorländer singled out the aspects of Kant's social philosophy which had been absorbed into the socialist idea, though they also applied to any form of radical democracy. Kant, for instance, opposed all hereditary privilege; he was against national oppression and standing armies and in favour of popular representation, the separation of Church and State, freedom under law, and a world political organization. He regarded revolution as legitimate if its aim was to secure freedom. He rejected the conservative idea that people should not be given freedom until they were mature enough to use it properly—as if they could ever learn to do so under a despotic system of government.

So far Kant was no more than a radical democrat, but, in the second place, Vorländer maintained that he had anticipated Marx's theory of progress by means of contradictions. Nature used antagonisms to bring about their resolution: the development of mankind was the result of the interplay of selfish impulses which, thanks to the mechanism of mutual limitation, led to increasing socialization. Wars, in the same way, would ultimately lead, in historical evolution, to the establishment of lasting peace; conflicts of all kinds brought home to men the necessity of a legal order within which political freedom could flourish. At the same time Kant was a pessimist who believed that evil was ineradicable and that, as he put it, nothing quite straight could ever be made out of the crooked wood of which man consisted. But this pessimism, which assumed that laws would always be necessary, did not, in Vorländer's view, conflict with Marxian historiosophy.

Most important, however, was the third group of arguments, showing that Kant's moral philosophy not only could but must be incorporated into scientific socialism. Vorländer recognized that Kant's mode of thought was rationalist while that of Hegel and Marx was historical, but he believed the two could be combined. Hegel's historicism had played an important part in the origin of Marxism, by providing a basis for the evolutionist view of history. Thanks to Darwin and Spencer, however, the theory of universal evolution now had better foundations in biology and did not need the aid of Hegelian metaphysics. What was harmful in the Hegelian tradition, on the other hand, was the rejection of the distinction between *Sein* and *Sollen*, what is and what ought to be. In Hegel's schema the notion of 'oughtness' appeared *post festum*, as an awareness of impotence. Marx had followed Hegel in ignoring the distinction, but without it there was no basis for the idea of socialism. Thus the theory of historical materialism was not thought through and lacked epistemological or moral foundations. The criticism of Kant by Marx and Engels was of minor importance, as they clearly did not know much about him: Engels's attack on the concept of the 'thing in itself' proved his complete misunderstanding of the problem. If Marx's theory was to form the consciousness of a social movement, it must represent socialism as an aim to be striven for: but Marxism failed to validate socialism as a goal. In general, the idea of progress involved evaluation, and there could be no theory of progress except from a teleological point of view. Kant's moral theory was thus a natural completion of Marxism. The categorical imperative laid down that desires and trends were morally good in so far as they could be included in a single order of ends. This of course was only a formal definition of the conditions that any moral precept must fulfil: concrete rules were by nature not categorical, but must vary according to historical circumstances. Marxism explained what actions were effective in achieving the aim which it shared with Kantianism, i.e. universal brotherhood and solidarity together with recognition of the irreducible value of every human individual. There was no contradiction here between Kant and Marx, and the Kantian moral doctrine could be introduced into Marxism without affecting any of the latter's basic premises. (Vorländer, like most Marxists of his time, understood historical materialism in a loose sense: economic conditions 'defined' consciousness but did not 'produce' it; human volition played a part in history, and there was interaction between the base and the superstructure.) All that was required was for Marxism to enunciate its own latent value-judgements, without which it was ineffectual and unconvincing.

These or similar arguments were used by all the Kantian Marxists: Ludwig Woltmann, Conrad Schmidt, Franz Staudinger, and the Austrian school. Their main drift was always the same: the scientific interpretation of society and history tells us what is or what will be; no historical or economic analysis can tell us what ought to be, yet we must have a measure by which to judge present conditions and determine our aims. The rightness of socialism is not due to the fact that its causes can be explained or that the working class is appointed to bring it about; things are not admirable simply because they cannot be otherwise than they are—as Staudinger put it, a rotten apple can only be the way it is, but it is rotten for all that.

The Kantians opposed the Darwinian or biological interpretation of man as a being denned by the sum of his 'natural' needs. If he can be fully explained within the natural order, they argued, there was no basis for socialism: nature knows nothing of freedom, and we cannot infer from the natural world that man ought to be free. If, on the other hand (so Staudinger continued), freedom is a postulate which is necessarily inherent in the idea of man, then we must also postulate a social order ensuring the same degree of freedom to everyone. This was impossible with private ownership of the means of production, for then one individual could decide whether another was to live or starve. Hence socialism was the logical consequence of the demand that man should be able to realize his own nature, which was rational and therefore free.

The neo-Kantian Marxists differed as to how far Kant's moral philosophy could or should be embodied in socialist doctrine. Vorländer and Woltmann were Kantists in the full sense, holding that Marx's theory of society should be completed by the whole of Kant's moral and epistemological philosophy. Conrad Schmidt, however, believed that while Kant's distinction between the order of will and that of reason must be maintained, his formal imperative was not a sufficient ground for ethics, which must be based on the totality of social needs defined by changing historical conditions. If we consider what enables man to realize himself as a free, rational being we find that no moral precepts can have absolute value, for different courses of action favour the attainment of the 'ultimate goal' in different circumstances. The Kantian ethic states that a moral duty must be performed simply because it is a duty and for no other reason; but to a socialist the only good consists in man and whatever is to man's advantage, and moral duty can only be defined by social needs. This viewpoint is already one of ethical utilitarianism, and departs fundamentally from Kantian doctrine.

The question of the relationship between Kant and socialism was debated for many years in all the German-language organs of social democracy (*Die Neue Zeit, Sozialistische Monatshefte, Vorwärts, Der Kampf*). In 1904 the centenary of Kant's death was commemorated by the entire working-class Press of Germany and Austria. The orthodox, particularly Kautsky, Mehring, and Plekhanov, saw in the glorification of Kant a drastic breach with Marxist tradition. Mehring and Kautsky accepted the view that a descriptive judgement was to be distinguished from an evaluative one, but they did not see why this should oblige Marxists to seek support in Kantian philosophy. Kant's social desiderata, they argued, could perfectly well be met within the framework of bourgeois democracy and were in no way specifically socialist. The fact that the socialist movement had its own ethical basis was clear enough, but gave no support to Kantian arguments: ethics in whatever form were defined by historical circumstances and were not subject to unchanging rules. The ideals of the working class were explained by history, and it could be shown that they were not merely utopian but were in line with the general course of social development. This was all men needed to know: in particular, Marxists had no need of Kant's unhistorical imperative or the absurd assumption of free will.

As we saw in discussing Kautsky's polemics, it did not occur to orthodox Marxists to put the question: given that certain ideals and values arise in society as the 'natural' product of interests, what motives other than interest can lead the individual to accept them? What ground have we for saying that the socialist ideal, besides being a product of the class situation of the proletariat, is also worthy of support? If, as Marx held, socialism is not only the cause of the working class in particular, but the fulfilment of humanity and the promised flowering of all specifically human potentialities, how can we manage without universal human values? How can we consistently refuse to believe that our moral postulates include non-historical factors that are not transient but belong to the permanent, unchanging idea of humanity? But, on the other hand, is it not contrary to the spirit of Marx's teaching and to his own words to maintain that any values are universal and do not depend on history for their validity?

This dispute, as already stated was insoluble in the ideological context in

which it took place. The Kantians had on their side the traditional distinction
between the order of facts and that of values, which the orthodox accepted
without drawing from it the proper logical conclusions. They for their part
could quote Marx's derisive remarks about non-historical values, and they
were rightly apprehensive of the social consequences of a doctrine that
involved moral standards and judgements independent of class and in effect
suggested that the fight for socialism should be based on universal values
rather than class interests. The Kantians admitted that Marx had refused to distinguish between facts and values, *Sein* and *Sollen*, but they regarded this as a
survival of Hegelianism which could be jettisoned without harm to the essence
of his doctrine. They did not realize that the absence of this distinction is fundamental to Marxism and that in consequence the whole argument on both
sides was being conducted in non-Marxist terms (historical determinism versus moralism). A few Marxists felt obscurely that the issues were wrongly formulated from the Marxist point of view, but none of them was able to clear the
matter up. This was done many years later by Lukács, who pointed out that
according to Marx (1) the working class comprehends social phenomena only
in the very act of revolutionizing the world; (2) in general, knowledge of society is the self-knowledge of a society; and (3) therefore the understanding of
the world and its transformation are not contrasted with each other (as in the
relationship between natural science and its technological application) but are
one and the same act, while the distinction between understanding and evaluation is a secondary abstraction that distorts the original unity.

5. The Austro-Marxists: biographical information

MAX ADLER (1873–1937), a lawyer by profession, spent his life in Vienna,
where in addition to practising as a barrister he wrote learned works and
engaged in party activity. He was not a leader of the organizing type and did
not stand for Parliament before the war, though he was a deputy for a short
time after it. His fellow socialists regarded him as a 'theoretician' in a somewhat pejorative sense, a scholar weaving a skein of argument for the intellectual pleasure of doing so. However, apart from his voluminous writings he was
one of the main founders of party education in Austria, and with Renner and
Hilferding set up a workers' school in Vienna, at which he taught. His books
and articles deal with all the vital problems of socialism in his day, but his main
concern was to consolidate the philosophical basis of Marxism, which he
believed had been much neglected in socialist literature. His philosophical
works, written in a heavy and complicated style, revert again and again to certain themes, in particular the 'social *a priori*' and the transcendental basis of
the social sciences. These matters are discussed in his first book *Kausalität und*

Teleologie im Streite um die Wissenschaft (1904) and recur in *Marxistische Probleme* (1913), *Das Soziologische in Kants Erkenntniskritik* (1924), *Lehrbuch der materialistischen Geschichtsauffassung*, Part I (1930), and the last of his works published during his lifetime, *Das Rätsel der Gesellschaft* (1936). Other permanent topics of his writing are state organization and democracy (*Demokratie und Rätesystem*, 1919; *Die Staatsauffassung des Marxismus*, 1922; *Politische und soziale Demokratie*, 1926), and the subject of religion is touched on incidentally in many of his works. The orthodox accused him of compromising with religion; Bauer wrote in a memoir that Adler could never reconcile himself to the idea that the human spirit was mortal, and that he sought in the Kantian theory of time and space justification for the belief in a timeless existence of the mind.

Throughout his life Max Adler belonged to the left wing of social democracy. During the war, unlike Viktor Adler, he remained a member of the minority group which condemned the opportunism of the 'social patriots'. His attitude to the October Revolution was similar to that of Rosa Luxemburg: he denounced Bolshevik despotism but believed in the value of the Soviets and thought that in altered circumstances the system in Russia would prove capable of democratic change.

Otto Bauer (1881–1938) was more of a political leader than Max Adler, but also made his name as an eminent theoretician. Born in Vienna, the son of bourgeois Jewish parents, he became a socialist at an early age and was soon one of the party's chief theorists and publicists. His first and also his most important theoretical work, *Die Nationalitätenfrage und die Sozialdemokratie* (1907), is the best treatise on nationality problems to be found in Marxist literature and one of the most significant products of Marxist theory in general. After the 1907 elections Bauer became secretary to the parliamentary socialist party; at the same time he taught at the workers' college and wrote for the party Press, especially *Der Kampf* and the *Arbeiterzeitung*. Called up at the outbreak of war, he served as a lieutenant for a few months and was then captured by the Russians. During his imprisonment, which lasted until the February Revolution, he wrote the philosophical work *Das Weltbild des Kapitalismus*, which was published in 1924. Returning to Austria in September 1917 he joined the anti-war wing of the party and, in expectation of the collapse of the monarchy, defended against Renner the principle of national self-determination. After the break-up he was for a short time Foreign Minister of Austria, but resigned when it became clear that there was no hope of the Anschluss with Germany. He was more hostile to the Bolshevik revolution than Adler, holding that the attempt to establish socialism in a semi-feudal country was virtually bound to lead, as in fact it did, to the despotism of a small minority, i.e. the political apparatus, over the proletariat and the rest of society (*Bolschevismus oder Sozialdemokratie?*, 1920).

Subsequently he reverted more than once to Russian questions, denouncing Stalinist terror, the annihilation of culture, and universal mutual spying as a system of government. In his last years, however, as the Fascist threat increased, he became less intransigent towards the Soviet Union. Even when most critical he had emphasized that he hoped to see democratic changes in Russia as the economic situation improved.

When the socialist movement broke in two after the First World War, Bauer did not identify with the reformist branch of social democracy but was one of those who sought to carry on the tradition of the socialist Left as established at the Zimmerwald Conference. The Austrian party was the main initiator of the short-lived organization known as the International Working Union of Socialist Parties, or more familiarly the 'Two-and-a-Half International'. This body, composed of a number of European socialist parties or groups, was founded at Vienna in February 1921 in the hope of mediating between social democrats and communists. Its secretary was Friedrich Adler, and among its leaders were Georg Ledebour (Germany) and Jean Longuet (France). Within two years it became clear that there was no hope of a reconciliation with the communists, and the Vienna Union was reabsorbed into the main social democratic organization.

Until 1934, when the counter-revolution took place in Austria, Bauer continued to be a popular and respected party leader and theorist. He believed that the socialists could in time achieve power without violence or civil war, and he tried to win over the peasants to socialism. In 1923 he published *Die österreichische Revolution*, a study of the fall of the Dual Monarchy. Unlike Renner, he did not believe that the socialists could, by taking part in coalition governments, bring about proletarian rule 'by degrees'. He had no wish, therefore, to share power with the Christian Social party, nor did the latter evince any desire for collaboration; when Bauer proposed to Dollfuss (Chancellor from 1932) a coalition against the Fascist threat, he met with a refusal. In 1933 the Austrian parliament was dissolved and the government's provocative actions drove the workers into a general strike: the short civil war which followed ended in the triumph of reaction and the suppression of the socialist party. Bauer fled to Czechoslovakia and, with a group of *émigrés*, endeavoured to save what was left of Austrian socialism by founding a new party. In May 1938 he moved to Paris, where he died soon after.

Karl Renner (1870–1950) came from a peasant family and, like Adler and Bauer, studied law in Vienna. He wrote works on the theory of the state and law and the national question: *Staat und Nation* (1899, under the pseudonym Synoptikus), *Der Kampf der österreichischen Nationen um den Staat* (1902, under the pseudonym Rudolf Springer), *Grundlagen und Entwicklungsziele der österreichisch-ungarischen Monarchie* (1904). In party politics he was, from

the outset, closer than Bauer to the German revisionists. He emphasized that
the working class should value partial gains and aim at playing an increasing
part in governing the state, not at violent revolution. More of a parliamentarist
than a party leader, he was in turn Chancellor, Minister of Home Affairs, and
Minister of Foreign Affairs of the first Austrian Republic, and sat in Parliament
until 1934. He survived Austrian Fascism, the Anschluss, and the War in political inactivity, and in 1945 became the first Chancellor of the post-war Republic; in the same year he was raised to the office of President, which he
occupied until his death.

Rudolf Hilferding (1877–1943), a doctor by profession, was perhaps the
most eminent Marxist writer on political economy during the period of the Second International. In 1904 he published in *Marx-Studien* his defence of Marx's
theory of value (*Böhm-Bawerks Marx-Kritik*), and in 1910 the classic *Das
Finanzkapital*, a general theory of the world economy in the imperialist era.
From 1906 he lived in Germany, where he taught in the Party school at Berlin
and edited the journal *Vorwärts*. During the war he belonged to the anti-war
group of socialists (the USPD), and with the rest of this group he rejoined the
SPD after 1918. He was German Finance Minister in 1923 and 1928, and a
member of the Reichstag. On Hitler's accession to power he emigrated and
lived in Switzerland and France. Caught by the Nazi police during the Second
World War, he died in the concentration camp at Buchenwald or, according to
other sources, committed suicide in a Paris prison.

▪ ▪ ▪

STRICTLY speaking, the term 'Austro-Marxism' denotes a group whose activities belong to the years 1904–14, but all its chief members were also active
throughout the interwar period. Their works are today largely forgotten,
though particular texts are revived from time to time; some historical studies
have been devoted to this variety of Marxism, which has perhaps made more
original contributions to the history of the doctrine than any other.

6. Adler: the transcendental foundation of the social sciences

ADLER, as we have said, endeavoured to apply Kantian transcendentalism to
the theoretical reconstruction of historical materialism. In his first work he set
out in a condensed form the theory which he maintained throughout his life,
amending or supplementing it from time to time. He began by criticizing the
neo-Kantians of the Baden school, i.e. Rickert and Windelband, and also
Stammler, Dilthey, and Münsterberg. The point on which he joined issue with
them was their view concerning the special methodology of the humanistic
sciences (*Geisteswissenschaften*) and in particular the legitimacy and necessity

of a teleological viewpoint in regard to them. (The term *Geisteswissenschaften* was used by Dilthey; Rickert spoke of *Kulturwissenschaften*, Windelband of 'idiographic' sciences, and Stammler of social sciences). The argument of the new school of thought was that natural science endeavours to reduce its object to what is universal in it, i.e. science is concerned with a particular phenomenon only as the exemplification of a timeless universal law. In this way physical science explains phenomena by reducing them to abstractions. The study of human affairs, on the other hand, is concerned with unique and unrepeatable phenomena, historical events and individuals, values and purposes. Its task is not to explain its object, but to understand it in terms of the motives and experiences of the human beings concerned. Human science is concerned with man as a *stellungnehmendes Wesen*, a being who adopts a certain attitude to events, and the human world cannot be described without reference to this motivational coefficient. Natural science, it is true, also studies man as an experiencing subject, but this naturalistic psychology is concerned with recurrent phenomena and regular associations, and is therefore no part of human science. There are laws of psychology, but a 'historical law' is a contradiction in terms. Moreover, according to Windelband and Rickert, the teleological viewpoint applies to natural science too, though in a restricted sense. All knowledge involves the adoption and rejection of judgements, and these activities are related to truth-values as a supreme objective. Cognition as a form of purposive human behaviour is concerned with values, and to recognize truth as a value is to recognize it as an object of general obligation: when I acknowledge a judgement I imply that it is everyone else's duty to acknowledge it too. No investigation in the field of natural science can arrive at this cognitive obligation, and the 'necessity' which truth imposes is not one of causation but of duty. The value of truth does not derive from science but is a precondition of it: it must therefore flow from an obligation founded in a consciousness transcending the individual. It is not the case that judgements are true because they tell us what reality is 'truly' like: on the contrary, we recognize as real that which ought to be acknowledged in judgements: truth is a value, and reality is relative to truth. The object of knowledge is constituted in a transcendental obligation. Again, it makes no sense to suppose that we know reality as it is in itself by means of representations, for we can only compare representations with one another and not with an object known in some other way. Existence is not an object of representation but is only the predicate of an existential judgement. It cannot therefore be said that our knowledge is directed towards Being, but only that the rules of thought furnish us with criteria for asserting or denying the existence of things. 'The being of objects is founded in obligation' (Rickert).

Adler's attack was directed against these arguments. He conceded that truth could not consist in conformity to an object 'given' independently of its constitution in the cognitive act, for we can know nothing of objects in this sense. 'That this world which is common to us all does not derive its objective form from the fact that "realities", unhappily unknown, are all about us and impart themselves in the form of "qualities", but that what we come firmly up against is nothing but our own mind, i.e. the invariable rule by which representations in it are associated—this is a thought which appears almost monstrous at first, but which finally becomes self-evident and allows us to repose in tranquillity' (*Kausalität und Teleologie*, p. 286). Adler also accepts the Kantian view that an object is a unity of representational associations and that space, time, and our own behaviour in the world are only possible thanks to forms of apperception. He regards this as perfectly consistent with Marx's doctrine, which is not one of naïve realism and has little but the name in common with materialism. But he disputes other points of the neo-Kantian theory of knowledge, in particular that the laws of thought can be regarded as moral commands or that the distinction between truth and falsehood, and not merely between the affirmation and denial of judgements, is rooted in obligation.

It seemed clear to Adler that Marx's doctrine had nothing to do with materialism as a metaphysical system: misunderstandings on this point were due to the misleading term 'historical materialism' and also to the fact that Marx felt a certain affinity with eighteenth-century materialism—not because he shared its view of the world, but because he saw it as an ally against barren idealistic speculation. Materialism had no foundation either in Marxism or in the natural sciences, which were ontologically neutral and had themselves demolished the unintelligible abstraction called 'matter'. The term 'historical materialism' had also encouraged the mistaken idea that Marx regarded economic development as a kind of soulless 'matter', of which human minds and wills and civilization were the mere passive 'reflection'. This led to the false criticism that Marxism ignored the individual and regarded social development as an autonomous process independent of human beings (Lorenz Stein), or that it treated economics as the only 'real' phenomenon and consciousness as an unnecessary duplication of it (Stammler). These, said Adler, were absurd charges, and none of the most orthodox Marxists, such as Cunow, Kautsky, and Mehring, had understood historical materialism in this manner. Marxism was a theory—the first scientific theory—of social phenomena, which it studied from the viewpoint of causal connections while fully realizing that in the world of man these connections are effected by purposive action and by the agency of human intentions, aims, and values. As a theory of this kind, based on experience, Marxism was neither logically nor historically bound up with any particular ontology, such as materialism, but was ontologically neutral like any other science. As to the basic epistemological question of the relation between experience and thought, Marx and Kant converged. The Kantian *a priori* categories were the components of experience that gave it universal validity. If the principles of the association of representations were not contained in experience itself, science would be impossible: this was Kant's view, and it was also Marx's. His criticism of political economy was a 'critique' in the Kantian sense, i.e. a search for instruments of cognition that would enable human knowledge to claim universal validity. This could be seen in Marx's 'Introduction' (the Introduction to *Grundrisse*, published in *Die Neue Zeit*), where he showed how the concrete could be reconstructed out of abstract notions, while emphasizing that this was not, as in Hegel, a description of how the concrete actually arose but only of how it came to be grasped in cognition. The concrete whole with which science was concerned was the product of thought, a conceptual creation and not the content of perception. Did Marx not say in Volume III of *Capital* that science would be unnecessary if the form of a phenomenon coincided with the 'essence'? Clearly the social sciences as Marx conceived them had their own *a priori* categories, the existence of which confirmed the Kantian critique. Marx himself did not observe this analogy, which showed that it was grounded in logic and was not a matter of intellectual borrowing.

Such, then, is the first sense of the 'social *a priori*'. In social investigation human thought presupposes synthesizing forms that are involved in the process of experience but do not derive from it: on the contrary, it is only through them that experience can have universal validity.

But this, Adler continues, does not mean that these formal *a priori* conditions of experience have the character of an obligation, as Rickert and Windelband maintain. Admittedly human acts, including cognitive ones, are purposive in their nature, and we strive after truth as a value. But the fact that truth presents itself to us as an object to be attained does not mean that the aspect of purpose is contained in the concept or definition of truth. If we regard something as true we ascribe to it universal validity, not merely validity for ourselves, and we expect others to acknowledge it; but this does not mean that its truth depends logically on this requirement of ours or on our affirmation of it. Experience may compel me to acknowledge certain judgements; but this is a logical compulsion, not a moral duty, for the latter would imply that I can perform it or not as I choose, whereas I cannot reject a judgement that my senses force upon me. The teleological view of the neo-Kantists rests on a confusion between the veracity that belongs to knowledge, and the desire for truth as an aspect of purposive behaviour: the former of these is in fact quite independent of the latter.

Adler thus adheres to the traditional concept of truth, which, while not presupposing any metaphysic of the world 'in itself', implies that cognitive acts do not constitute truth but ascertain it.

The fact, however, that in addition to 'contingent' truths (in Leibniz's sense:

i.e. those that we can imagine not being so, like all empirical truths) we also have knowledge of the 'necessary' truths of mathematics and logic, indicates that the mind to which this necessity appears must also be something necessary and not a mere contingent datum. And indeed, if we consider the matter, we find that it is impossible to conceive such a thing as 'the absence of consciousness'. It is erroneous to say that we know of a past in which there was no consciousness in the world, for the past devoid of consciousness cannot present itself except to consciousness. A conscious being cannot know what 'unconsciousness' is: the absence of consciousness cannot be a content of consciousness. This, however, is an intellectual necessity, not an ontological one: it does not mean that consciousness as a thing or substance is necessary, but that the content of all our knowledge necessarily includes consciousness.

Again, this necessary consciousness is not the empirical self or contingent subjectivity: it is consciousness in general, the transcendental unity of apperception. Contrary to the system of Hegel or Fichte, transcendental consciousness is not a metaphysical entity, an autonomous Being or 'spirit'. It is known to us only through the individual consciousness, as being that which enables the individual empirical consciousness to ascribe universality to its own content. Consciousness in general belongs to the ego, but is not personal: the ego is not the possessor of consciousness in general, but the form in which it manifests itself.

The theory of 'consciousness in general' points to the second sense of the 'social *a priori*'. When we discover in our own consciousness a claim to universality and the satisfaction of that claim, we discover at the same time the social character of our own ego. We find that the existence of other people, and therefore the social tie, does not require to be deduced from perception but is directly 'given' in the very manner in which our cognitive acts are performed. All empirical subjectivity is 'socialized' in its every act, and is able to perceive this without going outside itself: there is therefore no problem of solipsism, and no need to postulate a 'social fact' as something secondary to the immediate data of experience. Society is directly evident to the ego thanks to the latter's own transcendental components.

Thus the Marxian concept of man as a social being is seen to be best founded in the category of transcendental consciousness, which shows that socialization is not merely a historical fact but is in an integral part of the constitution of consciousness, an attribute of every individual *qua* human. The content of my ego presupposes the community of mankind—a fact already perceived, though not theoretically demonstrated, by Comte, who regarded individuality as a fiction and society as the only reality. Marx did not formulate his thoughts in this way, but he too believed that the content of every individual consciousness was necessarily socialized; language itself, in which that content is expressed, is of course a social inheritance. Kant's theory supplies this idea with an epistemological basis. There is a profound analogy between Kant's refutation of the apparent substantiality of the self, and Marx's critique of commodity fetishism and rejection of the 'reified' appearances of social phenomena. The life of a society is not secondary to that of the individuals composing it, but is a network of relationships comprehending those individuals. Man is a social being in his very essence, and not simply because he associates with others for reasons of instinct or calculation. Just as, in Marx's analysis, the apparent objectivity of commodities resolves itself into social relations, so the appearances of personal consciousness resolve themselves into a general consciousness (*das Bewusstsein überhaupt*) linking individuals with one another. Whether we know it or not, in communication with others we relate our thoughts to transcendental consciousness. A reality which cannot be directly perceived, but is accessible to critical analysis, is manifested in the relations between human beings, just as value is manifested in exchange-value.

To quote Adler once more:

Truth in respect of content (*die inhaltliche Wahrheit*) not only presupposes logically the intellectual compulsion of the individual consciousness in the sense explained above, but would also be unthinkable as a historico-social product, if it were not that the peculiar nature of human thought whereby it is both a separate, individual consciousness and also a manifestation of consciousness in general constitutes the transcendental ground which alone makes possible the interaction and co-operation of human beings in the process of bringing about the knowledge of truth. For it is only thus that what is intellectually necessary becomes universally valid, so that there is a community of human existence (*Verbundenheit menschlichen Wesens*) to which every empirical individual consciousness can be related, in its intercourse with others, as to a unity comprising them all. If, on the other hand, the individual in his concrete historical reality is regarded as something altogether prior to social life, there is no possible way in which he can achieve such a union with his fellow-man as to consider him as a subject and not an object. It is a complete misunderstanding—and indeed atrocious metaphysics, since it is essentially a revival of the notorious dogma that everything can come out of nothing—to suppose that the unity of the social tie can come about as the result of human beings living in communities, in such a way as to be the mere sum or integration of those individuals. In order to grasp the fundamental significance of the concept of 'consciousness in general', and also to bring out the specific novelty of Marx's basic idea of the socialization (*Vergesellschaftung*) of the individual, it cannot be sufficiently emphasized that the true problem of society does not originate in the association (*Verbundenheit*) of a number of human beings, but simply and solely in the individual consciousness. (*Kausalität und Teleologie*, p. 380)

This passage indicates, in somewhat involved language, the two basic concepts denoted by the term 'social *a priori*'. In the first place, knowledge cannot lay claim to universal, objective validity unless we accept the category of transcendental conciousness, providing every individual consciousness with a repertoire of 'necessary forms' for the organization of experience. Secondly, the social tie can only be understood if we regard it as grounded in the existence of the individual, not merely created as the answer to empirical needs. Each individual, as it were, bears the whole of humanity in his own self-consciousness. Transcendental consciousness thus performs a double function: it explains the unity of human beings and the tie between them, and thus the concept of 'man in society', and it shows how knowledge can be a general possession and a matter of obligation, not merely a collection of relative, contingent perceptions by a multiplicity of minds. On both these points Kant (at all events in the Marburg interpretation) and Marx (as interpreted by Adler) are at one. Transcendental consciousness, it should be added, is not a separate, substantive entity but is that part of each individual consciousness which has an impersonal character.

The universal validity of the moral law can be accounted for in a similar way: it too could not exist if it were not rooted in the 'general consciousness'.

It would seem that in Adler's view relations between people are logically prior to people themselves: this can be regarded as a particular exemplification of the general idea of the Marburg school which, in contrast to the common-sense or 'substantialist' view, regarded things as the product of relations and not the other way about.

All this, however, does not constitute an argument for the view that the social as opposed to the physical sciences should be based on teleology and not on causality. According to Adler the study of social phenomena is based on cause and effect like any other, even though the possibility of social relations and the 'form of social life' itself are presupposed before we can begin to study anything and cannot themselves be causally explained. But the primacy of 'consciousness in general' applies to physical science also: nature as an object of study is only possible on account of the formal regularities of thought. In the case of social phenomena it is clear enough that what happens involves human action, purposes, and values, but this is a form of causality, not a denial of it. We cannot distinguish nature from civilization on the ground that one is concerned with causes and the other with aims, or that the study of the latter is teleological, or that the first has to do with abstract laws and the second with unique occurrences. In both cases our study is objective, concerned with cause and effect and with discovering general rules; in both, the object is constituted by *a priori* conditions of knowledge. The only difference is that in humanistic studies we treat connections and events as consciously experienced, though they are causally conditioned as well.

As long as we are concerned only with what is simply given by the operation of consciousness in general, there comes into view a huge realm of existence that is given
simply as natural existence (*Naturdasein*); and conscious beings are part of this in
so far as they are merely considered as parts of nature. But when we turn our minds
to the question how this natural world is given, how it is conceived, judged, worked
upon and made use of, and how in all these respects it is possible for so many individuals, acting quite independently of one another, to achieve agreement and
mutual understanding even in their most hostile acts, then, in addition to the bare
natural fact that exists only for each particular act of knowledge and is therefore
isolated from all others, we become aware of that other great fact of the unique,
thorough-going community and unity (*der eigenartigen durchgängigen Verbundenheit und Ineinssetzung*) of human beings that know and act upon their knowledge.
(*Kausalität und Teleologie*, p. 427)

Adler's theory is not as clear as could be desired, but its general trend is
plain enough. Since the transcendental consciousness is not a 'spirit' in the
sense of an impersonal, self-existing substance, but exists only in the individual consciousness in such a way as to make it essentially identical with every
other, it might seem that it amounts to no more than the collectivity of judgements comprising the whole of 'necessary knowledge', i.e. synthetic *a priori*
judgements in the Kantian sense. If so, however, the question 'How does our
knowledge acquire the character of necessity?' (apart from that of analytical
judgements) has been formulated but not answered. If we reply that this necessity derives from the transcendental consciousness, and if this consciousness is
in fact nothing but a collection or repository of necessary judgements, then we
have not answered any question at all.

But this criticism of Adler's argument does not apply only to him. He is right
in holding, like all transcendentalists, that the universal validity of our knowledge, its certainty irrespective of contingent historical and biological facts, cannot be demonstrated empirically: as both Kant and Husserl maintain, there can
be no experimental epistemology. It follows that in the realm of empirical
knowledge we are condemned not only to uncertainty but also to the impossibility of finding out how much of our knowledge is valid and how much
depends on accidents of the human condition. The Marburg neo-Kantians
were aware of this, and they saw that the psychological interpretation of Kant
is no cure for the relativity of knowledge. But if so, it does not follow that we
have any other means of overcoming this relativism. We must also take it that
rationalism cannot justify the claim of knowledge to objectivity and must be
content with hypothetical and unverifiable theories of transcendental consciousness that only appear to provide a refuge from scepticism and relativism,
by introducing an arbitrary *deus ex machina* of epistemology.

Adler's ascription of transcendentalism to Marx is also highly questionable. True, the idea of 'socialized man' implied for Marx that the human individual as such was, as it were, a 'carrier' of social Being and only knew himself through society. But this does not imply any view as to how the socialization comes about. There is no ground for saying that according to Marx it cannot be explained historically but only by some kind of transcendental consciousness. As for the *a priori* conditions of our knowledge of society, it is true that Marx drew a distinction, which he never explained precisely, between the essence of a thing and a phenomenon; he also says that social processes cannot be theoretically reconstructed by accumulating single observations, but only by using conceptual instruments that precede observations. Marx does not explain, however, where these instruments are to come from or how their use is to be justified. To imagine that they are something in the nature of Kantian categories is quite arbitrary and is not an interpretation of Marx, but an introduction of quite different ingredients into his theory. Nor is there any analogy between Marx's analysis of commodity fetishism and Kant's critique of the substantive ego. Marx reduces the relations between commodities to relations between people, but this does not mean he thought that human beings were secondary to their own social ties. Individuals under capitalism were, in point of fact, dissolved amid the anonymous forces of communal life, but this was a criticism of capitalism and not something that had to endure for ever. Socialism, according to Marx, meant a return to individuality and the conscious treatment of one's own powers as belonging to society; but the object of this was to overcome the anonymous character of individual life resulting from alienation, i.e. from social processes escaping the control of 'real individuals'. Thus the critique of commodity fetishism had the opposite meaning to what Adler supposed.

Moreover, Adler's interpretation of the purposive character of social phenomena, and his critique of the neo-Kantists, are so expressed that it is not clear in what respect he disagrees with the purely naturalist interpretation of society, against which he is constantly protesting. If his argument is that social phenomena are subject to universal determinism in the same way as all others, while their peculiar character lies in the fact that they are experienced and that they present themselves as purposive actions, then these are propositions with which the most unbending 'mechanist' would agree. No one could deny that men experience the events they take part in or that their actions are governed by various motives, desires, and values. The radical determinist merely claims that this makes no difference to the fact that these motives, desires, and experiences are conditioned just as inevitably as all other events. Adler seems to accept this view, and consequently his statement that causality in human affairs operates 'through' the purposive actions of human beings does not differ from out-and-out 'mechanism'.

7. Adler's critique of materialism and the dialectic

IT IS clear that from the point of view of Engels's schema Adler counts as an 'idealist', at least in the sense in which Kant is so described. (The object of cognition is constituted in and by the act of cognition; transcendental consciousness is prior to any 'nature' that we can talk about intelligibly; the category of 'matter' is an absurdity.)

In all his philosophical writings Adler repeated the same thought: Marx's theory is a scientific reconstruction of social phenomena, and is ontologically neutral (or, as he calls it, 'positivist') in the same way as any other science. It is not based on any materialist metaphysic, which in any case is an untenable doctrine. Adler criticizes materialist philosophy at length in his *Lehrbuch der materialistischen Geschichtsauffassung*, where he argues on similar lines to Fichte. It is impossible to derive consciousness from 'physical motion', since physical motion is only given to us as the content of consciousness. Philosophy cannot take as its starting-point the question of the primacy of mind or nature, since Kant has taught us that reason cannot pronounce upon the world until it has examined its own right to do so. Our starting-point must be the 'critical' question of the possibility and validity of cognition. But, if we put this question without metaphysical prejudice, we see that any concept of reality that we can meaningfully create relates to reality constructed in conceptual forms: from no fact of experience can we deduce anything like the 'thing in itself'. In this sense it can be said that everything *is* consciousness, which does not mean that it is the content of the empirical self: on the contrary, the cognitive acts of the self are directed towards a reality that is common to all men, since the self participates in transcendental consciousness and is merely a form of the latter's activity. Here Adler joins issue with the materialism of Lenin, who seeks to refute idealism by arguing that the world existed before men and hence before the appearance of consciousness, and that consciousness is a function of the brain, which is a physical object. These, Adler retorts, are naïve and uncritical arguments. The existence of the world 'before' consciousness is given only in the form of a certain content of consciousness, and in the same way the brain is not known to us as the producer of our consciousness, but only indirectly through consciousness itself. The theory of 'reflection' is a trivial *petitio principii*. It first defines impressions as a reflection of the world, and then argues that since this is so, there must be a world to be reflected; but we cannot define impressions in this way without assuming some previous knowledge of the world.

Adler's argument is basically a repetition of the traditional themes of German idealism, and introduces no new features. It can be expressed as follows: if the world were 'given' in consciousness as a world that is completely independent of consciousness and does not presuppose it, it would be both given and not given. It is therefore a self-contradictory concept, or a concept that pretends not to be one.

It would seem that Adler, following the Marburg interpretation, rejects the category of the 'thing in itself' as superfluous and meaningless. To say that consciousness contains 'everything' is in his eyes (though he does not expressly say so) a tautology: whatever we know about the world, we know as an object of our knowledge. From this point of view, which is that of Fichte rather than Kant, the critical position amounts to maintaining that the world is a correlative to judgements about the world, which in their totality are termed consciousness-in-general. Adler expressly rejects as meaningless the question as to the origin of that which is contained in consciousness, for consciousness in fact comprises 'everything'.

Adler's transcendentalism, however, is not fully consistent. On the one hand, like Cohen and Natorp, he regards the transcendental consciousness as an autonomous world of 'truth' to which reality is relativized: a world which has no need of empirical human beings in order to exist, or rather to be 'valid'—for existence is only the predicate of an existential judgement, and consciousness-in-general is not a kind of Platonic realm of ideas, while its ontological status cannot even be an object of questioning. But, on the other hand, Adler frequently uses the concept of 'species-consciousness', which he identifies with transcendental consciousness. This, however, involves the existence of mankind as a differentiated species, and cannot lay claim to absolute validity. Thus Adler oscillates between anthropological relativism and transcendentalism in the true sense. The former viewpoint suffices when he is concerned, as he most often is, to show, or rather to state, that the community of mankind and the unity of the species have an epistemological basis, since all human beings share in the same impersonal form of the spirit. But it does not suffice when he also seeks to maintain that we are entitled, within certain limits anyway, to ascribe to our knowledge universal and absolute validity: this requires a world of necessary truths, the necessity of which does not depend on the empirical activity of the human mind. These, however, are two completely different purposes: to justify the humanistic faith in the unity of mankind, and to vindicate the claims of human knowledge to certainty. Adler's concept of transcendental consciousness is used to serve both purposes, which at times leads to confusion. This also gives rise to the double sense of the concept of the 'social *a priori*', which we have already mentioned and which Adler never clearly distinguished. On the one hand, this a *priori* is a collection of non-empirical categories, applicable in a particular way to the description of social phenomena; on the other hand, it is that part of the content of every individual consciousness in which the latter discovers itself as a member of the human species with the power of communicating with its fellows.

This confusion also affects Adler's interpretation of Marx. Marxism is a theory which offers a basis for belief in the perfect unity of human beings (which is what socialism is about) and also a method of discovering universally valid truths about social phenomena. There is, of course, no conflict between these aspects of Marxism, but it is often not clear which of them Adler is talking about.

Adler deserves a special place in the history of Marxism because, among other things, he was one of the few who tried to reinstate the dialectic in the Hegelian sense of an unceasing interplay between Being and thought about Being, instead of contenting themselves with the Engels-Plekhanov method of accumulating examples to show that in this or that sphere of reality 'quantitative changes lead to qualitative ones', or 'development is the result of a conflict of opposites'. However, Adler's exposition of the dialectic was highly abstract and un-related to the actual problems of the social sciences. *Marxistische Probleme*, the work in which he dealt especially with dialectical questions, did nothing to bring about a return of Marxism to Hegelian sources.

According to Adler, dialectical thought is its own object. In the dialectical movement every concept is understood in relation to its opposite—not by the ordinary comparison of one content with another, but by reason of the tendency of each towards self-cancellation. Our thought never embraces the whole of Being, but singles out particular aspects or qualities; consciousness, however, is aware of its own limitations and strives to overcome them by relating its own content to the concrete whole (*Totalität*), which is itself inexpressible. The mind is thus in a state of constant tension and must at once transcend every result that it achieves, aiming at the unattainable goal of a self-identity which would also mean identity with its object. But the law of the mind is not that of things: reality can be called dialectic only as the mind conceives it and not as it is 'in itself'. It is not clear, however, how Adler can make this distinction, since in his view the only reality we have contact with is that of thought. Later he apparently abandoned the critique of the 'dialectic of nature', having concluded that nature, being comprehended by thought, is no less 'dialectic' than thought itself.

8. Adler: consciousness and social being

ADLER, as we saw, regarded himself as a true adherent of the Marxian philosophy of history, but he rejected the term 'historical materialism' as based on a misunderstanding and as merely polemical in intent. He repeats all the current defences of Marxism against the charge that it 'takes no account' of human activity as a whole, that it regards social development as independent of human beings, etc. He emphasizes that the causal explanation of social phenomena is not in conflict with the existence of the human will. He overlooks, however, that the question is not whether men's acts are motivated but whether they are unequivocally determined by circumstances, while the objection that Marxism regards history as independent of human beings is aimed at historical determinism and not at the absurd idea that men and women behave no differently from stones. Like nearly all Marxists he fails to put the question clearly at this point, repeating merely that Marxism is not 'fatalistic', since it recognizes human initiative, and at the same time that science must regard all social processes as causally determined. This is a very weak explanation, for if human initiative in history is determined by circumstances it is only one of the many forms of universal causality, and the objection that men are 'only instruments' of an anonymous process has not been met; while if is not so determined, it is impossible to maintain the determinist position and belief in 'historical laws'.

However, Adler's specific contribution does not consist in general, unanalytical remarks about 'men making history'. His interpretation of historical materialism is distinguished by the attempt to call in question the whole traditional distinction between 'material' and 'spiritual' factors in the historical process.The general error of Marxists was, in his view, to oppose inanimate 'productive forces' and 'relations of production' to the spiritual 'superstructure', when it was clear that relations of production represented a system of conscious human behaviour and were thus no less spiritual than the superstructure itself. In the same way productive forces, if regarded not as lifeless objects but as elements in the social process, presupposed human consciousness on the part of the makers and users of tools. There were no factors in social life that were simply 'inanimate matter' and changed or developed of their own accord. Technique and economic phenomena were as much manifestations of the spirit as was ideology. Marx did not regard the superstructure as a passive reflection of 'objective' conditions, nor did he deny the autonomy of its features such as law, science, and religion. Consciousness was determined by 'social', not 'material', being, and 'social' implied 'spiritual'. What were called 'economic conditions' were spiritual phenomena at the lowest level of a particular phase of social development, i.e. those that were directly connected with the production and reproduction of human existence.

It is not clear exactly what is left of historical materialism after this interpretation. It would seem that in Adler's system the distinction, in social phenomena, between 'forms of consciousness' and 'objective' processes ceases to have any meaning, and so therefore does the basic idea of the materialist interpretation of history. Adler insists, however, that Marx's conception was that in the last resort the human spirit is the driving force of history. 'If we remember Marx's words: "With me the ideal is nothing else than the material world reflected by the human mind and translated into forms of thought" (*bei mir ist das Ideelle nichts andres als das im Menschenkopf umgesetzte und übersetzte Materielle*), we cannot fail to see that there is no economic causality that does not also take place inside the human head' (*Die Staatsauffassung des Marxismus*, p. 163). This, however, is extremely far-fetched, and distorts Marx's ideas out of recognition: what he meant was not that all economic phenomena take place in the human mind, but that what takes place in the mind can be explained economically.

9. What is and what ought to be

IN questions relating to ethics and their philosophical basis Adler repeats in his own fashion arguments that were the common property of all neo-Kantists, and from this point of view criticizes Kautsky's naturalism. If all historical processes are determined independently of the human will, then there is no place for ethics. It is meaningless to say that I 'ought' to do this or that, if everything I do is dictated by circumstances beyond my control. Nature knows neither good nor evil, and no empirical observation will enable us to find such a distinction in it. Hence Marxism as a theory of social phenomena is morally neutral. However, as beings endowed with mind and will we cannot avoid asking the questions 'What ought we to do?' and 'What is good?', and we are not helped to answer these by knowing what is regarded as right or good. Socialism cannot be considered as merely the result of the 'natural' development of phenomena, since if this is the case it does not follow that we ought to help in bringing it about, or regard it as an aim or ideal. Moral judgements cannot be derived from statements about biological or historical facts: they can only be based on recognizing the human will as a faculty of self-determination which is not a form of natural energy and which creates the principles of obligation autonomously—i.e. without regard to external considerations, whether of biology, religion, or utilitarianism.

In *Marxistische Probleme* and other works written before 1914 Adler treated ethical questions from a typically neo-Kantian standpoint. However, in an article of 1922 on the relation of Marxism to classic German philosophy he criticized the Kantists who held that socialism must be justified ethically as well as historically—a position that Adler himself had maintained until recently. His criticism, however, is extremely tenuous. He states that according to Marx socialism is based on purely empirical observation of the historical chain of causes and effects, and that its historical inevitability 'coincides' with its moral value. This coincidence is reflected in the concept of 'socialized man', who is impelled by social conditions to bring about what he regards as moral. Curiously, Adler fails to observe that this argument overlooks the Kantians' main objection, which he himself often used against Kautsky, viz.: how does 'socialized man' decide what is good or bad, and how does he find ethical grounds for his decision?

Bauer approached ethical questions on similar lines. In an article of 1905 entitled 'Marxismus und Ethik' he considers the problem of an unemployed worker who is offered pay in return for acting as a strike-breaker, and to whom it has to be explained that this is a wrong thing to do. The workman recognizes that his interests coincide generally with those of the proletariat as a whole, but he points out that in this particular case there is a conflict and he does not see why he should sacrifice his own interests for the sake of class solidarity. There is, says Bauer, no scientific answer to this question, for science does not pronounce moral judgements. The difference between Marxism and Hegelian idealism is precisely that the former does not identify 'natural' necessity with an obligation of the spirit, for it does not treat nature as a manifestation of the Idea. In the same way moral questions cannot be answered in terms of natural necessity: there must be special principles to guarantee the validity of value-judgements. Kant formulated such a principle in the shape of the formal categorical imperative, which does not tell us directly what we ought to do but provides a criterion for judging whether any particular moral rule is good or bad. Kant's ethical doctrine does not conflict with Marxism, but adds to it a moral foundation that is essential to all human beings. On the basis of the Kantian imperative we can prove that a proletarian who shows solidarity in fighting for the interests of his class is not in the same moral position as a strike-breaker; it would be impossible to show this, however, if morality had no more than a utilitarian basis. If I seek to find out not only which of the warring classes is historically most likely to win, but also which I should fight for, Marx's doctrine does not in itself tell me the answer. The orthodox are wrong in claiming that Kant's moral philosophy leads to class solidarity inasmuch as it formulates universal rules, unconnected with class-interest. On the contrary, it makes possible a moral distinction between bourgeois and proletarian interests and shows that we should opt for the latter because the particular interest of the proletariat stands for that of all humanity; if it did not, we should have no reason to take its side. The fact that the proletariat's cause is that of all mankind is known to us from Marx's analysis, and Kantian ethics cannot take the place of the historical and economic knowledge that we need in order to take moral decisions; but, on the other hand, such knowledge is not in itself capable of justifying a decision.

Bauer appears in the course of time to have altered his attitude to Kant and neo-Kantianism. In *Das Weltbild des Kapitalsmus* and in an article of 1937 on Adler he treats neo-Kantianism as an expression of philosophical reaction, analogous to the political attitude of the bourgeoisie in Bismarck's time. The defeat of liberalism was also the end of bourgeois materialism in Germany, and its philosophical counterparts were neo-Kantianism and empiriocriticism. The bourgeois intelligentsia sought to induce the proletariat to ally itself with the liberals, and their ideologists therefore underlined the merits and value of Marx's work, while interpreting it so as to eliminate the revolutionary content and reduce socialism to a moral postulate and nothing more. Bauer thus criticizes Kantianism from the very standpoint which he had condemned in orthodox Marxists, without meeting the objections that he himself formerly advanced.

10. The state, democracy, and dictatorship

THE Austro-Marxists were more agreed on philosophical questions than they were as regards the function of the state and the objectives of the political struggle of the proletariat. Renner's views on this subject, in particular, were close to Bernstein's and to those prevalent in German social democracy as a whole, owing in part to the Lassalle tradition. As Renner argued especially in his wartime and later articles, the evolution of capitalism towards imperialism had led to changes in the function of the state which gave the working class the opportunity to use the existing state machine to bring about socialist changes. Marx, in considering the state, had had in mind liberal capitalism, where the state organization refrains from interfering in production and trade. Imperialism had changed all this; the state itself had become a powerful instrument for the concentration of capital, and as a result capital had ceased to be cosmopolitan and become much more 'national'. State intervention was extending to more and more areas of economic life and this process was irreversible. The bourgeoisie was obliged in its own interest to increase the application of centralized control to industry, banking, and commerce, while working-class pressure had obliged the state to provide more social benefits and services. Thanks to class organizations the labour market was dominated by the collective action of the workers, who had it in their power to extract many concessions from capital, not only in short-term wage increases but in the form of permanent welfare institutions. It could not therefore be said that in capitalist society the state could never function in the interest of the proletariat. Experience had proved the contrary, and it was to be expected that private property would take on a more and more public character and that the working class would have increasing influence over its institutions. Thus it was no longer the case that the workers had an interest in weakening and destroying the state: on the contrary, they could use it as a lever to bring about socialist changes, and they ought to make it as strong and efficient as possible. This analysis led naturally to a general advocacy of the reformist path to socialism: Renner believed that a socialist society would develop as the workers gained more control over state institutions and as the proletariat succeeded more and more in obliging capital to perform public functions.

Bauer and Adler, however, were less optimistic. Bauer, it is true, agreed that it could not be said that the state was always an organ of the bourgeoisie and was completely subordinated to its interests; this, he pointed out, was contrary to many of Marx's own observations, for example about periods of joint control by the aristocracy and the bourgeoisie, or the state at a given moment becoming an autonomous force owing to an equilibrium in the class struggle. Marxism, he argued, did not exclude the possibility that the proletariat and the bourgeoisie might share the state power, though this would not diminish the antagonism between them: this was what happened in Austria after the fall of the monarchy. But where bourgeois property was threatened, the bourgeoisie preferred to hand over political power to dictators if by so doing it could preserve its economic privileges: witness the example of Fascism. Bauer, it appears, did not believe that the proletariat had to 'destroy the machinery of the state' before it could seize power, but he also did not believe that socialism could develop organically out of the existing state by the extraction of successive concessions from the bourgeoisie.

Adler's position on these questions was closest to the traditional doctrine of the revolutionary Marxists. His views on the state were summed up in *Die Staatsauffassung des Marxismus*, the starting-point of which is a critique of Hans Kelsen's *Sozialismus und Staat* (1920). Kelsen had attacked Marxism as an anarchist Utopia, arguing that the abolition of the state was an impracticable ideal: law must always be the organization of coercion *vis-à-vis* individuals, but it need not be for the purpose of maintaining economic exploitation. To suppose that legal coercion could ever be abolished was to imagine a moral transformation of humanity that there was absolutely no reason to expect. There was no choice between the state and a stateless society, but there was one between democracy and dictatorship.

Adler, on the basis of classical Marxist theory, combated these arguments at all points. The state, he contended, performed other functions than those of class oppression, but they were not essential or characteristic ones. The state was the historical form of human society that characterized all periods dominated by class antagonisms. More precisely, in communities that had not yet developed a class division, the state and society were the same: it was only later that the state became separate from society and an instrument of the interests of the privileged classes.

A particular form of the state, Adler goes on, is political democracy with its parliamentary institutions, universal suffrage, and civil liberties. Not only is political democracy not opposed to class dictatorship, but it presupposes it. The bourgeois state is a dictatorship of the bourgeoisie, and political democracy is the way in which that dictatorship is organized. Political democracy cannot create economic equality or cure social antagonisms. It is based on the will of the majority, a principle which presupposes conflicting interests.

The opposite of political democracy is social democracy—this distinction can also be found in anarchist literature, which Adler endorses to some extent, observing that socialists agree with anarchists as to the ultimate aim while differing as to the means of achieving it. Social or 'true' democracy (Adler, with his transcendentalist point of view, held that there was an 'objectively true' concept of democracy in tune with human nature) is the same thing as socialism. It presupposes the unity of society at least in the sense that when it prevails, the basic conflicts of interest due to class divisions will cease to exist. In this sense it signifies the abolition of the state. The state as a class organization will cease to exist, for there will be no more particular interests; various forms of organization that are necessary to social life will remain, but there will no longer be a bureaucracy alienated from society. The state will be built up from below, starting with small assemblies on a local or production basis. In general, the present centralizing tendency is a transitory one: the organization of the future will be a federation or an assemblage of corporations linked only by their common aims and interests.

The dictatorship of the proletariat is a necessary stage on the road towards a society of this kind, but it is not the same thing as social democracy. On the contrary, like the dictatorship of the bourgeoisie at the present time, it presupposes political democracy and majority rule. The dictatorship of the proletariat is a transitional form in which society has not yet attained the desired unity but is torn by particular interests, so that it requires political organizations, i.e. parties, to represent those interests, and the state to mediate between them. Parties, too, are a transitional institution and must disappear together with class divisions.

The transition from the present form of political democracy to a democratic dictatorship of the proletariat must take the form of a revolution, but Adler stresses that it need not be a violent one. Whether or not it can be effected by peaceful means and without violation of legality is a secondary point, and we cannot be certain exactly how events will develop. Adler, however, is against reformism in the sense of a belief that socialism can be achieved by gradual, organic change. The difference between capitalism and socialism is 'qualitative': one cannot simply ripen into the other. Socialists support reforms and fight for them, but they are always conscious that reforms are not a partial realization of socialism, but only a means of preparing for revolution.

In all this Adler is very close to German orthodox Marxism, and he shares with it the firm belief that socialism involves the removal of all conflicts of interest. Socialist freedom requires no institutions to ensure majority rule, for it is a 'true' freedom based on the 'principle of universalism': as in Rousseau's ideal society, it is not the will of the majority that counts, but the general will. Adler does not explain how the 'general will' can express itself without representative institutions, which, we are given to understand, will be superfluous. He merely states that socialists do believe, in spite of Kelsen, that human beings can change for the better: once class conflicts are done away with, socialist education will bring out the natural feeling of solidarity that will ensure harmony without compulsion.

Adler holds, in fact, that socialism is not only the ideal of a harmonious society, guaranteed by historical necessity, but also the reconciliation of empirical community life with the requirements of 'human nature', the transcendental unity of mankind which cannot find expression as long as class divisions breed inequality and injustice. He agrees not only with Rousseau but also with Fichte in believing that it is possible to restore to man his authentic essence, to make him once more what he really *is*—not merely what he would like to be, or must be by virtue of the 'laws of history'. Adler's philosophy thus postulates—this time in agreement with Marx but not with the orthodox of the Second International—a particular kind of reality that, though it is not empirically perceivable, already exists in some way, and is, as it were, the entelechy or 'truth' of humanity: the totality of the imperative demands of human nature, impelling the course of events towards a reconciliation of human essence with human historical existence. Adler's whole thought is centred on these two strictly correlated ideas: the unity of humanity as the transcendental constitution of consciousness, and the unity of humanity as an actual state of affairs which is the objective of the socialist movement.

Adler concedes, it is true, that the community of the future will not put an end to all tension, nor will it dry up the sources of development. Since, however, there will be general solidarity and freedom from material cares, we can expect that people will devote themselves with more fervour to the problems of art, metaphysics, and religion: this may give rise to fresh conflicts, but they will not be such as to disturb the basic solidarity of mankind. Here too Adler was in agreement with the general Marxist stereotypes: he believed in the absolute salvation of humanity and in a perfect harmony grounded in the moral consciousness of all members of society.

Adler dismisses the objection put forward by sociologists—Max Weber and especially Robert Michels—that any democracy, simply because it is a representative system, tends to evolve a bureaucracy which in time becomes an independent force, the master of the electorate instead of its servant. Michels in his classical work *Zur Soziologie des Parteiwesens in der modernen*

Demokratie (1914) concluded from a detailed analysis of the functioning of political parties, and especially the social democrats, that the emergence and autonomization of a political apparatus is an inevitable result of the democratic process within a party: consequently, he argued, democracy is bound to fall into an internal contradiction, or, in other words, perfect democracy is a theoretical impossibility. In the pursuit of its objectives the party creates a political machine which is virtually irremovable and can nearly always impose its will on the electors without violating the system of representation, while at the same time creating and furthering its own professional or factional interests. It can be expected that in future the oligarchic tendencies in democratic bodies will encounter more opposition from the masses than they to today; but such tendencies cannot be prevented from existing and recurring at all times, for they are rooted in the very nature of social organization.

Adler does not accept this 'law of oligarchy'. Under political democracy, he agrees, it is inevitable that autonomized 'apparatuses' will come into being, both in political parties and in the state: no party, not even the workers', is exempt from this danger. But under social democracy it can be averted, by education and by decentralizing the state. Hence Adler especially values workers' councils as institutions of direct control by producers over economic processes, and for the same reason he sharply criticizes Lenin and the Soviet state. The Bolsheviks, he says, have not established a dictatorship of the proletariat, but a party dictatorship over the proletariat and the whole of society—the terrorist rule of a minority, and a far cry from the predictions of Marx, to whom the dictatorship of the proletariat meant the rule of the entire working class in conditions of political democracy. Adler thus attacks the Bolsheviks from a position similar to that of Rosa Luxemburg, and at the same time criticizes Kautsky for wrongly opposing democracy to dictatorship.

Like the German centrists, Adler failed to provide an exact definition of the term 'revolution'. He agreed with Marx that the revolution must smash the existing state machine, but he also believed that it might, though not necessarily, be effected by legal and parliamentary means, without violation of the constitution. He did not make clear how these statements were to be reconciled. Like nearly all Marxists he was also vague in his description of the future socialist order. He saw no difficulty in arguing that on the one hand society would be linked by a unity of interests and aims and that production must therefore be centrally planned, while on the other hand socialism implied the maximum degree of decentralization and federalism. In these matters all Marxists were content with general formulas, declaring that they were not utopians and were not disposed to predict the details of socialist organization. They ignored, or answered in generalities, the objections of the anarchists, who showed more discernment in this particular sphere.

11. The future of religion

WHILE the Austro-Marxists were in general agreement with German orthodoxy on questions of the state, revolution, and democracy, both Adler and Bauer expressly differed from it as to the interpretation of religious faith. The orthodox, following Marx and Engels, regarded religion as the outcome of specific social conditions, oppression, ignorance, and 'false consciousness'. They advocated religious tolerance in state and party, but they were convinced that as exploitation and oppression were done away with and public enlightenment increased, religious beliefs were bound to die a natural death. As to the content of such beliefs, their incompatibility with the 'scientific outlook seemed too obvious to need discussing.

Adler did not accept these stereotypes, inherited by Marxism from the rationalists of the Enlightenment; he did not believe that men could ever do without religion, or that it was desirable that they should. In this respect too he was influenced by Kant, though he did not accept his view in every detail.

In Adler's opinion the evolutionist assertion that religious beliefs had grown up as a result of nature-worship was arbitrary and improbable, for there was no reason why concepts that bore no relation to experience should arise on a purely empirical basis. Religion was not a misinterpretation of experience, but resulted from the insoluble conflict between the natural and the moral order. Man was unable to resolve the contrast between his awareness of himself as a free, rational, purposive being and, on the other hand, the necessities of nature which restricted his freedom and spiritual expansion, brought upon him suffering and death, and created an impassable gulf between morality and happiness. No theoretical reflection and no empirical knowledge could reconcile these two orders of existence or provide a picture of the world as a synthetic whole (*Totalität*). This could only be done by religion, which, thanks to the idea of the divine Absolute, gave a universal meaning to the world of nature and the world of spirit, including scientific inquiry. This did not mean, however, that the idea of the Absolute could be inferred from empirical data or rational reflection. Religious concepts had a practical, not a theoretical, significance, which again did not mean that they were delusions but that they were arrived at by a practical route. Religion that purported to replace scientific knowledge was superfluous and was rightly criticized. The existing forms of religion were historical in character, but contained an unchanging nucleus which might one day be seen in its pure form as a 'rational religion' (*Vernunftreligion*)—not in the sense that its truth was proved by reason, but in the sense that it derived from man's practical attempts to define himself as a rational being, and not from any external revelation. Religion realized for the first time the primacy of practical reason, for it effected a synthesis between man as a part of nature and man as a moral and practical being, and conferred a meaning on human personality, to which nature is indifferent. God, as the absolute synthesis of Being, is not an object of theoretical proof but is the postulate of practical reason in the Kantian sense: not merely something we desire, for our desires may be illusions, but something required by our existence as free, morally oriented subjects. Genuine religion is thus 'subjective' in the sense that its proper meaning is related to human personality and cannot be based on an external revelation; but it is not subjective in the sense that it is an arbitrary caprice or an illusory compensation.

Adler's thoughts on religion, expressed, for example, in *Das Soziologische in Kants Erkenntniskritik* (1924), are based, it will be seen, on the opposition of 'nature' and 'spirit'; it is not clear how this is to be reconciled with the transcendentalist position which holds that everything is relative to the universal consciousness, and which thus leaves no room for nature conceived as indifferent and independent of consciousness. It would appear that Adler, on the one hand, wished to assert the perfect unity of the human species and evolved for this purpose his concept of transcendental consciousness, while on the other hand, realizing that this concept failed to allow for the unreplaceable value of the human individual, he sought to rescue the latter by means of the divine Absolute. He seems thus to have felt that a purely anthropocentric or even purely transcendentalist position was unsustainable, as it took no account of personal subjectivity. In this respect his hesitations are reminiscent of Brzozowski, except that Adler maintained his absolute transcendentalism to the end instead of trying to synthesize it with his *Vernunftreligion* and so repair the incoherence of his philosophy.

Otto Bauer did not go so far as Adler in the philosophical interpretation of religion, but he too diverged from the Marxist stereotypes. He believed that historical materialism did not imply any specific *Weltanschauung* or answer to the problem of religion or philosophical materialism. A world outlook could be interpreted as a function of class-interests: thus Calvinism was specially adapted to the needs of the bourgeoisie in the early stages of capitalism, while Darwinian materialism 'reflected' the laws of capitalist competition. The modern bourgeoisie was returning to religion, seeking in it a defence against threats to the social order. But church institutions, the clergy and their theological systems must be distinguished from the religious feeling which afforded consolation to the humiliated and oppressed. The socialist party should not profess or advocate an anti-religious outlook: it was fighting for clear political aims, not for the existence or non-existence of God. Nor should it be expected that the need for religion would die out in a socialist society. Men had a permanent need to seek for the hidden meaning of the world, and this could not be stifled. The expectation was rather that when religion was freed from social entanglements, that aspect of it would come to light which did not depend on passing circumstances but on the nature of the human spirit itself (*Sozialdemokratie, Religion und Kirche*, 1927).Unlike Adler, however, Bauer did not avow any religious convictions of his own, even in an abstract philosophical form.

12. Bauer: the theory of the nation

BAUER'S book on the question of nationality is seldom read nowadays, as may be seen from the fact that references to it in various encyclopedic works are generally incorrect. Yet it is the most important Marxist study in this field, and is based on a shrewd historical analysis.

Bauer criticizes a number of existing theories of the nation. Firstly, those of the spiritual type, which define it as the embodiment of a mysterious 'national soul', and secondly, materialist racial theories after the manner of Gobineau, based on the concept of a no less mysterious biological substance inherited by the national community: both these are metaphysical and therefore unscientific interpretations. Thirdly, voluntarist theories like that of Renan, which define a nation by the will to form a state: these are mistaken, because they imply that a people which is content to remain within a multinational state— like a large proportion of the Czechs—does not qualify as a 'nation'. Fourthly, empirical definitions which define a nation by enumerating various separate features such as language, territory, origin, customs, law, religion: these are unsatisfactory, because the individual features are not essential and play a different part at different times in forming the national life, so that by listing them we have not grasped the essence of the phenomenon.

What then is a nation? We can answer this question by taking the existing, clearly recognizable national units and examining the historical conditions that have given rise to them. Bauer does this with especial reference to the German nation, and arrives at the following conclusions.

The primary determinant of a nation is national character: this, however, itself requires explanation, and alters in the course of history. The factors that create and stabilize it are both natural and cultural. The physical community is defined not only by the existence of common forbears, but to a greater extent by the fact that conditions of life lead to a differentiated selection of physical types in accordance with the Darwinian law: certain characteristics are conducive to the survival of maritime peoples, others of hunters, etc. The inheritance of selected qualities is not contrary to historical materialism, but supplements it. As a result of shared conditions of life and natural selection there comes into being a cultural community which is, as it were, a piece of crystallized history. 'The nation is never anything but a community of destiny. This community, however, becomes effective on the one hand through the natural inheritance of qualities bred by the common destiny of the nation, and on the other by the transmission of a cultural patrimony the nature of which is determined by the nation's fate' (*Die Nationalitätenfrage*, p. 21). The existence of a national character does not consist merely in the fact that the individuals forming the nation are in some ways alike, but in the fact that historical forces have made them so.

In history up to the present time the national community has taken two forms. The first is the tribal link, which dissolves and is modified with ease; the second is the nation embodying a class society, especially since the beginnings of capitalism. The community of the early Germanic tribes and that of the medieval empire based on the ethos of chivalry differ from that created by specifically capitalist economic and cultural ties. Commodity production and trade, the improvement of communications, national literature, the post, newspapers, universal education and military service, democracy, the franchise, and finally the working-class movement—all these have successively contributed to uniting the isolated German peoples into a nation conscious of its unity. Even today, however, though less so than in the Middle Ages, participation in the national culture is reserved to the ruling classes. Peasants and workers are the backbone of the nation, but are culturally inactive. It is the business of the socialist movement to fight for the participation of all classes in the national culture.

Hence Bauer draws the inference, which is natural to his argument but contrary to the received Marxist opinion, that socialism not only does not obliterate national differences but reinforces and develops them by bringing culture to the masses and making the national idea the property of everyone. 'Socialism makes the nation autonomous, so that its fate is determined by its own will, and this means that in a socialist society nations will be increasingly differentiated, their qualities more sharply defined and their characters more distinct from one another' (*Die Nationalitätenfrage*, p. 92). Clearly, if the nation is (as Bauer finally describes it) 'a collectivity of human beings united by community of destiny in a community of character' (p. 118), then the more the people shares in deciding its own fate, the more evident and significant national characteristics will become. Socialism does not level out national differences, but enhances to an extreme degree the importance of the national principle in history.

This does not mean, however, that it intensifies national hatred or oppression. On the contrary, national hatred is a distorted form of class hatred, and national oppression is a function of social oppression. Hence the working class, fighting against all oppression, fights national oppression too, and in bringing about a socialist society it destroys the conditions that might revive national enmity and conflicts of national interest. The existence of many nations and national characters is part of the cultural wealth of mankind, and there is no reason to seek to diminish their number. In the preface to the second edition of his book (1922) Bauer refers to Duhem, who detected national peculiarities even in such a 'universal' field as physics: the British are more concerned with constructing easily visualized mechanical models regardless of theoretical consistency, while the French are more interested in uniformity of theory. Bauer relates this state of affairs to the different development of absolute monarchy in the two countries.

There is, then, no harm in the fact that the socialist movement itself is differentiated according to nationality, and it would be fatal to impose a uniform pattern on everyone. There is no conflict between proletarian internationalism and national variety. Members of the proletariat are linked together by a similarity of destiny, but not by a common destiny in the same sense as a nation. By destroying the conservative tradition and enabling every nation to decide its own affairs, socialism opens up entirely new prospects of the development of national consciousness and culture. The liberal bourgeoisie supported the right of nations to self-determination because the nations that were awakening and throwing off the yoke of absolutism provided it with new markets. The imperialist bourgeoisie, on the other hand, endeavours to subjugate undeveloped countries. The working class sometimes profits by imperialist policy, but the adverse consequences far outweigh the good, and in any case the racial and imperialist ideology is profoundly alien to socialism. 'When the capitalist class aims at creating a large multinational state under the dominion of a single nation, the working class takes up the old bourgeois idea of a free national state' (Die Nationalitätenfrage, p. 455).

Socialism, therefore, is on the side of national self-determination; but does this mean that the working class in multinational states should fight under the banner of separate statehood for each nation? This was a key question for the Austrian social democrats. Bauer used the same arguments as Rosa Luxemburg, though he was far from sharing her nihilist attitude to the national question. The fight for separate statehood was harmful to socialism because it linked the workers with the bourgeoisie. The right course was to work within the framework of existing states, demanding freedom for all nations to organize their spiritual and cultural life. 'A constitution that gives each nation the ability to develop its own culture, and that compels no nation to reconquer and reassert this right again and again in a fight for political power; a constitution that does not base the power of any nation on the rule of a minority over the majority—this is what the proletariat demands in the field of national policy . . . Each nation should govern itself and be free to meet its own cultural needs from its own resources: the state should confine itself to watching over those interests that are common to all its nations and are neutral as between them. In this way national autonomy and self-determination is necessarily the constitutional objective of the working class of all nations in the multinational state' (ibid., pp. 277–8).

Bauer considered, therefore, that in Austrian conditions the best course was to fight for complete national autonomy for all ethnic groups in the Monarchy, for the maximum enlargement of the powers of national institutions, and the maximum limitation of the functions of the state. In agreement with Renner, he contended that the national principle should not be based on territory. There were in Austria-Hungary many areas of mixed language and many linguistic enclaves, while migration to the towns and various economic factors caused incessant changes in the territorial basis of nationality. Consequently the personal principle should prevail, i.e. every citizen should choose his own national status. Each nation would set up its own organization and possess funds for the development of national culture, schooling in its own language, and institutions of all kinds. National self-governing bodies should be the foundation of the whole authority of the state. Generally speaking, a separate state for each nation would no doubt present some advantages, but granted complete freedom of national life, the interests of large states would prevail. Bauer was of course aware of the difference between the position of those peoples who lived wholly within the confines of the Monarchy, such as the Czechs, Hungarians, and Croats, and those who were divided by international frontiers, like the Poles, Ruthenes, Germans, and Serbs. He foresaw the possibility of an armed rising by the Poles in pursuit of national unity, but he thought this depended on events in Russia. If the revolution succeeded there, the Poles and other nations of the Russian empire would gain their autonomy and Austria-Hungary would have to accept a similar solution. If the revolution failed, the Poles might rise against the partitioning powers and bring about the dismemberment of the Monarchy. But the working class should not base its hopes on an imperialist war and the collapse of Austria-Hungary, for this would mean the victory of reaction in Russia and Germany. The struggle should be carried on on the basis of the existing state.

Bauer changed his mind, however, during the Balkan War, as he came to the conclusion that the Monarchy was bound to collapse owing to the strong pressure of the Slav nations for independence. During the war of 1914–18 he proclaimed the right of every nation to form a state of its own.

To sum up: Bauer shared the opinion of all Marxists that national oppression was a function of class oppression. He did not agree with them, however, that national differences would disappear in a socialist society, and he thought it a good thing that they should continue to exist. Unlike Lenin and Rosa Luxemburg, but like the Polish socialists of the PPS, he ascribed intrinsic value to the national community and thought this value should be defended. The Leninists, especially Stalin in 1913, attacked him on the ground that he did not come out firmly for the right of each nation to break away from the Monarchy, but confined his aim to self-determination in the form of cultural autonomy.

But there was no essential theoretical difference between them. Bauer maintained that the working class should not fight under the banner of national separatism and so did Lenin. Lenin, however, regarded national oppression as a destructive force of which the party should take advantage to overthrow the existing order. Bauer, who did not touch on this idea, was concerned to do away with national oppression, not to exploit it for party ends. He believed that in conditions of complete freedom and autonomy the problem of state separatism would cease to exist. There remained, of course, the question of the partitioned nations, especially Poland. Bauer did not take a clear line on this in his book, at any rate less so than Lenin, who endorsed the view that it would be a shameful farce if the Polish proletariat were to fight for the resurrection of the Polish state. Later, however, Bauer recognized not only Poland's right to independence but also, in contrast to Lenin's view, the real need for such independence. In the last resort the difference between him and Lenin was that to Lenin the national question was a tactical one of exploiting anti-Russian resentment, while national oppression would automatically disappear under socialism, whereas Bauer regarded nations as valuable in themselves and enriching human culture by their differences.

Renner, from this point of view, was much more of an Austro-Hungarian patriot. He also advocated cultural autonomy, but to the last opposed the idea that the socialist party should rest its hopes on the dissolution of the Monarchy. However, both he and Bauer emphasized that political democracy was a prerequisite to the solution of national conflicts, and that national oppression could not be done away with in conditions of despotism.

13. Hilferding: the controversy on the theory of value

HILFERDING'S controversy with Böhm-Bawerk epitomizes the whole range of problems connected with the Marxian theory of value and discussed during the period of the Second International. Eugen Böhm-Bawerk, the chief exponent of the 'psychological school' of economics, criticized Volume I of *Capital* in his *Geschichte und Kritik der Kapitalzinstheorien* (1884) and, after the publication of Volume III, produced a further criticism entitled *Zum Abschluss des Marxschen Systems* (1896: English translation, *Karl Marx and the Close of his System*, 1898). Hilferding believed that bourgeois political economy was no longer capable of forming integrated theories, but that the psychological school was an exception and was therefore worth noticing. Accordingly, in *Böhm-Bawerks Marx-Kritik* (*Marx-Studien*, vol. i, 1904) he summed up the Austrian economist's arguments against Marx and combated them from the orthodox standpoint.

According to Böhm-Bawerk, Marx had furnished no empirical or psychological grounds for his theory that labour constitutes value. Like Aristotle, he argued that as objects were exchanged they must possess some comparable, commensurate feature, and he arbitrarily assumed that this must consist in the labour input. In so doing Marx had made several errors. Firstly, he took into account only the products of labour; but the products of nature, such as land, were also exchanged, and accounted for quite a large part of the sum of trans-actions. Secondly, Marx entirely disregarded use-value, which was illegitimate since, as he himself emphasized, use-value was a condition of exchange-value. Thirdly, Marx assumed that apart from use-value an object consists of nothing but crystallized labour. But this ignores its scarceness in relation to demand, the fact that it is an object of need, the fact that it is or is not a natural prod-uct: why then should only one of its properties be the basis of value?

Moreover, Böhm-Bawerk continues, the category of value in Marx's sense is useless because it cannot be measured quantitatively apart from price, and one reason for this is that complex labour cannot, as Marx would have it, be reduced to a multiple of simple labour: forms of labour differ in quality and cannot be expressed in units of labour-time. The proposition that value gov-erns the terms of exchange thus cannot be empirically verified and affords no explanation of true economic processes.

In addition, Volume III of *Capital* contradicts Volume I, for in considering the origin of the average rate of profit Marx states that prices as a rule do not correspond to values, and that actual exchanges always take place at a rate dif-ferent from the proportionate input of socially necessary labour. Admittedly, Marx also says that these deviations are made up for on the global scale, i.e. that the sum total of all prices is equal to that of all values; but this is a tautol-ogy if we cannot define the relative values of any particular commodities. Since the concept of value does not explain the actual price relationship, it cannot serve any purpose in economic analysis.

In his rebuttal of this argument Hilferding tries to show that Böhm-Bawerk failed to understand Marx's theory of value and that his objections are either misconceived or do not lessen its utility.

As to the ignoring of use-value, Hilferding says that in the act of exchange use-value does not exist for the seller, so it would be hard for him to take it as the basis of price. According to Marx, as long as there is no commodity pro-duction and exchange is a casual and inessential phenomenon, objects are exchanged according to the will of their possessors, but in the course of time exchange-value becomes independent of use-value. Why then is labour the determinant of value? To this question Hilferding replies that objects acquire exchange-value only as commodities, i.e. when they are quantitatively con-fronted with others on the market: the possessors take part in the act of exchange not as human individuals but as embodiments of the over-all relations of production. The subject of economics is only the social aspect of commodities, i.e. their exchange-value, although the object itself is a 'unity' of exchange-value and use-value. The commodity expresses social relations, and hence the labour contained in it takes on a social character as necessary labour. In the exchange context people are not people in the psychological sense, and commodities are not objects defined by their qualities. But Marx endeavours to find the link between factors of production, and this link appears in the exchange process in a mystified form, as a link between things and not people. The commodity is defined quantitatively as the sum of the labour contained in it, and 'in the last resort' social changes can be reduced to the law of value. A theory which takes as its starting-point use-value, human needs, and the utility of objects seeks to explain social processes on the basis of the individual relation between the person and the thing; but it fails of its purpose, as it cannot on this basis discover any objective social measure or apprehend the real course of social development, which cannot be deduced from the relationship between an individual who wants something and the object that satisfies his want. In Marx's theory, by contrast, the principle of value 'causally dominates' the whole life of society. Within the total framework of social relations, things that are not commodities, such as land, may take on the character of commodities: man's control over natural forces enables him to obtain an exceptional amount of surplus value, and this privilege is expressed as the price of land. As for the attributes of commodities other than value, which Böhm-Bawerk mentions, they afford no basis for quantitative comparison.

As regards the reduction of labour to a common measure, Marx does indeed maintain that complex labour is a multiple of average simple labour, i.e. that involved in the expenditure of labour-power such as every human being on the average possesses. Different kinds of work depend on the degree of complexity, and the quantitative proportion between them is determined by the social process itself. Certainly there is no absolute measure by which complex labour could be reduced to simple labour independently of the market; but there is no need of this, for the purpose of economics is not to account for specific price-relations but to discover 'the laws of the social development of capitalism'. Absolute prices as they are given in experience are the starting-point of this investigation, but what it is concerned with are the laws of change, to which absolute prices are irrelevant: the important thing to note is that a change in the productivity of labour alters the relation between prices. Simple labour enters into complex labour in many ways, for example as labour expended in training complex labour-power, and so in the end complex labour can be conceived as the sum of simple labour. Böhm-Bawerk confuses the theoretical and the practical measurement of value: the latter is not possible, but the former is, and the only true measurer is the whole of society and the laws of competition that govern it. The idea that it is possible in practice to measure the value of particular commodities led to the utopian notion of a 'labour currency'; Marxism, however, is not concerned with fixing prices but with observing social laws.

Nor is it true, Hilferding continues, that Marx's theory of average profit refutes the theory of value. In Volume I of *Capital* he discusses equivalent exchange, but he does not say that actual exchange takes place at the rate determined by the proportionate input of socially necessary labour, and he is careful to point out that prices diverge from values. These divergences do not invalidate the law of value, but only 'modify' it. Economic theory is concerned to find out whether price-changes conform to a general tendency that can be expressed as a 'law': it is not concerned with the value of particular products. Marx's statement that the sum total of prices equals the sum total of values is not an empty one, for it enables us to conclude that all profit comes from production and not from circulation, and that the total volume of profit is identical with the total volume of surplus value. The argument that it is not only value that determines price is not a refutation of Marx, for Marx holds that when prices are given, their subsequent movement depends on the productivity of labour.

A careful reading of this controversy leads to the conclusion that Hilferding did not really answer Böhm-Bawerk's objections but was content to repeat the relevant arguments from *Capital*, so that his refutation is not convincing. Böhm-Bawerk's main arguments are three: (1) value in Marx's sense cannot be measured quantitatively, partly (but not solely) because there is no way of reducing different kinds of labour to a common measure; (2) prices depend on many factors, not only value, and we cannot ascertain the quantitative importance of value in relation to the others; (3) therefore the statement that value governs the movement of prices and social relations is both arbitrary (because it is not clear on what ground we are asked to believe that value is determined by labour-time) and scientifically useless, for it does not help us to explain the movement of prices, still less to foresee it. Hilferding accepts the first two points but denies that they affect Marx's theory, since it does not purport to explain actual terms of exchange but only to discover the general laws of change, and these are subordinate to the law of value.

We need only repeat here the remarks we have already made in discussing *Capital*. In the empirical sciences we generally define a law as a statement that in such and such particular conditions, such and such phenomena always occur. Clearly the statement that the value of a commodity is equal to the amount of socially necessary labour put into it is not a law but a definition of value. It could be proved that it was not an arbitrary definition if we were able to show that this particular attribute of commodities does govern actual price-changes; this latter proposition could then be called a law. But here is the real difficulty: price-changes depend on several factors—the average rate of profit, the supply-demand ratio, value, etc.—and we cannot ascertain their quantitative distribution. Hilferding evades the point by means of the formula 'in the last resort', which is familiar from historical materialism. Economic changes are determined in the last resort by the value of commodities; but what does this mean, if we accept that actual price-changes are *not* determined only by value? Hilferding only says that, other things being equal, changes in the productivity of labour produce price-changes: the producer who uses a technique more efficient than the average will make a higher profit. This is of course true, but it can be established independently of the so-called law of value and is generally known without the benefit of that law: the concept of value does no more to explain it than does the concept of production costs. If the cost of producing an article is lower because of improved technique, the producer stands to make a bigger profit. Price-changes resulting from changes in productivity can be explained without the aid of the concept of value. Value figures in these arguments as a *qualitas occulta* and is accounted for in the same fashion. Since we know it quantitatively only through prices, to say that 'as there are prices, there must be value' is no better than to say, like the character in Molière, that as we know by experience that opium puts people to sleep, we can deduce that it has soporific qualities. All phenomena connected with the movement of prices can be just as well explained without reference to value. That inefficient producers are driven out of business by larger, more efficient ones is well known and obvious, and is amply explained by the movement of prices: it is arbitrary to say that it is explained by the 'law of value', for this does not enable us to foresee price movements any better than we could without it. Hence the law of value is not a scientific statement that can be empirically verified or refuted.

The position is similar as regards the reduction of complex labour to units of simple labour. Hilferding's statement that this process takes place of its own accord in the movement of market prices, but that it cannot and need not be quantitatively expressed, means simply that price-changes are the empirical phenomenon and are not explained by the proportion between different kinds of labour. Hence the principle of reduction has no meaning that enables us to foresee or explain anything. As for the statement that value can be measured theoretically but not practically, its meaning is very obscure: it is hard to see what can be meant by saying that any magnitude cannot be measured in practice but only in theory.

The assertion that in days when there was hardly any commodity production the terms of exchange depended on the 'will' of individuals, but that afterwards they became subject to the law of value, is contrary to Engels's statement in the preface to Volume III of *Capital* that in primitive times goods were exchanged according to value, whereas the developed commodity economy introduced other factors regulating prices.

But the law of value has in fact another sense, as Hilferding explains. In economic theory as Marx understands it we are not concerned with actual terms of exchange but with the origin of profit. This theory does not explain the actual history of capitalism, but tells us that profit comes entirely from the workman's unremunerated labour, that capital does not create value, and that the only source of value is 'productive' labour (the definition of which, as we know, arouses numerous doubts). Since the 'real producers', i.e. the workers, have no power over the values they create, while all these values (including the value of labour-power) are exchanged according to the impersonal laws of the market, the 'law of value' as Marx conceives it is an economic description of the process of the universal alienation of capitalist society. It is an ideological, not a scientific category, and cannot be verified empirically. As a category of this kind it is of course significant and of importance to the doctrine; but it serves different purposes than the political economy which seeks to ascertain actual price movements, predict changes in the economic climate, and give practical advice for the conduct of economic affairs. Marx's theory of value is intended to be of practical importance too, but in quite a different sense. Its purpose is not to describe the quantitative relations between phenomena so that we can more easily influence events, but to unmask the anti-human character of a society in which production is entirely geared to the multiplying of exchange-value; to lay bare the 'alienation' of social life, and to throw light on the contradiction between man's requirements and his empirical existence. A theory of this kind is not so much an explanation as an ideological appeal, and must be understood as such. The controversy between Marxists and critics of the theory of value is thus insoluble, as the latter expect from a general economic theory something that Marx's doctrine is unable to provide.

Hilferding believes, it is true, that it is possible to deduce from the labour theory of value a 'law of changes' in capitalist society which would demonstrate the inevitability of socialism. He does not explain, however, how this is to be done. Marx believed in the necessity of socialism, but he did not indicate what features of the capitalist economy meant that socialism was certain to come about. It is not sufficient to say that capitalism suffers from an anarchical production system, undergoes periodical crises, and arouses the working class to revolt. All this does not prove that an economy of this kind which has existed, with whatever destructive consequences, for a considerable time cannot go on existing indefinitely: Marx ought to have shown that at a given moment the system is bound to break down, but the theory of value does not help to establish this conclusion.

14. Hilferding: the theory of imperialism

HILFERDING's *Finanzkapital* gives the impression of a plan to rewrite almost the whole of Marx's *Capital* so as to adapt it to altered economic conditions. He expounds Marx's theory of currency, credit, interest rates, and crises, but the most important part of his work is concerned with changes in the world economy since Marx's death: these changes are connected with the concentration of capital, but they are of a 'qualitative' nature and cannot be represented as a simple continuation of earlier processes.

The argument starts from the theory of value and the theory of the average rate of profit. Value in the strict sense, i.e. crystallized labour-time, cannot be expressed directly but is manifested in exchange as the quantitative ratio between prices. The fact that production is geared to profit means that exchange does not conform to the principle of 'equal pay for equal work' but to that of 'equal profit for equal capital': sale is effected at production prices, not according to value. The impossibility of directly expressing the value of commodities points up the utopian character of such doctrines as Rodbertus's socialism, in which society fixes the standard amount of labour-time for each product as a basis of exchange.

The dominance of profit as a motive in production leads naturally to the concentration of capital and to technical progress: the latter expresses itself economically in the constantly increasing proportion of constant capital in the organic composition of capital, and also in a change within constant capital itself: fixed capital increases faster than circulation capital. This means that the transfer of already invested capital is increasingly difficult: circulation capital can be transferred at will from one branch of production to another, but fixed capital is linked to the production process. It would thus be extremely hard for an average rate of profit to emerge if there did not exist, in the form of joint-stock companies and banks, the means of mobilizing capital on a large scale. The interests of banks, however, differ in some ways from those of individual capitalists. Competition which drives some firms out of business is not advantageous to the banks, though it is to the surviving firms. The banks therefore aim to prevent competition among their customers, and at the same time they are interested in a high rate of profit. In other words, the banks tend to create industrial monopolies.

One result of monopoly production is a change in the function of trade. In the period of the primary accumulation of capital trade plays a decisive role: it is the starting-point of the development of capitalism, and in the first phase, thanks to the credit system, it makes production dependent on itself. In a developed capitalist economy this dependence ceases, and production and trade are separate. Then, as capital becomes concentrated, trade loses its autonomy or even becomes superfluous as a distinct branch of economic life. Commercial capital thus decreases, and its share of profit is taken over by industrial capital. The merchant becomes increasingly the agent of syndicates and cartels.

The concentration of capital leads to the concentration of banks; but, reciprocally, the greater amount of capital is at the banks' disposal, the more they are able to bring about in their own interest the concentration of industrial capital. There is thus what would today be called a positive feedback. The banks accumulate the reserve capital of the capitalists and a large part of the cash resources of the non-producing classes: consequently the amount of capital available to industry is considerably greater than the total of industrial capital. This is advantageous to industry, but makes it highly dependent on bank capital. 'The bank capital, or capital in the form of money, which is thus in reality transformed into industrial capital, we call finance capital' (*Finanzkapital*, iii, 14).

Discussing the prospects of the cartellization of industry, Hilferding puts the question whether there is any impassable limit to this process, and answers that there is not. One can imagine the whole of capitalist production in the form of a universal cartel consciously regulating all productive processes. In such circumstances prices would be fixed conventionally and this would turn into a calculation which divided the total output between the cartel magnates and the rest of society. Money would cease to play a part in production, and the anarchy of the market would be done away with. Society would still be divided into antagonistic classes, but it would have a planned economy. Hilferding does not say that matters are bound to develop in this way, but that such is the tendency of the concentration of capital. In later years he came to regard this prospect as highly probable; he did not deduce that there was no hope for socialism, but he inclined to the view that socialism, by means of peaceful expropriation, could take over the machinery of capitalist planning almost ready-made.

However, as long as the process of concentration did not attain this hypothetical absolute form, crises were inevitable in the capitalist economy: production must go through cyclic stages of prosperity and depression. The possibility of crises was inherent in the very conditions of commodity production: the division of commodities into commodity and money, and the development of credit, meant that there could be a situation of insolvency due to marketing difficulties, and insolvency at any one point led to a natural chain reaction, for sales were the precondition of reproduction. Moreover, the urge to increase profit, which was the sole motive force of production, contained an inbuilt contradiction, as it also endeavoured to limit the consumption of the working class. This did not mean that crises were solely due to the low level of consumption by the workers and that, as Rodbertus's followers hoped, they could be cured simply by raising wages. An economic crisis, Hilferding explains, is a disturbance of circulation, but of a specifically capitalist kind, so that the laws of circulation as such do not account for it. Every industrial cycle begins with such accidental circumstances as the opening of new markets and new branches of production, important technical improvements, or the growth of population. These factors cause a rise in demand which spreads to other branches of production that are in some way or other dependent on the initial ones. The period of capital turnover is shortened, i.e. the amount that the businessman must invest decreases in relation to the production capital employed. But the conditions that favour technical progress at the same time produce a fall in the rate of profit and lengthen the period of capital turnover. At a certain stage, expanding production meets with insufficient demand and has to seek fresh markets. Meanwhile capital naturally flows into branches where the organic composition is at its highest, and thus the investments in those branches are larger than in others, where the rate of profit is lower. The resulting disproportion interferes with the whole process of commodity circulation: crises as a rule are most severe in the branches of production that are most technically advanced. This leads to a chain reaction of falling prices and profits. In addition, during boom periods prices and wages rise, but prices increase more rapidly than goods, for this is the condition of increased profit. Hence consumption cannot keep pace with production, and at a given moment the system breaks down. At that moment, owing to the huge demand for bank credit during the boom, the banks are unable to even out the disproportion by granting credits. There is an acute demand for ready money, but producers can obtain it only by realizing the cash value of their own products. Everyone wants to sell at once, with the result that nobody buys: prices collapse while huge stocks accumulate, and the upshot is bankruptcy and unemployment on a large scale.

Owing to the interdependence of capitalist agencies, crises in one country affect others by way of import restrictions, and depressions tend increasingly to be worldwide. The least vulnerable concerns are those with the largest amount of capital, for they can cut production drastically without going bankrupt. Hence crises are themselves a cause of the concentration of capital, for they tend to eliminate small producers and leave the giants holding the field.

The reign of finance capital also leads to a change in the function of the state and to the decline of bourgeois-liberal ideology. The size of the area in which finance capital can operate freely becomes of even greater importance. Finance capital requires a strong state which can protect it from foreign competition and, by political and military means, facilitate the export of capital. Imperialism is the natural result of the concentration of capital and the fight to maintain and raise the profit level. The ideal situation, of course, is one in which the metropolis gains political domination over new markets and territories providing a cheaper labour force: hence finance capital supports imperialist policy and the spread of capitalist production throughout the world. The ideological weapons of the liberal bourgeoisie are out of date. The ideals of free trade, peace, equality, and humanitarianism are replaced by doctrines sanctioning the expansion of finance capital: racism, nationalism, the ideal of state power, and the worship of force.

These developments have an important effect on the class composition of society. The old and sometimes mortal conflicts between the upper and lower bourgeoisie, between town and country or bourgeois and landowners, are less and less in evidence. Hilferding shows how the magnates of capital, as they gain control over the whole economic activity of the middle classes, create such a unity of interests that society tends more and more towards a class polarization between the workers and all the rest. The petty bourgeoisie has no longer any prospects beyond what large-scale capital allows it, and is forced to identify its interests with those of the cartels; it is also the class most receptive to imperialism and racism, to ideas of power and political expansion. Technical progress tends to reduce the working-class population, first relatively and later absolutely, while administrators, technicians, and production managers are required more and more. At the present time these classes are clearly dependent on capital, not only in the economic field but in that of ideas, and provide support for reactionary political movements. But their position is vulnerable: the demand for their talents is less than the supply, and there is already a tendency to streamline managerial techniques so as to limit or decrease their numbers. In course of time we may expect members of this class to throw in their lot with the proletariat, as they come to realize that their position and interests as salary-earners are essentially similar to those of the working class.

The reign of finance capital does not diminish class antagonism but intensifies it to the highest degree, while at the same time weeding out the class structure, so to speak, by eliminating intermediate political forces and arraying against each other the hostile forces of a financial oligarchy and the proletariat. The latter's economic organizations, fighting for better terms for the sale of labour-power, naturally evolve political organizations which go beyond the framework of bourgeois society. The coalescence of the state machine with finance capital is so obvious that the least conscious of the proletariat are aware of the antagonism between themselves and the whole existing system. The proletariat cannot, of course, oppose to imperialism the reactionary and senseless cry of a return to free trade and a liberal economy. At the same time, realizing as it does the inevitable tendency of the present system, the proletariat cannot support it even though its ultimate result is to bring about a proletarian victory. The proletariat's answer to imperialism can only be socialism. Imperialism and the reign of finance oligarchy greatly facilitate the political struggle and advance the prospects of socialism, not only by causing wars and political catastrophes that help to revolutionize the consciousness of the proletariat, but still more because they bring about the socialization of production to the utmost extent possible under capitalism. Finance capital has separated the management of production from ownership and created huge capital accumulations subject to unified control. Hence the expropriation of the financial oligarchy by the state, once the proletariat has gained power, is a comparatively easy task. The state need not and should not expropriate all medium-sized and small enterprises, which, in any case, are at the present time completely dependent on the magnates of finance. Finance capital has already performed most of the expropriation. The state has only to take over the big banks and industrial firms in order to control production; if it is working-class state it will use its economic power in the public interest and not to increase private profit. A single wholesale expropriation would be economically superfluous and politically dangerous.

At the end of his work Hilferding formulates the 'historical law' that 'In social formations based on class antagonisms, great social changes take place only when the ruling class has achieved the maximum concentration of its forces' (*Finanzkapital*, v. 25). This stage, he predicts, will soon be reached by bourgeois society, which will thus create the economic conditions for the dictatorship of the proletariat.

Hilferding's work had a greater influence on the development of Marxism than any other product of the Austrian school. It was in fact the most comprehensive attempt at a scientific analysis, from the Marxist point of view, of post-Marxian trends in the world economy. Hilferding was one of the first to point out the importance of the separation between capitalist ownership and production management, and to point out the increasingly significant role of managers and technicians. He also gave a lucid summary of the economic and political consequences of the new era of the concentration of capital.

His work is written from the standpoint of 'classical' Marxism, i.e. on the basis that concentration will lead finally to the polarization of classes and that the industrial proletariat is the battering-ram which will destroy the world of capital. He did not, however, draw the same conclusions from this analysis as Lenin subsequently did. Hilferding regarded capitalism as a worldwide system that would be destroyed owing to the exacerbation of class antagonism between the bourgeoisie and the proletariat. Lenin, from the same global point of view, concluded that the contradictions of imperialism would lead to its breaking down not at the points where economic evolution had gone furthest but at those where there was the greatest concentration and complexity of social conflicts. Other, non-proletarian demands—in particular those of the nationalities and the peasantry—must be present to constitute a reservoir of tension, and revolution was most probable where claims and dissensions were most numerous, rather than at the principal centres of finance capital. Hilferding believed in a proletarian revolution in the Marxian sense, as did Rosa Luxemburg, Pannekoek, and the whole of West European left-wing socialism; Lenin believed in a political revolution led by the party, supported by the proletariat but requiring in addition the impetus of other claims which it purported to represent and which it harnessed to its cause.

XIII

The Beginnings of Russian Marxism

1. Intellectual movements during the reign of Nicholas I

HISTORICAL DETERMINISM and the peasant question: these two headings sum up the history of the radical intellectual movement in nineteenth-century Russia, both in its pre-Marxist phases and in at least the first phase of the evolution of Marxism. The two questions were by no means independent of each other: the issue was whether and how far the theory of 'historical necessity' was reliable in general, and in particular what light it threw on the future of Russia—an overwhelmingly peasant country with a rudimentary industrial proletariat, governed by an autocracy and suffering, even after the 1861 reform, from many of the evils of feudalism.

The peculiarities of Russian Marxism are generally attributed to the special political and economic circumstances of the Empire, the effect of patterns created by pre-Marxist revolutionary movements, and the country's philosophical and religious tradition. There is no doubt much truth in these explanations, though they do not suffice to account for the spread of Russian Marxism in its Leninist form in other parts of the world after the October Revolution.

In considering the special character of Russian history emphasis has been laid not so much on political despotism as such but rather on its 'Oriental' nature: i.e. the far-reaching independence of the state and its bureaucracy *vis-à-vis* civil society, and its dominance over every social class including the most privileged. The Marxist thesis that state institutions in a class society are 'nothing but' organs of the privileged classes is harder to apply to Russia than to West European societies. In the nineteenth century some Russian historians, such as B. N. Chicherin, expressed the view, which is still held by some today, that the Russian state, far from being the outcome of previously existing class antagonisms, itself, as it were, created social classes from above. The Russian Marxists did not accept the theory of the autonomous nature of the Russian state in such an extreme form, but Plekhanov and Trotsky, for instance, agreed that the independence of the state apparatus in Russia was incomparably greater than elsewhere in Europe. Plekhanov in his historical analyses laid special emphasis on the 'Asiatic' features of the Russian autocracy: hence the importance he attached to decentralization in political programmes. Berdyaev wrote that Rus-

sia was a victim of the hugeness of her territory: the needs of defence and imperial expansion had led to the growth of a bureaucratic-military apparatus of
coercion which constantly thwarted the short-term interests of the possessing
classes and, from the time of Ivan the Terrible onwards, had consolidated itself
while brutally suppressing their aspirations. All major economic changes in Russian history have been effected from above by means of state power: this is true
of Peter the Great's time, of the reforms of Alexander II, and of industrialization and collectivization under Stalin. The essential feature of what is today
called totalitarianism—namely the principle that the whole life of society, especially economic and cultural activity, must not only be supervised by the state
but must be absolutely subordinated to its needs—has been characteristic of
Russia for centuries: it could not, of course, always be put into practice so effectively, but it was and is the constant basis of the activity of the state apparatus.
It follows from this principle that the state is the only legitimate source of any
social initiative, and that any organization or crystallization of social life that is
not imposed by the state is contrary to its needs and interests. It also follows
that the citizen is the property of the state, and that all his acts are either directed
by the state or are a challenge to its authority. Russian despotism created a society in which there was scarcely any middle term between servility and rebellion, between total identification with the existing order and absolute denial of
it. Hence it was only late in the day and with great difficulty that Russia assimilated the idea of freedom which had taken shape in Western Europe through
centuries of struggle between kings and barons, the nobility and the bourgeoisie—freedom which is defined by law and presupposes a legal order of society. In Russia social conditions were such that freedom was conceived only as
anarchy, as the absence of law, since law presented itself in scarcely any other
form than as the arbitrary will of a despotic ruler. Between absolutism and dis-
orderly peasant revolt it was difficult in the extreme to evolve an idea of freedom sanctioned and limited by law: revolutionary movements naturally slid into
the idea of a new form of totalitarianism (Pestel, Tkachov) or towards the anarchist vision of a society free from all laws and political institutions. Extremism
and maximalism, which are often singled out as characteristics of Russian culture, may be regarded as due to the history of a country which never produced
a strong middle class and whose stability always depended on the strength and
efficiency of a centralized bureaucracy and only to a very small degree on the
organic crystallization of interest-groups—a country in which to think about
social reforms in a natural manner was to think of revolution, and there was no
clear-cut dividing line between literary criticism and assassination.

The weakness of the towns and the minor role played by commerce for centuries impeded the growth of an independent intellectual culture. The emancipation of intellectuals, the cultivation of logical faculties, the power to reason

and debate, and the love of abstract analysis—all these are features of urban culture and are linked with commercial prosperity. The assertion of Moscow's supremacy and the destruction of Novgorod prevented the development of urban civilization, and the Orthodox religion helped to isolate Russia from the West. Russian Caesaro-Papism meant not only that the Eastern Church was the servant of Tsarist despotism, but also that the rulers claimed dominion over their subjects' souls: the Church was subordinated to the Tsardom in such a way as to give the latter unlimited authority over individual consciences, and the natural consequence was a system of state police supervision of citizens' thoughts. The rivalry between secular and ecclesiastical power which did so much to develop Western civilization was virtually absent in Russia: the Church identified itself with the state and allowed the latter to reign supreme in intellectual life. At the same time, Russia as a political organism was endowed with the Church's religious messianism. After the fall of Byzantium the Orthodox Church evolved the idea of Moscow as the 'Third Rome', the successor, appointed for all eternity, to the capital of Christendom that had been conquered by the Turks. Moscow as the centre of Orthodoxy and Moscow as the capital of the Tsars were one and the same: Orthodox messianism became indistinguishable from Russian messianism, and the Tsar was not only a political autocrat but the guardian of religious truth.

This, of course, is a simplified picture which does not apply equally to all periods of Russian history, but it helps to explain certain features of revolutionary Marxism in Russia.

It was natural in these circumstances that religious and philosophical thought in Russia did not develop on the same lines as in Western Europe. Russia did not go through a scholastic phase or develop the powers of logic and analysis, the classification and definition of concepts, the marshalling of arguments and counter-arguments, that were the legacy of medieval Christian philosophy in the West. On the other hand, Russia also had no part in Renaissance civilization and was not convulsed by the spirit of scepticism and relativism which left such deep marks on European culture. Both these deficiencies are glaringly evident in Russian philosophical thought from its beginnings in the Enlightenment period. Its exponents are literary men and intellectual amateurs, intrigued by social or religious questions but incapable of systematizing their thoughts, of analyzing concepts with laborious care or appraising the logical value of arguments. The philosophical writings of the greatest Russian thinkers are often fascinating from the rhetorical and literary points of view, full of passion and authentic feeling and free from 'scholasticism' in the pejorative sense: Russians did not ask what philosophy was for, they all knew its purpose. But as a rule their works are devoid of logical rigour, ill-constructed and inconsistent, shapeless, lacking in sequence and methodical subdivision.

At the same time we are struck by the absence of scepticism and relativism. There is plenty of scoffing but very little irony: a frenzy of denunciation, but little power of detachment; even the humour expresses rage and despair rather than merriment. The brilliance of the nineteenth-century Russian novel no doubt proceeds from the same causes as do the defects of Russian philosophy. Academic philosophy of the Western type did not really exist in Russia until the last quarter of the century, and had produced no works of the first rank when it was swept away by the Revolution.

It is noteworthy that the Russian philosophy which leads in a direct line to Russian Marxism has as its starting-point questions and alternatives similar to those that prompted Marx's early thinking and took the form of reflections on Hegel's philosophy of history. These discussions go back to the dark and forbidding era of Nicholas I. The young Vissarion Belinsky and the young Bakunin begin their philosophizing from the same celebrated phrase about the identity of the real and the rational which inspired and organized the critique of the Young Hegelians. Belinsky, who knew Hegel at second hand in a dilettante fashion, believed he had discovered the rationality of history even in its barbaric and despotic manifestations. It was possible, he thought, to come to terms with cruel reality if one grasped the insignificance of all that was individual, contingent, and subjective, and the greatness of historical Reason, craftily mocking at the desires and hopes of human beings. In articles written in 1839 Belinsky expounded his philosophy of reconciliation, or rather submission to the majesty of 'universality' embodied in an Asiatic satrapy. But within two years he had broken completely with this Hegelian, or rather pseudo-Hegelian, historiosophic masochism and had come to believe in the merit of the human individual as the sole intrinsic value, which must not be sacrificed to the Moloch of the historical *universale*. After his conversion to socialism and then to naturalism *à la* Feuerbach, Belinsky remained in the Russian tradition as the type of a mind oscillating between desperate fatalism and moralistic revolt, between the 'rationality' of the uncaring progress of the *Weltgeist* and the irrationality of the sentient individual, between 'objectivism' and sentimentalism.

The most important issue in Russian intellectual life under Nicholas I was that between Slavophils and Westernizers. Slavophilism was a Russian variant of Romantic philosophy in its opposition to the Enlightenment, rationalism, liberalism, and cosmopolitanism. The Slavophils (Ivan Kireyevsky, Alexey Khomyakov, Konstantin Aksakov, Yury Samarin) were in search of a philosophy to legitimize the Russian autocracy and the Eastern Church's claim to be the sole depositary of Christian truth. They idealized pre-Petrine Russia, especially the Russia of the first Romanovs, in which they discerned principles that could protect the nation from the pernicious imitation of Western liberalism and make it the spiritual leader of the world. For this purpose they elaborated the doctrine of 'community' (*sobornost*), the spiritual unity of society based on devotion to eternal truths and opposed to the mechanical, purely legal bond of interest that prevailed in Western Europe. The essence of the Russian spirit was freedom conceived as a result of the love of God, not the negative and unspiritual freedom of the liberals. Another essential feature was the integral development of the individual, in which human reason does not rely on its power of abstract thought but harmonizes its activity with living faith as the source of all spiritual values. This faith does not exist in the Roman Church, which maintains only the hierarchical unity of law, or in Protestant bodies, which have sacrificed the ideal of unity to a subjective love of freedom. In contrast to the West, whose intellectual culture and theology are based on confidence in the abstract power of logic, while its social organization takes for granted the antagonism of individual and class-interests, restrained only by the repressive force of law, the Russian spirit is that of a free organic union based on voluntary submission to divine truth and the unity of secular and religious authority.

The Westernizers did not have such a clearly defined social philosophy as the Slavophils. Westernism was the general name for the policy of 'Europeanizing' Russia: it went with the cult of natural science, an attachment to liberal principles, hatred of Tsarist despotism, and the conviction that only by taking the 'Western road' could Russia emerge from her backwardness and cultural stagnation. Although both the Slavophils and the Westernizers had roots in Russian tradition, symbolized respectively by Moscow and St. Petersburg, it is noteworthy that almost all the adherents of both schools were students of German philosophy and often defined their position with the aid of Hegelian categories. It might seem that in Nicholas I's time the conservatives had little enough reason to fear that Russia would be engulfed in a tide of liberalism. Nevertheless, despite the country's political and economic stagnation, Western ideas were beginning to seep through and find acceptance among the young, as witness the Petrashevsky discussion group. In the time of Alexander II and Alexander III, however, 'pure' versions of Slavophilism and Westernism became less important compared with trends which incorporated features of both in different ways and in varying proportions, as did all the variants of populism.

2. Herzen

ALEKSANDR IVANOVICH HERZEN (1812–70) was the first important advocate of a 'third solution', leaving room for Russia's own, non-capitalist way to social liberation and also for the values of Western liberalism. In his cult of science and hostility to religion and the autocracy he was sharply opposed to the Slavophil tradition, but his critique of capitalism was essentially in accordance with it.

As a schoolboy Herzen vowed hostility to Russian despotism, and he remained faithful to that vow. He settled in the West in 1847, and from 1855 published a periodical entitled *Polyarnaya Zvezda* (*The Pole Star*) and afterwards *Kolokol* (*The Bell*), which played a major part in animating the radical movement among the Russian intelligentsia. Like most intellectuals of his generation he went through a Hegelian phase, in which he attacked conservative interpretations of the 'rationality of the real' and upheld the dialectic as the principle of permanent negation and criticism of the existing order. He wrote some philosophical essays which, while they contain nothing original, played some part in propagating naturalist and anti-religious attitudes in Russia. His main influence, however, consisted in his critique of capitalism and hope of a specifically Russian road to socialism based on the traditional peasant community, the *mir* or *obshchina*.

Herzen was opposed to capitalism and Western civilization not because it bred poverty and exploitation but because it degraded people by the exclusive cult of material values: the universal ideal of prosperity crippled the personality, society became spiritually barren and was sunk in general mediocrity. As a rich member of the gentry, free from material cares and living in the comfort of Western capitals while he denounced the philosophy of wealth, Herzen was a suspect figure to some radicals, but he won much popularity with his appeal to a tradition that would enable Russia to achieve social justice while spurning capitalist values. He believed that the human personality was a supreme and intrinsic value, and that the purpose of social institutions was to enable it to develop and enrich itself spiritually in every way. Western civilization had the opposite effect, by standardizing all values and allowing the universal spirit of competition to destroy the spontaneous solidarity of all human beings. This was an attack on capitalism from the standpoint of aristocracy rather than socialism. However, Herzen had the people's cause at heart and was anxious not merely to preserve the values created by the privileged classes, but to extend them to everybody. The common ownership of land by the *mir* seemed to him to hold out the prospect of a new social order which would unite justice and equality with the voluntary solidarity of individuals, abolishing despotism but not replacing it by universal egoism and money-grubbing. In this way Herzen began a discussion that was to dominate Russian thinking for the next three decades: the question of Russia's road to socialism by way of the village commune.

Herzen has been invoked as a pioneer by populists, liberals, and Marxists. To the Marxists he was not only a denouncer of the autocracy but also a standard-bearer of the cult of science, an enemy to religion and the Orthodox Church and a philosopher who could, without much exaggeration, be called a materialist. Despite his hatred for despotism, however, it is hard to call him an ideologist

of revolution: he certainly was not one in the sense in which the next generation spoke of revolution, when it seemed hopeless to put any faith in a reform
of the existing system. Herzen did not get on with the revolutionaries of the
1860s: he disliked their primitivism and contempt for the non-utilitarian values of art and education, their dogmatism, intolerance, and cult of a revolutionary apocalypse, which they seemed to desire for its own sake and to which
they were prepared to sacrifice all existing values. A certain conservatism in
Herzen's thought made him aware of the danger of the fanatic belief in progress
that regards living generations as far less important than those still to come.

Although Herzen thought that Russia's situation was historically privileged
and that she could build a just society thanks to the tradition of the village
commune (which he mistakenly believed to be a survival of primitive communism), he did not link this with any nationalist messianism or with the idea of
Moscow as the future Mecca of humanity. He was a Russian patriot, but not a
chauvinist: in 1863 he offended a large part of public opinion by defending the
cause of the insurgent Poles. This was one reason, though not the only one, why
his star began to fade during the 1860s.

The death of Nicholas I and the defeat in the Crimea ushered in an era of
reforms which either caused fresh intellectual divisions or made it necessary
for old ones to be reformulated. With the abolition of serfdom and the grant of
land to the peasants in 1861, followed by reforms in the judicial system, the
army, and local government, the question of Russia's future under capitalism
ceased to be purely speculative and took on practical significance. Intensive
industrialization was still some thirty years away; the peasantry was encumbered with many remnants of serfdom, and economic questions were almost
purely agricultural in scope; but it was nevertheless clear to all that a period of
'modernization' had begun and that it was time to think about its possibilities
and dangers.

3. Chernyshevsky

THE writings of Nikolay Gavrilovich Chernyshevsky (1828–89) were much
more important to the radical intelligentsia of the sixties than those of Herzen.
Chernyshevsky was another of the chief inspirers of populism, though he is
not generally termed a populist in the strict sense. He also looked to the village commune for Russia's social regeneration, but he was more of a Westernizer than Herzen: he adopted in full the naturalist philosophy of Feuerbach
and presented it to the public in a work entitled *The Anthropological Principle
in Philosophy* (1860). He was a consistent exponent of Enlightenment-type
utilitarianism on a materialist basis. He believed that all human motives come
down in the last resort to a calculation of pleasures and pains and that egoism

is the sole driving force of human behaviour. This, however, did not mean that there could not be co-operation and solidarity, or acts of the kind described as self-sacrifice or disinterested aid: all such acts could perfectly well be interpreted as instances of the universal desire for pleasure and profit.

All these are traditional motifs, familiar from the history of utilitarian doctrine. From the same source Chernyshevsky derived his belief in rational egoism, i.e. the organization of communal life in such a way that all individual egoisms are satisfied in a general harmony. The conflict of egoisms is due to faulty social institutions and lack of education. Chernyshevsky accepted the basic values of liberalism: he desired the 'Europeanization' of Russia, the overthrow of the autocracy, political freedom, universal education, and the emancipation of the peasants. He also believed, however, that Russia could enjoy industrial progress and liberalism without extinguishing the communist flame that burnt on in the *obshchina*, and that the horrors of capitalist development could be avoided.

As disappointment ensued after the reform of 1861, Chernyshevsky laid increasing emphasis on revolutionary hopes. As time went on he lost interest in the village commune and devoted more attention in his writings to political developments and the need to overthrow the Tsardom by force. He was arrested in 1862 and sentenced to hard labour after two years' imprisonment. While in prison he wrote his celebrated novel *What is to be Done?*, which became the catechism of Russian revolutionary youth. It is a work of small literary value, didactic, boring, and pedantic, but all the more faithful to Chernyshevsky's doctrine that art, like science, had no intrinsic value but was to be judged by its immediate social utility. The novel succeeded in its purpose of instilling into revolutionary youth a spirit of asceticism, seriousness, devotion to the people's cause, and contempt for the moral conventions of their elders. It did much to popularize the moral 'style' of radical circles, marked by doctrinairism, fanaticism, sincerity and self-sacrifice, the cult of science, and the lack of a sense of humour. Lenin respected and admired Chernyshevsky all his life as the teacher who had introduced him to revolutionary ideology, and we may say that Lenin was an ideal specimen of the type which Chernyshevsky portrayed and which was not uncommon among the revolutionaries: an intellectual so exclusively devoted to the cause that any discussion which cannot be made to serve the revolution is no better than idle chatter, and values that cannot be put to use in the same way are merely food for aesthetes and dilettanti. Conversion to the revolutionary faith made it natural for many of the Russian intelligentsia, shocked and humiliated by poverty, ignorance, and oppression, to abandon all values that were peculiar to the privileged classes. Given the gigantic task of raising Russia out of her backwardness and barbarism, the cult of spiritual, aesthetic, or intellectual values that was so strong in Herzen's case seemed a betrayal of the revolutionary mission. Utilitarianism and materialism were, to speak, the natural expression of this attitude. The connection can be seen in Chernyshevsky and also in two writers who died young but were extremely popular in the 1860s: N. A. Dobrolyubov (1836–61) and D. I. Pisarev (1840–68). To the latter is attributed the remark that a pair of boots is worth more than all the works of Shakespeare.

Materialism—and this term can be applied to Chernyshevsky without reservation—thus had a clear political sense in Russia in the second half of the century. It of course involved hostility to the Church and religion, and thereby served in the fight against autocracy; at the same time, by seeming to justify a utilitarian philosophy of life, it was a negation of the culture and habits of the educated classes. Its votaries were able to brand all disinterested artistic and intellectual pursuits as idle amusements of the aristocracy, and to apply to all human thoughts and actions the key question: 'Whom does it profit?' In and after the sixties, as elsewhere in Europe, materialism was reinforced by the popularity of Darwinism. For the radicals, however, Darwinism was a two-edged sword. On the one hand, it gave opponents of religion scientific ground for saying that all human affairs could be explained in purely biological categories; on the other, especially as interpreted by Spencer, it suggested that human history and society could be explained in terms of natural selection, the struggle for existence, and the survival of the fittest. This latter consequence (as it was thought to be) of Darwinism was unwelcome to the revolutionaries on two grounds. In the first place, it might imply that the struggle for existence was an eternal law of nature, which put a stop to dreams of a perfectly harmonious future society. Secondly, if universally applied it introduced a kind of biological fatalism which condemned to sterility any individual efforts or moral endeavours. Whatever men may do, according to social Darwinism those who remain in possession of the field will finally be those who show most power of adaptation—not those whose sufferings are today most acute, or whose cause appears morally just. In this way scientism, utilitarianism, and materialism, which the revolutionaries adopted as weapons in the political struggle, appeared to show that the struggle had no purpose. Hence Chernyshevsky took from Darwinism the theory of the origin and mutation of species, but not the theory of natural selection; while later sociologists of the populist camp endeavoured to limit the Darwinian theory in various ways so as to avoid having to draw unwelcome conclusions.

4. Populism and the first reception of Marxism

THE radical movement which developed in Russia after 1861 bore the general title of populism (*narodnichestvo*). Historians differ as to the exact meaning and applicability of this term. In an article of 1898 entitled 'What heritage have we abandoned?' Lenin defined populism as consisting of three factors. In the first place, the populists (*narodniki*) considered capitalism in Russia a retrograde phenomenon and wished to halt its development. Secondly, they regarded the peasantry and especially the *obshchina* as a self-contained institution in the sense that it could not be analysed in terms of social class: they thus ignored class differences among the peasantry. Thirdly, they did not perceive the link between the intelligentsia and political institutions on the one hand and the class interests of Russian society on the other, and they thus imagined that the intelligentsia could be an independent force capable of imparting to history whatever course it chose. This account of populism, it will be seen, contains no reference to political strategy or policy *vis-à-vis* the autocracy. Those whom the Marxists combated under the name of populists in fact included both reformists and revolutionaries; some relied on terrorism, others on propaganda; they differed in their view of historical determinism, their attachment to the Slavophil or Westernizing tradition, and their attitude to Marxism. Most of the populist theoreticians were acquainted with Marxism and accepted some of its features, though none of them except Danielson styled himself a Marxist. The aspects of populism singled out by Lenin were those on which debate actually centred in the 1890s. He also characterized it from the point of view of class origin, as an ideology of small property-owners who wished to free Russian life from feudal constraint, but were frightened by the advance of capitalism which threatened to destroy their economic position. In the same article Lenin contrasted the populist tradition with that of the 'Enlightenment' writers of the sixties, such as Skaldin, who opposed all remnants of servitude and demanded political freedom, self-government, education, and the Europeanization of Russia: these writers represented the ideology of capitalist progress in a more or less pure form and did not realize the contradictions and antagonisms that the triumph of capitalism was bound to bring with it. Unlike the liberals of this stamp, the populists stood for a romantic Utopia: they realized what catastrophic results capitalism would bring, but they hoped to avert them by impossible dreams of a return to pre-capitalist forms of production and the preservation of the *obshchina* as the germ of the socialist future. The populists' merit, according to Lenin, was that they were the first to pose the question of the economic contradictions of capitalism in Russia, though they had no answer to offer except the reactionary idea of a golden age. From this point of view Lenin compared them to Sismondi, who, like them, represented the ideological interests of small owners threatened by the advance of capitalism. Like them, too, Sismondi denounced the poverty, exploitation, and anarchy of capitalist production, but had nothing to set against it except a return to craftsmanship and petty trading.

The view is held, for example by Richard Pipes, that populism in the sense defined by Lenin in this article never existed as a single intellectual or political movement. According to this view populism properly denotes a tendency which arose in the early 1870s and was based on the Bakuninist idea that it was not for the intelligentsia to impose socialism or any other doctrine on the people, but to support whole-heartedly the latter's wishes and aspirations and work for the revolution on the lines the people desired. This, it is argued, was a clearly anti-intellectual trend, involving no theory of socialism or attitude to the development of Russian capitalism, and was in fact the negation of political activity. The Marxists, and particularly Struve, are responsible for coining the term 'populism' to denote the opponents of capitalism and glorifiers of the peasant commune, but in this sense it was a political weapon and did not correspond to a historical reality. Other scholars, such as F. Venturi, A. Walicki, and Soviet historians, while not disputing that the populist ideology took many forms, use the term in the broad sense given to it by Marxist literature in the belief that it expresses the essence of the ideological controversy of the last quarter of the century in Russia, though in particular cases we may be in doubt as to whether this or that writer belongs to the populist camp.

The question is not of the first importance as far as the history of Marxist doctrine is concerned, but it is necessary to take note of the development of populism for two reasons. In the first place, populism in a broad sense was the first intellectual movement in Russia to be infiltrated by Marxism. Secondly, Marxism in Russia largely took shape through the controversy with populism and was for a long time dominated by the 'peasant question' and polemics with agrarian socialism. This accounts for certain features of the version of Marxism that finally prevailed in Russia, namely Leninism, and also for the fact that this version has since been particularly influential in parts of the world where the peasant question still dominates other social problems.

Populism in this broad sense developed around 1870 and was, in its different varieties, the chief form of social radicalism in the seventies and eighties: in the latter decade, however, orthodox Marxism made its appearance and created a new polemical situation.

The populists of varying shades were all agreed in identifying themselves with the cause of the Russian 'people', and devoted all their efforts to its emancipation. They differed, however, as to whether this meant emancipation by the people's own efforts, or whether there would have to be a revolution prepared and led by a conspiratorial organization. They agreed in believing that capitalism in Russia could only be a source of social degradation, and in hoping that the country could manage without it; but they differed in their general views of historical progress and determinism. They were united in despising political reforms and attaching no importance to liberal and constitutional slogans. These views determined the basic attitude of the populists towards Marx's theories.

They were glad to invoke his authority, but did so in a highly selective manner. They naturally welcomed his emphasis on the destructive effects of capitalist accumulation—exploitation, poverty, and spiritual degradation—and the anti-human consequences of the division of labour in its advanced form. They also gave a favourable reception to those parts of his theory which served to denounce 'formal' democracy, political liberties, and the whole liberal superstructure of capitalism and free competition. On the other hand, they rejected his view that capitalism was a tremendous historical advance and that the liberation of the working people must be preceded by the technological and social development that capitalism brought with it: in short, they rejected the Marxian-Hegelian theory of progress by contradiction, together with any suggestion that all countries had to go through the same historical evolution and endure the rigour and injustice of capitalist accumulation before they could embark on a socialist revolution. There were, of course, disputes among them as to the true meaning and degree of applicability of Marx's theory of capitalism, especially in the light of Russian conditions: the statements of Marx and Engels themselves on this point, taken together, were by no means unequivocal.

The three writers who did most to influence radical thinking in Russia in the 1870s were P. L. Lavrov, N. K. Mikhailovsky, and P. N. Tkachov. Pyotr Lavrov (1823–1900) aroused the intelligentsia to a sense of guilt vis-à-vis the people and an urge to expiate their privileges. His *Historical Letters*, published in the late sixties, and the periodical *Vperyod* (*Forward*), which appeared in Zurich in 1873–6 (he had fled from Russia in 1870), called on young members of the intelligentsia to work among the people and fan the flame of revolution. Under the combined influence of Lavrov and Bakunin there took place in 1872–4 the celebrated movement in which hundreds of young people went into the villages with the object of educating the peasants for socialism or, in the case of the Bakuninists, bringing their revolutionary instincts to the fore. The result of the pilgrimage was highly disappointing. No new Pugachovs and Stenka Razins made their appearance, nor did the peasants reveal a latent enthusiasm for socialism; they were more likely to denounce the agitators to the police than to heed their appeals. This did much to weaken Bakunin's influence, but it did not undermine the activity of Lavrov's followers, though they were obliged to change tactics.

Lavrov held that the intelligentsia could and must be the fount of revolutionary consciousness, but he did not believe that the Russian peasant was revolutionary and socialist by nature. His belief in the mission of the intelligentsia was of a moral and not a determinist character. He did not contend that there was any historical law which made it certain that Russia would adopt socialism; but he believed this could be brought about by an enlightened élite identifying itself morally with the people's cause. He demanded from the young intelligentsia self-sacrifice and a spirit of battle: their success would depend on the firmness of the people's will, not on ineluctable historical laws. Together with Mikhailovsky, Lavrov represented a viewpoint which was later called, in Russia, 'subjective sociology': viz. that social processes, unlike natural ones, are partly determined by subjective desires and ideals which animate people because they are thought to be right, not necessarily because they are expected to triumph. Our view that something is morally right cannot depend on whether we think it inevitable; and, as history is influenced by the fact that many people regard their own position as morally right, there is no reason to think that any universal laws, indifferent to human desires and ideals, are bound to impel the historical process in any particular direction. Lavrov shared the faith in the village commune as a possible nucleus of socialism in Russia, but he did not glorify the country's technical and economic backwardness; he thought the dissemination of socialist ideals among the toiling masses would lead to a revolution after which all problems of economic development could be solved. As to the struggle for a constitution and political freedom, it could only be a source of confusion and a waste of revolutionary energy. The basic elements of Lavrov's ideology—the denial of historical determinism and of the inevitability of capitalism in Russia, faith in the intelligentsia as the standard-bearer of socialism, the creative role of ideals in history, the village commune as the nucleus of socialism, indifference to the political struggle for 'liberalization'— these together form a stereotype which was to be the chief target of Marxist attack. Among pre-Marxist writers Lavrov contributed especially to awakening the revolutionary and socialist consciousness of the Russian intelligentsia. His attacks on religion as the fruit of ignorance, on law as the instrument of coercion by the privileged classes, on property as the result of theft, his emphasis on moral qualities and moral motivation among revolutionaries, his call for revolutionary asceticism and enlightenment for the people—all this went to form the radical ethos which prevailed in Russia for a long time and to a considerable extent inspired the social democratic intelligentsia.

N. K. Mikhailovsky (1842–1904) occupied a much more important place than Lavrov in the Marxists' anti-populist polemics. He was active as a writer for a longer period and was more influential, as he lived in Russia and wrote in the legal press, and, unlike Lavrov, he was not a revolutionary.

Mikhailovsky sought to integrate the peasant question in Russia into a social philosophy based on personalist and moralistic principles. In his books and articles in *Otechestvennye zapiski* (*Annals of the Fatherland*) and, in the 1890s, in his own periodical *Russkoye bogatstvo* (*Russia's Wealth*), he concentrated on analysing the social effects of capitalist economy and showing, with the aid of 'subjective sociology', that it was not historically necessary for Russia to tread the dolorous path of proletarianization and the class struggle. There were no inexorable laws of history independent of human ideals. In reasoning about society the question to ask was 'What is desirable?' and not 'What is necessary?': social processes were the work of people and depended, in part at least, on what people believed to be good. Social thought should be framed in normative categories, for values that were generally accepted were, for that very reason, a real social force. In general, no idea of progress could be formed without evaluative premises: it was not a question of pursuing the unrealizable ideals of a sociology free from value-judgements, but of examining critically the values underlying current theories of progress, viz. those of the positivists and Marxists.

Mikhailovsky's criticism was thus levelled at both Spencer and the Marxists. Spencer believed that progress was based on the unlimited differentiation of all forms of life, so that the development of the division of labour in society was progress *par excellence*. But this, said Mikhailovsky, was the reverse of the truth. If we start from the point of view of the good of the individual—and individuals are the only social reality—we see that the division of labour leads to spiritual degradation and destroys the possibility of the all-round development of the individual. This was also Marx's view. The object of life was not to develop one-sided aptitudes and increase production for its own sake, but to further the harmonious and many-sided development of personality. From this point of view the capitalist economy which favoured specialization for the sake of increased productivity was not an instance of progress but a cultural calamity. Capitalism signified pauperization of the spirit as well as the body: it broke the ties of solidarity and atomized society, universalizing the spirit of competition and struggle. Russia, however, had preserved in the village commune a form of social and productive organization which could bar the way to capitalism. The *obshchina* was based on simple, not complex, co-operation, and left the way open for all-round personal development: its members held their property in common and lived in a state of solidarity, not competition. In its present form it was not ideal, but the task was to remove the external obstacles that impeded its development and not to encourage disruptive factors in the name of abstract 'progress'. The Marxists, with their faith in the inevitability of capitalism in Russia, were in effect proclaiming a gospel of inactivity and capitulation, accepting the prospect that the great majority of the workers would be condemned to proletarianization, exploitation, and spiritual death. In acclaiming capitalism as progressive they were using a concept of progress in which the abstract idea of the common good was quite independent of the good of the individuals who made up society. But in reality all human values were personal values. There was no general good or perfect society that could be set up against the benefit of human individuals—for it is they and not society who feel and think, suffer and desire. The domination of impersonal values, even such as Justice or Science, over real individuals is contrary to anything that can properly be called progress.

Not without reason, the Marxists regarded Mikhailovsky as a Romantic critic of capitalism. In his attacks on it we recognize themes from Romantic literature, the utopian socialists, Rousseau and the anarchists, Saint-Simon and his followers, Stirner and Herzen. These attacks coincided on essential points with Marx's social philosophy (the pernicious consequences of the division of labour, the replacement of solidarity by competition, etc.), but the difference was that according to Marx humanity, to attain salvation, must first descend into the inferno of capitalism: the tyranny of money and machines over live human beings would end by destroying itself and enabling men to recapture their lost values. The question was, however, whether this applied to each country separately, or whether the fact that capitalism in some parts of the world had created the pre-conditions of socialism might not make it possible for others to avoid going through the full cycle. Marx himself had considered this point, and his well-known remarks on Russia afforded support in one important respect to the populists, who duly made use of them. In 1874 Engels, in controversy with Tkachov, expressed himself strongly against the idea that the socialist revolution could take place in a country without a proletariat, like Russia. He agreed, however, that the village commune might provide a nucleus of socialism if it survived until there was a proletarian revolution in the West: in other words there could only be a 'Russian road to socialism' if socialism first triumphed in its natural habitat, the highly industrialized countries. This idea is repeated in the preface by Marx and Engels to the Russian edition of *The Communist Manifesto* (1882): if a Russian revolution were to give the signal for the proletarian revolution in Western Europe, the village commune might be the nucleus of socialist changes. The populists were especially pleased with a letter which Marx wrote in 1877 to the editor of *Otechestvennye zapiski:* the letter was not sent, and was published in Russia only in 1886. In it Marx says clearly that the schemata of *Capital* apply to Western Europe and do not claim universal validity (though it must be observed here that there is no hint of this limitation in *Capital* itself). Therefore, Marx goes on, there is no necessary reason why Russia should follow in the footsteps of the West; but she will be obliged to do so if she continues on the course of 1861, for she will then lose her chance of separate, non-capitalist development. Marx expresses the same idea even more emphatically in a letter of March 1881 to Vera Zasulich and in his preparatory notes for this letter. (Neither Vera Zasulich nor Plekhanov thought fit to publish the letter, as they evidently feared it would give valuable ammunition to the populists: it came to light only after the Revolution.) Here he repeats that the argument of *Capital* does not in any way pre-judge the question of the *obshchina*, but adds that, having examined the matter, he believes that the latter can be a source of social regeneration if it is not destroyed by external pressure. Russia, thanks to its backwardness, is privileged socially as well as technologically. Just as it can adopt Western techniques in a ready-made, developed form without going through all the stages that have been necessary in the West, and was able to set up a banking and credit system that took centuries to establish in Western countries, so in the field of social evolution Russia can avoid the horrors of capitalism and develop the village commune into a universal productive system. Marx does not, of course, predict that this will necessarily be so, but repeats that Russia still has open to it the possibility of non-capitalist development. Altogether it may be said that on this crucial issue in Russian polemics at the time, Marx was much less of a Marxist than his Russian disciples. The latter, however, showed in the 1890s that the issue had become pointless, as by then no power could arrest the development of capitalism and the decline of the *obshchina*. Engels at this time reverted to his previous opinion and, in letters of 1892 and 1893 to Danielson, acknowledged that the *obshchina* was a lost cause. However, in a letter of 1885 to Vera Zasulich he supported the populist conspirators in another way by stating that Russia was in an exceptional situation in which a handful of people could, if they chose, bring about a revolution.

On this last point Engels was in agreement with Tkachov and his adherents. Pyotr Tkachov (1844–85) took part in underground activities from his early youth and was imprisoned more than once. From 1873 he lived abroad and became the chief ideologist of those populists who founded their hopes on a revolution brought about by terrorist conspiracy. Tkachov came to the conclusion, later formulated by Marx, that if Russia embarked on a capitalist course nothing could prevent its further development along this line, and the country would have to go through the same martyrdom as the West. But there was still time to avert this, for capitalism had not yet taken hold in Russia. The opportunity must therefore be seized to carry out a revolution at once and avoid the capitalist cycle of development. It was no good counting on the people's innate revolutionary instincts. The revolution could only be the work of a conscious, well-organized minority, an underground party with strict discipline and centralized command. The object of the revolution was the 'happiness of all', in particular the abolition of inequality and the destruction of élite cultures. Here Tkachov repeats themes from the totalitarian Utopias of the eighteenth century: the perfect society will suppress any possibility of exceptional individuals arising and will create equal conditions of life and education for all its members; a centralized authority of the enlightened *avant-garde* will plan every aspect of public life. Tkachov does not explain how the principle of equality can prevail in a society where the majority is subjected to the absolute, unfettered dictatorship of the revolutionaries, or how he reconciles hatred for élitism with the assumption of power by a revolutionary élite. His communism is of a homespun kind and displays no theoretical insight. But he is responsible, more than anyone else in Russia, for the idea of a centralized and disciplined party as the main organ of revolution. Historians have often emphasized his role as a precursor of Lenin on this point. The clandestine populist association founded in 1876 and known as Zemlya i Volya (Land and Liberty) owed its organizational ideas to Tkachov although it did not take over his social ideology. Lenin, while showing the greatest contempt for the populists especially in their later stages, had a high respect for the organizational traditions of the underground populist movement.

In the eyes of Marxist critics all the ideologists of populism were 'subjectivists', for they believed that the future of Russia could be decisively shaped by moral ideals spread by an enlightened élite (Mikhailovsky), socialist education of the people under the guidance of the intelligentsia (Lavrov), or the revolutionary will of an organized party (Tkachov). There remained, however, the question that Mikhailovsky put to the Marxists: if the scientific and completely unsubjective attitude consists in accepting what is said to be inevitable, i.e. whatever actually happens, how do the Marxists justify their own revolutionary activity? This question came to the fore later on, especially in the argument between the orthodox and the 'legal Marxists'. The populists, as it were, repeated in Russian terms the dilemma which had challenged Marx as a young man, between historical fatalism and a moralist Utopia. How can one justify theoretically and consistently the attitude of a revolutionary who desires to weigh up social phenomena in their practical, cause-and-effect relationships, not measuring them by arbitrary moral criteria, yet who does not wish to be a mere spectator or chronicler of events but believes that he can affect them by his own actions?

It should be noted that the populist doctrine in general, and the glorification of the village commune in particular, were not confined to moralists in search of a social ideal. The defence of the commune and the idea of bypassing capitalism in Russia also had purely economic foundations, as expounded, for example, by the populists Vorontsov and Danielson. These men were not political revolutionaries but, on the contrary, endeavoured to persuade the government that for the sake of economic and social progress it should cease to promote capitalist reforms and work for industrialization on different lines. They claimed to judge between the rural commune and capitalism from the standpoint of economic efficiency, while also pointing out the social consequences of each.

V. P. Vorontsov (1847–1918), in articles written in the seventies and published in book form in 1882, argued that capitalism in Russia was not only undesirable but impossible, at all events in a developed form. Russia could not follow the same path as the West, partly because its access to foreign markets was barred by stronger competitors, and also because it could not count on a home market large enough to permit the expansion of capitalist production. The development of capitalism so far was due less to natural conditions than to government protectionism—a policy that was ruinous and incapable of attaining its own aims, though it might well succeed in proletarianizing the peasantry. The home market could not expand sufficiently because capitalism, by destroying village crafts, was depriving the peasants of income with which to buy industrial products. The post-emancipation years had shown that land was passing into peasant hands on a large scale instead of its ownership being concentrated. Vorontsov was not an opponent of industrialization or a worshipper of primitive technology, but he believed that if the government went on fostering capitalism Russia would suffer from all the evils of the system without enjoying its benefits. The government should nationalize those branches of industry which required large-scale investment and should entrust small-scale industrial production to workers' co-operatives; at the same time it should remove the fiscal burdens and encumbrances which were breaking up the village commune, and should allow agriculture to develop freely on traditional lines. Vorontsov thus advocated a kind of state socialism under the aegis of the Tsarist government. The Marxists of course mocked this proposal, but, as R. Pipes observes, it is not very different from the principles of Lenin's New Economic Policy.

N. F. Danielson, the translator of *Capital* (1872) and a Marxist by conviction, also held that capitalism in Russia was bound to meet insuperable obstacles: it was in no position to conquer foreign markets, and was destroying its own home market by proletarianizing the peasants and bringing about mass unemployment. Russia's social needs could be met only by a 'popular' system in which the means of production belonged to the producers. Instead of being destroyed, the village commune should be made to adopt modern techniques and thus become the foundation of a socialist society.

The populist economists cared as little, or even less, about political freedoms and constitutions as most other members of the populist camp; but they set the whole of radical opinion against them by offering a programme of reforms whereby Russia might find salvation under the Tsar's auspices. In so doing, however, they raised new problems with which Marxist literature had to come to grips. In the nineties the question of markets was one of those most discussed in Marxist circles. In order to confute the populists it was necessary to prove that Russian capitalism was in a position to create a market sufficient for its own development. This problem was studied by all the chief Marxist writers, including Struve, Tugan-Baranovsky, Plekhanov, Lenin, and Bulgakov.

Almost immediately on its inception in the mid-seventies Zemlya i Volya was faced with the decision whether to concentrate on the political struggle or on socialist propaganda. The former meant in practice fighting for constitutional

liberties and for the liberalization of Russia on Western lines; but the populists'
dilemma was that this seemed incompatible with their socialist ideals. If Russia were to adopt a liberal and parliamentary system the prospect of socialism
would recede to an indefinite future, for it was hard to foresee a time when
socialism would triumph on the basis of popular representation. The adherents
of the traditional populist ideology therefore preferred a policy of revolutionary propaganda and education, while opposing both the idea of an alliance with
the liberals (who were few and far between at this time) and an attempt to take
over power by revolutionary force. Before long, in 1879, the organization split
into two groups. The advocates of the political struggle formed the People's
Will party (Narodnaya Volya) with a programme of terrorist action, while its
adversaries formed a group named Black Repartition (Chorny Peredel) to carry
on propaganda for the sharing-out of large estates among the peasantry. Unlike
the abstract ideals of socialism, this was calculated to appeal to the rural population, and the members of this group were thus faithful to the populist tradition of concentrating on issues understood by the people. Narodnaya Volya,
a small organization of fanatically brave and devoted terrorists, bequeathed the
legend of A. I. Zhelyabov and Sofya Perovskaya, who organized the assassination of Alexander II. It did not produce any theoretical works of importance;
its chief propagandist was Lyov Tikhomirov (1852–1923), who subsequently
recanted his revolutionary views and became an arch reactionary and monarchist. Zhelyabov and Perovskaya were hanged after the Tsar's murder on 1
March 1881; Zhelyabov declared in court that he was fighting for justice in
Christ's name, and before his execution he kissed the cross.

While the members of Narodnaya Volya held that the main revolutionary
task was to fight against the state, whose destruction would remove every hindrance to social liberation, the non-political adherents of Black Repartition
opposed the Blanquist idea of seizing power without the participation of the
masses. The repressions which followed the Tsar's murder effectively destroyed
the populist underground in both its forms. While the heroes of Narodnaya
Volya became a revolutionary legend, the Black Repartition movement produced the first outstanding ideologist of Russian Marxism in the person of
G. V. Plekhanov.

XIV

Plekhanov and the Codification
of Marxism

P LEKHANOV ranks with Kautsky in the importance of his role in the history of
Marxism and the dissemination of Marxist doctrine. He is generally, and
rightly, called the father of Marxism in Russia. Many populists had read Marx
and been influenced by him, but Plekhanov was the first Russian to adopt
Marxism as an integral, self-sufficient world-view, embracing all philosophical
questions and social theories and providing complete guidance for political
activity. Without exception, all Russian Marxists of Lenin's generation were
Plekhanov's pupils and acknowledged the fact. In addition, his writings were
influential far beyond Russia. He was not an original theoretician, nor did he
intend to be: he sought to remain faithful to the doctrine as he understood it,
and to defend it against all comers. He was an accomplished writer with a wide
knowledge of history, world literature, and social thought, though he was less
well acquainted with pure philosophy. He was also an excellent popularizer
and publicist. His mind was of a strongly dogmatic cast, and he was attracted
to all-embracing schemata. He did more, perhaps, than anyone to reduce
Marxism to a catechetical form: he wrote the first works which can be called
manuals of Marxism and which were in fact used as such. His major role in
Russian history is the more remarkable as he spent the whole of his Marxist
life in emigration, keeping in touch with Russian affairs through periodicals
and conversations with friends, and wrote of the mission of the Russian proletariat though he had no contact with actual workers. Nevertheless, he was the
true instigator of the Marxist movement in Russia, and consequently also of
Russian social democracy.

1. The origins of Marxist orthodoxy in Russia

G EORGE V ALENTINOVICH P LEKHANOV (1856–1918), the son of a landowner,
was born at Gudalovka in the Central Russian province of Tambov. He
attended the cadet school at Voronezh and in 1873 was enrolled at the Con-
stantine Military Academy in St. Petersburg. However, he abandoned the mili-

tary career after a few months and in 1874 entered the Mining Institute. Losing interest in his studies there, he was expelled after two years. During this period he imbibed the works of Chernyshevsky and other radical writers and met a number of revolutionaries, two of whom—Pavel Akselrod and Lyov Deutsch—were to be his closest collaborators and friends. At this time they were populists of the Bakunin persuasion. Plekhanov was a founder member of Zemlya i Volya and in 1876 was co-organizer and chief speaker at a demonstration in St. Petersburg against political persecution in Russia. He fled to Berlin to escape arrest, and returned in the middle of 1877 to embark on the career of a professional revolutionary. He worked for a time at Saratov organizing revolutionary groups and anti-Tsarist propaganda and composing Bakuninist manifestos and appeals. At this time he shared the populist contempt for political action to secure liberal and constitutional reforms, but he also opposed individual acts of terror as being ineffective and out of tune with the cult of the people. He was in this sense a 'classic' populist, and when the split came in 1879 he declared against the terrorists and became leader of the Black Repartition group, which concentrated on propaganda among the people in the belief that only a mass movement of peasants and workers could bring freedom to Russia. However, this activity was carried on only by a handful of conspirators and was soon stopped by police repression. The group still had a semblance of existence at the beginning of 1880, but early in that year its chief members—Plekhanov, Deutsch, and Vera Zasulich—were obliged to flee abroad.

Plekhanov, who was not to see Russia again until 1917, settled in Geneva. During his first two years there he was converted to Marxism, which does not mean that he was ignorant of it previously: like many other populists he was acquainted with Marxist doctrine and accepted many of its principles. From the articles he wrote as a populist we may infer that he subscribed to historical materialism and did not hold with 'subjective sociology', but considered that the general dependence of political and ideological systems on the economic base was compatible with the idea that Russia, owing to its special historical circumstances, might be able to avoid the Western path of development. In accordance with Bakunin's social philosophy, he argued in Marxist terms against the idea of a political struggle for the liberalization of Russia: as social development ultimately depended on the economic base, the aim should be a social and not a political revolution—not changes in the superstructure, but a transformation of the country's economic system. Plekhanov's conversion to Marxism was not a matter of coming to believe in the primacy of economic conditions as opposed to 'ideas', or in materialism as opposed to religion (he had lost his religious faith in early youth): it consisted in the adoption of three basic conclusions in regard to Russian conditions which were at variance with populist ideology. These were, first, that socialism must be preceded by a political revolution of a liberal-democratic kind; second, that Russia must go through a capitalist phase before she could be ready for a socialist transformation; and third, that that transformation must be carried through by the industrial proletariat and not by the 'people' in general, still less the peasantry. In short, Plekhanov's acceptance of Marxism represented a change in his idea of political strategy rather than a radical alteration of *Weltanschauung*.

Having embraced Marxism, Plekhanov remained faithful to it all his life. To some extent he altered his stand on particular questions affecting the tactics of social democracy in Russia (though he scarcely seemed aware that he had done so), but he derived from Marxism the intellectual satisfaction of a system that leaves practically nothing to contingency, making it possible to believe in the iron regularity of history and 'in principle' to foresee all future events. Having once attained confidence in the all-embracing system Plekhanov remained of the same mind on all theoretical questions, repeating the same truths again and again and, at most, supplementing them with fresh examples or applying them to new problems.

In Geneva, where he was beset with money troubles (he received help from Lavrov, and afterwards lived chiefly from his writings and occasional lectures), Plekhanov tried for a time to continue his populist activities: he published two numbers of a journal and made contact with what was left of the organization in Russia. His efforts came to nothing, however, both because the organization was so weak and because its members soon underwent a change of opinion in the direction of social democracy.

Having decided that the fight for democratic freedoms was the most urgent need in Russia, that it was by no means a matter of indifference what political system the exploited classes lived under, and that a change from absolutism to bourgeois democracy did not simply mean, as the populists contended, exchanging one exploiter for another, Plekhanov had to grapple with the question of the relationship of the workers' movement to the bourgeoisie. In his populist days he had maintained that the fight for political liberties was the affair of the bourgeois, and that if the revolutionary movement took any effective part in it it would merely be pulling the chestnuts out of the fire for its own exploiters. Having now decided that the fight for democracy was essential to the prospects of socialism, Plekhanov had to consider how it was possible to justify the alliance in this fight of two basically hostile classes, the bourgeoisie and the proletariat. This problem was the main object of his attention for the next few years.

In 1883 a small band of *émigré* converts to Marxism formed the Labour Emancipation Group—the first Russian social-democratic organization in the West European sense. It never became a political party, and in effect consisted only of its founders: Plekhanov, Deutsch, Vera Zasulich, and Akselrod, who had joined them in exile; yet in the first two years of its existence it created the ideological foundations of Russian social democracy. This was due principally to two works by Plekhanov, *Socialism and the Political Struggle* (1883) and *Our Differences* (1885), which marked the beginning of the breach between populism and the socialist revolutionary movement in Russia. The populists were wrong, said Plekhanov, to blame the Marxists on the ground that, as they held socialism to be a product of the evolution of capitalism, they must in Russia be allies of the bourgeoisie: the laws of history could not be bent by adjurations or the purest of revolutionary motives. The first task was to find out in what direction Russia was being impelled by inexorable economic necessity. Now it was clear that the village commune was doomed to disappear and could not form the basis of a socialist organization. Socialism in Russia, as in the West, could only be brought about by the contradictions of the capitalist economy which must soon overspread the country. Since the reforms of Alexander II Russia had embarked on capitalism and a money economy, and this could not be altered by dreams of a 'leap' from primitive, natural economy to communism. The capitalist differentiation of the peasantry had begun and was bound to continue, condemning millions to expropriation and proletarianization: land would be concentrated in the hands of a dwindling number of owners who would improve cultivation with modern techniques. Industry and transport were inevitably transforming Russia into a capitalist country subject to the normal laws of accumulation. Society was bound to be divided between the bourgeoisie and a growing army of the proletariat, and Russia's future would be decided by the struggle between them.

The development of Russian capitalism, however, was hampered by numerous survivals of feudalism and by the political autocracy. The bourgeoisie was interested in the Europeanization of Russia and the replacement of absolutism by liberal institutions. Russia's first need was not a socialist revolution but a bourgeois political one to sweep away the obstacles that the state superstructure opposed to the free expansion of capitalism. Despite populist dreams this revolution could not coincide with the socialist one, which presupposed an advanced state of industrial development and a well-organized, class-conscious proletariat. Russia must go through a capitalist era, which could not be avoided and ought to be welcomed. A bourgeois revolution was in the highest interest of the Russian proletariat, which needed a period of political freedom to organize itself and develop its strength for the socialist revolution of the future.

Hence the bourgeoisie and the proletariat, though basically antagonistic, had a common interest in seeking democratic changes in Russia. But—and this is especially important for Marxist strategy—although the next revolution would be a bourgeois one, it did not follow that it must be carried out by the bourgeoisie or even under its leadership. The weak and cowardly Russian bourgeoisie would not be equal to the task, and the bourgeois revolution could only take place under the leadership of the proletariat. This argument was attacked with especial vigour by the populists, who demanded to know why the proletariat should fight in order to give a clear field to its oppressors. But, said Plekhanov, this is a wrong way of putting the question. The proletariat has an interest in political freedoms and the abolition of the autocracy, as this is the precondition of its own victory. Moreover—and this is the second basic feature of social democratic strategy—in the struggle against absolutism the proletariat must not be a mere instrument in the hands of the bourgeoisie but an independent force, conscious of its own interests and how far they coincide with those of the capitalists, and also conscious that in proportion as capitalism succeeds in its objectives, the basic antagonism of the proletariat and the bourgeoisie will become more and more evident.

Daily experience, however, does not enable the workers themselves to develop a socialist consciousness and become fully aware of their position as a class. It is the task of the enlightened intelligentsia to act as their spiritual and political guide and open their eyes to the coming struggle. The proletariat must learn the lesson of bourgeois revolutions in the West, where, for lack of class-consciousness and organization, the workers shed blood in revolutionary upheavals which in the end profited only the bourgeoisie. The Russian proletariat can avoid this if it is imbued with socialist consciousness by an organized social-democratic movement; it cannot be helped, however, that after a bourgeois revolution the working class will not be the masters but will be in opposition to the system they have fought to establish. Basically Russia must follow the same development as the West, but there is reason to expect that on account of her very backwardness, capitalism will flourish and decay more rapidly than in Western Europe. By adopting advanced technology, learning from the experience of other countries, and possessing a ready-made theoretical basis, Russia may be able to shorten the cycle of development, but cannot bypass it altogether. Between the bourgeois and the socialist revolution there must be a period of capitalist exploitation. The social democratic movement should profit from the mistakes and defeats of the Western proletariat so as to avoid falling into the same errors and accelerate the course of events.

In the light of these predictions and recommendations, the whole populist ideology is revealed as a reactionary Utopia. The populists want Russia to enjoy the benefits of industrial development without its consequences in the form of rural proletarianization, the concentration of landownership, and the decline of the village commune. They also want socialism without its social preconditions, i.e. the class struggle between the proletariat and the bourgeoisie and the advanced technological, political, and social development that goes with capitalist society. These are self-contradictory demands and are contrary to the scientific, deterministic interpretation of social phenomena, which shows that the links between different aspects of social life and successive phases of development are matters of objective necessity, independent of human will.

Even if we suppose that a handful of revolutionaries by some chance or other seized power by a *coup d'état*, they could not introduce a socialist system because Russian capitalism is insufficiently developed. The result—so Plekhanov writes prophetically in *Our Differences*—would be 'a political abortion after the manner of the ancient Chinese or Persian empires—a renewal of Tsarist despotism on a communist basis'.

In both the works mentioned above Plekhanov showed himself to be an extreme Westernizer, as he remained throughout his life. Thanks to them Russian social democracy adopted an ideology of a basically 'European' type, reflecting the conviction that the schemata of Western development described by Marx were equally applicable to Russia. They laid the foundation of a strategy for Russian socialists which concentrated on political revolution of a liberal type. The programme included two paradoxical elements: that the proletariat should be the driving force of a bourgeois revolution, and that it was for the non-proletarian intelligentsia to instil socialist consciousness into the working class. The first of these propositions was not in conflict with Marx's doctrine, but it left open the question that was to confront socialists: if there has to be an alliance with other classes in a bourgeois revolution, should the proletariat's ally be the bourgeoisie (as might seem natural), or rather the peasantry or part of it? Twenty years later this question helped to split the Russian social democrats into two camps. As to the second premiss, it is debatable how far it is consistent with Marxist schemata; but this controversy too did not break out until later.

2. Dialectical and historical materialism

THANKS to their faith in the immutable laws of social development Plekhanov and his group were able to maintain their courage and hope during the long years when the revolutionary movement in Russia died out almost completely, and reaction appeared triumphant. The eighties were a time of discouragement and political retrogression. At this time Plekhanov gained the reputation of being the chief spokesman of Russian Marxism; his writings filtered through in small quantities only, but they did reach the few people who, in the nineties, were to lay the foundations of the social democratic movement in Russia itself. In 1889 Plekhanov was expelled from Switzerland as the result of an accidental explosion caused by a group of Russian terrorists with whom he had nothing to do; he moved to France, but was expelled again in 1894 for attacking the

French government in a speech at the congress of the International in Zurich. He then went to London, but was allowed shortly afterwards to return to Geneva. At the end of 1894 he published legally in Russia, under the pseudonym Beltov, a book originally entitled *In Defence of Materialism*, but renamed (in order to get past the censor) *A Contribution to the Question of the Development of the Monistic View of History*. This innocuous-sounding work established Plekhanov's position as the supreme authority in Russia on matters of Marxist doctrine, and was for years the main source from which the faithful imbibed their knowledge of its philosophical foundations. It contains almost everything that Plekhanov later repeated in his many works on philosophical and sociological questions. In addition to criticizing 'subjective sociology', chiefly in the writings of Mikhailovsky and Kareyev, and the populist Utopia of Russia's 'separate road', the work is a systematic exposition of Marxism and its theoretical sources, considered from the point of view of their merit in preparing the way for the materialist interpretation of history, and their idealistic 'errors' and 'inconsistencies'. In this field Plekhanov partly created, and partly followed Engels in popularizing, a large number of stereotypes which became part of the current coin of Marxism.

According to Plekhanov the basic categories and intellectual trends of Marxism were derived from the following sources, purged of their errors and contradictions.

Firstly, eighteenth-century materialism, especially the French materialism of Holbach and Helvétius. This had the merit that it explained spiritual phenomena by material ones; it discerned the source of all knowledge in sense-perception, and understood that human ideas and feelings are created by social environment. It fell into a vicious circle, however, in attributing changes in the environment to the influence of ideas. Moreover, it did not attain to an evolutionary view of history; it erred by 'fatalism' and had no knowledge of dialectical method.

Secondly, classical German philosophy, especially Hegel. In this and other works by Plekhanov, the picture of Hegel is mainly taken from Engels: it is much over-simplified and seems to be based on fragmentary and cursory reading. The dialectic is presented as a method of inquiry which considers all phenomena from the point of view of their development and interdependence, and in every form of life seeks to find the germ of that form's destruction and transformation into its opposite: it seeks everywhere to discover forces and attributes beyond those which appear at first glance. Development according to the 'triadic' schema is not, however, essential to Hegel's doctrine. The dialectic also discerns qualitative leaps in nature and society, arising from the accumulation of quantitative changes. In this way Plekhanov, like Engels, treats the dialectic as a method which can be abstracted from Hegelian philosophy, detached from idealist metaphysics, and applied to a materialist world-view. Hegel's other great merit is to have seen that human history is subject to laws independent of the will of the individual; however, in his eyes the necessity of history is of a spiritual nature and thus 'ultimately' coincides with freedom. Marxism transforms this idealistic world-view by showing that the necessities of history are rooted in material conditions of life, and that freedom consists of understanding the laws of history and taking advantage of them in order to act effectively.

Thirdly, utopian socialism. The utopians sought means of reforming society, but instead of studying inevitable consequences and laws of development they posed questions of a normative kind, asking what is good or desirable from the point of view of the requirements of human nature. By so doing they condemned themselves to sterility, for goodwill is powerless by itself to effect social changes.

Fourthly, the French historians of the restoration period. Guizot, Thierry, and Mignet had done much to interpret historical processes as struggles due to the differing material interests of social classes, and in this respect they paved the way for Marxism. But they remained bound to the idealist philosophy of history, ascribing social conflicts and forms of property, in the last resort, to unaltering human nature—whereas the latter postulate clearly cannot explain changing historical forms.

The defects of all these theories were finally cured by Marx's philosophy, which Plekhanov compares in importance to the Copernican revolution or to Darwinism. Like Copernicus, Marx laid the foundations of social science by introducing the idea of necessity, which is the basis of all scientific thinking, into the study of social phenomena. (In Hegel's philosophy of history, necessity was only a logical category. Plekhanov does not explain, however, in what sense Copernicus originated the theory of necessity in natural science.) But the comparison with Darwin is more significant. As Darwin explained the evolution of forms of life by the adaptation of species to changes in the environment (this is Plekhanov's idea of the essence of Darwinism), so Marx showed that human history can be explained by man's relations with external nature and especially his growing control over it by means of tools. Marx's historical monism is based on the premise that 'in the last resort' all historical changes are due to the development of tools, the ability to make which determines the character of the human species and the social bond of co-operation. The objection that technical change itself depends on human intellectual effort is invalid, for intellectual progress is in turn the result of technical progress: in this way cause and effect are constantly interchanging. At any given moment of history the level of productive forces determines the intellectual level of society, including technical inventions which make production more efficient still. Man is constantly being changed by external circumstances, and thus there is no such thing as unchanging human nature.

At a particular level of productive forces there come into being relations of production which in turn are the basis of political institutions, social psychology, and ideological forms. However, there is at all times a reciprocal influence: political institutions affect economic life; the economy and psychology of a society are two aspects of one and the same process, the 'production of life' or the struggle for existence, and both depend on the level of technology. Psychological attitudes adapt themselves to economic conditions, but 'on the other hand' the conflict of technology with relations of production produces changes in human psychology which precede economic changes. Thus Marxism cannot be reproached with one-sidedness, for it takes account of the whole multiplicity of mutual reactions in society.

Economic conditions are also the source of ideological creations, including science, philosophy, and art. True, one form of art may influence another, but the notion of 'influence' in itself explains nothing: different peoples can only influence one another artistically if their social conditions are similar.

History cannot be explained by the special role of outstanding geniuses. On the contrary, it is history that explains them: a genius is one who grasps the meaning of incipient social relations sooner than other people, and expresses in a more perfect way the tendency of a particular social class.

Since the necessity that governs the world is universal, freedom from the Marxist point of view—as in the philosphy of Spinoza or Hegel—is not a matter of enjoying a kind of margin within which causality does not operate, but of being able to control nature by understanding its laws. The measure of this control increases throughout history, and we have reached the point where it is possible to envisage 'the final triumph of mind over necessity, of reason over the blindness of law': this will be because men have learnt to govern social processes, over which they formerly had no power. (Plekhanov does not explain how mind can 'triumph' in this way if its activity is ruled by iron necessity, so that man's power over nature is determined by nature itself independently of human beings.)

Similar ideas to these are repeated in Plekhanov's many subsequent articles, books, and lectures, some of which have become classics of Marxist instruction even outside Russia: for example, *Fundamental Problems of Marxism* (1908), *The Role of the Individual in History* (1898), and *Contributions to the History of Materialism* (1896). All his theoretical writings are to some extent Polemics against those whom, at any particular moment, he regarded as most dangerous to the integrality and consistency of Marxist doctrine. This means that his adversaries were either close to Marxism or were desirous of reforming or revising it 'from within': after the populists came the German revisionists, then the neo-Kantians and the Russian school of empiriocriticism.

Unlike most West European Marxists, who saw no logical connection between Marxism as a theory of social development and any particular view of epistemological or metaphysical questions (Kautsky, too, came to believe in course of time that there was no such connection), Plekhanov insisted that Marxism was a complete and integral body of theory embracing all the main questions of philosophy. 'Dialectical materialism'—Plekhanov was apparently the first to use this term to denote the whole of Marxist philosophy—could not be separated from 'historical materialism', which was the application of the same principles and rules of thought to the investigation of social phenomena. This insistence on the integrality of Marxism was inherited from Plekhanov by Lenin, and became part of the ideology of the Soviet state. It is based on the premiss that social democracy cannot be neutral in any philosophical question, and that it possesses a comprehensive world-view which cannot be partially adopted without deforming each of its parts. Marxist philosophy as expounded by Plekhanov was a repetition, without attempt at further analysis, of Engels's formulas, generally in an exaggerated version. Materialism rests on the assertion which Marxism adopted from Feuerbach, that Being or matter is 'self-based', while all thought is a product of Being. However, dialectical materialism differs from Feuerbach in stating that the human subject is not merely passively aware of objects, but comes to know the world in the process of acting upon it. This does not mean, says Plekhanov, that men form or help to form the objects they become aware of, but only that the cognition of objects 'in themselves' takes place chiefly as a result of labour and not of contemplation. Materialism is an irrefutable theory confirmed by science, and all its modern critics—Croce, Schmidt, Bernstein—are only repeating arguments that were long ago demolished by Feuerbach. The dialectic is the theory of the development of the world with its interconnections, contradictions, and qualitative 'leaps', and these are demonstrated by modern science, for instance De Vries's theory of mutations (Plekhanov does not explain how biological mutations are prepared for by an accumulation of 'quantitative changes'). Qualitative changes are seen in the transformation of water into ice or steam, of a chrysalis into a butterfly, or again in arithmetic, as after the digit 9 we make a 'leap' into double figures. Plekhanov is full of such naïveties, and one of them is the idea that 'dialectical contradictions' are incompatible with formal logic: this recalls the contention of the Eleatic philosophers that motion is self-contradictory, as a moving body both is and is not in a given place. As rest is a particular case of motion, formal logic is a particular case of dialectical logic and 'applies' to reality treated as unchanging. A political revolution is an example of a qualitative leap; dialectical contradictions include the class struggle, etc.

All these arguments, which were to become part of the canon of dialectical materialism in Russia, are evidence of the shallowness of Plekhanov's philosophical education and the over-simplicity of his thought. In questions of historical materialism he shows better powers of analysis and knowledge of the subject. Here too, however, he is concerned above all to preserve his monistic faith in 'productive forces' as the all-sufficient motive power of history. However, following Engels, he takes issue with the statement that Marxism explains all historical processes in terms of a 'single factor', since, he contends, all 'factors' are only methodological abstractions: there is in reality one single historical process, and this is determined 'in the last resort' by technical progress. The phrase 'in the last resort', Plekhanov explains, means that in a given society we can distinguish 'intermediate stages' through which productive forces determine various features of social life—economic conditions, the political system, psychology, and ideology. In addition there is always the factor of interaction: the superstructure is determined by the base but afterwards reacts upon it; the base is constituted by the requirements of productive forces but itself affects those forces, and so on.

These ideas do not fit into a coherent whole. Like other Marxists of his time, Plekhanov cannot explain how the belief in productive forces as the ultimate cause of events is to be reconciled with the theory of interaction. If the 'higher stages' can initiate changes in the lower, it is not clear what becomes of historical 'monism' or how it can be said that the lower stages condition the higher 'in the last resort'; if changes cannot be so initiated, what is the meaning of 'interaction'? Again, it is not clear how it can be said that, for example, political institutions, ideologies, and property relations are 'only abstractions' used for purposes of argument, while at the same time making a substantive distinction between 'stages' and asserting, in addition, that everything depends on changes in the forces of production, as though for some reason these were not 'factors' like the others. In *Fundamental Problems of Marxism* Plekhanov adds for good measure that productive forces are determined by geographical conditions, so it would seem that, contrary to what is said elsewhere, these last are the real and ultimate cause of history. It is clear that Plekhanov, like many Marxists, wishes to maintain his belief in a single principle accounting for the whole of history, but not to part company with common sense which tells us that events are due in general to a variety of concurrent causes. Hence the numerous reservations which are meant to attenuate the rigour of the 'monistic' explanation, but in fact destroy it, as the vague expression 'in the last resort' finally loses its meaning when we also speak of 'interaction'. We are in fact thrown back on the common-sense view that important events are due to a multiplicity of forces whose relative strength cannot be calculated, including of course the level of technology in a society, its class structure and political system. But there is nothing specifically Marxist in this formulation, and therefore it is not one that can be uttered by true believers.

Plekhanov, like Kautsky, is also convinced that social processes can be studied in the same completely objective way as natural phenomena, human history being subject to universal laws of change—evolution, contradiction, qualitative leaps—in the same way as geological formations. He replies in this sense to Stammler's criticism that Marxists ignore the teleological character of human behaviour, and that when they urge mankind to co-operate with what they claim to be inevitable progress, it is as though they were to demand support for an eclipse of the sun which is bound to take place anyway without human aid. This criticism is groundless, Plekhanov says, because Marxists recognize that among the circumstances necessary to certain social processes are the purposive actions of human beings, their feelings, passions, and desires; they maintain, however, that such feelings and desires are necessarily determined by productive forces and the social conditions which these create. Plekhanov, however, seems to miss the point of Stammler's objection, as Kautsky did in the case of Bauer. It is one thing to reflect on past history, in which human feelings, purposes, and passions appear simply as psychological and social factors helping to shape the course of events; it is another to consider one's own share in processes whose future results one believes to be determined by irresistible historical forces. If an individual is considering what purpose to aim at or why he should take part in a given social movement, the statement that his aims, whatever they may be, are irrevocably determined by productive forces does not help him to make up his mind, any more than the statement that certain results of the historical process are inevitable. Plekhanov says that if I join a movement that I regard as historically necessary and certain to prevail, I am treating my own action as an indispensable link in that necessary process. But this is no answer to Stammler; for the belief that a movement is going to win is not in itself an argument for joining it, except to someone who wants to be on the winning side at all costs. This viewpoint, i.e. that of the long-sighted opportunist, is of course a possible one, but it is not the one Plekhanov is concerned with, and it does not answer the question what moral grounds exist for joining a movement that is certain to succeed. If there are no such grounds there is no reason why I should join it, and if there are, they must derive from some other source than the 'laws of history'. This was the neo-Kantist objection, which Plekhanov failed to understand. He regarded himself as a necessary link in the process of socialist change, implying that it could not take place without him: this may have been true in his case, but it conflicts with his own principles as to the historical role of the individual, and it still does not explain why he, or anyone else, should have taken upon themselves to be the necessary link.

To sum up the characteristics of Plekhanov's theoretical writing we may say that it is marked by an absolute conviction of historical necessity; the denial of any basic distinction between the study of nature and that of society; the belief that historical materialism is an 'application' of the rules of dialetical materialism, and an insistence on treating these two fields as part of a unique, indivisible whole; strong emphasis on the integrality of Marxism as the social democratic world-view, and the belief that social democracy as such must have a philosophical doctrine of its own; strong emphasis, also, on the importance of the philosophical tradition in the genesis of Marxism.

Plekhanov was one of the principal founders of that style of Marxist writing which Lenin adopted in a still cruder form and which recalls the polemics of religious sects. Having decided, on his conversion to Marxism, that it supplied the answers to all problems of philosophy and social development, Plekhanov never afterwards wrote as a man seeking for the solution of a theoretical problem, but as an adept defending an established doctrine. He uses any argument that comes to hand, the object being not to follow the discussion wherever it leads, but to knock the adversary down. He derides opponents who invoke any scientific authority (for Marxism bows to no authority outside itself), but he himself quotes any authority that may serve his turn, irrespective of whether he knows anything of the field in question, so that he constantly falls into factual error. He piles up examples to confirm the 'laws of dialectic' or of historical materialism without realizing the extent of the gap between a collection of mostly trivial instances (water turning to steam, biological mutations, etc.) and the general principle they are supposed to illustrate, for example that all processes consist of an accumulation of quantitative changes culminating in a qualitative leap. He does not observe that while it is easy to find examples, for instance, of particular cultural features which are due to the technical level of a society, or ideological ones which are due to class conflict, it is no less easy to find examples the other way round, for example technical development which is due to political institutions or political institutions due to ideological tradition. Such examples, however, do not prove any general theory of historiosophy beyond vague assertions that 'on the one hand' such and such circumstances account for such and such others, while 'on the other hand' the process may be reversed.

3. Marxist aesthetics

MUCH space is devoted in Plekhanov's writings and lectures to the discussion of art from the viewpoint of historical materialism: he was a pioneer in this field, along with Mehring and Lafargue. He was more at home in the history of art than in philosophy, and was able to support his argument with examples from diverse periods. Here too, however, there is a wide gap between his frequently accurate observation of the dependence of artistic activity on technical conditions and social conflict, and his general thesis that 'The artistic life of civilized nations is no less subject to necessity than that of primitive peoples. The only difference is that among civilized nations art no longer *directly* depends on technique and the means of production' (*Unaddressed Letters*, 1899–1900, i). He uses the accounts of various ethnographers to show that in primitive society art is connected with work either in the sense of imitating it (as in group dances, which, he says, serve to reproduce the 'pleasure' of working), or by aiding it (for example, musical rhythm), or again by association with such values as wealth or physical fitness, wherein the symbols that arouse such association come to be regarded as beautiful. In class societies, on the other hand, the dependence of art on productive forces is indirect, as art 'expresses' the ideals, feelings, and thoughts of this or that class. Eighteenth-century French comedy expressed popular discontent with the existing order, classical tragedy the ideals of the court and aristocracy, and so on. Plekhanov fails to notice that such observations as these are not specifically Marxist. The effect of class-interests and social changes on literary genres or styles of painting was known to many non-Marxist historians and critics, including some that Plekhanov himself quotes, such as Guizot, Taine, and Brunetière. What is essentially Marxist is not the recognition of such influences but the claim that they account for the whole of artistic creation, and that there is a necessary link between the state of class-relations in a given society and its artistic output. If this were taken seriously we should have to suppose that a keen enough mind could deduce the whole of a country's art and literature from its economic situation, i.e. that one could write the works of Shakespeare if one knew enough about the economy of Elizabethan England. Plekhanov, of course, does not say anything so absurd, but he fails to see that it would be a natural consequence of his theory. He is constantly endeavouring to show that artistic activity is wholly accounted for by class values and that the merits of a work of art should be judged by its content, which is also expressible in non-artistic language; at the same time, he wishes to preserve the distinction between ideological content and artistic presentation. Here again we are saved by the magic formula: 'in the last resort the value of a work of art is determined by the specific gravity of its subject-matter' (*Art and Social Life*, 1912). To know the genesis of a work of art, then, is to know the criteria of its artistic merit: these are not absolute, for everything changes, but they are objective, i.e. we can state with certainty what is or is not beautiful in the conditions of its time. The work is to be judged by the correspondence between its 'idea' and its 'form': the more closely they coincide, the more successful it is. But to be able to judge this we should have to know, independently of the actual work of art, what 'forms' are best suited to express the given idea; and Plekhanov does not suggest how we can acquire such knowledge. Nor is this all. It is not sufficient, we are told, for the form to correspond to the idea: for the work to be beautiful, the idea must be a 'true' one. We see here to what extent Plekhanov, partly of his own accord and partly under Chernyshevsky's influence, evolved the basic premises of what was to be called 'socialist realism'. Not that Plekhanov's own preferences were based on such criteria, or that he ascribed artistic merit to all works that 'expressed' ideas he believed in and to no others: on the contrary, his tastes were those of most educated people in his time, including a detestation of new trends in painting. But his theory laid the foundation for measuring artistic value by political utility.

Plekhanov believed that the slogan 'art for art's sake', and the idea that the main purpose of a work of art was to produce artistic values as an end in themselves, was itself the necessary product of a certain kind of social situation, that in which the creative artist feels isolated from society. This, he considered, was the state of affairs at the turn of the century. Impressionism and Cubism were a sign of bourgeois decadence: the former was superficial and did not look beyond the 'outer shell' of phenomena, the latter was 'nonsense raised to the third power'. The same applied to symbolist literature in Russia and abroad, for example Merezhkovsky, Zinaida Gippius, and Przybyszewski. In a typical passage Plekhanov wrote: 'Let us suppose the artist wants to paint a "Woman in a blue dress". If what he paints is like his subject, we call it a good picture. If, however, all we see on the canvas is a few stereometric figures tinted here and there, in a more or less primitive fashion, with layers of more or less diluted blue paint, we may call it a painting of whatever we like, but not a good picture.' (Ibid.)

There is of course nothing surprising in such naïvety: we know that after a certain age people cannot appreciate new artistic forms that are too unlike the ones they knew in youth, and reject them as extravagant and unnatural. But Plekhanov does not regard such judgements as mere expressions of his own taste, but as the inevitable logical consequence of the Marxist theory of society, and therefore as 'scientific' statements. From this point of view the influence of his writing, which virtually established the canons of Soviet aesthetic taste, was deplorable, even though he believed firmly in creative freedom for the artist and knew how barren art was when executed under compulsion, to please political masters or to present the world as it should be instead of as it is (cf. his criticism of Gorky's *The Mother*).

4. The struggle against revisionism

As THE result of rapid industrialization and the great famine of 1891–2 the nineties witnessed a revival of political activity in Russia; Marxism and social democratic ideology became the subject of widespread public debate. This was to some extent a triumph for Plekhanov as the chief exponent of the doctrine;

but the larger or smaller social democratic groups that came into existence in the cities produced new leaders and theorists who, while respecting Plekhanov as a teacher, were not prepared blindly to follow his advice in politics. He for his part did not bear opposition gladly and claimed absolute authority in all matters of doctrine and also of socialist policy in Russia. This state of affairs led to painful tension on some occasions, the best known of which was Lenin's disappointment at his meeting with the master in 1900.

In the late 1890s much of Plekhanov's energy was taken up by the controversy with Bernstein and the neo-Kantians. He was the first to launch a frontal attack on Bernstein and was, with Rosa Luxemburg, the most intransigent critic of revisionism: none of the Germans equalled in virulence these two *émigrés* from Eastern Europe. Unlike Rosa Luxemburg, however, he directed his attack at the philosophical bases of revisionism, which, again unlike most critics, he treated as a point of contention of the first order. Kantianism he regarded as an attempt to instil bourgeois mentality among social democrats: it taught, in the first place, that men could not know things 'in themselves', and it thus left room for religious faith, which had always been a means of spiritual enslavement of the oppressed classes. Secondly, the Kantists, in accordance with the theory of infinite progress, regarded socialism as an ideal which could be approached by degrees but never actually reached. They thus created a philosophical basis for reformism and opportunism, abandoning socialism as a practicable aim and revolution as the means to it. At the same time Plekhanov attacked the analyses of changes in capitalist society which Bernstein used to justify his departure from revolutionary Marxism. Even if the middle classes represented a growing proportion of the population as a whole, and the workers' lot was actually improving in absolute terms, this did not weaken the Marxist theory of intensifying class antagonism. Real wages might go up, but social inequalities still increased (the relative impoverishment of the proletariat). If the trade union mentality was spreading among the workers, this was not due to the class situation but to opportunistic leaders. In this matter Plekhanov argued on the same lines as Rosa Luxemburg and Lenin. The doctrine teaches that the working class is, by the nature of things, a revolutionary class; if shallow empiricism does not appear to bear this out, it cannot be due to any change in the workers' class situation but only to the machinations of renegades among the union and party leaders.

Plekhanov's other prinicipal target was Russian 'economism', which he regarded as a variant of Bernsteinian revisionism. Some of its advocates still paid lip-service, at least, to the 'final aim' of social democracy, but, in accordance with the classic tradition of populism, their approach to the workers was confined to immediate practical issues such as economic claims, to the neglect of political work, the struggle for constitutional freedoms, and the cultivation of a socialist consciousness among the proletariat. The 'economists' distrusted the idea of intellectuals leading the working-class movement: they believed that the latter should be composed of workers and not merely be working-class in name and ideology, and they held this to be the intention of Marx himself, who maintained that the proletariat could only be liberated by its own efforts. The 'economist' viewpoint was represented among the émigrés by S. N. Prokopovich and his wife E. D. Kuskova, but in Russia itself it enjoyed for a time a certain predominance over orthodox social democracy: it was expressed chiefly in the pages of the underground journal *Rabochaya Mysl'* (*Workers' Thought*), from 1897.

Plekhanov attacked the economists with similar arguments to those he had used against populism. Only socialism as a final aim gave meaning to the struggle for reforms and particular economic gains by the proletariat. A campaign which confined itself to these partial aims and could not, therefore, become a country-wide proletarian movement was not a fight for social democracy, and to regard it as a true workers' movement was to abandon Marxism. What Marxism required in Russian conditions was to fight for democratic freedoms that would provide a framework for the final battle, and to subordinate economic demands to the political struggle for socialism. If the 'economists' claimed that they represented the true consciousness of the Russian working class, then, as in the case of German reformism, it was their own fault that that consciousness was not evolving in a socialist direction.

Plekhanov thus stood for uncompromising orthodoxy against revisionism and economism. For some years he and Lenin were political allies; but the dispute over the editorship of *Iskra*, while it had much to do initially with Plekhanov's personal claim to supremacy among the social democrat émigrés, was also due to the fact that he thought Lenin over-conciliatory towards the economists and 'legal Marxists'. In the argument over the party programme drafted in 1902 there were no essential differences between the two men: Lenin wished to make Plekhanov's draft more precise and less abstract, but he did not object to its basic premises. At the Brussels–London Congress in the summer of 1903, at which the party split into Bolsheviks and Mensheviks, Plekhanov took Lenin's side as regards centralized forms of organization and also in the celebrated dispute over paragraph I of the Rules, which, as proposed by Lenin, defined a party member as one who personally participated in the work of a party organization—the object being to create a party of 'professional revolutionaries'. At the same Congress, in reply to a delegate who raised the question of the absolute value of democratic principles, Plekhanov made his celebrated speech declaring that the cause of the revolution was the supreme law for revolutionaries, and that if it should require the abandonment of any democratic principle, such as universal suffrage, it would be criminal to hesitate.

5. The conflict with Leninism

PLEKHANOV was thus a Bolshevik—but only for a short time, after which he allied himself once more with Akselrod, Martov, and others whom he had criticized at the Congress. Before long he was attacking Bolshevism and Lenin's idea of the party, accusing the Bolsheviks of ultracentralism and of aiming at absolute power and a party dictatorship over the proletariat. In numerous polemics he argued that Lenin's conception of the party, which made it completely independent of the spontaneous consciousness of the proletariat, meant that the role of the working class would be usurped by a party of intellectual professional revolutionaries: this party would become the sole source of political initiative, which was grossly at variance with Marx's theory of the class struggle. It was equally contrary to Marxism and to historical experience when Lenin declared that the working class could not attain to socialist consciousness by itself. This showed a lack of confidence in the workers and was idealistic to boot, as it implied that the class-consciousness of the proletariat was not the result of its living conditions ('being determines consciousness'), but must be the work of intellectuals.

Plekhanov's anti-Bolshevism, founded on classical Marxist schemata, grew more and more violent as time went on. Just as he had brought the same charges against the 'economists' as previously against the classical populists, namely that they showed excessive respect for spontaneity and neglected political activity, so now he attacked the Bolsheviks on the grounds for which he had condemned the terrorist branch of the populist movement. He accused them of Blanquism, Jacobinism, 'voluntarism', aiming to force social development by conspiratorial means and to bring about a revolution not by the operation of natural laws but at the behest of a handful of plotters. He maintained his own strategic viewpoint that the proletariat should co-operate with the bourgeoisie for democratic aims, and even the Revolution of 1905 did not alter his conviction, though he realized how uncertain such an alliance would be. Lenin, on the other hand, envisaged a bourgeois revolution followed immediately by a democratic-revolutionary dictatorship of the proletariat and peasantry. Plekhanov for his part did not regard the peasantry as a useful political ally. He seems to have thought that the proletariat could carry on the fight against the bourgeoisie and overtly aim at its destruction, while at the same time joining forces with it to overthrow the autocracy. This view rested on his dogmatic, anti-populist belief that the phases of development in Russia would be basically the same as in the West. His doctrinaire attitude and his hesitations considerably weakened his position as a social democratic leader after 1905. He continued to stand closer to the Mensheviks than to the Bolsheviks, while occasionally attempting, without success, to bridge the gulf between them.

Plekhanov held that the Bolsheviks had departed from Marxism in the philo-sophical sphere also. He regarded the attempts to introduce empiriocriticism into Marxist philosophy as a typical symptom of the basic Bolshevist attitude. The Bolsheviks despised or ignored the 'objective laws' of social development and believed in a revolution brought about by organization and strength of will: it was natural therefore that they should be attracted by a subjectivist philoso-phy which regarded the human mind as the 'active organizer' of the universe. This was indeed true of the empiriocritical philosophers in the Bolshevik camp, but it was far from meeting with Lenin's approval. The fight against empiriocrit-icism was the last occasion on which Lenin and Plekhanov found themselves in alliance.

Plekhanov spent the years after 1905 chiefly in writing on historical, philo-sophical, and aesthetic questions. He also began preparatory work on a long *His-tory of Russian Social Thought*, of which he was only to complete three volumes.

During the period from 1905 to 1914 Plekhanov's attitude to basic questions was close to that of the central group of the International. When war broke out he adopted a 'national' position like most members of that group, switching at once from anti-war slogans and proletarian internationalism to the defence of Russia's cause and that of the Entente. This of course did not mean that he had given up Marxism: as the Central Powers had attacked Russia the war was a defensive one, and support for it was in accordance with the resolutions of the International. Moreover, the defeat of Germany was in the interest of interna-tional socialism, as it would advance the revolutionary movement in both Ger-many and Russia. The rest of Plekhanov's patriotic activity—his call to national unity and a suspension of the class struggle—could be justified on the same grounds. In the result, he found himself on the extreme right wing of the social democratic movement.

The collapse of the autocracy, which had been awaited for decades, came in February 1917. Plekhanov returned to Russia at the end of March. He was received with enthusiasm, but it soon became clear that as a theoretician who had spent nearly forty years abroad he was unable to find his bearings in the new situation. His view was that, Tsarism having been swept away by a bour-geois revolution, there should now 'naturally' be a long period of constitutional and parliamentary rule; at the same time the war with Germany should be fought through to victory. In this he stood closer to the Provisional Government than to any socialist group. He continued, as a Marxist, to combat the idea of a socialist revolution in the near future: socialism could not be victorious in an economically backward country with a huge preponderance of peasants. He regarded the events of October as a deplorable error by the Bolsheviks, which might ruin all the achievements of the February Revolution. He died in a Finnish sanatorium on 30 May 1918, embittered and unreconciled to a situation which he himself had done a great deal to bring about, but which did not fit into his theoretical schemata.

S. H. Baron, the author of a basic work on Plekhanov, observes that his struggle against revisionism did much to facilitate the rise of Leninism, but that his subsequent opposition to Leninism brought him to a position close to the revisionists. The same author considers that the root cause of Plekhanov's political defeats was his unshakeable faith in the applicability of the West European pattern of development to Russia. He considered the Bolsheviks to be Bakuninists rather than Marxists: in this he was certainly right to some extent, on the basis of what Western Europe regarded as Marxist orthodoxy. But even though he correctly foresaw what would happen to a revolution carried out on Leninist principles, nevertheless the fact that it could succeed at all was inexplicable in terms of his social philosophy.

Soviet Russia, as was to be expected, condemns Piekhanov for his later political attitude but, following Lenin, applauds him as a Marxist theoretician. A complete edition of his writings was published shortly after his death; separate works have since appeared, dealing with philosophy but not politics (except for the early anti-populist treatises). In view of his controversy with the Bolsheviks he could not, of course, be ranked as a 'classic of Marxism' in terms of Soviet state ideology. None the less he remains one of the chief begetters of that ideology, which, under the name of Marxism-Leninism, in time succeeded—with the aid of the party, state, and police—in supplanting and destroying the Marxist idea.

XV

Marxism in Russia Before the
Rise of Bolshevism

In the 1890s Marxism became a subject of public debate in Russia and was an essential and influential part of the country's intellectual life. At this time, however, it was chiefly a movement of the intelligentsia. Contrary to the position in Western Europe, Marxism and socialism existed in Russia before there was a working-class movement. The reference here is to Marxism as a doctrine which defines itself as the mature consciousness of the working class and which is based on the Marxian analysis and critique of capitalist conditions, regarding capitalism as an essential phase of social progress and an independent workers' movement as the precondition of a socialist transformation. As already mentioned, Marxism had considerable influence on populist thinkers, but they made use of it chiefly to denounce the effects of capitalism, while hoping that Russia might avoid these by choosing a road of her own. Marxism as a social democratic ideology took shape, during the first ten years or so, largely in opposition to populism. The main subject of Marxist literature was the development of capitalism in Russia, and its main theme was that it was a utopian dream to seek to prevent it. The prospects of socialism depended on the working-class movement which would develop as the capitalist economy expanded, and which could fight effectively only in conditions of political freedom: the first objective for social democrats, therefore, was to carry out a democratic revolution and overthrow the autocracy.

It soon became clear, however, that when Marxism was no longer defined simply by opposition to populism, its application to the future of capitalism in Russia could be judged in different ways. To some of the intelligentsia Marxism was in effect a substitute for a liberal ideology, which the country did not otherwise possess. Those who thought in this way emphasized the need to introduce democratic freedoms, which they regarded as an end in themselves and not simply a means of developing the socialist movement. Interpreting Marx as they did, they expected a long period of capitalist conditions and regarded socialism either as a distant prospect with little practical meaning at the present time, or as a regulative moral norm. This was the attitude of the group whom their opponents later called 'legal Marxists', and who from the beginning advocated ideas similar in many respects to German revisionism. Most of them eventually abandoned Marxism and became liberal ideologists. The social democrats, on the other hand, linked the struggle for democracy with the coming fight for socialism by an organized movement of the proletariat.

The fact that Leninism eventually prevailed may suggest that pre-revolutionary Marxism in Russia should be studied entirely in relation to its Leninist variant. But the quarter-century was one of many-sided discussion in the fields of politics, philosophy, and social doctrine, and produced many variants of Marxism, some of which are more interesting than Lenin's from the theoretical point of view. At the same time it is hard to say that the perspective created by later events, and by what we know today of the historical consequences of Russian Marxism, is a false one. In describing a historical process we cannot really do so 'from the inside', i.e. treating each event in turn as if we knew no more of its effects than people did at the time. It is true to a certain extent that the history we write is that of the 'victors'. We can only judge the importance of events, including intellectual events, by their consequences, and every historical account must be based on a selection of what is most important. It is therefore legitimate to treat Leninism as the mainstream of twentieth-century Marxism, although when we compare Lenin's works with those of his Marxist opponents we often find the latter a good deal richer in theoretical content.

One of the events that animated ideological discussion and helped to crystallize the Marxist movement in Russia was the disastrous famine of 1891–2. Populist economists regarded it as a confirmation of their views and a proof of the horrors of capitalism, while the Marxists disputed this analysis. It was not only a question of economic causes, however, but of the whole range of social problems connected with Russia's future. Study groups of Marxists and Marxist sympathizers began to be formed in the ensuing years, chiefly among students. From these there soon emerged leaders who laid the foundations of Russian social democracy: Lenin, Struve, Potresov, Martov.

1. Lenin: early journalistic writings

If the greatness of historical figures is measured by the consequences that can be ascribed to their acts, Lenin must certainly rank as the greatest man of the twentieth century. The October Revolution was of course, like all revolutions, the result of many chances and coincidences; in particular it was made possible by the February Revolution and the resulting break-down of the Tsarist government machine. Yet hardly anyone, even Trotsky, has called in question that Lenin's presence and activity, in forming the Bolshevik party and at the time of the Revolution itself, was an indispensable condition of its outbreak and success. It is also beyond dispute that Lenin decisively influenced the character of the Soviet state as a historical formation of a completely new kind.

The subject of the present work is the history of Marxist doctrine and not of the socialist or communist movement; but in Lenin's case more than in any other it becomes clear that there is a certain artificiality in this distinction. From the outset of his political activity Lenin devoted himself, with extraordinary consistency and resolution, to a single cause and a single task. He was wholly absorbed in working for revolution in Russia, and all his theoretical works were subordinated to this end. Lenin was never a theorist in the sense of approaching questions in a spirit of intellectual curiosity and the disinterested quest for a solution. All questions, even epistemological ones, were potential instruments of the revolution, and all answers were political acts.

There is some controversy as to Lenin's intellectual and political development up to the time when he laid the foundations of Bolshevism. However, except for Soviet official hagiography most historians agree that as a young man he was strongly influenced by the tradition of populism in its terrorist form; that afterwards, until about 1899, he was a 'Westernizing' Marxist like Plekhanov; and that it was only in 1899–1902 that he worked out his own variant of Marxism, in which the populist tradition was again partly in evidence.

Vladimir Ilyich Ulyanov (he wrote under the pseudonym 'Lenin' from the end of 1901 onwards) was born on 22 April 1870 (10 April, Old Style) at Simbirsk, now Ulyanovsk. His father, Ilya Nikolayevich Ulyanov, was the provincial school inspector, a senior and well-paid member of the Tsarist bureaucracy: he seems to have been a loyal and conservative official. The children received a religious but unbigoted upbringing. The elder son Alexander, born in 1866, studied at St. Petersburg University and belonged to a clandestine group, inspired by Narodnaya Volya and claiming to be a terrorist branch of that organization, which plotted to assassinate the Tsar. The amateur conspiracy was discovered, and in May 1887 Alexander Ulyanov was hanged. Vladimir at this time was taking his final school examinations. His brother's death naturally aroused in him a sense of hatred for the authorities and an interest in the revolutionary cause. That autumn he entered the University of Kazan, whence he was expelled three months later for taking part in a demonstration against new regulations limiting the autonomy of universities and the freedom of students. He moved to his mother's estate at the village of Kokushkino and spent much time reading, particularly the works of Chernyshevsky, which impressed him greatly. In 1888 the family took a house in Kazan, but the brother of the would-be regicide was not allowed to resume his university studies. During his first and his second stay in Kazan Lenin was connected with local groups which sought to keep alive the Narodnaya Volya tradition. He had similar contacts in Samara, where he spent the next three years. Thanks to his mother's efforts he was allowed to become an extra-mural student at St. Petersburg University; he passed all the examinations in the course of a year, graduated at the end of 1891, and spent the next eighteen months or so in a lawyer's office at Samara. In the years around 1890 he read Marx and Plekhanov and became converted to Marxism as a doctrine that explained the mechanism of the capitalist economy and provided a theory of revolution, not brought about by terrorist conspiracy but by the expansion of capitalism and the developing class-consciousness of the proletariat.

In September 1893 Lenin moved to St. Petersburg and began his political apprenticeship in the industrial and intellectual capital of Russia. During the next two years he made his name in socialist circles as an expert on Marxism and became acquainted with many of his subsequent collaborators and opponents—Struve, Martov, Krzhizhanovsky, and Potresov. He also met Nadezhda Krupskaya, whom he was to marry in 1899 and who thereafter shared in all his literary and political activity. Martov (by his real name Yuly Osipovich Tsederbaum) was born at Constantinople in 1873, the son of well-to-do Jewish parents. He was brought up in Odessa and enrolled at St. Petersburg University in 1891, but was expelled for taking part in socialist discussion groups. He was arrested and spent some months in prison, after which he lived at Vilna. There he gained experience of propaganda among the workers, and on his return to St. Petersburg in 1895 he was able to help the socialist intelligentsia to make contact with the real proletariat. He urged that the social democrats, instead of expounding theory to the workers, should concentrate on immediate practical conflicts, especially the observance of factory legislation. This would soon awaken a spirit of solidarity among the workers and convince them that the state was on the side of the exploiters and that particular disputes were only instances of the antagonism between the workers and the system as a whole. The social democratic groups in St. Petersburg accordingly went to work among the proletariat on these lines.

The earliest of Lenin's writings date from 1893–5 and are chiefly aimed against the economic doctrines of the populists. The first, a review of a book by V. Y. Postnikov on *Peasant Farming in South Russia*, was rejected by the periodical to which it was sent. Postnikov's book spoke of the progress of capitalism in Russian agriculture and the differentiation of peasant incomes, and in this way furnished arguments against the populist ideology. In the same year Lenin also wrote an unpublished report for a discussion group on the market question. Here he joined issue with the populist economists for stating that capitalism was unable to create a home market in Russia as it was undermining its own position by proletarianizing the peasants and curtailing their purchasing power. Lenin argued that impoverishment and proletarianization did not prevent the market from increasing. The proletarianized peasants were obliged to sell their labour-power, and in this way created a market, while capitalism, as it developed, also created a market for means of production.

In 1894 Lenin wrote a dissertation of some length attacking the social philosophy of populism and particularly the views of Mikhailovsky and Krivenko. This work, entitled *What the 'Friends of the People' are and How they Fight the Social Democrats*, was hectographed and distributed to social democratic groups; its middle section has not been preserved. In it Lenin combats the 'subjective' and moralistic viewpoint of populist writers and contrasts it with Marxism as a scientific, determinist doctrine which does not ask any questions about what 'ought' to be but considers all social processes, including the phenomena of consciousness, as 'natural' events determined by the relations of production. 'Marx treats the social movement as a process of natural history, governed by laws not only independent of human will, consciousness and intentions, but, on the contrary, determining the will, consciousness and intentions of men . . . If the conscious element plays so subordinate a part in the history of civilization, it is self-evident that a critique whose subject is civilization can least of all take as its basis any form of, or any result of, consciousness' (*Collected Works*, vol. I, p. 166). There is no conflict between determinism, which rejects the 'stupid fable of free will', and the possibility of evaluating human acts or the role of the individual in history. All history consists of the acts of individuals; the question is in what conditions individual acts can be effective. Moreover, 'Everybody knows that scientific socialism never painted any prospects for the future as such: it confined itself to analysing the present bourgeois regime, to studying the trends of development of the capitalist social organization, and that is all' (ibid., p. 184).

On this point Lenin takes the same view as Plekhanov and the orthodox Germans: Marxism is a determinist interpretation of history which, by observing the present state of society, predicts how it will develop independently of human wishes, opinions, or values. Marxism can thus answer the question as to which human aspirations are in accordance with 'objective' trends and which are condemned to remain idle dreams. Like other orthodox Marxists, Lenin does not reply to the objection of the subjectivists and neo-Kantians that to know which of our actions are likely to succeed is not the same as having a reason for them: whence is this reason to be derived? By speaking of 'progress' we tacitly introduce a value-judgement, implying that the social process is not only necessary but deserves support; but this cannot follow from any mere descriptive analysis.

Lenin nevertheless uses the concept of progress, without explaining how it relates to a determinist historiosophy. He declares that capitalism is progressive as compared with Russian autocracy, and this clearly does not simply mean that the country is heading for a capitalist economy. However—and this is of fundamental importance in Lenin's eyes—capitalism in Russia and the future democratic changes associated with it are 'progressive' not in themselves but because they will facilitate the struggle of the working class to overthrow capitalism. He emphasizes that Marxists must call themselves social democrats and never forget the importance of 'democratism' and the struggle against feudalism, absolutism, and the Tsarist bureaucracy, since these must be overthrown before the bourgeoisie can be dealt with.

> That is why it is the direct duty of the working class to fight side by side with radical democracy against absolutism and the reactionary social estates and institutions—a duty which the Social-Democrats must impress upon the workers, while not for a moment ceasing also to impress upon them that the struggle against all these institutions is necessary only as a means of facilitating the struggle against the bourgeoisie, that the worker needs the achievement of the general democratic demands only to clear the road to victory over the working people's chief enemy, over an institution that is purely democratic by nature, *capital* . . . (*Collected Works*, vol. I, p. 291)

Lenin repeats this admonition several times, and its purport is clear. Democracy is not an end in itself; political freedom is mainly for the benefit of the bourgeoisie, but the working class has an interest in it as it will facilitate the struggle for socialism. This view presages an early breach between the social democrats and the 'legal Marxists', who regarded political freedoms as valuable in themselves and not merely weapons in the fight for the 'next stage' of history. Lenin from the beginning envisaged the struggle against absolutism in the context of the future victory of socialism, and only from this point of view did he take seriously anti-Tsarist activity or alliances with democratic forces. To measure the 'progressiveness' of social institutions it was not enough to compare different formations based on class antagonism: everything must be related to the final aim of socialism. On this point Lenin's eschatology is fully in accordance with Marx's ideas. Democratic institutions, and the political and cultural freedoms that go with the capitalist economy, are not values in themselves: their sense is entirely determined within the capitalist order.

Lenin agreed with Plekhanov at this time in holding that capitalism was bound to prevail in Russia. The populists, in his view, were involved in a contradiction on this point. They wished to do away with feudal survivals and yet preserve social institutions that could only exist by virtue of those survivals: to abolish the remaining restrictions of serfdom and feudal servitude, yet to avert the inevitable consequences of this process in the shape of the expropriation and class differentiation of the peasantry. They were reactionaries inasmuch as they wished to preserve institutions that progress condemned to be swept away, such as the attachment of the peasant to the soil.

The work quoted above clearly formulates the basic practical task to which

Lenin devoted the rest of his career: the organization of a socialist workers' party thanks to which the proletariat would not be a mere instrument of the bourgeoisie in the struggle against absolutism, but would be an independent body aware of its antagonism to capital as well as to the Tsardom. In forming the workers' party the intelligentsia would play only a subsidiary part: 'the role of the "intelligentsia" is to make special leaders from among the intelligentsia unnecessary' (ibid., p. 298). The proletariat was not only to form an independent movement but to lead the fight against absolutism. This last point is only indicated in general terms, but it figures in later writings as the key to Lenin's tactics.

In 1893–4, then, Lenin made his appearance on the political and intellectual scene of St. Petersburg as a Marxist in the classical Plekhanov sense. All the main elements of the social democratic outlook can be found in these early works: the assertion that historical inevitability is central to Marxism and that the latter has no room for evaluative elements; that the cause of capitalism has irrevocably prevailed in Russia; and that the task of social democracy is to help the workers organize an independent political movement which will lead all democratic forces in the fight against absolutism and thus clear the field for the future victory over capitalism.

The year 1895 is of especial importance both in Lenin's biography and in the history of Russian socialism. It is the date of Lenin's first journey abroad, his arrest, the creation of a social democratic organization in St. Petersburg, the first contacts between the social democratic intelligentsia and the workers, and Lenin's first conflict with Peter Struve and with what was later called 'legal Marxism'.

2. Struve and 'legal Marxism'

THE term 'legal Marxism' is applied to the writings of a group of Russian philosophers and economists who advanced Marxist ideas in the 1890s but who, almost from the beginning, took up an increasingly critical attitude towards essential features of orthodoxy, both in political economy and in the social field. None of the 'legal Marxists' were orthodox in the way that Plekhanov or Lenin was, and after 1900 they embraced political liberalism and, for the most part, Christian philosophy. In the nineties, however, they dominated the field of Marxist journalism in Russia. Their main differences from orthodoxy may be summed up in a few points. While accepting the principles of historical materialism, they held that it had no logical connection with philosophical materialism and was compatible with a spiritualist philosophy, or with positivism or Kantianism. They regarded Marxism as a scientific explanation of historical processes, but agreed with the neo-Kantians that it did not account for moral principles and that these must be derived from another source. They regarded political freedoms and democratic institutions as valuable in themselves, and were interested in the possibilities of political and economic reform under capitalism, not only from the point of view of the 'ultimate aim' but from that of the immediate interest of the workers, peasants, and intelligentsia and of cultural development. Marxism, to them, was rather a theory of society than a practical weapon: they were more interested in its cognitive value than its political function. They criticized Marx's theory of value, of the falling rate of profit, and the concentration of capital in agriculture. In some respects they anticipated German revisionism, and in others they endorsed its criticisms. They did much to popularize Marxism among the intelligentsia, but also to undermine its influence. They are regarded as the Russian counterpart of the revisionists, but the analogy is only partially valid. By the end of the century the legal Marxists were among the protagonists of the ideological struggle for liberal reforms: they existed as a group until Russian socialism and liberalism finally parted company.

The most eminent of the legal Marxists was Pyotr (Peter) Berngardovich Struve (1870–1944). Other members of the group were Nikolay Aleksandrovich Berdyayev (1874–1948), Mikhail Ivanovich Tugan-Baranovsky (1865–1919), Sergey Nikolayevich Bulgakov (1871–1944), and Semyon Ludwigovich Frank (1877–1944). The term 'legal Marxism' was mainly used, in a pejorative sense, by Lenin and others of the orthodox camp. As pointed out by R. Kindersley in the principal monograph on the subject, the term did not refer so much to the fact that they published books or articles that were allowed by the censorship (for so did Lenin), but rather to their 'legal' status as individuals, i.e. that they lived under their own names and did not as a rule carry on underground activity. The orthodox used the term, however, to suggest that the group regarded legal reformist activity as the only way to achieve social change in Russia.

Struve, whose father was governor of the province of Perm, entered St. Petersburg University in 1899 and studied first zoology, then law. He was a typical intellectual as opposed to a political figure, and became a Marxist for theoretical rather than political reasons. As a student he had a reputation for wide reading and expert knowledge of Western philosophy and sociology. Marxism attracted him by its scientific, unsentimental approach to social questions, its thoroughgoing determinism and the light it threw on social prospects in Russia. From his youth Struve was attracted by liberal ideas, and—as R. Pipes points out in his monograph—from the beginning he treated liberalism as an end and socialism as a means, whereas to orthodox Marxists it was the other way round. A convinced Westernizer, he saw Russia's future in terms of 'Europeanization' and believed that the working class would be the chief agent in this process. In 1890–1 he was the leader of a group which discussed social and philosophical questions. He was influenced at an early stage by neo-Kantian literature, and this was reinforced by a year spent at the University of Graz in 1891. Like all Marxists of his generation he began his writing career by attacking the populists on the peasant question and that of capitalism in Russia. In reviews and articles in 1892–3 he argued that class differentiation in the countryside and the development of a commodity economy were not only inevitable but salutary, and that capitalism had put an end to dreams of a barter economy and the maintenance of the village commune. In the autumn of 1894 his book *Critical Remarks on the Subject of Russia's Economic Development* was published in St. Petersburg. This was a Marxist work in the sense that Struve declared himself to be a historical materialist and criticized 'subjective sociology' from that point of view, renewing his attacks on populist economic theory and vain attempts to reverse the course of history; but in some important respects the book foreshadowed his future position as a revisionist. In the first place, he rejected the common Marxist view that the state is 'nothing but' an instrument of class oppression. On the contrary, it performed many necessary functions that were not tied to any particular class-interest: this was so under any social system, and would be the case when capitalism was superseded. Secondly, and more importantly, Struve was in favour of evolutionary socialism, developing out of the capitalist system by a process of gradual and continuous change; he thus also rejected the theory of the inevitable impoverishment of the working class. The book is not only a critique of the populist Utopia but also a hymn of praise to capitalism, not only because it contains the seeds of its own destruction and replacement by higher things, but because it represents enormous progress in every sphere: the productivity of labour, economic rationalization, political and cultural freedoms, and the socialization of life. The book ends with a sentence that became famous as the target of populist attacks: 'Let us admit our lack of culture and be schooled by capitalism.' The populists accused Struve of glorifying capitalism and of being a bourgeois ideologist; but he considered himself a Marxist and a social democrat, and for some years he and Lenin treated their differences of opinion as divergences within the social democratic movement. If the term 'legal Marxism' is intended to denote a clearly separate movement, aware of its separateness, this is to some extent a projection into the past of Lenin's attitude after he had broken with Struve. On the other hand, it is reasonable enough to regard the legal Marxists as forming a single group, since they showed certain common trends from the beginning, although for some years the differences between revolutionists and revisionists were less important than their joint opposition to populism.

In autumn 1895 Struve went to Switzerland, where he met Plekhanov, and then to Berlin, where he studied for some months. In the following year he and Potresov were sent to the congress of the International in London by a social democratic organization formed largely on the initiative of Martov and Lenin and named (after they had both been arrested) the League for the Liberation of the Working Class. Struve's contacts with the Fabians encouraged him to place his hopes in socialism evolving out of capitalism. At the beginning of 1897 he and Tugan-Baranovsky took over *Novoye Slovo*, a periodical previously published by liberal populists. Until its suppression nearly a year later this became the principal organ of Russian Marxism, publishing articles by Plekhanov, Lenin, Martov, and other leaders, and also a discussion between Struve and Bulgakov on Stammler's new book concerning historical materialism. Struve endeavoured to reconcile historical materialism with freedom on the lines of Kant's distinction between the empirical and the noumenal world, though he seems to confuse this distinction with that between physical and psychological reality. He declares that all ideals and evaluative experiences can be causally explained by social circumstances; however, since they present themselves psychologically as independent of such conditions and as possessing a reality of their own, this psychological reality cannot be described in entirely the same language as the world of phenomena, and we must therefore assume that there is some kind of independence as between historical conditions and human ideals. This reasoning is clumsy and unconvincing, but it shows the tension in Struve's mind between historical materialism and the desire to safeguard certain non-historical and non-relative values. Before long he resolved this tension by abandoning Marxism altogether.

In March 1898 a number of social democratic groups sent delegates to a meeting at Minsk which was intended to be the founding congress of the Russian Social Democratic Workers' party. It did not bring about the desired integration, and nearly all the participants, who were few in number, were arrested immediately after the meeting. However, it left behind it not only the name (and the numeration of party Congresses up to the present time, this being regarded as No. I) but also a manifesto drafted by Struve, though he was not present at the Congress itself. This stated that the immediate task of the working class was to achieve political freedoms; that in view of the weakness and cowardice of the bourgeoisie it was for the proletariat to overthrow the autocracy; but that the proletariat must continue to fight against the bourgeoisie for its own class aims and must preserve its separate identity as a class. All this was in accordance with Plekhanov's doctrine. However, the drafting of this programme for the nascent party was Struve's last act as a social democrat. Bernstein's book and articles confirmed his doubts as to the Marxist doctrine of revolution, though he rightly did not think much of Bernstein's criticism from the philosophical point of view. Before long he put forward similar conclusions with better arguments of his own. In 'Die Marxsche Theorie der sozialen Entwicklung' ('Marx's Theory of Social Development'), published in 1899 in

Archiv für soziale Gesetzgebung und Statistik, he attacked the notion of social revolution as contradictory and formulated his general objections to Marx's theory of society, though he continued to treat that theory with respect and even to call himself a Marxist.

Struve argued that Marx's theory of the pauperization and degradation of the working class had in its time been based on well-ascertained data. Apart from the fact, however, that later developments had shown that these did not necessarily represent a permanent trend, Marx in any case had failed to notice that if his theory were right on this point the outlook for socialism would be hopeless: for it could not be expected that a class condemned to increasing degradation of mind and body would be able to bring about the greatest revolution in history, including not only economic changes but the efflorescence of art and civilization. There was no reason to maintain that social antagonisms, especially the opposition between producers and the relations of production, must go on becoming more and more acute. On the contrary, the theory of the intensification of social contradictions and the universal collapse of capitalism conflicted with the other premises of historical materialism. It was wrong to think of the economy and the legal superstructure as two independent ontological realities, standing in a relationship of cause and effect or, as Stammler would have it, of content and form. Both these supposed entities were hypostases, intellectual creations and not real phenomena. What was real was the constant pressure of economic facts on legal ones, and a process of constant adaptation. Marx himself had admitted that the process of socialization went on uninterruptedly in a capitalist economy, but he assumed without proof that this must be accompanied by a steady increase in the 'capitalist' character of the legal system, so that the gap between the two abstract entities was bound to get wider. In reality the opposite was the case: socialist development took place within capitalist society in both the economic and the legal sphere, and the inevitable disharmony of these two became less and less acute as time went on. 'In a real society there is neither absolute antagonism nor absolute harmony between the economy and the law, but they constantly collide yet partially adapt to each other.' If the notion of a social revolution means anything it can only mean the slow process of social change which at some moment may, but need not, be accompanied by a political revolution; the process of socialist change takes place not by the continual increase of tension but by its gradual elimination. This view is in accordance with historical materialism, whereas the idea of a violent social revolution is contrary to it. The continuity of change is an epistemological condition of the intelligibility of the concept of change, whereas the idea of capitalism and socialism being opposed to each other in all respects and separated by an abrupt hiatus is quite unintelligible. As to the political revolution establishing a dictatorship of the proletariat, such a dictatorship becomes less likely or desirable, not more, as the proletariat grows in strength: for as the strength and social importance of the working class increase, so does the socialist element in the system of society.

This, it will be seen, is a repetition, on the empirical side, of Bernstein's argument to the effect that social reform under capitalism is itself the building of socialism. The 'epistemological' point, on the other hand, is decidedly far-fetched. Marx said that socialist conditions are prepared within the capitalist system by the growth of co-operation and concentration of the technological process of production, and he predicted that a political revolution, i.e. the seizure of power by the organized proletariat, was the necessary condition of a change in economic relations and especially the socialization of means of production. However this doctrine may be criticized, it does not appear to contain any logical inconsistency. The basic practical content of the social revolution was to be the violent expropriation of the capitalists, and it is hard to see why this should be logically impossible.

Struve's connection with the social democrats lasted for a year or two longer, but in 1901 it ceased in a welter of accusations and intrigue. For some time after Lenin and Martov returned from exile in Siberia they conducted involved negotiations with Struve with the object of collaborating on periodicals, existing or projected, but it was clear that the breach between them was too wide. Struve criticized, one after the other, various crucial points of social democratic ideology and Marxist philosophy, and in the end rejected them all. In 1899, following Böhm-Bawerk and the Russian 'economists', he criticized Marx's theory of value, stating that Marx had tried to combine in one concept two entirely different phenomena, the social fact of exploitation and the economic fact of exchange. If, as argued in Volume III of *Capital*, industry creates the average rate of profit, this simply means that economic realities do not correspond to the concept of value as defined by labour, for value is ultimately determined as a function of production costs; while value as in Volume I of *Capital* remains a purely metaphysical entity, of no use to political economy.

The estrangement was completed by Struve's philosophical criticism. True, he had never professed dialectical materialism after the fashion of Engels or Plekhanov: his views were those of a 'scienticist' and positivist, but his general determinist and empiricist outlook was in accordance with the way of thinking prevalent among Marxists. In 1900, however, he wrote a long introduction to Berdyayev's *Subjectivism and Individualism in Social Philosophy* (published in 1901) in which he expressly abandoned positivism for a Kantian transcendentalism on a religious basis. As values cannot be derived from experience, he argued, we must either fall into extreme relativism or accept that they have an ontological foundation and are not simply due to arbitrary, subjective decisions. The absoluteness of values implies the reality of the Absolute and the non-empirical: a substantive soul endowed with freedom, and a supreme Being. On this basis we can recognize the absolute value of personality, which is the foundation of liberal social philosophy. Liberalism in Struve's sense is above all a nominalist conception, rejecting the idea that any suprapersonal collective entity such as society or the state can claim to encroach upon the inalienable rights of the individual, his freedom and urge towards unlimited self-perfection.

Struve left Russia at the end of 1901 and in the following year settled in Stuttgart, where he edited the journal *Osvobozhdenie* (*Liberation*): this was not the organ of any political party, but was closely linked with the liberal movement that was taking shape in Russia, and was devoted to unmasking and combating the autocracy. From this time on Struve's activity as a writer and politician has no connection with the history of Marxism except that he was constantly under fire from the social democrats.

Of the other legal Marxist writers, Berdyayev had least in common with Marxism. As a student he belonged to social democratic groups, was arrested, and exiled for three years to Vologda, as were Bogdanov and Lunacharsky for the same reason. However, from the beginning of his career as a writer he stood much further from Marxism than did Struve. In the book referred to above he accepted the premises of historical materialism and the idea of the class struggle, but with reservations that were incompatible with even the loosest conception of Marxism. He believed that there must be an ontological repository of unchanging moral and logical values, and that historical circumstances, in particular the class struggle, govern the rules of cognition and obligation only in the sense that in each phase of history a different class is the exponent of those rules. Hence, while accepting the positivist argument that obligation cannot be deduced from empirical data, he endeavoured from the outset to base moral absolutism on other grounds. Of the former legal Marxists Berdyayev became the best known to the Western public, but this was after his expulsion from Soviet Russia and on account of his works attacking Communism and preaching a kind of Christian existentialism, based on faith in the absolute value of personality.

Tugan-Baranowsky, Bulgakov, and S. L. Frank were known in the 1890s chiefly as economists, the first-named being professionally the most qualified in this field. They were concerned to a large extent with the key question of markets and whether Russian capitalism was—as the populists denied—capable of creating a home market sufficient for its expansion. Tugan-Baranovsky argued that the viability and development of capitalism did not depend on the level of consumption, as the market for means of production expanded faster than that for consumption goods. Since, under capitalism, production and accumulation were ends in themselves, capitalism was in a position to create

its own conditions of compound reproduction and was not absolutely dependent on popular consumption. In that case, however, as Rosa Luxemburg had
pointed out, capitalism could apparently keep going indefinitely and there was
no economic reason to prophesy its overthrow. Tugan-Baranovsky worked out
a theory of crises to supplement Marx's arguments, but he did not in fact
believe that capitalism would collapse as a result of its crises or of the imbalance between production and the market. In this he was not at variance with
Lenin, who likewise did not hold that capitalism was certain to collapse owing
to the difficulty of finding outlets.

The economic revisionism of the legal Marxists centred on Marx's theory of
value. Their attack had no special political effects, but it struck at what the
orthodox regarded as the keystone of the doctrine. Since value in Marx's sense
was unmeasurable and did not in fact define the terms of exchange, so that
there was no logical transition from value to price, it followed, according to
Bulgakov, that value must be regarded purely as a social category of no importance in studying price movements, but essential to the broad analysis of capitalism. In this way, like Sombart, Bulgakov sought to protect the theory of
value by limiting its applicability. Frank, in *Marx's Theory of Value and its Significance* (1900), questioned the utility of Marx's concept if, as Marx himself
intended, it was supposed to denote not exchange-value but an intrinsic property of goods, whether marketed or not. In the end the legal Marxists either
rejected the category of value altogether, as being of no interest to economics
in so far as it differed from price, or adopted the theory of marginal utility
whereby value depends on the purchaser's sense of need, expressed as the
price he will pay for the last (marginal) unit of a commodity that he is disposed
to regard as useful.

The legal Marxists also attacked Marx's economic theory on other essential
points. Tugan-Baranovsky declared that the theory of the diminishing rate of
profit conflicted with other elements of the doctrine—the value of constant capital falls as the productivity of labour increases, so that the rate of profit may
be constant although productivity is rising—and also that it was contrary to factual observation. Bulgakov, like the German revisionists, criticized the theory
of concentration in agriculture.

In spite of all these criticisms Russian Marxism could be regarded as a single ideological camp, though with internal differentiations, as long as the Marxists held that the chief task of social democracy was to combat the populist idea
of a separate, non-capitalist road for Russia. Before the end of the century,
however, it was clear that the populist economic doctrine was losing ground in
the sense that appeals to stop capitalism developing were ineffectual, while
Marxists of all shades regarded the defence of the village commune as a hopeless cause. Thus, around 1900, what might have appeared secondary differ-

ences within Russian Marxism took on the aspect of a basic dispute, especially as they coincided in time with the debate over revisionism in Germany and the birth of a liberal movement in Russia. Marxism could no longer define itself simply as anti-populism. The relationship of social democracy to the bourgeoisie, the question of revolution, and the relation between the political and economic struggle of the working class became the paramount subjects of debate. In 1898–1900 three main trends may be discerned in Russian Marxism: revolutionary orthodoxy, revisionism or 'legal Marxism', and 'economism'. Before long, however, the legal Marxists went over to liberalism and ceased to count as revisionists. Bulgakov, Berdyayev, Frank, and Struve returned by different paths towards Christianity. They continued to play an important part in intellectual life as the contributors to three collections of essays, the first two of which–*Problems of Idealism* (1902) and *Landmarks* (1909)–are among the most significant events in the history of the Russian intelligentsia before the Revolution. The third, entitled *De Profundis*, was produced in 1918 but immediately confiscated, and was practically unknown for half a century: it depicted the revolutionary apocalypse as a national and cultural calamity.

It may seem strange that although revisionism made its appearance in Russia before there was an organized social democratic movement, it did not remain in existence for long, whereas it did so in Germany despite the opposition of an orthodox party establishment. However, German revisionism was the theoretical superstructure of a reformist struggle waged successfully for many years by an organized workers' movement. In Russia reformist ideas had a very fragile basis in political experience, and the idea of a wholesale and final revolution was deeply rooted in the minds of the radical intelligentsia. Moreover, while in Germany revisionism appeared from the beginning as a section of the social democratic movement existing alongside the liberals, in Russia it played for a time the part of the liberal movement with which it eventually merged, while the writers we have been considering regarded Marxism as a weapon against populist conservatism rather than a theory of global revolution. Marxism harmonized with the attitude of those who, having been inspired in their youth by the ideals of 'scientism', sought after a scientific interpretation of society as opposed to populist moralism; they also found in Marxism a promise of the triumph of capitalism and therefore of democratic and constitutional principles in Russia. Marxism proved that Russian absolutism was doomed by history, and this was probably more important to the legal Marxists than the prospect of socialism. When the Russian social democrats made it clear in the course of time that they regarded any alliance with liberalism as purely tactical, it became impossible to maintain a half-Marxist and half-liberal standpoint.

There is another important fact to be noted in the history of Russian revisionism. Because Marxism and social democracy made their appearance in

Russia independently of a workers' movement and were at the outset purely intellectual in character, Marxism took on a much more dogmatic and fanatical form than in the West, where it had constantly to adjust to the realities of labour politics. In Russia, where 'revolution' had been a word to conjure with for decades and where there was every reason to mistrust the prospects of reform, the tiny group of revolutionaries were naturally doctrinaire in the extreme, the more so as their convictions were of purely moral and intellectual origin and were not due to their being members of an oppressed class. In the resulting atmosphere theoretical problems were debated in terms of loyalty and treachery rather than simple truth and falsehood, and tactical questions were unvaryingly and solely related to the 'ultimate end'. Despite ideological differences the Russian socialists shared the mentality of populist conspirators rather than that of West European social democrats. It is significant that as soon as a Russian workers' movement came into existence there also appeared, though not for long, a variant of German revisionism in the shape of 'economism', i.e.. roughly speaking, a trade-unionist doctrine of non-political efforts to improve the workers' lot.

3. Lenin's polemics in 1895–1901

Up to 1899 Lenin was mainly absorbed by the controversy with populism, but the critique of legal Marxism, and later especially of economism, already figured prominently in his works. In 1895 his first printed article appeared in a miscellany published by Potresov, under the title *The Economic Content of Narodism [Populism] and the Criticism of it in Mr. Struve's Book*. This was an analysis of Struve's work on *Russia's Economic Development*: while critical in parts, it did not accuse Struve of treason and anti-Marxism but rather urged him to conform more strictly to the orthodox position. Apart from attacking the populists, Lenin's work contains some general theoretical remarks, and he reiterates his view of the progressiveness of capitalism: 'Yes, the Marxists do consider large-scale capitalism progressive—not, of course, because it replaces 'independence' [sc. of the peasantry] by dependence, but because it creates conditions for abolishing dependence' (*Works*, vol. 1, pp. 379–80). Criticizing Struve for opposing the idea of reform to that of the breakdown of capitalism, Lenin argues that one is a means to the other. His main criticism of Struve is that he is an 'objectivist'. He agrees with Sombart, whom Struve quotes, that 'in Marxism itself there is not a grain of ethics from beginning to end', since (as Lenin adds) 'theoretically, it subordinates the "ethical standpoint" to the "principle of causality"; in the practice it reduces it to the class struggle' (ibid., p. 421). He also agrees that scientific socialism rejects philosophy altogether: 'From the standpoint of Marx and Engels philosophy has no right to a separate, independent existence, and its material is divided among the various branches of positive science' (p. 418). In short, he understands the 'scientific' character of Marxism in the same way as Plekhanov and most of the orthodox Germans: Marxism is a non-evaluative, non-philosophical theory of social phenomena. Thus far Lenin is in agreement with Struve. But this formulation may suggest that Marxism confines itself to describing historical necessities and of itself offers no practical counsel, except of course as to the efficacy of certain actions. This was the difficulty of those who found it necessary to supplement the Marxist doctrine with a normative ethic derived from elsewhere, generally from Kant. Struve at this time had not gone so far, but confined himself to observing that Marxism was 'objective', i.e. descriptive only. To Lenin, however, this was unacceptable. An objectivist, in his view, was one who speaks only of the necessities involved by a particular social formation, and, by limiting himself to these, runs the risk of becoming an apologist for them simply as necessities. A materialist, on the other hand, does not so limit himself but goes on to explain what class forces are involved. 'Materialism includes partisanship, so to speak, and enjoins the direct and open adoption of the standpoint of a definite social group in any assessment of events' (ibid., p. 401).

From the theoretical point of view this is clumsy and unconvincing: for it is clear that to analyse 'historical necessities' in the light of the class structure of a society is not to go beyond a purely 'objective' description, and it is not explained why materialism as such should oblige us to anything or imply any active commitment. It is evident, however, that Lenin wished to avoid the dilemma propounded by the neo-Kantians: either Marxism describes the social process without telling us what human individuals should do about it, or it must be supplemented by normative ideas. Lenin, though he was unable to express his thought clearly, was endeavouring to bring out the essential point which was first elucidated by Lukács: Marxism does away with the dichotomy between facts and values, for it is identical with the self-knowledge of the working class; that class comprehends the social process in the very act of revolutionizing the world, so that in this one privileged case the understanding and the making of history appear as a single act. Lenin consistently ignored the neo-Kantian criticism and, being unable to examine the question properly, confined himself to summary statements like those quoted. He perceived vaguely, however, that it is the characteristic feature of Marxism that it is neither purely descriptive nor purely normative, nor a combination of descriptive and normative judgements, but claims to be at once a movement and an act of understanding—the self-awareness of the proletariat in the act of struggle. Knowledge of the world, in other words, is an aspect of changing it: theory and its practical application are one.

In 1895 Lenin went abroad for the first time and met in Geneva the founding

fathers of Russian Marxism, Plekhanov and Akselrod. The meeting was successful, though the *émigrés* had trouble convincing Lenin of the necessity of an
alliance with the liberal bourgeoisie. Soon after returning to Russia he was
arrested: police measures had been intensified owing to a wave of strikes in St.
Petersburg, which the social democrats had done much to instigate. He
remained in prison for a year and a half, writing appeals and pamphlets, and
was then sentenced to three years' exile at Shushenskoye in the Krasnoyarsk
area of Siberia, where he continued to study and write intensively. While in
prison he drafted a programme calling on the social democratic party to fight
for democratic freedoms and social legislation. The programme does not envisage the conquest of state power by the working class, but only a share in the
making of laws. The party is to help the workers develop class-consciousness
and to point out the objectives of the struggle; it must also explain to the workers that while they should support the bourgeoisie in the fight for political freedom, this is only a temporary alliance. In the summer of 1897 Lenin published
in *Novoye Slovo* a fresh attack on the populists entitled 'A Characterization of
Economic Romanticism', in which he compared their doctrine with that of Sismondi, the champion of small producers threatened by the expansion of capitalism, Sismondi might succeed in revealing the dire consequences of capitalist
accumulation, but he had nothing to set against it except a romantic, sentimental nostalgia for the pre-capitalist era. Like the populists he was no better than
a reactionary, for he dreamt of returning to the past instead of seeing that the
solution to the contradictions and injustices of capitalism lay in allowing it to
develop to the full. Lenin also reverted to the question of the home market,
anticipating to some extent the problems later raised by Rosa Luxemburg. It
was not true that capitalism was prevented from realizing surplus value by reason of the collapse of small owners and the resulting contraction of the market:
productive consumption offered capitalist production a wide field of expansion.

While in exile Lenin wrote a pamphlet on *The Tasks of the Russian Social
Democrats*, published in 1898 in Geneva, which defined the party's general strategy in regard to 'alliances' with other social forces. Social democrats were to
support all moves against the autocracy and to denounce all forms of oppression, whichever social groups were its victims. They should support protests
against national, religious, social, and class oppression, aiding the bourgeoisie
against the 'reactionary strivings of the petty bourgeoisie', and the latter in their
democratic demands upon the Tsarist bureaucracy. The party, however, was not
to consider itself a champion of the interests that it supported. Although it aided
the persecuted sectarians, it had no concern for their religious aspirations. To
support, in fact, meant simply to exploit. Social democracy was, in Lenin's view,
the only force that was engaged consistently and unreservedly against the autocracy: all others were irresolute or half-hearted. The party could and must act

as a centre for all the social energies which would one day bring absolutism to the ground, but at the same time it must have exclusively in view the interests of the proletariat as a separate class. 'The social democrats render this support in order to expedite the fall of the common enemy, but expect nothing for themselves from these temporary allies, and concede nothing to them' (*Works*, vol. 2, p. 334). 'Support for the democratic demands of the petty bourgeoisie certainly does not mean support of the petty bourgeoisie: on the contrary, it is precisely the development which political liberty will make possible in Russia that will, with particular force, lead to the destruction of small economy under the blows of capital' (*A Draft Programme of Our Party*, 1899; *Works*, vol. 4, p. 243). In a letter to Potresov, written from exile and dated 26 January 1899, Lenin says: 'to free all *fortschrittliche Strömungen* [progressive trends] from the rubbish of Narodism and agrarianism and to utilize all of them in this purified form. In my opinion 'utilize' is a much more exact and suitable word than *Unterstützung und Bundesgenossenschaft* [support and alliance]. The latter indicates the equality of these *Bundesgenossen* [allies], whereas they must (in this I fully agree with you) follow in the wake, sometimes even "with gnashing of teeth"; they have absolutely not grown so far as to reach equality and will never grow to reach it, owing to their cowardice, disunity etc' (*Works*, vol. 34, p. 30).

It is thus clear that Lenin from the outset regarded all political alliances as meaning simply the utilization of other groups for social democratic ends. Social democracy must rally around itself all forces that can in any way contribute to the break-up of the existing system, in the full awareness that that break-up is ultimately intended to destroy its 'allies' as well. From this point of view Lenin's attitude, and subsequently that of the whole Leninist movement, is identical whether it be a question of the bourgeoisie against absolutism, peasants against land-owners, religious sects aspiring to freedom, nationalities oppressed by Great Russian imperialism, or democratic institutions themselves. There is of course no mention of 'utilizing' the working class, for all these strategic rules are designed to enable that class, which is the *raison d'être* of the struggle, to attain its 'final aim'. Nevertheless, it soon became clear that as far as basic strategy was concerned the working class too, in Lenin's concept, was rather an instrument than a substantive agent.

While in exile Lenin also wrote a treatise on *The Development of Capitalism in Russia* (*Works*, vol. 3), which was published in 1899. This is his *magnum opus* against the populists, full of statistics and detailed analysis of the trends in agriculture and industry. It argues that Russian agriculture is in a state of commodity economy and shows all the signs of capitalist change: class differentiation, competition, and proletarianization on a large scale. In industry, Lenin depicts the process of concentration and the formation of a single country-wide market, sweeping away medieval forms of production and exchange.

While controversy with the populists played a diminishing role in intellectual life, unorthodox ideas were making their appearance among social democrats and were causing Lenin anxiety. He was roused to fury, as he himself states, by an article of Bulgakov's attacking Kautsky's recent analysis of the agrarian question. He was also disturbed by the growing popularity of Bernstein and the influence of neo-Kantianism, of which Struve and Bulgakov were to some extent the Russian spokesmen. He even began, as he wrote to Potresov on 27 June 1899, to study philosophy: he read Holbach and Hélvetius, and intended to apply himself to Kant. But he attached less importance to purely philosophical disputes at this time than subsequently. Meanwhile, besides theoretical revisionism the younger social democrats had taken up 'economism': Lenin reacted violently to the first signs of this movement, which attacked the very foundations of social democracy as he conceived it. In summer 1899, on receiving the document known as the 'Credo', drawn up by Kuskova and Prokopovich and setting out the 'economist' programme, Lenin wrote a sharp protest which was endorsed by sixteen other exiles, and was published next year at Geneva by the local organization of social democrats.

The 'Credo' called in question the desirability of a separate political workers' party in Russia, which its authors regarded as an artificial application of Western experience to quite different conditions. The workers' movement, they argued, should always aim at the point of least resistance: in the West it was much easier to carry on a political than an economic struggle, but in Russia it was the reverse. Marxists should therefore concentrate on helping the workers' economic struggle and should back up the liberal opposition, which would presumably be directed by non-socialist democratic forces. Lenin regarded this as a prescription for political suicide, and in reply set out principles that were generally accepted by the orthodox. The workers' movement must have its own political aims and an independent party to pursue them; it must organize opposition elements of every kind, while never forfeiting its independence or running the risk of becoming an instrument of bourgeois parties.

Russian 'economism' was, as it were, a revival of 'classic' (non-political, non-terrorist) populism, with the working class substituted for the peasantry. It maintained that intellectual leaders should concentrate on the most obvious and easily understood aspirations of the workers, viz. their economic aims, leaving it to the liberals to fight for freedom and themselves playing only an auxiliary role in the political battle. Economism as not revisionism as this term is used of Bernstein and his supporters, who had no intention of persuading the workers to abandon the political and parliamentary struggle; but it corresponded to the trade-unionist tendency which was strongly rooted in German social democracy and which was allied for a considerable period with the theoretical revisionists.

Lenin's alarm at this new deviation was well founded, for it dominated social democracy in Russia for about two years and won over a majority of the *émigrés*, leading to a split among their ranks. After 1900 the 'economists' declined in importance, but it was nevertheless largely in answer to them that Lenin wrote *What is to be Done?*, in which he laid the ideological foundations of Bolshevism.

Lenin's Siberian exile ended at the beginning of 1900, and in July of that year he went abroad for the purpose of organizing Russian social democrats into a united movement. The first step to be taken, as he had long believed, was to found a periodical which would act as a link between scattered groups and make it possible to create a real party. Such a periodical would of course have to be printed abroad and smuggled into Russia. The name chosen for it was *Iskra (The Spark)*.

The process of launching the paper was beset by quarrels that need not be gone into here. Lenin's meeting with Plekhanov was a disaster. In a posthumously published note on his encounter with the Geneva veterans he speaks bitterly of the older man's arrogance, though he (Lenin) had approached him with respect and admiration. Evidently Plekhanov was jealous of his authority among the Russian social democrats and vented his pride and intolerance on the young disciple. As Lenin put it, and as he was to remember for the future, 'An enamoured youth receives from the object of his love a bitter lesson—to regard all persons "without sentiment", to keep a stone in one's sling' (*Works*, vol. 4, p. 342).

In spite of these troubles the first number of *Iskra* was published in December 1900. It was printed successively in Leipzig, Munich, London, and Geneva, and had as its contributors the intellectual cream of Russian Marxism—Lenin, Plekhanov, Martov, Akselrod, Potresov, and Vera Zasulich.

The years 1901–3 marked a new stage in the development of Russain Marxism and Russian social democracy. During this time the foundations were laid of the Leninist variant of Marxism, the novelty and specific character of which were visible only by degrees. Up to now Lenin's ideological statements had been no different from those of Plekhanov or the Western orthodox Marxists, apart from the strong emphasis he laid on certain elements of the doctrine. Among these was the principle, which he repeated at every opportunity, that only the final aim—the conquest of political power by the proletariat—endows current actions with any meaning, and that social democrats may conclude any alliance and support any cause if by so doing they will bring the ultimate aim any closer. All other movements and social classes, human beings and ideologies, must be treated as subservient to the 'final revolution'.

XVI

The Rise of Leninism

1. The controversy over Leninism

THE CHARACTER of Leninism as a variant of Marxist doctrine has long been a subject of dispute. The question is, in particular, whether Leninism is a 'revisionist' ideology in relation to the Marxist tradition, or, on the contrary, a faithful application of the general principles of Marxism to a new political situation. The political bearing of this controversy is obvious. Stalinist orthodoxy, which on this point is still in force within the Communist movement, naturally takes the second view. Stalin maintained that Lenin added nothing to the inherited doctrine and took nothing away from it, but applied its principles unerringly, not only to Russian conditions but, most important, to the entire world situation. On this view Leninism is not a specifically Russian application of Marxism or one limited to Russian conditions, but a universally valid system of strategy and tactics for the 'new era' of social development, viz. that of imperialism and proletarian revolutions. Some Bolsheviks, on the other hand, regarded Leninism as more particularly an instrument of the Russian revolution, while non-Leninist Marxists argued that Lenin had been false to Marx's doctrine on many essential points.

The question, thus ideologically formulated, is in practice insoluble, like all such questions in the history of political movements or religious sects which have a strong inbuilt need of fidelity to their sources. It is natural and inevitable that the generations which come after the founders of the movement are confronted by questions and practical decisions that are not expressly foreseen in the existing canon, and that they interpret the canon in such a way as to justify their acts. In this respect the history of Marxism resembles that of Christianity. The result is generally to produce compromises of various kinds between doctrine and the demands of practice. New lines of division and conflicting political formations take shape under the immediate pressure of events, and each of them can find the support it requires in tradition, which is never perfectly integrated and consistent. Bernstein was indeed a revisionist in the sense that he openly rejected certain features of Marxist social philosophy and did not profess to be an inflexible custodian of the Marxian heritage on all points. Lenin, on the other hand, endeavoured to present all his acts and theories as the only possible or correct application of an existing ideology. He was not, however, a doctrinaire in the sense of preferring fidelity to Marx's text to the practical efficacy of the movement which he led. On the contrary, he had immense practical sense and the ability to subordinate all questions, whether of theory or tactics, to the single purpose of revolution in Russia and in the world. All questions of general theory had, in his view, already been settled by Marxism, and it was only necessary to draw intelligently on this body of doctrine to find the right solution for particular circumstances. In this he not only regarded himself as a faithful executor of the Marxist testament, but believed that he was conforming to the practice and tactics of European social democracy as exemplified more particularly in the German party. Up to 1914 he regarded German social democracy as a pattern and Kautsky as the greatest living authority on theoretical questions: he relied on him not only in theoretical matters but also on tactical Russian questions about which he himself knew a good deal more, such as the boycott of the Second Duma. In 1905 he wrote, in *Two Tactics of Social-Democracy in the Democratic Revolution*:

> When and where did I ever claim to have created any sort of special trend in international social-democracy, *not identical* [Lenin's italics] with the trend of Bebel and Kautsky? When and where have there been brought to light differences between me, on the one hand, and Bebel and Kautsky on the other—differences even slightly approximating in gravity to the differences between Bebel and Kautsky, for instance, at Breslau on the agrarian question? (*Works*, vol. 9, p. 66 n.)

The question whether Lenin was a 'revisionist' cannot be decided simply by comparing his writings with those of Marx or posing the unanswerable question as to what Marx would have done or said in this or that situation. Clearly Marx's theory is incomplete or ambiguous in many places, and could be 'applied' in many contradictory ways without manifestly infringing its principles. Nevertheless, the question of the continuity between Marxism and Leninism is not wholly without significance. It can best be considered, however, not in terms of 'fidelity' but rather by examining the general trend of Lenin's attempts, in the theoretical field, to 'apply' or supplement the Marxist heritage.

To Lenin, as we have said, all theoretical questions were merely instruments of a single aim, the revolution; and the meaning of all human affairs, ideas, institutions, and values resided exclusively in their bearing on the class struggle. It is not hard to find support for this attitude in the writings of Marx and Engels, who in many theoretical passages emphasized the transience and class-relatedness of all aspects of life in a class society. None the less, their specific analyses were generally more differentiated and less simplified than such 'reductionist' formulas might seem to imply. Both Marx and Engels had a considerably wider horizon of interest than that suggested by the question 'Is this good or bad for the revolution?'; to Lenin, on the other hand, this was the all-sufficient criterion as to whether a matter was important at all and, if so, how it should be decided. Marx and Engels had a sense of the continuity of civilization, and did not consider that all human values, including science, art, morals, and social institutions, were 'nothing but' instruments of class interests. Nevertheless, the general formulas in which they expressed their historical materialism lent themselves well enough to the use Lenin made of them. To Lenin philosophical questions had no meaning in themselves but were merely weapons in the political struggle: so were art and literature, law and institutions, democratic values and religious ideas. On this point he not only cannot be reproached with deviating from Marxism, but it can rather be said that he applied the principles of historical materialism more thoroughly than Marx. If law, for instance, is 'nothing but' a weapon in the class struggle, it naturally follows that there is no essential difference between the rule of law and an arbitrary dictatorship. If political freedoms are 'nothing but' an instrument used by the bourgeoisie in its own class-interest, it is perfectly fair to argue that communists need not feel obliged to uphold these values when they come to power. As science philosophy, and art are only organs of the class struggle, it can be seen that there is no 'qualitative' difference between writing a philosophical treatise and using fire-arms—the two are merely different weapons for different occasions and should be regarded in this light, whether used by friend or foe. These aspects of Lenin's doctrine became drastically evident after the Bolsheviks seized power, but they are expressed in his writings from the earliest years. Lenin often held the advantage in discussions with Marxists of other shades of opinion because of the devastating simplicity and consistency with which he applied the principles they had in common. When his adversaries were able to point out that he was in conflict with something Marx had actually said—for example, that 'dictatorship' did not signify a despotism unfettered by law—they were proving Marx's own inconsistency rather than Lenin's unorthodoxy.

None the less, on one or two essential points the innovations that Lenin introduced into the Russian revolutionary movement suggested considerable doubt as to his fidelity to Marxist tradition. In the first place, Lenin at an early stage advocated an alliance between the proletariat and the peasantry as the basic strategy for the 'bourgeois revolution', while his opponents contended that an alliance with the bourgeoisie would be more in accordance with the doctrine in this case. Secondly, Lenin was the first to see the national question as a powerful reservoir of energy that social democrats could and should use to further their cause, instead of merely an awkward hindrance. Thirdly, he formulated his own organizational rules and his own version of the attitude the party should adopt towards a spontaneous outbreak by the workers. On all these points he was criticized not only by reformists and Mensheviks but also by such a pillar of orthodoxy as Rosa Luxemburg. On all of them, too, his doctrine turned out to be exceedingly practical, and it can safely be said that on all three points his policy was necessary to the success of the Bolshevik revolution.

2. The party and the workers' movement. Consciousness and spontaneity

THE basic principles of Leninism as a separate political entity were formulated in 1901-3. These years saw the creation in Russia of the chief political groups which, while constantly at odds with one another, carried on the struggle against the Tsardom until the October Revolution: viz. the Bolshevik and Menshevik wings of social democracy, the social revolutionaries (S.R.s), and the constitutional democrats ('Kadets').

The principal organ in which Lenin's ideas gradually took visible shape was *Iskra*. Up to the Second Party Congress in 1903 the differences between Lenin and the rest of the editorial board were not of great consequence, and it was he who in fact gave the paper its tone: he edited it first in Munich and then in London, where he moved in the spring of 1902. *Iskra* was intended not only to combat revisionism and economism in Russian social democracy but to act as a link between groups which, despite the formal existence of the party, were still disunited as regards both ideology and organization: as Lenin put it, 'A newspaper is not only a collective propagandist and a collective agitator, it is also a collective organizer' ('Where to Begin', in *Works*, vol. 5, p. 22). *Iskra* in fact played a decisive part in preparations for the Congress, which, when it assembled, united the Russian social democrats into a single party and immediately split the party into two warring groups.

On the key question of the party's role Lenin laid the foundations of Bolshevik ideology in his conflict with economism, which he regarded as highly dangerous even though its influence was waning. The economists interpreted historical materialism as a theory of the primacy of the proletariat's economic struggle as compared with political aims (which, in the immediate future at any rate, were mainly the business of the Russian bourgeoisie), and they identified the working-class movement with a 'movement of workers' in the sense of a spontaneous struggle by the workers as a body. They emphasized the strictly class character of their own programme and attacked the *Iskra* group for touting after the intelligentsia and liberals, for exaggerating the importance of theory and ideology, and for giving too much weight to the common antagonism of all classes to the autocracy. Economism was a kind of Russian Proudhonism, or *ouvriérisme* as it was called. According to its adherents social democracy should be the organ, rather than the leader, of a true workers' movement.

In several articles and particularly in *What is to be Done?* (1902) Lenin attacked the economists for denying the party's role as a vanguard, and expressed in general terms his view on the importance of theory in the social democratic movement. The vital question for the prospect of revolution was, he argued, the theoretical consciousness of the revolutionary movement, and this could in no way be evolved by a spontaneous movement of workers. 'There cannot be a revolutionary movement without a revolutionary theory': this was even truer in Russia than elsewhere, since social democracy was in its infancy and since the task confronting the Russian proletariat was no less than to overthrow the bastion of European and Asiatic reaction. This meant that it was destined to be the vanguard of the world proletariat, and it could not perform this role without a proper equipment of theory. The economists spoke of the importance of 'objective' economic circumstances in social development, regarding political consciousness as an automatic consequence of economic factors and therefore denying it the right to initiate and activate social processes. But the fact that economic interests were decisive did not mean that the workers' economic struggle could itself assure them final victory, since the basic class interests of the proletariat could only be satisfied by a political revolution and a proletarian dictatorship. The workers, left to themselves, were not capable of attaining to consciousness of the fundamental opposition between their class as a whole and the existing social system.

> We have said that there could not have been social-democratic consciousness among the workers. It would have had to be brought to them from without. The history of all countries shows that the working class, exclusively by its own effort, is able to develop only trade-union consciousness, i.e. the conviction that it is necessary to combine in unions, fight the employers, and strive to compel the government to pass necessary labour legislation etc. The theory of socialism, however, grew out of the philosophic, historical and economic theories elaborated by educated representatives of the propertied classes, by intellectuals.' (*Works*, vol. 5, p. 375)

This was so in the West ('Marx and Engels themselves belonged to the bourgeois intelligentsia') and so it would be in Russia. Lenin appealed on this point to Kautsky, who wrote that the class struggle of the proletariat could not in itself create socialist consciousness: the class struggle and socialism were separate phenomena, and it was the task of social democracy to instil socialist consciousness into a spontaneous movement.

If the party regarded itself as merely the organ or servant of a spontaneous workers' movement, it could never be the instrument of a socialist revolution. It must be the vanguard and organizer, the leader and ideologist without which the workers could not advance beyond the horizon of bourgeois society or undermine its foundations. Here, however, Lenin adds a remark of decisive importance.

Since there can be no question of an independent ideology formulated by the working masses themselves in the process of their movement, the only choice is—either bourgeois or socialist ideology. There is no middle course—for mankind has not created a 'third' ideology, and in a society torn by class antagonisms there can never be a non-class or an above-class ideology . . . But the spontaneous development of the working-class movement leads to its subordination to bourgeois ideology . . . trade-unionism means the ideological enslavement of the workers by the bourgeoisie. Hence our task, the task of social-democracy, is *to combat spontaneity*. (*Works*, vol. 5, p. 384)

The doctrine of 'bowing to spontaneity', or *khvostizm* ('tailism'), is the chief target of Lenin's attack on the economists—Martynov, Kuskova, and others. The workers may fight to sell their labour-power on better terms, but the task of social democracy is to fight for the abolition of wage-labour altogether. The antagonism between the working class and the whole capitalist economic system can only be grasped by scientific thought, and until it is grasped there can be no general political struggle against the bourgeois system.

This fact, Lenin continues, leads to certain inferences as regards the relation between the working class and the party. In the economist view the revolutionary organization is no more or less than the organization of workers. But to be effective an organization of workers must be broadly based and as open as possible in its methods, and must have a trade-union character. The party cannot identify itself with a movement such as this, and there is no party in the world that is identical with the trade unions. On the contrary, 'the organization of the revolutionaries must consist first and foremost of people who make revolutionary activity their profession . . . In view of this common characteristic of the members of such an organization, all distinctions as between workers and intellectuals . . . must be effaced' (ibid., p. 452). Such a party of professional revolutionaries must not only gain the confidence of the working class and take over the spontaneous movement, but must make itself the centre of all forms of protest against social oppression, concentrating all the energies directed against the autocracy regardless of their origin or what class-interests they represent. The fact that social democracy is the party of the proletariat does not mean that it should be indifferent to the oppression and exploitation of other groups, even of the privileged classes. Since the democratic revolution, although bourgeois in content, is to be led by the proletariat, it is the latter's duty to rally all the forces that aim to overthrow the autocracy. The party must organize a general campaign of exposure; it must support bourgeois demands for political freedom, combat the persecution of religious sectarians, denounce the brutal treatment of students and intellectuals, support peasant claims, make itself felt in every sphere of public life, and unite the separate currents of indignation and protest into a single powerful stream which will sweep away the Tsarist order.

To cope with these requirements the party must be composed chiefly of professional revolutionaries—men and women who regard themselves, and are to be regarded, not as workers or intellectuals but simply as revolutionaries, and who devote their whole time to party activity. The party must be a small, centralized, disciplined organization on the lines of Zemlya i Volya in the seventies: in conspiratorial conditions it is impossible to apply democratic principles within the party, though it is natural to do so in overt organizations.

Lenin's idea of the party was much criticized as despotic, and some historians today believe that it contained in embryo the whole hierarchical, totalitarian structure in which the socialist system was subsequently embodied. It should be considered, however, in what respects his idea differed from those generally accepted at the time. He was accused of élitism and of desiring to substitute a revolutionary organization for the working class; it was even maintained that his doctrine represented the particular interests of the intelligentsia or of intellectuals, and that he wished to see political power entirely in their hands and not in those of the proletariat.

As regards the alleged élitism of treating the party as a vanguard, it should be noted that Lenin's position was no different from that generally accepted among socialists. The idea of a vanguard figures in *The Communist Manifesto*, whose authors describe the communists as the most conscious part of the proletariat, with no interests other than those of the class as a whole. The view that the workers' movement could not of itself evolve a revolutionary socialist consciousness, but must receive it from the educated intelligentsia, is one that Lenin shared with Kautsky, Victor Adler, and most of the social democratic leaders, who stressed their difference from the syndicalists on this point. Basically the thought expressed by Lenin is indeed a truism, since clearly no workman could have written *Capital* or the *Anti-Dühring*, or even *What is to be Done?* No one could dispute that the theoretical foundations of socialism must be laid by intellectuals and not by factory workers, and if this was all that was meant by the 'instilling of consciousness from outside', there was nothing to argue about. The proposition that the workers' party was something different from the whole working class was also generally accepted, and it cannot be shown that Marx identified the party with the proletariat, though it is true he never defined exactly what the party was. What was new in Lenin's thought was not the idea of the party as a vanguard, leading the working class and imbuing it with socialist consciousness. The novelty consisted, in the first place, in his statement that the spontaneous working-class movement must have a bourgeois consciousness, since it could not develop a socialist one, and no other kind existed. This does not follow from any of Kautsky's arguments quoted by

Lenin, nor from any of the premisses of Marxism. According to Lenin every social movement has a definite class character. Since a spontaneous workers' movement is incapable of a socialist consciousness, i.e. a proletarian one in the proper theoretical and historical sense of the term, it follows, curious as it may seem, that the workers' movement is a bourgeois movement unless it is subordinated to the socialist party. This is supplemented by a second inference: the working-class movement in the true sense of the term, i.e. a political revolutionary movement, is defined not by being a movement of workers but by possessing the right ideology, i.e. the Marxist one, which is 'proletarian' by definition. In other words, the class composition of a revolutionary party has no significance in determining its class character. Lenin consistently maintained this view, holding for instance that the British Labour Party was a bourgeois party although its members were working men, whereas a tiny group with no roots in the working class was entitled, so long as it professed the Marxist ideology, to declare itself the sole representative of the proletariat and the sole embodiment of proletarian consciousness. This is what Leninist parties have done ever since, including those which had not even minimal support among actual workers.

This does not mean, of course, that Lenin was indifferent to the composition of his own party or that he intended to build up a revolutionary organization consisting solely of intellectuals. On the contrary, he frequently insisted that there should be as high a proportion of workers in the party as possible, and he treated the intelligentsia with supreme contempt. The term 'intellectual' was a pejorative one in his vocabulary and was regularly used to signify 'irresolute, unreliable, undisciplined, consumed with individualism, capricious, up in the clouds', and so forth. (The party workers whom he most trusted were of working-class origin, such as Stalin and Malinovsky; the latter, as it turned out, was an Okhrana agent and rendered his masters invaluable service as one of Lenin's closest collaborators, made free of all the party's secrets.) There can be no question of Lenin having intended to 'substitute' intellectuals for workers, or having regarded them as the embodiment of socialist consciousness simply because they were intellectuals. That embodiment was the *party*, a body of a special kind in which, as we have seen, the distinction between intellectuals and workers was to disappear. The intellectual ceased to be an intellectual, and the workman to be a workman: both were components of a strictly centralized, disciplined revolutionary organization.

Thus, according to Lenin, the party with its 'correct' theoretical consciousness embodies the proletarian consciousness irrespective of what the real, empirical proletariat may think about itself or about the party. The party knows what is in the 'historical' interest of the proletariat and what the latter's authentic consciousness ought to be at any particular moment, although its empirical consciousness will generally be found lagging behind. The party represents that consciousness not because the proletariat agrees that it should, but because the party knows the laws of social development and understands the historical mission of the working class according to Marxist theory. In this schema the empirical consciousness of the working class appears as an obstacle, an immature state to be overcome, and never as a source of inspiration. The party is completely independent of the actual working class, except in so far as it requires its support in practice. In this sense Lenin's doctrine of party hegemony certainly means that in politics the working class can and must be 'replaced'—not by intellectuals, however, but by the party. The party cannot act effectively without proletarian support, but it is for the party alone to take political initiatives and to decide what the proletariat's aims shall be. The proletariat is incapable of formulating its own class aims, and if it tries to do so they will be bourgeois aims confined within the limits of capitalism.

It will thus be seen that it was not 'élitism', or the theory of socialist consciousness being introduced from outside into a spontaneous workers' movement, which made Lenin's party into the centralized, dogmatic, unthinking yet highly effective machine that it became, especially after the Revolution. The theoretical source, or rather justification, of that machine was Lenin's conviction that the party, by virtue of its scientific knowledge of society, is the one legitimate source of political initiative. This later became the principle of the Soviet state, where the same ideology serves to justify the party's monopoly of initiative in all fields of social life, its position as the sole fount of knowledge concerning society and therefore the sole proprietor of that society. It would of course be hard to maintain that the whole system of the totalitarian state was preformed, let alone consciously intended, in Lenin's doctrine as expressed in 1902; but the evolution of his party before and after the seizure of power confirms to some extent the Marxist or rather Hegelian belief in a 'logical order of things' embodied, although imperfectly, in the historical order. Lenin's premisses require us to believe that the interests and aims of a social class, the proletariat, can and indeed must be determined without that class having a say in the matter. The same, moreover, is true of the whole of society once it is ruled by that class and therefore presumably shares in its aims: once again the tasks, purposes, and ideology of the whole body are governed by the party's initiative and under its control. Lenin's idea of party hegemony developed naturally into that of the party's 'leading role' in a socialist society—i.e. into a despotism based on the principle that the party always knows better than the community itself what are the latter's interests, needs, and even desires: the people themselves may be too backward to understand these, but the party can divine them thanks to its scientific knowledge. In this way the notion of 'scientific socialism', opposed on the one hand to utopianism and on the other to a spontaneous workers' movement, became the ideological basis of a party dictatorship over the working class and the whole of society.

Lenin never abandoned his theory of the party. At the Second Congress he admitted that he had exaggerated slightly in *What is to be Done?*, but he did not say in what respect. 'We all know now that the "economists" bent the stick one way. To straighten matters out somebody had to bend it back the other way, and that is what I have done. I am convinced that Russian social-democracy will always vigorously straighten out whatever has been twisted by opportunism of any kind, and that therefore our stick will always be the straightest and the fittest' (speech on the party programme, 4 August 1902; *Works*, vol. 6, p. 491).

A further distinction must be made in considering how far *What is to be Done?* embodies the theory of the monolithic party. At this time and afterwards Lenin took it for granted that different views would be expressed within the party and that particular groups would be formed. He thought this natural but unhealthy, since in principle only one group could be in possession of the truth at a given time. 'Those who are really convinced that they have made progress in science would not demand freedom for the new views to continue side by side with the old, but the substitution of the new views for the old' (*Works*, vol. 5, p. 355). 'The much-vaunted freedom of criticism does not imply substitution of one theory for another, but freedom from all integral and pondered theory; it implies eclecticism and lack of principle' (ibid., p. 369). There can be no doubt that Lenin always regarded fractionalism and differences on essential points as a sign of disease or weakness in the party, though it was many years before he stated that all such manifestations should be cured by radical means, either by an immediate split or by expulsion from the party; only after the Revolution was there a formal ban on fractionalism. Even before the Revolution, however, Lenin did not hesitate to break with his colleagues over important matters. Believing as he did that all differences of view, not only on questions of major principle and strategy but also in matters of organization, in the last resort 'reflected' class antagonisms, he naturally regarded his opponents in the party as 'carriers' of some kind of bourgeois deviation or as symptoms of bourgeois pressure on the proletariat. As to the fact that he himself at all times represented the true and best-understood interests of the proletariat, Lenin never had the slightest doubt.

The theory of the party expounded in *What is to be Done?* was supplemented in Lenin's organizational proposals for the Second Congress, which met at Brussels after long preparation on 30 July 1903; it was afterwards transferred to London, where it sat until 23 August. Lenin attended from Geneva, where he had been living since the spring. The first and acutest point of difference concerned the celebrated paragraph I of the party Rules: Lenin wished membership to be confined to those who participated actively in one or other of the party organizations, whereas Martov proposed a looser formula admitting all who 'worked under the guidance and direction' of a party organization. This apparently trifling dispute led to a near split and to the formation of two groups which, as soon became clear, were divided not only on organizational matters but on many others. Lenin's formula, backed by Plekhanov, was rejected by a small majority. During the rest of the Congress, however, Lenin's supporters gained a slight predominance owing to the walk-out of two groups, the Bund (General Jewish Workers' Alliance) and the 'economists' representing the periodical *Rabocheye Delo*. The small majority which Lenin's group thus gained in the election to the Central Committee and the Party Council led to the coining of the famous terms 'Bolshevik' and 'Menshevik', after the Russian words for 'majority' and 'minority'. Their origin was thus fortuitous, but Lenin and his followers seized on the appellation 'Bolshevik' and clung to it for decades, suggesting as it did that throughout the party's later vicissitudes the Bolsheviks were the true majority group. Many who were unfamiliar with the history of the Congress, on the other hand, took the word to mean 'maximalist': the Bolsheviks themselves never suggested this interpretation.

The dispute over the membership clause in fact reflected two opposite ideas of party organization, about which Lenin had much to say at the Congress and in subsequent articles. In his opinion the effect of the 'loose' formula put forward by Martov, Akselrod, and Akimov was to allow any professor or schoolboy who might help the party, or any worker who came out on strike, to call himself a member. This would mean that the party lost all cohesion, discipline, and control over its own ranks; it would become a mass organization, built from below and not from above—a collection of autonomous units, unfit for centralized action. Lenin's idea was the exact opposite: strictly defined conditions of membership, rigid discipline, absolute control of the party authorities over its organizations, a clear dividing line between the party and the working class. The Mensheviks accused Lenin of adopting a bureaucratic attitude towards party life, of contempt for the working class, of dictatorial ambitions, and of wishing to subordinate the whole party to a handful of leaders. Lenin for his part wrote after the Congress (in *One Step Forward, Two Steps Back*, 1904; *Works*, vol. 7, p. 405 n.): 'Comrade Martov's fundamental idea—self-enrolment in the Party—was this same false "democracy", this idea of building the Party from the bottom upward. My idea, on the other hand, was "bureaucratic" in the sense that the Party was to be built from the top downwards, from the Party Congress to the individual Party organizations.'

Lenin had rightly perceived the fundamental importance of the dispute at the outset, and later on several occasions he compared it to the quarrel of the Jacobins and the Girondists. This was an apter parallel than the dispute between Bernstein's followers and German orthodoxy, for the Mensheviks' position was very close to the centre of German social democracy: they stood for a less centralized and 'military' organization and believed that the party should be a working-class one not only in name and ideology, but by including as many workers as possible and not being merely a staff of professsional revolutionaries. They thought the party should allow considerable autonomy to individual organizations and not deal with them exclusively by way of command. They accused Lenin of distrusting the working class, though they themselves accepted the doctrine of consciousness having to be instilled from outside it. It soon became clear that the Menshevik wing tended to adopt different solutions in other matters also: the dispute over a single paragraph of the Rules had in fact divided the party into two camps which, instinctively as it were, reacted differently to strategic and tactical issues. In every case the Mensheviks gravitated towards an alliance with the liberals, while Lenin proclaimed the peasant revolution and a revolutionary alliance with the peasants. The Mensheviks attached importance to legal forms of action and, when this became possible, to fighting by parliamentary means; Lenin for a long time opposed the idea of social democrats participating in the Duma, and subsequently treated it purely as a propaganda platform, putting no faith in any reforms it might enact. The Mensheviks emphasized trade-union activity and the intrinsic value of any improvements the working class might secure by legislation or by strike action; to Lenin, all such activity was valuable only in so far as it helped to prepare for the final conflict. The Mensheviks regarded democratic freedoms as valuable in themselves, while to Lenin they were only weapons that might serve the party in particular circumstances. On this last point Lenin quotes with approval a characteristic remark made at the congress by Posadovsky: 'Should we subordinate our future policy to certain fundamental democratic principles and attribute absolute value to them, or should all democratic principles be exclusively subordinated to the interests of our Party? I am decidedly in favour of the latter' (*Works*, vol. 7, p. 227). Plekhanov also supported this view, which illustrates how, at the very outset, the 'interest of the party' was exalted above all other considerations including the immediate interests of the class that the party was supposed to represent. Other writings by Lenin leave no doubt that he ascribed no value to 'freedom' as such, although his appeals and pamphlets are full of references to the 'fight for freedom'. 'They who serve the cause of freedom in general without serving the specific cause of proletarian utilization of this freedom, the cause of turning this freedom to account in the proletarian struggle for socialism, are, in the final analysis, plainly and simply fighters for the interests of the bourgeoisie' ('A New Revolutionary Workers' Association', article in *Proletary* (*The Proletariat*), June 1905; *Works*, vol. 8, p. 502).

In this way Lenin laid the foundation of what was to become the Communist Party—a party distinguished by ideological unity, efficiency, a hierarchic and centralized structure, and the conviction that it represents the interests of the proletariat whatever the proletariat itself may think: a party which deems its own interest to be automatically that of the working class and of universal progress, because it possesses the 'scientific knowledge' that entitles it to ignore, except for tactical purposes, the actual wishes and aspirations of the people it has appointed itself to represent.

The Mensheviks, like Rosa Luxemburg, regularly accused Lenin of Blanquism, plotting to destroy the existing order by a *coup d'état*, embracing the conspiratorial ideology of Tkachov, and striving for power regardless of 'objective' conditions. Lenin replied that his theory had nothing to do with Blanquism, that he wished to build up a party with real proletarian support and had no thought of a revolution carried out by a handful of conspirators. The Mensheviks claimed that he had an anti-Marxist faith in the decisive role of 'subjective factors', i.e. of revolutionary will-power. Historical materialism taught that revolutionary consciousness could not be artificially created by the party's efforts but depended on the ripening of social conditions. To attempt to provoke a revolution instead of waiting for economic events to bring about a revolutionary situation was to violate the laws of social development.

This criticism, though exaggerated, was not without foundation. Lenin, of course, was not a 'Blanquist' in the sense of envisaging a *coup d'état* which a small group of conspirators, properly prepared, could carry out at any moment. He realized that revolutions were elemental occurrences that could not be planned or produced at will. His view was that a revolution in Russia was inevitable, and that when it broke out the party must be prepared to direct it, to ride the wave of history and to seize power, sharing it initially with representatives of the revolutionary peasantry. He was not planning to cause a revolution, but to foster the growth of revolutionary consciousness and eventually take control of the mass movement. If the party was the 'subjective factor' in the revolutionary process—and this is how both Lenin and his opponents understood the matter—he was indeed of the opinion that the spontaneous uprising of the working class would come to nothing unless the party was there to give it shape and direction. This was an obvious corollary of the party's role as the only possible vehicle of socialist consciousness. The proletariat itself could not evolve that consciousness, and therefore the will to revolution could not be brought about simply by economic events but must be deliberately organized. The 'economists', the Mensheviks, and the left-wing German social democrats, all of whom expected economic laws to bring about a socialist revolution automatically, were following a disastrous policy, for this would never happen. It was no good appealing to Marx in the matter (according to Lenin, Rosa Luxemburg 'vulgarized and prostituted' Marx's doctrine). Marx did not say that socialist or any other consciousness arose automatically from social conditions, but only that conditions made its development possible. For the possibility to become a reality, the revolutionary idea and will must be present in the form of an organized party.

There is no certain answer as to which side in the dispute was interpreting Marx more accurately. Marx believed that social conditions gave rise to the consciousness which would in time transform those conditions, but that to be effective it must first take on an explicit and articulate form. Many texts of his can be quoted in support of the view that consciousness is 'nothing but' the reflection of an actual situation, and this appears to justify the *attentisme* of the orthodox view. But, on the other hand, Marx regarded his own writing as the expression or explicitation of a latent consciousness: in the first text in which he refers to the historic mission of the proletariat, he says: 'We must force these petrified relationships to dance by playing their own tune to them.' Somebody must play the tune—the 'relationships' cannot do so of their own accord. If the principle that 'social being determines consciousness' applies only to past history, in which social consciousness invariably took on 'mystified' forms, and ceases to be valid when the proletariat comes on the scene, then the doctrine that a vanguard is necessary to arouse consciousness is in accordance with Marx's teaching. The problem is then merely to identify the criteria by which we determine that conditions have ripened to the point at which the arousal is possible. Marxism gave no indication as to what these criteria were. Lenin often stated that the proletariat was (sc. 'in the nature of things') the revolutionary class; this however, did not mean that it would of itself develop a revolutionary consciousness, but only that it was capable of receiving it from the party. While Lenin, therefore, was not a 'Blanquist', he did believe that the party alone could and must be the initiator and source of revolutionary consciousness. The 'subjective factor' was not only a necessary condition of the advance to socialism (as all Marxists accepted, including the Mensheviks), but was the real creator of revolutionary consciousness, though it could not start a revolution without help from the proletariat. Although Marx himself never put the matter in these terms, there is insufficient ground for holding that Lenin's opinion on the point was a 'distortion' of Marxism.

3. The question of nationality

THE Second Congress also provided the occasion for taking a stand on the national question, which was a basic element in the politics of the Tsarist empire. The matter was raised by the Bund, whose claim to be recognized as the sole representative of the Jewish working population was rejected by a majority including Lenin. Like many others, including Kautsky and Struve, Lenin thought the Jews could not be considered a nationality, as they lacked a common language and a territorial base; but he also objected to the Bund proposal on grounds of principle, as it implied the creation of a federal party based on national criteria. In Lenin's view differences of origin, education, and occupation ought to be of no account in the party, and this was still more true of nationality. Centralization was to do away with all differences between party members, each of whom was to be the embodiment of the purest party spirit and nothing else.

The problem engaged Lenin's attention more and more as the subject peoples of the empire manifested their separatism in nationalist movements. He wished the party to denounce national oppression and use the question as a lever, among others, to unseat the autocracy. There is no doubt that Lenin hated Great Russian chauvinism and did his best to extirpate it within the party. At the end of 1901, apropos of the violation of Finland's modest autonomy by the Tsarist government, he wrote: 'We are still slaves to such a degree that we are employed to reduce other peoples to slavery. We still tolerate a government that suppresses every aspiration towards liberty in Russia with the ferocity of an executioner, and that furthermore employs Russian troops for the purpose of violently infringing the liberties of others' (*Iskra*, 20 November 1901; *Works*, vol. 5, p. 310).

There was no dispute among social democrats on the question of national oppression; but by no means all of them accepted the principle of self-determination, i.e. the right of each nationality to a separate political existence. The Austrian Marxists stood for national autonomy within the Dual Monarchy: each ethnic group was to have complete freedom of language, culture, education, publication, etc., but political independence was not expressly mentioned. Renner, Bauer, and their colleagues were incessantly troubled by national conflicts within the party: the Austro-Hungarian proletariat belonged to a dozen or more national groups, mostly not in clear-cut areas but jumbled up geographically, so that political separatism raised an inextricable problem of frontiers. As far as Russia was concerned, Lenin thought that cultural autonomy would not suffice and that self-determination would be no use unless it included the right to form separate states. He expressed this view on several occasions, and encouraged Stalin to do so in a pamphlet on the national question in 1913. The right of self-determination was the subject of a long dispute with SDKPiL, which on this account remained outside the Russian Social Democratic Workers' party for some time. Lenin's most determined adversary, as already mentioned, was Rosa Luxemburg, whose position on the matter, apart from the special circumstances of Poland, was stronger in terms of fidelity to Marx. In

Lenin's view all peoples were equally entitled to self-determination, and, unlike the founders of scientific socialism, he made no distinction between 'historical' and 'unhistorical' nations.

However, in theory at all events the dispute was not so violent as it might appear. Lenin acknowledged the right of self-determination, but from the beginning he made certain reservations: these account for the fact that within a short time after the Revolution, although Lenin's formulas remained unchanged, the 'right' in question became no more than an empty flourish, as indeed it was bound to do.

The first restriction was that although the party upheld the right to self-determination it did not commit itself to supporting all separatist aims: in many, indeed most, cases it found itself on the opposite side to the separatists. There was no contradiction in this, Lenin argued: the party might demand the legalization of divorce, but it did not follow that it wanted all married couples to split up.

> We, the party of the proletariat, must always and unconditionally oppose any attempt to influence national self-determination from without by violence or injustice. While at all times performing this negative duty of ours (to fight and protest against violence), we on our part concern ourselves with the self-determination of the *proletariat* in each nationality rather than the self-determination of peoples or nations . . . As to support of the demand for national autonomy, it is by no means a permanent and binding part of the programme of the proletariat. This support may become necessary for it only in isolated and exceptional cases. ('On the Manifesto of the Armenian Social-Democrats', *Iskra*, 1 February 1903; *Works*, vol. 6, p. 329)

The second restriction followed from the general principle that the party is interested in the self-determination of the proletariat and not of the people as a whole. Attacking the Polish Socialist party, Lenin wrote that in demanding Poland's independence unconditionally this party 'proves how weak in theoretical background and political activity is its link with the class struggle of the proletariat. But it is to the interests of this struggle that we must subordinate the demand for national self-determination . . . A Marxist can recognize the demand for national independence only conditionally' ('The National Question in our Programme', *Iskra*, 15 July 1903; *Works*, vol. 6, p. 456). The Polish question was crucial in these discussions for three reasons. First, Poland was the largest of the subjected nations of Europe; second, it was divided among three great Continental powers; and third, according to Marx, Polish independence would strike a decisive blow against reaction in the shape of the Tsarist autocracy and the other partitioning powers, Germany and Austria-Hungary. Rosa Luxemburg and Lenin both believed, however, that Marx's view on this point, if it had ever been valid, was out of date. Rosa Luxemburg ruled out the restoration of Polish independence as contrary to the economic tendencies of the Tsarist empire; in any case she regarded self-determination as a bourgeois invention designed to hoodwink the proletariat with the pretence of ideals common to a whole nation. Lenin was less firm on this point, though he rejected the idea that Polish social democrats should go for independence as an aim in itself irrespective of the party's interest. He quoted with full approval some remarks made by Mehring in 1902: 'Had the Polish proletariat desired to inscribe on its banner the restoration of a Polish class state, which the ruling classes themselves do not want to hear of, it would be playing an historical farce . . . If, on the other hand, this reactionary Utopia seeks to win over to pro-letarian agitation those sections of the intelligentsia and of the petty bour-geoisie which still respond in some measure to national agitation, then that Utopia is doubly untenable as an outgrowth of the unworthy opportunism which sacrifices the long-term interests of the working class to the cheap and paltry successes of the moment.' At the same time Lenin goes on to say: 'No doubt the restoration of Poland prior to the fall of capitalism is highly improb-able, but it cannot be asserted that it is absolutely impossible . . . And Russian social-democracy does not in the least intend to tie its own hands' (ibid., pp. 459–60).

Lenin's position is thus clear, and it is hard to see how he can ever have been represented, as he notoriously was, as a champion of political independence for all peoples. He was a convinced opponent of national oppression and proclaimed the right of self-determination, but always with the reservation that it was only in exceptional circumstances that social democracy could support political sep-aratism. Self-determination was at all times absolutely subordinate to the party's interests, and if the latter conflicted with the national aspirations of any peo-ple, the latter were of no account. This reservation in effect nullified the right of self-determination and turned it into a purely tactical weapon. The party would always try to utilize national aspirations in the struggle for power, but the 'interest of the Proletariat' could never be subordinated to the desires of a whole people. As Lenin wrote soon after the Revolution in his *Theses* on the Treaty of Brest-Litovsk, 'No Marxist, without renouncing the principles of Marxism and of socialism generally, can deny that the interests of socialism are higher than the interests of the right of nations to self-determination' (*Works*, vol. 26, p. 449). Since, however, the interest of the proletariat is by definition identical with the interest of the party, and its true aspiration can only be uttered through the party's mouth, it is clear that if the party comes to power it will be alone competent to decide questions of independence and separatism. This was inscribed in the party's programme in 1919, which stated that the level of his-torical development of each nation must decide the question as to who expresses its real will in the matter of independence. Since, as the party ideology also lays down, the 'will of the nation' is always expressed in the will of its foremost class, i.e the proletariat, while the latter's will is expressed in that of a centralized party representing the whole multinational state, it is clear that a particular nation has no power to determine its own destiny. All this is fully in accord with Lenin's Marxism and his interpretation of the right to self-determination. Once the 'interest of the proletariat' is embodied in the interest of a proletarian state, there can be no doubt that the interest and power of that state are superior to all national aspirations. The invasion and armed suppression, on one occasion after another, of nations seeking to be free was quite consistent with Lenin's views. His objections to the brutal methods applied in Georgia by Ordzhonikidze, Stalin, and Dzerzhinsky may have been due to a desire on his part to use as little cruelty as possible, but they did not affect the right of the 'proletarian state' to subjugate its neighbour: he saw nothing wrong in the fact that the Georgian people, with a social democratic government established by legal elections, was the object of an armed incursion by the Red Army. In the same way, the recognition of Poland's independence did not prevent Lenin, as soon as the Polish–Soviet war broke out, from forming the nucleus of a Soviet government for Poland—though it is true he believed, with almost incredible blindness, that the Polish proletariat would greet the invading Soviet troops as its liberators.

In short, on the presumption that the interest of the proletariat is the only absolute value and is identical with the interest of the party, whch has proclaimed itself the vehicle of the 'true' consciousness of the proletariat, the principle of national self-determination can be no more than a tactical weapon. Lenin was well aware of this, which is not to say that the principle was an unimportant part of his doctrine. On the contrary, his discovery of national aspirations as a powerful source of energy which the party could and should use in the fight for power was one of the most important features of his policy and did much to ensure its success, in opposition to the orthodox view that the Marxist theory of the class struggle made it unnecessary to pay specific attention to national problems. Lenin, however, was not only 'right' in the sense that his theory paid off: it was also in accordance with Marxism. Since the 'interest of the proletariat' is the supreme value, there can be no objection to exploiting national quarrels and aspirations in order to promote that interest, nor to the later policy of the Soviet state in supporting such aspirations in conquered and colonial territories in order to weaken the capitalist powers. On the other hand, Engels's distinction between 'historical' and 'unhistorical' nations, and Lenin's between the nationalism of great nations and that of small ones, do not seem to follow from the basic doctrine and may be regarded as bypaths, related to particular historical circumstances.

The principle of national self-determination in its 'pure' form, i.e. as an absolute right valid in all circumstances, is clearly contrary to Marxism, and from this point of view Rosa Luxemburg's position was easy to defend: the class division is paramount and is international, and there can be no national interests that are worth fighting for. But in the light of Lenin's far-reaching reservations, which reduced the principle to one of mere tactics, it is impossible to maintain that his defence of it was contrary to established doctrine. In other words, the dispute between him and Rosa Luxemburg on this issue was one of tactics and not of principle. National differences and national culture had no intrinsic value in Lenin's eyes but were, as he often repeated, essentially political weapons of the bourgeoisie. As he wrote in 1908, 'The proletariat cannot be indifferent to the political, social and cultural conditions of its struggle; consequently it cannot be indifferent to the destinies of its country. But the destinies of the country interest it only to the extent that they affect its class struggle, and not in virtue of some bourgeois "patriotism", quite indecent on the lips of a social democrat' (*Works*, vol. 15, p. 195). 'We do not support "national culture" but international culture, which includes only part of each national culture—only the consistently democratic and socialist content of each national culture . . . We are against national culture as one of the slogans of bourgeois nationalism. We are in favour of the international culture of a fully democratic and socialist proletariat' (ibid., vol. 19, p. 116). 'The right to self-determination is an exception to our general premise of centralization. This exception is absolutely necessary in view of reactionary Great-Russian nationalism; and any rejection of this exception is opportunism (as in the case of Rosa Luxemburg); it means foolishly playing into the hands of reactionary Great-Russian nationalism' (ibid., p. 501).

Lenin frequently expressed himself on these lines before and during the War; he quoted with emphasis the famous saying that the working man has no fatherland, and believed it quite literally. At the same time he was the only important social democratic leader who proclaimed the unrestricted right to self-determination and expressly applied it to the oppressed peoples of the Tsarist empire. At the end of 1914 he wrote a short article 'On the National Pride of the Great Russians' (*Works*, vol. 21), which was one of the texts most frequently reprinted and quoted as Russian communism came to be more and more permeated with chauvinism. Unlike all Lenin's other articles, in which he denounces and derides every form of 'patriotism' (always in quotation marks), he declares on this occasion that Russian revolutionaries love their language and country; that they are proud of their revolutionary traditions and for this reason desire the defeat of the Tsardom in every war, as the least harmful outcome for the working population; and that the interest of the Great Russians is in accordance with that of the Russian proletariat and of all others. This is the only text of its kind in Lenin's works, and diverges from the remainder in so far as it seems to regard national culture as valuable in itself and worth defending. In the light of Lenin's doctrine as a whole it gives the impression of an attempt, by watering down his views, to rebut the charge of treason that was levelled against the Bolsheviks at the time and to show that their policy deserved support on 'patriotic' grounds as well. Certainly it is hard to see how the defence of Great Russian national pride can be reconciled with the statement that 'the place of those who advocate the slogan of national culture is among the nationalist petty bourgeois, not among the Marxists' ('Critical Remarks on the National Question', *Works*, vol. 21, p. 25). However, the article of December 1914 is not at variance either with the principle of self-determination or with the restrictions Lenin imposed upon it.

4. The proletariat and the bourgeoisie in the democratic revolution. Trotsky and the 'permanent revolution'

ALL social democrats were agreed that Russia was on the eve of a bourgeois revolution which would sweep away the autocracy, establish democratic freedoms, give the land to the peasants, and abolish the relics of serfdom and personal dependence. But this left undecided several important questions, which to some extent involved the theoretical foundations of Marxist doctrine.

The idea that the proletariat would lead the coming revolution, as the Russian bourgeoisie was too weak and cowardly to do so, came from Plekhanov and was more or less common property among the social democrats, who from the beginning joined issue on this point with the populists and later the 'economists'. However, the Mensheviks did not adhere to this opinion consistently, but inferred from the bourgeois character of the revolution that the proletariat's natural allies in overthrowing the autocracy were the bourgeoisie and the liberal parties, and that after the revolution these latter would be in power and the social democrats would be in opposition.

On this point Lenin at an early stage declared for quite different tactics. The fact that the revolution would pave the way for capitalism in Russia did not mean that the bourgeoisie would hold political power after it, or that the social democrats ought to ally themselves with the liberals to bring it about. Lenin was guided in this not only by his inveterate hatred of the liberals, but mainly by his conviction that the peasant problem was the decisive element: this led him to condemn the adoption in Russia of any schema based on the experience of democratic revolution in the West. Unlike the orthodox Marxists he perceived the huge revolutionary potential that lay in the peasants' unfulfilled demands, and he urged the party to exploit this even though, from the traditional point of view, it might seem to involve a 'reactionary' programme of backing smallholders. (According to 'classic' patterns the concentration of property would speed the advance towards socialism, and the break-up of estates was therefore 'reactionary'.) Lenin, with his sharply practical, opportunist, undoctrinaire outlook, was less interested in Marxian 'correctness' and mainly, or exclusively, concerned with the political efficacy of the proposed tactics. 'Generally speaking,' he wrote,

> It is reactionary to support small property because such support is directed against large-scale capitalist economy, and consequently retards social development and obscures and glosses over the class struggle. In this case, however, we want to support small property not against capitalism but against serf-ownership . . . There are two sides to all things in the world. In the West, the peasant proprietor has already played his part in the democratic movement, and is now defending his position of privilege as compared with the proletariat. In Russia, the peasant proprietor is as yet on the eve of a decisive and nation-wide democratic movement with which he cannot but sympathize . . . In a historic moment like the present, it is our direct duty to support the peasants.
>
> Our principal immediate aim is to clear the way for the free development of the class struggle in the countryside, the class struggle of the proletariat, which is directed towards attainment of the ultimate aim of the international Social-Democratic movement, the conquest of political power by the proletariat and the laying of the foundations of a socialist society. ('The Agrarian Programme of Russian Social-Democracy', in *Zarya*, August 1902; *Works*, vol. 6, pp. 134, 148)

Lenin thus accepted the general notion of an 'alliance with the bourgeoisie', but immediately and fundamentally qualified it: not the liberal bourgeoisie which was prepared to come to terms with the monarchy, but the revolutionary, republican 'bourgeoisie', i.e. the peasants. This was the chief bone of contention between him and the Mensheviks, more important than the question of the party Rules; it was also the main theme of Lenin's *Two Tactics*, written after the Third Congress in 1905.

But it was a question not only of alliance during the revolution, but of power thereafter. Lenin proclaimed the slogan of rule by the proletariat and peasantry in the bourgeois society that the revolution was to establish. This society, he believed, would permit the unrestrained development of the class struggle and the concentration of property, but political power would be exercised by the proletariat and peasantry through their respective parties. With this in view the social democrats must cultivate peasant support and prepare a suitable agrarian programme. This too became a subject of dispute: Lenin proposed to go for the nationalization of all the land, emphasizing that this was not a specifically socialist measure and that it would gain peasant support while not undermining bourgeois society. Most Bolsheviks, like the S.R.s, favoured confiscating the big estates and church lands without compensation, and then partitioning them. The Mensheviks were for 'municipalizing' the expropriated lands, i.e. handing them over to local authorities. In an appeal *To the Rural Poor* in 1903 Lenin wrote: 'The social-democrats will never take away the property of the small and middle farmers who do not hire labourers' (*Works*, vol. 6, p. 397); but in the same pamphlet he stated that after the socialist revolution all means of production, including land, would be held in common. It was not clear how the 'rural poor' were expected to reconcile these two statements.

All social democrats regarded the distinction between the minimum and maximum programme as a matter of course, and all were concerned as to how social democracy would carry on the fight for the 'next stage' after the bourgeois revolution. None of them ventured to predict how long Russia's capitalist era would last. The Mensheviks, however, generally thought that it would take a whole historical epoch to assimilate Western democratic and parliamentary institutions, and that the transition to socialism was a remote prospect. Lenin, for his part, took seriously the principle, which was quite in the spirit of Marxism, that all tactics must be geared to the future socialist upheaval, and that the 'final aim' must be constantly kept in mind and govern all the party's acts. The question was: if the bourgeois revolution gave power to the people, i.e. the proletariat and peasantry, would they not inevitably seek to transform society in a socialist direction, so that the bourgeois revolution would grow into a socialist one? This problem came to the fore in the years just before the 1905 Revolution, and immediately after it in the writings of Parvus and Trotsky.

Leo Trotsky (Lyov Davidovich Bronstein) had made a name for himself in 1902–3 as a gifted exponent of Marxism in Russian *émigré* circles. Born in 1879 on 7 November (New Style) at Yanovka in the province of Kherson, the son of a Jewish farmer (of whom there were a few in the Ukraine), he went to school at Odessa and Nikolayev and became a Marxist at the age of 18. He studied mathematics for some months at Odessa University, but soon devoted himself to political work and was active in the South Russian Workers' Union, which although not purely social democratic was much influenced by Marxist ideas. He was arrested at the beginning of 1898, spent nearly two years in gaol, and was then sentenced to four years in Siberia. In prison and in exile he eagerly pursued his Marxist education, and in Siberia gave lectures and published articles in the legal Press. Escaping from banishment with a false passport in the name of Trotsky, under which he belongs to history, he joined Lenin in London in the autumn of 1902 and became a contributor to *Iskra*. At the Second Party Congress he was one of the majority which voted against Lenin's draft paragraph I, on the ground that Lenin was trying to turn the party into a close circle of conspirators instead of a working-class organization. He remained for a time in the Menshevik camp, but broke with it before long as he disapproved of the trend towards an alliance with the liberals. In 1904 he published in

Geneva a pamphlet entitled *Our Political Tasks*, which among other things attacked Lenin's conception of the party. He asserted that Lenin despised the people and the working class and was trying to substitute the party for the proletariat, which meant that in course of time the Central Committee would replace the party and a dictator would replace the Central Committee. This prophecy, which has been much quoted since, was based on the same premisses as Rosa Luxemburg's criticism of Lenin: the idea of a centralized, hierarchic party of professional revolutionaries was contrary to the fundamental Marxist principle that the working class can only be liberated by its own efforts.

For many years Trotsky acted mainly as an independent social democratic publicist, identifying with neither wing of the party but using his influence in the direction of restoring unity. In Munich he became a friend of Parvus (A. L. Helfand), a Russian Jew who had settled in Germany and belonged to the left wing of the German social democrats, and who is regarded as the true forerunner or originator of the theory of permanent revolution. His view was that the democratic revolution in Russia would bring to power a social democratic government which would of necessity endeavour to continue the revolutionary process towards socialism. Trotsky adopted this idea and expounded it in the light of the 1905 Revolution. Generalizing from that event, he stated that as the Russian bourgeoisie was so weak the coming revolution must be headed by the proletariat and therefore would not stop at the bourgeois stage. Russia's economic backwardness meant that the bourgeois revolution would be immediately followed by a socialist revolution. (This was similar to Marx's and Engels's forecast for Germany in 1848.) But, while in the 'first stage' the proletariat would be supported by the peasantry, in the socialist revolution it would have the mass of small owners against it. Being a minority in Russia, the proletariat would not be able to maintain itself in power unless aided by a socialist revolution in the West; but it was to be expected that the revolutionary process would spread promptly from Russia to Europe and to the rest of the world.

Trotsky's theory of 'permanent revolution' thus rested on the two propositions, which he frequently repeated in the coming years, that the bourgeois revolution in Russia would evolve continuously into a socialist one and that this would touch off a conflagration in the West. If it did not, the Russian revolution could not survive, as the proletariat would have to contend with overwhelming opposition from the peasant masses.

Until April 1917 Lenin did not believe that the first revolution would immediately develop into the second, and he contested Parvus's view that a social democratic government would come to power in the 'first stage'. Such a government could not last, he wrote in April 1905, because 'only a revolutionary dictatorship supported by the vast majority of the people can be at all durable . . . The Russian proletariat, however, is at present a minority of the population

in Russia' ('Social-Democracy and the Provisional Revolutionary Government', *Works*, vol. 8, p. 291). The social democrats should therefore reckon on
sharing power with the peasantry, which in its entirety was interested in overthrowing the autocracy, but not on an immediate transition to socialism. On
the other hand, Lenin wrote before the 1905 Revolution that the dictatorship
of the proletariat must be a dictatorship against and over the entire class of
peasant proprietors. This is clearly expressed in his *Notes* on Plekhanov's second draft of the party programme:

> The concept of 'dictatorship' is incompatible with positive recognition of outside
> support for the proletariat. If we really knew positively that the petty bourgeoisie will
> support the proletariat in the accomplishment of its, the proletariat's, revolution it
> would be pointless to speak of 'dictatorship', for we would then be fully guaranteed
> so overwhelming a majority that we could get on very well without a dictatorship . . .
> The recognition of the necessity for the dictatorship of the proletariat is most closely
> and inseparably bound up with the thesis of the Communist Manifesto that the pro-
> letariat alone is a really revolutionary class.
>
> The more 'indulgence' we show, in the practical part of our programme, towards
> the small producer (e.g. the peasant), the more 'strictly' must we treat these unreli-
> able and double-faced social elements in the theoretical part of the programme,
> without sacrificing one iota of our standpoint. Now then, we say, if you adopt this
> standpoint of ours you can count on 'indulgence' of every kind, but if you don't, well
> then don't get angry with us! Under the dictatorship we shall say about you: there is
> no point in wasting words where the use of power is required. (*Works*, vol. 6, pp. 51,
> 53 n.)

In accordance with these views Lenin wrote in 'Revision of the Agrarian
Programme' in 1906 that: 'The nearer the peasant uprising is to victory, the
more likely is the peasant proprietor to turn against the proletariat, the more
necessary is it for the proletariat to have its independent organization . . . The
rural proletariat must organize independently together with the town proletariat to fight for the complete socialist revolution' (W*orks*, vol. 10, p. 191). The
programme must therefore contain 'a precise definition of the next step the
movement can and should take to consolidate the peasants' gains and to pass
from the victory of democracy to the direct proletarian struggle for socialism'
(ibid., p. 192). At the party's 'unity congress' in April 1906 Lenin clearly took
the view that peasant resistance would defeat the revolution if there were not,
as he was sure there would be, a proletarian uprising in the West.

> The Russian revolution can achieve victory by its own efforts, but it cannot possibly
> hold and consolidate its gains by its own strength. It cannot do this unless there is a
> socialist revolution in the West. Without this condition restoration is inevitable,

whether we have municipalization, or nationalization, or division of the land: for under each and every form of possession and property the small proprietor will always be a bulwark of restoration. After the complete victory of the democratic revolution the small proprietor will inevitably turn against the proletariat; and the sooner the common enemies of the proletariat and of the small proprietors, such as the capitalists, the landlords, the financial bourgeoisie and so forth are overthrown, the sooner will this happen. Our democratic republic has no other reserve than the socialist proletariat in the West. (*Works*, vol. 10, p. 280)

This shows clearly how far Stalin exaggerated when he spoke later of a 'basic antagonism' between Leninism and the theory of permanent revolution. Stalin maintained against Trotsky that, in the first place, this theory implied distrust of the peasants as a revolutionary force, suggesting that as a class they would be enemies of the proletariat in the socialist revolution. Secondly, Trotsky called in question the possibility of building socialism in one country and did not believe that the revolution could preserve its achievement in Russia without an upheaval in the West. On both points, according to Stalin, Lenin and Trotsky were totally opposed from the outset. But in fact Lenin held before 1917, and was by no means alone in doing so, that even a democratic revolution in Russia, let alone a socialist one, could not maintain itself without a socialist revolution in the West. Lenin stressed the need to organize the rural proletariat, i.e. the landless peasants, whose interests, he believed, coincided with those of the town workers and who would therefore support a socialist revolution; but he realized before 1917 that the entire peasantry would turn against the proletariat at the 'second stage'. Finally, Lenin thought that although the 'first stage' could not lead to a socialist government it would inaugurate the 'direct proletarian struggle for socialism'. The theory of permanent revolution was contrary to Lenin's views only in so far as it suggested that the 'first stage' would lead at once to rule by the proletariat or its party. It was only later, when Lenin based his tactics on the class struggle in the countryside and put forward the doctrine of a dictatorship of the proletariat and the rural poor, that he was compelled to oppose a policy based on the theory of an unbridgeable gulf between the proletariat and the peasantry as a whole.

▪ ▪ ▪

THE theory of the party, the national question, and the relationship of the proletariat to the bourgeoisie and the peasantry—on these three points, even before the Revolution of 1905, Leninism took shape as a new formation within the socialist movement, although its novelty was not at first perceived by Lenin himself. Leninism envisaged a socialist movement allied with the peasantry but not with the urban bourgeoisie: the proletariat was to organize itself for a dem-

ocratic revolution in a semi-feudal country, in the hope of first sharing democratic power with the peasantry and then initiating the struggle for socialism
and a proletarian dictatorship against the bourgeoisie and the peasant proprietors. In all this the proletariat was to act under the leadership of the party—
the true keeper of the proletariat's consciousness—which, while it sought the
workers' support, considered itself 'proletarian' not by reason of that support
but because of its 'scientific' understanding of society. It was to be a centralized, hierarchical party, built around a core of professional revolutionaries, and
in its tactics and ideology independent of the 'empirical' proletariat. Its task was
to exploit all elements and forms of opposition and to channel all the energies—
whether national, social, religious, or intellectual—directed against the *ancien
régime*, but to use them for its own purposes and not to identify with them.
Thus it supported the liberal opposition to the Tsardom even though its own
future intent was to destroy liberalism. It supported the peasants against the
relics of feudalism, although its ultimate purpose was to deprive the peasants
of the right to own land. It supported religious sectarians against Orthodox persecution, although it professed atheism and intended to do away with 'religious
prejudices'. It supported national movements and aspirations to independence
in so far as they helped to disrupt the Empire, although its own purpose was to
abolish national states altogether. In short, it set out to make use of all destructive energies aimed against the present system, while intending eventually to
destroy, as separate social forces, all the groups that embodied those energies.
The party was to be a kind of universal machine, uniting social energies from
every source into a single current. Leninism was the theory of that machine,
which, aided by an extraordinary combination of circumstances, proved effective beyond all expectation and changed the history of the world.

XVII

Philosophy and Politics in the Bolshevik Movement

1. Factional struggles at the time of the 1905 Revolution

THE EFFECTS of the Second Congress were felt throughout the remaining life of the Russian social democratic movement. It became clear soon after the Congress that Lenin could not, as he had hoped, use the small majority he had gained in its latter stage to achieve control over the party. This was mainly because of Plekhanov's 'treachery'. The Congress had appointed an editorial board for the party journal: this body, which was at that time practically independent of the Central Committee and often more important in practice, consisted of Plekhanov, Lenin, and Martov, while the rest of the 'minority'—Akselrod, Vera Zasulich, and Potresov—were eliminated on a motion by Lenin. Martov, however, declined to function on the board as thus constituted, while Plekhanov broke with the Bolsheviks a few weeks later and, by the weight of his authority, succeeded in reconstituting the board with all four Menshevik members. This caused Lenin in his turn to resign; from then on *Iskra* became a Menshevik organ, and it was a year before the Bolsheviks were able to found one of their own.

The Congress was the occasion for an avalanche of articles, pamphlets, books, and leaflets in which the new-born factions exchanged insults and charges of disloyalty, intrigue, misappropriation of party funds, etc. Lenin's book *One Step Forward, Two Steps Back* was the most powerful piece of artillery fired in this campaign. It analysed all the important votes at the congress, defended the centralist idea of the party, and branded the Mensheviks as opportunists. In *Iskra*, on the other hand, articles by Plekhanov, Akselrod, and Martov accused the Bolsheviks of bureaucratic centralism, intolerance, Bonapartism, and plotting to subordinate genuine working-class interests to those of professional revolutionaries from the intelligentsia. Each side levelled the same charge against the other, that its policy was not a true expression of proletarian interests: but the charge missed its mark, as they meant different things by 'proletariat'. The Mensheviks had in mind an actual movement by actual workers, whom it was the party's role to assist to victory. To Lenin the actual, spontaneous workers' movement was by definition a bourgeois phenomenon, while the true proletarian movement was defined by the supremacy of proletarian ideology, that is to say of Marxism in its Leninist interpretation.

The Bolsheviks and Mensheviks continued to be, in theory, sections of a single party. The breach inevitably affected the party in Russia, but it was less evident there, as many leaders regarded the *émigré* squabbles as of little account, while working-class social democrats had hardly heard of them. The two factions jostled for influence in the underground organization and formed committees on every hand, while Lenin and his supporters pressed for a fresh congress to be held as soon as possible, to heal the split which was paralysing party action. Meanwhile Lenin created the organizational and ideological basis of the Bolshevik faction with the aid of new leaders and theorists such as Bogdanov, Lunacharski, Bonch-Bruyevich, Vorovsky, and others.

The 1905 Revolution came as a surprise to both factions, neither of which had anything to do with the first spontaneous outbreak. Of the *émigrés* who returned to Russia Trotsky, who did not belong to either group, played the most important part: he made his way to St. Petersburg at once, while Lenin and Martov did not return till November 1905, after the proclamation of an amnesty. The first stage of the revolution was linked with the formation, by the Petersburg workers, of trade unions that were in fact organized by the police, as if to confirm Lenin's warning of what would happen to the working class left to itself. The unions, however, which were under the patronage of Zubatov, chief of the Moscow Okhrana, got out of hand from the point of view of their organizers. Father Gapon, who took seriously his role as a leader of the working class, became a revolutionary as the result of 'Bloody Sunday' (9 January 1905), when the police fired on a crowd of peaceful demonstrators at the Winter Palace. This event touched off the crisis which was already coming to a head owing to defeats in the war with Japan, strikes in Poland, and peasant revolts.

In April 1905 Lenin summoned a Bolshevik congress in London which proclaimed itself to be a congress of the whole party and, for a time, set the seal on its division, passing anti-Menshevik resolutions and electing a purely Bolshevik Central Committee. However, as the Revolution progressed members of both factions in Russia co-operated with one another, and this helped towards a *rapprochement*. The spontaneous workers' movement created new bodies in the shape of workers' councils (Soviets). Bolsheviks inside Russia at first distrusted these as non-party organs which could not possess true revolutionary consciousness; Lenin, however, soon recognized them as the nucleus of workers' power in the future, and instructed his followers to join them and do their best to control them politically.

In October 1905 the Tsar issued a manifesto promising a constitution, civil liberty, freedom of speech and assembly, and an elected parliament, the Duma.

All the social democratic groups and the S.R.s denounced these promises as fraudulent and boycotted the elections. In the last two months of 1905 the revolution reached its peak; the revolt of the Moscow workers was suppressed in December. Bloody repressions followed in all the revolutionary centres of Russia, Poland, and Latvia, while reactionary bands inspired mass terror and pogroms. For some time after large-scale revolts were put down, local outbreaks and acts of violence took place and were stamped out by the authorities. Despite this ebb of the revolutionary tide, Lenin at first hoped for an early renewal of the struggle; but he finally accepted the need to work within the reactionary system, and stood out for social democratic participation in the elections to the Third Duma in mid-1907. On that occasion (cf. below), he was opposed by a majority of his own group, but supported by the Mensheviks.

As a result of the Revolution, the social democratic party was formally reunited. At the Stockholm Congress in April 1906—the Mensheviks had a considerable majority, but the old names were retained—organizational unity was restored in a form that lasted for the next six years, until Lenin brought about a final split in 1912. Ideological and tactical unity, however, were still lacking. The basic differences and mutual accusations continued, although for a time Lenin used less crude and insulting terms about the Mensheviks than previously. Each group interpreted the results of the Revolution as a confirmation of its own theories. Lenin argued that it was clear that the bourgeoisie (in this case the Kadets) was ready to come to terms with the Tsardom in return for trifling concessions and was more afraid of a popular revolution than of the autocracy. The Revolution had also shown, he contended, that the only force that could be counted on besides the proletariat was the peasantry, which at this stage was the natural ally of the social democrats. Some Mensheviks, on the other hand, thought the Revolution had failed because in its second phase the proletariat had been isolated by the excessive radicalism of its demands, which had alienated the bourgeoisie instead of turning it to account as an ally. Trotsky was led by the events of 1905 to formulate his theory of permanent revolution more precisely, arguing that a Russian revolution must at once evolve into a socialist phase and that it could touch off a socialist upheaval in the West.

Thus in the post-revolutionary period the old divisions remained and new problems confronted the two factions, who reacted according to their respective ideas. The Mensheviks were much more inclined to make use of the new parliamentary opportunities; Lenin's followers at first held out for a boycott, and when they finally agreed to be represented in the Duma they treated it as a sounding-board for revolutionary propaganda and not an instrument of social reform. The Mensheviks, though they took part in armed clashes during the Revolution, regarded an armed uprising as a last resort and were more interested in other forms of struggle, whereas to Lenin an uprising and the conquest of power by violence were the only possible way of achieving revolutionary aims. He was scandalized by Plekhanov's words 'We should not have taken up arms', and quoted them repeatedly to show what an opportunist the Mensheviks' ideological leader was. The Mensheviks favoured the most decentralized forms of government in the future republican state, and for this reason among others they proposed to make over confiscated lands to local government authorities, arguing that nationalization would mean strengthening the central power, which would be in the hands of the bourgeoisie. (The 'Asiatic' character of the Russian state was another reason why Plekhanov was in favour of decentralizing measures.) Lenin held to the plan for nationalization—i.e. not the confiscation of peasant land, or rural collectivization, but the transfer of 'absolute rent' to the state; in his view the post-revolutionary government would be one of the proletariat and peasantry, so the Menshevik argument had no force. Other Bolsheviks again, including the young Stalin, were for partitioning all the confiscated land: this was closest to what the peasants actually desired, and was finally inscribed in the programme. The Mensheviks, both in and outside the Duma, were inclined towards tactical alliances with the Kadets; Lenin denounced the Kadets as lackeys of the Tsardom and preferred to work with the peasants, represented after 1905 chiefly by the Labour Group (Trudoviki). The Mensheviks devised plans for a broad non-party organization of the proletariat in a general workers' congress, i.e. a nation-wide system of Soviets, whereas to Lenin this meant eliminating the party and replacing it, *horribile dictu*, by the proletariat. He also violently attacked Akselrod, Larin, and other advocates of the workers' congress, arguing that the Soviets were only of use for insurrectionary purposes. 'Soviets of workers' deputies and their unification are essential for the victory of the insurrection, but a victorious insurrection will inevitably create other kinds of organs' (from the symposium *Questions of Tactics*, Apr. 1907; *Works*, vol. 12, p. 332).

The next few years were filled with argument on these questions, especially the agrarian programme and relations with the Kadets. The Menshevik group was much more beset with doubts and was often irresolute in tactical matters, inclining to ascribe importance to legal institutions and broadly based proletarian organizations. Lenin wished the party to use every opportunity of legal activity, but to preserve its clandestine organization and to resist the blandishments of constitutionalism, parliamentarianism, and trade-unionism; all legal forms must be subordinate to the eventual aim of seizing power by force. At the same time Lenin was opposed to the S.R. policy of terrorism against individuals. He emphasized before 1905 that the party did not renounce terror as a matter of principle and that it was necessary in certain circumstances, but attacks on ministers and other public figures were premature and counter-productive, as they dissipated revolutionary forces and could not bring about any significant effect. In the latter part of the revolutionary period he crossed swords with the Mensheviks over 'expropriations', i.e. acts of armed robbery by terrorist groups for the purpose of replenishing party funds (Stalin in Transcaucasia was one of the chief organizers of this activity). The Mensheviks, and Trotsky, condemned this practice as unworthy and demoralizing, but Lenin defended it provided it was not exercised against individuals but against banks, trains, or state property. At the London Congress in the spring of 1907 'expropriations' were condemned by a Menshevik majority, against Lenin's opposition.

The party's ranks were much depleted by the period of reaction. After the 'unity congress' in September 1906 Lenin estimated its numbers at over 100,000. The delegates at the Congress represented about 13,000 Bolsheviks and 18,000 Mensheviks; the Bund re-joined, bringing in 33,000 Jewish workers; to these were added 26,000 Polish and Lithuanian social democrats and 14,000 Latvians, yet Trotsky in 1910 estimated the total at only 10,000. However, despite repressions, the post-revolutionary situation offered much wider opportunities for legal activity. At the beginning of 1907 Lenin moved to Finland, whence he re-emigrated at the end of the year. He proclaimed a boycott of the elections to the Second Duma, but not all social democrats obeyed, and 35 were elected. After about three months the Second Duma, like the first, was dissolved, whereupon Lenin abandoned the boycott policy and sanctioned his followers' participation in the Third Duma, not for the sake of social reform but to expose the delusions of parliamentarianism and to push the peasant delegates in a revolutionary direction. A few months previously, anyone who opposed the boycott showed, according to Lenin, that he had no conception of Marxism and was an arrant opportunist; now, anyone in favour of it was a self-confessed opportunist and ignoramus. Among the Bolsheviks there came into being a sub-group who criticized Lenin 'from the left', and whom he dubbed 'otzovists', i.e. 'recallists', for demanding the recall of the social democratic delegates from the Duma; while another group were nicknamed 'ultimatists' because they drafted an ultimatum to be addressed by the party to its deputies, mostly Mensheviks, on pain of recall if they did not obey. The distinction between the two sub-groups was not essential, but there was against Lenin a faction of revolutionary Bolsheviks who thought the party should have nothing to do with parliament but concentrate on direct preparation for the coming revolution. The most active member of this group, A. A. Bogdanov, had for years been Lenin's most faithful collaborator; he had played the main part in organizing Bolshevism inside Russia and can be regarded as the joint creator, with Lenin, of Bolshevism as a separate political movement. Among the other otzovists or ultimatists were several intellectuals—Lunacharsky, Pokrovsky, Menzhinsky—some of whom later reverted to Leninist orthodoxy.

The tactical controversy with the otzovists was intertwined in a curious fashion with a philosophical dispute which arose at this time in the social democratic camp and which drew from Lenin a treatise in defence of materialism, published in 1909. This dispute had a previous history which should be briefly described.

2. New intellectual trends in Russia

At the turn of the century the Russian intelligentsia showed a marked tendency to abandon positivism, scientism, and materialism, which had for so long been the dominant modes of thought. The same trend was seen throughout Europe, in philosophy and social thought as in poetry, painting, and drama. The typical free-thinking Russian intellectual of the last quarter of the century believed that science had the answers to all questions of social and individual life, that religion was a collection of superstitions maintained by ignorance and deceit, that the biologist's scalpel had annihilated God and the soul, that human history was irresistibly impelled by 'progress', and that it was the task of the intelligentsia to support progress against autocracy, religion, and oppression of all kinds. Historical optimism, rationalism, and the cult of science were the keynotes of evolutionary positivism à la Spencer, reinforced by the tradition of nineteenth-century materialism. Russian Marxism in its first stage duly gave pride of place to these positivistic elements of the inherited world-view. To be sure, the second half of the nineteenth century was not only the period of Chernyshevsky and Dobrolyubov, but also that of Dostoevsky and Solovyov. But the most dynamic and influential parts of the intelligentsia, and the great majority of the revolutionaries, whether populist or Marxist, accepted the rationalist and evolutionist catechism as a natural concomitant of their struggle against the Tsardom and the Church.

In the early 1900s, however, this outlook began to give place to a variety of intellectual attitudes in which it is hard to distinguish any common feature except that they rejected the scientistic, optimistic, and collectivist ideals of the previous century. In addition to academic philosophy in the style of Kant (A. I. Vvedensky) or Hegel (B. N. Chicherin), new works by non-academic philosophers struck a religious, personalist, and anti-scientistic note. Many Western philosophers were translated: not only Wundt and Windelband but also Nietzsche, Bergson, James, Avenarius, Mach, and even Husserl, together with Max Stirner, the prophet of egocentric anarchism. In poetry symbolism and 'decadence' flourished, and Russian literature was enriched by the names of Merezhkovsky, Zinaida Gippius, Blok, Bryusov, Bunin, Vyacheslav Ivanov, and Byely. Interest in religion, mysticism, oriental cults, and occultism was almost universal. Solovyov's religious philosophy experienced a revival. Pessimism,

Satanism, apocalyptic prophecies, the search for mystic and metaphysical depths, love of the fantastic, eroticism, psychology and self-analysis—all these merged into a single modernistic culture. Merezhkovsky, with Berdyayev and Rozanov, brooded on the metaphysic of sex; N. Minsky extolled Nietzsche, wrote religious poems, and co-operated with the Bolsheviks. Ex-Marxists returned to the Christian faith of their ancestors; a generation which had identified an interest in religion with obscurantism and political reaction gave place to a generation which regarded 'scientific' atheism as a symbol of naïve, narrow-minded optimism.

In 1903 there appeared *Problems of Idealism*, a collection of essays many of whose authors had recently been Marxists, but which condemned Marxism and materialism for their moral nihilism, contempt of personality, determinism, and fanatical pursuit of social values regardless of the individuals who made up society; they also attacked Marxism for its uncritical worship of progress and sacrifice of the present to the future. No ethical system, Berdyayev claimed, could be based on a materialist world-view, since ethics presupposed the Kantian distinction between what is and what ought to be. Moral norms cannot be deduced from experience, and the experimental sciences are therefore useless to ethics. For these norms to be valid there must be an intelligible world in which they have their being, other than the world of experience, and their validity also presupposes the free, 'noumenal' nature of man. Moral consciousness thus postulates freedom, the existence of God, and the immortality of the soul. Positivism and utilitarianism cannot provide man with absolute criteria of value. Bulgakov attacked materialism and positivism on the ground that they failed to solve metaphysical puzzles, regarded the world and human existence as the work of chance, denied freedom, and offered no criteria of moral value. The world and man's presence in it were only intelligible in the light of faith in the divine harmony, and social commitment could be based on nothing but a sense of religious duty. Only when our acts are given meaning by their relation to divinity can we speak of true self-realization and the integration of personality, which is the supreme human value.

Most of the authors of *Problems of Idealism* were agreed in holding that the validity of legal or moral norms presupposes a non-empirical world and that self-realization must not be sacrificed to the demands of society, since personality is an intrinsic and absolute value. Novgorodtsev emphasized the need for law to be based on *a priori* norms of justice; Struve criticized the ideal of equality in the sense of universal levelling and the elimination of personal differences. Most of the writers, especially S. L. Frank, invoked Nietzsche to support their personalist views, scanning his philosophy for condemnation of moral utilitarianism, eudaemonism, slave-morality, and the sacrifice of personal creativity to the 'welfare of the masses'. Struve, Berdyayev, Frank, and Askoldov all in some degree endorsed Nietzsche's attacks on socialism as a philosophy of mediocrity and the values of the herd; all regarded socialist ideals as designed to stamp out personal values for the sake of Man as an abstraction. All were sceptical of historical laws and criteria of progress derived from empirical history without the benefit of *a priori* moral norms; and all saw in socialism the prospect of abstract 'collective' values tyrannizing over personality.

Problems of Idealism was an important event in Russian cultural history, not because its ideas were especially novel but because it was a concerted attack on all the intellectual and moral stereotypes which the progressive intelligentsia had derived from nineteenth-century evolutionism and utilitarianism, and because it criticized Marxism not from the populist point of view, still less that of conservative orthodoxy, but from that of the most up-to-date, neo-Kantian, or Nietzschean philosophy. The key concepts that were accepted by revolutionists of every shade, and the main historiosophical dogmas of the 'progressive' intellectuals, were challenged by men who until recently had, at least to some extent, regarded them as their own. Atheism, rationalism, evolutionism, the categories of progress and causality, and the premisses of 'collectivist' morality—all these, it was claimed, did not represent the victory of reason over superstition but were symptoms of intellectual poverty. The new critics brought into the light of day everything in Marxism and socialism that was contrary to freedom and personal values, all doctrinaire schemes that enslaved the present to the future and self-realization to collective ideals. At the same time, without being fully aware of it, they brought to light the conflict between the absolute value of the individual and his development, and the desire for social change—a conflict especially obvious when the individual was extolled on Nietzschean lines. The Marxists, who regarded *Problems of Idealism* as nothing but a manifestation of bourgeois liberalism, were quick to emphasize those elements of the new movement which could be regarded as glorifying egocentrism or the morality of the *Herrenmensch* who despises the sufferings and aspirations of the masses. Lyubov Akselrod, who at this time was, with Plekhanov, the most vigorous defender of traditional Marxist philosophy, published in *Zarya*, under the pseudonym 'Orthodox', an exhaustive criticism of the new ideas from this point of view. She was able, as Lenin generally was not, to summarize the opposing arguments in a sober, factual manner; her reply, however, consists mainly of repeating hallowed formulas and trying to show that the cult of personal values as preached by Berdyayev, Frank, and Bulgakov is a glorification of egoism and a dissolvent of social obligation. Rehearsing the Marxist attack on religion as an instrument of oppression and inequality, she lays stress on the link between historical and philosophical materialism: in this as in all other respects she was a disciple of Plekhanov. The question was a live one in Marxist controversy: Max Zetterbaum had recently published a series of articles in

Die Neue Zeit arguing that historical materialism did not involve any particular ontological position and was compatible with Kantian transcendentalism. This view, popular among German and Austrian Marxists, was of course anathema to Plekhanov and 'Orthodox'. The 'mechanistic outlook', as she writes (accepting responsibility for this expression), is an integral interpretation of the world which includes pre-human history as well as that of mankind; there is room in it for a rational concept of progress: what is historically progressive is whatever tends towards the preservation of society and of individuals (she does not attempt to unravel the complications of this formula). There is no basic difference between the study of human history and the natural sciences: social science is just as 'objective' and just as much concerned with laws and repeatable phenomena as physical science.

This summary and over-simplified reply was made easier by the fact that the authors of the work criticized did not profess to be Marxists and defended idealism under its own name. It was harder to deal with those social democrats who were led astray by the new heresy and tried to combine the Marxist tradition with a socialist philosophy based on 'subjectivist' trends, and in particular on the empiriocritical brand of epistemology.

It is noteworthy that while attempts were also made in the West (especially by Viktor Adler's son Friedrich) to graft empiriocriticism on to Marxism, it is only in Russia that one can speak of a whole school of philosophers of this way of thinking, who exercised appreciable influence though only for a short time. Unlike many Western 'revisionists', this school did not contend that Marxism was philosophically neutral and could be combined with any epistemological theory, but sought, on the contrary, to adopt a philosophy in harmony with Marxist social theory and revolutionary strategy. In the same way as their orthodox critics, they endeavoured to create an integral picture of the world in which a particular philosophical doctrine and no other, would provide a basis for historical materialism and the theory of the revolution. In this respect they shared in the doctrinaire spirit which prevailed among Russian social democrats. What attracted them in empiriocritical philosophy was its scientistic and anti-metaphysical rigorism and its 'activistic' approach to epistemology. Both these characteristics seemed well in accord with the iconoclastic attitude of Marxism towards inherited philosophical 'systems', and with the revolutionary orientation of the Bolshevik wing of Russian social democracy.

3. Empiriocriticism

THIS term is associated with a fairly large number of philosophers and physicists, chiefly in Germany and Austria, among whom the most prominent names are those of Ernst Mach and Richard Avenarius. The two men worked independently of each other and their conclusions were not identical, but their thinking ran on similar lines although expressed in different terms.

The objective that Avenarius set himself was to demolish all philosophical concepts and explanations that turn the world into a mystery by postulating a difference between the phenomena we perceive and the 'true' reality which lies beneath or beyond them. Above all he sought to refute epistemological idealism, which derived from the distinction between 'mental impressions' and inaccessible 'things in themselves'. He also held that all agnostic doctrines were based on the same false distinction. If his ideas were fairly often interpreted, by Wundt among others, as a new variety of 'subjectivism' or even 'immanentism', this was due partly to a certain inconsistency in his argument and partly to the extreme complexity of his language, which bristles with neologisms and endeavours to make a clean sweep of all the traditional abstractions of philosophy.

The error which causes us to distinguish between the 'contents of the mind' and the thing itself, or between the subject's 'interior' and the object—this error, leading to all the aberrations of idealism and agnosticism, is due to an instinctive process which Avenarius calls 'introjection'. If we examine our perceptions without any philosophical prepossession, we do not find them mysterious. Philosophy, however, persists in telling us that our 'impression' or 'sensation', for example when we touch a stone, is something other than the thing itself (in this case the stone), and that the problem is how they are related to each other. If it were so we could never find the answer, for there is no way of comparing the likeness with the original and seeing whether they agree, whatever this may precisely mean. But the question is a false one. We do not have to do with the thing and the impression separately, and if we dichotomize the world in this way we condemn ourselves to barren speculation which can only result in our capitulating before the mystery of a world concealed by a veil of sensations, or embracing the idealist delusion that the world is nothing but a medley of 'mental states'. Introjection—i.e. the mental process by which, as it were, we 'take in' physical objects in the form of 'subjective' images or reflections—is due to a false, though historically inevitable, interpretation of our relations with the world. Since we rightly presume that other people's mental experience is similar to ours, and since we thus treat them as experiencing subjects and not as automata, we attribute to them a mental 'interior' similar to our own—a sort of container for their experiences, which we cannot ourselves directly perceive. Having thus dichotomized other people we do the same for ourselves, treating our own perceptions as mental states caused by outside stimuli but different from them. We thus divide the world into what is 'subjective' and what is 'objective', and then speculate on how the two are related. Hence, in due course, the distinction between the body and the immaterial soul, and all spiritualist and religious illusions. But the mistake of introjection can be avoided: I can recognize that another person is a cognizant subject like myself without making a distinction between his or my *for intérieur* and that which is external. Once we shake off the illusion that we have an 'inner consciousness' in which 'external objects' are mysteriously present—objects which exist independently of the fact that they are 'given', but which we cannot know in any other way—we are freed from all the traditional questions and categories of philosophy, the disputes between realism and spiritualism, and the insoluble problems inherent in the notions of substance, force, and causality.

However, the removal of the delusion does not solve the question of the 'act of cognition', which in the ordinary sense implies a distinction between the knower and the known. This relationship must now be defined in terms free from the error of introjection. The critique of introjection is the negative aspect of Avenarius's thought; its positive counterpart is the idea of 'principal co-ordination'. The content of my experience includes things, other people, and also myself, for the self that I experience directly is present in the same way as a thing, i.e. as the known and not the knower: it is not a subjective 'interior' transforming things into copies of themselves. At the same time, the self is irremovably present in experience as a relatively permanent part of it, and 'principal co-ordination' is the name given to the permanent conjunction of the 'term' and 'counter-term' of experience, which are equipollent and combined in such a way that neither is 'prior' to the other. The 'central term' is each separate human being, and the counter-term, i.e. what was formerly called the object of experience, is numerically identical for any number of central terms. Different people, in other words, perceive the same object: the counter-term does not multiply itself to match the number of 'subjects', and this rules out epistemological idealism. By removing the possibility of idealism and solipsism we also eliminate the problem of the 'thing in itself' hiding behind phenomena: for this would imply a counter-term that is not a counter-term since it is not 'given', and would therefore be self-contradictory. 'Principal co-ordination' does not, Avenarius continues, affect the sense we ascribe to scientific knowledge: for when we address ourselves to any object we create a situation of 'co-ordination', i.e. we include that object in a cognitive combination. We may think, for instance, that we are asking what the world was like when there was no one to perceive it, but in fact we are adding an imaginary observer to the scene and asking what the world would have been like then. We cannot raise a question about any part of the universe without embracing it in our act of inquiry and thus making it a counter-term of experience. We may say, and this is probably what Avenarius intended, that the act of inquiry cannot be eliminated from the content of the question, and therefore the situation of questioning is an instance of 'principal co-ordination'. It is impossible to put a question concerning 'independent' being, for the very act of uttering it establishes a dependence. To ask about 'being-in-itself' is to ask how we can know the world without creating a cognitive situation, that is to say without knowing it. In this sense all the traditional questions of epistemology and metaphysics, as posed by Descartes, Locke, Kant, and their successors, are seen to be wrongly framed and meaningless.

If human cognitive activity is understood in this light, Avenarius claims, its true biological significance becomes plain. Cognition is a form of behaviour comprising the reactions of the body to stimuli which constantly disturb our biological equilibrium, and the reactions have no other purpose than to restore it. Cognition, being simply a biological reaction, is not concerned with 'truth' in any transcendental sense or with discovering 'how things really are'. The predicates 'true' and 'false' do not belong to components of experience: like 'pleasant' and 'painful', 'good' and 'bad', 'beautiful' and 'ugly', they are related to a particular interpretation of experience, they are 'characters' and not 'elements'. Human ideas about the world, whether philosophical doctrines or religious beliefs, are to be interpreted biologically and not in relation to 'truth': they can without exception be genetically understood as the response of individuals or communities to needs occasioned by changes in the environment. This does not mean that the content of my knowledge is not valid for all mankind. Some features of biological existence are universal, and so therefore are certain 'truths' enunciated by human beings; but this universality refers to the human species and not to any transcendental validity of knowledge. From the purely biological point of view cognition is of course possible, but not a theory of it which would entitle us to claim that our knowledge is true 'objectively', i.e. independently of the act of cognition.

Although it was Avenarius's object to free philosophy from the dualism of 'mind' and 'matter' by reducing all Being to experience in which the self and the object are present on equal terms, he was unable to avoid drawing conclusions that brought him under suspicion of 'subjectivism' or inconsistency. If the self is not a subject but is something known, and if the 'central term' is inseparable from any account of experience, in what does the act of knowing consist? It would appear to be an experience which is nobody's, a situation in which something is 'given' not to anyone in particular but in general, an act of perception without a percipient. If I say that 'I see' something or other, this statement comprises 'me' as a grammatical and epistemological subject and implies that 'I', as the cognizant subject, am not on a par with the other components of the perceptual field: otherwise it would be truer to say that something 'is perceived' than that 'I' perceive it. But Avenarius's explanation is not clear: how could the category of subject be banished from the account of experience, and what is the difference between the 'central term' of the empiriocritics and the 'subject' in the ordinary sense? If we hold to the view that the self is only a component of the perceptual field it is not clear why 'principal co-ordination' happens at all, i.e. why the self must be present in every act of experience.

It is in fact hard to reconcile the two fundamental categories of 'introjection' and 'principal co-ordination'. The critique of introjection is intended to do away with the 'subject' as a superfluous construction and with the distinction between 'subjective' and 'objective' Being. Experience is left as an ontologically neutral zone, whose relation to 'being-in-itself' cannot be meaningfully inquired into. Epistemological aspirations are relinquished, and science is left to deal with its problems as they are, without ontological interpretation. This is how Mach understood the matter. If, however, we also adopt the theory of 'principal co-ordination', the subject, under a different name, reappears as a separate category, whose inevitable presence in experience can only be understood on the supposition that it is the knower and not the known—yet Avenarius rejects this supposition. If we accept both parts of his interpretation, the result may easily lead us into an absurdity: the self, as a component of experience on the same footing as things, is for some unintelligible reason the condition of the appearance of all its other components. The inadmissibility of this is clear when Avenarius identifies the 'central term' of co-ordination with the human nervous system—so that the latter, a physical object, is the condition of the presence of all other physical objects. Avenarius does not, of course, state this absurd conclusion, but it is hard to see how it can be avoided if both his basic tenets are maintained.

A second fundamental difficulty, to which Natorp and especially Husserl drew attention, is that of the physiological interpretation of cognitive values combined with the recognition of scientific knowledge as true in the everyday sense. If, as Avenarius says, truth is not part of experience but is a secondary interpretation of it, the whole purpose of scientific knowledge is reduced to biological utility. On this purely pragmatic view, what is 'true' is that which it is advantageous to accept in given conditions: some 'truths' may be universally valid, but this only means that they are advantageous in all circumstances because of the unaltering features of human species-life. But at the same time Avenarius bases his biological interpretation of knowledge on observations of the physiology of perception: he accepts these as valid or 'true' in the everyday sense, and thus seems to fall into a *petitio principii*. Hence, Husserl argued, the whole idea of 'biological epistemology' is an impossibility: we cannot find the meaning of all experience on the basis of certain particular data of experience which we tacitly regard as 'true' in the ordinary sense.

Avenarius sought to explode all the traditional questions of philosophy by doing away with 'subjectivity' as a superfluous construction, without which these questions would not arise. But his doctrine of 'principal co-ordination' thwarts the attempt and introduces a major inconsistency into the whole theory. The real achievement of his critique, for which the theory of 'co-ordination' is unnecessary, is to show the insuperable difficulties of treating the content of perception as consisting of copies or images of objects that are independent of the perceptual situation. His intention was to restore to cognitive acts their 'natural' character, unblurred by philosophical speculation. In the 'natural' conception of the world there was, in his view, no dichotomy between mind and matter, and cognition was not a process of storing images of things into a mental container. The critique of introjection was not meant to be a discovery of something new but a return to the naïve, immediate view of the world, in which cognitive acts would recover their true biological meaning; it was also in accordance with the basic principle of intellectual economy. In Avenarius's view, as in that of Mach, the principle of economy was not a general law of physics, as in Maupertuis, but signified, as in Spencer's philosophy, that any living organism, including the human brain, acts so as to attain its object with the minimum output of energy. The whole history of human thought exemplified this: the capitalization of knowledge proceeded by increasingly far-reaching generalizations and increasingly efficient ways of recording and transmitting acquired information. All abstract ideas were instruments of this process: so were human speech and writing, the laws of science, and the methods of mathematics. Scientific laws did not purport to reflect any particular facts in their every detail, but to express recurrent aspects of phenomena that were of biological importance: they were short cuts which saved effort in the manipulation of things. Metaphysical categories like 'thing', 'substance', 'spirit', and 'matter' were by-products of the same activity. They were useful in so far as they denoted certain relatively permanent combinations of qualities in experience, but when petrified in language our imagination was apt to treat them as metaphysical entities. The task of science, in accordance with the principle of economy, was to purge experience of such superfluous constructions.

Mach's philosophy is not open to the same charge of inconsistency as that of Avenarius, since it contains no equivalent of the principle of co-ordination. Mach was an experimental physicist and a historian of physics: he had a stronger sense than Avenarius of the relativity of knowledge, and did not believe in a one-way process of 'purifying' experience so as to achieve a definitive, uniform scientific world-picture. He regarded science as a biological instrument of the human species, developing in accordance with the principle of economy, and equally provisional and relative at each successive stage. Like Avenarius he took a pragmatic view of cognition, whether pre-critical perception or scientific hypotheses. This conception of knowledge left no room for metaphysics. The world consisted of collections of various qualities, which showed varying degrees of permanence and changed in a more or less predictable manner. These qualities or 'elements', perceived without prepossession, had no ontological significance; they were in themselves neither mental nor material; considered in relation to the human body they were sensations, while in their interdependence they appeared as things. These, however, were secondary interpretations: experience itself did not require us to attribute any ontological status to colours, sounds, pressures, time, or space. The actual content of knowledge, including the laws of science, comprised nothing that was not in experience. The purpose of science was to select, classify, and record concisely the results of experience, in accordance with the biological needs of the human species, and to facilitate manipulation and prediction; 'truth' in the transcendental sense was a superfluous addition and introduced nothing of value. All knowledge was experiential in origin and content, except for those parts of mathematics that were purely tautological and gave no information about the world. On this point Mach was faithful to the Humean tradition: all knowledge consists of the description of experience and of analytical judgements; there is no 'necessity' in it except of a linguistic kind, there are no synthetic *a priori* judgements.

Mach's ideas were basically a new version of Humean positivism, intended to free the human mind of an encumbering load of concepts, questions, and distinctions that were not rooted in experience but owed their existence to the inertia of language. He was not a 'subjectivist', treating material qualities as mental states, but sought to outlaw questions of the relationship between mental images and things in themselves, as the concepts they implied were not part of experience and were the fruit of philosophical prejudice. The world as man perceived it was selected and organized in a certain way under the pressure of biological needs. Although its primary features were found in experience, and although science, properly conceived, could add nothing to them, it could arrange experience by means of abstract concepts and laws so that the whole universe appeared under the aspect of a certain order; this order, however, was the work of human selection and was, in this sense, of our own making.

If we try to identify the common intention of Avenarius, Mach, and the many philosophers and physicists who thought like them, we find it to consist in a form of scientism and positivism, closely related to modernistic European culture. In their opposition to metaphysical preconceptions, whether materialist or religious, the empiriocritics sought to return to a direct, spontaneous, unphilosophical outlook on the world: to restore to man his 'natural' status as a cognitive being, freed from the abstract constructions of philosophy and religion and from the jugglery of language. They also held that the order of the universe which knowledge displays to us is not a 'real' order to be passively apprehended but is a product of man's adaptive power. The return to 'nature' and the idea that man is responsible for the order of the external world are characteristic of the intellectual life of the time. The anti-metaphysical scientism of the empiriocritics, and their biological, pragmatic view of knowledge, attracted Marxists in search of a new and more thoroughgoing interpretation of the universe in accordance with the revolutionary spirit.

4. Bogdanov and the Russian empiriocritics

THE principal Russian empiriocritics were the Bolsheviks Bogdanov, Lunacharsky, and Bazarov. There is, however, nothing specifically Bolshevik about their philosophy, although they themselves believed that their political and philosophical positions were closely connected. The same applies to the Mensheviks Yushkevich and Valentinov, and to the S.R. Viktor Chernov. All these were in search of a 'monistic' philosophy embracing the whole of experience and practical politics, but in a different way from that of Engels and Plekhanov, which seemed to them naïve, arbitrary, and unsupported by any analysis of the concepts they used.

The output of the Marxist empiriocritics is enormous and has not as yet been fully studied. Bogdanov was certainly the most important of them, both as a philosopher and as a politician. He was a doctor by profession but a man of varied learning, versed in psychology, philosophy, and economics, a novelist and one of the most active Bolshevik organizers and ideologists. In all his work he was obsessed with the monistic quest for a philosophy containing the key to every problem and explaining everything by a single principle.

Aleksandr Aleksandrovich Bogdanov (real name Malinovsky) was born at Tula in 1873. He studied natural science at Moscow, and medicine at Kharkov until 1899. He was a populist until 1896, when he became a social democrat together with Bazarov (Rudnev). In 1897 he published a popular Marxist handbook of economics, of which Lenin wrote a highly favourable review. This work presented a conspectus of all economic systems in a catechetic form and did much to create the conventional schemata of economic history which became part and parcel of Marxism-Leninism. In 1899, fascinated by the 'energism' of Wilhelm Ostwald, he published *Basic Elements of the Historical View of Nature*, which sought to construct a monistic world-view based on the concept of energy. In this work he displays the relativist tendency which he regarded as a corner-stone of Marxism: all truths are historical in the sense that they express man's biological and social situation; truth is a matter of practical applicability, not objective validity. He later took the view that energism was only a certain way of observing the world, but did not explain the 'stuff' it was made of and therefore could not satisfy the mind's monistic aspirations.

Arrested in Moscow in 1899 and sentenced to exile, Bogdanov lived in Kaluga and then Vologda until 1903. During this period he met Berdyayev, as well as Lunacharsky and other social democrat intellectuals. He was the inspirer and part-author of a collective work of 1904 entitled *An Outline of the Realist World-View*, and answer to *Problems of Idealism;* other contributors were Lunacharsky, Vladimir Fritche, Bazarov, and Suvorov. In 1904–6 Bogdanov published his three-volume *magnum opus, Empiriomonism,* an attempt to adapt the epistemology of Mach and Avenarius to historical materialism.

Bogdanov was a Bolshevik from 1903 onwards. Lenin, despite Bogdanov's heretical views on philosophy, maintained political ties with him for some years; he encouraged Lyubov Akselrod to write against empiriocriticism, but did not himself join the fray until the philosophical deviationists also opposed his policy towards the Duma. After the split in the social democratic party Bogdanov was Lenin's chief lieutenant in St. Petersburg; from 1906 he worked to rebuild the united organization there, and joined Lenin in Finland as one of the three Bolshevik members of the Central Committee. He opposed the participation of social democrats in the Duma elections, and was later an 'ultimatist'. The left-wing Bolsheviks who, with different degrees of firmness, rejected legal methods and pressed for the continuation of a directly revolutionary policy after 1907 were all more or less adherents of the empiriocritical philosophy. In 1909 Bogdanov and his friends were expelled from the Bolshevik Centre, and afterwards from the Central Committee. For a time the group published its own journal and, with financial help from Gorky—who, to Lenin's anxiety, sympathized with the unorthodox trend—founded a party school at Capri as a centre for the revival of revolutionary Bolshevism. The school functioned for some months in 1909, and again at Bologna in 1910–11. Besides Bogdanov its lecturers included Lunacharsky, Aleksinsky, Menzhinsky (a future head of the Ogpu), and occasionally Trotsky. Lenin was invited to give a lecture at the school, but declined. In 1911 Bogdanov's group disintegrated and he returned to Russia for good. He continued to pour out philosophical writings, seeking more and more generalized formulas in which to express his monistic views. Together with other deviationists he published two collective works: *Essays on the Philosophy of Marxism* (1908; Bogdanov, Bazarov, Berman, Lunacharsky, Yushkevich, Suvorov, and Helfand) and *Essays on the Philosophy of Collectivism* (1909; Bogdanov, Gorky, Lunacharsky, Bazarov). Among his own publications were *The Decline of Fetishism* (1910), which analysed 'fetishism' in general terms as a cognitive and social phenomenon; *The Philosophy of Living Experience* (1913), a popular account of empiriomonism; and *Tectology, a Universal Organizational Science* (1913; vol. ii, 1917). The last was an attempt to lay the basis of a universal science comprising philosophy, sociology, physics, and technology: it may be regarded as a forerunner of praxeology. In addition Bogdanov published manuals of economics that were much reprinted, and several dissertations on 'proletarian culture': he pursued this with vigour after the Revolution and was one of the chief ideologists of the institution known as 'Proletkult'.

During the war Bogdanov served at the front as an army doctor. He did not rejoin the party; in 1926 he was appointed director of the Haematological Institute in Moscow, and two years later he died as the result of a transfusion experiment on himself. Even this had its philosophical bearing: blood transfusion was, to him, a proof of the biological unity of mankind, and was thus linked with the 'collectivist' outlook.

An author who produced over fifty books and innumerable articles on all kinds of subjects could not be a philosopher of the first rank. He was also a bad writer: his principal work is diffuse, chaotic, vague, and repetitive. Nevertheless, he was the most influential expounder of 'proletarian philosophy', and for many years the whole Bolshevik party learnt economics from his books. As a philosopher he was superior to Lenin in all respects: erudition, knowledge of his subject, independence of thought, and skill in formulating problems. He also appears to have been an excellent organizer. He lacked, however, what Lenin possessed in full measure, the non-doctrinaire ability to change tactics in a new situation: like most ideologists, he was too consistent for his own good.

Bogdanov's 'empiriomonist' philosophy is based on three main ideas. All spiritual and mental activities are instruments of life in the biological and social senses; psychic and physical phenomena are alike from the ontic point of view; the life of the human race tends towards the integral harmony of all its manifestations. The first two ideas are found in Mach, but Bogdanov gives them a distinctive interpretation on the strength of which he calls his theory empiriomonism and not empiriocriticism. The third point is specifically connected with socialist doctrine.

According to Bogdanov, Mach's philosophy supports Marxism inasmuch as they both treat cognitive processes as instruments of man's fight for existence, and reject the possibility of ideas not derived from experience. The 'objectivity' of acts of cognition lies in the fact that they are valid for human societies and not only for the individual. This collective aspect distinguishes physical phenomena from 'subjective' ones. 'The objective character of the physical world consists in the fact that it exists not for me personally but for all, and has for everyone a definite meaning, the same, I believe, as it has for me' (*Empiriomonism*, i, 25). Nature is 'collectively organized experience'. Space, time, and causality are forms in which men co-ordinate their respective perceptions; but this co-ordination is not as yet complete. There are experiences, socially significant and with a social origin, which nevertheless conflict with other experiences. This is due to social antagonisms and the class division, which have the effect that human beings only understand one another within certain limits, while their discordant interests inevitably produce conflicting ideologies. In an individualistic society like ours each person's experience centres on himself, whereas in primitive communist societies the 'self' was merged in the community. In the society of the future it will be different again, when work is collectively organized and there will be no possibility of conflict between my own self and another's.

Work is genetically prior to all other forms of community life. However, when the immediate expenditure of energy in the fight with nature is supplemented by organizational forms to increase the efficiency of labour, these call into being ideological instruments including all modes of communication: language, abstract knowledge, emotions, customs, moral norms, laws, and arts. 'The ideological process constitutes all that part of social life that lies outside technical processes, beyond the immediate struggle of social man with external nature' (ibid. iii, 45). Science is not an ideology, for it develops as an immediate organ of technology. Ultimately, however, all forms of collective spiritual life, whether ideological or scientific, are subservient to the struggle for existence and have no significance apart from their function in that struggle. This subordination of all forms of life to the requirements of technology and increased efficiency is not yet visible to all, on account of ideological delusions which keep alive countless metaphysical fetishes; but it is becoming visible to the proletariat, and in the future it will be common to all mankind. 'The technical value of products, replacing the fetish of exchange value, is the sum of the social energy of human labour crystallized in those products. The cognitive value of an idea is its power to increase the volume of social energy of labour, by planning and "organizing" the forms of men's activity and the instruments they use. The "moral" value of human behaviour consists in increasing the social energy of labour by harmoniously uniting and concentrating human activity and by organizing it in the direction of maximum solidarity' (ibid. 135–6).

This purely pragmatic (but, it should be added, socially pragmatic) interpretation, according to which knowledge and the life of the mind generally are an assemblage of instruments whose 'ultimate' purpose is to assist technical progress, leaves no room for the concept of truth in the traditional sense, i.e. the conformity of our judgements to independent reality. The 'natural' world, in Bogdanov's view, is the result of the social organization of experience, and 'truth' means utility in the struggle for existence. This attitude, he claims, is strictly scientific, as it sweeps away all the metaphysical fetishes that have deluded philosophers and common men over the centuries. Having reduced the universe to collective experience, and cognitive values to socially useful ones, we have no need of such categories as 'substance' or 'thing in itself', or such specifications as 'spirit', 'matter', 'time', 'cause', 'force', etc. Experience contains nothing that answers to these concepts, and they are not required for the practical handling of objects.

Bogdanov's critique of the 'thing in itself' as a superfluity which can be eliminated from Kantian philosophy is based on a misunderstanding. Bogdanov and Mach, from whom he took this interpretation, appear to think that in Kant's view there is behind every phenomenal object a mysterious 'thing in itself' to which we have no access: if it be removed, the phenomena remain as they were and nothing has been lost except a 'metaphysical' construction. This, however, is a parody of Kant's thinking. What he held was that the 'phenomenon' is the mode in which things appear, so that they are immediately accessible to us, but organized in *a priori* forms. If the 'thing in itself' were removed, the phenomenon would be removed also. In short, the concept of a 'phenomenon' must mean something quite different for Bogdanov and Mach than it does for Kant, but they do not explain this meaning.

Mach's merit, according to Bogdanov, was that he broke with the dualism of 'mind' and 'matter' and introduced instead the concept of 'experience', in which phenomena appear as mental (psychical) or physical according to whether we connect them with one another or relate them to our own bodes. But Mach did not completely eradicate the dualism, as he retained these two aspects and did not explain why they should be different. The answer offered by expiriomonism is that the 'stuff' of mental and physical phenomena is identical; there is no area of 'subjectivity' in the universe, only the discordance between individual and collective experience, which is due to social causes and which history will in time remove.

We come here to the obscurest part of Bogdanov's philosophy. He appears to be saying that our thoughts, feelings, perceptions, acts of will, etc. are made of the same material as water or stones, but that this material is in some sense 'ultimate' and therefore cannot be defined: encompassing everything, it cannot be explained in terms of anything specific. In this respect, of course, Bogdanov's concept of 'experience' is on a par with all fundamental categories in all monistic doctrines, including 'matter' as understood by the materialists. Apart from this there is only the general idea that man's being is entirely a part of nature, that our subjectivity is no different in kind from the rest of the universe. In this sense the doctrine is a 'materialist' one, i.e. it reduces man to the functions prescribed by his position in nature and regards him as wholly explicable within the natural order. But the matter becomes more complicated when Bogdanov tries to describe this identity in his nebulous theory of 'substitution'.

This theory involves a psychophysical parallelism, not on the basis that mental and physical phenomena are 'two aspects' of a single process—for this involves the error of 'introjection', as though the body was the receptacle of the mind—but in the sense that there is a functional link between them analogous to that, for example, between the visual and tactile qualities of a single body. This is not a monism of 'substance', but a 'monism of the type of organization in accordance with which experience is systematized, a monism of the method of cognition' (*Empiriomonism* i, 64). Within the field of uniform 'experience' there is no problem of transition from inanimate to organic nature, for the whole of nature is an assemblage of homogeneous elements, and it is only our abstract thinking that calls parts of it 'inanimate', whereas they too are parts of our own life. This does not signify, however, that they have a 'psychical' character (for that would mean that they were valid only for the individual), but that there is in them a substratum of which we know nothing specific but which is related to their 'physical' aspect in the same way as mental phenomena are related to physiological ones in human beings. In human life physiological processes are the 'reflection' of direct experiences, and not the other way about. 'Physiological life is the result of the collective harmonization of the "external perceptions" of a living organism, each of which is the reflection of a single complex of experiences in another organism (or in itself). In other words, physiological life is the reflection of direct life in the socially organized experience of living subjects' (ibid. 145). Physical nature itself is derivative in relation to direct complexes which differ in their degree of organization; we must suppose that the world we perceive is of like nature to our experience, for otherwise we could not imagine the one affecting the other; we must therefore accept a kind of panpsychism, but without the assumption of different substances. Within the totality of experience, lower forms of organization 'corresponding to' the inorganic world precede higher ones corresponding to the human mind, and in this sense the 'priority' of nature *vis-à-vis* human existence remains valid. The following passage, though somewhat lengthy, is the most concise summary of Bogdanov's epistemology:

> 'The mental' and 'the physical' as forms of experience do not correspond to the concepts of 'mind' and 'nature'. The latter have a metaphysical sense and relate to 'things in themselves'; but we, discarding metaphysical 'things in themselves' as empty fetishes, place in their stead 'empirical substitution'. This substitution, which originates in each man's recognition of the psyche of others, pre-supposes that the 'basis' of the phenomena of physical experience consists of direct complexes organized in different degrees, including 'psychic' complexes. In recognizing that the physiological processes of the higher nervous centres, as phenomena of physical experience, are the reflection of psychic complexes which can also be 'substituted' for them, we also saw that all the physiological processes of life admit of the substitution of 'associative', i.e. psychic complexes; but in proportion as the physiological phenomenon is less complex and less highly organized, so also are the substitutes. We noted, further, that in the 'inorganic' world outside physiological life empirical substitution still takes place, but the 'direct complexes' that are to be substituted for inorganic phenomena have an organizational form that is not associative but of

another, lower kind: they are not 'psychical' combinations but are less definite, less complex and at a lower level of organization, which in the lowest, limiting phase appears simply as a chaos of elements.

Thus it is among the direct complexes that we substitute for physical experience that we must seek analogies for 'nature' and 'mind' in order to establish their mutual relation. But the very formulation of this question suggests the answer: 'nature', that is to say the inorganic and the simplest organic complexes, is genetically prior, while 'mind', i.e. the higher organic and associative complexes, and particularly those which constitute experience, are genetically secondary.

Thus our viewpoint, although not 'materialist' in the narrow sense, belongs to the same category as 'materialist' systems: it is an ideology of 'productive forces', of the technical process.' (*Empiriomonism*, iii, 148–9)

The obscurity and ambiguity of this philosophy is due to the fact that Bogdanov, unlike Mach, does not simply deny the validity of the 'metaphysical question' but, having declared it to be meaningless, then proceeds to try and solve it, which he cannot do without contradiction. His starting-point is a kind of collective subjectivism: the world is a correlative to the human struggle for existence, and it is no use ascribing any other meaning to it or inquiring as to its independent nature. Things are crystallizations of human projections, governed by practical ends; they make their appearance only within the horizon that biology determines for the human race; they are components of collective experience, which figures as the one absolute point of reference. Within the framework of this relativization 'mental' phenomena differ from physical ones only inasmuch as the latter are valid collectively and the former only for individuals. Having said this, Bogdanov then presents physiological phenomena as the 'reflection' of mental processes, which does not make sense in terms of the previous distinction. He goes on to seek analogies in the field of inanimate nature and thus falls into a kind of panpsychism; he tells us that it is not really panpsychism, as it does not presuppose any 'substance', but he does not explain its true nature. As a result, we are unable to fathom the meaning he attaches to the 'priority of experience in relation to the distinction of mental and physical phenomena. He uses the term 'mental' or 'psychical' in at least three senses, though he appears not to be aware of this: sometimes it means 'valid only for the individual', sometimes 'subjective' in the ordinary sense, and sometimes 'reflected in physiological processes'. This results in hopeless confusion, which there is little point in trying to remedy.

None the less, the main intention of Bogdanov's epistemology is clear: to do away with metaphysical 'fetishes', concepts without empirical correlates, and to preserve a strictly anthropocentric point of view in which the whole of reality is presented as the intentional correlate of human praxis. In this way he seeks to eliminate all 'substantial' entities, especially 'matter' and 'subject', and also 'time', 'space', 'causality', and 'force', as well as the concepts of 'truth' and 'objectivity' in the usual sense. The resulting picture, he claims, is strictly scientific, being free from metaphysics, and likewise humanistic, as it firmly relates all reality to human existence. In both respects this is in harmony with the intensions of Marxism, which is a scientistic, activistic, and socially pragmatic philosophy: it has no need of the category of individual subjectivity or truth in a transcendental sense, and relates the whole universe to human labour, thus making man the creator and organizer of the world. This, in Bogdanov's judgement, is true not of any form of Marxism but only of that embodied in the Bolshevik movement. He and the other Russian empiriocritics believed that their 'activist' epistemology was well attuned to the spirit of Bolshevism and to its general idea that the revolution would not break out of itself when economic conditions were ripe, but that it depended on the will-power of a group of organizers. Bogdanov, to whom 'organization' was an obsession, used the term with equal freedom in regard to party matters and the principles of epistemology.

Each of the Russian empiriocritics differed from the others in some respects. Some, like Valentinov, were strict Machists; others devised variant names for their ideas, such as Bogdanov's 'empiriomonism' and Yushkevich's 'empiriosymbolism'. However, they all agreed in emphasizing the anti-metaphysical, scientistic aspect of Marxism as opposed to the dualism of 'matter' and 'subject', and in envisaging the world in terms of human social praxis. The same viewpoint of collective subjectivism dictated their interpretation of Marx's *Theses on Feuerbach*.

5. *The philosophy of the proletariat*

BOGDANOV endeavoured to apply his theory directly to the prospect of socialism as a system under which all minds would at last share the same picture of the world, and even the separateness of the individual ego would disapear.

The philosophical basis of 'proletarian culture' was as follows. All human cognitive activity is directed to one end, namely man's success in the fight with nature. One can of course distinguish 'scientific' activities, which are directly concerned with technical efficiency, from 'ideological' ones, which perform the same function indirectly through the forms of social organization. This is not a distinction according to epistemological criteria of truth or falsehood, but only relates to the way in which the activities in question increase the productivity of labour. In both cases the principle holds good that 'truth is the living, organizing form of experience; it guides our activity and gives us a foothold in the battle for life' (*Empiriomonism*, iii, p. viii). In other words, the validity of the results of cognition does not consist in their being 'true' in the usual sense, but in the help they afford in the struggle for survival. We thus reach a position of extreme relativism: different 'truths' may be useful in different historical situations, and it is quite possible that any truth is valid only for a particular epoch or social class. Nor is there any epistemological reason to distinguish truth from emotions, values, or social institutions, all of which are equally to be judged according to how far they strengthen man in his fight with nature. At the same time, we can speak of the viewpoint of one class being 'superior' to another's, not as if it were 'true' in an absolute sense but because the social forces it represents are more conducive to technical progress.

According to Marx's theory, the division of labour led to the separation of organizational functions from executive ones, and in course of time to the division of classes. The managing class gradually ceased to perform any technical activity and became parasitic. Its ideology naturally mirrored this situation, evolving religious myths and idealist doctrines. Direct producers, on the other hand, are instinctively drawn to materialism: 'the technique of machine production, expressed in cognition, unfailingly produces a materialist outlook' (ibid. 129). The materialism of the 'progressive' bourgeoisie expressed their link with technical progress; but, being the outlook of a privileged class, it could not do without various metaphysical fetishes. The materialism of the proletariat, however, rejected metaphysics and took a purely scientific view of the world. The word 'materialism' was really a survival, and was appropriate to the new outlook only in the sense that it was anti-metaphysical and anti-idealist.

The proletariat, as the class destined to sweep away class antagonisms and restore to mankind the unity of labour, knowledge, and will, was the best embodiment of man's natural tendency to extend his power over nature. The proletariat was the standard-bearer of technical progress, which required the elimination of everything that opposed individuals to one another. In present-day society social antagonisms had reached their peak and it was almost impossible for the classes to come to terms or understand one another. 'The opposition of normative and cognitive ideologies is increasing and is dividing the classes into two societies that regard each other in the same way as they do the forces of external nature' (ibid. 138). In the society of the future, however, there would be a return to perfect unity. In the solidarity of close co-operation men would have no reason to oppose their ego to others', all individual experiences would be harmonized, there would be 'a single society with a single ideology' (ibid. 139). This ideology, it need hardly be said, would be that of empiriomonism, as the most radical thought-form eschewing the traditional fetishes of metaphysics.

No other Marxist, perhaps, carried the doctrine of the primacy of productive forces over ideology to such an extreme as Bogdanov; nor did any express so consistently the collectivist ideal and the hope that individuality would disappear in the perfect society. The Utopia of the absolute unity of society in all respects was, to Bogdanov, a natural consequence of his Marxist faith. As all forms of spiritual life are wholly determined by the division of classes, and indirectly by the technical level of society, and as technical progress was the sole criterion of 'truth' and required the elimination of class antagonisms, it was clear that socialism would abolish all differentiation between human beings, and that the subjective sense of difference would lose its *raison d'être* when it no longer had an economic basis in the conflict of individual interests. These conclusions of Bogdanov's, which are not to be found in Marx himself, are a link between the former's views and the totalitarian Utopias of the eighteenth century.

The same doctrinaire belief, inherited from Marxist tradition, in the ancillary function of culture and its absolute dependence on technology led Bogdanov to the theory of 'proletarian culture' (Proletkult) and the belief that it was the proletariat's mission to effect a clean break in cultural history. Since the classes were so estranged and hostile that they regarded one another as things and not people, they could not possibly have a common culture. The culture of the proletariat must borrow nothing from the tradition of the privileged classes but must make a Promethean effort to create *ex nihilo*, paying attention to its own needs and to nothing else whatever.

In a pamphlet entitled *Science and the Working Class* (1920) and in other writings Bogdanov proclaimed the slogan of 'proletarian science'. Marx, adopting the standpoint of the working class, had transformed economics; it was now time to recast all sciences in accordance with the proletarian world-view, not excluding, for example, mathematics and astronomy. Bogdanov did not explain what proletarian astronomy or integral calculus would be like, but he declared that if workers had difficulty in mastering the various sciences without long, specialized study it was chiefly because bourgeois scientists had erected artificial barriers of method and vocabulary so that the workers should not learn their secrets.

The theory and practice of Proletkult did not find favour with the Bolshevik leaders except Bukharin, who edited *Pravda* after the Revolution and supported Bogdanov's idea in its columns. Trotsky was against it, and Lenin criticized it sharply on several occasions. This was not so much because some of its advocates, including Bogdanov, had fallen into philosophical heresy, but because the idea seemed to Lenin an idle fantasy unconnected with the party's true objectives. In a country with a huge percentage of illiterates the need was to teach them reading, writing, and arithmetic (the ordinary kind, not a proletarian version) and give them an elementary idea of technology and organization, not to pull civilization up by the roots and start again from zero. In any case Lenin did not share the view of some Proletkult enthusiasts and their

Futurist allies that the art and literature of past ages should be scrapped by the working class.

It was of course impossible for Proletkult to adhere consistently to the principle of a 'clean break', either in theory or, still more, in actual artistic production. None the less, Bogdanov and others had raised a question which is neither trivial nor absurd from the point of view of Marxist doctrine. Given that culture is 'nothing but' an instrument of class-interests—and Marx afforded much foundation for this view—and that proletarian interests are in all respects contrary to those of the bourgeoisie, at any rate 'at the stage of socialist revolution', how was it possible to defend the idea of cultural continuity or of a universal culture for all mankind? Did it not logically follow from Marxism that the proletariat, in the struggle for socialism, must not take over any part of the existing heritage? The theoreticians of Proletkult were, however, in an ambiguous position. In opposition to those who spoke of an 'art for all mankind' they quoted historical examples to show that different classes and periods had developed their own artistic forms; it was natural, therefore, that the proletariat should evolve an art of its own reflecting its struggle and its historical mission. But, at the same time, they accepted the notion that art was common to humanity, although every class and every period gave it different forms according to its own tastes and interests. In effect, therefore, they agreed that there was a continuing cultural heritage to be added to by each generation—a view in accordance with common sense, but not with the theory that art is purely a matter of class interests.

Before the October Revolution these disputes were of no great practical importance, but it was different when the Soviet state had to decide on its cultural policy and what it meant by 'proletarian culture'. Lunacharsky, Lenin's first Commissar for Education, had to solve practical problems in this field, and Proletkult became, especially from 1917 to 1921, a fairly large organization devoted to the cultivation of revolutionary art and science among the workers. Lunacharsky showed moderation and tolerance, especially in comparison with the doctrinaire attitude of the revolutionary *avant-garde*. His belief in the dependence of art on social class did not blind him to artistic values, although—like most Marxist theoreticians on art, at all events educated ones—he had difficulty in accommodating his 'bourgeois' tastes to his 'proletarian' ideology. Thus, although he hoped to see an upsurge of proletarian art in the future, and explained its absence in the present by such evident facts as the workers' lack of education, he never shared the fanaticism of the Proletkult extremists. He pursued a policy of repression—mild enough at this stage—towards bourgeois artists and writers, but he realized that art would wither and die under police control. The period of his authority—from 1917 to 1929—is regarded as the golden age of Soviet culture, though it did not seem so to those who were harassed even then for producing works with insufficient revolutionary spirit. The artistic merit of the twenties may have been exaggerated, but there is no comparison between them and, for instance, Zhdanov's dictatorship over Soviet cultural life after the Second World War.

6. The 'God-builders'

ANATOLY VASILYEVICH LUNACHARSKY (1875–1933) is noted in the history of Russian Marxism not only for helping to spread the empiriocritical heresy and for his work as a literary critic and dramatist (not of the first rank) and art theoretician, but also for his plan, which especially infuriated Lenin, for a 'socialist religion'.

This plan, known as 'God-building' (*Bogostroitelstvo*), was a Marxist counterpart to the general increase of interest in religion after the 1905 Revolution, just as the empiriocriticism of the social democrats was a result of the permeation of the revolutionary intelligentsia by philosophic modernism. The movement is chiefly associated with the names of Lunacharsky and Gorky, and was a kind of reconstruction of the 'religion of humanity' expounded by Comte and especially Feuerbach.

Lunacharsky developed his idea of an anthropocentric Marxist religion in several articles and in a book entitled *Religion and Socialism* (1908, second volume 1911). G. L. Kline, an authority on the Russian religious tradition, observes that the God-builders adopted not only Feuerbach's deification of humanity but, perhaps in an even greater degree, Nietzsche's ideal of the superman.

The new religion was to be an answer not only to the 'God-seeking' movement (*Bogoiskatelstvo*) of Christian philosophers but also to the arid old-fashioned atheism of Plekhanov and the other orthodox Marxists, for whom the history of religion was summed up in the opposition between it and science. Lunacharsky and Gorky argued that historical religions were not a mere bundle of superstitions but were the expression, albeit ideologically false, of desires and feelings that socialism should take over and ennoble, not destroy. The new religion was purely immanent and had no need of belief in God, the super-natural world, or personal immortality, but it embraced all that was positive and creative in traditional faiths: the sense of community, man's yearning to transcend himself, a profound communion with the universe and the rest of mankind. Religion had always set out to reconcile men with their lives and give them a sense of the meaning of existence: this, and not metaphysical explanation, was its chief function. The old myths had collapsed, but men still sought to find a meaning in life; socialism opened up dazzling prospects and was able to inspire feelings of unity and enthusiasm that deserved to be called religious. Marx was not only a scholar, but equally a religious prophet. In socialist religion God was replaced by humanity, a superior creation in which the individual could find an object of love and worship: he could thus rise above his insignificant ego and experience the joy of sacrificing his own interest to the infinite increase of collective Being. Man's affective identification with humanity would liberate him from the fear of suffering and death, restore his dignity and spiritual strength, and enhance his creative abilities. The new faith was a premonition of the great harmony of the future: individual mortality was cancelled by collective immortality, and human actions thus acquired a meaning. The true creator of God was the proletariat, and its revolution was the fundamental act of God-building.

All this Promethean rhetoric and deification of humanity, with its stress on a future harmony as a surrogate of transcendence for the individual, was in effect a repetition of Feuerbach's philosophy, with anthropology considered as 'the secret' of theology. It added nothing to Marxist philosophy, and was merely an attempt to give emotional colour to 'scientific socialism'. As in Feuerbach, the words 'religion' and 'religious feeling' were used as mere ornaments and were unrelated to any actual religious tradition. 'God-building' was an attempt to assimilate the neo-Romantic vocabulary and to channel the religious inclinations of the intelligentsia, and religious emotion generally, into the service of socialism. Plekhanov and Lenin, however, condemned it as a dangerous flirtation with 'religious obscurantism', and after the Revolution Lunacharsky dropped the 'new style' and reverted to the traditional language of atheism. Thereafter 'God-building' had no discernible influence on Marxist ideology.

7. Lenin's excursion into philosophy

WHILE the Russian empiriocritics mostly considered themselves Marxists, they did not conceal their contempt for the naïve and uncritical 'common-sense' philosophy of Engels and Plekhanov. In a letter of 25 February 1908 to Gorky Lenin described the history of the dispute with Bogdanov and his allies: he wrote that in 1903 Plekhanov had spoken to him of Bogdanov's errors but had not thought them particularly dangerous. During the 1905 Revolution he (Lenin) and Bogdanov had tacitly ruled out philosophy as a neutral field. In 1906, however, Lenin had read the third volume of *Empiriomonism* and been intensely irritated by it; he sent some lengthy critical remarks to Bogdanov which, however, have not survived. When *Essays on the Philosophy of Marxism* appeared in 1908, Lenin's exasperation knew no bounds.

> Every article made me furiously indignant. No, no, this is not Marxism! Our empirio-critics, empirio-monists and empirio-symbolists are floundering in a bog. To try to

persuade the reader that 'belief' in the reality of the external world is 'mysticism' (Bazarov); to confuse in the most disgraceful manner materialism with Kantianism (Bazarov and Bogdanov); to preach a variety of agnosticism (empirio-criticism) and idealism (empirio-monism); to teach the workers 'religious atheism' and 'worship' of the highest human potentials (Lunacharsky); to declare Engels's teaching on dialectics to be mysticism (Berman); to draw from the stinking well of some French 'positivists' or other, of agnostics or metaphysicians, the devil take them, with their 'symbolic theory of cognition' (Yushkevich)! No, really, it's too much. To be sure, we ordinary Marxists are not well up in philosophy, but why insult us by serving this stuff up to us as the philosophy of Marxism! (*Works*, vol. 13, p. 450)

Plekhanov, who had been directly attacked by the empiriocritics, was the first in the orthodox camp to cross swords with them in defence of Engels's traditional materialism; he denounced their philosophy as 'subjective idealism', treating the whole universe as the creation of the perceiving subject. When splits occurred in the party Plekhanov—with some reason, given the situation of the Bolshevik intelligentsia—associated in his attack the Bolshevism of his opponents with their idealist doctrine. He maintained that Russian empiriocriticism was a philosophic attempt to justify Bolshevik 'Blanquism', a policy which flouted Marxist theory by seeking to hasten social development by violent means instead of letting it happen naturally. Bolshevik voluntarism was of a piece with the voluntaristic epistemology which regarded knowledge as an act of subjective organization and not an account of things as they existed independently of the human mind. Empiriocriticism, Plekhanov claimed, was contrary to the realism and determinism of Marxist doctrine in the same way as Bolshevik policy was contrary to Marxist historical determinism.

In defending his realist position against the Machists Plekhanov went so far as to admit that human perceptions were not 'copies' of objects but were signs of hieroglyphics. Lenin was not slow to reproach him for this, describing it as an inadmissible concession to 'agnosticism'.

Lyubov Akselrod ('Orthodox') also took up the cudgels on Engels's behalf in an article against Bogdanov published in 1904, in which she said that Lenin had encouraged her to write it eighteen months earlier. Conscious (as she said) of her duty to the party, she argued that Mach and Bogdanov treated objects as collections of impressions, thus making mind the creator of nature, in direct opposition to Marxism. This subjective idealism, which defined society by its consciousness, would lead 'with remorseless consistency' to social conservatism. As Marx had shown, the dominant consciousness was that of the ruling class, and consequently 'subjectivism' meant perpetuating the existing society and giving up thoughts of the future as idle and utopian.

In *Philosophical Essays* (1906) Lyubov Akselrod attacked not only Bogdanov but also Berdyayev, Struve, the Kantians, and philosophic idealism in general. The book contains almost everything that Lenin later wrote in his rebuttal of empiriocriticism; it is more concise than Lenin, but equally crude in tenor. Two main arguments are advanced in support of the view that the external world is 'reflected' in our perceptions or 'corresponds' to them. In the first place, we distinguish true and false perceptions, delusions and 'correct' observations, and we could not do this if reality and our sensations were one and the same. Secondly, everyone knows that things are not in our heads, but outside them. Kant's philosophy was a compromise between materialism and idealism: he preserved the concept of an external world, but under pressure from theology and mysticism he described that world as unknowable. The compromise, however, will not work: our knowledge has its source either in consciousness or in matter, there is no third possibility. Matter cannot be defined, for it is 'primal fact', the 'essence of all things', the 'beginning and sole cause of all phenomena', the 'original substance', etc. Matter is 'given in experience' and can be known by sensual perception. Idealism asserts that there is no object without a subject, but science has shown that the earth existed before man, so consciousness must be the product of nature and not a condition of it. All our knowledge, including mathematical knowledge, comes from experience, which consists of the 'reflection' of external bodies in our minds. To claim, as Mach does, that the world is man's creation is to make science impossible, for science presupposes an external world as the object of its study. Idealism leads to reactionary conclusions in politics. Mach and Avenarius regard man as the measure of the universe, and 'this subjective theory is of great objective value: it is easy to prove by it that the poor are rich and the rich poor, as everything depends on subjective experience' (*Philosophical Essays*, p. 92). Subjective idealism also leads infallibly to solipsism, since if everything is in 'my' imagination there is no ground for belief in the existence of other subjects. This is the philosophy of primitive man: the savage believes, literally, in everything that comes into his head, confusing dreams with reality, false perceptions with true ones, and thought with actual being, in the same manner as Berkeley, Mach, Struve, and Bogdanov.

In the same work Lyubov Akselrod defends determinism against Stammler, who objected that it was inconsistent to believe both in historical determinism and in revolutionary will-power. On this point too she echoes Plekhanov's counter-argument: it is human beings who make history, but their acts and the effectiveness of their intentions depend on circumstances outside their control. There is no difference between natural and historical necessity or, therefore, between the methods of the natural and social sciences. Bourgeois ideologists claim that only the present is real: in so doing they express the fears of a class that history has doomed to destruction, but to Marxists the future is 'real' in that it can be foreseen in the light of historical laws.

It should be added that Lyubov Akselrod and Plekhanov both indicate that the term 'reflection' should not be taken literally. Sensations are not 'copies' of things in the same sense as mirror-images, but in the sense that their content depends on the objects that produce them.

Lenin evidently thought that Plekhanov and 'Orthodox' had not refuted empiriocriticism as thoroughly as it deserved, and he therefore entered the fray himself although conscious that his philosophical education was fairly rudimentary. He spent most of 1908 working on the subject, including several months in London, where he studied at the British Museum. The result was published in Moscow in 1909 in the form of a book entitled *Materialism and Empiriocriticism: Critical Comments on a Reactionary Philosophy.*

In attacking empiriocriticism Lenin was not especially concerned with the objections of various philosophers to the doctrine on grounds of internal consistency. His object was to show that it did not succeed in avoiding the 'basic problem of philosophy', that of the priority of mind over matter or vice versa, but was a piece of verbal jugglery concealing out-and-out Berkeleyan idealism, and was therefore calculated to uphold religious spiritualism and the interests of the exploiting classes.

Lenin's argument is based on the principle of 'partisanship' (*partiinost'*) in philosophy. He uses this term in two different senses. In the first place it means that there can be no middle position between materialism and idealism as Engels defined these, and that philosophers who claim to have transcended the opposition are merely disingenuous idealists. Moreover, all the main questions of philosophy are ancillary to this one. Whether the world is knowable, whether determinism holds true, what are the criteria of truth and the significance of time and space—all these questions are special instances or an extension of the 'basic problem': any answer given to them is either materialistic or idealistic in tendency, and the choice between the two cannot be avoided.

Secondly, 'partisanship' means to Lenin that philosophical theories are not neutral in the class struggle but are instruments of it. Every philosophy is in the service of some class-interest, and in a society torn by the class struggle this cannot be otherwise, whatever the intentions of the philosophers themselves. It is no more possible to be a non-party man in philosophy than in direct political action: 'non-partisans in philosophy are just as hopelessly thick-headed as they are in politics' (*Materialism and Empiriocriticism* v. 5; *Works*, vol. 14, p. 286). 'Non-partisanship in philosophy is only wretchedly masked servility to idealism and fideism' (vi. 5; ibid., p. 355). Only materialism can serve the interests of the working class, and idealist doctrines are instruments of the exploiters.

Lenin does not discuss the relations between these two meanings of 'partisanship', nor does he consider whether the association of philosophies and classes can be projected into the past: for example, did the materialist Hobbes and the plebeian Christian sectaries represent the ideology of the oppressed classes and of property-owners respectively? He confines himself to arguing that at the present time the basic social antagonism between the proletariat and the bourgeoisie corresponds to the division of philosophers into the materialist and the idealist camp. The connection of idealism with political reaction is most clearly shown by the fact, which Lenin regards as obvious, that all forms of idealism and, particularly, epistemological subjectivism are buttresses of religious faith, either in practice or as a matter of logical consistency. It was hard for Lenin to corroborate this charge against the empiriocritics, who on the basis of their own philosophy attacked all forms of religious faith; Berkeley, however, was an easier target, as he held that belief in the reality of matter, which his theory denied, was the chief support of atheism. Anyway, said Lenin, the disputes among idealists were of trifling importance: there was no basic difference between Berkeley, Hume, Fichte, the empiriocritics, and Christian theologians. The attacks of Catholic philosophers on subjective idealism were mere family quarrels; similarly, the empiriocritics' opposition to religion was a fraud intended to lull the vigilance of the proletariat and lead it by different paths in the same direction as religious mythology. 'The subtle epistemological crotchets of a man like Avenarius remain a professorial invention, an attempt to form a small philosophical sect "of his own"; but, as a matter of fact, in the general circumstances of the struggle of ideas and trends in modern society, the objective part played by these epistemological artifices is in every case the same, namely to clear the way for idealism and fideism, and to serve them faithfully' (vi. 4; ibid., p. 341).

It was easy to see, therefore, that the empiriocritics were deceiving their naïve readers when they claimed to construct a picture of the world in which the elements of experience were ontologically neutral, neither 'psychical' nor 'physical'. Mach and Avenarius, who differed in nothing but their fraudulent terminology, and their brother-philosophers in Germany, Britain, and Russia purported to reduce the world to a collection of impressions, so that 'material reality' became merely the product of consciousness. If they had consistently followed out their theory they would have ended up in the absurdity of solipsism, regarding the whole world as the creation of an individual subject. If they did not state this conclusion it was because they desired to mislead the reader or feared to reveal the emptiness of their own doctrine. In any case they were lackeys of the clergy and unintelligible word-spinners, out to deceive the simpleminded and confuse the true philosophical issue, while the bourgeoisie took advantage of the people's bewilderment to maintain itself in power. 'Every one of us knows what is physical and what is mental, but none of us knows at present what that "third" is. Avenarius was merely covering up his tracks by this subterfuge, while *in fact* declaring that the self is the primary (central term) and nature (environment) the secondary (counter-term)' (iii. 1; ibid., p. 147).

But, Lenin continues, science enables us to refute this idealist nonsense. No educated person doubts that the earth existed before the appearance of mankind. But the idealist cannot admit this, for on his own premises he must hold that the earth and the whole physical world is a figment of the human mind. Contrary to the plain facts of science, he must argue that man came first and nature second. Moreover, we know that man thinks with his brain, which is a physical object; but the idealist cannot admit this either, since he regards all physical objects as the product of thought. It is clear, therefore, that idealism contradicts the most elementary scientific knowledge and is contrary to all progress, whether social or intellectual.

Having thus demolished idealism Lenin opposes to it the philosophy of the militant proletariat, i.e. dialectical materialism. A fundamental part of this is the theory of reflections or images, according to which sensations, abstract ideas, and all other aspects of human cognition are the reflection in our minds of actual qualities of the material world, which exists whether or not it is perceived by anyone. 'Matter is a philosophical category denoting the objective reality which is given to man by his sensations, and which is copied, reflected and photographed by our sensations while existing independently of them' (ii. 4; ibid., p. 130). As Lenin repeats again and again, it is literally a question of 'copying': our sensations are images of things, not merely effects or, as Plekhanov would have it, 'symbols'. 'Engels speaks neither of symbols nor of hieroglyphs, but of copies, photographs, images, mirror-reflections of things' (iv. 6; ibid., p. 232). Sensations are not a screen between us and the world but a link with it, a subjective imitation of it.

Dialectical materialism does not claim to solve the physical problems concerning the structure of matter, but that is not its business. It can accept all that physics tells us, 'for the sole property of matter with whose recognition philosophical materialism is bound up is the property of being an objective reality, of existing outside the mind' (v. 2; ibid., pp. 260–1).

On this last point Lenin is inconsistent, for he himself confidently answers various questions of physics: for example, he says that it is reactionary nonsense to claim that there can be more than three dimensions, and all forms of indeterminism are likewise nonsensical. As to matter being defined simply by its property of 'existing outside the mind', this was later a subject of dispute among Leninists, as it suggested that matter must be characterized by its relation to the experiencing subject, so that mind enters into the concept of matter as its correlative; in the same way Lenin uses 'objective' to mean 'independent of mind'. Elsewhere he says, following Lyubov Akselrod, that matter cannot be defined, as it is the broadest category of all and therefore cannot be expressed in particular terms; he does not attempt to reconcile this with the statement quoted above.

An essential part of the theory of reflection is the rejection of relativism and acceptance of the traditional idea of truth as conformity to reality. Truth, says Lenin, can be predicated of sensations, concepts, and judgements. We can say of any product of cognitive activity that it is true or false, i.e. a right or wrong 'reflection' of reality; that it presents the world as it is 'in itself', independent of our knowledge, or that it gives a distorted picture of the world. But the objectivity of truth does not conflict with its relativity, as Engels showed. The relativity of truth does not mean, as, for example, pragmatists argue, that the same judgement is true or false according to who pronounces it and in what circumstances, and what benefit accrues from assenting to it at the time. Science, as Engels pointed out, can never tell us with absolute certainty the limits within which its laws are valid, and consequently they are all liable to revision. This, however, does not change truth into falsehood or vice versa, but merely signifies that what was thought to be universally valid applies only in certain conditions. No truths are ultimately verified, and in that sense all are relative. All knowledge, too, is relative in the sense that we can never know all about the universe and that although our knowledge continues to expand it remains incomplete. But these reservations do not affect the concept of truth as conformity to reality. As Engels also said, the most effective criterion of truth, i.e. the best way to find out whether a judgement is true, is to put it to the test of practice. If we can apply to practical manipulations the discoveries we have made concerning natural relationships, the success of our actions will confirm that our judgements were the right ones, and failure will prove the opposite. The practical criterion can be applied equally in natural science and in social science, where our analysis of reality is confirmed if the political actions based on it are effective. This effectiveness is not 'utility' in the pragmatist sense: our knowledge is potentially useful because it is true, it is not true because it is useful. Marxist theory, in particular, has been signally confirmed by practice: the successes of the workers' movement based on it are the best proof of its validity.

Once we have recognized the objective nature of truth, the empiriocritical principle of 'economy of thought' is seen to be an idealist subterfuge, purporting to replace conformity with reality by an ill-defined criterion consisting in the economy of effort.

It is also clear that the empiriocritics' objections to Kant's philosophy are aimed 'from the right', i.e. from a more reactionary position than his. They challenge the distinction between the phenomenon and the noumenon, but they do so in order to show that the 'thing in itself' is superfluous, i.e. there is no reality independent of mind. Materialists, however, criticize Kant from the opposite point of view—not for recognizing that there is a world beyond phenomena, but for holding that we can know nothing about it. There is no difference, they contend, between the phenomenon and the thing in itself, inasmuch as there is no reality that cannot in principle be known; they condemn Kant's agnosticism, while recognizing the 'materialist element' in his idea of the reality of the world. From the materialist point of view reality may be divided into the known and the not yet known, but not into phenomena that can be known and 'things in themselves' that cannot.

As regards such categories as space, time, and causality, Lenin follows Engels's interpretation. Dialectical materialism does not regard causality as a functional dependence, but there is a true necessity in the relations between events. Practice is the best confirmation of the real necessity of the causal connection: whenever we observe a regular sequence of events and are able thereby to produce a desired consequence, we demonstrate that the cause-and-effect relation is not the work of our imagination but a real quality of the physical world. Such connections must, however, be understood dialectically: in cases where types of events and not merely single events are involved there is always a mutual interaction, though one element retains its primacy (not defined more closely) over the other. Time and space are neither the product of an organizing perceptual force, nor *a priori* forms of sensibility, nor antonomous entities independent of matter; they are objective qualities of physical being. Thus the relations of succession in time and arrangement in space are real properties of the world, but do not possess the status of independent metaphysical entities.

Lenin holds that dialectical materialism as expounded by him is not only an effective weapon in the practical sense but is also the only philosophy consistent with the present state of natural and social science. It is because the physicists themselves do not understand this that science is, or appears to be, in a crisis. 'Modern physics is in travail: it is giving birth to dialectical materialism' (v. 8; ibid., p. 313). Scientists must realize that dialectical materialism is the only way out of the trouble they have got into through ignorance of Marx and Engels. It will soon triumph even though some scientists oppose it, the reason for their attitude being that most of them are servants of the bourgeoisie, though they have achieved great things in specialized fields.

Lenin's book is of interest not for its own merits but for its influence on the development of philosophy in Russia. As philosophy it is crude and amateurish, based on vulgar 'commonsense' arguments eked out by quotations from Engels (only two sentences by Marx are quoted in the whole book) and unbridled abuse of Lenin's opponents. It shows complete failure to understand their point of view, and reluctance to make the effort to do so. It adds hardly anything to what is contained in the passages quoted from Engels and Plekhanov, the main difference being that Engels has a sense of humour and Lenin none. He makes up for it with cheap mockery and invective, decrying his adversaries as reactionary madmen and lackeys of the clergy. Engels's arguments are vulgarized and turned into cut-and-dried catechetical forms: sensations are 'copies' or 'mirror-reflections' of things, philosophical schools become 'parties', etc. The exasperation which pervades the book is typical of a primitive thinker who cannot understand how anyone of sound mind can seriously maintain (as Lenin supposes) that by the power of his own imagination he has created the earth, the stars, and the whole physical universe, or that the objects he is looking at are in his head when any child can see that they are not. In this respect Lenin's battle with idealism is similar to that of certain unsophisticated Christian apologists.

Lenin's attacks were answered by Bogdanov, Bazarov, and Yushkevich: the latter, in *Pillars of Philosophical Orthodoxy* (1910), attacked Plekhanov as a flat-footed ignoramus who had no more idea of philosophy than a gendarme. Both Plekhanov and Lenin, he declared, exemplified the decadence of Russian Marxism by their dogmatic self-assertion and inability to understand anyone's views but their own. Yushkevich was especially severe on Lenin's ignorance, his inability to write, and the coarseness of his language: he accused him of factual errors, of 'bringing the habits of the Black Hundred into Marxism', of not having read the books he quoted, etc. The definition of matter by its power to cause sensations was itself a capitulation to Machism—this applied to Plekhanov, and to Lenin who had copied from him. Neither Mach nor Berkeley had questioned the 'existence of the world': the question at issue was not its existence but the validity of categories like substance, matter, and spirit. The empiriocritics, said Yushkevich, had achieved a Copernican revolution by abolishing the dualism of mind and matter; they had changed nothing in man's natural relation to the world but, on the contrary, restored the spontaneous value of realism by freeing it from metaphysical fetishes. Lenin in fact confused epistemological realism with materialism (he repeats several times that materialism consists of recognizing 'objective material reality', 'independent of the subject'—but if so, nearly every Catholic philosopher is a materialist). The whole theory of 'reflection' was a repetition of the naïve pre-Democritean belief in images that detach themselves mysteriously from the object and strike upon one's eye or ear. No one can say what the 'similarity' is supposed to be between the 'thing in itself' and a purely subjective image of it, or how the copy can be compared with the original.

Materialism and Empiriocriticism had no particular influence before the Revolution or directly after it (though a second edition appeared in 1920). Later it was proclaimed by Stalin to be a fundamental epitome of Marxist philosophy, and for about fifteen years, together with a short work by Stalin himself, it was the chief source of philosophical learning in the Soviet Union. Slight as its value was, it represented one of the last points of contact between orthodox Leninist

Marxism and European philosophy. In later decades there was virtually no contact, even in the form of polemics, between Leninism and non-Marxist thought. The official Soviet criticism of 'bourgeois philosophy' took for granted that the latter in its various forms was a repetition of the idealist nonsense of Mach and Avenarius, which had been annihilated by Lenin's refutation.

The importance of Lenin's book, however, must be seen in the political context. It does not appear that when writing it he had any intention of 'enriching', supplementing, or—Heaven forbid—reforming Marxism. He was not in search of answers to any philosophical questions, for all the important ones had been solved by Marx and Engels; in his preface he mocks at Lunacharsky for saying 'Perhaps we have gone astray, but we are seeking.' Lenin was not seeking. He believed firmly that the revolutionary movement must have a clear-cut, uniform *Weltanschauung*, and that any pluralism in this respect was a grave political danger. He also believed that idealism of any kind was a more or less disguised form of religion, which was invariably used by exploiters to delude and stupefy the masses.

8. Lenin and religion

LENIN regarded religion as a key issue in the party's ideological activity, since the adversary was a mass phenomenon and not merely a group of theoreticians like the empiriocritics. His own attitude towards it was absolutely clear as a matter of philosophy, but his tactics were relatively flexible and changeable.

Lenin was brought up in an unbigoted religious atmosphere; he lost his faith at the age of fifteen or sixteen, before he had any contact with Marxism. From then on he took atheism for granted as scientifically self-evident, and at no time argued the case for it on merits. The problems of religion, in his view, presented no substantive difficulties but were matters of education, politics, and propaganda. In 'Socialism and Religion' (1905; *Works*, vol. 10) and some later writings he argues that religious beliefs are an expression of the impotence of the oppressed and poverty-stricken masses, an imaginary compensation for their sufferings—'spiritual booze', as he puts it (p. 83), coarsening in his usual way the language of Marx and Engels. At the same time religion and the Churches were a means of keeping the masses humble and submissive, an 'ideological knout' to keep the exploiters in power and the masses in a state of misery. The Orthodox Church was a glaring example of the conjunction of spiritual and political oppression. Lenin also laid stress on the need to exploit the repressive attitude of the regime towards religious sectarians. The party programme spoke from the outset of religious tolerance, the right of the individual to profess any faith he chose, and also the right to carry on atheistic propaganda; Church and State were to be separated, and the public teaching of religion abolished. But, unlike many Western social democrats, Lenin emphasized that while socialists might regard religion as a private matter vis-à-vis the state, it was not private so far as the party was concerned. In present conditions the party must tolerate believers in its midst (atheism did not figure expressly in its programme), but it was committed to carrying on anti-religious propaganda and educating its members to be militant atheists. The party could not be philosophically neutral: it was materialistic, therefore atheistic and anti-clerical, and this world-outlook could not be a matter of political indifference. However, anti-religious propaganda must be linked with the class struggle and not treated as an end in itself in the spirit of 'bourgeois free thought'.

Whatever his tactical concessions, Lenin was on political grounds an implacable opponent of religious belief. Hence the violence of his attack on the empiriocritics, whose philosophy coincided in part with that of the 'God-builders'. The latter were only trying to add rhetorical and sentimental trimmings to Marxism, but in Lenin's eyes they were engaged in a perilous compromise with religion. In his main philosophical work, in letters to Gorky, and on other occasions he argued that religion stripped of its cruder superstitions and using the language of social progress was even more dangerous than the besotted Orthodox Church which brutally proclaimed its union with Tsarist despotism. Religion in a humanist disguise was all the better able to conceal its class content and delude the unwary. Thus, while Lenin was prepared to compromise with believers on tactical grounds, his mind was firmly made up on the question of substance and he refused to admit any suggestion that the party's world-view could leave any room whatsoever for religious faith.

Lenin's position in these matters was in accordance with the Russian free-thinking tradition. The link between the Orthodox Church and the Tsarist bureaucracy was manifest. When the Soviet government came to power, most, though not all, churchmen were hostile to it. Owing to this and to the basic principles of Leninism, the fight against the Church soon took on wider dimensions than those indicated in the party's programmes. The government did not confine itself to expropriating Church estates and secularizing schools, measures which in any case were regarded as bourgeois reforms and not specifically socialist. The Church was in practice deprived of all public functions and prevented from teaching, publishing books and periodicals, and educating the clergy; monasteries and convents were for the most part dissolved. The treatment of religion as a private affair vis-à-vis the state could not apply in a one-party system in which party membership was, in the vast majority of cases, a precondition of state service. Persecution of the Church and the faithful varied in intensity according to political circumstances—it was much relaxed, for instance, during the war of 1941-5—but the principle that the socialist state must strive in every way to eradicate 'religious prejudices' has remained in force and is wholly in accordance with Lenin's doctrine. The separation of Church and State is only workable when the state is ideologically neutral and does not, as such, profess any particular world-view. The Soviet state, regarding itself as the organ of the proletariat and atheism as an essential feature of the one and only proletarian ideology, can no more accept the principle of disestablishment than, say, the Vatican with its similarly built-in ideology. Lenin and the other Marxists always held that there was no difference in this respect between a proletarian and a bourgeois state, both of which were bound to support a philosophy that represented the interests of the ruling class. But for this very reason the separation of Church and State, which Lenin used as a battlecry against the Tsardom, was contrary to his theory of the relations between ideology, classes, and the state and could not be maintained after the Bolsheviks seized power. On the other hand, the nature and scale of anti-religious measures was of course not prescribed by the doctrine and varied according to circumstances.

9. Lenin's dialectical Notebooks

APART from occasional passages in articles and speeches, Lenin wrote nothing further on purely philosophical subjects. (His article of 1921 on 'The Significance of Militant Materialism' is in the nature of a propaganda directive; that of 1913 on 'The Three Sources and Three Component Parts of Marxism' is a popular exposition and has no claim to originality.) However, there appeared posthumously in the Soviet Union a volume entitled *Philosophical Notebooks* (*Works*, vol. 38) consisting of extracts made by Lenin from various works and manuals, chiefly in 1914–15, together with approving or exasperated comments and some philosophical observations of his own. In certain cases it is not clear whether the notes are summaries of what he has read or represent his own position. The book is of interest inasmuch as the principal notes are concerned with the dialectic and to some extent tone down the crude formulas of *Materialism and Empiriocriticism*. They show, in particular, the influence of Lenin's wartime reading of Hegel's *Logic* and *Lectures on the Philosophy of History*. These convinced him that the Hegelian dialectic was of great importance in the development of Marxism: he even wrote that *Capital* could not be understood without a thorough study of Hegel's *Logic*, and added with irreproachable consistency: 'So, after half a century, no Marxist has yet understood Marx.' This *boutade* should not be taken literally, for it is hard to believe that Lenin did not think he himself had understood Marx until 1915, but it shows to what extent he was fascinated by Hegel's speculation.

As the *Notebooks* show, Lenin was most interested by the question of 'universality' and 'individuality' in Hegel's logic and by the dialectic considered as a theory of the 'unity and conflict of opposites.' He sought to discover in Hegel's dialectic the themes which could be taken over and used by Marxism after the transposition to a materialist basis. As to the question of abstraction and the relation between direct perception and 'universal' knowledge, Lenin emphasized everything in Hegel that was opposed to Kant's doctrine (for example, that the 'thing in itself was completely indefinite and was therefore nothing) and pointed out the autonomous cognitive function of abstract thinking: according to Lenin logic, dialectic, and the theory of knowledge were all the same thing. Whereas *Materialism and Empiriocriticism* concentrated on combating the subjective interpretation of sensations and seemed content to regard them as the source of all knowledge of the world, the *Notebooks* raise the question of abstractions that are contained in perception itself and introduce unending 'contradictions' into the cognitive process. Laws, and hence 'universality', are already contained in the particular phenomenon, and similarly the individual perception contains 'universal' elements, i.e. acts of abstraction. Nature is thus both concrete and abstract; things are what they are only in terms of conceptual knowledge, which apprehends them in their general regularity. The concrete cannot be grasped in its full concreteness by a particular act of perception. On the contrary, it reproduces itself only through an infinite number of concepts and general laws, so that it is never exhausted by cognition. Even the simplest phenomenon reveals the complexity of the world and the interdependence of all its components; but because all phenomena are thus interconnected, human knowledge is necessarily incomplete and fragmentary. In order to apprehend the concrete in all its particularity we should have to have absolute and universal knowledge of all the connections between phenomena. Every 'reflection' of the world suffers from internal contradictions which, as knowledge progresses, disappear and are replaced by new contradictions. The reflection is not 'dead' or 'inert', but by its fragmentary nature and contradictions gives rise to the increase of knowledge, which continues indefinitely but never reaches absolute finality. Thus truth manifests itself only as the process of the resolution of contradictions.

Since there is always a certain tension or 'contradiction' between the particular and the abstract components of knowledge, it is always possible in the cognitive process to absolutize the latter at the expense of the former, i.e. to think in idealist terms. Along with Lenin's emphasis on the 'universal' aspects of the 'reflection' (which is contrary to the description of it in his main philosophical work), this idea is a second important departure from the rough-and-ready interpretation of idealism as a fraud invented by the clergy and the bourgeoisie. Idealism, it now appears, has 'gnoseological sources': it is not just a mental aberration, but the absolutization or one-sided development of a real aspect of cognition. Lenin even remarks that wise idealism is closer to wise materialism than is foolish materialism.

The second important subject of the *Notebooks* is the 'conflict and unity of opposites'. The whole of the dialectic, Lenin claims, can be defined as the science of the unity of opposites. Among the sixteen 'elements of the dialectic' which he enumerates, the conflict of opposites appears in various forms as the main motif. Every single thing is the sum and unity of opposites, every property of things turns into its opposite; content 'conflicts' with form, features of lower stages of development are reproduced in higher ones by the 'negation of the negation', etc.

All these ideas are expressed in very brief and general terms and are therefore not suited to over-precise analysis. Lenin does not inquire how 'contradiction', a logical relationship, can be a property of objects themselves; nor does he explain how the introduction of abstractions into the content of perception fits into the theory of 'reflections'. It can be seen, however, that like Engels he regarded the dialectic as a universal method that could be expounded, irrespective of object, as a generalized 'logic of the world', and that he treated Hegel's logic as the raw material of a materialistic transformation. However, his remarks in general suggest an interpretation of Hegelianism that is less simplified than Engels's. The dialectic is not merely an assertion that 'everything changes', but an attempt to interpret human knowledge as a perpetual interplay between subject and object, in which the question of the 'absolute primacy' of either loses its sharpness.

The *Notebooks* were published mainly to serve the party in its critique of mechanistic materialism. While party philosophers used *Materialism and Empiriocriticism* to combat all doctrines suspected of idealism, they quoted the *Notebooks* to emphasize the difference between Marxism and mechanicism, especially in the campaign against Bukharin and his followers in the 1930s. There was of course no question of admitting that the two texts were in any way inconsistent with each other. Later, when the teaching of dialectical materialism in the Soviet Union departed from the schema laid down by Stalin, the *Notebooks* were used as the new basis and the sixteen 'elements' took the place of Stalin's 'four main features of the dialectic'. However, *Materialism and Empiriocriticism* is still revered as the philosophical foundation of Leninism, a status conferred on it by Stalin. It has had a deplorable effect in furnishing pretexts for the stifling of all independent philosophical thought and in establishing the party's dictatorship over science and culture in every sphere.

As Valentinov and others pointed out, the extreme obstinacy with which Lenin defended materialism was rooted not only in Marxism but in the tradition of the Russian materialists, especially Chernyshevsky, whose philosophy was a popularization of Feuerbach. Comment on these lines was also heard in the Soviet Union in the 1950s, but was condemned as it suggested that Leninism was a specifically Russian philosophy and not the infallible, universally valid continuation of Marxism.

Apart from the question of the influence of Russian sources, it is clear that Lenin's philosophy was closely linked with his political programme and the idea of a revolutionary party, and that he himself was fully aware of this. A party of professionals in which all theoretical questions were strictly subordinated to the struggle for power could not safely countenance philosophic pluralism or be neutral in ideological questions. For the sake of its own success it must possess a clearly defined doctrine or body of inexpugnable dogma, binding upon its members. Party discipline and cohesion demanded that any risk of laxity, vagueness, or pluralism in theoretical matters should be eliminated. That the ruling ideology must be strictly materialist was ensured by Marxist tradition and by the need to combat religious thought in all its forms as an obstacle to revolution, as well as to avoid an ontologically neutral philosophy. Lenin castigated, in friend and foe alike, any tendency to compromise even verbally with religion, or to side-step ontological questions on the ground that they were wrongly formulated or insoluble. Marxism, he believed, was a ready-made answer to all the major questions of philosophy and admitted of no doubts. Any attempt to shelve philosophical questions was a threat to the party's ideological unity. Thus his coarse, uncompromising materialism was not only the effect of a particular tradition but was part and parcel of his technique for action. The party must have the sole right to decide all ideological questions, and from this point of view Lenin well understood the danger that idealism presented to his political programme. The idea of totalitarian power, embracing every aspect of cultural life, was gradually taking shape in his mind and was eventually put into practice; it was well served by his philosophy, which was not concerned with investigating and solving problems but with imposing a dogmatic intellectual system on the socialist movement. In this way the fury of his philosophical attacks and lack of interest in others' arguments had their roots in his political doctrine.

Even for Leninists, however, *Materialism and Empiriocriticism* was ambiguous on two important points. Firstly, as already mentioned, Lenin held, unlike Engels and Plekhanov, that 'objectivity', i.e. independence of the subject, was the only attribute of matter that materialists as such were bound to recognize. This statement was evidently designed to free Marxist philosophy from any dependence on changing scientific theories, especially in physics: as 'matter' suffered no harm from any attributes that science might bestow or take away from it, science presented no danger to materialism. But this gain was achieved by emptying 'matter' of all content. If matter is defined simply by the fact of being something other than the perceiving subject, it is clear that this can equally be said of any 'substance' that is regarded as differing from the content of perception. 'Matter' becomes simply another term for 'everything', without implying any of the attributes—spatial, temporal, or dynamic—that we generally associate with 'materiality'. Secondly, this definition readmits the vague dualism that it purports to exclude. If everything 'outside' the subject is material, then either the subject itself is not material or we must extend the definition of matter to comprise subjective phenomena. The formula that 'matter is primary and mind secondary' appears to presuppose that mind and matter are different, and is thus contrary to materialist monism. Lenin's work does not answer these problems or deal with them consistently, and there is no point in trying to probe more closely: the obscurities of his text are not due so much to inherent philosophical difficulties as to Lenin's indolent and superficial approach and his contempt for all problems that could not be put to direct use in the struggle for power.

XVIII

The Fortunes of Leninism: from a
Theory of the State to a State Ideology

1. The Bolsheviks and the War

THE YEARS 1908–11 were a period of catastrophic decline and disintegration in the Russian social democratic movement. After the post-revolutionary repressions there was a temporary stabilization of the Tsarist regime, as civil liberties were considerably increased and attempts were made to base the weakened social structure on other foundations than the bureaucracy and the army. Stolypin, the Prime Minister, introduced reforms designed to create a strong class of peasantry with medium-sized holdings. These measures aroused the alarm of socialists, especially those of the Leninist persuasion, who realized that if the agrarian question could be solved under capitalism by means of reform, the revolutionary potential of the land-hungry masses would be irretrievably lost. In an article of 29 April 1908 entitled 'On the Beaten Track!' (*Works*, vol. 15, pp. 40 ff.) Lenin recognized that Stolypin's policy might succeed and might establish a 'Prussian road' of capitalist development in agriculture. If this happened, 'Marxists who are honest with themselves will straightforwardly and openly throw all "agrarian programmes" on the scrapheap altogether, and will say to the masses: "The workers have done all they could to give Russia not a Junker but an American capitalism. The workers call you now to join in the social revolution of the proletariat, for after the solution of the agrarian question in the Stolypin spirit there can be no other revolution capable of making a serious change in the economic conditions of life of the peasant masses."'

Stolypin's policy did not last long enough to bring about the hoped-for results, which might have completely altered the later course of events: Lenin wrote after 1917 that the Revolution could not have succeeded had the Bolsheviks not taken over the S.R. programme of confiscating the land and sharing it out to the peasants. Despite the assassination of Stolypin in 1911, for some years Russia was clearly moving in the direction of a bourgeois state with the rudiments of a constitutional monarchy. This development led to new divisions among the social democrats. In addition to the 'otzovists', i.e. those Bolsheviks who believed exclusively in illegal revolutionary action, Lenin at this time incessantly attacked the 'liquidators', a term more or less synonymous with the Mensheviks. He accused Martov, Potresov, Dan, and most of the other Menshevik leaders of wishing to liquidate the illegal party organization and replace it by a 'formless' legal assembly of workers, geared to a 'reformist' struggle within the existing order. The Mensheviks did not in fact wish to wind up the party's illegal activity, but they attached much more importance to peaceful methods and to the legal development of workers' organizations, hoping that when the autocracy was overthrown the social democrats would be in a similar position to their brothers in Western Europe. Meanwhile the old intra-party divisions continued to exist. The Mensheviks accepted the Austrian recipe for the national question ('ex-territorial autonomy'), while the Bolsheviks advocated self-determination including the right of secession. The Mensheviks maintained their links with the Bund and the Polish Socialists, both of which Lenin regarded as organs of bourgeois nationalism. However, Plekhanov, unlike most of the Menshevik leaders, was against the policy of the 'liquidators', and accordingly Lenin dropped his campaign of abuse and polemics against him and reverted to a kind of shaky alliance with the veteran of Russian socialism.

The various dissensions resulted in a new and final split in the party. In January 1912 the Bolshevik Conference at Prague declared itself to be a general party congress, elected its own Central Committee, and broke with the Mensheviks. Besides Lenin, Zinoviev, and Kamenev the Central Committee included Roman Malinovsky, the Okhrana agent, against whom Lenin was repeatedly warned by the Mensheviks: he called these warning 'the filthiest slander they could collect in the garbage heaps of the Black-Hundred newspapers' ('The Liquidators and Malinovsky's Biography', May 1914; *Works*, vol. 20, p. 204). Malinovsky was indeed an obedient executor of Lenin's orders, as the Okhrana had instructed him to be, and he had no ideological or political ambitions of his own. Shortly after the Prague Conference Stalin was co-opted on to the Central Committee at Lenin's instance, thus making his début in the field of Russian social-democratic politics.

Lenin spent the last two years before the outbreak of war at Cracow and the nearby resort of Poronin, whence it was easier to maintain contact with the organization in Russia. The Bolsheviks neglected no opportunity of legal action. From 1912 they published *Pravda* in St. Petersburg; the paper reappeared after the February Revolution and has been the party daily ever since. There were a few Bolshevik members of the Duma, who co-operated with the Mensheviks until forbidden to do so by Lenin.

The outbreak of war found Lenin at Poronin. Arrested by the Austrian police, he was set free a few days later thanks to the intervention of the PPS and the Vienna social democrats. He then returned to Switzerland, where he remained until April 1917, fulminating against the 'opportunist traitors' who had wrecked the International and working out directives for revolutionary social democracy in the new situation. Lenin was the first and only important leader of social democracy in Europe to proclaim the slogan of revolutionary defeatism: the proletariat in each country should endeavour to bring about the military defeat of its own government so as to turn the imperialist war into a civil war. Out of the ruins of the International, most of whose leaders had gone over to the service of the imperialists, there must be created a Communist International to direct the revolutionary struggle of the proletariat.

These appeals might well have seemed idle dreams, as only a handful of socialists were prepared to support them. Most social democrats took the view that they should suspend the class struggle and rally to the defence of their country. Among the Russians who thought in this way was Plekhanov, who, while continuing to profess himself a Marxist, whole-heartedly accepted the patriotic viewpoint. This sharply put an end to the truce between him and Lenin, and Plekhanov and Potresov were once more decried as 'clowns' and lackeys of the reactionary leader Purishkevich. Lenin took a similar view of all social-ist leaders who based their attitude on the principle of national self-defence, such as Hyndman in Britain and Guesde and Hervé in France: naturally there were no 'aggressors' among the belligerent powers. By degrees, however, anti-war groups were formed in all countries, mostly by socialists who had formerly occupied a central position: Bernstein, Kautsky, and Ledebour in Germany, Ramsay MacDonald in Britain. Here too belonged most of the former Men-sheviks, headed by Martov and Akselrod, and also Trotsky. For a time, despite their fundamental differences, Lenin's group sought to come to terms with these 'pacifists'. Owing principally to the efforts of Swiss and Italian socialists an inter-national conference was held at Zimmerwald in September 1915 and adopted a compromise anti-war resolution. Zimmerwald was regarded for a while as the embryo of a new international movement, but after the Russian Revolution the divergences between the centre and the Zimmerwald Left proved stronger than the conflict between the pacifists and the 'social chauvinists', as the defenders of their country at any price were called. The Zimmerwald Left, consisting of seven out of the thirty-eight delegates, in addition to signing the general reso-lution issued one of their own, calling on socialists to resign from imperialist governments and found a new revolutionary International.

At an early stage Lenin attacked the anti-war, pacifist social democrats almost as fiercely as he did the 'social chauvinists'. His main objections were, firstly, that the centrists wanted peace through international arbitration and agreement, not by waging a revolutionary war against their own governments. This meant a return to the pre-war order and a quest for peace by 'bourgeois' methods. The centrists were evidently lackeys of the bourgeoisie, and they failed to see that the only way to stop imperialist war was by a revolution that would at least overthrow the three great continental empires. Secondly, the pacifists wanted 'peace without annexations or indemnities', by which they meant only to cancel wartime annexations, thus preserving the old empires with all their nationalist oppression. The revolutionary objective must be, however, to invalidate all annexations and secure the right of all peoples to self-determination and, if they so desired, to form their own national states. Lenin was on strong ground in condemning socialists who inveighed against annexation and oppression, but only when perpetrated by their national enemies. The Germans were full of indignation at the treatment of subject nationalities in Russia, but said nothing about conditions in the Reich and Austria-Hungary; Russian and French socialists demanded freedom for the subjects of the Central Powers, but kept quiet about those of the Tsar. Finally, although the pacifists condemned chauvinism in words they could not make up their minds to break with the opportunists once and for all, but dreamed of reuniting with them and resurrecting the corpse of the International. This point is especially important. As on the occasion of all previous disputes and splits within the party, Lenin showed equal ferocity against his opponents and against 'appeasers' in his own camp, who hesitated to break completely with the opposition and thus sacrificed their principles to a hankering for organizational unity. The centrists condemned Lenin's attitude as fanatical and sectarian, and it is true that on several occasions it appeared to have reduced him to the leadership of a helpless, isolated group. In the end, however, he was proved right inasmuch as no other tactics could have produced such a centralized, disciplined party as the Bolsheviks, and at the critical moment a more loosely organized party could not have mastered the situation and seized power.

During his last years outside Russia Lenin wrote what is perhaps the most generally known of his works: *Imperialism, the Highest Stage of Capitalism* (published at Petrograd, 1917). This pamphlet—the economic portions of which contain nothing that is not to be found in Lenin's main sources, Hobson and Hilferding—was intended to serve as a theoretical basis for the new tactics that were to dominate the revolutionary party. Stressing the worldwide character and uneven development of imperialism, Lenin laid the foundation for the tactics which were soon to become binding on Communist parties: the right course was to support any movement tending to overthrow the system at any point, for any reasons and in the interests of any class: liberation in colonial countries, national or peasant movements, bourgeois national uprisings against the big imperialists. This was a generalization of the tactics he had been preaching in Russia for years: to support all claims and all movements against the Tsarist autocracy, so as to exploit their sources of energy and seize power at the critical moment. The victory of the Marxist party was the final aim, but it could not be achieved by the proletariat alone. Lenin soon came to the conclusion, in fact, that a revolution could not be carried out by the working class in its own name, without the support of other mass movements such as the nationalities or the peasants; in other words, a socialist revolution in the traditional Marxist sense was an impossibility. This discovery was the source of nearly all the successes of Leninism, and nearly all its failures.

The question of relations with the peasantry was at this time one of the main points of disagreement between Lenin and Trotsky. Up to the outbreak of war Trotsky lived chiefly in Vienna, where from 1908 onwards he edited his own journal *Pravda* (in 1912 he accused the Bolsheviks of stealing its title). He worked with the Mensheviks from time to time on various questions but did not join them, as he held different views of the coming revolution, prophesying that it would evolve into a socialist phase. He made repeated but unsuccessful efforts to restore party unity. From 1914 he belonged to the anti-war wing and joined Lenin in attacking 'social patriotism'; he also drafted the Zimmerwald Manifesto. Together with Martov he published a journal in Paris to which Lunacharsky and other leading social democratic intellectuals contributed. From the Second Congress until 1917, when he joined the Bolsheviks, he was the object of exceptional hostility on Lenin's part, whether or not they agreed on actual issues. Lenin described him, according to circumstances, as a noisy phrase-maker, a play-actor, an intriguer, a go-between, and a 'Yudushka' ('little Judas', a hypocritical character in Saltykov-Shchedrin's novel *The Golovlev Family*); he lost no opportunity of saying that Trotsky was a man without principle, dodging between one group and another and only caring that he should not be found out. In 1911 he wrote: 'It is impossible to argue with Trotsky on the merits of the issue, because Trotsky holds no views whatever. We can and should argue with confirmed liquidators and otzovists, but it is no use arguing with a man whose game is to hide the errors of both these trends; in his case the thing to do is to expose him as a diplomat of the smallest calibre' ('Trotsky's Diplomacy on a Certain Party Platform', 21 Dec. 1911; *Works*, vol. 17, p. 362). In 1914 he repeated the same idea: 'Trotsky, however, has never had any "physiognomy" at all: the only thing he does have is a habit of changing sides, of skipping from the liberals to the Marxists and back again, of mouthing scraps of catchwords and bombastic parrot phrases' ('The Break-Up of the "August" Bloc', 15 Mar. 1914; *Works*, vol. 20, p. 160). As for 'Trotskyism' itself: 'From the Bolsheviks Trotsky's original theory has borrowed their call for a decisive proletarian revolutionary struggle and for the conquest of political power by the proletariat, while from the Mensheviks it has borrowed "repudiation" of the peasantry's role' ('On the Two Lines in the Revolution', 20 Nov. 1915; *Works*, vol. 21, p. 419).

Trotsky in fact shared Lenin's view that the party must be the guiding force in the revolutionary struggle and not an adjunct to the bourgeoisie. Like Lenin, he was against both liquidators and otzovists, and he foresaw, sooner than Lenin, the 'revolution in two stages'. However, he did not believe in the revolutionary potential of the peasantry, and he thought the proletariat would prevail in Russia thanks to a general European revolution.

2. The Revolutions of 1917

ALTHOUGH the various socialist groups lived in the expectation of a revolution, the outbreak in February 1917 took place without their aid and came as a surprise to all of them. Some weeks before, Trotsky had settled in the United States in the belief that he was leaving Europe for ever. Lenin, in January 1917, gave a lecture in Zurich on the 1905 Revolution which contained the words: 'We of the older generation may not live to see the decisive battles of this coming revolution' (*Works*, vol. 23, p. 253). If any party had anything directly to do with the February Revolution it was the Kadets (liberals) in concert with the Entente governments. Lenin himself observed that the capitalists of France and Britain as well as of Russia wished to prevent the Tsar concluding a separate peace with the German Emperor, and had therefore conspired to remove him from the throne. The conspiracy coincided with a revolt of the masses, made desperate by hunger, defeat, and economic chaos. The Romanov dynasty, which had stood for three hundred years, collapsed overnight, and it was clear that no serious elements in society had been prepared to defend it. For eight months, for the first and last time in its history, Russia enjoyed complete political freedom: not thanks to any legal order, but chiefly because no social force was in command of the situation. The Provisional Government established by the Duma shared uncertain authority with the Councils (Soviets) of Workers' and Soldiers' Deputies, formed in imitation of 1905, but neither was in proper control of the armed masses of the big cities. The Bolsheviks for the time being were a small minority in the Soviets, and all parties were completely confused as to the course the revolution was taking.

Lenin arrived in Petrograd in April: the Germans had given him a safe conduct, together with a few dozen repatriates of various political parties. His adversaries used the pretext to brand him as a German agent. Lenin accepted German aid not, of course, in order to help the Kaiser's war but in the hope that revolution would spread from Russia to the rest of Europe. In *Letters from Afar*, written just before he left Switzerland, he formulated his basic strategy. As the Russian revolution was a bourgeois one, the task of the proletariat was to unmask the deceit of the ruling classes, who could not give the people bread, peace, and freedom; the order of the day was to prepare the 'second stage' of the revolution, which would give power to the proletariat supported by the indigent, semi-proletarian part of the peasantry. These maxims were developed, immediately after his return to Russia, in the famous 'April Theses'. No support for the war or the Provisional Government; power for the proletariat and the poor peasants, replacement of the parliamentary republic by a republic of Soviets, abolition of the police, army, and bureaucracy, all officials to be elective and removable; confiscation of large estates, Soviet control over all social production and distribution, re-establishment of the International, and adoption by the party of the designation 'Communist'.

These slogans, with their clear demand for an immediate transition to the socialist phase of the revolution, were opposed not only by the Mensheviks, who saw them as a complete denial of the socialist tradition, but also by many Bolsheviks. Lenin's firmness, however, prevented all hesitation. At the same time he made it clear to his followers that the Provisional Government could not be overthrown at once, as it was supported by the Soviets. The Bolsheviks must first gain control of the Soviets and get a majority of the working masses on their side, convincing them that the imperialist war could only be ended by a dictatorship of the proletariat.

In July Lenin revoked the slogan 'All power to the Soviets', having decided that the Bolsheviks could not gain a majority in them for the time being, and that the dominant Mensheviks and S.R.s had gone over to the counter-revolution and become the servants of Tsarist generals. The peaceful road to revolution was thus closed. The revocation of the slogan took place after the Bolshevik show of force which, though Lenin strenuously denied this in later years, was probably a first attempt to seize power. Threatened with arrest, Lenin fled from Petrograd and went into hiding in Finland, directing the party's activity and at the same time writing *The State and Revolution*—an extraordinary semi-anarchist blueprint for a proletarian state in which power was to be directly exercised by the whole people in arms. The basic ideas of this programme were not only soon falsified by the course of the Bolshevik revolution, but were derided by Lenin himself as anarcho-syndicalist fantasies.

General Kornilov's unsuccessful putsch increased the general confusion and made things easier for the Bolsheviks. Lenin's policy was for the party to aid in the resistance to Kornilov but not to drift into supporting Kerensky's government. As he wrote in a letter to the Central Committee on 30 August, 'The development of this war alone can lead *us* to power, but we must speak of it as little as possible in our propaganda, remembering very well that even tomorrow events may put power into our hands, and then we shall not relinquish it' (*Works*, vol. 25, p. 289).

In September the Bolsheviks gained a majority in the Petrograd Soviet, and Trotsky became its chairman. In October a majority of the Central Committee voted for an armed rising; Zinoviev and Kamenev dissented, and made their attitude publicly known. The seizure of power in Petrograd was comparatively easy and bloodless. The Congress of Soviets which assembled on the following day, with a Bolshevik majority, passed a decree on the land question and a decree calling for peace without annexations or indemnities. A purely Bolshevik government was in power and, as Lenin had promised, it had no intention of letting go.

There can be no doubt that Lenin's insurrectionary policy and all his calculations were based on the firm expectation that the Russian Revolution would touch off a world revolution or at least a European one. This view was in fact shared by all the Bolsheviks: there was no question of 'socialism in one country' for the first few years after the Revolution. In a farewell letter to Swiss workers in 1917 Lenin wrote that in view of Russia's agrarian character and the mass of unsatisfied peasant aspirations, a Russian revolution 'might', by reason of its scale, be the prelude to a world socialist revolution. But this 'might' soon disappeared from Lenin's speeches and articles, and for the next few years they are full of confidence that proletarian rule in Western Europe is just round the corner. In September 1917 he wrote: 'The maturing and the inevitability of the world-wide socialist revolution is beyond doubt . . . If the proletariat gains power it will have *every* chance of retaining it and of leading Russia until there is a victorious revolution in the West' ('The Russian Revolution and Civil War', *Works*, vol. 26, pp. 40–1). Almost on the eve of the October Revolution he wrote: 'Doubt is out of the question. We are on the threshold of a world proletarian revolution' ('The Crisis has Matured'; ibid., p. 77). After the Revolution he declared to the Third Congress of Soviets on 24 January 1918: 'Today we see that the socialist revolution is maturing by the hour in all countries of the world' (ibid., p. 471). In August 1918: 'We already see how frequent the sparks and explosions of the revolutionary conflagration in Western Europe have become, inspiring us with the assurance that the triumph of the world workers' revolution is not far off' (*Works*, vol. 28, p. 54). On 3 October 1918: 'The crisis in Germany has only begun. It will inevitably end in the transfer of political power to the German proletariat' (ibid., p. 101). On 3 November 1918: 'The time is near when the first day of the world revolution will be celebrated everywhere' (p. 131). On 6 March 1919, at the First Congress of the Third International: 'The victory of the proletarian revolution on a world scale is assured. The founding of an international Soviet republic is on the way' (p. 477). On 12 July 1919, at the party's Moscow Conference, he predicted that 'next July we shall welcome the victory of the world Soviet republic, and that victory will be full and irreversible' (*Works*, vol. 29, p. 493).

These prophecies were based not only on the observation of events, the 'rising tide of revolution' and the outbreaks in Bavaria, Hungary, and Estonia, but also on Lenin's conviction that the European war could only be stopped by overthrowing capitalism. In a speech on 3 July 1918 he said, as reported in *Pravda,* that 'the war was becoming hopeless. This hopelessness was an earnest that our socialist revolution had a very good chance of holding on until the world revolution broke out; and the guarantee of this was the war, which only the working masses could end' (ibid., vol. 27, p. 502). It is also beyond doubt that Lenin did not believe in the permanence of victory in one country. At the Third Congress of Soviets in January 1918 he said: 'The final victory of socialism in a single country is of course impossible' (ibid., vol. 26, p. 470). In an article on 12 March 1918: 'Salvation lies *only* along that road of world socialist revolution upon which we have set out' (ibid., vol. 27, p. 161). In a speech on 26 May 1918: 'We do not shut our eyes to the fact that in a single country, even if it were a much less backward country than Russia, even if we were living in better conditions that those prevailing after four years of unprecedented, painful, severe and ruinous war, we could not carry out the socialist revolution completely, solely by our own efforts' (ibid., p. 412). In a speech on 23 July 1918: 'Aware of the isolation of its revolution, the Russian proletariat clearly realizes that an essential condition and prime requisite for its victory is the united action of the workers of the whole world, or of several capitalistically advanced countries' (p. 545).

When these hopes were disappointed and it became clear that the European proletariat either did not wish to follow the Bolshevik example or would fail in its revolutionary attempts, and that the war could be brought to an end by other means than revolution, the party was confronted with the question of what to do with the power it had conquered. There was no question of giving up that power or, in practice, of sharing it with other socialist forces. (The short episode of the Left S.R.s was insignificant and did not deserve the description of 'participation in power'.) The dispute over 'socialism in one country' broke out after Lenin's death; Stalin in his fight with Trotsky completely falsified the background to the problem, but he was probably more faithful to Lenin's ideas than Trotsky. The point at issue was not whether socialism should or should not be built in a country that found itself in isolation for various historical reasons, but whether the building of socialism in Russia should be subordinated to the cause of world revolution or vice versa. This question was of decisive importance for the policy of the Soviet state, especially, but not only, its foreign policy and the fixing of goals for the Comintern. Trotsky could point to many statements by Lenin showing that he regarded the Russian Revolution as a prelude to world revolution, and Soviet Russia as the advance guard of the international proletariat. Naturally Lenin never disavowed anything he had said on the subject, and Stalin did not do so expressly either; instead, he misrepre-

sented the argument as though it was a question of whether socialism could be
built in one country, implying that Trotsky was abandoning the cause of socialism in Russia. As regards Lenin, it must be recognized that after the civil war
his attention was almost wholly taken up by the problems of peaceful construction, and in his last years his policy was that of a head of state and not the
leader of a world revolution. It is true that in a speech on 29 November 1920
he said: 'As soon as we are strong enough to overcome capitalism as a whole,
we shall immediately seize it by the scruff of the neck' (*Works*, vol. 31, p. 441),
and no doubt he really meant this; but when he wrote that 'Communism equals
the Soviets plus electrification of the whole country' he clearly meant the electrification of Russia and not of Western Europe. His change of front was not
accompanied by any express theoretical justification; Stalin's attempt to contrast Lenin's position with Trotsky's on this point was purely demagogic, as the
question did not exist in Lenin's day in the form in which Stalin put it. Stalin,
however, was not only more cautious than Trotsky in his estimate of the
prospects of world revolution, but also interpreted more logically Lenin's dictum that Soviet Russia was the advance guard of the revolution: for if Soviet
Russia is the world proletariat's most precious possession, clearly whatever is
good for the Soviet state is good for the world proletariat. There could of course
be a problem of what to do if the immediate interest of the Soviet state conflicted with the immediate interest of a revolutionary movement in another
country. But in such cases Stalin's strategy of never sacrificing Soviet interests
to the uncertain fortunes of a foreign revolution was in accordance with Leninist principles.

There is, indeed, no better proof that Lenin acted in this way than the history of the Treaty of Brest-Litovsk. This humiliating capitulation of the young
republic to the Germans was forced through by Lenin despite the infuriated
opposition of his own party and nearly the whole of Russia. To patriots outside
the Bolshevik party it was a national disgrace; to Bolsheviks, a betrayal of the
world revolution and a recantation of Lenin's frequent assurances before October 1917 that there could be no question of a separate peace with German imperialism. The treaty was a defeat, and Lenin never tried to pretend otherwise: he
was not in the habit, as Stalin later was, of representing every setback as a brilliant triumph. Lenin was fully conscious of the dilemma: as he explained to the
party, he must either save Bolshevik power by an ignominious peace, or wage
a revolutionary war against Germany with every likelihood that Russia would
be defeated and Bolshevik power destroyed. The lesson was a bitter one, as is
shown by the frequency of his references to the treaty during the rest of his life.
But his action in forcing the Central Committee to accept it despite the intial
opposition of a large majority (with Bukharin as one of its main leaders) was

the first clear instance of the policy later followed by Stalin: the interests of the Soviet state and Bolshevik power are paramount, and must never be put at risk for the sake of a problematical world revolution.

Almost immediately after the Revolution the question of the legitimacy of the new authority was unambiguously resolved in accordance with Leninist principles. The elections to the Constituent Assembly, preparations for which had been made before the Revolution, took place towards the end of November, and the Bolsheviks received about a quarter of the votes. This was the only instance in Russian history of an election held on a basis of equal, universal suffrage, and it took place when the popularity of the Bolsheviks was at its peak. The Assembly, when it met on 18 January 1918, was dispersed by armed sailors, and thus ended the history of Russian parliamentary democracy. Both before and after the dispersal of the Assembly Lenin repeatedly declared that to give it power signified a return to the rule of the bourgeoisie and the big landowners; in point of fact it had an S.R. majority, expressing the wishes of the peasant masses. In a speech on 14 December 1917 Lenin had said: 'We shall tell the people that their interests are superior to the interests of a democratic institution. We must not return to the old prejudices, which subordinate the interests of the people to formal democracy' (*Works*, vol. 26, p. 356). Again, on 26 December, he stated that: 'The slogan "All power to the Constituent Assembly!", which disregards the gains of the workers' and peasants' revolution ... has become in fact the slogan of the Cadets and Kaledinites and of their helpers ... Every direct or indirect attempt to consider the question of the Constituent Assembly from a formal, legal point of view, within the framework of ordinary bourgeois democracy and disregarding the class struggle and civil war, would be a betrayal of the proletariat's cause, and the adoption of the bourgeois standpoint' (pp. 381–2).

In saying this Lenin was only repeating his long-standing belief that it was none of the people's business to decide what its interests were. He had indeed no intention of 'returning to the old prejudices'; for a time, however, he believed that if a dictatorship had to be exercised against the peasantry, i.e. the bulk of the Russian people, it could still be a dictatorship supported by the great majority of the proletariat. This illusion too was dispelled before long. At the outset, however, the new state could count on support from a majority of the workers and peasants; otherwise it could not have survived the appalling hardships of the civil war, when, as Lenin freely admitted, the future of Soviet power more than once hung by a thread. The superhuman energy that the Bolshevik party displayed in those years, and the sacrifices it was able to elicit from the workers and peasants, saved Soviet power at the cost of economic ruin, immense human suffering, the loss of millions of lives, and the barbarization of society. In the last phase of the struggle the revolution encountered a further defeat in the Polish war, which finally destroyed the hope that the Soviet system could be transplanted to Europe at an early date.

As to the reasons for the success of the October Revolution, Lenin made no attempt to present the matter in traditional Marxist terms but referred to Russia's backwardness, the unsatisfied peasant demands, and the war situation. On 23 April 1919 he wrote: 'It was easier for the Russians to begin the great proletarian revolution, but it will be more difficult for them to continue it and carry it to final victory, in the sense of the complete organization of a socialist society. It was easier for us to begin, firstly, because the unusual—for twentieth-century Europe—political backwardness of the Tsarist monarchy gave unusual strength to the revolutionary onslaught of the masses. Secondly, Russia's backwardness merged in a peculiar way the proletarian revolution against the bourgeoisie with the peasant revolution against the landowners' (*The Third International and its Place in History*; *Works*, vol. 29, p. 310). On 1 July 1921, at the Third Congress of the Comintern, he put the matter even more clearly: 'We were victorious in Russia, and with such ease, because we prepared for our revolution during the imperialist war. That was the first condition. Ten million workers and peasants in Russia were under arms, and our slogan was: an immediate peace at all costs. We were victorious because the vast mass of the peasants were revolutionarily disposed against the big landowners.' Secondly, 'We were victorious because we adopted the agrarian programme of the Socialist-Revolutionaries instead of our own, and put it into effect. Our victory lay in the fact that we carried out the Socialist-Revolutionary programme' (*Works*, vol. 32, pp. 473, 475).

Lenin had indeed realized for a long time that if the Russian communists had to wait, like the Western parties, for the 'contradiction between relations of production and productive forces' to mature to the requisite point, they could say good-bye to the hope of a proletarian revolution. He was fully aware that the course of events in Russia bore no relation to the traditional Marxist schemata, though he did not consider the theoretical problem in all its bearings. The massive strength of the Russian revolution lay not in the class conflict between workers and bourgeoisie but in the aspirations of the peasants, the wartime débâcle, and the longing for peace. It was a communist revolution in the sense that it transferred state power to the Communist Party, but not in the sense of confirming Marxist predictions as to the fate of capitalist society.

3. The beginnings of socialist economy

THE economic history of Soviet Russia under Lenin is divided into two periods: that of 'War Communism' and, from the spring of 1921, the 'New Economic Policy' (N.E.P.). The term 'War Communism' was coined during the second period, and is misleading in that it suggests a temporary policy resulting from the civil war and the need to adopt extraordinary measures to feed the country in its state of economic ruin. History books not infrequently put the matter in this way and suggest, further, that the N.E.P. was planned in advance but could not be put into effect owing to the exceptional circumstances of the war: in other words, it was not a retreat and a confession of error, but a return to the previously chosen path from which the party had been temporarily forced to deviate.

In actual fact, both the course of events and Lenin's account of them make it clear that War Communism was thought of from the beginning as the economic system to be maintained until the 'complete victory of communism', while the N.E.P. was an admission of defeat. The key question in devastated Russia was of course the production of food, especially grain. War Communism consisted primarily of requisitioning from the peasants all food surpluses, or rather all foodstuffs that the local authorities or the requisitioning squads regarded as surplus. As it was impossible to calculate accurately the quantity of stocks and 'surpluses' on millions of small farms, the requisition system not only turned the peasant masses against the government and led to bribery and coercion on a vast scale, but ruined agricultural production and thus undermined the whole system of power. Lenin believed, however, that in a country of small farmers free trade in grain, as a principle rather than a temporary measure, was tantamount to the restoration of capitalism, and that those who proposed it in the name of economic recovery were no better than allies of Kolchak. In a speech on 19 May 1919 he referred to 'this historical epoch, when the struggle of the oppressed working people for the complete overthrow of capital *and the abolition of commodity production* [present author's italics] stands in the forefront' (*Works*, vol. 29, p. 352), and declared that free trade in grain was Kolchak's policy. On 30 July of that year, in a speech on the food situation, he re-emphasized the point stating that the question of free trade was decisive in the final battle with capitalism, and that 'there cannot be any concessions here, in this particular sphere', as free trade was the economic standby of Denikin and Kolchak. 'We know that one of the main sources of capitalism is freedom to trade in grain in the country, and it is this source that has been the ruin of all previous republics. Today the last, decisive battle against capitalism and against freedom to trade is being fought, and for us this is a truly basic battle between capitalism and socialism. If we win in this fight there will be no return to capitalism and the former system, no return to what has been in the past. Such a return will be impossible so long as there is a war against the bourgeoisie, against profiteering and against petty proprietorship' (ibid., pp. 525, 526). Similarly, in an article written but not published at this time, he wrote: 'Freedom to trade in grain is a return to capitalism, to the full power of the landowners and capitalists, to a savage struggle between people for profit, to the "free" enrichment of the few, to the poverty of the masses, to eternal bondage' (ibid., p. 570).

While, then, Lenin did not envisage an immediate transition to collective or state farming, he was in no doubt that rural production must from the outset be under direct state control and that free trade in commodities meant the ruin of socialism. His intention from the start was that agricultural production should be based on police coercion of the peasants and on the direct confiscation of produce in the form of quotas which were supposed (though this was impossible to work out in practice) to leave the peasants enough seed corn for the following year and a minimum on which to feed themselves.

The transition to N.E.P. was due to the catastrophic failure of this policy—a failure predicted by the Mensheviks and S.R.s, who for their pains had been denounced, imprisoned, and murdered as henchmen of the White Guards.

Lenin sounded the retreat at the party's Tenth Congress, in March 1921. He announced that small farming would have to go on for many years, and 'the unrestricted trade slogan will be inevitable ... It is apt to spread because it conforms to the economic conditions of the small producer's existence' (*Works*, vol. 32, p. 187). He acknowledged that in the nationalization of trade and industry the party had gone further than theoretical or practical considerations justified, and declared that 'we must satisfy the middle peasantry economically and go over to free exchange; otherwise it will be impossible—economically impossible—in view of the delay in the world revolution, to preserve the rule of the proletariat in Russia' (ibid., p. 225). As Lenin emphasized soon afterwards, the N.E.P. was meant as a serious long-term policy, consisting not only of replacing the appropriation of surpluses by a uniform grain tax, but of numerous other measures: wide concessions to foreign capital in Russia, aid to co-operatives, the leasing of state factories to private persons, relief to private traders and the distribution of state products through private merchants, greater independence and initiative for state enterprises as regards the use of financial and material resources, and the introduction of material incentives into production. 'Commodity exchange is brought to the fore as the principal lever of the New Economic Policy' (ibid., p. 433). Lenin made no secret of the fact that a disastrous error had been committed.

We expected—or perhaps it would be truer to say that we presumed without having given it adequate consideration—to be able to organize the state production and the state distribution of products on communist lines in a small-peasant country directly as ordered by the proletarian state. Experience has proved that we were wrong. It appears that a number of transitional stages were necessary—state capitalism and socialism—in order to *prepare*—to prepare by many years of effort—for the transition to communism. Not directly relying on enthusiasm, but aided by the enthusiasm engendered by the great revolution, and on the basis of personal interest, personal incentive and business principles, we must first set to work in this small-peasant country to build solid gangways to socialism by way of state capitalism. (*Pravda*, 18 Oct. 1921)

In attempting to go straight over to communism we, in the spring of 1921, sustained a more serious defeat on the economic front than any defeat inflicted upon us by Kolchak, Denikin or Pilsudski. This defeat was much more serious, significant and dangerous. It was expressed in the isolation of the higher administrators of our economic policy from the lower and their failure to produce that development of the productive forces which the programme of our Party regards as vital and urgent. The surplus-food appropriation system in the rural districts—this direct communist approach to the problem of urban development—hindered the growth of the productive forces and proved to be the main cause of the profound economic and political crisis that we experienced in the spring of 1921. (Address dated 17 Oct. 1921; *Works*, vol. 33, pp. 58, 63–4)

After the Brest treaty, the N.E.P. was a second major demonstration of Lenin's extraordinary ability to sacrifice doctrine to the retention of power. It excited less opposition in the party, as all could see that the country was on the brink of an abyss, but it was none the less a retreat towards capitalism—a case, as Lenin put it, of *reculer pour mieux sauter*. In the preceding years he had supposed that all important economic problems could be solved by police and military terror. This had been the Jacobins' policy; he believed that it had brought excellent results, but like them he found himself on the edge of a precipice, though he was able to draw back at the last moment. His economic directives during the period of War Communism were simple: they consisted of shooting, imprisonment, and intimidation. It turned out, however, that Marxist doctrine was quite right: economic life has its own laws, which cannot be set aside by terror; in time of famine and the breakdown of society, the execution of profiteers will not put an end to profiteering.

4. The dictatorship of the proletariat and the dictatorship of the party

THE new situation, however, brought about other changes that were bound to arouse dissension in the party. All the pre-Revolutionary promises had suddenly became scraps of paper. Lenin had undertaken to abolish the standing army and the police, to equalize the pay of high officials and specialists on the one hand and skilled workers on the other; he had promised that the people in arms would exercise direct rule. Directly after the Revolution, and long before N.E.P., it was evident that these were utopian dreams. An army with a cadre of professional officers had to be organized at once on a basis of rank and strict discipline, like any other army. Trotsky revealed his genius as the chief organizer of the Red Army, and was the main architect of victory in the civil war. The methods used were drastic enough—hostages were taken and executed, deserters and those who harboured them were shot, as were soldiers for offences against discipline, etc. But such methods would not have been possible without a large, trustworthy force under arms: to keep an army together by intimidation and terror there must be enough people willing to apply that terror in a situation where counter-terror is also powerful. It was necessary, immediately after the Revolution, to establish a force of political police, which was efficiently created by Feliks Dzerzhinsky. It soon became clear that production could not be organized without privileges for specialists, and that it could not be based on intimidation alone: as early as April 1918 Lenin recognized, in 'The Immediate Tasks of the Soviet Government', that it was necessary to 'compromise' in this respect and to depart from the principles of the Paris Commune. Lenin also proclaimed from the beginning of the Revolution that it was important to learn from the bourgeoisie (Struve in his time had been branded as a renegade for saying the same thing). Those who thought socialism could be built without learning from the bourgeois—so Lenin told the Central Executive Committee on 29 April 1918—had the mentality of Central African natives (*Works*, vol. 27, p. 310). In his writings and speeches he devoted more and more attention to 'civilization' (*kultura*), i.e. the technical and administrative skills necessary to run industry and the state. He emphasized that communists must stop being arrogant, must admit their ignorance and learn these skills from the bourgeoisie. (Lenin was always highly distrustful of communists except for the purpose of political agitation and fighting: in 1913, when he heard that Gorky had consulted a Bolshevik doctor, he wrote at once urging him to find a real doctor and not a 'comrade', who was sure to be an ass). In May 1918 he bethought himself of a better model than the Paris Commune, namely Peter the Great. 'While the revolution in Germany is still slow in "coming forth", our task is to study the state capitalism of the Germans, to spare no effort in copying it and not shrink from adopting *dictatorial* methods to hasten the copying of it. Our task is to hasten this copying even more than Peter hastened the copying of Western culture by barbarian Russia, and we must not hesitate to use barbarous methods in fighting barbarism' ('"Left-Wing" Childishness and the Petty-Bourgeois Mentality', *Works*, vol. 27, p. 340). The principle of unity of control in industry was soon introduced, and dreams of the collective administration of factories were condemned as a syndicalist deviation.

Thus the new society was to be built by means of increasing technical and administrative knowledge on the one hand, and coercion and intimidation on the other. The N.E.P. brought no relaxation of political and police terror, nor was it intended to. The non-Bolshevik Press was closed down during the civil war, and was never again permitted to appear. The opposition socialist parties, the Mensheviks and S.R.s, were terrorized and liquidated. The autonomy of the universities was finally suppressed in 1921. Lenin constantly repeated that the 'so-called freedom of the Press' was a bourgeois deceit, like freedom of assembly and the right to form parties, since in a bourgeois society the common people had no printing presses and no rooms in which to assemble. Now that the Soviet system had given these facilities to the 'people', the latter obviously could not allow the bourgeoisie to use them for deceptive purposes; and as the Mensheviks and S.R.s had sunk to the position of bourgeois parties, they too must submit to the dictatorship of the proletariat. The closure of Menshevik newspapers in February 1919 was justified by Lenin on the ground that 'the Soviet Government, right at the time of the last, decisive and sharpest armed clash with the landlord and capitalist troops, cannot put up with people who are unwilling to endure great sacrifices alongside the workers and peasants fighting for their just cause' (*Works*, vol. 28, p. 447). At the Seventh Congress of Soviets in December 1919 he declared that when Martov accused the Bolsheviks of representing a minority of the working class he was speaking the language of the 'wild beasts of imperialism'—Clemenceau, Wilson, and Lloyd George. The logical conclusion was that 'we have to be on the alert and to realize that the Cheka is indispensable!' (*Works*, vol. 30, p. 239).

The dissolution of non-Bolshevik organizations and periodicals, the expulsion from Russia (this clement measure was still employed) of hundreds of the country's chief intellectuals, purges in all cultural institutions, the atmosphere of terror in every walk of life—all this had the unplanned but natural effect that social conflicts came to be reflected within the Bolshevik party itself; and this in turn led to the application within the party of the same principle of despotic rule as the party exercised over the rest of society. The civil war had brought economic ruin and general exhaustion, and the working class, drained of its strength, was unresponsive to appeals to show the same enthusiasm and self-sacrifice in the cause of peaceful construction as it had on the field of battle. That the Bolsheviks represented the whole working class had been an axiom since 1918; it was unverifiable, as no institutions existed for the purpose. The proletariat, however, began to display anger and discontent, most forcefully in the Kronstadt rising of March 1921, which was suppressed with heavy bloodshed. The sailors of Kronstadt, like the great majority of the working class, were in favour of Soviet power, but they did not identify it with the despotism of a single ruling party: they wanted rule by the Soviets as opposed to party rule. Within the party itself, proletarian discontent was reflected in the strong 'workers' opposition', represented in the Central Committee by Aleksandr Shlyapnikov, Aleksandra Kollontay, and others. This group wanted economic management to be entrusted to a general organization of workers, i.e. trade unions; they called for the equalization of pay, and protested against despotic methods of control within the party. In short, they wanted the kind of 'dictatorship of the proletariat' that Lenin had written about before the Revolution. They believed that democracy for the workers and democracy within the party could be safeguarded even when there was no democracy for anyone else. Lenin and Trotsky no longer entertained any such illusion. They branded the 'workers' opposition' as an anarcho-syndicalist deviation, and its spokesmen were eliminated from party work on various pretexts, though they were not imprisoned or shot.

The episode gave rise to a general debate on the place and function of trade unions in the Soviet system. Three years earlier, in March 1918, Lenin had inveighed against the Mensheviks for saying that 'in the interests of preserving and strengthening the class independence of the proletariat the trade unions should not become state organizations ... This view was and is either a bourgeois provocation of the crudest kind or an extreme misunderstanding, a slavish repetition of the slogans of yesterday ... The working class is becoming and has become the ruling class in the state. The trade unions are becoming and must become state organizations which have prime responsibility for the reorganization of all economic life on a socialist basis' (*Works*, vol. 27, p. 215). The idea of turning the trade unions into state organizations followed logically from the theory of the proletarian dictatorship. Since the proletariat was identified with state power, it was clearly nonsense to imagine that the workers would have to defend their interests against the state. Trotsky held to this view, but Lenin changed his mind on both points in the above-quoted passage. Having decided in 1920 that the Soviet state was suffering from bureaucratic distortion, he attacked Trotsky for holding the views he had himself recently advanced, and declared that it was the business of the trade unions to defend the workers' state but also to defend the workers against their own state, or rather its abuses. At the same time he was violently opposed to the idea that the unions should take over the state's function of managing the economy.

Meanwhile Lenin took steps to prevent opposition groups from arising in future within the party. Rules were adopted prohibiting the formation of intra-party factions, and empowering the Central Committee to expel from its midst members who had been elected at the party congress. In this way, by a natural progression, the dictatorship first exercised over society in the name of the working class, and then over the working class in the name of the party, was now applied to the party itself, creating the basis for a one-man tyranny.

Another theme which becomes more and more prominent in Lenin's last years is that, just mentioned, of 'bureaucratic distortion'. He complains more and more frequently that the state apparatus is expanding indefinitely without need and at the same time is incapable of getting anything done, that every-thing is muddle and red tape, that civil servants refer the most trifling ques-tions to high party officials, and so on. It seems never to have occurred to Lenin that the root of these troubles lay in the fact that the whole system was based, as he constantly emphasized, on force and not on law. He demanded that peo-ple be imprisoned right and left for inefficiency, and then wondered why they were afraid to take decisions and referred them higher up whenever they could. He demanded vigilant supervision and exhaustive records, and yet was aston-ished at the amount of 'pen-pushing'. (His statement that 'socialism equals Soviet power plus electrification' is often quoted; less often his statement, just after the Revolution, that 'what socialism implies above all is keeping account of everything' (meeting of the Central Executive Committee, 17 November 1917; *Works*, vol. 26, p. 288).) He created a system in which, depending on the whim of a local party or police authority, any criticism might be regarded as counter-revolutionary and expose its author to imprisonment or death, and at the same time he urged the working people to be fearless in their criticism of the state apparatus. His diagnosis of the cancer of bureaucracy was a simple one: it was due to lack of education, 'culture' and administrative ability. There were two remedies, also simple: to imprison the inefficient, and to create new supervisory bodies of honest officials. He attached great importance to the Workers' and Peasants' Inspectorate (Rabkrin), headed by Stalin, which was appointed to supervise all branches of the administration and other supervisory bodies, and on the honesty of which, in his view, the success of the fight against bureaucracy ultimately depended. This body, besides adding to the burden of terror and issuing incompetent instructions in all directions, was used by Stalin, who became Secretary-General of the party in 1922, as a stick to beat his oppo-nents and a weapon in intra-party struggles. This, of course, Lenin did not fore-see. He had applied his 'final cure' to bureaucracy in the shape of an additional link in the bureaucratic chain which, as he well knew, was fastened upon the country irrevocably. The hierarchy grew and grew; it had powers of life and death over every citizen; it was at first directed by sincere communists, but in course of time absorbed a mass of careerists, parasites, and sycophants who, over the years, modelled the style of government in their own image.

The last two years of Lenin's life were overshadowed by physical infirmity due to sclerosis and a succession of strokes, despite which he continued fight-ing to the end. His famous 'Testament', consisting of notes written in Decem-ber 1922 and January 1923 in preparation for the party congress, was concealed from the Soviet public for the next thirty-three years. The notes express his feeling of helplessness at the difficulties of the state and the approaching strug-gle for power in the party hierarchy. He criticizes Stalin for concentrating excessive power in his own hands and for being high-handed, capricious, and disloyal, and therefore unfit to remain in the office of secretary-general. Lenin also enumerates the faults of Trotsky, Pyatakov, Zinovyev, and Kamenev, and criticizes Bukharin for un-Marxist views. He blames Ordzhonikidze, Stalin, and Dzerzhinsky for Great Russian nationalism and the brutality of the methods used in the invasion of Georgia. He speaks of the need to 'provide the non-Russians with a real safeguard against the truly Russian bully', and predicts that, given the 'apparatus which . . . we took over from tsarism and slightly anointed with Soviet oil', the promised freedom to secede from the Union 'will be a mere scrap of paper, unable to defend the non-Russians from the onslaught of that really Russian man, the Great-Russian chauvinist, in substance a rascal and a tyrant, such as the typical Russian bureaucrat is' (*Works*, vol. 36, pp. 605–6).

These appeals, warnings, and reproaches were of little practical importance. Lenin called for the protection of national minorities and the right of self-determination immediately after the Red Army, with his blessing, had invaded Georgia, with its democratically elected Menshevik government. He hoped to prevent factional strife by enlarging the Central Committee, as though its size could make any difference when he himself had virtually put an end to democracy within the party. He criticized all the main party leaders and called for Stalin's replacement, but who did he think should be the new secretary-general—Trotsky, with his 'excessive self-assurance', Bukharin, who was not a Marxist, Zinovyev or Kamenev, whose 'treason' in October 1917 was 'no accident', or Pyatakov, who could not be relied on in important political matters? Whatever Lenin's political intentions were, the 'Testament' today reads like a cry of despair.

Lenin died on 21 January 1924. (There is no evidence to support Trotsky's later suggestion that he was poisoned by Stalin.) The new state was to develop along the lines he had inculcated. His embalmed corpse, exhibited to this day in the mausoleum in Moscow, aptly symbolizes the new order which, he promised, was soon to embrace all mankind.

5. *The theory of imperialism and of revolution*

THE Bolshevik theory of imperialism was the work of Lenin and Bukharin: the latter was the first to formulate the basis of a strategy of revolution for the new historical era. Lenin in his work on imperialism—based for the most part, as already mentioned, on J. A. Hobson's *Imperialism* (1902) and R. Hilferding's *Finanzkapital* (1910)—enumerates five principal features distinguishing imperialism from pre-monopolistic capitalism: (1) the concentration of production and capital, leading to the domination of the world economy by big monopolies; (2) the fusion of bank and industrial capital and the consequent rise of a financial oligarchy; (3) the specially important role of the export of capital; (4) the division of the world among monopolistic leagues of international capitalists; (5) the completion of the territorial partition of the world among the great imperialist powers. This situation does not relieve the contradictions of capitalism, but intensifies them to the utmost; the inequalities of development within the system and the fierceness of competition not only do not reduce the likelihood of wars but make them increasingly inevitable. The last point is stressed by Lenin in his attack on Kautsky, who had argued that it was possible to foresee the world economic system passing into a phase of 'ultra-imperialism' in which the great powers and the great international cartels would stabilize the partition of the world and thus eliminate the risk of war. Kautsky put this forward as a general hypothesis and not something that was bound to occur, but Lenin was scandalized by the idea of capitalism without wars, a state of affairs in which revolutions too would be much less likely. Kautsky's 'stupid fable' was anti-Marxist and a symptom of opportunism: imperialism could not exist without wars, for there was no other way of regulating and eliminating the inequalities of world development. Hence, in his article 'The Military Programme of the Proletarian Revolution' (1916), Lenin drew the conclusion that socialism could not triumph simultaneously in all countries: the revolutionary process would begin in one or several countries, and this would lead to further conflicts and wars.

The connection between the prospects of revolution and the uneven development of the world economy, which at the same time constituted a single system, was expounded by Bukharin in books written during the war and in the first years after the Revolution. Imperialism, he explained, sought to overcome the anarchy of production and to organize a rational economy, with the state as a supervisory and regulating force; but it was unable to eliminate contradictions and competition, and hence to avoid imperialist wars. The capitalist system as a whole was ripe for socialist revolution; however, this was much less likely to break out in places where technological development had reached its height and where the bourgeoisie, thanks to its fat profits, was able to bribe the workers with high wages and dissuade them from revolution, than where the concentration of contradictions was greatest, i.e. on the fringe of the capitalist world, in back-ward, colonial, or semi-colonial countries. Thanks to the combination of intensive exploitation, national oppression, and peasant movements, these countries were the weakest link where the chain of the world system could be broken by force. Social movements in underdeveloped countries could not lead to the immediate establishment of socialism, but they were the natural allies of the proletariat in the advanced countries, and could create transitional social forms in which the achievement of bourgeois democratic objectives would coincide with the gradual and peaceful development towards socialism, based on the combined forces of workers and peasants.

By 1916, however, Lenin had taken the argument a stage further. In 'The Discussion on Self-Determination Summed Up' he wrote:

> To imagine that social revolution is *conceivable* without revolts by small nations in the colonies and in Europe, without revolutionary outbursts by a section of the petty bourgeoisie *with all its prejudices,* without a movement of the politically non-conscious proletarian and semi-proletarian masses against oppression by the landowners, the church and the monarchy, against national oppression, etc.—to imagine all this is to repudiate social revolution . . . Whoever expects a 'pure' social revolution will *never* live to see it . . . The socialist revolution in Europe *cannot be* anything other than an outburst of mass struggle on the part of all and sundry oppressed and discontented elements. Inevitably sections of the petty bourgeoisie and of the backward workers will participate in it—without such participation *mass* struggle is impossible, without it *no* revolution is possible—and just as inevitably will they bring into the movement their prejudices, their reactionary fantasies, their weaknesses and errors. But *objectively* they will attack *capital* (*Works*, vol. 22, pp. 355–6).

It is not clear whether Lenin was fully aware of the consequences of this theory or the extent to which it diverged from Marxist tradition. At all events, it laid down firmly that a socialist uprising could only take place when there were numerous unsatisfied claims and aspirations of the kind which Marxists assign to the 'bourgeois' phase of development, i.e. primarily those of the peasants and subject nationalities. This means that as capitalism approaches the situation, foreseen by Marx, in which society consists only of the bourgeoisie and the proletariat, a socialist revolution becomes less and less likely. Lenin's statement that unsatisfied peasant and national claims and the presence of 'survivals of feudalism' might assist the proletariat, reinforcing it with the energy of 'non-proletarian' demands, was of course not in conflict with the strategy of Marx and Engels, who adopted a similar position on various occasions, for example in their hopes for a proletarian revolution in Germany in 1848 or a Russian revolution in the seventies, or their view that the Irish question would strengthen the hand of the British working class. Marx and Engels, it is true, did not put forward any precise theory as to how such alliances would operate, nor was it clear how their hopes were to be theoretically reconciled with the general theory of socialist revolution. But the statement that a proletarian revolution could not happen at all without the reinforcement due to 'survivals of feudalism' was a novelty in Marxism and a complete departure from the traditional theory. Lenin was no doubt right when he accused the leaders of the Second International of being revolutionary in words and reformist in action. He alone thought seriously of the seizure of power, and, what is more, he thought of nothing else. His position was clear: power must be seized wherever it was politically possible to do so. He did not indulge in theoretical calculations as to whether productive forces had matured to the point of a socialist uprising; his calculations were all concerned with the power situation. He himself could rightly be accused of being a determinist in words and a Realpolitiker in action. Sometimes, though not often, he repeated the determinist catechism ('Everything that takes place in history takes place of necessity. That is elementary.'—'The Russian Brand of Südekum', 1 Feb. 1915; *Works*, vol. 21, p. 120), but this determinism only served to convince himself and others that the communist cause was historically bound to triumph; it was not applied to any specific political acts. He even jettisoned the idea, which had been regarded as one of the rudiments of Marxism, that all countries must go through the capitalist stage of development. At the Second Congress of the Comintern on 26 July 1920 he declared that backward peoples might bypass the capitalist 'phase' and proceed direct to socialism, with the aid of the proletariat in the advanced countries and of Soviet power. (Without this, indeed, it would have been hard to justify the exercise of Soviet authority over dozens of primitive tribes and small nations who belonged to the Russian Empire.)

Lenin, then, was not interested in 'economic ripeness', but only in the existence of a revolutionary situation. In an article of 1915 on 'The Collapse of the Second International' he defined the main features of such a situation as follows: (1) It is usually insufficient for 'the lower classes not to want' to live in the old way; it is also necessary that 'the upper classes should be unable' to live in the old way—popular discontent is not enough, there must also be a disintegration of the apparatus of government. (2) 'The suffering and want of the oppressed classes have grown more acute than usual', and (3) 'As a consequence of the above causes there is a considerable increase in the activity of the masses, who . . . are drawn . . . themselves into independent historical action.' But 'not every revolutionary situation gives rise to a revolution; revolution arises only out of a situation in which the above-mentioned objective changes are accompanied by a subjective change, namely the ability of the revolutionary class to take revolutionary mass action strong enough to break or dislocate the old government' (*Works*, vol. 21, pp. 213–14).

It is easy to see that the conditions prescribed by Lenin are most likely to occur in time of war and particularly of military defeat. Hence his anger at suggestions that capitalism might avoid wars and thus preclude, in all probability, the chance of a revolutionary situation arising. Hence, likewise, his desire that revolutionists should aim at their country's own defeat in the imperialist war and thus turn it into a civil one.

The fact that Lenin was wholly preoccupied by the question of political power meant that he was the only social democratic leader who was completely free from any vestige of what he called 'bourgeois pacifism'—the hope of abolishing wars without the revolutionary abolition of capitalism, and, when war had broken out, the attempt to bring it to an end by methods of international law. A symptom of bourgeois pacifism was the use of the concept of aggression, regardless of the class character of the war. War should be seen in terms of classes and not of states—it was not the collision of two state organisms, but a product of class interests. Lenin frequently quoted Clausewitz's remark that 'War is simply the continuation of policy by other means', and on the strength of this dictum the Prussian general of Napoleonic times is credited with formulating 'the main thesis of dialectics with reference to wars' (ibid., p. 219). War was a manifestation of conflict due to class interests, and the difference between warlike and peaceful means of resolving these conflicts was purely technical and had no political significance; war was 'simply' a way of attaining ends that could at other times be attained without it, and had no particular moral or political quality independent of class interests. It did not matter who was the aggressor, there was in fact no difference between offensive and defensive wars; all that mattered were the class interests underlying the military operations. Lenin's statements on this subject are numerous and perfectly clear, though not often quoted by his present-day disciples. 'It is absurd to divide wars into defensive and aggressive' (speech on 14 Oct. 1914; *Works*, vol. 36, p. 297). 'It is not the defensive or offensive character of the war, but the interests of the class struggle of the proletariat, or—to put it better—the interests of the international movement of the proletariat that represent the sole criterion for considering and deciding the attitude of the social-democrats to any particular event in international relations' ('Bellicose Militarism and the Anti-Militarist Tactics of Social-Democracy', Aug. 1908; *Works*, vol. 15, p. 199). 'As if the question were: Who was the first to attack, and not What are the causes of the war? What are its aims? Which classes are waging it?' (open letter to Boris Souvarine, Dec. 1916; *Works*, vol. 23, p. 198). 'The character of the war (whether it is reactionary or revolutionary) does not depend on who the attacker was, or in whose country the "enemy" is stationed; it depends on *what class* is waging the war, and what politics this war is a continuation of' (*The Proletarian Revolution and the Renegade Kautsky*, 1918; *Works*, vol. 28, p. 286).

It thus appears not only that 'aggression' is a fraudulent bourgeois concept serving to conceal the class character of wars, but that the working class organized in its own state has every right to wage war on a capitalist state, since by definition it represents the interests of the oppressed and has justice on its side. Lenin does not shrink from this conclusion. 'For instance, if socialism is victorious in America or in Europe in 1920, and Japan and China, let us say, then move their Bismarcks against us—if only diplomatically at first—we certainly would be in favour of an offensive revolutionary war against them' ('The Collapse of the Second International'; *Works*, vol. 21, p. 221 n.). In a speech on 6

December 1920 Lenin declared that war was bound to break out soon between the U.S.A. and Japan and that, while the Soviet state could not 'support' either against the other, it should 'play one off' against the other and exploit the war in its own interest (*Works*, vol. 31, p. 443). At the Seventh Party Congress in March 1918 he proposed a resolution to the effect that 'the Congress will empower the Central Committee of the Party both to break all the peace treaties and to declare war on any imperialist power or the whole world when the Central Committee of the Party considers that the appropriate moment for this has come' (*Works*, vol. 27, p. 120). This, it is true, was drafted in the atmosphere of Brest-Litovsk, but it is general in application and is wholly in accordance with Lenin's doctrine. As the proletarian state is by definition in the right *vis-à-vis* capitalist states, and since the question of aggression is beside the point in judging a war, it is clearly the right and duty of the former state to attack the latter for the sake of the world revolution whenever occasion offers— all the more so as peaceful coexistence between capitalism and socialism was, in Lenin's opinion, impossible. In the speech on 6 December 1920, already quoted, he declared: 'I said that we had passed from war to peace, but that we had not forgotten that war will return. While capitalism and socialism live side by side, they cannot live in peace' (*Works*, vol. 31, p. 457).

Such were the simple ideological foundations of the foreign policy of the socialist state. The new state by definition represented the leading force in history; whether attacking or defending itself, it was acting in the name of progress. International law, arbitration, disarmament talks, the 'outlawing' of war—all these were deceptions as long as capitalism existed, and afterwards they would not be necessary, for wars were as impossible under socialism as they were inevitable under capitalism.

6. Socialism and the dictatorship of the proletariat

ALTHOUGH Lenin's whole activity was subordinated to the struggle for the 'ultimate aim', i.e. the building of a socialist society, he did not concern himself before the war with specifying what that society would be like. His writings contain scattered references to familiar socialist ideas such as the collectivization of property, the abolition of wage-labour and of the commodity economy, etc., but he does not go into details. He did, however, explain before the Revolution what he meant by the 'dictatorship of the proletariat', and the terms in which he did so remained unaltered throughout his career. In *The Victory of the Cadets and the Tasks of the Workers' Party* (1906) he expressed himself several times with emphasis: 'Dictatorship means unlimited power based on force, and not on law' (*Works*, vol. 10, p. 216). 'Authority—unlimited, outside the law, and based on force in the most direct sense of the word—is dictatorship' (ibid.,

p. 244). 'The scientific term "dictatorship" means nothing more nor less than authority untrammelled by any laws, absolutely unrestricted by any rules whatever, and based directly on violence. The term "dictatorship" has *no other meaning but this*—mark this well, Cadet gentlemen' (ibid., p. 246).

To make clear that his views had not changed, Lenin repeated the above statements in 1920. Dictatorship was the 'directest form of coercion', and the dictatorship of the proletariat was the exercise of force by the proletariat against the exploiters it had overthrown. As to how that force would be organized, Lenin gave the answers in his pamphlet *The State and Revolution*, directed against the leaders of the Second International. On the eve of the creation of the Third International (which he had in mind as early as 1915), and in the hope that revolution would soon break out all over Europe, Lenin thought it necessary to expound once again the Marxist theory of the state and of the changes that socialism would involve in the functioning of state institutions.

According to Marx and Engels, Lenin points out, the state is the result of irreconcilable class antagonisms, but not in the sense that it harmonizes them or arbitrates between them; on the contrary, the state as such has hitherto always been the instrument whereby the possessing classes have coerced the oppressed classes. Its institutions cannot be neutral in the class conflict, but are only the legal expression of the economic oppression of one class by another. Since the whole function of the bourgeois state is to perpetuate the exploitation of the working class, the institutions and organs of that state cannot be used to emancipate the workers. The suffrage in bourgeois states is not a means of relieving social tension, let alone of enabling the oppressed classes to gain power: it is merely a way of maintaining the authority of the bourgeoisie. The proletariat cannot free itself except by destroying the state apparatus; this is the main task of the revolution, and must be clearly distinguished from the 'withering away' of the state in accordance with Marxist theory. The bourgeois state must be smashed here and now; the withering away applies to the proletarian state after the revolution, i.e. at a future time when all political authority will be done away with.

Lenin refers particularly to Marx's article on the Paris Commune and his *Critique of the Gotha Programme*, and also to essays and letters by Engels. Reformism in the socialist movement and the idea of using the bourgeois state to serve the interests of the proletariat are, he declares, contrary to the basis of Marxism: they are delusions or deceitful manoeuvres of opportunists who have renounced the revolution. The proletariat needs a state (this is where the anarchists go wrong), but it must be a state that tends to wither away and destroy itself. To overcome the resistance of the exploiters in the transitional period, the length of which cannot be foreseen, there must be a dictatorship of the proletariat which, unlike all previous forms of state, will be the dictatorship of the great majority of society over the remnants of the possessing classes. During this period the freedom of capitalists must be limited, while full democracy will be possible only when classes have been done away with altogether. During the transition the state will be able to function without difficulty, as the majority will have no trouble crushing the minority of exploiters and will have no need of a special police machine.

The experience of the Paris Commune serves to illustrate the general features of communist state organization. In such a state, the standing army will be disbanded and the people will be armed instead; all state officials will be elected and dismissed by the working people; the police as such will not be needed, as their functions, like those of the army, will be performed by the whole of the population that is capable of bearing arms. In addition, the organizational functions of the state will become so simple that they can be performed by anyone who knows how to read and write. No special skill will be required for the running of society in general, and there will therefore be no separate caste of officials; simple administration and accounting will be performed by all citizens in turn, at a wage equal to that of manual workers (Lenin lays great stress on this). Everyone will be in equal degree a servant of the state, paid on an equal basis and equally obliged to work. They will be alternately manual workers and officials, so that nobody will become a bureaucrat. Given the simplicity of administration, equality of pay, and the election and removability of public officers, there will be no risk of the formation of a parasitic caste of bureaucrats alienated from society. To begin with there must be political compulsion, but as the state withers away its functions will gradually lose their political character and become matters of pure administration. Orders will no longer be given from the top; necessary central planning will be combined with broad territorial autonomy. In 'Materials Relating to the Revision of the Party Programme', written in April-May 1917, Lenin spoke of 'public education to be administered by democratically elected organs of local self-government; the central government not to be allowed to interfere with the arrangement of the school curriculum, or with the selection of the teaching staffs; teachers to be elected directly by the population with the right of the latter to remove undesirable teachers', etc. (*Works*, vol. 24, p. 473).

The final objective is the complete abolition of the state and of all constraint; this will be possible as people get accustomed to the principles of voluntary coexistence and solidarity. Crimes and excesses are due to exploitation and poverty, and so will gradually disappear under socialism—this conviction of Lenin's was practically universal among socialists.

Lenin's Utopia, described in these terms while the European war was raging, may well seem astoundingly naïve to those who read it after fifty years of Soviet power; it had about as much to do with the state that was soon to come into existence as Thomas More's fantasies had with the England of Henry VIII. But it is a sterile exercise to point out the grotesque divergences between programmes and their 'fulfilment' half a century later. Lenin's Utopia is in general accord with Marx's ideas, but as compared with Lenin's own earlier writings, not to speak of the later ones, it presents one striking difference, viz. that it says nothing whatever about the party.

There is no reason to doubt that Lenin penned his fantasy in good faith; it should be recalled that when he did so he believed, wrongly, that there was about to be a world revolution. But he apparently did not perceive that the picture he drew was manifestly contrary to his own doctrine of revolution and of the party. The 'dictatorship of the majority' was supposed to be exercised through a political organization imbued with a scientific understanding of history; this qualification, which cuts across the idea of a 'transitional proletariat state', is not mentioned at all in *The State and Revolution*. At the time of writing the book Lenin evidently envisaged that the whole people, armed and liberated, would directly perform all functions of administration, economic management, the police, the army, the judiciary, etc. He also believed that restraints on freedom would apply only to the former privileged classes, while the workers and labouring peasants would be perfectly free to regulate their lives as they chose.

However, the nature of the system that developed after the Revolution was not merely the result of historical accidents connected with the civil war and the halting of the revolutionary movement outside Russia. The system, with all its despotic and totalitarian features (the distinction is important), was prefigured in its main lines by the Bolshevik doctrine as Lenin had worked it out over the years, though naturally the consequences were not fully realized or predicted.

The basic principle laid down by Lenin in different forms on many occasions since 1903 was that categories such as freedom and political equality were not intrinsic values but only instruments of the class struggle, and it was foolish to advocate them without considering what class interests they served. 'In practice the proletariat can retain its independence only by subordinating its struggle for all democratic demands, not excluding the demand for a republic, to its revolutionary struggle for the overthrow of the bourgeoisie' ('The Socialist Revolution and the Right of Nations to Self-Determination', Apr. 1916; *Works*, vol. 22, p. 149). Under the bourgeois system, the difference between a despotism and a democracy was only significant in so far as the latter facilitated the working-class struggle; it was a secondary difference, one of form only. 'Universal suffrage, a Constituent Assembly, a parliament are merely a form, a sort of promissory note, which does not change the real state of affairs' ('The State', lecture delivered on 11 July 1919; *Works*, vol. 29, p. 485). This is true *a fortiori* of the post-

revolutionary state. Since the proletariat is in power, no consideration is important in itself except the maintenance of that power; all organizational questions
are subordinate to the preservation of the dictatorship of the proletariat.

The dictatorship of the proletariat will—not provisionally, but permanently—
abolish the parliamentary system and the separation of the legislative power
from the executive. This is to be the main difference between the Soviet republic and a parliamentary regime. At the Seventh Congress of the Russian Communist Party (Bolshevik) in March 1918 Lenin presented a draft programme
embodying this principle: 'Abolition of parliamentarism (as the separation of
legislative from executive activity); union of legislative and executive state
activity. Fusion of administration with legislation' (*Works*, vol. 27, p. 154). In
other words, the rulers determine the laws by which they rule and are not controlled by anyone. But who are the rulers? In the same draft Lenin emphasizes
that freedom and democracy are not intended to be for all, but for the labouring and exploited masses and for the sake of their liberation. At the outset of
the Revolution Lenin hoped for support not only from the proletariat but from
the working peasants as opposed to the kulaks; but it soon became clear that
while the whole of the peasantry supported the Revolution against the big
landowners, they were much less enthusiastic for the next phase. The party
placed its hopes from the beginning on kindling the class struggle in the countryside, and tried to rouse the poor peasants and farm-labourers against the
richer peasants, *inter alia* by the so-called 'Committees of the Poor'. The results
were meagre, and it was clear that the common interest of the peasants as a
class was generally stronger than the conflict between poor peasants and
kulaks. Lenin soon began to speak for preference of 'neutralizing' the peasantry as a whole, and at the Tenth Party Conference in May 1921, on the eve of
N.E.P., he declared: 'We tell the peasants frankly and honestly, without any
deception: in order to hold the road to socialism, we are making a number of
concessions to you, comrade peasants, but only within the stated limits and to
the stated extent; and, of course, we ourselves shall be the judge of the limits
and the extent' (*Works*, vol. 32, p. 419).

The first 'transitional' slogan, that of the dictatorship of the proletariat and
the needy peasants, was never more than a delusion or a propaganda device.
The party in due course openly admitted that the dictatorship of the proletariat
was exercised over the whole peasantry, which thus had no say in deciding the
matters that concerned it most, though it was still an obstacle that had to be
taken into account. The situation was indeed obvious from the beginning: as
the November elections showed, if the peasants had had a share in power the
country would have been governed by the S.R.s, with the Bolshevik minority
in opposition.

The proletariat thus shared its dictatorship with nobody. As to the question of the 'majority', this never troubled Lenin much. In an article 'Constitutional Illusions' (Aug. 1917; *Works*, vol. 25, p. 201) he wrote: 'in time of revolution it is not enough to ascertain the "will of the majority"—you must *prove to be stronger* at the decisive moment and at the decisive place; you must *win* . . . We have seen innumerable examples of the better organized, more politically-conscious and better armed minority forcing its will upon the majority and defeating it.'

It was clear from the beginning, however, that the proletarian minority was to exercise power not in the manner described in *The State and Revolution*, but in accordance with the principle that the proletariat is 'represented' by the party. Lenin did not shrink from using the phrase 'dictatorship of the party'— this was at a time when the party still had to answer its critics and was some-times cornered into frankness. In a speech on 31 July 1919 he declared: 'When we are reproached with having established a dictatorship of one party and, as you have heard, a united socialist front is proposed, we say, "Yes, it is a dicta-torship of one party! That is what we stand for and we shall not shift from that position, because it is the party that has won, in the course of decades, the posi-tion of vanguard of the entire factory and industrial proletariat' (*Works*, vol. 29, p. 535). In a document on the trade unions in January 1922, after mentioning the 'contradictions' arising from the backwardness of the masses, he declared: 'The aforementioned contradictions will inevitably give rise to disputes, dis-agreements, friction, etc. A higher body is required with sufficient authority to settle these at once. This higher body is the Communist Party and the interna-tional federation of the Communist Parties of all countries—the Communist International' (*Works*, vol. 33, p. 193).

From the theoretical point of view the matter was elucidated by Lenin's famous pamphlet *'Left-Wing' Communism—an Infantile Disorder* (1920), from which it appeared that there was no problem at all.

The mere presentation of the question—'dictatorship of the party *or* dictatorship of the class; dictatorship (party) of the leaders, *or* dictatorship (party) of the masses?'— testifies to most incredibly and hopelessly muddled thinking . . . It is common knowledge that the masses are divided into classes . . . that as a rule and in most cases—at least in present-day civilized countries—classes are led by political parties; that political parties, as a general rule, are run by more or less stable groups com-posed of the most authoritative, influential and experienced members, who are elected to the most responsible positions, and are called leaders. All this is elemen-tary. All this is clear and simple. Why replace this with some kind of rigmarole, some new Volapük?

> The Russian Bolshevik . . . cannot help regarding all this talk about 'from above' *or* 'from below', about the dictatorship of leaders *or* the dictatorship of the masses, etc., as ridiculous and childish nonsense, something like discussing whether a man's left leg or right arm is of greater use to him. (*Works*, vol. 31, pp. 41, 49)

In thus ruling the issue out of court, Lenin implied that there was no problem about the relationship between a class and a party, or a party and its leaders, and that government by a handful of oligarchs can properly be called government by the class they claim to represent, although there is no institutional means of telling whether the class wants to have them as its representatives or not. Lenin's argument is so crude that it is difficult to believe he meant it seriously (in the above passage he was replying to the German Spartacists, who had criticized him on similar lines to Rosa Luxemburg); yet it harmonizes well enough with his general style of thought. Since nothing 'really' exists except class interests, any alleged problem concerning the independent interests of a governing group or apparatus is a false problem: apparatuses 'represent' classes, that is 'elementary' and everything else is 'childish nonsense'.

Lenin was quite consistent in such matters. According to *The State and Revolution* only an ignoramus or a crafty bourgeois could suggest that the workers are incapable of directly and collectively managing industry, the state, and the administration. Two years later, it turned out that only an ignoramus or a crafty bourgeois could suggest that the workers were capable of directly and collectively managing industry, the state, and the administration. Obviously industry requires single managers, and it is absurd to talk of 'collegiality'. 'Opinions on corporate management are all too frequently imbued with a spirit of sheer ignorance, a spirit of opposition to the specialists . . . We must get [the trade unions] to regard this task in the spirit of the fight against the survivals of the celebrated democracy. All these outcries against appointees, all this old and dangerous rubbish which finds its way into various resolutions and conversations must be swept away' (speech to Ninth Congress of R.C.P. (B.), 29 Mar. 1920; *Works*, vol. 30, pp. 458–9). 'Does every worker know how to run the state? People working in the practical sphere know that this is not true . . . We know that workers in touch with peasants are liable to fall for non-proletarian slogans. How many of the workers have been engaged in government? A few thousand throughout Russia and no more. If we say that it is not the Party but the trade unions that put up the candidates and administrate, it may sound very democratic and might help us to catch a few votes, but not for long. It will be fatal for the dictatorship of the proletariat' (speech to Congress of Miners, 23 Jan. 1921; *Works*, vol. 32, pp. 61–2). 'But the dictatorship of the proletariat cannot be exercised through an organization embracing the whole of that class . . . It can be exercised only by a vanguard that has absorbed the revolutionary energy of the class' (speech on 'The Trade Unions, the Present Situation and Trotsky's Mistakes', 30 Dec. 1921; ibid., p. 21).

It thus appears, thanks to a peculiar dialectic, that a proletarian government would be the ruin of the dictatorship of the proletariat—a perfectly plausible conclusion, given Lenin's interpretation of the latter term. It also appears that 'true' democracy means the abolition of all institutions that have hitherto been regarded as democratic. On this last point Lenin's language was not quite consistent: at times he extolled Soviet power as the highest form of democracy, since it meant rule by the people, while at others he stigmatized democracy as a bourgeois invention. This led to amusing contradictions, as in his speech to the Third Congress of Soviets on 25 January 1918: 'Democracy is a form of bourgeois state championed by all traitors to genuine socialism, who now find themselves at the head of official socialism and who assert that democracy is contrary to the dictatorship of the proletariat. Until the revolution transcended the limits of the bourgeois system, we were for democracy; but as soon as we saw the first signs of socialism in the progress of the revolution we took a firm and resolute stand for the dictatorship of the proletariat' (*Works*, vol. 26, p. 473). In other words, traitors to socialism assert that democracy is the opposite of dictatorship, but we have abandoned democracy for dictatorship, which is its opposite. Such awkwardnesses indicate that Lenin was conscious of the daily erosion of what few democratic institutions remained, but wished from time to time to invoke the virtuous-sounding name of democracy.

Directly after the Revolution the traditional democratic freedoms which the Bolsheviks had insistently demanded until they came to power turned out to be weapons of the bourgeoisie. Lenin's writings confirm this repeatedly as far as freedom of the Press is concerned. '"Freedom of the press" in bourgeois society means freedom for the *rich* systematically, unremittingly, daily, in millions of copies, to deceive, corrupt and fool the exploited and oppressed mass of the people, the poor' ('How to Guarantee the Success of the Constituent Assembly', 28 Sept. 1917; *Works*, vol. 25, p. 376). As against this, 'freedom of the press means that all opinions of *all* citizens may be freely published' (ibid., p. 377). This was so on the eve of the Revolution, but a few days after it things were different. 'Earlier on we said that if we took power, we intended to close down the bourgeois newspapers. To tolerate the existence of these papers is to cease being a socialist' (speech to the Central Executive Committee, 17 Nov. 1917; *Works*, vol. 26, p. 285). Lenin promised—and kept his word—that 'we shall not allow ourselves to be deceived by such high-sounding slogans as freedom, equality and the will of the majority' (*Works*, vol. 29, p. 351). 'At the present time, when things have reached the stage of overthrowing the rule of capital all over the world, or at all events in one country . . . all those who in such a political situation talk about "freedom" in general, who in the name of this freedom oppose the dictatorship of the proletariat, are doing nothing more nor less than aiding and abetting the exploiters, for unless freedom promotes the emancipation of labour from the yoke of capital, it is a deception' (speech on 19 May 1919; *Works*, vol. 29, p. 352). The point was put most clearly and concisely at the Third Congress of the Comintern: 'Until the final issue is decided on the general scale, this awful state of war will continue. And we say "*A la guerre comme à la guerre*; we do not promise any freedom, or any democracy"' (5 July 1921; *Works*, vol. 32, p. 495). The whole question of representative institutions, civil rights, the rights of minorities (or of the majority), control over government, constitutional problems in general—all these are silenced by the maxim *à la guerre comme à la guerre*, and the war is to go on until communism triumphs the world over. In particular, and this is the heart of the matter, the whole idea of *law* as a system of social mediation ceases to exist. Since law is 'nothing but' the instrument whereby one class oppresses another, there is clearly no essential difference between the rule of law and rule by direct compulsion; all that matters is which class has the upper hand. In a letter to D.I. Kursky in May 1922 Lenin wrote: 'The courts must not ban terror . . . but must formulate the motives underlying it, legalize it as a principle, plainly, without any make-believe or embellishment.' In an accompanying draft amendment to the Criminal Code he proposed the wording: 'Propaganda or agitation that objectively serves [variant: serves or is likely to serve] the interests of that section of the international bourgeoisie which refuses to recognize the rights of the communist system of ownership that is superseding capitalism, and is striving to overthrow that system by violence, either by means of foreign intervention or blockade, or by espionage, financing the press, and similar means, is an offence punishable by death, which, if mitigating circumstances are proved, may be commuted to deprivation of liberty, or deportation' (sc. from Russia: *vysylka za granitsu*) (*Works*, vol. 33, pp. 358–9). At the Eleventh Congress of the R.C.P.(B.) Lenin declared that the Mensheviks and S.R.s who maintained that the N.E.P. was a retreat towards capitalism and that this proved the bourgeois character of the revolution, would be shot for making such statements (ibid., pp. 282–3).

In this way Lenin laid the foundations of the legislation that distinguishes a totalitarian from a merely despotic system, the operative fact being not that it is severe but that it is spurious. A law may provide draconic penalties for small offences without being specifically totalitarian; what is characteristic of totalitarian law is the use of such formulas as Lenin's: people may be executed for expressing views that may 'objectively serve the interests of the bourgeoisie'. This means that the government can put to death anyone it chooses; there is no such thing as law; it is not that the criminal code is severe, but that it has no existence except in name.

As already mentioned, all this took place at a time when the party was not yet in full control and had sometimes to answer criticism. Paradoxically, the sharp and unambiguous formulas in which Lenin called for the use of terror and denied the possibility of democracy and freedom testified to the fact that freedom had not yet been completely eradicated. In the Stalin era, when there was no criticism from outside the party to contend with, the language of terror was replaced by that of democracy: especially in Stalin's later years, the Soviet system was presented as the supreme embodiment of popular rule and every kind of democratic freedom. In Lenin's day, however, the leaders had to answer socialist critics both in Russia and in the rest of Europe, who protested strongly at the idea that the dictatorship of the proletariat involved the destruction of democracy. Kautsky's onslaught on the Soviet system in his *Dictatorship of the Proletariat* (1918) drew a furious reply from Lenin: in *The Proletarian Revolution and the Renegade Kautsky* (1918) he repeated his attack on ignoramuses who talked of democracy irrespective of its class content, wilfully obscuring the fact that bourgeois democracy was for the bourgeoisie and proletarian democracy for the proletariat. Kautsky had argued that when Marx spoke of a 'dictatorship of the proletariat' he had in mind the class content of the regime and not its methods of government; democratic institutions, in Kautsky's view, were not only compatible with proletarian rule but were a condition of it. To Lenin all this was nonsense. Since the proletariat was governing, it must govern by force, and dictatorship was government by force and not by law.

7. Trotsky on dictatorship

KAUTSKY's next pamphlet, *Terrorism and Communism*, was answered by Trotsky in a work bearing the same title: an English translation appeared in 1921 as *The Defence of Terrorism*. This revealing work is in some ways even more emphatic than Lenin's utterances. Trotsky, who had foreseen in 1903 that Lenin's theory of the party would lead to a one-man tyranny, was completely converted to that theory by 1920. His pamphlet is noteworthy as containing the most general exposition, written when he was in power, of the theory of the state under a proletarian dictatorship, and also the most explicit account of what has come to be called the totalitarian system. True, the pamphlet was written during the civil war and the war with Poland (concerning which Trotsky says with remarkable naïvety: 'We hope for the victory, for we have every historical right to it'), but it clearly aspires to be a work of general theory; the many quotations from Trotsky's previous speeches show that he is not merely exaggerating his thesis in the heat of the moment. He presents the general principles of the dictatorship of the proletariat in the same way as Lenin. Bourgeois democracy is a cheat; serious issues in the class war are decided not by votes but by force; in time of revolution the right course is to fight for power and not wait foolishly for a 'majority'; to reject terror is to reject socialism (he who wills the end must will the means); parliamentary systems have had their day—they mainly reflected the interests of the intermediate classes, while in the revolutionary era it is only the proletariat and the bourgeoisie that count; talk of 'equality before the law', civil rights, etc. is, at the present day, nothing but metaphysical claptrap; it was right to disperse the Constituent Assembly, if only because the electoral system was overtaken by the rapid course of events, and the assembly did not represent the people's will; it was right to shoot hostages (*à la guerre comme à la guerre*); freedom of the Press could not be permitted, as it aided the class enemy and its allies, the Mensheviks and the S.R.s; it was idle to talk about 'truth' and who was right—this was not an academic debate, but a fight to the death; the rights of the individual were irrelevant nonsense, and 'as for us, we were never concerned with the Kantian-priestly and vegetarian-Quaker prattle about the "sacredness of human life"' (*The Defence of Terrorism*, p. 60). The Paris Commune had been defeated because of sentimental and humanitarian qualms; in a dictatorship of the proletariat the party must be the highest court of appeal and have the last word in all important matters; 'the revolutionary supremacy of the proletariat presupposes within the proletariat itself the political supremacy of a party, with a clear programme of action and a faultless internal discipline' (ibid., p. 100); 'the dictatorship of the Soviets became possible only by means of the dictatorship of the party' (p. 101).

Trotsky, however, answers questions that Lenin evaded or ignored. 'Where is your guarantee, certain wise men ask us, that it is just your party that expresses the interests of historical development? Destroying or driving underground the other parties, you have thereby prevented their political competition with you, and consequently you have deprived yourselves of the possibility of testing your line of action.' Trotsky replies: 'This idea is dictated by a purely liberal conception of the course of the revolution. In a period in which all antagonisms assume an open character, and the political struggle swiftly passes into a civil war, the ruling party has sufficient material standard by which to test its line of action, without the possible circulation of Menshevik papers. Noske crushes the Communists, but they grow. We have suppressed the Mensheviks and the S.R.s—and they have disappeared. This criterion is sufficient for us' (p. 101).

This is one of the most enlightening theoretical formulations of Bolshevism, from which it appears that the 'rightness' of a historical movement or a state is to be judged by whether its use of violence is successful. Noske did not succeed in crushing the German Communists, but Hitler did; it would thus follow from Trotsky's rule that Hitler 'expressed the interests of historical development'.

Stalin liquidated the Trotskyists in Russia, and they disappeared—so evidently Stalin, and not Trotsky, stood for historical progress.

From the principle of government by a vanguard it followed, of course, that

> the continuous 'independence' of the trade union movement, in the period of the proletarian revolution, is just as much an impossibility as the policy of coalition. The trade unions become the most important economic organs of the proletariat in power. Thereby they fall under the leadership of the Communist Party. Not only questions of principle in the trade union movement, but serious conflicts of organization within it are decided by the Central Committee of our party . . . [The unions] are the organs of production of the Soviet State, and assume responsibility for its fortunes—not opposing themselves to it, but identifying themselves with it. The unions become the organizers of labour discipline. They demand from the workers intensive labour under the most difficult conditions. (*The Defence of Terrorism*, p. 102)

The state is, of course, organized in the interest of the working masses; 'this, however, does not exclude the element of compulsion in all its forms, both the most gentle and the extremely severe' (ibid., p. 122). In the new society compulsion will not only not disappear but will play an essential part: 'The very principle of compulsory labour service is for the Communist quite unquestionable . . . The only solution of economic difficulties that is correct *from the point of view both of principle and of practice* [present author's italics] is to treat the population of the whole country as the reservoir of the necessary labour-power . . . The principle itself of compulsory labour service has just as *radically and permanently* [present author's italics] replaced the principle of free hiring as the socialization of the means of production has replaced capitalist property' (pp. 124–7). Labour must be militarized: 'we oppose . . . capitalist slavery by socially regulated labour on the basis of an economic plan, obligatory for the whole people and consequently compulsory for each worker in the country . . . The foundations of the militarization of labour are those forms of State compulsion without which the replacement of capitalist economy by the Socialist will for ever remain an empty sound . . . No social organization except the army has ever considered itself justified in subordinating citizens to itself in such a measure, and controlling them by its will on all sides to such a degree, as the State of the proletarian dictatorship considers itself justified in doing, and does' (pp. 129–30). 'We can have no way to Socialism except by the authoritative regulation of the economic forces and resources of the country, and the centralized distribution of labour-power in harmony with the general State plan. The Labour State considers itself empowered to send every worker to the place where his work is necessary' (p. 131). 'The young Socialist State requires trade unions, not for a struggle for better conditions of labour—that is the task of the social and State organization as a whole—but to organize the working class for the ends of production, to educate, discipline, distribute, group, retain certain categories and certain workers at their posts for fixed periods' (p. 132). To sum up, 'the road to Socialism lies through a period of the highest possible intensification of the principle of the State . . . The State, before disappearing, assumes the form of the dictatorship of the proletariat, i.e. the most ruthless form of State, which embraces the life of the citizens authoritatively in every direction' (p. 157).

It would be difficult indeed to put the matter more plainly. The state of the proletarian dictatorship is depicted by Trotsky as a huge permanent concentration camp in which the government exercises absolute power over every aspect of the citizens' lives and in particular decides how much work they shall do, of what kind and in what places. Individuals are nothing but labour units. Compulsion is universal, and any organization that is not part of the state must be its enemy, thus the enemy of the proletariat. All this, of course, is in the name of an ideal realm of freedom, the advent of which is expected after an indefinite lapse of historical time. Trotsky, we may say, provided a perfect expression of socialist principles as understood by the Bolsheviks. It should be noted, however, that we are not told clearly what, from the Marxist point of view, is to replace the free hiring of labour—which, according to Marx, is a mark of slavery, as it means that a man has to sell his labour-power on the market, i.e. treat himself as a commodity and be so treated by society. If free hiring is abolished, the only ways of inducing people to work and produce wealth are physical compulsion or moral motivation (enthusiasm for work). The latter was of course much extolled by both Lenin and Trotsky, but they soon found that it was chimerical to rely on it as a permanent source of effort. Only compulsion was left—not capitalist compulsion based on the necessity to earn a living, but sheer physical force, the fear of imprisonment, physical injury, and death.

8. Lenin as an ideologist of totalitarianism

Lenin, who in important practical matters was much less doctrinaire than Trotsky, departed from his own principles on at least two points. In the first place, he recognized that the trade unions had a part to play not only in the execution of planned production but also in defending the workers against the state—although previously, with true Marxist logic, he had maintained, like Trotsky, that this meant the working class defending itself against itself, which was absurd. Secondly, he admitted that the state was suffering from 'bureaucratic distortion', though it was not clear how this could fit into his mental scheme: on the face of things, from the viewpoint of class interests, capitalist bureaucracy was an instrument of oppression and socialist bureaucracy of liberation.

It does credit to his common sense that in both these matters he was able to sacrifice dogma to reality, but unfortunately he saw the light too late to do anything. In any case, for one word in favour of trade-union independence he uttered ten about the danger of syndicalism, and he had no cure for bureaucracy except more bureaucracy. Any illusion that the party itself could be an enclave of free speech and free criticism, suppressed in society at large, was doomed to early disappointment. Lenin himself, as we have seen, never regarded cliques or disputes within the party as a healthy sign. As early as 1910, at grips with the otzovists and the slogan of 'complete freedom of revolutionary and philosophical thought', he wrote: 'This slogan is thoroughly opportunist. In all countries this kind of slogan has been put forward in the socialist parties only by opportunists and in practice has meant nothing but "freedom" to corrupt the working class with bourgeois ideology. "Freedom of thought" (read: freedom of the press, speech and conscience) we demand from the *state* (not from a party) together with freedom of association' ('The *Vperyod* Faction', Sept. 1910; *Works*, vol. 16, p. 270). This, of course, referred to the bourgeois state. Once the authority of the state was identified with that of the party, the rules applying to freedom of criticism must evidently be the same for both. The *Gleichschaltung* of the party took longer, but was equally inevitable: the matter was settled in principle at the Tenth Congress, in March 1921, by Lenin's attack on factionalism and 'the luxury of studying shades of opinion', and his statement that 'we must make it quite clear that we cannot have arguments about deviations and that we must put a stop to that' (*Works*, vol. 32, pp. 177–8). For some years after Lenin's death it was impossible completely to prevent the overt formation of groups and 'platforms' within the party, or rather the party apparatus; but before long genuine or imaginary 'deviations' were dealt with by the punitive arm of the state, and the ideal of unity was achieved by police methods.

If it can be said, however, that Lenin's doctrine and the style of thought that went with it laid the foundations of the totalitarian system, this is not on account of the principles invoked to justify the use of terror and the stifling of civil liberties. Once the civil war begins, extreme measures of terrorism are to be expected from both sides. The extinguishing of civil liberties in order to maintain and strengthen the regime does not amount to totalitarianism unless accompanied by the principle that every activity—economic, cultural, etc.— must be completely subordinated to the aims of the state; that not only are acts against the regime forbidden and ruthlessly punished, but no political actions are 'neutral' and the individual citizen has no right to do anything that is not part of the state's purposes; that he is the state's property and is treated by it as such. The Soviet system, which took over these principles from Tsarist Russia and brought them to a far greater degree of perfection, is in this respect also the work of Lenin.

Lenin never believed in the possibility of impartiality or neutrality in any sphere of life, including philosophy. Anyone who claimed to belong to no party, or declared himself neutral, was a secret enemy. Attacking the railwaymen's union shortly after the Revolution, on 1 December 1917, Lenin told the Congress of Soviets of Peasants' Deputies: 'At a time of revolutionary struggle, when every minute counts, when dissent and neutrality allow the enemy to put in his word, when he will certainly be heard, and when no haste is made to help the people in their struggle for their sacred rights, I cannot call such a stand neutrality; it is not neutrality; a revolutionary would call it incitement' (*Works*, vol. 26, pp. 329–30).

There were no 'neutrals' in politics, or anywhere else. Whatever question Lenin was concerned with at any time, all that interested him was whether it was good or bad for the revolution or, afterwards, for the Soviet government. His four short articles on Tolstoy, written in 1910–11 after the latter's death, are a typical example. His central theme is the existence of 'two aspects' in Tolstoy's work: the first reactionary and utopian (moral perfection, charity towards all, and non-resistance to evil), the second 'progressive' and critical (description of the oppression and misery of the peasants, the hypocrisy of the upper classes and the Church, etc.). The 'reactionary' aspect of Tolstoy's doctrine was emphasized by reactionaries, but the 'progressive' aspect might afford 'useful material' for the purpose of arousing the masses, although the political struggle was already much wider in scope than Tolstoy's criticism. Lenin's article of 1905, 'Party Organization and Party Literature', was used for decades, and is still used, to justify ideologically the enslavement of the written word in Russia. It has been argued that it refers only to political literature, but this is not so: it relates to every kind of writing. It contains the words: 'Down with nonpartisan writers! Down with literary supermen! Literature must become part of the common cause of the proletariat, "a cog and a screw" of one single great Social-Democratic mechanism set in motion by the entire politically conscious vanguard of the entire working class' (*Works*, vol. 10, p. 45). For the benefit of 'hysterical intellectuals' who deplore this seemingly bureaucratic attitude, Lenin explains that there can be no mechanical levelling in the field of literature; there must be room for personal initiative, imagination, etc.; none the less, literary work must be part of the party's work and controlled by the party. This, of course, was written during the fight for 'bourgeois democracy', on the assumption that Russia would in due course enjoy freedom of speech but that literary members of the party would have to display party-mindedness in their writings; as in other cases, the obligation would become general when the party controlled the apparatus of state coercion.

Lenin's often-quoted speech to the Komsomol Congress on 2 October 1920 deals with ethical questions on similar lines. 'We say that our morality is

entirely subordinated to the interests of the proletariat's class struggle . . .
Morality is what serves to destroy the old exploiting society and to unite all the
working people around the proletariat, which is building up a new, a communist society . . . To a Communist all morality lies in this united discipline and
conscious mass struggle against the exploiters. We do not believe in an eternal
morality, and we expose the falseness of all the fables about morality' (*Works*,
vol. 31, pp. 291–4). It would be hard to interpret these words in any other sense
than that everything which serves or injures the party's aims is morally good or
bad respectively, and nothing else is morally good or bad. After the seizure of
power, the maintenance and strengthening of Soviet rule becomes the sole criterion of morality as well as of all cultural values. No criteria can avail against
any action that may seem conducive to the maintenance of power, and no values can be recognized on any other basis. All cultural questions thus become
technical questions and must be judged by the one unvarying standard; the
'good of society' becomes completely alienated from the good of its individual
members. It is bourgeois sentimentalism, for instance, to condemn aggression
and annexation if it can be shown that they help to maintain Soviet power; it
is illogical and hypocritical to condemn torture if it serves the ends of the power
which, by definition, is devoted to the 'liberation of the working masses'. Utilitarian morality and utilitarian judgements of social and cultural phenomena
transform the original basis of socialism into its opposite. All phenomena that
arouse moral indignation if they occur in bourgeois society are turned to gold,
as if by a Midas touch, if they serve the interests of the new power: the armed
invasion of a foreign state is liberation, aggression is defence, tortures represent the people's noble rage against the exploiters. There is absolutely nothing
in the worst excesses of the worst years of Stalinism that cannot be justified on
Leninist principles, if only it can be shown that Soviet power was increased
thereby. The essential difference between the 'Lenin era' and the 'Stalin era' is
not that under Lenin there was freedom in the party and society and that under
Stalin it was crushed, but that it was only in Stalin's day that the whole spiritual life of the peoples of the Soviet Union was submerged in a universal flood
of mendacity. This was due, however, not only to Stalin's personality but also,
if one may so put it, to the 'natural' development of the situation. When Lenin
spoke of terror, bureaucracy, or an anti-Bolshevik rising by the peasants, he
called these things by their names. Once the Stalinist dictatorship set in, the
party (though attacked by its enemies) had no mistakes whatever to its discredit, the Soviet state was flawless, and the people's love for the government
was unbounded. The change was natural in the sense that in a state where
every vestige of institutional control over the government had been done away
with, the latter's only justification was that, as a matter of foreordained principle, it embodied the interests and aspirations of the working people: this may

be called an ideological form of legitimacy, distinct from the charisma which belongs to a hereditary monarchy or from a properly elected regime. The omnipotence of the Lie was not due to Stalin's wickedness, but was the only way of legitimizing a regime based on Leninist principles. The slogan constantly met with during Stalin's dictatorship, 'Stalin is the Lenin of our day', was thus entirely accurate.

9. Martov on the Bolshevik ideology

TOGETHER with Kautsky and Rosa Luxemburg, Martov was the third eminent critic of Bolshevik ideology and tactics in the years immediately after the Revolution. His *World Bolshevism* (1923, in Russian), a collection of articles written chiefly in 1918–19, is probably the most important attempt to criticize Leninism from the Menshevik standpoint, i.e. it represents a social democratic view similar to Kautsky's. Martov claimed that the assumption of power by the Bolsheviks in Russia had little in common with the proletarian revolution as traditionally understood by Marxists. The successes of Bolshevism were not due to the maturity of the working class, but to its disintegration and the demoralization of war. The pre-war working class, educated in socialism for years or decades by the parties, had been depraved by the years of slaughter and altered in character by the influx of the rural element, a process which had taken place in all the belligerent nations. The former authority of ideas had vanished; crude, simple maxims were the order of the day; actions were dictated by direct material needs and the belief that all social questions could be solved by force of arms. The socialist Left had been defeated in its attempt, at Zimmerwald, to save what remained of the proletarian movement. The fact that Marxism had disintegrated during the war into 'social patriotism' on the one hand and Bolshevik anarcho-Jacobinism on the other was only a confirmation of the Marxist theory that consciousness depends on social conditions. The ruling classes, by means of their armies, were perpetrating mass destruction, pillage, forced labour, etc. In the midst of this general regression, world Bolshevism had arisen on the ruins of the socialist movement. Contrasting the promises in Lenin's *The State and Revolution* with post-Revolutionary reality, Martov nevertheless takes the view that the true sense of Bolshevism does not lie in the restriction of democracy: Plekhanov's old idea that the revolution should for a time deprive the bourgeoisie of electoral rights could have been applied if there had existed other forms of institutional democracy. The ideology of Bolshevism is based on the principle that scientific socialism is true and must therefore be imposed on the masses who, deluded by the bourgeoisie, cannot understand their own interests; for this purpose it is necessary to destroy parliament, the free Press, and all representative institutions. This doctrine, Martov says, is in accordance with a certain strain in the tradition of utopian socialism: measures similar to those of the Bolsheviks figured in the programme of the Babouvists, Weitling, Cabet, or the Blanquists. They are, however, contrary to dialectical materialism. From the principle that the working class is spiritually dependent on the society in which it lives, the utopians drew the inference that society must be transformed by a handful of conspirators or an enlightened élite, with the labouring masses playing the role of a passive object. But the dialectic view, expressed, for example, in Marx's third *Thesis on Feuerbach*, is that there is a constant interaction between human consciousness and material conditions, and that as the working class struggles to alter these conditions it changes itself and achieves spiritual liberation. The dictatorship of a minority cannot educate either society or the dictators themselves. The proletariat can only take over the achievements of bourgeois society when it becomes capable of taking the initiative as a class, and it cannot do so in conditions of despotism, bureaucracy, and terror.

The Bolsheviks, Martov continues, are not entitled to appeal to Marx's formulas concerning the dictatorship of the proletariat and the destruction of the former state machine. Marx attacked the electoral law in the name of universal eligibility and popular sovereignty, not the despotism of a single party. He called for the abolition of the anti-democratic institutions of the democratic state—police, standing army, centralized bureaucracy—but not the abolition of democracy as such: the dictatorship of the proletariat meant to him not a form of government but a particular kind of society. The Leninists, on the other hand, proclaim the anarchist slogan of smashing the state machine and are seeking at the same time to rebuild it in the most despotic form possible.

The dispute between Lenin and Martov thus ended at the point where it had begun in 1903. When Martov spoke of working-class rule he meant what he said, whereas in Lenin's view the working class left to itself could only produce bourgeois ideology, and to give it real power would amount to restoring capitalism. As Lenin wrote quite rightly in August 1921: 'The slogan "more faith in the forces of the working class" is now being used, in fact, to increase the influence of the Mensheviks and anarchists, as was vividly proved and demonstrated by Kronstadt in the spring of 1921' ('New Times and Old Mistakes in a New Guise'; *Works*, vol. 33, p. 27). Martov wanted the state to take over all the democratic institutions of the past and increase their scope; Lenin's state was communist only inasmuch as the communists had a monopoly of power in it. Martov believed in cultural continuity; to Lenin, the only 'culture' that should be taken over from the bourgeoisie consisted of technical and administrative skills. However, Martov was mistaken when he accused the Bolsheviks of expressing in their ideology the hunger of the demoralized masses for material goods. This view was occasioned by the mass plundering which marked the first phase of the Revolution; but neither Lenin nor any other Bolshevik leader regarded plundering as an expression of communist doctrine. On the contrary, Lenin maintained that increased labour productivity was the hallmark of socialist superiority, and he relied mainly, if not wholly, on technical progress to bring about socialism. He wrote, for instance, that if scores of regional electric power-stations were constructed—which, however, would take at least ten years—even the most backward parts of Russia would pass straight to socialism without any intervening stage (*The Tax in Kind*, May 1921; *Works*, vol. 32, p. 350). It was in fact the Bolsheviks who established the idea that global production indices are the basic evidence for the success of socialism; although of course not in so many words, they sanctified the principle of production for its own sake, irrespective of whether it makes life better for the producers, i.e. the whole working community. This was an important aspect, though not the only one, of the cult of state power as the supreme value.

10. Lenin as a polemicist. Lenin's genius

THE great bulk of Lenin's published work consists of attacks and polemics. The reader is invariably struck by the coarseness and aggressiveness of his style, which are unparalleled in the whole literature of socialism. His polemics are full of insults and humourless mockery (he had in fact no sense of humour at all). It makes no difference whether he is attacking the 'economists', the Mensheviks, the Kadets, Kautsky, Trotsky, or the 'workers' opposition': if his opponent is not a lackey of the bourgeoisie and the landowners he is a prostitute, a clown, a liar, a pettifogging rogue, and so on. This style of controversy was to become obligatory in Soviet writing on topics of the day, though in a stereotyped, bureaucratic form devoid of personal passion. If Lenin's opponent happens to say something he agrees with, the man is 'forced to admit' whatever it is; if a dispute breaks out in the enemy camp, one of its members has 'blurted out' the truth about another; if the author of a book or article does not mention something that Lenin thinks he ought to have mentioned, he has 'hushed it up'. His socialist adversary of the moment 'fails to understand the ABC of Marxism'; if, however, Lenin changes his mind on the point at issue, the one who 'fails to understand the ABC of Marxism' is he who maintains what Lenin was maintaining the day before. Everyone is constantly suspected of the worst intentions; anyone who differs from Lenin on the most trifling matter is a cheat, or at best a stupid child.

The purpose of this technique was not to satisfy any personal dislike, still less to arrive at the truth, but to achieve a practical object. Lenin himself confirmed this ('blurted it out', as he would have said of anyone else) on an occasion in 1907. On the eve of reunion with the Mensheviks the Central

Committee had brought Lenin before a party tribunal for 'impermissible' attacks on them: he had said in a pamphlet, among other things, that the St. Petersburg Mensheviks had 'entered into negotiations with the Cadet Party for the purpose of selling workers' votes to the Cadets', and had 'bargained with the Cadets to smuggle (*prolashchit*') their man into the Duma, in spite of the workers, with the aid of the Cadets'. Lenin explained his action to the tribunal as follows. 'The wording [i.e. that just quoted] is calculated to evoke in the reader hatred, aversion and contempt for people who commit such deeds. Such wording is calculated not to convince, but to break up the ranks of the opponent; not to correct the mistake of the opponent, but to destroy him, to wipe his organization off the face of the earth. This wording is indeed of such a nature as to evoke the worst thoughts, the worst suspicions about the opponent, and indeed, as contrasted with the wording that convinces and corrects, it "carries confusion into the ranks of the proletariat"' (*Works*, vol. 12, pp. 424–5). Lenin, however, is not expressing penitence for this. In his opinion it is right to incite to hatred instead of appealing to argument, unless the adversary is a member of the same party; and at the time of the remarks complained of, the Bolsheviks and Mensheviks were two separate parties on account of the split. He rebukes the Central Committee for 'remaining silent about the fact that at the time the pamphlet was written a united party did not exist in the organization from which it emanated (not formally, but in essence), and whose aims it served . . . It is wrong to write about Party comrades in language that systematically spreads among the working masses hatred, aversion, contempt, etc. for those who hold other opinions. But *one may and one must write* in that strain about an organization that has seceded. Why must one? Because when a split has taken place it is one's duty *to wrest* the masses from the leadership of the seceding section' (ibid., p. 425). 'Are there any limits to a permissible struggle stemming from a split? No Party standards set limits to such a struggle, nor can there be such limits, for a split implies that the Party has ceased to exist' (p. 428). We may thank the Mensheviks for provoking Lenin to this avowal, which is confirmed by the activity of his whole life: no holds are barred, and all that counts is to achieve one's object.

Unlike Stalin, Lenin was never actuated by motives of personal revenge: he treated people—and this, it should be emphasized, included himself—exclusively as political tools and instruments of the historical process. This is one of the most salient features of his personality. If political calculation so required, he could pelt a man with mud one day and shake hands with him the next. He vilified Plekhanov after 1905, but ceased to do so at once when he found that Plekhanov was opposed to the liquidators and the empiriocritics and was, with the prestige of his name, a valuable ally. Up to 1917 he hurled anathemas at Trotsky, but all this was forgotten when Trotsky became a Bolshevik and proved to be a highly gifted leader and organizer. He denounced the treachery of Zinoviev and Kamenev in publicly opposing the plan for an armed uprising in October, but afterwards he allowed them to occupy high positions in the party and the Comintern. When someone had to be attacked, personal considerations went by the board. Lenin was capable of shelving disputes if he thought it possible to agree on basic issues—for example, he overlooked Bogdanov's philosophical errors until the latter opposed him over the question of the party being represented in the Third Duma; but if the dispute concerned something he considered important at the time, he showed the adversary no mercy. He derided questions of personal loyalty in political quarrels. When the Mensheviks accused Malinovsky, one of the Bolshevik leaders, of being an Okhrana agent, Lenin rebutted these 'base slanders' with the utmost ferocity. After the February Revolution it came to light that they were true, whereupon Lenin attacked Rodzyanko, the president of the Duma. Rodzyanko, it appeared, had been informed of Malinovsky's role and had brought about his resignation from the Duma, but had not told the Bolsheviks (who at this time were covering Rodzyanko's party with abuse), on the ground, forsooth, that when he received the information from the Minister of the Interior he had given his word of honour not to reveal it. Lenin was full of pseudo-moral indignation at the fact that the Bolsheviks' enemies had abstained from helping them on the ridiculous pretext of 'honour'.

Another characteristic of Lenin's is that he often projected his hostility into the past in order to show that the opponent had always been a villain and a traitor. In 1906 he wrote that Struve had been a counter-revolutionary as early as 1894 ('The Victory of the Cadets and the Tasks of the Workers' Party'; *Works*, vol. 10, p. 265), although no one could have supposed this from Lenin's arguments with Struve in 1895, when they were still collaborating. For years Lenin regarded Kautsky as a theorist of the highest authority, but after Kautsky took up a 'centrist' position during the war Lenin denounced him for having shown 'opportunism' in a pamphlet of 1902 (*The State and Revolution*; *Works*, vol. 25, p. 479) and claimed that he had not written as a Marxist since 1909 (preface to a pamphlet by Bukharin, Dec. 1915; *Works*, vol. 22, p. 106). Throughout 1914–18, in his attacks on the 'social chauvinists', Lenin invoked the Basle Manifesto of the Second International, which called on parties to have nothing to do with the imperialist war; but after the final breach with the Second International it appeared that the Manifesto was a deception by 'renegades' (*Notes of a Publicist*, 1922; *Works*, vol. 33, p. 206). For many years Lenin insisted that he did not stand for any separate trend within the socialist movement, but that he and the Bolsheviks held to the same principles as the social democrats of Europe, especially Germany. But in 1920, in *'Left-Wing' Communism—an Infantile Disorder*, it was revealed that Bolshevism as a brand of political thought had existed since 1903, which indeed was the case. Lenin's retroactive view of history was of course nothing in comparison to the systematic falsification of Stalin's day, when it had to be shown at all costs that the current assessment of individuals and political movements was equally valid for all past years. In this respect Lenin only made a modest beginning, and often adhered to a rational mode of thought: for instance, he maintained to the end that Plekhanov had rendered great services in popularizing Marxism and that his theoretical works should be reprinted, although Plekhanov at the time was wholly on the side of the 'social chauvinists'.

Since Lenin was interested only in the political effect of his writings, they are full of repetitions. He was not afraid to repeat the same ideas again and again: he had no stylistic ambitions, but was merely concerned with influencing the party or the workers. It is noteworthy that his style is at its coarsest in factional dispute and when he is addressing party activists, but that he speaks to the workers in much milder terms. Some of his works addressed to them are masterpieces of propaganda, such as the pamphlet *Political Parties in Russia and the Tasks of the Proletariat* (May 1917), which gives a concise and lucid account of the position of the respective parties on the main questions of the hour.

In theoretical debates, too, he was more concerned to overwhelm the adversary with words and abuse than to analyse arguments in detail. *Materialism and Empiriocriticism* is an outstanding example, but there are many others. In 1913 Struve published a book entitled *The Economy and Prices*, in which he argued that value in Marx's sense, independent of price, was a metaphysical and non-empirical category and was economically superfluous. (This was not a new idea but had been put forward by many critics from Conrad Schmidt onwards.) Lenin commented in these terms: 'How can one help calling this most "radical" method most flimsy? For thousands of years mankind has been aware of the operation of an objective law in the phenomenon of exchange, has been trying to understand it and express it with the utmost precision, has been testing its explanations by millions and billions of day-by-day observations of economic life; and suddenly a fashionable representative of a fashionable occupation— that of collecting quotations (I almost said collecting postage stamps)—comes along and "does away with all this": "worth is a phantom"' ('Socialism Demolished Again', Mar. 1914; *Works*, vol. 20, p. 200). Lenin proceeds to explain: 'Price is a manifestation of the law of value. Value is the law of price, i.e. the generalized expression of the phenomenon of price. To speak of "independence" here is a mockery of science' (ibid., p. 201). Then the summing-up: 'Expelling laws from science means, in fact, smuggling in the laws of religion.' And the judgement: 'Does Mr. Struve really think he can deceive his readers and disguise his obscurantism with such crude methods?' (ibid., pp. 202, 204). This is a typical example of Lenin's treatment of an adversary. Struve had said that value cannot be calculated independently of price; Lenin says that to speak of independence is a mockery of science. There is no attempt to meet the real argument, which is drowned in a welter of verbiage and abuse.

It should be repeated, however, that Lenin did not exempt himself from this purely technical, instrumental attitude towards people and affairs. He had no thought of personal gain; unlike Trotsky for instance, he was in no way a *poseur* and was not given to theatrical gestures. He regarded himself as an instrument of the revolution and was unshakably convinced that he was in the right—so convinced that he was not afraid to stand alone, or almost alone, against his political opponents; he resembled Luther in the steadfastness of his belief that God, or rather History, spoke through his lips. He rejected with scorn the reproach, made, for example, by Ledebour at Zimmerwald, that he was calling on the Russian workers to shed blood while himself remaining safely in a foreign country. Such objections were absurd from his point of view, since it was to the advantage of the revolution that he should operate from abroad; given Russian conditions there could not be a revolution without the emigration. In any case no one could accuse him of personal cowardice. He was capable of assuming the heaviest responsibility, and always took up a clear-cut attitude in any dispute. He was certainly right in reproaching the leaders of all other socialist groups with being afraid to seize power. The others found it safer to put their faith in historical laws; Lenin, who was not afraid, played for the highest stakes and won.

Why did he win? Certainly not because he correctly foresaw the course of events. His prophecies and estimates were often wrong, sometimes glaringly so. After the defeat of 1905 he believed for a long time that another upsurge was imminent; when he realized, however, that the tide of revolution had subsided and that there would have to be long years of work in reactionary conditions, he immediately drew all the inferences from the situation. When Wilson was elected President of the United States in 1912 he declared that the two-party system in America was bankrupt *vis-à-vis* the socialist movement. In 1913 he stated no less categorically that Irish nationalism was extinct in the working class. After 1917 he expected a European revolution any day, and thought he could run the Russian economy by means of terror. But all his misjudgements were in the direction of expecting the revolutionary movement to be stronger, and to manifest itself earlier, than it actually did. They were fortunate errors from his point of view, since it was only on the basis of false estimates that he decided on an armed insurrection in October 1917. His mistakes enabled him to exploit the possibilities of revolution to the full, and were thus the cause of his success. Lenin's genius was not that of foresight, but of concentrating at a given moment all the social energies that could be used to seize power, and subordinating all his efforts and those of his party to this one aim. Without Lenin's firmness of purpose, it is unthinkable that the Bolsheviks could have succeeded. But for him they would have prolonged the boycott of the Duma beyond the critical moment; they would not have ventured on an armed uprising to secure power for themselves alone; they would not have signed the Treaty of Brest-Litovsk, and they might not, at the last moment, have adopted the New Economic Policy. In critical situations Lenin committed violence on the party, and his cause prevailed as a result. World communism as we know it today is truly his work.

Neither Lenin nor the Bolsheviks 'made' the Revolution. Since the turn of the century it had been clear that the autocracy was in a precarious state, though no 'historical laws' prescribed the manner of its downfall. The February Revolution was due to the coincidence of many factors: the war, peasant demands, memories of 1905, the conspiracy of the liberals, support from the Entente, the radicalization of the working masses. As the revolutionary process developed, the slogan was that of Soviet power, and those who supported the October Revolution wanted power for the Soviets, not for the Bolshevik party. But 'Soviet power' was an anarchist Utopia, the dream of a society in which the mass of the people, most of it ignorant and illiterate, would in permanent mass rallies decide all economic, social, military, and administrative questions. It can hardly be said that Soviet power was even overthrown. The slogan 'the Soviets without the communists' was frequently used in popular anti-Bolshevik revolts, but it meant nothing in practice and the Bolsheviks knew this. They were able to enlist support for themselves *as a Soviet government*, and to canalize the energies of the Revolution at a time when they were the only party prepared to govern single-handed.

None the less, the actual revolutionary process was much more Soviet than specifically Bolshevik, and for some years the culture, mood, and habits of the new society reflected the fact that it originated in an explosion in which the Bolsheviks were the best-organized force but were by no means a majority of society. The Revolution was not a Bolshevik *coup d'état*, but a true revolution of the workers and peasants. The Bolsheviks alone were able to harness it for their own ends; their victory was at once a defeat for the Revolution and a defeat for communist ideas, even in their Bolshevik version. Lenin described the dangers ahead with admirable clarity at the Eleventh Party Congress in March 1922 (the last he attended). Speaking of the communists' weakness *vis-à-vis* the culture inherited from Tsarist times, he said:

If the conquering nation is more cultured than the vanquished nation, the former imposes its culture upon the latter; but if the opposite is the case, the vanquished nation imposes its culture upon the conqueror. Has not something like this happened in the capital of the RSFSR? Have the 4,700 Communists (nearly a whole army division, and all of them the very best) come under the influence of an alien culture? True, there may be the impression that the vanquished have a high level of culture. But that is not the case at all. Their culture is miserable, insignificant, but it is still at a higher level than ours. (*Works*, vol. 33, p. 288)

This is one of Lenin's most penetrating observations on the state he had created. The slogan 'learn from the bourgeoisie' was put into practice in a way that was both tragic and grotesque. With enormous labour and only partial success the Bolsheviks set about assimilating, as they are still doing, the technical achievements of the capitalist world. With no labour at all, they adopted swiftly and completely the methods of government and administration of the Tsarist chinovniks. The revolutionary dreams have survived only in the form of phraseological remnants decorating the regime's totalitarian imperalism.

Selective Bibliography

I The Second International

Beer, Max, *Fifty Years of International Socialism*, London 1937.

Braunthal, J., *Geschichte der Internationale*, 2 vols., Hanover, 1961–3.

Cole, G. D. H., *A History of Socialist Thought*, vol. iii: *The Second International*, London, 1956.

Compere-Morel, A. C. A., *Encyclopédie socialiste, syndicale et coopérative de l'Internationale ouvrière*, 8 vols., Paris, 1912–13.

Van den Esch, Patricia, *La Deuxième Internationale*, Paris, 1957.

Haupt, G., *La Deuxième Internationale, 1889–1914. Étude critique des sources, essais bibliographiques*, Paris–La Haye, 1964.

Joll, James, *The Second International*, London, 1955

Settembrini, D., *Socialismo e rivoluzione dopo Marx*, Naples, 1974.

II German Orthodoxy

Kautsky: Works:

Karl Marx' ökonomische Lehren, Stuttgart, 1887.

Thomas More und seine Utopie, Stuttgart, 1888.

Die Klassengegensätze von 1789, Stuttgart, 1889.

Das Erfurter Programm in seinem grundsätzlichen Teil erläutert, Stuttgart, 1892, (many impressions; last edn. Hanover, 1964).

Die Vorläufer des neueren Sozialismus, Stuttgart, 1895.

Die Agrarfrage, Stuttgart, 1899.

Bernstein und das sozialdemokratische Programm. Eine Anti-Kritik, Stuttgart, 1899.

Ethik und materialistische Geschichtsauffassung. Ein Versuch, Stuttgart, 1906. (Eng. trans. Chicago, 1918).

Patriotismus und Sozialdemokratie, Leipzig, 1907.

Der Ursprung des Christentums, Stuttgart, 1908.

Der Weg zur Macht, Berlin, 1909.

Der politische Massenstreik, Berlin, 1914.

Demokratie oder Diktatur, Berlin, 1918.

Terrorismus und Kommunismus, Berlin, 1919.

Von der Demokratie zur Staatssklaverei, Berlin, 1921.

Die materialistische Geschichtsauffassung, Berlin, 1927.

On Kautsky:

Blumenberg, Werner, *Karl Kautsky's literarisches Werk*, The Hague, 1960 (bibliography).

Ein Leben für den Sozialismus. Erinnerungen an Karl Kautsky, Hanover, 1954.

Matthias, E., 'Kautsky und der Kautskyanismus', in *Marxismus-studien*, vol. ii, Tübingen, 1957.

Waldenberg, Marek, *Wzlot i upadek Karola Kautsky'ego* (*Kautsky's Rise and Decline*), vols. i and
ii, Cracow, 1972 (with a copious bibliography).

Mehring:
Mehring, Franz, *Gesammelte Schriften*, ed. T. Hoehle, H. Koch, and J. Schleifstein, East Berlin,
1960 ff.
Schleifstein, J., *Franz Mehring. Sein marxistisches Schaffen 1891–1919*, East Berlin, 1959.

Cunow:
Die Marxsche Geschichts-, Gesellschafts- und Staatstheorie, vols. i and ii,
Berlin, 1920–1.
Ursprung der Religion und des Gottesglaubens, Berlin, 1924.

III Rosa Luxemburg

Works:
Die industrielle Entwicklung Polens, Leipzig, 1898.
Sozialreform oder Revolution?, Leipzig, 1899.
Massenstreik, Partei und Gewerkschaften, Hamburg, 1906.
Die Akkumulation des Kapitals, Berlin, 1913 (Eng. trans. London, 1951).
(Junius) *Die Krise der Sozialdemokratie*, Zurich, 1916.
*Die Akkumulation des Kapitals oder was die Epigonen aus der Marxschen Theorie gemacht haben.
Eine Anti-Kritik*, Leipzig, 1921.
Einführung in die Nationalökomomie, hrsg. von P. Levi, Berlin, 1925.
Die Russische Revolution. Eine kritische Würdiging, Aus dem Nachlass hrsg. und eingel. von Paul
Levi, Berlin, 1932 (Eng. trans. Ann Arbor, 1961).
Politische Schriften, hrsg. und eingel. von Ossip K. Flechtheim, 3 vols., Frankfurt-Vienna, 1966–8.

In English:
Selected Political Writings, ed. R. Looker, London, 1972.

On Rosa Luxemburg:
Ciolkosz, Adam, *Róża Luxemburg a rewolucja rosyjska* (*Rosa Luxemburg and the Russian
Revolution*), Paris, 1961.
Fröhlich, Paul, *Rosa Luxemburg, Gedanke und Tat*, Paris, 1939 (Eng. trans. London, 1940).
Kowalik, Tadeusz, *Róża Luxemburg. Teoria akumulacji i imperializmu* (*Rosa Luxemburg. Theory
of Accumulation and of Imperialism*), Warsaw, 1971.
Nettl, J. P., *Rosa Luxemburg*, vols. i and ii, London, 1966 (with a copious bibliography).
Roland-Holst, Henriette, *Rosa Luxemburg: ihr Leben und Wirken*, Zurich, 1937.

IV Bernstein and Revisionism

Works:
Die Voraussetzungen des Sozialismus und die Aufgaben der Sozialdemokratie, Stuttgart, 1899
(many impressions; Eng. trans, by E. C. Harvey under title *Evolutionary Socialism*,
London, 1909).
Zur Geschichte und Theorie des Sozialismus, Berlin, 1901.
Der politische Massenstreik und die politische Lage der Sozialdemokratie in Deutschland, Breslau,
1905.
Geschichte der Berliner Arbeiterbewegung, 3 vols., Berlin, 1907–10.
Sozialismus und Demokratie in der grossen englischen Revolution, 2nd edn., Stuttgart, 1908; last
edn., Hanover, 1964.
Erinnerungen, Berlin, 1929.

On Bernstein:

Angel, Pierre, *Edouard Bernstein et l'évolution du socialisme allemand*, Paris, 1961.
Gay, Peter, *The Dilemma of Democratic Socialism*, London, 1952.
Meyer, Th., *Bernsteins konstruktiver Sozialismus*, Berlin-Bonn, 1977 (with a copious bibliography).

V–VII French Marxists

Jaurès:

Blum, L., *Jean Jaurès*, Paris, 1937.
Challaye, F., *Jaurès*, Paris, 1936.
Hampden, J., *Jean Jaurès*, 1943.
Jaurès, J., *Œuvres*, ed. Max Bonnafous, Paris (incomplete; 9 vols. appeared 1931–9).
Levy, Louis, *Anthologie de Jean Jaurès*, Paris, 1946.
Rappaport, C., *Jean Jaurès, l'homme, le penseur, le socialiste*, Paris, 1915.

Lafargue:

Lafargue, Paul, *Le Droit à la paresse*, Paris, 1883.
   Idéalisme et matérialisme dans la conception de l'Histoire, Lille, 1901.
   Le Déterminisme économique de Karl Marx, Paris, 1928 (1st edn., 1907).
   Critiques littéraires, Paris, 1936.
Varlet, J., (ed.), *Paul Lafargue, théoricien du marxisme*, Paris, 1933 (an anthology).
Stolze, G., *Paul Lafargue, théoricien, militant du socialisme*, Paris, 1937.

Sorel:

Sorel, Georges, *Les Illusion du progrès*, Paris, 1947 (1st edn., 1908).
   Réflexions sur la violence, Paris, 1908 (Eng. trans, with an introduction by E. A. Shils, Glencoe, Ill., 1950
   La Décomposition du marxisme, 1908 (2nd edn. Paris, 1910).
   Matériaux d'une théorie du prolétariat, Paris, 3rd edn., 1919.
Freund, M., *Georges Sorel. Der revolutionäre Konservatismus*, Frankfurt-on-Main, 1932.
Goriely, G., *Le Pluralisme démocratique de Georges Sorel*, Paris, 1962.
Horowitz, I. L., *Radicalism and the Revolt against Reason*, London, 1961.
Piron, G., *Georges Sorel*, 1927.
Roth, J. J., 'The Roots of Italian Fascism: Sorel and Sorelismo', in, *Journal of Modern History*, vol. 39, Mar. 1967.

VIII Antonio Labriola

Labriola, Antonio, *Della coscienza morale* (*On Moral Consciousness*), Naples, 1873.
   La concezione materialista della storia (*Materialist Concept of History*), 2nd edn., Bari, 1938.
   Scritii vari di filosofia e politico (*Various Writings on Philosophy and Politics*), Bari, 1906.
   Opere (*Works*), 3 vols., Milan, 1959.
dal Pane, Luigi, *Antonio Labriola. La vita e il pensiero* (*Antonio Labriola. Life and Thought*), Rome, 1935.

IX–XI Polish Marxists

Brzozowski, Stanisław, *Kultura i Życie* (*Culture and Life*), Lemberg, 1907.
   Idee (*Ideas*), Lemberg, 1910.
   Listy (*Letters*), ed. M. Sroka, vols. i and ii, Cracow, 1970.
Kelles-Krauz, Kazimierz, *Pisma Wybrane* (*Selected Writings*), vols. i and ii, Warsaw, 1962 (includes complete bibliography).

Kowalik, Tadeusz, *Krzywicki*, Warsaw, 1965.

Krzywicki, Ludwik, *Dzieła (Works)*, Warsaw, 1957 ff.

Stawar, A., *O Brzozowskim i inne szkice (On Brzozowski and other Essays)*, Warsaw, 1961.

Suchodolski, B., *Stanisław Brzozowski. Rozwój ideologii (Stanisław Brzozowski. Evolution of his Ideology)*, Warsaw, 1933.

Walicki, Andrzej, *Stanisław Brzozowski–drogi myśli (Stanisław Brzozowski–The Paths of Thought)*, Warsaw, 1977.

XII Austro-Marxists, Kantians in Marxism

Texts:

Adler, Max, *Kausalität und Teleologie im Streit um die Wissenschaft*, in *Marx-Studien*, vol. i, Vienna, 1904.

    Der Sozialismus und die Intellektuellen, Vienna, 1910.

    Marxistische Probleme, Stuttgart, 1913.

    Der soziologische Sinn der Lehre von Karl Marx, Leipzig, 1914.

    Politik und Moral, Leipzig, 1918.

    Demokratie und Rätesystem, Vienna, 1919.

    Die Staatsauffassung des Marxismus, Vienna, 1922 (last edn., Darmstadt, 1964).

    Das Soziologische in Kants Erkenntniskritik, Vienna, 1924.

    Kant und der Marxismus. Gesammelte Aufsätze zur Erkenntniskritik und Theorie des Sozialen, Berlin, 1925.

    Lehrbuch der materialistischen Geschichtsauffassung, vol. i, Berlin, 1930; vol. ii, Vienna, 1969.

    Das Rätsel der Gesellschaft, Vienna, 1936.

Bauer, Otto, *Die Nationalitätenfrage und die Sozialdemokratie*, Vienna, 1907.

    Grosskapital und Militarismus, Vienna, 1911.

    Nationalkampf oder Klassenkampf?, Vienna, 1911.

    Bolschewismus oder Sozialdemokratie?, Vienna, 1920.

    Das Weltbild des Kapitalismus, Jena, 1924.

    Sozialdemokratie, Religion und Kirche, Vienna, 1927.

    Eine Auswahl aus seinem Lebenswerk mit einem Lebensbild Otto Bauers, ed. Julius Braunthal, Vienna, 1961.

Cohen, H., *Kants Begründung der Ethik*, Berlin, 1877.

    Ethik des reinen Willens, Berlin, 1904.

Hilferding, R., *Böhm-Bawerks Marx-Kritik*, in *Marx-Studien*, vol. i, Vienna, 1904.

    Das Finanzkapital, Vienna, 1910.

Renner, Karl, *Staat und Nation*, Vienna, 1899.

    Mehrarbeit und Mehrwert, Vienna, 1902.

    Die soziale Funktion der Rechtsinstitute, Vienna, 1904.

    Der deutsche Arbeiter und der Nationalisms, Vienna, 1910.

    Staatswirtschaft, Weltwirtschaft und Sozialismus, Berlin, 1929.

Staudinger, F., *Ethik und Politik*, Berlin, 1899.

    Kulturgrundlagen der Politik, vols. i and ii, Jena, 1914.

Vorländer, K., *Kant und der Sozialismus*, Berlin, 1900.

    Kant und Marx. Ein Beitrag zur Philosophie des Sozialismus, Tübingen, 1911.

    Kant, Fichte, Hegel und der Sozialismus, Berlin, 1920.

    Marx, Engels und Lassalle als Philosophen, Berlin, 1921.

    Von Machiavelli bis Lenin, Leipzig, 1926.

Woltmann, L., *System des moralischen Bewusstseins*, Düsseldorf, 1898.

    Der historische Materialismus, Düsseldorf, 1900.

Austromarxismus, ed. H. J. Sandkühler und R. de la Vega, Frankfurt-Vienna, 1970 (an anthology).

Marxismus und Ethik, ed. R. de la Vega und H.-J. Sandkühler, Frankfurt, 1970 (an anthology).

Works on Austro-Marxism:

Heintel, Peter, *System und Ideologie. Der Austromarxismus im Spiegel der Philosophie Max Adlers*, Vienna-Munich, 1967.

Kautsky, Benedikt, *Geistige Strömungen im österreichischen Sozialismus*, Vienna, 1953.

Lesler, N., *Zwischen Reformismus und Bolschewismus. Der Austromarxismus als Theorie und Praxis*, Vienna-Frankfurt-Zurich, 1968.

Steiner, H., *Bibliographie zur Geschichte der österreischischen Arbeiterbewegung*, vols. i and ii, Vienna-Frankfurt-Zurich, 1967.

XIII–XVIII Russian Marxism

Akselrod, L., *Filosofskie ocherki (Philosophical Essays)*, St. Petersburg, 1906.

    (Ortodoks), *O 'problemakh idealizma' (On 'Problems of Idealism')*, Odessa, 1905.

Akselrod, P. B., *Istoricheskoe polozhenie i vzaimootnoshenie liberal'noy i sotsialisticheskoy demokratii v Rossii (Historical Situation and Mutual Relationship of Liberal and Socialist Democracy in Russia)*, Geneva, 1898.

    Rabochii klass i revolutsionnoe dvizhenie w Rossii (The Working Class and the Revolutionary Movement in Russia), St. Petersburg, 1907.

Avrich, P., *The Russian Anarchists*, Princeton, 1967.

Avtorchanov, A., *Proiskhozhdenie partokratii (The Origins of Partocracy)*, 2 vols., Frankfurt, 1973.

Baron, S. H., *Plekhanov. The Father of Russian Marxism*, Stanford, 1963.

Berdyaev, N., *The Origin of Russian Communism*, London, n.d.

Billington, J., *Michailovski and Russian Populism*, Oxford, 1958.

Bogdanov, A., *Empiriomonizm*, 3 vols., St. Petersburg, 1905.

    Vera i nauka (Faith and Science), Moscow, 1910.

    Kratkii kurs ekonomicheskoy nauki (Short Course of Economic Science), Moscow, 1897.

    Osnovnye elementy istoricheskogo uzglyada na prirodu (Essential Elements of the Historical View of Nature), St. Petersburg, 1899.

Conquest, R., *Lenin*, London, 1972.

Dan, F., *Proiskhozhdenie bolshevizma (The Origin of Bolshevism)*, New York, 1946.

Deutscher, I., *The Prophet Armed. Trotsky 1879–1921*, London, 1954.

Fomina, V. A., *Filosofskie vzglyady G. V. Plekhanova (Philosophical Views of Plekhanov)*, Moscow, 1955.

Grille, D., *Lenins Rivale. Bogdanov und seine Philosophie*, Cologne, 1966.

Haimson, L. H., *The Russian Marxists and the Origins of Bolshevism*, Cambridge, Mass., 1955.

Hare, R., *Portraits of Russian Personalities between Reform and Revolution*, London, 1959.

Iz glubiny. Sbornik statey o russkoi revolutsii (From the Depths. A Collection of Essays on the Russian Revolution), Paris, 1967 (1st edn. 1918)

Kindersley, R., *The First Russian Revisionists. A Study of 'Legal Marxism' in Russia*, Oxford, 1962.

Kline, G. L., *Religious and Anti-religious Thought in Russia*, Chicago, 1968.

Kucharzewski, J., *The Origins of Modern Russia*, New York, 1948.

Lenin, V. I., *Sochinenia (Works)*, 55 vols., 5th edn., 1959–65; English translation, London, 1960–70.

    Essentials of Lenin, London, 1947.

Lossky, N. O., *History of Russian Philosophy*, New York, 1969.

Lunacharsky, A. W., *Sobranie sochinenii (Collected Works)*, 8 vols., Moscow, 1963–7.

Martov, L., *Zapiski sotsial-demokrata (Notes of a Social-Democrat)*, Berlin, 1922

    Istoria rossiiskoi sotsial-demokratii (The History of Russian Social-Democracy), Moscow, 1923.

Mirovoy bolshevizm (World Bolshevism), Berlin, 1923.

Meyer, A., *Leninism*, New York, 1962.

Ocherki po filosofii marksizma. Filosofskii sbornik (Essays on the Philosophy of Marxism. A Philosophical Collection), St. Petersburg, 1908.

Ocherki filosofii kollektivizma (Essays on the Philosophy of Collectivism), St. Petersburg, 1909.

Parvus (A. L. Helphand), *Rossia i Revolutsia (Russia and Revolution)*, St. Petersburg, 1906.

Pipes, R., *Social Democracy and the St. Petersburg Labor Movement 1885–1897*, Cambridge, Mass., 1963.

    'Narodnichestvo: A Semantic Inquiry', in *Slavic Review*, Sept. 1964.

    Struve. Liberal on the Left 1870–1905, Cambridge, Mass., 1970 (with a complete bibliography).

    (ed.), *Revolutionary Russia*, Cambridge, Mass., 1968.

Plekhanov, G. V., *Sochinenia (Works)*, 26 vols., Moscow, 1922–7.

    Essays in the History of Materialism, London, 1934.

    Selected Philosophical Works, Moscow, 1961– .

    In Defence of Materialism, trans. A. Rothstein, London, 1947.

    The Role of the Individual in History, London, 1950.

    Art and Social Life, ed. A. Rothstein, London, 1953.

Problemy idealizma (Problems of Idealism), St. Petersburg, 1903.

Rosenberg, A., *A History of Bolshevism from Marx to the First Five-Year Plan*, London, 1934.

Schapiro, L., *The Communist Party of the Soviet Union*, London, 1960.

    and Reddaway, P. (eds.), *Lenin: the Man, the Theorist, the Leader*, London, 1967.

Scheibert, P., *Von Bakunin zu Lenin*, vol. i, Leiden, 1956.

Shub, D., *Lenin. A Biography*, New York, 1949 (New ed., London, 1966).

Struve, P. B., *Kriticheskie zametki k voprosu ob ekonomicheskom razvitii Rossii (Critical Remarks on the Question of Russia's Economic Development)*, St. Petersburg, 1894.

Treadgold, D. W., *Lenin and his Rivals, 1898–1906*, London, 1955.

Trotsky, L. D., *Sochinenia (Works)*, 21 vos., Moscow, 1925–7 (incomplete).

Ulam, A. B., *Lenin and the Bolsheviks*, London, 1965 (2nd edn., 1969).

Valentinov, N., *Filosofskie postroenia marksizma. Kriticheskie ocherki (Philosophical Bases of Marxism. Critical Essays)*, Moscow, 1908.

    E. Makh i Marksizm (E. Mach and Marxism), Moscow, n.d.

    Vstrechi s Leninym (Encounters with Lenin, with a foreword by L. Schapiro), London, 1968.

Vekhi. Sbornik statey o russkoi inteligentsii (Signposts. A Collection of Essays on the Russian Intelligentsia), Moscow, 1909 (reprinted Frankfurt, 1967).

Venturi, F., *Roots of Revolution*, London, 1960.

Walicki, A., *The Controversy over Capitalism. Studies in the Social Philosophy of Russian Populism*, Oxford, 1969.

    Rosyjska Filozofia i myśl społeczna od Oświecenia do marksizmu (Russian Philosophy and Social Thought from the Enlightenment to Marxism), Warsaw, 1973.

Wolfe, B. D., *Three Who Made a Revolution. A Biographical History*, New York, 1948.

Yassour, A., *Bogdanov et son œuvre*, in *Cahiers du monde russe et soviétique*, vol. x, 1969 (bibliography of Bogdanov's works)

    'Leçons de la révolution de 1905. La Controverse Lénine-Bogdanov', thesis, Paris, 1967 (not published except in Hebrew).

Yushkevich, P., *Stolpy filosofskoy ortodoksii (The Pillars of Philosophical Orthodoxy)*, St. Petersburg, 1910.

Zeman, Z. A. B. and Scharlam, W. B., *The Merchant of Revolution. The Life of A. L. Helphand (Parvus) 1867–1924*, London, 1965.

Zenkovsky, V. V., *A History of Russian Philosophy*, trans. G. L. Kline, 2 vols., New York, 1953.

BOOK THREE

THE BREAKDOWN

Preface

THE PRESENT VOLUME deals with the evolution of Marxism in the last half-century. Writing it has involved especial difficulties, one of which is the sheer bulk of the available literature: no historian can be fully acquainted with it, and it is therefore, so to speak, impossible to do everyone justice. Another difficulty is that I am not able to treat the subject with the desirable detachment. Many of the people mentioned in this volume I know or have known personally, and some of them are or were my friends. Moreover, in describing the controversies and political struggles in Eastern Europe in the later 1950s I am writing about events and issues in which I myself took part, so that I appear in the invidious role of a judge in my own cause. At the same time, I could not pass over these matters in silence. The upshot is that the most recent period, which is the one I know best from my own experience, is treated less fully than any other. The last chapter, which deals with this period, could be expanded into a further volume; but, setting aside the difficulties already mentioned, I am not convinced that the subject is intrinsically worthy of treatment at such length.

Bibliographical Note

Sources of quotations used in the text:

Adorno, Theodor W., *Negative Dialectics*, The Seabury Press, New York, 1972; Routledge & Kegan Paul, London, 1973.

Goldmann, L., *The Hidden God*, trans. Thody (International Library of Philosophy), Routledge & Kegan Paul, London, 1974.

Horkheimer, Max and Theodor W. Adorno, *Dialectic of Enlightenment*, trans. John Cummings, The Seabury Press, New York, 1972; Allen Lane, The Penguin Press, London, 1973.

Korsch, Karl, *Marxism and Philosophy*, trans. F. Halliday, New Left Books, London, 1970.

Lukács, George, *The Meaning of Contemporary Realism*, The Merlin Press, London, 1970.

Mao Tse-Tung, *Anthology of His Writings*, ed. Anne Fremantle, Mentor Books, New American Library, New York, 1962.

Four Essays on Philosophy, Peking, 1966; Collet's, London, 1967.

Quotations From Chairman Mao Tse-tung, ed. Stuart Schram, Pall Mall Press, London, 1968.

Mao Tse-tung Unrehearsed, ed. and trans. Stuart Schram, Pelican Books, London, 1974, and as *Chairman Mao Talks to the People*, Pantheon Books, New York, 1975.

Marcuse, Herbert, *One-Dimensional Man*, Routledge & Kegan Paul, London, 1964.

Five Lectures, Allen Lane, The Penguin Press, London, 1970.

Snow, Edgar, *The Long Revolution*, Hutchinson, London, 1973.

Stalin, Joseph, *Collected Works*, vols. 7 and 8, English ed., 13 vols., Lawrence & Wishart, London, 1953–5.

Trotsky, Leon, *Their Morals and Ours*, ed. George Novack, Pathfinder Press, New York, 1969.

In Defense of Marxism, New Park Publications, London, 1971; Pathfinder Press, New York, 1971.

Writings of Leon Trotsky, 1929–1940, 12 vols., Pathfinder Press, New York, 1971–7.

Wolff, Robert P., Barrington Moore, Jr., and Herbert Marcuse, *Critique of Pure Tolerance*, Jonathan Cape, London, 1969.

Zhdanov, A. A., *On Literature, Music, and Philosophy*, Lawrence & Wishart, London, 1950.

The First Phase of Soviet Marxism.
The Beginnings of Stalinism

1. What was Stalinism?

THERE IS no general agreement as to what the term 'Stalinism' connotes. It has never been used by the official ideologists of the Soviet state, as it would seem to imply the existence of a self-contained social system. Since Khrushchev's time the accepted formula for what went on in Stalin's day has been 'the cult of personality', and this phrase is invariably associated with two presuppositions. The first is that throughout the existence of the Soviet Union the party's policy was 'in principle' right and salutary, but that occasional errors were committed, the most serious of which was the neglect of 'collective leadership', i.e. the concentration of unlimited power in Stalin's hands. The second assumption is that the main source of 'errors and distortions' lay in Stalin's own faults of character, his thirst for power, despotic inclinations, and so on. After Stalin's death all these deviations were immediately cured: the party once more conformed to proper democratic principles, and that was the end of the matter. As to Stalin's errors, the most serious was the mass liquidation of Communists and especially of the higher party bureaucracy. In short, Stalin's rule was a monstrous but accidental phenomenon: there was never such a thing as 'Stalinism' or a 'Stalinist system', and in any case the 'negative manifestations' of the 'personality cult' fade into insignificance beside the glorious achievements of the Soviet system.

Although this version of events is doubtless not taken seriously by its authors or by anyone else, controversy still prevails as to the meaning and scope of the term 'Stalinism', which is in current use outside the Soviet Union even among Communists. The latter, however, whether critical or orthodox in their views, restrict its meaning to the period of Stalin's personal tyranny from the early 1930s to his death in 1953, and they blame the 'errors' of the time less on Stalin's own wickedness than on regrettable but unalterable historical circumstances: the industrial and cultural backwardness of Russia before and after 1917, the failure of the hoped-for European revolution, external threats to the Soviet state, and political exhaustion after the Civil War. (The same reasons, incidentally, are regularly advanced by Trotskyists to explain the degeneration of Russia's post-Revolutionary government.)

Those, on the other hand, who are not committed to defending the Soviet system, Leninism, or any Marxist historical schema generally regard Stalinism as a more or less coherent political, economic, and ideological system, which worked in pursuit of its own aims and made few 'errors' from its own point of view. Even on this basis, however, it may be debated how far and in what sense Stalinism was 'historically inevitable': i.e. was the political, economic, and ideological complexion of Soviet Russia already determined before Stalin's rise to power, so that Stalinism was only the full development of Leninism? The question also remains, how far and in what sense have all these characteristic features of the Soviet state persisted to the present day?

From the point of view of terminology it is of no special importance whether we confine the meaning of 'Stalinism' to the last twenty-five years of the dictator's life or extend it to cover the political system prevailing at the present time. But it is more than a purely verbal question whether the basic features of the system that took shape under Stalin have altered in the last twenty years, and there is also room for argument as to what its essential features were.

Many observers, including the present author, believe that the Soviet system as it developed under Stalin was a continuation of Leninism, and that the state founded on Lenin's political and ideological principles could only have maintained itself in a Stalinist form; such critics hold, moreover, that 'Stalinism' in the narrow sense, i.e. the system that prevailed until 1953, has not been affected in any essential way by the changes of the post-Stalinist era. The first of these points has been to some extent established in previous chapters, where Lenin was shown to be the creator of totalitarian doctrine and of the totalitarian state in embryo. Of course many events in the Stalin era can be attributed to chance or to Stalin's own peculiarities: careerism, lust for power, vindictiveness, jealousy, and paranoid suspicion. The mass slaughter of Communists in 1936–9 cannot be called a 'historical necessity', and we may suppose that it would not have taken place under a tyrant other than Stalin himself. But if, as in the typical Communist view, that slaughter is regarded as the true, 'negative' significance of Stalinism, it follows that the whole of Stalinism was a deplorable accident—the implication being that everything is always for the best under Communist rule until prominent Communists start being murdered. This is hard for the historian to accept, not only because he is interested in the fate of millions who were not party leaders or even party members, but also because the sanguinary terror on a huge scale which occurred in the Soviet Union at certain periods is not a permanent or essential feature of totalitarian despotism. The despotic system remains in force irrespective of whether, in a particular year, official murders are counted in millions or only in tens of thousands, whether torture is used as a matter of routine or only occasionally, and whether the victims are only workers, peasants, and intellectuals or include party bureaucrats as well.

The history of Stalinism, despite arguments over points of detail, is generally known and is adequately described in many books. As in the previous two volumes of this work, the main theme is the history of doctrine: political history will be dealt with cursorily, so far as is necessary to indicate the broad framework within which ideological life developed. In the Stalin era, however, the link between the history of doctrine and political events is much closer than before, since the phenomenon we have to study is the absolute institutionalization of Marxism as an instrument of power. This process, it is true, began earlier on: it goes back to Lenin's view that Marxism must be 'the party's world-outlook', i.e. that its content must be governed by the needs of the struggle for power at a particular moment. None the less, Lenin's political opportunism was to some extent restrained by doctrinal considerations; whereas in Stalin's day, from the early thirties onwards, doctrine was absolutely subordinated to the purpose of legitimizing and glorifying the Soviet government and everything it did. Marxism under Stalin cannot be defined by any collection of statements, ideas, or concepts: it was not a question of propositions as such but of the fact that there existed an all-powerful authority competent to declare at any given moment what Marxism was and what it was not. 'Marxism' meant nothing more or less than the current pronouncement of the authority in question, i.e. Stalin himself. For instance, up to June 1950 to be a Marxist meant, among other things, accepting the philological theories of N. Y. Marr, while after that date it meant rejecting them utterly. You were a Marxist not because you regarded any particular ideas—Marx's, Lenin's, or even Stalin's—as true, but because you were prepared to accept whatever the supreme authority might proclaim today, tomorrow, or in a year's time. This degree of institutionalization and dogmatization had never been seen before and did not reach its acme until the thirties, but its roots can be clearly traced in Lenin's doctrine: since Marxism is the world-view and instrument of the proletarian party, it is for the latter to decide what is Marxism and what is not, regardless of any objections 'from outside'. When the party is identified with the state and the apparatus of power, and when it achieves perfect unity in the shape of a one-man tyranny, doctrine becomes a matter of state and the tyrant is proclaimed infallible. Indeed, he really *is* infallible as far as the content of Marxism is concerned, for there is no Marxism but that which the party asserts in its capacity as the mouthpiece of the proletariat, and the party, having once achieved unity, expresses its will and its doctrine through the leadership embodied in the dictator's person. In this way the doctrine that the proletariat is historically the leading class and, in contrast to all other classes, the possessor of objective truth is transformed into the principle that 'Stalin is always right'. This, in fact, is not too grave a distortion of Marx's epistemology combined with Lenin's notion of the party as the advance guard of the workers' movement. The equation: truth = the proletarian world-view = Marxism = the party's world-view = the pronouncements of the party leadership = those of the supreme leader is wholly in accordance with Lenin's version of Marxism. We shall endeavour to trace the process by which this equation found final expression in the Soviet ideology which Stalin christened Marxism–Leninism. It is significant that he chose this term rather than speaking of Marxism *and* Leninism, which would have suggested two separate doctrines. The compound expression signified that Leninism was not a distinct trend within Marxism–as though there might be other forms of Marxism that were not Leninist–but was Marxism *par excellence*, the sole doctrine in which Marxism was developed and adapted to the new historical era. In actual fact Marxism–Leninism consisted of Stalin's own doctrine plus quotations selected by him from the works of Marx, Lenin, and Engels. It should not be supposed that anyone was free, in Stalin's day, to quote at will from Marx, Lenin, or even Stalin himself: Marxism–Leninism comprised only the quotations currently authorized by the dictator, in conformity with the doctrine he was currently promulgating.

In arguing that Stalinism was a true development of Leninism I do not mean to belittle Stalin's historical importance. After Lenin, and alongside Hitler, he certainly did more to shape the present-day world than any other individual since the First World War. Nevertheless, the fact that it was Stalin and not any other Bolshevik leader who became sole ruler of the party and state can be accounted for by the nature of the Soviet system. The view that his personal qualities, while they had a great deal to do with his victory over his rivals, did not themselves determine the main lines of the development of Soviet society is supported by the fact that throughout his earlier career he did not belong to the extremist wing of the Bolshevik party. On the contrary, he was something of a moderate, and in intra-party disputes he often stood on the side of common sense and prudence. In short, Stalin as a despot was much more the party's creation than its creator: he was the personification of a system which irresistibly sought to be personified.

2. The stages of Stalinism

IT IS a mania of Soviet historians to divide all epochs into stages; but the procedure is justified in some cases, especially where the delimitation is based on ideological grounds.

Since Stalinism was an international and not merely a Soviet phenomenon, its variations must be considered not only from the point of view of Russian internal policy and sectional strife, but also from that of the Comintern and international Bolshevism. There are, however, difficulties of correlating the respective periods, and also of nomenclature. Trotskyists and ex-Communists are in the habit of distinguishing 'leftist' and 'rightist' stages of Soviet history. The period immediately after 1917, dominated by the Civil War and by hopes of world revolution, is referred to as 'leftist' and is followed by the 'rightist' period of the N.E.P., when the party acknowledged the 'temporary stabilization of capitalism' in the world at large. Then comes a 'swing to the left' in 1928–9, when the party declared that this stabilization was at an end; the 'tide of revolution' set in once more, social democracy was denounced and combated as 'social Fascism', and Russia witnessed the beginning of mass collectivization and forced industrialization. This stage is supposed to have ended in 1935, when a 'rightist' policy was once more adopted under the slogan of a popular front against Fascism. These successive shifts of policy are associated with sectional and personal in-fighting among the Russian leaders. The rule of Stalin, Zinovyev, and Kamenev led to the political elimination of Trotsky; then Zinovyev and Kamenev were ousted in favour of Bukharin, Rykov, and Tomsky; then, in 1929, Bukharin was cast out and effective dissidence within the Bolshevik party came to an end.

This chronology is full of difficulties, however, even apart from the vague and arbitrary use of the terms 'left' and 'right'. As to the latter point, it is not clear why the slogan of 'social Fascism' was 'leftist' while the attempt to compromise with Chiang Kai-shek was 'rightist'; or why it was 'leftist' to persecute peasants on a vast scale but 'rightist' to use economic methods for political ends. It can of course be laid down that the more a policy involves terror, the more 'leftist' it is—this principle is frequently applied at the present day, and not only in Communist publications, but it is hard to see what it has to do with the traditional idea of 'leftism'. Apart from this, there is no clear correlation between changes in Comintern policy and the different phases of Soviet internal policy and ideology. The so-called 'leftist' assertion that European social democracy was a branch of Fascism was coined by Zinovyev and was current at least as early as 1924; the Comintern's fight against social democracy was intensified in 1927, long before the forced collectivization of the Russian peasantry was thought of. In 1935, when the campaign against social democracy was called off and clumsy efforts were made to patch up an alliance, there had already been a wave of mass political repression in the Soviet Union and another, more terrible one was about to commence.

In short, it makes no sense to present the history of the Soviet Union in terms of artificial criteria of 'left' and 'right', which in some cases lead to absurd results.

Nor is it correct to interpret changes in the Politburo as historical turning-points. During the period after Lenin's death certain political and ideological features became steadily more prominent, while others fluctuated in importance according to circumstances. The totalitarian character of the regime—i.e. the progressive destruction of civil society and absorption of all forms of social life by the state—increased almost without interruption between 1924 and 1953 and was certainly not diminished by the N.E.P., despite concessions to private ownership and trade. The N.E.P., as we saw, was a retreat from the policy of running the whole economy by means of the army and police, and was necessitated by the imminent prospect of economic ruin. But the use of terror against political opponents, the increased severity and intimidation within the party, the suppression of independence and enforcement of servility in philosophy, literature, art, and science—all this continued to be accentuated during the whole period of the N.E.P. From this point of view the thirties were only an intensification and consolidation of the process which began in Lenin's lifetime and under his direction. The collectivization of agriculture, with its countless victims, indeed constituted a turning-point; but this was not because it involved a change in the character of the regime or a 'swing to the left', but because it enforced the basic political and economic principle of totalitarianism in a single sector of key importance. It completely dispossessed the most numerous social class in Russia, established state control of farming once and for all, annihilated the last section of the community that was in any degree independent of the state, laid the basis for the oriental cult of the satrap with unlimited power, and, by means of famine, mass terror, and the death of millions, destroyed the spirit of the population and broke down the last vestiges of resistance. This was undoubtedly a milestone in the history of the Soviet Union, but it was no more than the continuation or extension of its basic principle, namely the extermination of all forms of political, economic, and cultural life that are not imposed and regulated by the state.

The Comintern, meanwhile, had been transformed in a few years into an instrument of Soviet foreign policy and espionage. Its policy twisted and turned in accordance with Moscow's assessment, correct or otherwise, of the international situation; but these changes had nothing to do with ideology, doctrine, or the difference between 'left' and 'right'. Similarly, it would be naïve to inquire whether, for instance, the Soviet Union's pact with Chiang Kai-shek or Hitler, the massacre of Polish Communists by Stalin, or Soviet participation in the Spanish Civil War, were in accordance with Marxism or betokened a 'leftist' or 'rightist' policy. All these moves can be judged in the light of how far they served to strengthen the Soviet state and increase its influence, but any ideological grounds adduced to defend them were invented for the purpose and have no bearing on the history of ideology, beyond showing how completely it was degraded to the role of an instrument of Soviet *raison d'état*.

Having said this, we may divide the history of the Soviet Union since Lenin's death into three periods. The first, from 1924 to 1929, is that of the N.E.P. During this time there was considerable freedom of private trading; political life no longer existed outside the party, but there were genuine disputes and controversies within the leadership; culture was officially controlled, but different trends of opinion and discussions were allowed within the bounds of Marxism and of political obedience. It was still possible to debate the nature of 'true' Marxism; one-man despotism was not yet an institution, and a fair proportion of society—the peasantry, and 'Nepmen' of all kinds—was not yet wholly dependent on the state from the economic point of view. The second period, from 1930 to Stalin's death in 1953, is marked by personal despotism, the almost complete liquidation of civil society, the subordination of culture to arbitrary official directives, and the regimentation of philosophy and ideology. The third period, from 1953 to the present, has features of its own which we shall consider in due course. As to which particular Bolshevik leader is in power, this is in general of minor importance. The Trotskyists, and of course Trotsky himself, regarded his removal from power as a historical turning-point; but there is no reason to agree with them and, as we shall see, it can well be maintained that 'Trotskyism' never existed, but was a figment invented by Stalin. The disagreements between Stalin and Trotsky were real to a certain extent, but they were grossly inflated by the struggle for personal power and never amounted to two independent and coherent theories. This is even more true of the disputes between Zinovyev and Trotsky, and the later conflict between Zinovyev and Trotsky on the one hand and Stalin on the other. Stalin's conflict with Bukharin and 'right-wing deviationism' was more substantial, but even this was not a dispute over principles but only as to the method and timetable for putting them into effect. The debate on industrialization in the twenties was certainly of great importance as regards practical decisions in industry and agriculture, and consequently the lives of millions of Soviet people, but it would be an exaggeration to see it as a basic doctrinal dispute or as involving the 'correct' interpretation of Marxism or Leninism. All the Bolshevik leaders without exception changed their attitude to the question so radically that it is pointless to speak of Trotskyism, Stalinism, or Bukharinism as coherent bodies of theory or variations of basic Marxist doctrine. (In this matter the historian of ideologies is interested in aspects that are, in themselves, secondary: doctrinal standpoints are of more significance to him than the fate of millions of people. This, however, is not a question of objective importance, but merely of professional concern.)

3. Stalin's early life and rise to power

UNLIKE the great majority of Bolshevik leaders, the future Communist ruler of All the Russias was, if not a proletarian, at any rate a man of the people. Joseph (Yosif) Dzhugashvili was born on 9 December 1879 in the small Georgian town of Gori. His father, Vissarion, was a shoemaker and drunkard, his mother illiterate. Vissarion moved to Tiflis, where he took a job in a shoe factory, and died there in 1890. His son attended the parish school at Gori for five years and was admitted in 1894 to the Theological Seminary at Tiflis—the only school in the Caucasus at which an able youth of his social condition could, in practice, receive further education. The Orthodox seminary was at the same time an organ of Russification, but, like many Russian schools, it was also a hotbed of political unrest, where Georgian patriotism flourished and socialist ideas were disseminated by many exiles from Russia proper. Dzhugashvili joined a socialist group, lost any interest he may have had in theology, and, in the spring of 1899, was expelled for failing to attend an examination. Traces of his seminary background can be discerned in his later writings, with their biblical tags and fondness for a catechetical style that lends itself well to propaganda. In articles and speeches he was in the habit of posing questions which he would then repeat verbatim in his answers: he also made his articles more assimilable by numbering each separate concept and statement.

From his seminary days onwards Stalin was associated with various rudimentary socialist groups in Georgia: the Russian Social Democratic party did not yet exist, though a formal decision to establish it was taken at the Minsk gathering in March 1898. For some months in 1899–1900 he worked as a clerk at the Tiflis geophysical observatory, after which he devoted himself entirely to political and propaganda activities, both legal and illegal. From 1901 he wrote articles for the clandestine Georgian socialist paper *Brdzola* (*The Struggle*) and spread propaganda among workers. Towards the end of that year he became a member of a committee to direct party work in Tiflis. In April 1902 he was arrested for organizing a workers' demonstration in Batum. He was sentenced to exile in Siberia, but escaped from his place of detention (or while on the way there) and was again in the Caucasus at the beginning of 1904, living as a member of the underground with forged papers. Meanwhile the Social Democratic party had held its second congress and had split into the Bolshevik and Menshevik factions. Stalin soon declared for the Bolsheviks and wrote pamphlets and articles supporting Lenin's idea of the party. The Georgian Social Democrats were nearly all Mensheviks: their leader was Noakh Zhordania, the most prominent Caucasian Marxist. During and after the 1905 Revolution Stalin worked for a time at Baku as a party activist with duties covering the whole Caucasus area.

It was some years, however, before he played a part in Bolshevik activities in Russia proper. He attended the party conference at Tammerfors in December 1905, and in April 1906 he was the only Bolshevik to attend the 'unity' congress at Stockholm (his credentials for so doing were disputed by the Mensheviks). However, until 1912 the real scene of his activity was the Caucasus. At Tammerfors he had his first meeting with Lenin, whose doctrine and leadership he never seriously challenged. At Stockholm, however, while siding with Lenin on all other questions, he took the line that the party programme should advocate the division of land among the peasants, and not its nationalization as Lenin contended.

Stalin's writings at this period contain nothing original or worthy of note: they are popular propaganda articles reproducing Lenin's slogans on current topics. Much space is given to attacking the Mensheviks, and there is of course criticism of the Kadets, the 'recallists' (otzovists), 'liquidators', anarchists, etc. The only article of any length, 'Anarchism or Socialism?', appeared in Georgian in 1906 (from 1905 onwards Stalin also wrote articles in Russian): it is a rather clumsy exposition of the Social Democratic world-view and its philosophical premises.

In 1906–7 Stalin is known to have been one of the organizers of 'expropriations', i.e. armed raids for the purpose of filling the party coffers. This activity was forbidden and condemned, despite Lenin's opposition, at the party's Fifth Congress in London in April 1907; but the Bolsheviks continued to practise it until it gave rise to a major scandal some months later.

In recent years several historians have examined allegations made originally by Zhordania and, after Stalin's death, by Orlov, a former high official of Soviet intelligence, to the effect that Stalin was in the service of the Okhrana (the Tsarist secret police) for some years after 1905. But the evidence for this charge is slight, and it is rejected by most historians, including Adam Ulam and Roy Medvedyev.

Between 1908 and the February Revolution Stalin spent most of his time in prison and exile, from which he escaped on every occasion except the last (1913–17). He acquired the reputation of a skilful, stubborn, and indefatigable revolutionary, and did his best to salvage the party's Caucasian organization during the calamitous years after 1907. Like many other leaders inside Russia he did not take a keen interest in the theoretical debates and squabbles among the émigrés. There is some evidence that he took a sceptical view of Lenin's *Materialism and Empiriocriticism* (which he afterwards extolled as the supreme achievement of philosophical thought), and that in the darkest days of 1910 he made genuine efforts to restore unity with the Mensheviks. In January 1912, when Lenin called an all-Bolshevik conference at Prague to set the seal on the breach with the Mensheviks, Stalin was in exile at Vologda. The conference elected a Central Committee of the party, to which Stalin was later co-opted at Lenin's suggestion, thus making his début on the all-Russian political scene.

After escaping from Vologda, Stalin was once more arrested and deported, and escaped again. In November 1912 he travelled outside Russia for the first time in his life, spending a few days at Cracow in Austrian Poland, where he met Lenin. He returned to Russia but in December went abroad again, this time to Vienna for six weeks—the longest period he was ever to spend on foreign soil. In Vienna he wrote for Lenin an article on 'Marxism and the National Question' which appeared in 1913 in the journal *Prosveshchenie* (*Enlightenment*), and which constitutes his earliest claim, and one of his principal ones, to celebrity as a theoretician. It does not add anything to what Lenin had said on the question, except for defining a nation as a community possessing a single language, territory, culture, and economic life—thus excluding, for example, the Swiss and the Jews. The article was written as an attack on the Austro–Marxists, especially Springer (Renner) and Bauer, and on the Bund (the General Jewish Workers' Union of Russia). As Stalin could read only Russian and Georgian he was probably helped by Bukharin, then in Vienna, to select quotations from the Austro–Marxist writers. In opposition to the latter's ideas of national cultural autonomy based on self-determination by the individual, Stalin argued for the right of national self-determination and political separation on a territorial basis. However, like Lenin, he emphasized that while the social democrats recognized the right of every people to form a state of its own, this did not mean that they would support separatism in every case; the deciding factor was the interest of the working class, and it must be remembered that separatism was often used as a reactionary slogan by the bourgeoisie. The whole debate was of course conducted on the assumption of a 'bourgeois revolution'. Like all socialists at that time, except Trotsky and Parvus, Stalin expected Russia to undergo a democratic revolution, followed by many years of bourgeois republican rule; but he held that the proletariat must take a leading part in bringing the revolution about, and not play second fiddle to the bourgeoisie or act merely as a servant of its interests.

The article on nationality was the last that Stalin wrote before the February Revolution. Soon after his return from Vienna, in February 1913, he was again arrested and sentenced to four years' deportation. This time he did not try to escape but remained in Siberia, reappearing in Petrograd in March 1917. For some weeks, until Lenin arrived, he was effectively in charge of the party in the capital city. Together with Kamenev he took over the editorship of *Pravda*. His attitude towards both the Provisional Government and the Mensheviks was a good deal more conciliatory than Lenin's, and he incurred the latter's censure by toning down the articles that Lenin was sending from Switzerland. However, after Lenin's return to Russia and the presentation of his 'April Theses' Stalin, with some hesitation, accepted the policy of working for a 'socialist revolution' and government by the Soviets. By contrast, during the first few weeks in Petrograd he was still writing in terms of a 'bourgeois revolution', peace with the Central Powers, confiscation of the big estates, and a policy of exerting pressure on the Provisional Government but not attempting its overthrow. Only after the July crisis, at the conference of the party organization in Petrograd, did Stalin speak clearly of transferring power to the proletariat and the poor peasantry; at this time the slogan 'All power to the Soviets' was abandoned, as the latter were dominated by Mensheviks and S.R.s. By the time of the October revolution Stalin was unquestionably among the chief party leaders, alongside Lenin, Trotsky (who joined the Bolsheviks in July 1917), Zinovyev, Kamenev, Sverdlov, and Lunacharsky. As far as we know he did not take part in the military organization of the uprising, but in Lenin's first Soviet government he was made Commissar for Nationalities. During the party crisis over the Treaty of Brest-Litovsk he supported Lenin against the 'left-wing Bolsheviks' who were pressing for a revolutionary war with Germany. However, he believed, as Lenin did, that the European revolution would break out any day, and that accepting the German peace terms was no more than a temporary tactical retreat.

As an expert on nationality affairs Stalin at this time made speeches to the effect that self-determination must be understood 'dialectically' (in other words, used as a slogan when it suited the party but not otherwise). At the Third Congress of Soviets at the beginning of 1918 he explained that self-determination, properly speaking, was for the 'masses' and not the bourgeoisie, and must be subordinated to the fight for socialism. In articles published in that year he emphasized that the secession of Poland and the Baltic States was a counter-revolutionary move and played into the hands of the imperialists, as these countries would form a barrier between revolutionary Russia and the revolutionary West; on the other hand, the struggle of Egypt, Morocco, or India for independence was a progressive phenomenon as it tended to weaken imperialism. All this was fully in accord with Lenin's doctrine and with party ideology. Separatist movements are progressive when directed against bourgeois governments, but once the 'proletariat' is in power national separatism automatically and dialectically changes its significance, since it is a threat to the proletarian state, socialism, and world revolution. Socialism, by definition, cannot practise national oppression, and thus what appear to be invasions are in fact acts of liberation—as, for instance, when the Red Army under Stalin's orders marched into Georgia, which at the time (1921) had a Menshevik government on a basis of representative democracy. Notwithstanding this, the slogan of national self-determination, which was never revoked, contributed largely to the Bolshevik victory in the Civil War, as the White commanders made no secret of the fact that their purpose was to restore Russia, one and indivisible, without any loss of her pre-Revolutionary territory.

Stalin played an important part in the Civil War, though his achievements were overshadowed by Trotsky's. The roots of the conflict between the two men no doubt go back to this period with its personal jealousies and recriminations—who did most to bring about victory at Tsaritsyn, whose fault was the defeat before Warsaw, etc.

In 1919 Stalin became Commissar for the Workers' and Peasants' Inspectorate. This institution, as we have seen, represented a desperate and hopeless attempt by Lenin to protect the Soviet system from the inroads of bureaucracy: the Inspectorate, composed of 'genuine' workers and peasants, had unlimited powers of supervision over all other branches of the state administration. Far from curing the situation it made things worse, since in the absence of any democratic institutions the Inspectorate became simply an additional tier of the bureaucratic edifice. Stalin, however, was able to make use of it to strengthen his control of the apparatus, and his tenure of the Commissarship was undoubtedly a factor that helped him in his rise to supreme power.

At this stage an important, though not original, observation should be made. In later years, when the whole history of the party was rewritten under Stalin's orders and for his own glorification, he was presented, or rather presented himself, as having been Lenin's 'second in command' from his early youth. In every field of action he was the leader, the chief organizer, the inspiration of his comrades, and so forth. (In a party questionnaire he claimed to have been expelled from the seminary for carrying on revolutionary activity; no doubt he discussed forbidden subjects while there, but in fact he was expelled for failing to attend an examination.) According to this fantastic version he was Lenin's closest confidant and helper from the very moment the party was founded; the infant socialist movement in the Caucasus had thriven under his brilliant leadership; later on, the whole party regarded him without question as the rightful and natural successor to Lenin, and so on. He was the brains of the Revolution, the architect of victory in the Civil War, the organizer of the Soviet state. In the hagiography composed by Beriya the year 1912 is singled out as the turning-point in the history of the Russian party, and therefore in the history of mankind, as it was then that Stalin became a member of the Central Committee.

On the other hand, Trotsky and the many other Communists who had reason to hate Stalin were at pains to belittle his role in the history of Bolshevism and to depict him as a second-rate *apparatchik* who, by a mixture of cunning and good fortune, managed in due course to climb on to a pedestal from which it proved impossible to dislodge him.

Neither of these versions can be accepted as the truth. Certainly, before 1905 Stalin was an obscure local figure and there were many in his own area who were more esteemed and played a more important part than he. None the less, by 1912 he had made himself one of the six or seven most prominent Bolshevik leaders, and in Lenin's last years—although less well known than Trotsky, Zinovyev, or Kamenev, and certainly regarded by no one as Lenin's 'natural' successor—he was one of a small group ruling over the party and Russia; and at the time of Lenin's death, in practice although not in theory he enjoyed greater power than anyone else in the country.

From the documents now available we know that even before the Revolution Stalin's comrades noticed qualities that later turned him into a pathological despot. Some were mentioned in Lenin's 'Testament': he was known to be brutal, disloyal, arbitrary, ambitious, envious, intolerant of opposition, a tyrant to his subordinates. Until he had wiped out the whole of the Bolshevik 'old guard', no one in the party took him seriously as a philosopher or theoretician: from this point of view he was outclassed not only by Trotsky and Bukharin but by a host of party ideologists. Everyone knew that Stalin's articles, pamphlets, and speeches contained nothing original and showed no sign that they were intended to: he was not a 'Marxist theoretician', but a party propagandist like hundreds of others. Later, of course, in the delirium of the 'personality cult', any scrap of paper he had ever written became an immortal contribution to the treasury of Marxism–Leninism; but it is perfectly clear that his whole reputation as a theoretician was nothing but a part of the ordained ritual and was forgotten within a short time of his death. If his ideological writings had been those of a man with no political claim to fame, they would scarcely deserve mention in a history of Marxism. But since, during his years of power, there was scarcely any other brand of Marxism than his, and since the Marxism of those days can hardly be defined except in relation to his authority, it is not only true but is actually a tautology to say that for a quarter of a century he was the greatest Marxist theoretician.

In any case, Stalin had many qualities that were useful to the party, and it was not only due to chance that he made his way to the top and eliminated his rivals. He was a tireless, shrewd, and efficient worker. In practical matters he knew how to disregard doctrinal considerations and discern clearly the relative importance of issues. He neither panicked (except in the first days of Hitler's invasion) nor lost his head from success. He was adept at distinguishing real from apparent power. He was a poor speaker and a dull writer, but he could say things in a plain way so that the ordinary party member could grasp them, and his pedantic habits of repetition and the numbering of points gave his exposés an appearance of force and clarity. He bullied subordinates, but he could use them as well. He knew how to adapt his style to different interlocutors, whether party members, foreign journalists, or Western statesmen, and could at will play the part of a strategist, an intrepid fighter for the proletarian cause, or the no-nonsense 'boss' of his country. He had the rare skill of contriving to receive the credit for all successes and to blame all failures upon others. The system he helped to establish enabled him to become a tyrant, but it must also be said that he worked long and hard to achieve that result.

Lenin undoubtedly valued Stalin's efficiency and powers of organization. Although Stalin occasionally disagreed with Lenin, he was always behind him at times of crisis. Unlike most of the front-rank Bolsheviks he had no 'intellectual' leanings, which Lenin could not endure. He was a matter-of-fact character who did not mind taking on hard and ungrateful tasks. And, although in a belated moment of vision Lenin realized what a dangerous man he had raised to the summit of power, there is some truth in Stalin's retort to his opponents when they at last decided to drag Lenin's 'Testament' out of the archives and invoke it against him. Yes, said Stalin, Lenin did accuse me of brutality, and I *am* brutal where the revolution is concerned—but did Lenin ever say that my policy was wrong? To this the opposition had no answer.

There is no reason to doubt that Stalin was Lenin's personal choice for Secretary-General of the party in April 1922, and there is no evidence that any of the other leaders objected to his nomination. It is quite true, as Trotsky afterwards pointed out, that nobody regarded the creation of this post and Stalin's appointment to it as signifying that he was to be Lenin's heir, or that the holder of the secretary-generalship would in practice be the supreme ruler of the Soviet party and state. All important decisions were still taken by the Politburo or the Central Committee, which ran the country through the intermediary of the Council of People's Commissars. The new office was not the highest individual post in the party hierarchy, and there was indeed no such post. The Secretary-General's function was to supervise the current work of the party bureaucracy, ensure coordination within the machine, control senior appointments, etc. With hindsight it is possible to see clearly that when all other forms of political life have been destroyed and the party is the only organized force in the country, the individual in charge of the party machine must become all-powerful. This is what actually happened, but no one perceived it at the time: the Soviet state was without precedent in history, and it is not astonishing that the actors on the political stage did not foresee the dénouement of the play. Stalin as Secretary-General was able to put his own men in the majority of local party posts and even central ones, except those of the highest rank, and his power was enhanced by the function of organizing conferences and congresses. This, of course, was a gradual process: the first few years still witnessed intra-party disputes and the formation of rival groups and opposition platforms, but as time went on these became more infrequent and tended to be confined to the very highest level.

As we have seen, during Lenin's lifetime there were opposition groups within the party, reflecting the discontent of some Communists at the increase in despotic and bureaucratic methods of government. The 'Workers' Opposition', whose best-known spokesmen were Aleksandr Shlyapnikov and Aleksandra Kollontay, believed in a literal 'dictatorship of the proletariat', i.e. that power should actually be exercised by the whole working class and not only by the party. They did not by any means advocate a return to state democracy, but they fondly imagined that the Soviet system could preserve democratic forms of life for the privileged minority, i.e. the proletariat, after having abolished such forms as far as the great majority were concerned, especially the peasants and intellectuals. Other opposition groups wanted to restore democracy within the party, though not for those outside it: they protested at the growing power of the bureaucracy, the system of nomination to all posts, and the reduction of intra-party discussions and elections to an empty ritual.

Such brands of Utopian criticism to some extent anticipated the 'critical' trends which made themselves felt within the Communist system after Stalin's death: the demand that democracy should prevail within the party although not outside it, or that power should be wielded by the whole proletariat or by workers' councils, though not, of course, by the rest of society. Apart from these ideas, however, there appeared in the early years a new version of Communism which in a sense prefigured Maoism, reflecting as it did the needs and interests of Asiatic peasant peoples. The author of this trend was Mir Sayit Sultan-Galiyev, a Bashkir by nationality and a teacher by profession. He became a Bolshevik soon after the October Revolution, and was one of the few intellectuals from the Muslim area of the Soviet Union who secured early recognition as an expert on the affairs of the Central Asian peoples. His conviction was, however, that the Soviet system did not solve any of the Muslims' problems but merely subjected them to a different form of oppression. The urban proletariat which had assumed dictatorial power in Russia was no less European than the bourgeoisie, and equally alien to the Muslim peoples. The basic conflict of the age was not between the proletariat and bourgeoisie of the developed countries, but between colonial or semi-colonial peoples and the whole industrialized world. Not only could Soviet power in Russia do nothing to liberate those peoples, but it would instantly begin to oppress them and pursue an imperialist policy under the red flag. The colonial peoples must unite against the hegemony of Europe as a whole, create their own parties and an International independent of the Bolshevik one, and combat Western colonizers as well as Russian Communists. They must combine anti-colonial ideology with Islamic tradition, and create one-party systems and state organizations backed by armed force. In accordance with this programme Sultan-Galiyev tried to form a Muslim party separate from the Russian one, and even an independent Tatar-Bashkir state. His movement was soon suppressed, conflicting as it did with both Lenin's ideology and the interests of the Bolshevik party and the Soviet state. Sultan-Galiyev was expelled from the party in 1923 and imprisoned as an agent of foreign intelligence: perhaps the first occasion on which this charge, which afterwards became a matter of routine in such cases, was levelled against a prominent party member. He was executed many years later, during the great purges, and his cause was soon forgotten. In a speech in June 1923 Stalin said that he had been arrested less because of his pan-Islamic and pan-Turkic views than because he had conspired against the party with the Basmach rebels of Turkestan. The episode is worth remembering on account of the striking resemblance between Sultan-Galiyev's ideas and subsequent Maoist doctrine, or some ideologies of the 'Muslim socialist' type.

As to those opposition groups which advocated democracy for the party or the proletariat, they were speedily and unanimously crushed by the leaders including Lenin, Trotsky, Stalin, Zinovyev, and Kamenev. The prohibition of splinter groups, and the right of the Central Committee to expel party members who joined them, were proclaimed at the Tenth Congress in 1921. It was indeed clear, as the defenders of party unity pointed out, that under a one-party system separate groups within the party were bound to become the mouthpieces of all social forces which would in the old days have formed parties of their own: hence, if 'factions' were allowed, there would virtually be a multi-party system. The inevitable conclusion was that a party ruling despotically must itself be despotically ruled, and that, having destroyed democratic institutions in society at large, it was idle to think of preserving them within the party, let alone for the benefit of the whole working class.

None the less, the process of transforming the party into a passive instrument in the hands of the bureaucracy took longer than the destruction of democratic institutions within the state, and was not completed until the late twenties. In 1922–3 there were strong currents of rebellion against the growing tyranny within the party, and no one was so skilful in repressing them as Stalin. Having successfully achieved control over the information that reached Lenin, who was ill and infirm, Stalin ruled the party with the aid of Zinovyev and Kamenev and systematically excluded Trotsky from power. The latter was in a losing position from an early stage, despite his oratorical skill and his prestige as the architect of victory in the Civil War. He did not dare to appeal to opinion outside the party, as this would have conflicted with the principle of Soviet power; and it proved easy to mobilize against him the party bureaucracy, which was the only active force in political life. Trotsky had joined the Bolsheviks at a late stage and was distrusted by the old-timers, who also disliked his excess of rhetoric and his haughty, arrogant manners. Stalin, Zinovyev, and Kamenev skilfully exploited all Trotsky's weaknesses: his Menshevik past, his hankering after the militarization of labour (a policy which Stalin never formulated in such despotic terms), his criticism of the N.E.P., his old quarrels with Lenin, and the charges that Lenin had trumped up against him in former times. As Commissar for the Armed Forces and a member of the Politburo he still appeared powerful, but by 1923 he was isolated and helpless. All his former tergiversations were turned against him. When he came to realize his situation he attacked the bureaucratization of the party and the stifling of intra-party democracy: like all over-thrown Communist leaders he became a democrat as soon as he was ousted from power. However, it was easy for Stalin and Zinovyev to show not only that Trotsky's democratic sentiments and indignation at party bureaucracy were of recent date, but that he himself, when in power, had been a more extreme autocrat than anyone else: he had supported or initiated every move to protect party 'unity', had wanted—contrary to Lenin's policy—to place the trade unions under state control and to subject the whole economy to the coercive power of the police, and so on. In later years Trotsky claimed that the policy, which he had supported, of prohibiting 'fractions' was envisaged as an exceptional measure and not a permanent principle. But there is no proof that this was so, and nothing in the policy itself suggests that it was meant to be temporary. It may be noted that Zinovyev showed more zeal than Stalin in condemning Trotsky—at one stage he was in favour of arresting him—and thus supplied Stalin with useful ammunition when the two ousted leaders tried, belatedly and hopelessly, to join forces against their triumphant rival.

4. Socialism in one country

THE doctrine of 'socialism in one country', formulated towards the end of 1924 against Trotsky and his idea of 'permanent revolution', was for a long time regarded as a major contribution of Stalin's to Marxist theory, with the corollary that Trotskyism constituted a rival body of coherent dogma—a view that Trotsky himself apparently came to share. In reality, however, there was no basic political opposition between the two men, let alone any theoretical disagreement.

As we have seen, the leaders of the October uprising believed that the revolutionary process would soon spread to the principal European countries, and that the Russian revolution had no hope of permanent success except as the prelude to world revolution. None of the Bolshevik leaders in the early days held or expressed any view other than this: some of Lenin's statements on the subject were so unequivocal that Stalin later had them expunged from his works. However, as hopes of a world revolution receded and the Communists failed in their desperate efforts to bring about an uprising in Europe, they also agreed that the task immediately before them was to build a socialist society, though no one knew exactly in what this ought to consist. Two basic principles continued to be accepted: that Russia had begun a process which, by the laws of history, must finally embrace the whole world, and that, as long as the West was in no hurry to start its own revolution, it was for the Russians to set about the socialist transformation of their own country. The question whether socialism could in fact be built once and for all was not seriously considered, as no practical consequences depended on the answer. When Lenin perceived, after the Civil War, that you could not make corn grow by issuing decrees or even by shooting peasants, and when he accordingly instituted the N.E.P., he was certainly concerned with 'building socialism' and was more interested in the internal organization of the state than in stirring up revolution abroad.

When Stalin, in the spring of 1924, published his article 'The Foundations of Leninism'—his first attempt to codify Lenin's doctrine after his own fashion— he reiterated points that were generally accepted, and attacked Trotsky for 'underestimating' the revolutionary role of the peasantry and holding that the revolution could originate in one-class rule by the proletariat. Leninism, he argued, was the Marxism of the age of imperialism and proletarian revolution; Russia had become the native country of Leninism because it was ripe for revolution owing to its relative backwardness and the many forms of oppression from which it suffered; and Lenin had foreseen the transformation of the bourgeois revolution into a socialist one. However, Stalin emphasized, the proletariat of a single country could not bring about final victory. In the autumn of the same year Trotsky published a collection of his own writings dating from 1917, with a preface designed to prove that he was the only statesman faithful to Leninist principles, and to discredit the then leaders, especially Zinovyev and Kamenev, for having shown a hesitant and even hostile attitude towards Lenin's insurrectionary plan. He also attacked the Comintern, of which Zinovyev was then the chief, for the defeat of the uprisings in Germany and for failing to exploit the revolutionary situation. Trotsky's criticism provoked a collective answer by Stalin, Zinovyev, Kamenev, Bukharin, Rykov, Krupskaya, and others, blaming him for all past errors and defeats, accusing him of arrogance and of quarrelling with Lenin, and belittling his services to the revolution.

It was at this time that Stalin constructed the doctrine of 'Trotskyism'. The idea of 'permanent revolution', formulated by Trotsky before 1917, presupposed that the Russian revolution would pass continuously into a socialist phase, but that its fate would depend on the world revolution which would also result from it; moreover, in a country with a huge peasant majority, the working class would suffer political destruction unless it were supported by the international proletariat, whose victory alone could consolidate that of the Russian workers. As the question of the 'transformation of the bourgeois revolution into a socialist one' had meanwhile lost its application, Stalin represented Trotskyism as signifying that socialism could not be definitively built in one country—thus suggesting to his readers that Trotsky's real design was to restore capitalism in Russia. In the autumn of 1924 Stalin declared that Trotskyism rested on three principles. Firstly, it did not recognize the poorest class of peasants as an ally of the proletariat; secondly, it accepted peaceful coexistence between revolutionaries and opportunists; and thirdly, it slandered the Bolshevik leaders. Later on, the essential feature of Trotskyism was declared to be the contention that, while it is possible to set about building socialism in one country, it is not possible to bring it to completion. In *Concerning Questions of Leninism* (1926) Stalin criticized his own theory of the spring of 1924, saying that a distinction must be drawn between the possibility of finally building socialism in one country and the possibility of finally protecting oneself against capitalist intervention. In conditions of capitalist encirclement there could be no absolute guarantee against intervention, but a fully socialist society could nevertheless be constructed.

The point of the controversy about whether socialism could be finally built in one country or not resided, as Deutscher well observes in his life of Stalin, in the latter's desire to transform the psychology of party workers. In proclaiming that the Russian revolution was self-sufficient he was less concerned with theory than with countering the demoralization produced by the failure of world communism. He wished to assure party members that they need not be troubled as regards the uncertain support of the 'world proletariat', since their own success did not depend on it; he wanted, in short, to create an atmosphere of optimism, without, of course, abandoning the consecrated principle that the Russian revolution was the prelude to a worldwide one.

It is possible that if Trotsky had been in charge of Soviet foreign policy and the Comintern in the 1920s he would have taken more interest than Stalin did in organizing Communist risings abroad, but there is no reason to think his efforts would have had any success. Naturally he used every defeat of Communists in the world to accuse Stalin of neglecting the revolutionary cause. But it is not at all clear what Stalin could have done if he had been actuated by the internationalist zeal which Trotsky accused him of lacking. Russia had no means of ensuring a German Communist victory in 1923 or a Chinese one in 1926. Trotsky's later charge that the Comintern failed to exploit revolutionary opportunities because of Stalin's doctrine of socialism in one country is completely devoid of substance.

Thus there is no question of two 'essentially opposite' theories, one asserting and the other denying that socialism could be built in one country. In theory everyone accepted the need to support world revolution and also the need to build a socialist society in Russia. Stalin and Trotsky differed to some extent as to the proportion of energy that ought to be devoted to one task or the other, and both men did their share to inflate these differences into an imaginary theoretical antithesis.

Still less is it possible to believe the assertion frequently made by Trotskyists that intra-party democracy was of the essence of their system. Trotsky's attacks on bureaucratic rule within the party began, as we have seen, when he himself was effectually deprived of power over the party apparatus; as long as he was still in power, he was one of the most autocratic champions of bureaucracy and of military or police control over the whole political and economic system. The 'bureaucratization' against which he later inveighed was the natural and inevitable result of destroying all democratic institutions in the state, a process into which Trotsky threw himself with zeal and which he never afterwards repudiated.

5. Bukharin and the N.E.P. ideology.
The economic controversy of the 1920s

THE controversy over Soviet economic policy in the 1920s was much more gen-uine than the issue of 'socialism in one country', which was rather a disguise for faction than a key to the solution of any practical or theoretical problem. Even the famous debate on industrialization, however, does not deserve to be presented as a clash between two opposite principles. All agreed that Russia must be industrialized: the point in dispute was the speed of the process and the connected issue, fraught with doom, of Soviet agriculture and the govern-ment's relations with the peasantry. These matters, however, were of funda-mental practical importance, and different points of view concerning them led to different political decisions of great importance to the whole country.

Bukharin, the chief ideologist of the N.E.P. (inaugurated in 1921), enjoyed great popularity in party circles and was regarded as a first-class theoretician. After the fall of Zinovyev and Kamenev in 1927 he became the most important man in the party after Stalin.

Nikolay Ivanovich Bukharin (b. 1888, d. 13 or 14 March 1938) belonged to the generation that entered the socialist movement during or shortly after the 1905 Revolution. Born and brought up in Moscow, a member of the intellec-tual class (his parents were teachers), he joined a socialist group while still at school and was a Bolshevik from the outset of his political career. He joined the party when just over eighteen, at the end of 1906, and carried out propa-ganda work in Moscow. In 1907 he enrolled at the University as a student of economics, but politics took up most of his time and he never completed the course. In 1908 he was already in charge of the small Bolshevik organization in Moscow. Arrested in autumn 1910 and sentenced to deportation, he escaped and spent the next six years as an *émigré* in Germany, Austria, and the Scan-dinavian countries, where his writings gained him the reputation of an expert Bolshevik theorist in the sphere of political economy. In 1914 he finished a work entitled *The Economics of the Rentier Class: the Austrian School's Theory of Value and Profit:* this was first published in full in Moscow in 1919, and an English version, *The Economic Theory of the Leisure Class*, appeared in 1927. The book is a defence of Marxian doctrine and an attack on the theory of value of the marginalists, especially Böhm-Bawerk. As the title suggests, Bukharin argued that the Austrian school of economic theory was an ideological expression of the mentality of the parasitic dividend-drawing bourgeoisie; as far as the defence of Marx goes, his work added nothing to Hilferding's earlier criticism. On the outbreak of war in 1914 he was deported from Vienna to Switzerland, where he worked on the economic theory of imperialism. At this time he was involved in controversy with Lenin, who accused him of 'Luxemburgist' errors over the national and peasant questions. Bukharin held, in the light of classic Marxist schemata, that the national question was becoming less and less important and that the purity of socialist class policies should not be sullied by doctrines of national self-determination, which was both utopian and contrary to Marxism. In the same way he disapproved of the party bidding for peasant support in its revolutionary policy, as Marxism taught that the class of small farmers was doomed to disappear anyway and that the peasantry was historically a reactionary class. (In the future, however, Bukharin was to be noted chiefly as an exponent of precisely the opposite 'deviation'.)

In Switzerland and afterwards in Sweden Bukharin wrote *Imperialism and World Economy*, first published in full in Petrograd in 1918; Lenin saw the manuscript and used it freely for his *Imperialism, the Highest Stage of Capitalism*. Bukharin himself made much use of Hilferding's analysis, but he also emphasized that as capitalism develops the economic role of the state grows in importance and leads to a new social form, that of state capitalism, i.e. an economy centrally planned and regulated on the scale of a national state. This meant the extension of state control to ever wider areas of civil society and the intensification of human slavery. The Moloch of the state was capable of functioning without internal crises, but only by encroaching on more and more aspects of private life. Bukharin, however, disagreed with Kautsky's and Hilferding's expectation of an 'ultra-imperialist' phase in which the necessity of war would be obviated by a centralized organization of the world economy: state capitalism, he thought, was feasible on a national scale but not on a global basis. Hence competition, anarchy, and crises would continue, but would take on increasingly international forms. It followed also—and here Bukharin agreed with Lenin, though for slightly different reasons—that the cause of the proletarian revolution must now be envisaged in the context of the international situation.

At a somewhat later date Lenin criticized the young Bukharin for his 'semi-anarchist' view that the proletariat would have no need of state power after the revolution—a utopian idea very similar to that expounded in Lenin's *State and Revolution* in 1917.

Towards the end of 1916 Bukharin went to the United States, where he held discussions with Trotsky and endeavoured to persuade the American Left of the rightness of the Bolshevik view on questions of war and peace. Returning to Russia after the February Revolution, he soon took his place among the party leaders and gave whole-hearted support to Lenin's 'April Theses'. During the crucial months before and after October he was chiefly active in Moscow as an organizer and propagandist. Soon after the Revolution he became editor-in-chief of *Pravda*, a position he held until 1929. Sharing the general view that the fate of the Russian revolution depended on whether it could set fire to the West, Bukharin stoutly opposed Lenin's policy of a separate peace with Germany. During the first dramatic months of 1918 he was one of the leaders of the 'Left Communists' who pressed for a continuance of the revolutionary war, despite Lenin's sober appraisal of the technical and moral condition of the army. Once peace was concluded, however, he stood by Lenin in all important economic and administrative questions. He did not support the left opposition's protest against the employment of 'bourgeois' specialists and experts in industry, or against the organization of the army on a basis of professional competence and traditional discipline.

During the period of 'War Communism' (a misleading term, as we have seen) Bukharin was the chief theoretical advocate of an economic policy based on coercion, requisitions, and the hope that the new-born state could manage without a market or a monetary system and would organize socialist production in no time. During the years before N.E.P., in addition to his work *Historical Materialism* which we shall discuss presently, he published two books expounding the party's economic policy: *The Economics of the Transition Period* (1920) and, with E. Preobrazhensky, *The ABC of Communism* (1919, English trans. 1922). These works enjoyed semi-official status as an authoritative account of Bolshevik policies at the time. Not only did Bukharin, like Lenin, jettison his utopian doctrine that the state would vanish immediately after the revolution, but he insisted on the necessity of an economic as well as a political dictatorship of the proletariat. He also reiterated his view regarding the evolution of 'state capitalism' in the advanced countries. (Lenin used this term to refer to private industry in socialist Russia, a fact which gave rise to some verbal misunderstanding.) Bukharin stressed the notion of 'equilibrium' as a key to the understanding of social processes. He argued that once the capitalist system of production has lost its equilibrium—as evidenced by the revolutionary process with its inevitable destructive consequences—this can only be restored by the organized will of the new state. Hence the state apparatus must take over all functions connected with the social organization of production, exchange, and distribution. In practice this means the 'statization' of all economic activity, the militarization of labour, and a general rationing system, in short the application of coercion throughout the economy. Under Communism there can be no question of the spontaneous working of the market; the law of value ceases to operate, as do all economic laws independent of human volition. Everything is subject to the planning power of the state, and political economy in the old sense ceases to exist. And, although the organization of society is essentially based on coercion *vis-à-vis* the peasants (compulsory requisition) and the workers (militarization of labour), there is clearly no exploitation of the working class, as it is impossible by definition for that class to exploit itself.

Bukharin, like Lenin, regarded the system of basing economic life on mass terror not as a transient necessity but as a permanent principle of socialist organization. He did not shrink from justifying all means of coercion and held, like Trotsky at the same period, that the new system called essentially for the militarization of labour—i.e. the use of police and military force to compel the whole population to work in such places and conditions as the state might arbitrarily decree. Indeed, once the market is abolished there is no longer any free sale of labour or competition between workers, and police coercion is therefore the only means of allocating 'human resources'. If hired labour is eliminated, only compulsory labour remains. In other words, socialism—as conceived by both Trotsky and Bukharin at this time—is a permanent, nation-wide labour camp.

Trotsky, it is true, had doubts for a time in 1920 as to the efficacy of an economy based on nothing but terror, and proposed that the requisition of grain should be replaced by a tax in kind. But he soon changed his mind, and during the N.E.P. period he was one of the chief opponents of a 'loose' economy with substantial concessions to the peasantry and with free trade as the principal mode of exchange between town and countryside.

Bukharin's views, on the other hand, evolved in the opposite direction. In 1920 the idea of a planned economy belonged to the realm of fantasy: Russia's industry lay in ruins, there was barely any transport, and the one pressing problem was how to save the towns from imminent starvation, not how to bring about a Communist millennium. When Lenin, in this catastrophic situation, beat a retreat from his economic doctrine and made up his mind to a long period of coexistence with a peasant economy, free trade in farm products, and the toleration of small-scale private industry, Bukharin likewise abandoned his earlier stand and became a fervent advocate and ideologist of the N.E.P., in opposition first to Trotsky and then to Zinovyev, Kamenev, and Preobrazhensky. From 1925 onwards he was Stalin's chief ideological supporter against the opposition. Like Lenin, he had come to recognize that the whole programme set out in *The Economics of the Transition Period* was a delusion; he did not concern himself with the millions of victims who had paid with their lives for the leaders' brief moment of frenzy.

Bukharin's arguments for returning to a market economy—while, of course, maintaining state ownership of the banks and main industries—were chiefly economic but to some extent also political. Throughout the N.E.P. period (1921–8) his economic utterances expressed the views of a substantial majority of the political leadership, including Stalin.

The main issue was how the state could influence the commodity market by economic means so as to achieve the desired level of accumulation and develop industry, in a situation where agriculture was almost entirely in the hands of small farmers. To obtain the necessary quantity of grain from the peasants under market conditions it was necessary to supply the countryside with an equivalent value of producer and consumer goods. In the ruined state of industry this was difficult if not impossible, but if it were not done the peasants would refuse to sell their produce, as there would be nothing they could buy with the proceeds. In addition it was a question how the 'proletariat', i.e. the Bolshevik party, could maintain its dominant position if the state economy was at the mercy of the peasants: as the market developed, their position would become stronger and they might in the end threaten the 'proletarian dictatorship'.

Preobrazhensky, who was regarded as a Trotskyist in economic affairs and who led the theoretical opposition to Stalin's and Bukharin's policy of concessions to the peasants, argued as follows. The principal task of a socialist state in its initial phase is to create a strong industrial base and ensure the necessary degree of accumulation. All other economic aims must be subordinated to the development of industry, and particularly the manufacture of industrial equipment. Capitalist accumulation was facilitated by plundering colonies; the socialist state has no colonies and must achieve industrialization from its own resources. State industry, however, cannot of itself create a sufficient basis of accumulation but must draw upon the resources of small producers, i.e. in practice the peasantry. Private holdings must be the object of internal colonization: Preobrazhensky admitted frankly that it was a matter of exploiting the peasant, extracting the maximum amount of surplus value from his labour to increase investment in industry. The 'colonization' process was to be achieved mainly by fixing the price of industrial products at a high level in relation to the prices paid by the state for farm produce. This must be reinforced by other forms of economic pressure on the peasantry, so as to extort the maximum aid to industry in the shortest possible time. The party leaders, on the other hand, were pursuing a policy which encouraged accumulation on the part of small producers and neglected industry, especially heavy industry, for the sake of the peasants' well-being. Moreover, the chief beneficiaries of this policy were the kulaks, the class of rural exploiters: for, as everything was being done to increase agricultural productivity regardless of the claims of industry, the relative strength of classes, and the dictatorship of the proletariat, naturally credits and facilities went by preference to those peasants who promised the biggest deliveries. This was bound to strengthen the kulaks, who, economically at first and soon politically too, would start to undermine the power of the proletariat. There could be no compromise between the two rival policies. Those who, like the existing government, wished to satisfy all the peasants' economic demands to induce them to sell grain would have to pursue a corresponding foreign trade policy and import consumer goods for the peasants instead of producer goods for industry. The whole trend of development would be distorted in the interest of a class other than the proletariat, and the result would be a threat to the existence of the socialist state.

Arguing on these lines, Preobrazhensky and the whole Left Opposition pressed for the collectivization of agriculture, though they did not explain clearly by what means it was to be achieved.

Trotsky argued on similar lines. As he wrote in 1925, if state industry developed at a slower rate than agriculture, the restoration of capitalism was inevitable. Agriculture must be mechanized and electrified so that it could be transformed into a branch of state industry: only thus could socialism purge the economy of alien elements and liquidate class divisions. But all this depended on industry being adequately developed. In the last resort, the triumph of a new form of society was a function of the productivity of labour in that society: socialism would win because it had the power eventually to achieve greater productivity than capitalism and a more efficient development of productive forces. Thus the victory of socialism depended on socialist industrialization. Socialism, indeed, had all the advantages on its side: technical advances could be brought into immediate and universal application, unhampered by the obstacles that private ownership created. The centralization of the economy prevented the waste which was due to competition; industry was not at the mercy of consumers' whims, and nationwide norms ensured a higher level of productivity. The complaint that centralization and standardization killed initiative and meant more monotonous work was nothing but a reactionary hankering for pre-industrial production. The whole economy must be transformed into a 'single, uniform, automatic mechanism', and for this purpose there must be an unremitting campaign against capitalist elements, i.e. small peasant producers: to abandon the fight was to acquiesce in the return of capitalism. Trotsky did not, like Preobrazhensky, speak of the 'objective law of socialist accumulation' and the need to extort the maximum amount of surplus value from the peasants for the sake of industrial investment, but his call for an economic offensive against capitalist elements came to the same thing. The opposition accused Bukharin of being basically in favour of a wealthy kulak class and a 'Thermidorean reaction': his policy, they claimed, would strengthen classes hostile to socialism and increase the specific gravity of capitalist elements in the economy. In reply Stalin, Bukharin, and their supporters declared that the call for 'super-industrialization' was unrealistic and that the opposition's policy would turn the bulk of the middle peasantry, not only the kulaks, against the regime; this would violate Lenin's sacred canon of an 'alliance between the proletariat and the poor and middle peasants' and would threaten the existence of the Soviet state. The opposition were constantly demanding that capitalist elements should be kept in check, but they did not say what should be done if increased government pressure—albeit economic only—deprived the peasantry of incentive, and how the state could then ensure food production and deliveries by any other method than a return to police coercion.

Bukharin's argument, supported at this time by Stalin, was that an out-and-out war by the state against the peasantry would be economically ineffective and politically disastrous, as the period of War Communism had sufficiently proved. The economic development of the country should depend not on the maximum exploitation of the peasantry but on preserving the market as a link between the state and rural economies and hence between the working class and the peasants. The rate of accumulation depended on the efficiency and rapidity of circulation, and it was to this that efforts should be directed. If the peasant were deprived of all his surpluses by coercion or economic means, he would produce no more than he could eat himself; hence to coerce the peasantry was against the manifest interest of the state and proletariat. The only way to increase farm production was to provide material incentives. Certainly, this would be to the kulaks' advantage; but the development of commercial co-operatives would make it possible to bring the whole peasantry, including kulaks, into a state-controlled system that would promote the growth of the economy as a whole.

The development of industry depended on the rural market; accumulation by the peasants meant increased demand for industrial products, and it was therefore in the whole country's interest to permit accumulation by peasants of all categories. Hence Bukharin's appeal to the peasants in 1925, 'Get rich!'—a slogan that was often quoted later as a glaring proof of his unorthodoxy. In his view the policy of declaring war on the better-off peasants and stirring up class conflict in the countryside would ruin not only agriculture but the whole economy. Poor peasants and farm labourers must be helped not by ruining the kulaks but by the state using the latter's resources, which it must first allow them to accumulate. Consumers' and marketing co-operatives would in time lead naturally to the development of producer co-operatives. The Trotskyist policy, on the other hand, would mean disaster in both agriculture and industry; it would alienate the whole peasantry from the state, and thus destroy the dictatorship of the proletariat. Moreover, the artificial raising of the price of industrial goods to a high level in order to exploit the countryside, as proposed

by Preobrazhensky and Pyatakov, would not only hit the peasants but the workers as well, since the bulk of these goods were consumed by the urban population. As for the opposition's attacks on bureaucratic degeneration in the
government machine, this danger indeed existed, but it would be a hundred
times worse if their policy towards the peasants were adopted. A return to the
methods of War Communism would mean creating a whole class of privileged
functionaries for the main purpose of coercing the countryside, and this huge
apparatus would be far more expensive than all the losses resulting from a lack
of organization in agriculture. The cure for bureaucracy was to encourage the
population to form voluntary social organizations in various spheres of life; the
remedy proposed by the opposition was the exact reverse of this, and would be
worse than the disease.

In this controversy with the Left Opposition Bukharin did not advocate any
steps that would have led to an extension of democracy within the state or
party. On the contrary, he attacked Trotsky, Zinovyev, and Kamenev as leaders
of faction and splitters of party unity. It was, he reminded them, the ABC of
Leninism that the dictatorship of the proletariat entailed the existence of a single ruling party and that that party must be united and not permit the existence
of 'fractions', which must lead to the development of separate parties. All the
oppositionists had been well aware of this until recently, and no one would be
deceived by their sudden transformation into democrats.

In the debate on industrialization both sets of adversaries, of course,
claimed that 'objectively' their opponents' policy would lead to the restoration
of capitalism. According to Bukharin, Preobrazhensky wanted the socialist
state to imitate capitalism in achieving accumulation by exploiting and ruining
small-scale producers. The dictatorship of the proletariat would be destroyed
if its basis, an alliance with the peasantry and especially the middle peasantry,
was undermined; meanwhile 'internal colonization' meant an attack not only
on the kulaks but on the whole countryside, if only because all sections of the
peasantry were equally affected by the ratio between industrial and agricultural
prices. Against this, the Left contended that the Stalin–Bukharin policy would
steadily increase the economic power of private owners, especially the kulaks,
and that the weakening of socialist industry and the working class could only
end by destroying the dictatorship of the proletariat. The opposition also held
that industry, and especially heavy industry, was the key to socialist development. Bukharin maintained, on the other hand, that the exchange of goods
between town and country was the main lever, that production was not an end
in itself but a means to consumption, and that the opposition were echoing
Tugan-Baranovsky's theory (in relation to the capitalist system) that there
could be an economy in which production goes on creating an ever-increasing
market for itself regardless of the volume of demand. As things then were in

Russia, rural accumulation was by no means contrary to the workers' interest but coincided with it. To this the opposition replied that there could be no identity of interest between exploiters and the exploited, and that since the kulak was an exploiter by definition, to assist him to accumulate wealth was to foster the class enemy.

In this way there took shape, as it were, two variants of Bolshevism, both, of course, constantly appealing to pronouncements by Lenin. Lenin had said that there must be an alliance with the middle peasantry, but he had also spoken of the danger presented by the kulaks. Roughly speaking, Bukharin's case was that the kulaks could not be abolished without at the same time destroying the middle peasants, while the opposition held that the middle peasants could not be aided without also aiding the kulaks: these were two ways of expressing the same fact, with opposite political intentions. The opposition looked for support among the many Communists who were indignant at the rise of a class of well-to-do 'Nepmen' while the workers were in a state of misery, and who took seriously and literally the slogans of egalitarianism and the dictatorship of the proletariat (so that it was natural for the Trotsky–Zinovyev group to make common cause eventually with the remnants of the old 'Workers' Opposition'). They were chiefly interested in the question of power, dictatorship, and heavy industry as an index of power; Bukharin, on the other hand, was concerned with effectively increasing welfare, and was prepared to tolerate the class of materially privileged Nepmen if their activity meant a better deal for the whole population, including the working class.

Throughout the debate, which was to decide the fate of millions of individuals, Stalin supported Bukharin's position but did not commit himself too completely, leaving it to Bukharin or Rykov to make the ideological declarations. He took note of Bukharin's blunder in inviting the peasants to 'get rich'—an expression that touched many Communists on the raw—but treated it as a slip of the tongue, not to be compared with the monstrous crimes of the opposition. Stalin never advanced too far in discussion, but it could be seen that up to 1928 there was no disagreement in economic policy between him and Bukharin: Stalin too repeated Lenin's words concerning the need for a lasting alliance with the middle peasants and attacked the 'ultra-Left' opposition for its 'revolutionary adventurism' and the shocking notion of 'internal colonization'. He got the upper hand in the political and organizational dispute with the opposition, not only thanks to his dominant position in the party machine but because it was easy to show how all the oppositionists were violating principles that they had recently been shouting from the house-tops. It was no trouble to prove that Trotsky's love of democracy was of extremely recent date, and when he and Zinovyev conspired together against Stalin the latter had only to quote the insults they had been hurling at each other the day before. As for democracy within the party, none of those who were now defending it could refer to his own past without embarrassment. As Stalin put it at the Fourteenth Congress in December 1925, 'Are not the comrades of the opposition aware that for us Bolsheviks formal democracy is an empty shell, but the real interests of the party are everything?' (*Works*, English ed, vol. 7, 1954, p. 394). A few months later he gave a more exact definition of party democracy: 'What does inner-Party democracy mean? Inner-Party democracy means raising the activity of the Party masses and strengthening the unity of the Party, strengthening conscious proletarian discipline in the Party' (Report to Leningrad party organization, 13 Apr. 1926; *Works*, English ed., vol. 8, 1954, p. 153). Stalin, however, was not so incautious as to speak of a 'party dictatorship', though neither Lenin nor, apparently, Bukharin shrank from this: instead he referred to the 'dictatorship of the proletariat under the party's leadership'. At a session of the Executive Committee of the Comintern of 7 December 1926, and on other occasions, he declared that Trotsky, by maintaining that socialism could not be built in one country, was inviting the party to relinquish power.

Trotskyist historians still brood regretfully over the events of the 1920s and speculate as to how Trotsky might have avoided various false moves and regained power by this or that political alliance or combination. It does not seem, however, that this was a real possibility at any time after 1923. Trotsky might indeed have made timely use, in public, of Lenin's 'Testament' to discredit Stalin; he not only failed to do so, but afterwards deprived himself of the possibility by denying the authenticity of the 'Testament' when it was published abroad. Possibly Stalin might have been overthrown in 1924, but this would have been of little benefit to Trotsky, as he was detested by the other leaders, who only showed readiness to conspire with him after they themselves were dislodged from power.

Economic and fiscal policy did not in fact remain unaltered during the N.E.P. period, but moved in the direction of increased pressure on the peasantry. Apart from Bukharin the advocates of N.E.P. in the top ranks of the party were Rykov, who succeeded Lenin as Premier, and Tomsky, in charge of the trade unions. Both these were prominent Bolsheviks in their own right and were by no means puppets of Stalin; however, from an early date Stalin brought into the leadership men like Molotov, Voroshilov, Kalinin, and Kaganovich, who signified nothing in themselves and showed him unquestioning obedience. The uncertainty and ambiguity of economic policy (even N.E.P. enthusiasts could not, in the last resort, altogether give up the idea of a 'class struggle in the countryside') led to an impasse from which there was no satisfactory way out. Substantial concessions to the peasants in 1925 led to an increase in farm production, but by 1927 the output of grain had still not reached its pre-1914 level, while the demand for food was increasing with the progress of industry and urbanization. Smallholders had little grain to dispose of, and the kulaks were not in a hurry to sell either, as there was nothing to buy with the money they received. Hence, in 1927, Stalin made up his mind to adopt extreme measures of confiscation and coercion. Bukharin at the outset approved this policy and revised his own programme in the direction of more planning, more investment in heavy industry, a greater degree of state interference with the market, and, finally, an 'offensive' against the kulaks. This was not enough to satisfy the Left Opposition, but the fact was of little consequence as their positions had meanwhile been destroyed.

The increased economic and administrative pressure on the peasants led to a drastic fall in deliveries and a worsening of the already serious food situation. Stalin talked more and more of the kulak danger and the growing strength of the class enemy, but in February 1928 he was still insisting that rumours of the abandonment of N.E.P. and the liquidation of the kulaks were counter-revolutionary twaddle. Barely four months later, however, he announced that the 'time was ripe' for the mass organization of collective farms. At the plenum of the Central Committee in July he endorsed all the theses of Preobrazhensky that he had till then violently attacked. Russia could only achieve industrialization by means of internal accumulation; the only solution was to fix prices at a level that would make the peasants pay through the nose for industrial goods. At the same time he continued to uphold the principle of a 'lasting alliance with the middle peasants' and averred that small-scale agricultural production was still a necessity. None the less, Bukharin, Rykov, and Tomsky rebelled against the new policy, whereupon Stalin branded them as a new, right-wing opposition: he informed the Politburo of this sad development at the beginning of 1929, and the world at large soon afterwards. (In the autumn of 1928 he had referred in speeches to the 'rightist danger' but declared that unanimity reigned in the Politburo.) The right-wing deviation consisted, it was explained, of slowing up industrialization, deferring collectivization to an indefinite future, re-establishing complete freedom of trade, and repudiating the use of 'extraordinary measures'—i.e. requisitions, arrests, and police pressure—against the kulaks. It soon appeared also that the 'Rightists' were in error concerning the international situation: they still believed in the stabilization of world capitalism, and refused to fight against the social democratic Left.

At this time also, Stalin made a number of speeches (the first in July 1928) in which he announced a new principle that was to add to his fame as a theoretician. This was that as Communism continued to advance, the class struggle and the resistance of the exploiters would become more and more violent. For the next twenty-five years this discovery served as the basis for wholesale repressions, persecutions, and massacres in the Soviet Union and the countries subjected to its rule.

Such was the setting for the mass collectivization of Soviet agriculture—probably the most massive warlike operation ever conducted by a state against its own citizens. Attempts to use coercion in moderation having proved fruitless, Stalin decided at the end of 1929 to embark at once on full collectivization, accompanied by the mass 'liquidation of the kulaks as a class'. A few months later, in March 1930, when this policy had already led to catastrophic results—the peasants destroyed grain and slaughtered livestock on a huge scale—Stalin decreed a temporary lull and, in an article 'Dizzy with Success', blamed the excessive zeal and haste of some party officials and the violation of the 'voluntary principle'. This caused the party and police apparatus to hesitate, with the result that numerous collective farms disbanded of their own accord. There was nothing for it but to revert to the policy of coercion, which turned the country into an inferno. Hundreds of thousands, and finally millions, of peasants, arbitrarily labelled 'kulaks', were deported to Siberia or other desolate areas; desperate revolts in the villages were bloodily suppressed by the army and police, and the country sank into chaos, starvation, and misery. In some cases the inhabitants of whole villages were deported or starved to death; in the mass convoys, hastily organized, thousands were done to death or succumbed to cold and privation; half-dead victims roamed the countryside vainly pleading for succour, and there were cases of cannibalism. To prevent the starving peasants from fleeing to the towns an internal passport system was introduced and unauthorized change of residence was made punishable with imprisonment. Peasants were not allowed passports at all, and were therefore tied to the soil as in the worst days of feudal-serfdom: this state of things was not altered until the 1970s. The concentration camps filled with new hordes of prisoners sentenced to hard labour. The object of destroying the peasants' independence and herding them into collective farms was to create a population of slaves, the benefit of whose labour would accrue to industry. The immediate effect was to reduce Soviet agriculture to a state of decline from which it has not yet recovered, despite innumerable measures of reorganization and reform. At the time of Stalin's death, almost a quarter of a century after mass collectivization was initiated, the output of grain per head of population was still below the 1913 level; yet throughout this period, despite misery and starvation, large quantities of farm produce were exported all over the world for the sake of Soviet industry. The terror and oppression of those years cannot be expressed merely by the figures for loss of human life, enormous as these are; perhaps the most vivid picture of what collectivization meant is in Vasily Grossman's posthumous novel, *Forever Flowing*.

It is widely held that in adopting the 'new course' and the policy of forced collectivization Stalin was simply taking over the Trotsky–Preobrazhensky programme after first eliminating its authors. This was Bukharin's charge from the outset, and it was believed by many of the former opposition who hastened to beg Stalin to pardon them on the ground that there was no longer any fundamental clash of policy. Those, such as Radek, who succeeded in this were able to serve the state for a few years longer, though they did not escape final destruction. Several Marxist thinkers have seen the situation in the same light, from Lukács to Roy Medvedyev. Trotsky, however (who was expelled from the Politburo in autumn 1926 and from the party a year later, deported to Alma Ata at the beginning of 1928, and exiled to Turkey with the consent of the Turkish Government in February 1929), did not share the view that Stalin's policy was identical with his own. The Stalinist bureaucracy, he wrote, had indeed been forced by opposition pressure to adopt left-wing objectives, but it had put them into effect in a ruthless and opportunist way. The opposition believed in collectivization, but not in mass coercion; the kulaks should have been checked and combated 'by economic means'. This was also the line subsequently taken by all Trotsky's followers.

Their contention, however, is a very weak one. Trotsky, it is true, never spoke of forced collectivization, but then neither did Stalin. Anyone who knew the history of those years only from Stalin's speeches and articles would unquestionably suppose that the peasants flocked into the collective farms for the sake of a better life, that the 'revolution from above' was greeted with unbridled joy, and that the only sufferers from stern measures were a handful of incorrigible saboteurs, enemies of the working people and of the government that infallibly expressed that people's interests. What is true is that Stalin put the opposition's programme into effect by the only possible means. All the economic inducements they suggested were tried before Stalin resorted to out-and-out coercion. Tax and price incentives, and a policy of limited terror, had been applied in the previous two years, but the only effect had been that grain deliveries fell and were likely to fall still further. No further means of economic pressure remained, and there were only two alternatives: either to go back to the N.E.P. in its full form and permit free trade, relying on the market to ensure food production and delivery, or to pursue the course already embarked on and eliminate the whole independent peasantry by the mass use of troops and police terror. In choosing the latter policy Stalin gave effect to the demands of the Left in the only feasible way.

Why did he do so? The first alternative was not excluded by any 'laws of history', and there was no fatal compulsion to take the second road. None the less, there was a logic in the Soviet system which operated strongly in the direction that was actually chosen. The ideology in force was far more consonant with a slave economy based on terror than with the return to market conditions, even under state control. As long as the bulk of the population was economically more or less independent of the state, and even kept the state in some degree of dependence on itself, the ideal of an indivisible dictatorship could not be fully realized. Marxist–Leninist doctrine taught, however, that socialism could only be built up by a completely centralized political and economic power. The abolition of private ownership of the means of production was the supreme task of humanity and the main obligation of the most progressive system in the world. Marxism held out the prospect of the merging or unification of civil society with the state through the dictatorship of the proletariat; and the only way to such unity was by liquidating all spontaneous forms of political, economic, and cultural life and replacing them by forms imposed by the state. Stalin thus realized Marxism–Leninism in the only possible way by consolidating his dictatorship over society, destroying all social ties that were not state-imposed and all classes, including the working class itself. This process, of course, did not take place overnight. It required, first, the political subjugation of the working class and then of the party: all possible nuclei of resistance had to be crushed, and the proletariat deprived of all means of self-defence. The party was able to do this because at the outset of its power it was supported by a large part of the proletariat. It was not simply that, as Deutscher emphasizes, the old working class, politically conscious and seasoned in battle, was decimated by the Civil War, and that post-war ruin and misery brought about a mood of apathy and fatigue. The party's success was also due to its using the period of proletarian support in two ways. In the first place, it systematically promoted the ablest members of the working class to privileged positions in the state service, thus turning them into a new ruling class; and secondly, it destroyed all existing forms of working-class organization, especially other socialist parties and trade unions, and saw to it that the material means of reviving such organizations were kept out of the workers' reach. All this was done at an early stage and quite efficiently. The working class was thus paralysed, and not only fatigue but the rapid progress of totalitarianism prevented it from subsequently taking effective action, in spite of occasional desperate attempts. In this sense it may be said that the Russian working class created its own despots, regardless of their individual class origins. In the same way the intelligentsia for many years laboured unconsciously to destroy itself by hesitancy and submission in the face of unremitting blackmail from the extreme left.

Thus was fulfilled the prophecy of the Mensheviks, who in 1920 compared the brave new world announced by Trotsky to the building of the Pyramids by Egyptian slaves. Trotsky, for many reasons, was ill suited to carry out his own programme; Stalin was Trotsky *in actu.*

The new policy meant the political downfall of Bukharin and his allies. At the outset of the controversy the Right still had firm political positions and fairly widespread support in the party; but it soon appeared that all their assets were nothing compared to the power of the Secretary-General. 'Rightist deviation' became the main target of attack by Stalin and his henchmen. The Bukharinites—the last opposition group in the party who fought for principles of government and not merely for personal power—were, in the course of 1929, thrust out of all the posts they occupied in the state bureaucracy. This did not signify by any means that the Left Opposition were restored to favour. None of them were brought back into their old posts, though Stalin took on a few for minor duties: the capable Radek was kept on for a few years as government panegyrist. The Bukharinites did not dare appeal to opinion outside the party, any more than the Leftists had done (though in their time there was more possibility of doing so). Nor did the Bukharinites even dare to organize 'fractional' activity: it was only a short time, after all, since the struggle with Trotsky and Zinovyev, in which they had inveighed against fractionalism and exalted party unity. As for one-party rule, it was questioned neither by the Left Opposition nor by the Right. All were prisoners of their own doctrine and their own past: all had worked with a will to create the apparatus of violence that crushed them. Bukharin's hopeless attempt to form a league with Kamenev was no more than a pitiful epilogue to his career. In November 1929 the deviationists performed a public act of penance, but even this did not save them. Stalin's victory was complete; the collapse of the Bukharinite opposition meant the triumph of autocracy in the party and in the country. In December 1929 Stalin's fiftieth birthday was celebrated as a major historical event, and from this point we may date the 'cult of personality'. Trotsky's prophecy of 1903 had come true: party rule had become Central Committee rule, and this in turn had become the personal tyranny of a dictator.

The destruction of the Soviet peasantry, who formed three-quarters of the population, was not only an economic but a moral disaster for the entire country. Tens of millions were driven into semi-servitude, and millions more were employed as executants of the process. The whole party became an organization of torturers and oppressors: no one was innocent, and all Communists were accomplices in the coercion of society. Thus the party acquired a new species of moral unity, and embarked on a course from which there was no turning back.

At this time also, what remained of independent Soviet culture and the intelligentsia was systematically destroyed: the regime was entering the phase of final consolidation.

Bukharin's personal fate from 1929 to his judicial murder in 1938 was of no consequence to the history of the Soviet Union or of Marxism. After his downfall he worked for a time as director of research under the Supreme Economic

Council and published occasional articles in which he tried—as Stephen F. Cohen points out in his excellent biography—to voice an occasional, muted note of criticism. He remained a member of the Central Committee and, after a further public recantation, became editor of *Izvestiya* in 1934. At the Writers' Congress in August of that year he made a speech which was 'liberal' for the times, and in 1935 he was effective chairman of the commission which drafted the new Soviet Constitution: this document, promulgated in 1936 and in force until 1977, is mainly if not wholly Bukharin's work. Arrested in February 1937, Bukharin was sentenced to death in the last of the series of monster show trials. His biographer calls him 'the last Bolshevik', a description which is true or false according to the meaning we attach to it. It is true if we mean by a Bolshevik one who accepted all the principles of the new order—the unlimited power of a single party, 'unity' within the party, an ideology excluding all others, the economic dictatorship of the state—and who also believed that it was possible, within this framework, to avoid despotism by an oligarchy or an individual, to govern without the use of terror, and to preserve the values that the Bolsheviks had championed during the struggle for power: namely, government by the working people or the proletariat, free cultural development, and respect for art, science, and national traditions. But if 'Bolshevik' means all this, it simply means a man incapable of drawing logical conclusions from his own premises. If, on the other hand, Bolshevik ideology is not just a matter of generalities but involves accepting the inevitable consequences of one's own principles, then Stalin was right to boast himself the most consistent of all Bolsheviks and Leninists.

II

Theoretical Controversies in Soviet
Marxism in the 1920s

1. The intellectual and political climate

As WE HAVE SEEN, the N.E.P. years from 1921 to 1929 were by no means a
period of freedom in the intellectual sphere. On the contrary, independent art,
literature, philosophy, and the humane sciences were subjected to ever-
increasing pressure. Nevertheless, in these fields too the subsequent years of
collectivization mark a turning-point, which may be defined as follows. During
the N.E.P. period writers and artists were required to show loyalty to the regime
and were not allowed to produce anti-Soviet work, but within these limits various trends were permitted and in fact existed. There were no exclusive canons
of art and literature; experimentation was allowed, and direct glorification of
the regime or its leader was not a *sine qua non* of publication. In philosophy
Marxism reigned supreme, but it was not yet codified, and it was by no means
universally clear in what 'true' Marxism consisted. Accordingly, controversies
continued, and there were convinced Marxists who genuinely sought to discover what was or was not consonant with Marxism. Moreover, the philosophers of the 1920s, although they left no works of particular importance, were
men of 'normal' intellectual background and, while loyal to the regime, did not
trouble themselves as to how it might react to their speculations.

For some years, too, private publishing firms were in operation. In 1918–20
non-Marxist works were still published—for example, those of Berdyayev,
Frank, Lossky, Novgorodtsev, and Askoldov—and one or two non-Marxist periodicals appeared, such as *Mysl i slovo* and *Mysl*. This shows how baseless was
the later argument that increased repression was necessary because of the
acute threat to Soviet power. The years of relative cultural freedom were those
of the Civil War, when the threat to the regime was much greater than subsequently (and, in the same way, a certain degree of relaxation in cultural matters took place in 1941 and after, when the country's fate hung in the balance).
In 1920, however, the university chairs of philosophy were suppressed, and in
1922 all non-Marxist philosophers, including those mentioned above, were
expelled from the country.

In art and literature the 1920s were marked by many valuable achievements. Outstanding writers who identified with the Revolution gave it a kind of authenticity by their work: these included Babel, the young Fadeyev, Pilnyak, Mayakovsky, Yesenin, Artem Vesyoly, and Leonov. Their creativity is proof of the fact that the Revolution was not a mere *coup d'état* but an explosion of forces truly present in Russian society. But other writers who by no means favoured the Soviet system were also active at this time, for example, Pasternak, Akhmatova, and Zamyatin. In the thirties all this came to an end. Indeed, it is hard to say whether it was safer in that period to identify with the Revolution or to be a 'bourgeois survival'. Many of the former class of writers were murdered (Babel, Pilnyak, Vesyoly) or committed suicide (Mayakovsky, Yesenin); of the second category some, such as Mandelshtam, died in labour camps, but others survived the years of persecution and heart-break (Akhmatova, Pasternak) or managed to emigrate (Zamyatin). Those who chose to become panegyrists of Stalin's tyranny (Fadeyev, Sholokhov, Olesha, Gorky) generally sacrificed their talent in the process.

The first years after the Civil War witnessed an upsurge in all forms of culture. The names of the great producers and directors—Meyerhold, Pudovkin, Eisenstein—belong to the world history of theatre and the cinema. Current Western fashions, especially of a more or less *avant-garde* type, were embraced eagerly and without fear of the consequences. Soviet adherents of Freud, such as I.D. Yermakov, stressed the materialist and determinist aspects of psychoanalysis; Trotsky himself showed a favourable interest in Freudianism. J. B. Watson's works on behaviourism appeared in Russian translation. As yet there were no ideological attacks on new developments in natural science. The theory of relativity was received with favour by commentators who argued that it confirmed dialectical materialism by asserting that time and space are forms of the existence of matter. 'Progressive' trends in education were also welcomed, especially Dewey's emphasis on the 'free school' as opposed to discipline and authority; at the same time Viktor M. Shulgin, for example, held out the prospect that schools would 'wither away' under Communism. It was indeed not incongruous with Marx's doctrine that all old-world institutions should be doomed to wither away: the state, the army, the school, nationality, and the family. Views such as these expressed a naïve *avant-garde* spirit of Communism which itself was destined soon to 'wither away' for good and all. Its adherents believed that a new world was coming into existence in which effete institutions and traditions, sanctities and taboos, cults and idols would collapse into dust before the triumphant power of Reason; the world proletariat, like another Prometheus, would create a new age of humanism. This iconoclastic fervour attracted many Western intellectuals of the literary or artistic *avant-garde*, such as the French surrealists, who saw in Communism the political embodiment of their own struggle against tradition, academism, authority, and the past in general. The cultural atmosphere of Russia in those years had an adolescent quality, common to all periods of revolution: the belief that life is just beginning, that the future is unlimited, and that mankind is no longer bound by the shackles of history.

The new regime made a strong effort to abolish illiteracy and promote education. The schools were soon used for ideological indoctrination, and the whole educational system was greatly expanded. Universities were founded right and left, but many did not last long, as the figures show: before the war Russia had 97 places of higher learning, in 1922 there were 278, but in 1926 there were again only half as many (138). At the same time 'Workers' Faculties' (*rabfaki*) were founded, providing crash courses to prepare workers for higher education. Initially, Soviet cultural policy under Lunacharsky was content with limited objectives. It was impossible to remove all 'bourgeois' scholars and teachers from academic institutions at a stroke, as this would have virtually put an end to learning and education. The universities, from the outset, were more subjected to political pressure than the Academy and research institutes, as is still the case today: there is naturally less strict control over bodies that are not engaged in teaching the young. In the 1920s the Academy of Sciences retained a considerable measure of autonomy, while the universities lost it at an early date, their governing bodies being packed with representatives of the Commissariat for Education and party activists from the Workers' Faculties. Professorial chairs were assigned to politically reliable individuals without academic qualifications; the enrolment of students was subjected to class criteria so as to exclude 'bourgeois' applicants, i.e. children of the old intelligentsia or the middle class. Stress was laid on 'vocational' education, in opposition to the old idea of a 'liberal' university with a fairly flexible curriculum: the object was to prevent the creation of an intelligentsia in the old sense, i.e. a class of people who wished not only to be skilled in their own profession but to enlarge their horizons, to acquire an all-round culture and form their own opinions on general topics. The education of the 'new intelligentsia' was to be confined as far as possible to strictly professional qualifications. The principles that still hold good today were introduced at an early date; however, the intensity of political pressure varied in different fields. At the outset there was practically no coercion as far as the content of natural science was concerned; in the humanities it was strongest in ideologically sensitive areas, namely philosophy, sociology, law, and modern history. Works by non-Marxists on the history of the ancient world, Byzantium, or old Russia were still allowed to appear in the 1920s.

As to the non-Russian peoples of the Soviet state, while their 'right of self-determination' soon proved to be a mere scrap of paper (as Lenin had predicted), they received the benefits of universal education through the medium of their own tongue, and Russification was not at first a significant factor. To sum up, although the general level of education inevitably suffered a good deal, the new regime did succeed in establishing a generally accessible school system for the first time in Russia's history.

For the first decade of Soviet power the universities were to a large extent influenced by academics of the old type, even though some faculties—especially history, philosophy, and law were completely 'reformed' or closed down. To form new teaching cadres and encourage the spread of orthodox learning the authorities created two party-based institutions: the Red Professors' Institute (1921) to train up replacements for the old intelligentsia in the universities, and, at an earlier date, the Communist Academy in Moscow. Both these bodies were supported by Bukharin as long as he remained in power, and were several times purged of 'left-wing' or 'right-wing' deviationists; they were disbanded in due course, when the party was in full control of all academic institutions and no longer needed a special training-ground to fill them with reliable staff. Another creation of this time was the Marx–Engels Institute, which studied the history of Communism and inaugurated a first-class critical edition of the works of Marx and Engels (the *M.E.G.A.* edition). Its director, D. B. Ryazanov, was dismissed from his post in the 1930s, like practically all genuine Marxist intellectuals, and probably fell a victim to the purge, though some say that he died a natural death at Saratov in 1938.

The principal Marxist historian of the 1920s was Mikhail N. Pokrovsky, an eminent scholar and a friend of Bukharin. He was for some years Deputy Commissar for Education under Lunacharsky, and was the first director of the Red Professors' Institute. He taught history in the classic Marxist style, endeavouring to show that detailed analysis invariably confirmed the general tenets of Marxism: the decisive role of technology and class conflicts, the subordinate importance of individuality in the historical process, and the doctrine that all nations went through essentially the same phases of evolution. Pokrovsky wrote a history of Russia that was much admired by Lenin, and had the good fortune to die in 1932, before the great purges. Subsequently, his views were branded as incorrect and he was accused of denying the 'objectivity' of historical science, for instance in the often-quoted statement that history is nothing but politics projected into the past. He was, however, a genuine historian and a conscientious sifter of evidence, unlike the party champions of 'scientific objectivity'. The accusations against him and his school were mainly connected with the growing influence of nationalism in state ideology and the cult of Stalin as the supreme authority on history: Pokrovsky, it was said, showed 'lack of patriotism' and his researches underestimated the role of Lenin and Stalin.

The charge was true in so far as Pokrovsky did not glorify the conquests of Tsarist Russia, as became *de rigueur* in later years, or extol the virtues and general superiority of the Russian people.

Party history was naturally subject to the strictest control from the very beginning. Nevertheless, there was no single authoritative version for many years, indeed not until the publication of the *Short Course* in 1938, and, as long as fractional strife continued, each group presented party history in the light most favourable to itself. Trotsky put about one version of the Revolution, Zinovyev another. Various manuals appeared, all of course written by party activists or historians under orders (for example, A. S. Bubnov, V. I. Nevsky, N. N. Popov), but not precisely the same in content. For some time the most authoritative version was that by E. Yaroslavsky, first published in 1923 and revised several times in accordance with power shifts among the leaders. Eventually it was replaced by a collective work with Yaroslavsky as editor, but despite all his efforts it was found to be marred by 'serious errors', i.e. it was not sufficiently laudatory of Stalin. Party history, in fact, was degraded to the status of a political weapon at an earlier date than any other branch of learning: from the outset, manuals of party history were nothing but manuals of self-praise. None the less, valuable material in this domain was also published in the twenties, chiefly in the form of memoirs and contributions to specialized journals.

The best-known Soviet expert on legal and constitutional theory in the 1920s was Yevgeny B. Pashukanis (1890–1938), who perished in the great purge like so many others. He was head of the department of legal studies in the Communist Academy, and his *General Theory of Law and Marxism* (published in a German translation in 1929) is regarded as typical of Soviet ideology of the period. His argument was that not only particular changing systems of legal norms, but the very form of law itself, i.e. the phenomenon of law as a whole, is a product of fetishistic social relationships and therefore, in its developed form, is a historical manifestation of the age of commercial production. Law was created as an instrument for the regulation of trade and was then extended to other types of personal relationship. It is therefore in accordance with Marxist theory to hold that in a Communist society law must wither away in the same manner as the state and other creations of commodity fetishism. Soviet law, currently in force, shows by its very existence that we are in a transitional period in which classes have not yet been abolished and survivals of capitalism are inevitably still present. There can be no such thing as a form of law peculiar to Communist society, as personal relationships in that society will not be mediated by juridical categories.

Pashukanis's theory was indeed strongly rooted in Marx's teaching and was in accordance with the interpretation of Marx advanced at the time by Lukács and Korsch; social democrats, on the other hand, such as Renner and Kautsky, regarded law as a permanent instrument for the regulation of relations between individuals. According to Lukács's argument in his analysis of reification, it follows from Marx's social philosophy that law is a form of the reified and fetishistic character of personal relations in a society dominated by commodity exchange. When social life returns to its unmediated form, human beings will not be obliged, or even able, to conduct their relationships through abstract legal rules; as Pashukanis emphasized, legal associations reduce individuals to abstract juridical categories. Law is therefore an aspect of bourgeois society, in which all personal associations take on a reified form, and individuals are only the puppets of impersonal forces—those of exchange-value in the economic process, or abstract legal rules in political society.

Similar conclusions were drawn from Marxist theory by another legal theoretician of the 1920s, Petr I. Stuchka, who contended that law as such is an instrument of the class struggle and must therefore exist as long as class antagonism continues: in socialist society it is an instrument for suppressing the resistance of hostile classes, and in a classless society there can be no further need for it. Stuchka, who represented Latvia in the Comintern, was for many years an officer in the Soviet secret police.

In literature and other areas less sensitive politically than party history, the state and party leaders for the most part saw no harm in allowing a certain pluralism within the limits of general loyalty to the regime. Neither Lenin, Trotsky, nor Bukharin sought to impose a strait-jacket on literature. Lenin and Trotsky were old-fashioned in their personal tastes and had no time for *avant-garde* literature or for Proletkult; Bukharin had some sympathy for the latter, but Trotsky, who published several articles on literary topics, stated flatly that there was not and could not be any 'proletarian culture'. The proletariat, he argued, could not produce any culture at the present time because it was not educated, and, as for the future, socialist society would not create a class culture of any sort but would raise the whole of human culture to new levels. The dictatorship of the proletariat was only a short, transient phase after which the glorious classless society would set in—a society of supermen, any one of whom could become the intellectual equal of Aristotle, Goethe, or Marx. In Trotsky's view it was wrong to canonize any particular literary style, or label creative forms as progressive or reactionary regardless of their content.

The imposition of a uniform pattern on art and literature and their transformation into media for the glorification of the state, the party, and Stalin was a natural effect of the development of totalitarianism; but the creative intelligentsia, or at least large sections of it, helped considerably in the process. During the time when various literary and artistic schools were in competition and were tolerated on condition of general loyalty to the regime, almost every one of them canvassed the party for support against its rivals: this applied especially to literature and the theatre. In this way writers and others seeking a monopoly for their views accepted and encouraged the baneful principle that it was for the party and state authorities to permit or prohibit this or that form of art. The destruction of Soviet culture was in part the work of its own representatives. There were, however, exceptions. For instance, the 'formalist' school of literary criticism flourished in the 1920s and was respected as an important humanistic trend; it was condemned at the end of the decade, but several of its members refused to bow to political pressure and police sanctions and had to be forced into silence. It is noteworthy that, as a result of this tenacity, formalism continued to exist as an underground current and reappeared twenty-five years later, during the partial thaw after Stalin's death, as a strong, untarnished intellectual movement, though of course some of its leaders had meanwhile died of natural causes or otherwise.

The twenties were also the period of the 'new proletarian morality'—a term which stands for a number of planned or spontaneous changes, not all in the same direction. On the one hand there was a continuing struggle against 'bourgeois prejudices': this was not specifically Marxist, but reflected the old Russian revolutionary tradition. It was seen, for instance, in the relaxation of legal forms concerning the family: marriage and divorce became rubber-stamp operations, discrimination between legitimate and bastard children was abolished, no restriction was placed on abortion. Sexual freedom was the rule among revolutionaries, as Alexandra Kollontay had long advocated as a matter of theory and as may be seen from Soviet novels of the period. The government was interested in these changes in so far as they tended to weaken parental influence and facilitate a state monopoly of education. Official propaganda encouraged all forms of collective education of even the youngest children, and family ties were often represented as simply another 'bourgeois survival': children were taught to spy on their parents and inform against them, and were rewarded when they did so. However, in this as in other aspects of life, such as schooling and the army, later years brought a marked change in the official outlook. Of the radical and iconoclastic ideals preached in the early years of the revolution, all were discarded except those which helped the state to exert absolute control over the individual. Hence the idea of collective education and reduction of parental authority to the minimum continued to hold sway, but an end was put to 'progressive' educational methods designed to promote initiative and independence. Strict discipline became once more the rule, and in this respect Soviet schools differed from Tsarist ones only in the immensely increased emphasis on indoctrination. In due course, puritanical sexual ethics were restored to favour. The first slogans to go were, of course, those relating to the democratization of the army. Trotsky, at the time of the Civil War, was well aware that an efficient army needs absolute discipline, a strict hierarchy, and a professional officer corps: dreams of a people's army based on brother-hood, equality, and revolutionary zeal were soon recognized to be utopian.

The state also set out from the beginning to destroy the influence of the Church and religion: this was manifestly in accord with Marxist doctrine and also with the state's object of destroying all independent education. We have already seen that, although the Soviet regime proclaimed the separation of Church and State, it has never succeeded, and cannot succeed, in making this principle a reality; for it would mean that the state took no interest in the reli-gious views of its citizens and assured them all of equal rights whether they belonged to any denomination or none, while the Church or Churches would be recognized as subjects of private law. Once the state had become an apanage of the party with its anti-religious philosophy, this separation was impossible. The party's ideology became that of the state, and all forms of religious life per-force became anti-state activity. The separation of Church and State means that believers and non-believers have equal rights and that the former have as much chance of exercising power as atheistic party members. It is sufficient to state this principle to realize how absurd it is in Soviet conditions. A state which from the outset professed adherence to a basic philosophy or ideology from which its legitimacy was derived could not be neutral *vis-à-vis* religion. Accord-ingly, throughout the twenties the Church was persecuted and prevented from preaching Christianity, though the intensity of the process varied at different times. The regime succeeded in persuading part of the hierarchy to give ground—it made no concessions on its own part, so one can hardly speak of a compromise—and in the later twenties, after many recalcitrant priests had been murdered, a fair proportion of those who remained professed loyalty and insti-tuted prayers for the Soviet state and government. By then, after innumerable executions, the dissolution of monasteries and convents, expropriations and deprivation of civil rights, the Church was only a shadow of what it had been. Nevertheless, anti-religious propaganda has remained to this day an important element in party education. The League of Militant Atheists, set up in 1925 under Yaroslavsky's leadership, harried and persecuted Christians and other believers in every possible way, and was supported by the state in doing so.

The most powerful educative force in the new society was, however, the sys-tem of police repression. Although this fluctuated in intensity, it was always the case that any citizen, at any time, could be subjected to repressive measures at the will of the authorities. Lenin had laid down that law in the new society must have nothing to do with law in the traditional sense, i.e. it must not be allowed to limit government power in any way. On the contrary, since law under any regime was 'nothing but' an instrument of class oppression, so the new order adopted a corresponding principle of 'revolutionary legality' which meant that the authorities did not have to bother with legal forms, rules of evidence, the rights of accused persons, etc., but could simply arrest, imprison, and do to death anyone who might seem to present even a potential danger to the 'dictatorship of the proletariat'. The Cheka, forerunner of the K.G.B., was empowered from the beginning to imprison anyone without the sanction of the judiciary, and decrees were issued immediately after the Revolution to the effect that various loosely defined categories of people—speculators, counter-revolutionary agitators, agents of foreign powers, etc.—were to be 'shot without mercy'. (It was not stated what categories were to be shot mercifully.) This meant in practice that local police authorities had absolute powers of life and death over every citizen. Concentration camps (the term was actually used) were set up in 1918, under the authority of Lenin and Trotsky, for various types of 'class enemy'. Initially these camps were used as places of punishment for political adversaries—Kadets, Mensheviks, and S.R.s, later Trotskyists and other deviationists, priests, former Tsarist officials and officers, and members of the property-owning classes, common criminals, workers who committed breaches of labour discipline, and recalcitrants of all kinds. Only after some years did the camps become an important factor in the Soviet economy by virtue of providing slave-labour on a massive scale. At different times the terror was directed especially against one or another social group, according to what the party chose to regard as the 'chief danger' of the moment; but from the outset the system of repression was completely above the law, and all decrees and penal codes served merely to authorize the use of arbitrary power by those who already possessed it. Show trials began at an early stage, for example, those of S.R.s and priests; a grim warning of things to come was the trial at Shakhty in May 1928 of some dozens of engineers working in the Donets coal basin, in which the evidence was trumped up from beginning to end and was based on extorted confessions. The victims, accused of sabotage and 'economic counter-revolution', were convenient scapegoats for the regime's economic set-backs, its organizational blunders, and the wretched state of the population. Eleven were sentenced to death and many to long terms of imprisonment. The trial was meant to serve as a warning to all members of the old intelligentsia that they could not expect indulgent treatment from the state. The record of the proceedings has been admirably analysed by Solzhenitsyn and presents a picture of the absolute degradation of legal concepts under the Soviet regime.

There is no evidence that any of the party leaders at any time protested or attempted to prevent repressions or obviously faked trials, as long as none of the victims was a Bolshevik. The opposition groups only began to complain when the terror affected their own members, who were devoted party activists; but by that time complaints were of no avail. The police apparatus was completely in the hands of Stalin and his helpers, and on the lower levels it took precedence of the party bureaucracy. It cannot be said, however, that the police ever controlled the party as a whole, for Stalin ruled supreme throughout the period as head of the party, not of the police; it was through the police, however, that he governed the party.

2. Bukharin as a philosopher

ONE of the distinguishing features of Communism was the conviction of the importance of philosophy in political life. From the very beginning, i.e. from Plekhanov's early writings, Russian Marxism showed the tendency to develop into an integral 'system', embracing and answering all questions of philosophy, sociology, and politics. Although individuals differed as to what the 'true' philosophy consisted in, they were all agreed that the party must and did have a clearly defined philosophical outlook, and that this outlook could tolerate no rival. There was virtually no counterpart in Russia to the philosophic 'neutralism' of so many German Marxists, which expressed itself in two logically independent propositions. The first of these was that Marxism, as a scientific theory of social phenomena, had no more need of philosophical premisses than any other science; the second, that the party was bound by a political programme and a historico-social doctrine, but that its members were free to adhere to any religion or philosophy they liked. Lenin violently attacked both these principles, and in so doing he was entirely representative of Russian Marxism.

Accordingly, the party authorities lost no time after the Revolution in concerning themselves with philosophical education. There was, however, as yet no codified philosophy. Apart from Marx and Engels, Plekhanov was regarded as the main authority; Lenin's work on empiriocriticism by no means enjoyed the status of a canonical text to which all were obliged to refer.

Bukharin was the first of the party leaders after Lenin who attempted a systematic exposition of the party's general philosophy and social doctrine. He was better equipped for the task than most others, as during the years in emigration he had studied non-Marxist sociological works such as those of Weber, Pareto, Stammler, and others. In 1921 he published *The Theory of Historical Materialism: a popular manual of Marxist sociology* (English translation, 1926). Unlike Lenin's *Empiriocriticism*, which was an attack on one particular heresy, Bukharin's work purported to give a general account of Marxist doctrine. For many years it was used as a basic text in the theoretical training of party cadres, and its importance lies in this fact rather than in its intrinsic merits.

Bukharin holds that Marxism is a strictly scientific, and the only scientific, comprehensive theory of social phenomena, and that it treats these phenomena as 'objectively' as any other science treats its proper subject-matter; hence Marxists are able correctly to foresee historical processes, which no one else can do. True, Marxism is also a class theory, as are all social theories; but it is a theory entrusted to the proletariat, which has wider mental horizons than the bourgeoisie, because its aim is to change society and it is therefore able to look into the future. Thus only the proletariat can produce, and has in fact produced, a 'true science' of social phenomena. This science is historical materialism, or Marxist sociology. (The term 'sociology' was not approved of by Marxists, and Lenin rejected it on the ground that 'sociology' as such—not merely this or that theory—was a bourgeois invention. However, Bukharin evidently wished to acclimatize a term already in use to denote a particular field of scientific inquiry.)

Historical materialism, Bukharin argues, is based on the premiss that there is no difference between the social and natural sciences in either methods of investigation or the causal approach to the object. All social processes are subject to invariable causal laws; despite the objections of such theorists as Stammler, the fact of human purpose makes no difference to this, as will and purpose are themselves conditioned like everything else. Theories of purposive action in either the natural or the social field, and all indeterminist theories, lead straight to the postulate of a Deity. Man does not have free will: all his actions are causally determined. There is no such thing as chance in any 'objective' sense. What we call chance is the intersection of two chains of causation, only one of which is known to us: the category of 'chance' is merely an expression of our ignorance.

As the law of necessity applies to all social phenomena, it is possible to predict the course of history. Such predictions are 'not yet' so exact that we can foretell the dates of particular events, but this is only because of the imperfectness of our knowledge.

The conflict between materialism and idealism in sociology is a particular instance of a basic philosophical controversy. Materialism asserts that man is a part of nature, that mind is a function of matter and thought an activity of the physical brain. All this is contradicted by idealism, which is nothing but a form of religion and has been effectively refuted by science. For who could take seriously the crazy theory of solipsism, or Plato's notion that there are no such things as people or pears, but only 'ideas' of them?

In the social sphere, then, the same question arises as to the primacy of spirit or matter. From the point of view of science, that is of historical materialism, material phenomena, namely productive activities, determine spiritual phenomena such as ideas, religion, art, law, etc. We must, however, take care to observe the way in which general laws operate in the social context, and not simply transpose the laws of natural science into social terms.

Dialectical materialism teaches that there is nothing permanent in the universe, but that all things are interconnected and affect one another. This is denied by bourgeois historians, who are at pains to argue that private property, capitalism, and the state are eternal. Changes in fact arise from internal conflicts and struggles, for, in society as everywhere else, all equilibrium is unstable and is eventually overthrown, and the new equilibrium must be based on new principles. These changes are effected by qualitative leaps resulting from the accumulation of quantitative changes. For instance, water is heated and, at a given movement, reaches boiling-point and turns into steam—a qualitative change. (We may note in passing that none of the 'classic Marxist writers', from Engels to Stalin, who repeated this example observed that water does not have to reach a temperature of 100° centigrade to evaporate.) Social revolution is a change of the same sort, and this is why the bourgeoisie rejects the dialectical law of change by qualitative leaps.

Specifically social forms of change and development depend on the interchange of energy between man and nature, that is to say on labour. Social life is conditioned by production, and social evolution by the increasing productivity of labour. The relations of production determine thought, but, as human beings produce commodities in mutual dependence on one another, society is not merely a collection of individuals but a true aggregate, every unit of which affects every other. Technology determines social development; every other factor is secondary. Geography, for instance, can at most affect the rate at which peoples evolve, but does not explain evolution itself; demographic changes depend on technology and not the other way about. As for racial theories of evolution, they were decisively refuted by Plekhanov.

'In the last resort' all aspects of human culture can be explained by technological change. The organization of society evolves according to the condition of productive forces. The state is an instrument of the ruling class and serves to maintain its privileges. How, for example, did religion come into being? Very simply: in primitive society there was a ruler of the tribe, and people transferred this concept to their own selves, thus arriving at the idea of a soul that rules the body; then they transferred the soul to the whole of nature and endowed the universe with spiritual qualities. Finally these fantasies were used to justify class divisions. Again, the idea of God as an unknown power 'reflects' the dependence of capitalists on fate, which they cannot control. Art is likewise a product of technical development and social conditions: savages, Bukharin explains, cannot play the piano, for if there is no piano one cannot play on it or compose works for it. Decadent modern art—impressionism, futurism, expressionism—expresses the decline of the bourgeoisie.

Despite all this the superstructure is not without importance: the bourgeois state, after all, is a condition of capitalist production. The superstructure affects the base, but at any given moment it is 'in the last resort' conditioned by the forces of production.

As for ethics, they are a product of the fetishism of class society and will vanish with it. The proletariat has no need of ethics, and the norms of behaviour that it creates in its own interest are technical in character. Just as a carpenter making a chair conforms to certain technical rules, so the proletariat builds communism on the basis of knowledge concerning the interdependence of members of society; but this has nothing to do with ethics.

In general, the whole dialectic may be reduced to an unending process of the disturbance and restoration of equilibrium. There is no longer any purpose in opposing the 'dialectical' to the 'mechanistic' view of phenomena, as in modern times mechanics has itself become dialectical: do we not learn from physics that everything affects everything else, and nothing in nature is isolated? All social phenomena can be explained by the conflict of opposing forces because of man's struggle with nature. (Bukharin seems to believe, nevertheless, that when communism is finally built, social equilibrium will be established once and for all. At present, however, we are in a revolutionary era, which inevitably involves a regression in technical matters.) Production relations are simply the co-ordination of human beings, considered as 'living machines', in the labour process. The fact that people think and feel while engaged in this process does not mean that production relations are spiritual in character: everything spiritual owes its existence to material needs and is subservient to production and the class struggle. It is not the case, for instance, as Cunow and Tugan-Baranovsky assert, that the bourgeois state performs functions that are for the benefit of all classes. True, the bourgeoisie is compelled in its own interest to organize activities in the sphere of public utility, for example, to build roads, maintain schools, and promote scientific knowledge; but all this is done purely from the point of view of the capitalist class-interest, and thus the state is nothing but an instrument of class domination.

Besides the 'law of equilibrium' Bukharin formulated in *Historical Materialism* several other laws of social life. One of these, the 'law of the materialization of social phenomena', was to the effect that ideologies and the various forms of spiritual life are embodied in things—books, libraries, art galleries, etc.—which have an existence of their own and become a point of departure for further evolution.

Bukharin's book is of an extremely simplistic kind, in some ways even more so than Lenin's *Empiriocriticism*. Lenin at least tried to argue, though his arguments were logically valueless, but Bukharin has not even this to his credit. The work is a series of 'principles' and 'fundamental points', enunciated dogmatically and uncritically, without any attempt to analyse the concepts used or to refute the objections to historical materialism that occur as soon as the doctrine is formulated and have repeatedly been advanced by critics. Bukharin's examples illustrate the level of his reasoning, as when he tells us that the dependence of art on social conditions is proved by the fact that no one can play the piano if there are no pianos. Other instances of primitive thought are the childish belief that science in the future will be able 'objectively' to predict the date of social revolutions in the light of technological development, or the 'scientific law' that people write books, or baseless fantasies on the origin of religion, etc. The characteristic feature of this 'manual', as of much subsequent Marxist literature, is its incessant use of the term 'scientific', and the insistent claim that its own statements possess this quality in an exceptional degree.

The mediocrity of Bukharin's book did not escape the notice of intelligent Marxist critics such as Gramsci and Lukács, who drew attention in particular to its 'mechanistic' tendency. Bukharin thought of society as a connected whole in which everything that happens can be explained by the current state of technology; people's thoughts and feelings, the culture in which they express them, and the social institutions they create, are all brought into being by the forces of production with the unalterable regularity of natural law. Bukharin does not explain clearly what he means by the 'law of equilibrium': we are told that equilibrium in society is constantly being disturbed and having to be restored, and that this equilibrium depends on the 'accordance' of production relations with the level of technology, but there is no indication of the criteria to be used in determining whether this accord exists at a given time. In practice, Bukharin seems to equate the disturbance of equilibrium with revolution or social upheaval of any kind. The 'law of equilibrium' thus appears to mean that crises and revolutions have occurred in history and will no doubt do so again. It did not enter Bukharin's head that the study of social phenomena is itself a social phenomenon and, as such, helps to bring about historical change: he believed that the 'proletarian science' of the future would be able to analyse and predict historical events in the same way as astronomy informs us of planetary movements.

Thanks to his political position Bukharin's standardized version of Marxism was long regarded as the most authoritative statement of the party's 'world-outlook', though it never became binding on the faithful in the way that Stalin's works were to do. *Historical Materialism* in fact contains almost everything that Stalin put into his own manual. Stalin did not mention the 'law of equilibrium', but he took over Bukharin's 'laws of the dialectic' (numbering them for good measure) and explained historical materialism as an 'application' or special case of the general principles of philosophical materialism. This approach, for which a basis can be found in Engels and especially Plekhanov, was presented by Bukharin as the essence of canonical Marxism.

Later, when Bukharin fell from grace and 'mechanism' was officially condemned, it became the task of party philosophers to show that there was a close connection between his 'mechanistic' errors and his right-wing deviation in politics, and that his ignorance of dialectic, which Lenin had justly blamed, was the root cause of his defence of the kulaks and opposition to collectivization. This kind of link between philosophy and politics, however, is quite baseless and artificial. The vague generalities in Bukharin's work do not provide any ground for specific political conclusions, except for such propositions as no one disputed then or later: for example, that the socialist revolution of the proletariat must eventually conquer the world, that religion must be combated, and that the proletarian state must foster the growth of industry. As for more precise conclusions, the most contradictory aims could be and were deduced with equal logic from the same theoretical formulas; doctrine, in fact, was ancillary to politics. If 'on the one hand' the base determined the superstructure, but 'on the other hand' the superstructure reacted upon the base, then to whatever extent and by whatever means the 'proletarian state' endeavoured to regulate economic processes, it would always be acting in accordance with the doctrine. Bukharin accused Stalin of disturbing the economic balance between town and countryside, but his 'law of equilibrium' supplied no clue as to when and in what conditions the existing equilibrium should be maintained or overthrown. Until final stabilization is attained under Communism, equilibrium will remain subject to disturbance, and such policies as Stalin's 'revolution from above', i.e. the forced expropriation of the peasantry, may be perfectly in accordance with the thesis of the general trend of society towards equilibrium: for the object of that policy was to eliminate 'contradictions' between state industry and private agriculture, and hence to remove factors of imbalance. Cohen rightly observes that Bukharin wrote his handbook at a time when he himself exemplified what was called in party language an extremely 'voluntaristic' attitude to economic phenomena: i.e. he believed that the whole of economic life could be perfectly well regulated by administrative and coercive means, and that after the victory of the proletariat all economic laws would be dialectically superseded. Later he abandoned his War Communism outlook and became the ideologist of the N.E.P.; but he made no alteration to the thesis of *Historical Materialism*, and it was therefore absurd to detect in that work the inspiration of his policy in 1929. Nor, for that matter, can the ideas of War Communism be deduced from it either: we can only say once again that such vague philosophical statements can be used to justify any policy or, which comes to the same thing, that they do not justify one more than another.

3. Philosophical controversies: Deborin versus the mechanists

INDEPENDENTLY OF Bukharin's intention, his book contributed to a lively dispute in the 1920s between two opposed camps, the 'dialecticians' and the 'mechanists'. The controversy was reflected in the pages of the monthly *Pod znamenem Marksizma* (*Under the banner of Marxism*): this journal, founded in

1922, played an important part in the history of Soviet philosophy and was one of the party's theoretical organs. (The first issue contained a letter from Trotsky, which, however, consisted merely of generalities.) The articles published were all by professed Marxists, but in the first few years readers were given sound information on contemporary philosophy outside Russia, for example, that of Husserl, and the general level of exposition was a great deal higher than in the standard philosophical writings of later years.

If the gist of the controversy were to be expressed in a single sentence, one might say that the mechanists represented the opposition of the natural sciences to philosophic interference, while the dialecticians stood for the supremacy of philosophy over the sciences and thus reflected the characteristic tendency of Soviet ideological development. The mechanists' outlook might be called negative, while the dialecticians ascribed immense importance to philosophy and regarded themselves as specialists. The mechanists, however, had a much better idea of what science was about. The dialecticians were ignoramuses in this sphere and confined themselves to general formulas about the philosophical need to 'generalize' and unify the sciences; on the other hand, they knew more than the mechanists about the history of philosophy. (Eventually the party condemned both camps, and created a dialectical synthesis of both forms of ignorance.)

The mechanists accepted Marxism but maintained that the scientific worldview had no need of a philosophy, as it merely represented the sum total of all the natural and social sciences. In one of the journal's first numbers there appeared an article by O. Minin, of whom nothing else is known, which was often quoted thereafter as an extreme example of the mechanists' anti-philosophical prejudice. The view expressed by Minin in a highly simplistic form was that feudal lords had used religion to further their class-interests and the bourgeoisie had similarly used philosophy; the proletariat, on the other hand, rejected both and drew all its strength from science.

In a more or less acute form, dislike of philosophy as such was typical of the whole mechanist camp. Its best-known adherents were Ivan I. Skvortsov-Stepanov (1870–1928) and Arkady K. Timiryazev (1880–1955), son of an eminent physiologist. Lyubov A. Akselrod, whose views we have discussed elsewhere, also professed a 'mechanist world-view', but, as a disciple of Plekhanov, she adopted a less extreme position than others of the group.

The mechanists, with some support from Engels's works, held that from the Marxist point of view there was no such thing as a 'science of sciences' which would dictate to particular sciences or claim a right to judge their findings. The dialectic as understood by the opposing camp was not only superfluous but contrary to scientific investigation: it consisted of introducing into the world-picture entities and categories unknown to science, a Hegelian inheritance that was equally alien to the scientific revolutionary spirit of Marxism and to the interests of socialist society. The natural aim of science was to explain all phenomena more and more precisely by reducing them to physical and chemical processes, whereas the dialecticians with their qualitative leaps, inner contradictions, etc. were doing the opposite: they were in effect confirming the alleged qualitative differences between various spheres of reality, by borrowing fictitious entities from the idealists. All changes could be finally reduced to quantitative terms, and the view that this did not apply, for example, to living phenomena was no more than idealistic vitalism. True, it was possible to speak of a struggle between contraries, but not in Hegel's sense of the internal disjunction of concepts: the struggle was between conflicting forces, as could be seen in physics, biology, or the social sciences without having to resort to any particular dialectical logic. Scientific investigation must be wholly based on experience, and all Hegel's dialectical 'categories' were irreducible to empirical data. The position of the dialecticians was clearly being undermined by the progress of natural science, which was proving slowly but surely that all processes in the universe could be expressed in physical and chemical terms. The belief in irreducible qualitative differences and the discontinuity of natural processes was nothing short of reactionary, as was the dialecticians' claim that 'chance' was something objective and not merely a term for our ignorance of particular causes.

The dialecticians' hand was much strengthened in 1925 by the publication of Engels's *Dialectics of Nature*, which provided ample ammunition against mechanism and philosophical nihilism and in favour of the demand for a philosophical and dialectical interpretation of the sciences. Even stronger support came in 1929 with the publication of Lenin's *Philosophical Notes*, which emphasized the need for a materialistic version of the Hegelian dialectic, enumerated a long list of dialectical 'categories', and declared that the principle of unity and the conflict between opposites was central to Marxism.

Of the two rival groups, the dialecticians were more numerous and better furnished with scientific institutions. Their leader and most active writer was Abram Moiseyevich Deborin (1881–1963). Born in Kovno, he joined the social democratic movement as a youth and was an *émigré* in Switzerland from 1903; he was at first a Bolshevik but afterwards joined the Menshevik group. After the Revolution he was for some years a non-party Marxist, but re-entered the party in 1928. In 1907 he wrote an *Introduction to the Philosophy of Dialectical Materialism*, which was not published until 1915; many times reprinted, it was a staple of Russian philosophical education in the 1920s. Although not a party member he lectured at the Communist Academy and the Red Professors' Institute and published several works. From 1926 he was chief editor of *Pod znamenem Marksizma*; from this time on the journal ceased to publish articles by the mechanists and became purely an organ of the dialecticians.

Although not an original writer, Deborin was well versed in philosophy. He expresses few ideas that cannot be found, for example, in Plekhanov, but compared to later Soviet philosophers he and his followers had a fair knowledge of the history of philosophy and were well able to turn it to polemical use.

Deborin's *Introduction* is a typical product of the Plekhanov school of Marxism. It contains no analysis of concepts but only a string of unsupported assertions, which are supposed finally to resolve all the problems that beset pre-Marxian philosophy. However, Deborin, like Plekhanov, emphasizes the link between Marxism and the whole of past philosophy, exalting the importance of Bacon, Hobbes, Spinoza, Locke, Kant, and especially Hegel in paving the way for dialectical materialism. He criticizes idealism, empiricism, agnosticism, and phenomenalism on the lines laid down by Engels and Plekhanov, as may be seen from the following extract.

> If, then, from the metaphysicians' point of view, everything is but nothing becomes, from the point of view of phenomenalism everything becomes but nothing is, i.e. nothing really exists. The dialectic teaches us that the unity of being and non-being is becoming. In concrete materialistic terms this means that the basis of everything is matter in a state of constant development. Thus changes are real and concrete, and, on the other hand, what is real and concrete is changeable. The subject of the process is absolutely real being, the 'substantive All' as opposed to the phenomenalistic Nothing . . . The contradiction between the quality-less, unchanging substance of the metaphysicians on the one hand, and, on the other, the subjective and changing states that are supposed to exclude the reality of substance, is resolved by dialectical materialism in the sense that substance, matter, is in a perpetual state of motion and change, that qualities or states have objective significance and that matter is the cause and the foundation, the 'subject' of qualitative changes and states. (*Introduction to the Philosophy of Dialectical Materialism*, 4th edn., 1925, pp. 226–7)

This passage is typical of Deborin's style in the book quoted and in his other works. 'Dialectical materialism teaches that . . .'; 'dialectical materialism takes over the correct portions' of this or that philosophy; subjective idealists are wrong because they do not recognize matter; objective idealists are wrong because they do not realize that matter is primary and mind secondary, and so forth. In every case a particular conclusion is stated, usually in extremely vague terms, and there is no attempt to support it by argument. It is not explained how we know that the phenomenalists are wrong, rather than their opponents; dialectical materialism tells us so, and that is all there is to it.

The opposition between the dialectic and 'metaphysics' is that the former teaches us that all things are connected and nothing is isolated; everything is in a state of constant change and development; this development is the result of real contradictions' inherent in reality itself, and takes the form of qualitative 'leaps'. Dialectical materialism states that everything is knowable, that there are no 'things in themselves' beyond our knowledge, that man comes to know the world by acting upon it, and that our concepts are 'objective' and comprehend 'the essence of things'. Our impressions are 'objective' too, that is to say they 'reflect' objects, although (here Deborin follows Plekhanov in the error denounced by Lenin) they do not resemble them; the congruity between impressions and objects lies in the fact that identities and differences in objects are matched by identities and differences in their subjective 'reflections'. This is what Mach and his Russian followers Bogdanov and Valentinov deny: according to them only psychic phenomena are real, so that the world 'outside us' does not exist. But in that case there are no laws of nature, and therefore nothing can be predicted.

Although their writings were dogmatic, simplistic, and of poor quality, Deborin and his followers had the merit of emphasizing historical studies and training up a generation of philosophers with a fair knowledge of classical literature; moreover, while stressing the 'qualitative' novelty of Marxism they also drew attention to its roots in tradition, especially the link with Hegel's dialectic. According to Deborin, dialectical materialism was a 'synthesis' of the Hegelian dialectic and the materialism of Feuerbach, wherein both these elements were transformed and 'raised to a higher level'. Marxism was an 'integral world-view' which comprised dialectical materialism as a general methodology of knowledge and also two more specific aspects, the dialectic of nature and the dialectic of history, otherwise historical materialism. As Engels had stated, the term 'dialectic' could be used in a three-fold sense. The 'objective' dialectic was the same thing as the laws or dialectical 'forms' of reality; 'dialectic' could also mean a description of those laws or, thirdly, a way of observing the universe, i.e. 'logic' in a broad sense. Changes were subject to a general regularity which applied equally to nature and to human history, and the study of this regularity, i.e. philosophy, was therefore a synthesis of all science. In order for scientists to be correctly oriented from the methodological point of view and to understand the meaning of their own observations they must recognize the primacy of philosophy, to which they supplied material for 'generalizations'. Thus Marxism called for a constant exchange between philosophy and the exact sciences: philosophy was empty without the 'material' provided by the natural and social sciences, but the sciences were blind without philosophy to lead them.

The purpose of this double requirement was clear enough. For philosophy to make use of the results of science meant, roughly speaking, that natural scientists must look for examples showing how natural objects undergo qualitative changes, and thus confirming the 'laws of the dialectic'. For philosophy to awaken the sciences to their own nature and preserve them from blindness meant that it was entitled to supervise their content and ensure that it conformed to dialectical materialism. Since the latter was synonymous with the party's world-view, Deborin and his school provided a justification for the party's supervision of the content of all sciences, natural as well as social.

Deborin claimed that all crises in natural science were due to the fact that physicists were not acquainted with Marxism and did not know how to apply dialectical formulas. He also believed, like Lenin, that the development of science would, spontaneously and continuously, lead to the emergence of Marxist philosophy.

For these reasons Deborin and his followers accused the mechanists of falling into pernicious error when they insisted on the autonomy of science and its independence of any philosophical premises. Materialism, thus conceived, had more in common with empiricist neutralism than with any ontological doctrine, and recalled Engels's remarks about the kind of materialism that is nothing more than the observation of nature without any outside element whatever. Natural science, Deborin maintained, must recognize a philosophical basis of some kind, and therefore any attempt to deprive philosophy of its guiding role, or to ignore it altogether, would mean in practice subjection to bourgeois and idealist doctrines. All philosophical ideas were class-based, either bourgeois or proletarian, and so by attacking philosophy the mechanists were supporting the enemies of socialism and the working class. As for denying the existence of 'qualitative leaps' and maintaining that all development is continuous, did not this amount to rejecting the idea of revolution, which was a leap *par excellence*? In short, the mechanists were not only wrong philosophically but were political revisionists as well.

The 'dialecticians' endowed Soviet Marxism with a stock of basic terms, statements, and dogmas which, even though their authors were later condemned, passed into the canon of state ideology and remained binding for decades. Part of their legacy was the attack on formal logic, which went far to bring about the collapse of logical studies in Russia. The dialecticians had no notion of what logic was concerned with or what its statements signified. They imagined, however, that as logic 'abstracts from the content of concepts' it must be contrary to the dialectic, for the latter requires us to study phenomena 'in the concrete' and 'in their mutual relations' (whereas logic isolates them) and also 'in motion' (which formal logic does not recognize). These absurdities were partly due to ignorance, but were partly based on some remarks by Engels. In an article of 1925 on Lenin, Deborin wrote that formal logic could not take account of the fact that the world was both uniform and manifold, and in *Dialectical Materialism and Natural Science* in the same year he declared that formal logic served only to build 'metaphysical systems' and had been put out of court by Marxism, since the dialectic taught that form and content must 'interpenetrate each other'. The sciences could not advance on the basis of formal logic, as each of them was only a 'collection of facts' and only Marxist dialectic could link these facts into a systematic whole. If the physicists would read Hegel instead of sticking to their 'crawling empiricism' they would soon see how the dialectic helped them to make progress and to overcome their various 'crises'. Engels, the creator of 'theoretical natural science', had, all along, absorbed the dialectic from Hegel.

Holding as he did that it was for philosophy to rule the sciences, Deborin was naturally incensed by Lukács's *History and Class-Consciousness*, which questioned the possibility of a dialectic of nature on the ground that the dialectic was an interaction of subject and object in progress towards unity. By taking this line, Deborin argued, Lukács had unmasked himself as an idealist who thought that cognition was the 'substance of reality'. In an article published in 1924 in the Austrian journal *Arbeiter-literatur* Deborin denounced Lukács's errors and his disrespectful attitude to Engels and therefore to Marx. What was more, Lukács had stated that Marxist orthodoxy consisted merely in acknowledging Marx's methods, whereas method, for a Marxist, was 'inseparably bound up with content'. As for Lukács's 'identity of subject and object', this was rank idealism and contrary to the express statements of Engels, Lenin, and Plekhanov. All the subject did was to 'reflect' the object, and to hold otherwise was to jettison 'objective reality'.

In attacking mechanism, 'crawling empiricism', and the autonomy of the sciences, and defending Hegel, 'qualitative leaps', and 'real contradictions', Deborin was supported by a large group of like-minded scholars and co-religionists. The most active of these were G. S. Tymyansky, who translated and commented on Spinoza's works (the commentary, though very schematic, was instructive and useful from the factual point of view); I. K. Luppol, an aesthetic philosopher and historian of philosophy; V. F. Asmus; N. A. Karev; I. I. Agol; and Y. E. Sten. Sten, as Medvedyev states in his book on Stalinism, gave Stalin lessons in philosophy in 1925–8 and tried to get him to understand the Hegelian dialectic. Most of the group, though not all, perished in the great purges of the 1930s.

In the later twenties, however, the dialecticians held the field and obtained complete control over Soviet philosophical institutions. At a conference of teachers of Marxism–Leninism in April 1929 Deborin presented his philosophical programme and repeated his denunciation of the heretics; the Communist Academy fully supported him and issued a decree condemning mechanism. Previously the conference itself, at Deborin's instance, had passed a resolution which confirmed the role of Marxism–Leninism as the theoretical weapon of the dictatorship of the proletariat, called for the application of Marxist methods in natural science, and condemned the mechanists for 'revisionism', 'positivism', and 'vulgar evolutionism'. The custom of deciding philosophical questions by voting at party assemblies, or gatherings subject to party control, was by this time well established and surprised nobody. The mechanists defended themselves in the discussion and even counter-attacked, charging their opponents with cultivating an 'idealist dialectic', seeking to impose imaginary schemata on nature, directing their fire against mechanism only and ignoring the problems raised by idealism, and diverting attention from the practical tasks imposed by the party. This defence was of no avail, however, and the mechanists were branded not only as schismatics but as representatives, in the philosophical field, of the 'right-wing deviation' which was just then being attacked by Stalin.

After this victory the Deborinists held sway in all institutions connected with teaching and popularizing philosophy or publishing philosophical works; but their triumph did not last for long. Despite all their efforts the 'dialecticians', it appeared, had not measured up to the party's expectations in philosophical matters. In April 1930, at a second philosophical conference in Moscow, Deborin and his group were attacked by a band of younger party activists from the Red Professors' Institute, who accused them of showing insufficient party spirit. This criticism was repeated in June in an article by M. B. Mitin, P. F. Yudin, and V. N. Raltsevich, which appeared in *Pravda* and was endorsed editorially, i.e. by the party authorities. The new critics called for a 'fight on two fronts' in philosophy as in party life, and accused the current philosophical leaders of being 'formalists' who overrated Plekhanov at Lenin's expense and sought to detach philosophy from party objectives. The dialecticians disputed the charge in vain. In December the party executive of the Red Professors' Institute had an interview with Stalin, who coined the expression 'Menshevizing idealism' to describe the Deborinist view. This label was officially applied from then on, and the executive passed a long resolution condemning, on the one hand, the mechanist and 'often Menshevizing' revisionism of Timiryazev, Akselrod, Sarabianov, and Varyash, and, on the other, the idealist revisionism of Deborin, Karev, Sten, Luppol, Frankurt, and others. The resolution stated that 'The whole theoretical and political outlook of the Deborinist group amounts essentially to a Menshevizing idealism, based on a non-Marxist, non-Leninist methodology and expressing a petty bourgeois ideology, as well as reflecting the pressure of hostile class forces surrounding the proletariat.' The group had 'distorted' the teaching of Lenin's article 'The Significance of Militant Materialism', 'separated theory from practice', and deformed and rejected 'the Leninist principle of party philosophy'; they had failed to recognize Leninism as a new stage in dialectical materialism, and in many ways made common cause with the mechanists while pretending to criticize them. Their publications contained 'Kautskyist' errors concerning the dictatorship of the proletariat, right-wing opportunist errors in cultural matters, Bogdanovist errors as regards collectivism and individualism, Menshevik errors as to the conception of productive forces and production relations, semi-Trotskyist errors concerning the class struggle, and idealist errors as to the interpretation of the dialectic. The Deborinists had unduly glorified Hegel; they had dissociated method from world-view, the logical from the historical, and had belittled Lenin's importance in questions of natural science. True, the chief danger of the moment was mechanist revisionism, as it furnished a theoretical basis for the right-wing deviation that sought to defend kulak interests within the party; but the struggle must be conducted unflinchingly on both fronts, as the two forms of revisionism really constituted a single block.

All these criticisms were further developed in a lecture at the Communist Academy by Mitin, who himself aspired at this time to become the leader of the 'philosophical front'. The lecture referred repeatedly to the links between 'Menshevizing idealism' and Trotskyism: to be sure, as the mechanists supplied a philosophical front for Bukharin and his pro-kulak deviation, it was natural to infer that the Deborinists, while pretending to be orthodox, were supporting the left-wing deviation of Trotskyism. According to Mitin, both groups had put about the vicious slander that in philosophical and theoretical matters Lenin merely echoed what Marx and Engels had said—as though Stalin had not proved that Lenin represented a qualitatively new stage in the history of Marxist theory by 'developing it, making it deeper and more concrete'! The deviationists had also neglected Lenin's principle that philosophy and all the sciences, including natural science, must be imbued with party spirit. Mitin quoted an article by Karev to the effect that while Plekhanov had made many political and philosophical mistakes his writings, as Lenin had testified, were among the best works of Marxist literature. This, said Mitin, showed that the Deborinists were taking up the cudgels for 'the whole Plekhanov, Plekhanov as a Menshevik'. They even dared to assert that Lenin was a pupil of Plekhanov in philosophy, whereas in reality he was the most consistent and orthodox Marxist after Marx and Engels. Plekhanov, on the other hand, did not understand the dialectic correctly, he was sunk in formalism, inclined to agnosticism, and influenced by Feuerbach, Chernyshevsky, and formal logic. The root of the Deborinists' errors, however, lay in 'separating theory from practice'. Their battle against the mechanists was a sham fight, as was shown by the fact that, although it had continued for years, not a single mechanist had admitted that he was mistaken! In fact there was little to choose between the two groups, as both the Menshevizing idealists and the Menshevizing mechanists took a disparaging view of Lenin's philosophy.

The purging of Soviet philosophy was completed by a decree of the party's Central Committee published in *Pravda* on 25 January 1931, which condemned the errors of *Pod znamenem Marksizma* and briefly summarized the criticisms already formulated.

Deborin, Luppol, and some other members of the group hastened to perform self-criticism and to thank the party for helping them to see the light. Sten, Luppol, Karev, Tymyansky, and many others perished in the purges of the 1930s. Deborin survived, though he was dismissed from the editorship of *Pod znamenem Marksizma* (the editorial board was in fact completely changed). He was not expelled from the party, and in subsequent years published many articles of irreproachable Stalinist orthodoxy. He survived into the Khrushchev era, and in the last years of his life worked for the rehabilitation of his many pupils and colleagues who had fallen victim to the purges. Asmus also survived into the post-war period (he died in 1975), and was subjected to further attack in the 1940s.

From 1931 onwards the history of Soviet philosophy under Stalin is largely a history of party ukases. In the next two decades a younger generation of careerists, informers, and ignoramuses monopolized the philosophical life of the country, or rather completed the extinction of philosophical studies. Those who made a career in this field generally did so by betraying their colleagues or parroting the party slogans of the moment. As a rule they knew no foreign languages and had no idea of Western philosophy, but they were more or less word-perfect in the works of Lenin and Stalin, from which their knowledge of the outside world was mainly derived.

The condemnation of 'Menshevizing idealists' and mechanists led to a flood of articles and dissertations whose authors echoed the party decrees and vied with one another in expressing indignation at the insidious plots of the philosophical saboteurs.

What was the real point of the whole discussion (if that is the right name for it)? Obviously it had nothing to do with any particular philosophical or even political outlook. The association of 'mechanism' with Bukharin's policy or of 'Menshevizing idealism' with Trotsky's was a fabrication of the most arbitrary kind: the condemned philosophers did not belong to any opposition groups, and there was no logical connection between their views and those of the oppositionists. (The accusers' argument ran that the mechanists 'absolutized the continuity of development' by denying 'qualitative leaps', and were therefore on the side of Bukharin, while the Deborinists overemphasized 'leaps' and thus represented the 'revolutionary adventurism' of the Trotskyists; but this is based on such flimsy analogies as not to be worth discussing.) The mechanists, it is true, invited condemnation by insisting on the independence of science *vis-à-vis* philosophy, which meant in practice denying the right of an infallible party to pronounce on the correctness of scientific theories and tell scientists what subjects they should investigate and what their results should be. No such charge, however, could be levelled against the Deborinists, who appeared to be Leninists of the purest type: Deborin at an early date recanted his Plekhanovian error concerning 'hieroglyphs' and attacked the mechanists for holding this doctrine, which contradicted the theory of reflection. The Deborinists paid due homage to Lenin, and the party spokesmen had the greatest trouble finding quotations to buttress their attacks, which therefore consisted almost entirely of vague, incoherent generalities: the Deborinists 'underestimated' Lenin, 'overestimated' Plekhanov, 'did not understand' the dialectic, lapsed into 'Kautskyism', 'Menshevism', etc. The point was not simply that the party proclaimed at this stage that such and such philosophical views were right and that the Deborinists had expressed views different from them. It was not the substance of any doctrine that was at issue: the official, canonical version of dialectical materialism that was later adopted was virtually indistinguishable from Deborin's. What counted, as indeed the accusations made plain, was the principle of 'party-mindedness', or rather its application—since, of course, the Deborinists accepted the principle itself. Feeble as the Deborinists' writings were from the intellectual point of view, they were genuinely interested in philosophy and did their best to prove the validity of the specific principles of Marxism and Leninism. They believed that their philosophy would help to build socialism, and for this reason they developed it to the best of their ability as a philosophy. But 'party-mindedness' under Stalin meant something quite different. Despite constant assurances, there was no thought of letting philosophy work out its own principles or discover truths that could be used or applied in politics. Philosophy's service to the party was to consist purely and simply in glorifying its successive decisions. Philosophy was not an intellectual process but a means of justifying and inculcating the state ideology in whatever form it might assume. This indeed was true of all the humane sciences, but the fall of philosophy was greater. The pillars on which all philosophical culture is based—logic and the history of philosophy—were swept away: philosophy was deprived of even the humblest technical support, in a way that did not apply altogether to the historical sciences, despite the extent of their corruption. The significance of Stalinism for philosophy does not lie in any particular conclusions that were forced upon it, but in the fact that servility became practically its whole *raison d'être*.

III

Marxism as the Ideology
of the Soviet State

1. *The ideological significance of the great purges*

THE 1930s in the Soviet Union witnessed the crystallization of a new version of Marxism as the official and canonical ideology of the totalitarian socialist state.

In the years following collectivization the Stalinist state went through a series of defeats and misadventures, while the population was subjected to one wave of repression after another. The enforcement of collectivization coincided with the beginning of the first five-year plan, which was officially dated from 1928 although not actually approved till the following year. According to the ideas formulated by Trotsky and Preobrazhensky and taken over by Stalin, the function of the enslaved peasantry was to supply surplus value for the rapid development of industry. From then on, the dogma of the primacy of heavy industry became a permanent part of the state ideology. The initial objectives were laid down arbitrarily, without any serious calculation, on the presumption that everything could be done by force and that 'there were no fortresses that Bolsheviks could not storm'. None the less, Stalin was constantly dissatisfied with production targets and kept boosting them to still greater heights. Most of the aims, of course, proved unattainable: even in heavy industry, to which the maximum human and financial effort was devoted, the results were sometimes half, a quarter, or an eighth of what they were supposed to be. The cure for this was to arrest and shoot statisticians and falsify their findings. In 1928–30 Stalin closed down almost all economic and statistical journals, and most statisticians of importance, including N. D. Kondratyev, were executed or thrown into gaol. It also became customary from this time on to calculate the national income in such a way as to count the same products two or three times, at different stages of manufacture, thus producing meaningless totals which were periodically vaunted as proof of the superiority of socialism. Figures for agriculture were systematically faked, as collectivization wrought more and more havoc in the countryside. How far Stalin or the other leaders were aware of the true state of the economy is not clear. Meanwhile the ranks of industrial workers were rapidly swelled by recruits from the rural sector. To compensate for the sufferings of society there were constant arrests and trials of engineers or agricultural experts on grounds of sabotage, i.e. failing to achieve impracticable norms. In 1932–3 there ensued a famine in which millions perished; by comparison the famine of 1891–2, which turned a whole generation of the intelligentsia into radicals and did much to foster the growth of Marxism, was a set-back of insignificant proportions. Stalinist propaganda repeated without ceasing that the country was full of wreckers and saboteurs, crypto-kulaks, disloyal intellectuals of the pre-war type, Trotskyists, and agents of the imperialist Powers. Starving peasants could be and were sentenced to concentration camps for stealing a handful of grain from the collective farm. The slave-labour camps proliferated and became an important factor in the state economy, especially in regions where conditions were most arduous, as in the mines and forests of Siberia.

Nevertheless, at the cost of indescribable suffering, exploitation, and oppression, amid the chaos of fictitious planning and the flood of official lies, Soviet industry did in fact progress, and the second five-year plan (1933–7) was much more realistic than the first. The fact that in those years the Soviet Union laid the basis of its present-day industrial power is still invoked by Communists as a historical justification of Stalinism, and many non-Communists take a similar view, believing that Stalinist socialism was necessary to enable backward Russia to modernize its industry with speed. Anticipating our argument to some extent, this may be answered as follows. The Soviet Union did indeed build up a considerable industrial base, especially in heavy industry and armaments, during the 1930s. It did so by methods of mass coercion and complete or partial enslavement, which had as side-effects the ruin of the nation's culture and the perpetuation of a police regime. In these ways Soviet industrialization was probably the most wasteful process of its kind in history, and there is no proof at all that progress could not have been achieved without human and material sacrifices on this scale. History records various methods of successful industrialization, all of which have been costly in social terms, but it is hard to point to any case in which the cost was as heavy as in socialist Russia. The further argument, often adduced, that the course followed by Western Europe could not have been repeated on the periphery of the industrial world because the big capitalist centres had already consolidated their position, is refuted by the example of 'peripheral' countries such as Japan, Brazil, and most recently Iran, which have all succeeded in industrializing themselves by means different from Russia's, albeit with considerable sacrifice. Russia before 1917 was a country of rapid and intensive industrialization, a process which the Revolution delayed for many years. The graph of industrial development rose markedly in the last two decades of Tsarist rule; it fell catastrophically after the Revolution, and it was a long time before the various indices (some recovering faster than others) once again reached their pre-war levels and continued to rise. The intervening period was one of social disintegration and the destruction of millions of lives, and it is mere fantasy to suggest that all this sacrifice was necessary to enable the country to resume its pre-Revolutionary development.

If one takes the view that historical processes have an immanent purpose independent of human intention, or a hidden meaning that is only discernible with hindsight, it must be said that the meaning of the Russian revolution did not consist in industrialization, but rather in the coherence and expansive energy of the Russian Empire: for in this respect the new regime has indeed been more efficient than the old.

After the resistance of all social classes—proletariat, peasantry, and intelligentsia—had been successively overcome, after all forms of social life not ordained by the state had been crushed out of existence, and the opposition within the party destroyed, it was time to subdue the last element that might—though it did not in practice—threaten the completeness of totalitarian rule under a single despot: namely the party itself, the instrument which had been used to stifle and destroy every other rival force in the community. The destruction of the party was achieved during the years 1935–9, and established a new record in the conflict between the Soviet regime and its own subjects.

In 1934 Stalin was at the height of his power. The party's Seventeenth Congress at the beginning of the year was an orgy of flattery and worship. There was no active opposition to the adored dictator, but there were many in the party, especially Old Bolsheviks, who paid him due honour but were not bound to him heart and soul. They had risen by their own efforts, not merely by his favour, and might therefore be a dangerous source of unrest or revolt in time of crisis. Hence, as a potential opposition, they must be destroyed. The first pretext for their extermination was the murder, on 1 December 1934, of Sergey Kirov, a secretary of the Central Committee and head of the party organization in Leningrad. Most historians, though not all, agree that the real author of the crime was Stalin, who at one stroke got rid of a possible rival and created a pretext for mass repression. The witch-hunt that followed was aimed in the first place at former oppositionists within the party, but soon also at the dictator's faithful servants. Zinovyev and Kamenev were arrested and sentenced to prison; mass executions took place in larger cities throughout the country, but especially in Leningrad and Moscow. The terror reached a paroxysm in 1937, the first year of the 'great purge'. August 1936 saw the first of the major show trials, at which Zinovyev, Kamenev, Smirnov, and others were sentenced to death; a second trial in January 1937 brought to light the 'treason' of Radek, Pyatakov, Sokolnikov, and others. In March 1938 the accused included Bukharin, Rykov, Krestinsky, Rakovsky, and Yagoda, the last-named having been head of the

N.K.V.D. (security service) in 1934–6 and organizer of the earlier purges. Shortly before, in 1937, Marshal Tukhachevsky and several other top army leaders were tried in secret and shot. The accused in all the public trials confessed to fantastic crimes, describing one after another how they had intrigued with foreign intelligence services, conspired to murder party leaders, offered parts of Soviet territory to the imperialist Powers, murdered and poisoned their fellow citizens, sabotaged industry, deliberately caused famines, etc. Almost all were sentenced to death and executed out of hand; a few who, like Radek, only received prison sentences were done to death soon after their trial.

The inferno of the great purges has often been described by historians, novelists, and memoir-writers. The show trials were only the visible fragment of a mass operation of genocide, with the party as its principal victim. Millions were arrested, hundreds of thousands executed. Torture, previously used sporadically and, as a rule, for the purpose of getting at the truth, now became a routine method of extracting thousands of false confessions to the most improbable crimes. (Torture had ceased to be a part of Russian judicial procedure in the eighteenth century, though it was afterwards used in exceptional circumstances such as the Polish insurrections or the 1905 Revolution.) Investigating officers were free to devise and inflict all manner of physical and mental suffering to induce people to admit to crimes which the persecutors well knew to be totally imaginary. Those few who did not succumb to such measures generally broke down when told that if they refused to confess their wives and children would be killed—a threat which was sometimes carried out. No one felt safe, for no degree of subservience to the tyrant was a guarantee of immunity. In some cases the party committees of whole regions were slaughtered and were followed into the grave by their own successors in office, whose hands still reeked from the execution. Among the victims were almost all the Old Bolsheviks, all Lenin's closest associates, former members of government and of the Politburo and the party secretariat, activists of every rank, scholars, artists, writers, economists, military men, lawyers, engineers, doctors, and—in due course, when they had done their stint—the agents of the purge themselves, whether senior officers of the security service or especially zealous party members. The officers' corps of the army and navy was decimated, a major cause of Soviet defeats in the first two years of the war with Germany. Quotas of arrests and executions were assigned to particular areas by the party authorities; if the police did not fulfil these they were liable to be executed themselves, if they did they might in time be brought to account for exterminating party cadres. (With a macabre humour typical of Stalin this charge was brought against some, such as Postyshev, who had distinguished themselves in the campaign of mass murder.) Those who performed their task badly might be shot for sabotage; those who did it too well might be suspected of showing zeal to cover up their own disaffection. (In a speech in 1937 Stalin said that many wreckers were doing precisely this.) The purport of the trials and investigations was to show that almost the whole original nucleus of the party, including Lenin's closest collaborators, were a band of spies, imperialist agents, and enemies of the people, whose one idea was and had always been to destroy the Soviet state. Before an astonished world, every imaginable crime was confessed to by the accused themselves at the great show trials. Of all the Grand Guignol victims Bukharin was the only one who, though he admitted general responsibility for the alleged crimes of the mythical counter-revolutionary organization, refused to confess to such damning charges as espionage and plotting to assassinate Lenin. While expressing penitence for all his misdeeds he added, in a phrase epitomizing the atmosphere of the trials, 'We rebelled by criminal methods against the joyfulness of the new life.' (Apparently Bukharin was not physically tortured, but was threatened with the murder of his wife and small son.)

The first effect of the purges was to create a desolation, not only in the party but in every aspect of life in the Soviet Union. The blood-bath accounted for a large majority of the delegates, for the most part loyal Stalinists, who had attended the Seventeenth Congress, which had done little but vote adulatory addresses to the leader. A whole series of eminent artists perished, and over a third of all Soviet writers. The whole country was in the grip of a monstrous fit of madness, induced apparently—but the appearance was deceptive—by the will of a single despot.

Foreign Communists in Russia fell victim to the purges also. The Poles suffered most: in 1938 a resolution of the Comintern dissolved the Polish Communist party (which was illegal in Poland) on the ground that it was a hotbed of Trotskyists and other enemies, and its cadres in the Soviet Union were decimated by arrests and executions. Almost all the leaders were imprisoned, and only a few regained their liberty some years later. The fortunate ones were those who could not make their way to Russia when summoned, as they were in prison in Poland. The few who actually disobeyed the summons were publicly declared to be agents of the Polish police, and were thus delivered into the latter's hands—a device frequently used in the thirties against 'deviationist' members of underground Communist parties in other countries. Besides Poles, victims of the purges were many Hungarian Communists (including Béla Kun), Yugoslavs, Bulgarians, and Germans; some of the latter who survived till 1939 were, in due course, handed over by Stalin to the Gestapo.

The concentration camps were full to bursting. Every Soviet citizen had got used to the fact that being arrested and sentenced to death or to an arbitrary and indefinite term of imprisonment had nothing to do with whether a man's work was good or bad, whether he did or did not belong to any kind of opposition, or even whether he did or did not love Stalin. The climate of atrocity brought about a kind of universal paranoia, a monstrous but unreal world in which all previous criteria, even those of 'ordinary' despotism, had ceased to be applicable.

Historians and others who, in later years, have sought to account for this unparalleled orgy of bloodshed and hypocrisy have posed questions that are not at all easy to answer.

In the first place, what could be the reason for such destructive frenzy when, to all appearances, there was no real threat to Stalin or the regime, and every possible source of revolt within the party could easily have been wiped out without mass slaughter? In particular, how could this be explained when it seemed obvious that the wholesale destruction of senior cadres would fatally weaken the state, both militarily and economically?

Secondly, why was there a complete lack of resistance when all members of the population were threatened, even those who carried out the atrocities most devotedly? Many Soviet citizens had displayed military courage and had risked their lives in battle: why did no one raise a hand against the tyrant, why did all go willingly to the slaughter?

Thirdly, granted that the victims of show trials were made to confess to non-existent crimes for propaganda reasons, why were such confessions extorted from hundreds of thousands or millions of lesser people of whom no one would ever hear? Why the tremendous effort to induce unknown victims to sign fantastic admissions which would be buried in police files and not used for any public purpose?

Fourthly, how was it that in those very years Stalin was able to raise the cult of his own personality to unprecedented heights? Why, in particular, did so many Western intellectuals, on whom there was no personal pressure, fall for Stalinism at this period and meekly swallow, or actively applaud, the Moscow chamber of horrors and the official explanation of it, whereas the lies and cruelty of the performance should have been obvious to everyone?

All these questions are relevant to an understanding of the peculiar function that Marxist-socialist ideology was beginning to exercise in the new system.

As to the first question, most historians believe that the main purpose of the great purges was to eliminate the party as a potential focus of political life, a force that might in some circumstances acquire a life of its own and not be merely an instrument in the ruler's hands. Isaac Deutscher, in his first book on the Moscow trials (published in Polish), advanced the remarkable theory that they were an act of revenge by the Mensheviks against the Bolsheviks!—this because the victims were nearly all Old Bolsheviks, while Vyshinsky, the chief prosecutor, was an ex-Menshevik, and the main party propagandist of those days, David Zaslavsky, had been a member of the Jewish Bund. This is as fanciful as the explanation that Deutscher afterwards put forward in the third volume of his life of Trotsky (*The Prophet Outcast*, 1963, pp. 306–7), namely that the higher Soviet bureaucracy were not content with their privileges, great though these were, because they could not accumulate wealth or bequeath it to their children, and there was therefore a risk, as Trotsky feared, that they would seek to destroy the system of social ownership. Stalin, according to Deutscher, was aware of this danger and used terror to prevent the new privileged class from consolidating itself and ruining the system. This, in effect, is a paraphrase of the Stalinist version that the victims intended to restore capitalism in Russia. However, in his life of Stalin (1949) Deutscher adopted what is more or less the general view of historians. Stalin wanted to destroy all possible alternative governments or party leaders; there was no longer an active opposition, but a sudden crisis might bring one to life, and he must therefore crush any possibility of a rival centre of power within the party.

This explanation may fit the Moscow trials, but it is less clear how it accounts for the mass character of the purge, affecting millions of unknown people who had no chance whatever of becoming alternative party leaders. The same objection applies to other theories sometimes advanced, such as Stalin's need to find scapegoats for economic failures, or his personal vengefulness and sadism—which certainly account for a great many individual cases, but hardly for the massacre of millions.

It may be said that the great purges were a macabre irrelevancy, in the sense that the purpose they served could quite well have been attained by other means. Yet they were, so to speak, part of the natural logic of the system. It was a question not only of destroying any actual or potential rivals but of wiping out the sole organism in which there were still any remnants, however faint and impotent, of loyalty to any cause other than the state and its leader—in particular, remnants of a belief in Communist ideology as a frame of reference and an object of worship, independent of the leader and the party's current directives. The object of a totalitarian system is to destroy all forms of communal life that are not imposed by the state and closely controlled by it, so that individuals are isolated from one another and become mere instruments in the hands of the state. The citizen belongs to the state and must have no other loyalty, not even to the state ideology. This may seem paradoxical, but it is not surprising to anyone who knows a system of this type from within. All forms of revolt against the ruling party, all 'deviations' and 'revisionism', fractions, cliques, rebellions—all alike had appealed to the ideology of which the party was the custodian. Consequently, that ideology had to be revised so as to make it clear to all that they were not entitled to appeal to it independently—just as in the Middle Ages unauthorized persons were not allowed to comment on the Scriptures, and the Bible itself was at all times *liber haereticorum*. The party was essentially an ideological body, that is to say one whose members were linked by a common faith and shared values. But, as always happens when ideologies are turned into institutions, that faith had to be vague and indefinite enough to be used to justify any political move while maintaining that there was no 'real' change of doctrine. Inevitably, those who took the faith seriously wanted to interpret it for themselves and to consider whether this or that political step was in accordance with Stalin's version of Marxism–Leninism. But this made them potential critics and rebels against the government, even if they swore fealty to Stalin; for they might always invoke yesterday's Stalin against today's and quote the leader's words against himself. The purge, therefore, was designed to destroy such ideological links as still existed within the party, to convince its members that they had no ideology or loyalty except to the latest order from on high, and to reduce them, like the rest of society, to a powerless, disintegrated mass. This was a continuation of the same logic that began with liquidating the liberal and socialist parties, the independent Press and cultural institutions, religion, philosophy, and art, and finally fractions within the party itself. Wherever there was any ideological link other than loyalty to the ruler, there was a possibility of fractionalism even if it did not actually exist. The object of the purge was to eradicate this possibility, and in that object it was successful; but the principles which dictated the hecatomb of the 1930s are still in force and have never been abandoned. Loyalty to Marxist ideology as such is still a crime and a source of deviations of all kinds.

Even so, the fact that the holocaust was not resisted by the Soviet public or even by the party seems to suggest that a purge was not necessary, at all events on that scale. The party, it would seem, was already close enough to the ideal condition of a 'sack of potatoes' (as Marx said of the French peasants), and was neither desirous nor capable of producing any centre of independent thought. On the other hand, we do not know whether, but for the purge, it might not have done so at a time of crisis, for example, in the most dangerous moments of the war with Germany.

This brings us to the second question: how is it that Soviet society was quite incapable of resistance? The answer seems to be that the party, outside the top leadership, was already incapable of organizing itself in any way independently of the apparatus. Like the rest of the population, it was reduced to a collection of isolated individuals; in the context of repression, as in every other sphere of life, the omnipotent state on the one hand confronted the lone citizen on the other. The paralysis of the individual was complete; and, at the same time, it could not be denied that the party was acting in accordance with the principles that had obtained since the beginning. All its members had taken part in mass acts of violence against the public, and when they themselves became victims of lawlessness there was nothing to which they could appeal. None of them had objected to fake trials and executions as long as the sufferers were not party members; all of them accepted, actively or passively, that 'in principle' there was nothing wrong in judicial murder. They all agreed, too, that at any given moment it was for the party leaders to decide who was a class enemy, a friend of the kulaks, or an imperialist agent. The rules of the game, which they had accepted, were being brought to bear against them, and they had no moral principles that might have fostered a spirit of resistance.

During the war, in one of Stalin's prisons, the Polish poet Aleksander Wat encountered an Old Bolshevik, the historian I. M. Stetlov, and asked him why all the protagonists of the Moscow trials had confessed to the most ludicrous charges. Stetlov replied simply: 'We were all of us up to the elbows in blood.'

As to the third question, it may at first seem that we have to do with collective hallucination. Even supposing Stalin had good reasons for massacring Communists, why was it necessary to make countless insignificant people confess under torture that they had plotted to sell Uzbekistan to the British, or been agents of Pilsudski, or tried to murder Stalin? But there was a grain of method even in this madness. The victims had to be not only destroyed physically or rendered harmless, but morally annihilated as well. It might have been thought that the N.K.V.D. agents could have signed the false confessions themselves and then finished off their tortured victims or sent them to camps on the ground of their 'admitted' guilt—except, of course, for the show-trial defendants who had to proclaim their crimes to the whole world; but these were only a tiny percentage of the whole. In fact, however, the police insisted on people signing their own confessions, and as far as is known they did not forge signatures. The effect was that the victims became accessories to the crimes committed against themselves, and participants in the universal campaign of falsification. Almost anyone can be forced by torture to confess to anything, but as a rule, in the twentieth century at least, torture is used to obtain true information. In the Stalinist system both the torturers and their victims knew perfectly well that the information was false; but they insisted on the fiction, as in this way everyone helped to build an unreal 'ideological' world, in which universal fiction took on the guise of truth.

A similar regime of organized make-believe prevailed in many other fields, for example, in the system of general 'elections'. It might have been thought that the government could have spared itself the trouble and expense of these performances, the absurdity of which was obvious to all; but they were important because they turned every citizen into a participant and co-author of the same fiction, the official 'reality' which, by that very fact, ceased to be completely spurious.

The fourth question again presents us with a baffling phenomenon. The information that reached the West from the Soviet Union was, of course, fragmentary and uncertain; the regime had done a thorough job of restricting contacts and limiting the flow of news in either direction; foreign travel by Soviet citizens was strictly controlled in the state interest, and any unauthorized communication to foreigners was treated as espionage or treason. Nevertheless, the Soviet state could not cut itself off entirely from the world. Some information about the police terror filtered through to the West, though nobody realized its scope. Moreover, the Moscow trials were prepared hastily and clumsily, and the contradictions and absurdities that emerged were pointed out in some Western newspapers. What, then, was the explanation for the indulgent attitude that Western intellectuals took up towards Stalinism, when they did not actively support it? The honest and incorruptible British socialists, Sidney and Beatrice Webb, visited the Soviet Union more than once during the height of the terror and produced an enormous book on the 'new civilization'. The Soviet system, they declared, was the embodiment of man's dearest longing for justice and happiness, in glaring contrast with Britain's corrupt and crumbling pseudo-democracy; they saw no reason to doubt the genuineness of the Moscow trials or the perfection of Russia's first 'democratic' government. Others who belauded the system and swallowed the fiction of the trials were Leon Feuchtwanger, Romain Rolland, and Henri Barbusse. Among the few who did not join in the chorus was André Gide, who visited the U.S.S.R. in 1936 and described his impressions. Naturally he saw nothing of the atrocities: he was surrounded by flattery and was only shown delusive achievements of the regime, but he realized that the façade concealed a system of universal mendacity. Some Polish writers also saw through the make-believe, as did the British journalist Malcolm Muggeridge (*Winter in Moscow*, 1934).

The reaction of Western intellectuals was a remarkable triumph of doctrinaire ideology over common sense and the critical instinct. True, the years of the purges were also those of the Nazi threat, and this may explain up to a point how many thinkers and artists brought up in a left-wing or liberal tradition saw in Russia the only hope of saving civilization from the menace that hung over it; they were prepared to forgive the 'proletarian state' a great deal if it could be relied on to provide a bulwark against Fascist barbarism. They were the more readily bamboozled because Nazism, unlike Stalinism, scarcely bothered to conceal its evil face from the world: it proclaimed openly that its intention was to create an all-powerful German giant, grinding other nations into the dust and reducing 'inferior races' to slavery. Stalin, on the other hand, continued to preach the socialist gospel of peace and equality, liberation of the oppressed, internationalism, and friendship among peoples. Westerners whose profession was to think critically found this verbiage more convincing than any facts: ideology and wishful thinking were stronger than the most manifest reality.

It is important to notice, in considering the purges, that Stalin's Russia was at no time governed by the police, nor was the police ever 'above the party':

this was an alibi used by would-be reformers after Stalin's death, who maintained that their task was to restore party supremacy. True, the police under Stalin could arrest and murder party members at will, but not on the highest level, where all such procedures had to be ordered or approved by the top party authorities and in particular by Stalin himself. Stalin used the police to rule the party, but he himself ruled both party and state in his capacity as party leader, not as a security chief: this point is well brought out by Jan Jaroslawski in his study of the party's functions in the Soviet system. The party, embodied in Stalin, did not abandon supreme power for a single moment. When the post-Stalin reformers demanded that the party should be above the police, they meant only that party members should not be arrested without the approval of the party authorities. But this had always been so, since even if the police at a certain level arrested party leaders of equal seniority, they did so under the eye of party leaders of a still higher grade. The police were an instrument in the party's hands. A police system in the strict sense, i.e. one in which the police have a completely free hand, did not and could not prevail in the Soviet state, as it would have meant that the party had lost power, and this could not happen without causing the whole system to collapse.

This also explains the special part played by ideology, both under Stalin and at the present day. Ideology is not simply an aid or adjunct to the system but an absolute condition of its existence, irrespective of whether people actually believe in it or not. Stalinist socialism created an empire ruled from Moscow, the basis of whose legality is entirely derived from ideology: in particular, from the doctrine that the Soviet Union embodies the interests of all working people and especially the working class everywhere, that it represents their desires and aspirations, and that it is the first step towards a world revolution that will liberate the toiling masses wherever they may be. The Soviet system could not do without this ideology, which is the sole *raison d' être* for the existing apparatus of power. The apparatus is essentially ideological and internationalist in character and could not be replaced by the police, the army, or any other institution.

This is not to say that the policy of the Soviet state at any given moment is determined by ideology; but the ideology must be there to justify it when required. Ideology is built into the system and consequently plays a quite different part in the Soviet Union as compared to states where the basic principle of legitimacy is derived from popular elections or the charisma of a hereditary monarchy.

A system of the Soviet kind enjoys the advantage that it does not have to justify its actions to the public: by definition, it represents their interests and desires, and nothing can alter this ideological fact. However, it is also exposed to a risk from which democratic structures are immune: namely, it is extremely sensitive to ideological criticism. This means, among other things, that the intelligentsia plays a part that is not paralleled elsewhere. A threat to the intellectual validity of the system, or the advocacy of a different ideology, represents a mortal danger. The totalitarian state can never become completely invulnerable or stamp out critical thought altogether. It may appear all-powerful, as it dominates all aspects of life, but it is also weak inasmuch as any crack in the ideological monolith is a threat to its existence.

It is hard, moreover, to maintain a system in which ideology is deprived of its own inertial movement and reduced to nothing more or less than the actual dictates of the state authority. The logic of Stalinism is that truth is what the party, i.e. Stalin, says at any given moment, and the effect of this is to empty ideology of its substance altogether. On the other hand, ideology must be presented as a general theory with a consistency of its own, and as long as this is done there is no guarantee that it may not acquire a momentum of its own and be used—as actually happened in the post-Stalinist period—against its chief spokesmen and sole authorized interpreters.

In the late 1930s, however, this danger appeared highly remote. The system had been brought to an almost ideal state of perfection, in which civil society hardly existed any more and the population seemed to have no other purpose than to obey the behests of the state personified in Stalin.

An essential instrument for the destruction of social ties was the universal system of spying on one's neighbour. Every citizen was under a legal and moral obligation to do so, and tale-bearing was the chief method of getting on in life. The continuing slaughter made room for many who aspired to join the privileged ruling class, and were prepared to demonstrate their fitness by destroying others. In this way, too, huge numbers of people became accessories to crime for the sake of personal advancement. The ideal of Stalinist socialism appeared to be a situation where everyone in the country (except Stalin) was an inmate of a concentration camp and also an agent of the secret police. It was hard to achieve this ultimate perfection, but the trend towards it in the 1930s was very strong.

2. Stalin's codification of Marxism

IN the thirties every branch of culture in the Soviet Union was strictly regimented, and independent intellectual life practically ceased to exist. Belles-lettres were gradually but effectively reduced to an adjunct of politics and propaganda, with the sole purpose of glorifying the system and its leader and unmasking 'class enemies'. In 1932, talking to a group of writers at Gorky's home, Stalin described authors in general as 'engineers of men's souls'; this flattering term duly became the official formula. Films and the theatre were treated in the same way, though the latter suffered less. A traditional repertoire of plays was allowed to subsist in so far as the authors, mostly classical Russian dramatists, could be described as 'progressive' or even 'partially progressive': this let in Gogol, Ostrovsky, Saltykov-Shchedrin, Tolstoy, and Chekhov, and even in the worst years excellent productions could be seen on the Russian stage. Novelists, poets, and film directors vied with one another in Byzantine adulation of Stalin: this reached its peak in the post-war years, but was already highly developed in the period we are considering.

However, repression and regimentation affected different spheres of intellectual life in different degrees. In the thirties there was a strong trend towards Marxist orientation in certain branches of science, especially theoretical physics and genetics, but this did not reach a climax until the late forties. Other subjects, however, which were particularly sensitive from the ideological point of view, such as philosophy, social theory, and history—especially the history of the party and of modern times generally—were not merely strait-jacketed in the thirties but were codified into completely Stalinist terms.

An important stage in the subjection of Soviet historiography was marked in 1931 by a letter from Stalin to the journal *Proletarian Revolution*, which the editorial board printed with an appropriate self-criticism. The letter upbraided them for publishing an article by Slutsky on relations between the Bolsheviks and the German social democrats before 1914, in which Lenin was criticized for failing to appreciate the danger of 'centrism' and opportunism in the Second International. After trouncing the journal for the 'rotten liberalism' of suggesting that Lenin 'failed to appreciate' anything, i.e. that he ever made a mistake, Stalin gave a complete history in outline of the Second International, which thereafter became a canonical text. His main concern was with the non-Bolshevik left wing of the International and with Trotsky. According to Stalin, while the socialist Left had done some service in the battle against opportunism, it had also made grievous mistakes. Rosa Luxemburg and Parvus had several times sided with the Mensheviks in party disputes, for example, over the party Rules, and in 1905 had devised the 'semi-Menshevik scheme of permanent revolution' that Trotsky later adopted, the fatal error of which was to reject the idea of an alliance between the proletariat and the peasantry. As for Trotskyism, it had long ceased to be part of the Communist movement and had become the 'advanced detachment of the counter-revolutionary bourgeoisie'. It was a monstrous lie to suggest that Lenin before the war did not understand that the bourgeois-democratic revolution was bound to develop into a socialist one, and that he afterwards picked up this idea from Trotsky. Stalin's letter (*Works*, English edn., vol. 13, 1955, pp. 86 ff.) laid down the rules of Soviet historiography once and for all: Lenin had always been right, the Bolshevik party was and had always been infallible, even though at times enemies crept into the fold and tried unsuccessfully to divert it from the correct path. All non-Bolshevik groups in the socialist movement had always been hotbeds of treason or, at best, breeding-grounds of pernicious error.

This judgement set the seal on Rosa Luxemburg's historical reputation, and also disposed finally of Trotsky. It was a few years longer, however, before all problems of history, philosophy, and the social sciences were settled once and for all. This was done in 1938 by the *History of the Communist Party of the Soviet Union (Bolsheviks), a Short Course* edited by an anonymous commission: Stalin was identified at the time only as the author of the celebrated section on 'Dialectical and Historical Materialism' (ch. IV), setting out the approved version of the party's world-view. After the war, however, it was officially stated that the whole book was by Stalin, and it was to have been republished as a volume in the series of his collected works, had not this been discontinued after his death. The exact genesis of the *Short Course* is not known: it was probably compiled in the main by a team of official writers and then revised by Stalin. His distinctive style is evident in several places, especially where he speaks of various traitors and deviationists as 'White Guard pygmies', 'contemptible lackeys of the Fascists', etc.

The fortunes of the *Short Course* are a remarkable episode in the history of the printed word. Published in millions of copies in the Soviet Union, it served for fifteen years as a manual of ideology completely binding on all citizens. The size of the editions could no doubt be compared only with those of the Bible in Western countries. It was published and taught everywhere without ceasing. In the upper forms of secondary schools, in all places of higher learning, party courses, etc., wherever anything was taught, the *Short Course* was the Soviet citizen's main intellectual pabulum. For any literate person it would have been an unusual feat to remain ignorant of it; most people were obliged to read it time and again, and party propagandists and lecturers knew it virtually by heart.

The *Short Course* set up a world record in another respect also. Among books with historical pretensions there is probably none that contains so high a proportion of lies and suppressions. As the title indicates, the book is a history of the Bolshevik party from its inception, but Chapter IV also introduces the reader to general questions of world history and expounds the 'correct' version of Marxist philosophy and social theory. Morals are drawn liberally from historical events and shown to have formed the basis of the actions of the Bolshevik party and the world Communist movement. The historical conclusions are simple: the Bolshevik party, under the brilliant leadership of Lenin and Stalin, unswervingly pursued from the outset the faultless policy which was crowned by the success of the October Revolution. Lenin is always depicted in the forefront of history, and Stalin directly after him. A few individuals of the second or third rank who were lucky enough to die before the great purges are briefly mentioned at appropriate points in the story. As for the leaders who actually helped Lenin to create the party, carry out the Revolution, and found the Soviet state, they are either not mentioned at all or are shown as double-dyed traitors and wreckers who crept into the party and whose whole career consisted of sabotage and conspiracy. Stalin, on the other hand, was from the beginning an infallible leader, Lenin's best pupil, his truest helper and closest friend. Lenin himself, the reader is given to understand, formed a plan for the development of humanity while he was still a youth, and each successive act of his life was a deliberate step in furtherance of that plan.

The *Short Course* not only established a whole pattern of Bolshevik mythology linked to the cult of Lenin and Stalin, but prescribed a detailed ritual and liturgy. From the time of its publication party writers, historians, and propagandists who touched on any part of its subject-matter were obliged to adhere to every canonical formula and to repeat every relevant phrase verbatim. The *Short Course* was not merely a work of falsified history but a powerful social institution—one of the party's most important instruments of mind control, a device for the destruction both of critical thought and of society's recollections of its own past.

From this point of view the book belongs squarely within the pattern of the totalitarian state created by Stalin. To bring the system to perfection and reduce civil society to a cipher it was necessary to root out all forms of life that were not state-controlled and might constitute a threat of any kind. It was also necessary to devise means of destroying independent thought and memory—an extremely difficult but important task. A totalitarian system cannot survive without constantly rewriting history, eliminating past events, personalities, and ideas and substituting false ones in their place. It was unthinkable in terms of Soviet ideology to say that a particular leader who had fallen a victim to the purge had once been a true servant of the party but had subsequently fallen from grace: anyone who was proclaimed a traitor in the end must have been one from the beginning. Those who were simply done to death without being branded as traitors became unpersons and were never heard of again. Soviet readers became used to seeing editions of books that were still on sale but from which the editor's or translator's name had been carefully erased. If, however, the author himself was a traitor, then the book disappeared completely from circulation and only a few copies remained in the 'prohibited' sections of libraries. This was so even if the book's content was irreproachably Stalinist: as in all magical thinking, an object connected in any way with the evil spirit was contaminated for ever and must be cast out and blotted from memory. Soviet citizens were allowed to remember the existence of a few traitors mentioned in the *Short Course* so as to include them in ritual comminations, but the rest of the satanic crew were supposed to be forgotten and no one dared to speak their names. Old newspapers and journals became unclean overnight if they contained photographs of traitors or articles written by them. Not only was the past constantly revised but—an important feature of Stalinism—everybody was supposed, on the one hand, to be aware of this and of the fairly simple way in which it was done, but, on the other, to say nothing about it on pain of the direst consequences. There were in the Soviet Union many other pseudo-secrets of this kind, i.e. matters that the whole population was intended to know about but never to mention. The labour camps were never spoken of in the newspapers, but it was an unwritten law that the citizen should know about them: not simply because such things could not be kept secret anyway, but because the government wanted people to be aware of certain facts of Soviet life while pretending to one another that no such facts existed. The object of the system was to create a dual consciousness. At public meetings, and even in private conversations, citizens were obliged to repeat in ritual fashion grotesque falsehoods about themselves, the world, and the Soviet Union, and at the same time to keep silent about things they knew very well, not only because they were terrorized but because the incessant repetition of falsehoods which they knew to be such made them accomplices in the campaign of lies inculcated by the party and state. It was not the regime's intention that people should literally believe the absurdities that were put about: if any were so naïve as to do so and to forget reality completely, they would be in a state of innocence *vis-à-vis* their own consciences and would be prone to accept Communist ideology as valid in its own right. Perfect obedience required, however, that they should realize that the current ideology meant nothing in itself: any aspect of it could be altered or annulled by the supreme leader at any moment as he might see fit, and it would be everyone's duty to pretend that nothing had changed and that the ideology had been the same from everlasting. (Stalin took care to emphasize that he himself, like Lenin, had not 'added' anything to Marxism but only developed it.) In order to realize that the party ideology at any given time was neither more nor less than what the leader said it was, the citizen had to possess a dual consciousness: in public he professed adherence to the ideology as an unchanging catechism, while in private or semi-consciously he knew that it was a completely adaptable instrument in the party's hands, i.e. Stalin's. He thus had to 'believe without believing', and it was this state of mind that the party sought to create and maintain in its own members and, as far as possible, in the whole population. Half-starved people, lacking the bare necessities of life, attended meetings at which they repeated the government's lies about how well off they were, and in a bizarre way they half-believed what they were saying. They all knew what it was 'right' to say, i.e., what was demanded of them, and in a curious way they confused this 'rightness' with truth. Truth, they knew, was a party matter, and therefore lies became true even if they contradicted the plain facts of experience. The condition of thus living in two separate worlds at once was one of the most remarkable achievements of the Stalinist system.

The *Short Course* was a perfect manual of false history and doublethink. Its lies and suppressions were too obvious to be overlooked by readers who had witnessed the events in question: all but the youngest party members knew who Trotsky was and how collectivization had taken place in Russia, but, obliged as they were to parrot the official version, they became co-authors of the new past and believers in it as party-inspired truth. If anyone challenged this truth on the basis of manifest experience, the indignation of the faithful was perfectly sincere. In this way Stalinism really produced the 'new Soviet man': an ideological schizophrenic, a liar who believed what he was saying, a man capable of incessant, voluntary acts of intellectual self-mutilation.

As we have mentioned, the *Short Course* contained a new exposition of dialectical and historical materialism—a complete Marxist catechism for a whole generation. This work of Stalin's did not really add anything to the simplified account of Marxism that might be found, for example, in Bukharin's manual, but it had the merit that everything was numbered and set out systematically: the exposé of Marxism, like the rest of the book, had a didactic purpose, and it was easy to assimilate and remember.

The passage begins by stating that dialectical materialism, the philosophy of Marxism, consists of two elements: a materialistic view of the world, and a dialectical method. The latter is distinguished by four principal features or laws. The first is that all phenomena are interlinked and that the universe must be studied as a whole. Second, everything in nature is in a state of change, movement, and development. Third, in all spheres of reality qualitative changes result from an accumulation of quantitative changes. Fourth, the law of the 'unity and struggle of opposites' states that all natural phenomena embody internal contradictions and that the 'content' of development is the conflict between those contradictions. This is seen in the fact that all phenomena have a positive and a negative aspect, a past and a future, so that the struggle takes the form of a conflict between new and old.

This account, it may be noticed, does not include the 'negation of the negation' of which Engels wrote, as did Lenin in his *Philosophical Notes*. The reason for the omission is not explained, but, at all events, the dialectic henceforth comprises four laws and no more. The contrary of dialectics is 'metaphysics'. Metaphysicians are bourgeois philosophers and scholars who deny one or more of the laws in question: thus they claim to judge phenomena in isolation and not in their mutual relations, they maintain that nothing develops, they do not recognize that qualitative changes arise from quantitative ones, and they reject the idea of internal contradictions.

The materialistic interpretation of nature embodies three principles. The first is that the world is by its nature material, and all phenomena are forms of matter in motion; the second, that matter or being is an 'objective reality' existing outside and independent of our mind; and the third, that everything in the world is knowable.

Historical materialism is presented as the logical consequence of dialectical materialism, a view for which support can be found in some statements by Engels, Plekhanov, and Bukharin. Since 'the material world is primary and mind is secondary', it follows that 'the material life of society' i.e. production and the relations of production, is also primary and is an 'objective reality', while the spiritual life of society is a secondary 'reflection' of it. The logical basis of this deduction is not explained. Stalin then quotes Marxist formulas concerning the base and superstructure, classes and the class struggle, the dependence of ideology (and all other forms of superstructure) on production relations, the wrongness of attributing social changes simply to geographical or demographic conditions, and the fact that history depends primarily on technological development. Then comes an account of the five main socio-economic systems: primitive-communal, slave-owning, feudal, capitalist, and socialist. The order in which these succeed one another is described as historically inevitable. Nothing is said about Marx's 'Asiatic mode of production': the probable reasons for this have been discussed elsewhere (vol. I, ch. XIV, pp. 350-1).

The enumeration of the five types of society and their application to the history of every country in the world presented Soviet historians with a major problem. It was no easy matter to discern the existence of a slave or feudal society among populations that had never heard of such phenomena. Moreover, as capitalism had been established by a bourgeois revolution and socialism by a socialist one, it was natural to suppose that previous transitions had taken place in a similar way. Stalin indeed wrote (or 'proved': in Soviet philosophy the two terms mean the same thing where the classics of Marxism–Leninism are concerned) that the feudal system emerged from the slave-owning one as the result of a slave revolution. He had in fact made the same point in an address on 19 February 1933: the slave-owning system was overthrown by a slave revolution, as a result of which feudal lords took the place of the old exploiters. This gave historians the additional problem of identifying the 'slave revolution' in every case of transition from slave-owning to feudalism.

Stalin's work was greeted by a chorus of ideologists as the supreme achievement of Marxist theory and a milestone in philosophical history. For the next fifteen years Soviet philosophy consisted of little but variations on the theme of its superlative merit. Every philosophical article and manual dutifully enumerated the four 'marks' of the dialectic and the three principles of materialism. Philosophers had little to do but to find examples showing that different phenomena were interrelated (a proof of Stalin's first law), or that things changed (a proof of the second), and so on. In this way philosophy was degraded to the status of a medium for incessant flattery of the supreme leader. Everyone wrote in exactly the same style; no writer could be distinguished from another by the form or content of his work. The same soporific clichés were repeated endlessly, with no attempt at independent thought: any such attempt, however timid and obsequious, would have exposed the author to immediate attack. To say anything of one's own in philosophy could only signify that one was accusing Stalin of having omitted something important; to write in a style of one's own was to show dangerous presumption by suggesting that one could express something better than he. Thus Soviet philosophical literature came to consist of heaps of waste paper reproducing in diluted form Chapter IV, Section 2 of the *Short Course*. Compared with this, even the polemics of the 'dialecticians' and 'mechanists' were an example of bold, creative, and independent thought. As for the history of philosophy, it became an almost forgotten subject. In the thirties a few translations of philosophical classics still appeared, but only of such authors as were classed, rightly or wrongly, as 'materialists' or had written against religion: the Soviet reader might thus occasionally see an anticlerical pamphlet by Holbach or Voltaire or, if he was lucky, something by Bacon or Spinoza. Hegel's works were also published, as he belonged to the canon of 'dialectical' writers. But for about forty years there was no chance of reading Plato, not to mention any more dangerous idealist. Professional philosophers quoted only the 'classics of Marxism–Leninism', namely Marx, Engels, Lenin, and Stalin: the chronological sequence was, of course, observed when the names were cited together, but in terms of frequency of quotation the order was precisely the reverse.

It might have seemed that the ideological situation resulting from the publication of the *Short Course* was one of final perfection; but the post-war years showed that it could still be improved upon.

It should not be supposed, however, that Marxism as codified by Stalin differed in any essential way from Leninism. It was a bald, primitive version, but contained scarcely anything new. Indeed, very little that is original can be found in any of Stalin's works before 1950, with two exceptions. The first, of which we have considered the import, was that socialism could be built in one country. The second was that the class struggle must become fiercer as the building of socialism progressed. This principle remained officially valid even after Stalin declared that there were no longer any antagonistic classes in the Soviet Union—there were no classes, but the class struggle was acuter than ever. A third principle, which Stalin seems first to have enunciated at a plenum of the Central Committee on 12 January 1933, was that before the state 'withered away' under Communism it must, for dialectical reasons, first develop to a point of maximum strength; but this idea had already been formulated by Trotsky during the Civil War. The second and third principles, in any case, were of no significance except as a justification of the system of police terror.

However, it should be emphasized once again that what mattered about Stalinist ideology was not its content—even though it was expressed in catechetical form—but the fact that there was a supreme authority from whose judgement on ideological matters there was no appeal. Ideology was thus completely institutionalized, and virtually the whole of intellectual life was subordinated to it. The 'unity of theory and practice' was expressed by the concentration of doctrinal, political, and police authority in Stalin's person.

Dialectical and historical materialism as expounded by Stalin amounted to an unimaginative, schematic version of Marxism according to Plekhanov, Lenin, and Bukharin: a philosophy with cosmic ambitions, proclaiming that the dialectic expressed universal 'laws' which governed every aspect of reality, and that human history was a special case of the application of these laws. This philosophy claimed to be 'scientific' in the same way as astronomy, and declared that social processes were as 'objective' and predictable as any other. In this respect it departed radically from the Marxian viewpoint as reconstructed by Lukács and Korsch, according to which, in the particular case of the proletarian consciousness, the social process and awareness of that process became one and the same, and knowledge of society coincided with the revolutionary praxis that transformed it. Stalin took over the popular naturalism which prevailed among Marxists of the Second International, and in which there was no room for the peculiar Marxian view of the 'unity of theory and practice'. True, this formula was acknowledged and emphasized at every opportunity by Stalin and his attendant philosophers; but its meaning was in effect reduced to the proposition that practice was superior to theory and that theory was ancillary to practice. In accordance with this view pressure was put on scholars—especially after the ideological reconstruction of the Academy of Sciences in the early thirties—to confine themselves to fields that might be of immediate profit to industry. This pressure applied to all the natural sciences and even, though less severely, to mathematics (Mathematical studies were scarcely ever 'supervised' ideologically in the Soviet Union, as even the omniscient high priests of Marxism did not pretend to understand them; consequently, standards were upheld and Russian mathematical science was saved from temporary destruction.) The 'unity of theory and practice', of course, applied to the humane sciences also, but in a slightly different sense. Broadly speaking, the natural sciences were harnessed to the demands of industry, and the humanistic sciences to those of party propaganda. History, philosophy, and the history of literature and art were supposed to 'serve the party and state', i.e. to buttress the party line and provide theoretical support for current decisions.

The demand that natural science should confine itself to subjects of immediate technical use was highly damaging to important branches of research, and
this very soon made itself felt in technology as well. Even more pernicious, however, were attempts to exercise ideological control over the actual results of scientific investigation, in the name of Marxist 'correctness'. In the thirties the
'idealist' theory of relativity came under fire from a band of philosophers and
half-baked physicists, led by A. A. Maksimov. The same period saw the rise of
Trofim D. Lysenko, whose mission was to revolutionize Soviet biological science in accordance with Marxism–Leninism and to explode the 'bourgeois' theories of Mendel and T. H. Morgan. Lysenko, an agronomist, had explored various
techniques of plant breeding and decided, early in his career, to develop them
into a universal theory of Marxist genetics. After 1935, together with his assistant I. I. Prezent, he attacked the modern genetic theory and claimed that hereditary influences could be almost completely eliminated by appropriate changes
in environment: genes were a bourgeois invention, as was the distinction
between genotype and phenotype. It was not hard to convince the party leaders and Stalin himself that a theory which rejected the 'immortal substance of
heredity' and proclaimed that living organisms could be altered to any desired
extent by environmental changes was in accordance with Marxism–Leninism
('everything changes') and was admirably suited to the ideology which maintained that human beings, especially 'Soviet man', could transform nature in
any way they had a mind to. So Lysenko rapidly secured party support and exercised a growing influence on research institutes, academicians, journals, etc.,
until, as we shall see, his revolutionary theory achieved a complete triumph in
1948. Party propaganda extolled his discoveries incessantly from about 1935
onwards, and those who objected that his experiments were scientifically worthless were soon put to silence. The eminent geneticist Nikolay I. Vavilov, who
refused to subscribe to the new theory, was arrested in 1940 and perished in
the Kolyma concentration camp. Most Soviet philosophers, as was to be
expected, joined in acclaiming Lysenko's views.

Today no one has any doubt that Lysenko was an ignoramus and a charla-
tan, and his career is an instructive example of how the Soviet system functions, not only with respect to science and culture but also in the economic and
administrative sphere. The self-destructive features that were to become still
more evident later on were already visible. As the party exercises unlimited
authority in every area of life, and the whole system is organized hierarchically
with a one-way chain of command, it follows that the career of any individual
depends on his obedience to authority and proficiency in the arts of flattery and
denunciation. It is fatal, on the other hand, to display initiative, a mind of one's
own, or even a minimal respect for truth. When the main object of those in
authority is to maintain and increase their power it is inevitable that the wrong

people will come to the top, both in science (especially if it is ideologically controlled) and in economic administration. Inefficiency and waste are built-in features of the Soviet system; economic development is hampered by both the promotion of the unfit and the wholesale restriction of information on grounds of politics and 'security'. Later attempts at rationalizing the economy have had some success, but only in so far as they departed from the totalitarian principle or the ideal of 'unity' which the Stalinist system brought to such perfection.

Another important feature of Soviet culture in the 1930s was the growth of Russian nationalism. This too is a phenomenon that reached its peak later on, but it was already discernible in the early thirties, when Stalin's speeches began to strike the note of a 'strong Russia' which could and must be created by socialism. The patriotic theme was stressed increasingly in propaganda, and Soviet and Russian patriotism coincided more and more. The glories of Russian history were revived in an appeal to national pride and self-sufficiency. Some nations, such as the Uzbeks, who had formerly written their language in Arabic script and were then given a Latin alphabet by the Soviet authorities, were now compelled to adopt a form of Cyrillic, so that three alphabets were used in a single generation. The idea of 'national cadres' exercising power in the non-Russian republics of the Union soon proved to be a fiction: in practice though not in theory, the top posts in the party and state administration were usually held by Russians appointed from Moscow. The ideology of state power became by degrees indistinguishable from that of Russian imperialism.

Marxism as the ideology of the Soviet state very soon ceased to be an independent factor in the determination of policy. Of necessity, its content had to be so vague and general as to justify any particular move in home or foreign affairs: N.E.P. or collectivization, friendship with Hitler or war with Hitler, any toughening or relaxation of the internal regime, and so on. And indeed, since the theory states that 'on the one hand' the superstructure is a creation and instrument of the base, but 'on the other' it also affects the base, it can be shown that any imaginable government policy for the regulation of the economy, or for controlling culture in a greater or less degree, is in accordance with Marxism. If 'on the one hand' individuals do not make history, but 'on the other' exceptional individuals who understand historical necessity do play an important part (and both points of view can be supported by quotations from Marx and Engels), then it is equally in accordance with Marxism to pay divine honours to the socialist despot or to condemn this practice as a 'deviation'. If 'on the one hand' all nations are entitled to self-determination, but 'on the other hand' the cause of world socialist revolution is paramount, then any policy, whether mild or severe, with the object of discouraging the national aspirations of the non-Russian inhabitants of the empire will be indubitably Marxist. Such in fact was the ambivalent basis of Stalin's Marxism, and its vague and contradictory tenets were alike put down to the 'dialectic'. From this point of view both the function and the content of official Soviet Marxism have remained the same since Stalin's death. Marxism has become simply a rhetorical dressing for the Realpolitik of the Soviet empire.

The rationale of this change was very simple: since the Soviet Union is by definition the bastion of human progress, whatever serves Soviet interests is progressive and whatever does not is reactionary. Tsarist Russia, like most other Powers in history, supported the aspirations of smaller peoples in order to weaken its own rivals, and the Soviet Union pursued this policy from the outset, but under a different guise. Even 'feudal' sheikhs and Asiatic princes, according to Stalin, played an 'objectively' progressive role in so far as they undermined the imperialist front. This was fully in accordance with Lenin's theory of world revolution, which admitted and even required the participation of non-socialist, non-proletarian, and, in Marxist terms, 'reactionary' forces. From a dialectical point of view the reactionaries immediately and dialectically became progressive if their efforts were hostile to the interests of other world Powers. In the same way it became axiomatic after 1917 that, as the Soviet Union was by definition the mainstay of the worldwide liberation movement, any armed incursion or seizure of foreign territory on its part was not an invasion but an act of liberation. Marxism thus provided the Soviet state with a repertoire of arguments that were far more useful as tools of imperialism than the clumsy and even absurd principles with which Tsarist Russia sought to justify its rule over alien peoples.

3. The Comintern and the ideological transformation of international Communism

IN the natural course of things, Stalinization spread throughout the world Communist movement. For the first decade of its existence the Third International was still a forum of discussion and conflict between different forms of Communist ideology, but thereafter it lost all independence and became an instrument of Soviet foreign policy, completely subordinated to Stalin's authority.

The various left-wing groups and fractions that emerged within social democratic parties during the First World War were not all pure Leninists, but all agreed in condemning the betrayal of the movement by the leaders of the Second International; they all rejected reformism, and sought to revive the traditional internationalist spirit. The October Revolution had created a new revolutionary stronghold, and most of these left-wingers believed that the world Communist revolution was imminent. In 1918 Communist parties were formed in Poland, Germany, Finland, Latvia, Austria, Hungary, Greece, and

Holland. In the next three years larger or smaller revolutionary parties, representing various minority groups, came into existence in all European countries. Despite many complicated disputes and schisms, there took shape in this way an international Communist movement inspired by Leninist principles.

In January 1919 the Bolshevik party issued a manifesto drafted by Trotsky and calling for the creation of a new International. A congress was held at Moscow in March, at which the project was approved by delegates of certain Communist parties and left-wing social democratic groups. The Third International was not actually set up until the Second Congress, in July–August 1920. From the beginning various parties developed internal divisions and departures from the Leninist norm. On the one hand were 'rightist' groups who hankered after a reconciliation with the social democrats from whom they had recently split off; on the other were 'leftist' or 'sectarian' deviationists who, as a rule, rejected compromise tactics or association with parliamentary politics. It was against this school of thought that Lenin wrote *'Left-Wing' Communism: an Infantile Disorder*. Given the belief prevalent among Communists that within a year the whole world, or at least Europe, would become a Soviet republic, 'leftist' tendencies were much stronger and more in evidence than 'reformist' ones.

The statutes of the Comintern marked a radical departure from the principles of the Second International, but harked back to the tradition of the First. They provided that the International was to be a single centralized party, of which the national parties were sections, and that its purpose was to use every means, including armed force, to bring about an international republic of Soviets, which, as the political form of the dictatorship of the proletariat, was the historically ordained prelude to the abolition of the state. The International was to hold annual congresses (biennial after 1924) and be governed in between times by its Executive Committee, which could expel 'sections' that disregarded its instructions and could require them to cast out groups or individuals for breaches of discipline. The theses adopted at the 1920 Congress included a firm rejection of parliamentarianism as a suitable form of the society of the future. Parliaments and all other bourgeois political institutions must be used only in order to destroy them; Communists must take part in elections for this purpose alone, and Communist deputies were responsible to the party alone and not to the anonymous mass of voters. The theses on colonial questions, drafted by Lenin, instructed Communists in colonial and backward countries to enter into temporary alliances with national revolutionary movements; at the same time Communists must remain independent, not allowing the national bourgeoisie to get hold of the revolutionary movement, but fighting from the outset for a Soviet republic; under their leadership the backward countries would achieve Communism without having to go through a capitalist stage.

The congress also issued a manifesto demanding unconditional support for the cause of the Soviet Union as being the cause of the whole International.

Another important document was a list of 'Twenty-One Conditions' which must be fulfilled by parties joining the Comintern, and which extended Leninist forms of organization to the whole Communist movement. The 'Conditions' provided that Communist parties must wholly subordinate their propaganda activities to decisions of the Comintern. The Communist Press was to be completely under party control. The 'sections' must resolutely combat reformist tendencies and, whenever possible, remove reformists and centralists from workers' organizations. They must also—this was specially emphasized—carry out systematic propaganda within their countries' armed forces. They must combat pacifism, support colonial liberation movements, be active in workers' organizations and especially trade unions, and make efforts to win peasant support. In Parliament, Communist deputies must subordinate their whole activity to revolutionary propaganda. Parties must be centralized to the maximum, observe iron discipline, and periodically purge their ranks of petty-bourgeois elements. They must unquestioningly support all existing Soviet republics. Each party's programme must be endorsed by a congress of the International or by its Executive Committee, and all decisions of congresses or the Executive Committee were binding on all sections. All parties must call themselves 'Communist', and those that were allowed by the laws of their country to function openly must, in addition, set up clandestine organizations for action 'at the decisive moment'.

In this way a centralized party operating on military lines became the prescribed mode of organization of the world Communist movement. However, Lenin and Trotsky, the creators of the International, did not envisage it as an instrument of Soviet state policy. The idea that the Bolshevik party itself was no more than a 'section' or branch of the world revolutionary movement was, at the outset, taken quite seriously. But the way in which the Comintern was organized, and the historical circumstances of its creation, soon dispelled such illusions. The Bolshevik party naturally enjoyed great prestige as the agent of the first successful revolution, and Lenin's personal authority was unshakeable. From the beginning Russia had a deciding voice in the Executive Committee, and the permanent representatives of other parties, residing in Moscow, gradually became Soviet functionaries. Internal struggles within the Soviet leadership were not only reflected in the International but eventually became its main concern. Each of the Bolshevik oligarchs who contended for power after Lenin's death naturally sought support among the leaders of fraternal parties, and the victories or defeats of international Communism were in turn exploited in fractional struggles in Moscow.

The first congresses of the International were held regularly in accordance with the statutes. The third took place in June–July 1921, the fourth in November 1922, and the fifth in June–July 1924. By this time Russia had been through the Civil War, the N.E.P. had entered its first phase, and Lenin had died. In accordance with Lenin's precepts, the International busied itself from the outset with revolutionary agitation in colonial and undeveloped countries. The Indian Communist Nath Roy argued that revolution in Asia should be the main objective of world Communism: the stability of capitalism depended on profits from colonial territories and it was there, not in Europe, that the future of humanity would be decided. A majority of the International, however, thought that Europe should still be the main focus of activity. The defeat of the Soviet armies before Warsaw in 1920 caused hopes of an early revolution to recede, but they did not fade completely. However, in March 1921 an attempt at revolution in Germany ended in fiasco, and the resolutions of the Third Comintern Congress in June were less optimistic as to the prospect of a world Soviet republic. The German uprising was condemned by Lenin and Trotsky and duly criticized by the congress. However, Paul Levi, the German communist leader, who had himself opposed the rising and was therefore expelled from the party shortly before the congress opened, was not rehabilitated; he was again condemned and his expulsion ratified. The new 'Leninist' style was clearly in full operation.

As the world revolution was hanging fire the Comintern leaders decided, against strong opposition from the 'leftist' minority, to adopt a 'united front' policy of co-operation with the socialists. Conversations were begun before the Fourth Congress in 1922, but came to nothing: the socialists suspected, with good reason, that the 'united front' was a ploy aimed at their destruction. A further abortive rising took place in Germany in October 1923; this time Heinrich Brandler, the new party leader, was made the scapegoat for a plan that had been wholly organized and initiated by the Comintern and the Bolshevik party. In 1924 Trotsky accused the Comintern, then under Zinoviev's direction, of failing to exploit the revolutionary situation by seizing power in Germany.

The Fifth Comintern Congress, held in mid-1924 at a time when the ruling triumvirate of Stalin, Zinoviev, and Kamenev was engaged in a crucial struggle with Trotsky, passed a resolution calling for the 'Bolshevization' of all member parties. This meant in theory that they should adopt the methods and style of the Russian party, but in practice that they should accept its authority in all matters. The congress itself showed that 'Bolshevization' was already well advanced: the Communists of all countries unanimously condemned Trotsky at the bidding of Stalin and his associates. In the following year there was a demonstration at the congress of the German Communist party of what Bolshevization meant, when the Soviet delegate Manuilsky, one of Stalin's chief henchmen in the Comintern, attempted to lay down the law as regards the membership of the Central Committee. As the German delegates refused to comply, Zinoviev, chairman of the Executive Committee, summoned them to Moscow and ordered them to get rid of their 'leftist' leaders, Ruth Fischer and Arkady Maslow, who had tried to maintain some semblance of autonomy *vis-à-vis* the Bolsheviks.

Another resolution of the Fifth Congress assessed the position of the social democrats, stating that their role, in collusion with the bourgeoisie, was to instil democratic and pacifist illusions in the working class. As capitalism decayed, social democracy came closer and closer to Fascism: the two were in fact aspects of a single weapon in the hands of capital. This was the genesis of the theory of 'social Fascism', which a few years later became the principal guideline of Comintern policy.

Four years elapsed between the Fifth and Sixth Comintern Congresses: Stalin was probably unwilling to call one until he had finally achieved victory over Trotsky and also Zinoviev, Kamenev, and their associates. Meanwhile the Comintern, in spite of its doctrine concerning 'social Fascism', made advances to the British trade unions which resulted in the formation, in 1925, of an Anglo-Russian committee to promote the unification of the world trade union movement. This, however, was short lived and unsuccessful. In 1926–7 the Comintern suffered a more serious set-back in China, where the small Communist party, on Moscow's instructions, had supported the revolutionary Kuomintang in its efforts to unify and modernize China and free it from Western domination. This, in Stalin's opinion, was a bourgeois nationalist movement and was not destined to lead at once at a dictatorship of the proletariat. The Soviet Union helped with arms and military and political advisers, and in the spring of 1926 the Kuomintang was even admitted to the Comintern as a 'sympathizing' party. However, when Chiang Kai-shek formed his government he excluded the Communists from any share in power, and in April 1927 he put down a Communist rising in Shanghai with many arrests and executions. Stalin, realizing too late that Chiang had anticipated the intentions of his 'allies' by getting his blow in first, attempted to save the situation by ordering an insurrection in Canton; this took place in December, but was quelled by another massacre. Trotsky blamed Stalin for these defeats, declaring that instead of accepting Chiang's leadership the Chinese Communists should have aimed at setting up a Soviet republic from the outset—though he did not explain how they could have prevailed against Chiang in the then state of their forces. However, the Comintern laid the blame on the Chinese party for pursuing a 'false policy', and its leader, Chen Tu-hsiu, was condemned and later expelled.

The Sixth Comintern Congress, in August 1928, put a final stop to attempts at co-operating with the socialists, which in any case had been feeble and unsuccessful. The congress declared that international social democracy and the trade unions under its control were the mainstay of capitalism, and Communist parties were ordered to concentrate all their efforts against the 'social Fascists'. The temporary stabilization of capitalism, it was proclaimed, had now come to an end, and a new revolutionary period was beginning. The Communist parties in various countries duly expelled 'Rightists' and 'conciliators' from the ranks, and the new purge claimed many victims among the leaders in Germany, Spain, the U.S.A. and elsewhere.

The fact that the German Communists, who represented a powerful political force, turned their fire against the socialists was a major cause of Hitler's accession to power. The party line was that Nazism could only be a transient episode and that by radicalizing the masses it would pave the way for Communism. Even after Hitler came to power, for a whole year the German Communists treated the socialists as their chief enemy; by the time they changed their minds, the party was already broken and helpless.

By the end of 1929, after the downfall of Bukharin (who had succeeded Zinovyev as chairman of the Executive Committee in 1926), Stalin was the unquestioned owner of the Bolshevik party and, through it, of international Communism. The Comintern lost all significance of its own and was merely a channel for the transmission of the Kremlin's orders to other parties. Its staff consisted exclusively of people loyal to Stalin and controlled by the Soviet police; among their tasks was to recruit intelligence agents for the Soviet Union. All the fraternal parties, after repeated purges, accepted without demur Moscow's changing directives, which for the most part were dictated by Soviet foreign policy. Stalin financed the parties generously and thus increased their dependence on himself. By the mid-thirties the Comintern was a mere façade, as it was no longer needed even for the purpose of securing obedience from foreign parties.

The Seventh and last Comintern Congress, held in Moscow in July–August 1935, proclaimed a new policy which had been foreshadowed for a year or more, that of the 'popular front' against Fascism. What had recently been condemned as 'rightist opportunism' now became the official line. All democratic forces, especially the socialists (the 'social Fascists' of two years earlier), as well as liberals and even conservatives if need be, were to rally under Communist leadership against the Fascist threat. Stalin's reason for this policy seems to have been his fear that France and the other Western countries would remain neutral if Hitler attacked Russia. France, in any case, was the main target of the 'popular front' policy: as far as Germany was concerned it could only apply to powerless *émigré* groups, and the Communist parties in other countries were too weak to affect events. In France the popular front was victorious at the election in May 1936, but the Communists refused to enter Léon Blum's government. In general the policy did not last long and produced few results. Although not officially revoked, it became a dead letter when Stalin decided to seek a *rapprochement* with Nazi Germany. Meanwhile the German Communist party, which had been smashed and driven underground, belatedly adopted Hitler's slogans of the unity of all Germans and the liquidation of the Polish Corridor.

The true character of the 'popular front' policy was shown up by the Civil War in Spain. Some months after Franco's rebellion, Stalin decided to intervene in defence of the republic. International brigades were formed, and besides military advisers the Soviet Union sent an army of political agents who purged the republican forces of Trotskyists, anarchists, and deviationists of all kinds.

International Communism was by now completely 'Bolshevized', and in any case non-Bolshevik forms of Communism had long ceased to signify. In the twenties individuals or groups who had been expelled from their parties or had seceded in protest against Comintern policy tried from time to time to organize a non-Soviet Communist movement, but these attempts never came to anything. The Trotskyists vegetated in small groups, appealing impotently to the 'internationalist conscience' of the world proletariat. The authority of the Bolshevik party, and the organizational principles accepted by all Communists, were such that until the 1950s no dissident group achieved any support or influence. World Communism marched obediently along the route prescribed by Stalin. The dissolution of the Comintern in May 1943 was a mere gesture to persuade Western public opinion of Soviet good will and democratic intentions. It had no other significance, as the Communist parties were so well trained and so dependent on the Soviet Union for their organization and finances that no special institution was necessary to keep them in line.

One effect of Stalin's dictatorship over world Communism was the gradual decline of Marxist studies. In the twenties, during the process of 'Bolshevization', the parties were dominated by various fractional and personal quarrels: these usually took the form of disputes over the correct interpretation of Lenin's political testament, but they had no permanent effect on doctrine apart from the gradual codification of Soviet-type orthodoxy. None the less, the revolutionary mood of the early twenties gave rise to several theoretical documents in which Marxist doctrine as transmitted by the orthodox thinkers of the Second International was subjected to a thorough revision. The most important of these are the writings of Lukács and Korsch, both of whom were stigmatized as 'ultra-leftist' by the Comintern. In different ways they attempted to reconstruct Marx's philosophy from the beginning, putting fresh life into the idea of the 'unity of theory and practice' and combating the scientistic outlook that prevailed among both the orthodox and the neo-Kantians. In various countries stalwarts of the previous generation still carried on traditions of undogmatic Marxism outside the Communist movement: Adler and Bauer in

Austria, Krzywicki in Poland, Kautsky and Hilferding in Germany. Their activity in those years did not, however, have much effect on the evolution of doctrine: some of them were content to repeat ideas and themes that had already been worked out, while others gradually fell away from Marxist tradition. Meanwhile theoretical work was paralysed by the Comintern's policy of polarizing the socialist movement by combating the social democrats. The latter became largely divorced from Marxism and lost the need for a single binding ideology; Marxism was practically monopolized by Soviet ideologists, and became more barren with every year that passed.

Only in Germany was there an important Marxist centre that did not identify with Communism: the Institut für Sozialforschung, founded at Frankfurt in 1923. Its members were at first strongly influenced by Marxist tradition, but the links weakened by degrees, and a pattern took shape which was later increasingly evident. On the one hand, Marxism became ossified as an institutionalized party ideology and, while politically effective, lost all philosophical value; on the other, it combined with quite different traditions to the point where it ceased to present a clear outline and became only one of many contributions to intellectual history.

Around the middle thirties, however, the Marxist movement in France revived to some extent. Among its leaders were scientists, sociologists, and philosophers, not all of whom were Communists: Henri Wallon, Paul Langevin, Frédéric Joliot-Curie, Marcel Prenant, Armand Cuvillier, and Georges Friedmann. These men were to play an important part in French intellectual life after the war, either as scholars who were politically committed to Communism (but not necessarily Marxist theoreticians) or as continuers of certain aspects of traditional Marxist theory, which had ceased to form a system but had penetrated intellectual life in a piecemeal fashion. The best-known orthodox Marxist in France between the wars was Georges Politzer, who was put to death during the occupation; he wrote a ferocious critique of Bergson and a popular handbook of Leninist dialectical materialism. In Britain J. B. S. Haldane, the well-known biologist and author of books on the origins of life on earth, endeavoured to prove the affinity of Marxism with modern science. Another Marxist was the American geneticist H. J. Muller. In both these cases, however, Marxism figured in aspects that were not specifically Marxist: in biology it appeared chiefly in the form of a general opposition to vitalism and finalism. Maurice Dobb, also in Britain, defended Marxist economic theory, especially in relation to the trade cycle.

On the left wing of the Labour party Harold J. Laski expounded in Marxist terms the theory of the state, the nature of authority, and the history of political ideas. In the later thirties he adopted the classic Marxist theory of the state as instrument which 'in the last resort' serves to enable one class to coerce another. He attacked contemporary liberalism as an ideology whose main purpose was to keep the exploited from being heard, and asserted that if the vital interests of the property-owning classes were threatened they would increasingly reject liberal forms of government and resort to naked force. The growth of Fascism in Europe was a natural result of the development of the bourgeois state; bourgeois democracy was in a state of decline, and the only alternative to Fascism was socialism. None the less, Laski was attached to traditional democratic liberties and believed that the proletarian revolution would leave them intact. The key to social development lay, he declared, in the attitude of the middle classes. John Strachey, at this time a Communist (he later became a social democrat), discussed the same problems from an orthodox Leninist viewpoint.

A gifted author, Christopher Caudwell (pseudonym of Christopher St. John Sprigg, 1907–37), was briefly prominent in British Marxism. His career as a Marxist and Communist lasted barely two years—he was killed fighting in the International Brigade in Spain—but in 1936 he produced a notable work entitled *Illusion and Reality: a Study of the Sources of Poetry*. Before becoming a Communist he wrote some detective stories and popular books on aviation. His poems were published posthumously, as were *Studies in a Dying Culture* (1938), a collection of essays on contemporary British literature and 'bourgeois culture' in general, and an unfinished work *The Crisis in Physics* (1939), a Leninist attack on idealism, empiricism, and indeterminism in modern scientific theory. In *Illusion and Reality*, the best known of his Marxist works, he attempted to correlate the history of poetry, including metrical changes, with different stages of social and technical evolution. At the same time he attacked the bourgeois idea which envisaged freedom as independence of necessity, whereas Engels had shown that freedom meant exploiting natural inevitability for human ends. The book devotes particular attention to English poetry from the sixteenth century onwards: Marlowe and Shakespeare stand for the heroic era of primary accumulation, Pope for mercantilism, and so on. Caudwell took the view (which is not specifically Marxist and can be found in earlier anthropological works) that poetry was originally only an element in the agricultural rites of primitive society, with the purpose of increasing production. Later on, in class societies, poetry, music, and the dance were disjoined from production, which meant the alienation of art; the function of socialism was to reverse this process and restore the unity of productive and artistic activities.

The intellectual life of Western Europe, and to some extent of the U.S.A., in the later thirties presented a curious picture. On the one hand, Stalinism was in full career, and some of its most repulsive features were laid bare for all the world to see; but, on the other, many intellectuals were attracted by Communism as the only alternative to Fascism and as a defence against it. All other political groupings appeared weak, irresolute, and helpless before the threat of Nazi aggression. Marxism seemed to many to uphold the tradition of rationalism, humanism, and all the old liberal ideals, while Communism was the political embodiment of Marxism and the best hope of containing the Fascist onslaught. Left-wing intellectuals were drawn towards Marxism by features that had indeed been present in it from the beginning but were not specifically Marxist. As long as Soviet Russia seemed to be the main force opposed to Fascism, these intellectuals endeavoured to identify Soviet Communism with Marxism as they understood it. In so doing they deliberately blinded themselves to the realities of Communist policy. Those who, like George Orwell, formed an idea of Communism in action from empirical facts instead of from doctrinaire assumptions met with hatred and indignation. Hypocrisy and self-delusion had become the permanent climate of the intellectual Left.

IV

The Crystallization of
Marxism–Leninism after the
Second World War

1. The wartime interlude

By the end of the 1930s Marxism had taken on a clearly defined form as the doctrine of the Soviet party and state. Its official name was Marxism–Leninism, which, as we have explained, meant nothing more or less than Stalin's personal ideology: it included bits of theory from Marx, Engels, and Lenin, but purported to be a single doctrine which the four 'classical' teachers had successively 'developed' and 'enriched'. In this way Marx was promoted to the rank of a 'classic of Marxism–Leninism' and a forerunner of Stalin. The true content of Marxism–Leninism was expounded in Stalin's writings, more particularly in the *Short Course*.

As we have seen, the characteristic feature of this ideology, which preeminently reflected the interests of the governing stratum of a totalitarian state, was its combination of extreme rigidity and extreme flexibility. These seemingly opposite qualities reinforced each other perfectly. The ideology was rigid in the sense that it was expressed in a collection of unchanging, cut-and-dried formulas which all were obliged to repeat without the slightest deviation; but the content of those formulas was so vague that they could be used to justify any state policy whatsoever, in all its phases and variations.

The most paradoxical effect of this function of Soviet Marxism was its partial self-liquidation during the Second World War.

In the second half of the thirties Europe was paralysed by the menace of Nazi aggression. During the crises which preceded the outbreak of war, the Soviet Union with Stalin at the helm pursued a skilful and subtle policy aimed at securing its position against threats from every side. The Western Powers' pusillanimous policy of appeasement made it difficult to foresee what would happen if Germany should attack her Eastern or Western neighbours. After the Anschluss and the subjugation of Czechoslovakia it was clear to most people that war was unavoidable. The German–Soviet non-aggression pact of August 1939 contained a secret protocol providing for the partition of Poland between the signatories and assigning Finland, Estonia, and Latvia to the Soviet sphere of interest (Lithuania was added to these in a modification of the agreement on 28 September). Germany invaded Poland on 1 September, the day after the Soviet Union ratified the pact, and on 17 September the Red Army marched in to 'liberate' the Polish Eastern territories, while the Soviet and German governments proclaimed that Poland had been annihilated once and for all. The aggressors concluded a secret agreement to aid each other in stamping out underground activity in the occupied territories. (During the period of Nazi–Soviet co-operation the Russians handed over some German Communists who were imprisoned in the U.S.S.R., including the physicist Alexander Weissberg: he survived the war, however, and was thus able to write one of the first documentary accounts of Stalin's purges.) The pact with Hitler brought about a transformation of Soviet state ideology. Attacks on Fascism, and the word 'Fascism' itself, disappeared from Soviet propaganda. The Western Communist parties, especially the British and French, were ordered to direct their whole propaganda against the war effort and to blame Western imperialism for the fight against Nazi Germany. The unsuccessful invasion of Finland revealed Russia's military weakness to the world and not least to Hitler, whose object from the beginning was to destroy his Soviet 'ally'. Still more catastrophic was the disarray of the Soviet Union immediately after the German invasion on 21 June 1941. Historians still debate the causes of its astonishing unpreparedness. The purging of the best army cadres, Stalin's military incompetence and refusal to heed warnings of an early attack, and the complete psychological disarmament of the Soviet people—a week before the invasion, the government publicly condemned rumours of war as 'absurd'—are among the reasons advanced for the series of defeats that brought the Soviet state to the brink of destruction.

The German–Soviet war brought about further ideological changes in the Soviet Union and the whole Communist world. The Western Communists no longer had to direct their fire against the anti-Nazi forces, but were free to treat Fascism as a 'natural' enemy. The Polish Communists, who until June 1941 had obediently accepted the abolition of the Polish state, reestablished their party and combated the Nazi invader, partly in the U.S.S.R. but mainly as an underground movement in German-occupied Poland. Apart from 'normal' cruelty and destruction, the war in Russia brought 'ideological' atrocities of its own: the mass deportation and murder of Poles, especially the intelligentsia, from Poland's Eastern territories; the massacre of Polish officers taken captive by the Russians; the resettlement en masse, while the struggle with Germany was still going on, of eight minority peoples of the U.S.S.R. and the dissolution of four autonomous national republics—those of the Volga Germans, the Crimean Tatars, the Kalmyks, and the Chechens and Ingushes. Countless lives were lost in these deportations, and the evacuated peoples were never to return to their native homes.

On the other hand, the war did much to relax the grip of ideology in Russia. With the nation struggling for dear life, Marxism proved worthless as a psychological weapon; it virtually disappeared from official propaganda, and Stalin appealed instead to Russian patriotism and the memory of such heroes as Alexander Nevsky, Suvorov, and Kutuzov. The Internationale ceased to be the Soviet anthem and was replaced by a hymn glorifying Russia. Anti-religious agitation was stopped, and the League of Militant Atheists was actually dissolved, while the clergy were invited to help maintain the spirit of patriotism.

Soviet propaganda since 1945 has represented the victory over Hitler as a triumph of socialist ideology, alive in the hearts of fighting men and of the whole Soviet people. The opposite would be closer to the truth: it was a necessary condition of victory, though of course not a sufficient one, that the nation should forget about Marxist ideology and be imbued with national and Patriotic sentiments. Apart from the efforts of the Soviet state and People, other factors played their part, including the vast quantity of U.S. military aid and the 'ideological' folly of Hitler, who, dazzled by his overwhelming success in the first months of the war, subjected the conquered territories to the full rigour of Nazi doctrine: instead of posing as a liberator in Byelorussia and the Ukraine, he brandished the scourge of racialism and treated the inhabitants as sub-men to be exterminated or enslaved for ever. (The Germans did not even disband the collective farms in conquered territory, as the system made it easier for them to commandeer produce.) The bestial cruelty of the Nazis convinced the whole population that there could be no greater evil than Hitlerism. The Red Army soldiers, who after the first reverses, showed outstanding courage and devotion, fought for their country's existence and not for Marxism–Leninism. Many in Russia hoped that the war would not only bring final victory over Nazism but also internal freedom or at least a relaxation of tyranny. It was natural to think so when ideological controls had been loosened so that every effort might be devoted to winning the war, but very soon after victory it was clear that such hopes were an illusion.

In spite of everything, various Marxist institutions continued to function throughout the war. The only important event in the sphere of Soviet philosophy was a decree of the party's Central Committee condemning errors in the third volume of a collective *History of Philosophy* edited by G. F. Aleksandrov: the authors, failing to keep abreast of the times, had over-praised Hegel's role as a philosopher and forerunner of Marxism–Leninism, without taking account of his German chauvinism. This condemnation was only one of many wartime acts of anti-German propaganda, but it helped to destroy Hegel's standing in the annals of Marxist–Leninist orthodoxy. In an interview with Soviet philosophers Stalin described Hegel as an ideologist of the aristocratic reaction to the French Revolution and French materialism, and from then on this assessment became obligatory in philosophical circles.

As the prospect of victory became a virtual certainty Stalin's policy, motivated throughout by the desire for conquest and territorial expansion, concerned itself with the post-war order in Europe and the world. By the Tehran and Yalta agreements the Western Allies gave the Soviet Union, in practice, a free hand in Eastern Europe. In addition to the outright annexation of the three Baltic States and the acquisition of territory from nearly all its neighbours, the Soviet Union, with the acquiescence of Churchill and Roosevelt, enjoyed a dominant position in Poland, Czechoslovakia, Hungary, Romania, Bulgaria, and, to a lesser extent, Yugoslavia. It was some years before Communist rule in these countries, and also in East Germany, was finally consolidated, but the result was a foregone conclusion.

Some historians argue that both the annexations and the imposition of Communism on countries occupied by the Red Army were not due to imperialist designs but to a concern for security which required the Soviet Union to surround itself as far as possible with 'friendly', or rather subservient, states. But this is a distinction without a difference, since as long as any states are not wholly subjected to the Soviet Union there can be no absolute guarantee of its security: to be perfectly effective, the 'defensive' process must continue until the whole world is under Soviet rule.

2. The new ideological offensive

AT the end of the war Soviet Russia had suffered immense casualties and was in a state of economic ruin; yet its position in the world, and consequently Stalin's personal prestige, had risen enormously. Stalin emerged from the turmoil of war as a great statesman, a brilliant strategist, and the destroyer of Fascism. Once the war was over and the Soviet conquests in Europe were assured, the dictator launched a new ideological offensive to reverse the pernicious effects of wartime 'liberalism', to teach the Russian people that the government had no intention of abating its power, and to compel those who, thanks to the war, had seen countries other than the homeland of the world proletariat to forget about such sights as quickly as possible. (A particularly drastic instance of this policy was the wholesale banishment to concentration camps of Soviet prisoners of war who had been freed and handed over by the Western Allies.) The terror and 'authenticity' of war, together with the relaxation of Marxist ideological criteria, had led to a certain cultural revival marked by the appearance of outstanding novels, for example, those of V. P. Nekrasov and A. A. Bek, as well as poems, films, and other works.

The remorseless ideological campaign that set in from 1946 onwards might be summed up in the maxim once used by Alexander II to the Poles: 'Point de rêveries!' The object was not only to restore ideological purity but to raise it to fresh heights, at the same time isolating Soviet culture from all contact with the outside world. Every form of intellectual life was affected in turn: literature, philosophy, music, history, economics, natural science, painting, architecture. The theme was the same in each case: to stop 'kowtowing to the West', to destroy every vestige of independence in thought and art, and to harness all forms of culture to the glorification of Stalin, the party, and the Soviet state.

The chief agent of this policy in 1946–8 was A. A. Zhdanov, a secretary of the Central Committee and a veteran of the war against cultural independence. It was he who, on behalf of the party, informed the All-Union Writers' Congress in August 1934 that Soviet literature was not only the greatest in the world but was the only creative and developing literature, while the whole of bourgeois culture was in a state of decay and corruption. Bourgeois novels were full of pessimism, their authors had sold out to capitalism and their heroes were mostly thieves, prostitutes, spies, and hooligans. 'The great body of Soviet authors is now fused with the Soviet power and the Party, having the aid of Party guidance and the care and daily assistance of the Central Committee and the unceasing support of Comrade Stalin.' Soviet literature must be optimistic, it must be 'forward-looking', and must serve the cause of the workers and collective farmers.

Zhdanov's first important move after the war was to attack two Leningrad literary journals, *Zuezda* (*Star*) and *Leningrad*. A resolution condemning these journals was passed by the Central Committee in August 1946. The main victims were the eminent poetess Anna Akhmatova and the humorist Mikhail Zoshchenko. Zhdanov made a speech at Leningrad in which he violently attacked both writers. Zoshchenko was a malevolent slanderer of the Soviet people: he had written a story about a monkey deciding that it would rather stay in its cage in the zoo than live at large in Leningrad, and this obviously meant that Zoshchenko wanted to reduce humanity to the level of monkeys. Even in the 1920s he had turned out unpolitical art devoid of party spirit, and had wanted nothing to do with the building of socialism: he was and remained 'a literary slum-rat, unprincipled and consciousless'. As for Akhmatova, she was a sex-crazed mystic longing for 'Catherine's good old days ... It would be hard to say whether she is a nun or a fallen woman; better perhaps say she is a bit of each, her desires and her prayers intertwined.' The fact that Leningrad journals printed such stuff showed that literary life was in a bad way. Many writers were imitating corrupt bourgeois literature, others were using history to escape from present-day themes, and one had even dared to parody Pushkin. The business of literature was to inspire young people with patriotism and revolutionary zeal. As Lenin had laid down, it should be political and imbued with party spirit: it should unmask the rottenness of bourgeois culture and show the greatness of Soviet man and the Soviet people, not only as they were today but as they would be in the future.

Zhdanov's clear injunctions set the course of Soviet literature for the next few years. Writers who were ideologically off-colour were forced to silence, if not worse. Even the most orthodox, like Fadeyev, revised their work to the new specifications. To be 'forward-looking' literature had, in practice, to describe the Soviet system not as it was but as ideology required it to be. This resulted in a flood of saccharine literature glorifying the party and extolling the beauties of Soviet life. The printed word was abandoned almost completely to time-servers and sycophants.

Music was not spared either. In January 1948 Zhdanov made a speech to a conference of composers, conductors, and critics, attacking the corruption of bourgeois music and calling for more of the patriotic Soviet variety. The immediate occasion was afforded by the opera *The Great Friendship* by the Georgian composer Muradeli. This work, with the best intentions, had shown the Caucasian peoples—Georgians, Lezgians, and Ossetes—as having fought the Russians directly after the Revolution, but soon becoming reconciled to the Soviet regime. Nothing of the kind, said Zhdanov: all these peoples had fought for Soviet power from the very beginning, shoulder to shoulder with the Russians. The only ones who had not were the Chechens and Ingushes, who—as Zhdanov did not mention on this occasion, but as everyone was well aware—had been deported *en masse* during the Nazi–Soviet war, while their autonomous republic was razed from the map. Not content with this example, Zhdanov launched a general attack on composers who sought inspiration in Western novelties instead of continuing the great Russian tradition of Glinka, Tchaikovsky, and Mussorgsky. Soviet music was 'lagging behind' other forms of ideology; composers were succumbing to 'formalism', departing from 'musical truth' and 'socialist realism'. Bourgeois music was anti-people, being either formalistic or naturalistic, but in any case 'idealistic'. Soviet music must serve the people: there was a need for operas, songs, and choral works, which some composers, tainted with formalism, looked down on as unimportant. Such composers looked askance at programme music, yet classical Russian music was mostly of this species. The party had already overcome reactionary and formalistic tendencies in painting and had re-established the healthy tradition of Vereshchagin and Repin, but music was still backward. The classic Russian heritage was unsurpassed, and composers must have a more sensitive 'political ear' as well as a musical one.

The results of this admonition were felt without delay. It suffices to compare Khachaturian's piano concerto, composed before Zhdanov's speech, with his violin concerto. Shostakovich, criticized for his Ninth Symphony among other works, made amends by composing an ode in praise of Stalin's forestry plan, and many other musicians repaired their ideological fences; the most favoured form of composition at this time was an oratorio in honour of the party, the state, and Stalin.

The campaign against literature and music reflected the general principles of Stalin's policy at the time, which was one of ideological intimidation and physical and moral rearmament against the eventuality of war. The doctrine was founded on a division of humanity into two camps: the corrupt and decadent world of imperialism, destined soon to collapse under the weight of its own contradictions, and the 'camp of peace and socialism', the bulwark of progress. Bourgeois culture was by definition reactionary and decadent, and anyone who looked for positive values in it was committing high treason and serving the interests of the class enemy.

3. The philosophical controversy of 1947

AFTER literature, it was the turn of philosophy to be disciplined. The occasion of the campaign was *History of West European Philosophy* by G. F. Aleksandrov, published in 1946. This was wholly orthodox in intent, full of quotations from the Marxist–Leninist classics and written in a spirit of true devotion to the party. It was a popular exposition of scant historical value, but paid ample attention to the 'class content' of the doctrines it described. The party, however, was incensed by the fact that it covered only Western philosophy and ended its survey in 1848, thus precluding a demonstration of the incomparable superiority of Russian philosophy. In June 1947 the Central Committee organized a large-scale discussion at which Zhdanov formulated directives for the benefit of philosophical writers. In the part of his speech devoted to Aleksandrov's book he declared that it showed a lack of party spirit; the author had failed to point out that Marxism represented a 'qualitative leap' in the history of philosophy and the beginning of a new era in which philosophy was a weapon of the proletariat in the struggle against capitalism. Aleksandrov suffered from corrupt 'objectivism': he had merely recorded the views of various bourgeois thinkers in a neutral spirit, instead of fighting ruthlessly for the victory of the one true, progressive Marxist–Leninist philosophy. The omission of Russian philosophy was itself a sign of deference to bourgeois tendencies. The fact that Aleksandrov's fellow philosophers had not themselves criticized these glaring defects, which were only revealed thanks to the personal intervention of Comrade Stalin, was a clear indication that all was not well on the 'philosophical front' and that philosophers were losing their Bolshevik fighting spirit.

The rules laid down by Zhdanov for future philosophical work in the Soviet

Union may be reduced to three. In the first place, it must be remembered once and for all that the history of philosophy was the history of the birth and development of scientific materialism, and of its conflict with idealism in so far as the latter had obstructed its development. Secondly, Marxism was a philosophical revolution: it had taken philosophy out of the hands of the élite and made it the property of the masses. Bourgeois philosophy had been in a state of decline and dissolution since the rise of Marxism, and was incapable of producing anything of value. The history of philosophy for the past hundred years was the history of Marxism. The compass to steer by in combating bourgeois philosophy was Lenin's *Materialism and Empiriocriticism.* Aleksandrov's book showed a spirit of 'toothless vegetarianism', as though the issue were not the class struggle but some kind of universal culture. Thirdly, the 'question of Hegel' had already been settled by Marxism and there was no need to return to it. In general, instead of digging about in the past philosophers should attend to the problems of socialist society and concern themselves with contemporary issues. In the new society there was no longer any class struggle, but there was still a fight of the old against the new; the form of this battle, and thus the motive force of progress and the chosen instrument of the party, was criticism and self-criticism. Such was the new 'dialectical law of development' of progressive society.

All the chief members of the 'philosophical front' took part in the debate, echoing the party directives and thanking Comrade Stalin for his creative contribution to Marxism and for correcting the errors of Soviet philosophy. Aleksandrov performed the ritual self-criticism, acknowledging that his work contained serious mistakes, but consoled by the fact that his colleagues had supported Comrade Zhdanov's criticism; he vowed unshakeable fidelity to the party, and promised to mend his ways.

During the debate Zhdanov opposed the idea of a special journal for philosophy (*Under the Banner of Marxism* had ceased publication three years before), arguing that the party monthly *Bolshevik* covered the ground perfectly well. Finally, however, he relented and agreed to the creation of *Problems of Philosophy*, the first number of which appeared shortly afterwards and contained a stenographic report of the debate. The first editor was V. M. Kedrov, who specialized in the philosophy of natural science and was a man of deeper culture than most Soviet philosophers. However, he committed the grave error of publishing in the second number of the journal an article by the eminent theoretical physicist M. A. Markov entitled 'The Nature of Physical Cognition', which defended the views of the Copenhagen school on the epistemological aspects of quantum physics. The article was attacked by Maksimov in the official weekly *Literary Gazette*, and Kedrov lost his post in consequence.

The 1947 debate left no room for doubt as to what Soviet philosophers were to write about and in what manner: the style of Soviet philosophy was thus fixed for many years. Zhdanov did not confine himself to repeating Engels's formula, which had long been paramount in Stalin's Russia, that the 'content' of the history of philosophy was the conflict between materialism and idealism. Under the new doctrine, its true content was the history of Marxism, i.e. the works of Marx, Engels, Lenin, and Stalin. In other words, it was not the business of historians of philosophy to analyse bygone theories or even elucidate their class origins: their studies must be teleological and wholly devoted to proving the superiority of Marxism–Leninism over all that had gone before, while 'unmasking' the reactionary functions of idealism. In writing about Aristotle, for instance, they had to show that he had 'failed to understand' this or that (for example, the individual and universal dialectic) or had 'wavered' reprehensibly between idealism and materialism. The effect of Zhdanov's formula was virtually to eliminate all differences between philosophers. There were materialists and idealists and those who 'wavered' or were 'inconsistent', and that was the end of it. Anyone who read the philosophical publications of those years would get the firm impression that the whole of philosophy consisted of the two rival assertions 'matter is primary' and 'spirit is primary', the former view being progressive and the latter reactionary and superstitious. St. Augustine was an idealist and so was Bruno Bauer, and the reader was left to suppose that their philosophies were more or less identical. Without quoting long extracts it would be hard to bring home the incredible primitiveness of the Soviet philosophical output of those years to anyone who has not examined it. In general historical studies went to the wall: scarcely any books on the history of philosophy were published, nor were translations of philosophical classics, except for Aristotle's *Analytics* and Lucretius' *De Rerum Natura*. The only history that was acceptable was that of Marxism or of Russian philosophy. The former consisted of diluted expositions of the four classics, while the latter was concerned with the 'progressive contribution' of Russian philosophy and its superiority to the Western brand: thus there were articles and booklets showing how Chernyshevsky outclassed Feuerbach and extolling Hertsen's dialectic, Radishchev's progressive aesthetics, Dobrolyubov's materialism, etc.

The ideological purge did not, of course, spare the study of logic, the position of which in Marxism–Leninism had been doubtful from the beginning. On the one hand, Engels and Plekhanov had spoken of the 'contradictions' inherent in all movement and development, and it appeared from their formulas that the principle of contradiction, and hence formal logic in general, could not claim universal validity. On the other hand, none of the classics had condemned logic unequivocally, and Lenin had enjoined that it be taught at the elementary level. Most philosophers took it for granted that 'dialectical logic' was a higher form of thought and that formal logic 'did not apply' to phenomena of movement; it was not clear, however, in what way and to what extent this 'restricted' logic was admissible. Philosophical writers unanimously condemned 'logical formalism', but none of them could explain the exact difference between this and 'formal logic', which was tolerated within narrow limits. In the late forties elementary logic was taught in the higher forms of secondary schools and in philosophical faculties; some textbooks also appeared, one by the jurist Strogovich and another by the philosopher Asmus. Apart from the ideological trimmings these were old-fashioned manuals, which scarcely went beyond Aristotelian syllogistics and ignored modern symbolic logic: they resembled the textbooks used in nineteenth-century high schools. Asmus's work, however, was violently attacked for lack of party spirit and for being apolitical, formalistic, and deficient in ideology: these criticisms were made in a debate organized by the Ministry of Higher Education in Moscow in 1948. The chief ground for the charge of neglecting politics was that in giving examples of syllogistic reasoning Asmus chose 'neutral' propositions devoid of militant ideological content.

Modern logic was a sealed book to the philosophers; it was not completely ignored, however, thanks to a small group of mathematicians, who concentrated on technical problems and took care not to get involved in philosophical discussions, which could only have spelt disaster to them. Thanks to their efforts translations of two excellent books on symbolic logic were published in 1948: Alfred Tarski's *Introduction to Mathematical Logic* and *The Foundations of Theoretical Logic* by Hilbert and Ackermann. Articles in *Problems of Philosophy* by otherwise unknown authors denounced these works as an 'ideological diversion'. Some improvement in this sphere was brought in 1950 by Stalin's essay on philology, as the defenders of logic invoked it to support their view that logic, like language, was classless, i.e. there was not a bourgeois and a socialist form of logic but a single one valid for all mankind. The status of formal logic and its relation to dialectical logic was debated several times in and after the Stalin era. Some maintained that there were two kinds of logic, formal and dialectical, which applied to different circumstances, the former representing a 'lower level of cognition'; others held that only formal logic was logic in the true sense and that it did not conflict with the dialectic, which provided other, non-formal rules of scientific method. As a whole, the attacks on 'formalism' contributed to depressing the general level of logical studies in the U.S.S.R., which was already extremely low.

Soviet philosophy reached its nadir in the last years of Stalin's rule. Philosophical institutions and periodicals were run by people whose only qualifications were servility, tale-bearing, and similar services to the party. The textbooks of dialectical and historical materialism that saw the light during those years are lamentable in their intellectual poverty. Typical examples are

Historical Materialism, edited by F. V. Konstantinov (1951) and *An Outline of Dialectical Materialism* by M. A. Leonov (1948): Leonov disappeared from circulation when it was discovered that his book was largely cribbed from the unpublished manuscript of another philosopher, F. I. Khaskhachikh, who was killed in the war. Other members of the 'philosophical front' besides those mentioned earlier were D. Chesnokov, P. Fedoseyev, M. T. Yovchuk, M. D. Kammari, M. E. Omelyanovsky (who, like Maksimov, was especially on the look-out for idealism in physics), S. A. Stepanyan, P. Yudin, and M. M. Rozental: these last two writers compiled an authoritative *Concise Dictionary of Philosophy* which ran through several editions and revisions.

It is safe to say that throughout the Stalin era there did not appear in the Soviet Union a single book on philosophy worth mentioning for its own sake and not merely as a pointer to the state of intellectual culture at the time, nor is there any philosophical writer whose name deserves to be recorded.

It should be added that in this period there were institutional mechanisms that cleansed philosophical works of all original ideas and all individuality of style. Most books were discussed before publication by one philosophical group or another, and it was the participants' duty to show party vigilance by pouncing on even the most timid attempts to exceed the bounds of the catechism in force. Sometimes several such operations were practised on the same text, and the result was that all the books were virtually identical. Leonov's case, mentioned above, is remarkable inasmuch as it might be thought that plagiarism could never have been detected, so closely did the authors' styles resemble one another.

4. The economic debate

At the same time as Zhdanov was dealing with the philosophers, economic science also underwent an ideological purge. The occasion was afforded in this case by Varga's book, published in 1946, on the effects of the Second World War on the capitalist economy. Jenő Varga (1879–1964), an eminent economist of Hungarian origin, had lived in the Soviet Union since the fall of Béla Kun's short-lived Communist republic and was the director of the Institute for World Economy, the purpose of which was to observe trends and predict crises in the capitalist system. In his book he sought to examine the permanent changes that the war had brought to the capitalist economy. It had obliged the bourgeois states to introduce a degree of economic planning and had vastly increased the functions of the state, especially in Britain and the U.S.A. The question of outlets for production had ceased to be decisive, and the struggle for markets was no longer a key factor in international affairs; the export of capital, however, had taken on greater importance. It was to be expected that overproduction in the U.S.A. and wartime destruction in Western Europe would combine to bring about a crisis situation which capitalism would seek to cure by the large-scale export of American capital to Europe. Varga's theories were debated in May 1947 and again in October 1948. His critics, and particularly K. V. Ostrovityanov, the chief economist of the Stalin era, accused him of believing that planning was possible under capitalism, of divorcing economics from politics, and of ignoring the class struggle. He had failed to perceive the general crisis of capitalism and, instead of emphasizing the power of capital over the bourgeois state, had made the mistake of supposing that the state was in control of capital. In addition Varga was accused of cosmopolitanism, kowtowing to Western science, reformism, objectivism, and underestimation of Lenin. The string of accusations was a conventional one, but the gist of Varga's book was indeed inimical to Stalinist ideology. His conclusion that capitalism had at its disposal more and more ways of remedying crisis situations, instead of fewer and fewer, was manifestly contrary to Lenin's teaching and to the party line for the past three decades, which held that the contradictions of capitalism were becoming more acute every day and that the universal crisis was more and more intense. Varga did not perform self-criticism after the first debate, but he finally did so in 1949; he was dismissed from his main functions, and the journal he edited was closed down. He was rehabilitated after Stalin's death, however, and repeated and developed his theses in a book published in 1964, in which he criticized Stalin and the dogmatic inability of Stalin's ideologists to recognize facts that conflicted with preconceived schemata. In a manuscript that was not published in Russia but reached the West after his death he went further still, maintaining that Lenin's plan of building socialism in Russia had proved a failure and that the bureaucratization of the Soviet system was in part due to Lenin's false prognoses.

5. Marxism–Leninism in physics and cosmology

A PARTICULARLY blatant example of aggressive Stalinism was the ideological invasion of the natural sciences. Apart from mathematics, which was left unscathed, the campaign of Marxist regimentation affected all branches of science in some degree: theoretical physics, cosmology, chemistry, genetics, medicine, psychology, and cybernetics were all ravaged by the interference which reached its peak in 1948–53.

Soviet physicists, for the most part, were not anxious to engage in philosophical discussions, but in some spheres they were unavoidable: neither the quantum theory nor the theory of relativity could be fully expounded without bringing out certain epistemological assumptions. The question of determinism, and that of the effect of observation on the object observed, obviously had philosophical bearings, and this was recognized in discussions throughout the world.

Soviet Russia and Nazi Germany were the two countries in which the theory of relativity was attacked and proscribed as contrary to official ideology. In the Soviet Union, as we have seen, the campaign started before the Second World War, but it was intensified in the post-war years. In Germany the indisputable argument against it was that Einstein was a Jew. In Russia this point was not raised, and the critics based their opposition on the teaching of Marxism–Leninism that time, space, and motion were objective and that the universe was infinite. Zhdanov in his address to the philosophers in 1947 inveighed against the disciples of Einstein who declared that the universe was finite. The philosophical critics also argued that, since time was objective, the relation of simultaneity must be absolute and not dependent on the frame of reference as the special theory of relativity maintained. In the same way motion was an objective property of matter, and therefore the path of a moving body could not be partly determined by the system of co-ordinates (an argument that of course applied against Galileo as well as Einstein). In general, since Einstein made temporal relations and movement dependent on the 'observer', i.e. on the human subject, he must be a subjectivist and thus an idealist. The philosophers who took part in these debates (A. A. Maksimov, G. I. Naan, M. E. Omelyanovsky, and others) did not confine their criticism to Einstein but attacked the whole of 'bourgeois science', their favourite targets being Eddington, Jeans, Heisenberg, Schrödinger, and all known methodologists of the physical sciences. Had not Einstein, moreover, admitted that he got his first ideas about relativity from Mach, whose obscurantist philosophy had been demolished by Lenin?

However, the essential point of the debate (which also touched, but only in a secondary fashion, on the general theory of relativity and the question of the homogeneity of space) did not reside in any 'contradiction' between the content of Einstein's theory and Marxism–Leninism. Marxist doctrine on time, space, and motion was not so precise that it could not be reconciled with Einsteinian physics without any special logical difficulty. It was even possible to contend that the relativity theory was a confirmation of dialectical materialism: this line of defence was adopted, in particular, by V. A. Fock, an eminent theoretical physicist, who at the same time produced scientific arguments for thinking that Einstein's theory was of limited validity. The campaign against Einstein—and indeed against most of the main achievements of modern science— had, however, two basic motives. In the first place, 'bourgeois versus socialist' meant practically the same as 'Western versus Soviet'. The state doctrine of Stalinism embraced Soviet chauvinism and demanded the systematic rejection of all the important achievements of 'bourgeois' culture, especially those dating from after 1917 when only one country in the world was the source of progress, while capitalism was in a state of decay and disruption. In addition to Soviet chauvinism there was a second motive. The simplistic doctrine of Marxism–Leninism coincided at many points with the common-sense everyday ideas of uneducated people: it was to these, for instance, that Lenin chiefly appealed in his attack on empiriocriticism. The theory of relativity, on the other hand, was undeniably to some extent an assault on common sense. The absoluteness of simultaneity, extension and motion, and the uniformity of space, are assumptions of everyday life that we accept as a matter of course, and Einstein's theory violated these in the same way as Galileo's paradoxical assertion that the earth revolves round the sun. Thus Einstein's critics were not only speaking for Soviet chauvinism but also for the ordinary conservatism that rejects theories inconsistent with the plain evidence of our senses.

The fight against 'idealism in physics' was also waged, with similar motives, against the quantum theory. The epistemological interpretation of quantum mechanics accepted by the Copenhagen school found favour with some Soviet physicists. The debate was triggered off by M. A. Markov's article of 1947, already mentioned. Markov followed Bohr and Heisenberg on two basic points which aroused the hostility of Marxist–Leninist philosophers. In the first place, as it is impossible simultaneously to measure the position and the momentum of microparticles, it is meaningless to say that a particle *has* a definite position and a definite momentum and that only a defect of observational technique prevents our measuring both at once. This point of view was in accord with the general empiric attitude of many physicists: the only real properties of objects are those that are empirically detectable, and to say that an object has a certain property but that there is no possibility of ascertaining it is either self-contradictory or meaningless. It must therefore be accepted that the particle does not have, simultaneously, a definite position and momentum, but that one or the other of these is attributed to it in the process of measurement. The second point of disagreement concerned the possibility of a literal description of the behaviour of micro-objects, which have different properties from macro-objects and therefore cannot be characterized in language evolved to describe the latter. Thus, according to Markov, theories describing microphysical phenomena are inevitably a translation into macrophysical terms: so that the microphysical reality that we know and can speak of meaningfully is partly constituted by processes of measurement and the language used to describe them. It followed that physical theories could not be spoken of as furnishing a copy of the universe under observation, and also, though Markov did not expressly say this, that the whole concept of reality, at least as far as microphysics was concerned, was inescapably relativized in respect of cognitive activity—which was manifestly contrary to Lenin's theory of reflection. Markov, therefore, was denounced by the new editors of *Problems of Phi-*

losophy as an idealist, an agnostic, and a follower of Plekhanov's theory of 'hieroglyphs', refuted by Lenin.

It should be emphasized that, unlike the theory of relativity, quantum mechanics really were hard to reconcile with materialism and determinism in the Marxist–Leninist sense. If it is meaningless to say that particles have certain unascertainable physical parameters which define their status, the doctrine of determinism seems untenable; if the very presence of certain physical properties presupposes the presence of measuring devices used to detect them, it becomes impossible to apply meaningfully the concept of an 'objective' world observed by physics. These problems are by no means imaginary: they were and are discussed by physicists quite irrespective of Marxism–Leninism. In the Soviet Union they were debated rationally by D. I. Blokhintsev and V. A. Fock, among others, and the discussion continued into the post-Stalinist era. In the sixties, when party ideologists had less say in determining the 'correctness' of scientific theories, it became clear that most Soviet physicists took the indeterminist view, including Blokhintsev, who had previously held out for latent parameters.

In general the so-called discussions of the Stalin period on the philosophical aspects of physics and other sciences were destructive and anti-scientific not because they treated of unreal problems but because in the confrontation–as was usually the case–of scholars on the one hand and party ideologists on the other, the latter were assured of victory by the support of the state and its police apparatus. Charges of advancing theories inconsistent, or suspected of inconsistency, with Marxism–Leninism could and sometimes did turn into charges under the criminal code. The great majority of ideologists were ignorant of the points at issue and skilled only in ferreting out statements at variance with the words of Lenin or Stalin. Scientists who did not believe that Lenin was the greatest authority in physics and all other subjects were 'unmasked' in the popular press as enemies of the party, the state, and the Russian people. The 'debate' often degenerated into a political witch-hunt; the police were brought into play, and the resulting condemnations had nothing to do with rational argument. Almost all branches of modern knowledge underwent this treatment, and the party authorities regularly backed the noisy ignoramuses against scholars and scientists. If the term 'reactionary' has any meaning, it is hard to think of a more reactionary phenomenon than Marxism–Leninism in the Stalin era, which forcibly suppressed everything new and creative in science and in every other form of civilization.

Chemistry was not spared either. The years 1949–52 witnessed attacks in philosophical journals, and also in *Pravda*, against structural chemistry and the resonance theory, propounded in the 1930s by Pauling and Wheland and accepted by some Soviet chemists, but now denounced as idealistic, Machist, mechanistic, reactionary, etc.

Still more sensitive ideological themes were involved in debates on the philosophical aspects of modern theories of cosmology and cosmogony, from which it appeared that all existing answers to the basic questions were unfavourable to Marxism–Leninism. Various theories of an expanding universe were hard to accept because they inevitably involved the question 'How did it start?' and suggested that the universe as we know it was finite and had a beginning in time. This in turn gave support to creationism (an inference accepted by many Western authors), and nothing worse could be imagined from the point of view of Marxism–Leninism. The supplementary theory that, while the universe went on expanding, the density of matter remained the same because new particles kept on coming into existence involved a process of constant creation *ex nihilo* and was thus contrary to the 'dialectic of nature'. Hence Western physicists and astronomers who argued for either of these two hypotheses were automatically written off as defenders of religion. The alternative theory of a pulsating universe, according to which the cosmos passes through alternative phases of expansion and contraction, was free from troublesome implications as regards a beginning in time, but it conflicted with the Marxist–Leninist doctrine of the unidirectional evolution of matter. A pulsating universe was a 'cyclic' one and could not be said to 'develop' or 'progress', as the 'second law of the dialectic' required. The dilemma was a difficult one: the unidirectional principle seemed to involve the idea of creation, while the opposite theory was contrary to the principle of 'endless development'. Those who took part in the cosmological discussions were, on the one hand, astronomers and astrophysicists (V. A. Ambartsumian, O. Y. Schmidt), who arrived at their conclusions by scientific methods and then tried to show that they were consonant with dialectical materialism, and, on the other, philosophers who judged the issue in terms of ideological orthodoxy. That the universe was unlimited by time and space, and that it must 'develop' eternally, were philosophical dogmas from which Marxism–Leninism could not possibly depart. In this way Soviet philosophers under the party's aegis dragooned men of learning in every field and did enormous harm to the cause of Soviet science.

6. Marxist–Leninist genetics

OF all the battles between Marxism–Leninism and modern science, the dispute over genetics attracted most attention in the outside world. The way in which the official state doctrine was used to solve the problem of heredity, and the destructive effect of the 'debate' generally, were indeed especially blatant. In the case of relativity and the quantum theory the champions of orthodoxy succeeded in holding up research and in obtaining certain condemnations, but they did not bring about the complete destruction of the opposition and the official and absolute prohibition of the theories complained of, as happened in the case of genetics.

We have already mentioned the pre-war phase of Lysenko's activity. The matter came to a climax in August 1948, at a debate in the Lenin Academy of Agricultural Sciences in Moscow. Here the 'Mendelist–Morganist–Weissmannists' were finally condemned and Lysenko's view endorsed by the party's Central Committee, as he himself announced to the meeting. His doctrine, which the party declared to be the only one consistent with Marxism–Leninism, was that heredity was 'ultimately' determined by environmental influences, so that in certain conditions traits acquired by individual organisms in the course of their lives could be inherited by their progeny. There were no genes, no 'unchanging substance of heredity', no 'fixed unalterable species', and there was in principle nothing to prevent science, especially Soviet science, from transforming existing species and creating new ones. Heredity, according to Lysenko, was merely a property of an organism consisting in the fact that it needed particular conditions in which to live and reacted in a particular way to its environment. An individual organism in the course of its life interacted with environmental conditions and turned them into characteristics of its own that could be transmitted to its progeny—which might in turn lose those characters or acquire new ones transmissible by heredity, as external conditions might determine. The adversaries of progressive science, who believed in an immortal hereditary substance, claimed in opposition to Marxism that mutations were subject to uncontrollable accident; but, as Lysenko argued at the Academy session, 'science is the enemy of chance' and is bound to assume that all processes of life are subject to rule and can be governed by human intervention. Organisms formed a 'unity with their environment', and therefore there was no limit in principle to the possibility of influencing an organism through its environment.

Lysenko presented his theory in the first place as a development of the ideas and experiments of the agronomist Michurin (1855–1935), and secondly as an example of 'creative Darwinism'. Darwin had gone wrong in so far as he did not recognize 'qualitative leaps' in nature and regarded the intra-species struggle (survival of the fittest) as the main factor in evolution; but he had explained evolution in purely causal terms, not resorting to teleological interpretations, and had brought out the 'progressive' character of evolutionary processes.

As to the empirical basis of Lysenko's theory, biologists today have no doubt that his experiments were scientifically worthless and were either faultily conducted or interpreted in a purely arbitrary manner. This, of course, did not affect the debate in the slightest. Lysenko emerged from the 1948 session as the unquestioned leader of Soviet biological sciences: the few disciples of idealistic, mystic, scholastic, metaphysical, bourgeois, formal genetics were irrevocably crushed. All institutions, journals, and publishing enterprises concerned with biology were put under the authority of Lysenko and his helpers, and for many years there was no question of any defender of the chromosome theory of heredity (*ex hypothesi* a Fascist, racist, metaphysician, etc.) being allowed to speak in public or appear in print. 'Creative Michurinist biology' reigned supreme, and the press was flooded with propaganda extolling Lysenko and denouncing the wicked plots of the Mendelist–Morganists. The glorious triumph of Soviet science was celebrated at innumerable meetings and congresses. The philosophers, of course, at once joined in the campaign, organizing sessions and passing resolutions against bourgeois genetics and writing a multitude of articles hailing the victory of progress over reaction. Humorous journals pilloried the adherents of idealistic genetics, and a song was written in praise of Lysenko, 'marching firmly in Michurin's traces and foiling the deceits of the Mendelist–Morganists'.

Lysenko's career continued for some years after 1948. Meanwhile, under his direction, some steppe areas were planted with forest belts to protect the fields against erosion, but the experiment proved a complete failure. In 1956, during the partial ideological thaw after Stalin's death, as a result of pressure from scientists he was removed from the presidency of the Academy of Agricultural Sciences. Some years later he was restored to his various posts owing to Khrushchev's favour, but not long afterwards, to the general relief, he finally disappeared from the scene. The losses that Soviet biology suffered from his ascendancy are incalculable.

7. General effect on Soviet science

THE Lysenko affair illustrates the considerable degree of fortuitousness in the history of the regime's battle with culture. It is easy to see that ideology was much more clearly involved in questions of cosmogony than in the matter of the inheritance of acquired characters. The theory that the universe had a beginning in time is hard to reconcile with dialectical materialism, but this is not obviously the case with the chromosome theory of heredity, and one can easily imagine Marxism–Leninism triumphantly proclaiming that this theory resoundingly confirmed the immortal ideas of Marx–Engels–Lenin–Stalin. Yet in fact the ideological struggle was especially acute in the case of genetics, and it was here that the party's intervention took its most brutal form, whereas the agitation over cosmogony was much milder. It is hard to find any logical explanation of the difference: much depended on accident, on who was in charge of the campaign, whether Stalin was interested in the point at issue, and so on.

Nevertheless, if we take a panoramic view of the history of those years we may perceive a certain gradation of ideological pressure, corresponding roughly to the hierarchy of the sciences established by Comte and Engels. Pressure was almost zero in mathematics, fairly strong in cosmology and physics, stronger still in the biological sciences, and all-powerful in the social and human sciences. The chronological order roughly reflected these degrees of importance: the social sciences were regimented from the outset, while biology and physics were not controlled until the last phase of Stalinism. In the post-Stalin era it was physics that first regained its independence; biology followed after a certain time, while the humanistic sciences remained under fairly strict control.

The fortuitous element in ideological supervision can also be seen in the case of psychology and the physiology of the higher nervous functions. The special feature here was that Russia was the birthplace of Ivan P. Pavlov, a scientist of world repute. Pavlov, who died in 1936, had several pupils who continued his experiments and were allowed to develop his theories independently of ideological pressure. Typically, the regime went to the opposite extreme and erected his theory into an official dogma from which physiologists and psychologists were forbidden to deviate. It is safe to say that if Pavlov had been British or American his ideas would have been sternly condemned by Soviet philosophers as mechanistic on the ground that they explained mental functions by conditioned reflexes: he would have been accused of 'reducing' the human mind to the lowest forms of nervous activity, ignoring the 'qualitative difference' between men and animals, and so forth. As it was, Pavlov's theory officially represented Marxism–Leninism in the field of neurophysiology, and the ideological invasion in this field was less devastating than elsewhere. None the less, the very fact that a theory, albeit based on serious scientific experiment, was erected into a state and party dogma inevitably had a cramping effect on further research.

A particularly astonishing example of ideology running counter to the interests of the Soviet state was the attack on cybernetics, the science of systems of control of dynamic processes. Cybernetic studies had made a major contribution to the development of automation in all technical fields and especially in military technology, economic planning, etc., yet the champions of Marxist–Leninist purity were able for a time completely to hold up the progress of automation in the Soviet Union. In 1952–3 a campaign was mounted against the imperialist 'pseudo-science' of cybernetics. There were indeed real philosophical or semi-philosophical problems involved: whether and how far social life could be described in cybernetic categories, in what sense mental activities were 'reducible' to cybernetic schemata, or, conversely, in what sense certain functions of artificial mechanisms could be equated with thought, and so on. But the real ideological danger was that cybernetics was a discipline of wide scope, developed in the West and claiming, rightly or wrongly, to be a *mathesis universalis*, a general all-embracing theory of dynamic phenomena: for this was precisely what Marxism–Leninism claimed to be. According to unofficial reports (not, of course, confirmed by any public information), it was the military who finally put a stop to the campaign against cybernetics, as they realized the practical importance of the subject and were strong enough to combat the obscurantist attacks which were damaging the fundamental interests of the Soviet state.

8. Stalin on philology

In the first few days of the Korean War, when international tension was at its height, Stalin added to his existing titles as the leader of progressive humanity, the supreme philosopher, scientist, strategist, etc., the further distinction of being the world's greatest philologist. (As far as is known, his linguistic attainments were confined to Russian and his native Georgian.) In May 1950 *Pravda* had published a symposium on the theoretical problems of linguistics and especially the theories of Nikolay Y. Marr (1864–1934). Marr, a specialist in the Caucasian languages, had endeavoured towards the end of his life to construct a system of Marxist linguistics and was regarded in the Soviet Union as the supreme authority in this field: linguists who rejected his fantasies were harassed and persecuted. His theory was that language was a form of 'ideology' and, as such, belonged to the superstructure and was part of the class system. The evolution of language took place by 'qualitative leaps' corresponding to qualitative changes in social formations. Before mankind developed spoken language it used the language of gesture, corresponding to the primitive classless society. Spoken language was a feature of class societies, and in the classless community of the future it would be replaced by a universal thought-language (of which, to be sure, Marr was unable to give much account). The whole theory showed signs of paranoid delusion, and the fact that it ranked for years as linguistic science *par excellence* and the only 'progressive' philological theory is eloquent testimony to the state of Soviet culture.

Stalin intervened in the debate with an article published in *Pravda* on 29 June, followed by four explanatory answers to readers' letters. He roundly condemned Marr's theory, declaring that language was not part of the superstructure and was not ideological in character. It was not part of the base either, but was directly 'linked' with creative forces. It belonged to society as a whole and not to particular classes: class-determined expressions were only a small fraction of the general vocabulary. Nor was it true that language developed by 'qualitative leaps' or 'explosions': it changed gradually, as some features died out and new ones came into being. When two languages competed the result was not a new composite language but the victory of one or other. As to the future 'withering-away' of language and its replacement by thought, Marr was fundamentally wrong: thought was linked with language and could not exist without it. People thought in words. Stalin took occasion to repeat the Marxist theory of the base and superstructure, making clear, firstly, that the base does not consist of productive forces but of relations of production, and secondly, that the superstructure 'serves' the base as its instrument. He went on to condemn in strong terms the monopoly position that Marrism had acquired by the suppression of free discussion and criticism—an 'Arakcheyev regime' (alluding to the despotic minister of Alexander I's reign) under which learning obviously could not develop properly.

The proposition that language was not a class matter and not part of the superstructure meant simply that French capitalists and French workers both speak French, and that the Russians went on speaking Russian after the Revolution. This discovery was hailed as a historic breakthrough in the history of philology and of other sciences. A wave of academic sessions and debates swept through the country, glorifying the new work of genius. In reality, although Stalin's remarks were no more than sensible truisms they served a useful purpose by clearing away Marr's absurdities, and they were of some benefit to the study of formal logic and semantics: advocates of these subjects could claim that they too were not part of the superstructure and that pursuing them did not necessarily turn one into a class enemy. As for Stalin's remarks about the 'auxiliary function' of the superstructure in relation to the base, these were a repetition of the basic doctrine, already well known to all, that culture in socialist countries was the handmaiden of 'political objectives' and must not lay claim to independence. It need hardly be said that Stalin's call for free discussion and criticism had no effect whatever in other cultural fields. The Marrists were ousted from the domain of linguistics (though it is not known that they suffered police repression), while elsewhere things remained as before.

9. Stalin on the Soviet economy

STALIN's last theoretical work was an article in the party journal *Bolshevik* in September 1952, entitled 'Economic Problems of Socialism in the U.S.S.R.' and intended as a basic document for the forthcoming Nineteenth Congress. Its main theoretical argument was that socialism too was subject to the 'objective laws of economics', of which advantage should be taken in planning and which could not be arbitrarily set aside. In particular the law of value applied under socialism—a statement which probably meant that money was in use in the Soviet Union, and that in running the economy account should be taken of profitability and the balancing of revenue and expenditure. The principle of the 'objectivity of the economic laws of socialism' was an implied condemnation of Nikolay Voznesensky, who was head of the State Planning Commission before the war and afterwards deputy Premier and a member of the Politburo. He had been shot as a traitor in 1950, and his book on the Soviet economy during the war with Germany was withdrawn from circulation. By implication it denied that socialism was subject to objective economic laws, maintaining instead that all economic processes were subordinate to the state's planning power. Stalin, however, in his defence of the law of value assured his readers that whereas capitalism was governed by the principle of maximum profit, the guiding rule of the socialist economy was the maximum satisfaction of human needs. (It was not clear how, as Stalin contended, the beneficent effect of socialism could be an 'objective law' independent of the will of the state planning authorities, and in particular how this 'law' could operate simultaneously with the 'law of value'.) Stalin's article also outlined a programme for the transition of the Soviet Union to the communist stage: for this it would be necessary to do away with the opposition between town and country and between physical and mental work, to raise collective farm property to the status of national property (i.e., in effect, to turn the collective farms into state farms), and to increase production and the general level of culture.

Stalin's thoughts on the perfect communist society of the future were a repetition of traditional Marxist motifs. As to the 'objective laws of economics', the only practical message that could be derived from the article was, apparently, that while those responsible for the economy endeavoured to satisfy the population's needs to the maximum, they should not lose sight of economic accountability.

10. General features of Soviet culture in Stalin's last years

THE peculiarities of Soviet cultural life at this period were not simply due to Stalin's idiosyncrasies. They might be summed up in a word by saying that the nation's culture was that of a parvenu—its every feature expressing almost to perfection the mentality, beliefs, and tastes of someone enjoying power for the first time. Stalin himself exemplified these peculiarities in a high degree, but they were also characteristic of the whole governing apparatus, which, while he reduced it to serfdom, continued to support him and maintain his supreme authority.

After successive purges and the extermination of the Bolshevik old guard and the former intelligentsia, the Soviet governing class consisted mainly of individuals of worker and peasant origin, very poorly educated and with no cultural background, athirst for privilege and filled with hatred and envy towards genuine 'hereditary' intellectuals. The essential trait of the parvenu is his incessant urge to 'make a show', and accordingly his culture is one of make-believe and window-dressing. A parvenu has no peace of mind as long as he sees about him representatives of the intellectual culture of the former privileged classes, which he hates because he is shut out from it, and which he therefore decries as bourgeois or aristocratic. The parvenu is a fanatical nationalist, wedded to the notion that his native country or milieu is superior to all others. His language is, in his eyes, 'language' *par excellence* (he generally knows no other), and he endeavours to convince himself and everyone else that his meagre cultural resources are the finest in the world. He detests anything that smacks of the *avant-garde*, cultural experimentation, or creative novelty. He lives by a restricted set of 'common-sense' maxims and is furious when they are challenged by anyone.

These features of the parvenu mentality can be recognized in the essential traits of Stalinist culture: its nationalism, the aesthetics of 'socialist realism', and even the system of power itself. The parvenu combines a peasant-like subservience to authority with an overmastering desire to share in it; once raised to a certain level in the hierarchy he will grovel to his superiors and trample on those beneath him. Stalin was the idol of parvenu Russia, the incarnation of its dreams of glory. The parvenu state must have a pyramid of power and a leader who is worshipped even while he scourges his subordinates.

As we have seen, Stalinist cultural nationalism developed gradually in the pre-war years, and after victory it took on gigantic proportions. In 1949 the Press launched a campaign against 'cosmopolitanism', a vice that was not defined but evidently entailed being anti-patriotic and glorifying the West. As the campaign developed, it was intimated more and more clearly that a cosmopolitan was much the same thing as a Jew. When individuals were pilloried and had previously borne Jewish-sounding names, these were generally mentioned. 'Soviet patriotism' was indistinguishable from Russian chauvinism and became an official mania. Propaganda declared incessantly that all important technical inventions and discoveries had been made by Russians, and to mention foreigners in this context was to be guilty of cosmopolitanism and kowtowing to the West. The *Great Soviet Encyclopedia*, published from the end of 1949 onwards, is an unsurpassed example of this half-comical and half-macabre megalomania. The historical section of the article on 'Motor Cars', for example, starts by saying that 'In 1751–2 Leonty Shamshugenkov (q.v.), a peasant in the Nizhny Novgorod province, constructed a self-propelling vehicle operated by two men.' 'Bourgeois', i.e. Western, culture was constantly attacked as a hotbed of corruption and decadence. Here, for example, is an extract from the entry on Bergson.

> French bourgeois philosopher—idealist, reactionary in politics and philosophy. B.'s philosophy of intuitionism, disparaging the role of reason and science, and his mystical theory of society serve as a basis for imperialist policies. His views present a

glaring picture of the decay of bourgeois ideology in the imperialist age, the grow-ing aggressiveness of the bourgeoisie in the face of increasing class contradictions and its fear of the intensified class struggle of the proletariat . . . In the period of the incipient general crisis of capitalism and the intensification of all its contradictions B. appeared as a rabid enemy of materialism, atheism and scientific knowledge, an enemy of democracy and the liberation of the toiling masses from class oppression, disguising his philosophy with pseudo-scientific trimmings . . . B. sought to present as a 'new' justification of idealism the view of ancient mystics and medieval theolo-gians, long since disproved by life, practice and science, concerning cognition by 'inner vision' . . . Dialectical materialism refutes the idealist theory of intuition by the indisputable fact that knowledge of the world and reality does not take place by some kind of supersensual means but through the socio-historical practice of humanity . . . B.'s intuitionism expresses the fear of the imperialist bourgeoisie before the inevitably looming collapse of capitalism, the urge to escape from the irrefutable implications of the scientific knowledge of reality and especially the laws of social development discovered by Marxist–Leninist science . . . An enemy of national sovereignty, B. advocated bourgeois cosmopolitanism, the rule of world capitalism, bourgeois religion and morality. B. favoured the cruel bourgeois dicta-torship and terrorist method of stifling the workers. Between the First and Second World Wars this militant obscurantist argued that imperialist wars were 'necessary' and 'beneficial' . . .

Here, again, is a portion of the entry on 'Impressionism':

Decadent trend in bourgeois art in the second half of the 19th century. I. was the result of the incipient decay of bourgeois art (see *Decadence*) and the break with pro-gressive national traditions. The adherents of I. advocated an empty, anti-popular programme of 'art for art's sake', rejected the truthful, realistic depiction of objective reality and claimed that the artist should record only his primary subjective impres-sions. . . . The subjective-idealist attitude of I. is related to the principles of contem-poraneous reactionary trends in philosophy–neo-Kantianism, Machism (q.v.) etc., which denied objectivity and the reliability of knowledge, divorced perception from reality and reason from impressions . . . Rejecting the criterion of objective truthful-ness, indifferent to mankind, social phenomena and the social functions of art, the adherents of I. inevitably produced works in which the picture of reality disintegrated and artistic form was lost . . .

The isolation of the Soviet Union from world culture was almost complete. Apart from a few propaganda works by Western Communists the Soviet reader was kept in total ignorance of what the West was producing in the way of nov-els, poetry, plays, films, not to speak of philosophy and the social sciences. The rich stores of twentieth-century painting in the Hermitage at Leningrad were kept in cellars so as not to corrupt the honest citizen. Soviet films and plays unmasked bourgeois scholars who served the cause of war and imperialism, and praised the unexampled joys of Soviet life. 'Socialist realism' reigned supreme: not, of course, in the sense of presenting Soviet reality as it actually was—that would have been crude naturalism and a kind of formalism—but in the sense of educating Soviet people to love their country and Stalin. The 'socialist realist' architecture of the period is the most permanent monument to Stalinist ideology. Here too the ruling principle was the 'primacy of content over form', though no one could explain how these were distinguished in architecture. The effect, in any case, was to produce pompous façades in a style of exaggerated Byzantinism. At a time when scarcely any dwellings were being built and millions of people in large and small towns were living in crowded squalor, Moscow and other cities were adorned with huge new palaces full of false columns and spurious ornament, of a size proportionate to the 'magnificence of the Stalin era'. This again was a typical parvenu style of architecture, which could be summed up in the motto: 'Big is beautiful.'

The keystone of the whole ideology was the cult of the Leader, which took on grotesque and monstrous forms at this period and has probably never been surpassed in history except by the later cult of Mao Tse-tung. Poems, novels, and films glorifying Stalin poured out in a constant stream; pictures and monuments of him decorated all public places. Writers, poets, and philosophers vied with one another in inventing new forms of dithyrambic worship. Children in crèches and kindergartens expressed heartfelt thanks to Stalin for their happy childhood. All the forms of popular religiosity were revived in a distorted shape: icons, processions, prayers recited in chorus, confession of sins (under the name of self-criticism), the cult of relics. Marxism in this way became a parody of religion, but one devoid of content. Here, chosen at random, is a typical exordium from a philosophical work of the time:

> Comrade Stalin, the great master of the sciences, has given a systematic exposition of the foundations of dialectical and historical materialism as the theoretical basis of Communism, in a study unsurpassed for its depth, clarity and vigour. The theoretical works of Comrade Stalin were admirably described by the Central Committee of the All-Union Communist Party (Bolsheviks) and the Council of Ministers of the USSR in an address to Comrade Stalin on his seventieth birthday: 'Great leader of science! Your classic works developing the theory of Marxism–Leninism in relation to the new age of imperialism, proletarian revolution and socialist victory in our country are a tremendous achievement of humanity, an encyclopedia of revolutionary Marxism. From these works Soviet men and women and leading representatives of the working people of all countries derive knowledge and confidence and new strength in the battle for the victory of the cause of the working class, finding in them answers to the

most burning problems of the contemporary struggle for Communism.' Comrade Stalin's brilliant philosophical work on *Dialectical and Historical Materialism* is a powerful means of knowledge and revolutionary transformation of the world and an irresistible ideological weapon against the enemies of materialism and the decaying ideology and culture of the capitalist world, doomed to inevitable overthrow. It is a new, supreme stage in the development of the Marxist–Leninist world-view . . . In his work Comrade Stalin has with unsurpassed clarity and conciseness expounded the basic features of the Marxist dialectical method and indicated their importance for the understanding of the regular development of nature and society. With the same depth, force, conciseness and party-political determination Comrade Stalin formulates in his work the basic features of Marxist philosophical materialism . . . (V. M. Pozner, *J. V. Stalin on the Basic Features of Marxist Philosophical Materialism*, 1950)

Stalin was extolled indirectly as well, through the great heroes of Russian history. Films and novels about Peter the Great, Ivan the Terrible, and Alexander Nevsky were made into tributes to his glory. (However, Eisenstein's film praising Ivan the Terrible and, at Stalin's express order, his *oprichnina* or secret police was not screened during Stalin's lifetime because it showed how the Tsar was obliged, albeit with a heavy heart, to cut off the heads of the most inveterate conspirators—even though the spectator is left in no doubt that they were double-dyed villains who merited no less, and that Ivan did the very least that could be expected of a prudent statesman.) Stalin, who was of low stature, was shown in films and plays as a tall, handsome man, considerably taller than Lenin.

The hierarchical structure of Soviet bureaucracy was seen in the fact that the cult of Stalin cast its shadow on lesser mortals. In many fields of life, though not in all, there was an individual who was known to be officially the 'greatest' in his line. Apart from the many instances in which Stalin himself held the top position—as philosopher, theoretician, statesman, strategist, economist, etc.—it was known, for example, who was the greatest painter, biologist, or circus clown. (The circus, incidentally had been ideologically reformed in 1949 by an article in *Pravda* which condemned bourgeois formalism in this domain. There were, it appeared, some performers who lapsed into cosmopolitan forms of humour, without ideological content, and tried simply to make people laugh instead of educating them to deal with the class enemy.)

During this period the falsification of history and pressure on the historical sciences reached a climax. It became the task of historians to show that the foreign policy of Tsarist Russia was essentially progressive, especially its conquests, which brought the blessings of Russian civilization to other peoples. The fourth edition of Lenin's works contained some new documents but suppressed others, including some unduly categorical remarks about the impossibility of building socialism in one country, and an enthusiastic preface to John Reed's *Ten Days That Shook the World*. Reed, who was in Petrograd during the October Revolution, had much to say about Lenin and Trotsky but did not mention Stalin at all, so that it was an unpardonable *gaffe* of Lenin's to commend his book to the world. The new edition also omitted, almost in their entirety, some very valuable historical comments and notes whose authors had perished in the purges. (This method of re-editing the past did not come to an end on Stalin's death: a few months later, when Beriya was put to death by the new leaders, subscribers to the *Great Soviet Encyclopedia* found a note in the next volume telling them to excise certain earlier pages with a razor blade and insert the new pages that accompanied the note. On turning up the place referred to, the reader found that it was the article on Beriya; the substitute pages, however, were not about Beriya at all but contained additional photographs of the Bering Sea.) Historical archives, without exception, were in the hands of the police, and access to them was strictly regulated, as it still is today. This often proved to be a wise measure: for instance, a woman journalist once discovered in old parish archives that Lenin's mother was of Jewish extraction, and even had the naïvety to attempt to publish this information in the Soviet Press.

This atmosphere naturally bred all kinds of scientific impostors who proclaimed their achievements in suitably patriotic language. Lysenko was the most famous, but there were many others. A biologist named Olga Lepeshinskaya announced in 1950 that she had succeeded in producing live cells from inanimate organic substances, and this was acclaimed by the Press as a proof of the superiority of Soviet science over the bourgeois kind. Soon, however, all her experiments turned out to be valueless. After Stalin's death a still more sensational article appeared in *Pravda* to the effect that a machine had been constructed in a Saratov factory which gave out more energy than it consumed—thus finally disposing of the second law of thermodynamics and at the same time confirming Engels's statement that the energy dispersed in the universe must also be concentrated somewhere (in the Saratov factory, to be specific). Soon afterwards, however, *Pravda* had to publish a shamefaced recantation—a sign that the intellectual atmosphere had already changed.

The written and spoken word faithfully reflected the atmosphere of Stalin's day. The purpose of public utterances was not to inform, but to instruct and edify. The Press contained only reports glorifying the Soviet system or discrediting the imperialists. The Soviet Union was immune not only from crime but from natural disasters: both were the unhappy prerogative of the imperialist countries. Virtually no statistics were published. Newspaper readers were used to gaining information from a special code that was known to all though never openly formulated: for instance, the order in which party dignitaries were named on this or that occasion was an index of how high they stood in Stalin's favour at that moment. On the face of things it might seem that 'Let us fight against cosmopolitanism and nationalism' was the same as 'Let us fight against nationalism and cosmopolitanism'; but as soon as the Soviet reader came across the latter formulation after Stalin's death he realized that 'the line had changed' and that nationalism was now the principal enemy. The language of Soviet ideology was composed of hints and not of direct statements: readers of leading articles in *Pravda* knew that their gist was usually contained in a single throwaway sentence amid the flood of clichés. It was not the content of particular statements that conveyed the meaning, but the order of words and the structure of the whole text. Bureaucratic monotony of language, an impersonal deadness, and an impoverished vocabulary became fixed canons of socialist culture. Many set phrases recurred automatically, so that from each word one could predict the next: 'the bestial face of imperialism', 'the glorious achievements of the Soviet people', 'the unshakeable friendship of the socialist nations', 'the immortal works of the classic authors of Marxism–Leninism'– countless stereotypes of this sort became the intellectual diet of millions of Soviet people.

Stalin's philosophy was admirably suited to the parvenu bureaucratic mentality, in both form and content. Thanks to his exposition anyone could become a philosopher in half an hour, not only in full possession of the truth but aware of all the absurd and nonsensical ideas of bourgeois philosophers. Kant, for instance, said it was impossible to know anything, but we Soviet people know lots of things, and so much for Kant. Hegel said that the world changes, but he thought the world consisted of ideas, whereas anyone can see that what we have around us are not ideas but things. The Machists said that the desk I am sitting at is in my head; but obviously my head is in one place and the desk in another. On these lines philosophy became the playground of every petty official, who had the satisfaction of knowing that by repeating a few common-sense truisms he had disposed of all philosophical problems.

11. The cognitive status of dialectical materialism

THE social function of 'diamat' and 'histmat', as they are familiarly called, and of Soviet Marxism–Leninism in general, consists in the fact that it is an ideology used by the governing bureaucracy to glorify itself and justify its policies, including those of imperialist expansion. All the philosophical and historical principles of which Marxism–Leninism is composed reach their culmination and final meaning in a few simple propositions. Socialism, defined as state ownership of the means of production, is historically the highest form of social order and represents the interests of all working people; the Soviet system is therefore the embodiment of progress and, as such, is automatically right against any adversary. The official philosophy and social theory are merely the self-praising rhetoric of the privileged Soviet ruling class.

We may, however, disregard the social aspect for a moment and consider dialectical materialism in its Stalinist form as a corpus of statements about the universe. Concentrating on the main aspects of 'diamat' and leaving aside the many critical remarks we have already made in connection with the views of Marx, Engels, and Lenin, we may make the following observations.

'Diamat' consists of assertions of different kinds. Some are truisms with no specific Marxist content, while others are philosophical dogmas that cannot be proved by scientific means. Others again are nonsense, while a fourth category consists of propositions that can be interpreted in different ways, and, according to their interpretation, fall into one or other of the first three classes.

Among the truisms are such 'laws of dialectic' as the statement that everything in the universe is somehow related, or that everything changes. No one denies these propositions, but they are of very little cognitive or scientific value. The former statement has, it is true, a certain philosophical bearing in other contexts, for example, the metaphysics of Leibniz or Spinoza, but in Marxism–Leninism it does not lead to any consequences of cognitive or practical importance. Everyone knows that phenomena are interconnected, but the problem of scientific analysis is not how to take account of the universal interconnection, since this is what we cannot do, but how to determine which connections are important and which can be disregarded. All that Marxism–Leninism can tell us here is that in the chain of phenomena there is always a 'main link' to be grasped. This seems to mean only that in practice certain connections are important in view of the end pursued, and others less important or negligible. But this is a commonplace of no cognitive value, as we cannot derive from it any rule for establishing the hierarchy of importance in any particular case. The same is true of the proposition that 'everything changes': cognitive value attaches only to empirical descriptions of particular changes, their nature, tempo, etc. Heraclitus' aphorism had a philosophical meaning in his day, but it soon sank into the category of common-sense, everyday wisdom.

The fact that truisms like these are represented as profound discoveries, known from no other source, led the adherents of Marxism–Leninism to proclaim that Marxism was confirmed by 'science'. Since the empirical and historical sciences are concerned generally with the fact that something changes or that it is connected with something else, it is safe to assume that each new scientific discovery will confirm the truth of 'Marxism' as thus understood.

Turning to the category of unprovable dogmas, the first of these is the main thesis of materialism itself. The analytical standard of Marxism philosophy is so low that this thesis is seldom clearly formulated, but its general implication is plain enough. As we have pointed out, the statement that 'the world is material by nature' loses all meaning if matter is defined, after Lenin's fashion, as mere 'objectivity' in abstraction from its physical properties, or, as Lenin also put it, as 'being, independent of consciousness'. For, leaving aside the fact that the concept of consciousness is thus included in the very concept of matter, the statement that 'the world is material' turns out to mean only that the world is independent of consciousness. But this, if applied to the whole universe, is manifestly false—since some phenomena, as Marxism–Leninism itself admits, are dependent on consciousness—and anyway it does not make the case for materialism, since, for example, according to religious ideas God, the angels, and devils are likewise independent of human consciousness. If, on the other hand, matter is defined by physical properties—extension, impenetrability, etc.—there is reason to think that some of these may not apply to micro-objects, which would thus prove not to be 'material'. In its earliest versions materialism assumed that all existent objects had the same properties as those of everyday life. Basically, however, its thesis was a negative one, namely that there was no reality essentially different from that which we perceive directly, and that the world was not created by a rational being. This was Engels's own formulation: the point at issue in materialism was whether or not God created the world. Clearly there can be no empirical proof that he either did or did not, and no scientific arguments can prove that God does not exist. Rationalism rejects the existence of God on the principle of the economy of thought (a principle which Lenin denied), not on the strength of any empirical information. This doctrine pre-supposes that we are only entitled to accept that something exists if experience compels us to do so. But this stipulation is itself debatable and rests on assumptions that are far from obvious. Without going into the issue here we may take note that the principle of materialism, thus reformulated, is not a scientific but a dogmatic statement. The same applies to 'spiritual substance' and the 'non-materiality of human consciousness'. Men have always known that consciousness is affected by physical processes: it did not take much scientific observation, for instance to discover that a man could be stunned by clubbing him over the head, and subsequent research into the mind's dependence on the body has added nothing essential to our knowledge on the point. Those who believe in a non-material substratum of consciousness do not maintain that there is no link between consciousness and the body (if they do, like Descartes, Leibniz or Malebranche, they have to devise complicated and artificial ways of accounting for the facts of experience): they assert only that while bodily processes can suspend the operation of the human spirit, they cannot destroy it—the body is a medium through which consciousness functions, but is not an essential condition of its functioning. This assertion cannot be proved empirically, but it cannot be disproved either. Nor is it the case, as Marxists claim, that the theory of evolution has refuted the argument for a non-material soul. If the human organism has evolved by mutation from lower forms of life, it does not logically follow that the soul does not exist. If it were so, there could not be such a thing as a consistent theory combing, on the one hand, a modern view of evolution and, on the other, a non-material substratum of consciousness, or even a teleological view of the world. But there have been several such theories, from Frohschammer through Bergson to Teilhard de Chardin, and it is far from clear that they involve any inconsistency. Christian philosophers have also found various ways of immunizing dogma from the theory of evolution, and while these may be open to objection it cannot be said that they are self-contradictory. Judged by the criteria of validity that are applied in scientific work, the materialist thesis is no less arbitrary in this respect than its opposite.

Among what I have called the nonsensical assertions of 'diamat' is the statement that impressions 'reflect' things in the sense of resembling them, as Lenin contended against Plekhanov. It is not clear what can be meant by asserting that a process taking place in the nerve-cells, or even the 'subjective' awareness of such a process, bears a 'resemblance' to those objects or processes in the outside world which, the theory informs us, are the cause of such changes in the nerve-cells. Another nonsensical statement (never specifically endorsed by Stalin, but advanced by Plekhanov and regularly repeated in expositions of Marxism) is that formal logic 'applies' to phenomena at rest, and dialectical logic to changes. This absurdity, which is not worth discussing, is simply the result of the Marxist–Leninists' ignorance and failure to understand the terms of formal logic.

Other assertions, as stated above, belong to one or other of the first three categories according to how one interprets them. Among these is the 'dialectical law' concerning 'contradictions'. If, as many Soviet textbooks inform us, this means that motion and change can be 'explained' by 'inner contradictions', it belongs to the class of meaningless statements, since 'contradiction' is a logical category denoting a relation between propositions, and it is impossible to say what is meant by 'contradictory phenomena'. (Impossible, at least, from the materialist point of view; in the metaphysics of Hegel, Spinoza, and some others who identify logical and ontological connections, the idea of Being involving a contradiction is not meaningless.) If, on the other hand, we interpret the statement as meaning that reality must be apprehended as a system of tensions and opposing tendencies, this seems to be no more than a truism with no specific consequences for scientific investigation or practical action. That many phenomena affect one another, that human societies are divided by conflict and discordant interests, that people's acts often bring about results they did not intend—these are all commonplaces, and to extol them as a 'dialectical method', the profundity of which contrasts with 'metaphysical' thinking, is only one more instance of the typical Marxist boastfulness which presents time-honoured truisms as momentous scientific discoveries imparted to the world by Marx or Lenin.

To this category also belongs the assertion, discussed in an earlier part of this work, that truth is relative. If this is no more than to say, as Engels noted, that in the history of science received opinions are often not abandoned altogether as a result of later research but that their validity is recognized as limited, there is no reason to dispute the accuracy of the statement, but it is in no way specifically Marxist. If, on the other hand, it means that 'we cannot know everything' or 'a judgement may be right in some circumstances but not in others', these again are ancient truisms. We did not, for example, need Marx's intellect to discover that rain is beneficial in time of drought but not in flood-time. This, of course, does not mean, as has often been pointed out, that the statement 'rain is beneficial' is true or false according to circumstances; it means that the statement is ambiguous. If it means 'rain is beneficial in all circumstances' it is clearly false; if it means 'in some circumstances', it is clearly true. If, however, we interpret the Marxist principle of the relativity of truth to signify that a statement, without changing its meaning, may be true or false according to circumstances, then this too belongs to the category of nonsense, assuming that, with Lenin, we take the traditional view of what constitutes truth. If, on the other hand, a 'truthful judgement' means the same as 'a judgement useful to the Communist party', then the principle of the relativity of truth once more becomes an obvious commonplace.

However, the question whether 'truth' should be understood genetically or in the traditional sense has never been clearly answered in the history of Marxism. As we saw, there are strong suggestions in Marx's works that truth should be understood as meaning 'validity' in relation to human needs. Lenin, however, was fairly explicit in his assertion of the traditional view that truth means 'conformity to reality'. Most manuals of 'diamat' follow him in this, but there are also frequent signs of the more pragmatic and political view that truth is that which 'expresses' social progress, in which case, of course, the criterion resides in pronouncements by the party authorities. The confusion is aided by the fact that Russian has two words for 'truth', *istina* and *pravda*, the former tending to express the traditional notion of that which *is*, while the latter, with moral overtones, suggests 'what is right and just' or 'what ought to be'. This ambiguity helps to blur the distinction between the traditional and the genetic concept of truth.

As to the principle of the 'unity of theory and practice', this too can be understood in different ways. Sometimes it is presented simply as a norm, signifying more or less that one should think only about matters of some practical use; in this case it does not fall into any of the above-mentioned categories, as they are not normative. Considered as a descriptive statement it may mean that people generally engage in theoretical reflection as a result of practical needs; this is true in a loose sense, but is not specifically Marxist. If, again, the unity of theory and practice means that practical success is a confirmation of the rightness of the thinking on which our actions are based, this is a criterion of truth which is acceptable as far as it goes, though it cannot be universal, since clearly in many fields of knowledge and science there is no such thing as practical verification. Finally, the principle can be understood in the specifically Marxian sense that thought is an 'aspect' of conduct and becomes 'true' by being aware of this fact. But this sense, which is examined in the chapters on Marx, Korsch, and Lukács, is practically absent from Soviet 'diamat'.

12. The roots and significance of Stalinism. The question of a 'new class'

THE debate, involving both Communists and adversaries of Communism, on the social roots and 'historical necessity' of Stalinism began soon after Stalin's death and has continued ever since. We cannot go into all its details here, but will note the principal points.

The problem of the causes of Stalinism is not the same as that of its inevitability, a question whose meaning in any case requires elucidation. Anyone who holds that every detail of history is determined by foregoing events obviously need not trouble to analyse the specific background of Stalinism, but must accept its 'necessity' as an instance of that general principle. The principle, however, is a metaphysical postulate that there is no good reason to accept. From any analysis of the course of the Russian revolution it can be seen that there was no fatal necessity about the outcome. During the Civil War there were many occasions when the fate of Bolshevik power hung by a thread, as Lenin himself bore witness, and no 'laws of history' determined what the result would be. It may be assumed that if the bullet aimed at Lenin in 1918 had been deflected by an inch or two and had killed him, the Bolshevik regime would have fallen; so it would have done if he had failed to persuade the party leaders to agree to the Treaty of Brest-Litovsk, and other such instances can easily be quoted. Speculation as to what would have happened in these hypotheses is of no importance at the present day and is bound to be inconclusive. The turning-points in the evolution of Soviet Russia—War Communism, the N.E.P., collectivization, the purges—were not due to 'historical laws' but were all consciously willed by the rulers, and there is no reason to think that they 'had to' happen or that the rulers could not have decided otherwise.

The only meaningful form in which the question of historical necessity can be put in this case is: are there rational grounds for thinking that the Soviet system, whose distinguishing features were the nationalization of means of production and the Bolshevik party's monopoly of power, could not have maintained itself by any means essentially different from those used and established by the Stalinist system of government? It can reasonably be argued that the answer to this question is in the affirmative.

The Bolsheviks achieved power in Russia on a programme of peace and land for the peasants, two slogans which were in no way specifically socialist, let alone Marxist; and the support they received was mainly support for that programme. Their objective, however, was world revolution and, when that proved unattainable, the building of socialism in Russia on the basis of single-party authority. After the devastation of the Civil War there were no active social forces other than the party which were capable of any initiative, but there was by this time the established tradition of a political, military, and police apparatus responsible for the whole life of society and especially production and distribution. The N.E.P. was a compromise between ideology and reality, arising from a recognition of the fact that the state could not cope with the economic regeneration of Russia, that attempts to regulate the whole economy by coercion were a catastrophic failure, and that help could only come from the 'spontaneous' operation of the market. The economic compromise was not meant to involve any political concessions, but to keep the power monopoly intact. The peasantry was still unsocialized, but the only force capable of initiative was the state bureaucracy: this class was the bulwark of 'socialism', and the further development of the system reflected its interests and urge for expansion. The winding-up of N.E.P. and the enforcement of collectivization were certainly not part of the design of history, but were dictated by the system and the interests of its only active element: the continuation of N.E.P. would have meant that the state and bureaucracy were at the peasants' mercy and that economic policy, including export, import, and investment plants, must largely be subordinated to their demands. We do not know, of course, what would have happened if, instead of collectivization, the state had chosen the alternative of returning to complete freedom of exchange and a market economy. The fears of Trotsky and the 'left wing' that this would have aroused political forces intent on overthrowing Bolshevik power were by no means without foundation. At the very least the bureaucracy's position would have grown weaker rather than stronger, and there was ground for believing that the building of a strong military and industrial state would have been postponed indefinitely. The socialization of the economy, even at enormous cost to the population, was in the bureaucracy's interest and in the 'logic' of the system. Stalin, the embodiment of the ruling class and of a state which had made itself virtually independent of society, performed acts which had occurred at least twice before in Russian history: he called into being a new bureaucratic caste independent of the organic divisions of society, and freed it from all subservience to the people as a whole, the working class, or, finally, the party's inherited ideology. This caste very soon destroyed all the 'Westernizing' elements in the Bolshevik movement, and used Marxist phraseology as a means of restoring and enlarging the Russian Empire. The Soviet system waged constant war against its own people, not because the latter showed much resistance, but chiefly because the ruling class needed a state of war and aggression to maintain its position. The permanent threat to the state from enemies on the look-out for the slightest weakness, foreign agents, conspirators, saboteurs, and other bogies is an ideological means of justifying the bureaucratic monopoly of power; the state of war inflicts damage on the ruling group itself, but this is part of the price of government.

We have already discussed the reasons why Marxism was a suitable ideology for this system, which was unquestionably a new phenomenon in history despite all the Russian and Byzantine traditions that are often invoked by historians and critics of Communism—the state's high degree of autonomy *vis-à-vis* the civil population, the moral and mental traits of the *chinovnik*, etc. Stalinism came into being as a continuation of Leninism, based on the Russian tradition and a suitably adapted form of Marxism. The importance of the Russian and Byzantine heritage is discussed by such writers as Berdyayev, Kucharzewski, Arnold Toynbee, Richard Pipes, Tibor Szamuely, and Gustav Wetter.

It does not follow from this that every attempt to socialize the means of production must necessarily result in a totalitarian society, i.e. one in which all organizational forms are imposed by the state and individuals are treated as state property. It is true, however, that the nationalization of all means of production and the complete subjection of economic life to state planning (however effective or ineffective that planning may be) practically amounts to a totalitarian society. If the basis of the system is that the central authority defines all the objectives and forms of the economy, and if the economy, including the work-force is subjected to over-all planning by that authority, the bureaucracy must become the only active social force and acquire undivided control over other aspects of life as well. Many attempts have been made to devise a means of socializing property without nationalizing it, by leaving the economic initiative in the hands of producers. The idea has been partially applied in Yugoslavia, but the results so far are too slight and ambiguous to give a clear picture of its success. The essential point, however, is that two mutually restrictive principles are always in play: the more economic initiative is left in the hands of particular socialized units of production, and the more independence those units enjoy, the greater will be the role of 'spontaneous' market laws, competition, and the profit motive. A form of social ownership that allowed full autonomy to production units would be a return to free-for-all capitalism, the only difference being that individual factory owners would be replaced by collective ones, i.e. producers' co-operatives. The more elements of planning there are, the more limited are the functions and competence of producers' collectives. However, the idea of economic planning has been accepted, though in different degrees, in all developed industrial societies, and the increase of planning and state intervention has meant an increased bureaucracy. The problem is not how to get rid of bureaucracy, which would mean destroying modern industrial civilization, but how to control its activity by means of representative bodies.

As far as Marx's intention is concerned, despite all the reservations that can be culled from his writings he undoubtedly believed that a socialist society would be one of perfect unity, in which conflicts of interest would disappear with the elimination of their economic basis in private property. This society, he thought, would have no need of bourgeois institutions such as representative political bodies (which inevitably gave rise to bureaucracies alienated from the public) and rules of law safe-guarding civil liberties. The Soviet despotism was an attempt to apply this doctrine in alliance with the belief that social unity can be produced by institutional means.

It would be absurd to say that Marxism was predestined to become the ideology of the self-glorifying Russian bureaucracy. Nevertheless, it contained essential features, as opposed to accidental or secondary ones, that made it adaptable to this purpose. In *Will the Soviet Union Survive Until 1984?* the Soviet historian Andrey Amalrik, who has been persecuted and imprisoned for his dissident views, compares the function of Marxism in Russia to that of Christianity in the Roman Empire. Just as the adoption of Christianity strengthened the imperial system and prolonged its life but could not save it from final destruction, so the assimilation of Marxist ideology has for a time preserved the Russian Empire but cannot avert its inevitable dissolution. One may accept Amalrik's theory in so far as it does not suggest that this was the point of Marxism from the beginning or that it was a conscious purpose of the Russian revolutionaries. Thanks to an unusual combination of circumstances, power in Russia was seized by a party professing Marxist doctrine. In order to stay in power the party was obliged successively to revoke all the promises contained in its ideology, which had no doubt been sincere in the mouths of its first leaders. The result was the creation of a new bureaucratic caste enjoying a monopoly of state power and devoted by nature to the tradition of Russian imperialism. Marxism became the prerogative of this caste and an effective instrument for the continuation of imperial policies.

In this connection many writers have discussed the question of a 'new class', i.e. whether 'class' is an appropriate designation for the governing circles of the U.S.S.R. and other socialist states. The point has been canvassed especially since the publication of Milovan Djilas's *The New Class* in 1957; but the discussion has a much longer history, some aspects of which have been noted in previous chapters. For example, Marx's anarchist critics, especially Bakunin, claimed that an attempt to organize society on the basis of his ideas must give rise to new privileged classes: the proletarians who were to replace the existing rulers would turn traitor to their own class and create a system of privileges that they would guard as jealously as their predecessors had done. This, Bakunin maintained, was inevitable because Marxism envisaged the continued existence of the state. Wacław Machajski, a Polish anarchist who wrote chiefly in Russian, drew far-reaching consequences from a modified version of this idea. He argued that Marx's idea of socialism specifically expressed the interests of intellectuals who hoped to attain a position of political privilege by means of the inherited social privilege of knowledge, which they already possessed. As long as the intelligentsia were able to give their children advantageous opportunities of acquiring knowledge there could be no question of equality, which was the essence of socialism. The working class, which was at present at the mercy of intellectuals, could only achieve its ends by depriving them of their chief capital, namely education. This argument, which to some extent recalled the syndicalism of Sorel, was based on the fairly obvious fact that in any society where there is both inequality of income and a strong correlation between education and social status, the children of the educated classes have a better chance than others of rising in the social hierarchy. This hereditary inequality could only be cured by destroying the continuity of culture and separating children from their parents in order to give them a completely uniform education: so that Machajski's Utopia would sacrifice both civilization and the family on the altar of equality. There were Russian anarchist groups who also detested education as a source of privilege. Machajski had followers in Russia, and for some years after the October Revolution the fight against his views was a recurrent propaganda theme: they were linked, not without cause, with 'syndicalist deviation' and the activities of the 'workers' opposition'.

The problem of the development of a new class under socialism was, however, also raised from another point of view. Some, like Plekhanov, argued that an attempt to build socialism before economic conditions were ripe for it must end in a new form of despotism. Others, like Edward Abramowski, spoke of the prior necessity of a moral transformation of society. They contended that the struggle for privilege of various kinds was bound to recur under a system of nationalized ownership, if Communism took over a society that had not been morally reformed and was still pervaded by the needs and ambitions inculcated by the old order. As Abramowski wrote in 1897, Communism in such conditions could only lead to a new class structure in which the old divisions were replaced by antagonism between society and a privileged bureaucracy, and which could only maintain itself by an extreme form of despotism and police rule.

Critics of the October Revolution pointed out from the beginning that a new system of privilege, inequality, and despotism was burgeoning in Russia; the term 'new class' was used by Kautsky as early as 1919. When Trotsky in exile developed his critique of the Stalinist regime he insisted, as did all orthodox Trotskyists after him, that there was no question of a 'new class' but only of a parasitical bureaucracy. He attached great importance to this distinction, even after coming to the conclusion that the regime could not be overthrown without a revolution. The economic basis of socialism, namely, public ownership of the means of production, was, he maintained, unaffected by the bureaucratic degeneration: consequently, there was no need for a social revolution, which had already taken place, but only for a political one which would sweep away the existing apparatus of government.

Trotsky, his orthodox followers, and other Communist critics of Stalinism denied the existence of a 'new class' on the ground that the privileges of the Soviet bureaucracy were not transmitted automatically from one generation to another, and that the bureaucrats did not personally own the means of production but only exercised collective control over them. This, however, turns the argument into a question of words. If 'class' is defined in such a way that one can only speak of a ruling and exploiting class when each of its members has a legal title, transmissible by inheritance, to the ownership of certain productive resources of society, then of course the Soviet bureaucracy is not a class. But it is not clear why the term should be restricted in this way. It was not so restricted by Marx. The Soviet bureaucracy has at its collective disposal all the productive resources of the state, though this fact is not embodied in any legal document but is simply a basic consequence of the system. Control over the means of production is essentially no different from ownership if the collective possessor is irremovable under the existing system and cannot be legally challenged by any rival. Since the owner is collective there is no individual inheritance, and no one can bequeath to his children a particular position in the political hierarchy. In practice, however, as has often been described, privilege is systematically inherited in the Soviet state. The children of the ruling group are clearly privileged from the point of view of opportunities in life and access to restricted goods and advantages of various kinds, and the group itself is very well aware of its superior position. The political monopoly and the exclusive control of means of production support each other and could not exist separately. The high incomes of the ruling group are a natural consequence of its exploiting role, but are not the same as exploitation itself, which consists in the right to dispose freely, without any control by the public, of the whole mass of surplus value which that public creates. The public has no say as to how or in what proportion resources are divided between investment and consumption, or what is done with the goods that are produced. From this point of view the Soviet class division is much more rigid and less sensitive to social pressure than any capitalist system of ownership, since in Russia there is no way in which different sections of society can express and pursue their interests through administrative and legislative bodies. True, the position of individuals in the hierarchy depends on the will and caprice of their superiors, or, in the palmy days of Stalinism, on the pleasure of a single despot. In this respect their position is not wholly secure: the situation is more like an Oriental despotism, where people in the higher ranks were equally at the tyrant's mercy and might be dismissed or executed from one day to the next. But it is not clear why this state of affairs should preclude the observer from speaking of a 'class', still less why it should be considered typically 'socialist' and a proof of the immense superiority of socialism to 'bourgeois democracy', as Trotsky's adherents claim. Djilas in his book drew attention to the variety of privileges enjoyed by the socialist ruling class, emphasizing that the monopoly of power was the basis of these privileges and not a consequence of them.

With the above qualifications, there is no reason why the socialist bureaucracy should not be termed an 'exploiting class'. Indeed, the description appears to be used increasingly often, and Trotsky's distinctions are seen to be more and more artificial.

James Burnham, after breaking with Trotsky, wrote in 1940 his celebrated book *The Managerial Revolution*, in which he argued that the establishment of a new class in Russia was only a particular instance of a universal process that was occurring and would continue to develop in all industrial societies. Capitalism, he thought, was going through the same evolution: formal property rights meant less and less, and power was gradually passing into the hands of those who actually controlled production, i.e. the managing class. This was an inevitable consequence of the nature of modern industry. The new élite was simply the present-day form of the division of society into classes, and class divisions, privilege, and inequality were natural phenomena of social life. Throughout history the masses had been used, under various ideological banners, to overthrow the privileged classes of the day; the result, however, was only to replace them with new masters who at once set about oppressing the rest of society no less efficiently than their predecessors. The despotism of the new class in Russia was not an exception, but an illustration of this universal law.

Whether or not Burnham was right in saying that all social life entailed despotism in some form, his remarks are far from an adequate description of Soviet reality. The rulers of post-Revolutionary Russia were and are not the industrial managers but the political bureaucracy. The former, of course, are an important section of society, and groups of them may be strong enough to affect decisions by higher authority, especially in their own fields. But the key decisions, including those on industrial investment, imports, and exports, are political and are taken by the political oligarchy. It is very implausible to suggest that the October Revolution is a special case of the transference of power to managers as a result of progress in technology and work organization.

The Soviet exploiting class is a new social formation which in some ways resembles the bureaucracy of Oriental despotisms, in others the class of feudal barons, and in others again the capitalist colonizers of backward countries. Its position is determined by the absolute concentration of political, economic and military power, to an extent never before seen in Europe and by the need for an ideology to legitimize that power. The privileges its members enjoy in the field of consumption are a natural consequence of its role in society. Marxism is the charismatic aura with which it invests itself in order to justify its rule.

13. European Marxism during the last phase of Stalinism

The history of Marxism in the countries which fell under Soviet control as a result of the war can be roughly divided into four phases. In the first phase, from 1945 to 1949, the 'people's democracies' still exhibited elements of political and cultural pluralism, which were gradually subdued by Soviet pressure. The second phase, from 1949 to 1954, saw the complete or almost complete *Gleichschaltung* of the 'socialist camp' as regards politics and ideology, and the far-reaching Stalinization of all aspects of culture. In the third phase, beginning in 1955, the most striking feature as far as the history of Marxism is concerned was the emergence of various 'revisionist', anti-Stalinist trends, chiefly in Poland and Hungary but later also in Czechoslovakia and to some extent in East Germany. This period effectively came to an end in about 1968, when, in most of the bloc countries at least, Marxism took on a petrified and sterile form, while remaining the official ideology of the ruling party.

The 'Stalinization' and 'de-Stalinization' of Eastern Europe proceeded in a different fashion in each country, in accordance with varying circumstances. In the first place, some of them—Poland, Czechoslovakia, Yugoslavia—had been on the Allied side in the war, while others were officially tied to the Axis. Poland, Czechoslovakia, and Hungary, which belonged historically to Western Christianity, had different cultural traditions from Romania, Bulgaria, and Serbia. East Germany, Poland, and Czechoslovakia had a tradition of serious philosophical studies dating back to the Middle Ages, which was lacking in other bloc countries. Finally, in certain countries there had been an active underground and guerrilla movement during the war, while in others, likewise under German occupation, the resistance was feeble and did not take the form of an armed struggle. In the former category were Poland and Yugoslavia, with the important difference that in Yugoslavia the Communists were the most active fighters whereas in Poland they were a small fraction of the total resistance movement, the backbone of which consisted of forces owing allegiance to the London Government. All these differences had an important bearing on postwar events in Eastern Europe and the evolution of Marxism in the respective countries: they affected the speed and depth of the ideological invasion and the manner in which Stalinism was later rejected. The only country whose liberation from the German invader was due in large measure to its own, Communist-controlled forces was Yugoslavia, and it was only there that the Communists exercised undivided power from 1945 onwards. Elsewhere—in Poland, East Germany, Czechoslovakia, Romania, and Hungary—social democratic or peasant parties were allowed to function during the initial post-war years.

It is quite possible that many of the East European Communist leaders believed at first that their countries would be independent states, building up socialist institutions in alliance with Russia but not under its direct control. Such illusions, however, were short-lived. For the first two years international relations were marked by traces of the wartime alliance: the Communist parties maintained a show of fidelity to the Yalta and Potsdam agreements, which provided for democratic institutions, multi-party governments, and free elections in Eastern Europe. The onset of the cold war, however, put a stop to any hopes that the area might develop independently of the Soviet Union. In 1946–8 the non-Communist parties were destroyed or forcibly 'united' with the Communists, the first to suffer this fate being the East German social democrats. From the beginning, even when there were still genuine elements of a coalition government, the Communists entrenched themselves in key positions of power, especially the police and army. Ubiquitous Soviet 'advisers' had the final say in key questions of government, and directly organized the most savage and blatant forms of repression. In 1949, after the programmed suppression of the non-Communist parties, after elections marked by fraud and violence and after the *coup* in Czechoslovakia, the East European Communists under Stalin's close control enjoyed virtually exclusive power. Yet at the very time when Stalinism was thus establishing itself in the satellite countries it met with its first serious defeat in the form of the Yugoslav schism.

One of the instruments used by Stalin to exact obedience from the ruling Communist parties of Eastern Europe, and from Communists elsewhere, was a weakened version of the Comintern known as the Communist Information Bureau or 'Cominform'. Set up in September 1947 (the Comintern had been dissolved in 1943), this body comprised representatives of all the ruling Communist parties of Eastern Europe except the Albanian and East German—i.e. the Soviet, Polish, Czechoslovak, Hungarian, Romanian, Bulgarian, and Yugoslav parties—as well as the French and Italians. Its orchestrator, under Stalin, was Zhdanov, and it was by his orders, for instance, that the Yugoslavs attacked the French and Italian Communists for not seizing power in their countries at the favourable juncture of 1944–5. (Their conduct had in fact been dictated by Stalin, but they nevertheless performed the appropriate self-criticism.) The Cominform's function was to transmit to Communists throughout the world the behests of Soviet policy disguised as unanimous resolutions of the principal parties. There were indeed signs that some East European parties really believed themselves entitled to act as sovereign governments: Czechoslovakia and Poland displayed a rash interest in the Marshall Plan, and Bulgaria and Yugoslavia put forward a plan for Balkan federation. All such displays of independence were swiftly crushed and the offending parties called to order. At a time when a third world war was at least not unthinkable, Communists outside the Soviet Union must again be taught that there was only one authority determining 'correct' policy and that the slightest deviation from its orders would have unpleasant consequences.

At the first session of the Cominform Zhdanov described the division of the world into two political blocs as the key factor in the international situation. The Cominform also launched an international journal, of course dominated by the Soviet Communist party, as a vehicle for the latter's propaganda directives. This journal was indeed the Cominform's chief activity: it held only two more sessions, in June 1948 and November 1949, both for the purpose of condemning the Yugoslavs. Friction between the Soviet and Yugoslav parties began in the spring of 1948; its immediate cause was the annoyance of Tito and his colleagues at the crude and arrogant interference of Soviet 'advisers' in Yugoslav internal affairs, especially the army and police. Stalin, outraged by this lack of internationalism, attempted to bring Yugoslavia to heel and no doubt thought it would be an easy task. In propaganda activity the Yugoslavs had until then shown extreme subservience to Russia; but they were masters in their own house, and it turned out that the Soviet Union was very poorly represented there. (One of the main bones of contention was the recruitment of Yugoslavs to the Soviet police and espionage network.) Apart from some individuals who were directly on the Soviet payroll the Yugoslavs had no thought of yielding, and the only way to reconvert them to internationalism appeared to be by armed invasion, which Stalin, rightly or wrongly, considered too risky a course.

The Yugoslav party was officially condemned at the second session of the Cominform, from which Yugoslavia's delegates were absent. The Belgrade leaders were declared to be anti-Soviet nationalists (on grounds that were not explained), and Communist Yugoslavs were called on to overthrow the 'Titoist clique' if it did not immediately toe the line. The quarrel with Yugoslavia became the main theme of the Cominform journal, and at the third and last session of that body Gheorghiu Dej, the Romanian party secretary, made a speech on 'the Yugoslav' Communist party in the grip of murderers and spies'.

From this it appeared that all the Yugoslav leaders had from time immemorial been agents of various Western intelligence services, that they had established a Fascist regime, and that their main policy was and always had been to stir up trouble for the Soviet Union and serve the interests of American warmongers. Taking their cue from this, the Communist parties of the world unleashed a hysterical anti-Yugoslav campaign. A macabre result of the schism was that the 'people's democracies' staged a series of judicial murders, clearly patterned on the Moscow show trials, to purge the local Communist parties of 'Titoist' or suspect elements. Many leading Communists fell victim to these trials, which took place in Czechoslovakia, Hungary, Bulgaria, and Albania. In Czechoslovakia the main trial, that of Slánský and others, took place in November 1952, shortly before Stalin's death, and was distinguished by clear overtones of anti-Semitism. This theme also came to the fore in the Soviet Union during Stalin's last years, culminating in the arrest, in January 1953, of a group of doctors, nearly all Jews, who were accused of plotting to murder party leaders and others; those of them who survived the tortures personally ordered by Stalin were released immediately after his death. In Poland Gomulka, the party secretary, and other prominent figures were imprisoned but were not tried or executed; some lesser functionaries were shot or subsequently done to death in prison. In East Germany arrests and trials followed the general pattern, though their victims were less well known. In the remainder of the bloc 'Titoists', 'Zionists', other imperialist agents, and Fascists who had 'wormed their way' into the party secretaryship or the Politburo confessed to being hirelings of foreign intelligence and were for the most part executed after show trials. It should not be supposed that all the victims were really 'Titoists' in the sense of wanting a Communist regime less dependent on Russia. This was true of some, but others were cast as traitors for arbitrary reasons. The general purpose was to terrorize the East European ruling parties and teach them what Marxism, Leninism, and internationalism really meant: namely, that the Soviet Union was absolute master of the nominally independent bloc countries, and that the latter must obediently execute its commands.

Despite the ferocity with which all forms of pressure except armed invasion were brought to bear, the Yugoslavs maintained their independence and made the first substantial breach in Stalinist Communism since the war. Immediately after the schism the Yugoslav party ideology differed from the Soviet only in emphasizing that Communist parties must be independent and condemning Soviet imperialism; the general principles of Marxism–Leninism remained in force in Yugoslavia and were no different from those observed in the Soviet Union. Before long, however, the bases of political doctrine underwent revision also and the Yugoslavs set out to create their own model of a socialist society, differing in important ways from the Russian one.

The Cominform by this time was little more than an instrument of anti-Yugoslav propaganda, and its *raison d'être* disappeared when, in the spring of 1955, Khrushchev decided to make peace with Belgrade; it was not actually dissolved, however, until April 1956. Since then, as far as is known, the Soviet party has not tried to create any institutionalized forms of international Communism but has contented itself with exercising, as far as possible, direct control over individual parties and from time to time calling conferences to adopt resolutions on world topics. These, however, have had less success than formerly: despite all their efforts the Soviet leaders have not managed to secure international condemnation of the Chinese Communist party in the same way as they did in the case of Yugoslavia.

The last years of Stalin's rule were marked by the Sovietization of doctrine throughout the Communist world. The effects of this varied from one bloc country to another, but the pressures and trends were generally the same.

Polish Marxism, as we have seen in earlier chapters, had its own tradition, quite independent of the Russian one. There was no single orthodox form of this tradition and no precise party ideology; Marxism was only one feature, and not a very important one, in the Polish intellectual scene. However, there were historians, sociologists, and economists who, while not professing any cut-and-dried doctrine, made some use of Marxist categories in their work; among these were Ludwik Krzywicki and Stefan Czarnowski (1879–1937), an eminent sociologist and historian of religion, who in his last years gravitated towards Marxism to some extent. (In an essay on proletarian culture he analysed the origins of a new mentality and a new type of art specifically related to the situation of the working class.) In the first years after 1945 these traditions were revived: the new Marxist thought, like the old, was not confined to any precise channels but appeared rather as a background to rationalism and to the habit of analysing cultural phenomena in terms of social conflict. This loose, uncodified Marxism was voiced by journals including the monthly *Myśl współczesna* (*Contemporary Thought*) and the weekly *Kuźnica* (*The Forge*). In 1945–50 the universities were re-created on pre-war lines and mostly with the same teaching staff; there were as yet no ideological purges in the educational field; many scientific books and journals published at this time had nothing to do with Marxism. The regime did not yet call itself a 'dictatorship of the proletariat', and the party ideology did not stress Communist themes but patriotic, nationalist, or anti-German ones. Soviet-type Marxism was very much in the background at this period; its chief spokesman was Adam Schaff, who wrote books and manuals expounding the Leninist–Stalinist version of dialectical and historical materialism, though these were in a less primitive style than their Soviet counterparts. Even in the worst years, it may be said in general that Marxism in Poland did not descend to the Soviet level: despite the encroachment of Russian models it retained some degree of originality and a timid respect for the canons of rational thought.

In 1945–9 political and police repression became more intense. For about two years after the war there was armed conflict with survivors of the underground army who had fought the German invader and refused to surrender to the new regime imposed by Russia. Persecution and frequent bloodshed marked the struggle against armed underground units and wartime political organizations, as well as against the peasant party and other legal non-Communist groups. Nevertheless, cultural pressure at this time was confined to purely political questions; Marxism was not yet enjoined as a compulsory standard in philosophy or the social sciences, and 'socialist realism' in art or literature was unknown.

In 1948–9 the party purged itself of 'right-wing nationalists'; the leadership was changed, political life was adjusted to Soviet norms, rural collectivization was decided on (though never carried out to any extent), and the regime was officially declared to be a form of proletarian dictatorship. In 1949–50 the political house-cleaning was followed by the Sovietization of culture. Many academic and literary journals were closed down, and others were given new editors. In the early fifties some 'bourgeois' professors were dismissed: the number, however, was not large, and although prevented from teaching or publishing they still drew their salaries and wrote books which they were able to publish a few years later, when times were less severe. Some members of philosophical faculties were left in their jobs but ordered to confine themselves to teaching logic; others again were given posts under the Academy of Sciences, where they did not come into contact with students. The curriculum of social science departments was revised, and chairs of sociology were replaced by chairs of historical materialism. A special party institute was set up to train cadres to take the place of 'bourgeois' professors in the ideologically sensitive departments of philosophy, economics, and history. In philosophy the organ of the Marxist 'offensive' was the journal *Myśl Filozoficzna* (*Philosophical Thought*). For a time Marxist philosophers concentrated on combating the non-Marxist tradition, especially the Lwów–Warsaw school of analytical philosophy: Kotarbiński, Ajdukiewicz, Stanislaw Ossowski, Maria Ossowska, and others. Many books and articles criticized various aspects of the tenets of this school. Another target was Thomism, which had a lively tradition centred on the Catholic University of Lublin. (This university—a fact unparalleled in the history of socialist states—was never suppressed and functions to this day, despite various measures of pressure and interference.) Many Marxists of the older and younger generation—Adam Schaff, Bronislaw Baczko, Tadeusz Kroński, Helena Eilstein, Władysław Krajewski—took part in these battles; so did the present author, who does not regard the fact as a source of pride. Another subject of study was the Marxist contribution to Polish culture in past decades.

The time is not ripe for a full appraisal of the cultural developments of those years, but it can be said that the enforced 'Marxification' had some redeeming features. Intellectual life certainly became poor and sterile, but the dissemination of Marxism led to some advantages despite the coercion that accompanied it. Besides destructive and obscurantist elements it introduced other features that were of intrinsic value and are to a greater or lesser extent part of the world's intellectual patrimony: for example, the habit of envisaging cultural phenomena as aspects of social conflict, of emphasizing the economic and technical background of historical processes and generally studying phenomena in terms of broad historical trends. Some new directions in humanistic studies, though ideologically motivated, led to valuable results, for example, in regard to the history of Polish philosophy and social thought. Useful work was done in publishing translations of philosophical classics and republishing standard works of Polish social, philosophical, and religious thought.

In the Stalinist years the state was quite generous in subsidizing culture, so that a good deal of rubbish was produced but also much work of permanent value. The general standard of education and access to universities soon rose considerably as compared with before the war. What was destructive was not universal instruction in Marxism but its use as an instrument of coercion and political mendacity. Marxism, even in a primitive and stereotyped form, still served in some measure to implant fruitful and rational ideas that were part of its tradition; but the seeds could only thrive in proportion as the oppressive uses of the doctrine were relaxed.

On the whole Stalinism in the strict sense did less harm to Polish culture than to that of the other bloc countries, and the harm it did was less irrevocable. There were several reasons for this. In the first place there was a spontaneous though largely passive cultural resistance and a deep-rooted distrust or hostility towards everything that came from Russia. There was also a certain half-heartedness or inconsistency about the imposition of Stalinist culture: Marxism never enjoyed an absolute monopoly of humanistic studies, and attempts to exert pressure on the biological sciences in Soviet style were weak and ineffective. The campaign for 'socialist realism' produced some worthless apologetics but did not destroy literature and the arts; the purges in institutions of higher learning were on a comparatively small scale; the proportion of prohibited books in libraries was lower than elsewhere. Moreover, cultural Stalinism in Poland was comparatively short-lived: it began in earnest in 1949-50, and was already declining in 1954-5. It is possible, though hard to prove, that another moderating factor was at work, namely the ill will that many veteran Communists felt towards Stalin, who had destroyed the pre-war Polish Communist party and murdered its leaders.

In the other countries under Soviet suzerainty, cultural Stalinization was for various reasons more thorough and more destructive. East Germany was under direct Soviet occupation, and the combination of Stalinism with the Prussian tradition produced a rigidly obscurantist atmosphere (relieved by the activity of Ernst Bloch, whom we shall discuss separately). Moreover, until 1961 it was not difficult to flee to West Germany, and among the four million who did so were many intellectuals, the loss of whom increased the desolation of their native territory. Czechoslovakia too suffered a relentless ideological purge, the consequences of which can still be felt today. For several years the cultural dictator was Zdeněk Nejedlý, originally a musical historian, who censored the arts with a heavy hand, 'emending' Czech literary classics and banning performances of works by the 'cosmopolitan' Dvořák, etc. His counterpart in Bulgaria was Todor Pavlov, a typical Marxist dilettante and pretender to omniscience, who wrote on biology, literature, philosophy, and other subjects; his best-known work, published before the war and translated into Russian, was a treatise on Leninist epistemology entitled *The Theory of Reflection*. The term 'reflection' was used here in a global sense to denote every kind of influence that one thing can exert on another, from mechanical causation onwards; human acts of perception and abstract thought were merely a special case of this 'reflection' at the highest level of the organization of matter. It happened that Mikhalchev, a veteran professor of philosophy at Sofia, had been a pupil of Rehmke (d. 1930), a German empiriocriticist of the second rank; hence for many years the chief task of Bulgarian Marxist philosophers was to 'combat Rehmkianism'.

In Hungary Marxism was in a stronger position from the beginning, thanks to some eminent philosophers of the older generation: J. Révai, B. Fogarasi, and G. Lukács. Révai was for some time the party representative in charge of Stalinizing Hungarian culture. Lukács was in a doubtful position throughout this period, though his books and articles during the last years of Stalinism were of irreproachable orthodoxy except for his book on Hegel, written before the war and published in German in 1948: this was completely un-Soviet in style and by no means conformed to the Stalin–Zhdanov formula.

In Western Europe the position of Marxists was somewhat different. All the Communist parties, it is true, obediently supported Stalin's line at any given time, glorifying Soviet policy and preaching the cult of the Leader; but neither in France, Britain, nor Italy did the Soviet pattern completely dominate Marxist theoretical writing on philosophy and the historical sciences. The deviation, however, was less in respect of content than of style and the method of argument.

In France the Communist movement developed with great impetus in the first few years after 1945. From the outset of the cold war the party maintained a tough attitude in major political and parliamentary affairs, sabotaging every government move irrespective of merits; in regional and municipal affairs, however, their policy was skilful and flexible. At the same time they developed elaborate and exclusive forms of cultural life on rather similar lines to those of the German social democrats before the First World War. The party ran many periodicals, including the theoretical journal *Pensée*, and numbered in its ranks many eminent men and women of national reputation: writers such as Aragon and Éluard, painters such as Picasso and Léger, scientists such as the Joliot–Curies. All this lent the Communist movement considerable prestige. A fair amount of philosophical literature was produced, some of it purely Stalinist, especially the party monthly *Nouvelle Critique*. This journal, for instance, launched a campaign against psychoanalysis, which was then a subject of increasing interest in France. Most of the contributors, as was to be expected, condemned it as a bourgeois doctrine, idealistic and mechanistic to boot, reducing social phenomena to individual psychology, and the human mind to biological impulses. Roger Garaudy, who was to be noted in the sixties as a champion of 'liberal' Communism, wrote books at this time that were purely Stalinist in content, although certainly more learned and better written than the Soviet output. One of these was *Grammaire de la liberté* (1950), arguing that the way to have freedom was to nationalize industry and abolish unemployment. In *Les Sources françaises du socialisme scientifique* (1948) Garaudy sought to prove that Communism was deeply and specifically rooted in French culture. He also wrote a book on Christianity, citing evidence of the obscurantism of the Catholic Church and its opposition to the advance of science.

A prolific writer of a somewhat different character, Henri Lefebvre, was known before the war as an anthologist of Marx and Hegel and author of books against nationalism and Fascism. In 1947 he published *Logique formelle et logique dialectique* and the interesting *Critique de la vie quotidienne;* later came a critique of existentialism (something no French Marxist philosopher in the fifties and sixties could avoid writing), then works on Descartes, Diderot; Rabelais, Pascal, Musset, Marx, and Lenin, also dissertations on painting and music. These works are all sketches rather than profound studies, but they contain original and useful observations. Lefebvre is a man of wide culture, especially in French terms; his writings are lively and ingenious, but he touches on too many themes to dwell for long on any of them. He had considerable influence on French Marxism because, among other things, he reverted frequently to Marx's early works, which Soviet Marxism practically ignored; he was particularly interested in the theme of 'total man'. It was largely thanks to Lefebvre that 'the young Marx' became a staple of French philosophy in the forties and early fifties. He also probably did most to popularize the Marxian term 'alienation', which (not that he intended this) became a favourite expression in French everyday language to designate a vaguely uncomfortable situation.

Somewhat apart from the main stream of party philosophy at this time is the work of Auguste Cornu, an outstanding historian of Marxism.

The evolution of French Marxism in the years of the break-up of Stalinist ideology was affected by the wave of Hegelianism and existentialism in the 1940s. The chief introducer of Hegel, especially the *Phenomenology of Mind*, to French readers was Alexandre Kojève, who expounded and commented on his philosophy before the war, and Jean Hyppolite. Neither was a Marxist or a Communist, but they both took a sympathetic interest in Marx's ideas and analysed them seriously, emphasizing the elements in Hegel's schemata that influenced Marx's thought. Both Kojève and Hyppolite did much to divert French philosophy from its traditional channels and interests. In particular they gave currency to the idea of Reason embodied in the historical process— an anti-Cartesian concept, since Descartes regarded history as essentially the realm of chance, outside the reach of philosophy and incapable of being rationalized except by means of consciously fictitious and artificial constructions, the *fabula mundi* as Descartes called it. In lectures published in 1947 Kojève presented the *Phenomenology* as a history of man's self-creation by dint of labouring and struggling; in the dialectic of master and servant he perceived the source of Marx's theory of the proletariat and the idea of work as the demiurge of history. Kojève and Hyppolite showed Marx's philosophy of history to be a continuation of the Hegelian dialectic of negation—evil, slavery, and alienation being the necessary means whereby mankind achieves self-understanding and liberation. Hyppolite emphasized in particular that, for Hegel as for Marx, Reason was not a transcendental observer of the world with its own rules independent of the course of history, but was itself a factor, aspect, or expression of history; and that the progress of mankind towards 'rationality' was not a matter of gradually assimilating ready-made rules of thought, but of a growing sense of community and acknowledgement of rationality in others. For that purpose it was necessary that human beings should cease to function as commodities, and this was Marx's principal message.

Sartre's existentialist philosophy, which had enormous success in France for several years after the war, was in its then form quite irreconcilable with Marxism. Sartre maintained that human existence was a vacuum of absolute freedom in an alien, inert world governed by natural determinants. This freedom was an intolerable burden from which man sought to escape, but could not do so without a breach of good faith. The very fact that my freedom is absolute and unlimited deprives me of every alibi and makes me a hundred per cent responsible for everything I do. My constant self-anticipation, in which this freedom is displayed, is the generator of time, which is the true form of human existence and which, like freedom, is the separate property of every one of us. For Sartre there is no such thing as collective, communal time, nor is there any freedom other than the natural, hopeless, and oppressive necessity for the individual to create himself without ceasing—a process in which he is unaided by God or any transcendental values, by historical tradition or by his fellow men. Since I am defined as empty freedom and pure negativity, every being outside myself appears to me as an attempt to limit my freedom. It follows that by the very nature of existence, ontologically as it were, human relations can only take the antagonistic form of attempting to annex other human beings as if they were things—and this applies in all contexts, in love as in political domination.

Clearly there was no common ground between Marxism in any form and a doctrine which precluded any notion of human community or shared time and reduced the whole of life to an irrational pursuit of one's own vacuity. Accordingly, French Communist intellectuals raised a hue and cry against existentialism. On the other hand, Sartre from an early stage sought to identify with the working class and the oppressed in general, so that his relations with the Communist party were marked by hesitation and ambiguity. He oscillated, in fact, between identification with the Communists and violent hostility towards them, in a complicated evolution that we cannot go into here. At every stage, however, he endeavoured to preserve his own reputation as a 'Leftist', and even to represent himself and his philosophy as the embodiment of 'Leftism' *par excellence*. Consequently, even when attacking the Communists and reviled by them he made a point of directing far more vehement attacks against the forces of reaction, the bourgeoisie, or the United States Government. Believing as he did that the Communist party represented the aspirations of the proletariat, with which he identified himself, he not only allied himself for a time with political Communism but hailed the Soviet Union, in the last phase of Stalinism, as humanity's best hope of liberation. His whole political activity was vitiated by fear of being in the typical situation of an intellectual condemning events that he has no power to influence; in short, his ideology was that of a politician *manqué*, cherishing unfulfilled ambitions to be on the 'inside'.

Merleau-Ponty, who collaborated with Sartre for a time, was from the outset more sceptical of Marxism and Communism, although his theory of freedom—namely, that it is always co-determined by actual situations and exists only through the obstacles it overcomes—was closer to Marxism than Sartre's idea of freedom as a vacuum. In *Humanisme et terreur* (1947) he discussed Communist terror and its possible historical justifications and argued that we can never know the full meaning of our actions because we do not know all their consequences, which are part of that 'meaning' and for which we are responsible willy-nilly; hence the historical process and our part in it are inevitably ambiguous and uncertain. It followed that violence might be historically justified if its ultimate effect was to do away with violence; but he did not lay down any rules for recognizing violence of this beneficent kind. As time went on, Merleau-Ponty became increasingly critical of Communism.

The style and content of Marxist writing in the West European countries naturally reflected their different cultural traditions. French Marxism was given to dramatic rhetoric, unctuous humanitarian phrases, and stirring revolutionary eloquence; it was impressionistic, logically untidy, but effective from the literary point of view. British Marxism preserved something of the empirical tradition: it was more down-to-earth and concerned with logical argument, better grounded in history and less fond of philosophical 'historicism'. Communism in Britain was very weak and never gained mass support among the working class; but it was not, as in some other countries, a purely intellectual movement, and always maintained links, tenuous though they might be, with the trade unions. Many intellectuals passed through the Communist party in the 1930s, and others did so after the war. Among Marxist philosophers of Communist persuasion were Maurice Cornforth and John Lewis. The former wrote a critique of logical empiricism and analytical philosophy entitled *Science versus Idealism* (1946), in which he defended the Engels–Lenin theory of knowledge and attacked 'logical atomism', the principle of the economy of thought and the reduction of philosophy to linguistic analysis. Lewis wrote, among other works, a critique of pragmatism. Benjamin Farrington made valuable contributions to history in the early post-war years, including a book on ancient Greek science in which he related philosophical doctrines to the contemporary state of technology.

While French Marxists laid stress on humanitarian phraseology and British ones on empirical and rationalist arguments, Italian Marxism, faithful to its own tradition, emphasized the note of 'historicism'. Even in the last years of Stalinism, Marxist philosophy in Italy was a long way from Leninist and Stalinist norms. In international affairs, however, the Italian Communist party, which, after the collapse of Fascism, recovered very quickly from twenty years of stagnation and inactivity, was no less submissive to the Soviet line than were comrades in other countries. Later, after 1956, Palmiro Togliatti (1893–1964) was to gain the reputation of being the most 'open-minded' of the Communist leaders and the most independent of Moscow, but there are no grounds for projecting this back into the Stalin era. At that time Togliatti faithfully conformed to every zigzag of Soviet policy; however, he had no difficulty in switching from rigid isolationism (described in party jargon as 'dogmatic', 'leftist', or 'sectarian') to the more flexible and effective 'popular front' policy. In cultural matters the Italians were generally less aggressive and abusive than Communists elsewhere, emphasizing the links between Marxism and native traditions and playing up 'positive' rather than reactionary elements in the latter. The publication in 1947–9 of Gramsci's *Notes from Prison* was a milestone in the history of Italian Communism, a source of inspiration enabling party intellectuals to accept a much more elastic version of Marxism than that permitted by the canons of Leninism. Prominent writers in the early fifties were Galvano della Volpe (1896–1968) and Antonio Banfi (1886–1957), who became Marxists and Communists fairly late in life and interpreted their new faith in the Italian spirit of universalist humanism. Della Volpe wrote a valuable book on Eckhart and a work on epistemology, *Logica come scienza positiva* (1950; 'logic' here means the theory of knowledge in general), in which he interpreted Marxism in anti-Hegelian and empiricist terms. Banfi emphasized the historical relativism of Marxism, as Labriola and Gramsci had done in Italy, or Sorel in France. On this interpretation Marxism was not so much a scientific account of the world, still less a system of metaphysics, but rather a historical expression of the current phase of man's self-creation, an articulation of the practical struggle for control over the conditions of human life.

To sum up, it may be said that the last years of Stalinism in Western Europe were not wholly fruitless as far as theoretical and historical works were concerned, but that the few books of any value (and even these would for the most part not be worth reading today for their own sake) were drowned in a flood of organized political mendacity, the blame for which rested on all Communist intellectuals of the world without exception. The French or Italian workers who joined the movement during those years generally took little interest in the Soviet system or the prospect of world revolution: they supported the party because it spoke out vigorously for their immediate claims and interests. The intellectuals, however, while they embraced Marxism and Communism as a universal doctrine, were well aware that the movement was wholly governed by Moscow and subordinated to Soviet political aims. They supported it nevertheless, and uncritically rejected all information (readily obtainable from books in the West, and from direct observation in the East European countries) that threw light on the true nature of the Soviet social system. They belauded this system whenever occasion offered, supporting it by word and deed and by their membership of the Communist parties. All of them took part in the farcical 'peace movement', which under its Orwellian title was a basic instrument of Soviet imperialism in the cold war years. All of them, without turning a hair, swallowed such fantastic inventions as the charge that the Americans were carrying on germ warfare in Korea. Any who entertained doubts of the perfection of the Soviet system told themselves that 'after all' Communism was the only, or the most effective, bulwark against Fascism, and must therefore be accepted a hundred per cent, without reservation. The psychological motives of this voluntary self-deception were various. Among them were a desperate need to believe that someone in the world embodied the age-old dreams of universal human brotherhood; the illusions of intellectuals concerning 'historical progress'; contempt for the democratic 'establishment', which in many West European countries had become thoroughly discredited between the wars; the longing for a master key to unlock all the secrets of the universe, including those of history and politics; the ambition to be on the crest of the wave of history, in other words on the winning side; the cult of force, to which intellectuals are especially prone. Desiring, as they believed, to be on the same side of the barricade as the deprived and persecuted of this world, the Communist intellectuals became the prophets of the most oppressive political system then existing, and willing agents of the huge and efficient apparatus of lies with which it sought to extend its power.

V

Trotsky

1. The years of exile

IN JANUARY 1929, after the Left Opposition in the Soviet Union had been almost entirely wiped out by repressive measures, its leader, Leon (Lev) Davidovich Trotsky, who had been in exile in Kazakhstan for a year, was deported to Turkey, where he took up his abode on Prinkipo Island in the Sea of Marmara. For a long time other countries were unwilling to admit to their territory a man reputed to be the most dangerous revolutionary in the world; during the four years he lived in Turkey Trotsky left it only once, to deliver a lecture in Copenhagen.

While in Turkey he wrote his vast *History of the Russian Revolution,* an analysis of the causes and development of the revolutionary process in which he sought to prove that history had confirmed the rightness of his predictions and especially the idea of 'permanent revolution': i.e. that the democratic revolution was bound to develop continuously into a dictatorship of the proletariat, and could only have been successful in that form. At this time he also wrote an autobiography and a huge number of articles, appeals, and letters for the purpose of supporting and developing the Left Opposition against Stalin, both in Russia and in the world at large. Within a few months of his deportation he founded a journal in Russian, the *Opposition Bulletin,* which continued to appear till the end of his life: it was published by his son, Leon Sedov, first in Germany and, after the Nazis came to power, in Paris. As with Trotsky's books in Russian, its main purpose was to promote the organization of an opposition movement in the Soviet Union; before long, however, police measures made it almost impossible to smuggle the journal into the country, and Trotsky's contacts with remnants of the Left in Russia were to all intents and purposes broken off.

At the same time Trotsky devoted a large part of his untiring energy to enlisting adherents in other countries. Small groups of dissident Communists existed here and there, and through them he hoped eventually to regenerate the Comintern and revive the spirit of true Bolshevism and Leninism in the Communist movement. These groups, under the collective title of the International Left Opposition, were active from 1930 onwards and regarded themselves as a fraction of the Comintern—an ideological fiction, since the Trotskyists had been expelled from the Comintern once and for all, and those who remained in Russia were mostly in camps and prisons. A meeting of Trotskyists from several countries was held in Copenhagen during their leader's stay there in November 1932, and a few months later a similar meeting took place in Paris. For some years Trotsky had firmly opposed the foundation of a Fourth International, as he held that Stalinism, having no social base, must collapse at any moment and that its only possible and natural heirs would be the 'Bolshevik Leninists', who would restore the Comintern to its true purpose. In 1933, however, after Hitler's accession to power, he decided that a new international revolutionary organ was necessary, and set about organizing his followers under a new banner. The Fourth International was officially set up at a congress in Paris in September 1938.

At the end of 1932 Trotsky formulated the strategy and ideology of the International Left Opposition in eleven points: (1) recognition of the independence of the proletarian party, and hence condemnation of the Comintern's policy of the 1920s in China (Communists joining the Kuomintang) and Britain (the Anglo-Russian trade union committee); (2) the international and therefore permanent character of the revolution; (3) the Soviet Union was still a workers' state despite its 'bureaucratic degeneration'; (4) condemnation of Stalin's policy, both in its 'opportunist' phase in 1923–8 and in its 'adventurist' phase in 1928–32; (5) Communists must work in mass organizations, especially trade unions; (6) rejection of the formula of the 'democratic dictatorship of proletariat and peasants' and of the possibility of its developing peacefully into a dictatorship of the proletariat; (7) the necessity for interim slogans during the struggle for the dictatorship of the proletariat, in cases where it was necessary to fight against feudal institutions, national oppression, or Fascism; (8) a united front with mass organizations, including social democrats, but not in an 'opportunist' form; (9) rejection of Stalin's theory of 'social Fascism'; (10) a distinction within the Communist movement between Marxists, the centre, and the Right; alliance with the Right against the centre (the Stalinists) was ruled out, and the centre should be supported against class enemies; (11) there should be democracy within the party.

Trotsky held to these principles until the end, but their full meaning only became clear in his more detailed analyses of the nature of the Soviet state, the concept of party democracy, and the idea of political alliances.

During his first years of exile Trotsky deluded himself that the opposition in Russia was a tremendous political force, that the Stalinist bureaucracy was increasingly losing its grip, and that the Soviet Communist party was polarizing rapidly into true Bolsheviks on the one hand and 'Thermidorians', i.e. advocates of a capitalist restoration, on the other. When it came to a clash between these two forces the bureaucracy would once more have to seek help from the Left if the Soviet system was to survive. Accordingly, Trotsky addressed letters and declarations to the Soviet leaders assuring them that the Opposition was prepared to join in the struggle against restoration and foreign intervention; he promised that he would not take revenge on his opponents, proposed an 'honourable agreement', and offered the Stalinists his aid against class enemies in the hour of mortal danger. Clearly, he imagined that when a crisis eventually came Stalin would beg him for help, and he would then name his conditions. This, however, was fantasy; Stalin and his followers had no intention of coming to terms with the Trotskyists, and would not ask them for aid under any circumstances. The Left Opposition in Russia did not gain in strength, as Trotsky thought it must by virtue of the laws of history, but was ruthlessly exterminated. When Stalin proclaimed the 'new course' of forced industrialization and collectivization the majority of oppositionists fell into line, recognizing that Stalin had taken over their policy; this applied, for example, to Radek and Preobrazhensky. Rakovsky, the most prominent Leftist after Trotsky, resisted longer than the rest, but after a few years of persecution he too capitulated. None of these ever again occupied a political post of any importance, and none escaped destruction in the Great Purge. Trotsky continued to believe that the opposition stood for the authentic forces of the proletariat as against the ruling bureaucracy, which lacked any social base; the opposition must therefore prevail in the end, and temporary defeats and persecutions could not destroy it. Repressions, he wrote, might be effective against a class condemned by history, but never against a 'historically progressive' class. In actual fact the Left Opposition vanished completely within a few years of Trotsky's exile, as a result of repression, slaughter, demoralization, and capitulation. It is true, however, that Stalin could hardly have done more to keep alive Trotsky's hopes and his belief in the potential strength of the opposition. The series of campaigns against 'Trotskyism', the show trials, and judicial murders might indeed have convinced an outside observer that 'Trotskyism' was still a powerful enemy of the Soviet state. Stalin in fact had an obsessive hatred of Trotsky and used his name as a symbol of universal evil, a stigma with which he branded adversaries of all descriptions or anyone whom he wished to destroy for any reason. In this way he coined portmanteau expressions—such as 'the Trotskyist-Rightist bloc', 'Trotskyist-Fascist', 'Trotskyist-imperialist', 'Trotskyist-Zionist'—to suit the purposes of his successive campaigns; the prefix 'Trotskyist' served much the same purpose as 'Jewish' in the mouth of anti-Semites who talk of 'the Jewish-Communist conspiracy', 'Jewish-plutocratic reactionaries', 'Jewish-Liberal corruption', etc. From the beginning of the thirties 'Trotskyism' had no specific meaning in Stalin's propaganda, but was simply an abstract emblem of Satanism. As long as Stalin was opposed to Hitler, Trotsky was pilloried as Hitler's agent; when Stalin and Hitler made friends, Trotsky became an agent of Anglo-French imperialism. In the Moscow show trials his name recurred *ad nauseam* as the victims, one by one, related how the arch-fiend in exile had impelled them to conspiracy, sabotage, and murder. This paranoid mythology of Stalin's purges was a constant reassurance to Trotsky himself: since he was so incessantly denounced, it must be that Stalin was genuinely afraid of the 'Bolshevik Leninists' who stood ready to dislodge him from the throne he had usurped. More than once Trotsky expressed the view that the Moscow trials had been organized in the hope that he, Trotsky, would be handed back to the Soviet police: Stalin, according to some, regretted that he had expelled his enemy instead of murdering him without further ado. Trotsky believed, too, that the last Comintern congress in 1937 was called for the sole purpose of meeting the Left Opposition threat. In short, the exiled leader played the part for which Stalin had cast him, but the duel took place largely in his own imagination. The International Left Opposition, like the Fourth International after it, was a cipher in political terms. Trotsky himself, of course, was a celebrated figure, but the movement which, according to the great laws of history, was bound to shake the foundations of the world at any moment proved to be an unimportant sect with virtually no impact on Stalinist parties anywhere.

A few Communists who were disillusioned by Stalinism or had been associated with Trotsky in the Comintern came out on his side, including Chen Tu-hsiu, the former head of the Chinese party. Intellectuals in various countries supported Trotsky as the embodiment of the true revolutionary spirit, which the Soviet leaders no longer represented. But sooner or later his adherents fell away, especially the intellectuals; Trotsky himself was largely responsible for this fact, as he demanded absolute obedience and tolerated no deviation from his own opinion on any subject. Apart from personal issues, his dictatorial manner, and astonishing belief in his own omniscience, the chief disagreement was over relations with the Soviet Union. Trotsky's insistence that the U.S.S.R. was still a dictatorship of the proletariat, and that the bureaucracy was not a class but only an excrescence on the healthy body of socialism, was a prime cause of argument and schism, as his views seemed increasingly out of touch with obvious reality. He remained obdurate, however, on this matter throughout his life, with the result that all the important intellectuals abandoned his cause: Souvarine in France, Victor Serge, Eastman, and, later, Hook, Shachtman, and Burnham in the U.S.A. He also lost the support of Diego Rivera, the well-known painter, who was his host in Mexico. The doctrinaire rigidity of Trotskyist groups caused them to break up incessantly and was one reason, though doubtless not the chief one, why the movement never became a political force. Trotsky himself, whenever the complete fruitlessness of his efforts was pointed out, had the same answer ready: Lenin in 1914 was almost completely isolated, and three years later he led the revolution to victory. What Lenin had done he, Trotsky, could do, as he too represented the profound tendencies of historical development. This belief inspired all his activity and political analyses, and was the source of his indomitable hope and energy.

As to the empirical evidence on which Trotsky based his hopes of an early victory of the Left in Russia, from today's viewpoint it appears amazingly slight. One or two minor Soviet diplomats quitted their posts and remained in the West; Trotsky cited this repeatedly as a proof that the Stalinist party was breaking up and that 'Thermidorian elements' and traitors to the revolution were coming to the fore, which must mean that the true Bolsheviks on the other side of the barricade were also gaining in strength. At the outbreak of war in 1939 he read in a newspaper that someone in Berlin had painted on a wall the slogan 'Down with Hitler and Stalin, long live Trotsky!' This filled him with encouragement, and he wrote that if there ever had to be a black-out in Moscow under Stalin, the whole city would be plastered with such notices. Later he read that a French diplomat had told Hitler that if France and Germany went to war, Trotsky would be the only victor; this too he quoted triumphantly in several articles as proof that even the bourgeoisie understood how right he was. He was unshakeably convinced that the war must end in a world revolution in which the true Bolsheviks, i.e. the Trotskyists, would be victorious. His article on the foundation of the Fourth International ended with the prophecy that 'During the next ten years the programme of the Fourth International will be the guide of millions, and these revolutionary millions will know how to storm earth and heaven' (*Writings of Leon Trotsky, 1938–1939*, ed. N. Allen and G. Breitman, 1974, p. 87).

In the summer of 1933, after long efforts, Trotsky finally secured permission to live in France, subject to various police restrictions. He stayed at different addresses for two years, his personal situation growing more and more dangerous: all the Stalinist parties were loudly hostile, and terrorist operations of the Soviet police were on the increase. In June 1935 he was granted asylum in Norway, where he wrote perhaps the best-known of his books, *The Revolution Betrayed:* a general analysis of the Soviet system, its degeneration and prospects, and an appeal for the overthrow of Stalin's bureaucracy by revolution. At the end of 1936 the Norwegian Government got rid of their awkward guest by sending him to Mexico, where he spent the rest of his life. Much of his energy during this period was devoted to unmasking the forgeries of the Mosocw trials, in which he was denounced as the master-mind behind all the conspiracies, sabotage, and acts of terrorism perpetrated by the accused. Through the efforts of Trotsky's friends an international commission of inquiry was set up under the chairmanship of John Dewey, the American philosopher and educationist; this body visited Mexico and took evidence from Trotsky himself, and in due course concluded that the trials were a complete fabrication.

Trotsky lived in Mexico for over three and a half years. The local Stalinists organized a campaign of persecution, and in May 1940, together with Soviet agents, made an armed attack on his house. Trotsky and his wife miraculously escaped alive, but not for long: an agent of the Soviet police, posing as a visitor, struck him down on 20 August. His son Leon, who acted as his father's representative in Europe, died in Paris in 1938, probably poisoned by Soviet agents. Another son, Sergey, who never left Russia or engaged in politics, disappeared in Stalin's prisons. Trotsky's daughter Zina committed suicide in Germany in 1933.

During his eleven years of exile Trotsky published innumerable articles, pamphlets, books, and manifestos; he issued instructions, advice, and appeals at every turn, either to the world proletariat as a whole or to the workers of Germany, Holland, Britain, China, India, and America. Inasmuch as all these documents were read only by a handful of true believers and had not the slightest influence on events, one might be inclined to dismiss Trotsky's activity as a game with toy soldiers. But the fact remains that the assassin's ice-pick was not a toy and that Stalin devoted much energy to destroying Trotskyism throughout the world—a purpose in which he was largely successful.

2. Trotsky's analysis of the Soviet system, the bureaucracy, and 'Thermidor'

ALL Trotsky's analyses are based on the conviction that his and Lenin's policies were unfailingly right, that the theory of permanent revolution was abundantly borne out by events, and that 'socialism in one country' was a pernicious error. In an article on 'Three Concepts of the Russian Revolution' (1939) he argued as follows. The Populists believed that Russia could bypass capitalism altogether; the Mensheviks thought the Russian revolution could only be of a bourgeois character, so that there could be no question at that stage of a dictatorship of the proletariat. Lenin then put forward the slogan of a democratic dictatorship of the proletariat and peasantry in the hope that a revolution conducted under this banner would give the impulse for a socialist victory in the West, which would make possible a rapid transition to socialism in Russia. Trotsky's own view was that the programme of the democratic revolution could only succeed in the form of a dictatorship of the proletariat, but that the latter could only maintain itself if the revolution spread to Western Europe. In 1917 Lenin took the same line, as a result of which the proletarian revolution was successful in Russia. As Trotsky shows at length in his *History of the Revolution*, none of the Bolsheviks doubted that the Russian proletariat could only conquer if it was supported by the Western proletariat, and the pernicious idea of 'socialism in one country' did not enter anyone's head until it was invented by Stalin at the end of 1924.

How did it happen, then, that Trotsky's unquestionably correct policy, which was also Lenin's from 1917 onwards, resulted in government by a 'parasitic bureaucracy', and that Trotsky himself was driven from power and branded as a traitor? The answer was to be found in an analysis of the degeneration of Soviet power and 'Thermidorianism'.

During the first years of his exile Trotsky took the view that Stalin and his group occupied the 'centre' of the Russian political spectrum and that the chief danger to the revolution came from the 'Right'—then represented by Bukharin and his followers—and counter-revolutionary elements which threatened a 'Thermidorian reaction', i.e. the restoration of capitalism. Accordingly, Trotsky offered to support Stalin against counter-revolution. Stalin, he thought, had made too many concessions to the Right, with the result, as seen in the successive trials of the 'Industrial party' and the Mensheviks, that saboteurs and enemies of the people had occupied the highest posts in the state planning organization and were deliberately slowing up industrialization. (Trotsky believed implicitly in the guilt of the accused, and it did not occur to him for a moment that these trials might be fabrications; he only began to wonder years afterwards, when his own misdeeds and those of his friends were proved by equally strong evidence in the great show trials.) In the early thirties Trotsky also spoke of 'Bonapartism' in the Stalinist regime. In 1935, however, he observed that in the French Revolution Thermidor had come first and Napoleon afterwards; the order should be the same in Russia, and, as there was already a Bonaparte, Thermidor must have come and gone. In an article entitled 'The Workers' State, Thermidor, and Bonapartism' he amended his theory somewhat. He stated that the Thermidorian reaction had taken place in Russia in 1924 (i.e. when he himself was finally removed from power); it was not, however, a capitalist counter-revolution but a seizure of power by the bureaucracy, which had begun to destroy the advance guard of the proletariat. The dictatorship of the proletariat had been preserved, as the state still owned the means of production, but political power had passed into the hands of the bureaucrats; the Bonapartist system must soon collapse, however, as it was contrary to the laws of history. A bourgeois counter-revolution was possible, but it could be avoided if the true Bolshevik elements were properly organized. Trotsky added, however, that he had in no way altered his view as to the working-class character of the Soviet state, but was merely expressing the historical analogy with more precision; in France, too, Thermidor was not a return to the *ancien régime*. The Soviet bureaucracy was not a social class, but a caste which had deprived the proletariat of its political rights and introduced a brutal despotism. Its existence in its present form, however, depended on the system of state ownership, the supreme achievement of the October Revolution, which the bureaucracy was obliged to defend and did defend in its own way. It was therefore the duty of the world proletariat to defend the Soviet Union unconditionally as the bastion of world revolution, while at the same time fighting against Stalinist degeneration (Trotsky did not explain in detail how these aims could be combined in practice). By 1936 he came to the conclusion that Stalinism could not be overthrown by reforms and internal pressures: there must be a revolution to remove the usurpers by force. That revolution would not alter the system of ownership, and would therefore not be a social revolution but a political one. It would be carried out by the advance guard of the proletariat, embodying the traditions of true Bolshevism which Stalin had destroyed.

The theory of 'socialism in one country' was responsible for all the bureaucracy's failures at home and abroad. It meant abandoning hope of world revolution and hence of Russia's main support in the world proletariat. Socialism in one country was impossible, i.e. it could be started but not completed: in a state closed within itself, socialism was bound to degenerate. The Comintern, which until 1924 had pursued a correct policy aimed at stirring up world revolution, had been transformed by Stalin into an instrument of Soviet policy and espionage, reducing the worldwide Communist movement to a state of degeneracy and impotence.

Trotsky made many attempts to explain how it was that the political power of the proletariat had been destroyed and the bureaucracy had gained control and introduced (as he later put it more than once) a totalitarian system of government. These attempts, contained in various books and articles, do not form a consistent argument. At times he maintained that the chief cause of degeneration was the delay in the outbreak of world revolution: the West European proletariat did not assume its historic mission in time. On the other hand, he maintained equally often that the defeat of revolution in Europe was the fault of the Soviet bureaucracy. It thus remained in doubt which phenomenon was the cause and which the effect—though later, as he pointed out, they aggravated each other. In *The Revolution Betrayed* we are told that the social basis of the growth of the bureaucracy was the faulty policy of the N.E.P. years, which favoured the kulaks. If so, one would expect that the liquidation of the kulaks and forced industrialization under the first five-year plan would at least have weakened the bureaucracy if not destroyed it; in fact precisely the opposite happened, and Trotsky nowhere explains why this was so. Later in the same book he says that the bureaucracy was originally an organ of the working class but that later, when it became involved in the distribution of goods, it began to place itself 'above the masses' and to claim privileges. This does not explain, however, whether and in what way the system of privilege could have been avoided, and why the working class, which was truly in charge, permitted such a thing to happen. Still in the same work, Trotsky says that the main cause of bureaucratic government was the slowness of the world proletariat to fulfil its historic mission. In an earlier pamphlet, *Problems of Development of the U.S.S.R.* (1931), he gives other reasons: the weariness of the Russian proletariat after the Civil War, the collapse of illusions fostered in the heroic days of the Revolution, the defeat of revolutionary outbreaks in Germany, Bulgaria, and Estonia, and the bureaucracy's betrayal of the Chinese and British proletariat. In an article in the following year he stated that the war-weary workers handed over power to the bureaucracy for the sake of order and reconstruction; but he did not explain why these tasks could not have been carried out by 'true Bolshevik-Leninists' under his own leadership.

From all these explanations one clear argument emerges, namely that Trotsky himself did not contribute in the smallest measure to the establishment of a bureaucratic regime, and that the bureaucracy had nothing in common with the dictatorship of the first six years after the Revolution, but was its exact contrary. The fact that the party apparatus exercised absolute power during those years had, it seems, nothing to do with the regime of Stalin and his clique, since the party in those days was the 'advance guard of the proletariat', while Stalin's subsequent apparatus represented nothing and no one. In that case, we may ask, why could not the proletariat shake off the clique of usurpers who lacked any social backing? Trotsky has an answer to this too: the proletariat does not rebel against Stalin's government (elsewhere, however, we read that it is in constant rebellion) because it fears that in the present situation a proletarian revolution might lead to the restoration of capitalism.

It is not clear from Trotsky's arguments whether there was any means of avoiding such a disastrous outcome. It seems, on the whole, that there was not, since otherwise Trotsky and his group, who invariably pursued the right policy and 'expressed' the true interests of the proletariat, would surely have prevented the bureaucracy taking over. If they did not prevent it, it was because they could not; and if the bureaucracy continued to maintain itself without any visible social foundation, this must surely be due to the operation of historical laws.

3. Bolshevism and Stalinism. The idea of Soviet democracy

TROTSKY thus took every opportunity to emphasize that there was no continuity between true Bolshevism or Leninism, that is to say Trotsky's own ideology and politics on the one hand, and Stalinism on the other. Stalinism was not only not the true heir of Leninism, but a glaring contradiction of it. In an article of 1937 he takes issue with Mensheviks and anarchists who were saying: 'We told you so from the beginning.' Not at all, replies Trotsky. The Mensheviks and anarchists predicted that despotism and the stifling of the Russian proletariat would come as a result of Bolshevik government; they have indeed come, but as a result of Stalin's bureaucracy, which has nothing to do with true Bolshevism. Again, Pannekoek and some German Spartacists say that the Bolsheviks set up a dictatorship of the party instead of a dictatorship of the proletariat, and that Stalin established a bureaucratic dictatorship on that basis. This is not the case either. The proletariat could not take over state power except through its own vanguard, in which the working masses' aspirations to freedom were crystallized.

In this article as in many others, Trotsky was obliged to answer the objections frequently raised by his adversaries and also by such supporters as Serge, Souvarine, and Burnham. Surely, they pointed out, the Bolsheviks had from the beginning, with Trotsky's active participation, liquidated all Russian political parties including the socialists; they had themselves forbidden the formation of groups within the party, had destroyed the freedom of the press, had bloodily suppressed the Kronstadt revolt, and so forth.

Trotsky answered these objections many times, and always in the same way: the actions complained of were right and necessary and in no way infringed the healthy foundations of proletarian democracy. In a letter to the workers of Zurich, published in August 1932, he wrote that the Bolsheviks had certainly used force to destroy the anarchists and Left S.R.s (other parties are not even mentioned in this context), but they did so in defence of the workers' state, and therefore their action was right; the class struggle could not be carried on without violence, the only question was which class the violence was exercised by. In a pamphlet of 1938, *Their Morals and Ours*, he explained that it was absurd to compare Communism with Fascism, as the resemblance in their methods was 'superficial' and related to secondary phenomena (for example, the abolition of general elections); what mattered was the class in whose name such methods were used. Trotsky, it was objected, had taken hostages, including children, from the families of political opponents, and was now indignant when Stalin did the same thing to Trotskyists. But, he replied, there was no true analogy, for what Trotsky did was necessary to fight the class enemy and bring victory to the proletariat, whereas Stalin was acting in the interests of the bureaucracy. In a letter of 1940 to Shachtman he agrees that the Cheka originated and functioned when he was in power—of course it did, but it was a necessary weapon against the bourgeoisie, whereas now Stalin was using it to destroy 'true Bolsheviks', so there was no proper comparison. As to the suppression of the Kronstadt revolt, how could a proletarian government be expected to give up an important fortress to reactionary peasant soldiers, among whom there might be a few anarchists? As to the forbidding of party groups, this was absolutely necessary, for when all non-Bolshevik parties were liquidated the antagonistic interests that were still present in society were bound to seek expression in different tendencies within the one party.

It is clear from this that for Trotsky there was no question of democracy as a form of government, or of civil liberties as a cultural value: from this point of view he was faithful to Lenin and did not differ from Stalin. If power was wielded by the 'historically progressive' class (through its vanguard, of course), then by definition this was an authentic democracy, even if oppression and coercion in every form were otherwise the order of the day; for all this was in the cause of progress. But from the moment that power was taken over by a bureaucracy that did not represent the interests of the proletariat, the same forms of government automatically became reactionary and therefore 'anti-democratic'. In an article of 1931 entitled 'The Right–Left Bloc' Trotsky wrote: 'What we mean by the restoration of party democracy is that the real revolutionary proletarian core of the party win the right to curb the bureaucracy and to really purge the party: to purge the party of the Thermidorians in principle as well as their unprincipled and careerist cohorts who vote according to command from above, of the tendencies of tail-endism as well as the numerous factions of toadyism, whose title should not be derived from the Greek or Latin but from the real Russian word for toady in its contemporary, bureaucratized and Stalinized form. This is the reason we need democracy' (*Writings of Leon Trotsky, 1930–1931*, ed. G. Breitman and S. Lovell, 1973, p. 57). It is thus clear that by 'democracy' Trotsky means government by Trotskyists, expressing the historical aspirations of the proletariat.

In an article of December 1939 Trotsky again answers the question whether he himself was not responsible for the liquidation of all political parties except the Bolsheviks. Certainly, he replies, and it was quite right to do so. 'But,' he goes on, 'one cannot identify the laws of civil war with the laws of peaceful periods'–and then, it clearly having occurred to him that in that case the liquidated parties should have been re-legalized after the Civil War, he adds: '[or] the laws of dictatorship or the proletariat with the laws of bourgeois democracy' (*Writings of Leon Trotsky, 1939–1940*, ed. N. Allen and G. Breitman, 1973, p. 133).

In a statement dating from the end of 1932 we read: 'Every regime must be judged first and foremost according to its own rules. The regime of the proletarian dictatorship cannot and does not wish to hold back from infringing the principles and formal rules of democracy. It has to be judged from the standpoint of its capacity to ensure the transition to a new society. The democratic regime, on the other hand, must be judged from the standpoint of the extent to which it allows the class struggle to develop within the framework of democracy' (*Writings of Leon Trotsky, 1932–1933*, 1972, ed. G. Breitman and S. Lovell, p. 336).

In short, it is right to be indignant and to attack democratic states when they infringe the principles of democracy and freedom, but one must not treat a Communist dictatorship in this way, because it does not recognize democratic principles; its superiority lies in the promise to create a 'new society' in the future.

In *The Revolution Betrayed* we are even told that Stalin's constitution, by proclaiming universal suffrage, made it clear that there was no longer a dictatorship of the proletariat. (Trotsky also remarks that by introducing the secret ballot Stalin evidently wished to purge his regime of corruption to some extent. Incredible as it may seem, he evidently took Stalin's elections at face value.)

Thus, while Trotsky constantly attacked Stalin and his regime and demanded a return to 'Soviet democracy' and 'party democracy', it is clear in the light of his general principles that 'democracy' signifies the rule of those whose policy is 'right': it does not mean that the 'rightness' of a policy is determined as the result of different groups contending for popular support. In *The Revolution Betrayed* he writes of the need to regain freedom for 'Soviet parties', starting with the Bolsheviks (i.e. Trotsky and his followers); but it not clear which other parties qualify as 'Soviet'. Since only the genuine vanguard of the proletariat is to exercise power, that vanguard must also have the right to decide which parties are 'Soviet' and which are counter-revolutionary. In Trotsky's eyes, the upshot seems to be that socialist freedom means freedom for Trotskyists and no one else.

The same arguments apply to cultural freedom. Trotsky sometimes expressed indignation at the gagging of art and science by Stalin's regime. In *The Revolution Betrayed* he recalled that in 1924 he himself had formulated rules for the dictatorship of the proletariat in art and literature: the sole criterion was to be whether a work was for or against the Revolution, and beyond that there should be perfect freedom. In July 1932 he wrote that there should be freedom in art and philosophy, 'eliminating pitilessly only that which is directed against the revolutionary tasks of the proletariat' (*Writings, 1932–1933*, p. 279). This, however, is the same principle that prevailed under Stalin: the party authorities decide what is 'directed against the revolutionary tasks of the proletariat' and must therefore be 'pitilessly eliminated'. Freedom thus defined has never been infringed in the Soviet state. Of course, under such a general formula the degree of repression and regimentation of culture may be greater or less according to various political circumstances, and in the twenties it was certainly less than in the thirties. Since, however, the principle is that the rulers decide in every case what manifestations of culture are in accordance with their political needs, no degree of repression and enslavement can possibly offend against the dictatorship of the proletariat. The whole question reduces once again to the same pattern: if Trotsky had been in charge he would not, of course, have allowed freedoms that he thought dangerous to his authority; Stalin behaved in the same way, and in both cases it was a matter of self-interest. The whole difference comes down to this, that Trotsky believed himself to 'represent the historical interests of the proletariat', while Stalin believed that he, Stalin, did so.

In *Their Morals and Ours* Trotsky endeavoured to refute the objection of those of his followers who claimed that his rule of morality was simply 'What is good for me is right' and that in his view the end justified the means. To this he replied that if the means were to be justified by something other than the aims evolved by history, that something could only be God. In other words his questioners were falling into religiosity, just as the Russian revisionists Struve, Bulgakov, and Berdyayev had done; they tried to combine Marxism with some kind of morality superior to class, and ended up in the bosom of the Church. Morals in general, he declared, were a function of the class struggle. At the present time morality could be in the interest of the proletariat or in that of Fascism, and, obviously, warring classes might sometimes use similar means; the only important question was which side they benefited. 'A means can be justified only by its end. But the end in its turn needs to be justified. From the Marxist point of view, which expresses the historical interests of the proletariat, the end is justified if it leads to increasing the power of man over nature and to the abolition of the power of man over man' (*Their Morals and Ours*, 1942, p. 34). In other words, if a policy is conducive to technical progress (the power of man over nature), any means which furthers that policy is automatically justified; it is not clear, however, why Stalin's policy should in that case be condemned, since it certainly raised the country's technical level. As to the abolition of the power of man over man, Trotsky himself enunciated the principle (which Stalin took over) that before this power can be abolished it must be increased to the highest degree; Trotsky reiterated this view in an article in June 1933. But in future things will be different. The 'historical aim' is embodied in the proletarian party, which therefore decides what is moral and what is immoral. As to Souvarine's remark that, as Trotsky's party does not exist, he must regard himself alone as the embodiment of morality, the prophet replies once again by pointing to Lenin's example—he too stood alone in 1914, and what happened after that?

In a sense the critics' objection was invalid: Trotsky did not maintain that what served his party's interests was morally good, and what injured them was morally bad. He held simply that there were no such things as moral criteria, but only criteria of political efficacy: 'Problems of revolutionary morality are fused with the problems of revolutionary strategy and tactics' (ibid., p. 35). To say that a thing was good or bad in itself, irrespective of political consequences, was tantamount to believing in God. It was meaningless to ask, for instance, whether it was right in itself to murder the children of one's political opponents. It had been right (as Trotsky says elsewhere) to kill the Tsar's children, because it was politically justified. Why then was it wrong for Stalin to murder Trotsky's children? Because Stalin did not represent the proletariat. All 'abstract' principles of good and bad, all universal rules of democracy, freedom, and cultural values were without significance in themselves: they were to be accepted or rejected as political expediency might dictate. The question of course then arises why anyone should side with the 'vanguard of the proletariat' rather than with its opponents, or identify himself with any aims whatever. Trotsky does not answer this question, but merely says that 'The end flows naturally from the historical movement' (ibid., p. 35). This presumably means, though he does not say so clearly, that we must first find out what is historically inevitable, and then support it for no other reason than that it is inevitable.

As for democracy within the party, Trotsky is quite categorical about this also. In Stalin's party, when his own group was in opposition, he naturally demanded free intra-party discussion and even freedom to form 'fractions'. On the other hand, he defended the prohibition of fractions enacted by himself and others at the Tenth Congress in 1921, on the ground that it was an 'extraordinary measure'. It is hard to interpret this otherwise than as meaning that it is right to prohibit fractions when they are wrong, but that Trotsky's group must not be prohibited because it expresses the interest of the proletariat. During his exile he also endeavoured to impose 'true Leninist' principles on the small groups of his adherents: he unceasingly condemned all variations from his own statements, ordered the exclusion of all who resisted his authority on any subject, and proclaimed the doctrine of Communist centralism at every turn. He denounced Souvarine's group of 'Communist democrats' in Paris, saying that their very name showed that they had broken with Marxism (on which point he may have been right). He reprimanded Naville's group when, in 1935, they proclaimed a programme of their own within the Left Opposition. He condemned Luciano Galicia, the leader of the Mexican Trotskyists, who forgot about centralism and demanded full freedom of opinion within the Fourth International. He lashed out furiously at the American Trotskyist Dwight Macdonald, who had said that all theory must be treated with scepticism: 'He who propagates theoretical scepticism is a traitor' (*Writings, 1939–1940*, p. 341). He pronounced irrevocable sentence on Burnham and Shachtman when they finally came to doubt that the Soviet Union was a workers' state, and talked of Soviet imperialism in invading Poland and in the war with Finland. On this occasion he refused to agree to a referendum within the American Trotskyist party (which, with about a thousand members according to Deutscher, seems to have been the biggest contingent in the Fourth International) on the ground that party policy was not 'simply an arithmetical total of local decisions' (*In Defence of Marxism*, 1942, p. 33). The fact that this absolutism caused his movement to shrink and to become more and more like a tiny religious sect, convinced that its members and they only were destined to salvation, did not worry Trotsky at all—once more, what about Lenin in 1914? He also shared Lenin's 'dialectical' view that the true or 'underlying' majority did not consist of those who happened to be in larger number but of those who were right or stood for historical progress. He seems to have genuinely believed that the working masses of the world were on his side in their inmost hearts, even though they did not yet know it; for the laws of history made clear that this must be so.

Trotsky's attitude to the problems of national oppression and self-determination was on similar lines. His writings contain a few references to Stalinist suppression of the national aspirations of the Ukrainians and other peoples; at the same time he emphasized that no concessions must be made to Ukrainian nationalists, and that true Bolsheviks in the Ukraine must not form a 'people's front' with them. He went so far as to say that the Ukrainians, divided as they were among four states, constituted an international problem no less crucial than, in Marx's opinion, the Polish question had been in the nineteenth century. But he saw nothing reprehensible in the socialist state bringing the 'proletarian revolution' to other countries by means of armed invasion. In 1939–40 he explained indignantly to Shachtman and Burnham that the Soviet invasion of Poland coincided with the revolutionary movement in that country, that the Stalinist bureaucracy had given a revolutionary impulse to the Polish proletariat and peasantry, and that in Finland too the war with the Soviet Union had awakened revolutionary feelings. True, this was a revolution of a 'special kind', since it was introduced at the point of the bayonet and did not spring from the depths of popular feeling, but it was a genuine revolution all the same. Trotsky's knowledge of what was happening in Eastern Poland and Finland was based, of course, not on any empirical data but on the 'laws of history': the Soviet state, degenerate though it was, represented the interests of the popular masses, and therefore the latter must support the invading Red Army. On this point Trotsky certainly cannot be accused of deviating from Leninism: as the 'true' national interest coincides with that of the vanguard of the proletariat, it follows that wherever the vanguard is in power (albeit in a state of 'bureaucratic degeneration') the right of national self-determination has been realized, and the masses must support this state of affairs, for so the theory requires.

4. Criticism of Soviet economic and foreign policy

SINCE, in theory at least, industrialization and the future agricultural policy were a vital issue to the Left Opposition in the Soviet Union, Trotsky was in an awkward position when it turned out that Stalin had taken over all the opposition's policies, and had done so in an intensified form. He solved the difficulty by declaring that Stalin had indeed carried out the opposition's aims but had done so in a bureaucratic and ill-considered manner. 'The Left Opposition began with the struggle for the industrialization and agrarian collectivization of the Soviet Union. This fight is won in a certain sense, namely in that, beginning with 1928, the whole policy of the Soviet government represents a bureaucrat-ically distorted application of the principles of the Left Opposition' (*Writings of Leon Trotsky, 1933–1934*, ed. G. Breitman and B. Scott, 1972, p. 274). The bureaucracy 'had been compelled' to carry out these measures in its own inter-est, by the logic of government, and although it had performed the historical tasks of the proletariat in a distorted manner, the changes in themselves were 'progressive'; moreover, it was leftist pressure that had forced Stalin to change his tune. 'Between the creative forces of the revolution and the bureaucracy there exists a profound antagonism. If the Stalinist apparatus constantly comes to a halt at certain limits, if it finds itself compelled even to turn sharply to the left, this occurs above all under the pressure of the amorphous, scattered, but still powerful elements of the revolutionary party' (*Writings, 1930–1931*, p. 224). As to collectivization, Trotsky criticized the haste and lack of economic prepa-ration and emphasized that the Stalinists were wrong in regarding the kolkhozes as socialist institutions: they were no more than a transitional form. What was more, collectivization turned out to be a step towards the restoration of capi-talism. In *The Revolution Betrayed* Trotsky wrote that Stalin had annulled the nationalization of the land by giving it to the kolkhozes, and by allowing the peasants to cultivate private plots on the side he had strengthened the element of 'individualism'. Thus, when Soviet agriculture lay in ruins and millions of peasants were starving to death, or were kept alive only by the permission they had at last received to maintain private plots, Trotsky's chief concern was the danger of 'individualism' that this represented. He even held that the fight against the kulaks was insufficiently thorough, as Stalin had given them a chance to organize in the kolkhozes and, after the first liquidation campaign, had made further substantial concessions which must lead to renewed class differentia-tion in the countryside. (This was Trotsky's line in 1935, when he perceived a 'swing to the right' in Stalin's foreign policy and therefore looked for symptoms of a similar turn in Soviet internal affairs.)

On several occasions, in *The Revolution Betrayed* and elsewhere, Trotsky condemned the 'barbarous' introduction of piece-work into Soviet industry. It was hard to tell from his arguments, however, whether he thought material incentives to productivity should be replaced by police compulsion or revolu-tionary zeal, and, in the latter case, how that zeal was to be evoked.

As to Stalin's foreign policy, Trotsky harped on the theme that international revolution was being abandoned for the sake of 'socialism in one country':

hence the revolution had been 'successively betrayed in Germany, China, and Spain. (The Spanish Civil War, according to Trotsky, was 'essentially' a proletarian struggle for socialism.) He did not say whether the Red Army should have been sent to aid the German Communists in 1923 (as he himself had vainly tried to do in 1920), or to aid the Chinese in 1926. In general Trotsky opposed the policy of supporting the 'national bourgeoisie' in undeveloped countries. This policy was often quite successful in weakening the great capitalist Powers; Trotsky, however, thought it pernicious on the ground that in colonial territories, as elsewhere, the tasks of the 'bourgeois revolution' could only be performed under Communist leadership, which would bring the revolution continuously into a socialist stage. It was, for instance, absurd to suppose that India could gain its independence otherwise than by a proletarian revolution; this was absolutely ruled out by the laws of history. The example of Russia showed that the only possibility was a 'permanent revolution' led from the outset by the proletariat, i.e. the Communist party. Trotsky regarded Russian models as absolutely binding on all countries of the world, and he therefore had ready-made answers to all their problems whether or not he knew anything about their history or specific conditions.

Trotsky did not dispute that Communists in a revolutionary period must make use of transitional aims before they could control the situation completely. Thus in a letter of August 1931 to the Chinese Trotskyists he wrote that the idea of a national assembly must not be dropped from their programme, because when the support of the poor peasants was being canvassed 'the proletariat will have to convoke a national assembly in order not to arouse the mistrust of the peasantry and in order not to provide an opening for bourgeois demagogy' (*Writings, 1913–1931*, p. 128). On the other hand, we read elsewhere that it would be a fatal mistake to repeat Lenin's pre-1917 slogan of a 'dictatorship of the proletariat and peasantry'. At the outset of the Russian revolution the government was referred to as representing the proletariat and the poor peasantry. As to this, Trotsky writes: 'True, subsequently we called the Soviet government worker and peasant. But by this time the dictatorship of the proletariat was already a fact, the Communist Party was in power, and consequently the name Workers' and Peasants' Government could not give rise to any ambiguity or grounds for alarm' (ibid., p. 308). In short, once the Communists were in power there could be no harm in fictitious and deceptive names.

Trotsky's supporters and admirers, such as Deutscher, have often emphasized, as a fact greatly to his credit, that he opposed the slogan of 'social Fascism'. It is true that he criticized this slogan because it cut off the Communists from the working masses in the social democratic parties, but he does not seem to have had any real policy to suggest as far as the social democrats were concerned. He wrote that there could be no question of permanent co-operation with organizations which did not break radically with reformism and which sought to regenerate social democracy. At the same period, before Hitler's accession to power, he blamed the Stalinists simultaneously for talking of 'social Fascism' and for capitulating to the social democrats. In June 1933, just after the Nazi victory, he declared that there could be no thought of a united front with the German social democrats, who were Hitler's lackeys. But Trotsky's indignation was aroused in earnest by the change of Soviet policy in 1934-5. Stalinism had at last shown its Rightist countenance: the Stalinists were allying themselves with the renegades of the Second International and, worse still, were talking of peace and international arbitration and dividing states into democratic and Fascist as if that were the important difference. They spoke of Fascism threatening world war, yet as Marxists they must know that imperialist war had an 'economic foundation'. They even accepted at Geneva a formula defining the aggressor in terms which would apply equally to all wars, including those between capitalist states. This was a surrender to bourgeois pacifism: Marxists could not be opposed to all wars in principle, they left that sort of cant to Quakers and Tolstoyans. Marxists judged war from the class point of view' and were not interested in bourgeois distinctions between the aggressor and his victim; their principle was that a war in the interests of the proletariat, be it aggressive or defensive, was a just war, while a war between imperialists was a crime.

In reality all Trotsky's earlier appeals for a change of attitude towards the social democrats were illusory and could have borne no fruit even if he had been in power: for he seems to have imagined that it was possible to maintain ideological 'purity' *vis-à-vis* the social democrats while at the same time soliciting their help in particular circumstances. When Stalin, to prevent France coming to terms with Nazi Germany, launched the policy of the 'popular front' and an anti-Fascist alliance with the socialists, he realized that he must pay a price, at all events in propaganda terms, if his policy was to be successful. Trotsky, on the other hand, thought it possible to form an anti-Nazi front with the socialists while denouncing them at every turn as impostors, agents of the bourgeoisie, traitors to the working class, and lackeys of imperialism—the only taboo epithet being 'social Fascists'. It is evident that if he had been in charge of the Comintern at that time, his policy would have been even less successful than Stalin's.

Trotsky was indeed a true adherent of Lenin's opinion that (as the latter repeated many times during the war and the Revolution) reliance on international treaties, arbitration, disarmament, and so on was idle reactionary chatter. It did not matter who was the aggressor, but which class was waging the war. The socialist state, representing the interests of the world proletariat, was 'right' in every war, regardless of who began it, and could not seriously consider itself bound by treaties with imperialist governments. Stalin was concerned with the security of the Soviet state, not with world revolution, and therefore had to present himself on various occasions as an advocate of peace and a champion of international law and democracy. Trotsky, however, believed that the main elements of the situation were still as he had seen them in 1918: on one side the imperialists, on the other the socialist state and the world proletariat waiting for the right slogans to unleash a revolution. Stalin, the exponent of Realpolitik, did not believe in the 'rising tide of revolution', and used the European Communist parties as instruments of Soviet policy. Trotsky was the advocate of incessant 'revolutionary war', and his whole doctrine was based on the conviction that the world proletariat was, in the nature of things and by the laws of history, tending towards revolution, and that only the erroneous policy of the Stalinist bureaucracy prevented this innate trend from taking effect.

5. Fascism, democracy, and war

How doctrinaire and unrealistic Trotsky's political thinking was in the 1930s may be judged from his remarks on the coming war and his recommendations for action in the face of the Fascist threat.

A few days after the outbreak of war he wrote: 'I do not see the slightest reason for changing those principles in relation to world war which were elaborated between 1914 and 1917 by the best representatives of the workers' movement under the leadership of Lenin. The present war has a reactionary character on both sides. Whichever camp is victorious, humanity will be thrown far behind' (*Writings, 1939–1940*, p. 85). These words—written after the German invasion of Poland and the Anglo-French declaration of war, but before the Soviet invasion of mid-September—were an epitome of Trotsky's views on the subject of a war among capitalist states such as Nazi Germany, Fascist Italy, Poland, France, Britain, and the U.S.A. For many years he repeated indefatigably that it was a fatal illusion and a capitalist trick to suggest that there was or could be a front of 'democratic' states against Fascism, or that it made any difference whether victory went to Hitler or to a coalition of the Western democracies, since neither side had nationalized its factories. The proletariat of the belligerent countries, instead of helping their reactionary governments to fight Hitler, should rise against them as Lenin had urged during the First World War. The cry of 'national defence' was in the highest degree reactionary and anti-Marxist; what was at issue was a proletarian revolution, not the defeat of one bourgeoisie by another.

In a pamphlet of July 1934 entitled *War and the Fourth International* Trotsky wrote:

The sham of national defence is covered up wherever possible by the additional sham of the defence of democracy. If even now, in the imperialist epoch, Marxists do not identify democracy with fascism and are ready at any moment to repel fascism's encroachment upon democracy, must not the proletariat in case of war support the democratic governments against the fascist governments? Flagrant sophism! We defend democracy against fascism by means of the organizations and methods of the proletariat. Contrary to Social Democracy we do not entrust this defence to the bourgeois state ... Under these conditions, the support by a workers' party of "its" national imperialism for the sake of a fragile democratic shell means the renunciation of an independent policy and the chauvinistic demoralization of the workers ... The revolutionary vanguard will seek a united front with the working-class organizations—against its own 'democratic' government—but in no case unity with its own government against the hostile country. (*Writings, 1933–1934*, pp. 306–7)

The Third International, Trotsky emphasized in an article in 1935, had always combated pacifism, not only social-patriotism, and had always condemned talk of disarmament, arbitration, the League of Nations, etc.; yet today it was endorsing all these bourgeois policies. When *L'Humanité* called for the defence of 'French civilization' it showed that it had betrayed the proletariat and was taking a nationalist stand, inviting workers to help their own government to fight German imperialism. Wars were the product of capitalism, and it was senseless to argue that the chief danger at present was from Nazism. 'On this road one quickly arrives at the idealization of French democracy as such, counterposed to Hitler Germany' (*Writings of Leon Trotsky, 1934–1935*, ed. G. Breitman and B. Scott, 1971, p. 293).

A year before the war Trotsky declared that democracy and Fascism were simply two alternative instruments of exploitation—the rest was all a deceit.

Really, what would a military bloc of imperialist democracies against Hitler mean? A new edition of the Versailles chains, even more heavy, bloody and intolerable ... The Czechoslovakian crisis revealed with remarkable clarity that fascism does not exist as an independent factor. It is only one of the tools of imperialism. 'Democracy' is another of its tools. Imperialism rises above them both. It sets them in motion according to needs, at times counterposing them to one another, at times amicably conciling [*sic*] them. To fight against fascism in an alliance with imperialism is the same as to fight in an alliance with the devil against his claws or horns. (*Writings, 1938–1939*, p. 21)

In short, there was no such thing as a fight between democracy and Fascism. International treaties took no account of such pseudo-antagonisms: the British might conclude a pact with Italy, the Poles with Germany. No matter who the contending parties were, the coming war would bring about an international proletarian revolution—such was the law of history. Humanity would not endure the war longer than a few months; rebellions against national governments, led by the Fourth international, would break out on every hand. In any case the war would at once wipe out all traces of democracy, so that it was absurd to talk about the defence of democratic values. In reply to a Trotskyist group in Palestine who suggested that Fascism was the chief threat to be resisted at that time and that it was wrong to preach defeatism in countries combating it, Trotsky wrote that their attitude was no better than social-patriotism. For all true revolutionaries, the chief enemy was always at home. In another letter, of July 1939, he declared: 'The victories of fascism are important, but the death agony of capitalism is more important. Fascism accelerates the new war, and the war will tremendously accelerate the revolutionary movement. In case of war every small revolutionary nucleus can and will become a decisive historic factor in a very short time' (*Writings, 1938–1939*, p. 349). The Fourth International would play the same part in the coming war as the Bolsheviks had in 1917, but this time the downfall of capitalism would be complete and final. 'Yes, I do not doubt that the new world war will provoke with absolute inevitability the world revolution and the collapse of the capitalist system' (ibid., p. 232).

When war actually came it did not alter Trotsky's opinion on these matters, but strengthened it. In the manifesto of the Fourth International, published in June 1940, he declared that 'A socialist who comes out today for the defence of the "fatherland" is playing the same reactionary role as the peasants of the Vendée who rushed to the defence of the feudal regime, that is of their own chains' (*Writings, 1939–1940*, p. 190). It was pointless to talk of defending democracy against Fascism, for Fascism was a product of bourgeois democracy, and it was not any 'fatherland' that had to be defended, but the interests of the world proletariat. 'But the first to be vanquished in the war will be the thoroughly rotten democracy. In its definitive downfall it will drag down with it all the workers' organizations which served as its support. There will be no room for reformist unions. Capitalist reaction will destroy them ruthlessly' (ibid., p. 213). '"But isn't the working class obliged in the present conditions to aid the democracies in their struggle against German fascism?" This is how the question is put by broad petty-bourgeois circles for whom the proletariat always remains only an auxiliary tool for this or that faction of the bourgeoisie. We reject this policy with indignation. Naturally there exists a difference between the political regimes in bourgeois society, just as there is a difference in comfort between various cars in a railway train. But when the whole train is plunging into an abyss, the distinction between decaying democracy and murderous fascism disappears in the face of the collapse of the entire capitalist system ... The victory of the imperialists of Great Britain and France would be no less frightful for the ultimate fate of mankind than that of Hitler and Mussolini. Bourgeois democracy cannot be saved. By helping their bourgeoisie against foreign fascism, the workers could only accelerate the victory of fascism in their own country' (ibid., p. 221).

Here, again, is Trotsky's advice to the Norwegian workers at the time of Hitler's invasion. 'Should the Norwegian workers have supported the "democratic" camp against the fascist? . . . In reality this would be the crudest kind of blunder . . . In the world arena we support neither the camp of the Allies nor the camp of Germany. Consequently we have not the slightest reason or justification for supporting either one of their temporary tools within Norway itself' (*In Defense of Marxism*, p. 172).

Accordingly, if the workers of Poland, France, or Norway had read Trotsky's proclamations and obeyed them they would have turned their arms against their own governments at the time of the Nazi invasion, as it made no difference whether they were ruled by Hitler or their own bourgeoisie; Fascism was an instrument of the bourgeoisie, and it was an absurdity to talk of all classes forming a common front against Fascism. Lenin in the same way, had preached defeatism in the First World War, and lo, the revolution had broken out. Trotsky, it should be observed, thought it very likely that the war would be one of all capitalist states against the Soviet Union, as the former were united by class-interest. If, however, the Soviet Union were allied with one capitalist Power against another, the war could only be a very short one, as a proletarian revolution would at once break out in the defeated capitalist state, as in Russia in 1917, and the two hostile Powers would then unite against the fatherland of the proletariat.

Thus, for Trotsky, the general upshot of the war was a foregone conclusion. Capitalism would finally collapse, Stalinism and Stalin would be swept away, the world revolution would break out, the Fourth International would instantly gain ascendancy over the workers' minds and appear as the final victor. As he wrote in reply to the criticisms of Serge, Souvarine, and Thomas: 'All the parties of capitalist society, all its moralists and all its sycophants will perish beneath the debris of the impending catastrophe. The only party that will survive is the party of the world socialist revolution, even though it may seem non-existent today to the sightless rationalizers, just as during the last war the party of Lenin and Liebknecht seemed to them non-existent' (*Their Morals and Ours*, p. 47). In addition Trotsky made many detailed predictions with complete assurance. It was, for instance, absolutely impossible for Switzerland to avoid being dragged into the war; democracy could not survive in any country, but must by an 'iron law' develop into Fascism; if Italian democracy were restored it could only last a few months before being swept away by the proletarian revolution. As Hitler's army consisted of workers and peasants it was bound eventually to ally itself with the peoples of the occupied countries, for the laws of history taught that the bonds of class were stronger than any other.

As to the general nature of the Fascist danger, Trotsky put forward a very interesting analysis in August 1933. 'Theoretically, the victory of fascism is undoubtedly evidence of the fact that democracy has exhausted itself; but politically the fascist regime preserves democratic prejudices, recreates them, inculcates them into the youth and is even capable of imparting to them, for a short time, the greatest strength. Precisely in this consists one of the most important manifestations of the reactionary historic role of fascism' (*Writings, 1932–1933*, p. 294). 'Under the yoke of the "fascist" dictatorship the democratic illusions were not weakened, but became stronger' (ibid., p. 296). In other words, the threat of Fascism lies in the fact that people subjected to it long for democracy, and thus democratic prejudices are preserved instead of being dispelled; Hitler is dangerous because he makes it harder to destroy democracy.

Shortly before his death Trotsky reaffirmed his predictions as to the development of the war and at the same time put the question, in a rhetorical vein, as to what would happen if they were not fulfilled; he answered that it would signify the bankruptcy of Marxism.

> If this war provokes, as we firmly believe, a proletarian revolution, it must inevitably lead to the overthrow of the bureaucracy in the USSR and the regeneration of Soviet democracy on a far higher economic and cultural basis than in 1918 . . . If, however, it is conceded that the present war will provoke not revolution but a decline of the proletariat, there remains another alternative: the further decay of monopoly capitalism, its faster fusion with the state, and the replacement of democracy, wherever it still remains, by a totalitarian regime. The inability of the proletariat to take into its hands the leadership of society could actually lead under these conditions to the growth of a new exploiting class from the Bonapartist fascist bureaucracy. This would be, according to all indications, a regime of decline, signalizing the eclipse of civilization. An analogous result might occur in the event that the proletariat of advanced capitalist countries, having conquered power, should prove incapable of holding it and surrender it, as in the USSR, to a privileged bureaucracy. Then we would be compelled to acknowledge that the reason for the bureaucratic relapse is rooted not in the backwardness of the country and not in the imperialist environment, but in the congenital incapacity of the proletariat to become a ruling class. Then it would be necessary in retrospect to establish [*sic*] that in its fundamental traits the present USSR was the precursor of a new exploiting regime on an international scale . . . However onerous the second perspective may be, if the world proletariat should actually prove incapable of fulfilling the mission placed upon it by the course of development, nothing else would remain except only to recognize that the socialist

programme, based on the internal contradictions of capitalist society, ended as a Utopia (*In Defence of Marxism*, pp. 8–9)

This is an unusual argument to find in Trotsky's works. Naturally he states with confidence that the pessimistic second alternative is an unreal one, and he continues to believe that world revolution is inevitable, not merely as a general proposition but as a result of the war in progress. But the mere fact that he envisages another hypothesis seems to point to a certain hesitation, if we compare the above passage with the absolute confidence in victory that he expresses elsewhere.

Trotsky did not admit the idea that capitalism might be capable of reforming itself. Roosevelt's 'New Deal' seemed to him a desperate and reactionary attempt, foredoomed to failure. He believed, moreover, that the United States, having reached the highest stage of technical development, was already ripe for Communism. (In an article of March 1935 he promised the Americans that when they did go Communist their production costs would be cut by eighty per cent, and in 'The U.S.S.R. in Wartime', written shortly before his death, he declared that with a planned economy they could soon raise their national income to 200 billion dollars a year, and so ensure prosperity for all.) In *The Revolution Betrayed* we read that if anyone supposed that capitalism could thrive for more than a decade or two he must, by the same token, believe that socialism in the Soviet Union made no sense and that the Marxists had misjudged their historical moment, for the Russian revolution would in that case stand as a mere episodic experiment like the Paris Commune.

6. Conclusions

FROM the perspective of today, Trotsky's literary and political activity in the 1930s gives an impression of extreme wishful thinking: it is an unhappy mixture of unfulfilled prophecies, fantastic illusions, false diagnoses, and unfounded hopes. Of course it is not of the first importance that Trotsky failed to foresee the course of the war: many people in those days made predictions, most of which were belied by events. What is important and characteristic, however, is that he invariably presented his speculations as scientifically exact prognoses, based on a profound dialectic and understanding of great historical processes. In fact his prophecies were partly founded on hopes that history would vindicate his judgement, and partly on doctrinaire deductions from supposed historical laws which he believed must come into play sooner rather than later. One wonders what would have happened if Stalin had foreseen the outcome of the war and had taken his revenge on Trotsky not by killing him but by letting him live to see the collapse of all his hopes and prophecies, not a single one of which came true. The war was an anti-Fascist war; no proletarian revolution took place in Europe or America, apart from the Soviet conquest of Eastern Europe; the Stalinist bureaucracy was not swept away, but became immeasurably stronger, as did Stalin himself; democracy survived, and was restored in West Germany and Italy; most of the colonial territories gained their independence without a proletarian revolution; and the Fourth International remained an impotent sect. If Trotsky had seen all this, would he have admitted that his pessimistic hypothesis had proved to be the right one and that Marxism was an illusion? We cannot tell, of course, but his mentality would probably not have allowed him to draw such an inference; he would no doubt simply have noted that the operation of the laws of history had again been somewhat delayed, but would have remained firm in his belief that the great moment was at hand.

Trotsky, as a true doctrinaire, was insensitive to everything that was happening around him. Of course he followed events closely and commented on them, and did his best to obtain accurate information about the Soviet Union and world politics. But the essence of a doctrinaire is not that he does not read newspapers or collect facts: it consists in adhering to a system of interpretation that is impervious to empirical data, or is so nebulous that any and every fact can be used to confirm it. Trotsky had no need to fear that any event might cause him to change his mind, as his basic premises were always in the form 'on the one hand . . . on the other hand', or 'admittedly . . . but nevertheless'. If Communists suffered a set-back anywhere in the world, it confirmed his diagnosis that the Stalinist bureaucracy (as he had always said) was leading the movement to ruin. If there was a Communist success it also confirmed his diagnosis: the working class had shown, despite the Stalinist bureaucracy, that it was still full (as he had always said) of revolutionary spirit. If Stalin made a 'rightist' move it was a triumph for Trotsky's analysis: he had always predicted that the Soviet bureaucracy would degenerate into reaction. But if Stalin made a swing to the left it was also a triumph for Trotsky, who had always declared that the revolutionary vanguard in Russia was so strong that the bureaucracy must take account of its wishes. If a Trotskyist group in some country increased its membership, that was of course a good sign: the best elements were beginning to understand that true Leninism was the right policy. If, on the other hand, a group dwindled in size or underwent a split, this too confirmed the Marxist analysis: the Stalinist bureaucracy was stifling the consciousness of the masses, and in a revolutionary era unstable elements always desert the battlefield. If Soviet Russia scored economic success it confirmed Trotsky's argument: socialism, supported by the consciousness of the proletariat, was gaining ground in spite of the bureaucracy. If there were economic set-backs or disasters, Trotsky was right again: the bureaucracy, as he had always said, was incompetent and lacked the support of the masses. A mental system of this kind is watertight and immune from correction by the facts. Obviously, various forces and conflicting tendencies are at work in society, and different ones prevail at different times; if this commonplace truth is erected into a philosophy, there is no danger of its being empirically refuted. Trotsky, however, like many other Marxists, imagined that he was conducting scientific observations with the aid of an infallible dialectical method.

Trotsky's attitude to the Soviet state is psychologically understandable: it was to a large extent his own creation, and it is not surprising that he could not admit the idea that his offspring had degenerated beyond recall. Hence the extraordinary paradox which he repeated incessantly and which, in the end, even faithful Trotskyists found hard to swallow: the working class had been politically expropriated, robbed of all its rights, enslaved and trampled on, but the Soviet Union was still a working-class dictatorship, since the land and factories were the property of the state. As time went on, more and more of Trotsky's adherents left him on account of this dogma. Some, noting the obvious analogies between Soviet Communism and Nazism, had pessimistic forebodings as to the inevitability of totalitarian systems throughout the world. The German Trotskyist Hugo Urbahns concluded that state capitalism would become universal in one form or another. Bruno Rizzi, an Italian Trotskyist who in 1939 published a book in French on 'world bureaucratization', held that the world was moving towards a new form of class society, in which individual ownership was replaced by collective ownership vested in a bureaucracy, as exemplified by the Fascist states and the Soviet Union. Trotsky opposed such ideas furiously: it was nonsense to suggest that Fascism, the organ of the bourgeoisie, could expropriate its own class in favour of a political bureaucracy. Similarly, Trotsky broke with Burnham and Shachtman when they came to the conclusion that it no longer made any discernible sense to call the Soviet Union a 'workers' state'. Shachtman pointed out that under capitalism economic and political power could be separate, but that this was impossible in the Soviet Union, where property relations and the proletariat's participation in political power were dependent on each other; the proletariat could not lose political power and continue to exercise an economic dictatorship. The political expropriation of the proletariat meant the end of its rule in every other sense, and it was therefore absurd to maintain that Russia was still a workers' state; the ruling bureaucracy was a 'class' in the true meaning of the term. Trotsky to the end firmly opposed this conclusion, reiterating his single argument that the implements of production in the Soviet Union belonged to the state. This, of course, no one denied. The dispute was psychological rather than one of theory: to recognize that Russia had created a new form of class society and exploitation would have meant admitting that Trotsky's life-work had been in vain, and that he himself had helped to bring about the exact opposite of what he intended. This is a kind of inference that few are prepared to draw. For the same reason Trotsky maintained tooth and nail that when he was in power the Soviet Union and the Comintern had been above reproach in every way: it was a true dictatorship of the proletariat, a true proletarian democracy, with genuine support from the working masses. All repressions cruelties, armed invasions, etc. were justified if they were in the interest of the working class, but this had nothing to do with Stalin's later measures. (In exile Trotsky maintained that there was no religious persecution in Russia—the Orthodox Church had simply been deprived of its monopoly power, which was right and proper. On this point he was obliged to defend the Stalinist regime, as it had not deviated in any way from Lenin's policy.) Trotsky never suggested that the armed incursions carried out by the new-born Soviet state in Lenin's day might have been wrongful. On the contrary, he repeated many times that the revolution could not alter geography; in other words, the Tsarist frontiers ought to be preserved or restored, and the Soviet regime had every right to 'liberate' Poland, Lithuania, Armenia, Georgia, and the other border states. He maintained that if it had not been for bureaucratic degeneration the Red Army in 1939 would have been welcomed as a liberator by the working masses of Finland; but he did not ask himself why in that case, when he was in power and there was no 'degeneration', the working masses of Finland, Poland, or Georgia had failed to greet their liberators with enthusiasm in accordance with the laws of history.

Trotsky did not concern himself with philosophical questions. (Towards the end of his life he did try to expound his views on dialectics and formal logic, but it was clear that all the logic he knew consisted of fragments recollected from high school and from youthful studies of Plekhanov, all of whose absurdities he repeated. Burnham advised Trotsky to drop the subject, pointing out that he knew nothing of modern logic.) Nor did he attempt any theoretical analysis of the foundations of Marxism. It was sufficient for him that Marx had shown that the decisive feature of the modern world was the struggle between the bourgeoisie and the proletariat, and that this was bound to end in the victory of the proletariat, a worldwide socialist state, and a classless society. He did not concern himself to discover on what these prophecies were based. Being convinced of their truth, however, and of the fact that he as a politician embodied the interests of the proletariat and the deep-seated trend of history, he maintained unswervingly his faith in the final outcome.

At this point we should answer an objection. It may be said that the complete inefficacy of Trotsky's efforts and of his International do not invalidate his analysis, since a man may be right even if most or all of his fellows disagree with him, and *force majeure* is not an argument. Here, however, we may recall Oscar Wilde's remark (in *The Soul of Man under Socialism*) that whether force is an argument depends on what one wants to prove; and we may add, in the same line of thought, that force is an argument if the point at issue is whether one is strong or not. The fact that a theory is rejected by everyone or almost everyone, as has happened more than once in the history of science, does not prove that it is wrong. But it is a different matter with theories that have an inbuilt self-interpretation to the effect that they are an 'expression' of great historical tendencies (or of the will of Providence); that they embody the true consciousness of the class which is destined soon to triumph, or that they constitute a revelation of truth, and that therefore, simply as theories (or as 'theoretical consciousness'), they must inevitably prevail over all others. If a theory of this kind fails to secure recognition, its failure is an argument against it on its own premises. (On the other hand, success in practice is not necessarily an argument in its favour. The early victories of Islam were not a proof that the Koran was true, but a proof that the faith inspired by it was a powerful rallying-point because it corresponded to essential social needs; in the same way, Stalin's successes did not prove that he was 'right' as a theorist.) For this reason the failure of Trotskyism in practice, unlike the rejection of a scientific hypothesis, is also a theoretical failure, that is to say a proof that the theory as Trotsky conceived it was wrong.

Trotsky, with his dogmatic cast of mind, did not contribute to the theoretical elucidation of any point of Marxist doctrine. But he was an outstanding personality, endowed with immense courage, will-power, and endurance. Covered with obloquy by Stalin and his henchmen in all countries, persecuted by the most powerful police and propaganda machine in the world, he never faltered or gave up the fight. His children were murdered, he was driven out of his country and hunted down like an animal, and was finally done to death. His amazing resistance to every trial was the result of his faith and by no means conflicted—on the contrary—with his unshakeable dogmatism and inflexibility of mind. Unfortunately, the intensity of a faith and the willingness of its adherents to undergo persecution for it are no proof that it is intellectually or morally right.

Deutscher says in his monograph that Trotsky's life was 'the tragedy of the precursor'; but there is no good reason to maintain this, and it is not clear what he is supposed to have been the precursor of. He contributed, of course, to unmasking the forgeries of Stalinist historiography, and to refuting the lies of Soviet propaganda concerning conditions in the new society. But all his predictions as to the future of that society and of the world turned out to be wrong. Trotsky was not unique in criticizing Soviet despotism, nor was he the first to do so. On the contrary, he criticized it much more mildly than the democratic socialists, and he did not object to it *qua* despotism but only to its ultimate aims, which he diagnosed on ideological principles. The opposition that has found expression in Communist countries since Stalin's death has no connection with Trotsky's writings or thoughts, either factually or in the minds of the critics themselves. His ideas play no part at all in the 'dissident' movement in those countries, even among the dwindling band of those who attack the Soviet system from a Communist viewpoint. Trotsky did not offer any alternative form of Communism or any doctrine different from Stalin's. The main thrust of his attack, against 'socialism in one country', was merely an attempt to continue a certain tactical line which had become unfeasible for reasons that had nothing to do with Stalin. Trotsky was not a 'forerunner' but an offshoot of the revolution, thrown off at a tangent to the course which it followed in 1917–21, but which it subsequently had to abandon for both internal and external reasons. It would be more exact to call his life the tragedy of an epigone, rather than that of a forerunner; but this is not an adequate description either. The Russian revolution changed course in certain respects, but not in all. Trotsky advocated ceaseless revolutionary aggression and endeavoured to convince himself and others that if he had been running the Soviet state and the Comintern, the whole world would have been set ablaze without delay; his reason for so believing was that Marxist historiosophy taught him that such were the laws of history. However, the Soviet state was obliged by events to alter course on this point, and Trotsky did not cease to upbraid its leaders on that account. As far as the internal regime was concerned, however, Stalinism was the natural and obvious continuation of the system of government established by Lenin and Trotsky. Trotsky refused to recognize this fact and persuaded himself that Stalin's despotism bore no relation to Lenin's; that coercion, police repression, and the devastation of cultural life were due to a 'bureaucratic' *coup d'état* and that he himself bore no vestige of responsibility for them. This desperate self-delusion is psychologically explicable. What we have here is not merely the tragedy of an epigone, but that of a revolutionary despot entangled in a snare of his own making. There was never any such thing as a Trotskyist theory—only a deposed leader who tried desperately to recover his role, who could not realize that his efforts were vain, and who would not accept responsibility for a state of affairs which he regarded as a strange degeneration, but which was in fact the direct consequence of the principles that he, together with Lenin and the whole Bolshevik party, had established as the foundations of socialism.

VI

Antonio Gramsci:
Communist Revisionism

GRAMSCI is probably the most original political writer among the post-Lenin generation of Communists. His relation to Leninism was and still is a subject of controversy. Italian Communists such as Togliatti generally represent him as a Marxist–Leninist *pur sang*, or at any rate claim that whatever is original in his doctrine is a complement to Leninism and never a denial of it. To some extent this interpretation is prompted by tactical motives: when Italian Communists invoke the authority of Gramsci to justify their deviations from the Soviet ideological model, it is convenient to emphasize that they are basically of one mind with the tutelary genius of the Communist movement. Gramsci himself never called Lenin's authority into question, and it is not clear how far he was aware that his own writings—which consist for the most part of unfinished essays and notes from prison, often fragmentary, elliptical, and ambiguous—could serve as the basis for an alternative type of Communism, differing from Lenin's in some essential points.

Although Gramsci's writings do not amount to a coherent theory but rather to a vague and embryonic sketch, some aspects of them are clear and original enough to justify the view that they constitute an independent attempt to formulate a Communist ideology, and not merely an adaptation of the Leninist schema. An indirect confirmation of this is the frequency with which seekers after a more democratic and 'open' version of socialism—especially Communists and ex-Communists—turn to Gramsci for inspiration, and also the acute difficulties and resistance that occur when attempts are made to introduce his ideas to Communist parties outside Italy, especially ruling parties.

Although Gramsci died in 1937 his writings really belong to the history of post-Stalinist Marxism, as it was only in the fifties and sixties, after the publication of a six-volume edition of his letters and notes from prison, that his ideas began gradually to be canvassed in ideological disputes. His position *vis-á-vis* Leninist–Stalinist orthodoxy is somewhat like that of Rosa Luxemburg: lip-service is paid to him as a martyr in the Communist cause, but his writings are more embarrassing than useful. As to the articles he published up to 1926, before his imprisonment, their significance is only apparent in the light of his prison writings. Without this completion, the articles in question would be chiefly material for a history of the Italian Communist movement, but could not be said to constitute an original body of theory. From the point of view of Marxist doctrine, the prison writings are the essential part of his work.

1. Life and works

ANTONIO GRAMSCI (1891–1937), who became the leader of the Italian Communist party, was born in the village of Ales in Sardinia, the son of a petty official. As the result of a childhood accident he was hunchbacked and physically underdeveloped. Owing to political intrigues his father went to prison for some years, which reduced the family to destitution. The son had to work at various casual jobs while still a small boy, but he completed secondary school at Cagliari and in autumn 1911 won a scholarship to Turin University (as did Palmiro Togliatti in the same year).

As a freshman at University, Gramsci was not yet a socialist in the full sense. His horizon was to some extent limited by Sardinian regionalism: his fellow islanders, not without cause, regarded the neglect and poverty from which they suffered as owing, in some measure at least, to the privileges enjoyed by the expanding industry of northern Italy. The grievances of impoverished villagers and exploited miners found an outlet in separatist and regionalist tendencies rather than in socialism, which had scarcely taken root in Sardinia at that time.

Before long, however, Gramsci's studies and the industrial environment of Turin led him to take an interest in national politics. He took a humanistic course and was especially attracted by linguistics: throughout his life he took a lively interest in what is nowadays called socio-linguistics, the study of the effect of social situations on linguistic change. He no doubt joined the socialist party around the end of 1913, as did his Turin friends Angelo Tasca, Umberto Terracini, and Palmiro Togliatti, who were in due course to play a key part in the formation of the Communist party.

Gramsci broke off his university education in the spring of 1915, by which time he had acquired an extensive knowledge of history and philosophy. As for all Italian intellectuals of that generation, his philosophical teacher *par excellence* was Benedetto Croce. Gramsci was certainly not a Crocean in the literal sense, but the writings of the Italian Hegelianist introduced him to the realm of European philosophical problems. He admired Croce's critique of positivism and, for a time at least, hoped that Italian Marxism might be based on a critical assimilation of Croce, subjecting the latter to the same treatment as Marx performed on Hegel. In later years Gramsci became increasingly critical towards Croce, as the latter became more and more anti-Marxist; but he never ceased to recognize that Crocean philosophy had played a huge part in Italian intellectual life, even when he was chiefly concerned to point out its 'reactionary' effects.

In the same way, even when he had completely broken with Sardinian localism in favour of the orthodox Marxist class interpretation of Italian affairs, he never abandoned the theme of the Italian South and the peculiar importance of the opposition between it and the North in Italian history, past and present.

The 1913 elections and the European war turned Gramsci into a professional politician. From the end of 1914 he began to write for the Italian socialist press, and from 1916 he was a co-editor of the Piedmont edition of *Avanti*, for which he wrote political notes and reviewed books and plays, as well as helping to educate and organize the Turin workers. Although it is hard to ascribe to him a definite philosophical attitude at this time, it is clear from various occasional remarks that he did not share the faith, then popular among socialists, in the beneficent operation of 'historical laws' that would assure humanity of a socialist future; he did not believe in the natural inevitability of progress, but was inclined to place more reliance on human will-power and the force of ideas than was permitted by the orthodoxy of his day. No doubt he was already to some extent influenced by the activism of Sorel, with whose views he never identified himself but to whom his interpretation of Marxism owed a great deal.

By 1917, when revolutionary riots broke out in Turin, Gramsci was already one of the city's socialist leaders. His personal view of Marxism was expressed in an article of November 1917, often quoted today, on the October Revolution in Russia, entitled 'The Revolution against *Das Kapital*'. In it he observed that the Bolsheviks had won victory in Russia despite Marx's belief that that country would first go through a phase of Western-type capitalism. The Bolsheviks' revolutionary will had overthrown Marx's schema, but it had drawn strength from what was alive in Marxism and from elements which, though sullied by the intrusion of positivism, were a continuation of German and Italian idealism.

In May 1919 there appeared the first number of *L'Ordine Nuovo*, a weekly edited by Gramsci, Togliatti, Tasca, and Terracini, which was to play an important part in the ideological training of the future Italian Communist party. On October of that year the Socialist Party held a congress at Bologna at which it decided by a large majority to join the Third International. The party was divided into hostile groups and was far from meeting Lenin's requirements from the Comintern point of view, but the Soviet leader regarded Gramsci and his friends as closest to the Bolshevik orientation. An extreme left faction led by Amadeo Bordiga held that the party should eschew all parliamentary activity, which only dulled the revolutionary will of the working class: Communists must have nothing to do with bourgeois institutions and must prepare for an immediate struggle for power, eliminating from their ranks any who did not share this view. Both the centre of the party and its right wing rejected this policy of 'abstentionism', and the Right disapproved of seizing power by violence. In these controversies the *Ordine Nuovo* group was chiefly distinguished by its advocacy of workers' councils: this became the dominant idea of the movement, and Gramsci its most eloquent exponent.

Workers' councils came into being during the big strikes in Turin in 1919 and 1920, in part spontaneously and in part as a result of *Ordine Nuovo* propaganda. Gramsci held that they were a completely new form of social organization and that their functions must not be confused either with those of the trade unions, which were to improve working conditions under capitalism, or with those of the Socialist party, which were parliamentary and ideological. The councils were the proper means of enabling all the workers of a factory, regardless of party allegiance, religion, etc., to shoulder the task of organizing production; they were the germ of the future workers' state, the main organ of the dictatorship of the proletariat. They should be elected by all the wage-earners of a given plant without exception, so as to take over the functions of capitalists in the factories and, in due course, the organization of the state.

Gramsci thought that workers' councils were the Italian counterpart of the Russian experience, and no doubt imagined (at any rate before his visit to Moscow) that the Soviet system embodied the same idea of a real transference of power to the workers. 'All power to the Soviets' was indeed in line with Lenin's doctrine in *State and Revolution,* but not with Russian reality. Gramsci's view, in addition, betrays the strong influence of Sorel's idea that it was the task of the real producers not only to manage production but to organize the whole of social life. The society of the future would, so to speak, take its pattern from the shop-floor; in addition to being autonomous organs of production, the councils would be the matrix of a new proletarian culture, and would bring about the spiritual transformation of the working class.

For different reasons, this doctrine was unacceptable to both the anti-parliamentary Communist Left and the centre and Right. The Left held that the true purpose of socialist revolution was to destroy the institutions of political power by force and to set up new central bodies operating in the name of the proletariat: from this point of view, though not in its avowed anti-parliamentarianism, it agreed with Lenin. The Right identified proletarian rule with domination by the Socialist party, backed by a majority of society and exercising authority by democratic means. Both factions considered that Marxist doctrine precluded the idea of a dictatorship of the proletariat in the sense of direct rule by the workers—whose proper place was the factory, not Parliament or party headquarters. The reformists wanted representative democracy with a socialist majority, while the Left called for a dictatorship of the party; Gramsci, however, imagined a society in which every process of life was subject to control by the whole mass of producers, whose economic, political, and cultural liberation must advance simultaneously.

Despite Gramsci's hopes, the series of strikes accompanied by workers' occupation of the factories and the establishment of workers' councils did not develop into a nation-wide movement. In the spring of 1920 the Turin workers were forced to return to work on their employers' terms. Gramsci was almost alone in his stubborn defence of the councils as the basic weapon of the emancipation of the proletariat.

He was not alone, however, in fighting to create a Communist party in the true, Leninist sense of the term. *L'Ordine Nuovo* declaimed incessantly against reformism and the irresoluteness of the party leadership, complaining that despite the Bologna decisions the party had remained a purely parliamentary institution with no single will of its own, and had abandoned the idea of a proletarian revolution. After another, unsuccessful attempt by the Turin workers to occupy the factories in August–September 1920 the Communist group, in accordance with Lenin's wishes, decided to transform itself into a separate party. The anti-parliamentary faction reluctantly gave up the principle of 'abstentionism', which was in conflict with the formal directives of the Comintern. In November the Communists issued a separatist manifesto, and at the next congress of the Socialist party, at Livorno in January 1921, the split was effected: the Communists secured about one-third of the votes and set up the Italian Communist party. Gramsci (now chief editor *of L'Ordine Nuovo*, which had become a daily) was a member of the first Central Committee, which was dominated by Bordiga's followers. A controversy at once broke out within the party, the main issue being whether and how far the Communists should seek alliance with other Socialist parties: this question became increasingly critical as Fascism began manifestly to gain ground in Italy. Gramsci favoured a policy of broad alliances, and this fitted in with the change of Comintern policy as the Bolsheviks realized that the 'tide of revolution had ebbed'. In May 1922 Gramsci went to Moscow as the Italian party's representative on the Executive Committee of the Comintern; he remained there a year and a half, and took part in the Fourth Comintern Congress in November 1923. Meanwhile Mussolini had carried out his 'march on Rome'. The Comintern withdrew its support from Bordiga, who, in accordance with his 'purely class' attitude, saw no essential difference between bourgeois democracy and Fascism and opposed the 'united front' policy. Numerous arrests deprived the Communist party of its leadership, and Gramsci was recognized as head of the party by the Comintern. At the end of 1923 he left Moscow for Vienna, from where he tried to revive the Italian party, at that time torn by fractional strife. He arrived back in Italy in May 1924, was elected to Parliament and thus enjoyed personal immunity for the time being. The party was in a state of extreme weakness and disorganization. After a long struggle Gramsci defeated Bordiga's faction (the latter was in prison, but was still able to dominate local groups) and, at a congress held at Lyons in January 1926, gained a majority for his policy of forming a united front to restore democracy in Italy. The Communists, together with other anti-Fascist groups, had seceded from Parliament in June 1924, but they now decided to return and use what was left of parliamentary institutions for propaganda purposes. These manoeuvres were of little avail against the increasingly repressive measures of the Fascist government. Gramsci was arrested in November 1926, and in the following June was sentenced to imprisonment for twenty years and four months. Confined successively in various towns, he was permitted after a time to write and to receive books. The rest of his life was spent, as far as his weak health and prison conditions allowed, in reading and writing notes which constitutes one of the most original contributions to twentieth-century Marxism.

It was undoubtedly thanks to his imprisonment that Gramsci was able to remain a member of the Communist party. He escaped being expelled from it or condemned by the International precisely because he was almost completely cut off from party contacts. He read newspapers and received belated accounts of political developments from relatives who visited him, but he himself had no influence on events. Shortly before his arrest he sent a letter to the Bolshevik leaders in which he took the side of the then majority (Stalin and Bukharin) against Trotsky but expressed disquiet at the ferocity of their intestine conflicts accusing the Bolsheviks in scarcely veiled terms of forgetting their duty to the international proletariat and jeopardizing the whole of Lenin's work. At the same time, being convinced that the wrong class could not fight unless it were allied with the peasantry, he was against Trotsky's programme of forced industrialization at the peasants' expense. Togliatti, who had taken Gramsci's place as Italian representative in the Comintern, had decided to support Stalin through thick and thin, as he did for the next thirty years, and Gramsci was alone in his criticism of Moscow. However, at the turn of the year 1928–9 Stalin switched the policy of the Comintern and the Bolshevik party in a direction completely opposite to Gramsci's views. The idea of a united front was abandoned, the attack was concentrated against social democracy ('social Fascism'), it was announced that the world revolution was imminent and that Communists must be prepared for a direct transition to the dictatorship of the proletariat; Bukharin fell, and Stalin set about the mass collectivization of Soviet agriculture. Togliatti organized a purge of refractory elements in what was left of the Italian party (one of the victims was Angelo Tasca). Gramsci expressed opposition to the new Comintern policy and sympathy with the expelled 'deviationists' in a conversation with his brother, who visited him in prison; however, as Gramsci's biographer Giuseppe Fiori has shown, the brother gave

Togliatti a false account of what was said, and thus saved Gramsci from certain condemnation by the party authorities and the Comintern.

Towards the end of 1933 Gramsci was allowed to move to a private clinic under police supervision, and at the end of the next year, when already in very poor health, he was temporarily released. He worked until the middle of 1935 and was then moved to a hospital in Rome, where he died in April 1937.

In addition to letters, Gramsci wrote nearly three thousand pages in prison. All these writings were published after the Second World War; the first edition of the letters, in 1947, was abridged by the Italian Communists for political reasons. The various notes written in 1929–35 were collected into six further volumes: *Il materialismo storico e la filosofia di Benedetto Croce* (1948), *Gli intellettuali e l'organizzazione della cultura* (1949), *Il risorgimento* (1949), *Note sul Machiavelli, sulla politica e sullo Stato moderno* (1949), *Letteratura e vita nazionale* (1950), *Passato e presente* (1951). Some of his earlier articles and pamphlets were also reprinted.

The prosecutor who declared at Gramsci's trial that 'this brain must be put out of action for twenty years' achieved the exact opposite of what he intended. If Gramsci had been allowed to pass the Fascist years in exile he would inevitably have become one of the many outcasts of Communism—unless he had gone to Moscow, when he would certainly have been done to death—and would have spent the rest of his days in a barren defence of his political actions for the benefit of a non-existent public. Thanks to the imprisonment which cut him off willy-nilly from current affairs, he was obliged to work on more theoretical and fundamental topics. As a result we have his interesting notes, containing among other things an attempt at a Marxist philosophy of culture whose originality and breadth of view cannot be denied.

2. The self-sufficiency of history; historical relativism

THE main theme of Gramsci's reflections is that which dominated Marx's early writings: the question of the relation of human thoughts, feelings, and will to 'objective' social processes. Few other Marxists expressed so emphatically the viewpoint generally known as historicism (in one sense of that term) in contrast to transcendentalism. The essence of this view is that the meaning and 'rationality' of all human behaviour and every product of human activity, including works of the mind such as philosophy and science, is manifested only in relation to the 'global' historical processes of which they are part. In other words, the 'truth' of philosophy or science is 'truth' in a socially pragmatic sense: what is true is that which, in a particular historical situation, expresses the real developmental trend of that situation. Neither philosophies nor sciences can be judged by any other criteria than those we use to judge social institutions, religious beliefs, emotions, or political movements. This anti-positivist and anti-scientistic relativism of Gramsci's was no doubt rooted in his Crocean studies, but he believed it to be the quintessence of Marxism—or of 'the philosophy of praxis', a term which he generally used in his prison notes to elude the censor, but which was also an accurate description from his point of view. Marxism, in particular, was also 'true' in this historical sense, i.e. it expressed the 'truth' of its times better than any other theory. Ideas could not be understood outside their social and historical context, irrespective of function and origin; there was thus no such thing as 'scientific philosophy' in the sense in which most Marxists used this term, i.e. a philosophy that 'reflected' reality as it was, regardless of whether we knew it or not. But, in the same way, there was no such thing as 'scientific science', i.e. science that merely described the universe as it was, independent of man. 'If we are to escape solipsism and also the mechanistic conceptions implied in the idea of thought as a receptive and ordering activity, we must pose the question "historically" (*storicisticamente*), at the same time basing our philosophy on "will" (in the last analysis, practical or political activity)—but a rational, not an arbitrary will, realizing itself in so far as it corresponds to objective historical necessities: that is to say, in so far as it is identical with the progressive actualization of universal history. If that will is represented initially by a single individual only, its rationality is attested by the fact that it becomes accepted permanently by the bulk of mankind and is thenceforward a culture, a matter of "common sense", a conception of the world, with an ethic in conformity with its structure' (*Opere*, vol. 2, 1949, pp. 22–3). In other words, the rightness of an idea is confirmed by, or perhaps actually consists in, the fact that it prevails historically—a view irreconcilable with the usual one that truth is truth no matter whether or when it is known, or who regards it as true and in what way. 'Ideas are not born of other ideas, philosophies do not beget other philosophies, but these are the ever-new expression of real historical development . . . Every truth, even though it may be universal and expressible in an abstract formula of the mathematical type . . . owes its efficacy to being expressed in the language of particular, concrete situations; if it cannot be so expressed it is a Byzantine, scholastic abstraction, a pastime for phrase-mongers' (*Opere*, vol. 7, 1952, p. 63). Gramsci, it is true, disclaims the imputation of relativism, but it is not clear how he can be acquitted of being a historical relativist. Criticizing Bukharin, he says: 'To think of a philosophical statement as being true in a particular historical period, i.e. as the necessary, inseparable expression of a particular historical activity or praxis, but as being overtaken and "nullified" [*vanificata*] in a subsequent period—to think this without falling into scepticism or moral and ideological relativism, in other words to take an historicist view of philosophy, is a somewhat arduous and difficult mental enterprise' (*Il materialismo storico, Opere,* vol. 2, p. 133). It is hard to get more than this out of Gramsci as far as the epistemological sense of 'truth' is concerned. But the basic thought is clear: it amounts to reducing all products of the mind to a historical function, and refusing to distinguish sharply between science and 'non-scientific' forms of mental activity. 'According to the theory of praxis it is clear that human history is not explained by the atomistic theory, but that the reverse is the case: the atomistic theory, like all other scientific hypotheses and opinions, is part of the superstructure' (ibid., p. 162). What was thus 'clear' to Gramsci was not so to the majority of Marxists, who rather took the opposite view that the scientific explanation of the universe accumulates historically as the advance of 'truth' in the everyday sense, and that 'science', unlike religious belief, art, or political opinions, is thus not part of the 'superstructure': on this view Marxism itself, as a scientific theory, can be vindicated 'objectively', i.e. independently of the fact that it also performs political functions as the weapon of the working class.

By virtue of this 'absolute historicism' (Gramsci's phrase), all the concepts by which our knowledge of the world is organized are related primarily not to 'things' but to relations between the users of those concepts. 'Matter is thus not to be considered in itself [*come tale*] but as it is socially and historically organized for production; in the same way, natural science is to be regarded essentially as an historical category, a human relationship' (ibid., p. 160). The same applies to the idea of 'human nature': as Gramsci repeats many times, there is no such thing as unchanging human nature, but only historically variable social relationships. He appears to reject the common-sense view that all historical changes occur within the limits set by relatively permanent biological and physical circumstances, by which man finds the universe to be governed. In this respect Gramsci reverts to the idea of 'pure historicism' which is present in Marx but was almost completely discarded from evolutionist interpretations in the style of Engels. (Before Gramsci, only Brzozowski attempted to conceive Marxism in this radically anti-scientistic way, though such tendencies can be found in Labriola in a less radical form.) For Gramsci nothing exists but the changing form of human 'praxis': all meaning derives from praxis and is related to it. Questions and answers are meaningful only in so far as they can be integrated in the human process of self-creation. In this sense human history is indeed the absolute boundary of knowledge.

For the same reason Gramsci, more than any other Marxist, rejected the view that the whole realm of the 'superstructure' is an expression of the 'truly real' aspects of social life, i.e. relations of production. The very distinction between 'base' and 'superstructure' seemed to him inessential. He repeated more than once, especially in controversy with Croce, that it was absurd to tax Marxists with holding that the 'superstructure' was a world of mere appearances or a 'less real' side of life than production relations. In the various aspects of the 'super-structure' social classes became aware of their position and opportunities, and were able to change the social conditions of which they thus became conscious. This was a continuous process, and there was therefore no point in talking of a clear 'primacy' of the base or debating which came 'first', still less in postu-lating a one-way determinism whereby the 'base' created the 'superstructure' it required. If any form of 'superstructure' could be called a mere appearance, this only meant that it had outlived its historical function and was no longer capa-ble of organizing social forces: this might apply to philosophical or religious doctrines or artistic trends as well as to scientific theories.

3. Critique of 'economism'. Prevision and will

GRAMSCI uses the terms 'fatalistic', 'deterministic', and 'mechanistic' almost without distinction and always with reference to views that he considers radi-cally opposed to Marxist doctrine. He does not dispute that there is a strong strain of determinism in the history of Marxism, but he attributes this to the historical circumstances of the early phase of the workers' movement. As long as the oppressed class does not possess the initiative but is restricted mainly to defensive action, it is apt to develop the compensatory idea that it is bound to triumph sooner or later because of 'historical laws', and that history is 'objec-tively' on its side. This is a primitive, quasi-religious faith, necessary in the early stages and comparable to fatalistic theories of predestination in Chris-tianity. It reached its height in German idealism in the proposition that free-dom is the awareness of necessity (Gramsci appears to interpret Hegel's formula in a stoic sense); it is in fact nothing more than the cry 'It is God's will.' Throughout history fatalistic beliefs have functioned as the ideology of dependent groups, and so it was in the early days of the workers' movement. However, once the proletariat is no longer condemned to a defensive attitude but becomes aware of its social position and able to take the initiative, it no longer needs to believe in a historical providence watching over its fate: any such belief is henceforth a hindrance, to be jettisoned as quickly as possible.

The philosophy of praxis cannot, by its very nature, rely on the operation of 'historical laws' as the agents of social change, as hidden deities using human beings to bring about their ends. Certainly the working class, when it reaches the level of consciousness at which it is able to take the initiative, encounters historical circumstances which cannot be arbitrarily altered: the rejection of determinism does not mean that in any given situation human will-power can achieve whatever it likes and is subject to no limits at all. But the question which of several possible developments will take place is not prejudged by any laws of history, for history is nothing but human praxis and therefore includes will. 'It may be said', Gramsci writes, 'that the economic factor (understood in the immediate, Judaic sense of historical economism) is only one of several ways in which the basic historical process manifests itself (factors of race, religion etc.); but it is this basic historical process that the philosophy of praxis seeks to explain, and this is why it is a philosophy, an "anthropology" and not a mere canon of historical research' (*Passato e presente, Opere*, vol. 7, pp. 183–4). Gramsci does not explain what he means by the 'basic historical process' of which economic changes, like cultural ones, are no more than a particular manifestation. It is clear, however, that he regards evolutionist and determinist theories of history, and likewise the principle of the causal 'primacy' of production relations *vis-à-vis* cultural phenomena, as a complete misconception of Marxism.

Since the historical process is indivisible and merely 'expresses' itself in different aspects of social life, it is impossible to maintain the 'technological' conception of the relationship between theory and practice which is also current among Marxists, i.e. the view that it is the task of theoreticians to provide practical politicians with effective plans of action based on a 'scientific' and 'objective' analysis of social processes. Gramsci protests against the idea that theory is instrumental or ancillary to practice. Important social processes occur thanks to the development of class-consciousness, and this is impossible without organization and intellectuals. Political action and awareness of that action, its direction and purpose, are not two separate phenomena but aspects of a single one, and it is difficult to speak of any 'primacy'. Intellectuals as such are participants in social 'praxis', and politicians as such are theoreticians. Accordingly, Gramsci declares that Lenin rendered a service to philosophy by improving the theory and practice of politics. This is in line with Gramsci's view of the 'unity of theory and practice', but at the same time it appears to deny Lenin the title of a philosopher in the strict sense; Gramsci in fact makes no mention of Lenin's philosophical views.

For the same reason, in Gramsci's view, there is no point in separating historical prognoses from the acts by which they are fulfilled. The act of foreseeing coincides with the act of realizing what is foreseen. 'In reality we can predict "scientifically" only the struggle but not its concrete phases, which are bound to be the result of conflicting forces in constant movement: these can never be reducible to fixed quantities, because quantity in them is always transforming itself into quality. In fact we "foresee" to the extent that we are active, bringing a conscious effort to bear and thus contributing materially to the result "foreseen". Prevision is thus not an act of scientific cognition but the abstract expression of an effort, the practical way in which a collective will is created. How, indeed, could prevision be an act of cognition? We can only know what is or has been, not what will be—for this does not exist, and is therefore by definition unknowable. Thus prevision can only be a practical act' (*Il materialismo storico*, p. 135).

Thus, in Gramsci's view, we do not know social processes by 'observing' them from outside; there is in fact no such observation. Cognition is an 'aspect' or 'expression' of social development, on the same footing as economic changes. (Gramsci expressly denies that economic development can be 'reduced' to the improvement of productive forces: in his *Notes on Machiavelli* (*Opere*, vol. 5) he joins issue with Achille Loria as the spokesman of this pseudo-Marxist 'economism'.) In the same way he rejects the traditional distinction between Is and Ought, as it was found in Kant and the neo-Kantians but also among Marxists of 'positivist' tendency. Ought is the form in which men express their desires, hopes, and wishes: it is therefore a part of social reality, as good as any other. It is as real as that which is; it is in fact inchoate action, just as all cognition is a form of practical action. Indeed, from the point of view of a philosophy in which 'praxis' is the most general category, the distinction between Is and Ought does not arise, any more than it does in pragmatism.

It does not follow, however—and this is an important point in Gramsci's argument—that people's thoughts are simply a perfect, unblemished reflection of their social position and practical activity. If this were so, one could not speak of false consciousness, ideological mystification, or the gradual development of class awareness, for consciousness would always be absolutely transparent; but we know that matters are otherwise. Gramsci frequently points out that there is a contradiction between what people profess and what they implicitly acknowledge, as revealed in their behaviour; and this contradiction is the rule rather than the exception. People have, as it were, two conflicting attitudes or sets of standards, those they proclaim and those expressed in their acts. Which of these is the individual's 'true' attitude? Gramsci clearly inclines to think that what matters is what people do, even if their words belie it: as far as the 'unity of theory and practice' is concerned, real consciousness is expressed in deliberate social behaviour, whereas any utterances to the contrary are merely verbal and 'superficial'. Gramsci does not discuss particular instances, but we can see what he is driving at: an outstanding example is the situation in which the dependent classes verbally acknowledge the principles inculcated by Church and education and tending to uphold class domination—in particular, the principle of the sanctity of property—but at the same time behave in practice as if they did not take these principles seriously, for instance when factories are occupied by the workers.

Gramsci did not develop or particularize these observations, however, and their exact purpose is not clear. That people say one thing and do another is a fairly commonplace truth, even in the form which accepts that they are not acting out of hypocrisy or bad faith but are really incapable of understanding their own motives, the reasons for their acts, and the extent to which they conflict with acknowledged principles. This kind of inconsistency is in no way a prerogative of the oppressed but is at least equally characteristic of the privileged classes, as seventeenth-century moralists pointed out. Nor does it follow from the divergence that the principles governing actual behaviour are 'more real' than those that are professed but not practised; indeed, it is not clear what this statement would mean. The most we can infer from the fact that the inconsistency is so prevalent is that moral rules are chiefly a means of compelling people to behave in ways contrary to their natural inclinations—a state of things which applies to all fields of moral behaviour and not only those related to the class struggle. The influence of verbally acknowledged standards on actual conduct varies along a continuous spectrum, and it is therefore of doubtful utility to speak of two kinds of *Weltanschauung*, the explicit and the implicit. Least of all, however, should we assume that in case of divergence it is the 'implicit' view expressed in action that deserves approval, and not the other. The sanctity of property is violated in practice not only by the oppressed but just as much by the privileged; not only in acts pertaining to the class struggle, but in individual cases of theft and extortion. No doubt Gramsci's real point was simply that social classes often pursue their interests in ways contrary to the accepted norms of the culture to which they belong: but to establish this undoubted fact there is no need to invoke a theory of 'two *Weltanschauungen*'.

As we have seen, in Gramsci's view Marxism was not a 'scientific' account of social reality from which practical rules can be deduced for effective political action, but was an expression of the class-consciousness of the proletariat and an aspect or component of its practical struggle. Accordingly, he argued, there was no point in dividing it into 'philosophical', 'sociological', and 'political' aspects. Philosophy, he frequently stated, might either be synonymous with history or the social process, or it might be the theoretical awareness of that process and thus an inseparable part of it. Sociology as such was a foredoomed attempt to apply characteristic modes of scientific thought to social phenomena, in the hope that these would prove amenable to law and would be as predictable as the revolutions of the planets. But this idea was no more than a relic of mechanism. There was no 'Marxist sociology' and there were no 'sociological laws'. What people thought about social phenomena was itself a social phenomenon, an expression of their initiative or passivity towards the world. The 'philosophy of praxis', in particular, was an act of self-knowledge of the proletariat as it assumed the role of an initiator of great historical processes: it was thus not a mere description of reality, but a practical act. In this respect, though not in all others, Gramsci's critique of 'mechanism' coincides with Lukács's.

Gramsci endeavoured by all possible means to minimize or obliterate the distinction between thought and behaviour. Since specifically human behaviour was always more or less conscious, and since, on the other hand, the most refined forms of philosophical, theoretical, and scientific thought were nothing but ways in which human beings became socially aware of their own practice, and were consequently themselves part of that practice, it followed that everything in human behaviour was in some way 'philosophical'; everyone had a philosophy of his own, though he could not necessarily express it properly.

These views of Gramsci's were called in question more than once, by Marxists and others. On the one hand, he emphasized the unique role of intellectuals in forming class-consciousness and organizing the class struggle; on the other hand, he often spoke as if the difference between implicit and theoretical consciousness was of no importance—everyone was a philosopher, because he acted consciously; philosophy was nothing but a name for the historical process, the sum of all human actions. It was easy to infer from this that it made no real difference whether a person simply performed an act or whether he could give a coherent account of why he did so: in other words, a working man who took some action to defend his interests was as much a 'theoretician' as Marx, who tried to evolve from such acts a universal theory of history. This view would lead to complete theoretical nihilism, which Gramsci in fact disavowed, thus showing himself to be inconsistent. His concern was to present theory as a mere 'aspect' of behaviour, with no special status. But it is impossible to argue from behaviour to theoretical consciousness: the fact that a snail's behaviour obeys biological laws does not mean that the snail is aware of them. Human behaviour, indeed, is always more or less conscious, but because human beings are very often unaware of their true motives or the causes of their actions, they are not essentially different from snails in this regard. The notion of 'theoretically implicit consciousness' turns out to be self-contradictory.

4. Critique of materialism

TOTAL historicism and the view that collective praxis is the only absolute reality, determining whether any philosophical question or answer is meaningful or not, is a denial of materialism, since it is a denial of any metaphysic whatever. From this point of view Gramsci was consistent, and his aim was to restore the original Marxist intuition which had been obscured by the naïveties of Engels and Lenin. His anti-metaphysical standpoint is most clearly seen in an extended critique of Bukharin's *Theory of Historical Materialism*, first published in 1921 and later translated into French; but he repeated the same ideas many times on other occasions. If, indeed, everything we have to do with is manifested to us only in connection with our practical activities, there is no point in inquiring about the universe 'in itself'. According to Gramsci, Marxism teaches that 'there is no "reality" existing in and for itself [*per sè stante, in sè e per sè*] but only in historical relation to human beings who modify it' (*Opere*, vol. 2, p. 23). Elsewhere we read:

> Is it supposed that there can be an objectivity outside history and outside human-ity? But who is to judge of such objectivity? Who can adopt the viewpoint of the 'uni-verse in itself', and what would such a viewpoint mean? It may very well be held that we have to do here with a residue of the idea of God, particularly the mystical notion of an unknown God . . . 'Objective' always means 'humanly objective', which may correspond exactly to 'historically subjective', i.e. 'objective' would mean 'universal subjective'. Man possesses objective knowledge in so far as knowledge is real for the whole human race *historically* unfied in a unitary cultural system . . . The concept of 'objectiveness' in metaphysical materialism is apparently intended to mean an objectivity that exists outside us as well as within us; but when we say that a certain reality would exist even if man did not, we are either using metaphor or falling into a kind of mysticism. We can know reality only in relation to mankind, and since man is historical development [*divenire*, 'becoming'], so the same is true of knowledge, reality, objectivity, etc. (*Opere*, vol. 2, pp. 142–3)

There is no need to demonstrate that these ideas are the precise contrary of the materialist metaphysics of Engels and Lenin. Gramsci, however, occasion-ally appeals to Engels and specifically to his statement that the materiality of the universe is proved by the historical development of science and philoso-phy. According to Gramsci this statement somehow incorporates the history of science into the very concept of materiality: that is to say, the development of knowledge did not so much prove the 'materiality of the universe' as create it. This view comes out most clearly in his critique of Lukács, who rejected Engels's idea of the 'dialectic of nature' on the ground that dialectic, being a process of the unification of subject and object, could only apply to human his-tory. Gramsci appears to defend Engels, arguing that Lukács presupposes dual-ism as between nature and man; if the history of nature is included in the history of mankind, there is no reason why dialectic should not apply to nature also. This reasoning not only does not rehabilitate Engels's materialism but emphasizes Lukács's 'historical subjectivism', as it subsumes natural history into human history and not the other way about. On this interpretation Marx-ism turns out to be collective solipsism, a world-picture that is made wholly rel-ative to human social practice.

In Gramsci's eyes materialism, far from being the contrary of religion, is the direct outcome of religious superstition; it is like primitive common sense, the apparent 'obviousness' of which only conceals a lack of critical thought.

The broad public does not even believe that there can be such a problem as whether the outside world exists objectively: one has only to put the question thus to be greeted by an outburst of irrepressible, Gargantuan laughter. The public 'believes' that the outside world is objectively real, but the question arises: what is the origin of that 'belief, and what is the critical value of the term 'objectively'? It is in fact a belief of religious origin, even if the person in question has no religious feelings. Because all religions have always taught that the world, nature, the universe were created by God before he created man, so that man came upon the world ready-made, catalogued and defined once and for all, this belief has become a cast-iron tenet of 'common sense' and lives on as sturdily as ever, even though religious feelings have become dulled or extinguished. And consequently, to appeal to common-sense experience in order to laugh subjectivism out of court is a kind of 'reactionary' device, an implicit return to religious sentiment; as we see Catholic writers and speakers resort to the same means to bring about the same effect of corrosive ridicule. (*Opere*, vol. 2, p. 138)

Gramsci's allusions are clear. He grew up at a time when Catholic philosophy was dominated by the battle with modernism and its 'idealist' doctrines, when the easiest way to rout an adversary for the benefit of an uneducated audience was to claim that the idealists held that 'that table there' did not exist or was a mere appearance, whereas any child could see that they were wrong. Lenin's polemic against 'idealism' was on the same level, and it is not surprising that analogies presented themselves.

Gramsci was well aware of the crudeness of the forms in which Marxism was most commonly taught and preached. To some extent he regarded this as unavoidable or at any rate understandable: Marxism was, after all, a world-view for the proletariat, who were a socially dependent group, and in its everyday forms it could not rise far above the level of popular superstition and everyday commonsense. But in this shape it could not effectively challenge the ideologies of the educated classes: it could only score cheap, illusory victories against its most primitive adversaries. If Marxists wanted to make real headway in the intellectual field they must tackle opponents of substance and make a genuine attempt to understand the latter's views.

Gramsci was one of the few Marxists who attempted to restore historical 'immanentism' or anti-metaphysical 'collective subjectivism' as the true philosophical content of Marxism, at a time when corroborative evidence was sparse. (Marx's early writings, above all the 1844 Paris Manuscripts, were published while Gramsci was in prison, and he cannot have read them; the *Theses on Feuerbach* were the chief available material for the philosophical interpretation of Marxism.) In this respect his ideas are completely incompatible with Leninist orthodoxy.

5. Intellectuals and the class struggle. The concept of hegemony

In the search for forms in which the new class, striving to dominate social life, might or should organize its own culture, Gramsci frequently addressed himself to the history of the Roman Church. He seems to have been impressed by the ideological strength of Christianity, and he laid particular stress on the care taken by the Church at all periods to prevent an excessive gap developing between the religion of the learned and that of simple folk, and to preserve the link between the teaching imparted to the faithful at all levels. Gramsci indeed maintained that the link was purely 'mechanical', but he recognized that the Church had had enormous success in the struggle for mastery over men's consciences. If the working class was to meet the demands of the situation which enabled it to create a new culture and a new system of power, it must also create new forms of intellectual work and a new interrelation between politics and economic production on the one hand and, on the other, the activity of those intellectuals who took the side of the proletariat.

The proletariat needed 'organic' intellectuals (one of Gramsci's favourite and most frequent adjectives): that is to say, intellectuals who did not simply describe social life from outside in accordance with scientific rules, but who used the language of culture to 'express' the real experiences and feelings which the masses could not express for themselves. In order to understand those experiences, they must feel the same passions as the masses. Gramsci used the term 'intellectuals' in a wide sense, practically equivalent to 'intelligentsia' or the whole educated class. On the one hand, each of the 'main' social classes developed its own intellectual stratum; on the other, intellectual work united people into a single stratum which preserved the continuity of culture through the ages and was bound by a certain solidarity. The fact that intellectuals appeared to form a separate *métier* of their own, as opposed to being the mouthpieces of a particular class standpoint, inclined them towards idealistic philosophies which asserted the complete autonomy of intellectual activity. The victory of the working class was impossible without a cultural victory, and for this it needed to evolve an intellectual stratum which could express the actual experiences of the masses with conviction and in educated language. This applied to philosophy as well as literature, both of which could not really be explained by their own historical 'logic', but 'expressed' the distinctive social relationships of a given epoch. It did not follow that, for instance, literature could be reduced to political propaganda. On the contrary, a work of art was a work of art not because of its moral or political content but because of the form with which that content was identified; an extra-artistic intention governing the artist's work could not in itself produce a work of any value. Hence it was no use trying to produce an artificial culture without intellectuals who themselves truly shared the values of the working class.

Just because the historical process was a single whole, neither cultural activities nor intellectuals had any autonomous significance. It followed that the 'organic' character of intellectual and artistic work was also a condition of cultural achievement.

Gramsci believed that the working class was on the way to creating its own original culture, quite different from that of the bourgeoisie: it would destroy bourgeois myths and prejudices and set up for the first time truly universal spiritual values. It is not clear from Gramsci's arguments how far he expected cultural continuity to be broken by the proletarian revolution. He did not talk the language of the Russian radicals of Proletkult, but he insisted that the new culture must be 'quite different' from the old. Such language admits of any desired conclusion as regards the manner and extent to which the old culture is to be destroyed.

However, and this was an important point in Gramsci's argument, the workers could only win if they achieved cultural 'hegemony' before attaining political power. The concept of hegemony is important in Gramsci's writings, but it is used in varying senses. Occasionally he seems to identify it with political power exercised by coercion, but as a rule he distinguishes the two concepts, so that hegemony signifies the control of the intellectual life of society by purely cultural means. Every class tries to secure a governing position not only in public institutions but also in regard to the opinions, values, and standards acknowledged by the bulk of society. The privileged classes in their time secured a position of hegemony in the intellectual as well as the political sphere; they subjugated the others by this means, and intellectual supremacy was a precondition of political rule. The main task of the workers in modern times was to liberate themselves spiritually from the culture of the bourgeoisie and the Church and to establish their own cultural values in such a way as to attract the oppressed and intellectual strata to themselves. Cultural hegemony was a fundamental and prior condition of attaining political power. The working class could only conquer by first imparting its world-view and system of values to the other classes who might be its political allies: in this way it would become the intellectual leader of society, just as the bourgeoisie had done before seizing political control.

No oppressed class in history had yet succeeded in doing this. The typical situation was that of a gulf between mass culture and the intellectuals; a particularly striking example, with far-reaching consequences, was the divergence between Renaissance humanism and the Reformation. The latter was a mass movement, the former a purely intellectual critique. In the last analysis, Gramsci believed, humanism and the Renaissance were reactionary. Modern intellectual liberalism was analogous to the humanistic critique, and Marxism to the Reformation. Croce was the modern equivalent of Erasmus, with his vacillation, irresolution, and constant gravitation towards the political establishment. His critique of Catholic modernism, while ostensibly based on the same grounds as his opposition to Catholicism in general, had 'objectively' aided the Jesuits to combat modernism. (The Jesuits had conducted their campaign much more skilfully than the 'integralists' favoured by Pius X, who interpreted 'modernism' so widely as to estrange many intellectuals from the Church, while affording the real modernists greater room for manoeuvre.) Croce's conservative and liberal reformism was based on the Hegelian doctrine that every synthesis preserves elements of thesis and antithesis: he claimed to judge the conflict from the standpoint of an arbiter who could foresee the future synthesis and the contribution to it of each of the present contestants. But it was not in fact possible to know this, and the object of any conflict was to destroy the adversary and not to save him for a future synthesis. In practice Croce's philosophy amounted to constant attempts to moderate and assuage the conflict, which only helped to confirm the hegemony of the bourgeoisie. His critique of Catholicism had a most important effect, but a reactionary one: by detaching the intellectuals of southern Italy from the Church he estranged them from the peasant masses, associated them with national bourgeois and then with cosmopolitan culture, and finally made them spiritual vassals of the bourgeoisie. As the intellectual leader of Italian liberalism, Croce did much to deepen the gulf between the educated classes and the people and to prevent the development of a new proletarian culture. His anti-Catholicism and his anti-Marxism (or rather his pronounced revisionism) went hand in hand; the former cut the intelligentsia off from the peasantry, the latter from the working class.

Gramsci dreamed of a Marxism that would be a kind of synthesis of humanism and the Reformation, avoiding the natural crudity of a popular world-view but preserving its appeal to the masses while acquiring the ability to solve complex cultural problems. It would be 'a culture that, in Carducci's words, would synthesize Robespierre and Kant, politics and philosophy, into a dialectical unity within a social group, no longer merely French or German but European and world-wide' (*Opere*, vol. 2, p. 200). Croce was right in saying that one must not take away people's religion without giving them something that satisfied the same needs, but he admitted despite himself that idealistic philosophy could not fill the bill. Marxism must indeed take the place of previous world-views, but it could only do so if it met the same spiritual needs as they had—in other words, people must be able to recognize it as an expression of their own experience.

The question arises whether Gramsci's idea of a new proletarian culture differed from that of Lenin, who emphasized that culture was 'ancillary' to political objectives. On the one hand, Gramsci regarded cultural hegemony, achieved by purely ideological means, as a prior condition of attaining political power, whereas for Lenin that attainment of power was a purely technical question: power could and must be seized whenever circumstances allowed. On the other hand, we read in Gramsci's *Notes on Machiavelli:* 'If it is the case that every type of state must go through a phase of economic-corporative primitivism, we must infer that the content of the political hegemony of the new social group that has established the new type of state must be chiefly of an economic order: it is a matter of reorganizing the structure and the real relations between human beings and the economic world of production. The superstructural elements are bound to be exiguous, provisional and contentious, but with scattered elements of "planning". The cultural aspect, above all, will be negative, directed towards criticism of the past, obliterating it from memory and destroying it; the lines of construction will as yet be outlines only, rough sketches that can and must be revised at any moment to conform to the new structure that is being built' (*Opere*, vol. 5, pp. 132–3).

It is difficult to read these words in any but the obvious sense that, as far as culture is concerned, the new proletarian state will concentrate on destroying the heritage of the past, relegating the question of new values to an uncertain future. In this vital matter, as in several others, Gramsci's notes are lacking in order and consistency.

6. Organization and mass movement. The society of the future

THERE is no doubt that Gramsci, unlike Lenin, took a highly sensitive view of the difference between, on the one hand, the proletariat as the real subject of the political struggle and the subsequent building of socialism, and, on the other, the political organization which was to direct these processes. He never sidestepped such questions, as Lenin did, by saying that the masses were led by the party and the party by its leaders, that this was how things must be and that there was no problem about it. Gramsci wanted the political movement of the working class to be a movement of real workers, not of professional politicians seeking support from the working class. In this respect many of his arguments coincide with the criticisms of Rosa Luxemburg.

Gramsci's thoughts on the role of the party, and his critique of party bureaucracy, first appeared in his journalistic writings at the time of *L'Ordine Nuovo* and were aimed chiefly at the bureaucratic and 'inorganic' type of political leadership practised by the German and Italian social democrats. 'The Party', he wrote,

> identifies itself with the historical consciousness of the popular masses and governs their spontaneous, irresistible movement; this government is disembodied, it oper-

ates through millions of spiritual ties, it is an irradiation of authority (*prestigio*) that can only become an effective government at certain supreme moments ... The Party is the upper hierarchy of that irresistible mass movement: it exercises the most effective of dictatorships, that which is born of prestige, the conscious and spontaneous acceptance of an authority that is acknowledged to be indispensable for the success of the work in hand. Woe betide us if, through a sectarian conception of the Party's function in the revolution, we should try to turn it into a material hierarchy, to fix in mechanical forms of immediate power the governing apparatus of the moving masses, to constrict the revolutionary process into Party forms. If that happens we may succeed in diverting part of mankind from its course and in 'dominating' history, but the true revolutionary process will escape from the control and influence of the Party, which will unconsciously become an organ of conservatism. (Article of 27 Dec. 1919, quoted in *2000 Pagine di Gramsci*, ed. Ferrata and Gallo, 1964, vol. 1, pp. 446–7)

'The Communist Party is the instrument and historical form of the process of inward liberation whereby the workman is changed from an executor to an initiator: instead of a mass he becomes a guide and leader, instead of an arm—a brain and a will' (article of 4 Sept. 1920, ibid., p. 491).

Gramsci's many references to the 'dialectical unity' in which the spontaneous movement from below combines with the planned, organized activity of the party are not specific enough to form an articulate theory. However, his main point is clearly that the political organization should be subordinate to the real aspirations of the working class and should not be allowed to claim that it expresses those aspirations by virtue of its own 'scientific' omniscience, regardless of what the empirical 'masses' actually think. A party for which the 'masses' are only an object of tactical manoeuvres and not a source of inspiration is doomed to degenerate into a clique of professionals and to become a reactionary force. This view is reflected in two important aspects of Gramsci's thought: his idea of the revolution, and the role he assigns to workers' councils.

As we have seen, Gramsci does not regard the revolution as a mere technical question of seizing power, an operation that the political machine can and should carry out whenever circumstances are favourable. The proletarian revolution is not only a question of political opportunity but also of cultural and technical conditions: the spiritual emancipation of the working masses and the attainment of a level of social development such that a socialist transformation can be effective. As he wrote in *L'Ordine Nuovo*, the revolution is not proletariat and Communist simply because it transfers power to people who call themselves Communists, or because it abolishes the institutions of the old regime. It is proletariat and Communist when it liberates existing productive forces, strengthens the initiative of the proletariat, and establishes a society the development of which is accompanied by the disappearance of class divisions and the withering away of state institutions. It must find on the scene forces that are capable of transforming the apparatus of production from an instrument of oppression into an instrument of liberation. In this context the Communist party must be a party of the masses spontaneously seeking to throw off their bonds, and not a Jacobin-type party using the masses for its own ends.

Gramsci's attitude in this matter was certainly that of a Communist and not a reformist social democrat. When he spoke of 'economic maturity' he did not mean, as did orthodox members of the Second International, that socialists must wait until the state of productive forces developed to a point at which the working class could attain power by parliamentary means. He was of course convinced, like all Marxists, that socialism grew out of the conflict between the level of technology and existing production relations which barred the way to further technical progress, so that socialist revolution could be effective only in a state of highly developed capitalism; but he did not try to define this situation more closely, and probably did not think it possible to do so in the abstract. He did not believe, however, in the attainment of power by parliamentary means. The political revolution must, he considered, be a movement of the masses, aware of their desire for liberation and intellectually mature enough to take charge of the whole machinery of production, not through a political apparatus but of their own accord.

For the same reason, the idea of workers' councils played a dominant role in his thoughts at the time of *L'Ordine Nuovo*. They could not, he argued, be replaced by the party or the trade unions, but were the true form of the organization of a communist society of producers and were the principal organ of liberation of the proletariat. They did not make the party superfluous, however: it would continue to have its place as an agent of organization and communist education. But the councils, besides looking after production, were the true organ of the dictatorship of the proletariat. Arising in a capitalist society, they were a model of the proletarian state of the future, and thus opened a new era of human history. The party was not to be their 'ready-made superstructure', nor was its function to supervise them: its task was to aid the liberation of the proletariat and bring the day of revolution closer.

In short, Gramsci believed literally in 'government by councils' as distinct from government by the party. He thus shared the view which Lenin set out in *State and Revolution* but repudiated immediately after seizing power, and which oppositionists in the Bolshevik party vainly tried to reassert for some years afterwards.

Like all Communists, Gramsci was convinced that the parliamentary system of government was done for and could not provide a model for the state of the future. However, he emphasized in his *Notes on Machiavelli* that this did not mean he favoured bureaucratic government. It remained a question whether a representative system could be devised which was neither parliamentary nor bureaucratic. In the *Notes on Machiavelli*, as opposed to his articles in *L'Ordine Nuovo*, Gramsci does not appear to think that workers' councils provide the answer. (They are not mentioned in his prison writings.)

While Gramsci's critique of bureaucratic centralism in 1919–20 was apparently chiefly directed against the parties of the Second International, his prison writings on the subject seem clearly to be aimed against Communism in its Leninist form. 'The predominance of bureaucratic centralism in the state is a sign that the governing group is saturated and is turning into a narrow clique whose object is to safeguard its own petty privileges, restraining or even stifling the development of opposing forces, even when those forces are in accord with the basic interests of the ruling elements . . . The pathological manifestations of bureaucratic centralism are due to a lack of initiative and responsibility at the base, that is to say the political backwardness of peripheral forces, even when these are homogeneous with the dominant territorial group' (*Opere*, vol. 5, pp. 76–7). In his remarks about the 'latter-day Prince'—for the modern counterpart of the *Principe* is no other than the political party, the organization of a collective will—he repeatedly criticizes totalitarian parties that degenerate into a privileged caste to which mass movements and mass initiative are not a source of strength but a threat. It is hard to know exactly how far Gramsci was aware of the course of events in Russia which led to absolute control by the party bureaucracy and the destruction of all democratic elements, whether political or industrial. But his criticism is so general and fundamental that it is hard to doubt that he had in mind not only Fascism but Soviet Communism. Noting that the ruling party also exercises police power, he observes: 'A party's police function may be either progressive or regressive. It is progressive when it aims at keeping dispossessed reactionary forces within the bounds of legality and raising the backward masses to the level of the new legality. It is regressive when it aims at restraining the living forces of history and maintaining an outdated, anti-historical legality that has become a mere empty shell . . . When the party is progressive it functions "democratically" (in the sense of democratic centralism); when it is regressive it functions "bureaucratically" (in the sense of bureaucratic centralism). In the latter case the party is merely an executive, not a deliberating body; accordingly it is technically a policing organ, and its title of a "political party" is no more than a mythological metaphor' (ibid., p. 26). The reference to 'dispossessed reactionary forces' clearly indicates that he is talking about the Communist party in power and not the Fascists; and it is hard to imagine that when he spoke of the degeneration of that party he had in mind only an abstract possibility and not the process that was actually going on, and of which he was more or less well informed. At the same time he certainly still believed that Communism could be realized in the form described (as he thought) by Marx, i.e. a system in which the mass of producers exercised direct control over production and political life, and which still paid honour to Marx's principle that the educator must likewise be educated.

Like Sorel, whom he criticized but from whom he learnt much, Gramsci believed that a socialist society meant extending to the whole of social life the principles that governed a democratically organized production plant: it should be a community of producers in which political rule and economic authority conditioned and supported each other. Like Marx, he believed that socialism would in time obliterate the difference between civil society and the state, or rather would cause the first to absorb the second, while the police functions of the state would wither away and become unnecessary. On this point he did not differ from Marxists of any other shade of opinion. He speculated concerning the schools of the future, which on the one hand would not be based on the 'Jesuit', 'mechanical' system of learning by rote, but on the other hand would not pretend that all learning was child's play. They would encourage pupils to show initiative and independence and would at the same time provide all-round education with emphasis on knowledge for its own sake, rather than prematurely forcing pupils into vocational specialization.

7. Summary

IF we compare Gramsci's Communist doctrine with Lenin's we find certain basic differences which are logically interconnected.

In the first place, unlike either Lenin or the materialists and evolutionists of the Second International, Gramsci rejects Engels's brand of materialism, which interprets human history as a modified continuation of natural history, and he rejects the idea of knowledge as a copy or 'reflection' of some reality independent of man, and of praxis as a method of testing the truth of hypotheses. Gramsci's position is one of species subjectivism and historical relativism. All reality that can be meaningfully spoken of is a component of human history, including reality as observed by science. Consequently, human history is the impassable frontier of human knowledge. Not only are there no such things as universal natural laws of which history is a special case, but nature itself is part of human history, for it is known to us only in relation thereto. Thus human praxis determines the meaning of all components of knowledge, and (contrary to Lukács's view) there is no fundamental distinction between scientific and humanistic knowledge, for all knowledge is in fact humanistic.

Secondly, it follows that all cognition is an expression of the actual historical consciousness of social groups, and no distinction can be drawn between social consciousness on the one hand and the 'scientific' or 'objective' knowledge of scholars on the other, although one can distinguish more and less primitive forms of consciousness. Consequently—and this is a crucial difference—Gramsci rejects the idea of 'scientific socialism', i.e. the doctrine (accepted by both Kautsky and Lenin, and in a modified form by Lukács) that socialist theory must be evolved by intellectuals outside the workers' movement and then injected into that movement as its 'correct' and 'authentic' class-consciousness. True, socialist theory does not come into being without the aid of intellectuals, who are a necessary element in socialism; but it is no better than a doctrinaire pastime unless it expresses the actual experience of the working class.

Thirdly, it also follows that Gramsci takes a different view of the party. On pain of degenerating into a body of professional politicians fighting for jobs, it must not regard itself as the repository of a 'scientific world-view' elaborated outside the empirical consciousness of the proletariat. It must not be a party of manipulators, using tactical and demagogical means to achieve a temporary advantage and finally grasping the opportunity to exercise dictatorial power. The party can of course do these things, but if it does it will turn into a reactionary privileged clique. To be able to perform the tasks associated with the conquest of power by the proletariat, it must identify itself with the latter's real aspirations and organize them or 'express' them in its ideology.

Hence, fourthly, Gramsci's interpretation of the revolution. It is not, in his view, a mere technical act of seizing power, a *coup d'état* enabling the Communists to impose their will on society. Communist revolution is a mass process in which the toiling masses, backed by the 'democratic confidence' of all working classes, take over economic and political leadership, in their own name and not through a separate political entity. Workers' councils are the proper instrument of this process, the object of which is to transform society so as to render superfluous all forms of political rule, to prevent the recurrence of class divisions, and to bring about the withering-away of the state and the unification of society. A revolution in this sense cannot take place unless it is preceded by a large measure of spiritual emancipation of the working class, transforming it from an object of the political process into a subject and initiator.

On all these points, which are clearly linked together, Gramsci's idea of Communism conflicts with Lenin's—except the idea of government by workers' councils, which Lenin took up briefly and discarded almost at once, and which was contrary to his basic political doctrine of dictatorship by the party as the repository of 'scientific socialism'. The idea of 'scientific socialism' and the manipulative conception of the party's role were common to Lenin and the social democrats, with the important difference that the latter believed in representative democracy, whereas rule by naked force was one of Lenin's chief theoretical tenets. In addition, the social democrats, in the name of historical determinism, maintained that the revolution could not take place until such time as the forces of production had reached the proper stage of development, whereas Lenin was resolved to seize power the moment political circumstances enabled him to do so. Gramsci did not believe in historical determinism or in 'laws of history' using the human will as their instrument, but he also rejected the Blanquist or Jacobin notion of a political *coup* as a purely technical operation. He believed that the human will was not governed by any historical necessity, but he naturally did not regard it as completely unfettered. Socialist revolution was for him a matter of will—but it must be the will of the masses, who aspired to organize production themselves and had no desire to transfer their rights to self-appointed 'scientific' guardians.

Gramsci was a Communist and not a social democrat inasmuch as he excluded the possibility of attaining power by parliamentary means and also rejected parliamentarism in a socialist society (though, like Lenin, he accepted participation in the parliamentary struggle in certain situations). He also envisaged the radical expropriation of the bourgeoisie, the collectivization of all means of production, and the eventual abolition of the state, and looked forward to a society of perfect unity. Yet his idea of Communism was different from Lenin's both philosophically and politically, though he was probably not fully aware of this. One may say that Gramsci provided the ideological nucleus of an alternative form of Communism, which, however, has never existed as a political movement, still less as an actual regime.

It can thus be seen why the exponents of modern 'humanist' or 'democratic' trends in Communism, as well as various forms of revisionism, seek encouragement in Gramsci's writings. The main theme of internal criticism in the Communist movement is that of the socialist bureaucracies, which claim the right to rule by force on the ground that they embody the 'true' desires and aspirations of the working class, not because the workers have elected them democratically but because they are the holders of an infallible scientific theory. The criticism of 'scientific socialism', in the sense of that term which identifies it with the self-glorification of the ruling bureaucracies, comes very close to Gramsci's ideas and explains the popularity of his writings in revisionist circles. Whether his variant of Communism is as practicable as Lenin's (which has proved practicable beyond any shadow of doubt) is another question, which we shall consider later.

VII

György Lukács: Reason in the Service of Dogma

LUKÁCS's personality and his role in the history of Marxism are, and no doubt will be for a long time, a matter of lively controversy. It is agreed, however, that he was the most outstanding Marxist philosopher during the period of Stalinist orthodoxy. Indeed, we may go further and say that he was the only one: he alone expressed the fundamental tenets of Leninism in the language of the German philosophical tradition and, unlike the unsophisticated Marxists of his day, he wrote in a manner that enabled at least some Western intellectuals to digest his thoughts. But it is a matter of dispute whether he was a true philosopher of Stalinism, an intellectual exponent of that particular system, or rather, as some would have it and as he himself often suggested in later times, a kind of Trojan horse—an ostensibly orthodox disciple who, under the pretence of Stalinism, was in fact purveying a 'genuine', non-Stalinist form of Marxism.

The question is indeed extremely complicated. Lukács joined the Communist party unexpectedly, at a comparatively late stage of his intellectual life: he was thirty-three and had published a number of works unconnected with Marxism, although critics, as usual, have been at pains to show that his thought developed on consistent lines throughout. During the rest of his life (he lived to be eighty-six) he remained faithful to the Communist cause through various political upheavals and ideological changes. He was frequently condemned and attacked by orthodox Stalinists and frequently submitted to party discipline, recanting his previous opinions only to disavow or modify the recantation when times became easier. Thus his works are full of palinodes, retractions, withdrawals of retractions, and reinterpretations of earlier writings, particularly in forewords and epilogues to reprints of his books that appeared in the 1960s.

From the beginning of his Marxist career to the end of his life Lukács professed fidelity to Lenin and Leninism, and the question how far he was a 'Stalinist philosopher' depends in part on the more general question of the relationship between Leninism and Stalinism. The quotations from Stalin and flattering remarks about him that occur in Lukács's writings (though much less often than in the average ideological output of the time) are not a decisive argument, as for many years practically every work published in the Soviet Union or its dependencies was studded with references to Stalin and his glorious intellect. This applied even to manuals of physics, cookery books, and so on, though it was still possible to distinguish between ritual homage and genuinely Stalinist works: there was not really any such thing as 'Stalinist physics'. On the other hand, we cannot accept without reservation Lukács's later assurances that he was always critical of Stalinism but for tactical reasons conformed to the party line: for one who objects in private but joins in the public chorus of praise is not an objector, but a eulogist pure and simple. Thus the question can only be decided by examining the content of Lukács's writings and the political significance of his comments and actions at various times.

Lukács's voluminous works are devoted for the most part to questions of aesthetics and literary criticism; but it would be wrong to say that he was a critic first and foremost and a philosopher only in a lesser degree. In accordance with his conception of Marxism he always endeavoured to relate even the most detailed questions to the 'totality' of great social processes and the past and future history of mankind. This attitude, he believed, was as essential to Marxism as it was to Hegelianism, and accordingly he approached all questions from the standpoint of a philosopher.

Lukács's work has generally been considered in the context of international Marxism or German philosophy: most of his books were written in German and are concerned with the history of German culture. In recent years attention has also been drawn increasingly to the Hungarian 'background' of his philosophy and the important part played in his development by the Hungarian cultural tradition. However, the predominantly German strain in his work is clear when it is studied as an element in the history of Marxism; and he was certainly far better acquainted with the language, literature, and philosophy of Germany than with those of any other country besides his native Hungary, where he spent the beginning and end of his life.

1. Life and intellectual development. Early writings

GYÖRGY LUKÁCS (1885–1971), the son of a banker, was born at Budapest, where he attended grammar school and university, graduating in 1906. From his schooldays onwards he belonged to socialist groups under the aegis of the left-wing social democrat Ervin Szabó (1877–1918). Szabó was not an orthodox Marxist but an exponent of anarcho-syndicalism, and it was mainly through him that Lukács for a time came under the influence of Sorel. From his earliest years Lukács was attracted by the modernist, anti-positivist outlook that prevailed at the turn of the century: he sought a 'global', all-embracing world-view, free from the inhibitions of positivism and empiricism but also capable of opposing the national, conservative, and Christian tradition. In short, he was in quest of a new metaphysic, like a great many of his contemporaries in all parts of Europe. In the same spirit he helped to found a theatrical group devoted to producing works by the new philosophical dramatists—Ibsen, Strindberg, and Gerhart Hauptmann. Despite difficulties and opposition this group maintained itself for four years, from 1904 to 1908. In 1906 and again in 1909–10 Lukács continued his studies in Berlin, where he attended the lectures of Simmel among others. Kantianism was then dominant in German universities, and young philosophers naturally fell under its influence. Lukács was attracted by versions of Kantianism which concentrated on the philosophy of history and the methodology of the social sciences and which sought to go beyond the 'critical' point of view (in Kant's sense of the term): i.e. they did not accept that the theory of knowledge must logically take precedence of all metaphysical questions, a view which meant in effect that the latter could not be framed correctly or would remain insoluble. Lukács returned to Germany in 1913 and studied at Heidelberg: he attended the lectures of Rickert, Windelband, and others, and made the acquaintance of Max Weber, Stefan George, Emil Lask, and Ernst Bloch.

From 1906 onwards he wrote articles for Hungarian literary magazines: some of these were republished in his first book, which appeared in Hungarian in 1910 and in German in the following year, entitled *Die Seele und die Formen*. Like other early works by Lukács, this is a kind of philosophic essay on literary themes. Goldmann discerns in it a 'tragic Kantianism' with a phenomenological slant: Lukács's concept of 'form', he believes, corresponds to the 'significant structure' of the phenomenologists, but the approach is one of 'static structuralism', i.e. the quest for meaning independent of any consideration of genesis or historical change. Lukács, in fact, argues that every literary work should be regarded as an attempt to give form to the author's soul or sense of life. The attempt is natural and inevitable, but the form itself connotes an acceptance of the imperfect, a limitation of the content that it aims to express. It is as though the very process of artistic creativity, the attempt to subdue the spirit to forms, reveals our basic inability to achieve a true synthesis of the internal and the external, subjectivity and expression. Lukács opposes altogether the kind of artistic culture that only tries to depict the contingency of life and pays no heed to its 'essence': he thus rejects naturalism as firmly as impressionism. At the same time he appears to hold that the search for meaning and essence brings to light the inescapable tragedy of life, the individual's dependence on invisible and unintelligible powers that break out into insoluble conflicts. He is as far removed as possible from 'aestheticism', if by that is meant faith in the absolute autonomy of form *vis-à-vis* the genesis of a work: forms are a way of imparting unity to the world, but where spiritual life itself is impoverished and chaotic, the perfection of forms cannot restore its value. According to Lukács, modern artistic culture either seeks after 'abstract' form, i.e. it apes the perfection of past forms that will not accommodate a new content, or else it tries to reject form altogether; in either case the attempt does not signify a crisis of form as such, but only the weakness and spuriousness of the 'life' which seeks to express itself in art.

In *Die Theorie des Romans*, written at Heidelberg in 1914–15 and published in 1916 in the *Zeitschrift für Ästhetik und allgemeine Kunstwissenschaft* (and in book form in 1920), Lukács appeared to have reached a less pessimistic and fatalistic standpoint. Looking back in the 1950s he described this work as reactionary in all respects—idealistic, mystical, etc. Nevertheless, it is regarded today as one of his most important achievements. L. Congdon in his study points out the profound effect that Lukács's reading of Dostoevsky and Kierkegaard had on his development during the 1914–18 War. At that time he believed that the novel as a literary genre was an expression of the world in which relations between individuals were mediated by social forms and institutions, or 'reified' as he would have said at a later date. The very existence of the novel bore witness to a cultural disease, the inability of human beings to communicate directly. Dostoevsky's greatness lay in the fact that he had succeeded in portraying human relationships that were not determined by social or class conditions—so that in this sense, paradoxical as it might seem, his works were not novels at all. In the discussion of Dostoevsky's 'Utopia' there could certainly be discerned an anticipation of questions that were to occupy Lukács's attention in his subsequent Marxist works: questions as to the possibility of a society which, in accordance with Marx's romantic vision, would sweep away all social and institutional obstacles and enable human beings to meet one another as individuals, not representatives of anonymous forces. However, *Die Theorie des Romans* makes no mention of Marxism, though it shows the influence of Dilthey and Hegel: Lukács regards literary forms as the expression of changing historical totalities, each of which in turn seeks to achieve self-consciousness in artistic creation. In accordance with Hegel's philosophy of history, art is the realm of the objectivization of the 'spirit of the age', and its significance cannot be reduced to mere form; on the other hand, it has its own autonomy and is not simply a function of philosophy or science. The 'intellectualist' view of artistic creation is thus no less mistaken than romantic faith in the privileged position of art in creating a universal synthesis of human thought and activity.

Lukács's writings in his last pre-Marxist years show that, in his aesthetic studies as in other fields, he was absorbed by ethical problems: the contradiction between the decisions of individuals and the results of their acts, the conflict between the need for expression and the self-limiting function of expression, the conflict between the need for direct communication and the social forms that make it impossible. During the war, besides his unfinished essay on Dostoevsky, Lukács wrote a study (also unfinished) of Kierkegaard as a critic of Hegel. As Congdon points out, Lukács's conversion to Communism may itself have been the result of his seeing the situation in terms of Kierkegaard's 'either–or': a state of conflict in which there is no possibility of synthesis between two sets of values, and in which the individual must therefore choose between them.

After returning to Budapest in 1915 Lukács was among the leaders of an intellectual circle, and subsequently an independent study centre, where young intellectuals seeking philosophical and moral answers to the problems of war-torn Europe attempted to give expression to their feelings of despair and hope. Several of Lukács's comrades in this endeavour were to become eminent in different cultural spheres: Karl Mannheim, Zoltán Kodály, Arnold Hauser, Béla Bartók, and Michael Polanyi. The general atmosphere was left-wing, but not such as to encourage Bolshevik sympathies. Consequently, Lukács's friends were surprised when he joined the Communist party immediately after its foundation, at the end of 1918, especially as he had published an article a few days earlier asserting that the Bolsheviks had no rational ground for maintaining that the conflict-free society of the future could be brought about by dictatorship and terror. Apparently, however, he believed—as did many of those who became Communists as a result of the war and the collapse of the Second International—that Bolshevism was the only practical alternative for those who refused to accept, actively or passively, the system which was responsible for the horrors of war and the threat to civilization itself.

In any case, from then on Lukács accepted Communism whole-heartedly as a moral, intellectual, and political solution. Despite various philosophical adventures, he completely identified himself with the Communist movement for the rest of his life. He believed that Marxism was the final answer to the problem of history, that Communism guaranteed the final reconciliation of all human forces and the free play on all human possibilities; that the conflict between the individual and society, between one person and another, between contingent existence and 'essence', morality, and law, had 'in principle' been resolved, and that it remained only to unite oneself in practice with the historical movement which promised that the synthesis would without fail be realized.

For some time it looked as though the hope of a European Communist revolution would come true at an early date. A few months after the overthrow of the Dual Monarchy a Soviet republic was set up in Hungary under Béla Kun (who subsequently lost his life in a Russian gaol, a victim of Stalin's terror); it lasted from the end of March to the end of July 1919. Lukács joined the government as deputy to the Commissar for Education (Zsigmond Kunfi, a social democrat and theoretician close to the Austrian Marxists). The brief Communist dictatorship was followed by savage mass repression, but most of the leaders escaped abroad. Lukács, after a few weeks of clandestine activity in Budapest, reached Vienna, where he was arrested for a short time; he was saved from extradition, partly owing to a protest by a group of writers including Thomas and Heinrich Mann.

Thereafter he led the life of a political *émigré*, carrying on theoretical and propaganda work and involved in the incessant quarrels of his Hungarian fellow exiles. These disputes had no practical effect on the situation in Hungary but, as is usually the case, aroused bitter passions among the *émigrés* with their rival plans for revolution. Lukács belonged at this time to the so-called Communist Left; in 1920-1 he edited a journal *Kommunismus*, of similar tendency, which was once criticized by Lenin for its anti-parliamentary standpoint.

In 1919-22 Lukács wrote a number of theoretical essays, published in book form in 1923 as *Geschichte und Klassenbewusstsein* (*History and Class-Consciousness*: English trans. 1971). This is considered his *magnum opus*, although he declared more than once that in some respects at least it no longer represented his views. At all events, among all his works it is this one which gave rise to most controversy and left the deepest traces on the Marxist movement: In it he emphasized the importance of the Hegelian sources of Marxism and also put forward an original interpretation of the whole of Marx's philosophy, in which the category of 'totality' was presented as the foundation of Marxist dialectic. He set out to show that the chief philosophical disputes among the Marxists of the Second International had been conducted from positions alien to Marx's ideas, and in particular that the orthodox line had continued to ignore the essential feature of dialectical materialism, namely the interaction of the object and subject of history in the movement towards unity. His work was largely directed against the evolutionist or positivist interpretations of Marxism that dominated the Second International, and was designed to supply a philosophical basis for the revolutionary, Leninist theory of socialism and the party. On two points, however, Lukács parted company with Leninism: he criticized Engels's idea of the dialectic of nature as basically contrary to the theory of the dialectic itself, and he disputed the theory of 'reflection' which Lenin had declared to be the essence of Marxist epistemology.

It was not surprising, therefore, at a period when Communist ideology was hardening into dogmatic form, that Lukács's book was sharply attacked in the most official manner possible, namely at a session of the Third International. At the Fifth Comintern Congress in Moscow in July 1924 Zinoviev, then chairman of its Executive Committee, denounced Lukács's work as a harmful revisionist attack on Marxism; this view was endorsed by Bukharin. At the same time Zinoviev attacked Antonio Graziadei, who had recently published a book criticizing Marx's theory of value, and also Karl Korsch. His condemnation of Lukács was expressed in general terms, without any specific charges, and it may be doubted whether he had in fact read the offending work. Soon, however, more reasoned attacks were delivered by philosophers such as A. M. Deborin, N. Luppol, and L. Rudas. Lukács is not known to have performed any self-criticism at the time, but he did so in 1933; he also repeated in several later works that he regarded *History and Class-Consciousness* as erroneous and reactionary, at least on the two points mentioned above. The book disappeared without trace from Communist annals and was only rediscovered after Stalin's death. It had its effect, however, on non-Communist German Marxists, and today it is regarded as one of the most important theoretical documents in the history of Marxism.

Other theoretical works by Lukács in the early post-war years include an article 'Tactics and Ethics', published in Hungarian in 1919, and essays on Lassalle (1925) and Moses Hess (1926) in *Archiv für die Geschichte des Sozialismus und der Arbeiterbewegung*: the former was occasioned by an edition of Lassalle's letters, the latter by the republication of Hess's writings and the appearance of a life of him by Theodor Zlocisti. In 1924 Lukács published a short book on Lenin, written immediately after the latter's death (*Lenin. Studie über den Zusammenhang seiner Gedanken*). All these works were concerned with the same broad theme as *History and Class-Consciousness*: the Marxist conception of history as an integral whole, and the resolution of the traditional dilemmas of freedom and necessity, what is and what ought to be. In 1925 Lukács published a critical review of Bukharin's manual of historical materialism.

Up to 1928 Lukács was actively involved in controversies among Hungarian Communist groups, and in that year he drew up a fractional programme to be presented at the next party congress. This document, known after Lukács's pseudonym as the 'Blum theses', was severely criticized by the majority group under Béla Kun, and afterwards by the Comintern Executive in an open letter to the Hungarian Communists.

The 'Blum theses' (first published, in an abridged form, in 1956) are sometimes quoted today as a proof that in the Stalin era Lukács consistently opposed what was later euphemistically called 'sectarianism', and that he advocated a 'popular front' of the kind proposed by the Comintern at its last congress in 1935, after the set-backs of the early 1930s. In actual fact, Lukács's opposition to Béla Kun's policy in the twenties was of a very limited kind. Far from proposing joint action with the social democrats against Horthy's regime in Hungary, Lukács maintained that social democracy was 'on the road to Fascism' and could not be regarded as a democratic opposition: he subscribed, in fact, to the designation 'social Fascism' which was one of the more fantastic symptoms of Communist paranoia in the late twenties and early thirties. He also declared, in accordance with the slogans of the new era, that the battle was not between democracy and Fascism but between class and class. On the other hand, he put forward the controversial formula of a 'democratic dictatorship' of the proletariat and peasantry as a transitional stage leading to the dictatorship of the proletariat, while making it clear that there was no question of co-operating with the bourgeoisie or the social democrats to build up democracy. In this way he sought to apply certain of Lenin's pre-revolutionary maxims to Hungary. The Comintern, on the other hand, envisaged an immediate transition to the dictatorship of the proletariat, i.e. to a Communist monopoly of power, and it condemned the 'Blum theses' as advocating a policy of 'liquidation'. The whole dispute had no effect whatever on events in Hungary, then or later, and from this point of view it did not matter what ideas were worked out by a handful of powerless *émigrés*. However, the result of the condemnation was that Lukács hastily recanted in order to avoid expulsion from the party, and from then on withdrew from political activity and confined himself to theoretical work.

In the thirties and during the Second World War Lukács published very little. In 1930–1 he spent some time in Moscow, where he worked in the Marx-Engels Institute and became acquainted with Marx's early manuscripts, which had still not appeared in print. After returning to Berlin he wrote a few articles for *Die Linkskurve*, including an important essay on literature and politics entitled 'Tendenz oder Parteilichkeit?' (1932). When Hitler came to power he returned to the Soviet Union and stayed in Moscow till the end of the war, working at the Institute of Philosophy of the Academy of Sciences. The intensive studies of those years bore fruit in numerous publications after 1945. Among these were *Der junge Hegel*, finished before the war but published only in 1948; *Goethe und seine Zeit* (1947); *Essays über Realismus* (1948: on realism in literature); studies of Russian literature (*Der russische Realismus in der Weltliteratur*, 1949); *Thomas Mann* (1949); *Deutsche Realisten des neunzehnten Jahrhunderts* (1951); *Balzac und der französische Realismus* (1952); *Existentialisme ou marxisme?* (1948); a history of irrationalist German philosophy as a source of Nazism (*Die Zerstörung der Vernunft*, 1954); and a study of the historical novel (*Der historische Roman*, 1955).

Throughout this period Lukács's position as a Communist ideologist and Marxist was ambiguous. He remained a party member and did his best to conform scrupulously to each new phase of the 'ideological struggle'. Nevertheless, when the Stalin line hardened from 1949 onwards and repression intensified in the 'peoples' democracies', Lukács again came under fire, the attacks being led by J. Révai, then cultural dictator of Hungary. Once more Lukács bowed to the party's judgement and performed self-criticism. His books continued to appear—mostly in the G.D.R., in German—but in party circles they were considered rather suspect, unduly 'liberal' and not a hundred per cent Marxist.

A new turn of events came with the upheavals of 'de-Stalinization' in 1956, triggered off by the Twentieth Congress of the Soviet Communist party and Khrushchev's famous speech about Stalin's 'mistakes'. Lukács was one of those in Hungary who criticized the 'distortions' of the Stalin era; he belonged to the 'Petőfi Circle', which played an important part in the ideological ferment that preceded the Hungarian uprising. Lukács directed his main attack against ideological 'dogmatism' and the primitive attitude towards literary and philosophical questions in the Stalin era. When the Hungarian anti-Stalinist movement reached its height with the formation of Imre Nagy's government in October 1956, Lukács was co-opted on to the party's Central Committee and for a few days held the post of Minister of Culture. After the Soviet invasion he was deported to Romania with the rest of Nagy's government, most of whom were murdered by the Soviets; Lukács, one of the few survivors, returned to Budapest in the spring of 1957. He soon became the target of fresh attacks, in which his former pupil J. Szigeti played a prominent part. He sought to resume party membership, but was not allowed to as he refused to perform self-criticism on this occasion; apparently, however, he was readmitted in 1967, the condition being waived. In any case, to the end of his life he maintained the belief that socialism, begun in Russia and continued in Eastern Europe, would liberate itself from the aftermath of Stalinist 'distortions' and return to the path of 'true' Marxism. He stated in an interview that the worst socialism was better than the best capitalism. In the political field he whole-heartedly endorsed the Soviet policy of 'coexistence' and opposed Chinese 'dogmatism'. His scholarly activity after the uprising was mainly devoted to problems of Marxist aesthetics. In 1957 he published an essay 'Über die Besonderheit als Kategorie der Ästhetik', and in 1963 a two-volume work *Die Eigenart des Ästhetischen*. As the cultural pressure eased in Hungary in the sixties he enjoyed more reasonable conditions of work and publication facilities. A volume celebrating his eightieth birthday appeared in West Germany in 1965.

In addition to his aesthetic studies he embarked on a basic handbook of Marxist doctrine: this work, nearly completed, appeared posthumously under the title *Zur Ontologie des gesellschaftlichen Seins*, as part of a fourteen-volume edition of his works published by the firm of Luchterhand.

Lukács died at Budapest in 1971. In the previous decade interest in his ideas increased rapidly, as is shown by the number of books, articles, and discussions concerning them, and also by numerous translations and new editions of his works themselves. Attacks from the Stalinist angle practically ceased; on the other hand, he was criticized by some (Deutscher, Adorno, Lichtheim) as a

Stalinist writer and ideologist. Discussion has centred mainly on his literary and aesthetic views and his conception of the dialectic, especially in *History and Class-Consciousness*. His posthumous work did not arouse great interest and must have disappointed those who looked for new ideas on the interpretation of Marxism: it is a conventional exposé of historical materialism, with Lukács's customary attacks on empiricism and positivism. On the other hand, he broke fresh ground in 1964 and 1969 in articles on Solzhenitsyn, whom he hailed as the harbinger of a great renewal of socialist realism.

Lukács left a number of disciples in Hungary who have tried, with greater or less fidelity, to continue his work and range of interests. In Western Europe perhaps the most zealous advocate of his philosophy was Lucien Goldmann, whose work requires special notice.

2. The whole and the part: critique of empiricism

BOTH in 'Tactics and Ethics' and in *History and Class-Consciousness* Lukács puts the question 'What is orthodox Marxism?' and replies that this concept does not involve the acceptance of any particular tenet. An orthodox Marxist does not, as such, owe allegiance to any specific view and may criticize Marx's ideas so long as he remains faithful to the essence of Marxism, namely the dialectical method. 'Method' does not mean here a set of rules for intellectual operations, as it does in logic, but a particular way of thinking which includes awareness that in thinking about the world it is also helping to change it, being at the same time a practical commitment. The Marxian dialectic is not merely a way of perceiving or describing social reality, or even indicating how it should be described: it is the mainspring of social revolution and does not exist outside the revolutionary process, of which, as method, it forms an integral part.

This conception of method, Lukács argues, involves regarding the social universe as a single whole of 'totality'. His vew that this is the key to Marxist theory did not alter from 1919 to 1971. The text that he quotes most often is probably the introduction to the *Grundrisse*, in which Marx expounds his view of the primacy of the abstract over the concrete. Marxism, according to Lukács, would be impossible if it did not involve the principle that the social 'totality' cannot be reconstructed by accumulating facts. Facts do not interpret themselves: their meaning is only revealed in relation to the whole, which must be known in advance and is thus logically prior to the facts. In this respect Marx follows Hegel. 'We thus understand the fundamental assertion of the dialectical method, the Hegelian theory of the concrete concept. This theory states, in brief, that the whole is prior to its parts: the part must be interpreted in the light of the whole and not vice versa' ('Tactics and Ethics', p. 25). The concrete must not be contrasted with phenomena that can only be apprehended by the

mind, since for both Marx and Hegel the concrete itself can only be so apprehended, as a single aspect of the whole. 'This absolute primacy of the whole,
its unity over and above the abstract isolation of its parts—such is the essence
of Marx's conception of society and of the dialectical method' (ibid., p. 27).

Thus Marx's theory of revolution and socialism can be based only on a
global understanding of society that cannot be achieved by any detailed, factual analysis. This is why opportunists and revisionists always appeal to facts,
knowing that there is no logical transition from facts to the revolutionary transformation of society. Empiricism is the ideological foundation of revisionism
and reformism in the workers' movement. 'And every orthodox Marxist who
realizes that the moment has come when capital is only an obstacle to production, and that it is time to expropriate the exploiters, will reply in the words of
Fichte, one of the greatest of the classical German philosophers, when vulgar
Marxists adduce "facts" that appear to contradict the process: "So much the
worse for the facts!"' (ibid., p. 30).

Lukács does not appear to have used this phrase elsewhere in his attacks on
empiricism, but his attitude on the point remained unchanged. In *History and
Class-Consciousness* he emphasizes that a theory which simply takes account
of facts as they are directly given is, by the same token, locating itself within
capitalist society. But to understand the meaning of facts is to situate them in
a 'concrete whole' and to discover the 'mediation' between them and the whole,
which of course is not directly given. The truth of the part resides in the whole,
and if each part is properly examined the whole can be discerned in it. The
whole is the vehicle of the 'revolutionary principle', in social practice as well as
in theory. There is only one single science, embracing the whole of human history—politics, economics, ideology, law, etc.—and it is that whole which gives
meaning to every separate phenomenon. Did not Marx say that a spinning-
jenny in itself is only a spinning-jenny, and that it becomes capital only in particular social conditions? No direct perception of a machine can reveal its
function as capital: that can only be seen by considering the whole social
process of which it forms a part. Facts are not the final reality but are artificially
isolated aspects (*Momente*) of the whole: the over-all trend of historical evolution is more real than the data of experience.

But—and this is the next fundamental point—the 'whole' is not simply a state
of affairs comprising all the particulars of reality at a given moment. It must be
understood as a dynamic reality, involving a certain trend, its direction, and its
results. It is in fact identical with present, past, and future history—but a future
which is not simply 'foreseen' like a fact in nature, but which is created by the
act of foreseeing it. Thus the 'whole' is anticipatory, and present facts can only
be understood in relation to the future.

This is particularly important in distinguishing the revolutionary from the reformist viewpoint in the socialist movement. In the eyes of reformists the significance of the current social and political struggle of the working class is exhausted in its immediate consequences. For Marx, on the other hand, each fragment of the actual struggle, including the workers' fight for economic betterment, only derives meaning from the prospect of revolution. Such was the dialectic and revolutionary attitude of those leaders, like Lenin and Rosa Luxemburg, who combated opportunism and revisionism and always kept in view the 'final goal'. In his essay on Rosa Luxemburg Lukács especially praises her power of 'global' analysis. She saw the phenomenon of accumulation not as an isolated occurrence but as part of the process leading unavoidably to the proletarian revolution, and was thus able to show that it could not continue indefinitely but must bring about the collapse of capitalism. Opportunists like Otto Bauer were unable to think in terms of an integral historical process, and as a result they surrendered to capitalism, seeking only to cure its 'bad aspects' by ethical means. Once the integral viewpoint is abandoned, capitalism does indeed seem invincible, as the peculiar laws governing its economy appear to be 'given' as unalterable facts and laws of nature, which may be turned to use but cannot be nullified. A global view, on the other hand, shows capitalism to be a historical and transient phenomenon, and is therefore the vehicle of revolutionary consciousness.

In his book on Lenin, Lukács again uses the notion of *Totalität* to describe the core of Lenin's doctrine and the secret of its greatness. Lenin was the one genius who discerned the revolutionary trend of the age independently of particular facts and events, or rather in the facts themselves, and united all current issues, even the smallest, in a single great socialist perspective. He knew that the global process was more real than any of its details, and despite all appearances he saw that the hour for revolution had already struck. From the economic point of view he added nothing to the theory of imperialism, but he surpassed Hilferding by his brilliant success in integrating economic theory with current political developments.

The interrelated concepts of the 'whole' and of 'mediation' apply to all spheres of social inquiry, and play a prominent part in Lukács's view on literature. By 'mediation' he means any kind of subordinate totality into which observed facts and phenomenon must be fitted before they are integrated into the universal whole, the global historical process of past, present, and future. Frequently, however, he also uses 'mediation' to mean the intellectual process which relates the concrete to the whole. Whereas inability to think globally enslaves us to given situations and prevents our transcending the existing order of society, so that in terms of socialism we end up as reformists and revisionists, on the other hand those who overlook the need for 'mediation' are in danger of succumbing to the primitive error of lumping all phenomena together in a single undifferentiated whole, ignoring the specific character of various aspects of life and culture. An example of an ideology taking account of totality but not of mediation can be found in Nazism as it later revealed itself. In addition, almost all the artistic trends condemned by Lukács can be described as deficient either in 'mediation' or in a sense of totality. Naturalism confines itself to direct description and fails to reach the level of integral social criticism; symbolism creates only 'subjective' wholes, while the various forms of decadence exalt partial experience into eternal metaphysical truth, and thus likewise fall short of an integral view. In socialism the lack of a sense of 'mediation' results in sectarianism, i.e. inability to grasp the particular functions of subordinate interrelations: for instance, the claim that the tasks of art in socialist society should be determined solely by its propaganda value overlooks the mediating role of specifically aesthetic criteria. The main burden of Lukács's later criticism of Stalinism was that it lacked 'mediation' by failing to appreciate the diversity of means involved in the building of socialism, and by reducing art and science to a purely political role.

A special case, within Marxism, of failure to understand the nature of 'totality' and 'mediation' is afforded by all reductionist interpretations which take for granted the one-way determination of certain factors in history by other such factors. As the whole is always prior to its parts, so the determination of parts by the whole is more fundamental than that of some parts by others. In his last work Lukács contends that the maxim 'social being determines consciousness' has nothing to do with what is called economism. This maxim 'does not link the world of forms and the content of consciousness with the economic structure in a directly productive relationship, but links it with the whole of social being. The determination of consciousness by social being is thus of a purely general kind. Only vulgar Marxism, from the Second International to the age of Stalin and after, claimed to establish a direct, unqualified causal link between the economy, or even particular aspects of it, on the one hand and ideology on the other' (*Zur Ontologie des gesellschaften Seins*, 'Die ontologischen Grundprinzipien von Marx', p. 39). In other words, the basic dependence in social life is not between the base and the superstructure but between social being (or 'the whole', i.e. everything) and particular elements of the whole.

3. The subject and object of history. Theory and practice. What is and what ought to be. Critique of neo-Kantianism and evolutionism

NEVERTHELESS—and this is the next fundamental quality of dialectical thinking emphasized by Lukács in his *magnum opus*—the dialectic is not simply a scientific method that can be transferred at will from one object to another, nor is it independent of the subject who applies it. For in both Hegel's and Marx's theory it is, as already explained, an active constituent of the social reality to which it is applied as a method, and not simply a way of apprehending that reality. It is the expression of history ripening towards the final transformation, and is also the theoretical consciousness of the social agent, namely the proletariat, by which that transformation is to be brought about. In other words, it is not the case that anyone, independent of his political status and social commitment, can adopt the dialectical method and successfully apply it to any object that he may choose. For the dialectic does not exist outside the revolutionary struggle of the proletariat: it is the self-awareness of that struggle and a component of it.

The dialectic presupposes the conception of society as a whole; and only the social agent which is itself a 'whole'—i.e. Marx's 'universal class', the proletariat—can perceive the 'whole' in isolated phenomena. In accordance with Hegel's principle, 'the truth is the subject'; i.e., in the present case, the truth concerning the historical process can be revealed only from the viewpoint of the class whose revolutionary initiative is destined radically to transform the whole of social life and to abolish the class society.

Marxism is not, as the theoreticians of the Second International would have it, a scientific description of historical reality that anyone can accept if he applies logical rules correctly. It is nothing else than the theoretical consciousness of the working class as it matures towards revolution; and the class-consciousness of the proletariat is not a mere reflection of an independent historical process, but is the indispensable driving force of that process. Unlike all previous revolutions, the agents of which did not understand what they were doing and fell victim to illusions, the proletarian revolution, as a matter of principle, cannot be brought about without the complete, un-mystified self-awareness of the proletariat in regard to its position in society and the destiny it is called on to fulfil.

The proletariat is thus privileged by history, not only in the sense that it is called on to achieve the radical upheaval that will once and for all abolish class divisions, exploitation, and social conflict, the separation of individual from social being, alienation, false consciousness, and the dependence of humanity on impersonal historical powers. In addition to all this the proletariat is privileged from the epistemological point of view, inasmuch as its historical role entails the complete understanding of society: only it can apprehend history as a whole, for only in its actions is the totality truly realized as a revolutionary movement. The proletariat's self-awareness coincides with its awareness of history as a whole; theory and practice coincide, as the proletariat transforms the world in the process by which it arrives at a mature understanding of the world. In this particular case the understanding and transformation of reality are not two separate processes, but one and the same phenomenon.

For this reason both the neo-Kantians in the Marxist movement and their evolutionist adversaries were at fault in distinguishing between the 'pure science' of history and the 'socialist ideal' deriving, as a kind of moral imperative, from arbitrarily established values. Since subject and object coincide in the knowledge of society; since, in this case, science is the self-knowledge of society and, by the same token, a factor in determining its situation at any stage of history; and since, in the case of the proletariat, this self-knowledge is at the same time a revolutionary movement, it follows that the proletariat cannot at any point disjoin its 'ideal' from the actual process of realizing it. Socialism is not a state of affairs waiting for humanity and guaranteed by the impersonal laws of history, nor is it a moral 'imperative': it is the self-knowledge of the proletariat, an aspect of its actual struggle.

In this way Marxism resolves the dilemma that perplexed the theoreticians of the Second International. Both the evolutionists and the neo-Kantians supposed that Marx's theory was an account of 'inevitable' historical laws and that, as a scientific doctrine, it contained no normative element. The neo-Kantians inferred that the necessary normative factors or ideals must be imported from Kantian moral philosophy. To this the orthodox replied that Marxism must be content with historical description, and that it was both impossible and unnecessary to demonstrate that socialism was desirable as well as inevitable. According to Lukács, however, both parties were arguing from essentially un-Marxist positions, as they followed Kant in taking for granted the dualism of 'what is' and 'what ought to be', whereas Hegel and Marx after him had overcome that dualism. Marxism is not a mere description of the world but the expression and self-knowledge of a social process by which the world is revolutionized, and thus the subject of that self-knowledge, i.e. the proletariat, comprehends reality in the very act of transforming it. The division of social life into 'objective' processes outside human control, and the impotent awareness that merely observes or moralizes, is a characteristic and inevitable attitude of classes which, even if in their own day they may have represented over-all progress, were not and are not universal classes in the same sense as the proletariat—that is to say, they cannot rise to an understanding of history as a whole, being fettered to their own particular interests. The proletariat, however, as its particular interest coincides with that of humanity as a matter of principle and not merely by a temporary accident, truly embodies the unity of the subject and object of history. In the revolutionary activity of this class history achieves self-knowledge: historical necessity appears, and must appear, as free action, free because fully conscious. The 'objective' process and awareness of it are one and the same: there is no difference between social 'being', that which actually is, and the theoretical or moral consciousness of the class which is the agent of that process. Subject and object, freedom and necessity, the fact and the norm are no longer opposed but are aspects of a single reality. This puts an end to the Kantian dilemma of how obligation can be deduced from empirical facts, and likewise to the dilemma of 'scientism'.

In the same way there is no longer a conflict between voluntarism and determinism, or human will and scientific prediction. Since awareness of society as a whole is not simply information that anyone can acquire but is the self-knowledge of actual revolutionary praxis, it follows that there is no such thing in Marxism as 'objective' prediction based on historical laws and independent of the will that governs future changes. The act of foreseeing coincides with the act of effecting what is foreseen: the proletariat knows the future in the act of creating it, not after the fashion of a weather forecast where the changes that actually happen are unaffected by anything the forecaster can do.

This unity of the object and subject of history, of the cognitive and normative aspects of consciousness, is, Lukács argues, the most precious legacy of Hegelianism to Marxism. This does not mean, of course, that it was taken over in a directly Hegelian form. Hegel could not have discovered the identity of the object and subject in history itself, as in his time there was no real historical basis for it. Consequently, he transferred the identity into the extra-historical sphere of reason, and ascribed to Mind the role of a demiurge in the evolution of history. Thus he could not, although it was his aim to do so, overcome finally the dualism of object and subject: it was left to Marx to achieve this.

In the same line of thought it is clear that there cannot in principle be anyone who is a mere 'theoretical Marxist', i.e. who recognizes the validity of Marx's social theory and historical predictions but takes no part in making them come true. To be precise, such an attitude is possible, but it is not a Marxist attitude. A Marxist must be someone who plays a practical part in the movement that gives effect to the theory, for the theory is itself nothing but the self-awareness of the movement.

This viewpoint is a basis for the criticism of many different trends within Marxism and also in non-Marxist socialism. Lukács, as we have seen, used it to refute the theoreticians of the Second International, both orthodox and neo-Kantian, but also Marx's predecessors and contemporaries. Lassalle, for instance, was not a Marxist, as he revised Hegel from a Fichtean standpoint, modifying the contemplative theory of history by an 'activist' element introduced from outside in the guise of will or moral consciousness. Thus, instead of rebutting Hegelianism, he reverted to a pre-Hegelian position. In the same way Lukács argues in his study of Hess that Cieszkowski's or Hess's philosophy of action did not surmount the dualism of theory versus practice, but eternalized it in the dualism of the socialist movement and its philosophical consciousness: philosophy, in Hess's system, was not the product and self-awareness of the class movement, but a kind of wisdom, independent of party, which it behoved the movement to acquire. Finally, Hess preached a moral Utopia which, while ostensibly criticizing Hegel's 'contemplative' attitude, rejected that part of his thinking which came close to Marxism, namely the conviction that philosophy is an expression of its own time and cannot transcend the limits of the age. Hegel's refusal to look into the future was 'reactionary', but 'from the methodological point of view' it was extremely realistic in rejecting utopianism and in regarding philosophy as the expression of an era and not as Mind entering history from outside it. Marx rebutted the contemplative viewpoint, not by supplementing historical knowledge with arbitrary norms or utopian constructions, but by discerning the future as a real trend already active in the present.

4. Critique of the 'dialectic of nature' and the theory of reflection. The concept of reification

As THE dialectic consists of the interaction of the historical subject and object in the movement towards unity, it follows that Engels's idea of the 'dialectic of nature' is untenable; indeed, on this point Lukács accuses Engels of culpable misapprehension of the spirit of Marxian dialectic. If the dialectic denotes a mere system of ready-made natural laws ascertained by man, we are still in the realm of 'predestined' reality and the idea of knowledge as purely contemplative. The 'laws of dialectic' turn out to be an unalterable property of nature: we can discover them and use them, but this 'external' knowledge of nature and its exploitation by human technology have nothing to do with dialectic as understood by Marx and Hegel. The dialectic loses its revolutionary character, and the unity of theory and practice can be conceived only in a contemplative bourgeois, reified sense—the technical exploitation of the world as it exists, not the collective subject taking possession of the world by revolutionary action. Historical materialism, on the other hand, shows us the world as a product of human activity, but one which men have so far treated as something alien, failing to realize that they themselves are its creators. Pre-Marxist philosophy with its dichotomy between knowledge and praxis was obliged to see the world as a collection of crystallized 'data', and praxis as a set of arbitrary ethical precepts and technical devices. By contrast, when, as in the class-consciousness of the proletariat, the subject's self-awareness coincides with knowledge of the whole—when social being is recognized as man-made and subject to conscious regulation by the organized community—then the dichotomy ceases to exist and the dilemma of empiricism versus utopianism is resolved. What Engels called 'practice' (experimentation, technology) does not transform man into a conscious creator of reality, but only increases his mastery of the environment; technical progress does not itself break the bounds of the bourgeois system. Man, exploiting the laws of nature that he has discovered, does not cease to be an 'object' of history. He only becomes a 'subject' when he assimilates and identifies with the external world, abolishing the state of affairs in which that world is a mere datum and knowledge is no more than perception or contemplation. The idea of the unity of subject and object cannot survive if the dialectic relates to external nature.

For the same reason, knowledge cannot be regarded as the mere 'reflection' of a pre-existing reality. In criticizing this idea Lukács does not expressly join issue with Lenin, but he clearly attacks his philosophy. From the point of view of the dialectic as Lukács understands it, to treat cognition as the 'reflection' of the external world in mental experience is to perpetuate the dualism of thought and being and to assume that they are fundamentally alien to each other. If, however, cognition signifies taking possession of the world in a process of revolutionary change, and if understanding and changing the world are a single indivisible act of the liberated consciousness of the proletariat, it no longer makes sense to speak of knowledge as a process whereby an already existing world duplicates itself in the passive human consciousness. The process of thought is not dialectic unless it is part of the historical process of transforming its object.

The 'contemplative' notion of reality, which leaves no room for the unity of theory and practice or the subject's creative role, is linked by Lukács—a point on which he lays special weight in *History and Class-Consciousness*—with 'reification' as a typical feature of the mystified consciousness of capitalist society. The term 'reification' was not used by Marx and in fact owes its currency to Lukács himself, but the idea is thoroughly Marxian: the analysis of 'commodity fetishism' in Volume I of *Capital* is really an analysis of the reified consciousness. The bourgeoisie, by virtue of its social situation, must have a false consciousness: it is contrary to its interests to understand the nature of economic crises and the transient historical character of the system in which it plays the dominant role. In a society which subordinates production entirely to the increase of exchange-value, and in which relations between human beings are crystallized in object-values and themselves take on the character of objects, individuals themselves turn into things. A man is no longer a specific individual but part of a huge system of production and exchange; his personal qualities are merely an obstacle to the complete uniformity and rationalization of the productive mechanism. He is a mere unit of labour force, an article to be bought and sold according to the laws of the market. One result of the omnipotence of exchange-value is the rationalization of legal systems, disregard for tradition, and the tendency to reduce individuals to juridical units. Rationalization is applied to technology and the organization of labour, leading to increasing specialization and the particularization of productive activity; the individual is more and more spiritually crippled and confined to a narrow range of skills by the division of labour. Everything is specialized, activities become partial and fragmented, the unity of society becomes unintelligible and unattainable. Bourgeois philosophy endorses this tyranny of reification and has neither the power nor the desire to rise to an understanding of the whole. All it understands is either empirical reality, from which no 'whole' is capable of emerging, or, on the other hand, normative ethics or arbitrary Utopias which, by definition, have nothing to do with 'facts'. Bourgeois rationalism, which extols mathematics as the most perfect form of knowledge, has no interest in phenomena beyond what is calculable and predictable and can therefore be exploited technically. Anything that might symbolize the 'whole' is banned from the domain of scientific knowledge and labelled an unknowable 'thing in itself.' The contradiction between the irrationality of 'facts' and the desire to apprehend the whole led to the idealist dialectic, which sought to restore the unity of subject and object by denying objectivity altogether; it ascribed creativity to the subject, but, being unable to conceive this creativity as revolutionary practice, endowed it with a moral and internal form.

Reification, in short, cannot be overcome within the terms of bourgeois consciousness. Only when the proletariat, which is a mere commodity in bourgeois society, becomes aware of its own situation will it be able to understand the social mechanism as a whole. The consciousness of the proletariat may be thought of as the acquisition of self-knowledge by a commodity. In the proletariat's situation the process of reification, the transformation of men and women into things, takes on an acute form. When the proletariat becomes aware of itself as a commodity it will at the same time understand, and rebel against the reification of all forms of social life. Its awakened subjectivity will liberate the whole of humanity from the thraldom of objects; its self-knowledge is not a mere perception of the world as it is, but a historical movement of emancipation, and for consciousness of this kind there can be no question of a mere 'reflection' of reality.

Does this argument mean that from the point of view of liberated consciousness the problem of 'truth' in the traditional sense, i.e. the correspondence of judgement with reality, no longer arises, or that truth is relative to social class or to the human species? Lukács's answer to this question is vague and ambiguous. He disclaims an 'anthropological' or pragmatist conception of truth, since, as he says, pragmatism makes man the measure of things but cannot dialectically transform man himself: instead of considering the subject in his interaction with the object, it raises him to the status of a deity. Marxism, on the other hand, does not declare truth to be relative to the individual or the species, but claims that the meaning of different truths is apparent only in the social process. Thought is a factor in the progress of history, and history is the development of forms of objectivity.

This explanation is by no means clear. If, as Lukács says, truth is attainable only from a particular (class) point of view, we may still ask: is it nevertheless inherently true, i.e. the description of a given state of affairs independently of whether it is perceived or not? Lukács, however, appears to consider this a wrongly framed question, as it presupposes a 'contemplative' and 'reified' consciousness outside the object. It is not clear how we can avoid the conclusion that in his view not only is truth revealed solely from a particular class angle, but that nothing is true at all except in the class-consciousness that is identical with the practical revolutionary movement—in other words, participation in the movement equals possession of the truth, which is of course more than saying that it is a condition of possessing the truth. If we accept Lukács's premisses, how can we avoid concluding that truth is relative to class, or that nothing is true at all without the qualification 'for the working class? If for this phrase we substitute 'for future humanity, freed from false consciousness', we are still involved in a species-based relativism which excludes 'truth' in the traditional sense. There are good reasons for holding that this position is in accordance with the doctrine of the early Marx, but it cannot be described as anything but species relativism.

When Lukács speaks of the 'unity of subject and object' in the cognitive process, or the 'unity of theory and practice', he generally uses terms applicable to all knowledge and all objects, but it would seem that he has in mind the object of human and social sciences, namely human history and man as a social being. As a disciple not only of Hegel but also of Dilthey and Windelband, he no doubt wished to maintain the principle of the fundamentally different character of humanistic knowledge ('the humanistic coefficient', as Znaniecki called it) and to emphasize that in awareness of human realities the subject is present in a different way than in the natural sciences, as the act of knowing is a component of the known reality and alters its character. The subject in question is always a collective subject, more precisely a social class. Sometimes, however, owing to his vagueness and disregard of logic, Lukács used expressions suggesting that the 'object' that tends towards unity with the 'subject' is the whole universe, including non-human nature. Yet his real purpose was to distinguish between man and nature and not 'unify' them. To treat the world of human behaviour and historical processes as a reality no less 'given' and 'objective' than stones and stars is to permit one's consciousness to become 'reified'. For the proletarian consciousness there is no such thing as a social universe that exists in itself and whose nature must first be learnt like that of any other object, so that we may then apply technical devices to it for a purpose that must then be irrationally prescribed by moral imperatives. A technological attitude to social phenomena, which treats them as a mere object of political engineering and in which the human agent is purely subjective and inspired by moral laws alone, is a bourgeois delusion—though Engels did not escape it when he extended the dialectic to nature and described social laws as no less objective than the laws governing the formation of geological deposits. Once the proletariat comes on the scene, conscious of its role in production and in the dynamic unity of history, 'historical laws' are identified with human will, and freedom becomes identical with historical necessity.

For the same reason Lukács makes no distinction between bourgeois and Marxist sociology, maintaining that sociology as such is inevitably part of bourgeois ideology. Its task is to study social phenomena 'objectively', i.e. as objects accessible to the observer irrespective of his participation in them. This presumed separation of subject and object is the *raison d'être* of sociology, and therefore Lukács regards 'Marxist sociology' as a contradiction in terms. His criticism of Bukharin in 1925 was based on the same ground. Bukharin had reverted to mechanistic materialism, which sought to interpret social processes in the same way as natural ones, regarding natural science as the model of all knowledge instead of criticizing it as a product of bourgeois consciousness. In this way Bukharin rejected historical materialism in favour of a 'contemplative' epistemology and sought to find in technology the 'objective' forces governing history, as though technology was an independent motive force and not a factor in social conditions.

Lukács's criticism, aimed directly at Engels and implicitly at Lenin, naturally aroused the wrath of orthodox Russian Marxists. Deborin wrote an article branding Lukács as an idealist in his views of nature and society. As to the alleged contradiction between Marx and Engels, Deborin and all others who took up the question pointed triumphantly to the preface to the second edition of the *Anti-Dühring* (1885), in which Engels said that Marx had read and approved his work before it went to press. The idea of the identity of subject and object, Deborin argued, was the purest idealism, as Lenin had himself shown. Consciousness 'reflected' reality, and in denying this Lukács was repeating the absurdities of Mach. All in all, Deborin's rebuttal was primitive and unskilful, and Lukács did not hasten to recant his errors. In 1933, in an article 'Mein Weg zu Marx', he withdrew his criticism of the theory of reflection and the dialectic of nature, but only in general terms and without going into the substance of the dispute. In the following year, however, in an article in *Pod znamenem Marksizma* (*Under the Banner of Marxism*) entitled 'The Significance of [Lenin's] *Materialism and Empiriocriticism* for the Bolshevization of Communist Parties', he made an act of abject self-criticism ascribing his deviation to residual influences of syndicalism and idealism. *History and Class-Consciousness*, he declared, was an idealistic work, and as idealism was the ally of Fascism and of its social democratic hangers-on, his error was dangerous in practice as well as in theory. Fortunately, the Bolshevik party under the leadership of Comrade Stalin was fighting indomitably for the purity of Marxism–

Leninism, steering a steady course with Lenin's work as its infallible compass. Lukács repeated his recantation several times in similar terms, blaming his mistake either on 'revolutionary impatience' (though it is hard to see how this would lead to denying the dialectic of nature) or on his Hegelian and syndical-ist background. After Stalin's death he tempered his self-criticism to a great extent. In the preface to a new edition of his book in 1967 he admitted to hav-ing neglected Marx's distinction between objectivization and alienation and, in consequence, pushed too far his own theory of the identity of subject and object (i.e. presumably by suggesting that all 'objectivity' ceased to exist in the prole-tarian consciousness, and not only the 'alienated' object). As, however, labour itself was necessarily a process of 'objectivization', it could not be said that all objectivity disappeared in the revolutionary process, and therefore it was wrong completely to exclude 'reflection' from the act of cognition.

In short, Lukács did not deliver a clear judgement on his early work. He cer-tainly did not abandon his theory of totality and mediation, or (with the qualifi-cation explained above) his critique of reification; and he held to his view of the basic distinction between humanistic and natural science. He apparently con-tinued to regard it as a merit of his book that it had drawn attention to the Hegelian sources and aspects of Marx's dialectic. The upshot of his revised the-ory seems to be that in the revolutionary movement object and subject coincide, but only to a certain degree; it remains true that the cognition of social reality is itself a part of that reality, and that the proletarian consciousness revolutionizes the world in the very act of understanding it. It can also still be maintained that Marxism has overcome the dilemma of freedom versus necessity, facts versus values, will versus foreknowledge; but it is not the case that this does away with objectivity altogether. This being Lukács's final position, are we to take it sim-ply as meaning that he wished to exclude the idea that all reality, including exter-nal nature and the objectified material products of human labour, was subsumed into conscious revolutionary praxis—in other words, that he desired to limit the identity of subject and object to the sphere of social processes (of course only in the liberated consciousness of the proletariat) and not extend it to the extra-human world? If so, this would not mean a significant departure from his orig-inal thesis but rather a restatement of it; the book, as we saw, could be read as meaning that he had in mind 'objectivity' in general and not merely that of his-torical processes, but this would seem to be due to a want of logical discipline rather than to a considered theory.

5. Class-consciousness and organization

It might seem that the glorification of the class-consciousness of the proletariat as a force which not only transforms social institutions but also, in so doing, resolves all problems of philosophy, art, and the social sciences, was related in Lukács's mind to the real proletariat and not its 'organized' expression, i.e. the party: that is to say, his view of the revolution would be that of Rosa Luxemburg rather than Lenin. In fact, however, his works from 1919 onwards leave no doubt that he held firmly to Lenin's conception of the party and that his whole theory of class-consciousness formed a logical basis for that conception.

The 'proletarian consciousness' is not to be understood as that of the empirical working class, nor as a sum or average of individual consciousnesses. There must always be a gap between the empirical consciousness of actual workers and the 'true' class-consciousness of the proletariat. The former will never quite catch up with the latter, yet it is this 'true' consciousness that is the motive power of history, and its vehicle is the party—a special form of social existence, a necessary mediator between the spontaneous workers' movement and the totality of history. What individual workers think, either unanimously or in the main, is simply of no significance as to the content of the proletarian consciousness. The latter is embodied in the party, and it is only in and through the party that the spontaneous movement can apprehend its own meaning, since it is powerless of itself to rise to a conception of the whole. Thus the unity of theory and practice, of necessity and freedom, are truly realized only in the party's revolutionary will.

Expounding this view in *History and Class-Consciousness*, Lukács showed (without saying so explicitly) that Lenin's theory of the party was not a logical concomitant of Lenin's philosophy but was fully in accord with Marx's humanistic relativism and the theory of all-absorbing 'praxis', whereby epistemological and metaphysical problems are deprived of content. Lukács reiterated this view in his book on Lenin and several later works. The party is the visible embodiment of class-consciousness, the sole guarantor of the correct political orientation of the proletariat and the sole exponent of its 'real' will. Lukács does not, of course, infer from this, any more than Lenin did, that the party can do everything in practice without the proletariat, or that the latter's aid is not important to it. The point is merely that the proletariat's 'real' interest, its will, desires, and aspirations and also its theoretical consciousness, are quite independent of the desires, feelings, thoughts, and awareness of the empirical working class.

We thus see the political importance for Lukács of the critique of empiricism. As long as we remain on an empirical footing all our knowledge of the proletariat comes from observing actual workers: we cannot comprehend the totality of history, as the empirical state of human consciousness is merely an index of its immaturity. It can be seen that Lukács's theory of the unity of theory and practice is logically better suited to Lenin's idea of the party than is Lenin's own philosophy. For it is hard, on the basis of the theory of 'reflection', to defend the assertion that the party, embodying the 'true' consciousness of the proletariat, is right notwithstanding any empirical evidence which might refute its doctrine. This proposition, on the other hand, follows smoothly from the idea of 'totality' and its corollary, 'so much the worse for the facts'. The all-embracing totality brings into 'dialectical unity' facts and values, knowledge and will, freedom and necessity. The proletariat therefore, embodied in the party, is *theoretically* right on the strength of its social position and historical mission; or rather its theoretical rightness is the same as its progressive function, and no other criteria are to the purpose. Politically, this is a more convenient philosophy than Lenin's, for, once granted that the party is in possession of the practico-theoretical 'whole', there is no need to seek any further justification. As the proletariat is privileged in the cognitive sense thanks to its social role, and as the genesis of its consciousness guarantees that that consciousness is right, true, and unmystified, so, assuming further that the proletarian consciousness is embodied in the party, we arrive at the desired conclusion: the party is always right. Lukács, of course, does not formulate it in so many words—neither did Lenin or even Stalin—but it is the ideological foundation of Communist training and has been accepted in practice by all Communist intellectuals.

By the end of the Stalin era the epistemologically privileged position of the proletariat was reduced for practical purposes to the view that Comrade Stalin was always right. Lukács provided a better theoretical foundation for belief in the infallibility of the party than anyone before him, Lenin included. In 'Tactics and Ethics' he had already stated that 'it is the great achievement of Russian Bolshevism to incorporate, for the first time since the Paris Commune, the consciousness of the proletariat and its self-knowledge in terms of world history' (p. 36). In the nature of things, Bolshevism was the truth of the present age—a belief that Lukács never renounced. Even if it turned out in after days that the party or its leader had made mistakes, it was still true that the party was 'dialectically' right and that it was a moral and intellectual duty to stand by it, mistakes or no. Thus, when Lukács followed the new leaders in noticing Stalin's 'mistakes', he still maintained that he had been right to defend those mistakes at the time. This was indeed the typical, classical standpoint of Communist ideologists, backed up by Lukács's philosophy: the party might be 'formally' wrong but not 'dialectically' so. To oppose its politics and ideology was in all circumstances a political mistake and therefore a cognitive error, since the party embodied the historical consciousness in which the movement of history and awareness of that movement were merged into one.

Lukács also had no doubt that the dictatorship of the proletariat was and ought to be realized as the dictatorship of the party. Thus in his book on Lenin he condemned the ultra-Leftists (or 'workers' opposition' in the Bolshevik party) who regarded the Soviets (workers' councils) as the permanent forms of class organization and sought to establish them in place of the party and trade unions. The Soviets, Lukács argued, were naturally designated organs of the struggle against the bourgeois government in the revolutionary period, but those who wished to endow them with state power after the revolution simply did not understand the difference between a revolutionary and a non-revolutionary situation, in short they were thinking 'un-dialectically'. The party's role after a successful revolution was greater and not less than before, one reason being that in the post-revolutionary period the class struggle, far from abating, became inevitably more and more acute. This doctrine as to the role of the Soviets differs to some extent from that expressed in Lukács's main work, where he said that it was their function to liquidate the bourgeois distinction between executive, legislative, and judicial powers and to be an instrument of 'mediation' between the immediate and ultimate interests of the proletariat. This might suggest that Lukács ascribed to the Soviets functions which, according to Lenin, belonged exclusively to the party (although other references to the party in *History and Class-Consciousness* do not support this view). However, in his work on Lenin he corrects any such ultra-leftist errors and makes it clear that after a victorious revolution the Soviets can be dispensed with. From that time on, it would appear, the task of abolishing the bourgeois separation of powers devolves on the party—in other words, the latter makes the laws, carries them out, and judges offenders without aid or supervision from any quarter: In this way, in 1924, Lukács proclaimed a world-view purged of any remnants of syndicalism.

6. Critique of irrationalism

LUKÁCS's chief work was devoted, in effect, to providing Leninism with a better philosophical basis than Lenin himself had offered. In this sense Lukács could be called an inconsistent Leninist, encumbered to some extent by the typical shortcomings of the intellectual. While accepting Bolshevik policy without question he imagined that, as a philosopher, he could be a better Bolshevik than the party leaders, expounding their theoretical position in a more coherent and convincing manner.

His later philosophical works show, however, that he understood the true nature of fidelity to Leninism–Stalinism: what was required was not to devise justifications of one's own for the party's decisions and doctrines at any given time, but to support them and act upon them in practice. The few works of pure philosophy which he published in the thirties and forties evince an almost complete assimilation to Stalinism. It is true that Lukács's erudition distinguished him at all times from run-of-the-mill ideologists of Stalinism, who were all ignoramuses. Whether he wrote about Goethe, Dilthey, or Hegel, he obviously knew what he was talking about and had the subject at his fingers' ends. It was this, rather than what he actually wrote, that infuriated his orthodox critics. To some extent, moreover, he preserved an individual style of writing. This was suspect in the Stalin era, when everybody wrote in the same way and no two philosophers could be distinguished on stylistic grounds. Monotonous clichés and an impoverished vocabulary were the order of the day, and to have a style of one's own was practically an ideological deviation. In this respect Lukács was an imperfect Stalinist, but he made up for it in many others.

An important document of this period is *Die Zerstöirung der Vernunft* (*The Destruction of Reason*), a work which Adorno called 'The Destruction of Lukács's Reason'. This is a history of irrationalist philosophy, chiefly in Germany, from Schelling and the Romantics to Heidegger ('the Ash Wednesday of parasitic subjectivism') and the existentialists, with the primary purpose of revealing the ideological sources of Nazism. Schelling, who substitutes incommunicable intuition for rational dialectic; Schopenhauer, who proclaims the incurable absurdity of mankind and history and sees the world as governed by irrational will; and Kierkegaard, who glorifies irrational faith and places it above reason—these are the prophets of the first period, ending in 1848. Nietzsche is the chief ideologist of the second period, in which the class struggle of the proletariat becomes the dominant feature of social life: his negation of history, contempt for the common people, and unabashed pragmatism are devoted to the service of the bourgeoisie, which he extols as the 'master race'. Philosophic irrationalism reaches its height in the imperialist age from 1890 onwards: neo-Kantian formalism and agnosticism are replaced by attempts to create a new all-embracing world-view, but one based on intuition and impervious to rational analysis. The objective validity of science itself is questioned, as it is regarded as the product of irrational historical or instinctive forces. This period is ushered in by Dilthey's 'philosophy of life' (*Lebensphilosophie*), which leads directly to Nazi ideology. It opposes positivism, but does so from the point of view of the irrationality of history and the subjectivity of culture. It also criticizes capitalism, but from the outdated standpoint of reactionary Romanticism; it attacks democracy and sets out in quest of a new organic unity that eventually found its embodiment in the Fascist state.

What makes *The Destruction of Reason* an essentially Stalinist work is not, of course, the fact that it seeks the origins of Nazism in German philosophy. There is nothing specifically Marxist, let alone Stalinist, in such a line of thought, which has been pursued by many historians and writers, including Thomas Mann. The typically Stalinist feature of Lukács's work is the contention that since Marxism came on the scene, all non-Marxist philosophy has been reactionary and irrationalistic. In this way the whole of German philosophical culture outside Marxism is condemned as an intellectual apparatus preparing the way for Hitler's assumption of power in 1933. Everybody was a herald of Nazism in one way or another. Clearly, Lukács's conception of irrationalism is not only vague, indefinite, and absurdly wide, but in many respects it is almost directly contrary to the usual conception of the term. In epistemology the word 'irrationalist' is generally applied to doctrines which hold that the most perfect forms of cognition cannot be expressed in language but are achieved only in particular incommunicable acts. Some of the thinkers listed by Lukács were certainly irrationalists in the true sense, but it does not follow that they paved the way for Nazism. Lukács, however, calls everyone an irrationalist who was not an orthodox Marxist. If Max Weber, as a sociologist, analysed the character of the charismatic leader, it proves that this was required of him by the age which produced the charismatic Führer. If the analytical philosophers deny that the world can be apprehended as a whole and confine themselves to observing isolated fragments, they are by the same token falling into irrationalism, as is Mannheim when he emphasizes the part played by extra-cognitive factors in the formation of social theories. Irrationalists are all those who hold that any elements or aspects of being are outside the range of discursive knowledge; all who discover irrational forces in human behaviour; all who do not believe in historical laws; all who profess subjective idealism; and all who do not accept that the meaning of the 'totality' of history can be scientifically ascertained. In other words, the irrationalists and (consequently) allies of Nazism are all who do not believe in the 'dialectical reason' that Lukács took over from Hegel—reason being regarded as capable of comprehending the whole of history and human society, including its Communist future, and thus giving significance to the present. Or, to put it in yet another way, all philosophers who do not profess Communism in its current orthodox form, i.e. Stalinism, are irrationalists and therefore Nazis 'objectively' if not by actual conviction. The whole history of German and indeed European culture, including Croce, Windelband, Bergson, and the analytic philosophers, is seen as imbued with the immanent purpose of ensuring Hitler's triumph. All non-Marxist philosophers of the nineteenth and twentieth centuries were engaged in the destruction of 'reason', that is to say of the belief that there is a historic 'totality' which includes the future and to which Marxism provides the key by predicting the expropriation of the bourgeoisie and a worldwide Communist dictatorship. It would be hard indeed to find a more striking example of anti-rationalism than that afforded by Lukács's own philosophy of blind faith, in which nothing is proved but everything asserted *ex cathedra*, and whatever does not fit the Marxian schemata is dismissed as reactionary rubbish.

Lukács's polemic against existentialism, published in 1948, is another outstanding specimen of Stalinist philosophy, embodying all the main points of the Lenin–Stalin–Zhdanov catechism. Philosophy must be either idealistic or materialistic, there is no third way; subjective idealism leads to solipsism, the philosophy of madmen, while objective idealism invents imaginary ideas or spirits governing the world. Either spirit or matter must be primary: those who claim to stand above the opposition between the two are deceivers or self-deceived. Lenin's *Materialism and Empiriocriticism* provides unanswerable arguments to refute all idealists, whether his immediate opponents or those, like the existentialists, who have come on the scene later. The latter seek to reconstruct the whole of being on the basis of pure consciousness, although science has long since exploded such nonsense—even though natural scientists, for lack of Marxist education, have not yet grasped the fact that all the achievements of science point to the triumph of dialectical materialism.

Existentialism or Marxism? is perhaps the most flagrant example of Lukács's intellectual degradation: it is indistinguishable in style and content from the standard products of Soviet philosophy under Stalin, including the ritual advice to physicists, of whose subject Lukács knew nothing.

There is no indication that Lukács ever disavowed his works of this period; *The Destruction of Reason* was republished unchanged after Stalin's death, in 1954.

7. *The whole, mediation, and mimesis as aesthetic categories*

LUKÁCS's main ambition was to lay the foundations of a Marxist aesthetic. His many works in this field are concerned variously with literary theory and criticism and with general aesthetics. However, even when he tries to establish categories relating to all forms of art his information is chiefly drawn from the history of literature, especially drama and the novel, and it is not always clear how his doctrine is to be applied outside this sphere. His works on aesthetics—apart, of course, from those written before he was a Marxist—can be treated as a single whole, as his views on theory, and even on particular writers and artistic trends, do not seem to have undergone any change from the 1920s to his last years.

Certain general observations by Lukács on the 'nature' of art have no specifically Marxist content. He states that art, unlike science, is anthropomorphic in character, being concerned with social conditions. For this reason art is essentially hostile to religion, even if its immediate purpose is to serve as an adjunct to faith or worship: for, whatever the artist's intention, art itself is a thing of this world. Historically, art is rooted in magic practices, but it differs from them in that its purpose is to arouse particular feelings and attitudes, which in magic is only a secondary or subordinate aim. Art offers images of reality, but these are charged from the outset with an emotional content and imply an active attitude towards the world they describe. All art conveys cognitive values: it increased man's knowledge of himself and therefore of the world. It enables people to step outside immediate practical reality and rise to an understanding of the sense of the universe. It should not therefore be treated as a mere entertainment or distraction: it plays a major part in man's spiritual evolution, being a means by which he creates himself and becomes aware of his own species-nature.

Hence, although art cannot be reduced to purely cognitive functions—since, unlike science, it presents the world in the form of images and in such a way that their transmission entails an act of evaluation—it is nevertheless a 'reflection' of reality, based on a particular form of imitation or mimesis. This is not a mere passive copying of the world, but involves selection and a certain degree of universalization. By means of individual images, art presents a view of the world that lays claim to universality: in this sense the 'individual' and the 'universal' are presented, in the work of art, as a single unity.

It has often been objected to Lukács—as to all others who speak of art in terms of 'reflection' or 'mimesis'—that, even if we know roughly what these expressions mean in relation to a play, a novel, or a figurative painting, it is not at all clear how a piece of music or architecture, or an ornament, can be said to 'reflect' reality. Lukács maintains, however, that mimesis is a category applicable to all artistic phenomena. Music, for instance, conveys emotions that are aroused by social conditions, and thus 'reflects', albeit indirectly, the historical links between human beings. Architecture likewise expresses human attitudes and needs by organizing space in a particular way. Ornaments imitate natural figures and present them in a form that expresses human attitudes towards them. Such explanations as these have often struck Lukács's critics as artificial, and they also call in question the real meaning of the idea of reflection or mimesis. If a piece of music reflects the world by expressing emotions, and if these emotions must in some way be connected with social life, then to say that art 'reflects' reality would seem to mean simply that it is influenced by the various phenomena and interconnections of social life; but this is so general and obvious a statement as not to be of much use. In any case, it is clear that when Lukács is talking about works of literature he uses the term 'reflection' in a much stronger sense. Not only do social conditions affect artistic production, which nobody would deny, but works of art present an image of reality from which the reader or spectator can learn something about that reality and recognize its 'structure' or its internal conflicts.

Lukács is in fact seeking to define art in such a way as to justify the conclusion that only 'realistic' works truly deserve the name of art; his condemnation of artistic 'decadence' is likewise based on this conclusion. But again, it is not at all clear how music, architecture, or even lyric poetry can be judged from the point of view of 'realism'. If the term 'mimesis' denotes any kind of dependence of a work of art on social phenomena, then certainly all art must be imitative and also 'realistic'; but in that case the notions of mimesis and realism have lost their meaning. Lukács's main concern is with drama and the novel, to which they are undoubtedly more applicable; but here again he seems to use 'mimesis' in two different senses, a descriptive and a normative. In the former sense any novel or play in some measure reflects the world, social conditions, and conflicts, and every work of art is socially committed: it takes one side or the other in regard to the basic issues of the day, irrespective of how far the author is aware of his involvement or the real significance of his work (often he does not understand it). In the normative sense, however, 'mimesis' is the quality of a work that imitates reality 'correctly', presenting the problems of its time as they 'truly' are; the author of such a work, of course, is on the 'right' or progressive side. This seems to be the sense in which Lukács uses the term 'mimesis' most frequently.

The same is true of the notion of 'totality' as applied to literature. Every literary work reflects in some way the totality of social life, since when we adopt an attitude towards the world, even a reactionary one, it is necessarily related to the world as a whole—not because we so intend, but because all human affairs are linked together and by engaging in a particular conflict we are also engaged, willy-nilly, in a universal one. But, more often than not, Lukács also uses 'totality' in a normative sense. 'Genuine' works of literature are those which seek to mirror the world as a whole, and it is for the critic or ideologist to ensure, as far as he may, that the work embodies a true reference system giving significance to its component parts and subordinating them to an over-all artistic purpose. In this sense 'totality' is not simply an attribute of all literature but an ideal to be aimed at in socialist art. Lukács, however, does not clearly formulate the distinction.

The demand that art should reflect 'totality' is aimed primarily against naturalism—the idea that it suffices to describe reality in terms of direct observation, simply recording what happens or what meets the eye. Literature, thus limited, cannot convey the meaning of events, which only reveals itself in relation to the whole: it requires conceptual understanding and not mere observation. But—and this is the nub of the argument, as Lukács urged in his dispute with Bloch on the subject of expressionism and realism—the totality of our society, or capitalism as an integrated system, is the true though invisible reality governing every single individual phenomenon. He who is able to make sense of the smallest details of human life by relating them to the whole can alone be said to depict social reality as it truly is, and to practice 'mimesis' in the normative sense of the term. Since this universality and sense of the whole requires a prior understanding of the nature of society such as only Marxism can provide, it follows that in the present age only a Marxist, in the sense in which Lukács understands this term, can possess the qualifications of a good writer.

This, of course, does not mean that to be a good writer it suffices to master the conceptual understanding of the principle of totality. To create a work of art he must be able not only to relate the parts to the whole but also to present the whole in terms of individual images. Art is subject not only to the principle of wholeness but also to that of speciality (*Besonderheit*). This is the artistic counterpart of 'mediation' and is, in Lukács's view, the basic category of aesthetic analysis. Taking experience as its point of departure, art endeavours to find the type in the individual, the universal in particular phenomena. Lukács's 'speciality' may be defined, it seems, as this process whereby a writer transforms individual experiences into types or images of universal validity, so that they become the medium through which the reader apprehends the social whole. To say that art is subject to the category of 'speciality' does not mean that its place is 'in between' the universality of science and the immediacy of day-to-day experience, but that it reflects universality in particular images. In these images the universal and the individual do not appear separately but in a state of unity, and it may thus be said that art subsumes the two elements (in Hegel's sense of *aufheben*), or synthesizes them into aspects of a single phenomenon.

The relative prominence of the individual and the universal varies in different types of literature and different schools of art. Drama is, by its nature, more universal than the novel. Naturalism tends towards the individual, while allegory emphasizes the universal.

As several critics have pointed out, the view that an artist, at least in some forms of art, makes use of images to present 'typical' phenomena (i.e. not necessarily frequent or everyday ones, but such as reveal the salient features of their age or of this or that social milieu) is not specifically Marxist, and was often advanced by pre-Marxist or non-Marxist thinkers. Indeed, it seems to be a common-sense viewpoint as long as it is not applied to all kinds of art and is not erected into an arbitrary rule, so that art which does not 'typify' in this way is stigmatized as not being art in the 'good' sense. Lukács, however, violates both these provisos. As to the specifically Marxist element in his theory, it consists in relating everything to the 'totality' considered as a social system defined by Marxist categories, i.e. capitalism or socialism as the case may be.

However, the category of 'totality' figures in Lukács's aesthetics in other contexts also. Not only is art supposed to reveal the totality of society, but it is a means whereby man himself strives to achieve 'totality' as his mode of being— i.e. to become a complete and harmonious personality, not impaired by any one-sided preoccupations. The kind of art which favours this aspiration or helps men to become conscious of it is truly humanistic art, but it can only be such if it aims to be in advance of its time. In other words, it is the business of art not only to describe reality but to foresee it. In an article 'Es geht um Real-ismus' Lukács says that Marx considered Balzac a prophetic writer, as he cre-ated characters of a type that existed only in embryo in his time but developed later, under the Second Empire. In the same way, Lukács says, Gorky antici-pated types that did not exist when he wrote his first novels. Writers have this faculty because they are able to perceive trends and foresee their outcome. It is not clear on this basis, however, in what way the Stalinist literature of social-ist realism was at fault when it set out to describe not what was but what ought to be, as correctly anticipated by 'Marxist-Leninist science'; for that literature presumably conformed to Lukács's ideal pattern in that it used scientific analy-sis to discern the shape of future events.

8. Realism, socialist realism, and the avant-garde

FROM several of Lukács's arguments it may be inferred that the only literature that deserves to be called realistic is that which relates human life to the 'whole' as understood by Marxism. However, Lukács distinguishes two forms of realism: critical and socialist. To the former category belong practically all the great writers of the past; and, at least as far as the nineteenth century is con-cerned, it makes no difference what their conscious world-outlook was. Balzac, Scott, and Tolstoy were reactionary in their political views, but they created great works owing to their skill in painting a realistic picture of the world they lived in. There was, according to Lukács, a 'contradiction' between their liter-ary performance and their political attitudes. It is not clear, however, in what this 'contradiction' lay. On the contrary, it would seem that Balzac's legitimist and aristocratic outlook was fully in harmony with his critique of post-Revolu-tionary society, just as Tolstoy's emphasis on the virtues of country life and undogmatic religion were fully consonant with his attack on the Church and the privileged classes. The only 'contradiction', in fact, seems to be between these writers' world-outlook and Marxist doctrine.

Critical realism, in Lukács's view, is an attribute of writers who, while they did not manage to achieve a Communist outlook, strove to record accurately the conflicts of their time and did not confine themselves to particular events, but described great historical movements through the medium of individual destinies. They were not mere naturalists, but neither were they allegorists or metaphysicians: they did not retreat from the world into the isolation of the individual psyche, nor did they elevate particular mental or spiritual events to the status of a timeless, eternal, unalterable human condition. Such realists were Balzac, Tolstoy, and the other great Russians of his day and, in more recent times, Anatole France, Bernard Shaw, Romain Rolland, Feuchtwanger, and, above all, Thomas Mann.

Lukács observes more than once that realistic art generally comes to the fore in advanced countries or those that are going through a period of social and economic growth. In cases where this does not apply, he explains that backward countries may sometimes produce great literature as an attempt to break out of their very backwardness. These arguments are not peculiar to Lukács but are often found in Marxist writing. If 'advanced' countries like eighteenth-century France produce 'advanced' literature, this is a clear confirmation of historical materialism; if backward countries like nineteenth-century Russia produce 'advanced' literature it is again a confirmation of historical materialism, as in such cases ideology makes up for the deficiencies of the 'base'.

Contrasted with realism is the whole of modernist and *avant-garde* literature: naturalism, expressionism, surrealism, etc. Examples of this decadent form of art are the works of Kafka, Joyce, Musil, Montherlant, Samuel Beckett, and others. The decisive shortcoming of all modernist literature is its inability to grasp the 'totality' and to perform the act of mediation. A writer is not to blame for depicting loneliness, for example, but he must show it to be a fatal consequence of capitalism; Kafka, however, presents us with 'ontological loneliness' as though it were a permanent human condition of universal validity. He paints what is immediately before his eyes and fails to penetrate to the 'whole' which alone gives it meaning, and in this he resembles the naturalists. In the same way, the world may be realistically described as being in a state of chaos and panic, but only if this is shown to be due to the horrors of capitalism. If, as in Joyce, the hero's spiritual life and perception of time disintegrate without cause and without hope of remedy, the universe so depicted must be false, and the work of art a bad one.

Lacking a historical perspective, *avant-garde* art presents situations as permanent when they are in fact conditioned by history and social forms, and endows them with a 'transcendental' quality. (It may be remarked that Lukács uses terms like 'transcendental' and 'mystic' in an arbitrary and vaguely pejorative way, regardless of their meaning in philosophical tradition: all we can gather is that they denote something bad.) The great characters of literature, from Achilles and Oedipus to Werther and Anna Karenina, are all social beings—for man himself is a social being, as Lukács reminds us with a reference to Aristotle; but the heroes of modernist literature are wrenched from their social and historical background. The narrative becomes purely 'subjective', or else, as with Beckett and Montherlant, animal man is contrasted with social man: this corresponds to Heidegger's condemnation of society (*das Man*) and leads to Nazi racism of the Rosenberg type. (All these examples are in *The Meaning of Contemporary Realism*, first published in 1958; English trans.

1963.) Modernist literature, in short, is not an enrichment of art but a negation of it.

The acme of literature, however, consists in socialist realism. 'The perspective of socialist realism is, of course, the struggle for socialism ... Socialist realism differs from critical realism, not only in being based on a concrete socialist perspective, but also in using this perspective to describe the forces working towards socialism *from the inside*' (*The Meaning of Contemporary Realism*, p. 93). Critical realists have from time to time depicted contemporary political struggles and created socialist heroes; but socialist realists portray these from within and identify with the forces of progress. The greatness of socialist realism lies in the fact that the historical totality of the movement towards socialism is evident in every facet of the work. To this category belong some at least of Gorky's novels, Sholokhov's *And Quiet Flows the Don*, and the works of Aleksey Tolstoy, Makarenko, and Arnold Zweig.

To avoid misjudgement it should be pointed out that Lukács had a thorough knowledge of European literature and was perfectly well aware of the difference between great and mediocre works. His aversion to modernist writers such as Proust, Kafka, and Musil—in fact almost everyone later than Thomas Mann—does not have to be explained by ideology: most people find it hard to come to terms with literature radically different from what they were used to in their youth. His dislike of the *avant-garde* was certainly genuine, though it was sometimes based on amazingly primitive arguments. As to socialist realism, the examples he cited were all outstanding or at least meritorious: he did not refer to hack writers of the Stalinist period whose works have long since been pulped. The result is that it is not easy to find citations by him of works of socialist realism dating from the 1930s and after, though he frequently speaks in general terms of the flourishing state of Soviet literature under Stalin. At a period when literature was in fact completely crushed, when many prominent writers died in concentration camps and when almost the only works published were servile panegyrics in honour of the Great Leader, written by mediocrities and devoid of literary merit, Lukács accounted as follows for the absence of modernist art in Russia: 'As proletarian rule became stronger, as socialism penetrated the Soviet economy more deeply and universally, and as the cultural revolution affected the toiling masses on a broader and deeper front, so avant-garde art has been driven out by an increasingly conscious realism. The decline of expressionism is due in the last analysis to the maturity of the revolutionary masses' ('Es geht um den Realismus'). In other words, Lukács ascribed to revolutionary maturity what he well knew to be the work of police repression. It is worth noting that although Lukács does not quote much from Stalin as a rule, he indulges in many interpretations of this kind. Typical examples can be found in the article 'Tendenz oder Parteilichkeit?', in which he objects to the description of socialist art as 'tendentious'. Literature should not be 'tendentious', but it should be 'true to the party'. By 'tendentious' literature we mean a kind which eclectically mingles 'pure art' with alien political elements introduced from without. This procedure (to be observed in Mehring) signifies the 'primacy of form over content'; it is a Trotskyist view of art, which opposes the purely aesthetic components of a work to political ones which are essentially non-aesthetic. True revolutionary writers, however, refuse to distinguish between art and its political message. Their works are imbued with party spirit, which means that they convey a correct Marxist understanding of the movement of reality towards socialism and present a harmonious integration of individual description and historical perspective.

Lukács continued to be involved with socialist realism till the end of his career as a critic. During the 'thaw' after Stalin's death he wrote a few essays touching on the literature of the previous period. He observed that Stalinism suffered from a lack of 'mediation' in culture as in other fields; Stalinist literature had become abstract and schematic instead of describing the real conflicts of socialist society; it attempted to portray general theoretical truths directly instead of through the medium of images based on reality. It had overlooked the specific nature and claims of art and had subordinated it to propaganda. Optimism had become schematic instead of historical. The heroes of Stalinist fiction displayed no qualities typical of the new society. Lenin's article of 1905 on party literature, which—as Krupskaya had testified—was concerned only with political writings, had been applied to all literature and turned into a general code of conduct for artists. Critical realism had been buried prematurely, and the notion of decadence had been so widened as to condemn all the more recent products of that school.

Despite these criticisms, however, Lukács never renounced the view that socialist realism was 'basically' and 'historically' a higher form of art than any of its predecessors, nor did he revise the criteria for defining it: relationship to the 'whole', optimism, 'partyism' (*Parteilichkeit*), Marxist orthodoxy, and identification with the forces of revolution. There is no reason to suppose that his book on realism, a purely Stalinist work, did not reflect his later views with equal accuracy.

The most astonishing expression of Lukács's ideas on socialist realism, however, is contained in his articles on Solzhenitsyn. He greeted the latter's novels as the first signs of a renaissance of socialist realism because, he said, the accounts of life in the camps presented day-to-day events as symbols of a whole era. Solzhenitsyn was not a mere naturalist, but related phenomena to the social 'whole'—and, Lukács adds for good measure, he could not be accused of intending to restore capitalism in Russia. His weakness was, however, that he criticized Stalinism from a plebeian and not a Communist viewpoint, and his art would suffer if he did not overcome this. In short, Lukács advised Solzhenitsyn to become a Communist for the sake of his literary development; but he failed to cite any example of a good writer who had become still better as a result of embracing Communism.

It seems a pathetic end to Lukács's aesthetic doctrine that in his closing years, after Russian culture had been devastated by two decades of Stalinism, of which he had been an eminent spokesman, he should have discovered 'socialist realism' in the work of a convinced and passionate adversary of Communism—for there could be no doubt that this was Solhenitsyn's position from the beginning: it is irrelevant that Lukács did not live to read *The Gulag Archipelago*. Lukács's verdict on Solzhenitsyn is a symbol of the nullity of his whole theory of literature.

9. The exposition of Marxist mythology. Commentary

LUKÁCS was, beyond doubt, an outstanding interpreter of Marx's doctrine, and rendered great service by reconstructing it in a completely different way from that followed by the previous generation of Marxists. Besides emphasizing Marx's profound debt to the Hegelian dialectic as the interplay of subject and object seeking identity, he was the first to show clearly that, in the dispute among Marxists between neo-Kantians and evolutionists, both sides were arguing from non-Marxian positions; and that Marx believed in a dialectic in which the understanding and transformation of the world were one and the same process, so that the dilemmas of freedom versus necessity, facts versus values, and will versus prediction lost their meaning. The questions that the theorists of the Second International put to Marx missed the point of his philosophy, as they presupposed an 'objective' historical process governed by its own laws; whereas, as Lukács showed, in the historically privileged case of the working class the 'objective' process coincided with the development of awareness of that process, so that free action and historical inevitability became one and the same thing. Lukács certainly formulated a radically new and, I believe, correct interpretation of Marx's philosophy, and from this point of view his achievement seems unquestionable.

However, the fact that Lukács interpreted Marx afresh and more accurately than anyone before him does not mean that he was right to adopt Marx's belief in the unity of theory and practice, freedom and necessity. Despite his intention, his work had the effect of revealing the mythological, prophetic, and utopian sense of Marxism which had eluded Marx's more scientistic followers. The blurring of the distinction between descriptive and normative elements is in fact characteristic of the way in which a myth is apprehended by believers: narration and precept are not distinguished, but are accepted as a single reality. That which the myth commands, or holds up to be worshipped and imitated, is not presented as a separate conclusion but is directly perceived as part of the story. To understand a myth rightly is not only to understand its factual content but to accept the values implied in it. In this sense a disciple understands the myth differently from an outside observer—a historian, anthropologist or sociologist—he understands the myth in the act of self-commitment and, in this sense, it is right to say that it can be understood only 'from within', by an act of practical affirmation. Such, in Lukács's view, is the position with Marxism. A non-Marxist cannot understand it properly, as to do so requires actual participation in the revolutionary movement. Marxism is not simply a theory *about* the world, which can be accepted by anyone whether or not he approves the values of the political Marxist movement; it is an understanding of the world that can only be enjoyed within that movement and in political commitment to it. Marxism in this sense is invulnerable to rational argument: outsiders cannot understand it correctly, and therefore cannot criticize it effectively. Thus, as Lukács showed, the Marxist consciousness obeys the epistemological rules appropriate to a myth.

At the same time Lukács pointed out the prophetic character of that consciousness, in that it does away with the distinction between will and prediction. A prophet does not speak with his own voice but with the voice of God or History; and neither God nor History 'foresees' any thing in the way that human beings foresee events over which they have no influence. With God, the act of foreseeing is identical with the act of creating the thing foreseen, and the same is true of the ultimate History in which the subject and object of action are identified with each other. (God never acts from without, but always immanently.) The historical subject that has identified its own consciousness with the historical process no longer distinguishes between the future it foresees and the future it creates.

The historical subject, as understood by Lukács, embodies the Utopian consciousness *par excellence*. This consciousness appears in that very part of the doctrine that is directed against Utopian socialism, particularly in Marx's belief, elucidated and emphasized by Lukács, that socialism must not be treated either as an ordinary moral command, the result of an evaluative process, or as a matter of 'historical necessity'. If the distinction between facts and values, between an act of pure cognition and one of moral affirmation, is not present in the proletarian consciousness, it is because socialism is not simply desirable or simply necessary, nor even both at once: it is a 'unity' of the two, a state of things that realizes the essence of humanity—but an essence that already exists, not the arbitrary precept of a moralist. The socialist future of the world is not something that we desire as a matter of preference or that we foresee on the basis of a rational analysis of historical tendencies: it is something which already exists as a Hegelian reality of a higher order, which cannot be empirically perceived but is more real than all empirical facts. In the same way Lukács's 'totality' is real but non-empirical. Thus when speaking of the socialism of the future we need not use either normative language or the language of scientific prediction. Socialism is the meaning of history and is therefore already present in today's events. The typical utopian ontology presents the future not as something desired or expected but as the *modus* of being of the present day. It is Lukács's undoubted merit to have revealed this ontology, of Hegelian and Platonic origin, as a basic feature of Marxism.

In so doing, however, Lukács gave Marxism an irrational and anti-scientific form. His conception of 'totality' protects it in advance from any rational or empirical criticism: for the totality cannot be deduced from any accumulation of facts or empirical arguments, and if the facts appear to be contrary to it, it is they that are wrong. This being so, it may be asked how we can possibly know the totality, or know that we know it. Lukács replies that we can know it by means of a correct dialectical 'method'; but on investigation it proves that this method consists precisely in relating all phenomena to the whole, so that we must know the latter before we can start. The method, and knowledge of the whole, presuppose each other; we are in an elementary vicious circle, the only way out of which is to assert that the proletariat possesses the whole truth by virtue of its privileged historical position. But this is only an apparent escape, for how do we know that the proletariat is thus privileged? We know it from Marxist theory, which must be right because it alone comprehends the whole: so we are back in the vicious circle again.

The only recourse is to say that the whole is not to be discovered by pure scientific observation but only by active participation in the revolutionary movement. This, however, involves a genetic criterion of truth: Marxism is true because it 'expresses' the proletarian consciousness, and not the other way about. But this is merely a criterion of authority: the truth must be recognized as such not because it is supported by ordinary scientific arguments but because it emanates from a historically privileged class, and we know that class to be so privileged because we are told so by the theory of which it is the exponent. Moreover, the mythology of the proletariat as an infallible class is reduced in Lukács's theory to pure party dogmatism. The content of class-consciousness is decided not by the class itself but by the party in which its historical interest is embodied: so the party is the source and criterion of all truth. Q.E.D.

On this basis the unity of theory and practice, of facts and values turns out to be simply the primacy of political commitment over intellectual values: an assurance given by the Communist movement to its members that they possess the truth by virtue of belonging to the movement. Lukács's Marxism implies the abandonment of intellectual, logical, and empirical criteria of knowledge, and as such it is anti-rational and anti-scientific.

10. Lukács as a Stalinist, and his critique of Stalinism

As ALREADY mentioned, Lukács always considered himself a true disciple of Lenin, and his criticisms of Stalinism after 1956 were made on the basis that Stalin had distorted Lenin's principles. His speeches, interviews, and articles on the subject give a fairly exact idea of his opinions on the Stalinist past. In a postscript of 1957 to 'Mein Weg zu Marx' he wrote: 'At the beginning of the imperialist era Lenin developed the question of the significance of the subjective factor and in so doing extended the bounds of classical theory. Stalin turned this into a system of subjectivist dogmas. It was a tragedy that with his great talent, rich experience, and unusual quickness of mind he did not break out of the vicious circle or even perceive clearly the error of subjectivism. It also seems to me tragic that his last work begins with a well-founded criticism of economic subjectivism, while at the same time it does not occur to him that he himself was the spiritual father and patron of that subjectivism' (*Schriften zur Ideologie und Politik*, ed. Ludz, 1967, pp. 652–3).

Stalin, then, was a tragic subjectivist; and, as we have seen, Lukács elsewhere states that the Stalin era suffered from a lack of 'mediation' in cultural policy. It was wrong to lump together all non-Communist forces (the theory of 'social Fascism'), and to say that there was no longer any place in literature for critical realism. It was wrong, too, to stifle all discussion *within the party*, and to subject oppositionists to police repression. However, as Lukács stated in a letter to Alberto Carocci published in 1962, it did not follow that the victims of Stalin's purges, such as Trotsky and his followers, should be rehabilitated politically. In principle, Stalin was right as against Trotsky, but Stalin himself subsequently pursued a Trotskyist policy instead of a Leninist one. It was a mistake to subordinate the whole of culture to propaganda aims, regardless of its intrinsic values. An especially pernicious effect of Stalinism was the degradation of Marxist theory. The task now was to restore confidence in Marxism, to reconstruct its intellectual values, to overcome dogmatism and subjectivism, and to re-establish Leninist principles of socialist organization and Marxist thought.

As to the causes of Stalinism, Lukács confines himself to generalities about the backwardness of Russia and the havoc wrought by the years of war, revolution, and civil war.

Lukács at no time questioned the Leninist foundations on which the whole edifice of Stalinism was reared. He did not question the principle of one-party dictatorship and the abolition of the 'bourgeois' division of authority into legislative, executive, and judicial: in other words, he accepted that the governing party should be subject to no form of public control and that socialism ruled out competition between independent political forces. In short, he accepted despotism in principle, although he later criticized some of its extreme manifestations. He was one of those Communists, numerous in the late 1950s, who believed that democracy could exist within the ruling Communist party although it had been abolished for the rest of the community. This delusion, however, did not last long, and the experience of Stalinism showed clearly that the liquidation of democracy in the state was bound to lead, in a short time, to the liquidation of democracy within the ruling party: the process, indeed, began under Lenin and with his encouragement. The reason is that when state democracy is abolished it is inevitable, whatever anyone's intentions, that groups within the party will, if they are allowed, become advocates of other, non-party forces and reflect various social pressures. In other words, intra-party democracy, in which sects are permitted to exist, is essentially the same as a multi-party system, with the revival under one name or another of the political organisms that the party has just destroyed. Thus, if the party bureaucracy is to remain all-powerful within the state, democracy within the party can be no more than a pious wish.

The same holds good in the field of culture. In an interview published in *Szabad Nép* on 14 October 1956, a few days before the Hungarian uprising, Lukács stated that different artistic trends should be allowed to exist in a socialist state, but that there could be no question of ideologies freely competing, and that, for example, the teaching of philosophy in universities must be exclusively carried on by Marxists (*Schriften*, p. 634). But this is precisely the Stalinist principle of government: for if it is laid down that only Marxists have the right to teach, there must be an authority to decide who is and who is not a Marxist; and this authority can only be the ruling party, i.e. the party bureaucracy. If the party says somebody is not a Marxist, then by definition he is not. Hence the principle of a Marxist monopoly is identical with the Stalinist system, and from this point of view it is not clear how that system was at fault in its cultural policy.

In the late 1950s, when the political and ideological ferment in Eastern Europe was at its height, Lukács was one of the most timid and cautious critics of Stalinism, never questioning its basic principles but only certain manifestations. However, phenomena such as mass terror and the extermination of political adversaries are not a necessary feature of totalitarian Communism: it may resort to such means in case of need, but it may also do without them. Nor is it incompatible with the system for ideological discussions to take place 'within Marxism': as a matter of fact such discussions took place even in the worst years, and Stalin often called for 'a frank discussion'. All that the Stalin-

ist system requires is acceptance of the principle that the limits of discussion
and of cultural freedom are fixed at any given time by the party (i.e. the party
bureaucracy), which cannot be subject to any higher authority. Lukács
accepted this principle, and at no time called it in question.

During the war, when Stalin played on anti-German nationalism and, among
other things, described Hegel as the philosopher of the aristocratic reaction
against the French Revolution, Lukács, we may believe, was unable to swallow
such nonsense, and the publication of his book on Hegel was consequently
held up for some years. There is no reason to doubt that he rejected Stalin's
views on Hegel, but here again what counted with him was the political justification. In the postscript, already quoted, to 'Mein Weg zu Marx' he declared
that although he thought Stalin wrong on many points he did not engage in
opposition, not only because it was physically impossible to do so but because
any opposition could easily have degenerated into support for Fascism. In
short, Stalin might have made mistakes, but he, Lukács, had been right not to
oppose Stalinism. But this avowal, dating from 1957, is a clearer proof of
Lukács's actual Stalinism than any glorification of Stalin during his lifetime.
The argument is that it was right to support Stalin and Stalinism without reservation, even while harbouring, internally and invisibly, objections to the party's
current policy. But Stalinism demanded no loyalty other than that expressed in
outward obedience, and the burden of Lukács's argument is precisely to justify
such obedience. As long as the world is torn by the struggle between capitalism and socialism, and if socialism is assumed on philosophical grounds to be
an essentially superior system irrespective of any empirical facts, then clearly
any internal opposition to socialism as it exists at a given time is a blow struck
in favour of the enemy. Any public criticism, however mild, of the system and
its leaders is exploited in some way by the adversary—a fact which, ever since
Soviet Russia came into existence, has been effectively used to silence real,
imaginary, or potential critics by branding them as allies of imperialism. What
is notable in Lukács's case is not that he submitted to this form of blackmail
but that he provided a theoretical justification for it, in full accord with his rule
of thinking in terms of the 'whole' and of comprehensive systems.

This rule of Lukács's, in fact, is tantamount to a general justification of the
typical Communist contempt for facts. Communism is defined in theoretical
terms as a higher form of society which will do away with the division of labour,
introduce 'true' freedom and equality, abolish exploitation, lead to a blossoming of culture, and so on. All these truths are valid *a priori*, whatever the actual
face of Communism may be. The most repellent forms of totalitarian despotism, oppression, and exploitation cannot detract from its superiority: at most
it may be conceded in after years, when the party allows a measure of criticism,
that there have been occasional mistakes or that 'survivals of capitalism' were

at work. The superiority of socialism is absolute and is not susceptible to empirical proof or disproof. Lukács's achievement is to have elevated the practice of contempt for facts as compared with 'systems' to the dignity of a great theoretical principle, of which Marxism can be justly proud.

In Stalin's day Lukács glorified the Soviet system as the supreme embodiment of freedom, maintaining that, with the exploiters overthrown, work had become identical with pleasure, as Marx had promised; that socialism had replaced 'apparent and superficial freedom' by the genuine variety, and that only under the new system did writers enjoy true contact with the people. All this is in no way surprising: these are the regular clichés of Stalinist propaganda. (A good example is the article 'Frei oder gelenkte Kunst?', published in 1947, which abounds in stock phrases contrasting Soviet freedom with capitalist corruption.) But even in Lukács's later writings there is no suggestion that his views on these matters had changed. In *The Meaning of Contemporary Realism* he wrote: 'In socialist society the individual will enjoy greater freedom to choose a place for himself in society than under capitalism ("freedom" being understood here, of course, as conscious acceptance of historical necessity—a necessity which subsumes much that is apparently arbitrary)' (p. 112). Thus true, superior socialist freedom is still made to consist in accepting historical necessity. On this definition it may be wondered whether the mind of men could conceive a system (under Communist party rule, of course) so despotic that it did not qualify to be regarded as an embodiment of the highest freedom.

In the same way Lukács's aesthetic doctrine, at least in its specifically Marxist features and especially in regard to socialist and critical realism and *avant-garde* literature, is a perfect theoretical justification of Stalin's cultural policy. Lukács, in fact, forged the conceptual instruments of cultural despotism. If socialist realism is 'basically' the highest form of art for historio-sophical reasons, and if its characteristic feature is that the author relates particulars to the 'whole', i.e. the battle for socialism, and identifies with those who are fighting that battle, then clearly the socialist state must foster and encourage the type of art in which its own interests are expressed. Literature and painting whose main function was to glorify Stalin are really in terms of Lukács's doctrine, true examples of socialist realism; in general he was well aware of the difference between good and bad art, but in the last resort what mattered was the content, i.e. in this case ideological values or the relation to the 'whole'.

Lukács also helped to popularize the deplorable misuse of the term 'dialectical' either to express a commonplace (as that two phenomena interact on each other, or that in observing an object various circumstances should be taken into account, or that a certain judgement may be right in some conditions and wrong in others), or as a knock-down argument enabling the user to dismiss empirical facts and maintain that 'superficially' things may appear thus and so, but 'dialectically' the case is the exact opposite. In his book on Lenin, for example, he accuses the reformists of having an 'un-dialectic conception of the nature of a majority', from which it would appear that the 'dialectical' sense of this term is the opposite of what common sense or common arithmetic understands by it. (Since Communism has never, in any situation, had a majority of the people on its side, it is certainly convenient to maintain that it nevertheless commanded a majority in the deeper, dialectical sense—an irrefutable statement in the light of the theory that Communism necessarily stands for the true interests of humanity.) In this and similar cases the term 'dialectical' is designed to convey that its user is in possession of a special, profound, infallible method of observing and understanding the world. In an interview given in October 1969 (English text in the *Cambridge Review*, 28 January 1972) Lukács even stated that 'in Lenin there existed a dialectical unity of patience and impatience'.

▪ ▪ ▪

Lukács was an extremely important figure in the history of Marxism not only by virtue of his contribution to the interpretation of Marx's thought, or because he showed how the latter's philosophy could be used to justify the self-glorification of Communist bureaucracies, or again because he originated or revived certain concepts which have had a strong influence on the shape of Marxism at the present day. Besides all this he is important as an outstanding representative of those intellectuals who identified with the totalitarian system, denied their own intellectual values for the purpose, and evolved a theoretical justification of that denial. Lukács is depicted in literature as the Jesuit Naphta in Thomas Mann's *The Magic Mountain:* a highly intelligent character who needs authority, finds it, and renounces his own personality for its sake. Lukács in fact was a true intellectual, a man of immense culture (unlike the vast majority of Stalinist ideologists), but one who craved intellectual security and could not endure the uncertainties of a sceptical or empirical outlook. In the Communist party he found what many intellectuals need: absolute certainty in defiance of facts, an opportunity of total commitment that supersedes criticism and stills every anxiety. In his case, too, the commitment was such as to afford its own assurance of truth and invalidate all other intellectual criteria.

From the time of his identification with Communism and Marxism Lukács *knew* that all problems of philosophy and the social sciences had been solved in principle and that the only remaining task was to ascertain and proclaim the true content of Marx's and Lenin's ideas, so as to bring about a correct understanding of the received canon. He gave no further thought to the question whether the Marxian 'totality' was itself a true one and how its truth could be proved. Consequently, his works, as we have pointed out, are a collection of dogmatic statements and not of arguments. Having once and for all found a standard of truth and accuracy, he applied it to one object after another: the philosophy of Hegel or Fichte, Goethe's poetry, or Kafka's novels. His dogmatism was absolute, and almost sublime in its perfection. In his critique of Stalinism he did not step outside its fundamental bases.

Lukács is perhaps the most striking example in the twentieth century of what may be called the betrayal of reason by those whose profession is to use and defend it.

VIII
Karl Korsch

In THE EARLY 1920s Karl Korsch was a well-known figure in the Marxist move-ment. After his expulsion from the Communist party in 1926, however, his name almost completely disappeared from circulation, though he remained active in politics and as a writer for over a quarter of a century. Posthumously, in the six-ties, he was again officially mentioned, and some translations and new editions of his works were published. At present he enjoys the deserved reputation of having made some of the most interesting contributions to the interpretation of Marxism.

Together with Lukács he was the most eminent of those who tried to recon-struct Marx's original philosophy, or rather anti-philosophy, in opposition both to the evolutionism and scientism of the Marxists of Kautsky's generation and also to the neo-Kantian revisionists, and by so doing to furnish a correct basis, which in time became an anti-Leninist one, for the revolutionary strategy of the class struggle. Korsch's reconstruction is important for several reasons. In the first place, it made clear the Hegelian origin of Marxist dialectic. Secondly, it revived the almost forgotten early Marxist conception of the unity of theory and practice. Thirdly, it emphasized the purely negative aspect of Marxism as the consciousness of the proletariat, making a complete break with all traditional forms of life in bourgeois society including the state, law, ethics, philosophy, and science. In some respects the Utopian radicalism of this reconstruction is reminiscent of Sorel. Whether or not Korsch identified with Marxism as rein-terpreted by him, his version is certainly one of the most fruitful attempts to consider Marx from the point of view of *The German Ideology* rather than the *Critique of the Gotha Programme*.

1. Biographical data

KARL KORSCH (1886–1961) was born near Hamburg, the son of a civil servant. He studied law and philosophy at different universities, received his doctorate in law at Jena in 1910, and in 1912 went to London for further studies. He joined the Fabian Society, and, as his biographers observe, the ideas of British socialism made a permanent impression on his mind, even during his later ultra-revolutionary phase. While fundamentally opposed to all reformism he nevertheless maintained that both revolutionaries and British reformists were truly devoted to socialism and that they recognized the importance of subjective factors, unlike the orthodox leaders of the Second International, who relied on the beneficent effects of historical determinism.

In the First World War Korsch served for a time as an officer, but was reduced to the ranks for expressing anti-war sentiments. He joined the anti-war group of German socialists (the USPD) and was among the left-wing members of the social democratic party who formed the German Communist party (KPD) in 1920. He took an active part in the revolution of November 1918, and in 1923 was Minister of Justice in the short-lived revolutionary government of Thuringia. In the same year he became a professor at Jena University, a post he occupied until Hitler's accession to power. From 1924 he was a Communist member of the Reichstag, and for a year he also edited the party's theoretical journal, *Die Internationale*. At that time he published theoretical articles and reviews, including two short essays on the dialectic, and also what is perhaps his most important work, *Marxismus und Philosophie*, published in 1923 in *Archiv für Geschichte des Sozialismus und der Arbeiterbewegung* (English trans., *Marxism and Philosophy*, 1970). These writings caused him to be regarded within the party as an 'ultra-Leftist', a revisionist and an idealist, for which errors he and Lukács were condemned by Zinoviev at the Fifth Comintern Congress in July 1924. (Later, in July 1926, he received a mention from Stalin himself, who described him at a plenum of the Central Committee as an 'ultra-Leftist' theoretician who believed that the Soviet state had reverted to capitalism and that Russia needed a new revolution.)

While identifying with Communism, Korsch from the first had reservations as to the principles of the Third International, especially the organizational forms which placed the whole Communist movement in the hands of a professional apparatus and also subordinated the worldwide structure to the dictates of Moscow. Like other 'left-wing' deviationists he held that the party was no substitute for the revolutionary potential of the true proletariat. He finally came to believe that the Comintern was an instrument of counter-revolution and that the Soviet system was a proletarian dictatorship exercised not by the proletariat, but over it. He was expelled from the party in the spring of 1926, after which time he wrote and spoke as an independent Marxist. In 1930 he republished *Marxismus und Philosophie* with an extensive commentary; earlier, in 1929, he wrote a long and violent attack on Kautsky, whose *magnum opus*, *Die materialistische Geschichtsauffassung*, appeared in 1927. In 1932 he published an edition of *Das Capital* with an introduction, and in 1931 he wrote an essay, not published at the time, on the crisis of Marxism. In the 1930s he still considered himself a Marxist, but continued to criticize Kautsky and

Lenin, whose philosophies, he believed, had much in common despite their political differences. He also insisted more and more strongly that Marxism in the form inherited from the nineteenth century did not adequately express the consciousness of the modern proletariat, and that there was need for a new theory which would be a continuation but also a revision of Marxist doctrine. He put forward these views in *Karl Marx* (1938) and in articles entitled 'Why I am a Marxist' (1935) and 'Leading Principles of Marxism: a Restatement' (1937).

When Hitler came to power in 1935 Korsch emigrated to Denmark, where he lived for two years, and then to England. In 1936 he moved to the U.S.A., where he spent the rest of his life. The first political writer to draw attention to his importance as an interpreter of Marx was no doubt Iring Fetscher in the late fifties; in the next two decades he was the subject of a fairly large body of literature.

2. Theory and practice. Movement and ideology. Historical relativism

THE essence of Marxism, Korsch repeatedly emphasized, was the practical interpretation of human consciousness; but this had been completely eliminated from the positivist version of Marxism which dominated the Second International.

All Marxists, to be sure, subscribed to the doctrine of the 'unity of theory and practice'; but they usually meant by it—and Engels's writings tended to confirm this interpretation—that practice was 'the basis of knowledge and the touchstone of truth'. It followed, in the first place, that practical considerations for the most part determined the range of the cognitive interests of human beings, that technical needs and material interests were the strongest incentive in the advance of science, and that people were deluded if they supposed that a disinterested thirst for information played any part in the extension of knowledge. (This last might be taken either as a historical judgement or as a normative precept.) In the second place, the current view meant that practical efficacy was the best confirmation of the hypotheses on which action is based. These two opinions, which were logically independent of each other, were applied both to the natural and to the social sciences. It might be observed that irrespective of whether or to what extent the 'unity of theory and practice', thus understood, was a reality, it was quite compatible with the traditional or transcendental conception of truth as consisting in the conformity of our judgement with a state of affairs completely independent of our cognitive activity. In other words, the unity of theory and practice, thus understood, did not conflict with what Marx called the 'contemplative' conception of knowledge. The cognitive act—irrespective of the stimuli that provoked it, or of how the accuracy of its content was determined—was still the 'passive' assimilation of a ready-made universe.

In Korsch's view, however, the point of Marxism was not to supplement the traditional interpretation of cognition with observations regarding the motivation of cognitive acts and the verification of judgements, but to subject that interpretation to a radical change. Marxism was concerned particularly—though, as will appear, not exclusively—with knowledge of the social universe. Theoretical knowledge was not a mere 'reflection' of the social movement but a part, aspect, or expression of it; it must be interpreted as an essential component of the movement itself, and thus it was 'good' or 'true' in so far as it expressed the movement adequately and was aware that it did so. This applied above all to Marxism itself, which was an 'expression' of the class struggle of the proletariat and not a 'science' as understood by the positivists. This interpretation derived from Hegelian sources, for had not Hegel said that philosophy must be the intellectual expression of its own age?

It was the essence of Marxism to have drawn the fullest possible conclusions from this point of view. Above all, as Korsch argued at length in *Marxism and Philosophy*, Marxism was not a new philosophical doctrine but the abolition (*Aufhebung*) of philosophy. To abolish philosophy, however, does not simply mean to despise or abandon it or dismiss it as an illusion, as Mehring would have us do. For the very reason that philosophy was an 'expression' of the historical process, it could not be done away with by ignoring it or by the exercise of philosophy itself, but only by means of a revolutionary and practical critique of society, whose existing philosophy dwelt in a 'mystified' consciousness. Bourgeois society was an indissoluble whole (*Totalität*) and could only be attacked as such. The forms of consciousness of bourgeois society 'can only be abolished in thought and consciousness by a simultaneous practico-objective overthrow of the material relations of production themselves, which have hitherto been comprehended through these forms' (*Marxism and Philosophy*, p. 81). The fact that society is a *Totalität* means, in particular, that capitalist relations of production are what they are, only in conjunction with their ideological superstructure. In so far as Marxism is a theoretical and practical attack on that society, an expression of the movement that is to destroy it, it is also a philosophical critique. 'Eventually, it aims at the concrete abolition of philosophy as part of the abolition of bourgeois social reality as a whole, of which it is an ideal component' (ibid., p. 68). This is the correct understanding of Marx's important concept of a 'Critique of Political Economy'—the sub-title of *Das Capital* in the original: not merely an academic criticism of economic doctrines, but a practical attack on society through one of its main components, namely the economic ideologies which serve to perpetuate capitalist exploitation.

If we consider social realities as a whole, we perceive the concurrence

(*Zusammenfallen*) of reality and the theoretical forms that express it. They cannot exist separately, although the mystified bourgeois consciousness falsely imagines itself to be an external analysis of the social scene and not a part of it. Marxism, while unmasking this illusion, sees itself as a practical phenomenon, the expression and component of a social movement revolutionizing the present system.

Although Korsch regards ideologies as a necessary element in the social whole, he emphasizes that they are by no means 'on a level' with economic phenomena. On the contrary, he says, there are three degrees of reality: firstly, economics, which are the 'one true reality', secondly, the state and law, which are reality in an ideological disguise, and thirdly, 'pure ideology (pure nonsense), which is unreal and without an object' (ibid., p. 12).

In social affairs, the act of investigation coincides with its object—such is the Hegelian interpretation adopted by Marxism. From this point of view Korsch likens the Marxist theory of society to the view of Clausewitz (also a Hegelian) that the theory of war is not a matter of external observation but is part of war itself. If we lose sight of this identity, we cannot grasp the Hegelian-Marxist sense of the dialectic. The dialectic is not simply a 'method' applicable at will to any object. It would seem that in Korsch's view it is altogether impossible to expound the materialistic dialectic as a collection of statements or precepts of investigation. As an expression of the revolutionary movement of the working class it is part of that movement and not a mere theory or 'system'. 'The materialist dialectic of the proletariat cannot be learnt in the abstract, or from so-called examples, as a separate "science" with its own "subject-matter". It can only be *concretely* applied in proletarian revolutionary practice and in the theory which is a real, immanent part of that revolutionary practice' ('Über materialistische Dialektik', in *Marxismum und Philosophie*, p. 117)

This approach, it may be noted, involves a radical epistemological relativism. If philosophy and theories of society are 'nothing more than' the intellectual expression of practical social movements and interests, it must be inferred that they cannot be evaluated except from the point of view of whether they reflect those movements adequately, and whether the movements themselves are 'progressive' or not. In other words, no theory is true in itself in the sense of giving a correct description of the world, i.e. 'reflecting' it accurately; the question of 'truth' in the ordinary sense is meaningless, and theories are 'good' or 'valid' in so far as they are 'progressive' and conscious of their own origins. It follows that Marxism is 'true' only in the sense that at the present stage of history it articulates the consciousness of the 'progressive' movement and is aware of that fact, and furthermore that a theory which is true at one time may be false at another by reason of a change in its social function. For instance, the doctrines of the 'progressive bourgeoisie' were true as long as the bourgeoisie was progressive, but subsequently became reactionary and therefore false; and the same might one day be true of Marxism. Korsch in fact accepts all these conclusions, though he does not state them clearly enough. He states that it is the essence of dialectical materialism to regard *all* theoretical truths as strictly *diesseitig* (this-worldly), a term which is to be understood as the opposite of 'transcendental'. 'All truths with which we as human, this-worldly beings are or have ever been concerned are likewise human, this-worldly, and transient (*vergänglich*)' (article of 1922, 'Der Standpunkt der materialistischen Geschichtsauffassung', in *Marxismus und Philosophie*, p. 153). No truths are immutable in themselves; what we call truths are the instruments of practical action by social classes. Korsch's theory is thus a kind of collective pragmatism which completely alters the nature of Marxism as a 'science'. On several occasions he joins issue with both Hilferding and Kautsky, who asserted that Marxism was only a theory of the laws of social development and did not, as such, involve any social commitment or value-judgements, but could be accepted even by those who did not share the objectives of the socialist movement. In Korsch's view this separation of theory from practice, of doctrinal truth from the revolutionary movement, was a complete distortion of Marxism. Since Marxism is simply the class-consciousness of the revolutionary proletariat, it can only be recognized in the act of practical commitment to that movement; there can in principle be no such thing as 'purely theoretical' Marxism.

What is more, the doctrine of relativism, historicism, and the rejection of the idea of 'truth' in the ordinary sense applies not only to the social sciences but also to natural science. There is no basic difference in this respect between our knowledge of nature and of society. Historical and natural reality are 'one and the same universe': both are part of the process of human life, and they are linked on the economic plane and specifically in material production. All natural circumstances—biological, physical, geographical—affect our lives not directly but through the intermediary of productive forces, and thus present themselves to us as social and historical phenomena. The whole universe as known to us is a social universe: as far as we are concerned, there is no such thing as nature independent of history and wholly external to us.

Thus not only the social but the natural sciences are historical and practical 'expressions' of a particular social 'totality' and of class-interests. The revolutionary movement, in abolishing society as we know it, abolishes not only its philosophy but all other sciences. Korsch maintains that when the present order is overthrown even mathematics will have to be transformed; though he adds that it would be foolish for a Marxist to claim that a new, Marxist mathematics can be put into operation at the present time. In general, he contends, the function of Marxism is chiefly negative: it is a component of the movement to destroy bourgeois society, not a collection of new sciences to replace the existing ones.

While Korsch extends the 'class viewpoint' to cover natural science, he does not share Lukács's view of the dialectic of nature. Since knowledge of nature, no less than knowledge of society, is part of a social, practical attitude, there is no ground for asserting that nature as we know it is not 'dialectical', for it too is a human creation. On this point Korsch's view appears to be the same as Gramsci's.

The proletarian revolutionary movement ends by 'abolishing' all the economic, social, and ideological forms of bourgeois society. It does not create a new philosophy or sociology, but abolishes both these things along with all other sciences, the state, law, money, the family, ethics, and religion. Korsch, for instance, criticizes Pashukanis for writing about 'socialist ethics': Communism has no ethics of its own, but does away with ethics as a form of consciousness. He does not, however, explain exactly how the 'abolition' of ethics or science is to come about, but confines himself to vague generalities for which he finds some support in equally general observations by Marx. Marx believed that in time to come there would be 'a single science' embracing all aspects of reality, and that people would be so integrated as to express the whole of their social being equally in all forms of activity and thought; as in the utopias of Cieszkowski and Hess, thought and action would in some mysterious way coincide. One can imagine that in such a society there would indeed be no room for ethics as a collection of general norms regulating communal life, since every individual would experience himself immediately as a 'social being': that is to say, he would identify spontaneously with the 'whole', and would need no 'abstract' norms or rules for this purpose. This, it would seem, is what both Korsch and Lukács meant by the 'abolition' of all bourgeois institutions: the elimination of all 'reified' forms of life, i.e. all instruments or agencies which in any way mediate between individuals. The society of the future would consist of individuals with a permanent, indestructible awareness of their identity with the community; they would also themselves be perfectly integrated, having overcome the division of labour and recognizing no difference between thought, feeling, and conduct. As we have shown earlier, this Messianic era of the perfect integration of all human powers is the essence of Marx's Utopia, and Korsch deserves credit for reviving awareness of it.

3. Three phases of Marxism

THE question arises, however: how is it that this essential feature of Marx's interpretation of the world was overlooked for decades and replaced by evolutionist, determinist, and positivist scientism? Korsch seeks to explain this aberration in terms of historical materialism, that is to say he tries to explain the history of Marxism itself on Marxist principles.

His view is that Marxism has gone through three clearly differentiated stages, corresponding to three phases of the development of the workers' movement. He defines this chronology in similar terms in several essays, and most fully in the introduction to the second edition of *Marxismus und Philosophie*. The first phase corresponds to the first few years of the formation of Marx's thought, from 1843 to 1848, when revolutionary theory was taking shape as the consciousness of the proletariat directly based on an actual class struggle: the unity of theory and practice was not a mere slogan but a reality. After June 1848, however, the situation changed as capitalism entered upon a new phase of development and expansion. For the rest of the nineteenth century Marxism could only develop as a theory, and, despite the theoretical achievements of Marx and Engels, scientific socialism did not and could not exist in the sense of class-consciousness actually assimilated and created by the proletariat. Theory became independent of the revolutionary movement, and this altered its content. Especially after Marx's death, his ideas increasingly took on the character of a 'system', supposedly based on purely scientific values. This form of Marxism divorced from revolution became the dogmatic ideology of the orthodoxy of the Second International. Marx himself was not free from guilt in the matter of stripping Marxism of its revolutionary content, especially in the *Critique of the Gotha Programme*; but the main cause lay in objective political conditions, which simply did not permit the theory to function as 'only the expression' of an actual movement. More and more, Marxists treated scientific socialism as the sum of different sciences—economics, sociology, history, philosophy—with no 'direct relation' to the class struggle: that is to say, these sciences theorized about the class struggle but were not themselves part of it. Only around the turn of the century came the third phase, with attempts to revive the 'subjective aspect' of Marxism as a proletarian theory of the class struggle. This change was due to three main developments: trade union reformism, revolutionary syndicalism, and Bolshevism. The tendency of all these was to shift the attention of theorists from the economic laws of capitalism to the 'subjective activity of the working class', and thus to restore Marxism to its proper function as the intellectual superstructure of the actual class movement. Leninist Communism, however, did not radically overcome the dogmatism of the Second International. Theory was still regarded as a 'reflection' of the external world, not an expression of the activity of the proletariat; thus both Lenin and Kautsky took the view that theory came into existence independently of the workers' movement and was then instilled into it from outside. Lenin, moreover, treated theory simply as a practical tool in the technical sense, a statement being 'true' or 'false' according as it served the party's interest. Korsch repeated this last objection several times, though it is not clear at first sight in what way Lenin's utilitarian attitude towards theory differed from his own opinion that Marxism was defined by its function in the class struggle and not by its content alone. It appears, however, that Korsch took the view that a revolutionary theory must be the 'expression' of a movement, and not an instrument forged outside the movement by leaders or theoreticians. Although he does not use these terms, it may be said that in his view the historical meaning of a theory is determined by its origin and not by its actual function.

However, as Korsch observed in 1931, none of the main forms of theoretical activity in which the 'subjective aspect' of Marxism was revived was appropriate to the needs of the class struggle of the proletariat in its current phase. There was a clear divergence between Russian Communism and the position of Western theoreticians of the revolution such as Lukács, Pannekoek, and Korsch himself. Leninism had proved to be an adequate theoretical form for the anti-imperialist struggle in countries on the periphery of the capitalist world, but the working class in the developed capitalist countries needed a new basis of theory which Marxism in its inherited form could not provide. Korsch therefore abandoned his original hope that it was sufficient to return to authentic Marxism to restore the revolutionary consciousness of the modern proletariat. He did not, however, formulate a theory of his own as a substitute, supplement, or revision of Marxism; it cannot be inferred from his writings what such a theory would have been like, or how it would have differed from traditional Marxism.

4. Critique of Kautsky

It is quite understandable that from the point of view of Korsch's interpretation of Marxism the whole of Kautsky's theoretical work must have seemed a perfect and classical specimen of the aberration into which Marxism fell when it lost touch with the revolutionary movement. Korsch's violent attack on Kautsky's *magnum opus* is thus essentially a reaffirmation of his own position. He objected to Kautsky not so much as a reformist (reformism based on the actual struggle of the trade unions was in Korsch's view a higher form of Marxism than 'orthodox' evolutionism) but rather as a naturalist and Darwinist who regarded historical materialism as the application to human history of the general principles of organic evolution. The main points of his attack are as follows.

Firstly, he observes, Kautsky treats Marxism as a purely scientific theory, the truth of which has nothing to do with its class function and can be established by universally recognized criteria of scientific accuracy. This, however, amounts to emptying Marxism of its revolutionary content and reverting to 'mystified' bourgeois objectivism.

Secondly, Kautsky replaces the dialectic by a general epistemology borrowed from Mach and based on the principle that thoughts must correspond to facts and to one another. As for the dialectic of nature, which was of importance to Marx and Engels only in so far as it figured in the dialectic of history, Kautsky presented it as a collection of universal laws of development, of which human history is a particular example. His standpoint is that of nineteenth-century scientific materialism or popular Darwinism, summed up in the view that man is an animal and is subject to all the laws of species evolution; all history is explained by adaptation to the environment, and all human behaviour by biological instincts. Kautsky, seeking to deduce eternal laws of history from biology, is really trying to perpetuate the specific features of bourgeois society, and is incapable of perceiving that society as a historical interrelated whole which can only be, and must be, abolished as the totality of its component parts. It is not surprising that in treating society as an objective process subject to natural laws, and constructing his theory in isolation from its 'subjective' base, Kautsky is obliged, like the neo-Kantians, to reassert the distinction, which Marx resolved, between what is and what ought to be—thus resorting to idealistic normativism as a complement to the materialism of natural science.

Thirdly, Kautsky's theory of the state is absolutely contrary to Marxism. He regards the state as the permanent and highest form of social existence, and democracy as the supreme achievement of history. The state, in his view, accounts for existing relations of production, and not vice versa. As to the origin of the state, Kautsky, in opposition to Engels, invokes the hypotheses of violence and conquest. States, he says, were usually formed by warlike nomads raiding peaceful settlements; today, however, democratic state forms are gradually prevailing everywhere. Thus Kautsky abandons the whole theory of the state as an instrument of oppression and exploitation, in favour of a bourgeois theory of democratic progress. Instead of the revolutionary abolition of the state he thinks only of its further democratization, and he is thus an advocate of bourgeois statehood. The abolition of the state, of money, and of the division of labour—all these ideas, which belong to the essence of Marxism, he treats as an anachronistic Utopia. He believes that the class struggle of the proletariat can henceforth be carried on within the framework of the bourgeois state and its democratic institutions, and he rejects on principle the idea of revolutionary violence.

All in all, Kautsky is an example of a degenerate form of Marxism, perverted in such a way as to impose a brake on the class struggle.

Korsch's analysis is itself typical of Communist criticism: one can see from it why Korsch is outraged by Kautsky, but it does not give reasons why we should agree with the former rather than the latter on any particular point. When, for instance, Kautsky argues that as a matter of history states were generally created by conquest, and by a particular form of conquest, Korsch does not dispute the statement or advance new historical facts, since facts do not interest him: he only remarks indignantly that Kautsky is in disagreement with Engels (which Kautsky was well aware of, and himself emphasized). Similarly, Kautsky tried to give practical reasons why prophecies about the abolition of the state, law, money, and the division of labour were unreal; Korsch does not try to refute these arguments, but only repeats that Kautsky's critique empties Marxism of its revolutionary content. The whole of his attack is devoid of argumentative force or theoretical substance, and is merely a restatement of his own interpretation of Marxism.

Korsch's indifference to empirical argument is indeed admirably suited to his whole doctrine. Since a theory, as he constantly repeats, can only be the intellectual expression of a social movement, whether or not it is conscious of performing this function, it is pointless to judge it by any universal criteria of scientific accuracy: one either sides with the bourgeoisie or with the proletariat, and everything else follows automatically from that commitment. Rational cognitive criteria cease to exist, and the act of political identification takes the place of theoretical reflection. By professing Marxism in this form, Korsch perhaps expressed more clearly than anyone else the latent anti-intellectualism of Marxism and Communism.

5. *Critique of Leninism*

IN the first half of the 1920s Korsch was an avowed Leninist, as may be seen from his article 'Lenin und die Komintern' (1924), from his reviews of Lukács's book on Lenin and of articles by Stalin. In particular he took Lenin's side against Rosa Luxemburg on the question of the party and 'spontaneity'. His support was stated in general terms, however, and it is clear that from the beginning he was opposed to the substitution of party control for the Soviets, and believed in the direct dictatorship of the working class as a whole. It is also clear, though he did not say so at that time, that his whole reconstruction of Marxism as an expression of proletarian consciousness was incompatible with Lenin's 'theory of reflection'.

Soon after breaking with the Communist party Korsch made a clear statement of his disagreement with Leninism. He repeated several times that from the theoretical point of view there was little or no difference between the Leninists and the orthodox of the Second International. Both believed in Marxism as a 'science' and as the true reflection of reality, whereas it was in fact the class self-awareness of the revolutionary movement and, as such, was an aspect of that movement and not merely an objective account of empirical facts. The separation of subject and object, theory and practice, was exactly the same in Lenin's case as in Kautsky's. Lenin had also abandoned the Marxist idea of the abolition of philosophy and had tried to create a new doctrine which preserved Hegel's cognitive absolutism while substituting 'matter' for 'spirit'. This was no more than a terminological device; true Marxism knew nothing of any absolute, or of any transcendental epistemology. Lenin had failed to understand the dialectic; he had situated the dialectical movement in the external world—nature or society—ignoring the fact that knowledge is not a mere copy or reflection of the objective process, but an active element in it. Hence pure theory and pure practice were as much divorced in his thinking as in any positivism, and so were the method and content of knowledge. As a result, the Leninists had created a system in which the doctrine invented by them independently of the class struggle was used as an instrument of ideological dictatorship over science and art.

There was a close link between Lenin's philosophical positivism and Soviet despotism: for, once it was accepted that the theory was not an expression of the actual workers' movement but a 'scientific' doctrine claiming to possess 'objective truth' on grounds independent of the movement, this doctrine became a despotic ideology enabling the party apparatus to exercise a dictatorship over the proletariat.

Korsch finally reached the conclusion that the Soviet state was a totalitarian counter-revolutionary system, a form of monopoly state capitalism which had no more than verbal links with Marxism and was closer to Fascist totalitarianism than to a proletarian dictatorship as understood by Marx.

6. A new definition of Marxism

In a brief essay or declaration of 1935 entitled 'Why I am a Marxist' Korsch reformulated the main features of Marxist doctrine in four points, as follows.

Firstly, all the tenets of Marxism are particular, not general (as official Soviet doctrine would have it). Marxism does not comprise any general theory of the relation between the 'base' and the 'superstructure'; Engels's statements about 'mutual influence' are valueless, as we cannot establish any quantitative criterion of measurement. The only statements that are valid are particular descriptions of particular phenomena at a given stage of history.

Secondly, Marxism is critical and not positive. It is neither a science nor a philosophy, but a theoretical and practical critique of existing society, and is therefore itself a kind of praxis. However, the proletariat must be able to distinguish between true and false scientific claims, and therefore Marxism consists of 'exact, empirically verifiable knowledge', no less precise than that of natural science.

Thirdly, the subject of Marxism is capitalist society in the period of its decline, including everything that throws light on the historical character of existing relations of production. Fourthly, its purpose is not to contemplate the world but to change it, and theory is 'subordinated' to revolutionary aims.

The first of these points, it will be seen, is a drastic limitation of the scope of Marxism: it would be very hard to show that Marx never made general statements about the interdependence of various aspects of social life, but was content to observe particular historical phenomena. As to the second point, it is not clear how the general rule of empiricism can be reconciled with the notion of a theory which (as Korsch apparently continued to maintain) is only the expression of an actual social movement. If Marxism is subject to criteria of empirical verification in the same way as any other science, its validity must depend on whether it satisfies those criteria and not on how adequately it expresses a particular class-interest. In that case, the fact that Marxism serves as a political instrument is logically irrelevant to its value or content; it can be professed by anyone who thinks it meets the requirements of scientific accuracy, whether or not he accepts the values of socialism and the workers' movement. But in this same statement Korsch explicitly rejects that viewpoint, which was characteristic of the theoreticians of the Second International. Thus his revised version of Marxism still appears to contain an incurable contradiction.

IX

Lucien Goldmann

1. Life and writings

GOLDMANN, as we have mentioned, was the most active exponent of Lukács's ideas in France, and he endeavoured to reduce the latter's doctrine to methodical rules and even to a codified system. He also showed, in studies on Jansenism, how these rules might be applied to historical research. His chief interest was the methodology of the humanistic sciences, and his work on the history of philosophy and literature was conceived from the outset as a demonstration of method rather than as a description.

Lucian Goldmann (1913–70), a Romanian Jew, was born in Bucharest, where he initially studied law. Afterwards he studied philosophy, Germanic philology, and economics, at Vienna and Lwów in 1933, and in Paris from 1934 onwards. During the Nazi occupation he moved to Switzerland, where he worked for a time as assistant to the psychologist Jean Piaget, an association that had a marked effect on his later work and habits of thought. He attempted on many occasions to show that Piaget's 'genetic epistemology' agreed in the main, as to its theoretical basis and results, with his own theory of 'genetic structuralism', and that the latter, properly understood, was nothing but the dialectical method evolved by Hegel, Marx, and the young Lukács, although Piaget's results were achieved experimentally and were not due to any philosophical inspiration. Goldmann prepared a doctoral thesis on Kant at Zurich; after the war he returned to Paris and lived there till his death, working in the Centre national de recherche scientifique and later in the École pratique des hautes études. In 1952 he published a short book on humanistic methodology entitled *Sciences humaines et philosophie*, and in 1955 his principal work, *Le Dieu caché. Étude sur la vision tragique dans les 'Pensées' de Pascal et dans le théâtre de Racine* (English trans., *The Hidden God*, 1964). The purpose of this book was to show how the observation of significant 'structures of consciousness', related to the specific situations of social classes, could be of use in understanding cultural phenomena and bringing to light aspects that would otherwise remain unexplored.

In subsequent years Goldmann did not publish any large work, but he produced numerous essays and addresses which were collected in the volumes

Recherches dialectiques (1959), *Pour une sociologie du roman* (1964), and *Marxisme et sciences humaines* (1970). He also wrote *Racine* (1956) and *Situation de la critique racinienne* (published posthumously in 1971). For many years he was a zealous expounder of the dialectic. His flowing white locks and bear-like silhouette were familiar to participants in innumerable congresses and humanistic symposia, at which, in a bass voice and passionate, somewhat aggressive tones, he would expatiate time and again on the principles of genetic structuralism as exemplified particularly in Pascal and Racine.

Unlike Lukács, whose disciple he considered himself to be, Goldmann was not politically active; he was never a Stalinist and at no time belonged to any party, except for a Trotskyist group which he joined for a few months in early youth. He was, however, a convinced socialist, and in his last years took a lively interest in workers' councils as a new form of socialist development in Western society.

2. *Genetic structuralism*, Weltanschauung, *and class-consciousness*

As MENTIONED above, Goldmann regarded the names of Hegel, Marx, Lukács, and Piaget as four milestones in the history of the dialectical method and the interpretation of social phenomena. Thanks to the methods they had worked out, humanistic science was able to overcome the traditional opposition, emphasized, by the neo-Kantians, between explanation and understanding, to free itself from the dichotomy of facts and values, and finally to combine the historical and genetic viewpoint with the structural one. The main ideas of genetic structuralism are as follows.

The first task of humanistic science is to identify its object correctly. It is not obvious, nor a matter of simple common sense, how the subjects of study are to be defined or singled out: whether they should consist, for instance, of an individual person, a work of art or philosophy, a whole cultural era, philosophy in the technical sense, or painting considered as a distinct activity. According to dialectical thought, no empirical facts are significant in themselves: their meaning only comes to light when they are combined into a whole or structure of some kind. For the student of civilization these structures consist of human behaviour patterns involving an interdependence of intellectual activity and its products, of moral and aesthetic values and the actions intended to give effect to them. The observer is not bound by the limitations that restrict people's understanding of their own behaviour; on the contrary, it is his business to understand them better and more consistently than they do themselves, and this applies also to the interpretation of artistic and philosophical works. His task is to discover the 'significant structures' that alone give meaning to particular facts, ideas, and values. 'Facts concerning man always form themselves into significant global structures, which are at one and the same time practical, theoretical and emotive, and these structures can be studied in a scientific manner, that is to say they can be both explained and understood, only within a practical perspective based upon the acceptance of a certain set of values' (*The Hidden God*, p. ix).

The dialectic is based on the principle that cultural activities are not the work of individuals but of social groups, and particularly of classes as historically privileged communities. Cultural achievements are to be considered as the response of these groups to 'global' situations, which they are designed to affect in a way favourable to the group interest. Thus the genetic interpretation of a work of art or philosophy must not be related to the personal qualities of its creator, for this would leave out of account the community, which is the true begetter of civilization. Nor is it correct to study the 'influence' of tradition on the individual thinker, writer, or artist, for it is he who, as it were, selects the influence he will undergo in order to express the aspirations of his class. In short, genetic explanation means explanation in the light of a social situation, not of some immanent cultural 'logic' or individual psychology.

So far, Goldmann does not go beyond the standard rules of historical materialism. He goes on to argue, however, that by formulating these rules more specifically it is possible to resolve all the traditional dilemmas of humanistic methodology. He attaches particular importance to the distinction, scarcely noticed by Marx but developed by Lukács, between actual and potential class-consciousness: the latter is called by Lukács *zugerechnetes Bewusstsein*, and by Goldmann *conscience possible*. Lukács states in *History and Class-Consciousness* that by relating the empirical consciousness of a social class to the 'totality' of the historical process we can discover not only what that class actually thinks, feels, and desires, but also what it would think, feel, and desire if it had a clear, unmystified understanding of its position and interests. The dialectic, in other words, enables us to discover the full extent of the potential consciousness of a particular class in particular historical conditions; and this conception according to Goldmann, provides the key to the study of civilization. Potential consciousness is not a fact, but a theoretical construction. It can and does happen, however, that outstandingly gifted members of a class transcend the average and express that class's aspirations or interests in a more perfect form, thus converting potential into actual consciousness.

Thus an observer sufficiently skilled in dialectic can discover what form of consciousness is perfectly appropriate to a particular group, or what this archetypal consciousness might be or ought to have been. Goldmann claimed specifically to have analysed the Jansenist consciousness in this way.

However, the explanation of cultural phenomena by class origin does not mean 'reducing' culture to economic behaviour. On this point, too, Goldmann agrees with Lukács. Human communities are integral wholes, and only by abstraction do we distinguish different 'factors' and spheres of life. There is not really any separate history of economics, politics, religion, philosophy, or literature: there is a single concrete historical process, manifesting itself in various forms of behaviour. The true subject of humanistic study is not a cause-and-effect relation between economics and culture. The 'primacy' of economics in Marx's theory is not a law of history; it merely reflects the fact that human beings through the ages have had to devote most of their time to satisfying elementary material needs. Under socialism they will no longer have to. Hence cultural activities are neither mere 'effects' or by-products of economic history, nor are they simply means of pursuing other interests and aspirations which, supposedly, are the only real ones. On the contrary, class structures may be studied through their expression in literature or philosophy.

If we accept that all human behaviour has a meaning, but that it is revealed not in the motives of individuals but only in the more or less conscious endeavours of large social groups, then, according to Goldmann, we no longer need distinguish between explanation and understanding as two separate, independent modes of investigation. 'Understanding' is not, as Dilthey would have it, a matter of imitative experience (*Nacherlebnis*) or empathy. 'Understanding presents itself to us as a purely intellectual approach based on a description, as exact as possible, of the significant structure', while 'explanation is simply the integration of that structure, as a constitutive and functional element, in a structure that directly comprises it' (*Marxisme et sciences humaines*, pp. 65–6). There is a hierarchy of structures; when we describe an inferior structure we 'understand' it, i.e. we grasp its meaning; when we include it in a larger structure we understand that structure, and at the same time we explain the lesser by the greater. There is thus no difference between the two methods, but only in the scope of the object: the act of explaining a particular structure, and understanding one superior to it in the hierarchy, is one and the same.

A 'structure' is not necessarily a harmonious whole. On the contrary, it usually presents internal contradictions owing to the fact that the values pursued by a given class are mutually incompatible, or unattainable in the historical circumstances of the time, or that attempts to realize them bring about opposite results to those intended. A structure is thus not only an orderly system, but a complex of tensions as well.

While non-genetic structuralism (especially that of Lévi-Strauss) confines itself to constructing internally connected wholes, and while genetic structuralism of the Freudian type considers only the psychological genesis of the meanings under observation, genetic structuralism as developed by Marx, Lukács, and Piaget (and of course Goldmann himself) regards individuality only as a manifestation of collective tensions, struggles, and aspirations.

In addition to surmounting the distinction between explanation and comprehension, genetic structuralism makes it possible to resolve the dichotomy of facts and values. The 'wholes' or structures that are the object of our study are an indissoluble complex of practical and mental activities, moral and aesthetic attitudes. Intellectual activity presupposes such evaluative acts, which cannot in fact be separated from purely cognitive ones. Reality always presents itself as a field for practical activity; perception at every level selects its object in accordance with human values and desires, and is always, as it were, incipient action. There is simply no such thing as pure, disinterested contemplation. Acts of cognition must and can only be understood as a particular 'aspect' of man as a practical being. Thus humanist studies, conscious of this 'integrality' of all human behaviour, cannot without distortion distinguish between purely intellectual activity and evaluative attitudes.

Piaget helped to illustrate this practical character of mental activity by showing that all cognitive structures—for instance, the concepts and rules of logic, arithmetic, and geometry—arise, on both the ontogenetic and the phylogenetic level, from the convergence of various circumstances, including human communications, language, and practical habits formed in early childhood. Piaget showed experimentally, as it were, that our intellectual 'structuralization' of the world cannot be explained by transcendental norms of rationality, but derives from social and practical circumstances. Cognitive norms are instruments of communal life and practice; they therefore comprise evaluative and practical elements, and could not be framed without them.

For the genetic structuralist the object of study *par excellence* is the world-view (*vision du monde, Weltanschauung*) or pattern of aspirations, feelings, and ideas that unites the members of a group (generally a social class) and opposes them to other groups. This unitary principle is so important that, Goldmann argues, it is wrong for the humanist to study art or literature, philosophical or theological ideas as separate subjects. The world-view must be studied through all forms of expression and not only, for instance, in its discursive philosophical aspect. Hence, too, the history of philosophy, art, or literature is not a proper object of study in itself. The historian of Jansenism must investigate that phenomenon or world-view as a whole, so as to reveal the common ideological inspiration behind the writings of Pascal and Racine and the painting of Philippe de Champaigne. Thus Goldmann seeks to reorganize humanistic studies so as to subordinate them in their entirety to the study of large communities and the cultural monuments created by them.

All these rules are not so unambiguous that a mere statement of them suffices to indicate how they should be applied. It may be useful, therefore, to show how this is done in *Le Dieu caché*, although the subject of that work is somewhat too particular as far as our own argument is concerned.

3. The tragic world-view

ALTHOUGH Goldmann considered himself a Marxist, he never adopted the simplistic division of the history of philosophy into two trends labelled 'materialism' and 'idealism'. He saw the units of historical meaning quite differently, and attached particular importance to the 'tragic world-view', as he perceived it in Jansenism and to some extent in the works of Kant.

The tragic world-view in the seventeenth century was, he believed, an attempt to rediscover a global picture of the world that had been shattered by the inroads of rationalism and empiricism. These doctrines, which reflected the ambitions of the *tiers état*, had destroyed the idea of human fellowship and the ordered conception of the universe, replacing them by the notion of the rational individual and the concept of unlimited space. The new world-view called in question the traditional hierarchy and sought to transform society into a collection of free, equal, autonomous, and isolated units. In philosophy and literature its champions were Descartes and Corneille. Cartesianism eliminated all sources of morality outside the individual; there was no room for God in its world, or for the universe considered as a beneficent order. The tragic world-view had to take account of these effects of rationalism, which already dominated the intellectual life of Europe. It attempted to counter the new spirit, as it were, from within: it accepted reason, but disputed its monopoly; and it insisted that there was a God, while admitting that he was not directly present in nature. Science having concealed God from human eyes, the tragic world-view produced the idea of a *deus absconditus*. Pascal's God is at the same time always present and always absent. He is a spectator of human life, but his presence cannot be confirmed by reason. He is no longer man's helper nor even (as for Descartes) a guarantor of the validity of knowledge; he is a judge and nothing more.

Rationalism had shaken the foundations of order in the world. The tragic view expressed the consciousness of those who could not efface the results of rationalism but were ill at ease in an ambiguous world, deserted by Providence and deprived of clear moral laws. The tragic view admits no gradation between perfection and nothingness. The eye of the hidden God deprives the world of all its value, but precisely since he is hidden, the empirical world is the only one we can perceive directly, and it is therefore everything to us as well as nothing. Those who hold this view are the victims of a constant inner conflict: they can neither flee from the world nor live in it so as to realize transcendent values. The only consistent attitude they can adopt is to live in the world while constantly refusing allegiance to it. This was the attitude of Pascal when he wrote the *Pensées*, and of Racine at the time of *Phèdre*.

Jansenism was not a single unified movement, though its adherents shared certain characteristics and values: the doctrine of efficacious grace, anti-Molinism, rejection of the *dieu des philosophes*, aversion to mysticism, defence of Jansen, and the anti-historical rejection of the world. Goldmann distinguished four main variants of the Jansenist attitude. The first (Martin de Barcos, Pavillon, the Racine of *Andromaque* and *Britannicus*) stood for complete rejection of the world, from which it took refuge in contemplation. The second sought to reform the world by remaining in it and discriminating between good and evil (Arnauld, Nicole, Pascal in the *Provincial Letters*). The third attempted to compromise with the world (Choiseul, Arnauld d'Audilly). The fourth, and the most consistent, accepted the tragic situation: it remained in the world while denying the world, and expressed man's uncertainty and helplessness in the extreme form of the *pari*, the wager that applied not only to salvation but to the very existence of God (Pascal's *Pensées*, Racine's *Phèdre*).

In the tragic predicament in which God deprives the world of all value and yet, by his absence, obliges man to regard it as his only good, the human outlook is reduced to a permanent paradox, constantly denying and affirming the same proposition: for man's life is lived among antagonistic values, none of which can eliminate the others. It is part of the tragic consciousness to feel that one lives for the realization of values that cannot be realized completely—and therefore not at all, for those who believe in 'all or nothing'. Man can turn only to God, but God does not answer him. Thus the true utterance of the tragic consciousness is a monologue, a voice crying in the wilderness. The *Pensées* are a monologue of this kind, not an apologetic treatise.

Pascal and Racine represent Jansenism in a consummate form, expressing fully what others say by halves, and thus they exemplify the maximum 'potential consciousness' of the community to which they belong. It is a class-consciousness, that of the *noblesse de robe* during the transition to absolute monarchy, when the former was being more and more displaced from its social fastnesses by the new royal bureaucracy. While depriving it of its *raison d'être*, however, the monarchy was still its economic mainstay, and hence the consciousness of the *noblesse de robe* took on a tragic and paradoxical form; the new political trends were strange and hostile to it, but it could not aspire to alter them radically. This confusion and perplexity found its literary and philosophical expression in Jansenism—the ideology of a class driven into less and less favourable positions, and bound up with a system that maintained it on the one hand and destroyed it on the other.

In the tragic consciousness there is no place for mysticism. On the contrary, God appears as an infinitely remote being. He cannot be reached in mystic unity but only in prayer, which stresses the distance that mysticism seeks to annihilate.

Pascal reached the zenith of tragic consciousness in 1657, immediately after the date of the *Provincial Letters*. He denied the value of all worldly knowledge, yet went on with scientific research; he refused to compromise with authority, yet declared his obedience to the Church. He did not believe that truth and righteousness could triumph in this world, but he proclaimed that the whole of life should be devoted to fighting for them. This attitude also conditioned his literary style: in the world of tragedy no statement is true and no action is right unless accompanied by another which contradicts it. To this extent Pascal is also an exponent of dialectical thought, although his dialectic is static and tragic: there is no synthesis, no escape from the clash of opposites. In Pascal's world man lives between two extremes, but he does not feel this as a natural position (as in Thomist philosophy), because both extremes attract him equally and seem equally right, so that he lives in a state of constant tension. He cannot accept finitude, and he sees infinity as unattainable; he affirms himself only through his own weakness and incapacity for synthesis. He yearns for 'wholeness', but perceives that his yearning is in vain. In the last resort Pascal cannot recognize any basic principles of cognition, either the *cogito* or the rules of empiricism, but falls back on the *raisons du cœur*, on a practical faculty as the only trustworthy guide. In this respect too he anticipates dialectical thought; his dialectic reaches its acme in the *pari*, where a question fundamental to human destiny, the existence of God, is decided not by theoretical reasoning but by a gambler's throw. Pascal knows that reason left to itself is helpless, and he thus knows, as it were, that cognitive activity is only an 'aspect' of the complete man. Since not only God's will but his very existence are hidden from us we are forced to take the risk of wagering on this cardinal question, and the situation that makes this necessary does not depend on our own will. The *pari* is an act of hope, a practical act to decide a theoretical question. It is similar in this to Kant's practical reason, which decides metaphysical questions in reliance on the possibility of a supreme good, and also to Marx's invocation of the classless society: it is by no means scientifically proved that there is bound to be such a society, but by believing in it we commit ourselves actively to its cause.

Neither the past nor the future play a part in Pascal's dialectic: only the present, which is constantly passing away, and the nostalgic sense of eternity. Society is full of evil, and no rules of justice can be discerned in it, but we are condemned to live in the world of men although we have no hope that it will change radically for the better. Pascal's social conservatism and his paradoxical contempt for all the values of law, custom, and social hierarchy are both consequences of the tragic world-view.

In this analysis of Goldmann's we have an example of the construction of historical categories which explain structures of consciousness in relation to the class situation. Such categories, if properly devised, make it possible to give a uniform sense to phenomena without isolating them from their historical sources, and thus they satisfy the demands of both structuralist thought and genetic interpretation. By constructing such conceptual aids we provide ourselves with the means of interpreting a wide range of phenomena. Having seen Jansenism to be the ideology of the *noblesse de robe*, we can also see libertinism as the ideology of the *noblesse de cour*, expressed for example in Molière's plays. *Le Misanthrope* is an attack on Jansenism; *Dom Juan*, while accepting libertinism in principle, is also a partial critique of it and a reassertion of *la mesure*.

4. Goldmann and Lukács. Comment on genetic structuralism

GOLDMANN, as already mentioned, regarded himself as a disciple and continuer of Lukács's work, especially the early Lukács of *Die seele und die Formen* and *History and Class-Consciousness*. (In Goldmann's view the basic elements of the dialectic as Lukács subsequently developed them can already be found in his pre-Marxist work.) In fact, however, Goldmann adopted only part of Lukács's theory, omitting other features which Lukács himself regarded as fundamental. Goldmann attempted to put into effect the concept of historical 'totality'; he believed that scientific observation must lead to the discovery of class-consciousness as it ought to be, were it fully consistent; that the dialectical method made it possible to resolve the dichotomy of facts and values, understanding and explanation; that cognitive acts were always involved in practical attitudes, so that it was impossible to isolate an element of pure theoretical contemplation in human behaviour; and, accordingly, that there were no absolute criteria of knowledge, no basic judgements. In all these ideas he was faithful to Lukács. But he was not interested in what Lukács regarded as an essential point, namely the mythology of the proletariat as the repository of the liberated absolute consciousness, nor did he hold that that perfect consciousness was embodied in the Communist party. All these questions were quite alien to him, and consequently in all specific matters he was much less dogmatic than Lukács. His general view, which he repeated many times, was that the Marxist critique of 'reification' in capitalist society was fully applicable at the present day. The transformation of all human products and individuals into goods comparable in quantitative terms; the disappearance of qualitative links between people; the gap between private and public life; the loss of personal responsibility and the reduction of human beings to executors of tasks imposed by a rationalized system; the resulting deformation of personality, the impoverishment of human contacts, the loss of solidarity, the absence of generally recognized criteria of artistic work, 'experimentation' as a universal creative principle; the loss of authentic culture owing to the segregation of the different spheres of life, in particular the domination of productive processes treated as an element independent of all others—these were all features of the consumption-oriented society. On the other hand, Goldmann believed that historical development had invalidated another part of Marx's analysis, namely the pauperization of the proletariat and the growth of revolutionary consciousness. Capitalism had managed to provide the workers with a relatively secure and satisfactory life, and there was therefore no reason to expect that their revolutionary mood and aspirations would reach an explosive pitch as forecast by the early Marxists. On this point Goldmann disagreed with Lukács, and it is an essential one: Lukács would not have been Lukács without his faith in the revolutionary consciousness of the proletariat.

For similar reasons Goldmann did not fully accept Lukács's aesthetic theory. He did not believe in 'socialist realism' as the 'highest phase' of culture. Unlike Lukács he was keenly alive to new trends in literature and art, and was a sympathetic critic of such authors as Gombrowicz, Robbe-Grillet, Jean Genet, and Nathalie Sarraute, whose work is diametrically opposed to anything that could be called 'socialist realism'. In these writers too he looked for a 'structure' which corresponded to particular social phenomena, whether or not they themselves intended or even perceived the correspondence: for instance, Robbe-Grillet's *Les Gommes* revealed the self-regulating mechanism of capitalist society, while the same author's *La Jalousie* was about reification.

In this sense Goldmann can be called a moderate Lukácsist, which is as much as to say that he was not a Lukácsist at all: he only adopted certain categories of Lukács's which he thought useful in studying the history of the dialectic and of civilization generally.

Goldmann's political views also had little in common with Communist dogmatism. As we have seen, he did not believe in a proletarian revolution taking place as the classical doctrine had predicted. He believed, however, that the most important need was for a new social order which would free the world from 'reified' structures and restore a sense of authenticity and human solidarity. He was particularly interested in the movement for workers' self-government (*autogestion ouvrière*), which Serge Mallet sought to place on a theoretical basis, and in Yugoslav experiments in this sphere. He thought this movement might lead in time, without violent revolutionary shocks, to a reunification of economic and cultural life; that it might give the workers a new sense of responsibility and of belonging to the community, and re-forge the links which capitalism had broken by quantifying all human values. But he did not define socialism in institutional terms, nor in terms of increased consumption. To

him, the main features of the socialist ideal were spiritual values, the direct-
ness of social ties, and the responsibility of the individual. He did not believe
in any laws of history guaranteeing that the ideal would be realized; it was a
duty to wager on it, but there was no certainty of a pay-off.

As Goldmann was much less burdened with the dogmatic heritage of Marxism than was Lukács, his historical studies are a good deal less schematic. *Le
Dieu caché* is certainly an interesting investigation; many points in it may be
criticized by historians of the seventeenth century, but it nevertheless draws
attention to aspects of Jansenism that may well repay further study. This does
not mean, however, that we can accept Goldmann's methodological rules without reservation, or that their meaning is absolutely clear.

In particular, the doctrine of 'potential consciousness' seems extremely
doubtful. To accept it as a tool of historical research implies that we can deduce
from the situation of a particular class what its consciousness would have been
if it had corresponded perfectly to that situation. This, however, is a fantasy.
Even if we suppose with Goldmann—contrary to the evidence of history, to
common sense, and even to Marx—that every world-view stands in a one-to-one
correspondence with the class situation in which it arises, the deduction would
still be impossible, for we should also have to know the general laws according
to which particular class situations always produce particular forms of ideology,
art, philosophy, or religion. We do not know any such laws and we never shall,
for the possibility of doing so is excluded by the nature of the subject under
examination, which is the whole process of history, unique and unrepeatable.
There can be no law which says that 'Whenever conditions are exactly as they
were in France in the middle of the seventeenth century they will produce the
doctrines of Gassendi, Descartes, Pascal, etc.' To formulate the idea of seeking
such 'laws' suffices to demonstrate its absurdity.

Goldmann believed, however, that it was possible in this way to argue from
the historical situation of a class to its intellectual and artistic production, and
that he had done so in one instance at least. To believe that such a feat is possible does not necessarily mean that the class situation 'produces' corresponding cultural phenomena; a more modest postulate will suffice, namely that the
two spheres are not causally related but that there is a one-to-one correspondence between them. If we believe this, however, we must also believe that the
deduction can be made in the opposite direction, for example that from Pascal's *Pensées* we could reconstruct the economic and political history of France
in his day. But in any case it is easy to see that the one-to-one correspondence
is pure fantasy. If it were fully ascertainable it would mean that we could reconstruct the works of art and philosophy *ex nihilo*, from a mere knowledge of the
class situation in the society which produced them: thus from what we knew of
the position of the *noblesse de robe* in Mazarin's time we should be able to write

the *Pensées* even if we had never read or heard of them. No less than this is required for a confirmation of the theory of 'potential consciousness'. (Goldmann did indeed maintain that he had deduced the existence of Martin de Barcos from a general analysis of Jansenism: he had inferred that there must have been such a person, and had discovered afterwards that he was right.) Goldmann endeavoured to interpret all Pascal's ideas without exception, and even his forms of expression, as the reflection of a specific class-consciousness: this, he maintained, accounted for the fact that the *Pensées* were unfinished (though it is also true that Pascal died while writing them), that they are a collection of fragments and not a coherent treatise, that Pascal was a Catholic and not a Protestant (though in any case he was born and brought up a Catholic), and so on. Explanations of this kind are ingenious, but they do not add up to more than an intellectual *tour de force*.

Goldmann says, it is true, that in investigating the phenomena of consciousness we must distinguish 'essential' from accidental features. This seems to imply that only the former can be explained by the class situation or correlated with it; but it is not clear how we are supposed to make the distinction. We must either, it would seen, decide *a priori* what the world-view of a particular class must be, or else beg the question by classifying as 'essential' the features that can in fact be explained by the class situation.

Since, however, Goldmann believes that almost everything to do with a given *Weltanschauung* can be correlated with the class situation of its 'collective subject', his analyses ignore all the other social and psychological circumstances that in fact play a part in the creation of a philosophy. In holding that Jansenism is directly related to the class whose aspirations it somehow 'expresses', he leaves out of account such antecedent facts as the existence of the Church and the relatively autonomous way in which conflicts within it were fought out, either in matters of dogma or, for example, the organizational differences between the secular and regular clergy. In the same way he completely ignores the immanent logic of the development of philosophy and theology, as well as individual, biographical, and psychological factors.

In the last resort Goldmann falls a victim to a highly simplified and selective interpretation of Marxism. His object is to discover 'significant structures', which may be described as units of historical 'meaning'; this latter term, as many of his remarks indicate, is to be taken as signifying an unconscious or semi-conscious purposiveness, a kind of lower-grade purposive action such as that we attribute to animals. But he lays down quite arbitrarily that a 'unit of meaning' can only consist of a social class with a particular set of values and aspirations which are due to its position, and that these values and aspirations are the only possible frame of reference for studying the history of civilization. To justify this method it must be assumed that all human behaviour of importance, especially intellectual and artistic creation, is 'in the last resort' an expression of class-interests, anything else being mere chance or secondary rationalization. This may be in accordance with some of Marx's more simplistic formulas, but it is not borne out by the facts. We know that in practice all kinds of circumstances contribute to the formation of a world-view, and that all phenomena are due to an inexhaustible multiplicity of causes. To interpret Pascal in terms of individual psychology is certainly possible, and no less certainly inadequate; the same could be said of an interpretation relating his ideas purely to theological controversies, and it is equally inadequate to interpret him in terms of social class. To say this is not to hold out the hope that a complete, all-round synthesis of the truth could ever be formulated; doubtless it could not. But, while the attempt to interpret Pascal in class terms may be interesting and instructive, it does not require to be supported by a methodology which asserts dogmatically and gratuitously that there is no other way to interpret Pascal (or any other cultural figure), and that this method explains everything that is worth explaining. 'Genetic structuralism' of this kind cannot account for the continuity and permanence of any cultural achievements: if the meaning of Pascal's work is exhausted by the fact that it reflects the position of the *noblesse de robe* in seventeenth-century France, how is it that anyone at the present day, including Lucien Goldmann, can be interested in Pascal or find his work relevant to themselves? This continuity and permanence require us to suppose that, irrespective of the changing circumstances and class struggles that contribute to the creation of cultural values, there is a universal history of culture that is beyond class. The same spiritual needs, the same uncertainties and anxieties recur time and again in history, though their expression is affected by historical and psychological factors of all kinds.

Again, it does not seem that we are any closer to resolving the dichotomy of facts and values, despite Goldmann's assurances that, following Marx and Lukács, he has provided a key to this awkward problem. His writings contain no logical analysis of the difficulty, and no attempt to answer the questions raised by traditional positivism or by Max Weber. A clear distinction must, however, be made between values as studied by the sociologist and psychologist, and values as a concealed assumption of investigative method. If we accept Goldmann's view that in studying philosophies we always find practical motives embedded in intellectual processes, this does not imply anything as to the prospect of 'surmounting' the dichotomy of value-judgements and descriptive judgements. What is more, to suppose that all our descriptions are concealed value-judgements and that they regularly reflect class-aspirations is a dangerous habit of mind and may lead to intellectual nihilism, since it means that we cannot judge human thought by any purely intellectual criteria of empiricism or logic: all cultural achievements will seem equally permeated by class-interest, from the crudest political propaganda to the sublimest products of the intellect. Nor will there be any universal rules enabling us to discuss philosophical or scientific questions independently of class attitudes. Even if we agree with Marx that man is a practical being and that his mind is at the service of practical needs, we must still make some further distinctions. For, granted that we select phenomena on practical grounds at the level of elementary perception, and that the increase of knowledge is also largely governed by practical circumstances, it does not follow that there are no universal logical and empirical criteria (universal to the human species, not necessarily in a transcendental sense) for the evaluation of human knowledge and intellectual activity; and such criteria can be well enough distinguished from those by which we make moral or aesthetic judgements. To maintain that in all fields of culture, including scientific work, we have to do only with 'global' complexes of values, emotions, and practical behaviour, and that these complexes are only intelligible when correlated with social class, is to preclude the application of logic and the verifiability of scientific results, and to reduce everything to a single undifferentiated 'class-interest'.

Goldmann certainly did much to revive Marxism in France, and gave an example of ingenuity in applying Marxist rules of interpretation to Jansenism. His historical analyses were less schematic than his general methodological principles; but these principles do not remove the doubt as to the value of the Marxist understanding of the history of civilization.

X

The Frankfurt School
and 'Critical Theory'

The term 'Frankfurt school' has been used since the 1950s to denote an important German para-Marxist movement, the history of which goes back to the early twenties and is associated with that of the Institut für Sozialforschung. One may speak here of a 'school' in a rather stricter sense than in the case of other trends within Marxism, though as usual there are doubts as to whether and how far particular individuals belong to it. There is, at all events, a clearly continuous mode of thought spanning two intellectual generations; the pioneers are no longer alive, but they have left successors in the field.

The abundant academic and publicistic output of the Frankfurt school covers multifarious domains of humanistic science: philosophy, empirical sociology, musicology, social psychology, the history of the Far East, the Soviet economy, psychoanalysis, the theory of literature and of law. In the present short account there can of course be no question of commenting on this output as a whole. The school is characterized, in the first place, by the fact that it treats Marxism not as a norm to which fidelity must be maintained, but as a starting-point and an aid to the analysis and criticism of existing culture; hence it has made free use of many non-Marxist sources of inspiration such as Hegel, Kant, Nietzsche, and Freud. Secondly, the school's programme was expressly non-party: it did not identify with any political movement, in particular Communism or social democracy, towards both of which it has often expressed a critical attitude. Thirdly, the school was clearly influenced by the interpretation of Marxism evolved by Lukács and Korsch in the 1920s, especially the concept of 'reification' as an epitome of the problems of the modern world. However, it can in no way be regarded as a school of Lukács's disciples; for its members—and this is the fourth important point—have always emphasized the independence and autonomy of theory and have opposed its absorption by all-embracing 'praxis', even though they were also engaged in criticizing society with a view to transforming it. Fifthly—and here again the Frankfurt school differs basically from Lukács—while accepting Marx's position as to the exploitation and 'alienation' of the proletariat, it did not identify with the latter in the sense of regarding its existing class-consciousness, let alone the dictates of the Communist party, as an *a priori* norm. It emphasized the universality of 'reification' as a process affecting all strata of society, and came to be more and more doubtful of the proletariat's revolutionary and liberating role, so that in the end it jettisoned this part of Marx's doctrine altogether. Sixthly, although profoundly 'revisionist' *vis-à-vis* orthodox versions of Marxism, the school regarded itself as a revolutionary intellectual movement; it rejected the reformist position and maintained the need for a complete transcendence of society, while admitting that it had no positive Utopia to offer, and even that in present conditions a Utopia could not be created.

The period of the school's development was also that of the rise, victory, and fall of Nazism, and much of its output was concerned with relevant social and cultural problems such as racial prejudice, the need for authority, and the economic and ideological source of totalitarianism. Almost all the chief members of the school were middle-class German Jews; only a few had any real cultural links with the Jewish community, but their origin no doubt had some influence on the range of topics in which the school was interested.

In philosophy the Frankfurt school took issue with logical empiricism and positivist trends in the theory of knowledge and the methodology of science; also with pragmatism, utilitarianism, and, later, German existentialism. Its members attacked the 'mass society' and the degradation of culture, especially art, through the increasing influence of the mass media. They were pioneers in the analysis and aggressive criticism of mass culture and in this respect were successors of Nietzsche, defenders of élite values. They combined these attacks with criticism of a society in which the means whereby a professional bureaucracy could manipulate the masses were becoming more and more effective: this applied both to Fascist and Communist totalitarianism and to the Western democracies.

1. Historical and biographical notes

THE Institut für Sozialforschung (Institute for Social Research) was founded by a group of young intellectuals at Frankfurt at the beginning of 1923. The funds were provided by the family of one of their number, Felix Weil, but the Institute was officially a department of Frankfurt University. The principal founders and early members were as follows.

Friedrich Pollock (1894–1970), an economist, later known for the first serious analysis of planned economy in Soviet Russia (*Die planwirtschaftlichen Versuche in der Sowjetunion 1917–1927*, 1929).

Carl Grünberg (1861–1940), the Institute's first director, was of a different intellectual background from most of its members. An orthodox Marxist of the older generation, he specialized in the history of the workers' movement and from 1910 edited the *Archiv für die Geschichte des Sozialismus und der Arbeiterbewegung*.

A central figure in the Institute, and its director from 1930, was Max Horkheimer (1895–1973), a psychologist and philosopher by training, a pupil of Hans Cornelius and author of works on Kant.

Another of the earliest members was Karl Wittfogel (b. 1896), then a member of the Communist party and afterwards known as the author of works on Chinese history (*Wirtschaft und Gesellschaft Chinas*, 1931; *Oriental Despotism*, 1957). He worked with the Institute for a few years only; his importance in the history of Marxism is that he explored the question, on which Marx had barely touched, of the 'Asiatic mode of production'. He cannot, however, be regarded as a typical representative of the Frankfurt school.

Another scholar who, besides Horkheimer, made a decisive contribution to the formation of an individual school of philosophy at Frankfurt was Theodor Wiesengrund-Adorno (1903–1970), who, however, did not join the Institute until the late twenties. A philosopher, musicologist, and composer, he obtained his doctorate with a study of Husserl and then wrote a thesis on Kierkegaard's aesthetics; after 1925 he studied composition and musicology at Vienna. Horkheimer and Adorno between them may be regarded as the embodiment of the Frankfurt school.

Leo Lowenthal (b. 1900), who also joined the Institute rather late, made a significant contribution to its ideology with works on the history and theory of literature.

In the 1930s, after the Institute left Germany, it was joined by Walter Benjamin (1892–1940), one of the most eminent German literary critics between the wars. His work, however, is not important as a contribution to the development of Marxism: of all the well-known writers of the Frankfurt school, he was least connected with the Marxist movement.

Other Communists besides Wittfogel were Karl Korsch, of whom we have written separately, and Franz Borkenau, who is known chiefly for works attacking Communism after his break with the party. His book on the rise of capitalism (*Der Übergang vom feudalen zum bürgerlichen Weltbild*, 1934) may, however, be regarded as a product of the Frankfurt school, as it analyses the connection between the spread of the market economy and rationalist philosophy, a theme typical of those studied by the Institute.

Henryk Grossman (1881–1950), a Polish Jew, worked with the Institute from the late 1920s but was not a typical member: he belonged to traditional Marxist orthodoxy, and devoted himself to economic analyses for the purpose of confirming Marx's predictions of the falling profit rate and the collapse of capitalism.

In the early thirties the Institute was joined by Herbert Marcuse, to whom we devote a separate chapter on account of his later activity, and Erich Fromm, afterwards one of the best-known heretics among erstwhile Freudians.

From 1932 the Institute published the *Zeitschrift für Sozialforschung (Journal for Social Research)*, which was its principal organ and in which many of its basic theoretical documents first appeared. After the move to the United States the *Journal* was continued for two years (1939–41) under the title *Studies in Philosophy and Social Sciences*.

When the Nazis came to power at the beginning of 1933 the Institute was, of course, unable to continue functioning in Germany. A branch had previously been founded in Geneva, to which some of the German members now moved. Another branch was set up in Paris, where the *Journal* continued to appear. Adorno spent the first few years of emigration at Oxford, and in 1938 moved to the United States, where almost all the Institute's members arrived sooner or later (Fromm being the first). Wittfogel was in a concentration camp for some months, but was finally released. The *émigrés* set up the International Institute for Social Research at Columbia University, which continued the Frankfurt projects and started new ones on similar lines. Walter Benjamin, who lived in Paris from 1935, fled from the Nazis in September 1940 and committed suicide on the Franco-Spanish border. Horkheimer and Adorno spent the war years in New York and Los Angeles; they returned to Frankfurt in 1950 and 1949 respectively, and took up professorships at the University there. Fromm, Marcuse, Lowenthal, and Wittfogel remained in America.

. . .

THE fundamental principles of the Frankfurt school, applying both to epistemology and to the critique of civilization, were formulated by Horkheimer in a series of articles in the *Journal*, most of which were republished in 1968 under the title of *Kritische Theorie* (two volumes, edited by A. Schmidt). The most general and programmatic of these articles, written in 1937, was entitled 'Traditionelle und kritische Theorie'. Others discussed various philosophical questions, for example the relation of critical theory to rationalism, materialism, scepticism, and religion; we also find critiques of Bergson, Dilthey, and Nietzsche, and essays on the role of philosophy, the concept of truth, and the specific nature of the social sciences. Horkheimer's use of the term 'critical theory' was apparently meant to emphasize three aspects of his philosophical approach. Firstly, independence *vis-à-vis* existing doctrines, including Marxism; secondly, the conviction that civilization was irremediably diseased and needed a radical transformation, not merely partial reform; and thirdly, the belief that the analysis of existing society was itself an element of that society, a form of its self-awareness. Horkheimer's thought was permeated by the Marxist principle that philosophical, religious, and sociological ideas can only be understood in relation to the interests of different social groups (but not that everything 'in the last resort' comes down to class-interest), so that theory is a function of social life; on the other hand, he defended the autonomy of theory, and there is an unresolved tension between these two viewpoints. Horkheimer defends Hegelian Reason against the empiricists, positivists, and pragmatists; he is convinced that we can ascertain truths which cannot be expressed either as empirical hypotheses or as analytical judgements; but, it would seem, he does not accept any theory of a transcendental subject. He opposes scientism, i.e. the view that the methods actually used in natural science constitute all the intellectual equipment we need in order to achieve cognitive results of any value. To this view he has at least two objections: firstly, that in social matters, unlike natural science, observation is itself an element in what is observed, and secondly, that in all fields of knowledge the operation of Reason is required in addition to empirical and logical rules; yet the principles governing Reason are not sufficiently elucidated and it is not clear whence we are to derive them.

These thoughts of Horkheimer's essentially foreshadow such later works of the Frankfurt school as Adorno's *Negative Dialectics:* he is clearly at pains to avoid all 'reductionist' formulas in dealing with either traditionally Hegelian or traditionally Marxist questions. The subjectivity of the individual cannot be fully described in social categories and resolved into its social causes, nor can society be described in psychological terms; the subject is not absolutely prior, nor is it a mere derivative of the object; neither the 'base' nor the 'superstructure' is manifestly primary; 'phenomenon' and 'essence' are not presented independently of each other; praxis cannot absorb theory, nor vice versa; in all these cases we have to do with mutual interaction. These thoughts are not so precise, however, as to provide a basis for methodological rules that would preserve us at once from all the temptations of 'reductionism', dogmatism, idealism, and vulgar materialism. In all cases of interaction we have to do with the partial autonomy of factors affecting one another, but the boundaries of this autonomy are not clearly drawn. By emphasizing the need for constant 'mediation' Horkheimer apparently seeks to guard his position against all 'reductionist' traditions.

It is also clear, both from Horkheimer and from other writings of the Frankfurt school, that the critical theory associated empiricist and positivist doctrines with the cult of technology and technocratic tendencies in social life. One of the school's main themes is that the world is threatened by the progress of technology served by a science which is essentially indifferent to the world of values. If scientistic rules and restrictions are to govern all cognitive activity in such a way that it cannot generate value-judgements, then the progress of science and technology is bound to lead to a totalitarian society, the increasingly successful manipulation of human beings, the destruction of culture and of personality. Hence the importance of Hegelian Reason (*Vernunft*), which, as opposed to understanding (*Verstand*), can formulate 'global' judgements, prescribing the ends to be followed and not only the means of achieving ends that are themselves determined irrationally. A scientistic culture cannot and will not do this, as it presupposes that ends cannot be determined scientifically and must therefore be a matter of caprice. It does not appear, however, that Horkheimer or any other member of the Frankfurt school can explain how the same cognitive faculty can determine both ends and means, or how we proceed from observing phenomena to understanding the hidden 'essence' which teaches us not only what man empirically is but also what he would be if he fully realized his own nature.

In combating the phenomenalistic standpoint of the positivists, the Frankfurt school followed in the footsteps of the young Marx and were animated by the same interest. Their object was to ascertain what man really was and what were the requirements of true humanity—its essential aims, which could not be empirically observed nor yet arbitrarily determined, but must be discovered. The members of the school seem to have held that something is 'objectively' due to man by reason of his very humanity, and in particular that he is entitled to happiness and freedom. However, they tended to reject the young Marx's view that humanity is realized in the process of work, or that work in itself, in the present or in the future, could reveal the 'essence of humanity' and bring it to full perfection. It is nowhere clear in these arguments how faith in the paradigm of humanity is to be reconciled with the belief that man is determined by his self-creation in history. Nor is it clear how the statement that intellectual activity cannot exceed the bounds of historical praxis is to be squared with the demand for a 'global' criticism in which the totality of that praxis is opposed by theory or Reason.

All these elements of the critical theory are already present in the 1930s, in Horkheimer as in Marcuse or Adorno. The last-named studied the question of subjectivity and the object, and the problem of 'reification', chiefly in the context of Kierkegaard's philosophy and of musical criticism. The commercialization of art under monopoly capitalism was a recurrent theme of his; jazz music as a whole appeared to him a symptom of this degradation. His main point was that in a mass culture art loses its 'negative' function, i.e. that of representing a Utopia above and beyond existing society. It was not so much the 'politicization' of art that he objected to as, on the contrary, the replacement of its political function by passive, mindless enjoyment.

As to the work of Walter Benjamin, this cannot be wholly summed up in terms of the history of Marxism. Among his many writings on philosophy and literary criticism few can be described as showing a Marxist background. Nevertheless, he was for a long time an adherent of historical materialism in his own sense of the term, and went through a period of attraction towards Communism, though he never joined the party. He seems to have tried to graft historical materialism on to his own theory of culture, which had nothing to do with Marxism and which he had worked out beforehand. Gershom Scholem, his close friend and one of the greatest present-day authorities on the history of Judaism, emphasizes that Benjamin had at all times a strong mystical streak, and also that he had read very little Marx. Benjamin had a lifelong interest in the hidden meanings of words, which led him to study the language of magic, the cabbala, and the origins and functions of speech in general. He seems to have regarded historical materialism as a possible clue to the secret meaning of history, but his own speculations led to the view that it was a special case or application of a more general theory connecting human behaviour with a general 'mimetic' impulse in nature. In any case his thoughts on history had nothing to do with a theory of universal progress or determinism. He was impressed, on the other hand, by the dialectic of uniqueness and recurrence in history, mythology, and art. What seems to have attracted him in Communism was not the idea of regularity in history but rather that of discontinuity (hence his interest in Sorel). In *Theses on the Idea of History* (*Thesen über den Begriff der Geschichte*), written a few months before his death, he remarked that nothing had been so disastrous to the German workers' movement as the belief that it was swimming with the stream of history. Especially harmful and suspect, in his opinion, were versions of Marxism that regarded history as the progressive conquest of nature, seen as an object of exploitation—a view which he thought redolent of technocratic ideology. History, he wrote in the same *Theses*, was a construction, the scene of which was not empty, undifferentiated time but time filled by the *Jetztzeit*—the existence of bygone events, constantly revived in the present. This idea of unfading 'presentness' recurs in several places in his work. Benjamin had a strong, conservative sense of the permanence of the past, which he endeavoured to reconcile with a revolutionary faith in the discontinuity of history. He connected this latter idea with the Jewish Messianic tradition, holding, contrary to Marxist doctrine, that purely immanent eschatology was impossible; the *eschaton* could not manifest itself as a natural continuation of the course of events up to the present but, like the advent of the Messiah, presupposed a hiatus in time. But the discontinuous and catastrophic nature of history could not deprive the past of its meaning-generating significance. From Benjamin's various reflections, vague and ambiguous as they are, on the disappearance of the ancient links between art on the one hand and myth and ritual on the other it can be seen that he did not by any means consider this rift to be a source of pure gain: he seems to have believed that something essential must be salvaged from the mythical heritage of mankind if culture was to survive. He also apparently believed that there was a pre-existing treasury of the senses which human language and art did not create, but revealed; language, he held, conveys meaning not by virtue of convention and chance, but by a kind of alchemic affinity with objects and experience. (In this connection he was interested in Marr's speculations on the origin of language.) The purely instrumental view of language, characteristic of positivism, seemed to him of a piece with the general breakdown of inherited meaning in a civilization heading towards technocracy.

It does not seem that Benjamin had much in common with Marxism, despite his occasional professions. He was certainly linked with the Frankfurt school by his interest in various forms of cultural decadence resulting from the commercialization of art. He may for a time have believed more than other members of the school in the liberating potential of the proletariat, but the latter was in his view not so much the organizer of new relations of production, as the standard-bearer of a new culture which might one day restore the values that were perishing as the influence of myths declined.

The triumph of Nazism, with its catastrophic effect on German culture, naturally turned the attention of the Frankfurt school to investigating the psychological and social causes of the astonishing success of totalitarianism. Both in Germany and later in the United States the Institute carried out empirical studies for the purpose of investigating attitudes that found expression in the desire for authority and readiness to submit to it. In 1936 a collective work, *Studien über Autorität und Familie*, was published in Paris, based on theoretical argument as well as empirical observation; its main authors were Horkheimer and Fromm. Horkheimer sought to explain the growth of authoritarian institutions in terms of the decline and transference of family authority and the correspondingly increased importance of political institutions in the 'socialization' of the individual. Fromm interpreted the need for authority in psychoanalytical terms (the sado-masochistic character); he did not, however, share Freud's pessimism as to the inevitable conflict between instincts and the demands of communal life, or the permanently repressive role of culture. The Frankfurt writers sought to illuminate the phenomenon of Nazism from many sides and to discover its psychological, economic, and cultural roots. Pollock discussed Nazism in terms of state capitalism, of which he saw another example in the Soviet regime: both systems presaged a new era of domination and oppression based on state direction of the economy, autarkic tendencies, and the elimination of unemployment by coercion. Nazism was not a continuation of the old capitalism but a new formation in which the economy was deprived of its independence and subordinated to politics. Most writers of the school thought that the prospects of individual freedom and authentic culture were poor in view of contemporary trends, the growth of state control over the individual, and the bureaucratization of social relationships. Nazi and Soviet totalitarianism were not, they believed, historical aberrations but symptoms of a universal trend. Franz Neumann, however, in a book of 1944, took a more traditionally Marxist view: he held that Nazism was a form of monopoly capitalism and could not cope with the typical 'contradictions' of that system, so that its duration was bound to be limited.

In the United States the school continued to produce studies of social psychology designed to elucidate the causes that brought about and maintained attitudes, beliefs, and myths characteristic of totalitarian systems. These included a volume on anti-Semitism and a collective work, by Adorno and others, *The Authoritarian Personality* (1950), based on the results of projective tests and questionnaires. This was a study of the correlation between different personality traits of those inclined to welcome and revere authority, and the link between the existence and strength of these traits and such social variables as class, upbringing, and religion.

Adorno and Horkheimer remained extremely active to the end of their lives, publishing works in post-war America and Germany which are regarded as classic documents of the Frankfurt school. Among these are a joint work, *Dialektik der Aufklärung* (1947), Horkheimer's *Eclipse of Reason* (1947) and his *Zur Kritik der instrumentellen Vernunft* (1967). Adorno, besides numerous works on musicology (*Philosophie der neuen Musik*, 1949; *Dissonanzen: Musik in der verwalteten Welt*, 1956; *Moments Musicaux*, 1966), published *Negative Dialektik* (1966), the philosophical summa of the school, also a critique of existentialism (*Jargon der Eigentlichkeit: zur deutschen Ideologie*, 1964) and essays on the theory of culture, some of which were collected in *Prismen* (1955). He also edited, with Scholem, a two-volume edition of Benjamin's writings (1955). His unfinished *Ästhetische Theorie* was published posthumously in 1973. English translations of three of the above works (*Dialectic of Enlightenment*; *Negative Dialectics*; *The Jargon of Authenticity*) also appeared in 1973.

In the following sections I shall try to describe more fully some of the main points of the 'critical theory', without keeping to chronological order. I shall leave Adorno's musicology out of account, not because it is unimportant but because of my own incompetence in this sphere.

2. Principles of critical theory

THE RULES of 'critical' as opposed to 'traditional' theory were formulated in Horkheimer's programmatic essay of 1937, the main ideas of which are as follows.

In studies of social phenomena up to the present it has normally been assumed either that these should be based on the ordinary rules of induction and should aim at formulating general concepts and laws, expressed quantitatively as far as possible, or else that, as phenomenologists believe, it is possible to discover 'essential' laws independent of empirical results. In both cases the state of things under observation was separate from our knowledge about it, just as the subject-matter of natural science was furnished to it 'from outside'. It was also believed that the development of knowledge was governed by its own immanent logic, and that if some theories were discarded in favour of others this was because the former involved logical difficulties or proved incompatible with new data of experience. In reality, however, social changes were the most powerful agent of alterations in theory; science was part of the social process of production, and underwent change accordingly. Bourgeois philosophy had expressed its misguided faith in the independence of science in various transcendentalist doctrines which prevented people realizing the social genesis and social functions of knowledge; they also maintained a picture of knowledge as an activity that consisted of describing the world as it was but not of going beyond it or criticizing it, since this required evaluative judgements which science could not supply. The world of science was a world of ready-made facts which the observer sought to reduce to order, as though perception of them was quite independent of the social framework within which it took place.

For critical theory, however, there is no such thing as 'facts' in this sense. Perception cannot be isolated from its social genesis; both it and its object are a social and historical product. The individual observer is passive *vis-à-vis* the object, but society as a whole is an active element in the process, although unconsciously so. The facts ascertained are in part determined by the collective praxis of human beings who have devised the conceptual instruments used by the investigator. Objects as we know them are partly the product of concepts and of collective praxis, which philosophers, unaware of its origin, mistakenly petrify into a pre-individual transcendental consciousness.

Critical theory regards itself as a form of social behaviour and is aware of its own functions and genesis, but this does not mean that it is not a theory in the true sense. Its specific function is that it refuses to accept implicitly, as traditional theory does, that the rules of existing society—including the division of labour, the place assigned to intellectual activity, the distinction between the individual and society—are natural and inevitable. It seeks to understand society as a whole, and for that purpose it must in some sense take up a position outside it, although on the other hand it regards itself as a product of society. It criticizes society by analysing its categories. Existing society behaves as a 'natural' creation independent of the will of its members, and to understand this is to realize the 'alienation' to which they are subject. 'Critical thought is motivated today by the endeavour genuinely to transcend the situation of tension, to remove the opposition between the purposiveness, spontaneity, and rationality of the individual and the labour conditions on which society is based. It implies the conception that man is in conflict with himself until he recovers this identity' (*Kritische Theorie*, ed. A. Schmidt, vol. ii, p. 159).

Critical theory recognizes that there is no absolute subject of knowledge, and that subject and object do not yet coincide in the process of thinking about society, although that process is in fact society's self-knowledge. Their coincidence lies in the future; it cannot, however, be the result of mere intellectual progress, but only of the social process which will make humanity master of its fate again by stripping social life of its quasi-natural, 'external' character. This process involves a change in the nature of theory, the function of thought and its relation to the object.

Horkheimer's view, it will be seen, is here close to Lukács's: thought about society is itself a social fact, theory is inevitably part of the process it describes. But the essential difference is that Lukács believed that the complete unity of the subject and object of history, and thus the unity of social praxis and the theory that 'expresses' it, was realized in the class-consciousness of the proletariat; whence it followed that the observer's self-identification with the class outlook of the proletariat (sc. the Communist party line) was a guarantee of theoretical correctness. Horkheimer explicitly rejects this, declaring that the situation of the proletariat offers no guarantee in the matter of knowledge. Critical theory is in favour of the liberation of the proletariat, but it also wishes to preserve its independence, and refuses to commit itself to passive acceptance of the proletarian viewpoint; otherwise it would turn into social psychology, a mere record of what the workers thought and felt at any given moment. Precisely because it is 'critical', theory must remain autonomous *vis-à-vis* every existing form of social consciousness. Theory conceives itself as an aspect of praxis devoted to creating a better society; it retains a militant character, but it is not simply activated by the existing struggle. Its critical attitude to the 'totality' of the social system is not a matter of value-judgements superimposed on theoretical findings, but is implicit in the conceptual apparatus inherited from Marx: such categories as class, exploitation, surplus value, profit, impoverishment, and crises 'are elements of a conceptual whole, the purpose of which is not to reproduce society as it is but to change it in the right direction' (ibid., p. 167). Theory thus has an active and destructive character in its own conceptual framework, but has to take account of the fact that it might be in opposition to the actual consciousness of the proletariat. Critical theory, following Marx, analyses society in the light of abstract categories, but it does not forget at any stage that, *qua* theory, it is a criticism of the world it describes, that its intellectual act is at the same time a social act, that it is thus a 'critique' in the Marxian sense. Its subject is a single, particular historical society: the capitalist world in its present form, which impedes human development and threatens the world with a return to barbarism. Critical theory looks forward to another society in which

men and women will decide their own fate and not be subject to external necessity; in so doing it increases the likelihood of such a society coming about, and
it is aware of this fact. In the future society there will be no difference between
necessity and freedom. The theory is in the service of human emancipation and
happiness and the creation of a world fitted to human powers and needs, and
it declares that mankind has potentialities other than those manifested in the
existing world.

As can be seen, the main principles of 'critical theory' are those of Lukács's
Marxism, but without the proletariat. This difference makes the theory more
flexible and less dogmatic, but also obscure and inconsistent. Lukács, by identifying theory with the class-consciousness of the proletariat, and this in turn
with the wisdom of the Communist party, clearly defined his criteria of truth:
namely, in the observation of society, truth does not proceed from the application of general scientific rules that are valid also in natural science, but is
defined by its origin; the Communist party is infallible. This epistemology at
least has the merit of being consistent and perfectly clear. But in 'critical theory' we do not know how genetic criteria are to be combined with the intellectual autonomy of the theory and whence the rules governing its correctness are
to be derived, since it rejects 'positivist' criteria but also refuses to identify with
the proletariat. On the one hand, Horkheimer repeats (in 'Der Rationalis-
musstreit in der gegenwärtigen Philosophie', 1934) Feuerbach's statement that
it is man who thinks, and not the Ego or Reason; in so doing he emphasizes
that both the rules of scientific procedures and the stock of concepts used in
science are a creation of history, the outcome of practical needs, and that the
content of knowledge cannot be divorced from its social genesis—in other
words, there is no transcendental subject. On this basis it might seem that the
theory is 'good' or correct because it stands for 'social progress', or that intellectual value is defined by social function. But, on the other hand, the theory
is supposed to retain its autonomy *vis-à-vis* reality; its content must not be
derived from any identification with an existing movement, and it must not be
pragmatistic in terms even of the human species, let alone a social class. It is
not clear, therefore, in which sense it claims to be true: because it describes
reality as it is, or because it 'serves the interests of the liberation of humanity'?
The clearest answer that Horkheimer offers is perhaps the following: 'The open
dialectic does not, however, lose the imprint of truth. The discovery of limitations and one-sidedness in one's own thought and that of others is an important aspect of the intellectual process. Both Hegel and his materialist
successors rightly emphasized that this critical, relativist approach is part of
knowledge. But certainty and the affirmation of one's own conviction do not
require us to imagine that the unity of concept and object has been achieved
and that thought can come to a stop. The results obtained from observation and

inference, methodical research and historical events, everyday work and the political struggle, are true if they stand up to the cognitive means at our disposal (*den verfügbaren Erkenntnismitteln standhalten*)' ('Zum Problem der Wahrheit', ibid., vol. i, p. 246). This explanation is far from being unambiguous. If it means that critical theory, whatever the social circumstances in which it is evolved, is in the last resort subject to the rules of empirical verification and is judged as true or false accordingly, then it is no different epistemologically from the theories it condemns as 'traditional'. If, however, something more is meant, namely that in order to be true a theory must stand the empirical test and be 'socially progressive' as well, then Horkheimer fails to tell us what to do if these two criteria conflict. He merely repeats generalities about truth not being 'supra-historical' and about the social conditioning of knowledge, or what he calls the necessary 'social mediation' between a concept and its object; he assures us that the theory is not 'static', that it does not 'absolutize' either the subject or the object, and so on. All that is clear is that 'critical theory' refuses to accept Lukács's party dogmatism and seeks to maintain its status as theory while also refusing to acknowledge empirical criteria of verification. In other words, it exists by virtue of its own ambiguity.

Critical theory, thus understood, also comprises no specific Utopia. Horkheimer's predictions are confined to trite generalities: universal happiness and freedom, man becoming his own master, the abolition of profit and exploitation, etc. We are told that 'everything' must be changed, that it is not a matter of reforming society but of transforming it, but we are not told how this is to be done or what will be put in its place. The proletariat no longer ranks as the infallible subject of history, though its liberation is still an objective of the theory. Since, however, the latter does not claim to be the effective lever of general liberation, there is nothing clearly left of it except the conviction that it constitutes a higher mode of thought and will contribute to the emancipation of mankind.

Horkheimer's remarks on the social preferences and interests involved in the conceptual apparatus used by various theories of society are certainly true, though they were not new even in his day. But the fact that the social sciences reflect different interests and values does not mean, as Horkheimer seems to think (following Lukács, Korsch, and Marx), that the difference between empirical and evaluative judgements has been 'transcended'.

In this sense the 'critical theory' is an inconsistent attempt to preserve Marxism without accepting its identification with the proletariat and without recognizing the class or party criteria of truth, but also without seeking a solution of the difficulties that arise when Marxism is truncated in this manner. It is a partial form of Marxism, offering no replacement for what it leaves out.

3. Negative dialectics

THERE IS, as far as I am aware, no summarized version of what is regarded, no doubt rightly, as the most complete and general exposition of Adorno's thought, namely *Negative Dialectics*. Probably it would be impossible to compile such a summary, and probably Adorno was well aware of this and deliberately made it so. The book may be called an embodied antinomy: a philosophical work that sets out to prove, by example or argument, that the writing of philosophical works is impossible. The difficulty of explaining its content is not only due to its extremely intricate syntax, which is evidently intentional, or the fact that the author uses Hegelian and neo-Hegelian jargon without any attempt to explain it, as though it were the clearest language in the world. The pretentious obscurity of style and the contempt that it shows for the reader might be endurable if the book were not also totally devoid of literary form. It is in this respect a philosophical counterpart to the formlessness that manifested itself some time earlier in the plastic arts, and later in music and literature. It is no more possible to summarize Adorno's work than to describe the plot of an 'anti-novel' or the theme of an action painting. It can no doubt be said that the abandonment of form in painting did not lead to the destruction of art, but actually liberated pure painting from 'anecdotic' work; and, similarly, the novel and drama, although they consist of words, have survived the loss of form (which can never be complete) to the extent that we are able to read Joyce, Musil, and Gombrowicz with understanding. But in philosophical writing, the dissolution of form is destructive in the highest degree. It may be tolerable if it is due to the author's attempt to catch fleeting 'experience' in words and to make his work directly 'expressive', like Gabriel Marcel; but it is hard to endure a philosopher who continues to deal in abstractions while at the same time contending that they are a meaningless form of discourse.

With this reservation we may try to give an idea of Adorno's argument. The main theme that pervades his book and is expressed, for example in his critique of Kant, Hegel, and the existentialists appears to be as follows. Philosophy has always been dominated by the search for an absolute starting-point, both metaphysical and epistemological, and in consequence, despite the intentions of philosophers themselves, it has drifted into a search for 'identity', i.e. some kind of primordial being to which all others were ultimately reducible: this was alike the trend of German idealism and positivism, of existentialists and transcendental phenomenologists. In considering the typical traditional 'pairs' of opposites—object versus subject, the general versus the particular, empirical data versus ideas, continuity versus discontinuity, theory versus practice—philosophers have sought to interpret them in such a way as to give primacy to one concept or the other and so create a uniform language by means of which everything can be described: to identify aspects of the universe in respect of which all others are derivative. But this cannot be done. There is no absolute 'primacy': everything philosophy is concerned with presents itself as interdependent with its opposite. (This, of course, is Hegel's idea, but Adorno claims that Hegel was afterwards untrue to it.) A philosophy which continues in traditional fashion to strive to discover the 'primal' thing or concept is on the wrong track, and, moreover, in our civilization it tends to strengthen totalitarian and conformist tendencies, by seeking order and invariability at any cost. Philosophy in fact is impossible; all that is possible is constant negation, purely destructive resistance to any attempt to confine the world within a single principle that purports to endow it with 'identity'.

Thus summarized, Adorno's thought may seem desperate or sterile, but it does not seem that we have done it an injustice. It is not a dialectic of negativity (which would be a metaphysical theory), but an express negation of metaphysics and epistemology. His intention is anti-totalitarian: he is opposed to all ideas that serve to perpetuate a particular form of domination and reduce the human subject to 'reified' forms. Such attempts, he argues, take on a paradoxical 'subjectivist' form, especially in existentialist philosophy, where the petrification of the absolute individual subject as the irreducible reality involves indifference to all social relationships that increase the enslavement of man. One cannot proclaim the primacy of this monadic existence without tacitly accepting everything that lies outside it.

But Marxism too—especially in Lukács's interpretation, though he is not expressly mentioned in this context—serves the same totalitarian tendency under colour of criticizing 'reification'. 'The remaining theoretical inadequacy in Hegel and Marx became part of historical practice and can thus be newly reflected upon in theory, instead of thought bowing irrationally to the primacy of practice. Practice itself was an eminently theoretical concept' (*Negative Dialectics*, p. 144). Adorno thus attacks the Marxist–Lukácsist 'primacy of practice', in which theory is dissolved and loses its autonomy. In so far as his opposition to the 'philosophy of identity' is turned against the anti-intellectualism of Marxism and its all-absorbing 'practice', he defends the right of philosophy to exist; he even begins his book with the statement that 'Philosophy, which once seemed obsolete, lives on because the moment to realize it was missed' (p. 3). At this point Adorno clearly departs from Marxism: there may, he argues, have been a time when Marx's hopes for the liberation of humanity by the proletariat and the abolition of philosophy by its identification with 'life' were realistic, but that time has passed. Theory must abide in its autonomy, which of course does not mean that theory in its turn has any absolute 'primacy'; nothing whatever has 'primacy', everything depends on everything else and, by the same token, has its own measure of 'substantiality'. 'Practice' cannot fulfil the tasks of theory, and if it claims to do so it is simply the enemy of thought.

If there is no absolute primacy it is also the case, in Adorno's opinion, that all attempts to embrace the 'whole' by means of reason are bootless and serve the cause of mystification. This does not mean that theory must resolve itself wholly into particular sciences as the positivists would have it: theory is indispensable, but for the present it cannot be anything but negation. Attempts to grasp the 'whole' are based on the same faith in the ultimate identity of everything; even when philosophy maintains that the whole is 'contradictory' it retains its prejudices concerning 'identity', which are so strong that even 'contradiction' can be made their instrument if it is proclaimed to be the ultimate foundation of the universe. Dialectic in the true sense is thus not merely the investigation of 'contradiction', but refusal to accept it as a schema that explains everything. Strictly speaking, the dialectic is neither a method nor a description of the world, but an act of repeated opposition to all existing descriptive schemata, and all methods pretending to universality. 'Total contradiction is nothing but the manifested untruth of total identification' (p. 6).

In the same way there is no epistemological absolute, no single unchallengeable source of wisdom; the 'pure immediacy' of the cognitive act, if it exists, cannot be expressed except in words, and words inevitably give it an abstract, rationalized form. But Husserl's transcendental ego is also a false construction, for there are no acts of intuition free from the social genesis of knowledge. All concepts are ultimately rooted in the non-conceptual, in human efforts to control nature; no concepts can express the whole content of the object or be identified with it; Hegel's pure 'being' proves in the end to be nothingness.

The negative dialectic can, as Adorno says, be called an anti-system, and in that sense it appears to coincide with Nietzsche's position. However, Adorno goes on to say that thought itself is negation, just as the processing of any substance is a 'negation' of its form as presented to us. Even the statement that something is of a certain kind is negative inasmuch as it implies that that something is not of another kind. This, however, reduces 'negativity' to a truism; it is not clear how there could be any philosophy that is not 'negative' in this sense, or whom Adorno is arguing against. His main intention, however, appears to be a less truistic one, namely to put forward no definite answers to the traditional problems of philosophy but to confine himself to exploding philosophy as it is today, since by its urge towards 'positiveness' it inevitably degenerates into acceptance of the *status quo*, namely the domination of man by man. The bourgeois consciousness at the time of its emancipation combated 'feudal' modes of thought but could not bring itself to break with 'systems' of all kinds, since it felt that it did not represent 'complete freedom'—from this observation of Adorno's we gather that he stand for 'complete freedom' as against 'systems'.

In his critique of 'identity' and 'positiveness' Adorno continues a traditional motif taken over by the Frankfurt school from Marx: the critique of a society which, being subject to the domination of 'exchange-value', reduces individuals and things to a common level and a homogeneous anonymity. A philosophy which expresses and affirms that society cannot do justice to the variety of phenomena or the interdependence of different aspects of life; on the one hand it homogenizes society, on the other it reduces people and things to 'atoms'—a process in which, Adorno observes, logic plays its part also: on this point he is faithful to the tradition of recent Marxist philosophy, which inveighs against logic while ignoring its modern developments.

Science, too, it appears, is a party to the general conspiracy of civilization against man, as it identifies rationality with measurability, reduces everything to 'quantities', and excludes qualitative differences from the scope of knowledge; Adorno does not suggest, however, that a new 'qualitative' science is ready and waiting to take over.

The upshot of his critique is not to defend relativism, for that too is part of 'bourgeois consciousness'; it is anti-intellectual (*geistesfeindlich*), abstract, and wrong, because what it treats as relative is itself rooted in the conditions of capitalist society: 'the alleged social relativity of views obeys the objective law of social production under private ownership of the means of production' (p. 37). Adorno does not say what 'law' he refers to, and, true to his contempt for bourgeois logic, does not reflect on the logical validity of his criticism.

Philosophy in the sense of a 'system' is impossible, he argues, because everything changes—a statement he enlarges on as follows. 'The invariants, whose own invariance has been produced (*ein Produziertes ist*), cannot be peeled out of the variables as if all truth were then in our possession. Truth has coalesced with substance, which will change; immutability of truth is the delusion of *prima philosophia*' (p. 40).

On the one hand, concepts have a certain autonomy and do not emerge simply as copies of things; on the other, they do not enjoy 'primacy' as compared with things—to agree that they do would mean accepting bureaucratic or capitalist government. 'The principle of dominion, which antagonistically rends human society, is the same principle which, spiritualized, causes the difference between the concept and its subject matter (*dem ihm Unterworfenen*)' (p. 48). Hence nominalism is wrong ('The concept of a capitalist society is not *a flatus vocis*'—p. 50 n.), and so is conceptual realism: concepts and their objects subsist in a constant 'dialectical' association, in which primacy is obliterated. In the same way positivist attempts to reduce knowledge to that which is simply 'given' are misguided, as they seek to 'dehistoricize the contents of thought' (p. 53).

Anti-positivist attempts to reconstruct an ontology are no less suspect; for ontology as such—not any particular ontological doctrine—is an apologia for the *status quo*, an instrument of 'order'. The need for an ontology is genuine enough, since the bourgeois consciousness has replaced 'substantial' by 'functional' concepts, treating society as a complex of functions in which everything is relative to something else and nothing has a consistency of its own. Nevertheless, ontology cannot be reconstructed.

At this point, as at many others, the reader may well wonder how Adorno intends his propositions to be applied. What are we to do if ontology and the lack of it are both bad and are both likely to involve us in the defence of exchange-value? Perhaps we should not think of these questions at all, but declare ourselves neutral in philosophical matters? But Adorno will not have this either: it would be a surrender of another kind, an abandonment of reason. Science, just because it puts faith in itself and refuses to seek self-knowledge by any methods other than its own, condemns itself to being an apologia for the existing world. 'Its self-exegesis makes a *causa sui* of science. It accepts itself as given and thereby sanctions also its currently existing form, its division of labour, although in the long run the insufficiency of that form cannot be concealed' (p. 73). The humanistic sciences, dispersed in particular inquiries, lose interest in cognition and are stripped of their armour of concepts. Ontology, which comes to science 'from outside', appears with the abruptness of a pistol-shot (in Hegel's phrase) and does not help them to acquire self-knowledge. In the end we do not know how to escape from the vicious circle.

Heidegger's ontology not only does not cure this state of affairs, but proposes something even worse. Having eliminated from philosophy both empiricism and Husserl's concept of the *eidos*, he seeks to apprehend Being—which, after this reduction, is pure nothingness; he also 'isolates' phenomena and cannot conceive them as aspects (*Momente*) of the process of manifestation; in this way phenomena are 'reified'. Heidegger, like Husserl, believes that it is possible to proceed from the individual to the universal without 'mediation', or to apprehend Being in a form unaffected by the act of reflection. This, however, is impossible: Being, however conceived, is 'mediated' by the subject. Heidegger's 'Being' is constituted, not simply 'given': 'We cannot, by thinking, assume any position in which that separation of subject and object will directly vanish, for the separation is inherent in each thought; it is inherent in thinking itself' (p. 85). Freedom can be sought only by observing the tensions that arise between opposite poles of life, but Heidegger treats these poles as absolute realities and leaves them to their fate. On the one hand he accepts that social life must be 'reified', i.e. he sanctions the *status quo*, while on the other he ascribes freedom to man as something already gained, thus sanctioning slavery. He attempts to rescue metaphysics, but wrongly supposes that what he is trying to rescue is 'immediately present'. All in all, Heidegger's philosophy is an example of *Herrschaftswissen* in the service of a repressive society. It calls on us to abandon concepts for the sake of a promised communion with Being—but this Being has no content, precisely because it is supposed to be apprehended without the 'mediation' of concepts; basically it is no more than a substantivization of the copula 'is'.

It would seem that, speaking in as general terms as possible, the main thrust of Adorno's attack on Heidegger's ontology lies in the Hegelian contention that the subject can never be wholly eliminated from the results of metaphysical inquiry, and that if we forget this and attempt to place subject and object 'on opposite sides' we shall fail to comprehend either one or the other. Both are inseparable parts of reflection, and neither has epistemological priority; each is 'mediated' by the other. Similarly, there is no way of apprehending by cognition that which is absolutely individual—what Heidegger calls *Dasein* or *Jemeinigkeit*. Without the 'mediation' of general concepts, the pure 'this thing here' becomes an abstraction; it cannot be 'isolated' from reflection. 'But truth, the constellation of subject and object in which both penetrate each other, can no more be reduced to subjectivity than to that Being whose dialectical relation to subjectivity Heidegger tends to blur' (p. 127).

The passage in which Adorno comes closest to explaining what he means by 'negative dialectics' is as follows: 'In a sense, dialectical logic is more positivistic than the positivism that out-laws it. As thinking, dialectical logic respects that which is to be thought—the object—even where the object does not heed the rules of thinking. The analysis of the object is tangential to the rules of thinking. Thought need not be content with its own legality; without abandoning it, we can think against our thought, and if it were possible to define dialectics, this would be a definition worth suggesting' (p. 141). It does not appear that we can infer more from this definition than that the dialectic need not be cramped by the rules of logic. In another passage we are indeed told that it is freer still: for 'Philosophy consists neither in *vérité's de raison* nor in *vérités de fait*. Nothing it says will bow to tangible criteria of any "being the case": its theses on conceptualities are no more subject to the criteria of a logical state of facts than its theses on factualities are to the criteria of empirical science' (p. 109). It would be hard indeed to imagine a more convenient position. The negative dialectician declares, firstly, that he cannot be criticized from either the logical or the factual point of view, as he has laid down that such criteria do not concern him; secondly, that his intellectual and moral superiority is based on his very disregard of these criteria; and thirdly, that that disregard is in fact the essence of the 'negative dialectic'. The 'negative dialectic' is simply a blank cheque, signed and endorsed by history, Being, Subject, and Object, in favour of Adorno and his followers; any sum can be written in, anything will be valid, there is absolute liberation from the 'positivist fetishes' of logic and empiricism. Thought has transformed itself dialectically into its opposite. Anyone who denies this is enslaved to the 'identity principle', which implies acceptance of a society dominated by exchange-value and therefore ignorant of 'qualitative differences'.

The reason why the 'identity principle' is so dangerous, according to Adorno, is that it implies, firstly, that each separate thing is what it is empirically, and secondly, that an individual object can be identified by means of general concepts, i.e. analysed into abstractions (an idea of Bergson's, whom Adorno, however, does not mention). The task of the dialectic, on the other hand, is firstly to ascertain what a thing is in reality, not merely to what category it belongs (Adorno does not give examples of an analysis of this kind), and secondly to explain what it ought to be according to its own concept, although it is not yet (an idea of Bloch's, to whom Adorno also does not refer in this context). A man knows how to define himself, while society defines him differently in accordance with the function it assigns to him; between the two modes of definition there is an 'objective contradiction' (again no examples given). The object of the dialectic is to oppose the immobilization of things by concepts; it takes the position that things are never identical with themselves; it seeks out negations, without assuming that the negation of a negation signifies a return to the positive; it recognizes individuality, but only as 'mediated' by generality, and generality only as an aspect (*Moment*) of individuality; it sees the subject in the object and vice versa, practice in theory and theory in practice, the essence in the phenomenon and the phenomenon in the essence; it must apprehend differences but not 'absolutize' them, and it must not regard any particular thing as a starting-point *par excellence*. There cannot be a point of view that presupposes nothing, such as Husserl's transcendental subject; the delusion that there can be such a subject is due to the fact that society precedes the individual. The idea that there can be a spirit which comprises everything and is identical with the whole is as nonsensical as that of a single party in a totalitarian regime. The dispute as to the primacy of mind or matter is meaningless in dialectical thinking, for the concepts of mind and matter are themselves abstracted from experience, and the 'radical difference' between them is no more than a convention.

All these precepts concerning the dialectic should, in Adorno's opinion, serve definite social or political ends. It even appears that criteria of practical action can be deduced from them. 'For the right practice, and for the good itself, there really is no other authority than the most advanced state of theory. When an idea of goodness is supposed to guide the will without fully absorbing the concrete rational definitions, it will unwittingly take orders from the reified consciousness, from that which society has approved' (p. 242). We thus have a clear practical rule: firstly there must be an advanced (*fortgeschritten*) theory, and secondly, the will must be influenced by 'concrete rational definitions'. The object of practice, thus enlightened, is to do away with reification which is due to exchange-value; for in bourgeois society, as Marx taught, the 'autonomy of the individual' was only apparent, an expression of the contingency of life and the dependence of human beings on market forces. It is hard to gather from Adorno's writings, however, what non-reified freedom is to consist of. In describing this 'complete freedom' we must not, in any case, use the concept of self-alienation, as it suggests that the state of freedom from alienation, or the perfect unity of man with himself, has already existed at some former time, so that freedom can be achieved by going back to the starting-point—an idea which is reactionary by definition. Nor is it the case that we know of some historical design that guarantees us a joyful future of freedom and the end of 'reification'; up to now there has been no such thing as a single process of universal history: 'history is the unity of continuity and discontinuity' (p. 320).

There can be few works of philosophy that give such an overpowering impression of sterility as *Negative Dialectics*. This is not because it seeks to deprive human knowledge of an 'ultimate basis', i.e. because it is a doctrine of scepticism; in the history of philosophy there have been admirable works of scepticism, full of penetration as well as destructive passion. But Adorno is not a sceptic. He does not say that there is no criterion of truth, that no theory is possible, or that reason is powerless; on the contrary, he says that theory is possible and indispensable and that we must be guided by reason. All his arguments go to show, however, that reason can never take the first step without falling into 'reification', and it is thus not clear how it can take the second or any further steps; there is simply no starting-point, and the recognition of this fact is proclaimed as the supreme achievement of the dialectic. But even this crucial statement is not clearly formulated by Adorno, nor does he support it by any analysis of his concepts and maxims. As with many other Marxists, his work contains no arguments but only *ex cathedra* statements using concepts that are nowhere explained; indeed, he condemns conceptual analysis as a manifestation of positivist prejudices to the effect that some ultimate 'data', empirical or logical, can provide philosophy with a starting-point.

In the last resort Adorno's argument boils down to an assortment of ideas borrowed uncritically from Marx, Hegel, Nietzsche, Lukács, Bergson, and Bloch. From Marx he takes the statement that the whole mechanism of bourgeois society is based on the domination of exchange-value, reducing all qualitative differences to the common denominator of money (this is Marx's form of romantic anti-capitalism). From Marx also comes the attack on Hegelian philosophy for subjecting history to an extra-historical *Weltgeist* and asserting the primacy of 'that which is general' over human individuals, substituting abstractions for realities and thus perpetuating human enslavement. Again from Marx comes the attack on Hegel's theory of subject and object, in which the subject is defined as a manifestation of the object, and the object as a subjective construction, thus producing a vicious circle (but it is not clear how Adorno avoids this vicious circle, as he denies absolute 'priority' to either subject or object). Adorno departs from Marx, on the other hand, in rejecting the theory of progress and historical necessity and the idea of the proletariat as the standard-bearer of the Great Utopia. From Lukács comes the view that all that is evil in the world can be summed up in the term 'reification' and that perfected human beings will cast off the ontological status of 'things' (but Adorno does not say what the 'de-reified' state will be like, still less how it will be attained). Both the Promethean and the scientific motif of Marxism are discarded, and there remains only a vague romantic Utopia in which man is himself and does not depend on 'mechanical' social forces. From Bloch, Adorno derives the view that we possess the idea of a Utopia 'transcending' the actual world, but that the especial virtue of this 'transcendence' is that it cannot, in principle, have any definite content at the present time. From Nietzsche comes the general hostility to the 'spirit of the system' and the convenient belief that a true sage is not afraid of contradictions but rather expresses his wisdom in them, so that he is forearmed against logical criticism. From Bergson comes the idea that abstract concepts petrify changeable things (or, as Adorno would say, 'reify' them); Adorno himself, on the other hand, contributes the hope that we can create 'fluid' concepts that do not petrify anything. From Hegel, Adorno takes the general idea that in the cognitive process there is a constant 'mediation' between subject and object, concepts and perception, the particular and the general. To all these ingredients Adorno adds an almost unparalleled vagueness of exposition: he shows no desire whatever to elucidate his ideas, and clothes them in pretentious generalities. As a philosophical text, *Negative Dialectics* is a model of professorial bombast concealing poverty of thought.

The view that there is no absolute basis for human reasoning can certainly be defended, as is shown by sceptics and relativists who have propounded it in various forms. But Adorno not only adds nothing to this traditional idea but obscures it by his own phraseology (neither subject nor object can be 'absolutized'; perceptions cannot be 'abstracted' from concepts; there is no absolute 'primacy' of practice, etc.), while at the same time imagining that this 'negative dialectic' can lead to some practical consequences for social behaviour. If we do try to extract intellectual or practical rules from his philosophy, they reduce to the precepts: 'We must think more intensively, but also remember that there is no starting-point for thought' and 'We must oppose reification and exchange-value'. The fact that we can say nothing positive is not our fault and not Adorno's, but is due to the domination of exchange-value. For the present, therefore, we can only negatively 'transcend' existing civilization as a whole. In this way the 'negative dialectic' has provided a convenient ideological slogan

for left-wing groups who sought a pretext for root-and-branch destruction as a
political programme, and who extolled intellectual primitivism as the supreme
form of dialectical initiation. It would be unjust, however, to accuse Adorno of
intending to encourage such attitudes. His philosophy is not an expression of
universal revolt, but of helplessness and despair.

4. Critique of existential 'authenticism'

EXISTENTIALISM was clearly the main competitor of the Frankfurt school as
regards the critique of 'reification', and was far more influential as a philosophy. German thinkers rarely used the term, but on the face of it the intention
of their anthropological theories was the same: to express in philosophical language the contrast between the self-determining consciousness of the individual and the anonymous world of social ties conforming to rules of their own.
Thus, in the same way as the attacks on Hegel by Marx, Kierkegaard, and
Stirner contained a common element, namely their critique of the primacy of
impersonal 'generality' over real subjectivity, so the Marxists and existentialists
were on common ground in criticizing the social system which confined
human beings to socially determined roles and made them dependent on
quasi-natural forces. The Marxists, following Lukács, called this state of things
'reification' and ascribed it, as did Marx, to the all-powerful effect of money as
a leveller in capitalist conditions. Existentialism did not concern itself with
explanations such as the class struggle or property relationships, but it too was
fundamentally a protest against the culture of developed industrial societies,
reducing the human individual to the sum of his social functions. The category
of 'authenticity' or 'authentic being' (*Eigentlichkeit*), which plays an essential
part in Heidegger's early writings, was an attempt to vindicate the irreducible
identity of the individual subject as against the anonymous social forces
summed up in the term 'the impersonal' (*das Man*).

Adorno's attack on German existentialism was thus perfectly understandable: he wished to assert the claim of the Frankfurt school to be the sole
fighter against 'reification', and to prove that existentialism, while appearing
to criticize reification, in reality endorsed it. This is the purpose of *Jargon der
Eigentlichkeit: zur deutschen Ideologie* (1964), in which he joins issue principally with Heidegger but also with Jaspers and occasionally Buber, Bollnow,
and others. Adorno accepts the idea of 'reification' and the Marxist view that
it results from the subjection of human beings to exchange-value, but he
rejects the idea of the proletariat as the saviour of humanity and does not
believe that 'reification' can be done away with simply by nationalizing means
of production.

The main points of Adorno's attack on existentialism are as follows.

Firstly, the existentialists have created a deceptive language, the elements of which are intended, by some peculiar 'aura', to arouse a magic faith in the independent power of words. This is a rhetorical technique which precedes any content and is merely designed to make it appear profound. The magic of words is supposed to take the place of an analysis of the true sources of 'reification' and to suggest that it can be cured simply by incantations. In reality, however, words cannot directly express irreducible subjectivity, nor can they generate 'authentic being': it is quite possible to adopt the watchword of 'authenticism' and believe that one has escaped from reification, while in fact remaining subject to it. Moreover—and this seems to be the essential point—'authenticism' is a purely formal catchword or incantation. The existentialists do not tell us in what way we are to be 'authentic': if it suffices simply to be what we are, then an oppressor and murderer is doing his duty by being just that. In short (though Adorno does not put the point in these words), 'authenticism' does not imply any specific values and can be expressed in any behaviour whatsoever. Another deceptive concept is that of 'authentic communication' as opposed to the mechanical exchange of verbal stereotypes. By talking of authentic communication the existentialists seek to persuade people that they can cure social oppression simply by expressing thoughts to one another, and conversation is thus turned into a substitute for what should come after it (Adorno does not explain what this is).

Secondly, 'authenticism' cannot in any case be a cure for reification because it is not interested in its sources, namely the rule of commodity fetishism and exchange-value; it suggests that anyone can make his own life authentic, while society as a whole continues to be under the spell of reification. This is a classic case of distracting people's attention from the real causes of heir slavery, by conjuring up the illusion that freedom can be realized in the individual consciousness without any change in the conditions of communal life.

Thirdly, the effect of existentialism is to petrify the whole area of 'non-authentic' life as a metaphysical entity which cannot be done away with but can only be resisted by an effort confined to one's own existence. Heidegger, for instance, speaks of empty, everyday chatter as a manifestation of the reified world, but he regards it as a permanent feature, not realizing that it would not exist in a rational economy that did not squander money on advertising.

Fourthly, existentialism tends to perpetuate reification not only by distracting attention from social conditions but by the way in which it defines existence. According to Heidegger, individual human existence (*Dasein*) is a matter of self-possession and self-reference. All social content is excluded from the idea of authenticity, which consists of willing to possess oneself. In this way Heidegger actually reifies human subjectivity, reducing it to a tautological state of 'being oneself', unrelated to the world outside.

Adorno also attacks Heidegger's attempts to investigate the roots of language, which he regards as part of a general tendency to glorify bygone times, Arcadian rusticity, etc., and consequently as related to the Nazi ideology of 'blood and soil'.

Adorno's criticism follows the main lines of conventional Marxist attacks on 'bourgeois philosophy': existentialism makes a pretence of fighting reification but in fact aggravates it by leaving social problems out of account and promising the individual that he can have 'true life' by simply deciding to 'be himself'. In other words, the objection is that the 'jargon of authenticity' contains no political programme. This is true, but the same could be said of Adorno's own jargon of reification and negation. The proposition that we must constantly set our faces against a civilization subject to the levelling pressures of exchange-value does not itself imply any specific rule of social behaviour. The case is different with orthodox Marxists, who maintain that reification with all its baneful consequences will cease when all factories are taken over by the state; but Adorno specifically rejects this conclusion. He condemns society based on exchange-value without giving any indication of what an alternative society would be like; and there is something hypocritical in his indignation at the existentialists' failure to provide a blueprint for the future.

Adorno is certainly right in saying that 'authenticism' is a purely formal value from which no conclusions or moral rules can be deduced. It is dangerous, moreover, to set it up as the supreme virtue, since it affords no moral protection against the idea that, for example, the commander of a concentration camp can, by behaving as such, achieve perfect fulfilment as a human being. In other words, Heidegger's anthropology is amoral inasmuch as it contains no definition of values; but is 'critical theory' in any better case? True, it includes 'reason' and 'freedom' among its basic concepts. But we are told little of 'reason' in its higher dialectical form except that it is not bound by the trivialities of logic or the cult of empirical data, and as regards 'freedom' we are chiefly told what it is not. It is neither bourgeois freedom, which enhances reification instead of curing it, nor is it freedom as promised and realized by Marxism–Leninism, for that is slavery. Clearly, it must be something better than these, but it is hard to say what. We cannot anticipate Utopia in positive terms; the most we can do is negatively to transcend the existing world. Thus the precepts of critical theory are no more than a call to unspecified action, and are just as formal as Heidegger's 'authenticism'.

5. Critique of 'enlightenment'

ALTHOUGH Horkheimer's and Adorno's *Dialectic of Enlightenment* consists of loose and uncoordinated reflections, it contains some basic ideas which can be reduced to a kind of system. Written towards the end of the Second World War, the book is dominated by the question of Nazism, which, in the authors' view, was not simply a monstrous freak but rather a drastic manifestation of the universal barbarism into which humanity was falling. They attributed this decline to the consistent operation of the very same values, ideals, and rules that had once lifted mankind out of barbarism, and that were summed up in the concept of 'enlightenment'. By this they did not mean the specific eighteenth-century movement to which the term is usually applied, but the 'most general sense of progressive thought . . . aimed at liberating men from fear and establishing their sovereignty' (*Dialectic of Enlightenment*, p. 3). The 'dialectic' consisted in the fact that the movement which aimed to conquer nature and emancipate reason from the shackles of mythology had, by its own inner logic, turned into its opposite. It had created a positivist, pragmatist, utilitarian ideology and, by reducing the world to its purely quantitative aspects, had annihilated meaning, barbarized the arts and sciences, and increasingly subjected mankind to 'commodity fetishism'. The *Dialectic of Enlightenment* is not a historical treatise but a collection of haphazardly chosen and unexplained examples to illustrate various forms of the debasement of 'enlightened' ideals; after some introductory remarks on the concept of enlightenment it includes chapters on Odysseus, the marquis de Sade, the entertainment industry, and anti-Semitism.

Enlightenment, seeking to liberate men from the oppressive sense of mystery in the world, simply declared that what was mysterious did not exist. It aspired to a form of knowledge that would enable man to rule over nature, and it therefore deprived knowledge of significance, jettisoning such notions as substance, quality, and causality and preserving only what might serve the purpose of manipulating things. It aimed to give unity to the whole of knowledge and culture and to reduce all qualities to a common measure; thus it was responsible for the imposition of mathematical standards on science and for creating an economy based on exchange-value, i.e. transforming goods of every kind into so many units of abstract labour-time. Increased dominion over nature meant alienation from nature, and likewise increased domination over human beings; the theory of knowledge produced by enlightenment implied that we know things in so far as we have power over them, and this was true in both the physical and the social world. It also signified that reality had no meaning in itself but only took its meaning from the subject, while at the same time subject and object were completely separate from each other. Science ascribed reality only to what might occur more than once—as if in imitation of the 'repetition principle' that governs mythological thinking. It sought to contain the world within a system of categories, turning individual things and human beings into abstractions and thus creating the ideological foundations of totalitarianism. The abstractness of thought went hand in hand with the domination of man by man: 'The universality of ideas as developed by discursive logic, domination in the conceptual sphere, is raised up on the basis of actual domination' (p. 14). Enlightenment in its developed form regards every object as self-identical; the idea that a thing may be what it is not yet is rejected as a relic of mythology.

The urge to enclose the world in a single conceptual system, and the propensity to deductive thinking, are especially pernicious aspects of enlightenment and are a menace to freedom.

> For enlightenment is as totalitarian as any system. Its untruth does not consist in what its romantic enemies have always reproached it for: analytical method, return to elements, dissolution through reflective thought; but instead in the fact that for enlightenment the process (*Prozess*) is always decided from the start. When in mathematical procedure the unknown becomes the unknown quantity of an equation, this marks it as the well-known even before any value is inserted. Nature, before and after the quantum theory, is that which is to be comprehended mathematically ... In the anticipated identification of the wholly conceived and mathematized world with truth, enlightenment intends to secure itself against the return of the mythic. It confounds thought and mathematics ... Thinking objectifies itself to become an automatic, self-activating process ... Mathematical procedure becomes, so to speak, the ritual of thinking ... it turns thought into a thing, an instrument. (*Dialectic of Enlightenment*, pp. 24–5)

Enlightenment, in short, will not and cannot grasp what is new; it is only interested in what is recurrent, what is already known. But, contrary to the rules of enlightenment, thought is not a matter of perception, classification, and counting; it consists in 'the determinate negation of each successive immediacy' (*bestimmende Negation des je Unmittelbaren*) (ibid., p. 27)—i.e., presumably, in advancing beyond what is to what may be. Enlightenment turns the world into a tautology, and thus reverts to the myth which it sought to destroy. By restricting thought to 'facts' which must then be arranged in an abstract 'system', enlightenment sanctifies what is, that is to say social injustice; industrialism 'reifies' human subjectivity, and commodity fetishism prevails in every sphere of life.

The rationalism of enlightenment, while enhancing man's power over nature, also increased the power of some human beings over others, and by this token it has outlived its usefulness. The root of the evil was the division of labour and, along with it, the alienation of man from nature; domination became the one purpose of thought, and thought itself was thereby destroyed. Socialism adopted the bourgeois style of thinking, which regarded nature as completely alien and thus made it totalitarian. In this way enlightenment embarked on a suicidal course, and the only hope of salvation seems to consist in theory: 'true revolutionary practice (*umwälzende Praxis*) depends on the intransigence of theory in the face of the insensibility (*Bewusstlosigkeit*) with which society allows thought to ossify' (p. 41).

According to the *Dialectic of Enlightenment* the legend of Odysseus is a prototype or symbol of the isolation of the individual precisely because he is fully socialized. The hero escapes from the Cyclops by calling himself 'Noman': to preserve his existence, he destroys it. As the authors put it, 'This linguistic adaptation to death contains the schema of modern mathematics' (p. 60). In general the legend shows that a civilization in which men seek to affirm themselves is only possible through self-denial and repression; thus, in enlightenment, the dialectic takes on a Freudian aspect.

The perfect epitome of eighteenth-century enlightenment was the marquis de Sade, who carried the ideology of domination to its utmost logical consequence. Enlightenment treats human beings as repeatable and replaceable (hence 'reified') elements of an abstract 'system', and this too is the meaning of de Sade's way of life. The totalitarian idea latent in enlightenment philosophy assimilates human characteristics to interchangeable commodities. Reason and feeling are reduced to an impersonal level; rationalist planning degenerates into totalitarian terror; morality is derided and despised as a manœuvre by the weak to protect themselves against the strong (an anticipation of Nietzsche); and all traditional virtues are declared inimical to reason and illusory, a view already implicit in Descartes's division of man into an extended and a thinking substance.

The destruction of reason, feeling, subjectivity, quality, and nature itself by the unholy combination of mathematics, logic, and exchange-value is especially seen in the degradation of culture, a crying example of which is the modern entertainment industry. A single system dominated by commercial values has taken over every aspect of mass culture. Everything serves to perpetuate the power of capital—even the fact that the workers have attained a fairly high standard of living and that people can find clean homes to live in. Mass-produced culture kills creativity; it is not justified by the demand for it, since that demand is itself part of the system. In Germany at one time the state at least protected the higher forms of culture against the operation of the market, but this is now over and artists are the slaves of their customers. Novelty is anathema; both the output and the enjoyment of art are planned in advance, as they must be if art is to survive market competition. In this way art itself, contrary to its primal function, helps to destroy individuality and turn human beings into stereotypes. The authors lament that art has become so cheap and accessible, for this inevitably means its degradation.

In general their concept of 'enlightenment' is a fanciful, unhistorical hybrid composed of everything they dislike: positivism, logic, deductive and empirical science, capitalism, the money power, mass culture, liberalism, and Fascism. Their critique of culture—apart from some true observations, which have since become commonplace, on the harmfulness of commercialized art—is imbued with nostalgia for the days when the enjoyment of culture was reserved to the élite: it is an attack on the 'age of the common man' in a spirit of feudal contempt for the masses. Mass society was attacked from various quarters even in the last century, by Tocqueville, Renan, Burckhardt, and Nietzsche among others; what is new in Horkheimer and Adorno is that they combine this attack with an onslaught on positivism and science, and that, following Marx, they discern the root of the evil in the division of labour, 'reification', and the domination of exchange-value. They go much further than Marx, however: the original sin of enlightenment, according to them, was to cut man off from nature and treat the latter as a mere object of exploitation, with the result that man was assimilated to the natural order and was exploited likewise. This process found its ideological reflection in science, which is not interested in qualities but only in what can be expressed quantitatively and made to serve technical purposes.

The attack, it can be seen, is essentially in line with the romantic tradition. But the authors do not offer any way out of the state of decadence: they do not say how man can become friends with nature again, or how to get rid of exchange-value and live without money or calculation. The only remedy they have to offer is theoretical reasoning, and we may suspect that its chief merit in their eyes is to be free from the despotism of logic and mathematics (logic, they tell us, signifies contempt for the individual).

It is noteworthy that whereas socialists formerly denounced capitalism for producing poverty, the main grievance of the Frankfurt school is that it engenders abundance and satisfies a multiplicity of needs, and is thus injurious to the higher forms of culture.

The *Dialectic of Enlightenment* contains all the elements of Marcuse's later attack on modern philosophy, which allegedly favours totalitarianism by maintaining a positivist 'neutralism' in regard to the world of values and by insisting that human knowledge should be controlled by 'facts'. This strange paralogism, equating the observance of empirical and logical rules with fidelity to the *status quo* and rejection of all change, recurs again and again in the writings of the Frankfurt school. If the supposed link between positivism and social conservatism or totalitarianism (the authors treat these as one and the same!) is studied in the light of history, the evidence is all the other way: positivists, from Hume onwards, were wedded to the liberal tradition. Clearly, there is no logical connection either. If the fact that scientific observation is 'neutral' towards its object and abstains from evaluation implies that it favours the *status quo*, we should have to maintain that physio-pathological observation implies approval of disease and a belief that it should not be combated.

Admittedly, there is an essential difference between medicine and social science (though the remarks of the Frankfurt philosophers in this context purport to apply to all human knowledge). In the social sciences, observation itself is part of the subject-matter, if that is taken to include the entire social picture. But it does not follow that a scientist who abstains as far as he can from value-judgements is an agent of social stability or conformism; he may or may not be, but nothing can be inferred in this respect from the fact that his observation is 'external' and uncommitted. If, on the other hand, the observer is 'committed' not only in the sense of having some practical interest in view but also in regarding his cognitive activity as part of a certain social practice, he is more or less obliged to regard as true whatever seems conducive to the particular interest with which he identifies, i.e. apply genetic, pragmatic criteria of truth. If this principle were adopted, science as we know it would disappear and be replaced by political propaganda. Undoubtedly, various political interests and preferences are reflected in various ways in social science; but a rule which sought to generalize such influences instead of minimizing them would turn science into a tool of politics, as has happened with social science in totalitarian states. Theoretical observation and discussion would completely forfeit their autonomy, which is the reverse of what the Frankfurt writers would wish, as they indicate elsewhere.

It is also true that scientific observation does not of itself produce aims; this is the case even if some value-judgements are implicit in the rules prescribing the conditions under which certain statements or hypotheses become part of science. The canons of scientific procedures are not, of course, infringed by the fact that the investigator wants to discover something that will serve practical ends, or that his interest is inspired by some practical concern. But they are infringed if, on the pretext of 'overcoming' the dichotomy of facts and values (and the Frankfurt writers, like many other Marxists, are constantly boasting of having done this), the truth of science is subordinated to the criteria of any interest whatsoever; this simply means that anything is right which suits the interests with which the scientist identifies himself.

The rules of empirical observation have evolved for centuries in the European mind, from the late Middle Ages onwards. That their development was somehow connected with the spread of a market economy is possible, though certainly not proved; on this as on most other subjects, the proponents of 'critical theory' offer only bare assertions, devoid of historical analysis. If there actually is a historical link, it still by no means follows that these rules are an instrument of 'commodity fetishism' and a mainstay of capitalism; any such assumption is in fact pure nonsense. The writers we are discussing seem to believe that there is, at any rate potentially, some alternative science which would satisfy the demands of human nature, but they cannot tell us anything about it. Their 'critical theory' is in fact not so much a theory as a general statement that theory is of great importance, which few would deny, and a plea for a critical attitude towards existing society, which we are invited to 'transcend' in thought. This injunction, however, makes no sense as long as they cannot tell us in what direction the existing order is to be transcended. From this point of view, as we have already noted, orthodox Marxism is more specific, as it does at least claim that once the means of production are publicly owned and the Communist party installed in power, only a few minor technical problems will stand in the way of universal freedom and happiness. These assurances are completely refuted by experience, but at least we know what they mean.

The *Dialectic of Enlightenment* and other works of the Frankfurt school contain many sound remarks on the commercialization of art in industrial society and the inferiority of cultural products dependent on the market. But the authors are on very doubtful ground when they say that this has led to the degradation of art as a whole and of the artistic enjoyment open to people in general. If this were so it would mean that, for instance, country folk in the eighteenth century enjoyed some higher forms of culture, but that capitalism gradually deprived them of these and substituted crude, mass-produced objects and entertainments. It is not obvious, however, that eighteenth-century rustics enjoyed higher artistic values, in the form of church ceremonies, popular sports and dances, than television offers to present-day workers. So-called 'higher' culture has not disappeared, but has become incomparably more accessible than ever before, and is undoubtedly enjoyed by more people: while it is highly unconvincing to argue that its dramatic formal changes in the twentieth century are all explicable by the domination of exchange-value.

Adorno, who refers to the degradation of art in many of his writings, seems to think that the present situation is hopeless, i.e. that there is no source of strength which would enable art to revive and perform its proper function. On the one hand, there is 'affirmative' art, which accepts the present situation and pretends to find harmony where there is only chaos (for example, Stravinsky); on the other, there are attempts at resistance, but, as they have no roots in the real world, even geniuses (for example, Schönberg) are forced into escapism, shutting themselves up in self-sufficient realms of their own artistic material. The *avant-garde* movement is a negation, but for the present at least it can be nothing more; as far as it goes it is true for our time, unlike mass culture and bogus 'affirmative' art, but it is a feeble and depressing truth, expressive of cultural bankruptcy. The last word of Adorno's theory of culture is apparently that we must protest, but that protest will be unavailing. We cannot recapture the values of the past, those of the present are debased and barbarous, and the future offers none; all that is left to us is a gesture of total negation, deprived of content by its very totality.

If the foregoing is a true account of Adorno's work, not only can we not regard it as a continuation of Marx's thought, but it is diametrically opposed to the latter by reason of its pessimism: failing a positive Utopia, its final response to the human condition can only be an inarticulate cry.

6. Erich Fromm

ERICH FROMM (b. 1900), who has lived in the U.S.A. since 1932, began as an orthodox Freudian but is primarily known as a co-founder of the 'culturalist' school of psychoanalysis, together with Karen Horney and Harry Sullivan. This school departed so radically from the Freudian tradition (except for sharing the same general field of interest) as to leave little of the original bases of psycho-analytical anthropology, the theory of culture, and even the theory of neuroses. Fromm may be regarded as a cousin of the Frankfurt school, not only because he belonged to the Institut für Sozialforschung and published articles in the *Journal,* but also in view of the content of his work. He shared the conviction of his Frankfurt colleagues that the Marxian analyses of reification and alien-ation were still valid and were vital to the solution of the basic problems of modern civilization. Like the others, he did not agree with Marx as to the lib-erating role of the proletariat; alienation, in which he was specially interested, was a phenomenon affecting all social classes. He did not, however, share Adorno's negativism and pessimism. Although he had no faith in historical determinism and did not expect the laws of history to bring about a better social order, he was convinced that human beings had an immense creative potential which could be brought into play to overcome their alienation from nature and one another and to establish an order based on brotherly love. Unlike Adorno, he believed it possible to define in broad lines the character of a social life in harmony with human nature. Again, unlike Adorno, whose books are full of pride and arrogance, Fromm's writings are imbued with good-will and faith in the human capacity for friendship and co-operation; it was for this reason, perhaps, that he found Freudianism unacceptable. He may be called the Feuerbach of our time. His books are simple and readable; their didactic and moralistic intention is not concealed, but is expressed plainly and straightforwardly. Whatever their immediate subject—the theory of character, Zen Buddhism, Marx, or Freud—all are inspired by critical and constructive thought. Among the titles are *Escape from Freedom* (1941), *Man for Himself* (1947), *The Sane Society* (1955); *Zen Buddhism* and *Psychoanalysis* (with D. T. Suzuki and R. de Martino, 1960), and *Marx's Concept of Man* (1961).

Fromm believes that Freud's theory of the unconscious opened up an extremely fertile field of inquiry, but he rejects almost completely the theory of anthropology based on the libido and the purely repressive functions of culture. Freud held that the human individual can be defined by the instinctual energies that inevitably oppose him to others; the individual is antisocial by nature, but society exists to give him a measure of security in return for the limitation and repression of his instinctive desires. Unsatisfied desires are channelled into other, socially permitted areas and are sublimated into cultural activity; however, culture and social life continue to police the impulses that cannot be destroyed, and the cultural products that are created as a substitute for unfulfilled desires help to curb those impulses still further. Man's position in the world is hopeless inasmuch as the satisfaction of his natural cravings would mean the ruin of civilization and the destruction of the human race. The conflict between the demands of instinct and the communal life which is necessary to human beings can never be resolved, nor can the complex of causes which incessantly drive them into neurotic solutions. Sublimation in the form of creative activity is only a substitute, and moreover it is only available to the few.

To this Fromm replies that Freud's doctrine is an illegitimate universalization of a particular limited historical experience, and, moreover, is based on a false theory of human nature. It is not the case that an individual can be defined by the sum of his instinctive desires, directed exclusively towards his own satisfaction and consequently hostile to others. Freud talks as if, by giving something of himself to others, a man parts with a piece of wealth that he might have kept; but love and friendship are an enrichment and not a sacrifice. Freud's view is a reflection of particular social conditions causing the interests of individuals to conflict with one another; but this is a historical phase, not a necessary effect of human nature. Egoism and egocentricity are not protective but destructive of the individual's interests, and they spring from self-hatred rather than self-love.

Fromm concedes that man is equipped with certain permanent instincts, and that in this sense one can speak of unchanging human nature. He even holds that the contrary view, that there are no anthropological constants, is a dangerous one, as it suggests that human beings are infinitely malleable and can adapt to any conditions, so that slavery, if properly organized, could last for ever. The fact that people do rebel against existing conditions shows that they are not infinitely adaptable, and this is a ground for optimism. But the main thing is to ascertain which human traits are really constant and which are a matter of history; and here Freud went badly wrong, mistaking the effects of capitalist civilization for unalterable characteristics of the human race.

In general, Fromm continues, human needs are not confined to individual satisfaction. People need links with nature and with one another—not just any links, but such as to give them a sense of purpose and belonging to a community; they need love and understanding, and they suffer when isolated and deprived of contact. A human being also needs conditions in which he can make full use of his abilities: he is not born simply to cope with conditions and dangers, but to engage in creative work.

For this reason the development of the human species, or the self-creation of man, has been a history of conflicting tendencies. Ever since man freed himself from the natural order and thus became truly human, the need for security and the creative urge have often been opposed to each other. We want freedom, but we are also afraid of it, for freedom signifies responsibility and the absence of security. Consequently, men take refuge from the burden of freedom in submission to authority and in closed systems; this is an inborn tendency, though a destructive one, a false escape from isolation into self-renunciation. Another form of escape is hatred, in which man tries to overcome his isolation by blind destruction.

On the basis of these views, Fromm distinguishes psychological types or orientations which differ from Freud's in that they are explained in terms of social conditions and family relationships and not merely by the distribution of the libido; moreover, unlike Freud, he expressly labels them good or bad. Characters are formed from infancy by the child's surroundings and the system of punishments and rewards that it encounters. The 'receptive' type is characterized by compliance, optimism, and passive benevolence; people of this kind are adaptable but lack creative power. The 'exploitative' type, on the contrary, is aggressive, envious, and inclined to treat others purely as a source of profit to itself. The 'hoarding' type expresses itself less in active aggression and more in hostile suspicion; it is stingy, self-centred, and inclined to sterile fastidiousness. Another unproductive type is the 'marketing' orientation, which derives satisfaction from adapting itself to prevailing fashions and customs. Creative characters, on the other hand, are neither aggressive nor conformist, but seek contact with others in a spirit of kindness combined with initiative and a measure of non-conformity. This is the best combination of all, as their non-conformity does not degenerate into aggression, while their desire for co-operation and capacity for love does not sink into passive adaptation. These various characters correspond to the typology previously worked out by Freudians, especially Abraham, but Fromm's explanation of their origin emphasizes not the infant's successive sexual fixations but the part played by the family circle and the values current in society.

Capitalist society as developed in Europe in the last few hundred years has liberated huge creative possibilities in human beings, but also powerful destructive elements. Men have become aware of their individual dignity and responsibility, but have found themselves in a situation dominated by universal competition and conflict of interests. Personal initiative has become a decisive factor in life, but increased importance also attaches to aggression and exploitation. The sum total of loneliness and isolation has grown beyond measure, while social conditions cause people to treat one another as things and not as persons. One of the delusive and dangerous remedies against isolation is to seek protection in irrational authoritarian systems such as Fascism.

In Fromm's view his radical revision of Freudianism has a Marxist complexion, both because it explains human relationships in terms of history and not of defence mechanisms and instinctual energy, and because it is based on value-judgements in harmony with Marx's thought. Fromm regards the Manuscripts of 1844 as the fundamental exposition of Marx's doctrine; he insists that there is no essential change between that work and *Capital* (on which point he joins issue with Daniel Bell), but he considers that the *élan* of the early texts is somewhat lost in the later works. The central issue, he contends, is that of alienation, representing the sum of human bondage, isolation, unhappiness, and misfortune. Totalitarian doctrines and Communist regimes have in his view nothing in common with Marx's humanistic vision, the chief values of which are voluntary solidarity, the expansion of man's creative powers, freedom from constraint and from irrational authority.

Marx's ideas are a revolt against conditions in which men and women lose their humanity and are turned into commodities, but also an optimistic profession of faith in their ability to become human once again, to achieve not only freedom from poverty but freedom to develop their creative powers as well. It is absurd to interpret Marx's historical materialism to signify that people are always actuated by material interests. On the contrary, Marx believed that they forfeited their true nature when circumstances compelled them to care for nothing but such interests. To Marx, the main problem was how to free the individual from the shackles of dependence and enable human beings to live together in amity once more. Marx did not hold that man must be eternally the plaything of irrational forces beyond his control; on the contrary, he maintained that man could be the master of his fate. If, in practice, the alienated products of human labour turned into anti-human forces, if people were enthralled by false consciousness and false needs and if (as both Freud and Marx held) they did not understand their own true motives, all this was not because nature had so ruled forever. On the contrary, a society dominated by competition, isolation, exploitation, and enmity was a contradiction of human nature, which—as Marx believed no less than Hegel or Goethe—found its true satisfaction in creative work and fellowship, not in aggression or passive adaptation. Marx wanted men to return to unity with nature and among themselves, thus bridging the gulf between subject and object; Fromm, who especially stresses this motif from the 1844 Manuscripts, observes that Marx is in agreement here with the whole tradition of German humanism and also with Zen Buddhism. Of course Marx wanted to see an end to poverty, but he did not want consumption to increase indefinitely. He was concerned with human dignity and freedom; his socialism was not a matter of satisfying material needs but of creating conditions in which men could realize their own personalities and be reconciled with nature and one another. Marx's themes were the alienation of labour, the loss of meaning in the labour process, the transformation of human beings into commodities; the basic evil of capitalism, in his view, was not the unjust distribution of goods but the degradation of mankind, the destruction of the 'essence' of humanity. This degradation affected everyone, not only the workers, and accordingly Marx's message of emancipation was universal and did not only apply to the proletariat. Marx believed that human beings could understand their own nature rationally and, by so doing, free themselves from false needs that conflicted with it; this they could do for themselves, within the historical process, without any help from extra-historical sources. In maintaining this, Fromm believes, Marx was in line not only with Utopian thinkers of the Renaissance and Enlightenment but also with chiliastic sects, the Hebrew prophets, and even Thomism.

In Fromm's view the whole question of human liberation is summed up in the word 'love', which implies treating others as an end and not a means; it also signifies that the individual does not give up his own creativity or lose himself in the other's Personality. Aggressivity and passivity are two sides of the same Phenomenon of degradation, and must both be replaced by a system of relations based on fellow-feeling without conformism and creativity without aggression.

As this summary indicates, Fromm's endorsement of Marx rests on a true interpretation of his humanistic outlook, but is nevertheless highly selective. Fromm does not consider the positive functions of alienation or the role of evil in history; to him as to Feuerbach, alienation is simply bad. Moreover, Fromm adopted from Marx only the ultimate idea of the 'whole human being', the Utopia of reunion with nature and perfect solidarity among mankind, helped and not hindered by individual creativity. He endorses this Utopia, but ignores all that part of Marx's doctrine which tells us how to bring it about—his theory of the state, the proletariat, and revolution. In so doing he has chosen the most acceptable and least controversial aspects of Marxism: for anyone would agree that people should live on good terms and not cut one another's throats, and that it is better to be free and creative than stifled and oppressed. In short, Fromm's Marxism is little more than a series of trite aspirations. Nor is it clear from his analysis how men came to be dominated by evil and alienation, or what ground there is for hoping that healthy tendencies will in the end prevail over destructive ones. Fromm's ambiguity is typical of utopian thought in general. On the one hand, he professes to derive his ideal from human nature as it actually is, although it is not at present realized—in other words, it is man's true destiny to develop his personality while living in harmony with others; but, on the other hand, he is aware that 'human nature' is also a normative concept. Clearly, the concept of alienation (or the de-humanization of man) and also the distinction between false and true needs must, if they are to be more than mere arbitrary norms, be based on some theory of human nature as we know it from experience, albeit in an 'undeveloped' state. But Fromm does not explain how we know that human nature requires, for instance, more solidarity and less aggression. It is true that people are in fact capable of solidarity, love, friendship, and self-sacrifice, but it does not follow that those who display these qualities are more 'human' than their opposites. Fromm's account of human nature thus presents an ambiguous mixture of descriptive and normative ideas, which is likewise characteristic of Marx and many of his followers.

Fromm did much to popularize the idea of Marx as a humanist, and was undoubtedly right to combat the crude and primitive interpretation of Marxism as a 'materialistic' theory of human motives and short cut to despotism. But he did not discuss the relationship between Marxism and modern Communism, saying merely that Communist totalitarianism was contrary to the ideals of the 1844 Manuscripts. His picture of Marx is thus almost as one-sided and simplistic as the one he criticizes, which presents Marxism as a blueprint for Stalinism. As for the pre-established harmony between Marxism and Zen Buddhism, it is based on a few sentences in the Manuscripts about a return to union with nature. These are no doubt consonant with the young Marx's apocalyptic idea of a total and absolute reconciliation of everything with everything else, but it is an exaggeration to regard them as part of the hard core of Marxist doctrine. Fromm in fact retains only that part of Marx's doctrine which he held in common with Rousseau.

7. Critical theory (continued). Jürgen Habermas

HABERMAS (b. 1929) ranks as one of the chief living German philosophers. The titles of his principal books—*Theorie und Praxis* (1963), *Erkenntnis und Interesse* (1968), *Technik und Wissenschaft als 'Ideologie'* (1970)—indicate his main philosophical interests. His work comprises an anti-positivist analysis of all kinds of links between theoretical reasoning—not only in the historical and social sciences, but also in natural history—and the practical needs, interests, and behaviour of human beings. It is not, however, a sociology of knowledge, but rather an epistemological critique designed to show that no theory can be properly based on the criteria propounded by the positivist and analytical schools, that positivism always contains assumptions dictated by non-theoretical interests, but that it is possible to find a viewpoint from which practical interest and the theoretical approach coincide. These are topics that certainly fall within the sphere of interest of the Frankfurt school; but Habermas displays more analytical precision than his mentors of the previous generation.

Habermas takes up Horkheimer's and Adorno's theme of the 'dialectic of the Enlightenment'—the process whereby Reason, striving to emancipate mankind from prejudice, by its own inner logic turns against itself and serves to maintain prejudice and authority. In the classic period of the Enlightenment, represented by Holbach, Reason saw itself as a weapon in the social and intellectual battle against the existing order, and it upheld the essential virtue of boldness in attack. Evil and falsity were one and the same in its eyes, and so were liberation and truth. It did not seek to dispense with evaluation, but declared openly the values by which it was guided. Fichte's Reason, which based itself on the Kantian critique and therefore could not invoke the oracle of empiricism, was nevertheless also conscious of its own practical character. The acts of understanding and of constituting the world coincided in it, as did Reason and Will; the practical interest of the self-liberating ego was no longer separate from the theoretical activity of Reason. For Marx too, Reason was a critical power, but, in contrast to Fichte's view, its strength was not rooted in moral consciousness but in the fact that its emancipating activity coincided with the process of social emancipation; the critique of false consciousness was at the same time a practical act of abolishing the social conditions to which false consciousness was due. Thus the Enlightenment in Marx's version expressly maintained the link between Reason and interest. However, with the progress of science, technology, and organization that link was broken; Reason gradually lost its emancipating function, while rationality was more and more restricted to technical efficiency, no longer proposing aims but merely organizing means. Reason took on an instrumental character, abandoning its meaning-generating function to serve the ends of material or social technology; the Enlightenment turned against itself. The delusion that Reason was independent of human interests was sanctioned as the epistemology of positivism, as a scientific programme free from value-judgements and thus incapable of performing emancipative functions.

Habermas, however, like the rest of the Frankfurt school, is not concerned with the 'primacy of practice' in Lukács's sense or in that of pragmatism. He is concerned with a return to the idea of praxis as distinct from technique, i.e. restoring the concept of Reason aware of its practical functions, not subject to any aims imposed 'from outside' but somehow comprising social aims by virtue of its own rationality. He therefore seeks an intellectual faculty which can synthesize practical and theoretical reason, as it is capable of identifying the sense of objects and thus neither can nor will be neutral as regards aims.

The essence of Habermas's critique, however, lies in his contention that such neutrality has not been, and never could be, actually attained, and that positivist programmes and the idea of theory liberated from value are therefore an illusion of the Enlightenment in its stage of self-destruction. Husserl rightly argued that the so-called facts or objects posited by natural science as ready-made reality, unconstructed things-in-themselves, are in fact organized in a primal, spontaneously created *Lebenswelt*, and that every science takes over from pre-reflective reason a repertoire of forms dictated by various practical human interests. He was wrong, however, in supposing that his own idea of a theory purged of these practical residua might later be used for practical ends; for phenomenology cannot propose any cosmology, any idea of universal order, and such an idea is indispensable if theory is to have a practical purpose. The natural sciences, Habermas goes on, are constituted on the basis of technical interest. They are not neutral in the sense that their content is uninfluenced by practical considerations; the material they are prepared to admit to their store is not a reflection of facts as they exist in the world, but an expression of the effectiveness of practical technical operations. The historico-hermeneutic sciences are also in part determined by practical interests, though in another way: in their case the 'interest' consists in preserving and enlarging the possible area of understanding among human beings, so as to improve communication. Theoretical activity cannot escape from practical interest: the subject–object relationship must itself involve some degree of interest, and no part of human knowledge is intelligible except in relation to the history of the human race, in which these practical interests are crystallized; all cognitive criteria owe their validity to the interest by which cognition is governed. Interest operates in three spheres or 'media'—work, language, and authority—and to these types of interest correspond respectively the natural, the historico-hermeneutic, and the social sciences. In self-reflection, however, or 'reflection on reflection', interest and cognition coincide, and it is in this realm that 'emancipative reason' takes shape. If we cannot discover the point at which reason and will, or the determination of ends and the analysis of means, coincide, we are condemned to a situation in which, on the one hand, we have an apparently neutral science and, on the other, fundamentally irrational decisions as to ends: the latter cannot then be rationally criticized, each is as good as any other.

Habermas does not go so far as Marcuse in criticizing science: he does not claim that the very content of modern science, as opposed to its technical application, serves anti-human ends, or that modern technology is inherently destructive and cannot be used for the good of humanity, but must be replaced by technology of a different kind. To say this would only make sense if we could propose alternatives to existing science and technology, which Marcuse is unable to do. All the same, science and technology are not wholly innocent in respect of their applications, when these take the form of weapons of mass destruction and the organization of tyranny. The point is that modern productive forces and science have become elements of the political legitimation of modern industrial societies. 'Traditional societies' based on the legality of their institutions on mythical, religious, or metaphysical interpretations of the world. Capitalism, by setting in motion the self-propelling mechanism of the development of productive forces, has institutionalized the phenomenon of change and novelty, overthrown the traditional principles of the legitimation of authority, and replaced them by norms corresponding to those of equivalent commercial exchange—the rule of mutuality as the basis of social organization. In this way property relations have lost their directly political significance and become production relations governed by the laws of the market. The natural sciences began to define their scope in terms of technical application. At the same time, as capitalism evolved, state intervention in the field of production and exchange became more and more important, with the result that politics ceased to be only part of the 'superstructure'. The political activity of the state— represented as a purely technical means of improving the organization of public life—tended to merge with science and technology, which were supposed to serve the same purpose; the dividing line between productive forces and the legitimation of power became obscured, in contrast to the capitalism of Marx's day when productive and political functions were clearly separate. Thus Marx's theory of the base and superstructure began to be out of date, as did his theory of value (having regard to the enormous importance of science as productive force). Science and technology took on 'ideological' functions in the sense that they produced an image of society based on a technical model, and technocratic ideologies which deprive people of political consciousness (i.e. awareness of social aims), by implying that all human problems are of a technical and organizational character and can be solved by scientific means. The technocratic mentality makes it easier to manipulate people without violence and is a further step towards 'reification', blurring the distinction between technical activity, which in itself has nothing to say about aims, and specifically human relationships. In a situation where state institutions have a powerful influence on the economy, social conflicts too have changed their character and bear less and less resemblance to class antagonism as Marx understood it. The new ideology is no longer merely an ideology but is merged with the very process of technical progress; it is harder to identify, with the result that ideology and real social conditions can no longer be contrasted as they were by Marx.

The increase of productive forces does not itself have an emancipating effect; on the contrary, in its 'ideologized' form it tends to make people apprehend themselves as things, and to obliterate the distinction between technology and praxis—the latter term signifying the spontaneous activity in which the acting subject determines his own goals.

The purpose of Marx's critique was that people should become truly subjects, i.e. that they should rationally and consciously control the processes of their own lives. But the critique was ambiguous inasmuch as the self-regulation of social life could be understood as either a practical or a technical problem, and in the latter case it could be thought of as a manipulative process similar to the technical handling of inanimate objects—which is what happens under both capitalist planning and bureaucratic socialism. In this way reification is not cured but aggravated. True emancipation, on the other hand, is the return to 'praxis' as a category involving the active participation of everyone in the control of social phenomena; in other words, people must be subjects and not objects. For this purpose, as Habermas observes, there must be an improvement of human communication, free discussion of existing power systems, and a fight against the de-politicization of life.

The critique of Marx in *Knowledge and Interest* goes perhaps even further. Habermas says there that Marx finally reduced the self-creation of the human species to the process of productive work, and in so doing prevented himself from fully understanding his own critical activity: for reflection itself appears in his theory as an element of scientific work in the same sense in which it is related to natural science, that is to say it is modelled on patterns of material production. Thus critique as a praxis, as subjective activity based on self-reflection, did not fully take shape in Marx's work as a separate form of social activity. In the same book Habermas criticizes scientism, Mach, Peirce, and Dilthey, and argues that the forms of methodological self-knowledge of the natural or historical sciences also reflect an understanding of their cognitive status and of the interest behind them. He points out, however, the 'emancipative' potential of psychoanalysis, which in his opinion makes it possible to attain a viewpoint in which the operation of reason and the interest and emancipation coincide in self-reflection, or, to put it otherwise, the cognitive and the practical interest become identical. Marx's schema cannot provide a ground for such unity, as he reduced the specific characteristic of the human species to the capacity for instrumental (as distinct from purely adaptive) action, which meant that he could not interpret the relations between ideology and authority in terms of distorted communication, but reduced them to relations stemming from human labour and the battle with nature. (Habermas's thought is not quite clear on this point, but he apparently has in mind that in psychoanalysis, auscultation is also therapy—the patient's understanding of his own situation is at the same time a cure for it. This is not correct, however, if it suggests that the act of understanding is the whole cure, for according to Freud the essence of the therapeutic process consists in transference, which is an existential and not an intellectual act.) In Marx's theory the coincidence does not take place: the interests of reason and emancipation do not combine to form a single practico-intellectual faculty. If this is Habermas's argument, his interpretation of Marx is at variance with Lukács's judgement (which I believe to be correct) that the essential feature of Marxism consists in the doctrine that the act of understanding the world and the act of transforming it achieve identity in the privileged situation of the proletariat.

Habermas does not clearly define his key concept of 'emancipation'. It is evident that, in the spirit of the whole tradition of German idealism, he is seeking for a focal point at which practical and theoretical reason, cognition and will, knowledge of the world and the movement to change it, all become identical. But it does not appear that he has actually found such a point or shown us how to arrive at it. He is right in saying that the criteria of epistemological evaluation must be understood as an element in the history of the human species, in which the processes of technical progress and the forms of communication both appear as independent variables; that none of the rules by which we determine what is cognitively valid is grounded transcendentally (in Husserl's sense); and that positivist criteria of the validity of knowledge are based on evaluation related to human technical abilities. But it does not follow that there is or can be a vantage-point from which the distinction between knowledge and will can be seen as eliminated. It may be that, in some cases, acts of self-understanding by individuals or societies are themselves part of the practical behaviour leading to 'emancipation', whatever this term means. But the question will always remain: by what criteria are we to judge the accuracy of that self-understanding, and on what principle do we decide that 'emancipation' consists in one state of affairs rather than another? On the second point we cannot avoid making a decision that goes beyond our knowledge of the world. If we believe that we can become endowed with some higher spiritual power which distinguishes between good and bad and, in the same act, determines what is true and what is false, we are not effecting any synthesis but are simply replacing the criteria of truth by criteria of an arbitrarily established good: i.e. we are returning to individual or collective pragmatism. 'Emancipation' in the sense of a union between analytical and practical reason is, as we have seen, only possible in instances of religious illumination, where knowledge and the existential act of 'commitment' do indeed become one. But there is nothing more dangerous to civilization than to suppose that the operation of reason can be wholly founded on such acts. It is indeed true that analytical reason, or the whole body of rules by which science functions, cannot provide its own basis; the rules are accepted because they are instrumentally effective, and if there are any transcendental norms of rationality they are not known to us. Science can function without concerning itself with the existence of such norms, for science is not to be confused with scientistic philosophy. Decisions as to good and evil and the meaning of the universe cannot have any scientific foundation; we are bound to make such decisions, but we cannot turn them into acts of intellectual under-standing. The idea of a higher reason synthesizing these two aspects of life can only be realized in the realm of myth, or remain a pious aspiration of German metaphysics.

■   ■   ■

ANOTHER member of the younger generation of the Frankfurt school is Alfred Schmidt, whose book on Marx's concept of nature (1964) is an interesting and valuable contribution to the study of this complicated question. Schmidt argues that Marx's concept contains ambiguities thanks to which it has been interpreted in conflicting ways (nature as a continuation of man, the return to unity, etc.; contrariwise, man as a creation of nature, defined by his attempts to cope with its alien forces). Schmidt contends that Marx's doctrine cannot in the last resort be interpreted as an unequivocally monistic 'system', but that Engels's materialism was in line with an essential aspect of Marx's thought.

Iring Fetscher, undoubtedly one of the most eminent historians of Marxism, can only be regarded as a member of the Frankfurt school in the very broad sense that his works show him to be receptive to those aspects of Marxism in which the writers of the school are interested. His great achievement is to have expounded lucidly the different versions and possible interpretations of the Marxian inheritance, but his own philosophical position does not appear to be based on the typical ideas of the Frankfurt school such as the negative dialec-tic and emancipating reason. Apart from their welcome clarity, his works are characterized by the restraint and open-mindedness of the historian.

8. Conclusion

WHEN we consider the place of the Frankfurt school in the evolution of Marx-ism, we find that its strong point was philosophical anti-dogmatism and the defence of the autonomy of theoretical reasoning. It freed itself from the mythology of the infallible proletariat and the belief that Marx's categories were adequate to the situation and problems of the modern world. It also endeavoured to reject all elements or varieties of Marxism that postulated an absolute, primary basis of knowledge and practice. It contributed to the analy-sis of 'mass culture' as a phenomenon that cannot be interpreted in class cate-gories as Marx understood them. It also contributed to the critique of scientistic philosophy, by drawing attention (though in fairly general and unmethodical terms) to the latent normative assumptions of scientific programmes.

The Frankfurt philosophers were on weak ground, on the other hand, in their constant proclamation of an ideal 'emancipation' which was never prop-erly explained. This created the illusion that while condemning 'reification', exchange-value, commercialized culture, and scientism they were offering something else instead, whereas the most they were actually offering was nostalgia for the pre-capitalist culture of an élite. By harping on the vague prospect of a universal escape from present-day civilization, they unwittingly encouraged an attitude of mindless and destructive protest.

In short, the strength of the Frankfurt school consisted in pure negation, and its dangerous ambiguity lay in the fact that it would not openly admit this fact, but frequently suggested the opposite. It was not so much a continuation of Marxism in any direction, as an example of its dissolution and paralysis.

XI

Herbert Marcuse: Marxism as a Totalitarian Utopia of the New Left

MARCUSE DID NOT become a well-known figure outside academic circles until the late 1960s, when he was acclaimed as an ideological leader by rebellious student movements in the U.S.A., Germany, and France. There is no reason to suppose that he sought the spiritual leadership of the 'student revolution', but when the role devolved upon him he did not object. His Marxism, if that is the right name for it, is a curious ideological mixture. Originating in the interpretation of Hegel and Marx as prophets of a rationalist Utopia, it evolved into a popular ideology of 'global revolution' in which sexual liberation played a prominent part, and in which the working class was rudely displaced from the centre of attention to make way for students, racial minorities, and the lumpenproletariat. In the seventies Marcuse's importance has faded considerably, but his philosophy is still worth discussing, less on account of its intrinsic merits than because it coincided with an important, though perhaps ephemeral, tendency in the ideological changes of our time. It also serves to illustrate the amazing variety of uses that can be made of Marxist doctrine.

As far as his interpretation of Marxism goes, Marcuse is generally considered as a member of the Frankfurt school, to which he is linked by his negative dialectic and faith in the transcendental norms of rationality. Born in Berlin in 1898, he belonged in 1917–18 to the Social Democratic party, but left it, as he afterwards wrote, following the murder of Liebknecht and Rosa Luxemburg; since then he has not belonged to any political party. He studied at Berlin and Freiburg im Breisgau, where he took his doctor's degree (under Heidegger's supervision) with a dissertation on Hegel. His *Hegels Ontologie und Grundzüge einer Theorie der Geschichtlichkeit* was published in 1931. Before emigrating from Germany he also wrote a number of articles clearly indicating the future course of his thought; he was one of the first to draw attention to the importance of Marx's Paris Manuscripts, immediately after their publication. He emigrated after Hitler's accession to power, spent a year in Switzerland, and then moved permanently to the United States. He worked until 1940 in the Institute for Social Research set up by German *émigrés* in New York, and during the war served in the Office of Strategic Services—a fact which, when it became known in later years, helped to destroy his popularity with the student movement. He taught in various American universities (Columbia, Harvard, Brandeis, and from 1965 San Diego), and retired in 1970. In 1941 he published *Reason and Revolution*, an interpretation of Hegel and Marx with particular reference to the critique of positivism. *Eros and Civilization* (1955) was an attempt to erect a new Utopia on the basis of Freud's theory of civilization, and also to refute psychoanalysis 'from within'. *Soviet Marxism* appeared in 1958, and in 1964 he published perhaps the most widely read of his books, a general critique of technological civilization entitled *One-Dimensional Man*. Some minor writings also attracted much attention, especially 'Repressive Tolerance' in 1965 and a series of essays dating from the fifties and sixties and published in 1970 under the title *Five Lectures: Psychoanalysis, Politics and Utopia*.

1. Hegel and Marx versus positivism

MARCUSE has a range of perennial targets comprising 'positivism' (defined in a highly personal way), technological civilization based on the cult of work and production (but not of consumption and luxury), American middle-class values, 'totalitarianism' (so defined as to make the United States a signal example of it), and all the values and institutions associated with liberal democracy and toleration. According to Marcuse, all these objects of attack constitute an integral whole, and he is at pains to demonstrate their fundamental unity.

Marcuse follows Lukács in attacking positivism for its 'worship of facts' (an expression not defined more closely), which prevents us from discerning the 'negativity' of history. But, unlike Lukács, whose Marxism concentrates on the dialectic between subject and object and the 'unity of theory and practice', Marcuse lays most stress on the negative, critical function of reason, providing standards whereby any given social reality can be judged. He agrees with Lukács in emphasizing the link between Marxism and the Hegelian tradition, but differs completely from him as to its nature: the essential basis of Hegelian and Marxian dialectic, according to Marcuse, is not the movement towards the identity of subject and object, but towards the realization of reason, which is at the same time the realization of freedom and happiness.

In his articles published in the 1930s Marcuse already took the view that reason is the fundamental category providing a link between philosophy and human destiny. This idea of reason developed on the basis of the conviction that reality is not 'directly' reasonable but can be reduced to rationality. German idealist philosophy made reason the supreme court of appeal, judging empirical reality by non-empirical criteria. Reason in this sense presupposes freedom, as its pronouncements would be meaningless if men were not completely free to judge the world they live in. Kant, however, transferred reality to the internal sphere, making it a moral imperative, while Hegel in his turn confined it within the bounds of necessity. But Hegel's freedom is only possible thanks to the operation of reason whereby man is aware of his real identity. Thus Hegel appears in the history of philosophy as a champion of the rights of reason revealing to human beings their own truth, i.e. the imperative demands of authentic humanity. The self-transforming operation of reason creates the dialectic of negativity which opens up new horizons at every stage of history, advancing beyond the empirically known possibilities of that stage. In this way Hegel's work is a summons to perpetual nonconformity and a vindication of revolution.

However—and this is one of the main contentions of *Reason and Revolution*—the demand that reason should rule the world is not a prerogative of idealism. German idealism rendered a service to civilization by combating British empiricism, which forbade men to go beyond 'facts' or appeal to *a priori* rational concepts, and which *consequently* supported conformism and social conservatism. But critical idealism regarded reason as located only in the thinking subject, and did not succeed in relating its demands to the sphere of material social conditions: it was left to Marx to achieve this. Thanks to him, the postulate of the realization of reason became a postulate of the rationalization of social conditions in accordance with the 'true' concept or true essence of humanity. The realization of reason is at the same time the transcendence of philosophy, its critical function being thus fully discharged.

Positivism, which is not so much a denial of critico-dialectical philosophy as of philosophy altogether (for philosophy in the true sense has always been antipositivist), is based on accepting the facts of experience and thus affirming the validity of every situation that actually occurs. In positivist terms it is impossible rationally to designate any objectives: these can only be the result of arbitrary decisions, with no foundation in reason. But philosophy, whose business it is to seek the truth, is not afraid of utopias, for truth is a Utopia as long as it cannot be realized in the existing social order. Critical philosophy must appeal to the future and therefore cannot base itself on facts but only on the demands of reason: it is concerned with what man can be and with his essential being, not his empirical state. Positivism, by contrast, sanctifies every compromise with the existing order and abdicates the right to judge social conditions.

The spirit of positivism is exemplified in sociology—not of any particular school, but sociology itself, as a branch of knowledge governed by Comtean rules. Sociology of this kind deliberately confines itself to noting and describing social phenomena, and if it does go so far as to investigate the laws of communal life, it refuses to go beyond such laws as it finds actually in operation. Hence sociology is an instrument of passive adaptation, whereas critical rationalism derives from reason itself the strength with which it demands that the world be subject to reason.

What is more, positivism is not only equivalent to conformism but is the ally of all totalitarian doctrines and social movements; its main principle is that of order, and it is ready at all times to sacrifice freedom to the order which authoritative systems provide.

It is clear that Marcuse's whole argument rests on the belief that we can know, independently of empirical data, the transcendental demands of rationality according to which the world must be judged; and also that we know what constitutes the essence of humanity, or that a 'true' human being would be like as opposed to an empirical one. Marcuse's philosophy can only be understood on the basis of the transcendality of reason, with the proviso that reason 'manifests itself' only in the historical process. This doctrine, however, is based on both historical and logical fallacies.

Marcuse's interpretation of Hegel is almost exactly the same as that of the Young Hegelians attacked by Marx. Hegel is presented simply as the advocate of supra-historical reason, evaluating facts by its own criteria. We have seen more than once how ambiguous Hegel's thought is in this respect; but it is a parody of his ideas to ignore the anti-utopian strain completely and reduce his doctrine to a belief in transcendental reason telling men how to achieve 'happiness'. In addition, it is more than misleading to depict Marx as a philosopher who transferred the categories of Hegelian logic into the realm of politics. Marcuse's argument ignores all the essential features of Marx's critique of Hegel and of the Hegelian Left. In his zeal to present Hegel as a champion of freedom against any kind of authoritarian regime, he makes no mention of Marx's criticism of Hegel's 'reversal of subject and predicate', whereby the values of individual life are made to depend on the requirements of universal reason. Yet this criticism, regardless of how far it was based on a true interpretation, was the point of departure for Marx's Utopia, and it is flouting history to ignore it for the sake of depicting a harmonious transition from Hegel to Marx. The picture is further distorted by the suppression of Marx's critique of the Young Hegelians and their Fichtean interpretation of Hegel. Marx's account of his own philosophical position was based first and foremost, on his emancipation from the Young Hegelian faith in the sovereignty of supra-historical reason— the very faith which Marcuse seeks to ascribe to Marx.

These distortions enable Marcuse to assert that modern totalitarian doctrines have nothing to do with the Hegelian tradition but are the embodiment of positivism. In what, however, does positivism consist? Marcuse is content with the label of 'fact-worship', and lists as its chief proponents Comte, Friedrich Stahl, Lorenz von Stein, and even Schelling. This, however, is a confusion of ideas for the sake of an arbitrary, unhistorical exposition. Schelling's 'positive philosophy' has nothing but the name in common with historical positivism. Stahl and von Stein were in fact conservatives, and so was Comte in a sense. But Marcuse sets out to depict as 'positivists' all supporters of a given social order, and then to proclaim, in the teeth of obvious facts, that all empiricists, i.e. all who wished to subject theory to the test of facts, were automatically conservatives. Positivism in the historical sense—as opposed to the sense in which Schelling and Hume can scarcely be distinguished—embodies the principle, among others, that the cognitive value of knowledge depends on its empirical background: so that science cannot draw a line between the essential and the phenomenal, in the manner of Plato or Hegel, nor can it enable us to say that a given empirical state of things is inconsistent with a true concept of those things. Positivism, it is true, does not provide us with a method for determining the norm of a 'true' human being or a 'true' society. But empiricism by no means obliges us to conclude that existing 'facts' or social institutions must be supported simply because they exist: on the contrary, it expressly denies such a conclusion, regarding it as logically nonsensical on the same ground as that which forbids us to deduce normative judgements from descriptive ones.

Not only is Marcuse wrong in proclaiming a logical link between positivism and totalitarian politics, but his assertion of a historical link is directly contrary to the facts. The positivist outlook which developed and flourished in Britain from the late Middle Ages onwards, and without which we would not have modern science, democratic legislation, or the idea of the rights of man, was from the beginning inseparably linked with the idea of negative freedom and the values of democratic institutions. It was Locke and his successors, not Hegel, who founded and disseminated the doctrine of human equality, based on the principles of empiricism, and the value of individual freedom under the law. The twentieth-century positivists and empiricists, especially the analytical school and the so-called logical empiricists, not only had nothing to do with Fascist trends but, without exception, opposed them in no uncertain terms. Thus there is no logical or historical link whatever between positivism and totalitarian politics—unless, as some of Marcuse's remarks suggest, the word 'totalitarian' is to be understood in a sense as remote from the usual one as the word 'positivism'.

On the other hand, both logical and historical arguments speak with much greater force in favour of a connection between Hegelianism and totalitarian ideas. It would, of course, be absurd to say that Hegel's doctrine leads to the commendation of modern totalitarian states, but it would be less absurd than to say the same thing of positivism. A deduction of this kind could be made from Hegelianism by stripping it of many important features, but from positivism no such deduction could be made at all: all that can be done is to assert without proof, as Marcuse does, that positivism means fact-worship, therefore it is conservative, therefore totalitarian. It is true that the Hegelian tradition played no essential part as a philosophic basis of non-Communist totalitarianism (Marcuse says nothing of the Communist variety in this context); but, when he comes to the instance of Giovanni Gentile, Marcuse simply declares that although Gentile used Hegel's name he actually had nothing in common with him, but was close to being a positivist. Here we have a confusion of the 'question of right' and the 'question of fact', as Marcuse seeks to rebut the possible objection that Hegelianism was, as a matter of fact, used as a justification of Fascism. It is no answer to this objection to say that it was used improperly.

In short, the whole of Marcuse's critique of positivism, and most of his interpretation of Hegel and Marx, are a farrago of arbitrary statements, both logical and historical. These statements, moreover, are integrally bound up with his positive views on the global liberation of mankind and his ideas on happiness, freedom, and revolution

2. Critique of contemporary civilization

BEING in possession of transcendental norms, or the normative concept of 'humanity' as opposed to empirical human destiny, Marcuse examines the question why and in what respects our present civilization fails to correspond with this model. The basic determinant of the authentic concept of mankind is 'happiness', a notion which includes freedom and which Marcuse claims to find in Marx—although Marx does not actually use it and it is not clear how it can be deduced from his writings. In addition to the empirical fact that human beings seek 'happiness', we must begin by acknowledging that happiness is their due. To discover why they fail to assert this claim, Marcuse takes as his starting-point Freud's philosophy of civilization. He accepts this to a large extent as far as the interpretation of past history is concerned, but calls it in question as regards the future; Freud, in fact, observed that there is no law which says that human beings are entitled to happiness or certain to obtain it. Freud's theory of instinct and the three levels of the psyche—the id, the ego, and super-ego—explains the conflict between the 'pleasure principle' and the 'reality principle' which has governed the whole development of civilization. In *Eros and Civilization* and in three lectures analysing and criticizing Freud's theory of history, Marcuse considers whether and how far that conflict is necessary. His arguments may be summarized as follows.

According to Freud there is an eternal, inevitable clash between civilized values and the demands of human instincts. All civilization has developed as a result of society's efforts to repress the instinctive desires of individuals. Eros, or the life-instinct, was not originally limited to sexuality in the reproductive sense: sexuality was a universal characteristic of the human organism as a whole. But, in order to engage in productive work, which in itself gives no pleasure, the human race found it necessary to confine the range of sexual experience to the genital sphere and to restrict even this narrowly conceived sexuality to the minimum. The store of energy thus released was devoted not to pleasure but to the struggle with man's surroundings. In the same way the other basic determinant of life, Thanatos or the death-instinct, was transformed in such a way that its energy, directed outwards in the form of aggression, could be used to overcome physical nature and increase the efficiency of labour. As a result, however, civilization necessarily took on a repressive character, as instincts were harnessed to tasks that were not 'natural' to them. Repression and sublimation were conditions of the development of culture, but at the same time, according to Freud, repression gave rise to a vicious circle. As labour came to be regarded as good in itself and the 'pleasure principle' was wholly subordinated to increasing its efficiency, human beings had to fight down their instincts unremittingly for the sake of these values, and the sum total of repression increased with the advance of civilization. Repression was a self-propelling mechanism, and the instruments produced by civilization to lessen the suffering arising from repression themselves became organs of repression in a still higher degree. In this way the advantages and freedoms procured by civilization are paid for by increasing the loss of freedom, especially by the growing volume of alienated labour—the only kind of labour that our civilization permits.

Marcuse takes note of this theory but modifies it in an essential respect, thus rebutting Freud's pessimistic predictions. Civilization, he says, has as a matter of fact developed by repressing instincts, but there is no law of biology or history which requires this to be so forever. The process of repression was 'rational' in the sense that, as long as basic commodities were scarce, men could only live and improve their condition by diverting their instinctual energies into 'unnatural' channels so as to further material production. But, once technology made it possible to satisfy human needs without repression, this became an irrational anachronism. Since unpleasant work can be reduced to a minimum and there is no threat of a scarcity of goods, civilization no longer requires us to thwart our instincts: we can allow them to revert to their proper function, which is a condition of human happiness. 'Free time can become the content of life and work can become the free play of human capacities. In this way the repressive structure of the instincts would be explosively transformed: the instinctual energies that would no longer be caught up in ungratifying work would become free and, as Eros, would strive to universalize libidinous relationships and develop a libidinous civilization' (*Five Lectures*, p. 22). Production will cease to be regarded as a value in itself; the vicious circle of increasing production and increasing repression will be broken; the pleasure principle and the intrinsic value of pleasure will come into their own, and alienated labour will cease to exist.

Marcuse makes it clear, however, that in speaking of 'libidinous civilization' and the return of instinctual energy to its proper functions he does not have in mind 'pansexualism' or the abolition of sublimation, whereby, according to Freud, men have found an illusory satisfaction of their frustrated desires in cultural creativity. The liberated energy will not manifest itself in a purely sexual form but will eroticize all human activities; these will all be pleasurable, and pleasure will be recognized as an end in itself. 'Incentive to work are no longer necessary. For if work itself becomes the free play of human abilities, then no suffering is needed to compel men to work' (ibid., p. 41). In general there will be no need for social control of the individual, whether through institutions or in an internalized manner—and these, according to Marcuse, are both features of totalitarianism. There will thus no longer be any 'collectivization' of the ego: life will be rational and the individual will once more be fully autonomous.

This 'Freudian' aspect of Marcuse's Utopia presents obscurities at all its vital points. Freud's theory was that the repression of instincts was necessary not only to liberate the energy needed for production but also to make possible the existence of any social life at all in the specifically human sense. Instincts are directed towards the satisfaction of purely individual desires; the death-instinct, according to Freud, can either work towards self-destruction or be transformed into external aggression; man ceases to be an enemy to himself, only in so far as he becomes an enemy to others. The only way to prevent the death-instinct becoming a permanent source of enmity between each human being and all his fellow humans is to force its energies into other channels. The libido is likewise asocial, as it treats other human beings only as possible objects of sexual satisfaction. In short, the instincts not only have no power, left to themselves, to create human society or form the basis of a community, but their natural effect is to make such a community impossible. Leaving aside the difficult question how, in that case, societies can ever have come into existence, the situation is, in Freud's view, that the society which does exist can only maintain itself by numerous taboos, commands, and prohibitions, which keep the instincts under control at the price of unavoidable suffering.

Marcuse does not address himself to this question. He seems to agree with Freud that the suppression of instincts has been necessary 'up to now', but holds that it has been an anachronism since the abolition of scarcity. But, while disputing Freud's theory of the eternal conflict between instincts and civilization, he accepts the view that instincts are essentially devoted to satisfying the individual's 'pleasure principle'. It is not clear, in view of this, how the 'libidinous civilization' can maintain itself and what forces will keep human society in being. Does Marcuse hold, in opposition to Freud, that man is naturally good and inclined to live in harmony with others, and that aggression is an accidental aberration of history which will disappear along with alienated labour? He does not say so, and inasmuch as he accepts the Freudian concept and classification of instincts, he expressly suggests the contrary. Even if he were right in asserting that 'in principle' mankind has plenty of everything and that there is no essential problem about the satisfaction of material needs, it is still not at all clear what forces are to maintain the new civilization in which all instincts have been liberated and allowed to revert to their native channels. Marcuse seems to be unconcerned with these problems, as he is interested in society chiefly in so far as it constitutes a barrier to instinct, i.e. to individual satisfaction. He seems to believe that as all questions of material existence have been solved, moral commands and prohibitions are no longer relevant. Thus when Jerry Rubin, the American hippie ideologist, says in his book that machines will henceforth do all the work and leave people free to copulate whenever and wherever they like, he is expressing, albeit in a primitive and juvenile way, the true essence of Marcuse's Utopia. As to Marcuse's qualifications of the notion of eroticism, they are too vague to convey any tangible meaning. What could the eroticization of the whole man signify, except his complete absorption in sensual pleasures? The utopian slogan is void of content; nor can we see how Marcuse imagines that the Freudian sublimation would remain in force after all the factors that brought it about had ceased to operate. According to Freud sublimation, expressed in cultural creativity, is only an illusory, ersatz satisfaction of instinctual appetites that civilization does not permit us to gratify. This theory can be and has been criticized, but Marcuse does not attempt to do so. He seems to assume that cultural creativity has in the past been an ersatz as described by Freud, but that it will nevertheless go on in the future although there will be no need for such sublimation.

Marcuse's whole inversion of Freud's theory seems to have no intelligible purpose other than a return to pre-social existence. Marcuse, of course, does not spell out this conclusion, but it is not clear how he can avoid it without contradiction. His reliance on Marx at this point is extremely dubious. Marx thought that the perfect society of the future would be so constituted that each individual would treat his own powers and abilities as direct social forces, thus removing the conflict between individual aspirations and communal needs. But Marx, on the other hand, did not hold Freud's view as to the nature of instincts. One cannot without contradiction maintain that men are instinctively and inevitably enemies of one another, and yet that their instincts must be liberated so that they can live together in peace and harmony.

3. 'One-dimensional man'

MARCUSE, however, also criticizes modern civilization, especially that of America, in terms that do not necessarily involve Freud's philosophy of history but revert to the theme of his Hegelian studies, i.e. the transcendental norms of rationality as they affect the problem of human liberation. *One-Dimensional Man* is a study of this kind.

The prevailing civilization, he argues, is one-dimensional in all its aspects: science, art, philosophy, everyday thinking, political systems, economics, and technology. The lost 'second dimension' is the negative and critical principle— the habit of contrasting the world as it is with the true world revealed by the normative concepts of philosophy, which enable us to understand the true nature of freedom, beauty, reason, the joy of living, and so on.

The philosophical conflict between dialectical and 'formal' thinking goes back to Plato and Aristotle: the former extolled the importance of normative concepts with which to compare the objects of experience, while the latter developed 'sterile' formal logic and thus 'separated truth from reality'. What we need now, according to Marcuse, is to return to the ontological concept of truth as being not merely a characteristic of propositions, but reality itself: not empirical, directly accessible reality, but of a higher order, that which we perceive in universals. The intuition of universals leads us into a world which, though non-empirical, exists in its own way and ought to exist. 'In the equation Reason = Truth = Reality . . . Reason is the subversive power, the "power of the negative" that establishes, as theoretical and practical Reason, the truth for men and things—that is, the conditions in which men and things become what they really are' (*One-Dimensional Man*, p. 123). The truth of concepts is grasped by 'intuition', which is 'the result of methodic intellectual mediation' (p. 126). This truth is normative in character, and in it Logos and Eros coincide. This is beyond the scope of formal logic, which tells us nothing about the 'essence of things' and restricts the sense of the word 'is' to purely empirical statements. But when we make statements like 'virtue is knowledge' or 'man is free', 'if these propositions are to be true, then the copula "is" states an "ought"', a desideratum. It judges conditions in which virtue is *not* knowledge', etc. (p. 133). Thus the word 'is' has a twofold meaning, an empirical and a normative, and this duality is the subject of all genuine philosophy. Or again, one may speak of 'essential' and 'apparent' truths: dialectic consists in maintaining the tension between what is essential, or what ought to be, and what appears (i.e. facts); accordingly, dialectic is a critique of actual conditions and a lever of social liberation. In formal logic this tension is banished and 'thought is indifferent towards its objects' (p. 136), and this is why true philosophy developed beyond it. Dialectic cannot in principle be formalized, as it is thought determined by reality itself. It is a critique of direct experience, which perceives things in their accidental shape and does not penetrate to the deeper reality.

The Aristotelian mode of thought, which confines knowledge to direct experience and to the formal rules of reasoning, is the basis of all modern science, which deliberately ignores the normative 'essence' of things and relegates the question of 'what ought to be' to the realm of subjective preference. This science and the technology based on it have created a world in which man's rule over nature goes hand in hand with enslavement to society. Science and technology of this kind have indeed raised living standards, but they have brought oppression and destruction in their wake.

> Scientific-technical rationality and manipulation are welded together into new forms of social control. Can one rest content with the assumption that this unscientific outcome is the result of a specific societal *application* of science? I think that the general direction in which it came to be applied was inherent in pure science even where no practical purposes were intended . . . The quantification of nature, which led to its explication in terms of mathematical structures, separated reality from all inherent ends and, consequently, separated the true from the good, science from ethics . . . The precarious ontological link between Logos and Eros is broken, and scientific rationality emerges as essentially neutral . . . Outside this rationality, one lives in a world of values, and values separated out from the objective reality becomes subjective. (*One-Dimensional Man*, pp. 146–7.)

Thus, Marcuse continues, the ideas of goodness, beauty, and justice are deprived of universal validity and relegated to the sphere of personal taste. Science tries to concern itself only with what is measurable and can be put to technical use; it no longer asks what things are, only how they work, and proclaims itself indifferent to the purpose they are used for. In the scientific world-picture things have lost all ontological consistency, and even matter has somehow disappeared. Socially, the function of science is basically conservative, as it affords no ground for social protest. 'Science, *by virtue of its own method* and concepts, has projected and promoted a universe in which the domination of nature has remained linked to the domination of man' (ibid., p. 166). What is required is a new, qualitative, normative science which 'would arrive at essentially different concepts of nature and establish essentially different facts' (ibid.).

This deformed science, leading to the enslavement of man, finds its philosophical expression in positivism, and particularly analytical philosophy and operationalism. These doctrines reject all concepts that do not bear a 'functional' sense or make it possible to foresee and influence events. Yet such concepts are the most important of all, as they enable us to transcend the world as it is. Worse still, positivism preaches tolerance of all values and thus displays its own reactionary character, as it countenances no restrictions of any kind in regard to social practice and value-judgements.

Given the predominance of this functional attitude to thought, it follows that society must be composed of one-dimensional beings. It becomes a victim of false consciousness, and the fact that most people accept the system does not make it any more rational. A society of this kind (by which Marcuse means chiefly America) can absorb all forms of opposition without injury to itself, as it has emptied the opposition of its critical content. It is capable of satisfying a host of human needs, but these needs are themselves bogus: they are foisted on individuals by interested exploiters, and they serve to perpetuate injustice, poverty, and aggression. 'Most of the prevailing needs to relax, to have fun, to behave and consume in accordance with the advertisements, to love and hate what others love and hate, belong to this category of false needs' (p. 5). As to which needs are 'true' and which are false, no one can decide this except the individuals concerned, and that only when they are rescued from manipulation and external pressure. But the modern economic system is devised to multiply artificial needs in a condition of freedom which is itself an instrument of domination. 'The range of choice open to the individual is not the decisive factor in determining the degree of human freedom, but *what* can be chosen and what *is* chosen by the individual' (p. 7).

In this world people and things are reduced, without exception, to a functional role, deprived of 'substance' and autonomy. Art is likewise involved in the universal degradation of conformism, not because it abandons cultural values but because it includes them in the existing order. Higher European culture was once basically feudal and non-technical, moving in spheres independent of commerce and industry. The civilization of the future must recover that independence by creating a second dimension of thoughts and feelings, upholding the spirit of negation, and restoring universal Eros to its throne. (At this point Marcuse for once gives a practical instance of what he means by 'libidinous civilization', pointing out that it is much more comfortable to make love in a meadow than in an automobile on a Manhattan street.) The new civilization must also be opposed to liberty as we know it, for 'inasmuch as the greater liberty involves a contraction rather than extension and development of instinctual needs, it works *for* rather than *against* the status quo of general repression' (p. 74).

4. The revolution against freedom

Is THERE a way out of the system which multiplies bogus needs and offers the means of satisfying them, and which binds the multitude under a spell of false consciousness? Yes, says Marcuse, there is. We must completely 'transcend' existing society and strive for a 'qualitative change'; we must destroy the very 'structure' of reality so that people can develop their needs in freedom; we must have a new technology (not simply a new application of the present one) and recapture the unity of art and science, science and ethics; we must set free our imaginations and harness science to the liberation of mankind.

But who is to do all this when a majority of the people, and especially of the working class, are absorbed by the system and are not interested in the 'global transcendence' of the existing order? The answer, according to *One-Dimensional Man*, is that 'underneath the conservative popular base is the substratum of the outcasts and outsiders, the exploited and persecuted of other races and other colours, the unemployed and the unemployable. They exist outside the democratic process . . . The fact that they start refusing to play the game may be the fact which marks the beginning of the end of a period' (pp. 256–7).

It appears, then, that the lumpenproletariat of the racial minorities of the United States is the section of humanity ordained above all others to restore the unity of Eros and Logos, to create the new qualitative science and technology, and to free mankind from the tyranny of formal logic, positivism, and empiricism. However, Marcuse explains elsewhere that we can also count on other forces, namely students and the peoples of economically and technically backward countries. The alliance of these three groups is the chief hope for the liberation of humanity. Student movements of revolt are 'a decisive factor of transformation', though in themselves insufficient to bring it about (see 'The Problems of Violence and the Radical Opposition', in *Five Lectures*). Revolutionary forces must use violence, because they represent a higher justice and because the present system is itself one of institutionalized violence. It is absurd to talk of confining resistance within legal limits, for no system, not even the freest, can sanction the use of violence against itself. Violence is justified, however, when the aim is liberation. It is, moreover, an important and encouraging sign that the students' political revolt is combined with a movement towards sexual liberation.

Violence is inevitable because the present system afflicts the majority with a false consciousness from which only a few can liberate themselves. Capitalism has devised such means of assimilating all forms of culture and thought that it can disarm its critics by turning their criticism into an element of the system: what is needed, therefore, is criticism by violence, which cannot be thus digested. Freedom of speech and assembly, tolerance, and democratic institutions, are all means of perpetuating the spiritual dominance of capitalist values. It follows that those endowed with a true and unmystified consciousness must strive for liberation from democratic freedoms and tolerance.

Marcuse has no hesitation in drawing this conclusion, which he expresses perhaps with most clarity in his essay on 'Repressive Tolerance' (in *A Critique of Pure Tolerance* by Robert Paul Wolff and others, 1969). In the past, he argues, tolerance was a liberating ideal, but today it is an instrument of oppression, as it strengthens a society which, with the assent of the majority, builds nuclear arsenals, pursues imperialist policies, and so on. Tolerance of this kind is a tyranny of the majority against liberationist ideals; moreover, it tolerates doctrines and movements that ought not to be tolerated, as they are wrong and evil. Every particular fact and institution must be judged from the point of view of the 'whole' to which they belong, and since in this case the 'whole' is the capitalist system, which is inherently evil, freedom and tolerance within the system are likewise evil in themselves. Therefore a true, deeper tolerance must involve intolerance towards false ideas and movements. 'The tolerance which enlarged the range and content of freedom was always partisan—intolerant toward the protagonists of the repressive status quo' (p. 99). When it is a question of establishing a new society (which, as it belongs to the future, cannot be described or defined except as the contrary of the present one), indiscriminate tolerance cannot be permitted. True tolerance 'cannot protect false words and wrong deeds which demonstrate that they contradict and counteract the possibilities of liberation' (p. 102). 'Society cannot be indiscriminate where the pacification of existence, where freedom and happiness themselves are at stake: here, certain things cannot be said, certain ideas cannot be expressed, certain policies cannot be proposed, certain behaviour cannot be permitted without making tolerance an instrument for the continuation of servitude' (ibid.). Freedom of speech is good, not because there is no such thing as objective truth, but because such truth exists and can be discovered; hence freedom of speech cannot be justified if it is shown to be perpetuating untruth. Such freedom assumes that all desirable changes can be effected through rational discussion within the 'system'; but in fact everything that can be achieved in this way serves to corroborate the system. 'A free society is indeed unrealistically and undefinably different from the existing ones. Under these circumstances, whatever improvement may occur "in the normal course of events" and without subversion is likely to be an improvement in the direction determined by the particular interests which control the whole' (p. 107). Freedom to express various opinions is bound to mean that the opinions expressed will reflect establishment interests, because of the establishment's power to form opinion. True, the mass media describe the atrocities of the modern world, but they do so in an impassive, impartial manner. 'If objectivity has anything to do with truth, and if truth is more than a matter of logic and science, then this kind of objectivity is false, and this kind of tolerance inhuman' (p. 112). To combat indoctrination and develop the forces of liberation 'may require apparently undemocratic means. They would include the withdrawal of toleration of speech and assembly from groups and movements which promote aggressive policies, armament, chauvinism, discrimination on the grounds of race and religion, or which oppose the extension of public services, social security, medical care, etc. Moreover, the restoration of freedom of thought may necessitate new and rigid restrictions on teachings and practices in the educational institutions' (p. 114), as those enclosed within these institutions have no real freedom of choice. If it is asked who is entitled to decide when intolerance and violence are justified, the answer depends on which cause is to be served thereby. 'Liberating tolerance ... would mean intolerance against movements from the Right and toleration of movements from the Left' (pp. 122–3). This simple formula epitomizes the kind of 'tolerance' that Marcuse advocates. His object, he declares, is not to set up a dictatorship but to achieve 'true democracy' by combating the idea of tolerance, on the ground that the vast majority cannot form right judgements when their minds are deformed by democratic sources of information.

Marcuse did not write from a Communist standpoint but rather from that of the 'New Left', which broadly shared his ideas. His attitude to existing forms of Communism was one of mixed criticism and approbation, expressed in highly vague and ambiguous terms. He uses the words 'totalitarian' and 'totalitarianism' in such a way that they would fit the U.S.S.R. as well as the U.S.A., but generally disparages the latter as compared with the former. He recognizes that one system is pluralistic and the other based on terror, but does not regard this as an essential distinction: '"totalitarian" here is redefined to mean not only terroristic but also pluralistic absorption of all effective opposition by the established society' (*Five Lectures*, p. 48). '"Totalitarian" is not only a terroristic political coordination of society, but also a non-terroristic economic-technical coordination which operates through the manipulation of needs by vested interests' (*One-Dimensional Man*, p. 3). 'In the realm of culture, the new totalitarianism manifests itself precisely in a harmonizing pluralism, where the most contradictory works and truths peacefully coexist in indifference' (ibid., p. 61). '... is there today, in the orbit of advanced industrial civilization, a society which is not under an authoritarian regime?' (ibid., p. 102).

Terror, in short, can either be exerted by terror or by democracy, pluralism, and tolerance. But when terror is exercised for the purpose of liberation there is a promise that it will come to an end, whereas terror in the form of freedom lasts forever. On the other hand, Marcuse repeatedly expresses the view that the Soviet and capitalist systems are growing more alike, as types of the same process of industrialization. In *Soviet Marxism* he sharply criticizes Marxist state doctrine and claims that the system based upon it is not a dictatorship of the proletariat but a method of speeding up industrialization by means of a dictatorship over the proletariat and peasantry, the Marxist ideology being skewed for this purpose. He realizes the primitive intellectual level of the Soviet version of Marxism and the fact that it serves purely pragmatic aims. On the one hand, he believes that Western capitalism and the Soviet system show marked signs of converging in the direction of increased centralization, bureaucracy, economic rationalization, regimented education and information services, the work ethos, production, etc. On the other hand, however, he sees more hope for the Soviet system than for capitalism because, in the former, bureaucracy cannot become completely entrenched or perpetuate its interests: 'in the last resort' it must take second place to over-all technical, economic, and political aims which are incompatible with a system of government by repression. In a state based on class, rational technical and economic development conflicts with the interests of the exploiters. The same situation occurs in Soviet society, as the bureaucracy tries to exploit progress for its own ends, but there is a possibility of the conflict being resolved in the future, which is not the case with capitalism.

5. Commentary

WHILE Marcuse's early works may be regarded as expressing a version of Marxism (based, it is true, on a false Young Hegelian interpretation of Hegel), his later writings, though they frequently invoke the Marxist tradition, have little in common with it. What he offers is Marxism without the proletariat (irrevocably corrupted by the welfare society), without history (as the vision of the future is not derived from a study of historical changes but from an intuition of true human nature), and without the cult of science; a Marxism, furthermore, in which the value of liberated society resides in pleasure and not in creative work. All this is a pale and distorted reflection of the original Marxist message. Marcuse, in fact, is a prophet of semi-romantic anarchism in its most irrational form. Marxism, it is true, contains a romantic strain—a yearning for the lost values of pre-industrial society, for unity between man and nature and direct communication among human beings, and also the belief that man's empirical life can and should be reconciled with this true essence. But Marxism is not itself if it is stripped of all other elements than these, including its theory of the class struggle and all its scientific and scientistic aspects.

However, the main point about Marcuse's writing is not that he professes to be a Marxist despite clear evidence to the contrary, but that he seeks to provide a philosophical basis for a tendency already present in our civilization, which aims at destroying that civilization from within for the sake of an apocalypse of the New World of Happiness of which, in the nature of things, no description can be given. Worse still, the only feature of the millennium that we can deduce from Marcuse's work is that society is to be ruled despotically by an enlightened group whose chief title to do so is that its members will have realized in

themselves the unity of Logos and Eros, and thrown off the vexatious authority of logic, mathematics, and the empirical sciences. This may seem a caricature of Marcuse's doctrine, but it is hard to extract anything more from an
analysis of his writings.

Marcuse's thought is a curious mixture of feudal contempt for technology,
the exact sciences, and democratic values, plus a nebulous revolutionism
devoid of positive content. He bemoans the existence of a civilization which
(1) divorces science from ethics, empirical and mathematical knowledge from
values, facts from norms, the description of the universe from insight into its
normative essence; (2) has created 'sterile' logic and mathematics; (3) has
destroyed the unity of Eros and Logos and does not understand that reality
contains its own unrealized 'standard', so that by intuition we can compare it
with an objective norm of itself; and (4) has staked everything on technological progress. The destructive effects of science are inherent in its content and
are not simply due to its social misapplication. This perverted civilization must
be opposed by a dialectic which upholds the 'unity' of knowledge and values
and transcends reality by invoking its normative essence. Those who have
achieved this higher wisdom, untainted by logic and the rigours of empiricism,
are entitled for that reason to use violence, intolerance, and repressive measures against the majority who form the rest of the community. The élite in
question consists of revolutionary students, the illiterate peasantry of economically backward countries, and the lumpenproletariat of the U.S.A.

On basic points Marcuse gives no indication of what his actual claims are.
How do we tell, for instance, that the true essence of humanity is revealed by
one particular intuition and not another? or how do we know which models and
normative concepts are the right ones? There is and can be no answer to these
questions: we are at the mercy of arbitrary decisions by Marcuse and his followers. In the same way, we do not know what the liberated world is going to
look like, and Marcuse expressly says that it cannot be described in advance.
All we are told is that we must completely 'transcend' existing society and civilization, carry out a 'global revolution', create 'qualitatively new' social conditions, and so on. The only positive conclusion to be drawn is that whatever
tends to destroy existing civilization is praiseworthy: there is no reason to suppose, for instance, that the burning of books, which happened in various university centres in the U.S.A., was not a good way to start the revolutionary
process of 'transcending' the corrupt world of capitalism in the name of a
higher reason *à la* Plato or Hegel.

Marcuse's attacks on science and logic go hand in hand with attacks on
democratic institutions and 'repressive tolerance' (the opposite of 'true' tolerance, i.e. of repressive intolerance). The principles of modern science, which
clearly distinguishes normative acts and evaluations from logical thought and

empirical method, are in fact closely linked with the principles of tolerance and free speech. Scientific rules, whether formal or empirical, define an area of knowledge within which disputants can appeal to shared principles and, in due course, agree on this basis which theories or hypotheses are acceptable. In other words, science has evolved a code of thought, consisting of deductive and probabilistic logic, which imposes itself coercively on the human mind and creates a sphere of mutual understanding among all who are prepared to recognize it. Beyond this sphere lies the realm of value, where discussion is also possible, but only in so far as certain specific values, unprovable by the laws of scientific thought, are recognized by those concerned; yet basic values cannot be validated with the help of rules governing scientific thought. These simple principles enable us to distinguish between the fields to which compelling laws apply and those in which there are no such laws and mutual tolerance is therefore necessary. But if it is required that our thought be subject to the intuition of normative 'essences', and if it is declared that only on this condition can it be truly called thought and conform to the demands of higher reason, this amounts to a proclamation of intolerance and thought control, as the exponents of a particular idea are not obliged to defend their opinion by invoking the common stock of logical and empirical rules. To inveigh against 'sterile' formal logic (and all Marcuse tells us about logic is that it is sterile) and against the natural sciences with their quantitative orientation (sciences of which Marcuse certainly knows nothing, any more than he does of economics and technology) is simply to exalt ignorance. Human thought developed and produced science by enlarging the area of knowledge that was not subject to arbitrary judgement, thanks to the Platonic distinction between knowledge and opinion, *episteme* and *doxa*. This distinction, of course, leaves no room for an ultimate, all-embracing synthesis in which thoughts, feelings, and desires are merged in a higher 'unity'. Such an aspiration is only possible when a totalitarian myth claims supremacy over thought—a myth based on 'deeper' intuition, so that it does not have to justify itself, but assumes command over the whole of spiritual and intellectual life. For this to be possible, of course, all logical and empirical rules have to be declared irrelevant, and this is what Marcuse purports to do. The object he strives after is a unified body of knowledge which despises such trivial aims as technological progress, and whose merit is to be one and all-embracing. But there can only be such knowledge if thought is allowed to shake off the external compulsions of logic; moreover, since each person's 'essential' intuition may be different from that of others, the spiritual unity of society must be based on other foundations than logic and facts. There must be some compulsion other than the rules of thought, and that must take the form of social repression. In other words, Marcuse's system depends on replacing the tyranny of logic by a police tyranny. This is corroborated by all historical experience: there is only one way of making a whole society accept a particular world-view, whereas there are different ways of imposing the authority of rational thought, provided the rules of its operation are known and acknowledged. The Marcusian union of Eros and Logos can only be realized in the form of a totalitarian state, established and governed by force; the freedom he advocates is non-freedom. If 'true' freedom does not mean freedom of choice but consists in choosing a particular object; if freedom of speech does not mean that people can say what they like, but that they must say the right thing; and if Marcuse and his followers have the sole right to decide what people must choose and what they must say, then 'freedom' has simply taken on the contrary of its normal sense. In these terms a 'free' society is one that deprives people of freedom to choose either objects or ideas except at the behest of those who know better.

It should be noted that Marcuse's demands go much further than Soviet totalitarian Communism has ever done, either in theory or in practice. Even in the worst days of Stalinism, despite universal indoctrination and the enslavement of knowledge to ideology, it was recognized that some fields were neutral in themselves and subject only to logical and empirical laws: this was true of mathematics, physics, and also technology except for one or two brief periods. Marcuse, on the other hand, insists that normative essences must prevail in every domain, that there must be a new technology and a new qualitative science of which we know nothing whatever except that they *are* new; they must be freed from the prejudices of experience and 'mathematization'—i.e. attainable without any knowledge of mathematics, physics, or any other science—and must absolutely transcend our present knowledge.

The kind of unity that Marcuse craves for and which he imagines to have been destroyed by industrial civilization has in fact never existed: even primitive societies, as we know, for example, from Malinowski's work, distinguished the mythical from the technical order. Magic and mythology have never taken the place of technique and rational effort, but only complemented them in spheres over which mankind has no technical control. The only possible forerunners of Marcuse are the theocrats of the Middle Ages and early Reformation who sought to eliminate science or deprive it of independence.

Neither science nor technology, of course, offers any basis for a hierarchy of aims and values. Aims-in-themselves, as opposed to means, cannot be identified by scientific methods; science can only tell us how to attain our ends and what will happen when we do attain them, or when a certain course of action is followed. The gap here cannot be bridged by any 'essential' intuition.

Marcuse combines contempt for science and technology with the belief that we must strive for higher values because all the problems of material welfare have been solved and commodities exist in plenty: to increase the amount can only serve the interests of capitalism, which lives by creating false needs and instilling a false consciousness. In this respect Marcuse is typical of the mentality of those who have never had to trouble themselves to obtain food, clothing, housing, electricity, and so on, as all these necessities of life were available ready-made. This accounts for the popularity of his philosophy among those who have never had anything to do with material and economic production. Students from comfortable middle-class backgrounds have in common with the lumpenproletariat that the technique and organization of production are beyond their mental horizon: consumer goods, whether plentiful or in short supply, are simply there for the taking. Contempt for technique and organization goes hand in hand with a distaste for all forms of learning that are subject to regular rules of operation or that require vigorous effort, intellectual discipline, and a humble attitude towards facts and the rules of logic. It is much easier to shirk the laborious task and to utter slogans about global revolution transcending our present civilization and uniting knowledge and feeling.

Marcuse of course repeats all the usual complaints about the destructive effect of modern technology and the spiritual impoverishment that results from a utilitarian approach to life in which the individual amounts to no more than the function he performs. These are not his own invention, but are long-standing truisms. The important point, however, is that the destructive effects of technology can only be combated by the further development of technology itself. The human race must work out scientifically, with the aid of 'sterile' logic, methods of social planning to neutralize the adverse consequences of technological advance. For this purpose it must foster and establish values that make life more endurable and facilitate the rational consideration of social reforms, namely the values of tolerance, democracy, and free speech. Marcuse's programme is the exact opposite: to destroy democratic institutions and tolerance in the name of a totalitarian myth, subjecting science and technology (not only in practical application, but in their theoretical aspects as well) to a nebulous 'essential' intuition which is the exclusive property of philosophers hostile to empiricism and positivism.

There could hardly be a clearer instance of the replacement of Marx's slogan 'either socialism or barbarism' by the version 'socialism equals barbarism'. And there is probably no other philosopher in our day who deserves as completely as Marcuse to be called the ideologist of obscurantism.

XII

Ernst Bloch: Marxism as a
Futuristic Gnosis

I N T H E R E A L M of philosophy, Bloch's writings are certainly the most extravagant of the peripheral manifestations of Marxism. He stands alone in his attempt
to graft on to the inherited doctrine a complete metaphysic, cosmology, and
speculative cosmogony in a gnostic and apocalyptic style, inspired by the most
varied sources. Although we use the word 'graft' as an interpretation of Bloch's
intent, he himself believed that he was piecing together the fragments of Marx's
thought so as to reveal its hidden metaphysical meaning: a picture of the world
tending towards a universal synthesis of all forces and factors, not only social
phenomena but the cosmos as a whole. According to this philosophy the significance of being is revealed only in acts directed towards the future. Such acts,
of which 'hope' is the most general description, are both cognitive and affective, but they are also the actual creation of the hoped-for reality, a movement
of the universe towards its own entelechy. Bloch's works are in fact prophetic
appeals, couched in an aphoristic and poetic prose which derives from the literary tradition of German expressionism. His style, involved and bristling with
neologisms, is indigestible reading for anyone not familiar with the oddities of
German philosophical language, which have flourished exuberantly from the
days of Meister Eckhart to those of Heidegger, not forgetting Böhme and Hegel.
Besides a fondness for unusual words and linguistic combinations, Bloch took
over Heidegger's device of turning adverbs, conjunctions, etc. into nouns: *das
Wohin, das Wozu, das Woher, das Nicht, das Noch-nicht, das Dass*, and so forth.
Some critics regard him as a master of German prose; others consider his style
artificial and pretentious, concealing poverty of thought beneath a welter of
baroque ornamentation. Certainly at times the reader feels as though he were
amid the fumes of an alchemist's laboratory, and when he reduces the poetic
verbiage to everyday terms he may find it sterile and commonplace. Nevertheless, Bloch's metaphysical constructions should not be ignored. Interest in his
philosophy has tended to increase of late; some theologians, even, have found
inspiration in it, and, what is relevant to our own purpose, for most of his life
he considered himself to be a full-blown Marxist.

1. Life and writings

ERNST BLOCH (1885–1977), the son of assimilated Jewish parents, was born at Ludwigshafen. His intellectual development coincided with the modernist or neo-Romantic revolt against positivism and evolutionism. This revolt took the form of both unorthodox variants of Kantianism and *Lebensphilosophie*, allied with Bergsonian trends and with an interest, fostered by Oriental lore, in the hermetic, occult, and gnostic tradition and in non-dogmatic, uncodified expressions of the religious instinct. From 1905 onwards Bloch studied under Lipps at Munich and Külpe at Würzburg. His doctoral thesis on Rickert's philosophy, published in 1909 as *Kritische Erörterungen über Rickert und das Problem der modernen Erkenntnistheorie*, contained the germ of important later themes. In particular it called for a new utopian theory of knowledge (and even, according to Bloch, a new logic) which would apply to things not as they actually are but only as they may become. This theory would not be based on the principle of identity and the formula 'S is P', but would address itself to the latent potentialities and future destiny of objects, allowing room for the operations of fancy and dealing in propositions of the type 'S is not yet P'. It would thus provide for elements that are as yet wholly or partially latent, in the human mind, and thus for the expression of the unconscious.

Bloch continued his studies at Berlin, where his philosophical mentor was Simmel. He also studied physics and was interested in a wide range of humanistic subjects: poetry, painting, music, and drama. He absorbed socialist ideas, though as far as is known he did not join any political party. During the 1914–18 War he became a Marxist, but in a restricted sense. His utopian ideas on metaphysics and the theory of knowledge were not expressed at this time as a reconstruction of Marx's thought; instead, he added Marxism to them as a separate political ideology. This is especially clear in the first important book on which he worked during the war, published in 1918 as *Geist der Utopie* (a second, revised edition appeared in 1923). By this time, in Bloch's usage, the word 'Utopia' had lost the pejorative sense which it bore for Marx and the whole Marxist tradition. Bloch, on the contrary, held that Marxism was insufficiently utopian, and that it was not bold enough in anticipating a world that was inherently possible although not immediately so. This utopian boldness was present, on the other hand, in the tradition of chiliastic popular movements and especially German revolutionary anabaptism, the subject of Bloch's next book (*Thomas Münzer als Theologe der Revolution*, 1921). Mot of the ideas that he was to develop throughout his life are contained in *Geist der Utopie*: like his subsequent works, it does not itself define a Utopia except in very general terms, but is a summons to utopian thought. Its argument is that man is a utopian subject, a focus of unrealized possibilities which it is the task of philosophy to awaken into life. The primacy of practical reason is thus valid in philosophy, not in Kant's sense but in the sense that philosophy's task is not merely to describe what is, but to contribute to the emergence of a world that is still latent and cannot be born without human initiative. Our souls contain strata of the not-yet-conscious, of our own hidden future and that of all being: we are not yet what we really and essentially are, and the universe itself has not yet attained its own essence and its own calling. What that essence and destiny are cannot be ascertained by empirical observation and scientific rules, but our imagination is capable of encompassing the world which may be, though it is not yet.

Bloch thus follows the Platonists in believing that things have a 'truth' of their own which does not coincide with their actual empirical existence but which can be discovered. In his view, however, this 'truth' is not actually in being anywhere, but can be made actual by the human will and human activity. We are able to discover this form within us: Utopia is contained in our actual experience, but it consists in a complete transformation of the universe, a grand apocalypse, the descent of the Messiah, a new heaven, and a new earth. Utopian philosophy is not eschatology in the sense of merely awaiting the *eschaton*, but is a way of attaining it; it is not a contemplation but an action, an act of the will rather than of reason. Everything we were promised by the Messianism of past ages, there is a possibility of actuating by our own power. There is no God to guarantee that we shall succeed: God himself is part of the Utopia, a finality that is still unrealized.

In *Geist der Utopie* Bloch followed the tradition of Jewish apocalyptic literature, which he combined with vague ideas of socialism and anarchism: it is not clear what the world which has attained salvation is to be like, except that it will be a realm of freedom with no need for mediating institutions such as the state and politics. Here Bloch conformed to Marx's ideas, but in so general a form as to preserve no more of Marxism than can be found in Thomas Münzer's sermons. The comparison, moreover, seems to be to Marx's disadvantage: he is reproached for putting too much faith in the impersonal mechanism of history, whereas the Utopia can only be brought about by human will. Thus the early Bloch's respect for Marx's views is similar to that we have seen in Sorel, and is basically different from any of the standard versions of Marxism.

In the twenties and until Hitler's accession to power Bloch lived in Germany as an independent writer, occupying no academic post. He was a friend of Walter Benjamin and also of Lukács, though he criticized the latter for the schematic and purely 'sociological' interpretation of the world in *History and Class-Consciousness*, and also for his dogmatic condemnation of expressionist literature. In these years Bloch also published a collection of essays entitled *Durch die Wüste* (1923), attacking the utilitarianism, nihilism, and pragmatism of bourgeois civilization, and *Spuren* (1930), a rambling work inspired by various anecdotes and legends. Forced to emigrate in 1933, he spent some time in Switzerland, Paris, and Prague. In 1935 he published *Erbschaft dieser Zeit*, a critique of Nazism and an analysis of its cultural sources. In this work he identified himself wholly with Marxism and also with political Communism, though he never joined any Communist party or accepted the Stalinist version of Marxism which was then in force. He supported Stalin, however, at the critical period of the great purges and the Moscow trials.

In 1938 Bloch emigrated to the United States, where he spent the war years, writing for *émigré* German periodicals and preparing his *magnum opus*, *Das Prinzip Hoffnung*. Returning to Europe in 1949, he affirmed his solidarity with Stalinist socialism by accepting an appointment as Professor of Philosophy at Leipzig. He spent the next twelve years in East Germany and, especially in the early part of this period, repeatedly professed his absolute political loyalty to the regime. At this time he published a book on Hegel (*Subjekt–Objekt. Erläuterungen zu Hegel*, 1951); a short essay on Avicenna, whose thousandth anniversary according to the Muslim calendar was then being celebrated ('Avicenna und die Aristotelische Linke', 1952); an essay on Thomasius ('Christian Thomasius. Ein deutscher Gelehrter onhe Misere', 1953); and three volumes of *Das Prinzip Hoffnung* (1954, 1955, 1959), a revision and enlargement of the text as originally written. As a non-party Marxist whose political loyalty was unquestioned, Bloch received rewards and tokens of respect from the authorities; his idiosyncratic interpretation of Marxism was tolerated despite the strict Stalinist orthodoxy of philosophical teaching and literature in East Germany at that time. Every now and then, however, articles attacking him were published by official party philosophers, and the attacks were intensified after the Twentieth Congress of the Soviet Communist party in 1956: this event gave rise to passionate discussions throughout Eastern Europe, and Bloch, albeit in cautious and fairly abstract terms, evinced a definite sympathy for 'liberal' or 'revisionist' ideas. Thus it was that, two years after a Festschrift in honour of his seventieth birthday, a collective work was published denouncing him for 'revisionism', 'idealism', 'mysticism', flirting with religion, and voicing anti-Marxist demands for greater cultural freedom in the G.D.R. In 1956 a group of his pupils and collaborators were imprisoned for 'revisionist' plans of party and political reform, and Bloch himself was forbidden to teach, though publication of the third volume of *Das Prinzip Hoffnung* was finally allowed. Bloch had become increasingly disillusioned with East European socialism, and, happening to be in West Berlin in the summer of 1961, when the Berlin wall was erected, he resolved to join the millions who were fleeing from the G.D.R. to West Germany. Although seventy-six years old he was offered a university chair at Tubingen, where he lived till his death. Having broken politically with the

Soviet system, he became the advocate of a renewal of Communism. Besides republishing several earlier works he published in these years *Naturrecht und menschliche Würde* (1961), an attempt to salvage the concept of natural law in Marxist terms, also *Tübinger Einleitung in die Philosophie* (two vols., 1963–4), *Atheismus im Christentum* (1968), and numerous articles and essays. He received many honours and awards, and the firm of Suhrkamp embarked on a sixteen-volume edition of his works from 1959 onwards.

Throughout his life Bloch was a typical example of what may be called an academic thinker, whose knowledge of political reality was mainly derived from books. He had a vast knowledge of literature and philosophy, but his powers of analysis were extremely poor. His frequent political statements, both during his Stalinist and anti-Stalinist days, were naïve, vague, and stereotyped, mere echoes of current slogans and clichés. It is clear that he had no conception of economics. Throughout his life he remained a literary man deeply versed in books, dreaming of a perfect world yet unable to explain how it was to be created, or even what form its perfection was to take.

2. *Basic ideas*

BLOCH's writings consist to a large extent of self-contained aphorisms expressed in one or a few sentences, and conveying in a concise form the essence of his philosophy. Here are some examples:

> Der Mensch ist dasjenige, was noch vieles vor sich hat. Er wird in seiner Arbeit und durch sie immer wieder umgebildet. Er steht immer wieder vorn an Grenzen, die keine mehr sind, indem er sie wahrnimmt, er überschreitet sie. Das Eigentliche ist im Menschen wie in der Welt ausstehend, wartend, steht in der Furcht, vereitelt zu werden, steht in der Hoffnung, zu gelingen. (*Das Prinzip Hoffnung*, Suhrkamp ed., pp. 284–5)
>
> (Man is he who has much before him. He is constantly transformed in and through his work. He is always reaching boundaries that are boundaries no longer: as he perceives them, so he passes beyond them. That which is genuine in man and in the world waits and endures, in the fear of frustration and the hope of success.)

> Von früh auf will man zu sich. Aber wir wissen nicht, wer wir sind. Nur dass keiner ist, was er sein möchte, scheint klar. Von daher der gemeine Neid, nämlich auf diejenigen, die zu haben, ja zu sein scheinen, was einem zukommt. Von daher aber auch die Lust, Neues zu beginnen, das mit uns selbst anfängt. Stets wurde versucht, uns gemäss zu leben. (Ibid., p. 1089)
>
> (From our earliest days we try to find ourselves. But we do not know who we are. All that seems clear is that no one is what he would like to be. Hence our usual envy of others who seem to have, or even to be, what is rightly ours. But hence also the joy

of starting something new that begins with us. We have always tried to live in accordance with our own being.)

Ich bin. Aber ich habe mich nicht. Darum werden wir erst. Das Bin ist innen. Alles Innen ist an sich dunkel. Um sich zu sehen und gar was um es ist, muss es aus sich heraus. (*Tübinger Einleitung*, i, 11)

(I am, but I do not possess myself. Thus we are still in course of becoming. The 'am' is within us, and whatever is within is in darkness. In order to perceive itself and what is around it, it must come out of itself.)

This is a typical sample of Bloch's ideas, and of his characteristic lack of precision. Most of his imposing volumes consist of variations on the same theme; their repetitiveness is almost without parallel. From the aphorisms quoted above, an outline of his doctrine may be constructed.

The universe, and man in particular, are not finite but contain many possibilities. No objective laws, operating independently of man, decide which possibilities will be finally realized. The eventualities are either total destruction or perfection. Perfection consists in the identity of empirical existence with the hidden 'essence' of man and the universe. We must not, however, speak of this as a 'return', since that would suggest that perfection was realized in some golden age of the past, so that the subsequent history of the cosmos and mankind has been a decline and not an ascent: The truth is that our essence, with which we may or may not succeed in identifying, awaits its own fulfilment. This depends on human will and on our ability to surmount the successive barriers that life places in our way; and the condition of our success is to maintain a positive attitude towards the future, in other words a state of hope. Hope is an affective quality but it is also something more: it embodies a particular kind of knowledge, revealing to us the world as it is capable of being. Moreover, it is an attribute of the whole of being, as the urge towards goodness and perfection which pervades the universe is expressed in the orientation of the human mind. Cosmic destiny is fulfilled by human activity. The future, which does not yet exist, is not mere nothingness but has its own peculiar ontological status as a real possibility latent in things and human attitudes. The task of philosophy is to arouse this slumbering utopian potential of mankind.

To indicate how Bloch develops this thought we shall take *Das Prinzip Hoffnung* as a basis, since this work appears to include all his important ideas and concepts.

3. Greater and lesser day-dreams

FROM the dawn of history, Bloch observes, in all cultures and at all stages of individual and social development, men have dreamt of a better and brighter life, of superhuman powers and a world without care, suffering, and struggle: in short they have, more or less skilfully, constructed various kinds of Utopia. We find the germ of such utopias in children's dreams, fairy-tales, and popular legend—in such archetypes as Aladdin's lamp, seven-league boots, magic carpets, Fortunatus's cap, or the ring of Gyges. At the lowest level these daydreams relate simply to immediate private ends such as wealth, glory, or sexual satisfaction: we do not seek to change the world, but only to get more out of it for ourselves. At the higher level, in revolutionary utopias, our attitude is the reverse. We refuse to allow that one man's happiness should be bought at the cost of another's misfortune or enslavement; we want not only a better world than the present, but a paradisal state in which there is no longer any evil, misfortune, or suffering. 'Whereas the negative emotions of expectation (*die negativen Affekte der Erwartung*) and their utopian images are oriented towards hell as their ultimate end (*ihr Unbedingtes*), the positive emotions of expectation [i.e. hope]—are oriented no less absolutely towards paradise' (*Das Prinzip Hoffnung*, p. 127).

In other words, the positive or what Bloch calls the 'concrete' Utopia is the expectation of absolute perfection, the Hegelian consummation of history: it is the will having as its object the Totum, Ultimum, or *eschaton*. Bloch insists that there are only two possibilities, all or nothing, absolute destruction and nothingness or absolute perfection; there is no middle term. 'Nothingness too is a utopian category, though an extremely anti-utopian one . . . nothingness, in the same way as a positive Utopicum: one's native home (*Heimat*) or the All are present only as an objective possibility' (p. 11). 'Since the historical process is undetermined inasmuch as its trend and outcome are as yet unrealized, its final upshot (*Mündung*) may be either Nothing or All, total failure (*das Umsonst*) or total success' (p. 222).

The expressions Totum, Ultimum, Optimum, *summum bonum*, *eschaton*, the All, being (*das Sein*), and *Heimat* all mean the same thing. *Heimat* represents being-in-oneself, man's complete reconciliation with himself and the universe, the elimination of all that is negative, the final state (*Endzustand*) in which all alienation is overcome. The utopian will, according to Bloch, is not a matter of endless endeavour or endless progress: it aspires to actual fulfilment within a finite time.

The history of civilization is one of innumerable utopias, not only great all-embracing ones but partial ones as well; all of them, however, have reflected the human desire for absolute goodness. Utopian dreams can be found in poetry and drama, music and painting. There are architectural utopias, geographical ones such as Eldorado or Eden, medical ones such as the dream of eternal youth or the final abolition of disease and physical disability. Sport is a kind of Utopia, in which people try to overcome the natural limitations of the human frame. Dancing, fairs, circuses—even these are expressions of man's constant yearning for perfection, unconscious though it often is. Finally there are the elaborate blueprints of a perfect world in utopian literature, in the chiliastic visions of the Middle Ages and the sixteenth century, in the whole history of religion with its Messianic expectations and ideas of salvation, the Saviour, and heaven.

Man, according to Bloch, is essentially Utopia-minded, believing in a perfect world and anticipating the future with undying hope. There is scarcely any aspect of culture that is not pervaded by this irresistible utopian energy, and we would therefore expect it to have left a strong mark on the history of philosophy. In fact, however, almost the whole of European philosophy before Marx turned away from the future and culpably fixed its eyes on the past; it was content to interpret the existing world instead of planning a better one and teaching men how to create it. It is not clear why philosophy distinguished itself thus negatively from other branches of culture. 'Plato's theory that all knowledge is nothing but *anamnesis*, the recollection of something once seen—this version of knowledge centred on the past (*Ge-wesenheit*) has since been repeated incessantly' (p. 158). Even doctrines which contained projections of a final state of perfection did not really envisage the future: their Ultimum was a false one, as it was always realized initially in the Absolute. Such philosophies, including Hegel's, did not recognize the Novum: they had no notion of real change and orientation towards the future. 'Throughout Judaeo-Christian philosophy, from Philo and Augustine to Hegel, the Ultimum is related only to the Primum and not to the Novum, so that what finally comes about is only a repetition of what was in the beginning—something already fulfilled, which has meanwhile become lost or alienated' (p. 233). Thus pre-Marxian philosophy recognized an Ultimum but knew of no true novelty in the world, as it assumed an initially realized Absolute. Perfection or salvation was represented as the return to a lost paradise, not the conquest of a possible one.

It might seem that Bloch would at least approve of twentieth-century attempts to describe a real Novum, such as we find in the metaphysics of Bergson or Whitehead. This is not so, however. In Bergson, it appears, the 'new' is an abstraction, a mere negation of repetition; moreover, his whole philosophy is not one of anticipation, but is Impressionistic and liberal-anarchic. From some of Bloch's remarks it would seem that not only philosophy but the whole of human knowledge before Marx was fettered to the past, capable only of describing it and not of looking to the future. Capitalism intensified this attitude by turning all objects into commodities and thus bringing about the 'reification' of thought: reified thought, reduced to the form of commodities, expresses itself as fact-worship or 'crawling empiricism'. On this point Bloch more or less follows Lukács and the Frankfurt school. 'The fetishism of facts' and 'shallow empiricism', devoid of imagination and fettered to 'isolated' phenomena, are incapable of apprehending the 'whole' or of grasping the 'essential' in the course of history (*was wesentlich geschieht*) (p. 256).

All these comments on philosophy, past and present, add up to casual condemnation with no attempt at analysis. Bloch devotes somewhat more attention to psychoanalysis, which from his point of view is the negation of the future *par excellence*. Bloch, as we have seen, is concerned to replace the category of the unconscious by the 'not yet conscious', that which is latent within us in the form of anticipation but is not yet articulate. But in all versions of psychoanalysis, whether Freud's or those of his more or less faithful disciples, the unconscious derives from accumulations of the past and contains nothing new. This backward orientation is even more evident in Jung, the 'psychoanalytical Fascist', who interprets the whole human psyche in terms of collective prehistory and proclaims 'hatred of intelligence' as the only remedy for the ills of modern life. Freud, being a liberal, sought to bring the unconscious into the light of day, whereas Jung wants to thrust our consciousness back beneath the surface. As for Adler, he in a simply capitalist way considers the will to power as the fundamental human impulse (p. 63). In any case, all forms of psychoanalysis are backward-looking, which is accounted for by the fact that they express the consciousness of the bourgeoisie, a class without a future.

The revolutionary utopias of past ages reflected humanity's desire for perfection and even the knowledge that it was possible; post-Marxian Utopias are, without exception, reactionary. Wells's 'bourgeois democratic Utopia', for instance, 'is coated with a moral veneer, a simulacrum of human rights, as if the capitalist whore could once more become a virgin'; but 'freedom as the Utopia of Western capitalism is chloroform, nothing else' (p. 682).

4. Marxism as a 'concrete Utopia'

MARXISM, and it alone, has given humanity a full and consistent perception of the future. What is more, Marxism is wholly future-oriented: it recognizes the past only in so far as it is still alive and is therefore part of the future. Marxism has achieved the 'discovery that concrete theory-practice is strictly bound up with the observed mode of objective-real possibility' (p. 236). Marxism is a science, but one that has overcome the dualism of being and thought, of what is and what ought to be; it is both a theory of the future paradise and a praxis which brings it about.

Marxism is an all-embracing Utopia, but, unlike the dreams of previous ages, it is a concrete and not an abstract one. The phalansteries or the New Harmony were types of an abstract Utopia; Marx's concrete Utopia contains no exact predictions concerning the society of the future, but it opposes to the old fantasies 'an actively conscious participation in the immanent historical process of the revolutionary transformation of society' (p. 725). 'The point of a concrete Utopia is to understand precisely the dream concerning it, a dream rooted in the historical process itself' (p. 727). In short, what makes a Utopia concrete is that we can give no exact account of it—a truly classic instance of *lucus a non lucendo*.

Although Bloch declares that the supreme good, or the Totum, has been scientifically analysed, all we learn of it in his works is contained in a few phrases borrowed from Marx: it will be a classless society, a realm of freedom in which there will be no alienation, and so on. It will also mean the reconciliation of man with nature: Bloch mentions several times, as of key importance, the sentences about the 'humanization of nature' from Marx's Paris Manuscripts of 1844. For a Utopia cannot be 'concrete' unless it embraces the 'whole', i.e. the universe; as long as our imagination restricts itself to the organization of society and ignores nature, it is no better than 'abstract'.

Marxism is an act of hope, embodying knowledge of the anticipated world and the will to create it. This will and this knowledge have their counterpart, not in empirical reality but in the higher and more real 'essential' order. Unlike empiricist philosophy, Marxism, rightly understood, includes the ontology of that which is not yet (*Ontologie des Noch-Nicht*). 'Expectation, hope, intention towards possibilities that have not yet materialized—all this is not only a mark of human consciousness but, when rightly understood and regulated, is a fundamental determinant within objective reality as a whole. Since Marx there has been no possible inquiry into truth and no realism of decision that did not take account of the subjective and objective content of hope in the universe' (p. 5). 'The not-yet-conscious in man thus belongs wholly to that part of the external world that has not yet happened, not yet emerged or manifested itself. The not-yet-conscious communicates and interacts with what has not yet happened' (p. 12). 'Until reality has been completely determined, as long as it still embodies open possibilities in the form of new beginnings and new areas of development, we cannot absolutely reject a Utopia on the basis of purely factual reality . . . A concrete Utopia finds its counterpart in emergent reality (*Prozesswirklichkeit*), the counterpart of the mediated Novum . . . The anticipating elements are themselves a component of reality' (pp. 226–7).

We thus find in Bloch the typical neo-Platonic and Hegelian concept of non-empirical reality, which, however, in this case is not a perfection already actualized somewhere, like the Platonic ideas, nor a mere arbitrary normative construction, but which, as an anticipation, is invisibly present in the empirical world. Bloch himself does not invoke Hegel or the neo-Platonists in this content, but rather the Aristotelian concept of entelechy and the 'creative matter' of Aristotle's followers. The world, he believes, has a kind of immanent purposiveness whereby it evolves, out of incomplete forms, complete ones. These forms are both natural and normative. However, Bloch does not seem to be aware that his use of the concepts of energy, potentiality, and entelechy differs from Aristotle's in one major respect. These concepts are more or less intelligible when applied to particular objects and processes—a plant evolving a complete form hidden in a seed, for instance—but they cease to be intelligible when applied to being as a whole. Aristotle used them, in fact, to describe the empirical processes of development in the organic world and in purposive human activity. Bloch's concepts, however, relating to the entelechy of the whole universe, owe nothing to empirical observation: they merely express a speculative belief in the tendency of the universe towards a perfection about which we can predicate nothing. We do know, however, according to Bloch, that any objections to the hope of absolute perfection that may be raised on the basis of existing scientific knowledge are invalid *a priori*, because 'facts' have no ontological meaning and may be ignored without hesitation: what matters are the premonitions of the anticipating fancy. Thus Marxism, as Bloch understands it, need not be constrained in any way by our present state of knowledge. That a barley corn will grow into an ear of barley is something we can rationally expect on the basis of experience; that the present not very perfect universe is destined, by virtue of an immanent natural purpose, to turn into a perfect one is clearly not only unprovable, but hard to imagine with any degree of plausibility. Bloch is aware of this and of the fact that the existing rules of scientific thought give no support to his idea of the Ultimum; instead, he invokes the aid of imagination, artistic inspiration, and enthusiasm. This would not be out of the way if he considered himself a poet, but he contends that the anticipating fancy is a science in its own right—not an ordinary one, but a science of a superior kind, free from the irksome constraints of logic and observation.

It is not sufficient to say, however, that the 'essence of the universe' is in a 'not yet manifested state' (p. 149), so that the possibilities inherent in it are, as it were, a task to be accomplished, a latent desire, an 'objective fantasy' of Being as a whole. It is also important that this task can be accomplished only through the will and consciousness of mankind, and not simply by the force of cosmic laws. The human race, in fact, is not merely an executant of the universe's intentions, the instrument of a blind mysterious providence; it also wields a power of decision. Man can choose whether to bring the universe to perfection or destruction—there is, as already stated, no middle way—and which the outcome will be is not determined in advance. Thus man is in a sense the guide of the universe, bearing on his shoulders not only the weight of human history but that of Being as a whole. This idea is typical of neo-Platonism, but Bloch, with enviable self-assurance, ascribes it to Marx. In the *Tübinger Ein-*

leitung (p. 231) he quotes Marx as saying that 'man is the root of all things'; what Marx actually wrote, at the age of twenty-five, was that 'man himself is the root of man', which is obviously quite different.

Since Bloch's Ultimum, or paradise, is not simply the final state of the world as it must be, but has to be realized by human will, it is never clear in what sense the present really 'contains' the future—in what sense our 'knowledge' of the future world relates to that world, and how far it is merely an act of will. From this point of view his concept of a higher or 'essential' reality is no less ambiguous than the similar concept of the surrealists. In surrealist philosophy it is not clear whether the world to which we have access through special hallucinatory experiences is a ready-made reality to which they provide the key, or something we create even as we become aware of it. However, this ambiguity does not matter in the case of the surrealists, since their philosophy is only an offshoot of their art. Bloch, on the other hand, purports to be using the language of discursive philosophy, in which the ambiguity of basic concepts is suicidal.

Bloch is excusable on this point to the extent that his ambiguities are those of the Hegel–Marx tradition in general. As we saw in the case of Lukács, it is characteristic of this tradition to blur the distinction between foreseeing the future and creating it. It is here that prophets and scientists part company. When a scientist foretells occurrences, accurately or otherwise, he relies on observation of the past and on the belief that he understands the interrelations of events; he does not claim to know the future, since such knowledge is impossible, but only to foresee it with greater or less probability. A prophet, on the other hand, does not 'foresee' anything: the source of his knowledge of the future is not the past but the future itself, which in a mysterious way is already present to him, with an ontological status of its own. Bloch speaks of a reality which 'is not yet', but which he emphatically distinguishes from nothingness or pure negation. The 'not' certainly implies a lack, but it is a lack of *something* and therefore represents a striving towards that something, a creative desire by which the world is pervaded; it must be opposed to nothingness and not to the All (*Das Prinzip Hoffnung*, pp. 356-7). The subjective counterpart of the 'not yet', namely 'not-yet-awareness', is not to be regarded as pure negation but rather as an urge of the mind to become conscious of a certain object. Bloch refers to Leibniz's 'little perceptions' to explain what he has in mind: a kind of inarticulate knowledge which is none the less knowledge, a paradoxical state in which we know something that we do not know, or that we know potentially but not actually.

In this way the prophet is in an extremely convenient position. On the one hand, he does not have to give reasons for his predictions, as he makes it clear in advance that they are not based on pedestrian empiricism, that he scorns the tyranny of facts and logic. On the other hand, he delivers his prophecies with the utmost assurance, based on his special power of perceiving what is somehow already present although it has not yet occurred. His knowledge is higher and far more certain than the scientist's, and he does not have to explain its source or the reasons for it: anyone who demands explanations is a self-confessed exponent of 'reified consciousness' and a slave to 'crawling empiricism'.

Clearly, the self-styled prophet, enjoying this freedom of intellectual manœuvre, can promise whatever comes into his head, while assuring us that his promises are based on a superior type of knowledge. Bloch, while making the proviso that the social organization of the future Utopia cannot be described in advance, speaks of an entirely new kind of technology effecting a radical change in our lives. Capitalism, he explains, has created a technology based on a purely quantitative and mechanistic conception of nature as opposed to a qualitative approach. In the future we shall enjoy a miraculous technology which he calls 'non-Euclidean' (ibid., pp. 775 ff.). Leaving the details of the technical revolution to be worked out by others, he nevertheless assures us that if it were not for imperialism we should already be able to irrigate the Sahara and the Gobi desert, and turn Siberia and the Antarctic into pleasure resorts, at the cost of 'a few hundredweight of uranium and thorium'. 'Non-Euclidean technology' will restore man's intimacy with nature and make possible a 'qualitative' attitude towards it which 'abstract capitalism' (Bloch's own phrase) is incapable of achieving. Nor should we bother about the law of increasing entropy, as the techniques of the future will take care of that also.

5. Death as an anti-Utopia. God does not yet exist, but he will

BLOCH's anticipations become even bolder when he deals with the problem of death and the 'subject of nature'. The third volume of *Das Prinzip Hoffnung* gives an extended account of ancient Egyptian, Greek, Jewish, Buddhist, Hindu, and Christian ideas on immortality, after which Bloch puts forward the following conclusions. The belief of traditional religions in immortality or the transmigration of souls is pure fantasy, but it is a manifestation of the utopian will and of human dignity. In the materialist dialectic, on the other hand, 'the universe is not bounded by Newton's mechanics' (p. 1303).

> Dialectical as opposed to mechanistic materialism acknowledges no boundaries, no negations prescribed by an alleged 'natural order' ... The utopian final aim of its practice is the humanization of nature ... Here as everywhere else, Communist cosmology [*sic*] is the realm of problems related to the dialectical mediation between man and his labour on the one hand and a possible subject of nature on the other ... The word 'No' can never be pronounced from the outset: if nature contains no positive

answer to the problems of our destiny, it also contains none that are, once and for all, negative ... No one knows what is in the universe outside the range of human labour, that is to say in unmediated nature; we do not know whether any subject or agency is at work there, and if so, of what kind it is ... All this depends on the development and prospects of human power, and hence, more precisely, on the development and unfolding horizons of Communism. (*Das Prinzip Hoffnung*, pp. 1382–3)

The kernel of human existence (*der Kern des Existierens*) has not yet fully displayed itself, and therefore it is 'exterritorial vis à vis the process of becoming and transformation' (ibid., p. 1390); if the world developed to a state of complete frustration (*zu einem absoluten Umsonst*), then and only then would death penetrate to the core of nature which lies in the human heart.

In so far as this argument can be understood, it may be summarized by saying that all the promises of traditional religion as to immortality are vain, but when we have built Communism we shall somehow overcome the problem of death. To put it as kindly as possible, this must be the most frivolous promise that has ever been uttered in the name of a political movement. It is paralleled only by the last of Bloch's utopian hopes—the eventual creation of God, as to which he argues as follows.

The kernel of all religion is the attainment of the kingdom of absolute human perfection. Hence, if the aim of religion is pushed to its furthest extent, it is seen to require the elimination of God as an entity limiting human powers, the removal of such limitation being implicit in all religious Utopias. Here, it would seem, Bloch is simply following Feuerbach, who held that the truth of religion is atheism: if we try to express exactly what people want from religion, it turns out to be the non-existence of God.

> The intention of religion concerning the Kingdom conceived in its fullest sense, presupposes atheism ... Atheism excludes the *Ens perfectissimum* (which is what was meant by 'God') from the creation and evolution of the world, defining it not as a fact but as the only thing it can be, viz. the supreme utopian problem, the problem of finality. The place assigned in particular religions to what was called 'God' was ostensibly filled by the hypostasis of God, and when this is discarded the vacant place continues to exist, as the ultimate projection of a radical utopian intention ... The place corresponding to the God of olden times is not itself nothing ... Authentic, i.e. dialectical materialism does away with the transcendence and reality of any hypostasis of God, but it does not exclude what was meant by the *Ens perfectissimum* from the real Utopia of the kingdom of freedom, the final content of the qualitative process ... The Utopia of the kingdom destroys the fiction of God the Creator and the hypostasis of God in heaven, but it does not destroy the ultimate dwelling-place where the *Ens perfectissimum* preserves the abyss of its latent unfrustrated possibility. (*Dans Prinzip Hoffnung*, pp. 1412–13)

Thus religion, according to Bloch, does not simply terminate in the absence of religion but leaves a legacy in the shape of the final problem of perfected being. Instead of a ready-made heaven in the 'next world', we have the command to create a new heaven and a new earth. However, mindful of Lenin's scornful attitude to the 'God-builders' in the Russian social-democratic movement, Bloch makes it clear that he does not regard the world as a machine for the production of a supreme being, but that when God is removed we shall still possess the 'total content of the hope' to which the name 'God' was formerly given. This vague language seems to mean only that the perfect Being will emerge under Communism. Elsewhere this perfect Being is called the 'possible subject of nature' or the *Dass-Antrieb* (urge towards 'thatness'). To understand this last expression it should be realized that in Bloch's vocabulary 'thatness' represents either a state of things or a purpose ('in order that. . .'); he makes full use of this ambiguity, but it is probably simplest to read *das Dass* as signifying a purposive process or the awareness of an aim. In this way Communism will achieve the creation of God, which is more than all the religions of the world have done. Bloch's philosophy is in the last resort a theogony, a fantastic projection of the God that is to be: 'the true Genesis is not in the beginning but at the end' (p. 1628).

6. Matter and materialism

THE picture of a world whose 'essence' embodies a Utopia or fantasy, and which is imbued with the purpose of attaining divine perfection, is on the face of it very different from traditional materialism, and it is understandable that it should be attacked by orthodox Leninists. Bloch himself maintains, however, that his philosophy is nothing but a continuation of dialectical materialism and in particular that it is based on materialism in Engels's sense—i.e. that it 'explains the universe in terms of itself' and presupposes no other reality than what is material.

In 'Avicenna and the Aristotelian Left' and in other works Bloch invokes the concept of creative matter which was present in the Aristotelian tradition and was taken over, he claims, by Marxism. Strato, Alexander of Aphrodysias, Avicenna, Averroës, Avicebron, David of Dinant, and finally Giordano Bruno evolved the concept of matter as a process, containing a diversity of forms and a permanent possibility of further development: any new thing that happens is not due to a force outside the universe, but is the manifestation of a potentiality residing in matter itself. There is no distinction between matter and form: forms are latent or manifest attributes of the single substratum, *natura naturans*.

In his lecture 'Zur Ontologie des Noch-Nicht-Seins' Bloch gives the following explanation purporting to be the definition of matter.

It is not a mere mechanical lump but—in accordance with the implicit sense of Aristotle's definition—it is both being-according-to-possibility (*kata to dynaton*, i.e. that which determines every possible historical phenomenon in accordance with conditions and with historical materialism), and also being-in-possibility (*dynamei on*, i.e. the correlative of that which is objectively and really possible or, ontically speaking, the possibility-substrate of the dialectical process). ('Sie ist nicht der mechanische Klotz, sondern—gemäss dem implizierten Sinn der Aristotelischen Materie-Definition—sowohl das Nach-Möglichkeit-Seiende (*kata to dynaton*), also das, was das jeweils geschichtlich Erscheinenkönnende bedingungsmässig, historisch-materialistisch bestimmt, wie das in- Möglichkeit-Seiende (Sein) (*dynamei on*), also das Korrelat des objektiv-real-Möglichen oder rein seinshaft: das Möglichkeits-Substrat des dialektischen Prozesses'.)

He goes on to say that 'inorganic nature, no less than human history, has its Utopia. This so-called inanimate nature is not a corpse but a centre of radiation, the abode of forms whose substance has not yet come into being.'

Thus, according to Bloch, matter is not characterized by any physical properties but simply by the fact of 'creativity' or immanent purpose. It is easy to point out that in that case 'materialism' means no more than that the world is subject to change and may develop in many unexpected ways. Matter is merely used as a term denoting 'all that is', and has all the divine attributes except complete actuality. In these nebulous arguments we do indeed hear echoes of Giordano Bruno, as well as of Böhme and Paracelsus. Matter is the *Urgrund*, an indeterminate *universum* out of which anything may come; thus conceived, it is indistinguishable from the God of pantheism. To say that 'all is matter' is a tautology, since matter is a synonym for 'all'—not only all that is actual, but all that is possible as well. It is not surprising, therefore, when Bloch tells us that 'matter' includes dreams, subjective images, aesthetic experiences, and the aesthetic qualities of the external world (which, it appears, are contained in nature but become actual through aesthetic perception). If God is possible his coming into existence involves no threat to materialism, since by definition he will be 'material' also.

What we have here is really not an assertion of materalism but of monism: the doctrine that there is one single substratum of all possible phenomena, including human subjectivity and all its products. Since the substratum in question has no qualities of its own and all we know of it is that it is 'creative' and contains all possibilities within itself, Bloch's monistic theory is likewise devoid of content. All that can exist, we are told, is material, and matter equals all that can exist.

Nevertheless, on two points at least Bloch's cosmology and metaphysics are regarded by him as supporting Marxism and, more precisely, the Leninist version thereof.

In the first place, not only does the universe embody an immanent purpose but, at least in the higher stages of evolution, it requires the participation of human subjectivity to realize its utopian potentialities or actualize its self-anticipations. Man is a product of matter, but since he appeared on the scene he has been, as it were, in charge of its further development: he is the head of creation, as in the theogony of Plotinus and Eriugena or the old neo-Platonist philosophy. That which is 'not yet conscious' in us is correlated, in an undefined way, with the 'not yet' of nature itself; the subjective 'not yet' is to become explicit through our efforts, thus making manifest the essence of the universe. Consequently, man cannot assume that the laws of evolution, whether consciously perceived or not, will ensure that the world becomes a better place. In terms of politics this means that the perfect world of the future can only be brought about by the conscious will of man. This is the metaphysical justification for Bloch's criticism of the 'fatalism' or determinism of the Second International, and for his allegiance to Leninist Marxism, which insists that revolutionary will plays a decisive part in the revolutionary process.

Secondly, the same metaphysic provides a bulwark against revisionism. As the future of the world is summed up in the dilemma 'all or nothing', if we do not want man and the universe to be destroyed we must go for the first alternative. Not only must the world be seen in terms of a movement evolving higher and higher forms, but it is intelligible only from the standpoint of final perfection. Metaphysics and social activity must alike be aimed at the *eschaton*, the complete and irreversible fulfilment of cosmic destiny, a synthesis of all the forces of being. Hence Bernstein is an enemy to Marxism when he preaches a revisionist programme of gradual or incomplete reforms lacking the horizon of ultimate perfection: the inspiration of the final goal is an inseparable part of Marxist philosophy, which on this fundamental point inherits the apocalyptic outlook of radical Anabaptism (*Das Prinzip Hoffnung*, pp. 676–9). Accordingly, one of Bloch's main criticisms of East European socialism in later years was that the party leaders promised various short-term advantages and improvements in lieu of the great utopian prospects offered by socialism.

7. Natural law

A SPECIAL FEATURE of Bloch's philosophy is his attempt to combine Marxism with a theory of natural law. His ideas on this subject are set out in several works, particularly *Naturrecht und menschliche Würde*. The idea that man has certain rights by nature, and that no positive law can deprive him of these without ceasing to be law in the true sense, has played a large part in utopian thought from ancient times to the present. It gave rise to the theory of the social contract, the principle of popular sovereignty, and the doctrine that tyranny

may be lawfully resisted. Unlike utopias in the classical sense, theories of natural law were inspired by the notion of human dignity rather than happiness or
economic efficiency. In Bloch's view, while they paved the way to bourgeois
democracy they contained elements of universal validity, not confined to that
or any other political system. Marxism is in a sense the heir of Locke, Grotius,
Thomasius, and Rousseau, not only of the utopians: for Communism is concerned not only with abolishing poverty but also with putting an end to the
humiliation of man. The theories of natural law also partook of utopianism, as
they contained anticipations of the notion of a supreme good. We also read in
Naturrecht und menschliche Würde that the socialist Utopia comprises 'bourgeois' freedoms such as those of the press, assembly, and free speech. However,
Bloch emphasizes that 'true' freedom involves the abolition of the state, and
that ideals can only be fully realized in the stateless socialist society. When that
comes there will be no more conflict between the individual and the community; freedom and happiness will not limit each other, compulsion will no
longer be needed, and there will be universal brotherhood. It is not clear, however, why such a perfect society should need laws at all, and what would be the
point of 'natural rights' which there was no occasion to assert against anyone,
as all would be living in a state of spontaneous solidarity.

8. Bloch's political orientation

IT WAS already clear in the 1930s, long before he took up his abode in the G.D.R.,
that although Bloch was not a member of any party, his political sympathies
were wholly on the side of Stalinism. Not only did he proclaim the socialist
Utopia, but he maintained that although the *summum bonum* was not fully in
existence anywhere, it was already taking shape in the Soviet Union. *Das Prinzip
Hoffnung* is full of passages that bear unambiguous testimony to its author's
politics, as he loses no opportunity of praising the superiority of the new order:
his expressions of this kind are mostly clichés without any probative force, but
they are embedded in his philosophy in such a way as to seem organically linked
with it. In particular he lays stress on the class interpretation of Utopia. We are
told, for instance, that the petty-bourgeois idea of Utopia is egoistic, while the
proletarian one is disinterested (pp. 33–4); concerning Utopias of longevity,
Bloch does not fail to point out that they are impossible under capitalism but
will be realized under socialism. Monopolistic capitalism has degraded man's
utopian aspirations by exploiting them in order to popularize record achievements out of which it derives profit (p. 54). Heidegger, it appears, is a propagandist for death at the behest of imperialism (p. 1365), and when he talks about
fear and boredom 'he reflects, from the petty-bourgeois standpoint, society
under monopoly capitalism, the normal state of which is perpetual crisis' (p.

124). Psychoanalysis, as we have seen, explains the human psyche by reference to the past because it arose in a society that has no future. Apropos of the utopian role of dancing, Bloch does not omit to mention that under capitalism it has a stultifying effect, as it is intended to dull people's senses and make them forget oppression, whereas the new 'socialist love of the fatherland' has revived the beauty of folk-dancing (pp. 456–8). Some of his remarks in this line sound like a downright parody of Stalinist propaganda. The book is full of ideological clichés such as: 'Socialism, as the ideology of the revolutionary proletariat, is nothing but true consciousness applied conceptually to the movement of events and the rightly understood trend of reality' (p. 177). Capitalist art and literature, we are told elsewhere, use the 'happy ending' to make up for the hopelessness of life in conditions of exploitation, whereas socialism 'has and maintains its own kind of happy ending' (p. 516). In the context of sport we hear about the degeneration of the human physique in an 'alienated society based on the division of labour' (p. 525); as to the prolongation of life and combating the effects of age, the Soviet Union has made progress in this direction for reasons which capitalism cannot afford to acknowledge (p. 535). Bloch cannot mention Malthus without adding that his spiritual descendants are 'American murderers' and that present-day Malthusianism is due to the imperialists' desire to practise genocide and exterminate the unemployed (p. 543). Capitalist freedom means freedom for the worker to starve, while in the 'land where socialism is being built' every effort is directed towards the abolition of violence (p. 1061). Under capitalism, moreover, there can be no such thing as true friendship, since the whole of life is dominated by buying and selling, whereas socialism is paving the way for universal friendship among all peoples (pp. 1132–3).

It is quite possible that Bloch inserted these nonsensical and servile propaganda phrases when revising *Das Prinzip Hoffnung* in the G.D.R. in the 1950s, and that they were a *sine qua non* of publication at the time. None the less, we must suppose that he believed them then and later, as they also figure in reprints published after he settled in West Germany.

In political speeches and articles written after 1961 (some of which are collected in a small volume entitled *Widerstand und Friede. Aufsätze zur Politik*, 1968) Bloch took up a position in favour of democratic socialism, though in very vague and general terms; he also condemned Stalinism in vague language, declaring that Marxism needs to be renewed, adapted to changing circumstances, and so on. Expressions of this sort had some meaning in Eastern Europe in 1955–6, but by the early sixties they had already become sterile clichés.

It would be unfair to say, however, that Bloch's identification with Leninism as a political doctrine and Stalinism as a political system is an organic and integral part of his metaphysical theory. That theory does not entail any specific political consequences or directives for self-commitment, and nothing of the kind could be deduced from *Das Prinzip Hoffnung* if the Stalinist trimmings were simply removed from its text. In this respect Bloch's case is on a par with that of Heidegger and his temporary identification with Nazism, though Heidegger was less outspoken and his philosophical works are not decked out with political moralizing in the same way. In their political utterances both men used their own characteristic concepts to buttress their loyalty to a totalitarian dictatorship, but the concepts themselves did not point in one direction more than another. The identification might equally have been the other way round: Bloch's category of 'hope' might have been used to glorify Nazism, and Heidegger's 'authenticity' (*Eigentlichkeit*) might have served the cause of Communist propaganda. Both concepts were vague and formal enough to be used in this way; neither theory contains any inbuilt moral restriction to inhibit such use, or prescribes any specific course of political action. It may be urged that this is not a valid objection to any metaphysic, since the latter has no duty to provide political directives, nor does its value depend on the political use made of it; such conclusions are not the necessary business of philosophy. But neither Bloch nor Heidegger can be defended on these lines, since they themselves claimed that their metaphysical doctrine, or philosophic anthropology, had and ought to have the practical purpose, not only of explaining the world but of showing how men must behave, and with what forces they must ally themselves in order to live worthily. The objection that a philosophical doctrine does not clearly suggest any particular way of life or social commitment is valid if the doctrine in question makes practical claims and purports to be normative, not merely descriptive. Heidegger's aggressive and arrogant phenomenology of existence has been of incomparably greater importance to twentieth-century philosophy, and has provided infinitely more stimulus to culture, than Bloch with his obscure and convoluted style; but they have this in common, that they both sought to erect a metaphysical foundation for practical life in the world and not merely for contemplation. For this purpose they devised respectively the obscure and purely formal categories of *Eigentlichkeit* and *Hoffnung*, which turn out to be applicable in any way one chooses.

9. Conclusion and comments

THE present writer cannot claim to assess the merits or defects of Bloch's German prose. As a philosopher, Bloch must be termed a preacher of intellectual irresponsibility. He cannot be credited with inventing a Utopia, still less a 'concrete' one: we turn with relief from his works to Fourier's 'abstract' Utopia with its quaint particularities. Bloch does no more than urge us to have utopian thoughts, and to speculate on a future that he himself makes no attempt to delineate.

Like many other Marxists, Bloch does not trouble to substantiate his assertions but merely proclaims them. On the rare occasions when he puts forward
an argument, it usually reveals his logical helplessness. For instance, he says
there is no such thing as unchanging human nature, because even such a universal phenomenon as hunger has taken different forms in the course of history, in that people at different times have preferred different foods (*Das
Prinzip Hoffnung*, pp. 75–6). The reader who endeavours to follow his arguments generally finds that they consist of truisms and tautologies, disguised in
verbiage of intolerable complexity. Here are some examples:

'Wir leben nicht, um zu leben, sondern weil wir leben, doch gerade in
diesem Weil oder besser: diesem leeren Dass, worin wir sind, ist nichts
beruhigt, steckt das nun erst fragende, bohrende Wozu' ('Zur Ontologie des
Noch-Nicht-Seins'). ('We do not live in order to live but because we live. But
in this "because", or rather in the empty "that" in which we live, there is no
reassurance, but rather the full challenge of the tormenting "why?"') In other
words, people often wonder what life is about.

Again: 'Es gäbe kein Heraufkommen in Zukunft, wenn das Latente schon
erschienen wäre, und es gäbe ebenso kein Vergehen in Vergangenheit, wenn
das in ihr Erschienene, bereits zur Erscheinung Gelöste dem Überhaupt in der
Tendenz entspräche' (ibid.). ('There would be no ascent into the future if that
which is latent had already appeared, and no lapse into the past if that which
appeared and was released in it corresponded to the "altogetherness" of the
trend'.) This seems to mean that if nothing changed, nothing would change.

Or again: 'Das Wirkliche ist Prozess; dieser ist die weitverzweigte Vermit-
tlung zwischen Gegenwart, unerledigter Vergangenheit und vor allem:
möglicher Zukunft' (*Das Prinzip Hoffnung*, p. 225). ('The real is a process; this
process is the widely ramified mediation between the present, the undisposed-
of past and, above all, the possible future'.) It is hard to detect in this any meaning beyond the commonplace statement that the world is subject to change.

Bloch's incapacity for analysis is raised to the rank of a theoretical virtue in
his frequent wholesale condemnations of 'positivism', the 'fetishism of facts',
and 'positivist logic'. Like Lukács, he adopts the slogan 'so much the worse for
the facts' (*Tübinger Einleitung*, p. 114), declaring that it signifies the 'primacy
of practical reason' and the need for 'humanization' of the world and of the
'logic of philosophy'.

It should perhaps be pointed out that I am not criticizing Bloch for his
attack on positivism in general or for refusing to accept the concept of a 'fact'
as something self-evident, requiring no argument. Bloch, however, is not a
philosophical critic. It suffices to compare his contemptuous phrases about the
'fetishism of facts' with the rational discussions among positivists themselves

concerning the concept of a 'fact', or to compare the penetrating critique of positivism in Volume I of Jaspers's *Philosophy*, or in the works of the phenomenologists Husserl and Ingarden, with Bloch's invective against 'crawling empiricism'.

What disqualifies Bloch's philosophy is not that it is wrong but that it lacks content. There is certainly no harm in fantasies about a better future or dreams of invincible technology used to promote human happiness. The trouble with his fantastic projections is not that we cannot tell how to bring them about, but that we are not told in what they consist. Roger Bacon, Leonardo, and Cyrano de Bergerac dreamt of flying-machines, which were impossible with the technology of those days, but if men had not dreamed of them at a time when they could not be constructed, very likely they would never have evolved the technology to make their dreams come true. In this sense utopian projections are a necessary part of life. Unlike those 'concrete' visions, however, Bloch's Utopia is the dream of a perfect world, the nature of whose perfection is a closed book to us. He tells us that the technology of the future will be 'non-Euclidean', but he does not explain what this means, except that it will be 'qualitative' and will restore the harmony between man and nature (capitalism, according to Bloch, is incapable of producing 'true technology').

What is peculiar to Bloch is not that he fantasizes about a better future but that, firstly, his fantasy lacks content; secondly, he believes that it can and must include final perfection within its scope (philosophy has to embrace the whole of future time); and thirdly, he claims that his generalities are a higher form of scientific thought, beyond the grasp of those who worship facts or practise formal logic.

Bloch's thought is a medley of the most varied traditions: neo-Platonic gnosis, the naturalism of the Renaissance and after, modernistic occultism, Marxism, romantic anti-capitalism, cosmic evolutionism, and the theory of the unconscious. Traces of romantic anti-capitalism can certainly be found in Marx and are very strong among the German Marxists or para-Marxists of Bloch's generation, including the Frankfurt school and Marcuse (not Lukács). Bloch maintains that his attacks on capitalism have nothing to do with romantic conservatism, but in fact they are closely linked. He laments that capitalism has killed the beauty of life, mechanized personal relationships, and replaced the aesthetic values of everyday life by purely utilitarian ones. He calls aeroplanes 'mock birds' and believes that nature contains altogether new forms of technology, about which, however, he can only tell us that they will be quite different and will have no harmful consequences.

The core of Bloch's philosophical writing is the idea of transforming 'hope' into a metaphysical category, so that hope becomes a quality of being. This is a kind of inversion of Gabriel Marcel's 'metaphysic of hope', where hope is not an emotional state but a form of existence touched by the grace of God. Bloch, on the other hand, believes that although hope is part of being, it is actualized by human activity. Man does not receive it from nature, still less from God; he activates the hope that is latent in being, and awakens the God asleep in nature. From the point of view of Christian philosophy, Bloch's idea must represent the acme of the sin of pride.

Although his ontologizing of hope cannot be deduced from any Marxist source, Bloch helped in one way to throw light on Marxism by revealing its neo-Platonic roots, which were hidden to Marx himself. He pointed out the link between Marx's belief in the prospect of man's complete reconciliation with himself, and the neo-Platonic gnostic tradition that found its way into Marxism through Hegel. He emphasized the soteriological strain which was blurred in Marx and could therefore be neglected and overlooked, but which set the whole Marxian idea in motion: namely the belief in the future identification of man's authentic essence with empirical existence, or, more simply, the promise *eritis sicut dei*. In this sense Bloch was right to connect Marxism with the gnostic sect that worshipped the serpent in Genesis, maintaining that it and not Jehovah was the true guarantor of the Great Promise. Bloch helped to reveal an essential facet of Marxism which had previously been noticed only in criticisms, for the most part ineffectual, by Christian writers. To this extent his work has not been in vain.

Bloch's philosophy may also be more favourably viewed if we consider not its intrinsic merits but its relation to intellectual conditions in the G.D.R. and Eastern Europe as a whole under the destructive pressure of Stalinism with its levelling influence. Bloch's thought is not only richer, more varied, and many-sided than the cardboard schemata of Soviet dialectical materialism: it also has the virtue that one cannot imagine it being transformed into a party dogma or a 'world-view' imposed by the state. Its very vagueness preserves it from being used as a rigid catechism. In some essential points it diverges so far from Marxist–Leninist schemata as to be irreconcilable with official doctrine. Above all it implies a certain rehabilitation of religion, and this not only in the historical sense that certain forms of religion may in past ages have 'played a progressive role for their time. This formula is acceptable to Marxism–Leninism, but Bloch goes further: in his view religion has a permanent indestructible root, which in some undefined way must be preserved in futuristic Marxism. Religion therefore must not be treated as a mere collection of superstitions, arising from the ignorance of former times or the search of oppressed peoples for illusory consolation. Although Bloch, like all orthodox Leninist–Stalinists, condemned all non-Marxist philosophy of Marx's day and after, he sought to include in the Marxist tradition certain aspects of the intellectual culture of past ages which stood in very low repute with his orthodox fellow Marxists: among these were several elements of Christianity and also Leibnizian philosophy, the doctrine of natural law and various strands of neo-Platonism. Philosophers in the G.D.R. who had undergone Bloch's influence could no longer swallow Marxist–Leninist schemata without question. In this respect, too, his ideas played a part in combating the dogmatic state ideology of East European socialism.

XIII

Developments in Marxism
Since Stalin's Death

1. *'De-Stalinization'*

Joseph Vissarionovich Stalin died of an apoplectic stroke on 5 March 1953. The world had scarcely assimilated the news when his successors, jockeying for power among themselves, inaugurated the process misleadingly known as 'de-Stalinization'. This reached its peak almost three years later, when Nikita Khrushchev announced to the Soviet Communist party, and soon to the whole world, that he who had been the leader of progressive humanity, the inspiration of the world, the father of the Soviet people, the master of science and learning, the supreme military genius, and altogether the greatest genius in history was in reality a paranoiac torturer, a mass murderer, and a military ignoramus who had brought the Soviet state to the verge of disaster.

The three years that had elapsed since Stalin's death had been full of dramatic moments, of which we may briefly mention a few. In June 1953 a revolt of East German workers was crushed by Soviet troops. Soon afterwards it was officially announced that Lavrenty Beriya, one of the key men in the Kremlin and head of State Security, had been arrested for various crimes (news of his trial and execution did not come until December). Around the same time (though the West heard of this much later and unofficially) the inmates of several Siberian concentration camps rebelled; although brutally suppressed, these revolts probably helped to bring about a change in the repressive system. The cult of Stalin was much abated within a few months of his death; in the 'theses' proclaimed by the party to celebrate its fiftieth anniversary in July 1953 his name was mentioned only a few times and was not accompanied by the usual dithyrambs. In 1954 there was some relaxation in cultural policy, and in the autumn it became clear that the Soviet Union was preparing for a reconciliation with Yugoslavia, which meant recanting the charges of 'Titoist conspiracy' that had been the pretext for executing Communist leaders throughout Eastern Europe.

Since the cult of Stalin and his irrefragable authority had for many years been the linchpin of Communist ideology throughout the world, it was not surprising that its reversal led to confusion and uncertainty in all Communist parties and stimulated increasingly sharp and frequent criticism of the socialist system in all its aspects—economic absurdities, police repression, and the enslavement of culture. This criticism spread throughout the 'socialist camp' from the end of 1954 onwards; it was most vehement in Poland and Hungary, where the revisionist movement, as it was called, developed into a wholesale attack on all aspects of Communist dogma without exception.

At the Twentieth Congress of the Communist Party of the Soviet Union in February 1956 Khrushchev made his famous speech on the 'cult of personality'. This took place at a closed session, but in the presence of foreign delegates; the speech was never printed in the Soviet Union, but its text was made known to some party activists and was published shortly afterwards by the U.S. State Department. (Among the Communist countries Poland seems to have been the only one where the text was distributed in print 'for internal use' by trusted party members; the Western Communist parties for a long time refused to acknowledge its authenticity.) In it Khrushchev gave a detailed account of Stalin's crimes and paranoiac delusions, the torture, persecution, and murder of party officials, but he did not rehabilitate any members of the opposition movements: the victims whose names he cited were irreproachable Stalinists like Postyshev, Gamarnik, and Rudzutak, not the dictator's former opponents like Bukharin and Kamenev. Nor did Khrushchev make any attempt at a historical or sociological analysis of the Stalinist system. Stalin had simply been a criminal and a maniac, personally to blame for all the nation's defeats and misfortunes. As to how, and in what social conditions, a blood-thirsty paranoiac could for twenty-five years exercise unlimited despotic power over a country of two hundred million inhabitants, which throughout that period had been blessed with the most progressive and democratic system of government in human history—to this enigma the speech offered no clue whatever. All that was certain was that the Soviet system and the party itself remained impeccably pure and bore no responsibility for the tyrant's atrocities.

The bombshell effect of Khrushchev's speech in the Communist world was not due to the amount of new information it contained. In the Western countries a good deal of literature was already available, both of an academic kind and in the form of first-hand accounts, describing the horrors of the Stalin system in fairly convincing terms, and the details cited by Khrushchev did not alter the general picture or add a great deal to it; while in the Soviet Union and its dependent countries both Communists and non-Communists knew the truth from personal experience. The disruptive effect of the Twentieth Congress on the Communist movement was due to two important peculiarities of that movement: the Communist mentality, and the party's function in the system of government.

Not only in the 'socialist bloc', where the authorities used every means to prevent information seeping in from the outside world, but also in the democratic countries, the Communist parties had created a mentality that was completely immune to all facts and arguments 'from outside', i.e. from 'bourgeois' sources. For the most part Communists were victims of magic thinking, according to which an impure source contaminates the information that comes from it. Anyone who was a political enemy on fundamental issues must automatically be wrong on particular or factual questions. The Communist mind was well armed against the incursions of fact and rational argument. As in mythological systems, truth was defined in practice (though not, of course, in ideological manuals) by the source from which it emanated. Reports which had caused no tremor as long as they appeared in 'bourgeois' books or newspapers had the effect of a thunderclap when confirmed by the Kremlin oracle. What were yesterday the 'despicable lies of imperialist propaganda' suddenly became the appalling truth. Moreover, the fallen idol did not simply leave a pedestal to be occupied by someone else. Stalin's dethronement meant not only the collapse of one authority, but that of a whole institution. Party members could not pin their hopes on a second Stalin coming to repair the errors of the first; they could no longer take seriously the official assurances that although Stalin had been bad, the party and the system were immaculate.

Secondly, the moral ruin of Communism momentarily shook the entire system of power. The Stalinist regime could not exist without the cement of ideology to legitimize party rule, and the party apparatus at this time was sensitive to ideological shocks. Since, in Leninist–Stalinist socialism, the stability of the whole power system depends on that of the governing apparatus, the confusion, uncertainty, and demoralization of the bureaucracy threatened the whole structure of the regime. De-Stalinization proved to be a virus from which Communism never recovered, though it made shift to adapt itself, at all events in temporary fashion.

In Poland, although social criticism and 'revisionist' tendencies were already far advanced at the time of the Twentieth Congress, that Congress and Khrushchev's speech greatly accelerated the dissolution of the party; it emboldened critics to attack the system more openly, and so far weakened the governing apparatus that social discontent, which had accumulated for years and was kept down by intimidation, came more and more clearly to the surface. In June 1956 there was a workers' rising at Poznań; though touched off by immediate economic hardship it reflected the pent-up hatred of the whole working class for the Soviet Union and the Polish Government alike. The revolt was quelled, but the party was demoralized and disoriented, rent by faction and undermined by 'revisionism'. In Hungary the situation reached a point where the party collapsed completely, the population went into open rebellion, and the government announced that it was withdrawing from the Soviet military camp (the Warsaw Pact); the Red Army intervened to crush the revolt, its leaders were mercilessly dealt with, and almost all the government team of October 1956 were put to death. Poland escaped invasion at the last moment, owing in part to the fact that the former party leader Władysław Gomulka, who had escaped with his life during the Stalin purges, came forward as a providential figure to avert the explosion, his background of political imprisonment serving to gain the confidence of the population. The Russian leaders, at first highly mistrustful, decided in the end—quite rightly, as it turned out—that although Gomulka had taken over without Kremlin sanction he would not prove too disobedient, and that invasion would be a greater risk. The 'Polish October', as it was called, far from ushering in a period of social and cultural renewal or 'liberalization', stood for the gradual extinction of all such attempts. In 1956 Poland was, relatively speaking, a country of free speech and free criticism, not because the government had planned it so but because they had lost control of the situation. The October events started a process of reversal, and the margin of freedom which still remained grew less year by year. Of the rural co-operatives that had been compulsorily set up, the great majority were soon disbanded; but from October 1956 onwards the party machine regained its lost positions step by step. It repaired the dislocation of government, imposed restrictions on cultural freedom, put a brake on economic reform, and reduced to a purely decorative role the workers' councils that had formed spontaneously in 1956. Meanwhile the invasion of Hungary and the wave of persecution that followed there struck terror into the other 'people's democracies'. In East Germany a few of the more active 'revisionists' were locked up. De-Stalinization led in the end to brutal repressions, but the devastation throughout the bloc was such that the Soviet system could never be the same as before.

The term 'de-Stalinization' (like the term 'Stalinism') was never officially used by the Communist parties themselves, which spoke instead of 'correcting errors and distortions', 'overcoming the cult of personality', and 'returning to Leninist norms of party life'. These euphemisms were meant to convey the impression that Stalinism had been a series of regrettable errors committed by the irresponsible Generalissimo but had nothing to do with the system itself, and that it sufficed to condemn his ways in order to restore the pre-eminently democratic character of the regime. But the terms 'de-Stalinization' and 'Stalinism' are misleading for other reasons than those which precluded their use in the official vocabulary of Communist countries. The Communists eschewed them because 'Stalinism' gave the impression of a system and not of accidental deviations arising from the ruler's faults of character. But, on the other hand, the term 'Stalinism' also suggests that the 'system' was bound up with Stalin's personality, and that his condemnation was the signal for a radical change in the direction of 'democratization' or 'liberalization'.

Although the background to the Twentieth Congress is not known in detail, it is clear in retrospect that certain features of the system that had prevailed for twenty-five years could not be maintained without Stalin and the inviolable authority he had wielded. Since the great purges Russia had lived under a regime in which none of the most privileged members of the party and government, even the Politburo, could be sure from one day to the next whether they would be suffered to live or be destroyed at the tyrant's whim, by the mere lifting of his infallible finger. It is not surprising that after Stalin's death they were anxious that no successor of his should get into the same position. The condemnation of 'errors and distortions' was a necessary part of the unwritten mutual security pact among the party leaders; and in the Soviet Union, as in the other socialist countries, intra-party conflicts were henceforth settled without the deposed oligarchs losing their lives. The system of periodic massacre had certainly had its merits from the point of view of political stability, making faction impossible and ensuring the unity of the apparatus of power; but the price of that unity was one-man despotism and the reduction of all members of the apparatus to the conditions of slaves whose very tenure of life was uncertain, though they enjoyed privileges as the custodians of other slaves whose condition was more abject still. The first effect of de-Stalinization was the replacement of mass terror by selective terror which, though still of considerable scope, was not completely arbitrary as it had been under Stalin. Soviet citizens henceforth knew more or less how to avoid prison and the concentration camp, whereas previously there had been no rules at all. One of the important events of Khrushchev's era was the liberation of millions from the camps.

Another effect of the change was that various moves were made towards decentralization, and it became easier for rival political groups to form in secret. There were also attempts at economic reform, which improved efficiency to some extent; however, the dogma of the primacy of heavy industry was upheld (except for a brief interlude under Malenkov), and no steps were taken to make production more responsive to mass demand by releasing market mechanisms. Nor was there any substantial improvement in agriculture, which despite frequent 'reorganizations' remained in the miserable state to which it had been reduced by collectivization.

All the changes, however, did not amount to 'democratization' but left unimpaired the foundations of Communist despotism. The abandonment of mass terror was important for human security, but it did not affect the state's absolute power over the individual; it did not confer on citizens any institutional rights, or infringe the state and party monopoly of initiative and control in all spheres of life. The principle of totalitarian government was upheld, whereby human beings are the property of the state and all their aims and actions must conform to its purposes and needs. Although various departments of life resisted absorption, so that the process was never complete, the whole system operated, as it still does, to enforce state control to the utmost degree possible. Indiscriminate terror on a vast scale is not a necessary and permanent condition of totalitarianism; the nature and intensity of repressive measures may be affected by various circumstances; but under Communism there can be no such thing as the rule of law, in which law acts as an autonomous mediator between the citizen and the state, and deprives the latter of its absolute power *vis-à-vis* the individual. The present repressive system in the Soviet Union and other Communist countries is not simply a 'survival of Stalinism' or a regrettable blemish that may be cured in time without a fundamental change in the system.

The only Communist regimes in the world are of the Leninist–Stalinist pattern. On Stalin's death the Soviet system changed from a personal tyranny to that of an oligarchy. From the point of view of state omnipotence this is a less effective system; it does not, however, amount to de-Stalinization, but only to an ailing form of Stalinism.

2. Revisionism in Eastern Europe

FROM the second half of the 1950s the term 'revisionism' was used by the party authorities and official ideologists in Communist countries to stigmatize those who, while remaining party members or Marxists, attacked various Communist dogmas. No precise meaning was attached to it, or indeed to the label of 'dogmatism' affixed to party 'conservatives' who opposed the post-Stalin reforms, but as a rule the term 'revisionism' connoted democratic and rationalist tendencies. As in former times it had been applied to Bernstein's critique of Marxism, party functionaries took to linking the new 'revisionism' with Bernstein's views, but the connection was remote and insubstantial. Few of the active 'revisionists' were especially interested in Bernstein; many problems that had been at the centre of ideological debate around 1900 were no longer topical; some of Bernstein's ideas that had aroused furious indignation at the time were now accepted by orthodox Communists, such as the doctrine that socialism might be achieved by legal means—a purely tactical change, but none the less important ideologically. 'Revisionism' did not come from reading Bernstein but from living under Stalin. However vaguely the term was used by party leaders, however, there was in the fifties and sixties a genuine, active political and intellectual movement which, operating for a time within Marxism or at least using Marxist language, had a highly disruptive effect on Communist doctrine.

In 1955–7, as Communist ideology disintegrated, attacks on the system were widespread. The typical feature of this period was that Communists, while not the only critics of existing conditions, were the most active and conspicuous ones, and on the whole the most effective. There were several reasons for this predominance. In the first place, as the revisionists belonged to the 'establishment' they had much easier access to the mass media and to unpublished information. Secondly, in the nature of things they knew more than other groups about Communist ideology and Marxism, and about the state and party machine. Thirdly, Communists were used to the idea that they should take the lead in everything, and the party did, after all, include a number of members endowed with energy and initiative. Fourthly, and this was the chief reason, the revisionists, at least for a considerable time, used Marxist language: they appealed to Communist ideological stereotypes and Marxist authorities, and made a devastating comparison between socialist reality and the values and promises to be found in the 'classics'. In this way the revisionists, unlike others who opposed the system from a nationalist or religious point of view, not only addressed themselves to party opinion but awakened an echo in party circles; they were listened to by the party apparatus and thereby contributed to its ideological disarray, which was the principal condition of political change. They used party language to some extent because they still believed in Communist stereotypes, and to some extent because they knew it would be more effective; the proportion as between faith and deliberate camouflage is hard to estimate at this distance of time.

In the wave of criticism which affected all aspects of life and gradually undermined all the sanctities of Communism, some demands and viewpoints were peculiar to the revisionists while others were common to them and non-party or non-Marxist opponents of the regime. The principal demands put forward were as follows.

In the first place, all the critics called for a general democratization of public life, the abolition of the system of repression and the secret police, or at least the subordination of the police to a judiciary acting in accordance with law and independence of political pressure; they demanded freedom of the Press, sciences, and arts, and the abolition of preventive censorship. The revisionists also called for intra-party democracy, and some of them demanded the right to form 'fractions' within the party. From the beginning there were differences among the revisionists on these points. Some demanded democracy for party members without advancing any more general claims, appearing to believe that the party could be a democratic island in a non-democratic society; they thus accepted, expressly or by implication, the principle of the 'dictatorship of the proletariat', i.e. of the party, and imagined that the ruling party could afford the luxury of internal democracy. In time, however, most of the revisionists came to see that there could be no democracy for the élite only; if intra-party groups were allowed to exist they would become the mouthpieces of social forces which were otherwise denied utterance, so that a system of 'fractions' within the party would become a substitute for a multi-party system. It was necessary to choose therefore between the free formation of political parties, with all its consequences, and dictatorship by one party, which involved dictatorship within that party.

Important among democratic objectives was the independence of trade unions and workers' councils. The cry 'All power to the councils' was even heard—not very loudly, it is true, but the idea of workers' councils independent of the party, which could not only bargain with the state over questions of pay and working conditions but also play an effective part in industrial management, was frequently advanced in both Poland and Hungary; later on, the example of Yugoslavia was quoted. Workers' self-government went naturally with the decentralization of economic planning.

An important reform desired by non-party critics was freedom of religion and an end to persecution of the Church. The revisionists, who were for the most part anti-religious, stood aside from this question; they believed in the separation of Church and State and did not support the demand, which was wide-spread in those years, for the reintroduction of religious education into schools.

The second category of demands universally put forward related to state sovereignty and equality among members of the 'socialist bloc'. In all the bloc countries Soviet supervision was extremely thorough in many spheres; the army and police in particular were under specific and direct control, and the duty to follow the elder brother's example in everything was the foundation of state ideology. The whole population felt keenly the humiliation of their country, its dependence on the Soviet Union, and the latter's unscrupulous economic exploitation of its neighbours. While, however, the Polish population as a whole was strongly anti-Russian, the revisionists generally invoked traditional socialist principles and avoided the language of nationalism. A frequent demand by both revisionists and others was for the abolition of the privileges enjoyed by the bureaucracy, not so much in matters of pay but in the extra-legal arrangements that freed them from the hardships of everyday life—special shops and medical facilities, housing priorities, and so on.

The third main area of criticism was economic management. There was, it should be noted, scarcely any call for the restoration of industry to private hands; most people were used to the idea that it should be publicly owned. They demanded, however, the cessation of compulsory agricultural collectivization; a reduction in the extremely burdensome investment programme; an enlargement of the role of market conditions in the economy; profit-sharing by workers; rationalized planning and the abandonment of unrealistic all-embracing plans; a reduction in the norms and directives that hampered enterprise; and concessions to private and co-operative activity in the field of services and small-scale production.

In all these matters revisionist demands coincided with those of the population in general; the revisionists, however, used socialist and Marxist arguments instead of nationalist and religious ones, and they also put forward aspirations relating to party life and Marxist studies. In this respect, like other heretics in history, they appealed for a 'return to the sources', i.e. they based their criticism of the system on Marxist tradition. More than once, especially in the early stages, they invoked Lenin's authority, searching his writings for texts in support of intra-party democracy, the participation of the 'broad masses' in government, and so on. In short, the revisionists for a time opposed Lenin to Stalinism, as survivors of the movement still do from time to time. They did not have much intellectual success, as the discussions made it increasingly clear that Stalinism was the natural and legitimate continuation of Lenin's ideas; but politically their arguments were of some importance, as we have seen, in helping to disrupt Communist ideology by appealing to its own stereotypes. The peculiarity of the situation was that both Marxism and Leninism spoke a language full of humane and democratic slogans which, while they were empty rhetoric as far as the system of power was concerned, could be and were invoked against that system. By pointing out the grotesque contrast between Marxist–Leninist phraseology and the realities of life, the revisionists laid bare the contradictions of the doctrine itself. The ideology became detached, as it were, from the political movement of which it had been a mere façade, and began to live a life of its own.

While, however, attempts to hold fast to Leninism were soon abandoned by most of the revisionists, the hope of a return to 'authentic' Marxism lasted much longer.

The main issue that divided the revisionists from their party colleagues was not the fact that they criticized Stalinism; at that time, especially after the Twentieth Congress, hardly any party members defended it with all its aberrations. Nor did the difference even lie chiefly in the extent of their criticism, but rather in their rejection of the official view that Stalinism was a 'mistake' or a 'distortion' or a series of 'mistakes and distortions'. Most of them held that the Stalinist system had made few mistakes from the point of view of its social functions, that it was a fairly coherent political system in itself, and that the roots of the evil must therefore be sought not in Stalin's personal faults or 'mistakes' but in the nature of Communist power. They believed for some time, however, that Stalinism was curable in the sense that Communism could be restored or 'democratized' without questioning its foundations (though it was far from clear what exactly were basic features and what were accidental ones).

But, as time went on, the revisionists saw more and more clearly that this position too was untenable: if the one-party system was a necessary condition of Communism, then Communism was unreformable.

It appeared, however, for some time yet that Marxist socialism was possible without Leninist political forms, and that Communism might be attacked 'within the framework of Marxism'. Hence many attempts were made to reinterpret the Marxist tradition in an anti-Leninist sense.

The revisionists began by requiring that Marxism should subject itself to the normal rules of scientific rationality, instead of relying on the monopolistic power of censorship, police, and privilege. They argued that such privilege inevitably led to the degeneration of Marxism and deprived it of vitality; that Marxism must be able to defend its existence by the empirical and logical methods universally accepted by science; and that Marxist studies were withering away because Marxism had been institutionalized into a state ideology immune from criticism. It could only be regenerated by free discussion in which Marxists would have to defend their positions by rational argument. The critics attacked the primitiveness and sterility of Marxist writings, their inadequacy to the main problems of the present age, their schematic and ossified character, and the ignorance of those who were regarded as the chief exponents of the doctrine. They attacked the poverty of the conceptual categories of Leninist–Stalinist Marxism and the simplistic attempts to explain all culture in terms of the class struggle, to reduce all philosophy to 'the conflict between materialism and idealism', to turn all morality into an instrument for the 'building of socialism', and so on.

As far as philosophy is concerned, the revisionists' main objective may be defined as the vindication of human subjectivity in opposition to Leninist doctrine. The main points of their attack were as follows.

In the first place, they criticized Lenin's 'theory of reflection', arguing that the sense of Marx's epistemology was entirely different. Cognition did not consist of the object being reflected in the mind, but was an interaction of subject and object, and the effect of this interaction, co-determined by social and biological factors, could not be regarded as a copy of the world. The human mind could not transcend the manner in which it was associated with being; the world as we know it is partially man-made.

Secondly, the revisionists criticized determinism. Neither Marx's theory nor any factual considerations justified a determinist metaphysic, especially as far as history was concerned. The idea that there were unalterable 'laws of history' and that socialism was historically inevitable was a mythological superstition which might have played a part in stirring up enthusiasm for Communism but was none the more rational for that. Chance and uncertainty could not be excluded from past history, still less from predictions of the future.

Thirdly, they criticized attempts to deduce moral values from speculative historiographical schemata. Even if it were supposed, wrongly, that the socialist future was guaranteed by this or that historical necessity, it would not follow that it was our duty to support such necessities. What is necessary is not for that reason valuable; socialism still needs a moral foundation, over and above its being allegedly the result of 'historical laws'. For the idea of socialism to be restored, a system of values must first be re-created independently of historiosophical doctrine.

All these criticisms had the common aim of restoring the role of the subject in the historical and cognitive process. They were combined with a criticism of the bureaucratic regime and the absurd pretentions of the party apparatus to superior wisdom and knowledge of 'historical laws' and, on the strength of this, to unrestricted power and privilege. From the philosophical point of view, revisionism soon broke completely with Leninism.

In the course of their criticism the revisionists naturally appealed to various sources, some Marxist and some not. In Eastern Europe some part was played by existentialism, especially the works of Sartre, as many revisionists were attracted by his theory of freedom and the subject's irreducibility to the status of a thing. Many others found inspiration in Hegel, while those who were interested in Engels's philosophy of science brought analytical philosophy to bear on his and Lenin's 'dialectic of nature'. The revisionists read Western critical and philosophical literature about Marxism and Communism: Camus, Merleau-Ponty, Koestler, Orwell. Marxist authorities of the past played only a secondary role in their discussions and criticisms. Trotsky was scarcely mentioned; some interest was taken in Rosa Luxemburg for her attacks on Lenin and the Russian revolution (but an attempt to publish her book on that subject in Poland was unsuccessful); among philosophers Lukács was popular for a while, chiefly on account of his theory of the historical process in which subject and object tend towards identity. Somewhat later, Gramsci became an object of interest: his works contained the outline of a theory of knowledge completely opposed to Lenin's, together with critical reflections on Communist bureaucracy, the theory of the party as an advance guard, historical determinism, and the 'manipulative' approach to socialist revolution.

Further reinforcement came at this time from the Italian Communists. Palmiro Togliatti, who had till then enjoyed the deserved reputation of a dyed-in-the-wool Stalinist, went on record after the Twentieth Congress with a criticism of the Soviet leaders, moderate as to language but important in its consequences. He accused them of casting the whole responsibility for Stalinism on to Stalin and failing to analyse the causes of bureaucratic degeneration, and ended with an appeal for 'polycentrism' in the world Communist movement, i.e. an end to Moscow's hegemony over the other parties.

Revisionism in Poland, where the critical movement in the 1950s went much further than in the rest of Eastern Europe, was the work of a numerous group of party intellectuals—philosophers, sociologists, journalists, men of letters, historians, and economists. It found expression in the specialized Press and in literary and political weeklies (especially *Po prostu* and *Nowa Kultura*), which played an important part until they were suppressed by the authorities. Among the philosophers and sociologists who were frequently attacked as revisionists were B. Baczko, K. Pomian, R. Zimand, Z. Bauman, M. Bielińska, and the present writer, who was singled out as the chief culprit. Economists who advanced revisionist theories were M. Kalecki, O. Lange, W. Brus, E. Lipiński, and T. Kowalik.

In Hungary the chief centre of revisionism was the 'Petőfi Circle' in Budapest, which included some of Lukács's disciples. Lukács himself took a prominent part in its discussions, but both he and his followers emphasized their fidelity to Marxism much more strongly than the Polish revisionists; Lukács called for freedom 'within the framework of Marxism' and did not question the principle of single-party rule. It may be—this is only a supposition—that the much more orthodox character of Hungarian revisionism was the reason why it became so detached from the movement of popular discontent that the revisionists were unable to keep the attack on the party within bounds; the result was a mass protest, expressly anti-Communist in character, leading to the collapse of the party and to Soviet invasion. This caused a shock not only in Poland, where it became obvious at once that ideas of a 'democratized' Communist system were fairy-tales, but also among Western Communists: some of the smaller parties split up, while others lost the support of many intellectuals. Among Communists throughout the world the invasion of Hungary provoked various dissident movements and attempts to reconstruct the movement and its doctrine on non-Soviet lines. In Britain, France, and Italy many works were published on the possibility or otherwise of democratic Communism; the 'New Left' of the sixties was largely inspired by these sources.

The revisionist movement in Hungary was destroyed by the Soviet invasion. In Poland it was combated over a period of years by various, relatively mild forms of repression: the closure of periodicals or enforced dismissal of contributors who refused to toe the line, the temporary banning of publication by individual writers, intensified censorship in all branches of culture. The main reason, however, why Polish revisionism gradually declined was not the use of such measures but the disintegration of party ideology, undermined by revisionist criticism.

As an attempt to renew Marxism by returning to its 'sources'—chiefly the young Marx and his idea of the self-creation of humanity—and to reform Communism by curing its repressive and bureaucratic character, revisionism could be effec-

tive only as long as the party took the traditional ideology seriously and the apparatus was in some degree sensitive to ideological questions. But revisionism itself
was a major cause of the fact that the party lost its respect for official doctrine
and that ideology increasingly became a sterile though indispensable ritual. In
this way revisionist criticism, especially in Poland, cut the ground from under
its own feet. Writers and intellectuals continued their manifestations, protests,
and attempts to put political pressure on the authorities, but there were less and
less inspired by truly revisionist, i.e. Marxist, ideas. In the party and bureaucracy the importance of Communist ideology was manifestly declining. Instead
of people who, even if they had taken part in the atrocities of Stalinism, were
in their way loyal Communists and attached to Communist ideals, the reins of
power were now held by cynical, disillusioned careerists who were perfectly
aware of the emptiness of the Communist slogans they made use of. A bureaucracy of this kind was immune to ideological shocks.

Revisionism itself, on the other hand, had a certain inner logic which, before
long, carried it beyond the frontiers of Marxism. Anyone who took seriously the
rules of rationalism could not be interested any longer in the degree of his own
'loyalty' to Marxist tradition, or feel any inhibition about using other sources
and theoretical stimuli; Marxism in its Leninist–Stalinist form was such a poor
and primitive structure that on close analysis it practically disappeared. Marx's
own doctrine certainly afforded more food for the mind, but in the nature of
things it could not provide answers to questions that philosophy and the social
sciences had raised since Marx's day, nor could it assimilate various important
conceptual categories evolved by twentieth-century humanistic culture.
Attempts to combine Marxism with trends originating elsewhere soon deprived
it of its clear-cut doctrinal form: it became merely one of several contributions
to intellectual history, instead of an all-embracing system of authoritative
truths among which, if one looked hard enough, one could find the answer to
everything. Marxism had functioned for decades almost entirely as the political ideology of a powerful but self-contained sect, with the result that it was
almost completely cut off from the external world of ideas; when attempts were
made to overcome this isolation it generally proved too late—the doctrine collapsed, like mummified remains suddenly exposed to the air. From this point
of view, orthodox party members were quite right to fear the consequences of
trying to breathe fresh life into Marxism. Revisionist appeals which seemed to
be the merest common sense—Marxism must be defended in free discussion by
the intellectual methods universally applied in science, its ability to solve modern problems must be analysed without fear, its conceptual apparatus must be
enriched, historical documents must not be falsified, and so on—all proved to
have catastrophic results: instead of Marxism being enriched or supplemented,
it dissolved in a welter of alien ideas.

   In Poland revisionism lived on for a time but became less and less important ideologically as compared with other forms of opposition. It was represented in the early sixties by Kuro ń and Modzelewski, who put forward a
Marxist and Communist political programme. Their analysis of Polish society
and government, which led them to the conclusion that a new exploiting class
had come into existence in the Communist countries and could only be overthrown by a proletarian revolution, was arrived at on traditional Marxist lines.
It cost them several years' imprisonment, but their resistance helped to form a
students' opposition movement leading to fairly widespread riots in March
1968. This, however, had little to do with Communist ideology: most of the students protested in the name of civic and academic liberties, but did not interpret these in any specifically Communist or even socialist sense. After the riots
were crushed the government launched an attack in the cultural field (closely
linked with the struggle between rival party cliques at that time), and in so
doing revealed that its main ideological principle was anti-Semitism.
   The year 1968, which was also that of the Soviet invasion of Czechoslovakia,
virtually marked the end of revisionism as a separate intellectual trend in
Poland. At present the opposition which articulates itself in various forms
makes scarcely any use of Marxist or Communist phraseology, but finds fully
adequate expression in terms of national conservatism, religion, and traditional
democratic or social-democratic formulas. Communism has ceased in general
to be an intellectual problem, remaining simply a matter of government power
and repression. The situation is a paradoxical one. The ruling party still officially professes Marxism and the Communist doctrine of 'proletarian internationalism'; Marxism is a compulsory subject in all places of higher learning,
manuals of it are published and books are written about its problems; yet this
state ideology has never been in such a lifeless condition as now. No one in
practice believes in it, neither the rulers nor the ruled, and both are aware of
this fact; yet it is indispensable, since it constitutes the main foundation of the
legitimacy of the regime, as the dictatorship of the party is based on the claim
that it 'expresses' the historical interests of the working class and the people.
Everyone knows that 'proletarian internationalism' is nothing but a phrase to
cover the fact that the East European countries are not masters of their own
affairs, and that the 'leading role of the working class' simply means dictatorship by the party bureaucracy. Consequently, the rulers themselves, when they
wish to arouse at least some degree of response from the population, appeal less
and less to the ideology that exists only on paper, and instead use the language
of *raison d'état* and national interest. Not only is the official ideology lifeless,
but it is no longer clearly formulated as it was in Stalin's day, since there is no
authority competent to do so. Intellectual life continues, though harassed by
censorship and various police restrictions, but Marxism plays next to no part in

it, although state support maintains it artificially in being and immune from criticism. In the field of ideology and the humanistic sciences the party can only act negatively, by means of repression and prohibitions of all kinds. Even so, the official ideology has had to forfeit a large part of its former universalist claims. Marxism, of course, may not be criticized directly, but even in philosophy works appear which completely ignore it and are written as if it had never existed. In sociology a certain number of orthodox treatises are regularly published, mainly to secure an attestation of their authors' political reliability, while at the same time many other works fall into the category of ordinary empirical sociology, using the same methods as in the West. The scope permitted to such works is of course limited: they may deal with changes in family life or working conditions in industry, but not the sociology of power or of party life. Severe restrictions are imposed, for purely political rather than Marxist reasons, on the historical sciences, especially where recent history is concerned. The Soviet rulers seem to be firmly convinced that they represent the continuation of Tsarist policy, and hence the study of Polish history, which for two centuries was dominated by relations with Russia, the Partitions, and national oppression, is subject to a multitude of taboos.

To a certain extent one may still speak of revisionism in the context of Polish economic studies, where it takes the form of practical recommendations for increased efficiency. The best-known authors in this field are W. Brus and E. Lipiński, who both invoke the Marxist tradition but in a form closer to social democracy. They argue that the faults and inefficiency of the socialist economy cannot be cured by purely economic means, as they are tied up with the repressive political system. Economic rationalization therefore cannot succeed without political pluralism, i.e. in practice without abolishing the specifically Communist regime. Nationalization of the means of production, Brus contends, is not the same as public ownership, since the political bureaucracy has a monopoly of economic decision; a truly socialized economy is incompatible with political dictatorship.

To a somewhat lesser degree Władysław Bieńkowski may be classed as a revisionist: in works published outside Poland he analyses the causes of social and economic deterioration under bureaucratic governments. He appeals to the Marxist tradition, but goes beyond it in examining the autonomized mechanisms of political power independent of the class system (in Marx's sense of 'class').

Similar tendencies connected with the decline of Communist faith, the reduced vitality of Marxism and its transformation into a political rite can be observed, though in varying degrees, in all the Communist countries.

In Czechoslovakia 1956 was a much less important year than in Poland and Hungary, and the revisionist movement was late in developing, but the general trend was the same as elsewhere. The best-known revisionist among Czech economists is Ota Šik, who in the early sixties advanced a typical programme of reform: increased influence of the market on production, greater autonomy of enterprises, decentralized planning, an analysis of political bureaucracy as the cause of socialist economic inefficiency. Although political conditions were more difficult than in Poland, a revisionist group of philosophers also came into being. Its best-known member was Karel Kosik, who in *Dialectics of the Concrete* (1963) put forward a number of typically revisionist issues: a return to the idea of praxis as the most general category in the interpretation of history; the relativity of ontological questions *vis-à-vis* anthropological ones, the abandonment of materialist metaphysics and of the primacy of the 'base' over the 'superstructure'; philosophy and art as co-determinants of social life and not merely its products.

The economic crisis in Czechoslovakia at the beginning of 1968 precipitated political change and the replacement of the party leadership. This at once let loose an avalanche of political and ideological criticism, dominated by revisionist ideas. The proclaimed objectives were the same as they had been in Poland and Hungary: abolition of the repressive police system, legal guarantees of civic freedom, the independence of culture, democratic economic management. The demand for a multi-party system, or at least the right to form different socialist parties, was not directly put forward by those of the revisionists who were party members, but figured constantly in the discussions.

The Soviet occupation in August 1968 and the mass repressions that followed had the effect of almost completely stifling Czechoslovak intellectual and cultural life, which still presents a highly depressing picture even in comparison with the other bloc countries. On the other hand, precisely because the reform movement in Czechoslovakia did not disintegrate of itself but was suppressed by force of arms, the country offers a more fertile soil for revisionist ideas. It may be imagined that, if the invasion had not taken place, the reform movement begun under Dubček and supported by the great majority of the population might eventually have brought about 'socialism with a human face' without shaking the foundations of the system. This of course is a matter of speculation, and depends on what exactly is regarded as fundamental. What does seem clear, however, is that if the reform movement had continued and had neither been suppressed by invasion nor, as in Poland, had disintegrated from fear of invasion, it must soon have led to a multiparty system, thus destroying the Communist party dictatorship and therefore destroying Communism as that doctrine conceives itself.

East Germany, where the system of repression was generally more thorough than elsewhere, did not witness any widespread revisionist movement, but was none the less shaken by the events of 1956. The philosopher and literary critic Wolfgang Harich put forward a democratic programme of German socialism, which earned him several years' imprisonment. Some well-known Marxist intellectuals left the country (Ernst Bloch, Hans Mayer, Alfred Kantorowicz). The strict regimentation of ideas made any attempt at revisionism extremely difficult, as it still does, but occasionally a reformist voice was heard. In philosophy the most important name in this connection is that of Robert Havemann, a professor of physical chemistry with an interest in philosophical questions, who, unlike many other revisionists, remained a convinced Marxist throughout. In essays and lectures, published of course in West Germany, he sharply criticized the party dictatorship in science and philosophy and the custom of deciding theoretical questions by bureaucratic decree; in addition he attacked the doctrine of dialectical materialism and the official norms of Communist morality. He did not, however, criticize Marxism from a positivist standpoint but, on the contrary, wished to return to a more 'Hegelianized' version of the dialectic. He maintained that the chief enemy of Marxism was mechanistic materialism, which was generally taught under the name Marxism. He attacked the Leninist version of determinism as morally dangerous and incompatible with modern physics. Following Hegel and Engels he postulated a dialectic that was not merely a description but an aspect of reality, including logical relations; in this way, like Bloch, he tried to justify a finalistic attitude within the terms of dialectical materialism. He condemned the Stalinist enslavement of culture, and declared that the philosophical negation of freedom in the mechanistic doctrine that usually passed for Marxism went hand in hand with the destruction of cultural freedom under Communism. He called for the rehabilitation of 'spontaneity' as a philosophic category and as a political value, but at the same time emphasized his fidelity to dialectical materialism and Communism. Havemann's philosophical writings are less precise than one might expect from a chemist.

In the U.S.S.R. there was no revisionism to speak of in philosophy, but some economists proposed reforms aimed at the rationalization of management and distribution. Official Soviet philosophy was little affected by de-Stalinization, while the unofficial variety soon lost all contact with Marxism. In official philosophy the principal change was that the schemata of dialectical materialism were no longer taught after the exact pattern of Stalin's booklet. The textbook published in 1958 followed Engels in distinguishing three laws of the dialectic (including the negation of the negation), not four; materialism was expounded first and the dialectic second, a reversal of Stalin's order. The dozen or so 'categories' of the dialectic enumerated in Lenin's *Philosophical Notes* provided the basis of a newly arranged schema. Soviet philosophers held several discussions on the time-honoured theme of the 'relation of the dialectic to formal logic', the majority view being that there was no conflict between the two, as their subject-matter was different; some also challenged the theory that 'contradictions' might occur in reality itself. Hegel ceased to personify the 'aristocratic reaction to the French Revolution'; henceforth it was correct to speak of his 'limitations' and also his 'merits'.

All these inessential and superficial changes made no breach in the structure of the Leninist–Stalinist 'diamat'. None the less, Soviet philosophy enjoyed some benefit from de-Stalinization, though less than other disciplines. A younger generation came on the scene and, of its own accord—since there were hardly any qualified teachers except a few chance survivors from Stalin's purges—began to look into Western philosophy and logic, to study foreign languages, and finally even to explore non-Marxist Russian traditions. In the first years after Stalin's death it was clear that the young philosophers were most attracted by Anglo-Saxon positivism and the analytical school. The treatment of logic became more rational and less subject to political control. The five-volume *Philosophical Encyclopedia* published in the 1960s is on the whole better than the output of Stalin's day: the main ideological articles, especially those relating to Marxism, are on the same level as before, but there are also many concerned with logic and the history of philosophy which are written on sensible lines and are not merely dictated by state propaganda. Thanks to the younger philosophers' efforts to renew contact with European and American thought, a few modern works have been translated from Western languages. Timid and cautious attempts to 'modernize' Marxism were perceptible for a time in *Philosophical Science (Filosofskie Nauki)*, which began to appear in 1958. On the whole, however, publications did not reflect the mental changes that were taking place. The backwoodsmen trained in Stalin's day continued to decide which of the younger men should be allowed to publish or teach in universities, and naturally favoured their own kind. However, some of the younger and better educated philosophers found ways of expressing themselves in other fields that were less strictly controlled.

On the whole, however, philosophy, the first discipline to be destroyed by Communism, was also the slowest to revive, and the results so far are extremely meagre. Other branches of learning recovered in more or less the opposite order to that in which they were originally 'Stalinized'. Within a few years of the dictator's death the natural sciences virtually ceased to be ideologically regulated, though the choice of research subjects continued to be strictly controlled, as it still is. In physics, chemistry, medical, and biological research the state provides material resources and lays down the purposes for which they are used, but it no longer insists that the results shall be orthodox from the Marxist point of view. The historical sciences are still closely controlled, but here too areas of less political sensitivity are less subject to regulation. For some years theoretical linguistics were relatively free and revived the tradition of the Russian formalistic school, but eventually the state intervened here also by closing some institutions, having noticed that they were being used as an outlet for various unorthodox ideas. On the whole, however, the period from 1955 to 1965 was one of considerable and often successful efforts to revive Russian culture after years of devastation; this applies to literature, painting, drama, and films as well as historiography and philosophy. In the second half of the sixties increasing pressure was again brought to bear on suspect individuals and institutions. Unlike the situation in Eastern Europe, Marxism in the Soviet Union showed hardly any signs of reanimation. Among the clandestine or semi-clandestine ideological developments which were especially lively from about 1965 onwards, Marxist trends were scarcely noticeable: instead we find the most varying tendencies, including Great Russian chauvinism (often in a form that might be called 'Bolshevism without Marxism'), the national aspirations of the oppressed non-Russian peoples, religion (specifically Orthodox or broadly Christian or Buddhist), and traditional democratic ideas. Marxism or Leninism accounts for only a small fraction of the general opposition, but it does exist, its best-known Soviet spokesmen being the brothers Roy and Zhores Medvedyev. The former, a historian, is the author of some valuable works, including a general analysis of Stalinism on a large scale. This contains much information not known from elsewhere and certainly cannot be regarded as an attempt to palliate the horrors of the Stalinist system; nevertheless, like the author's other works, it is based on the view that there is a clear break between Leninism and Stalinism and that Lenin's plan for the socialist society was completely distorted and deformed by Stalin's tyranny. (The present writer, as will be clear from previous chapters of this work, takes exactly the opposite view.)

In the last two decades the ideological situation in the Soviet Union has gone through changes in many ways similar to those that have occurred in the other socialist countries. Marxism is practically extinct as a doctrine, though it performs a useful service in justifying Soviet imperialism and the whole internal policy of oppression, exploitation, and privilege. As in Eastern Europe, the rulers have to resort to other ideological values than Communism if they wish to find common ground with their subjects. As far as the Russian people itself is concerned the values in question are those of chauvinism and imperial glory, while all the peoples of the Soviet Union are susceptible to xenophobia, especially anti-Chinese nationalism and anti-Semitism. This is all that remains of Marxism in the first state in the world to be constituted on allegedly Marxist principles. This nationalist and to some extent racist outlook is the true, unavowed ideology of the Soviet state, not only protected but inculcated by means of allusions and unprinted texts; and, unlike Marxism, it awakens a real echo in popular feeling.

There is probably no part of the civilized world in which Marxism has declined so completely and socialist ideas have been so discredited and turned to ridicule as in the countries of victorious socialism. It can be said with little fear of contradiction that if freedom of thought were allowed in the Soviet bloc, Marxism would prove to be the least attractive form of intellectual life throughout the area.

3. Yugoslav revisionism

YUGOSLAVIA's special role in the evolution of Marxism lies in the fact that we have to do here not only with individual philosophers or economists professing revisionist ideas, but with what may be called the first revisionist Communist party and even the first revisionist state.

After her excommunication by Stalin Yugoslavia was in a difficult situation, both economically and ideologically. At first her official ideology did not depart from the Marxist–Leninist model except for one important point: by asserting their sovereignty in the face of Soviet imperialism the Yugoslavs rejected Soviet claims to ideological supremacy and attacked the elder brother's Great Power chauvinism. Before long, however, the Yugoslav party began to devise its own model of socialism and its own ideology, loyally Marxist in intent but concentrating on workers' self-government and socialism without bureaucracy. The formation of this ideology and the corresponding economic and political changes extended over many years. In the early 1950s the party leaders were already talking of the danger of bureaucratization and criticizing the Soviet system as a degenerate type of state in which the extreme centralization of power had killed what was most valuable in the socialist ideal, namely the self-determination of the working people and the principle of public ownership as distinct from nationalization. The party leaders and theoreticians drew an increasingly sharp distinction between state socialism on Soviet lines and an economy based on workers' self-government, in which the collectives did not simply fulfil production norms imposed by the authorities but themselves decided all questions of production and distribution. By successive measures of reform industrial management was more and more entrusted to bodies representing the workers themselves. The state's economic functions were curtailed, and party doctrine pointed to this as a sign of the withering-away of the state in accordance with Marxist theory. At the same time state control of cultural life was relaxed, and 'socialist realism' ceased to be a canon of artistic merit.

The programme approved by the party at its Sixth Congress in April 1958 set out the official version of socialism based on self-government. It is an unusual type of party document for those years, being concerned with theory as well as propaganda. It distinguished the nationalization of the means of production from their socialization, and emphasized that the concentration of economic management in the hands of the bureaucracy led to social degeneration and was a brake on socialist development. It also led to a fusion between the state and the party apparatus, and instead of the state withering away it would become increasingly powerful and bureaucratic. In order to build socialism and put an end to social alienation it was necessary to transfer production to the producers, i.e. into the hands of workers' associations.

It was evident from the beginning that if workers' councils were to have unlimited authority in each individual production unit the result would be a system of free competition differing from the nineteenth-century model only in the ascription of ownership to particular concerns; no economic planning would be possible. Accordingly, the state reserved to itself various basic functions concerning the investment rate and the distribution of the accumulation fund. The reforms of 1964–5 further reduced the powers of the state without abandoning the idea of planning; the state was to regulate the economy chiefly through the nationalized banking system.

The economic and social effects of the Yugoslav model of workers' self-government were and still are the subject of much discussion and lively disagreement, both in Yugoslavia and among economists and sociologists throughout the world. If the system is not to be a bureaucratic fiction it requires a con-siderable extension of market relations and increased influence of the market on production, and this predictably soon led to certain undesirable consequences as the normal laws of accumulation took effect once more. The gap between more and less economically developed parts of the country tended to grow wider instead of narrowing; pressure on wages threatened to push down the investment rate below what was socially desirable; competitive conditions led to the appearance of a class of rich industrial managers whose privileges excited popular discontent; the market and competition caused an increase in inflation and unemployment. The Yugoslav leaders and economists are aware that self-government and planning tend to limit each other and can only be reconciled by compromise, but the terms of the compromise are a matter of constant dispute.

It is true, on the other hand, that the Yugoslav economic reforms were accompanied by an expansion of cultural and even political freedom well beyond anything that occurred in the rest of Eastern Europe, let alone the Soviet Union. To call this a sign of the 'withering-away of the state', however, was at no time anything but an ideological fiction. The state voluntarily restricted its own economic power—an unusual event—but it did not give up its monopoly of political initiative or the use of police methods to deal with opposition. The situation is a curious one: Yugoslavia still enjoys more freedom of the spoken and written word than other socialist countries, but it is also subject to harsh police measures. It is easier than elsewhere to publish a text attacking the official ideology, but it is also easier to be put in prison for doing so; there are many more political prisoners in Yugoslavia than in Poland or

Hungary, yet in those countries the police control of cultural matters is more severe. Single-party rule has not been infringed in any way, and to call it in question is a punishable offence. In short, the elements of pluralism in social life extend as far as the ruling party thinks proper. Yugoslavia has gained much from its reforms and from being excluded from the Soviet camp, but it has not become a democratic country. As to workers' self-government, its pros and cons are still a matter of controversy; at all events it is a new phenomenon in the history of Communism.

The question of self-government and de-bureaucratization also has a philosophical aspect. From the early 1950s there has been in Yugoslavia a large and dynamic group of Marxist theoreticians, discussing questions of epistemology, ethics, and aesthetics and also the political problems connected with changes in Yugoslav socialism. From 1964 onwards this group published a philosophical journal, *Praxis* (closed down by the authorities in 1975) and organized annual philosophical debates on the island of Korčula, attended by many scholars from different countries. The group has concentrated on typically revisionist themes such as alienation, reification, and bureaucracy; its philosophical orientation is anti-Leninist. Most of these philosophers, whose literary output is very large, were partisan fighters in the Second World War; some of the principal names are G. Petrović, M. Marković, S. Stojanović, R. Supek, L. Tadić, P. Vranicki, D. Grlić, M. Kangrga, V. Korać, and Z. Pesić-Golubović.

The main object of this group, who are perhaps the most active circle of Marxist philosophers in the world today, is to restore Marx's humanistic anthropology in its radical opposition to Leninist–Marxist 'diamat'. Most or all of them reject the 'theory of reflection' and seek, following Lukács and Gramsci to some extent, to establish 'praxis' as a fundamental category in relation to which not only other anthropological concepts but also ontological questions are secondary. Their starting-point is thus the early Marxian idea that man's practical contact with nature determines the meaning of metaphysical problems and that cognition is the effect of eternal interaction between subject and object. From this point of view historical determinism cannot hold its ground if it posits that anonymous 'laws of history' in the last resort determine the whole of human behaviour; we must take seriously Marx's saying that people make their own history, and not transform it, on evolutionist lines, into the statement that history makes people. The *Praxis* philosophers criticized Engels's definition of freedom as 'understood necessity', pointing out that it does not leave room for the active, spontaneous human subject. They thus took up the revisionist idea of the 'vindication of subjectivity', linking their analysis with the critique of Soviet state socialism and support for workers' self-government as the true path of socialist development in accordance with Marx's doctrine. At the same time, however, while emphasizing that socialism requires the active management of the economy by producers and not by a party bureaucracy call-ing itself the 'advance guard of the working class', they were aware that economic self-government, if carried too far, produces inequalities which are contrary to the idea of socialism. Orthodox Yugoslav Communists accused the *Praxis* group of wanting to have it both ways, by instituting full self-government but abolish-ing the market so as to avoid inequality. The Yugoslav revisionists seem to be divided on this matter, but their writings often strike a utopian note, express-ing the conviction that it is possible to do away with 'alienation', to assure everyone of full control over the results of their actions, and to remove the conflict between the need for planning and the autonomy of small groups, between individual interests and long-term social tasks, between security and technical progress.

The *Praxis* group played an important part in disseminating a humanistic version of Marxism not only in Yugoslavia but in the international philosophi-cal world; they also contributed to reviving philosophical thought in Yugosla-via, and were an important centre of intellectual resistance to autocratic and bureaucratic forms of government in that country. As time went on they came increasingly into conflict with the state authorities; nearly all their active mem-bers were finally expelled or resigned from the Communist party, and in 1975 eight of them were removed from their posts at Belgrade University. Their writ-ings appear to reflect increasing scepticism as to the Marxian Utopia.

Milovan Djilas, one of the leading Yugoslav Communists in the forties and fifties, cannot be regarded as a revisionist. His ideas on the democratization of socialism were condemned by the party as far back as 1954, and his later works (including the famous *New Class*, which we have already discussed) cannot be considered Marxist even in the loosest sense. Djilas completely gave up utopian ways of thought, and has many times pointed out the links between the origi-nal Marxist doctrine and its political realization in the form of bureaucratic despotism.

4. Revisionism and orthodoxy in France

FROM the second half of the 1950s lively discussions went on among French Marxists, with revisionist tendencies partly drawing support from existentialism and partly in conflict with it. Existentialism as expounded by both Heidegger and Sartre had one essential feature in common with Marxist revisionism, namely its emphasis on the opposition between irreducible human subjectivity and thing-like forms of existence; at the same time, it pointed out that human beings had a constant tendency to flee from subjective, i.e. free and independ-ent, existence into a 'reified' state. Heidegger developed an elaborate system of categories wherewith to express the drift into 'unauthenticity' and anonymity, the urge to identify with impersonal reality. In the same way Sartre's analyses of the opposition between 'being-in-itself' and 'being-for-itself', and his passionate denunciation of the *mauvaise foi* which hides our freedom from us and causes us to shun responsibility for ourselves and for the world, were in full accord with revisionist attempts to restore Marxism as a philosophy of subjectivity and freedom. Marx, and Kierkegaard in his own way, had both protested against what they saw as Hegel's attempt to merge human subjectivity into impersonal historical being; from this point of view the existentialist tradition coincided with what the revisionists regarded as Marx's fundamental doctrine.

At a later stage Sartre ceased to identify Marxism with the Soviet Union and French Communism, but at the same time he came decidedly closer to identifying himself with Marxism. In *Critique de la raison dialectique* (1960) he put forward a revision of existentialism and also his own interpretation of Marxism. This long and amorphous work contains some points which clearly indicate that hardly a shadow remained of Sartre's former existentialist philosophy. In it he stated that Marxism was a contemporary philosophy *par excellence* and that for purely historical reasons it could be criticized only from a pre-Marxist, i.e. reactionary, standpoint, just as in the seventeenth century Locke and Descartes could be criticized only from a scholastic point of view. For this reason Marxism was invincible, and particular manifestations of it could only be validly criticized 'from the inside'.

Leaving aside the absurd contention as to the historical 'invincibility' of Marxism (according to Sartre's argument, Leibniz's criticism of Locke and Hobbes's of Descartes must have been based on scholastic positions!), the *Critique* is interesting as an attempt to find room within Marxism for 'creativity' and spontaneity, abandoning the 'dialectic of nature' and historical determinism but preserving the social significance of human behaviour. Conscious human acts are not presented simply as projections of freedom producing human 'temporality', but as movements towards a 'totalization', their sense being co-determined by existing social conditions. In other words, the individual is not absolutely free to determine the meaning of his acts, but neither is he a slave to circumstances. There is a possibility of the free fusion of many human projects constituting a Communist society, but it is not guaranteed by any 'objective' laws. Social life does not only consist of individual acts rooted in freedom, but is also a sedimentation of history by which we are limited. It is, in addition, a fight with nature, which imposes its own obstacles and causes social relationships to be dominated by scarcity (*rareté*), so that every satisfaction of a need can be a source of antagonism and makes it more difficult for human beings to accept one another as such. People are free, but scarcity deprives them of particular choices and to that extent diminishes their humanity; Communism, by abolishing scarcity, restores the freedom of the individual and his ability to recognize the freedom of others. (Sartre does not explain how Communism abolishes scarcity; on this point he takes Marxist assurances on trust.) The possibility of Communism lies in the possibility of the voluntary combination of many individual projects in a single revolutionary purpose. The *Critique* gives a description of groups engaged in common action without infringing the freedom of any of the individuals concerned—a vision of revolutionary organization intended to replace the discipline and hierarchy of the Communist party and to harmonize individual freedom with effective political action. The account, however, is so generalized as to ignore the real problems of such harmonization. All that can be seen is that Sartre envisaged the objective of devising a form of Communism free from bureaucracy and institutionalization, the latter in all its forms being contrary to spontaneity and a cause of 'alienation'.

Apart from many superfluous neologisms it does not appear that the *Critique* contains any new interpretation of Marxism; as regards the historical character of perception and knowledge, and the negation of the dialectic of nature, Sartre follows in Lukács's footsteps. As to reconciling spontaneity with the pressure of historical conditions, the work seems to tell us little except that freedom must be safeguarded in revolutionary organization and that there will be perfect freedom when Communism has done away with shortages. Neither of these ideas is especially new in the Marxist context; what would have been new is an explanation of how these effects are to be achieved.

Revisionism in the strict sense, i.e. as expressed by philosophers deriving from the Communist tradition, did not coincide with 'Sartrism', but in some ways it showed existentialist inspiration.

This brand of revisionism took several forms. In the late forties some dissident Trotskyists including C. Lefort and C. Castoriadis formed a group called Socialisme ou barbarie, with a periodical of the same name. This group rejected Trotsky's view that the Soviet Union was a workers' state that had degenerated, but argued that it was ruled by a new class of exploiters who collectively owned the means of production. They traced this new form of exploitation to Lenin's theory of the party, and wished to revive the idea of workers' self-government as the true form of socialist rule; the party was not only superfluous, but ruinous to socialism. This group introduced French thinkers to ideas which became crucial from the late fifties onwards: workers' self-government, non-party socialism, and industrial democracy.

A more philosophic type of revisionism was represented by the journal *Arguments*, published from 1956 by a group of philosophers and sociologists who had mostly resigned or been expelled from the Communist party: Kostas Axelos, Edgar Morin, Pierre Fourgeyrollas, François Châtelet, and Jean Duvignaud, also Henri Lefebvre, who was expelled from the party in 1958. This group did not use the typical language of Communist philosophy but sought to combine the Marxist themes of alienation and reification with categories drawn from psychoanalysis, biology, and modern sociology; none of them claimed to be true Marxists. Axelos, who was a kind of Heideggerist with Marxist tendencies, criticized Marx for interpreting human existence in terms of technology; Joseph Gabel, in a book on false consciousness, pointed out similarities between the social and psychiatric symptoms of 'reification'; Châtelet, in a book on early Greek historiography, discussed the connection between the urge to write history and awareness of making it; Fougeyrollas criticized Marx's reduction of 'alienation' to class and economic conditions. In general this group took the view that Marx's categories were inadequate for the analysis of society at its present technological level, and that they failed to reflect man's 'planetary' situation, the biological conditions of existence, and non-economic sources of alienation. Lefebvre, without disavowing the Marxian Utopia of the 'complete man', about which he had written much when a Communist, turned his attention to the specific forms of 'reification' which arise in a consumer society in conditions of relative welfare, increasing leisure, and increasing urbanization. Like many other neo-Marxists he maintained that if 'emancipation' has a meaning it relates primarily to shaking off the oppressive rules of capitalist society as they are internalized in consciousness. He appears, however, to have ceased to believe that alienation could be completely overcome. He resumed, in a new version, his 'critique of everyday life', declaring that this, as opposed to productive activity, was the sphere in which human isolation, mechanization, and mutual incomprehension were most acute, and which was therefore the proper scene for a true revolution that would expand human potentialities.

Most of the French revisionists abandoned the belief that the working class, thanks to its special historical mission, would become the liberator of humanity; their scepticism on this point, coinciding with the critique of the Frankfurt school, removed from their philosophy what is certainly the corner-stone of Marxism. For this reason, when the word 'revolution' occurs in their writings it is not to be taken in the Marxist sense; it denotes a revolution in people's feelings, their way of life, or their mutual relations, rather than the seizure of political power by this or that 'advance guard'. After a few years it became clear that none of the revisionists of this group except perhaps Lefebvre could be called a Marxist in any tangible sense, although concepts or themes from the Marxist tradition appear from time to time in their writings.

As to Roger Garaudy, who for many years was the party's chief philosophical spokesman, in the late 1950s he began by following the general course of de-Stalinization. In *Perspectives de l'homme* (1959) he offered a humanistic interpretation of Marx and made friendly gestures towards existentialists, phenomenologists, and even Christians. In *D'un réalisme sans rivages* (1963) he interpreted literary realism on broad enough lines to afford a welcome to Proust and Kafka. The tactical purpose of these books was fairly clear; they were in line with the Communist party's efforts to emerge from the intellectual isolation it had imposed upon itself. But Garaudy pushed his humanistic interpretation to the point of criticizing the Soviet system and denouncing the invasion of Czechoslovakia. Expelled from the party in 1970 after a series of quarrels and accusations, he published the relevant documents in the same year under the ambitious title *Toute la vérité*; in this book he presents himself as a Communist anxious to renew the party and cure it, for efficiency's sake, of ideological sclerosis.

In the second half of the 1960s, when the fashion in Paris changed from existentialism to structuralism, attention turned to a completely different interpretation of Marxism put forward by the French Communist Althusser. One reason for the popularity of structuralism was that it originated as a method of linguistics, which was regarded as the only humanistic discipline capable of evolving more or less exact 'laws'; the hope was now entertained that a 'scientific' status could be conferred on other humanistic studies, which had hitherto been sadly deficient in this respect. Lévi-Strauss was the first French advocate of a structural, non-historical approach to humanistic studies, paying little attention to the individual but concentrating on the analysis of a system of signs as they operated in the myths of primitive societies; the 'structure' of that system was not consciously devised by anyone and was not present to the minds of its users, but could be discovered by the scientific observer. In two successive works— *Pour Marx* (1965) and *Lire le Capital* (1966, with E. Balibar)—Althusser endeavoured to show that Marxism could provide a structuralist method of investigation from which human subjectivity and historical continuity were consciously excluded. He directed his attack against 'humanism', 'historicism', and 'empiricism', and claimed that Marx's intellectual development had undergone a distinct break in 1845, at the time of *The German Ideology*. Before that date Marx was still enslaved to Hegel and Feuerbach and described the world in 'humanistic' and 'historicist' categories (such as alienation), having in mind concrete human individuals; afterwards, however, he discarded this ideological approach and evolved a strictly scientific theory, which alone is genuine Marxism (why the later Marx is more genuine than the earlier, Althusser does not explain). This Marxism, which is most fully expounded in *Capital* and whose methodology is set out in the Introduction to the *Grundrisse*, rejects the idea that the historical process can be described in terms of the actions of human subjects. As with all scientific works, according to Althusser, the subject of *Capital* is not actual reality but a theoretical construct, all elements of which are dependent on the whole. The essence of historical materialism is not that it makes certain aspects of historical reality dependent on others (the superstructure and the base respectively), but that each of them depends on the whole (an idea of Lukács's, to whom Althusser does not refer in this context). Every sphere has its own rhythm of change, however; they do not all develop evenly, and at any given moment they are at different stages of evolution. Althusser does not define 'ideology' and 'science', merely stating that science cannot be bounded by any 'external' criteria of truth, as the positivists would have it, but creates its own 'scientificity' in its own 'theoretical practice'. Having thus disposed of the problem of what constitutes a science, he declares that Marx's analysis of capitalist society is not concerned with human subjects but with production relations, which determine the functions of the people involved in them. (It is true, we may observe, that *Capital* treats individuals as mere embodiments of functions determined by capital movements, but this is merely a repetition of Marx's earlier observation that capital in fact reduces them to units of wealth or labour-power, this being the 'dehumanizing' effect that Communism promises to abolish. Thus we have to do not with a universal methodical rule but with a critique of the anti-humanist nature of exchange-value.)

The subject of observation, then, is 'structure' (a term used incessantly in these books, but nowhere explained) and not its individual human elements. By 'humanism' Althusser seems to mean a theory which reduces the historical process to individual acts, or which sees in human individuals the same species-nature multiplied through many examples, or which explains historical change in terms of human needs and not impersonal 'laws'. 'Historicism' (though Althusser does not explain this term either) apparently consists in treating all forms of culture, and science in particular, as relative to changing historical conditions, in Gramsci's manner, and thus belittling the special dignity and 'objectivity' of science. In true Marxism, however, science does not belong to the 'superstructure'; it has its own rules and its own evolution, it constructs objective conceptual wholes and is not an 'expression' of class-consciousness; thus Lenin was right in saying that it must be brought into the working-class movement from outside and cannot come into existence as a mere element or product of the class struggle. For it is an essential fact that the different aspects of social life develop unevenly (a point which Althusser claims to find in Mao Tse-tung) and do not all express the same *Zeitgeist* in the same way. Each of them is relatively autonomous, and the social 'contradictions' that culminate in revolution are always the product of conflicts arising from these 'inequalities'. To this last phenomenon Althusser gives the name 'super-determination', meaning apparently that particular phenomena are determined not only by an existing complex of conditions (for example, capitalism) but also by the developmental rhythm of the aspect of life in questions; thus, for example, the state of science depends on the previous history of science as well as on the entire social situation, and the same is true of painting, etc. This seems a highly innocuous conclusion, a repetition of Engels's remarks about the 'relative independence of the superstructure'. Althusser observes on occasion, again following Engels, that in spite of 'super-determination' the situation is always governed by production relations 'in the last resort', but he does not add anything to make Engels's vague statement more precise. The upshot is simply that particular cultural phenomena are generally due to a variety of circumstances, including the history of the aspect of life they belong to and the present state of social relations. We are not told what is so 'scientific' about this obvious truth, why it is a revolutionary discovery of Marxism, or how it helps us to account for any particular fact, let alone predict the future. Nor does Althusser explain how we can compare two different fields, for example sculpture and political theory, in order to show that they are or are not at the same stage of development. This could only be done on the assumption that we can deduce from historical laws what conditions in the realm of sculpture would correspond to a given state of 'production relations'; but Althusser does not suggest any way of making such a deduction. (The idea that party leaders were capable of making it has always been highly convenient in Communist countries, where ideological persecution was held to be justified because the existing state of social consciousness 'lagged behind' production relations; the rulers, it was implied, knew what form that consciousness should take so as to be in conformity with the 'base'.)

Later Althusser came to believe that the epistemological turning-point in Marx's views around 1845 was not so clearly defined as he had thought, since regrettable traces of humanism, historicism, and Hegelianism were still to be found in *Capital*. Only two of Marx's writings, the letter known as the *Critique of the Gotha Programme* and some notes in the margin of Adolph Wagner's book on political economy, were completely free from the ideological taint. At this point we begin to wonder if Marxism existed at all in Marx's day, or whether it was left to Althusser to invent it.

The popularity of Althusser's view especially in the later sixties was not a matter of politics, as his books do not lead to any specific political conclusion. A more important point was that he opposed the tendency among Marxists to make advances to existentialists, phenomenologists, or Christians, thus diluting their own philosophy and depriving it of its uniqueness. Althusser stood for ideological 'integralism' and the assurance that Marxism was a self-sufficient doctrine, a hundred per cent scientific and needing no assistance from outside. (The mythology of 'science' has always played a tremendous part in Marxist propaganda. Althusser is constantly proclaiming how scientific he is, and many other Marxist writers do likewise. It is not a habit of real scientists, or of humanistic scholars.) Apart from a few neologisms, Althusser did not make any fresh contribution to theory. His work is merely an attempt to revert to ideological austerity and doctrinal exclusivism, a belief that Marxism can be preserved from the contamination of other ways of thought. From this point of view it is a return to old-fashioned Communist bigotry, but at the same time it bears witness to the directly opposite process which set in as a result of the post-Stalinist 'thaw'. Just as, before the First World War, the 'infection' of Marxism by current intellectual fashions led to such phenomena as neo-Kantian Marxism, anarcho-Marxism, Marxist Darwinism, empiriocritical Marxism, and so on, in the same way Marxists of the past two decades, desperately trying to make up for their long isolation, have resorted to various ready-made or popular philosophies, so that we have Marxism tempered by Hegelianism, existentialism, Christianity, or, as in Althusser's case, structuralism. Other causes of the vogue for structuralism which made itself felt in the humanistic sciences in the late fifties are a separate subject, which we shall not discuss here.

▪ ▪ ▪

REVISIONISM as we have described it was only one of several manifestations of the post-Stalinist disintegration of Marxism. Its importance was that by its critical attitude it contributed much to the decline of ideological faith in the Communist countries and to showing up the intellectual as well as the moral destitution of official Communism. At the same time it drew attention to neglected aspects of Marxist tradition, and gave an impulse to historical studies. The values and aspirations to which it gave currency are by no means extinct and are still prominent in the democratic opposition in Communist countries, but are not usually expressed in a specifically revisionist context; that is to say, the criticism of Communist despotism is conducted more and more seldom, and with less and less effect, in terms of 'purging Communism of abuses', 'reforming Marxism', or 'going back to the sources'. To fight against despotic regimes it is not, after all, necessary to prove that they are contrary to Marx's or Lenin's ideas (and in the case of Lenin the contradiction is especially hard to prove anyway); such arguments were appropriate to the particular situation of the 1950s, but they have now lost much of their importance. Similarly, in philosophy the vindication of human subjectivity against 'historical laws' or the 'theory of reflection' does not need to be based on Marxist authorities and can get on better without them. In this sense revisionism has largely ceased to be a live issue; but this does not affect the continuing value of some of its ideas and critical analyses.

5. Marxism and the 'New Left'

THE so-called New Left is also a complex of phenomena witnessing, on the one hand, to the universalization of Marxist phraseology and, on the other, to the disintegration of the docctrine and its inadequacy to modern social problems. It is hard to define the common ideological features of all groups and sects which claim to belong to the New Left or are considered by others to form part of it. A group of this name with revolutionary aspirations arose in France in the later fifties (the Parti Socialiste Unifié grew out of it to some extent), and similar groups were formed in Britain and other countries. The movement was catalysed by the Soviet Twentieth Congress and, perhaps to a still greater degree, by the invasion of Hungary and the Suez crisis of 1956; its literary organs in Britain were the *New Reasoner* and the *University and Left Review*, which later merged into the *New Left Review*. The New Left condemned Stalinism in general and the invasion of Hungary in particular, but its members differed among themselves as to how far the 'degeneration' of the Soviet system was inevitable and whether there was any prospect of the political, moral, and intellectual renewal of the existing Communist parties. At the same time they emphasized their fidelity to Marxism as the ideology of the working class, and some even professed allegiance to Leninism. They also took care to differentiate their criticism of Stalinism from that of the social democrats or the Right, and to avoid being classed as 'anti-Communist'; they were at pains to preserve a revolutionary and Marxist ethos and to match their criticism of Stalinism with renewed attacks on Western imperialism, colonialism, and the arms race.

The New Leftists contributed to the ferment in the Communist parties and to the general revival of ideological discussion, but they do not appear to have worked out any alternative model of socialism except in very general terms. The designation 'New Left' was claimed by various dissidents who sought to revive 'true Communism' outside the existing parties, as well as bigger and smaller Maoist, Trotskyist, and other groups. In France the name *gauchiste* is generally used by groups who emphasize their opposition to all forms of authority, including Leninist 'advance guard' parties. The post-Stalinist years saw a certain revival of Trotskyism, and this led to the formation of numerous splinter groups, separate 'internationals', etc. In the sixties the term 'New Left' was generally used in Europe and North America as a collective label for student ideologies which, while not identifying with Soviet Communism and often expressly disavowing it, used the phraseology of worldwide anti-capitalist revolution and looked chiefly to the Third World for models and heroes. So far these ideologies have not produced any intellectual results worth the name. Their characteristic tendencies may be described as follows.

Firstly, they maintain that the concept of a society's 'ripeness' for revolution is a bourgeois deceit; a properly organized group can make a revolution in any country and bring about a radical change of social conditions ('revolution here and now'). There is no reason to wait; existing states and governing élites must

be destroyed by force, without arguing about the political and economic organization of the future—the revolution will decide these in its own good time.

Secondly, the existing order deserves destruction in all its aspects without
exception: the revolution must be worldwide, total, absolute, unlimited, all-
embracing. As the idea of total revolution began in the universities, its first
blows were naturally directed against 'fraudulent' academic institutions,
against knowledge and logical skills. Periodicals, pamphlets, and leaflets
declared that revolutionaries must not get into discussion with teachers who
asked them to explain their demands or terminology. There was much talk of
'liberation' from the inhuman oppression that required students to pass exams
or to learn one subject rather than another. It was also a revolutionary duty to
oppose all reforms in the universities or in society: the revolution must be universal, and all partial reforms were a conspiracy of the establishment. Either
everything or nothing must be changed, for, as Lukács, Marcuse, and the
Frankfurt school had taught, capitalist society was an indivisible whole and
could only be transformed as such.

Thirdly, the working class could not be relied on, as it had been irre-
deemably depraved by the bourgeoisie. At the present time students were the
most oppressed members of society, and therefore the most revolutionary. All
were oppressed, however: the bourgeoisie had introduced the cult of labour,
and the first duty was therefore to stop work—the necessities of life would be
forthcoming in some way or another. One disgraceful form of oppression was
the prohibition of drugs, and this too must be fought against. Sexual liberation,
freedom from work, from academic discipline and restrictions of all kinds, universal and total liberation—all this was the essence of Communism.

Fourthly, the patterns of total revolution were to be found in the Third
World. The heroes of the New Left were African, Latin American, and Asian
political leaders. The United States must be transformed into the likeness of
China, Vietnam, or Cuba. Apart from leaders of the Third World and Western
ideologists interested in its problems, like Frantz Fanon and Régis Debray, the
student New Left especially admired negro leaders in the United States who
advocated violence and black racialism.

While the ideological fantasies of this movement, which reached its climax
around 1968–9, were no more than a nonsensical expression of the whims of
spoilt middle-class children, and while the extremists among them were virtually indistinguishable from Fascist thugs, the movement did without doubt
express a profound crisis of faith in the values that had inspired democratic
societies for many decades. In this sense it was a 'genuine' movement despite
its grotesque phraseology; the same, of course, could be said of Nazism and
Fascism. The sixties brought into the public view acute problems which

humanity can only solve, if it can at all, on a worldwide basis: over-population, environmental pollution, the poverty, backwardness, and economic failures of the Third World; at the same time it has become clear that owing to predatory and contagious nationalism the likelihood of effective global action is very small. All this, together with political and military tension and fears of a world war, not to mention various symptoms of crisis in the educational field, has brought about a general atmosphere of insecurity and a feeling that present remedies are ineffectual. The situation is one of a kind frequently met with in history, where people feel they have got into a blind alley; they long desperately for a miracle, they believe that a single magic key will open the door to paradise, they indulge chiliastic and apocalyptic hopes. The sense of universal crisis is intensified by the speed of communication, whereby all local problems and disasters are at once known all over the world and merge into a general sense of defeat. The New Left explosion of academic youth was an aggressive movement born of frustration, which easily created a vocabulary for itself out of Marxist slogans, or rather some expressions from the Marxist store: liberation, revolution, alienation, etc. Apart from this, its ideology really has little in common with Marxism. It consists of 'revolution' without the working class; hatred of modern technology as such (Marx glorified technical progress and believed that one reason for the impending breakdown of capitalism was its inability to sustain such progress—a prophecy that could not be repeated today with absurdity); the cult of primitive societies (in which Marx took scarcely any interest) as the source of progress; hatred of education and specialized knowledge; and the belief in the American lumpenproletariat as a great revolutionary force. Marxism, however, did have an apocalyptic side which has come to the fore in many of its later versions, and a handful of words and phrases from its vocabulary sufficed to convince the New Left that it was possible at a stroke to transform the world into a miraculous paradise, the only obstacles to this consummation being the big monopolies and university professors. The chief complaint of the New Left against official Communist parties was and is that they are not revolutionary enough.

In general we have a situation today in which Marxism provides ideological pabulum for a wide range of interests and aspirations, many of them unconnected with one another. This is a long way, of course, from the medieval type of universalism in which all conflicting human interests and ideas clothed themselves in the garb of Christianity and spoke its language. The intellectual panoply of Marxism is only used by certain schools of thought, but they are quite numerous. Marxist slogans are invoked by various political movements in Africa and Asia and by countries striving to emerge from backwardness by methods of state coercion. The Marxist label adopted by such movements or applied to them by the Western Press often means no more than that they receive war material from the Soviet Union or China, and 'socialism' sometimes means little more than that a country is ruled despotically and that no political opposition is allowed. Scraps of Marxist phraseology are used by various feminist groups and even so-called sexual minorities. Marxist language is least frequently met with in the context of defending democratic freedoms, though this does sometimes occur. Altogether Marxism has achieved a high degree of universality as an ideological weapon. Russia's interests as a world Power, Chinese nationalism, the economic claims of French workers, the industrialization of Tanzania, the activities of Palestine terrorists, black racialism in the United States—all express themselves in Marxist terms. One cannot seriously judge the Marxist 'orthodoxy' of every one of these movements and interests: the name of Marx is often invoked by leaders who have heard that Marxism means having a revolution and taking power in the people's name, this being the sum total of their theoretical knowledge.

There is no doubt that this universalization of Marxist ideology is due first and foremost to Leninism, which showed itself able to direct every existing social claim and grievance into a single channel and use the impetus thus provided to secure dictatorial power for the Communist party. Leninism raised political opportunism to the dignity of a theory. The Bolsheviks rose to victory in circumstances irrelevant to any Marxist schema of 'proletarian revolution'; they prevailed because they used as a lever the aspirations and desires that were actually present in society, i.e. chiefly national and peasant interests, although from the point of view of classical Marxism these were 'reactionary'. Lenin showed that those who wish to seize power must take advantage of every crisis and every manifestation of discontent, regardless of doctrinal considerations. In a world situation in which, despite all Marxist prophecies, nationalist feelings and aspirations are the most powerful and active forms of ideology, it is natural for 'Marxists' to identify with them whenever nationalist movements are strong enough to disrupt the existing power structure.

Since, however, the various interests throughout the world which use Marxist language are often opposed to one another, the universality of Marxism, looked at in another way, amounts to its disintegration. In the holy war between the Russian and Chinese empires, both sides can invoke Marxist slogans with equal right. In this situation schisms are bound to occur, such as those which rent the international Communist movement in the years after Stalin's death. It is noticeable, moreover, that the various schisms express tendencies which were already present in embryonic form in the twenties, but disappeared under the pressure of Stalinism or survived only in marginal forms. These included elements of what later became Maoism (Sultan-Galiyev, Roy), Communist reformism (represented today by various West European parties, especially those of Italy and Spain), the idea of workers' councils exercising the dictatorship of the proletariat, and the ideology of 'left-wing' Communism (Korsch, Pannekoek). All these ideas, in somewhat altered forms, have reappeared at the present day.

An important manifestation of Marxism in the last fifteen years or so is the ideology of industrial self-government. This is not genetically derived from Marxism, however, but rather from anarchist and syndicalist traditions represented by Proudhon and Bakunin. The idea of factory management by the workers was canvassed by British guild socialists in the nineteenth century without any impetus from Marxism. Socialists, like anarchists, already realized at that time that the nationalization of industry would not in itself do away with exploitation, and, on the other hand, that the complete economic autonomy of individual firms would mean the restoration of capitalist competition with all its consequences; they therefore proposed a mixed system of parliamentary democracy and representative industrial democracy. Bernstein also concerned himself with the question, and after the October Revolution the cry for industrial democracy was raised by the Communist Left Opposition both in the Soviet Union and in the West. After Stalin's death the issue was revived, partly on account of the Yugoslav experiment. One of the first to take it up in France was the ex-Communist Serge Mallet, author of *La Nouvelle Classe ouvrière* (1963). Mallet analysed some social consequences of the automation of industry, pointing out that skilled technicians were increasingly important as an 'advance guard' of the working class, but in a new sense of this phrase, namely that of carrying on the struggle for democratic control of production. In that struggle the old distinction between economics and politics disappeared; the prospects of socialism were not connected with the hope of a worldwide political revolution preluded by the economic claims of the proletariat, but with the extension of democratic methods of organizing production, in which skilled wage-earners could play an essential part.

The question of the possibility and prospects of industrial democracy has come to be of key importance in discussions on democratic socialism; it has in itself nothing in common with the apocalyptic dreams of the New Left as inspired by Marcuse or Wilhelm Reich, and is historically and logically independent of Marxism.

A by-product of the revival of ideological discussion since Stalin's death has been the increased interest in the history and theory of Marxism, expressed in a profusion of academic literature. The fifties and sixties saw the production of many valuable works of this kind, by a wide variety of authors. These include declared adversaries of Marxism (Bertram Wolfe, Zbigniew Jordan, Gustav Wetter, Jean Calvez, Eugene Kamenka, Inocenty Bocheński, John Plamenatz, Robert Tucker) and others whose attitude to it is critical but favourable (Iring Fetscher, Shlomo Avineri, M. Rubel, Lucio Coletti, George Lichtheim, David

McLellan), as well as a smaller number of orthodox Marxists of one school or another (Auguste Cornu, Ernst Mandel). Many studies were devoted to the origins of Marxism and particular aspects of its doctrine; there is a wealth of literature on Lenin and Leninism, Rosa Luxemburg, Trotsky, and Stalin. Some Marxists of an earlier generation, like Korsch, were rescued from oblivion. All the old interpretive problems were revived, and some new ones made their appearance. There was discussion of Marx's relationship to Hegel, that of Marxism to Leninism, the 'dialectic of nature', the possibility of a 'Marxist ethic', historical determinism and the theory of value. Themes related to Marx's early views—alienation, reification, praxis—continue to be the object of debate. The profusion of works directly or indirectly related to Marxism is such that of recent years a degree of satiety has become noticeable.

6. The peasant Marxism of Mao Tse-tung

THE CHINESE revolution is indisputably one of the most important events of twentieth-century history, and its doctrine, known as Maoism, has accordingly become one of the chief elements in the contemporary war of ideas, irrespective of its intellectual value. Measured by European standards the ideological documents of Maoism, and especially the theoretical writings of Mao himself, appear in fact extremely primitive and clumsy, sometimes even childish; in comparison, even Stalin gives the impression of a powerful theorist. However, judgements of this kind must be made with some caution. Those who, like the present writer, do not know Chinese and have only a scanty and superficial knowledge of China's history and culture doubtless cannot grasp the full meaning of these texts, the various associations and allusions perceptible to a reader acquainted with Chinese thought; in this respect one must rely on the views of experts, who, however, do not always agree. More than elsewhere in this book, the remarks that follow are based on second-hand information. It may, however, be stated at the outset that despite the theoretical and philosophical claims of Maoism it is first and foremost a collection of practical precepts, which in some ways have proved highly effective in the Chinese situation.

What is nowadays called Maoism, or in China 'the Thought of Mao Tse-tung', is an ideological system whose origins date back several decades. Some characteristic features of Chinese as opposed to Russian Communism were already visible in the late 1920s. It was only after the Chinese Communists' victory in 1949, however, that their ideology, including in particular Mao's utopian vision, began to take on a definite form, and some very important aspects developed only in or after the late fifties.

Maoism in its final shape is a radical peasant Utopia in which Marxist phraseology is much in evidence but whose dominant values seem completely alien to Marxism. Not surprisingly, this Utopia owes little to European experience and ideas. Mao never left China except for two visits to Moscow when he was already head of the new state; as he himself declared, he knew next to nothing of any foreign language, and his knowledge of Marx was probably also fairly limited. For instance, while laying claim to Marxist orthodoxy he was in the habit of saying that everything had two sides, a good and a bad; he would presumably not have done so if he had known that Marx derided this form of dialectic as pettybourgeois nonsense. Again, if he had known that Marx referred to the 'Asiatic mode of production' he would probably have discussed it too, whereas there is no mention of it in his works. His two philosophical essays—'On Practice' and 'On Contradiction'—are a popular and simplified exposition of what he had read in the works of Stalin and Lenin, plus some political conclusions adapted to the needs of the moment; to put it mildly, much good will is needed to perceive any deep theoretical significance in these texts.

This, however, is not the essential point. The importance of Chinese Communism does not depend on the intellectual level of its dogmas. Mao was one of the greatest, if not the very greatest, manipulator of large masses of human beings in the twentieth century, and the ideology he used for the purpose is significant by reason of its effectiveness, not only in China but in other parts of the Third World.

Communism in China was a continuation of the revolutionary events that began with the overthrow of the Empire in 1912 and were the outcome of developments going back several decades, particularly the Taiping rebellion of 1850–64 (one of the bloodiest civil wars in history). Mao was the main architect of the second phase of the revolution, which, as in Russia, did not orginate under Communist auspices but what Lenin would have called 'bourgeois democratic' ones: the sharing-out of large estates to the peasants, the liberation of China from foreign imperialists, and the abolition of feudal institutions.

Mao Tse-tung (1893–1976) was the son of a well-to-do farmer in Hunan Province. He attended a village school, where he learnt the elements of the Chinese literary tradition and acquired a taste for learning that carried him on to secondary school. At an early age he joined Sun Yat-sen's revolutionary republican party, the Kuomintang. After fighting for a time in the republican army he resumed his studies until 1917; during these years he also wrote poetry. Later he worked in the University library at Peking. At this time he was a nationalist and a democrat with socialist leanings, but not a Marxist.

The Kuomintang's objectives were to free China from Japanese, Russian, and British imperialism, to set up a constitutional republic, and to improve the peasants' lot by economic reforms. After a fresh outbreak of unrest in 1919 the first Marxist group was formed in Peking, and in June 1921, under the aegis of a Comintern agent, this group of a dozen members, including Mao, founded the

Chinese Communist party. On the Comintern's instructions the party at first co-operated closely with the Kuomintang and tried to gain support from China's embryonic proletariat (in 1926 urban workers represented one in 200 of the population). After Chiang Kai-shek's massacre of Communists in 1927, after unsuccessful attempts to stage an insurrection and to reach an *entente* with the breakaway left wing of the Kuomintang, the Communists changed their policy and branded their ex-leader Chen Tu-hsiu as a 'right-wing opportunist'. Though decimated, the party continued to concentrate its efforts on reaching the workers, but Mao at an early stage advocated switching to the peasants and organizing a peasant army. Both groups within the party, however, emphasized anti-imperialist and anti-feudal objectives; there was scarcely any sign of a specifically Communist outlook. Mao set about organizing an armed peasant movement in his native province of Hunan, and in the areas it conquered this force expropriated big landowners, liquidated traditional institutions, and set up schools and co-operatives.

For the next two decades Mao lived in the countryside, away from urban cen-tres. He soon became not only an outstanding organizer of peasant guerrillas but also the unchallenged leader of the Chinese Communist party and the only such leader in the world who did not owe his position to Moscow's endorse-ment. For twenty years, a period full of remarkable victories and dramatic defeats, he fought in extremely difficult conditions against the Kuomintang and the Japanese invader, siding for a time with the former against the latter. The Communists organized the bases of their future state in the territory they occu-pied, but continued to emphasize the 'bourgeois democratic' character of their revolution and to call for a 'popular front' including not only all the peasants and workers but also the lower middle-class and the 'national' bourgeoisie, i.e. those who were not in league with the imperialists. The party continued to take this line for the first few years after its victory in 1949.

In 1937, during the period of guerrilla warfare, Mao delivered two philo-sophical lectures to the party's military school at Yenan, which at the present day constitute almost the whole of the philosophical education available to the Chinese people. In the lecture 'On Practice' he states that human knowledge springs from productive practice and social conflict, that in a class society all forms of thought without exception are class-determined, and that practice is the yardstick of truth. Theory is based on practice and is its servant; human beings perceive things with their senses and then form concepts by means of which they comprehend the essence of things they cannot see. In order to know an object one must bring practical action to bear on it: we know the taste of a pear by eating it, and we understand society only by taking part in the class struggle. The Chinese began by fighting imperialism on the basis of 'superfi-cial, perceptual knowledge', and only afterwards reached the stage of rational knowledge of the internal contradictions of imperialism and were thus able to fight it effectively. 'Marxism emphasizes the importance of theory precisely and only because it can guide action' (*Four Essays on Philosophy*, 1966, p. 14). Marxists must adapt their knowledge to changing conditions or they will fall into right-wing opportunism; while, if their thinking outstrips the stages of development and they mistake their imagination for reality, they will fall victims to pseudo-Leftist phrase-mongering.

The lecture 'On Contradiction' is an attempt to explain the 'law of the unity of opposites' with the aid of quotations from Lenin and Engels. The 'metaphysical' outlook 'sees things as isolated, static and one-sided' (ibid., p. 25) and regards movement or change as something imposed from without. Marxism, however, lays down that every object contains internal contradictions and that these are the cause of all change, including mechanical motion. External causes are only the 'condition' of change, while internal causes are its 'basis'. 'Each and every difference already contains contradiction, and difference itself is contradiction' (p. 33). Different spheres of reality have their characteristic contradictions, and these are the subject-matter of the different sciences. We must always observe the particular features of every contradiction, so as also to perceive the 'whole'. A thing turns into its opposite: for instance, the Kuomintang was revolutionary at first but then became reactionary. The world is full of contradictions, but some are more important than others, and in every situation we must discern the main contradiction from which the other, secondary ones derive—for example, in capitalist society, that between the bourgeoisie and the proletariat. We must understand how to unravel and overcome contradictions. Thus 'at the beginning of our study of Marxism, our ignorance of or scanty acquaintance with Marxism stands in contradiction to knowledge of Marxism. But by assiduous study, ignorance can be transformed into knowledge, scanty knowledge into substantial knowledge' (pp. 57–8). Things turn into their opposites: landowners are dispossessed and turn into paupers, while landless peasants become landowners. War gives way to peace, and peace again to war. 'Without life there would be no death; without death there would be no life. Without "above" there would be no "below"; without "below" there would be no "above" . . . Without facility there would be no difficulty; without difficulty there would be no facility' (p. 61). A distinction must also be drawn between antagonistic contradictions such as those between hostile classes, and non-antagonistic ones such as that between a right and a wrong party line. The latter can be resolved by correcting errors, but if this is not done they may turn into antagonistic contradictions.

A few years later, in 1942, Mao delivered an address to his followers on 'Art and Literature'. Its main points are that art and literature are in the service of social classes; that all art is class-determined; that revolutionaries must practise forms of art that serve the cause of revolution and the masses; and that artists and writers must transform themselves spiritually so as to help the masses in their struggle. Art must not only be good artistically but also politically right. 'All dark forces which endanger the masses of the people must be exposed, while all revolutionary struggles of the masses must be praised—this is the basic task of all revolutionary artists and writers' (*Mao Tse-tung, An Anthology of his Writings*, ed. Anne Fremantle, 1962, pp. 260–1). Writers are warned not to be led astray by so-called love of humanity, for there can be no such thing in a society divided into hostile classes: 'love of humanity' is a slogan invented by the possessing class.

Such is the gist of Mao's philosophy. It is, as may be seen, a naïve repetition of a few commonplaces of Leninist–Stalinist Marxism. Mao's originality, however, lay in his revision of Lenin's strategic precepts. This, and the peasant orientation of Chinese Communism, were the essential causes of its victory. The 'leading role of the proletariat' remained in force as an ideological slogan, but throughout the revolutionary period it meant little more than the leading role of the Communist party in organizing peasant guerrillas. Mao not only emphasized that in China, unlike Russia, the revolution came from the country to the town, but he saw the poor peasantry as a natural revolutionary force and—in opposition to both Marx and Lenin—expressly stated that social strata were revolutionary in proportion to their poverty. He firmly believed in the revolutionary potential of the peasantry, not only because the proletariat in China was such a small class, but for reasons of principle. His slogan of 'encirclement of the city by the country' was opposed as far back as 1930 by the then party leader, Li Li-san. The 'orthodox' revolutionaries at that time, obedient to Comintern directives, pressed for the strategy followed in Russia, with the main emphasis on strikes and revolts by workers in big industrial centres, peasant warfare being regarded as a side-line. It was Mao's tactics that proved effective, however, and in after years he emphasized that the Chinese revolution had been victorious in spite of Stalin's advice. Soviet material aid to the Chinese Communists in the thirties and forties seems to have been of no more than a token character. Possibly—this is merely a speculation, not based on direct evidence—Stalin realized that if Communism were victorious in China he could not hope in the long run to keep five hundred million people in subjection to the Soviet Union, and therefore quite rationally preferred to see China weak, divided, and ruled by quarrelling military cliques. The Chinese Communists, however, continued to profess loyalty to the Soviet Union in all their official statements, and in 1949 Stalin had no choice but to proclaim his delight at the new Communist victory and do his best to turn his formidable neighbour into a satellite.

The Sino–Soviet conflict was not due to any ideological heresy but to the independence of the Chinese Communists and the fact that, as we may suppose, the Chinese revolution was contrary to the interests of Russian imperialism. In an article of 1940, 'On New Democracy', Mao wrote that the Chinese revolution was 'essentially' a peasant revolution based on peasant demands and that it would give power to the peasantry; at the same time he emphasized the need for a united front against Japan comprising the peasants, workers, lower middle class, and patriotic bourgeoisie. The culture of the new democracy, he declared, would develop under the leadership of the proletariat, i.e. the Communist. In short, Mao's programme at that time was similar to 'first-stage' Leninism: a revolutionary dictatorship of the proletariat and peasantry, led by the Communist party. He repeated the same thing in a speech of June 1949, 'On the People's Democratic Dictatorship', though he laid more emphasis then on the 'next stage', in which the land would be socialized, classes would disappear, and 'universal brotherhood' ensue.

The first few years after the Communist victory seemed to be a period of unruffled Sino–Soviet friendship, with the Chinese leaders paying deferential homage to their elder brother, although, as became known afterwards, serious friction developed at the very first inter-state negotiations. At that time it was hard to speak of a clearly differentiated Maoist doctrine. As Mao himself was to point out on several occasions, the Chinese had no experience of economic organization and therefore copied Soviet models. Only with time did it come to light that these models were, in some important respects, contrary to the ideology which was perhaps already latent in the Chinese revolution but had not yet expressed itself in an articulate form.

After 1949 the Chinese traversed at high speed several stages of development, each accompanied by a further advance towards the crystallization of Maoism. In the fifties it appeared that the country was retracing the course of Soviet evolution at an accelerated rate. Large holdings of land were divided among needy peasants; private industry was tolerated within limits for a few years, but in 1952 it was subjected to strict control, and in 1956 it was completely nationalized. Agriculture was collectivized from 1955, first by means of co-operatives but soon in a 'highly developed' form of public ownership, though peasants were allowed to keep private plots. At this time the Chinese, following the Russians, maintained the absolute priority of heavy industry. The first economic plan (1953–7), which was intended to enforce strictly centralized planning and give a powerful stimulus to industrialization at the expense of the countryside, introduced several features of Soviet Communism: an expanded bureaucracy, a deepening of the cleavage between town and countryside, and a highly repressive system of labour laws. Inevitably, it became clear that rigorous central planning was an impossibility in a country of small peasant holdings. The change of administrative methods which followed, however, was not confined to various forms of planning decentralization but found expression in a new Communist ideology in which production targets and modernization took second place, while the main stress was on breeding a 'new type of man' embodying the real or supposed virtues of rural life.

For a time it even seemed that this stage would involve some relaxation of cultural despotism. This delusion was connected with the short-lived 'hundred flowers' campaign launched by the party in May 1956–i.e. after the Soviet Union's Twentieth Congress–and endorsed by Mao himself. Artists and scholars were encouraged to exchange their ideas freely; all schools of thought and artistic styles were to compete with one another; the natural sciences, in particular, were declared to have no 'class character', and in other fields progress was to be the result of unfettered discussion. The 'hundred flowers' doctrine aroused the enthusiasm of East European intellectuals, who were experiencing the ferment of de-Stalinization in their own countries. Many people thought for a brief period that the most backward country of the socialist bloc from the economic and technical point of view had become the champion of a liberal cultural policy. These illusions lasted barely a few weeks, however, as the Chinese intellectuals were emboldened to criticize the regime in no uncertain terms, and the party at once reverted to its normal policy of repression and intimidation. The inner history of the whole episode is not clear. From some articles in the Chinese Press, and from a speech by Teng Hsiao-ping, the party's Secretary-General, to the Central Committee in September 1957 it might be thought that the 'hundred flowers' slogan was a ruse to induce 'anti-party elements' to come forward so that they might be more easily destroyed. (Teng declared that the party allowed weeds to grow as a deterrent example to the masses; they would then be pulled up by the roots and used to fertilize Chinese soil.) It may be, however, that Mao really believed for a time that the Communist ideology could hold its own in a free discussion among Chinese intellectuals. If so, his illusion was clearly dispelled almost at once.

China's failure to industrialize after the Soviet pattern probably caused or precipitated the political and ideological changes of the next decade, which the world observed with some bewilderment. At the beginning of 1958 the party under Mao's leadership announced a 'great leap forward' which was to work miracles of productivity in the ensuing five years. The targets for industrial and agricultural production, which were to multiply by factors of 6 and 2.5 respectively, put even Stalin's first five-year plan in the shade. These fantastic results were to be achieved, however, not by Soviet methods but by inspiring the population with creative enthusiasm, on the principle that the masses could do anything they set their minds to and must not be hampered by 'objective' obstacles invented by the bourgeoisie. All sectors of the economy without exception were to undergo dynamic expansion, and the perfect Communist society was just round the corner. Farms organized on the lines of Soviet kolkhozes were to be replaced by communes on a hundred per cent collective basis: private plots were abolished, communal meals and housing were introduced wherever possible; the Press carried reports of special establishments where married couples attended at regular intervals and in due order of priority to carry out their patriotic duty of begetting the next generation. One celebrated feature of the 'great leap' was the smelting of steel in a multiplicity of small village furnaces.

For a short time the party leaders basked in a statistical paradise (a false one, as was later admitted), but soon the whole project proved a complete fiasco, as had been predicted both by Western economists and by Soviet advisers in China. The 'great leap' resulted in a catastrophic fall in the standard of living because of the high accumulation rate; it involved enormous waste and filled the towns with workers from the countryside who soon proved redundant and had to go back to their fields amid general chaos and famine. The years from 1959 to 1962 were a period of set-backs and misery, owing not only to the failure of the 'great leap' but to disastrous harvests and the virtual breaking-off of economic relations with the Soviet Union; the sudden withdrawal of Soviet technicians brought many major projects to an abrupt standstill.

The 'great leap' reflected the development of the new Maoist tenet that the peasant masses could do anything by the power of ideology, that there must be no 'individualism' or 'economism' (i.e. material incentives to production) and that enthusiasm could take the place of 'bourgeois' knowledge and skills. The Maoist ideology began at this time to take on a more definite form. It was formulated in public statements by Mao and also, more explicitly, in utterances that were divulged only later in the turmoil of the 'cultural revolution'; some of these have been published in English by the eminent Sinologist Stuart Schram (*Mao Tse-tung Unrehearsed*, 1974, cited hereafter as Schram).

At the Lushan party conference in July–August 1959 Mao made a speech of self-criticism (of course not published at the time) in which he admitted that the 'great leap' had been a defeat for the party. He confessed that he had no idea of economic planning, and that it had not occurred to him that coal and iron do not move of their own accord but have to be transported. He took responsibility for the policy of rural steel smelting, declaring that the country was heading for catastrophe and that he now saw it would take at least a century to build Communism. The 'great leap', however, had not been entirely a defeat, as the leaders had learnt from their errors; everybody made mistakes, even Marx, and in such matters it was not only economics that counted.

The Sino–Soviet dispute, which became public knowledge in 1960, was due above all to Soviet imperialism and not to differences, though these did exist, as to Communist ideals and methods. The Chinese, while ardent in their professions of loyalty to Stalin, were not disposed to accept the status of an East

European 'people's democracy'. An immediate cause of contention arose over nuclear weapons, which the Russians were prepared to make available to the Chinese only on condition that they retained control over their use; other issues that need not to be enumerated here included Soviet policy towards the U.S.A. and the doctrine of 'coexistence'. The extent to which the conflict was one of two empires and not merely two versions of Communism is shown by the fact that the Chinese unreservedly approved the Soviet invasion of Hungary in 1956 and—twelve years later, after the breach—violently condemned the invasion of Czechoslovakia, although from the Maoist point of view Dubček's policy must have seemed arrant 'revisionism' and the 'Prague spring' with its liberal ideas was manifestly more 'bourgeois' than the Soviet system. Later, when the quarrel between two factions in China brought the country to the verge of civil war, it was clear that both of them were equally anti-Soviet in the basic sense, i.e. from the point of view of Chinese interests and sovereignty.

At the first stage of the conflict with Moscow, however, the Chinese showed that they attached importance to ideological differences and hoped, by creating a new doctrinal model, to supplant the Russians as leaders of world Communism or at least to gain a considerable following at Moscow's expense. As time went on they seem to have decided that instead of urging the world to follow China's example they could achieve better results by directly attacking Soviet imperialism. The 'ideological battle', i.e. the public exchange of insults between the Chinese and Soviet leaders, has continued since 1960, its intensity varying according to the international situation; but it has plainly become a conflict between rival empires for influence in the Third World, with each adversary resorting to *ad hoc* alliances with this or that democratic state. Chinese Marxism in its adapted form has become the ideological mainstay of Chinese nationalism, in the same way as happened previously with Soviet Marxism and Russian imperialism. Thus two powerful empires face each other, each laying claim to Marxist orthodoxy and each more hostile to the other than to the 'Western imperialists'; the development of 'Marxism' has led to a situation in which the Chinese Communists attack the United States Government chiefly on the ground that it is not sufficiently anti-Soviet.

The struggle within the Chinese Communist party went on in secret from 1958 onwards. The main issue was between those who favoured a Soviet type of Communism and those who endorsed Mao's formula for a new, perfect society; the former, however, were not 'pro-Soviet' in the sense of wanting to subject China to the dictates of Moscow. The specific points at issue may be summed up as follows.

Firstly, the 'conservatives' and 'radicals' had different ideas as to the army: the former wanted a modern army based on discipline and up-to-date technology, while the latter held to the tradition of guerrilla warfare. This was the cause of the first purge in 1959, among whose victims was the army chief P'eng Te-huai.

Secondly, the 'conservatives' believed in pay differentials and incentives more or less on the Soviet pattern, with the emphasis on cities and big heavy-industry plants, while the 'radicals' preached egalitarianism and relied on mass enthusiasm for the development of industry and agriculture.

Thirdly, the 'conservatives' believed in technical specialization at all levels of the educational system, so as to train doctors and engineers who could in time rival those of the developed countries. The 'radicals', on the other hand, emphasized ideological indoctrination and believed that if this were success-ful, technical skills would somehow come of themselves.

The 'conservatives', logically enough, were prepared to seek scientific knowledge and technology either from the Russians or from Europe and Amer-ica, while the 'radicals' contended that scientific and technical problems could be solved by reading the aphorisms of Mao Tse-tung.

The 'conservatives' were, in general, party bureaucrats of the Soviet type, concerned for the technical and military modernization and economic devel-opment of China, and believing in the strict hierarchical control of the party apparatus in every sphere of life. The 'radicals' seemed to place considerable faith in utopian fantasies of an impending Communist millennium; they believed in the omnipotence of ideology and direct coercion by the 'masses' (under party leadership, however) rather than by a professional apparatus of repression. As regards their geographical base, the 'conservatives' were appar-ently centred in Peking and the 'radicals' in Shanghai.

Both groups, of course, appealed to Mao's ideological authority, which was unshakeable from 1949 onwards; in the same way, all factions in the Soviet Union in the 1920s had invoked the authority of Lenin. The difference was, however, that in China the father of the revolution was still alive and not only favoured the 'radical' group but had in effect created it, so that its members were better off ideologically than their rivals.

They did not, however, enjoy the advantage in all respects. As a result of the set-backs of 1959–62 Mao had to cope with strong opposition among the party leaders, and his power seems to have been appreciably limited. Some, indeed, believe that he exercised no real authority from 1964 onwards; but the secrecy of Chinese politics is such that all assessments of this kind are uncertain.

The principal 'conservative' was Liu Shao-ch'i, who took over the state pres-idency from Mao at the end of 1958 and who, in the 'cultural revolution' of 1965–6, was denounced and execrated as an arch-fiend of capitalism. He was the author of a work on Communist education which, with two other booklets of his, was staple party reading from 1939 onwards. A quarter of a century later this faultless exposition of Marxist–Leninist–Stalinist–Maoist doctrine suddenly turned out to be a poisonous well of Confucianism and capitalism. The malign influence of Confucius, according to a host of critics, was visible in two main points. Liu had stressed the ideal of Communist self-perfection instead of a merciless class struggle, and he had depicted the Communist future as one of harmony and concord, whereas according to Mao's teaching tension and con- flict were the eternal law of nature.

The struggle for power which broke out within the party at the end of 1965 and brought China close to civil war was thus not only one between rival cliques but between two versions of Communism. The 'cultural revolution' is generally reckoned as beginning with an article inspired by Mao and published in Shanghai in November 1965, which condemned a play by Wu Han, the vice- mayor of Peking, on the ground that under the guise of an historical allegory it attacked Mao for dismissing P'eng Te-huai from the post of Minister of Defence. This unleashed a campaign against 'bourgeois' influences in culture, art, and education and a call for a 'cultural revolution' to restore the country's revolutionary purity and prevent a return to capitalism. The 'conservatives', of course, echoed this objective, but tried to interpret it so as not to disturb the established order and their own positions. The 'radicals', however, managed to secure the dismissal of P'eng Chen, the party secretary and mayor of Peking, and to gain control of the chief newspapers.

In the spring of 1966 Mao and his 'radical' group launched a massive attack on the most vulnerable seats of 'bourgeois ideology', namely, the universities. Students were urged to rise against the 'reactionary academic authorities' who, entrenched in bourgeois knowledge, were opposing Maoist education. Mao, it was pointed out, had long proclaimed that in places of education half the time should be devoted to learning and half to productive work, that staff appoint- ments and the admission of students should depend on ideological qualifica- tions or 'links with the masses', not academic attainments, and that Communist propaganda was the most important feature of the curriculum. The Central Committee now called for the elimination of all who 'took the capitalist road'. As the bureaucracy paid lip-service to his ideas but sabotaged them in practice, Mao took a step which no Communist leader anywhere had ventured on before him, by appealing to the mass of unorganized youth to destroy his adversaries. The universities and schools began to form Red Guard detachments, storm troops of the revolution which were to restore power to the 'masses' and sweep aside the degenerate party and state bureaucracy. Mass meetings, processions, and street fighting became a feature of life in all the bigger cities (the country- side was largely spared). Mao's partisans skilfully exploited the discontent and frustration caused by the 'great leap' and directed it against bureaucrats who were blamed for economic failure and accused of wanting to restore capitalism. For several years the schools and universities ceased functioning altogether, as the Maoist groups assured pupils and students that by virtue of their social origin and fidelity to the Leader they were the possessors of a great truth unknown to 'bourgeois' scholars. Thus encouraged, bands of young people bullied professors whose only crime was their learning, ransacked homes in search of proofs of bourgeois ideology, and destroyed historical monuments as 'relics of feudalism'. Books were burnt wholesale; the authorities, however, had prudently closed the museums. The battle-cry was equality, popular sovereignty, and liquidation of the privileges of the 'new class'. After some months the Maoists also directed their propaganda to the workers. This proved a more difficult target, as the better paid and more stable section of the working class were not anxious to fight for wage equality or to make further sacrifices for the Communist ideal; however, some of the poorer workers were mobilized for the 'cultural revolution'. The result of the campaign was social chaos and a collapse in production; different factions among the Red Guard and the workers soon began to fight one another in the name of 'true' Maoism. Many violent clashes took place, with the army intervening to restore order.

It is clear that Mao could not have taken such a dangerous step as to call in non-party forces to destroy the party establishment if it were not for the fact that he himself, as the infallible source of wisdom, stood above all criticism, so that his opponents could not attack him directly. Like Stalin in former years, Mao was himself the embodiment of the party and could therefore destroy the party bureaucracy in the name of party interests.

For this reason, no doubt, the cultural revolution was a period in which the cult of Mao, already inflated to an extraordinary degree, took on such grotesque and monstrous forms as even to surpass—impossible though this might have seemed—the cult of Stalin in the years just before his death. There was no field of activity in which Mao was not the supreme authority. Sick people were cured by reading his articles, surgeons carried out operations with the aid of the 'little red book', public meetings recited in chorus the aphorisms of the greatest genius that humanity had ever produced. The adulation reached such a point that extracts from Chinese newspapers glorifying Mao were reprinted without comment in the Soviet Press for the amusement of its readers. Mao's most faithful aide and successor-designate, the army chief Lin Piao (who, however, soon 'proved' to be a traitor and a capitalist agent) laid down that ninety-nine per cent of the material used in Marxist–Leninist studies must be taken from the Leader's works; in other words, the Chinese were not to learn even about Marxism from any other source.

The purpose of the orgy of praise was, of course, to prevent critics at any time from undermining Mao's power and authority. In conversation with Edgar Snow (as the latter relates in *The Long Revolution*, 1973, pp. 70, 205) he remarked that Khrushchev probably fell 'because he had no cult of personality at all'. Later, after Lin Piao's disgrace and death, Mao sought to lay the blame on him for the degeneration of the cult. In April 1969, however, at the party congress which marked the end of the cultural revolution, Mao's position as leader and that of Lin Piao as his successor were officially written into the party statutes—an event without precedent in the history of Communism.

The 'little red book' of *Quotations from Chairman Mao Tse-tung* also came into prominence at this time. Prepared initially for army use, and with a preface by Lin Piao, it soon became universal reading and the basic intellectual diet of all Chinese. It is a kind of popular catechism containing everything the citizen ought to know about the party, the masses, the army, socialism, imperialism, class, etc., together with a good deal of moral and practical advice: thus it lays down that one should be brave and modest and not daunted by adversity, that an officer should not strike a soldier, that soldiers should not take goods without paying for them, and so on. Here is a selection of its precepts: 'The world is progressing, the future is bright, and no one can change this general trend of history' (*Quotations* . . . , 1976, p. 70). 'Imperialism will not last long because it always does evil things' (p. 77). 'Factories can only be built one by one. The peasants can only plough the land plot by plot. The same is even true of eating a meal . . . It is impossible to swallow an entire banquet in one gulp. This is known as a piecemeal solution' (p. 80). 'Attack is the chief means of destroying the enemy, but defence cannot be dispensed with' (p. 92). 'The principle of preserving oneself and destroying the enemy is the basis of all military principles' (p. 94). 'We should never pretend to know what we don't know' (p. 109). 'Some play the piano well and some badly, and there is a great difference in the melodies they produce' (p. 110). 'Every quality manifests itself in a certain quantity, and without quantity there can be no quality' (p. 112). 'Within the revolutionary ranks it is necessary to make a clear distinction between right and wrong, between achievements and shortcomings' (p. 115). 'What is work? Work is struggle' (p. 200). 'It is not true that everything is good; there are still shortcomings and mistakes. But neither is it true that everything is bad, and that too is at variance with the facts' (p. 220). 'It is not hard for one to do a bit of good. What is hard is to do good all one's life and never do anything bad' (p. 250).

The convulsions of the cultural revolution went on until 1969, and at a certain stage the situation was clearly out of control: various factions and groups emerged from the ranks of the Red Guards, each with its own infallible interpretation of Mao. Ch'en Po-ta, one of the chief ideologists of the revolution, often invoked the example of the Paris Commune. The only stabilizing factor was the army, which Mao prudently did not encourage to hold mass discussions or to attack its own bureaucratized leaders. The army restored order when local clashes became too violent, and it was noticeable that the provincial commanders were not over-eager to assist the revolutionaries. As the party apparatus had disintegrated to a large extent, the army's role naturally increased greatly. After the removal and political liquidation of several prominent figures including Liu Shao-chi, Mao used the army to curb the revolutionary extremists, many of whom were sent to farm labour by way of re-education. The altered composition of the party leadership as a result of the struggle seemed to most observers to be a compromise solution which did not give a clear victory to any one faction. The 'radicals' were defeated only after Mao's death.

As we have seen, the years between 1955 and 1970 witnessed the development of a Maoist ideology which constitutes a new variant of Communist doctrine and practice, differing from the Soviet version in several important respects.

The theory of permanent revolution is basic in Mao's thought, as he declared in January 1958 (Schram, p. 94). In 1967, when the cultural revolution was in progress, he stated that this was only the first revolution in a series of indefinite length, and that it should not be thought that after two, three, or four of them everything would be well. Mao seems to have believed that stabilization always leads inevitably to privilege and the emergence of a 'new class'; this calls for periodical shock treatment in which the revolutionary masses destroy the germs of bureaucracy. Thus apparently there can never be a definitive social order without classes or conflicts. Mao often repeated that 'contradictions' were eternal and must eternally be surmounted; one of his charges against the Soviet revisionists was that they did not speak of contradictions between the leaders and the masses. One of Liu Shao-chi's errors was to believe in the future harmony and unity of society.

Mao's disbelief in a harmonious Communist social order is clearly at variance with the traditional Marxist Utopia. He went further still, however, in his speculations about the distant future: as everything changed and must perish in the long run, Communism was not eternal and neither was humanity itself. 'Capitalism leads to socialism, socialism leads to communism, and communist society must still be transformed, it will also have a beginning and an end . . . There is nothing in the world that does not arise, develop and disappear. Monkeys turned into men, mankind arose; in the end, the whole human race will disappear, it may turn into something else, the earth itself will also cease to exist' (Schram, p. 110). 'In the future, animals will continue to develop. I don't believe that men alone are capable of having two hands. Can't horses, cows, sheep evolve? Can only monkeys evolve? . . . Water has its history too. Earlier still, even hydrogen and oxygen did not exist' (pp. 220–1).

In the same way, Mao did not think that China's Communist future was guaranteed. A generation in time to come might choose to restore capitalism; but if so, its posterity would overthrow capitalism once again.

Another essential departure from orthodox Marxism was the cult of the peasantry as the mainstay of Communism, whereas to European Communists they were a mere auxiliary force in the revolutionary struggle and were otherwise despised. At the Ninth Party Congress in 1969 Mao declared that when the people's army conquered cities it was a 'good thing' because otherwise Chiang Kai-shek would have continued to hold them, but a 'bad thing' because it led to corruption in the party.

The cult of the peasantry and of rural life explains most of the characteristic features of Maoism, including the cult of physical labour as such. The Marxist tradition regards manual labour as a necessary evil from which men will be gradually freed by technological progress, but for Mao it has a nobility of its own and is of irreplaceable educational value. The idea of pupils and students spending half their time in physical labour is not motivated so much by economic needs as by its function in the forming of character. 'Education through work' is a universal value, closely connected with the egalitarian ideal of Maoism. Marx believed that the difference between physical and mental labour would eventually disappear, and that there ought not to be one set of people working exclusively with their brains while others used muscle only. The Chinese version of Marx's ideal of the 'complete man' is that intellectuals must be made to fell trees and dig ditches, while university teachers are recruited from the ranks of barely literate workers; for, Mao declared, even illiterate peasants understand economic matters better than intellectuals can do.

But Mao's theory goes further still. Not only must scholars, writers, and artists be deported to work in the villages or to educative labour in special institutions (i.e. concentration camps), but it must be realized that intellectual work can easily lead to moral degeneration and that people must at all costs be prevented from reading too many books. This thought recurs in various forms in many of Mao's speeches and conversations. In general he seems to have held that the more people knew, the worse they were. At a conference at Chengtu in March 1958 he stated that throughout history young people with little knowledge had had the better of learned men. Confucius, Jesus, Buddha, Marx, and Sun Yat-sen had been very young and had not known much when they began to form their ideas; Gorky had only two years' schooling; Franklin sold newspapers in the streets; the inventor of penicillin had worked in a laundry. According to a speech of Mao's in 1959, in the reign of Emperor Wu-ti the Premier, Che Fa-chih, was illiterate, but he produced poetry; however, Mao added that he himself was not opposed to combating illiteracy. In another speech in February 1964 he recalled that there had only been two good emperors of the Ming dynasty, both illiterate, and that when the intellectuals took over the country it had gone to rack and ruin. 'It is evident that to read too many books is harmful' (Schram, p. 204). 'We shouldn't read too many books.

We should read Marxist books, but not too many of them either. It will be enough to read a dozen or so. If we read too many, we can move towards our opposites, become bookworms, dogmatists, revisionists' (p. 210). 'Emperor Wu of the Liang dynasty did pretty well in his early years, but afterwards he read many books, and didn't make out so well any more. He died of hunger in T'ai Ch'eng' (p. 211).

The moral of these historical reflections is clear: intellectuals must be sent to work in the villages, teaching hours in schools and universities must be cut (Mao declared several times that they were too long at all stages of education), and admissions must be subject to political critieria. The last point was and is a matter of violent dispute within the party. The 'conservatives' argue that at least certain minimum academic criteria should apply to admissions and the conferring of degrees, while the 'radicals' hold that nothing ought to count except social origin and political consciousness. The latter view is clearly in line with the ideas of Mao, who in 1958 twice remarked with satisfaction that the Chinese were like a blank sheet of paper on which one could draw any picture one liked.

This deep mistrust of learning, professionalism, and the whole culture created by the privileged classes illustrates clearly the peasant origins of Chinese Communism. It is as far as can be from Marx's doctrine and the tradition of European Marxism, including Leninism, although at the outset of the Russian revolution there were symptoms of a similar hatred of education, especially in the Proletkult movement. In China, where the gulf between the educated élite and the masses seems formerly to have been deeper than in Russia, the idea that illiterates are naturally superior to scholars seems a perfectly natural outcome of the revolution from below. In Russia, however, hostility to education and professionalism was never a feature of the party programme. The party, of course, wiped out the old intelligentsia and set itself to turn humanistic studies, art, and literature into tools of political propaganda; but at the same time it proclaimed a cult of expertise and developed an educational system based on a high degree of specialization. The technical, military, and economic modernization of Russia would have been utterly impossible if the state ideology had exalted ignorance for its own sake and warned against reading too many books. Mao, however, seems to have taken it for granted that China would not and could not modernize itself in the Soviet manner. He often warned against 'blind' imitation of other countries. 'Everything we copied from abroad was adopted rigidly, and this ended in a great defeat, with the party organizations in the White areas losing one hundred per cent of their strength and the revolutionary bases and the Red Army losing ninety per cent of their strength, and the victory of the revolution being delayed for many years' (Schram, p. 87). On another occasion he observed that the copying of Soviet models had had fatal effects: he himself had for three years been unable to eat eggs and chicken soup, because some Soviet journal had said that it was bad for one's health.

Thus Maoism expresses not only the traditional hatred of peasants for an élite culture (a familiar feature, for example, in the history of the sixteenth-century Reformation), but also the traditional xenophobia of the Chinese and their mistrust of everything that came from abroad and from the white man, who had generally stood for imperialist encroachment. China's relations with the Soviet Union could only reinforce this general attitude.

For the same reason the Chinese sought for a new method of industrialization; this ended in the fiasco of the 'great leap forward', but the ideology behind it was not abandoned. Mao and his followers believed that the building of socialism must begin with the 'superstructure', i.e. the creation of a 'new man'; that ideology and politics must have priority as far as the rate of accumulation is concerned; and that socialism is not a matter of technical progress and welfare but of the collectivization of institutions and human relationships, from which it follows that ideal Communist institutions can be created in technically primitive conditions. For this, however, it is necessary to abolish all the old social links and the conditions that produce inequality: hence the Chinese Communists' zeal to destroy family ties, which are especially resistant to nationalization, as well as their campaign against private motivation and material incentives ('economism'). Rewards are still, of course, to some extent differentiated on grounds of skill and the type of work performed, but considerably less so, it would appear, than in the Soviet Union. Mao held that if people were properly educated they would work hard without special inducement, and that 'individualism' and a desire for one's own satisfaction were a pernicious survival of the bourgeois mentality and must be eradicated. Maoism is a typical instance of the totalitarian Utopia in which everything must be subordinated to the 'general good' as opposed to that of the individual, though it is not clear how the former can be defined except by the latter. Mao's philosophy made no use of the concept of the 'good of the individual', which plays an important part in Soviet ideology, and it also eschewed humanistic language in all its forms. Mao expressly condemned the notion of the 'natural rights of man' (Schram, p. 235): society consists of hostile classes and there can be no community or understanding between them, nor are there any forms of culture independent of class. The 'little red book' tells us (p. 15) that 'We should support whatever the enemy opposes and oppose whatever the enemy supports'—a sentence that probably no European Marxist would have written. There must be a complete break with the past, with traditional culture, and with anything that might bridge the gap between the classes.

Maoism, according to the Leader's repeated pronouncements, is the 'application' of Marxism to specifically Chinese conditions. As may be seen from the foregoing analysis, it is more accurately described as the use of Lenin's technique of seizing power, with Marxist slogans serving as a disguise for ideas and purposes that are alien or contrary to Marxism. The 'primacy of practice' is, of course, a principle rooted in Marxism, but it would be hard indeed to defend in Marxist terms the deduction that it is harmful to read books and that the illiterate are naturally wiser than the learned. The substitution of the peasantry for the proletariat as the most revolutionary class is flagrantly at variance with the whole Marxist tradition. So is the idea of 'permanent revolution' in the sense that class conflicts are bound to recur unceasingly and must therefore be resolved by periodical revolutions. The idea of abolishing the 'opposition' between mental and physical work is Marxist, but the cult of manual labour as the noblest human occupation is a grotesque interpretation of Marx's Utopia. As to the peasant being the supreme representative of the 'complete man' unspoilt by the division of labour, this idea may sometimes be met with among the Russian populists of the last century, but is again diametrically opposed to the Marxist tradition. The general principle of equality is undoubtedly Marxist, but it is hard to suppose that Marx would have seen it as embodied in the policy of packing off intellectuals to the rice-fields. To make a somewhat anachronistic comparison, from the point of view of Marxian doctrine we may regard Maoism as belonging to the type of primitive Communism which, as Marx put it, has not only not overcome private ownership but has not even reached it.

In a certain limited sense Chinese Communism is more egalitarian than the Soviet variety; not, however, because it is less totalitarian, but because it is more so. It is more egalitarian inasmuch as wages and salaries are less differentiated; certain symbols of hierarchy, such as army badges of rank, have been abolished, and in general the regime is more 'populist' than in the Soviet Union. In keeping the population under control a more important part is played by institutions organized on a territorial or place-of-work basis, and the role of the professional police is correspondingly less. The system of universal espionage and mutual denunciation seems to work through local committees of various kinds and is openly treated as a civic duty. It is true, on the one hand, that Mao enjoyed far more popular support than the Bolsheviks ever have done, and therefore trusted more in his own strength than they: this is seen not so much in his repeated injunctions to let people speak out (for Stalin also took this line on occasion) as in the risk he took during the cultural revolution in inciting young people to overthrow the existing party apparatus. But, on the other hand, it is clear that during the whole chaotic period he kept in his hands the instruments of power and coercion which enabled him to restrain the excesses of those who followed his advice. On many occasions Mao preached the gospel of 'democratic centralism', and it is not clear that his interpretation differed in any way from Lenin's. The proletariat governs the country through the party, the party's operations are based on discipline, the minority obeys the majority, and the whole party obeys the central leadership. When Mao declares that centralism is 'First of all . . . a centralization of correct ideas' (Schram, p. 163), there can be no doubt that it is the party which decides whether an idea is correct or not.

In February 1957 Mao delivered an address 'On the Correct Handling of Contradictions among the People', which is another of the main texts on which his reputation as a theorist is based. In it he declares that we must distinguish carefully between contradictions among the people and contradictions between the people and its enemies. The latter are resolved by dictatorship, the former by democratic centralism. Among 'the people' freedom and democracy prevail, 'But this freedom is freedom with leadership and this democracy is democracy under centralized guidance, not anarchy . . . Those who demand freedom and democracy in the abstract regard democracy as an end and not a means. Democracy sometimes seems to be an end, but it is in fact only a means. Marxism teaches us that democracy is part of the superstructure and belongs to the category of politics. That is to say, in the last analysis it serves the economic base. The same is true of freedom' (*Four Essays on Philosophy*, pp. 84–6). The chief practical conclusion drawn from this is that contradictions among the people must be handled by a skilful combination of education and administrative measures, whereas a conflict between the people and its enemies has to be solved by dictatorship, i.e. by force. However, as Mao indicates elsewhere, 'non-antagonistic' contradictions among the people may in time turn into antagonistic ones if the proponents of incorrect views refuse to admit their error. This can hardly be read otherwise than as a warning to Mao's party opponents that if they acknowledge the truth promptly they will be pardoned, but if not, they will be declared class enemies and treated as such. As regards conflicting views among the people, Mao enumerates six criteria (ibid., pp. 119–20) for distinguishing right from wrong. Views and actions are right if they unite the people instead of dividing it; if they are beneficial and not harmful to socialist construction; if they help to consolidate and not weaken the people's democratic dictatorship; if they help to strengthen democratic centralism; if they help to support the leading role of the Communist party; and if they are beneficial to international socialist unity and the unity of the peace-loving peoples of the world.

In all these precepts concerning democracy, freedom, centralism, and the leading role of the party there is nothing contrary to Leninist–Stalinist orthodoxy. There does, however, seem to be a difference in practice: not in the sense imagined by many Western enthusiasts for Maoism, that in China the 'masses' rule, but in the sense that government has a more consultative air because the party has more methods of ideological manipulation at its command than have the Soviet leaders. This has been due to the long-continued presence of the father of the revolution, whose authority was unquestioned, and to the fact that China is a pre-eminently rural society, confirming as it were Marx's saying that the peasants' leader must also be their lord. In a situation in which the classes representing the old culture have been practically destroyed and the channels of information are even more strictly controlled than in the Soviet Union (the 'centralization of correct ideas', as Mao put it), it is possible, without infringing the powers of the central government, for many questions of local politics or production to be settled by local committees instead of by the official government apparatus.

'Egalitarianism' is certainly one of the most important features of Maoist ideology; it is based, as we have seen, on a tendency to eliminate pay differentials and on the principle that all must perform a certain amount of manual work (though the leaders and chief ideologists seem to be exempt from this requirement). This does not, however, signify any trend towards equality in the political sense. In modern times, access to information is a basic asset and a *sine qua non* of real participation in government; and in this respect the Chinese population is more deprived even than that of the Soviet Union. In China everything is secret. Practically no statistics are publicly available; meetings of the Central Committee and organs of state administration are often held in complete secrecy. The idea that the 'masses' control the economy, in a country where no one outside the top hierarchy even knows what the economic plans are, is one of the most extravagant fantasies of Western Maoists. The information about foreign countries that the citizen can glean from official sources is minimal, and his cultural isolation is almost complete. Edgar Snow, one of the most enthusiastic observers of Chinese Communism, reported after a visit in 1970 that the only books available to the public were textbooks and the works of Mao; Chinese citizens could go to the theatre in groups (practically no individual tickets were sold), or they could read newspapers which told them next to nothing about the outside world. On the other hand, as Snow remarked, they were spared the stories of murders, drugs, and sexual perversion on which Western readers are nourished.

Religious life has been practically destroyed; the sale of objects used in religious worship is officially forbidden. The Chinese have done away with many aspects of the democratic façade that have survived in the Soviet Union, such as general elections or a public prosecutor's department independent of the police authorities: the latter, in practice, administer both 'justice' and repression. The extent of direct coercion is not known; nobody can even make a rough guess at the number of inmates of concentration camps. (In the Soviet Union much more is known about these matters, which is one effect of a certain relaxation since Stalin's death.) The difficulties with which experts contend are illustrated by the fact that estimates of China's population vary by some forty to fifty million.

The ideological influence of Maoism outside China derives from two main sources. In the first place, since the breach with the Soviet Union the Chinese leaders have divided the world not into the 'socialist' and 'capitalist' camps but rather into rich and poor countries; the Soviet Union is placed in the former category and is, moreover, according to Mao, the scene of a bourgeois restoration. Lin Piao sought to apply on an international scale the old slogan of the Red Chinese army concerning the 'encirclement of the cities by the countryside'. China's example certainly has a definite attraction for Third World countries. The achievements of Communism are manifest: it has freed China from foreign influence and, at a huge cost, set it on the path of technical and social modernization. The nationalization of the whole of social life has, as in other totalitarian countries, brought with it the abolition or alleviation of some of the chief plagues that afflict mankind, especially in backward agrarian countries: unemployment, regional starvation, and beggary on a vast scale. Whether the Chinese pattern can in fact be imitated successfully, for example, in the countries of black Africa, is a question beyond the scope of this work.

The other source of the ideological influence of Maoism, especially in the sixties, was the acceptance by some Western intellectuals and students of the utopian fantasies that constituted the façade of Chinese Communism. At that time Maoism endeavoured to project itself as the universal solution of all human problems. Various leftist sects and individuals seem to have seriously believed that it was the perfect cure for the ills of industrial society, and that the United States and Western Europe could and should be revolutionized on Maoist principles. At a time when the ideological prestige of Soviet Russia had collapsed, utopian longings fixed themselves on the exotic East, the more easily because of the general ignorance of Chinese affairs. For those in search of a perfect world and a sublime, all-embracing revolution, China became the Mecca of a new dispensation and the last great hope of revolutionary war—for had not the Chinese rejected the Soviet formula of 'peaceful coexistence'? Many Maoist groups were sadly disappointed when the Chinese to a large extent dropped their revolutionary proselytizing and turned to more 'normal' forms of political rivalry, having evidently ceased to hope that Maoism could become a real force in Europe or North America. It is indeed the case that Maoism in the Western countries had no significant effect on the position of the existing Communist parties: it caused no schism of any consequence and remained the property of small splinter groups. Nor did it have any noteworthy success in Eastern Europe, except for the special case of Albania. Accordingly, the Chinese changed tactics and, instead of offering Maoism as a sovereign remedy of equal value to Britain, the United States, Poland, and the Congo, concentrated on unmasking Russian imperialism and seeking alliances, or at all events a measure of influence, on the basis of a common interest in checking Soviet expansion. It seems, indeed, that this is a much more promising course, though it is a straightforward political one and not a matter of Maoist ideology; as far as Marxist language is still used in prosecuting this policy, it is decorative rather than essential.

From the point of view of the history of Marxism, Maoist ideology is noteworthy not because Mao 'developed' anything but because it illustrates the unlimited flexibility of any doctrine once it becomes historically influential. On the one hand, Marxism has become the instrument of Russian imperialism; on the other, it is the ideological cement or superstructure of a huge country striving to overcome its technical and economic backwardness by other means than the ordinary operation of the market (of which, in many cases, it is virtually impossible for backward countries to take advantage). Marxism has become the motive force of a strong, highly militarized state, using force and ideological manipulation to mobilize its subjects in the cause of modernization. Certainly, as we have seen, there were important elements in the Marxist tradition which served to justify the establishment of totalitarian governments. But one thing is beyond doubt: Communism as Marx understood it was an ideal for highly developed industrial societies, not a method of organizing peasants to create the rudiments of industrialization. Yet it has turned out that this aim can be achieved by means of an ideology in which vestiges of Marxism are blended with a peasant Utopia and the traditions of Oriental despotism—a mixture that describes itself as Marxism *par excellence* and that works with a certain efficiency.

The obfuscation of Western admirers of Chinese Communism is scarcely believable. Intellectuals who cannot find words strong enough to condemn U.S. militarism go into ecstasies over a society in which the military training of infants begins in their third year and all male citizens are obliged to do four or five years' military service. Hippies are enamoured of a state which enforces severe labour discipline without holidays and upholds a puritanical code of sexual morals, not to speak of drug-taking. Even some Christian writers speak highly of the system, although religion in China has been ruthlessly stamped out. (It is of little importance here that Mao seems to have believed in an after life. In 1965 he mentioned twice to Edgar Snow that he was 'soon going to see God' (Snow, op. cit., pp. 89 and 219–20); he said the same thing in a speech in

1966 (Schram, p. 270), and also in 1959 (ibid., p. 154), when he referred humorously to his future meeting with Marx.)

The Chinese People's Republic is obviously a factor of enormous importance in the modern world, not least from the point of view of containing Soviet expansionism. This, however, is a matter which has little to do with the history of Marxism.

Epilogue

MARXISM has been the greatest fantasy of our century. It was a dream offering the prospect of a society of perfect unity, in which all human aspirations would be fulfilled and all values reconciled. It took over Hegel's theory of the 'contradictions of progress', but also the liberal-evolutionist belief that 'in the last resort' the course of history was inevitably for the better, and that man's increasing command over nature would, after an interval, be matched by increasing freedom. It owed much of its success to the combination of Messianic fantasies with a specific and genuine social cause, the struggle of the European working class against poverty and exploitation. This combination was expressed in a coherent doctrine with the absurd name (derived from Proudhon) of 'scientific socialism'—absurd because the means of attaining an end may be scientific, but not the choice of the end itself. The name, however, reflected more than the mere cult of science which Marx shared with the rest of his generation. It expressed the belief, discussed critically more than once in the course of the present work, that human knowledge and human practice, directed by the will, must ultimately coincide and become inseparable in a perfect unity: so that the choice of ends would indeed become identical with the cognitive and practical means of attaining them. The natural consequence of this confusion was the idea that the success of a particular social movement was a proof that it was scientifically 'true', or, in effect, that whoever proved to be stronger must have 'science' on his side. This idea is largely responsible for all the anti-scientific and anti-intellectual features of Marxism in its particular guise as the ideology of Communism.

To say that Marxism is a fantasy does not mean that it is nothing else. Marxism as an interpretation of past history must be distinguished from Marxism as a political ideology. No reasonable person would deny that the doctrine of historical materialism has been a valuable addition to our intellectual equipment and has enriched our understanding of the past. True, it has been argued that in a strict form the doctrine is nonsense and in a loose form it is a commonplace; but, if it has become a commonplace, this is largely thanks to Marx's originality. Moreover, if Marxism has led towards a better understanding of the economics and civilization of past ages, this is no doubt connected with the fact that Marx at times enunciated his theory in extreme, dogmatic, and unacceptable forms. If his views had been hedged round with all the restrictions and reservations that are usual in rational thought, they would have had less influence and might have gone unnoticed altogether. As it was, and as often happens with humanistic theories, the element of absurdity was effective in transmitting their rational content. From this point of view the role of Marxism may be compared to that of psychoanalysis or behaviourism in the social sciences. By expressing their theories in extreme forms, Freud and Watson succeeded in bringing real problems to general notice and opening up valuable fields of exploration; this they could probably not have done if they had qualified their views with scrupulous reservations and so deprived them of clearcut outlines and polemical force. The sociological approach to the study of civilization was expounded by writers before Marx, such as Vico, Herder, and Montesquieu, or contemporary but independent of him, such as Michelet, Renan, and Taine; but none of these expressed his ideas in the extreme, onesided, dogmatic form which constituted the strength of Marxism.

As a result, Marx's intellectual legacy underwent something of the same fate as Freud's was to do. Orthodox believers still exist, but are negligible as a cultural force, while the contribution of Marxism to humanistic knowledge, especially the historical sciences, has become a general underlying theme, no longer connected with any 'system' purporting to explain everything. One need not nowadays consider oneself or be considered a Marxist in order, for instance, to study the history of literature or painting in the light of the social conflicts of a given period; and one may do so without believing that the whole of human history is the history of class conflict, or that different aspects of civilization have no history of their own because 'true' history is the history of technology and 'production relations', because the 'superstructure' grows out of the 'base', and so forth.

To recognize, within limits, the validity of historical materialism is not tantamount to acknowledging the truth of Marxism. This is so because, among other reasons, it was a fundamental doctrine of Marxism from the outset that the meaning of a historical process can be grasped only if the past is interpreted in the light of the future: that is to say, we can only understand what was and is if we have some knowledge of what will be. Marxism, it can hardly be disputed, would not be Marxism without its claim to 'scientific knowledge' of the future, and the question is how far such knowledge is possible. Prediction is, of course, not only a component of many sciences but an inseparable aspect of even the most trivial actions, although we cannot 'know' the future in the same way as the past, since all prediction has an element of uncertainty. The 'future' is either what will happen in the next moment or what will happen in a million years; the difficulty of prediction increases, of course, with distance and with the complication of the subject. In social matters, as we know, predictions are especially deceptive, even if they relate to the short term and to a single quantifiable factor, as in demographic prognoses. In general we forecast the future by extrapolating existing tendencies, while realizing that such extrapolations are, always and everywhere, of extremely limited value, and that no developmental curves in any field of inquiry extend indefinitely in accordance with the same equation. As to prognoses on a global scale and without any limitation of time, these are no more than fantasies, whether the prospect they offer is good or evil. There are no rational means of predicting 'the future of humanity' over a long period or foretelling the nature of 'social formations' in ages to come. The idea that we can make such forecasts 'scientifically', and that without doing so we cannot even understand the past, is inherent in the Marxist theory of 'social formations'; it is one reason why that theory is a fantasy, and also why it is politically effective. The influence that Marxism has achieved, far from being the result or proof of its scientific character, is almost entirely due to its prophetic, fantastic, and irrational elements. Marxism is a doctrine of blind confidence that a paradise of universal satisfaction is awaiting us just round the corner. Almost all the prophecies of Marx and his followers have already proved to be false, but this does not disturb the spiritual certainty of the faithful, any more than it did in the case of chiliastic sects: for it is a certainty not based on any empirical premises or supposed 'historical laws', but simply on the psychological need for certainty. In this sense Marxism performs the function of a religion, and its efficacy is of a religious character. But it is a caricature and a bogus form of religion, since it presents its temporal eschatology as a scientific system, which religious mythologies do not purport to be.

We have discussed the question of continuity between Marxism and its embodiment in Communism, i.e. Leninist–Stalinist ideology and practice. It would be absurd to maintain that Marxism was, so to speak, the efficient cause of present-day Communism; on the other hand, Communism is not a mere 'degeneration' of Marxism but a possible interpretation of it, and even a well-founded one, though primitive and partial in some respects. Marxism was a combination of values which proved incompatible for empirical though not for logical reasons, so that some could be realized only at the expense of others. But it was Marx who declared that the whole idea of Communism could be summed up in a single formula—the abolition of private property; that the state of the future must take over the centralized management of the means of production, and that the abolition of capital meant the abolition of wage-labour. There was nothing flagrantly illogical in deducing from this that the expropriation of the bourgeoisie and the nationalization of industry and agriculture would bring about the general emancipation of mankind. In the event it turned out that, having nationalized the means of production, it was possible to erect on this foundation a monstrous edifice of lies, exploitation, and oppression.

This was not itself a consequence of Marxism; rather, Communism was a bastard version of the socialist ideal, owing its origin to many historical circumstances and chances, of which Marxist ideology was one. But it cannot be said that Marxism was 'falsified' in any essential sense. Arguments adduced at the present day to show that 'that is not what Marx meant' are intellectually and practically sterile. Marx's intentions are not the deciding factor in a historical assessment of Marxism, and there are more important arguments for freedom and democratic values than the fact that Marx, if one looks closely, was not so hostile to those values as might at first sight appear.

Marx took over the romantic ideal of social unity, and Communism realized it in the only way feasible in an industrial society, namely, by a despotic system of government. The origin of this dream is to be found in the idealized image of the Greek city-state popularized by Winckelmann and others in the eighteenth century and subsequently taken up by German philosophers. Marx seems to have imagined that once capitalists were done away with the whole world could become a kind of Athenian *agora*: one had only to forbid private ownership of machines or land and, as if by magic, human beings would cease to be selfish and their interests would coincide in perfect harmony. Marxism affords no explanation of how this prophecy is founded, or what reason there is to think that human interests will cease to conflict as soon as the means of production are nationalized.

Marx, moreover, combined his romantic dreams with the socialist expectation that all needs would be fully satisfied in the earthly paradise. The early socialists seem to have understood the slogan 'To each according to his needs' in a limited sense: they meant that people should not have to suffer cold and hunger or spend their lives staving off destitution. Marx, however, and many Marxists after him, imagined that under socialism all scarcity would come to an end. It was possible to entertain this hope in the ultra-sanguine form that all wants would be satisfied, as though every human being had a magic ring or obedient jinn at his disposal. But, since this could hardly be taken seriously, Marxists who considered the question decided, with a fair degree of support from Marx's works, that Communism would ensure the satisfaction of 'true' or 'genuine' needs consonant with human nature, but not whims or desires of all kinds. This, however, gave rise to a problem which no one answered clearly: who is to decide what needs are 'genuine', and by what criteria? If every man is to judge this for himself, then all needs are equally genuine provided they are actually, subjectively felt, and there is no room for any distinction. If, on the other hand, it is the state which decides, then the greatest emancipation in history consists in a system of universal rationing.

At the present time it is obvious to all except a handful of New Left adolescents that socialism cannot literally 'satisfy all needs' but can only aim at a just distribution of insufficient resources—which leaves us with the problem of defining 'just' and of deciding by what social mechanisms the aim is to be effected in each particular case. The idea of perfect equality, i.e. an equal share of all goods for everybody, is not only unfeasible economically but is contradictory in itself: for perfect equality can only be imagined under a system of extreme despotism, but despotism itself presupposes inequality at least in such basic advantages as participation in power and access to information. (For the same reason, contemporary *gauchistes* are in an untenable position when they demand more equality and less government: in real life more equality means more government, and absolute equality means absolute government.)

If socialism is to be anything more than a totalitarian prison, it can only be a system of compromises between different values that limit one another. All-embracing economic planning, even if it were possible to achieve—and there is almost universal agreement that it is not—is incompatible with the autonomy of small producers and regional units, and this autonomy is a traditional value of socialism, though not of Marxist socialism. Technical progress cannot coexist with absolute security of living conditions for everyone. Conflicts inevitably arise between freedom and equality, planning and the autonomy of small groups, economic democracy and efficient management, and these conflicts can only be mitigated by compromise and partial solutions.

In the developed industrial countries, all social institutions for the purpose of evening out inequalities and ensuring a minimum of security (progressive taxation, health services, unemployment relief, price controls, etc.) have been created and extended at the price of a vastly expanded state bureaucracy, and no one can suggest how to avoid paying this price.

Questions such as these have little to do with Marxism, and Marx's doctrine provides virtually no help in solving them. The apocalyptic belief in the consummation of history, the inevitability of socialism, and the natural sequence of 'social formations'; the 'dictatorship of the proletariat', the exaltation of violence, faith in the automatic efficacy of nationalizing industry, fantasies concerning a society without conflict and an economy without money—all these have nothing in common with the idea of democratic socialism. The latter's purpose is to create institutions which can gradually reduce the subordination of production to profit, do away with poverty, diminish inequality, remove social barriers to educational opportunity, and minimize the threat to democratic liberties from state bureaucracy and the seductions of totalitarianism. All these efforts and attempts are doomed to failure unless they are firmly rooted in the value of freedom—what Marxists stigmatize as 'negative' freedom, i.e. the area of decision which society allows to the individual. This is so not only because freedom is an intrinsic value requiring no justification beyond itself, but also because without it societies are unable to reform themselves: despotic systems, lacking this self-regulating mechanism, can only correct their mistakes when these have led to disaster.

Marxism has been frozen and immobilized for decades as the ideological superstructure of a totalitarian political movement, and in consequence has lost touch with intellectual developments and social realities. The hope that it could be revived and made fruitful once again soon proved to be an illusion. As an explanatory 'system' it is dead, nor does it offer any 'method' that can be effectively used to interpret modern life, to foresee the future, or cultivate utopian projections. Contemporary Marxist literature, although plentiful in quantity, has a depressing air of sterility and helplessness, in so far as it is not purely historical.

The effectiveness of Marxism as an instrument of political mobilization is quite another matter. As we have seen, its terminology is used in support of the most variegated political interests. In the Communist countries of Europe, where Marxism is the official legitimation of the existing regimes, it has virtually lost all conviction, while in China it has been deformed out of recognition. Wherever Communism is in power, the ruling class transforms it into an ideology whose real sources are nationalism, racism, or imperialism. Communism has done much to strengthen nationalist ideologies by using them to seize power or hold on to it, and in this way it has produced its own gravediggers. Nationalism lives only as an ideology of hate, envy, and thirst for power; as such it is a disruptive element in the Communist world, the coherence of which is based on force. If the whole world were Communist it would either have to be dominated by a single imperialism, or there would be an unending series of wars between the 'Marxist' rulers of different countries.

We are witnesses and participators in momentous and complicated intellectual and moral processes, the combined effects of which cannot be foreseen. On the one hand, many optimistic assumptions of nineteenth-century humanism have broken down, and in many fields of culture there is a sense of bankruptcy. On the other hand, thanks to the unprecedented speed and diffusion of information, human aspirations throughout the world are increasing faster than the means of satisfying them; this leads to rapidly growing frustration and consequent aggressiveness. Communists have shown great skill in exploiting this state of mind and channelling aggressive feelings in various directions according to circumstances, using fragments of Marxist language to suit their purpose. Messianic hopes are the counterpart of the sense of despair and impotence that overcomes mankind at the sight of its own failures. The optimistic belief that there is a ready-made, immediate answer to all problems and misfortunes, and that only the malevolence of enemies (defined according to choice) stands in the way of its being instantly applied, is a frequent ingredient in ideological systems passing under the name of Marxism—which is to say that

Marxism changes content from one situation to another and is cross-bred with other ideological traditions. At present Marxism neither interprets the world nor changes it: it is merely a repertoire of slogans serving to organize various interests, most of them completely remote from those with which Marxism originally identified itself. A century after the collapse of the First International, the prospect of a new International capable of defending the interests of oppressed humanity throughout the world is less likely than it has ever been.

The self-deification of mankind, to which Marxism gave philosophical expression, has ended in the same way as all such attempts, whether individual or collective: it has revealed itself as the farcical aspect of human bondage.

New Epilogue

THERE IS LITTLE to add, in this Epilogue to the Epilogue, to the few sentences written in the New Preface. After all that has happened in the last decades, we cannot foresee the possible vicissitudes of Marxism (assuming there is something to foresee) in its various, mutually unrecognisable incarnations or the future fate of communist ideology and its institutional bodies—although corpses may be a better word. Communism in its Leninist–Stalinist version seems to have been crushed; 'capitalism'—i.e., the market—seems to be continuing its triumphant conquest of the world. Let us not forget, however, that the most populous country on earth, China, now experiencing a flamboyant, dazzling expansion of the market (accompanied both by gigantic corruption and by an extremely high rate of growth), is in some important respects continuing its insane Marxist past—a past which, unlike the post-Stalinist Soviet Union, it never officially repudiated. Maoist ideology may be dead there, but the state and the Party still exert strict control over the way people think; independent religious life is persecuted and stifled, as is, of course, political opposition. Despite the existence of numerous non-governmental bodies, the law does not exist as an independent organ (law, in the proper sense, can be said to exist only if a citizen can take legal action against the state organs and have a chance of winning); there are no civil liberties and no freedom of opinion. Instead there is slave labour on a mass scale, concentration camps (in which it takes place), and the brutal repression of national minorities, of which the barbaric destruction of Tibetan culture is the best known but by no means the only example. This is not a Communist state in any recognisable sense but a tyranny that grew out of a Communist system. Numerous academics and intellectuals extolled its glory when it was at its most savage, destructive, and foolish. This fashion seems to have ended. Whether this country will ever adopt the norms of Western civilization is uncertain; the market favours development in this direction but by no means guarantees it.

Will Russian imperialism return, after the demise of the Soviet regime? It is not inconceivable—we can observe a certain amount of nostalgia for the lost empire—but if it does, Marxism will have nothing to contribute to this rebirth.

Whatever the proper definition of capitalism, the market, combined with the rule of law and civil liberties, seems to have obvious advantages in assuring a tolerable level of material well-being and security. And yet, despite these social and economic benefits, 'capitalism' is continually attacked, from every side. These attacks have no coherent ideological content; they often use revolutionary slogans even though no one can explain what the revolution in this context is supposed to mean. There is some remote relationship between this vague ideology and communist tradition, but if traces of Marxism can be discovered in anti-capitalist rhetoric, it is a grotesquely distorted kind of Marxism: Marx championed technical progress and his attitude was strongly Eurocentric, including a lack of interest in the problems of underdeveloped countries. The anti-capitalist slogans we hear today contain a poorly articulated fear of rapidly growing technology, with its possibly sinister side effects. No one can be certain whether our civilisation will be able to cope with the ecological, demographic, and spiritual dangers it has caused or whether it will fall victim to catastrophe. So we cannot tell whether the present 'anti-capitalist', 'anti-global ist', and related obscurantist movements and ideas will quietly fade away and one day come to seem as pathetic as the legendary Luddites at the beginning of the nineteenth century, or whether they will maintain their strength and fortify their trenches.

But we may safely predict that Marx himself will become more and more what he already is: a chapter from a textbook of the history of ideas, a figure that no longer evokes any emotions, simply the author of one of the 'great books' of the nineteenth century—one of those books that very few bother to read but whose titles are known to the educated public. As for my three, newly combined volumes, in which I tried to sum up and assess this philosophy and its later ramifications (provoking the fury—very predictable but less widespread than I had expected—of Marxists and Leftists), they may perhaps be useful to the dwindling number of people still interested in the subject.

Selective Bibliography

Adorno, T. W. (with M. Horkheimer), *Dialektik der Aufklärung*, Amsterdam, 1947 (Eng. trans. J. Cumming, London, 1973).

Prismen, Frankfurt, 1955 (Eng. trans. S. and S. Weber, London, n.d.).

Einleitung in die Musiksoziologie, Frankfurt, 1962.

Jargon der Eigentlichkeit, Frankfurt, 1964 (Eng. trans. K. Tarnowski and F. Will, London, 1973).

Negative Dialektik, Frankfurt, 1966 (Eng. trans. E. B. Ashton, London, 1973).

Ahlberg, R., '*Dialektische Philosophie*' *und Gesellschaft in der Sowjetunion*, Berlin, 1960 (good bibliography).

Aleksandrov, G. F., *Istoria zapadnoevropeyskoy filosofii* (*History of West European Philosophy*), Moscow, 1946.

(ed.), *Dialektichesky materializm* (*Dialectical Materialism*), Moscow, 1954.

Althusser, L., *Pour Marx*, Paris, 1965 (Eng. trans. B. Brewster, London, 1969).

Lire le Capital, 2 vols., Paris, 1965 (Eng. trans. B. Brewster, London, 1970).

Lénine et la philosophie, 2nd edn. Paris, 1972 (Eng. trans. B. Brewster, London, 1971).

Arendt, H., *The Origins of Totalitarianism*, Cleveland, 1958.

Aron, R., *L'Opium des intellectuals*, Paris (Eng. trans. T. Kilmartin, New York, 1962).

D'une sainte famille à l'autre: essais sur les marxismes imaginaires, Paris, 1969.

Avtorkhanov, A., *Tekhnologia vlasti* (*The Technology of Power*), 2nd ed., Frankfurt, 1973.

Axelos, K., *Marx, penseur de la technique*, Paris, 1961.

Baczke, B., *Weltanschauung, Metaphysik, Entfremdung. Philosophische Versuche*, Frankfurt, 1969.

Bahr, E., *Ernst Bloch*, Berlin, 1964.

Bauer, R. A., *The New Man in Soviet Psychology*, Cambridge, Mass., 1952.

Bauman, Z., *Towards a Critical Sociology*, London and Boston, 1976.

Baumann, G., 'Die Schlüssel-Gewalt der Erkenntnis. Ernst Blochs philosophische Haltung der "konkreten Utopie"', thesis, Louvain, 1974.

Benjamin, W., *Schriften*, ed. Th. W. Adorno and G. Scholem, 2 vols., Frankfurt, 1955.

Illuminations: Essays and Reflections, ed. H. Arendt, New York, 1968.

Benseler, F. (ed.), *Festchrift zum achtzitgsten Geburtstag von Georg Lukacs*, Neuwied, 1965 (comprehensive bibliography).

Berdiaev, N., *Wahrheit und Lüge des Kommunismus*, Darmstadt, 1953.

Les Sources et le sens du communisme russe, Paris, 1938.

Besançon, A., *Court traité de soviétologie à l'usage des autorités civiles, militaires et religieuses*, Paris, 1976.

Bienkowski, Wl., *Motory i hamulce socjalizmu* (*Driving Forces and Brakes of Socialism*), Paris, 1969.

Blakeley, T. J., *Soviet Philosophy*, Dordrecht, 1964.

Bloch, E., *Gesamtausgabe*, 16 vols., Frankfurt, 1959 ff.

Man on his Own, trans. E. B. Ashton, New York, 1970 (an anthology).

On Karl Marx, trans. J. Maxwell, New York, 1971 (a selection from *Das Prinzip Hoffnung*).

Atheism in Christianity, trans. J. T. Swann, New York, 1972.

Bochenski, I. M., *Der sowjetrussische dialektische Materialismus*, 2nd edn. Berne, 1956 (Eng. trans. Dordrecht, 1953).

Bociurkiw, B. R. and J. W. Strong (eds.), *Religion and Atheism in the USSR and Eastern Europe*, Toronto, 1975.

Borkenau, F., *European Communism*, London, 1953.

Brus, W., *The Market in a Socialist Economy*, London, 1972.

The Economics and Politics of Socialism, London, 1973.

Brzezinski, Z., *The Permanent Purge: Politics in Soviet Totalitarianism*, Cambridge, Mass., 1956.

The Soviet Bloc: Unity and Conflict, Cambridge, Mass., 1967.

Bukharin, N., *Teoria istoricheskogo materializma*, Moscow, 1921 (Eng. trans. *Historical Materialism*, New York, 1928; Ann Arbor, 1969).

(with E. Preobrazhensky), *The ABC of Communism*, London, 1924 and 1969.

Imperialism and World Economy, New York, 1929.

Burnham, J., *The Managerial Revolution*, New York, 1941.

Bütow, H. G., *Philosophie und Gesellschaft im Denken Ernst Blochs*, Berlin, 1963.

Carmichael, J., *Trotsky: An Appreciation of his Life*, New York, 1975.

Caute, D., *Communism and the French Intellectuals*, New York, 1964.

Chambre, H., *Le Marxisme en Union Soviétique*, Paris, 1955.

Chang, P. H., *Radicals and Radical Ideology in China's Cultural Revolution*, New York, 1973.

Chatelet, F., *Logos et praxis. Recherches sur la signification théorique du marxisme*, Paris, 1962.

Ch'en, J., *Mao and the Chinese Revolution*, London and New York, 1965.

Cohen, S. F., *Bukharin and the Bolshevik Revolution: A Political Biography 1888–1938*, New York, 1973 (copious bibliography).

Congdon, L., 'Lukács's Road to Marx', *Survey*, no. 2/3, 1974.

Conquest, R., *The Great Terror: Stalin's Purge of the Thirties*, London, 1968.

Cranston, M., *The Mask of Politics*, London, 1973.

Dahm, H., *Die Dialektik im Wandel der Sowjetphilosophie*, Cologne, 1963.

Daniels, R. V. (ed.), *A Documentary History of Communism*, 2 vols., New York, 1960.

The Conscience of the Revolution. Communist Opposition in Soviet Russia, Cambridge, Mass., 1960.

Daubier, J., *Histoire de la révolution culturelle prolétarienne en Chine*, 2 vols., Paris, 1971.

Deborin, A. M., *Vvedenie v filosofiyu dialekticheskogo materializma* (*Introduction to the Philosophy of Dialectical Materialism*), Petrograd, 1916; 4th edn. 1925.

Lenin kak myslitel (*Lenin as Thinker*), Moscow, 1924.

and N. Bucharin, *Kontroversen über dialektischen und mechanistischen Materialismus*, Einl. von Oskar Negt, Frankfurt, 1969.

De George, R. T., *Patterns of Soviet Thought*, Ann Arbor, 1966.

The New Marxism, New York, 1968.

Desan, W., *The Marxism of J.-P. Sartre*, New York, 1965.

Desanti, J., *Phénoménologie et praxis*, Paris, 1963.

Deutscher, I., *Stalin. A Political Biography*, rev. edn., Harmondsworth, 1966.

Marxism in Our Time, London, 1972.

The Prophet Armed. Trotsky 1879-1921, London, 1954.

The Prophet Unarmed. Trotsky 1921-1929, London, 1959.

The Prophet Outcast. Trotsky 1929-1940, London, 1963.

Djilas, M., *The New Class. An Analysis of the Communist System*, New York, 1957.

The Unperfect Society. Beyond the New Class, New York, 1969.

Dobb, M., *Soviet Economic Development since 1917*, New York, 1966.
Draper, T., 'The Strange Case of the Comintern', *Survey*, summer 1972.

Erhlich, A., *The Soviet Industrialization Debate 1924–1928*, Cambridge, Mass., 1960.

Fedoseev, P. N. *et al.* (eds.), *Filosofskie problemy sovremennogo estestvoznania (Philosophical Problems of Contemporary Natural Sciences)*, Moscow, 1959.
Fetscher, I., *Von Marx zur Sowjetideologie*, Frankfurt, 1957.
Fiori, G., *Vita di Antonio Gramsci*, Bari, 1965 (Eng. trans. New York, 1971).
Fischer, E., *Kunst und Koexistenz. Beitrag zu einer modernen marxistischen Aesthetik*, Hamburg, 1970.
Fischer, L., *The Life of Stalin*, London, 1953.
Fischer, R., *Stalin and German Communism*, Oxford, 1948.
Fitzpatrick, S., *The Commissariat of Enlightenment. Soviet Organization of Education and the Arts under Lunacharsky*, Cambridge, 1970.
Flechtheim, O. K., *Bolschewismus 1917–1967*, Vienna–Frankfurt–Zurich, 1967.
    Weltkommunismus im Wandel, Cologne, 1965.
Fougeyrollas, P., *Le Marxisme en question*, Paris, 1959.
Frank, P., *La Quatrième Internationale*, Paris, 1969.
Fromm, E., *Fear of Freedom*, London, 1942.
    Man for Himself, New York, 1947.
    The Sane Society, New York, 1955.
    Marx's Concept of Man, New York, 1961.

Gabel, J., *La Fausse Conscience*, Paris, 1962.
Garaudy, R., *Le Communisme et la morale*, Paris, 1945.
    Une Littérature des fossoyeurs, Paris, 1948.
    L'Église, le communisme et les chrétiens, Paris, 1949.
    Perspectives de l'homme: Existentialisme, pensée catholique, marxisme, Paris, 1961.
    Dieu est mart: Étude sur Hegel, Paris, 1962.
Giusti, V., *Il pensiero di Trotzky*, Firenze, 1949.
Goldmann, L., *Le Dieu caché*, Paris, 1954.
    Recherches dialectiques, Paris, 1959.
    Marxisme et sciences humaines, Paris, 1970.
Graham, L. R., *Science and Philosophy in the Soviet Union*, London, 1971 (copious bibliography).
Gramsci, A., *Il materialismo storico e la filosofia di Benedetto Croce*, Turin, 1948.
    Gli intellettuali e l'organizzazione della cultura, Turin, 1949.
    Il Risorgimento, Turin, 1949.
    Note sul Machavelli, sulla politica e sullo stato moderno, Turin, 1949.
    Litteratura e vita nazionale, Turin, 1950.
    Passato e presente, Turin, 1951.
    The Modern Prince and Other Writings, London, 1957.
    Scritti giovanili, Turin, 1958.
    2000 pagine di Gramsci, ed. G. Ferrate and N. Gallo, Milan, 1964.
Grossmann, H., *Das Akkumulations- und Zusammenbruchgesetz des kapitalistischen Systems*, Leipzig, 1929.

Habermas, J., *Theorie und Praxis*, Neuwied and Berlin, 1963.
    Erkenntnis und Interesse, Frankfurt, 1968.
    Technik und Wissenschaft als 'Ideologie', Frankfurt, 1968.
    (ed.), *Antworten auf Herbert Marcuse*, Frankfurt, 1968.

Haldane, J. S. B., *The Marxist Philosophy and the Sciences*, New York, 1939.

Harrington, M., *Socialism*, New York, 1971.

Havemann, R., *Dialektik ohne Dogma?*, Hamburg, 1964.

    Antworten, Fragen, Antworten, Munich, 1970.

    Rückantworten an die Hauptverwaltung 'Ewige Wahrheiten', Munich, 1971.

Heller, A., 'Lukács Esthetics', *New Hungarian Quarterly*, no. 24, 1966.

    'Jenseits der Pflicht. Das Paradigmatische der Ethik der deutschen Klassik im Oeuvre von G. Lukács', *Revue Internationale de Philosophie*, no. 106, 1973.

Hirszowicz, M., *Komunistyczny Lewiatan (The Communist Leviathan)*, Paris, 1973.

Hobsbawm, E. J., *Revolutionaries: Contemporary Essays*, London, 1973.

Horkheimer, M., *Kritische Theorie*, ed. Alfred Schmidt, 2 vols., Frankfurt, 1968.

    Eclipse of Reason, New York, 1947.

    Zur Kritik der instrumentellen Vernunft, Frankfurt, 1967.

Hudson, W., 'The Utopian Marxism of Ernst Bloch', thesis, Oxford, 1975.

Hyppolite, J., *Studies on Marx and Hegel*, New York, 1969.

Istituto Giangiacomo Feltrinelli, *Storia del Marxismo contemporaneo*, Milan, 1974.

Jaffe, P. J., 'The Varga Controversy and the American CP', *Survey*, summer 1972.

Jager, A., *Reich ohne Gott. Zur Eschatologie Ernst Blochs*, Zurich, 1969.

Jay, M., *The Dialectical Imagination. A History of the Frankfurt School and the Institute of Social Research 1923–50*, London, 1953 (copious bibliography).

Johnson, C. (ed.), *Change in Communist System*, Stanford, 1970.

Joravsky, D., *Soviet Marxism and Natural Science 1917–1932*, London, 1932.

Jordan, Z. A., *Philosophy and Ideology. The Development of Philosophy and Marxism–Leninism in Poland since the Second World War*, Dordrecht, 1963 (excellent bibliography).

Kamenev, L., E. Preobrajensky, N. Boukharine, and L. Trotsky, *La Question paysanne en URSS de 1924 à 1929, présentation par M. Fichelson et A. Derischenbourg*, Paris, 1973.

Karev, N., *Za materialisticheskuyu dialektiku (For the Materialist Dialectics)*, Moscow, 1930.

Karsch, S., *Théorie et politique: Louis Althusser*, Paris, 1974.

Kedrov, B. M., *o kolichestvennykh i kachestvennykh izmeneniakh v prirode (On the Qualitative and Quantitative Chances in Nature)* Moscow, 1946.

    O proizvedenii Engelsa 'Dialeklika prirody' (On Engels's Work 'Dialectics of Nature'), Moscow, 1954.

Khaskhachikh, F. I., *o poznavaemosti mira (On The Knowability of the World)*, Moscow, 1952.

Kline, G. L. (ed.), *Soviet Education*, New York, 1957.

Kołakowski, L., *Marxism and Beyond*, 2nd edn. London, 1971.

    Der revolutionäre Geist, Stuttgart, 1972.

    Marxismus–Utopie und Anti-Utopie, Stuttgart, 1974.

    and S. Hampshire (eds.), *The Socialist Idea: A Reappraisal*, London, 1974.

Kolbanovsky, V. N., *Dialektichesky materializm i sovremennoe estestvoznanie (Dialectical Materialism and Contemporary Natural Science)*, Moscow, 1964.

Konstantinov, F. V. (ed.), *Istorichesky materializm (Historical Materialism)*, Moscow, 1951.

Korey, W., *Zinoviev on the Problem of World Revolution 1919–1922*, Colorado Univ. Press, 1960.

Korsch, K., *Marxismus und Philosophie*, hg. und eingel. von E. Gerlach, 5th edn., Vienna, 1972 (Eng. trans. London, 1970).

    Die materialistische Geschichtsauffassung und andere Schriften, hg. E. Gerlach, Frankfurt, 1971.

    Three Essays on Marxism, Introduction by P. Breines, New York and London, 1972.

Kosik, K., *Die Dialektik des Konkreten*, Frankfurt, 1967.

Krasso, N. (ed.), *Trotsky: The Great Debate Renewed*, St. Louis, 1972.

Kruczek, A., 'Sultan-Galijew po 50 latach' ('Sultan-Galiev after 50 years'), *Kultura*, no. 9, 1973.

Kusin, V. V. (ed.), *The Czechoslovak Reform Movement 1968*, London, 1973.

Labedz, L. (ed.), *Revisionism. Essays on the History of Marxist Ideas*, London, 1961.

Lacroix, J., *Marxisme, existenlialisme, personnalisme*, Paris, 1949.

Lazitch, B., *Les Partis communistes d'Europe 1919–1955*, Paris, 1956.

   (ed.), *The Comintern—Historical Highlights*, London, 1966.

   Lénine et la IIIème Internationale, Neuchâtel, 1951.

Lefebvre, H., *A la lumière du materialisme dialectique*, i: *Logique formelle, logique dialectique*, Paris, 1947.

   La Pensée de Karl Marx, Paris, 1947.

   Problèmes actuels du marxisme, Paris, 1957.

   La Somme et le reste, Paris, 1959.

   Critique de la vie quotidienne, 2 vols., Paris, 1962.

Lemberg, E., *Ideologie und Gesellschaft. Eine Theorie der ideologischen Systeme*, Stuttgart, 1971.

Leonhard, W., *The Three Faces of Marxism*, New York, 1974.

Leonov, A. M., *Ocherk dialekticheskogo materializma (An Outline of Dialectical Materialism)*, Moscow, 1948.

Lewin, M., *Russian Peasants and Soviet Power: A Study of Collectivisation*, Evanston, Ill., 1958.

   Political Undercurrents in Soviet Economic Debates: From Bukharin to the Modern Reformers, Princeton, 1974.

Lewytzkyj, B., *Politische Opposition in der Sowjetunion 1960–1972*, Munich, 1972.

Lichtheim, G., *Marxism in Modern France*, New York and London, 1966.

   'From Marx to Hegel. Reflections on Georg Lukacs, T. W. Adorno and Herbert Marcuse', *TriQuarterly*, no. 12, 1968.

   Lukács, London, 1970.

Lieber, H. J., *Die Philosophie des Bolschewismus in den Grundzügen ihrer Entwicklung*, Frankfurt, 1957.

Liften, R. J., *Revolutionary Immortality: Mao Tse-tung and the Chinese Cultural Revolution*, London, 1969.

Lobkowicz, N., *Das Widerspruchsprinzip in der neueren sowjetischen Philosophie*, Dordrecht, 1960.

   Marxismus—Leninismus in der CSR, Dordrecht, 1962.

Losky, N. O., *Dialektichesky materializm v SSSR (Dialectical Materialism in the USSR)*, Paris, 1934.

Lowenthal, R., *World Communism. The Disintegration of a Secular Faith*, New York, 1966.

Ludz, P. C, *Ideologiebegriff und marxistische Theorie. Ansätze zu einer immanenten Kritik*, Opladen, 1976.

Lukács, G., *Schriften zur Literatursoziologie*, ausgew. und eingel. von Peter Ludz, 2nd edn. Neuwied, 1963.

   The Meaning of Contemporary Realism, London, 1963.

   The Historical Novel, Boston, 1963.

   Werke, 14 vols., Neuwied, 1964–73.

   Schriften zur Ideologie und Politik, ausgew. und eingel. von Peter Ludz, Neuwied, 1967.

   Solzhenitsyn, London, 1970.

   History and Class-Consciousness, London, 1971.

Lunacharsky, A. V., *Sobranie sochinenii (Collected Works)*, 8 vols., Moscow, 1963–7.

MacIntre, A., *Marcuse*, London, 1970.

McKenzie, K. E., *Comintern and the World Revolution 1928–1943*, New York, 1964.

Maksimov, A. A. *et al.* (eds.), *Filosofskie voprosy sovremennoy fiziki (Philosophical Problems of Contemporary Physics)*, Moscow, 1952.

Mallet, S., *La Nouvelle Classe ouvrière*, Paris, 1963.

Mandel, E., *Traité d'économie marxiste*, 2 vols., Paris, 1962.

Mao Tse-tung, *An Anthology of his Writings*, ed. A. Fremantle, New York, 1962.

    Four Essays on Philosophy, Peking, 1966.

    Mao Tse-tung Unrehearsed: Talks and Letters 1956–71, ed. and introduced by Stuart Schram, London, 1974.

Marcuse, H., *Reason and Revolution*, New York, 1941; 2nd edn. 1954.

    Eros and Civilization, Boston, 1955.

    Soviet Marxism, New York, 1958.

    One-dimensional Man, Boston, 1964.

    (with P. Wolff and Barrington Moore, Jr.), *A Critique of Pure Tolerance*, Boston, 1967.

    Negations, Boston, 1968.

    Five Lectures, Boston, 1970.

Marie. J.-J., *Staline*, Paris, 1967.

Markovic, M., *Dialektik der Praxis*, Frankfurt, 1971.

    From Affluence to Praxis, Ann Arbor, 1974.

Martinet, G., *Les Cinq Communismes*, Paris, 1971.

Mascolo, D., *Le Communisme: Révolution et communication ou la dialectique des valeurs et des besoins*, Paris, 1953.

Matteuci, A. G., *Antonio Gramsci e la filosofia della prassi*, Milan, 1951.

Medvedev, R., *Let History Judge: The Origins and Consequences of Stalinism*, New York, 1973.

Mehnert, K., *Der Sowjetmensch*, Stuttgart, 1958.

    Moscow and the New Left, Berkeley, 1975.

Merleau-Ponty, M., *Humanisme et terreur. Essai sur le problème communiste*, Paris, 1947 (Eng. trans. Boston, 1969).

    Les Aventures de la dialectique, Paris, 1955 (Eng. trans. Evanston, 1973).

Meszaros, I., *Lukács' Concept of Dialectic*, London, 1972.

Meyer, A. G., *The Soviet Political System. An Interpretation*, New York, 1965.

Micaud, C. A., *Communism and the French Left*, London, 1963.

Mills, C. W., *The Marxists*, London, 1969.

Mitin, M. and I. Razumovsky (eds.), *Dialektichesky i istorichesky materializm (Dialectical and Historial Materialism)*, 2 vols., Moscow, 1932–3.

Moltmann, J., *Theologie der Hoffnung*, Munich, 1964.

Morawski, S., 'Mimesis—Lukács' Universal Principle', *Science and Society*, winter 1968.

Morin, E., *Autocritique*, Paris, 1959.

Naville, P., *Psychologie, marxisme, matérialisme*, Paris, 1948.

    L'Intellectuel communiste, Paris, 1956.

Nollau, G., *International Communism and World Revolution*, New York, 1961.

Nove, A., *An Economic History of the USSR*, London, 1969.

    Stalinism and After, London, 1975.

Oglesby, C. (ed.), *The New Left Reader*, New York, 1969.

O polozhenii v biologicheskoy nauke. Stenografichesky otchet sessii Vsesoyznoy Akademii selskokhozyaistvennykh nauk im. V. I. Lenina 31 yulya–7 augusta 1947 (On the Situation in Biological Science. Stenographic report of the session of the Soviet Academy of Agricultural Science). Moscow, 1958.

Papaioannou, K., *L'Idéologie froide. Essai sur le dépérissement du marxisme*, Paris, 1967.
Parkinson, G. H. R. (ed.), *Georg Lukács: The Man, his Work and his Ideas*, New York, 1970.
Petrovic, G., *Philosophie und Revolution*, Hamburg, 1971.
   Marx in the Mid-twentieth Century, New York, 1967.
Politzer, G., *Principes fondamentaux de philosophie*, Paris, 1954.
Pollock, F., *Die planwirtschaftlichen Versuche in der Sowjetunion 1917–1927*, Leipzig, 1929.
Poster, M., *Existential Marxism in Postwar France*, Princeton, 1975 (good bibliography).
Pozzolini, A., *Che cosa ha veramente detto Gramsci*, Rome, 1968 (Eng. trans. London, 1970).
Preobrazhensky, E., *The New Economics*, London, 1965.

Ratschow, C. H., *Atheismus im Christentum? Eine Auseinandersetzung mit Ernst Bloch*, Gütersloh, 1971.
Roberts, P. C, *Alienation and Soviet Economy*, Albuquerque, 1971.
Rosenberg, A., *A History of Bolshevism from Marx to the First Five-Year Plan*, London, 1934.
Rothberg, A., *The Heirs of Stalin: Dissidence and the Soviet Regime*, Ithaca, 1972.
Rozental, M. M., *Voprosy dialektiki v 'Kapitale' Marksa* (*Problems of Dialectics in Marx's 'Capital'*), Moscow, 1955.
   and P. Yudin, *Kratky filosofsky slovar* (*Short Philosophical Dictionary*), Moscow, 1939; 5th edn. 1963.
Rubinshtein, S. L., *O myshlenii i putyakh ego issledovania* (*On Thinking and the Ways of Investigating it*), Moscow, 1958.
   Bytie i soznanie (*Existence and Consciousness*), Moscow, 1957.

Sakharov, A. D., *Thoughts on Progress, Peaceful Coexistence and Intellectual Freedom*, New York, 1968.
Sartre, J.-P., *Critique de la raison dialectique*, Paris, 1960.
   'Problème du marxisme', *Situations VI*, Paris, 1964.
Schapiro, L., *The Communist Party of the Soviet Union*, London, 1960.
Schmidt, A., *Der Begriff der Natur in der Lehre von Marx*, Frankfurt, 1962.
Schram, S. R., *Mao Tše-tung*, Harmondsworth, 1967.
Schwartz, B. I., *Chinese Communism and the Rise of Mao*, Cambridge, Mass., 1951.
Shachtman, M., *The Bureaucratic Revolution: The Rise of the Stalinist State*, New York, 1962.
Sinclair, L., *Leon Trotsky: A Bibliography*, Hoover Institute Press, 1972.
Skilling, H. G., *Czechoslovakia's Interrupted Revolution*, Princeton, 1976.
Skolimowski, H., *Polski marksizm* (*Polish Marxism*), London, 1969.
Snow, E., *China's Long Revolution*, London, 1974.
Soubise, L., *Le Marxisme après Marx*, Paris, 1967.
Souvarine, B., *Staline. Aperçu historique du bolchevisme*, Paris, 1935.
Stalin, I. V., *Sochinenia* (*Works*), vols. 1–13, Moscow, 1946 ff. (not completed); Eng. trans. 1954 ff.
   Marksizm i voprosy yazykoznania, Moscow, 1950 (*Marxism and Problems of Linguistics*), Eng. trans. New York, 1951.
   Ekonomicheskie problemy sotsializma v SSSR (*Economic Problems of Socialism in the USSR*), Moscow, 1952.
Stojanovic, S., *Critique et avenir du socialisme*, Paris, 1971.

Tamburano, G., *Antonio Gramsci: La vita, il pensiero, l'azione*, Manduria, 1963.
Tigrid, P., *Amère révolution*, Paris, 1977.
Todd, E., *La Chute finale. Essai sur la décomposition de la sphère soviétique*, Paris, 1976.
Tökes, R. (ed.), *Dissent in USSR: Politics, Ideology and People*, Baltimore and London, 1975.
Treadgold, D. W. (ed.), *The Development of the USSR*, Seattle, 1964.

Trotsky, L., *The History of the Russian Revolution*, 3 vols., New York, 1932.
    In Defense of Marxism (Against the Petty-bourgeois Opposition), New York, 1942.
    Their Morals and Ours, New York, 1942.
    Writings, 1929–1940, ed. G. Breitman, B. Scott, N. Allen, S. Lovell, New York, 1971 ff (contains
        the articles and speeches written in exile, no major works).
    The Revolution Betrayed, New York, 1972.
Tucker, R. C., *Stalin as Revolutionary, 1879–1929. A Study in History and Personality*, New York,
        1973.
    (ed.), *Stalinism. Essays in Historical Interpretation*, New York, 1977.
    The Soviet Political Mind, rev. edn. New York, 1971.

Ulam, A. B., *Stalin: The Man and His Era*, New York, 1973.
Unseld, S. (ed.), *Ernst Block zu Ehren*, Frankfurt, 1965.

Vacca, G., *Lukács o Korsch?*, Bari, 1969.
Vranicki, P., *Mensch und Geschichte*, Frankfurt, 1968.

Weinberg, E. A., *The Development of Sociology in the Soviet Union*, London and Boston, 1974.
Wetter, G. A., *Der dialektische Materialismus. Seine Geschichte und sein System in der
        Sowjetunion*, 5th edn. Freiburg, 1960; Eng. trans. New York, 1958 (copious bibliography).
    Soviet Ideology Today, New York, 1966.
Wilson, D., (ed.), *Mao Tse-tung in the Scales of History*, Cambridge, 1977.
Wolfe, B. D., *An Ideology in Power*, London, 1969.
Wolff, K. H. and Barrington Moore, Jr. (eds.), *The Critical Spirit: Essays in Honor of Herbert
        Marcuse*, Boston, 1967.

Zhdanov, A. A., *On Literature, Music and Philosophy*, London, 1950.
Zitta, V., *Georg Lukacs' Marxism: Alienation, Dialectics, Revolution*, The Hague, 1964.

Index

About the Author

Leszek Kołakowski was born in Radom, Poland, in 1927. A philosopher, historian, and essayist, Kołakowski earned his doctorate from Warsaw University in 1953, later becoming a professor and chairman of its section on the history of philosophy. An orthodox Marxist at first, he eventually became disillusioned with Stalinism, writing a short, incisive critique of the Party line, "What Is Socialism?" which drove the increasingly outspoken and critical professor into exile. Teaching at both the University of California at Berkeley and Oxford, Kołakowski has received numerous academic honors for his thirty books and other writings in four different languages. He is most famous for the three-volume opus on institutional and theoretical Marxism that you hold in your hand. In 2002, Kołakowski was awarded the first million-dollar John W. Kluge prize by the Library of Congress, which is given for lifetime achievement in the humanities and social sciences—areas of scholarship for which there are no Nobel Prizes.